Football Outsiders Almanac 2009

THE ESSENTIAL GUIDE TO THE 2009 NFL AND COLLEGE FOOTBALL SEASONS

Edited by Aaron Schatz

With Dr. Benjamin Alamar, Bill Barnwell, Jason Beattie, Will Carroll,

Bill Connelly, Doug Farrar, Brian Fremeau, Ned Macey, Sean McCormick,

Bill Moore, Mike Tanier, Vince Verhei, Robert Weintraub, Mark Zajack

Copyright 2009 Football Outsiders, Inc.

ISBN 1448648459

Contents

Introduction

This is the fifth time I've written an Introduction to a Football Outsiders preseason annual, but this one feels a little different.

The differences are pretty obvious, starting with the title on the cover: *Football Outsiders Almanac*, rather than *Pro Football Prospectus*. Some of you are reading this on your computer screens, rather than on paper. If you do have a paper copy, you'll find there's no publisher imprint on the back cover.

In the past, the main purpose of the Introduction was to attract readers who might be browsing at their local bookstore. This year, there isn't the same need to explain ourselves to people. You aren't browsing at your local bookstore, because this book isn't available at your local bookstore. If you are reading this, you've already bought the book online, either through our Web site or Amazon.com.

Still, a handful of readers will still be new to our work. Perhaps a friend told you about our book, or you heard me on the Bill Simmons podcast, or read about us in Peter King's Monday Morning Quarterback column. In that case, let me explain what makes Football Outsiders analysis different.

Football Outsiders is not founded on the idea that statistics are all-encompassing or can tell us everything about football. Everybody who writes about football uses both statistics (whether they be basic yardage totals or more advanced stats like ours) and scouting (whether scouting reports by professionals or just their own eyes). The same goes for us, except that the statistics portion of our analysis is far more accurate than what you normally see from football coverage. Those numbers are based on two ideas:

1) **Conventional football statistics are heavily dependent on context.** If you want to see which teams are good and which are bad, which strategies work and which do not, you first need to filter out that context. Down and distance, field position, the current score, time left on the clock, the quality of the opponent — all of these elements influence the objective of the play and/or its outcome. Yet, the official NFL stats add together all yardage gained by a specific team or player without considering the impact of that particular yardage on wins and losses.

A close football game can turn on a single bounce of the ball. In a season of only 16 games, those effects can have a huge impact on a team's win-loss record, thus obscuring the team's true talent level. If we can filter out these bits of luck and random chance, we can figure out which teams are really more likely to play better for the rest of the season, or even in the following season.

2) **On any one play, the majority of the important action is not tracked by the conventional NFL play-by-play.** That's why we started the Football Outsiders game charting project four years ago. A cadre of football-obsessed volunteers watches every single game and adds new detail to our record of each play. We know how many pass rushers teams send on each pass, how often teams go three-wide or use two tight ends, how often teams use a play-fake or a zone blitz, and which defensive backs are in coverage, even when they don't get a tackle in the standard play-by-play.

All of this makes *Football Outsiders Almanac 2009* very similar to the four editions of *Pro Football Prospectus* which came before. So why the name change, and why aren't we in bookstores?

For those who don't know, our first four books were published through an agreement with Prospectus Entertainment Ventures, the company that owns Baseball Prospectus (as well as the expansion projects Basketball Prospectus and Puck Prospectus). It was PEV that had the publishing contract (first with Workman, then Plume). This year, for various reasons, Plume decided they no longer wanted to publish books related to other sports besides baseball. Other publishers were interested in doing our book, but by the time Plume made their decision, it was too late to get on the publication schedule for 2009.

And so, we launched our first foray into self-publishing. We don't yet know if this is a one-shot deal, or whether we'll be back in stores with a more conventional book in 2010. We also want to make clear that, despite the change in title, we are still buddies with the Prospectus guys and we'll look for other ways to partner with them in the future (and you'll notice Will Carroll is still crossing over and writing in this book, including an essay about injury rehabilitation and contributions to a number of the skill player comments).

There is one big difference inside this book, and it does explain part of the name change: the disappearance of the word "Pro." With *Football Outsiders Almanac 2009*, we've continued to expand our coverage of college football. I'm lucky enough to have found Brian Fremeau and Bill Connelly, two men who have devoted tons of free time to breaking down NCAA play-by-play and drive stats. In past books, we looked at the best games on the college schedule. Last year, we added a projected Top 25. This year, we expand to full coverage of Division I-A (a.k.a. the "FBS"), with stats and commentary on every team from the six BCS conferences as well as the top independents and teams from the mid-majors.

Look around the Internet, and you'll probably find more statistical analysis of college football than pro football. However, almost all that analysis is about ranking teams 1 to 120. That's nice, but football is a chess game with 22 pieces at a time, not two. Just like with our NFL coverage, the goal of our college previews is to focus as much as possible on "why" and how," not just "which team is better." We break things down to offense and defense, pass and run, clutch situations ("late and close") compared to all plays.

As for the NFL, all the material from previous editions of *Pro Football Prospectus* is still here in *Football Outsiders Almanac*. We start off with "Pregame Show" (reviewing the most important research we've done in past books) and "Statistical Toolbox" (explaining all our stats, including the new, improved version 6.0 of our main DVOA metric). Once again, we preserve the ridiculousness of the NFL for posterity with another version of "The Year in Quotes;" look at the importance of injury by ranking the record of all 32 medical staffs; and introduce you to some of the more promising (and lesser-known) young bench players with our third annual list of Top 25 Prospects chosen in the third round or later.

Each NFL team gets a full chapter covering what happened in 2008 and our projections for the upcoming season. Are there reasons to believe that the team was actually better or worse than its record last year? What did the team do in the offseason, and what does that mean for the team's chances to win in 2009? Each chapter also includes all kinds of advanced statistics covering 2008 performance and strategic tendencies, plus detailed commentary on each of the major units of the team: Offensive line, defensive front seven, defensive secondary, special teams, and coaching staff.

"Skill players" (by which we mean "players who get counted in fantasy football") get their own section in the back of the book. We list the major players at each position alphabetically, along with commentary and a 2009 KUBIAK projection that will help you win your fantasy football league. We also have the most accurate projections anywhere for two fantasy football positions that people wrongly consider impossible to predict: kickers and team defense.

In the back of the book, you'll find a number of extra essays including a look at red zone consistency from season to season, analysis of the Miami Dolphins' Wildcat formation, and the introduction of a new stat called "Playmaker Score," which helps forecast which highly-drafted wide receivers are likely to succeed or fail.

With all that content, we're pretty proud of our first self-published book. We hope it helps you raise your level of football expertise, win arguments with your friends, and conquer your fantasy football league. If you are primarily an NFL fan, we hope the expanded college football coverage helps you enjoy pigskin on Saturdays more than ever before. Most importantly, we hope you enjoy reading our book as much as we enjoy writing it every year.

Aaron Schatz
Relaxing (finally) in Harwich Port, MA
June 26, 2009

P.S. Don't forget to visit FootballOutsiders.com every day for fresh coverage of the NFL and college football, plus the most intelligent football discussion threads on the Internet.

Statistical Toolbox

In the six years since Football Outsiders launched online, we have introduced a number of new statistics unlike any that had been used to measure the National Football League in the past. We've gradually improved the accuracy of the original statistics and introduced some new ones, in particular a number of metrics that would not be possible without the Football Outsiders game charting project, which is explained later in this introduction. Our statistical palette contains a wide variety of colors with which to paint a picture of the NFL. What follows is an explanation of all the statistics you'll find in this book: how we calculate them, what the numbers mean, and what they tell us about why teams win or lose football games. We've done our best to present these numbers in a way that makes them easy to understand. This explanation is long, so feel free to read some of it, flip around the rest of the book, and then come back. It will still be here.

DEFENSE-ADJUSTED VALUE OVER AVERAGE (DVOA)

One running back runs for three yards. Another running back runs for three yards. Which is the better run?

This sounds like a stupid question, but it isn't. In fact, this question is at the heart of nearly all of the analysis in this book.

Several factors can differentiate one three-yard run from another. What is the down and distance? Is it third-and-2, or second-and-15? Where on the field is the ball? Does the player get only three yards because he hits the goal line and scores? Is the player's team up by two touchdowns in the fourth quarter and thus running out the clock, or down by two touchdowns and thus facing a defense that is playing purely against the pass? Is the running back playing against the porous defense of the Raiders, or the stalwart defense of the Vikings?

Conventional NFL statistics value plays based solely on their net yardage. The NFL determines the best players by adding up all their yards no matter what situations they came in or how many plays it took to get them. Now, why would they do that? Football has one objective — to get to the end zone — and two ways to achieve that, by gaining yards and achieving first downs. These two goals need to be balanced to determine a player's value or a team's performance. All the yards in the world won't help a team win if they all come in eight-yard chunks on third-and-10.

The popularity of fantasy football only exacerbates the problem. Fans have gotten used to judging players based on how much they help fantasy teams win and lose, not how much they help *real* teams win and lose. Typical fantasy scoring further skews things by counting the yard between the one and the goal line as 61 times more important than all the other yards on the field (each yard worth 0.1 points, a touchdown worth 6). Let's say Anquan Boldin catches a pass on third-and-15 and goes 50 yards but gets tackled two yards from the goal line, and then Tim Hightower takes the ball on first-and-goal from the two-yard line and plunges in for the score. Has Tim Hightower done something special? Not really. When an offense gets the ball on first-and-goal at the two-yard line, they are going to score a touchdown five out of six times. Hightower is getting credit for the work done by the passing game.

Doing a better job of distributing credit for scoring points and winning games is the goal of **DVOA**, or Defense-adjusted Value Over Average. DVOA breaks down every single play of the NFL season, assigning each play a value based on both total yards and yards towards a first down, based on work done by Pete Palmer, Bob Carroll, and John Thorn in their seminal book, *The Hidden Game of Football*. On first down, a play is considered a success if it gains 45 percent of needed yards; on second down, a play needs to gain 60 percent of needed yards; on third or fourth down, only gaining a new first down is considered success.

We then expand upon that basic idea with a more complicated system of "success points," improved over the past four years with a lot of mathematics and a bit of trial and error. A successful play is worth one point, an unsuccessful play zero points, with fractional points in between (for example, eight yards on third-and-10 is worth 0.54 "success points"). Extra points are awarded for big plays, gradually increasing to three points for 10 yards (assuming those yards result in a first down), four points for 20 yards, and five points for 40 yards or more. Losing three or more yards is -1 point. Interceptions average -6 points, with an adjustment for the length of the pass and the location of the interception (since an interception tipped at the line is more likely to produce a long return than an interception on a 40-yard pass). A fumble is worth anywhere from -1.7 to -4.0 points depending on how often a fumble in that situation is lost to the defense — no matter who actually recovers the fumble. Red zone plays are worth 25 percent more for teams (and 10 percent more for players), and there is a bonus given for a touchdown that acknowledges that the goal line is significantly more difficult to cross than the previous 99 yards (although this bonus is no where near as large as the one used in fantasy football).

(Our system is a bit more complex than the one in *Hidden Game* thanks to our subsequent research, which added a larger penalty for turnovers, the fractional points, and a slightly higher baseline for success on first down. The reason why all fumbles are counted, no matter whether they are recovered by the offense or defense, is explained in the essay "Pregame Show.")

Every single play run in the NFL gets a "success value" based on this system, and then that number gets compared to the average success values of plays in similar situations for all players, adjusted for a number of variables. These include down and distance, field location, time remaining in game, and the team's lead or deficit in the game score. Teams are always compared to the overall offensive average, as the team made its own choice whether to pass or rush. When it comes to individual players, however, rushing plays are compared to other rushing plays, passing plays to other passing plays, tight ends to tight ends, wideouts to wideouts, and so on.

Going back to our example of the three-yard rush, if Player A gains three yards under a set of circumstances in which the average NFL running back gains only one yard, then Player A has a certain amount of value above others at his position. Likewise, if Player B gains three yards on a play on which, under similar circumstances, an average NFL back gains four yards, that Player B has negative value relative to others at his position. Once we make all our adjustments, we can evaluate the difference between this player's rate of success and the expected success rate of an average running back in the same situation (or between the opposing defense and the average defense in the same situation, etc.). Add up every play by a certain team or player, divide by the total of the various baselines for success in all those situations, and you get VOA, or Value Over Average.

Of course, the biggest variable in football is the fact that each team plays a different schedule against teams of disparate quality. By adjusting each play based on the opposing defense's average success in stopping that type of play over the course of a season, we get DVOA, or Defense-adjusted Value Over Average. Rushing and passing plays are adjusted based on down and location on the field; passing plays are also adjusted based on how the defense performs against passes to running backs, tight ends, or wide receivers. Defenses are adjusted based on the average success of the offenses they are facing. (Yes, technically the defensive stats are actually "offense-adjusted." If it seems weird, think of the "D" in "DVOA" as standing for "opponent-Dependent" or something.)

The biggest advantage of DVOA is the ability to break teams and players down to find strengths and weaknesses in a variety of situations. In the aggregate, DVOA may not be quite as accurate as some of the other, similar "power ratings" formulas based on comparing drives rather than individual plays, but, unlike those other ratings, DVOA can be separated not only by player, but also by down, or by week, or by distance needed for a first down. This can give us a better idea of not just which team is better, but why, and what a team has to do in order to improve itself in the future. You will find DVOA used in this book in a lot of different ways — because it takes every single play into account, it can be used to measure a player or a team's performance in any situation. All Pittsburgh third downs can be compared to how an average team does on third down. Matt Leinart and Kurt Warner can each be compared to how an average quarterback performs in the red zone, or with a lead, or in the second half of the game.

Since it compares each play only to plays with similar circumstances, it gives a more accurate picture of how much better a team really is compared to the league as a whole. The list of top DVOA offenses on third down, for example, is more accurate than the conventional NFL conversion statistic because it takes into account that converting third-and-long is more difficult than converting third-and-short, and that a turnover is worse than an incomplete pass because it eliminates the opportunity to move the other team back with a punt on fourth down.

One of the hardest parts of understanding a new statistic is interpreting its scale, or what numbers represent good performance or bad performance. We've made that easy with DVOA. In all cases, 0% represents league-average. A positive DVOA represents a situation that favors the offense, while a negative DVOA represents a situation that favors the defense. This is why the best offenses have positive DVOA ratings (last year, San Diego led the league at +24.1%) and the best defenses have negative DVOA ratings (with Pittsburgh number one at -26.9%). For teams, the best and worst ratings tend to be around +/-30%; for players, they tend to be around +/- 45%. Because league average is determined across multiple years, no single year will average exactly 0%. This gives DVOA the added benefit of being able to show us how the scoring environment has fluctuated from year to year. Last year's total league DVOA on offense was 4.8%, the highest season on record and the third straight year where the league DVOA increased. It was below 0% in both 2003 and 2005.

Team DVOA totals combine offense and defense by subtracting the latter from the former because the better defenses will have negative DVOA ratings. (Special teams performance is also added, as described later in this essay.)

Does it work? Using correlation coefficients, we can show that only actual points scored are better than DVOA at indicating how many games a team has won (Table 1) and DVOA is a does a better job of predicting wins in the coming season than either wins or

points scored in the previous season (Table 2).

(Correlation coefficient is a statistical tool that measures how two variables are related by using a number between 1 and -1. The closer to -1 or 1, the stronger the relationship, but the closer to 0, the weaker the relationship.)

DEFENSE-ADJUSTED YARDS ABOVE REPLACEMENT (DYAR)

After using DVOA for a few months, we came across a strange phenomenon: well-regarded players, particularly those known for their durability, had DVOA ratings that came out around average. The reason is that DVOA, by virtue of being a percentage or rate statistic, doesn't take into account the cumulative value of having a player producing at a league-average level over the course of an above-average number of plays. By definition, an average level of performance is better than that provided by half of the league and the ability to maintain that level of performance while carrying a heavy work load is very valuable indeed. In addition, a player who is involved in a high number of plays can draw the defense's attention away from other parts of the offense, and, if that player is a running back, he can take time off the clock with repeated runs.

Let's say you have a running back who carries the ball 300 times in a season. What would happen if you were to remove this player from his team's offense? What would happen to those 300 plays? Those plays don't disappear with the player, though some might be lost to the defense because of the associated loss of first downs. Rather those plays would have to be distributed among the remaining players in the offense, with the bulk of them being given to a replacement running back. This is where we arrive at the concept of replacement level, borrowed from our partners at Baseball Prospectus. When a player is removed from an offense, he is usually not replaced by a player of similar ability. Nearly every starting player in the NFL is a starter because he is better than the alternative. Those 300 plays will typically be given to a significantly worse player, someone who is the backup because he doesn't have as much experience and/or talent. A player's true value can then be measured by the level of performance he provides above that replacement level baseline, totaled over all of his run or pass attempts.

Table 1: Correlation of Various Stats to Wins, 2000-2008

Stat	Offense	Defense	Total
Points Scored/Allowed	.73	-.69	.92
DVOA	.67	-.52	.85
Yards Gained/Allowed	.54	-.46	.69
Yards Gained/Allowed per Play	.51	-.40	.72

Table 2: Correlation of Various Stats to Wins Following Year, 2000-2008

Stat	Correlation
DVOA	.34
Point Differential	.26
Yards per Play Differential	.25
Wins	.25
Yardage Differential	.23

INTRODUCING DVOA v6.0

One of this offseason's big projects at Football Outsiders was another round of improvements on our DVOA formula. We want to discuss those changes here, but beware: This may get a little technical.

The biggest change in DVOA v6.0 is that offense and defense are no longer judged on the same baseline. This is related to the specific adjustments and additions made to the formula, particularly these three:

1) DVOA now includes more penalties. Originally, DVOA only included passes and runs. In 2007, with DVOA v5.0, we added defensive pass interference and began to count intentional grounding with yards lost (rather than just as a regular incomplete pass.) Now, we add in the two offensive penalties which have both the highest correlation to wins and the most consistency from year-to-year: false starts and delays of game. Yes, that's right, delay of game really has a higher correlation to wins and losses than holding, offensive pass interference, or any number of other penalties. DVOA only counts false starts and delays of game on offense, so fourth down delays when a team is trying to draw the defense offside don't count, and neither do those penalties for when a guy spikes the ball after the play or breathes on the official wrong or whatever.

However, there is no correlation between the defense on the field and the frequency of false starts and delays of game. Therefore, we could only count these changes on the offensive side of DVOA. That required a big change: separate baselines for offense and defense. The average for "success points" in any given situation is now lower on offense because of the possibility of a penalty. This also means that offensive plays come in three categories: Instead of just rushing and passing, there are also penalties. So on defense, all pass plays and run plays from 2002-2007 total to 0% DVOA, but on offense they do not, because you have to add in false starts and delays of game (which are all negative plays) to get 0% DVOA as the average. Therefore, you may notice that team DVOA for both pass offense and run offense will seem higher than in past years. (This is not an issue with defensive pass interference or intentional grounding, since we count both of those as pass plays.)

2) Once we split offense and defense, we were able to change the way we counted aborted plays such as dropped snaps and incomplete backwards

lateral passes. These plays now only count as negative for the offense, and defenses do not receive a "bonus" just because the quarterback can't hold onto the ball.

3) DVOA v6.0 improves the way we adjust for teams playing from behind or with a lead in the fourth quarter. These adjustments are different for offense and defense. We also added an adjustment for the final two minutes of the first half when the offense is not near field-goal range.

Other improvements in DVOA v6.0 include:

• Red zone plays (for team DVOA) are now worth 25 percent more than other plays, rather than 20 percent.

• Offense gets a slight penalty and defense gets a slight bonus for games indoors.

• Defensive pass interference for less than the needed yards now gets the proper first-down bonus.

• Adds penalty for a safety, beyond just the penalty for lost yardage.

For most teams, the new version of DVOA only makes a small change to their rating. The average team since 1995 saw its rating change by 2.7 percent. However, a handful of teams did see their ratings change significantly, and the biggest improvement belonged to a team from the 2008 season. The Jacksonville Jaguars had a total DVOA of -8.5% in the final ratings posted on Football Outsiders in 2008. In the new DVOA v6.0, their total DVOA is 1.9%, more than 10 percentage points higher — although because the old version of DVOA had a big gap between the 19th and 20th best teams of 2008, their rating actually only goes up two spots, from 22nd to 20th overall. Nonetheless, this higher DVOA rating helps to explain why our projection for Jacksonville in 2009 may be better than most fans expect.

Here's a look at which teams saw their DVOA change the most with the new version of the system:

Biggest Changes between DVOA 5.0 and DVOA 6.0

DVOA higher with version 6.0				DVOA lower with version 6.0			
Year	Team	Old	New	Change	Year	Team	Old	New	Change
2008	JAC	-8.5%	1.9%	10.3%	1999	STL	45.8%	34.3%	-11.5%
2003	NYJ	-5.7%	4.0%	9.8%	2005	MIN	-7.2%	-18.0%	-10.8%
1997	PIT	18.4%	27.6%	9.2%	2001	STL	38.5%	28.9%	-9.6%
1999	DEN	1.0%	8.9%	7.8%	2007	DET	-19.9%	-29.2%	-9.3%
1999	NYJ	1.8%	8.8%	7.1%	2006	STL	-5.0%	-13.8%	-8.8%
2000	ARI	-44.3%	-37.9%	6.4%	1999	JAC	34.8%	26.5%	-8.3%
2002	ARI	-42.0%	-35.8%	6.2%	1997	SEA	-1.4%	-8.9%	-7.5%
2002	KC	19.5%	25.4%	5.9%	1998	ATL	26.3%	19.0%	-7.3%
2008	WAS	4.6%	10.4%	5.8%	2004	MIN	-0.5%	-7.7%	-7.2%
1995	GB	10.5%	16.3%	5.8%	1998	SEA	6.5%	-0.4%	-6.9%

Of course, the *real* replacement player is different for each team in the NFL. Over the past two years, the second-string running back in Jacksonville (Maurice Jones-Drew) had a much higher DVOA than the first-string back (Fred Taylor). In 2007, Ryan Grant started the year as the fifth-string running back for the Giants and ended the year with a 12.4% DVOA for Green Bay. On other teams, the drop from the starter to the backup can be even greater than the general drop to replacement level. Imagine if Peyton Manning broke his leg, for example. The choice to start an inferior player or to employ a sub-replacement level backup, however, falls to the team, not the starter being evaluated. Thus we generalize replacement level for the league as a whole as the ultimate goal is to evaluate players independent of the quality of their teammates.

Our estimates of replacement level were re-done during the 2008 season and are computed differently for each position. For quarterbacks, we analyzed situations where two or more quarterbacks had played meaningful snaps for a team in the same season, then compared the overall DVOA of the original starters to the overall DVOA of the replacements. We did not include situations where the backup was actually a top prospect waiting his turn on the bench, since a first-round pick is by no means a "replacement-level" player.

At other positions, there is no easy way to separate players into "starters" and "replacements," since unlike at quarterback, being the starter doesn't make you the only guy who gets in the game. Instead, we used a simpler method, ranking players at each position in each season by attempts. The players who made up the final 10 percent of passes or runs were split out as "replacement players" and then compared to the players making up the other 90 percent of plays at that position. This took care of the fact that not every non-starter at running back or wide receiver is a freely available talent. (Think of Jerious Norwood or Devery Henderson, for example.)

As noted earlier, the challenge of any new stat is to present it on a scale that's meaningful to those attempting to use it. Saying that DeAngelo Williams' runs were worth 84.3 success value points over replacement in 2008 has very little value without a context to tell us if 84.3 is good total or a bad one. Therefore, we translate these success values into a number called "Defense-adjusted Yards Above Replacement," or DYAR. For example, DeAngelo Williams led all running backs in 2008 with 385 rushing DYAR.

PROBLEMS WITH DVOA AND DYAR

Football is a game in which nearly every action requires the work of two or more teammates — in fact, usually 11 teammates all working in unison. Unfortunately, when it comes to individual player ratings, we are still far from the point at which we can determine the value of a player independent from the performance of his teammates. That means that when we say, "In 2008, Earnest Graham had a DVOA of -8.5%," what we are really saying is "In 2008, Earnest Graham, playing in Jon Gruden's offensive system with the Tampa Bay offensive line blocking for him and Jeff Garcia selling the fake when necessary, had a DVOA of -8.5%."

DVOA is limited by what's included in the official NFL play-by-play or tracked by the Football Outsiders game charting project (introduced below). Because we need to have the entire play-by-play of a season in order to compute DVOA and DYAR, these metrics are not yet ready to compare players of today to players throughout the league's history. As of this writing, we have processed 15 seasons, 1994 through 2008, and we add seasons at a rate of roughly two per year (the most recent season, plus one season back into history.)

SPECIAL TEAMS

The problem with a system based on measuring both yardage and yardage towards a first down is what to do with plays that don't have the possibility of a first down. Special teams are an important part of football and we needed a way to add that performance to the team DVOA rankings. Our special teams metric includes five separate measurements: field goals and extra points, net punting, punt returns, net kickoffs, and kick returns.

The foundation of most of these special teams ratings is the concept that each yard line has a different value based on the likelihood of scoring from that position on the field. In Hidden Game, the authors suggested that the each additional yard for the offense had equal value, with a team's own goal line being worth -2 points, the 50-yard line 2 points, and the opposing goal line 6 points. (-2 points is not only the value of a safety, but also reflects the fact that when a team is backed up in its own territory, it is likely that its drive will stall, forcing a punt that will give the ball to the other team in good field position. Thus, the negative point value reflects the fact that the defense is more likely to score next.) Our studies have updated this concept to reflect the actual likelihood that the offense or defense will have the next score from a given position on the field based on actual results from the past few seasons. The line that represents the value of field position is not straight, but curved, with the value of each yard increasing as teams approach either goal line.

Our special teams ratings compare each kick or punt to league average based on the point value of the position of the kick, catch, and return. We've determined a league average for how far a kick goes based on the line of scrimmage for each kick (almost always the 30-yard line for kickoffs, variable for punts) and a league average for how far a return goes based on both the yard line where the ball is caught and the distance that it traveled in the air.

The kicking or punting team is rated based on net points compared to average, taking into account both the kick and the return if there is one. Because the average return is always positive, punts that are not returnable (touchbacks, out of bounds, fair catches, and punts downed by the coverage unit) will rate higher than punts of the same distance that are returnable. (This is also true of touchbacks on kickoffs.) There are also separate individual ratings for kickers and punters that are based on distance and whether the kick is returnable, assuming an average return in order to judge the kicker separate from the coverage.

For the return team, the rating is based on how many points the return is worth compared to average, based on the location of the catch and the distance the ball traveled in the air. Return teams are not judged on the distance of kicks, nor are they judged on kicks that cannot be returned. As explained below, blocked kicks are so rare as to be statistically insignificant as predictors for future performance and are thus ignored. For the kicking team they simply count as missed field goals, for the defense they are gathered with their opponents' other missed field goals in Hidden value (also explained below).

Field goal kicking is measured differently. Measuring kickers by field goal percentage is a bit absurd, as it assumes that all field goals are of equal difficulty. In our metric, each field goal is compared to the average number of points scored on all field goal attempts from that distance over the past decade, with adjustments for rule changes such as the introduction of the

special-teams-use-only "k-ball" in 1999. The value of a field goal increases as distance from the goal line increases. Kickoffs, punts, and field goals are then adjusted based on weather and altitude. It will surprise no one to learn that it is easier to kick the ball in Denver or a dome than it is to kick the ball in Buffalo in December. Because we do not yet have enough data to tailor our adjustments specifically to each stadium, each one is assigned to one of four categories: Cold, Warm, Dome, and Denver. There is also an additional adjustment dropping the value of field goals in Florida (because the warm temperatures allow the ball to carry better) and raising the value of punts in San Francisco (because of those infamous winds).

Once we've totaled how many points above or below average can be attributed to special teams, we translate those points into DVOA so the ratings can be added to offense and defense to get total team DVOA.

There are three aspects of special teams that have an impact on wins and losses, but don't show up in the standard special teams rating because a team has little or no influence on them. The first is the length of kickoffs by the opposing team. The other two are field goals against your team, and punt distance against your team. Research shows no indication that teams can influence the accuracy or strength of field-goal kickers and punters, except for blocks. As mentioned above, although blocked field goals and punts are definitely skillful plays, they are so rare that they have no correlation to how well teams have played in the past or will play in the future, thus they are included here as if they were any other missed field goal or botched punt, giving the defense no additional credit for their efforts. The value of these three elements is listed separately as "Hidden" value.

The 2007 Chicago Bears proved to be an important exception to the general fact that a team has no influence on opposing kickoffs and punts. Changes in special teams over the past two seasons attempt to correct for this by giving Chicago net value rather than no value on a kickoff that was not returned because it was deliberately kicked short to avoid Devin Hester. We also did this with a handful of kickoffs against Cleveland and the New York Jets. This doesn't fully compensate for the impact of Hester on the kicking game, but it is a more accurate measure of the value Chicago got from special teams (and it was less of an issue in 2008).

Special teams ratings also do not include two-point

conversions or onside kick attempts, both of which, like blocks, are so infrequent as to be statistically insignificant in judging future performance.

PYTHAGOREAN PROJECTION

The Pythagorean projection is an approximation of each team's wins based solely on their points scored and allowed. This basic concept was introduced by baseball analyst Bill James, who discovered that the record of a baseball team could be very closely approximated by taking the square of team runs scored and dividing it by the sum of the squares of team runs scored and allowed. Statistician Daryl Morey later extended this theorem to professional football, refining the exponent to 2.37 rather than 2.

Until recently, Pythagorean projections did a remarkable job of predicting Super Bowl champions. From 1988 through 2004, 11 of 16 Super Bowls were won by the team that led the NFL in Pythagorean wins, while only seven were won by the team with the most actual victories. Super Bowl champions that led the league in Pythagorean wins but not actual wins include the 2004 Patriots, 2000 Ravens, 1999 Rams, and 1997 Broncos.

Over the last four seasons, as readers know, the results of the postseason haven't quite looked like the results of the regular season, and so this rule has — temporarily or permanently, nobody is quite sure — gone out the window. The two championship Steelers teams were fifth (2005) and third (2008) in Pythagorean wins. The 2006 Colts set a mark for the fewest Pythagorean wins of any Super Bowl champion (9.6), a mark then shattered by the Giants the following season (8.6). The 2008 Arizona Cardinals had the fewest Pythagorean wins of any conference champion in history (8.0) and last year was the first season since 1995 where neither conference champion led its conference in Pythagorean wins during the regular season.

Nonetheless, while its value as a postseason predictor seems to have gone down, the Pythagorean projection is still a valuable predictor of year-to-year improvement. Teams that win a minimum of one full game more than their Pythagorean projection tend to regress the following year; teams that win a minimum of one full game less than their Pythagorean projection tend to improve the following year, particularly if they were at or above .500 despite their underachiev-ing. The 2006 Jacksonville Jaguars, for example, finished 8-8 but had 10.8 Pythagorean wins, one of the larger differences in recent history. The following year, they improved to 11-5. In 2009, this trend suggests improvement from Philadelphia, San Diego, and New Orleans.

ADJUSTED LINE YARDS

One of the most difficult goals of statistical analysis in football is isolating the degree to which each of the 22 men on the field is responsible for the result of a given play. Nowhere is this as significant as in the running game, in which one player runs while up to nine other players — including wideouts, tight ends, and a fullback — block in different directions. None of the statistics we use for measuring rushing — yards, touchdowns, yards per carry — differentiate between the contribution of the running back and the contribution of the offensive line. Neither do our advanced metrics DVOA and DYAR.

We do, however, have enough play-by-play data amassed that we can try to separate the effect that the running back has on a particular play from the effects of the offensive line (and other offensive blockers) and the opposing defense. A team might have two running backs in its stable: RB A, who averages 3.0 yards per carry, and RB B, who averages 3.5 yards per carry. Who is the better back? Imagine that RB A doesn't just average 3.0 yards per carry, but gets exactly 3 yards on every single carry, while RB B has a highly variable yardage output: sometimes 5 yards, sometimes -2 yards, sometimes 20 yards. The difference in variability between the runners can be exploited not only to determine the difference between the runners, but the effect the offensive line has on every running play.

At some point in every long running play, the running back passes all of his offensive line blocks as well as additional blocking backs or receivers. From there on, the rest of the play is dependent on the runner's own speed and elusiveness and the speed and tackling ability of the opposing defense. If Frank Gore breaks through the line for 50 yards, avoiding tacklers all the way to the goal line, his offensive line has done a great job—but they aren't responsible for the majority of the yards gained. The trick is figuring out exactly how much they *are* responsible for.

For each running back carry, we calculated the probability that the back involved would run for the specific yardage on that play based on that back's average yardage per carry and the variability of their yardage from play to play. We also calculated the probability that the offense would get the yardage based on the team's rushing average and variability using all backs *other* than the one involved in the given play, and the probability that the defense would give up the specific amount of yardage based on its average rushing yards allowed per carry and variability. For example, based on his rushing average and variability, the probability in 2004 that Tiki Barber would have a positive carry was 80 percent, while the probability that Giants would have a positive carry without Barber running was only 73 percent.

A regression analysis breaks the value for rushing yardage into the following categories: losses, 0-4 yards, 5-10 yards, and 11-plus yards. In general, the offensive line is 20 percent more responsible for lost yardage than it is for positive gains up to four yards, but 50 percent less responsible for additional yardage gained between five and ten yards, and not at all responsible for additional yardage past ten yards.

By applying those percentages to every running back carry, we were able to create **Adjusted Line Yards**, a statistic that measured offensive line performance. (We don't include carries by receivers, which are usually based on deception rather than straight blocking, or carries by quarterbacks, which are almost always busted passing plays unless they involve Vince Young.) Those numbers are then adjusted based on down, distance, situation, opponent and — new for 2009 — whether or not a team is in the shotgun. (Because defenses are generally playing pass when the quarterback is in shotgun, the average running back carry from shotgun last year gained 5.6 yards, compared to just 4.1 yards on other carries.) The adjusted numbers are then normalized so that the league average for Adjusted Line Yards per carry is the same as the league average for RB yards per carry (in 2008, 4.25 yards).

The NFL distinguishes between runs made to seven different locations on the line: left/right end, left/right tackle, left/right guard, and middle. Further research showed no statistically significant difference between how well a team performed on runs listed as having gone up the middle or past a guard, so we separated runs into just five different directions (left/right end, left/right tackle, and middle). Note that there may not

be a statistically significant difference between right tackle and middle/guard either, but pending further research (and for the sake of symmetry) we still list runs behind the right tackle separately. These splits allow us to evaluate subsections of a team's offensive line, but not necessarily individual linesmen, as we can't account for blocking assignments or guards who pull towards the opposite side of the line after the snap.

SUCCESS RATE

Success rate is a statistic for running backs that measures how consistently they achieve the yardage necessary for a play to be deemed successful. Some running backs will mix a few long runs with a lot of failed runs of one or two yards, while others with similar yards-per-carry averages will consistently gain five yards on first down, or as many yards as necessary on third down. This statistic helps us differentiate between the two.

Since Success Rate compares rush attempts to other rush attempts, without consideration of passing, the standard for success on first down is slightly lower than those described above for DVOA. In addition, the standard for success changes slightly in the fourth quarter when running backs are used to run out the clock. A team with the lead is satisfied with a shorter run as long as it stays in bounds. Conversely, for a team down by a couple of touchdowns in the fourth quarter, four yards on first down isn't going to be a big help.

The formula for Success Rate is as follows:

• A successful play must gain 40 percent of needed yards on first down, 60 percent of needed yards on second down, and 100 percent of needed yards on third or fourth down.

• If the offense is behind by more than a touchdown in the fourth quarter, the benchmarks switch to 50 percent, 65 percent, and 100 percent.

• If the offense is ahead by any amount in the fourth quarter, the benchmarks switch to 30 percent, 50 percent, and 100 percent.

The league-average Success Rate in 2008 was 46.8 percent. Success Rate is not adjusted based on defenses faced, and is not calculated for quarterbacks and wide receivers who occasionally carry the ball.

SIMILARITY SCORES

Similarity scores were first introduced by Bill James to compare baseball players to other baseball players from the past. It was only natural that the idea would spread to other sports as statistical analysis spread to other sports. NBA analyst John Hollinger has created his own version to compare basketball players, and we have created our own version to compare football players.

Similarity scores have a lot of uses, and we aren't the only football analysts who use them. Doug Drinen of the website Footballguys.com has his own system that is specific to comparing fantasy football performances. The major goal of our similarity scores is to compare career progressions to try to determine when players have a higher chance of a breakout, a decline, or — due to age or usage — an injury (much like Baseball Prospectus's PECOTA player projection system). Therefore we not only compare numbers such as attempts, yards, and touchdowns, but also age and experience. We often are looking not for players who had similar seasons, but for players who had similar two- or three-year spans in their careers.

Similarity scores have some important weaknesses. The database for player comparison begins in 1978, the year the 16-game season began and passing rules were liberalized (a reasonable starting point to measure the "modern" NFL), thus the method only compares standard statistics such as yards and attempts, which are of course subject to all kinds of biases from strength of schedule to quality of receiver corps. For our comparisons, we project full-season statistics for the strike years of 1982 and 1987, although we cannot correct for players who crossed the 1987 picket line to play more than 12 games.

If you are interested in the specific computations behind our similarity scores system, we have listed the standards for each position online at http://www.footballoutsiders.com/stats/similarity.php.

KUBIAK PROJECTION SYSTEM

Most "skill position" players whom we expect to play a role this season receive a projection of their standard 2009 NFL statistics using the KUBIAK projection system. KUBIAK takes into account a number of different factors including expected role, performance over the past two seasons, age, height, weight, his-torical comparables, and projected team performance on offense and defense. When we named our system KUBIAK, it was a play on the PECOTA system used by our partners at Baseball Prospectus — if they were going to name their system after a long-time '80s backup, we would name our system after a long-time '80s backup. Little did we know that Gary Kubiak would finally get a head coaching job the very next season. After some debate, we decided to keep the name, although discussing projections for Houston players can be a bit awkward.

To clear up a common misconception among our readers, KUBIAK projects individual player performances only, not teams.

2009 WIN PROJECTION SYSTEM

In this book, each of the 32 NFL teams receives a **2009 Mean Projection** at the beginning of its chapter. These projections stem from three equations that forecast 2009 DVOA for offense, defense, and special teams based on a number of different factors, including the previous two years of DVOA in various situations, improvement in the second half of 2008, recent draft history, coaching experience, injury history, specific coaching styles, and the combined tenure of the offensive line.

These three equations produce precise numbers representing the most likely outcome, but also produce a range of possibilities, used to determine the probability of each possible offensive, defensive, and special teams DVOA for each team. This is particularly important when projecting football teams, because with only 16 games in a season, a team's performance may vary wildly from its actual talent level due to a couple of random bounces of the ball or badly timed injuries. In addition, the economic structure of the NFL allows teams to make sudden jumps or drops in overall ability more often than in other sports.

To project wins, Dr. Benjamin Alamar created a simulation that plays out the entire schedule for each team using random draws of DVOA for each team's offense, defense, and special teams to calculate a final score for each game in each season. The values and frequencies of these DVOA rating are based on the projection equations described above. This game-by-game simulation also accounts for home-field advantage, warm-weather or dome-stadium teams playing in the cold after November 1, and several other variables that can affect the outcome of each game. We ran the simulation 10,000 times, producing 10,000 unique seasons representing the full range of possibilities for each team in 2008. We then compared the results to the historical probability that a certain win total would be achieved in a 16-game NFL season, adjusting the simulation to produce a more realistic number of 16-, 15-, 1- and 0-win seasons, as these are historically very low probability.

The resulting possible win totals are then separated into five categories:

• On the Clock (0-3 wins)
• Loserville (5-6 wins)
• Mediocrity (7-8 wins)
• Playoff Contender (9-10 wins)
• Super Bowl Contender (11+ wins)

The percentage given for each category is dependent not only on how good we project the team to be in 2009, but the level of variation possible in that projection, and the expected performance of the teams on the schedule. Each variable has a different impact on the variability of the projection. For example, offenses that were better through the air in 2008 have more variation in their 2009 projections than offenses that were better on the ground. Defensive improvement in the second half of last season leads to less variation, while a rookie kicker or punter leads to more variation.

In response to reader requests, we also list the mean projection for each team. We do not expect any teams to win the exact number of games in their mean projection, however—particularly since no team can win 0.8 of a game (although in his early Tampa days, Jon Gruden tested the idea that he might will his team to win fractional games by getting to the office as early as humanly possible).

FOOTBALL OUTSIDERS GAME CHARTING PROJECT

Each of the formulas listed above relies primarily on the play-by-play data published by the NFL. When we began to analyze the NFL, that was all that we had to work with. Just as a television broadcast has a color commentator who gives more detail to the facts related by the play-by-play announcer, so too we need some color commentary to provide contextual information that breathes life into these plain lines of numbers and text. The Football Outsiders Game Charting Project is our attempt to provide color for the simple play-by-play.

Providing color to 512 hours of football is a daunting task. To put it into perspective, there were more than 54,000 lines of play-by-play information in the 2008 NFL season and our goal is to add several layers of detail to nearly all of them. We recruited more than 50 volunteers to collectively chart each week's NFL games. Unfortunately, we do not have access to the coaches' film the NFL provides to the 32 teams. That tape includes a sideline and end zone perspectives for each play, and shows all 22 players at all times. Only NFL teams and NFL Films are allowed to have access to the film, and the only place it is ever shown to the public is on NFL Network or ESPN's *NFL Matchup*. Anyone who has watched *Matchup* knows the benefit of watching coaches' film. It is easy to see the type of coverage being run and the cause-and-effect of certain actions taken on the field; the end zone perspective enables the identification of individual linemen.

Without access to coaches' film, we had to chart games using regular broadcast footage. Broadcast footage is not as definitive, but it served our purposes. In the end, we have data on nearly every play from the past four NFL seasons. A handful of plays are missing due to technical difficulties—for example, many games were charted using Direct TV Short Cuts, which would occasionally skip a play to fit the 30-minute window.

Through trial-and-error, we have narrowed our focus to charting things both traceable and definitive. We are limited by the camera angles on standard television broadcasts and the time constraints of our volunteers. Charting a game, and rewinding to make sure mistakes are minimized, can take two to three hours. More than a couple of these per week can be hazardous to one's marriage. Our goal was to provide comprehensive information while understanding that our charters were doing this on a volunteer basis.

We want to emphasize that all data from the charting project is unofficial. (For this reason, we will usually mention the charting project when using this data in comments later in the book.) Other sources for football statistics may keep their own measurements of yards after catch or how teams perform against the blitz. Our data will not necessarily match theirs. However, any other group that is publicly tracking this data is also working off the same television broadcast footage, and thus will run into the same issues of difficulty. No one outside of the league can get official game film from the NFL.

The Football Outsiders game charting project tracks the following information:

FORMATION: For each play, charters recorded the number of running backs, wide receivers, and tight ends. The formation was recorded in the moment prior to the snap. Therefore, it does not include any pre-snap motion. Formations have become more fluid in recent years, so these numbers should not be considered gospel. Because television cameras do not always show player numbers, we told our game charters to mark formations based on appearance, not personnel. It can be hard to tell where to draw the distinction between an H-back and an offset fullback, or between a flex tight end and a slot receiver. We did not want a hard and fast rule that any tight end standing up off the line becomes a slot receiver, because that's not the way defensive coordinators think when they send in their personnel in response. In addition, once the Dolphins unveiled the Wildcat in Week 3, we asked charters to mark whenever a team ran a direct snap to a non-quarterback or other "Wildcat" type play.

RUSHERS AND BLOCKERS: "Blitz" is a rather ubiquitous word in football, and a standard definition is difficult to nail down. Rather than asking charters to determine when a team was blitzing, we asked them to record the number of blockers and rushers on passing plays. Counting rushers was easy, but counting blockers proved to be an art as much as a science. Offenses base their blocking schemes on how many rushers they expect. A running back or tight end's assignment may depend on how many pass-rushers cross the line at the snap. Therefore, an offensive player was deemed to be a blocker if he engaged in an actual block, or there was some hesitation before running a route. A running back that immediately heads out into the flat is not a blocker, but one that waits to verify that the blocking scheme is working and then goes out to the flat would, in fact, be considered a blocker.

In 2008, for the first time, we also asked charters to mark down when a defense used a "zone blitz." This was defined as any play where at least one down lineman dropped into pass coverage while at least one linebacker or defensive back rushed the passer.

QUARTERBACK ACTION: In passing situations, the charters recorded the movement of the quarterback. This consisted of three items:

• Marking plays which began with a play-action fake, including a fake end-around or a flea flicker.

• Marking when the quarterback left the pocket. Charters marked rollouts and bootlegs. (A rollout has the quarterback moving behind his blockers, while a bootleg has the quarterback moving one way and his blockers the other, usually in connection with a play-action fake.) Charters also marked when a quarterback run past the line of scrimmage was a sneak, a draw, or a scramble. We asked the charters to differentiate between designed runs and plays on which the quarterback originally intended to pass, although this is often a judgment call.

• Marking a defender with a "hurry" if he clearly caused the quarterback to rush his motion or leave the pocket after originally setting up in the pocket to throw. If the quarterback stood tall and delivered the pass with defenders in his face, this was not a hurry. Charters were allowed to list two names if necessary, and could also attribute a hurry to Overall Pressure or list a play as a Coverage Scramble when the quarterback wasn't under pressure but ran because there were no open receivers.

PASS DETAILS: We divided all pass yardage into two numbers: distance in the air and yards after catch. You will see much of this information throughout the team chapters and in each of the individual player tables. Distance in the air was based on the distance from the line of scrimmage to the place where the receiver either caught or was supposed to catch the pass. We did not count how far the quarterback was behind the line or horizontal yardage if the quarterback threw across the field. All touchdowns were counted to the goal line, so that distance in the air added to yards after catch always equals the official yardage total kept by the league. Charters also marked screen passes and tried to differentiate between passes to running backs that were standard pass routes, swing passes, or dumpoffs.

DEFENDERS: The NFL play-by-play lists tackles and, occasionally, tipped balls, but it does not definitively list the defender on the play. Charters were asked to determine which defender was primarily responsible for covering either the receiver at the time of the throw or the location to which the pass was thrown, regardless of whether the pass was complete or not.

Every defense in the league plays zone coverage at times, some more than others, which leaves us with the question of how to handle plays without a clear man assigned to that receiver. We gave charters three alternatives:

• We asked charters to mark passes that found the holes in zone coverage as Hole in Zone, rather than straining to assign that pass to an individual defender. We asked the charter to also note the player who appeared to be responsible for that zone, and these defenders are assigned half credit for those passes. Some holes were so large that no defender could be listed along with the Hole in Zone designation.

• Charters were free to list two defenders instead of one. This could be used for actual double coverage, or for zone coverage in which the receiver was right between two close defenders rather than sitting in a gaping hole. When two defenders are listed, ratings assign each with half credit.

• Screen passes and dumpoffs are marked as Uncovered unless a defender (normally a linebacker) is obviously shadowing that specific receiver on the other side of the line of scrimmage.

Since we began the charting project four years ago, nothing has changed our analysis more than this information on pass coverage. However, we want to be upfront: It was often the most difficult information to chart. Broadcast camera angles often do not show the set up of the secondary, making it impossible to identify before the play if there is man coverage. On passes longer than a few yards, the camera won't show the receiver until the pass is in the air. The sideline view of network cameras makes seeing the specific numbers on some jerseys difficult. (At this point, we would like to give a big shout out to all the defensive backs with dreadlocks that come out of their helmets, making them easier to identify.) Zone coverage makes things even twice as difficult. That being said, reviewing tape kept mistakes to a minimum and, if two cornerbacks might have been confused for one other once or twice, such mistakes tend to cancel out.

INCOMPLETE PASSES: Quarterbacks are evaluated based on their ability to complete passes. However, not all incompletes should have the same weight. Throwing a ball away to avoid a sack is actually a valuable incomplete, and a receiver dropping an otherwise quality pass is hardly a reflection on the quarterback. Therefore, our charters marked the reason for every incomplete pass. Possible entries included Overthrown, Underthrown, Thrown Away, Tipped/Batted at Line, Hit in Motion (indicating the quarterback was hit as his arm was coming forward to make a pass), Defensed, Dropped, and a few others. Defensed was listed when the pass was incomplete as the direct result of actions by the defender. That action can include balls tipped or batted in coverage or hard hits that jar a ball loose. We also ask charters to track dropped interceptions by defenders.

(Note: Our count of passes defensed will be different from the unofficial totals kept by the league, as explained below in the section on Defensive Secondary tables.)

ADDITIONAL DETAILS: Charters marked each quarterback sack with one of the following terms: Blown Block, Coverage Sack, QB Fault, or Blitz/Overall Pressure. Blown Blocks were listed with the name of a specific offensive player who allowed the defender to come through. Coverage Sack denotes when the quarterback has plenty of time to throw but cannot find an open receiver. QB Fault represents "self sacks" listed without a defender, such as when the quarterback drops back, only to find the ball slip out of his hands with no pass-rusher touching him.

All draw plays were marked, whether by halfbacks or quarterbacks.

An additional column called Extra Comment allowed the charters to add any description they wanted to the play. These comments might be good blitz pickup by a running back, a missed tackle, a great hit, a description of a pass route, an angry tirade about the poor camera angles of network broadcasts, or a number of other possibilities.

Finally, we asked the game charters to mark when a mistake was made in the official play-by-play. The most common mistake was for an official scorer not to mark a quarterback hit, since that has only been tracked in the official play-by-play for two seasons. Other mistakes included incorrect names on tackles, penalties, or intended receivers, as well as missing direction on runs or passes, or the absence of the "scramble" designation when a quarterback ran on a play that began as a pass. Thanks to the diligence of our volunteer game charters and a friendly contact at the league office, the NFL corrected over 300 mistakes in the official play-by-play based on the data collected by our game charters.

ACKNOWLEDGEMENTS: None of this would have been possible without the time spent by all the volunteer game charters. There are some specific acknowledgements at the end of the book, but we want to give a general thank you here to everyone who has helped collect data over the last four seasons. Without your unpaid time, the task of gathering all this information would have been too time-consuming to yield anything useful. If you are interested in participating in next year's charting project, please e-mail your contact information to Bill Moore at charting@football-outsiders.com. Please make sure to mention where you live, what team you follow, and whether or not you have the Sunday Ticket package.

How to Read the Team Summary Box

Here is a rundown of all the tables and stats that appear in the 32 team chapters. Each team chapter begins with a box in the center of the page that gives a summary of our statistics for that team, as follows:

2008 Record gives each team's actual win-loss record. **Pythagorean Wins** gives the approximate number of wins expected last year based on this team's raw totals of points scored and allowed, along with their NFL rank. **DVOA** gives the team's total DVOA rating, with rank. **Offense**, **Defense**, and **Special Teams** list the team's DVOA rating in each category, along with NFL rank. Remember that good offenses and special teams have positive DVOA numbers, while a negative DVOA means better defense, so the lowest defensive DVOA is ranked number one (Pittsburgh).

Variance measures a team's consistency over the 2008 season. Teams are ranked from most consistent (Washington, first) to least consistent (Oakland, 32nd).

2009 Mean Projection gives the average number of wins for this team based on the 2009 Win Projection System described earlier in this chapter. The next few lines give the team's chances of finishing in the five different win categories.

Projected Average Opponent gives the team's strength of schedule for 2009 based not on last year's record but on the median projected DVOA for each opponent. A positive schedule is harder, a negative schedule easier. Teams are ranked from the hardest projected schedule (Denver, first) to the easiest (New England, 32nd for the second straight season). This strength of schedule projection does not take into account which games are home and which are away, or the timing of the bye week.

You'll also find a table with the team's 2009 schedule placed within each chapter. A handful of teams have a graph showing their week-to-week performance by single-game DVOA, along with a trendline with a longer-term view of when they were improving and declining. After the essays come statistical tables and comments related to that team and its specific units.

WEEKLY PERFORMANCE

The first table gives a quick look at the team's week-to-week performance in 2008. (Table 3) This includes the playoffs for those teams that made the postseason, with the four weeks of playoffs numbered 18 (wild card) through 21 (Super Bowl). All other tables in the team chapters represent regular-season performance only unless otherwise noted.

Looking at the first week for the Buffalo Bills in Week 1, the first five columns are fairly obvious: The Bills beat Seattle at home in Week 1, 34-10. **YDF** and **YDA** are net yards on offense and net yards against the defense. These numbers do not include penalty yardage or special teams yardage. **TO** represents the turn-

Table 3: 2008 Bills Stats by Week

Wk	vs.	W-L	PF	PA	YDF	YDA	TO	Total	Off	Def	ST
1	SEA	W	34	10	338	252	+2	47%	9%	-22%	16%
2	@JAC	W	20	16	285	243	0	36%	19%	-14%	3%
3	OAK	W	24	23	378	247	-2	-3%	14%	6%	-11%
4	@STL	W	31	14	277	380	+1	-17%	-14%	15%	11%
5	@ARI	L	17	41	287	373	-4	-65%	-33%	37%	4%
6	BYE										
7	SD	W	23	14	370	263	+3	68%	45%	-23%	-1%
8	@MIA	L	16	25	339	358	-3	-15%	-4%	11%	0%
9	NYJ	L	17	26	292	297	-2	-60%	-39%	18%	-4%
10	@NE	L	10	20	168	370	-1	-16%	-31%	6%	22%
11	CLE	L	27	29	334	337	-4	-15%	-18%	27%	30%
12	@KC	W	54	31	444	462	+5	-4%	16%	38%	17%
13	SF	L	3	10	350	195	0	-17%	-10%	-10%	-17%
14	MIA	L	3	16	163	295	-2	-66%	-63%	6%	3%
15	@NYJ	L	27	31	306	372	-2	-18%	-5%	33%	20%
16	@DEN	W	30	23	275	532	+2	10%	9%	15%	15%
17	NE	L	0	13	276	241	-1	-5%	-11%	-9%	-4%

over margin. Unlike other parts of the book in which we consider all fumbles as equal, this only represents actual turnovers: fumbles lost and interceptions. So, for example, the Bills forced three more turnovers than the Chargers when they beat San Diego in Week 7, then turned the ball over three more times than the Dolphins when Miami beat Buffalo in Week 8.

Finally, you'll see **DVOA** ratings for this game: Total DVOA first, then offense (**Off**), defense (**Def**), and special teams (**ST**). Note that these are DVOA ratings, adjusted for opponent. This is one reason why the Bills are listed with negative DVOA for their wins over Oakland and St. Louis early in the season.

TRENDS AND SPLITS

Next to the week-to-week performance is a table giving DVOA for different portions of a team's performance, on both offense and defense. Each split is listed with the team's rank among the 32 NFL teams. These numbers represent regular season performance only.

Total DVOA gives total offensive and defensive DVOA in all situations. **Unadjusted VOA** represents the breakdown of play-by-play considering situation but not opponent. A team whose offensive DVOA is higher than its offensive VOA played a harder-than-average schedule of opposing defenses; a team with a lower defensive DVOA than defensive VOA player a harder-than-average schedule of opposing offenses.

Weighted Trend lowers the importance of earlier games to give a better idea of how the team was playing at the end of the regular season. The final four weeks of the season are full strength; moving backwards through the season, each week is given less and less weight until the first three weeks of the season, which are not included at all. **Variance** is the same as noted above, with a higher percentage representing less consistency. This is true for both offense and defense: Tampa Bay, for example, had the league's most consistent offense (4.3%

variance) but the league's *least* consistent defense (15.3% variance).

Passing and **Rushing** are fairly self-explanatory. Note that rushing includes all rushes, not just those by running backs, including quarterback scrambles that may have began as pass plays.

The next three lines split out DVOA on **First Down**, **Second Down**, and **Third Down**. Third Down here includes fourth downs on which a team runs a regular offensive play instead of punting or attempting a field goal. **First Half** and **Second Half** represent the first two quarters and last two quarters (plus overtime), not the first eight and last eight games of the regular season. Next comes DVOA in the **Red Zone**, which is any offensive play starting from the defense's 20-yard line through the goal line. The final split is **Late and Close**, which includes any play in the second half or overtime when the teams are within eight points of each other in either direction. (Eight points, of course, is the biggest deficit that can be made up with a single score, a touchdown and two-point conversion.)

FIVE-YEAR PERFORMANCE

This table gives each team's performance over the past five seasons. (Table 4) It includes win-loss record, Pythagorean Wins, **Estimated Wins**, points scored and allowed, and turnover margin. Estimated wins are based on a formula that estimates how many games a team would have been expected to win based on 2008 performance in specific situations, normalized to eliminate luck (fumble recoveries, opponents' missed field goals, etc.) and assuming average schedule strength. The formula emphasizes consistency and overall DVOA as well as DVOA in the most important specific situations: red zone defense, first quarter offense, and performance in the second half when the score is close. The next columns of this table give total DVOA along with DVOA for offense, defense, and special teams, and the rank for each among that

Table 4: Detroit Lions Five-Year Performance

Year	W-L	Pyth	Est W	PF	PA	TO	Total	Rk	Off	Rk	Def	Rk	ST	Rk	Off AGL	Rk	Def AGL	Rk
2004	6-10	6.4	7.7	296	350	+4	-9.0%	21	15.0%	10	-11.7%	5	-2.4%	25	24.6	12	7.8	30
2005	5-11	5.2	5.8	254	345	+1	-22.5%	27	-18.5%	29	-0.3%	19	-4.3%	32	7.3	25	29.8	5
2006	3-13	5.6	5.6	305	398	-9	-22.1%	31	-13.4%	28	11.4%	28	2.7%	6	12.5	23	14.9	14
2007	7-9	5.7	6.3	346	444	-1	-29.2%	30	-9.5%	24	16.7%	32	-3.0%	23	24.5	10	4.7	31
2008	0-16	2.8	2.3	268	517	-9	-48.4%	32	-20.6%	30	29.2%	32	1.4%	14	44.3	6	60.7	1

season's 32 NFL teams.

The final four columns of the Five-Year Performance table are new in 2009 and give the **Adjusted Games Lost** for starters on both offense and defense. (Our total for starters here includes players who take over as starters due to another injury, such as Matt Cassel, as well as important situational players who may not necessarily start, such as Robert Mathis or Maurice Jones-Drew.) Adjusted Games Lost was introduced in *Pro Football Prospectus 2008*; it gives a weighted estimate of the probability that players would miss games based on how they are listed on the injury report. Unlike a count of "starter games missed," this accounts for the fact that a player listed as questionable who does in fact play is not playing at 100 percent capability. Teams are ranked from the most injuries (2008: Seattle on offense, Detroit on defense) to the fewest (2008: New York Giants on offense, Miami on defense).

INDIVIDUAL OFFENSIVE STATISTICS

Each team chapter contains a table giving passing and receiving numbers for any player who either threw five passes or was thrown five passes, along with rushing numbers for any players who carried the ball at least three times. These numbers also appear in the player comments at the end of the book (except for wide receiver rushing attempts). By putting them together in the team chapters we hope we make it easier to compare the performances of different players on the same team.

Players who are no longer on the team are marked with an asterisk. New players who were on a different team in 2008 are in italics. Changes should be accurate through mid-June. Rookies are not included.

All players are listed with DYAR and DVOA. Passing statistics then list total pass plays (**Plays**), net yardage (**NtYds**), and net yards per pass (**Avg**). These numbers include not just passes (and the positive yardage from them) but aborted snaps and sacks (and the negative yardage from them). Then comes average yards after catch (**YAC**) as determined by the game charting project. This average is based on charted receptions, not total pass attempts. The final three numbers are completion percentage (**C%**), which does not include aborted snaps or sacks, passing touchdowns (**TD**), and interceptions (**Int**).

Sample Passing Table

Player	DYAR	DVOA	Plays	NtYds	Avg	YAC	C%	TD	Int
Shaun Hill	180	-2.4%	313	1912	6.1	4.4	63.7%	13	8
J.T. O'Sullivan*	-414	-37.3%	257	1594	6.2	6.7	58.4%	8	11
Damon Huard	-228	-54.7%	90	414	4.6	4.0	62.5%	2	4

Rushing statistics start with DYAR and DVOA, then list rushing plays and net yards along with average yards per carry and rushing touchdowns. The final two columns are fumbles (**Fum**) — both those lost to the defense and those recovered by the offense — and Success Rate (**Suc**), explained earlier in this chapter. Fumbles listed in the rushing table include all quarterback fumbles on sacks and aborted snaps, as well as running back fumbles on receptions, but not wide receiver fumbles.

Sample Rushing Table

Player	DYAR	DVOA	Plays	Yds	Avg	TD	Fum	Suc
Tim Hightower	-79	-20.5%	143	400	2.8	10	1	37%
Edgerrin James*	46	0.0%	133	515	3.9	3	1	44%
J.J. Arrington*	44	31.2%	30	188	6.3	1	0	43%
Anquan Boldin	13	-9.7%	9	67	7.4	0	1	--

Receiving statistics start with DYAR and DVOA and then list the number of passes thrown to this receiver (**Plays**), the number of passes caught (**Catch**) and the total receiving yards (**Yds**). Yards per catch (**Y/C**) includes total yardage per reception, based on standard play-by-play, while yards after catch (**YAC**) is based on information from our game charting project. Finally we list total receiving touchdowns, and catch percentage (**C%**), which is the percentage of passes intended for this receiver that were caught. Wide receivers, tight ends, and running backs are separated on the table by horizontal lines.

Sample Receiving Table

Player	DYAR	DVOA	Plays	Ctch	Yds	Y/C	YAC	TD	C%
Steve Smith	365	22.7%	129	78	1421	18.2	5.5	6	60%
Muhsin Muhammad	160	6.1%	107	65	923	14.2	4.9	5	61%
D.J. Hackett	-20	-21.7%	28	13	190	14.6	6.1	0	46%
Dwayne Jarrett	1	-11.8%	19	10	119	11.9	2.9	0	53%
Jeff King	-7	-10.7%	34	21	195	9.3	3.8	1	62%
Dante Rosario	13	-0.9%	31	18	209	11.6	3.3	1	58%
DeAngelo Williams	-1	-14.5%	30	22	121	5.5	6.7	2	57%
Jonathan Stewart	-37	-49.5%	17	8	47	5.9	6.1	0	47%

An important note: Individual numbers in the team tables will differ from individual numbers in the player comments. The team tables feature our numbers, which are edited to remove plays such as kneeldowns, Hail Marys, and clock-stopping spikes, and include aborted snaps as passes rather than rush attempts. The tables in the player comment chapters at the end of the book contain the official NFL totals.

STRATEGIC TENDENCIES

The Strategic Tendencies table presents a mix of information garnered from both the standard play-by-play and the Football Outsiders game charting project. It gives you an idea of what kind of plays teams run in what situations and with what personnel. Each category is given a league-wide Rank from most often (1) to least often (32) except as noted below. The sample table shown here lists the NFL average in each category for 2008.

The first column of strategic tendencies lists how often teams ran in different situations. These ratios are based on the type of play, not the actual result, so quarterback scrambles count as "passes" while quarterback sneaks and draws count as "runs."

The first three entries are self-evident: **Runs** on **all plays**, in the **first half**, and on **first down**. **Runs, second-and-long** is the percentage of runs on second down with seven or more yards to go, giving you an idea of how teams follow up a failed first down. **Runs, power situations** is the percentage of runs on third or fourth down with 1 or 2 yards to go, or at the goal line with 1 or 2 yards to go. **Runs, behind 2H** tells you how often teams ran when they were behind in the second half, generally a passing situation. **Pass, ahead 2H** tells you how often teams passed when they had the lead in the second half, generally a running situation.

In each case, you can determine the percentage of plays that were passes by subtracting the run percent-age from 100 (the reverse being true for "Pass, ahead 2H," of course).

The second column gives information about offensive formations and strategy, as tracked by our game charters.

3+ WR/4+ WR: Plays with three or more wide receivers, and plays with four or more wide receivers. This may include a player normally identified as a tight end or running back lining up as a wide receiver.

2+ TE: Plays with multiple tight ends, including "H-backs."

Single back: Plays with only one running back, no matter the mixture of tight ends and wide receivers.

Play-action: The percentage of pass plays (including quarterback scrambles) which began with a play-action fake to the running back. This percentage does not include fake end-arounds unless there was also a fake handoff.

Max protect: The percentage of this team's passing plays (including quarterback scrambles) on which blockers outnumber pass rushers by at least two, with a minimum of seven blockers.

Outside pocket: The percentage of this team's passing plays in which the quarterback was listed as leaving the pocket on a rollout, bootleg, or unplanned scramble, no matter whether the play ended with a pass attempt, sack, or scramble for positive yardage.

The third column shows strategies used by the **Defense**.

Rush 3/Rush 4/Rush 5: The percentage of pass plays (including quarterback scrambles) on which our game charters recorded this team rushing the passer with three or fewer defenders, four defenders, or five defenders. These percentages do not include goal-line plays on the one- or two-yard line.

Rush 6+/Rush 7+: The percentage of pass plays (including quarterback scrambles) on which our game charters recorded this team rushing the passer with six or more defenders, as well as seven or more defenders. These are the only two of the pass-rush categories which overlap — plays included in "Rush 7+" are all included in "Rush 6+" as well. Again, these percentages do not include goal-line plays.

Sample Strategic Tendencies Table

Run/Pass		Rank	Offense		Rank	Defense		Rank	Other		Rank
Runs, all plays	44%	16	3+ WR	52%	16	Rush 3	6.3%	16	2+ RB, Pct Runs	61%	16
Runs, first half	44%	16	4+ WR	12%	16	Rush 4	63.9%	16	1 RB/2 TE, Pct Runs	51%	16
Runs, first down	51%	16	2+ TE	26%	16	Rush 5	21.3%	16	1RB/3+WR, Pct Runs	27%	16
Runs, second-long	39%	16	Single back	57%	16	Rush 6+	8.5%	16	Zone Blitz	4%	16
Runs, power sit.	65%	16	Play action	17%	16	Rush 7+	1.7%	16	Go for it on 4th	1.00	16
Runs, behind 2H	32%	16	Max protect	8%	16	Sacks by LB	26.3%	16	Offensive Pace	30.8	16
Pass, ahead 2H	42%	16	Outside pocket	12%	16	Sacks by DB	8.7%	16	Defensive Pace	30.8	16

Sacks by LB/Sacks by DB: The percentage of this team's sacks that came from linebackers and defensive backs. To figure out the percentage of sacks from defensive linemen, simply subtract the sum of these numbers from 100 percent.

The fourth column has data on run strategies that doesn't fit in the first column, and other assorted statistics.

2+ RB, Pct Runs: When this offense came out with two or three running backs, how often did they run the ball, as opposed to passing? Two running backs usually means a fullback and a halfback, but not necessarily. The percentage of runs does not include quarterback scrambles.

1 RB/2 TE, Pct Runs: The percentage of running plays when this offense came out with two tight ends and only one running back.

1 RB/3+ WR, Pct Runs: The percentage of running plays when this offense came out with three or four wide receivers and only one running back.

Zone blitz: The percentage of pass plays where this defense ran a zone blitz.

Go for it on fourth: This is the Aggressiveness Index (AI) introduced by Jim Armstrong in *Pro Football Prospectus 2006*, which measures how often a team goes for a first down in various fourth down situations compared to the league average. A coach over 1.00 is more aggressive, and one below 1.00 is less aggressive. Coaches are ranked from most aggressive to least aggressive.

Offensive Pace: Situation-neutral pace represents the seconds of game clock per offensive play, with the following restrictions: no drives are included if they start in the fourth quarter or final five minutes of the first half, and drives are only included if the score is within six points or less. Teams are ranked from quickest pace (Seattle, 26.9 seconds) to slowest pace (Miami, 33.7 seconds).

Defensive Pace: Situation-neutral pace based on seconds of game clock per defensive play. This is a representation of how a defense was approached by its opponents, not the strategy of the defense itself (an issue discussed in the Indianapolis chapter of *PFP 2006*). Teams are ranked from quickest pace (San Francisco, 29.0 seconds) to slowest pace (Cleveland, 32.2 seconds).

Veteran readers may notice that an entry from previous years, "CB1 on WR1," is missing. For a variety of reasons (injuries, zone coverage, player roles changing during the season), very few teams actually had one player who was easily identified as the "number one cornerback" for most of the season. Therefore, the

numbers for this metric would have been fairly useless. We hope to bring it back in 2010.

Following each strategic tendencies table, you'll find a series of comments highlighting interesting data from that team's charting numbers. This includes DVOA ratings split for things like different formations, draw plays, or play-action passing. Please note that all DVOA ratings given in these comments are standard DVOA with no adjustments for the specific situation being analyzed, and the average DVOA for a specific situation will not necessarily be 0%. For example, the average DVOA on play-action passes in 2008 was 28.2%, while the average DVOA when the quarterback was hurried (but not sacked) was -37.2%.

HOW TO READ THE OFFENSIVE LINE TABLES

The offensive line tables list the last three years of Adjusted Line Yards and other statistics for each team (Table 5).

The first column gives standard yards per carry by each team's running backs (**Yds**). The next two columns give Adjusted Line Yards (**ALY**) followed by rank among the 32 teams.

Then come three other rushing statistics. **Power** gives the percentage of runs in "power situations" that achieved a first down or touchdown. Those situations include any third or fourth down with one or two yards to go, and any runs in goal-to-go situations from the two-yard line or closer. Unlike the other rushing numbers on the Offensive Line table, Power includes quarterbacks.

10+ Yards gives the percentage of a team's rushing yards that came more than 10 yards past the line of scrimmage. A team with a high ranking in Adjusted Line Yards but a low ranking in 10+ Yards is heavily dependent on its offensive line to make the running game work. A team with a low ranking in Adjusted Line Yards but a high ranking in 10+ Yards is heavily dependent on its running back breaking long runs to make the running game work, and therefore tends to have a less consistent running attack.

Stuff gives the percentage of runs that are stuffed for zero or negative gain. In past years, we had a more complex definition of being "stuffed," but we've simplified things for 2009. Since being stuffed is bad, teams are ranked from stuffed least often (New England, 1st) to most often (Cincinnati, 32nd).

Table 5: Minnesota Vikings Offensive Line

Year	Yards	ALY	Rank	Power	Rank	10+ Yds	Rank	Stuff	Rank	Sacks	ASR	Rank	False	Cont.
2006	4.20	4.25	13	68%	12	16%	14	18%	18	43	7.7%	22	20	36
2007	5.44	4.18	13	76%	2	32%	1	22%	28	38	8.6%	28	21	42
2008	4.63	4.13	12	73%	8	25%	4	19%	21	43	8.9%	28	16	32

Year	LE	Rank	LT	Rank	Mid	Rank	RT	Rank	RE	Rank
2006	2.95	26	4.79	6	4.29	15	4.46	5	5.07	5
2007	4.64	9	4.17	20	4.27	9	4.04	21	3.45	26
2008	4.27	15	4.69	7	4.06	19	3.59	27	4.33	8

The next two columns give Adjusted Sack Rate (**ASR**) and its rank among the 32 teams. Some teams allow a lot of sacks because they throw a lot of passes; Adjusted Sack Rate accounts for this by dividing sacks and intentional grounding by total pass plays. It is also adjusted for situation (sacks are much more common on third down, particularly third-and-long) and opponent, all of which makes it a better measurement than raw sack totals. Remember that quarterbacks share responsibility for sacks, and two different quarterbacks behind the same line can have very different Adjusted Sack Rates. Particularly if one is named Rob Johnson.

The final two columns in the first part of the table are new for 2009. **False** gives the number of false starts, which is the offensive penalty which best correlates to both wins and wins the following season. This total includes false starts by players other than offensive linemen, but it does not include false starts on special teams. False starts in 2008 ranged from 10 to 32, with the NFL average at 19.1. Finally, Continuity Score (**Cont.**) tells you how much continuity each offensive line had from game-to-game in that season. It was introduced in the Cleveland chapter of *Pro Football Prospectus 2007*; Continuity score starts with 48 and then subtracts:

• The number of players over five who started at least one game on the offensive line;

• The number of times the team started at least one different lineman compared to the game before; and

• The difference between 16 and that team's longest streak where the same line started consecutive games.

The perfect Continuity Score is 48, achieved in 2008 by Arizona, Chicago, Denver, Houston, and both New York teams. The lowest Continuity Score belonged to Detroit (21) and the NFL average was 34.

The second part of the Offensive Line table gives Adjusted Line Yards in each of the five directions with rank among the 32 teams. Note that the league average is higher on the left than the right. Specifically in 2008, the league average was 4.16 on left end runs (**LE**), 4.18 on left tackle runs (**LT**), 4.14 on runs up the middle (**MID**), 4.10 on right tackle runs (**RT**), and 3.90 on right end runs (**RE**).

HOW TO READ THE DEFENSIVE FRONT SEVEN TABLES

Defensive players make plays. Plays aren't just tackles—interceptions and pass deflections change the course of the game, and so does the act of forcing a fumble or beating the offensive players to a fumbled ball. While some plays stop a team on third down and force a punt, others merely stop a receiver after he's caught a 30-yard pass. We still cannot measure each player's opportunities to make a tackle. We can measure a linebacker's opportunities in pass coverage, however, thanks to the Football Outsiders game charting project.

DEFENSIVE LINEMEN: Defensive linemen are listed in the team chapters if they made at least 15 plays during the 2008 season. Players are listed with the following numbers:

Age: The player's age, listed simply as the difference between birth year and 2009. Players born in January and December of the same year will have the same listed age.

Position (**Pos**): The player's position on the line.

Plays (**Plays**): The total defensive plays including tackles, pass deflections, interceptions, fumbles forced, and fumble recoveries. This number comes from the official NFL gamebooks and therefore does not include plays on which the player is listed by the Football Outsiders game charting project as in coverage, but does not appear in the standard play-by-play. Special teams tackles are also not included.

Table 6: Jacksonville Jaguars Defensive Line

Defensive Line	Age	Pos	Plays	TmPct	Rk	Stop	Dfts	Overall Stop%	Rk	AvYd	Rk	Pass Rush Sack	Hit	Hur	vs. Run Runs	St%	Yds	vs. Pass Pass	St%	Yds
John Henderson	30	DT	46	7.0%	7	37	10	80%	20	1.8	32	2.0	2	2	38	76%	2.3	8	100%	-0.1
Paul Spicer*	34	DE	36	4.8%	57	32	9	89%	5	0.9	19	3.5	4	4	29	86%	1.7	7	100%	-2.4
Rob Meier	32	DT	30	4.3%	49	25	12	83%	8	0.7	8	2.0	3	3	27	81%	1.1	3	100%	-3.0
Reggie Hayward	30	DE	27	3.6%	79	26	20	96%	1	-1.3	2	4.5	7	6	17	94%	-0.2	10	100%	-3.1
Derrick Harvey	23	DE	20	2.7%	--	18	10	90%	--	0.1	--	3.5	4	5	11	82%	0.5	9	100%	-0.4
Tony McDaniel*	24	DT	19	4.1%	--	15	2	79%	--	2.2	--	0.5	1	1	15	80%	2.8	4	75%	0.0

Percentage of Team Plays (**TmPct**): The percentage of total team plays involving this defender. The sum of the percentages of team plays for all defenders on a given team will exceed 100 percent, primarily due to shared tackles. This number is adjusted based on games played, so an injured player may be fifth on his team in plays but third in **TmPct**.

Stops (**Stop**): The total number of plays which prevent a "success" by the offense (45 percent of needed yards on first down, 60 percent on second down, 100 percent on third or fourth down).

Defeats (**Dfts**): The total number of plays which stop the offense from gaining first down yardage on third or fourth down, stop the offense behind the line of scrimmage, or result in a fumble (regardless of which team recovers) or interception.

Stop Rate (**StpRt**): The percentage of all Plays that are Stops.

Average Yards (**AvYds**): The average number of yards gained by the offense when this player is credited with making the play. Note that passes defensed count as zero yards.

Sack: Standard NFL sack totals.

Hit: To qualify as a quarterback hit, the defender must knock the quarterback to the ground in the act of throwing or after the pass is thrown. We have listed hits on all plays, including those cancelled by penalties. (After all, many of the hardest hits come on plays cancelled because the hit itself draws a roughing the passer penalty.) Small adjustments are made to the hit totals based on the tendencies of certain official scorers to inconsistently mark hits.

Hurries (**Hur**): The number of quarterback hurries recorded by the Football Outsiders game charting project. This includes both hurries on standard plays and hurries that force an offensive holding penalty that cancels the play and costs the offense yardage. Because our game charters are not entirely consistent, hurries are adjusted based on which FO game charter was doing the game in question (although these ad-justments are smaller than in past seasons).

Finally, we split our stats for defensive linemen into **Run** plays and **Pass** plays. Pass plays include sacks, tackles after completions, and pass deflections. We list separate Stop Rate for passes (**PaStp**) and runs (**RuStp**) as well as separate average yards for passes (**PaYds**) and runs (**RuYds**).

Defensive linemen are ranked by percentage of team plays, Stop Rate, and average yards. The lowest number of average yards earns the top rank (negative numbers indicate the average play ending behind the line of scrimmage). Except for pass-rush specialists, most linemen do not have enough pass plays to make separate rankings of pass and run statistics viable. Defensive ends are ranked if they made 24 or more plays during 2008 (with an exception made to rank Tennessee's Kyle Vanden Bosch). There are 93 defensive ends who qualify. Defensive tackles are ranked if they made 20 or more plays during 2008, with 74 players ranked.

LINEBACKERS: Linebackers are listed in team chapters if they made at least 20 plays during the season. Most of the stats for linebackers are the same as those for defensive linemen. The listings of both total plays and percentage of team plays are based on standard play-by-play. Average yards on the left side of the table is also based on standard play-by-play, and gives us a good indication of which linebackers play closer to the line of scrimmage, and which players drop into coverage.

Linebackers are ranked in percentage of team plays, and also in Stop Rate and average yards for running plays specifically. Linebackers are ranked in these standard stats if they made at least 46 plays during the 2008 season. Outside, inside (3-4), and middle (4-3) linebackers are all ranked together, with 99 players ranked in total. This does mean a handful of starting linebackers are not ranked, primarily outside linebackers who didn't play a full season.

The final five columns in the linebacker stats come from the Football Outsiders game charting project.

Table 7: New England Patriots Linebackers

Linebackers	Age	Pos	Plays	TmPct	Rk	Stop	Dfts	Stop%	AvYd	Sack	Hit	Hur	Runs	St%	Rk	Yds	Rk	Tgts	Suc%	Rk	AdjYd	Rk
						Overall				**Pass Rush**			**vs. Run**					**vs. Pass**				
Jerod Mayo	23	ILB	130	17.6%	6	55	12	42%	5.9	0.0	1	3	74	54%	94	4.1	79	38	59%	17	5.1	20
Tedy Bruschi	36	ILB	77	12.9%	34	48	5	62%	3.0	0.0	1	3	66	65%	47	2.7	17	5	43%	--	4.7	--
Mike Vrabel*	34	OLB	66	9.0%	78	47	15	71%	2.2	4.0	7	9	49	76%	12	1.9	3	18	63%	8	5.1	18
Adalius Thomas	32	OLB	36	8.7%	--	26	9	72%	1.6	5.0	3	4	20	80%	--	2.9	--	15	58%	--	5.6	--
Gary Guyton	24	ILB	28	4.1%	--	16	6	57%	5.4	0.0	1	4	17	65%	--	4.8	--	12	56%	--	5.1	--
Pierre Woods	27	OLB	27	4.9%	--	16	7	59%	4.9	1.0	2	2	15	73%	--	3.0	--	8	41%	--	5.9	--
Junior Seau*	40	ILB	21	11.4%	--	13	3	62%	3.4	0.0	0	1	17	76%	--	2.6	--	7	27%	--	14.6	--

Targets (**Tgts**): The number of pass plays on which our game charters listed this player in coverage.

Success Rate (**Suc%**): The percentage plays of targeting this player on which the offense did not have a successful play. This means not only incomplete passes and interceptions, but also short completions which do not meet our baselines for success (45 percent of needed yards on first down, 60 percent on second down, 100 percent on third or fourth down). This year, unlike in our two previous books, Success Rate is adjusted for the quality of the receiver covered.

Adjusted Yards per Pass (**PaYd**): The average number of yards gained on plays on which this defender was the listed target, adjusted for the quality of the receiver covered.

These stats are explained in more detail below, in the section on secondary tables. Plays listed with two defenders or as "Hole in Zone" with this defender as the closest player count only for half credit in computing both Success Rate and Average Yards per Pass. Eighty-nine linebackers are ranked in the charting stats, with a minimum of 16 charted passes. As a result of the different thresholds, some linebackers are ranked in standard stats but not charting stats, or vice versa.

FURTHER DETAILS: Just as we did in the offensive tables, players who are no longer on the team are marked with asterisks, and players who were on other teams last year are in italics. Other than the game charting statistics for linebackers, defensive front seven player statistics are not adjusted for opponent.

Numbers for defensive linemen and linebackers unfortunately do not reflect all of the opportunities a player had to make a play, but they do show us which players were most active on the field. A large number of plays could mean a strong defensive performance, or it could mean that the linebacker in question plays behind a poor part of the line. In general, defensive numbers should be taken as information that tells us what happened on the field in 2008, but not as a strict, unassailable judgment of which players are better than others — particularly when the difference between two players is small (for example, players ranked 20th and 30th) instead of large (players ranked 20th and 70th).

After the individual statistics for linemen and linebackers, the Defensive Front Seven section contains a table that looks exactly like the table in the Offensive Line section. The difference is that the numbers here are for all opposing running backs against this team's defensive front. As we're on the opposite side of the ball, teams are now ranked in the opposite order, so the number one Defensive Front Seven is the one that allows the fewest adjusted line yards (Baltimore), the lowest percentage in Power situations (Pittsburgh), and has the highest Adjusted Sack Rate (Dallas). Directions for Adjusted Line Yards are given from the offense's perspective, so runs left end and left tackle are aimed at the right defensive end and (assuming the tight end is on the other side) weak side linebacker.

HOW TO READ THE SECONDARY TABLES

The first few columns in the secondary tables are based on standard play-by-play, not game charting. Age, Total Plays, Percentage of Team Plays, Stops, and Defeats are computed the same way they are for other defensive players, so that the secondary can be compared to the defensive line and linebackers. That means that Total Plays here includes passes defended, sacks, tackles after receptions or on runs, tipped passes, and interceptions, but not pass plays on which this player was in coverage but was not given a tackle or passed defense by the NFL's official scorer.

The middle four columns address each defensive back's role in stopping the run. Average Yardage and

Table 7: Cleveland Browns Defensive Secondary

Secondary	Age	Pos	Plays	TmPct	Rk	Stop	Dfts	Yds	Rk	St%	Rk	Tgts	Tgt%	Rk	Dist	Suc%	Rk	AdjYd	Rk	Yds	PD	Int
				Overall					vs. Run							vs. Pass						
Brandon McDonald	24	CB	90	10.6%	15	41	18	6.1	34	64%	13	86	23.2%	8	13.2	46%	56	8.7	73	8.6	16	5
Eric Wright	24	CB	78	9.2%	33	37	14	8.4	57	74%	4	82	22.1%	17	11.2	46%	60	7.9	53	7.8	13	3
Brodney Pool	25	FS	70	8.8%	53	24	15	7.9	58	37%	50	36	10.4%	4	12.2	50%	45	8.6	53	8.6	5	3
Sean Jones*	27	SS	60	9.4%	44	24	8	8.0	60	49%	18	15	5.2%	64	11.7	46%	62	9.1	56	9.5	4	4
Mike Adams	28	FS	43	5.8%	71	6	4	7.9	57	17%	75	16	4.8%	69	17.2	28%	78	13.1	76	12.7	2	2
Terry Cousin*	34	CB	29	3.4%	--	10	6	7.6	--	22%	--	30	8.1%	--	8.1	44%	--	7.9	--	7.8	2	1
Abram Elam	28	SS	63	7.6%		18	9	7.2	43	32%	61	21	4.4%	70	11.5	50%	48	10.3	67	10.1	4	1
Roderick Hood	28	CB	54	7.4%	60	23	5	15.2	81	17%	77	85	22.0%	18	12.6	45%	61	8.0	54	7.7	13	1
Corey Ivy	32	CB	47	6.4%	67	23	14	6.3	38	44%	42	49	11.2%	76	11.3	49%	47	7.5	43	7.3	2	0
Hank Poteat	32	CB	40	5.9%	--	16	6	7.6	--	63%	--	29	7.5%	--	6.0	50%	--	6.7	--	6.2	3	2

Year	Pass D Rank	vs. #1 WR	Rk	vs. #2 WR	Rk	vs. Other WR	Rk	vs. TE	Rk	vs. RB	Rk
2006	4	-23.6%	2	28.6%	30	-20.2%	7	-2.8%	17	-18.9%	10
2007	13	-32.3%	1	28.9%	31	5.0%	23	-10.4%	7	7.6%	25
2008	13	-19.6%	2	31.0%	29	-0.4%	22	-16.6%	5	3.8%	14

Stop Rate for running plays is computed in the same manner as it is for defensive linemen and linebackers.

The third section of statistics represents data from the game charting project:

Targets (**Trgt**): The number of pass plays on which our game charters listed this player in coverage. This number gives full credit to all passes, including those on which two defenders are listed and those listed as "Hole in Zone" with this player as the closest zone defender (both of those count as half credit in the other stats below). We do not count pass plays on which this player was in coverage, but the incomplete was listed as Thrown Away, Tipped at Line, or Hit in Motion.

Target Percentage (**Tgt%**): The number of plays on which this player was targeted divided by the total number of charted passes against his defense, not including plays listed as Uncovered. Like Percentage of Team Plays, this metric is adjusted based on number of games played.

Distance (**Dist**): The average distance in the air beyond the line of scrimmage of all passes targeted at this defender. It does not include yards after catch, and is useful for seeing which defenders were covering receivers deeper or shorter.

Success Rate (**Suc%**): The percentage of plays targeting this player on which the offense did not have a successful play. This means not only incomplete passes and interceptions, but also short completions which do not meet our baselines for success (45 percent of needed yards on first down, 60 percent on second down, 100 percent on third or fourth down). Defensive pass interference is counted as a failure for the defensive player, similar to a completion of equal yardage (and a new first down).

Average Yards per Pass (**PaYd**): The average number of yards gained on plays on which this defender was the listed target.

Passes Defensed (**PD**): This is our count of passes defensed, and will differ from the total found in NFL gamebooks. Our count includes:

• All passes listed by our charters as Defensed.

• All interceptions, or tipped passes leading to interceptions.

• All passes defensed listed in the NFL gamebooks for games which remain uncharted.

• Any pass on which the defender is given a pass defensed by the official scorer, and the game charter listed a reason for incomplete which can be hard to differentiate from a pass defensed, including: Dropped, Miscommunication, and Catch Out of Bounds.

Our count of passes defensed does not include passes marked as defensed in the official gamebooks but listed by our charters as Overthrown, Underthrown, or Thrown Away. It also does not include passes tipped in the act of rushing the passer.

Interceptions (**Int**): Standard NFL interception total.

Cornerbacks need 40 charted passes or eight games started to be ranked in the defensive stats, with 83 cornerbacks ranked in total. Safeties are ranked if they had either 16 charted passes or at least 12 charted passes with at least 12 run tackles. Seventy-eight safeties are ranked in total, with strong safeties and free safeties ranked together.

Just like the front seven, the secondary has a table of team statistics following the individual numbers. This table gives DVOA figured against different types of receivers. Each offense's wide receivers have had one receiver designated as number one, and another as number two. (Occasionally this is difficult, due to injury or an amorphous wide receiver corps like last year's Jaguars, but it's usually pretty obvious.) The other receivers form a third category, with tight ends and running backs as fourth and fifth categories. The defense is then judged on the performance of each receiver based on the standard DVOA method, with each rating adjusted based on strength of schedule. (Opponents with Randy Moss and Larry Fitzgerald as top receivers, for example, are tougher than an opponent with Johnnie Lee Higgins as its number one receiver.) **Pass D Rank** is the total ranking of the pass defense, as seen before in the Trends and Splits table, and combines all five categories plus sacks and passes with no intended target.

The defensive secondary table should be used to analyze the defense as a whole rather than individual players. The ratings against types of receivers are generally based on defensive schemes, not specific cornerbacks — although there are exceptions, like the team in our sample, the Oakland Raiders — and the ratings against tight ends and running backs are in large part due to the performance of linebackers.

HOW TO READ THE SPECIAL TEAMS TABLES

The special teams tables list the last three years of kick, punt, and return numbers for each team.

The first two columns list total special teams DVOA and rank among the 32 teams. The next two columns list the value in actual points of field goals and extra points (**FG/XP**) when compared to how a league average kicker would do from the same distances, adjusted for weather and altitude, and rank among the 32 teams. Next, we list the estimated value in actual points of field position over or under the league average based on net punting (**Net Punt**), and rank that value among the 32 teams. That is followed by the estimated point values of field position for punt returns (**Punt Ret**), net kickoffs (**Net Kick**), and kick returns (**Kick Ret**) and their respective ranks.

The final two columns represent the value of **"Hidden"** special teams, plays which throughout the past decade have usually been based on the performance of opponents without this team being able to control the outcome. We combine the opposing team's value on field goals, kickoff distance, and punt distance, adjusted for weather and altitude, and then switch the sign to represent that good special teams by the opponent will cost the listed team points, and bad special teams will effectively hand them points. We have to give the qualifier of "usually" because, as explained above, certain returners like Devin Hester and Josh Cribbs will affect opposing special teams strategy. Nonetheless, the "hidden" value is still "hidden" for most teams, and they are ranked from the most hidden value gained (Tennessee, 20.4 points) to the most value lost (St. Louis, -16.6 points). The best and worst individual values for kickers, punters, and returners are listed in the statistical appendix at the end of the book.

ADMINISTRATIVE MINUTIAE

Receiving statistics include all passes intended for the receiver in question, including those that are incomplete or intercepted. The word "passes" refers to both complete and incomplete pass attempts. When rating receivers, interceptions are treated as incomplete passes with no penalty.

For the computation of DVOA and DYAR, passing statistics include sacks as well as fumbles on aborted snaps. We do not include kneeldown plays or spikes for the purpose of stopping the clock. Some interceptions which we have determined to be "Hail Mary" plays that end the first half or game are counted as regular incomplete passes, not turnovers.

All mentions of yards after catch, hurries, hits, blitzes, and screens come from the Football Outsiders game charting project and may be different from totals compiled by other sources.

Unless we say otherwise, when we refer to third-down performance in this book we are referring to a combination of third down and the handful of rushing and passing plays that take place on fourth down (primarily fourth-and-1).

Aaron Schatz

Special Teams

Year	DVOA	Rank	FG/XP	Rank	Net Punt	Rank	Punt Ret	Rank	Net Kick	Rank	Kick Ret	Rank	Hidden	Rank
2005	7.2%	1	3.6	11	7.5	5	0.4	12	3.8	12	27.2	1	8.9	4
2006	5.9%	2	8.5	4	16.1	1	6.6	3	-2.0	25	5.5	6	-2.2	16
2007	4.1%	6	5.9	4	7.2	4	11.3	3	-2.2	19	2.1	14	-1.4	17

Pregame Show

In the six years since we launched FootballOutsiders.com, we've done a lot of primary research on the National Football League, and we reference that research in many of the articles and comments in *Football Outsiders Almanac 2009*. New readers may come across an offhand comment in a team chapter about, for example, the idea that fumble recovery is not a skill, and wonder what in the heck we are talking about. We can't repeat all our research in every new edition of *Football Outsiders Almanac*, so we start each year with a basic look at some of the most important precepts that have emerged from Football Outsiders research. You will see these issues come up again and again throughout the book.

You can also find this introduction online at http://www.footballoutsiders.com/pregame.php, along with links to the original research in the cases in which that research appeared online instead of (or as well as) in print.

You run when you win, not win when you run.

If we could only share one piece of anti-conventional wisdom with you before you read the rest of our book, this would be it. The first article ever written for Football Outsiders was devoted to debunking the myth of "establishing the run." There is no correlation whatsoever between giving your running backs a lot of carries early in the game and winning the game. Just running the ball is not going to help a team score; it has to run successfully.

There are two reasons why nearly every beat writer and television analyst still repeats the tired old school mantra that "establishing the run" is the secret to winning football games. The first problem is confusing cause and effect. There are exceptions — usually involving the Indianapolis Colts without Bob Sanders — but, in general, winning teams have a lot of carries because their running backs are running out the clock at the end of wins, not because they are running wild early in games.

The second problem is history. Most of the current crop of NFL analysts came of age or actually played the game during the 1970s. They believe that the run-heavy game of that decade is how football is meant to be, and today's pass-first game is an aberration. It was actually the game of the 1970s that was the aberration. The seventies were far more slanted towards the run than any era since the arrival of Paul Brown, Otto Graham, and the Cleveland Browns in 1946. Optimal strategies from 1974 are not optimal strategies for 2009.

A sister statement to "you have to establish the run" is "team X is 5-1 when running back John Doe runs for at least 100 yards." Unless John Doe is ripping off six-yard gains Adrian Peterson-style, the team isn't winning because of his 100-yard games. He's putting up 100-yard games because his team is winning.

A great defense against the run is nothing without a good pass defense.

This is a corollary to the absurdity of "establish the run." With rare exceptions, teams win or lose with the passing game more than the running game — and by stopping the passing game more than the running game. Ron Jaworski puts it best: "The pass gives you the lead, and the run solidifies it." The reason why teams need a strong run defense in the playoffs is not to shut the run down early; it's to keep the other team from icing the clock if they get a lead. You can't mount a comeback if you can't stop the run.

Note that "good pass defense" may mean "good pass rush" rather than "good defensive backs."

Running on third-and-short is more likely to convert than passing on third-and-short.

On average, passing will always gain more yardage than running, with one very important exception: When a team is just one or two yards away from a new set of downs or the goal line. On third-and-1, a run will convert for a new set of downs 36 percent more often than a pass. Expand that to all third or fourth downs with 1 or 2 yards to go, and the run is successful 40 percent more often. With these percentages, the possibility of a long gain with a pass is not worth the tradeoff of an incomplete that kills a drive.

This is one reason why teams have to be able to both run and pass. The offense also has to keep some semblance of balance so they can use their play-action fakes, and so the defense doesn't just run their nickel and dime packages all game. Balance also means that teams do need to pass occasionally in short-yardage situations; they just need to do it less than they do now. Teams pass roughly 60 percent of the time on third-and-2 even though runs in that situation convert 20 percent more often than passes. They pass 68 percent of the time on fourth-and-2 even though runs in that situation convert twice as often as passes.

Standard team rankings based on total yardage are inherently flawed.

When you open your newspaper on Sunday morning, you'll see that the little agate-type previews of each game list team rankings by total yardage. That is still how the NFL "officially" ranks teams, but these rankings rarely match up with common sense. That is because total team yardage may be the most context-dependent number in football.

It starts with the basic concept that rate stats are generally more valuable than cumulative stats. Yards per carry says more about a running back's quality than total yardage, completion percentage says more than just a quarterback's total number of completions. The same thing is true for teams; in fact, it is even more important because of the way football strategy influences the number of runs and passes in the game plan. Poor teams will give up fewer passing yards and more rushing yards because opponents will stop passing once they have a late-game lead and will run out the clock instead. For winning teams, the opposite is true. Did Tampa Bay really have a better passing game than Atlanta did last year? Or did Tampa Bay have more passing yards because they threw the ball 128 more times than the Falcons did?

Total yardage rankings are also skewed because some teams play at a faster pace than other teams. Last year, Tampa Bay had 100 more total yards than Indianapolis, but that's not because Tampa Bay was the better offense. The Colts ran only 144 offensive drives last year, compared to 183 offensive drives for the Buccaneers.

A team will score more when playing a bad defense, and will give up more points when playing a good offense.

This sounds absurdly basic, but when people consider team and player stats without looking at strength of schedule, they are ignoring this. In 2004, Carson Palmer and Byron Leftwich had very similar num-bers, but Palmer faced a much tougher schedule than Leftwich did. Palmer was better that year, and better in the long run. Last year, Michael Turner had two games with at least 200 rushing yards — they came against the defenses ranked 31st (Detroit) and 32nd (St. Louis) in DVOA against the run. Jamal Lewis had four games with fewer than 50 rushing yards, but all four came against teams ranked sixth in run defense DVOA or higher (Baltimore, Philadelphia, Pittsburgh, and Tennessee).

If their overall yards per carry are equal, a running back who consistently gains yardage on every play is more valuable than a boom-and-bust running back who is frequently stuffed at the line but occasionally breaks a long highlight-worthy run.

Our brethren at Baseball Prospectus believe that the most precious commodity in baseball is outs. Teams only get 27 of them per game, and you can't afford to give one up for very little return. So imagine if there was a new rule in baseball that gave a team a way to earn another three outs in the middle of the inning. That would be pretty useful, right?

That's the way football works. You may start a drive 80 yards away from scoring, but as long as you can earn 10 yards in four chances, you get another four chances. Long gains have plenty of value, but if those long gains are mixed with a lot of short gains, you are going to put the quarterback in a lot of difficult third-and-long situations. That means more punts and more giving the ball back to the other team rather than moving the chains and giving the offense four more plays to work with.

The running back who gains consistent yardage is also going to do a lot more for you late in the game, when the goal of running the ball is not just to gain yardage but to eat clock time. If you are an Arizona fan watching your team with a late lead, you don't want to see three straight Tim Hightower stuffs at the line followed by a punt. You want to see a game-icing first down.

A common historical misconception is that our preference for consistent running backs means that "Football Outsiders believes that Barry Sanders was overrated." Sanders wasn't just any boom-and-bust running back, though; he was the greatest boom-and-bust runner of all time, with bigger booms and fewer busts. Our play-by-play database currently goes back to 1994, but Sanders ranked second in DYAR three times (1994, 1996, and 1997).

Rushing is more dependent on the offensive line than people realize, but pass protection is more dependent on the quarterback himself than people realize.

Some readers complain that this idea contradicts the previous one. Aren't those consistent running backs just the product of good offensive lines? The truth is somewhere in between. There are certainly good running backs who suffer because their offensive lines cannot create consistent holes, but most boom-and-bust running backs contribute to their own problems by hesitating behind the line whenever the hole is unclear, looking for the home run instead of charging forward for the four-yard gain that keeps the offense moving.

As for pass protection, some quarterbacks have better instincts for the rush than others, and are thus better at getting out of trouble by moving around in the pocket or throwing the ball away. Others will hesitate, hold onto the ball too long, and lose yardage over and over.

Note that "moving around in the pocket" does not necessarily mean "scrambling." In fact, a scrambling quarterback will often take more sacks than a pocket quarterback, because while he's running around trying to make something happen, a defensive lineman will catch up with him.

Shotgun formations are generally more efficient than formations with the quarterback under center.

Over the past two seasons, offenses have averaged 5.9 yards per play from shotgun, but just 5.1 yards per play with the quarterback under center. In 2006, the difference was even greater, with 6.4 yards per play from shotgun and just under 5.0 yards per play with the quarterback under center. This wide split exists even if you analyze the data to try to weed out biases like teams using shotgun more often on third-and-long, or against prevent defenses in the fourth quarter. Shotgun offense is more efficient if you only look at the first half, on every down, and even if you only look at running back carries rather than passes and scrambles.

Clearly, NFL teams have figured the importance of the shotgun out for themselves. Over the past three seasons, the average team has gone from using shotgun 19 percent of the time to 32 percent of the time. Before 2007, no team had ever used shotgun on more than half its offensive plays; last year, three teams did. It is likely that if teams continue to increase their usage of the shotgun, defenses will adapt and the benefit of the formation will become less pronounced.

A running back with 370 or more carries during the regular season will usually suffer either a major injury or a loss of effectiveness the following year, unless he is named Eric Dickerson.

Terrell Davis, Jamal Anderson, and Edgerrin James all blew out their knees. Larry Johnson broke his foot. Earl Campbell and Eddie George went from legendary powerhouses to plodding, replacement-level players. Shaun Alexander broke his foot *and* became a plodding, replacement-level player. This is what happens when a running back is overworked to the point of having at least 370 carries during the regular season.

The "Curse of 370" was expanded in *Pro Football Prospectus 2005*, and now includes seasons with 390 or more carries in the regular season and postseason combined. Research also shows that receptions don't cause a problem, only workload on the ground.

Plenty of running backs get injured without hitting 370 carries in a season, but there is a clear difference. On average, running backs with 300 to 369 carries and no postseason appearance will see their total rushing yardage decline by 15 percent the following year and their yards per carry decline by two percent. The average running back with 370 or more regular-season carries, or 390 including the postseason, will see their rushing yardage decline by 35 percent, and their yards per carry decline by eight percent.

(Just to be clear, 370 carries is not an automatic line where all backs over the mark are guaranteed to get injured; it just happens to be a handy marker that estimates the point where overuse becomes a much larger problem.)

Wide receivers must be judged on both complete and incomplete passes.

We don't yet know enough to precisely parse the blame for incomplete passes, but we know that wide receiver catch rates are as consistent from year to year as quarterback completion percentages. Since 2001, Hines Ward has never had caught fewer than 59 percent of intended passes, whether from Kordell Stewart, Tommy Maddox, or Ben Roethlisberger. Plaxico Burress, playing with the same quarterbacks as well as with Eli Manning, has never caught more than 58 percent of intended passes, and in three different years had a catch rate below 50 percent.

The total quality of an NFL team is three parts offense, three parts defense, and one part special teams.

There are three units on a football team, but they are not of equal importance. Our DVOA ratings provide good evidence for this. The special teams ratings are turned into DVOA by comparing how often field position on special teams leads to scoring compared to field position and first downs on offense. After figuring out these numbers, the top ratings for special teams are roughly one-third as high as the top ratings for offense or defense.

Offense is more consistent from year to year than defense, and offensive performance is easier to project than defensive performance. Special teams is less consistent than either.

Nobody in the NFL understands this concept better than Indianapolis Colts general manager Bill Polian. Both the Super Bowl champion Colts and the four-time AFC champion Buffalo Bills of the early 1990s were built around the idea that if you put together an offense that can dominate the league year after year, eventually you will luck into a year where good health and a few smart decisions will give you a defense good enough to win a championship. (As the Colts learned in 2006, you don't even need a year, just four weeks.) Even the New England Patriots, who are led by a defense-first head coach in Bill Belichick, have been more consistent on offense than on defense since they began their run of success in 2001.

Field-goal percentage is almost entirely random from season to season, while kickoff distance is one of the most consistent statistics in football.

This theory, which originally appeared in the *New York Times* in October 2006, is one of our most controversial, but it is hard to argue against the evidence. Measuring every kicker from 1999 to 2006 who had at least ten field goal attempts in each of two consecutive years, the year-to-year correlation coefficient for field-goal percentage was an insignificant .05. Mike Vanderjagt didn't miss a single field goal in 2003, but his percentage was a below-average 74 percent the year before and 80 percent the year after. Adam Vinatieri, supposedly the best kicker in the game, has never has never had two straight seasons with accuracy better than last year's NFL average of 85 percent.

On the other hand, the year-to-year correlation coefficient for kickoff distance, over the same period as our measurement of field-goal percentage and with the same minimum of ten kicks per year, is .61. The same players consistently lead the league in kickoff distance, particularly Neil Rackers, Olindo Mare, Josh Brown, and Stephen Gostkowski.

Recovery of a fumble, despite being the product of hard work, is almost entirely random.

Stripping the ball is a skill. Holding onto the ball is a skill. Pouncing on the ball as it is bouncing all over the place is not a skill. There is no correlation whatsoever between the percentage of fumbles recovered by a team in one year and the percentage they recover in the next year. The odds of recovery are based solely on the type of play involved, not the teams or any of their players.

Fans like to insist that specific coaches can teach their teams to recover more fumbles by swarming to the ball. Chicago's Lovie Smith, in particular, is supposed to have this ability. However, in Smith's first three seasons as head coach of the Bears, their rate of fumble recovery on defense went from a league-best 76 percent in 2004 to a league-worst 33 percent in 2005, then back to 67 percent in 2006.

Fumble recovery is equally erratic on offense. In 2007, the St. Louis Rams fumbled 19 times on offense, but recovered 11 of those fumbles. Last year, the Rams had fewer fumbles on offense (17) but more turnovers because they only recovered five of those fumbles.

Fumble recovery is a major reason why the general public overestimates or underestimates certain teams. Fumbles are huge, turning-point plays that dramatically impact wins and losses in the past, while fumble recovery percentage says absolutely nothing about a team's chances of winning games in the future. With this in mind, Football Outsiders stats treat all fumbles as equal, penalizing them based on the likelihood of each type of fumble (run, pass, sack, etc.) being recovered by the defense.

Other plays that qualify as "non-predictive events" include blocked kicks and touchdowns during turnover returns. These plays are not "lucky," per se, but they have no value whatsoever for predicting future performance.

Field position is fluid.

As discussed in the Statistical Toolbox, every yard line on the field has a value based on how likely a team is to score from that location on the field as opposed to from a yard further back. The change in value from one yard to the next is the same whether the team has the ball or not. The goal of a defense is not just to prevent scoring, but to hold the opposition so that the offense can get the ball back in the best possible field position. A bad offense will score as many points as a good offense if it starts each drive five yards closer to the goal line.

A corollary to this precept: The most underrated aspect of an NFL team's performance is the field position gained or lost on kickoffs and punts. This is part of why Devin Hester has such an impact on the game, even when he isn't returning a kickoff or punt for a touchdown.

Teams which are strong on first and second down, but weak on third down, will tend to improve the following year. Teams which are weak on first and second down, but strong on third down, will tend to decline the following year.

We discovered this when creating our first team projection system in 2004. It said that the lowly San Diego Chargers would have of the best offenses in the league, which seemed a little ridiculous. But looking closer, our projection system treated the previous year's performance on different downs as different variables, and the 2003 Chargers were actually good on first and second down, but terrible on third.

Teams get fewer opportunities on third down, so third-down performance is more volatile — but it's also is a bigger part of a team's overall performance than first or second down, because the result is usually either very good (four more downs) or very bad (losing the ball to the other team with a punt). Over time, a team will play as well in those situations as it does in other situations, which will bring the overall offense or defense in line with the offense and defense on first and second down.

This trend is even stronger between seasons. Struggles on third down are a pretty obvious problem, and teams will generally target their offseason moves at improving their third-down performance ... which often leads to an improvement in third-down performance. Teams significantly affected by this trend in 2009 include Dallas, Green Bay, and Baltimore (offense better on third downs in 2008), Chicago (defense better on third downs in 2008), and Pittsburgh (offense worse on third downs in 2008).

Injuries regress to the mean on the seasonal level, and teams that avoid injuries in a given season tend to win more games.

There are no doubt teams with streaks of good or bad health over multiple years. However, teams who were especially healthy or especially unhealthy, as measured by our Adjusted Games Lost (AGL) metric, almost al-ways head towards league average in the subsequent season. Furthermore, injury — or the absence thereof — has a huge correlation with wins, and a significant impact on a team's success. Last year alone, six of the seven least-injured teams in the league made the playoffs. Teams with a high number of injuries — which last year included Seattle, Cincinnati, St. Louis, and, surprisingly, Baltimore — are a good bet to improve the following season.

By and large, a team built on depth is better than a team built on stars and scrubs.

Connected to the previous statement, because teams need to go into the season expecting that they will suffer an average number of injuries no matter how healthy they were the previous year. The Redskins went into 2007 with a Super Bowl-quality starting lineup, and finished 5-11 because they had no depth. You cannot concentrate your salaries on a handful of star players because there is no such thing as avoiding injuries in the NFL. The game is too fast and the players too strong to build a team based around the idea that "if we can avoid all injuries this year, we'll win."

Running backs usually decline after age 28, tight ends after age 29, wide receivers after age 30, and quarterbacks after age 32.

This research was originally done by Doug Drinen of footballguys.com in 2000. In recent years, a few players have had huge seasons above these general age limits (most notably Tiki Barber and Tony Gonzalez), but the peak ages Drinen found a few years ago still apply to the majority of players.

As for "non-skill players," research we did in 2007 for *ESPN The Magazine* suggested that defensive ends and defensive backs generally begin to decline after age 29, linebackers and offensive linemen after age 30, and defensive tackles after age 31. However, because we still have so few statistics to use to study linemen and defensive players, this research should not be considered definitive.

The future NFL success of quarterbacks chosen in the first two rounds of the draft can be projected with a high degree of accuracy by using just two statistics from college: games started and completion percentage.

This theory was introduced in *Pro Football Prospectus 2006* and further refined in *Pro Football Prospectus 2007*. The projection created by these stats is known as the Lewin Career Forecast, after the creator of the theory, David Lewin.

Scouts expected players such as Kyle Boller (48 percent), Jim Druckenmiller (54 percent) and Ryan Leaf (54 percent) to suddenly figure out how to complete passes once they hit the NFL. It isn't surprising that it didn't happen. Having a high completion percentage (above 60 percent or so) is no guarantee of success, especially if it was done in a small number of games in a fluky system (Tim Couch being a strong example), but it is a prerequisite for it. Games started are important because the more film that exists of a player in game conditions, the easier it is to find weaknesses that might come out against different opponents or different schemes. When scouts don't get sufficient information, they place too much weight on "measureables" and off-field workouts, and make mistakes like Couch (26 starts), Leaf (24 starts) or Akili Smith (19 starts).

The Lewin Career Forecast only applies to the first two rounds because it assumes that with enough game film to judge, scouts can accurate identify players who are "system quarterbacks" and will not succeed in the NFL, and those players appropriately fall on draft day (Graham Harrell being a good example from 2009).

Championship teams are generally defined by their ability to dominate inferior opponents, not their ability to win close games.
Football games are often decided by just one or two plays — a missed field goal, a bouncing fumble, the subjective spot of an official on fourth-and-1. One missed assignment by a cornerback or one slightly askew pass that bounces off a receiver's hands and into those of a defensive back five yards away and the game could be over. In a blowout, however, one lucky bounce isn't going to change things. Championship teams beat their good opponents convincingly and destroy the cupcakes on the schedule.

Aaron Schatz

The Year In Quotes

Best Quotes From Elementary School

I haven't been in second grade since I don't know when.
— Redskins quarterback **Jason Campbell**, reacting to being back in a second grade classroom with the seven-year-old winner of the NFL's Take a Player to School Sweepstakes

Jim Zorn once told me the first pass he threw to a cheerleader, he gave her a bloody nose. So I want to be careful of that.
— **Campbell**, not wanting to repeat the mistake of his head coach while playing catch with the second-graders

This week we come back and play the Cowboys, so you know what time it is. I'm gonna teach y'all at a young age to hate the Cowboys.
— Redskins cornerback **Fred Smoot**

Best Quotes For Trent Edwards To Read

He bought me dinner a couple of times and so we just went from there. Now we're dating.
— Cowboys quarterback **Tony Romo**, on his relationship with Terrell Owens

I think really the thing is Tony gets me.
— Cowboys wide receiver **Terrell Owens**

Mom, You're Not Helping

He's hurting inside and out. But he will be fine if people are prayerful and help my baby boy out. He is a young man. He just needs a lot of love and support.
— **Felicia Young**, mother of Titans quarterback Vince Young, after her son indicated he didn't want to play football anymore

You're Not Helping Either

I know if I was a first-round pick and didn't have any court cases and I got $25 million up front, I wouldn't be worried about what y'all say about me.
— Cowboys cornerback **Adam "Pacman" Jones**, on Young's situation

Best List Of Things You Are Not Allowed To Do

He can't be in a car and get shot. He can't be someplace where somebody spills some coffee on him. He can't be someplace at night. That's in the future, but now he can't be there.
— Cowboys owner and general manager **Jerry Jones** on cornerback Adam Jones

Best Quote About A Head Injury

That was the first time I ever had a concussion test. You know what's funny, you take the test when you're fine so that way they can compare the answers. I did better after the head injury than I did before.
— Steelers safety **Ryan Clark**, after his collision with Ravens running back Willis McGahee in the AFC Championship game

You Can Take The Players Off The Love Boat, But You Can't Take The Love Boat Out Of The Players

I'm like a fine wine, a Cabernet-Merlot-Shiraz blend. It can do a lot of things. It gets better as you open it up and let it get out there and air out, filtrate, do all those things. I don't even need a decanter, just let me go out there and run. Pour me in your mouth, suck it up and enjoy the run.
— Vikings safety **Darren Sharper**

I grew up on a horse ranch. My dad trained horses for 30 years. I like to rock the cowboy hat. People seem to like it too. I'm either wearing a baseball hat or a cowboy hat. You know the tight jeans, you can't wear boots with baggy jeans plus you got to use the tools in your toolbox and let's be honest, I've got a phenomenal ass!
— Vikings defensive end **Jared Allen**

Best Quote About Team Chemistry

Think of the anatomy. Brains, eyes, ears, nose. You know there's got to be some [sphincters] over here to have the whole anatomy. My point is this team is made up of that. By golly, when you start picking that part out and saying, "They don't have a team," you're missing the point.
— Cowboys owner **Jerry Jones**

Best Awkward Quarterbacking Quotes

I know I was asked a question yesterday, is that the guy who who's going to be the quarterback at the end of the week? That's something that is ongoing. You don't crown a guy king and then the king doesn't have any clothes on and you say, "Hey, he's still the king."
— Vikings head coach **Brad Childress**, on deciding whether to continue starting quarterback Tavaris Jackson

Do you guys believe that happened? I said a second ago, if I watched a movie and that happened I'd be like, "OK, that's not really real. That's not going to happen in real life. A team would take care of that situation and get a win, even if by a couple of points." It's not funny, but I almost want to just laugh about it because it's so unbelievable.
— Texans tight end **Owen Daniels**, on the "Sage Rosenfels-led" loss to the Colts

When they started blowing the whistle, I was like, "Did we false start or were they offsides or something?" And I looked, and I was just like, "You're an idiot."
— Lions quarterback **Dan Orlovsky**, regarding running out of the back of the end zone for a safety

I just wasn't going to sit back there and try to hold the ball and be stupid and give them points, and then I ended up giving them points.
— **Orlovsky**

Best Quote About Punting

I want him to punt the ball in the right direction. I'm expected to win games. He's expected to punt the ball in the right direction. I'm not trying to be funny.
— Packers head coach **Mike McCarthy**, on what he expected from new punter Jeremy Kapinos

The Year In Ocho Cinco

A lot of people look at Chad Johnson and say he's crazy and he does a lot of stuff, but I don't think people really understand how smart I really am.
— Bengals wide receiver **Chad Ochocinco**

Ochocinco? If I was going to take all the legal steps for a name change I would go with something way cooler than Ochocinco.
— Redskins tight end **Chris Cooley**

Oucho? I like Oucho. Oucho Cinco. That's great. He's Oucho right now, I saw him with that shoulder brace on the sideline looking real dejected yesterday. Baltimore took it to those guys. We'll just see how that shoulder is. Tell him to get his shoulder right. Oucho Cinco.
— Titans linebacker **Keith Bulluck**

I think (the trade demand) might be part of why my production is down this year. To rant and rave in the offseason like that and to come back and expect to be productive or expect them to use me the same way they used me in the past is very unlikely. That's like me talking about you guys in a negative way and then me expecting you all to be my No. 1 fan. I made my bed. I have to lay in it. I've apologized about it a million times to my team, my organization, my fans … I wouldn't say it's somewhat of a punishment, but you open your mouth and this is what you get, and I understand that.
— **Ochocinco**

The Year In Herm: Herm's Last Hurrah

He was with us last year and … we still went 4-12.
— Chiefs head coach **Herm Edwards**, when asked if he regretted the trade that sent defensive end Jared Allen to the Vikings

If he goes in and plays well and we win some games it would be great. It would be good for us, good for him, good for everybody … (Jets) have a number four and we have a number four. It's just two different number fours. You never know.
— **Herm**, on new starting quarterback, Tyler Thigpen

We think whoever we put in there gives us the best chance to win and it happens to be Tyler this week.
— **Herm**

I'm going to tell him, "you don't have to be Brett Favre, 'cause there is only one of them."
— **Herm**

No. We lost. No. We lost. That's all you take. We lost the game.
— **Herm**, on whether he can take anything away from a loss

We were able to score points, and it became a game of just playing football. That was good to see for us.
— **Herm**, on playing football in a football game

Sometimes you get pigeon-holed as a coach. Well this guy thinks like this. I think this, I want to score points, I've always said that. How you do it is how you do it.
— **Herm**

I kept asking my wife about 1 o'clock [A.M.], "We won, right?" She said, "Yeah, you won, honey."
— **Herm**

The Year In Marty B

He says it all the time: "Jason doesn't like me."
— Cowboys tight end **Jason Witten**, quoting rookie tight end Martellus Bennett

It's not that I don't like him. It's just that I'm letting him figure it out. He's got to figure it out first, and once he does, obviously that's where I come along.
— **Witten**

I'm not going to be [bleep-ing] doing this all the [bleep-ing] time. You've got to know what the [beep] to do.
— **Witten**

A lot of stuff I take from him, but when it comes to the way I move and the way I do things, it's still me. I've been doing it like that for 21 years. I've been pretty productive
— Cowboys tight end **Martellus Bennett**, regarding the effect of Witten's tutelage

You can get your first kiss from Oprah, or you can get your first kiss from Halle Berry. Oprah gave me the first kiss. This was Halle Berry right here.
— **Marty B**, comparing his first career touchdown late in a humiliating loss to the Rams to his leaping

grab over Redskins safety Chris Horton, giving the Cowboys the lead

T.O. and those guys know I'm the best dancer on the team and they always get mad at my selections in the end zone. They want me to do my best stuff. But they need to be patient.
— **Marty B**

I guess women have to let go at times too but it just doesn't seem right, but if they do then it shouldn't smell or make a sound. I mean come on if you were on a date with Angelina Jolie a lunch date eating spaghetti and pancakes or whatever it is people eat in Hollywood and as she's feeding you she farts. Do you let her slide because of her beauty or call her out?
— **Marty B**, as written on his blog

The Year In Groins

We are very sorry that we showed a penis on our website all day yesterday.
— Redskins tight end **Chris Cooley**, apologizing on his blog for mistakenly posting a picture of his unit

I know, but it's within the locker room, not with the nation but you know, it's not too bad. I didn't just get out the pool.
— Vikings tight end **Visanthe Shiancoe**, after the local Fox station's postgame locker room coverage caught him adjusting his towel

Is it all over the Internet?
— **Shiancoe**, who was then told that there was an unedited clip on Youtube

How'd it look?
— **Shiancoe**

Dude grabbed my [expletive]. I told that dude, "You're lucky I'm trying to do better because I would have got 15 (yards) for kickin' your [expletive]." He grabbed them and squeezed them … If you want somebody to let the ball go, grab their [expletive]. I'll sure let go after that.
— Cowboys cornerback **Adam Jones**, on becoming closely acquainted with Browns defensive back Nick Sorensen at the bottom of the pile after muffing a punt

Best Quote That Could Have Been About Groins

His balls come a lot faster. I ain't seen no balls like that. Kurt's ball gets there, but not like that. It messed with me a little bit as far as my technique. I played cautious.
— Cardinals rookie cornerback **Dominique Rodgers-Cromartie** comparing Brett Favre's balls to Kurt Warner's balls

It's Always Sunny In Philadelphia

You know what, though, they're good shots. They've been practicing. You could see them coming in; they were leading the bus. It was good egging.
— Redskins tight end **Chris Cooley**, on the egging of his team bus by Eagles fans

Oh yeah, they just come raining down when you pull in there. You know, I don't know how many we got hit with, but it looked like a hailstorm.
— Redskins center **Casey Rabach**

They were lighting it up.
— Redskins wide receiver **Devin Thomas**

I'm talking about the middle of the bus, like, bam-mmm, like busted and everything. I ain't never been thrown eggs at. I mean, at Philly, they throw everything.
— Redskins defensive tackle **Kedric Golston**

It must have been one of those big ones too, an ostrich egg.
— **Golston**

It was crazy, though, because the egg was actually thrown in front of the bus. It was like a quarterback almost; you throw it to where the receiver's gonna be at. I was very impressed.
— Redskins wide receiver **Malcolm Kelly**

Very impressed. If they ever had a replacement [team] in Philly, they'd have to get that dude for quarterback, because he hit that thing on point.
— **Thomas**

We didn't get no eggs. I just know we got flipped off. By everybody, kids and everything.
— Redskins running back **Rock Cartwright** on his bus

You've got the six-year olds flipping you off, and the dad's patting them on the back.
— **Rabach**

They give us the bird, we wave. The universal greeting, I guess, for Philly.
— Redskins fullback **Mike Sellers**

Grandma's mooning you.
— Offensive tackle **Jon Jansen**

I've had some old ladies moon us, oh yeah.
— **Jansen**

It's hard to tell from the backside, to tell you the truth.
— **Rabach**

Oh, you can tell. When it's an old lady, you can tell.
— **Jansen**

Sons Of Buddy Ryan Quote Of The Year

(Expletive), look at this … I've got gray. I've got it. This is the National (expletive) Football League, you're not going to be on point every week. Am I pissed off about (last) Monday night? You're (expletive) right. But it's on me and (expletive) it, enough's enough.
— Oakland defensive coordinator **Rob Ryan**, on the N(F-ing)FL

Honorable Mention For Sons Of Buddy Ryan Quote

The message to the rest of the league is "Hey, the Jets are coming. We're going to give you everything we got, and that's going to be, I think, more than you can handle."
— Jets new head coach **Rex Ryan**, on how he wants his new team to play

You've heard of the KISS philosophy, which is Keep It Simple Stupid. That's for somebody else. Ours is a KILL philosophy.
— **Ryan**

The Year In Samurai Mike

Our formula is this: We go out, we hit people in the mouth, No. 1.
— 49ers head coach **Mike Singletary**, revealing the first step of his formula for winning

I told him that he would do a better job for us right now taking a shower and coming back and watching the game than to go out on the field.
— **Singletary**, on why he sent tight end Vernon Davis to the locker room with 10 minutes left in a game

We are not a charity. We cannot give them the game.
— **Singletary**, on his team's performance against the Seahawks

I voted a while ago in my mind.
— **Singletary**, when asked by reporters whether he voted on Election Day

They Are Who They Thought They Were

You're talking about a Cardinals team that's not the Cardinals of old. People don't understand that. You can't take them lightly. I know people (including teammates) asked me about them, and I said the same thing: "They're not the same Cardinals."
— Cowboys guard and former Cardinal, **Leonard Davis**, on his old team in mid-October

We beat a 4-0 team last week (Buffalo) like they were stealing something from us. Today, we treated America's Team like they were stealing something from us. We can beat anybody in the country. Our time is now.
— Cardinals linebacker **Karlos Dansby**

Whatever we have to do, if we're operating the way we operated today, we're going to win football games and that's what this is all about.
— Cardinals quarterback **Kurt Warner**, after the regular season loss to the Panthers

We talk so much ... my wife thinks sometimes I'm having an affair with Coach Haley.
— Cardinals quarterback **Kurt Warner**, on his relationship with offensive coordinator Todd Haley

Mine, too.
— **Haley**, indicating his wife is onto them as well

I remember the coach, he was like "Do you know the three-point stance?" I was like "No, but I can tell you how to steal a Buick Regal."
— Cardinals defensive tackle **Darnell Dockett**, on starting to play football in eighth grade, as a way to avoid trouble

He takes these protein shakes where he's trying to keep himself healthy, but when it comes out we all suffer. It's nasty.
— Cardinals defensive tackle **Bryan Robinson**, regarding Dockett's nickname "Fart Box"

He hit me in the head like 15 times. I watched a replay and he was going so crazy a referee literally had to pick him up and pull him back. When we got to the sideline, I said, "Man, what are you hitting me in the head for?" He's like, "Man, I was just excited." I told him I had a headache and to leave me alone.
— Cardinals defensive end **Antonio Smith**, who suffered a celebratory attack from Dockett, after recording a safety against the Falcons

A lot of people, coming into this game, said that we were the worst playoff team to ever get in ... and I think we rallied around that.
— Cardinals Coach **Ken Whisenhunt**

We heard it all, from, "Same old Cardinals" to "They should have to give up their playoff spot." But what happened today shows ... I can say this now: We are who I thought we were.
— Cardinals defensive end **Bertrand Berry**

Give Obama a high five and go get some tattoos together.
— **Dockett**, describing the perfect ending to his ideal Super Bowl

Best Quotes Endorsing The Sun Tzu Pee-Wee Coaching Clinic

I was mad at my son's pee-wee game the other day. They was losing 27-0, and there was two minutes left. They had the twos [second-stringers] in the game and we was trying to stop them. They got to fourth down, and [the opposing coach] brought back in the ones and they break a touchdown. I mean, these are kids, 33-0.
— Dolphins linebacker **Joey Porter**

What was the point of scoring the extra touchdown for? This was the Super Bowl game. You already won. The kids is already crying. Why would you do that?
— **Porter**

Seriously, I went up to the coach. I was pissed off. I just wanted to understand. What is the point? You just won. What's the difference in 27-0 or 33-0? Seven- and

eight-year-olds. He just said "That's life." That's a reminder to let you know how people think. So you can't never let your guard down, even in pee-wee football.
— **Porter**

The Year In Chilly And His Mustache

It's kind of like going out to find a girlfriend. The minute you go out to find a girlfriend that you want to make a wife, that's a bad thing to do. You've got to just let it happen. What I'm saying with Sharp, you better just let it happen. You don't want to force the issue because that would probably be a bad thing.
— Vikings head coach **Brad Childress**, explaining his theory on safety Darren Sharper, without an interception for the season, despite being the active NFL leader with 53 career picks

Hopefully, my wife doesn't see this.
— **Childress**

I had a vodka as big as your head last night.
— **Childress**, on how he celebrated his team being in first place

We can meet on the 50-yard line and we can go at it.
— Jags wide receiver and former Viking **Troy Williamson**, on his desire to duke it out with the Vikings head coach

Do you need my reach? I'm not like a woman; I'll give you my weight. It's 190 pounds of twisted steel and rompin', stompin' dynamite.
— **Childress**, in response to Williamson

Coach Childress is a tough-minded guy. And he has a badass mustache. I put my money on whoever has a kickass mustache.
— Vikings defensive end **Jared Allen**

The Year In Hair

Today is Mustache Monday. It's for the throwback game. Every day we go to meetings and we go by these beautiful pictures and we admire these guys' mustaches.
— 49ers quarterback **Shaun Hill**

Every single day that we walk through here, you just can't help but admire John Ayers' mustache.

It's awesome.
— **Hill**, on the 49ers' late 'stache star

If they can grow those [bleeps] in a week, they some bad guys.
— Redskins cornerback **Fred Smoot**, on the Niners' mustache plan

I started four weeks ago. How bad is that?
— **Hill**, on his own mustache-growing endeavors

It doesn't matter, I'm gonna jam his mustache to the ground.
— **Smoot**, on whether he'd be intimidated by a receiver with lip fur

We might have an edge; our heads might be a little lighter.
— Redskins wide receiver **Antwaan Randle El**, upon hearing that most of the 49ers had grown mustaches in advance of Sunday's game

I would say no, it didn't make me a better football player, but I looked a lot cooler. I mean, I kind of felt like Magnum P.I, to be honest with you.
— Redskins tight end **Todd Yoder**, on sporting a mustache last season

They have bad hair. They don't know how to cook.
— Chargers defensive end **Jacques Cesaire**, on why he dislikes the Broncos

They have bad teeth.
— **Cesaire**

What else don't I like about them? They watch *Dr. Quinn, Medicine Woman*. Who does that? Who watches *Dr. Quinn, Medicine Woman*? That's what I want to know. I heard the Denver Broncos watch it. I'm just sayin'.
— **Cesaire**

My biggest complaint with him is that he looks like Ringo Starr, you know? I'm just not feeling his haircut.
— **Cesaire**, on his feelings regarding Broncos quarterback Jay Cutler

Supercuts.
— **Cesaire**, when asked what he would say to Cutler should he sack him

Um what's up with Flacco's eyebrows? Do you think you could tweeze 'em out a little bit? I can't even watch him on TV.

— Redskins tight end **Chris Cooley** interviewing Ravens linebacker Terrell Suggs, asking him to weigh in on quarterback Joe Flacco's preponderance of mislaid facial hair

I think so definitely, for the simple fact that, you know he's gonna be the face of our franchise. He's gotta look like … he's gotta clean that thing up. Everybody loves the quarterback. You know look … like I said. Look at Tom Brady, he's been on *GQ* magazine like 7 times … on the cover. You know … you know whenever he's big he's big. He's dated all the hot actresses, all the hot models. If Flacco even wanna compete to that he's gonna have to clean that thing up a little bit.

— Ravens linebacker **Terrell Suggs**, on Flacco's monobrow

I mean he's not that ugly, but he looks like a caveman with his eyebrows.

— **Cooley**, on the tragedy of the Flacco visage

Yeah, you know you gotta trim the eyebrows up just a little bit.

— **Suggs**, with a cure for the countenance

The Year In Blache

Honestly, for me, I've got to get in some people's rear ends. And it starts in the mirror.

— Redskins defensive coordinator **Greg Blache**, describing a predilection for do-it-yourself proctology

We're not what people think we are, we're not who we think we are right now. We're probably the worst 6-2 defense in the NFL, if there is such a stat kept.

— **Blache**, not only dropping a reverse Denny Green on you, but asking for a stat!

(Ed. note: There were only two 6-2 teams in the league: Carolina's defense was tenth and Washington's was … 11th! Blache was right!)

Those folks are terrorists with the double-move. I don't think they can go to the bathroom straight.

— **Blache**, on the Eagles receivers

Well you know, first of all we're not that good. We're a blue-collar team, and we have to recognize that. We're not going to come in and blow anybody out. We've got to focus and prepare and do the details whoever we play. If it's the Lost Sisters of the Poor, we have to focus on details. And we came in here today and made some STUPID mistakes early on, and actually played like the south end of a northbound skunk, to be quite candid.

— **Blache**, on the performance of his defense … after a win

The great craftsmen have great detail and great pride in it. We don't do that. We're just kind of guys with sledgehammers and pickaxes right now, and to be a real good football team and to be what we want to be, we've got to be a little bit more detailed than that.

— **Blache**

In my job, nobody cares how shallow the water is, I've got to get the boat to shore. All right? I've got to get the boat to shore, and right now, I've got some guys I don't feel like they're stroking their oars as well as they should on a consistent basis, and if they're not, and I'm the guy there with the horn, then it's on my shoulders. It's on my watch. And I'm not a very happy camper today. And when I'm not happy, I can make a lot of other people unhappy, too.

— **Blache**

You have this stomach where it's up in the top of your throat, and you've got heartburn and everything else. You're thinking, "This is really, really foolish," because I'm worrying about things I can't control. I was worrying about mice turds, and there's just mounds of elephant dung around.

— **Blache**

Like I told them, I thought they needed some emotional and attitudinal Viagra. We needed to get a little spike out of them today.

— **Blache**

I'm gonna go home and congratulate my wife on her great decision of who she married, and have a cocktail, and get a couple hours before I have to get up and get on the 49ers in the morning.

— **Blache**

In my opinion, Shawn Springs could be a male model. Shawn Springs is clean. He is. Of the big guys, you've

got to think about Cornelius Griffin. For a big man, Griff dresses like a pimp daddy sometimes. He really does. He's pretty darn clean.
— **Blache**

I don't believe in politics. I learned as a kid: Santa Claus, the Easter Bunny and politics.
— **Blache**

The Year In Stats

You've got some real good stats there. You know he's 3-0 as a starter, how about that?
— Buccaneers head coach **Jon Gruden** when asked about quarterback Brian Griese's low ranking in several statistical categories

You look at the sack total for yourself and you wish you had some.
— Jets linebacker **Vernon Gholston**

You've got a chance in this league, the way onside kicks are, you've got a pretty good chance of getting it. About 50-50.
— Chargers head coach **Norv Turner**, on the odds of recovering an onside kick, leading to a Chargers win in Kansas City

(Bleep) no. It's not real high.
— Chargers special teams coach **Steve Crosby**, critiquing Norv's estimate (Actual success rate of expected onside kicks, 2000-2005: 16.6 percent.)

We still have a chance to go 4-12.
— Titans linebacker **Keith Bulluck**, on the Titans' 4-0 start

We don't worry about numbers here. Statistics are for losers. I'm not a stat guy. I'm not interested in them, because you can do anything you want with numbers, you can manipulate them, and work around with them. Look at all the financial [problems] we're having in Wall Street right now. That's all those guys lying and playing with numbers. And now all of us are suffering. So I don't believe in numbers, because any crook can play with numbers … It angers me. You know? That's the whole thing, people play with numbers.
— Redskins defensive coordinator **Greg Blache**, responding to a question about the defensive line, and presumably, a number

Financial Planning Quote Of The Year

I'm about to go dig a hole in my back yard and put it in my back yard where I can see it. I don't like this stock stuff. I don't like not being able [to rely on] this bond and that bond. Everything's funny. I don't trust nothing.
— Dolphins linebacker **Joey Porter**, with sage advice on dealing with the financial crisis

Quote Of The Year

What has made us consistent is our consistency.
— Patriots fullback **Heath Evans**

Compiled by Mark Zajack

Arizona Cardinals

The 2008 Arizona Cardinals were, by almost any measure, one of the worst teams ever to play in a Super Bowl. They lost seven games during the regular season, more than any Super Bowl team except the 1979 Rams. They benefited from playing in an easy division, going 6-0 against the lowly 49ers, Seahawks, and Rams; outside their division, they went just 3-7. They were only 1-4 against playoff teams, and were also blown out by non-playoff squads like the Jets and the Patriots. They were just 21st in our DVOA rankings, ten spots below 6-10 Green Bay. Most expected a one-and-done playoff finish, but instead the Cardinals put together three straight wins to reach the Super Bowl, where they briefly led in the fourth quarter before falling behind at the end. (In fact, Arizona had a much higher single-game DVOA than Pittsburgh, despite losing.)

Arizona's postseason run was nothing new — the Cardinals were the fourth team this decade to sneak into the playoffs after an average regular season, only to get hot enough to reach the league's championship game. For the previous three teams to pull this off — the 2001 Patriots, 2003 Panthers, and 2007 Giants — the Super Bowl appearance proved to be a sign of a long-term turnaround, not just a month-long hot streak that faded away. On the other hand, our numbers currently have Arizona with the third-fewest mean projected wins for 2009.

CARDINALS SUMMARY

2008 Record: 9-7

Pythagorean Wins: 8.0 (18th)

DVOA: -3.2% (21st)

Offense: 9.9% (15th)

Defense: 9.4% (23rd)

Special Teams: -3.7% (28th)

Variance: 22.9% (28th)

2008: Once thought to be dead in the water, the old man from Arizona marshals the troops for a soaring comeback that ends one step from the promised land.

2009: The old man tries to stay relevant while his younger, better-looking running mate waits to get off the bench and take leadership of this party.

2009 Mean Projection: 5.6

On the Clock (0-3): 24%

Loserville (4-6): 42%

Mediocrity (7-8): 18%

Playoff Contender (9-10): 12%

Super Bowl Contender (11+): 3%

Projected Average Opponent: 6.2% (3rd)

Why do the Cardinals have such a low projection? The system is fairly complex, but there are some clear obvious warning signs, starting with the fact that Kurt Warner is now 38 years old. Only two quarterbacks have topped 3,600 yards or 25 touchdowns at that age or older: Brett Favre and Warren Moon. Yes, Warner is a special quarterback, but most special quarterbacks — including guys like Joe Montana, John Elway, and Dan Marino — were essentially done when they passed 37. It's nigh-impossible to find comparable passers to Warner who are older than 34; the best comparisons include Steve Beuerlein in 1997-99, Rich Gannon in 2001-02, and Ken Anderson in 1981-82. Beuerlein and Anderson both declined the following year, and Gannon fell off the cliff. Further, a Warner injury seems likely; he's yet to make it through a full 16-game slate in consecutive seasons, so it would not be a surprise if Matt Leinart was forced onto the field at some point in 2009. While we still believe that Leinart can develop into an effective NFL starter, there's no indication that he would match Warner's 2008 performance.

Another major warning sign is the health of the offensive line. The Cardinals trotted out the same five offensive linemen in every game last season, including the playoffs. It's doubtful they'll be that lucky two years in a row. When the inevitable happens and a

2009 Cardinals Schedule

Week	Opp.	Week	Opp.	Week	Opp.
1	SF	7	at NYG	13	MIN
2	at JAC	8	CAR	14	at SF (Mon.)
3	IND	9	at CHI	15	at DET
4	BYE	10	SEA	16	STL
5	HOU	11	at STL	17	GB
6	at SEA	12	at TEN		

tackle or guard limps to the sideline, who will come in? The Cardinals have no promising youngsters on their bench; none of the backup linemen on the team was drafted any higher than the fourth round.

There are potential issues on the defensive side of the ball as well. The loss of Antonio Smith opens up a spot for second-year defensive end Calais Campbell, but now who will play if Campbell gets hurt? Defensive tackle Darnell Dockett was a fearsome pass-rusher on the interior, but he wants a new deal and may hold out. Cornerback Dominique Rodgers-Cromartie looked no different in the Super Bowl than he did the rest of the season: like a talented, but inexperienced cover corner who still struggles with tackling and run coverage.

In addition, both of last year's coordinators are now in Kansas City after Todd Haley took a promotion and Clancy Pendergast got forced out by politics. Losing both coordinators isn't the end of the world, but teams that replace their coordinators do tend to regress in the subsequent season.

Will Arizona be the first Super Bowl surprise team this century to fall back to the bottom, or will they move on to greater heights like their predecessors? What did those teams have in common with each other, and does Arizona share similar traits? Before we can answer that question, we have to look back at these other teams.

The 2001 Patriots went 11-5 and won the AFC East despite finishing with a middling 7.7% DVOA, third in the division behind the 11-5 Dolphins (8.9%) and the 10-6 Jets (13.0%). They beat the St. Louis Rams, the best team in the league by both win-loss record and DVOA, to win Super Bowl XXXVI. The Patriots averaged 7.3 wins between 1998 and 2000. After the Super Bowl, the Patriots became something of a dynasty, averaging more than 12 wins a season over the next seven campaigns, including five playoff berths and three more Super Bowl appearances (two of which we are going to discuss right now).

The 2003 Panthers went 11-5, but finished the regular season with a DVOA of 0.8%: 17th in the league, and right below the 5-11 Jaguars. They narrowly lost 32-29 to the Patriots, by then one of the league's best teams, in Super Bowl XXXVIII. Before that Super Bowl, the Panthers had been one of the league's worst teams, putting up six consecutive non-winning seasons, averaging fewer than six wins a year. Since then, although they haven't matched the Patriots' success, they've never been worse than 7-9, and have reached the playoffs twice in five seasons.

The 2007 Giants went 10-6 to earn a Wild Card berth, but DVOA was not impressed; the Giants had a DVOA rating of 1.1%, 16th in the NFL and last in their division. Then came the playoffs, the four straight road wins, David Tyree's helmet catch, and the most unlikely Super Bowl championship ever. In the four years prior to that Super Bowl, the Giants posted only one winning season (they did make the playoffs at 8-8 in 2006; they lost their only playoff game). They've played just one season since, but it was highly successful, producing a league-high 12 wins and a top seed in the playoffs. Another playoff bid in 2009 seems likely.

So what were the traits these teams shared, and how do the Cardinals stack up?

YOUTH AT QUARTERBACK: There's a lot of variation in the rosters of these teams, with virtually no pattern of age or experience at any position on the field — with one exception.

The common bond between the Patriots, Panthers, and Giants is at the quarterback position. Tom Brady was only 24 when he played in his first Super Bowl; Eli Manning, 26. Jake Delhomme was 28, but still in his first year as a starter. In each of those cases, the

Table 1: The Fantastic Four

Team	Rush O	Rank	Pass O	Rank	Rush D	Rank	Pass D	Rank	S. Teams	Rank	Variance	Rank
2001 Patriots	-4.3%	17	12.2%	10	3.9%	28	-11.6%	11	2.5%	6	12.1%	6
2003 Panthers	-3.8%	20	-0.4%	17	-10.3%	10	-4.6%	12	0.6%	17	5.3%	1
2007 Giants	12.3%	4	-3.0%	22	-8.9%	9	3.4%	15	-0.7%	19	8.2%	3
2008 Cardinals	-9.6%	28	29.7%	8	-3.7%	15	21.9%	25	-3.7%	28	22.9%	28

playoffs were breakout performances for the signal-callers. When healthy, each has been the quarterback on his team since the Super Bowl. And each has been better since the Super Bowl season than they were before it.

The Cardinals do have a talented young quarterback, but he has spent most of the past two seasons on the bench. After a reasonably successful rookie season in 2006 (20th in the league with a DVOA of -1.2%), Matt Leinart opened the 2007 as Arizona's starter — technically. In reality, Leinart was rotating in and out of the lineup with Kurt Warner, with the two splitting playing time fairly evenly. Then in Week 5 of that season, Leinart suffered a broken collarbone against St. Louis. Warner has started every game since then, with Leinart only coming in for garbage time.

If the Cardinals are in the playoffs in 2011, however, it will be Leinart, not Warner, who is leading them. Should Arizona fans be worried about Leinart getting stale on the shelf? Not really — some of the league's most successful passers spent several years holding clipboards. Philip Rivers spent two years backing up Drew Brees, who spent a year backing up Doug Flutie. Tony Romo spent two seasons on the bench in Dallas, watching Vinny Testaverde and Drew Bledsoe take the field. Aaron Rodgers, Matt Hasselbeck, and Aaron Brooks backed up Brett Favre for a combined six seasons. Matt Cassel spent three seasons on the bench behind Tom Brady. Leinart's an unusual case in that he started as a rookie before being relegated to second-string, but by no means does that signal an end to his career — just ask Warner, who was benched early in Leinart's rookie season but worked his way back into the lineup and has since gone from Hall of Fame longshot to Canton favorite.

Quarterback is the most important position on the field, and a young, established starter frees up the front office to dedicate draft picks and free agent acquisitions to other positions. These surprise Super Bowl teams have not drafted a quarterback in the first round since their initial playoff runs, but they have taken players like Vince Wilfork, Jerod Mayo, Logan Mankins, DeAngelo Williams, and Jeff Otah. With Leinart at the ready, the Cardinals shouldn't need to worry about a quarterback for a long, long time.

BALANCE: Our first three surprise teams were jacks of all trades, masters of none. In the five basic phases of the game — rush and pass offense, rush and pass defense, and special teams — they were usually out-side the top five, but also outside the bottom five. This across-the-board competence allowed them to look for values in free agency and the draft, rather than reaching or overspending for players that "fit a need" in the draft and in free agency.

The Cardinals don't fit here. Their pass offense was eighth in the league, but their pass defense was 25th, and their rush offense and special teams were both 28th. We've already seen the ramifications of this: With impact defenders like Rey Maualuga, James Laurinaitis, and Louis Delmas available, Arizona selected Ohio State running back Beanie Wells with their first-round draft pick. While Wells was a fine value where he was taken and should be a productive starter from Day One in Arizona, the team really had no option but to draft him. Worse, if another team had traded in front of Arizona to steal Wells, the Cardinals would have been looking at another year with no running game. Here again, we see how weakness in a certain area can handcuff a team for years to come.

For at least the first part of 2009, expect Wells to back up incumbent Tim Hightower. NFL rules forbid Wells from participating in voluntary workouts until Ohio State's academic period ends on June 13, so he missed two weeks of practice time in May and June. Cardinals coach Ken Whisenhunt noted that Wells would have a lot of catching up to do when training camp began. Since both Wells and Hightower do their best work running up the middle behind a bruising fullback, it will be interesting to see if the Cardinals alter their philosophy and use more power formations in 2009.

COMMITMENT TO LINE PLAY: In the five years leading up to their Super Bowl appearances, all four of these squads made heavy investments on both sides of the line, spending at least four first- or second-round draft picks on linemen on both sides of the ball. Those draft picks — including Richard Seymour, Julius Peppers, Mathias Kiwanuka, and Osi Umenyiora on defense, and Matt Light, Jordan Gross, and Chris Snee on offense — were producing in the Super Bowl, and for years beyond.

The Cardinals had a pair of recent first-day linemen starting in the Super Bowl: tackle Levi Brown and guard Deuce Lutui. A third, defensive end Calais Campbell, will likely be starting in 2009. While none of these players has been dominating yet in their young careers, the Cardinals would certainly be worse off without them in the lineup.

Figure 1: 2008 ARI Weekly DVOA Performance

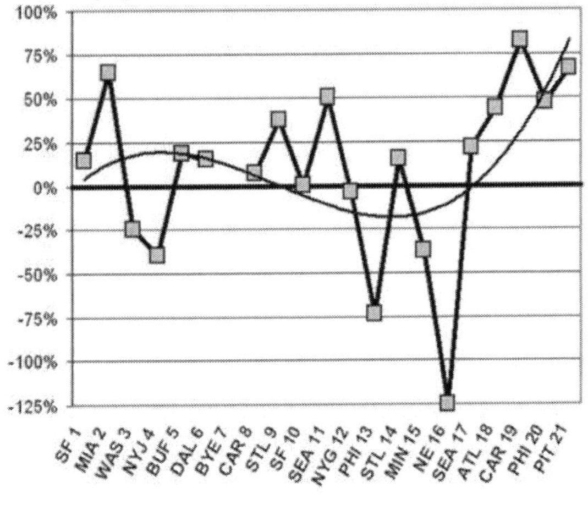

FRESH COACHING STAFFS: Bill Belichick, John Fox, and Ken Whisenhunt each led his team to the Super Bowl two years after taking charge. Tom Coughlin was in his fourth year with the Giants, but he didn't reach the Super Bowl until he changed his coaching style. Once a tyrannic despot who drove his players out of football and onto TV sets, Coughlin didn't win a championship until he learned to treat his players with a gentler hand.

While it's important to have stability on top of a franchise, it's also true that coaches have a limited shelf life. The Patriots and Panthers extended that shelf life for Belichick and Fox by winning so early in their careers, and now the Cardinals have done the same for Whisenhunt.

The Cardinals won't have to worry about a stale coaching staff in 2009, not with the loss of both co-ordinators to Kansas City. It will be up to Whisenhunt and new defensive coordinator Bill Davis to get Arizona back to the playoffs.

CONSISTENCY: Here is the one trait where our three prior examples were exceptional: According to our Variance statistic, the Patriots, Panthers, and Giants were each among the most consistent teams in football in the years of their Super Bowl run. The Panthers were especially steady, topping the NFL in 2003. That played a big part in their postseason success — since they rarely played much worse than their very best football, they were poised to conquer enemies who showed up with anything less than their A game.

And then there are the Cardinals. In 2008 they ranked 28th in Variance. To be perfectly blunt, there were signs that this team flat-out quit last year, especially on defense. When down by more than one score, a defense that usually played respectably would fold up its tents, putting up a 37.1% DVOA, worse than every team except Denver. How bad is a 37.1% DVOA? Consider that the Lions' defense posted a DVOA of 29.2% last season, and that's by far the worst we have on record. When the going got tough, the Cardinals died, and early deficits turned into blowouts.

Need more evidence? After a Week 11 win over Seattle, the Cardinals stood at 7-3, with a four-game lead over the 3-7 49ers. With the division all but won, they promptly lost four out of five games, including three by 21 points or more. (See Fig. 1) The pass defense in particular laid down like dogs: Eli Manning, Tarvaris Jackson, Donovan McNabb, and Matt Cassel combined for 14 touchdowns and no interceptions in those losses. Over the last six weeks of the season, Arizona's best DVOA against the pass was 17.7% against Seattle, when they allowed 250 yards and a pair of touchdowns to Seneca Wallace. Their other games were much worse, ranging all the way up to 90.1% against Minnesota.

It's possible that the end-of-season collapse was a natural reaction when the Cardinals clinched a playoff spot so early — and one that allowed them to be rested and refreshed for the playoffs. Attempting to turn your players' intensity off and on, however, is a dangerous gambit. Whisenhunt himself acknowledged this after his team's lousy effort in a 47-7 loss to New England last December. "I think we have some players that probably think they can turn it on for the play-off game," Whisenhunt told the *East Valley Tribune*. "That's something that we've talked about. That's not something you can do." You can get away with subpar effort and mental lapses when you're the only halfway decent team in your division. With competition certain to be tougher down the line, the onus is on Whisenhunt to keep the Cardinals at their best.

If Whisenhunt and Arizona can make annual playoff contention a reality, it will be a Herculean feat. Before last season, the Cardinals had made the playoffs just six times in 88 seasons. They could have the talent to double that number over the next decade or so, but only if they learn to keep their foot on the gas pedal. Otherwise, last year's playoff run will be seen as a one-time oddity, not the start of something great.

Vince Verhei

2008 Cardinals Stats by Week

Wk	vs.	W-L	PF	PA	YDF	YDA	TO	Total	Off	Def	ST
1	@SF	W	23	13	285	291	+5	15%	1%	-14%	0%
2	MIA	W	31	10	445	236	0	64%	29%	-33%	3%
3	@WAS	L	17	24	313	323	-2	-25%	15%	32%	-8%
4	@NYJ	L	35	56	468	373	-6	-40%	2%	30%	-11%
5	BUF	W	41	17	373	287	+4	19%	31%	11%	-1%
6	DAL	W	30	24	276	374	-2	15%	-2%	3%	21%
7	BYE										
8	@CAR	L	23	27	425	351	-1	7%	23%	12%	-4%
9	@STL	W	34	13	510	231	+3	38%	25%	-17%	-4%
10	SF	W	29	24	374	336	+3	0%	25%	-3%	-27%
11	@SEA	W	26	20	458	196	+1	50%	1%	-46%	4%
12	NYG	L	29	37	371	321	-2	-4%	19%	15%	-7%
13	@PHI	L	20	48	260	437	-3	-74%	-13%	53%	-8%
14	STL	W	34	10	335	308	+2	15%	11%	2%	6%
15	MIN	L	14	35	316	396	-1	-37%	20%	40%	-17%
16	@NE	L	7	47	186	514	-2	-126%	-82%	34%	-10%
17	SEA	W	34	21	457	330	+1	21%	20%	1%	2%
18	ATL	W	30	24	357	250	+2	44%	13%	-36%	-4%
19	@CAR	W	33	13	360	269	+5	83%	10%	-73%	-1%
20	PHI	W	32	25	369	454	+2	47%	60%	15%	2%
21	PIT	L	23	27	407	292	-1	66%	74%	10%	2%

Trends and Splits

	Offense	Rank	Defense	Rank
Total DVOA	9.9%	15	9.4%	23
Unadjusted VOA	10.0%	15	6.2%	19
Weighted trend	6.6%	19	11.9%	24
Variance	7.3%	19	9.1%	27
Average opponent	0.4%	32	5.3%	18
Passing	29.7%	8	21.9%	25
Rushing	-9.6%	28	-3.7%	15
First down	14.4%	6	-5.0%	8
Second down	7.5%	17	11.0%	21
Third down	4.3%	18	32.6%	32
First half	-1.7%	22	9.8%	20
Second half	21.3%	6	9.0%	22
Red Zone	9.5%	12	5.6%	21
Late and close	18.6%	11	6.6%	19

Five-Year Performance

Year	W-L	Pyth	Est W	PF	PA	TO	Total	Rk	Off	Rk	Def	Rk	ST	Rk	Off AGL	Rk	Def AGL	Rk
2004	6-10	6.8	5.0	284	322	+1	-22.3%	29	-22.8%	30	-2.0%	15	-1.4%	21	3.5	32	26.9	12
2005	5-11	6.0	6.3	311	387	-11	-11.9%	22	-11.3%	22	-1.7%	17	-2.3%	26	23.7	10	17.3	11
2006	5-11	6.0	6.2	314	399	+3	-19.5%	28	-8.8%	25	5.7%	24	-5.0%	32	5.8	29	14.2	16
2007	8-8	8.1	6.3	404	399	-7	-11.6%	23	-2.7%	19	5.2%	20	-3.8%	26	26.0	8	37.2	5
2008	9-7	8.0	7.4	427	426	0	-3.2%	21	9.9%	15	9.4%	23	-3.7%	28	23.5	19	14.3	25

Strategic Tendencies

Run/Pass		Rank	Offense		Rank	Defense		Rank	Other		Rank
Runs, all plays	33%	32	3+ WR	69%	4	Rush 3	6.2%	13	2+ RB, Pct Runs	61%	16
Runs, first half	36%	31	4+ WR	38%	1	Rush 4	56.9%	27	1 RB/2 TE, Pct Runs	48%	21
Runs, first down	41%	30	2+ TE	13%	31	Rush 5	28.5%	3	1RB/3+WR,Pct Runs	19%	28
Runs, second-long	23%	32	Single back	68%	7	Rush 6+	8.4%	16	Zone Blitz	1%	30
Runs, power sit.	45%	31	Play action	7%	32	Rush 7+	2.0%	9	Go for it on 4th	1.24	5
Runs, behind 2H	15%	32	Max protect	6%	24	Sacks by LB	32.3%	10	Offensive Pace	29.2	4
Pass, ahead 2H	52%	3	Outside pocket	6%	29	Sacks by DB	8.1%	17	Defensive Pace	31.3	26

Arizona's opponents only used shotgun 28 percent of the time, 28th in the league, even though the Cardinals had the NFL's largest gap between DVOA against shotgun plays and DVOA against plays with the quarterback under center. This continues a pattern that has now existed for three seasons:

Table 2: Arizona vs. Shotgun, 2006-08

Year	DVOA vs. Shotgun	DVOA vs. Other	Difference	Rank	Pct Shotgun	Rank
2006	50.4%	0.4%	49.9%	3	12%	27
2007	34.1%	-1.1%	35.2%	1	21%	31
2008	51.1%	3.8%	54.9%	1	28%	28

New England blew out Arizona by using predominantly shotgun formations, even in a snowstorm. When the Pittsburgh Steelers marched down the field to win Super Bowl XLIII, Ben Roethlisberger was in shotgun on every play. Why on earth aren't Arizona's opponents using shotgun all the time? ● Twenty-two percent of passes against Arizona were thrown to non-starting receivers, the highest percentage in the league. ● The Cardinals' defense had an Adjusted Sack Rate of only 1.8 percent on third down, lower than any defense except Kansas City. ● The Cardinals struggled against screen passes (57.5% DVOA, 26th in the NFL) after having the best defense in the league against screens in 2007. Consequently, they faced more RB screen passes than any other defense. ● On offense, the Cardinals used screen passes on 11.5 percent of third downs, the highest rate in the league. Half of these were running back screens, half wide receiver screens. ● 19 percent of Arizona's running plays were marked as draws, the highest rate in the league (NFL average: 7.6 percent). ● Arizona passed more often than any other team in second-and-long — probably because they were so awful when they ran the ball, with a league-low -43.1% DVOA. ● Arizona used a tight end on only 58 percent of offensive plays; every other team used a tight end on at least 73 percent of plays.

Passing

Player	DYAR	DVOA	Plays	NtYds	Avg	YAC	C%	TD	Int
Kurt Warner	1404	22.4%	631	4476	7.1	5.1	67.8%	30	12
Matt Leinart	-26	-23.9%	31	248	8.0	6.5	51.7%	1	1

Rushing

Player	DYAR	DVOA	Plays	Yds	Avg	TD	Fum	Suc
Tim Hightower	-79	-20.5%	143	400	2.8	10	1	37%
Edgerrin James*	46	0.0%	133	515	3.9	3	1	44%
J.J. Arrington*	44	31.2%	30	188	6.3	1	0	43%
Anquan Boldin	13	-9.7%	9	67	7.4	0	1	--
Kurt Warner	-12	-63.1%	3	11	3.7	0	0	--
Jason Wright	16	8.2%	23	85	3.7	0	0	39%

Receiving

Player	DYAR	DVOA	Plays	Ctch	Yds	Y/C	YAC	TD	C%
Larry Fitzgerald	402	19.7%	154	96	1431	14.9	4.7	12	62%
Anquan Boldin	269	13.9%	126	89	1038	11.7	6.1	11	71%
Steve Breaston	239	14.1%	113	77	1006	13.1	3.0	3	68%
Jerheme Urban	88	8.5%	51	34	448	13.2	4.7	4	67%
Early Doucet	12	-4.4%	17	14	90	6.4	3.8	0	82%
Ben Patrick	-3	-9.5%	18	11	104	9.5	4.1	1	61%
Leonard Pope	-14	-23.2%	13	9	77	8.6	1.8	0	69%
Stephen Spach	-19	-53.3%	6	2	15	7.5	5.5	0	33%
Anthony Becht	-31	-48.7%	11	6	39	6.5	3.2	0	55%
Tim Hightower	10	-10.2%	50	34	245	7.2	6.7	0	68%
J.J. Arrington*	81	23.3%	40	30	254	8.5	9.4	1	75%
Edgerrin James*	1	-12.6%	18	12	85	7.1	4.8	0	67%
Terrelle Smith*	-14	-46.9%	6	2	24	12.0	7.5	0	33%
Jason Wright	-17	-22.5%	37	22	155	7.0	5.5	2	59%
Dan Kreider	-19	-96.8%	5	0	0	0.0	0.0	0	0%

Offensive Line

Year	Yards	ALY	Rank	Power	Rank	10+ Yds	Rank	Stuff	Rank	Sacks	ASR	Rank	False	Cont.
2006	3.34	3.95	23	56%	26	4%	32	21%	28	36	6.3%	14	25	32
2007	3.70	4.28	9	65%	14	8%	32	15%	2	24	4.7%	9	29	39
2008	3.60	3.68	30	58%	29	15%	25	20%	26	28	4.4%	8	16	48

Year	LE	Rank	LT	Rank	Mid	Rank	RT	Rank	RE	Rank
2006	4.04	17	3.88	26	4.12	21	3.68	30	3.39	25
2007	3.74	21	4.34	13	4.22	10	4.71	3	4.15	12
2008	4.14	18	3.67	26	3.28	31	4.23	14	4.22	9

This unit was blessed with great health in 2008, as all five regulars started every game. If there is an injury here in 2009, it will likely come on the right side. Left tackle Mike Gandy hasn't missed a game in four years; left guard Reggie Wells, three. That's the good news. The bad news is that the Cardinals' line appears to have been built inside-out. Usually you look for strong run blocking from your guards and center, and strong pass blocking from your tackles. The Cardinals' interior linemen — Wells, center Lyle Sendlein, and right guard Deuce Lutui — combined for 5.5 blown blocks leading to sacks or hurries last season, an above-average performance considering Arizona attempted more passes than any team except New Orleans. Only 10 left tackles allowed more sacks on blown blocks than Gandy's 5.5, though, and Levi Brown's eight tied for the highest total among right tackles. On the other hand, the team was terrible running up the middle last season, and much better running to either side. The problem does not lie with fullback Terrelle Smith, who impressed our game charters with his blocking ability last season. (The same can not be said for all Arizona backs; Tim Hightower's poor pass protection, coupled with poor running, had him glued to the bench by the end of the season, and led to the drafting of Beanie Wells.)

Defensive Front Seven

Defensive Line	Age	Pos	Plays	TmPct	Rk	Stop	Dfts	Stop%	Rk	AvYd	Rk	Sack	Hit	Hur	Runs	St%	Yds	Pass	St%	Yds
						Overall						Pass Rush			vs. Run			vs. Pass		
Darnell Dockett	28	DT	50	6.4%	18	40	20	80%	24	2.1	40	4.0	14	7	38	79%	2.4	12	83%	1.0
Antonio Smith*	28	DE	37	4.7%	59	26	14	70%	70	1.8	46	3.5	10	4	29	72%	1.8	8	63%	1.9
Travis LaBoy	28	DE	31	4.9%	53	19	8	61%	89	3.3	86	4.0	3	4	26	54%	4.2	5	100%	-1.8
Bertrand Berry	34	DE	25	3.6%	77	16	7	64%	86	1.4	35	5.0	4	7	11	55%	3.3	14	71%	0.0
Calais Campbell	23	DE	22	2.8%	--	14	3	64%	--	4.2	--	0.0	1	2	16	69%	2.9	6	50%	7.5
Bryan Robinson	35	DE	20	2.6%	93	13	5	65%	82	2.3	66	1.0	1	2	15	73%	1.2	5	40%	5.4
Gabe Watson	26	DT	20	3.7%	59	16	4	80%	22	1.8	26	1.0	0	0	18	78%	2.5	2	100%	-5.0

Linebackers	Age	Pos	Plays	TmPct	Rk	Stop	Dfts	Stop%	AvYd	Sack	Hit	Hur	Runs	St%	Rk	Yds	Rk	Tgts	Suc%	Rk	AdjYd	Rk
						Overall				Pass Rush			vs. Run					vs. Pass				
Karlos Dansby	28	OLB	124	15.8%	16	73	26	59%	5.1	3.5	0	5	80	69%	30	3.6	59	29	40%	75	8.6	86
Gerald Hayes	29	ILB	97	12.4%	40	57	15	59%	4.1	1.0	2	4	60	65%	48	3.2	39	24	47%	57	6.8	57
Chike Okeafor	33	OLB	61	7.8%	84	40	15	66%	3.0	4.5	8	14	41	66%	43	3.0	29	18	41%	73	8.0	76
Clark Haggans	32	OLB	20	3.7%	--	12	2	60%	4.7	1.0	1	2	9	67%	--	3.6	--	7	78%	--	3.8	--

Year	Yards	ALY	Rank	Power	Rank	10+ Yds	Rank	Stuff	Rank	Sack	ASR	Rank
2006	4.23	4.22	18	66%	17	17%	21	20%	12	38	6.0%	23
2007	3.86	3.91	10	78%	32	16%	15	18%	18	37	6.0%	20
2008	3.94	4.15	15	70%	24	13%	7	17%	22	31	5.4%	23

Year	LE	Rank	LT	Rank	Mid	Rank	RT	Rank	RE	Rank
2006	3.20	6	4.48	18	4.64	28	4.30	19	4.34	20
2007	3.58	9	3.39	4	3.84	7	5.03	30	3.78	10
2008	4.91	27	4.02	12	4.60	29	2.75	1	4.13	19

The Cardinals got to the Super Bowl with a hybrid defense that switched back and forth between a 4-3 and a 3-4, but new defensive coordinator Bill Davis appears to be installing a more conventional 3-4 set. The plan is to play 332-pound Gabe Watson at nose tackle, but as of mid-May he was still being held out of drills with a bad knee. If he can't go, it'll be Alan Branch, taken by the Cardinals with the first pick in the second round in 2007. The ends will be second-year man Calais Campbell and Darnell Dockett, the most disruptive Arizona lineman over the past two seasons. He was held out of spring drills with a mysterious hamstring injury that may be related to his hunt for a new contract. With Travis LaBoy released in April, depth will be provided by Bryan Robinson, who started 15 games last year at tackle but is too small to play the nose in a pure 3-4.

Lining up at inside linebacker will be do-it-all player Karlos Dansby, the front seven's leading playmaker who rarely leaves the field. The other insidebacker will be Gerald Hayes, who is better against the pass than against the run, where our charters noted him being blocked out of plays and missing tackles. Strongside backer Chike Okeafor started every game after missing all of 2007 with a torn biceps. Expect him to rush the passer more this season. As a defensive end, he had at least six sacks every year between 2002 and 2006. The other outside backer will be Clark Haggans, who played mostly special teams in his first year in Arizona, but started 57 games in Pittsburgh's 3-4 from 2004 to 2007. Veteran Bertrand Berry will back up both Okeafor and Haggans. The

Cardinals added depth for this unit by using a second-round pick on Connecticut's Cody Brown, who will move to a rush-linebacker position in Arizona's 3-4 defense. Brown is quick, agile, and surprisingly strong in pass coverage for a player who was primarily playing defensive end in college, although he needs to learn a wider variety of pass rush moves if he wants to get past the NFL's better offensive tackles.

Defensive Secondary

				Overall					vs. Run					vs. Pass										
Secondary	Age	Pos	Plays	TmPct	Rk	Stop	Dfts	Yds	Rk	St%	Rk	Tgts	Tgt%	Rk	Dist	Suc%	Rk	AdjYd	Rk	Yds	PD	Int			
Antrel Rolle	27	FS	94	12.0%	13	28	8	7.5	48	34%	57	33	8.0%	22	11.9	40%	71	9.9	64	9.6	4	1			
Adrian Wilson	30	SS	78	10.6%	29	43	15	4.2	6	62%	5	32	8.1%	19	8.7	59%	20	6.4	12	6.5	7	2			
Dominique Rodgers-Cromartie	23	CB	58	7.4%	59	27	17	5.7	29	33%	59	74	17.8%	45	10.6	53%	34	6.7	33	6.5	18	4			
Roderick Hood*	28	CB	54	7.4%	60	23	5	15.2	81	17%	77	85	22.0%	18	12.6	45%	61	8.0	54	7.7	13	1			
Aaron Francisco	26	FS	42	5.4%	73	18	9	6.5	33	48%	20	13	3.0%	77	9.5	74%	1	4.0	2	3.9	3	0			
Eric Green*	27	CB	37	5.8%	--	16	4	5.0	--	36%	--	37	11.0%	--	13.5	54%	--	9.4	--	9.4	6	1			
Ralph Brown	31	CB	26	3.3%	--	12	7	1.0	--	67%	--	34	8.2%	--	8.7	53%	--	6.8	--	6.4	5	1			
Bryant McFadden	28	CB	48	9.7%	27	25	10	6.0	33	80%	1	51	17.6%	48	9.4	51%	39	6.4	26	5.7	9	2			

Year	Pass D Rank	vs. #1 WR	Rk	vs. #2 WR	Rk	vs. Other WR	Rk	vs. TE	Rk	vs. RB	Rk
2006	26	13.5%	28	1.5%	14	23.7%	27	-5.1%	15	9.3%	24
2007	21	16.4%	26	22.6%	28	-18.7%	9	-14.9%	3	-0.4%	17
2008	23	19.8%	27	-0.8%	15	16.7%	27	14.6%	22	1.6%	13

Adrian Wilson, longtime FO binky, remains one of the game's elite run support safeties. Still, it must be said that his numbers show only the value of the plays he made, not those he missed; our charters noted a surprisingly high number of missed tackles. He turns 30 during the upcoming season, but safeties are not running backs, and he should be productive for a few more years. While Wilson is close to the line, former cornerback Antrel Rolle is playing a deep free safety, which partially explains why his Success Rate on pass plays is so low. Dominique Rodgers-Cromartie was made a full-time starter in Week 9 of his rookie season. He showed flashed of brilliance, but struggled with consistency and often looked awful trying to tackle opposing runners. One guy who didn't struggle with tackles is Bryant McFadden, formerly of the Steelers and the league's top cornerback on rushing plays in 2008. The nickelback will once again be Ralph Brown; he's led Arizona cornerbacks in Adjusted Yards per Pass over the past two years (although he also covers the shortest routes).

Special Teams

Year	DVOA	Rank	FG/XP	Rank	Net Kick	Rank	Kick Ret	Rank	Net Punt	Rank	Punt Ret	Rank	Hidden	Rank
2006	-5.0%	32	-2.8	21	0.6	17	-3.5	22	-20.0	31	-3.8	29	-7.1	25
2007	-3.8%	26	-6.9	29	6.1	7	-4.8	24	-21.2	32	4.7	7	8.2	8
2008	-3.7%	28	2.1	13	-9.1	29	-1.8	19	-6.5	25	-6.5	28	4.0	8

Arizona once again struggled to put together a decent coverage team, a sign of poor depth across the roster. The problem was especially notable on kickoffs, where Neil Rackers was slightly above average by himself, but the Cardinals' coverage teams were worst in the league by a wide margin. At punter, the Cardinals released Dirk Johnson during the season, choosing instead to go with Ben Graham, who had already been cut by both the Saints and the Jets. He was close to league average in punt value, but in his four games with Arizona, his coverage teams allowed returns of 33 yards to Derek Stanley of the Rams and 28 yards to Wes Welker of the Patriots, plus an 82-yard touchdown to Bernard Berrian of the Vikings. Graham will return in 2009, hopefully with better support. The draft might help, as Cody Brown and third-round safety Rashad Johnson are both considered strong tacklers on special teams.

Things weren't much better for the Cardinals when their opponents were kicking; primary return man Steve Breaston was one of the league's worst on both punt and kickoff returns. J.J. Arrington fared much better, returning one kickoff for a touchdown against Dallas, but he's gone now. Sixth-round running back LaRod Stephens-Howling could get a shot at return duties.

Coaching Staff

It was a newsworthy couple of weeks after the Super Bowl for Arizona. First, offensive coordinator Todd Haley left to take the head coach position in Kansas City. Shortly thereafter, defensive coordinator Clancy Pendergast was fired. The termination was a long time coming; Cards coach Ken Whisenhunt had wanted to make the move as soon as he took the job, but was talked out of it by management. Pendergast's position in Arizona will be filled by Bill Davis, a 17-year NFL coaching veteran who had been the Cardinals' linebackers coach. He also has previous coordinator experience, running San Francisco's defense in 2005 and 2006. Those defenses switched between 4-3 and 3-4 formations, as the Cardinals have done in recent years. Under Davis, the 49ers rarely used big blitzes of six or more defenders, but they did send a lot of defensive backs after opposing quarterbacks. In 2006, five different San Francisco defensive backs had at least one sack. Adrian Wilson enters 2009 with 18.5 career sacks — expect that number to climb. One important task for Davis is improving Arizona's performance in the red zone. The Cardinals surrendered a touchdown on 63.6 percent of opponents' red zone drives, ranking 28th in the league.

Whisenhunt himself will call the plays on offense. It's hard to knock a coach who got his team to the Super Bowl, and Whisenhunt deserves credit for creative schemes on both sides of the ball that mask the weaknesses and accentuate the strengths of his roster. On the other hand, the Cardinals did experience a severe second-half lull that might have cost them a playoff berth in a more competitive division, and Whisenhunt can sometimes get cute just for cuteness' sake. For example, defensive backs Antrel Rolle and Dominique Rodgers-Cromartie both saw playing time on offense, where the Cardinals were not exactly hurting for playmakers.

Atlanta Falcons

Let's explain the Falcons' 2008 season in terms owner Arthur Blank, the man who built the Home Depot chain, can understand. Blank wanted to build a palatial McMansion in downtown Atlanta. He hired several contractors who created snazzy exteriors. But the building's foundation was a rotting hulk, prone to collapse from within. No one Blank hired was willing to address that problem. So his building remained unpalatable to the masses.

Finally, Blank tired of being ripped off by flashy but insubstantial work. He brought in some employees who tore down the entire structure and started anew. The edifice they built wasn't very showy, but it was stable and strong. And it turned out that people much preferred it to the old version.

Here endeth the metaphor. Anyone else have a hankering to go buy some sheetrock?

2007 was an extended nightmare for Blank. It isn't hyperbolic to suggest that it was among the worst seasons ever suffered by a franchise. After years of humiliation at the hands of well-paid employees like Jim Mora, Bobby Petrino, and most notoriously Michael Vick, Blank finally wised up. He tried to hire the ultimate franchise re-booter, Bill Parcells, but the Tuna preferred South Beach to the Dirty South. Blank turned instead to a branch of the Parcells tree, Thomas Dimitroff. Dimitroff was Bill Belichick's college scouting director in New England, and had worked for the Pats coach

when Belichick headed the Cleveland Browns. Dimitroff was a member of Cleveland's grounds crew.

Resodding the "Mistake By The Lake" apparently offers a man plenty of quality thinking time. Dimitroff brought a coherent plan for team building to Georgia. His first move was to hire Mike Smith as head coach.

Several highly rated assistant coaches had interviewed with Blank already — but USC coach Pete Carroll was the sexy name in the mix. Dimitroff convinced Blank to forego the banner headlines Carroll would create and hire the little known Smith, who was defensive coordinator in Jacksonville.

Dimitroff and Smith quickly shed the roster of veterans they deemed surplus to requirements. DeAngelo Hall, Alge Crumpler, and Rod Coleman were among those long-time Falcons let go, while even young players like 2006 second-round pick Jimmy Williams and 2008 fourth-round pick Martrez Milner were given one way flights out of ATL.

Of course, clearing out roster spots and salary cap space doesn't do an organization any good unless they find better players to fill that space, so it was essential that Dimitroff and Smith hit on the third overall pick. The debate ended up being between the safer pick, LSU defensive tackle Glenn Dorsey, and the high risk, high reward option of Boston College quarterback Matt Ryan. Ryan's completion percentage in his final year at B.C. raised

---

FALCONS SUMMARY

2008 Record: 11-5

Pythagorean Wins: 9.7 (10th)

DVOA: 5.6% (16th)

Offense: 12.9% (10th)

Defense: 10.6% (25th)

Special Teams: 3.3% (7th)

Variance: 19.0% (23rd)

2008: Rookie GM, coach, and quarterback pole vault over low expectations and into the playoffs.

2009: That bar is set much higher, and the team is weighted down by almost certain regression.

2009 Mean Projection: 6.6

On the Clock (0-3): 10%

Loserville (4-6): 39%

Mediocrity (7-8): 29%

Playoff Contender (9-10): 18%

Super Bowl Contender (11+): 4%

Projected Average Opponent: -1.6% (23rd)

2009 Falcons Schedule

Week	Opp.	Week	Opp.	Week	Opp.
1	MIA	7	at DAL	13	PHI
2	CAR	8	at NO (Mon.)	14	NO
3	at NE	9	WAS	15	at NYJ
4	BYE	10	at CAR	16	BUF
5	at SF	11	at NYG	17	at TB
6	CHI	12	TB		

issues about his accuracy at the pro level, yielding comparisons to a list of busts that only require one name to identify them: Akili, Leaf, Joey, Couch.

Despite much local clamoring for Dorsey, whom all of Georgia had watched dominate the SEC, the Atlanta brain trust staked their entire regime on Ryan. The move went to show that Dimitroff may have studied at the feet of the master, but had the *huevos* to trust his own instincts and make the unpopular, perilous decision.

The rest, of course, is history. Based on the system we used to rank the top quarterback seasons of all-time in our book *Pro Football Prospectus 2005*, Ryan had the finest rookie season of any quarterback since the 1970 AFL-NFL merger. (see Table 1 below). He threw for a 62-yard touchdown on his very first official pass. Ryan's defining moment came in mid-October against the Bears. Trailing by a point with six seconds to play, Ryan delivered a picture-perfect corner route pass to Michael Jenkins, who skipped out of bounds with a single tick left. The ensuing field goal gave Atlanta a heartstopping win.

Ryan parachuted into the perfect situation for a rookie signal-caller. Atlanta signed Michael Turner, who answered all questions about his ability to be a franchise back. The offensive line pulled off a stunning about-face that mirrored that of the team overall. The receiving corps performed admirably. Ryan was seldom asked to win games with his arm. And when he needed to make plays, he consistently did so. Few rookies at any position have entered the league looking and playing with such confidence — that is a compliment both to Ryan and the coaches that prepared him so well.

Of course, sports are all about that most ruthless and cynical question — "What have you done for me lately?" Ryan's effectiveness tailed off at the end of the season. His DVOA over the final five games (including the wild-card contest) plummeted from 36.8% to 8.2%. Ryan's DYAR over the same stretch fell from 83.7 per game to 22.2. He threw two critical interceptions in Atlanta's loss at Arizona in the wild-card playoff game. In fairness, the Falcons won three of the final four regular season games despite Ryan's decline, putting themselves on the brink of the division title.

The Falcons should throw it around more this season, due to Ryan's maturity and a desire to reduce Turner's workload. But while KUBIAK projections see Ryan throwing more touchdowns, it also sees a drop in completion percentage, net yards per pass, and DVOA.

Of course, the Falcons now have a mitigating factor to those projections, in the form of a 6-foot-5 freakish athlete with tractor beams for hands. The acquisition of future Hall of Fame tight end Tony Gonzalez before the draft cranked up the expectations meter in Atlanta. The sole obvious need on offense was a pass-catching tight end to provide Ryan a safety valve and red zone target. The fact that the team traded for the best one ever — at the low, low cost of only a 2010

Table 1: Top 10 Rookie Quarterbacks Since 1960 (27 or Younger)

Player	Year	Team	G	Actual Comp	Att	C%	PaYd	Yd/At	TD	INT	RuYd	Translated to 04-08 Environment Comp	Att	C%	PaYd	Yd/At	TD	INT	RuYd
Greg Cook	1969	CIN	11	106	197	54%	1854	9.4	15	11	148	170	261	65%	2657	10.2	17	8	170
Matt Ryan	2008	ATL	16	265	434	61%	3440	7.9	16	11	104	262	435	60%	3544	8.2	17	12	109
Ben Roethlisberger	2004	PIT	14	196	295	66%	2621	8.9	17	11	144	200	299	67%	2533	8.5	16	11	135
Dennis Shaw	1970	BUF	14	178	321	55%	2507	7.8	10	20	210	288	437	66%	3448	7.9	13	16	238
Jim Kelly	1986	BUF	16	285	480	59%	3593	7.5	22	17	199	310	481	65%	3465	7.2	22	13	190
Dan Marino	1983	MIA	11	173	296	58%	2210	7.5	20	6	45	189	305	62%	2135	7.0	19	4	44
Joe Flacco	2008	BAL	16	257	428	60%	2971	6.9	14	12	180	254	429	59%	3061	7.1	15	13	188
Charlie Batch	1998	DET	12	173	303	57%	2178	7.2	11	6	229	185	304	61%	2145	7.1	11	6	181
Fran Tarkenton	1961	MIN	14	157	280	56%	1997	7.1	18	17	308	248	383	65%	2459	6.4	19	11	242
Byron Leftwich	2003	JAC	15	239	418	57%	2819	6.7	14	16	108	246	420	59%	2870	6.8	15	15	101

For methodology, see http://www.footballoutsiders.com/stats/qbmethod

second-round pick — burnished Dimitroff's reputation around town to Schuerholzian levels. Credit too should go to Gonzalez for being thoroughly professional about his trade request, unlike Chad Ochocinco, for example. As Mike Florio of Pro Football Talk pointed out, when a player "mans up" and doesn't try to bitch his way out of town, the likelihood of being accommodated increases exponentially.

Gonzalez's presence should help the rest of the receivers keep their numbers from dropping off dramatically. Roddy White and Michael Jenkins were excellent in 2008. White has solidified himself as a true number one receiver. He is blazingly fast, and has gotten over the dropsies that plagued him when Vick was hurling thunderbolts in his direction. Jenkins has settled in as the possession-oriented number two. Speedy Harry Douglas will love drafting off the attention-getting Gonzalez in the slot. With no precedent to work from, our projection system doesn't have a variable for "added the best tight end in history."

The power running game instituted by Smith and offensive coordinator Mike Mularkey was executed to perfection by the resurgent line, fullback Ovie Mughelli, and Turner. The Vick-and-Petrino-era Falcons attempted to exploit the speedy Georgia Dome carpet, and built a small, agile squad. Smith determined that hitting the other guy harder is an effective style indoors and out, and was rewarded with 152.7 rushing yards per game, second-most in the league.

Table 2: Matt Ryan's Hope: Teams Since 1978 That Improved by 7+Wins

Team	Years	Year 1	Year 2	Δ Wins	Year 3	Δ Wins
MIA	2007-2009	1-15	11-5	+10	--	--
IND	1998-2000	3-13	13-3	+10	10-6	-3
PIT	2003-2005	6-10	15-1	+9	11-5	-4
STL	1998-2000	4-12	13-3	+9	10-6	-3
SD	2003-2005	4-12	12-4	+8	9-7	-3
CHI	2000-2002	5-11	13-3	+8	4-12	-9
NYJ	1996-1998	1-15	9-7	+8	12-4	+3
IND	1991-1993	1-15	9-7	+8	4-12	-5
CIN	1987-1989	4-11	12-4	+8	8-8	-4
ATL	2007-2009	4-12	11-5	+7	--	--
BAL	2005-2007	6-10	13-3	+7	5-11	-8
NO	2005-2007	3-13	10-6	+7	7-9	-3
NO	1999-2001	3-13	10-6	+7	7-9	-3
ATL	1997-1999	7-9	14-2	+7	5-11	-9
SD	1991-1993	4-12	11-5	+7	8-8	-3
DEN	1990-1992	5-11	12-4	+7	8-8	-4
DET	1979-1981	2-14	9-7	+7	8-8	-1
Average				7.9		-3.9

However, Atlanta's rushing DVOA was only 3.4%, 13th best in the NFL. Before adjustment, Atlanta was fifth best, which speaks to the easy schedule Atlanta played in 2008. Six division games against the 12th (Tampa), 20th (New Orleans), and 24th (Carolina) rated rush defenses helps. Atlanta's schedule replaces the AFC West with the AFC East in 2009 (including a season-opening test of Year Two strength against Miami), and the NFC North with the powerful NFC East.

This brings us to our pessimistic projection for the team in 2009. Whether Ryan falls off a little or a lot, the history of fast turnarounds suggests that reality comes to town in Year Two. Since 1978, 17 different teams have improved by seven or more wins (not counting the 1982 strike season). We don't know yet about this year's Falcons and Dolphins, but the other teams declined by an average of four wins the following season (Table 2). Only the 1998 Jets built on their huge improvement, and they had Bill Parcells growling from the sideline.

The Falcons certainly don't have history on their side — incredibly, the franchise has never posted back-to-back winning seasons in its 43-year existence. Fans need only go back a decade to find a steep fall after a dramatic rise. The 1998 Falcons leapt from 7-9 to 14-2 and a trip to the Super Bowl. The 1999 Falcons crashed to an ugly 5-11 campaign, thanks in large part to injuries to quarterback Chris Chandler and All-Pro running back Jamal Anderson.

Ah, yes, injuries. The Falcons ranked fifth in the league in Adjusted Games Lost (the similarly rags-to-riches Dolphins were fourth). Rookie tackle Sam Baker was the only key player to miss significant time. The excellent health is unlikely to repeat itself. If Ryan and Turner go down, the team could easily extend that historic run of mediocrity.

Assuming the stars stay off injured reserve, the most likely culprit in Atlanta's regression is the defense. The Falcons actually improved in defensive DVOA from 2007, but context is everything — on a contender, the failure to find any consistency, especially against the run, cost the team dearly. Atlanta released several defenders in the offseason, including long-serving linebacker Keith Brooking. Starters Michael Boley and Domonique Foxworth were allowed to sign elsewhere.

The 2009 unit will be young and inexperienced, with a notable lack of depth. Newcomers are the key. First-round draft choice Peria Jerry is this year's Dorsey, a stud defensive tackle from the SEC. Linebacker Mike Peterson, an old favorite of Smith's, was brought over from Jacksonville to further bulwark against the division's potent running games. Another rookie, William Moore, is the presumptive starting safety opposite Erik Coleman.

The only certainties on defense are John Abraham, a destructive pass rushing force off the edge, and Curtis Lofton, who had a superb rookie season at middle linebacker. Everywhere else, question marks dot the landscape. Smith, a longtime defensive coach, will have to call upon all his wiles to achieve respectability on that side of the ball.

Surprisingly, the feeling in Atlanta is less one of grateful surprise over last season's achievements than one of unfinished business. Remember, Atlanta only played in the wild-card game because Steve

Smith latched onto a desperation heave in double coverage in the regular season finale. The ensuing field goal cost Atlanta a division title, a week off, and at least one home playoff game. The collapse in the desert left a bitter taste, one that was only mildly alleviated by Arizona's Super Bowl run. Big things are expected this season, not least by the team itself.

Even if the Falcons take an almost inevitable step back in 2009, the feeling that Dimitroff is in full control and has a long-term plan is palpable, a rare feeling for Birds fans. For what seems like the first time ever, the franchise is imbued with professionalism. The football operation promises to be simply but smartly designed, well executed, and within budgetary constraints. Kind of like Home Depot.

Robert Weintraub

2008 Falcons Stats by Week

Wk	vs.	W-L	PF	PA	YDF	YDA	TO	Total	Off	Def	ST
1	DET	W	34	21	474	316	+1	22%	64%	44%	3%
2	@TB	L	9	24	234	311	-1	-56%	-42%	17%	4%
3	KC	W	38	14	378	301	+2	65%	26%	-34%	5%
4	@CAR	L	9	24	268	401	0	-27%	-2%	29%	4%
5	@GB	W	27	24	370	408	0	4%	27%	25%	1%
6	CHI	W	22	20	376	361	0	-14%	12%	30%	4%
7	BYE										
8	@PHI	L	14	27	335	432	-2	-9%	12%	23%	2%
9	@OAK	W	24	0	453	77	+1	91%	23%	-79%	-11%
10	NO	W	34	20	521	521	+3	68%	40%	-16%	12%
11	DEN	L	20	24	361	332	-1	-48%	-11%	28%	-8%
12	CAR	W	45	28	392	408	-1	29%	34%	24%	19%
13	@SD	W	22	16	348	201	-3	58%	5%	-41%	11%
14	@NO	L	25	29	414	414	-1	-23%	17%	35%	-5%
15	TB	W	13	10	373	325	-2	-17%	-13%	-1%	-5%
16	@MIN	W	24	17	222	356	+4	19%	16%	6%	9%
17	STL	W	31	27	417	408	-3	-21%	5%	38%	13%
18	@ARI	L	24	30	250	357	-2	-23%	-23%	13%	13%

Trends and Splits

	Offense	Rank	Defense	Rank
Total DVOA	12.9%	10	10.6%	25
Unadjusted VOA	12.0%	10	11.9%	25
Weighted trend	11.9%	12	10.4%	22
Variance	5.9%	10	5.8%	17
Average opponent	5.0%	9	5.6%	19
Passing	36.9%	4	11.9%	17
Rushing	3.5%	19	9.0%	25
First down	18.2%	2	0.4%	18
Second down	3.4%	20	31.9%	32
Third down	17.9%	12	-2.1%	10
First half	13.0%	12	9.7%	19
Second half	12.7%	13	11.4%	25
Red Zone	-1.6%	25	-1.8%	15
Late and close	11.0%	17	20.5%	28

Five-Year Performance

Year	W-L	Pyth	Est W	PF	PA	TO	Total	Rk	Off	Rk	Def	Rk	ST	Rk	Off AGL	Rk	Def AGL	Rk
2004	11-5	8.1	8.0	340	337	+2	-5.0%	17	-9.4%	24	-0.4%	17	4.0%	6	5.7	30	10.0	27
2005	8-8	8.3	7.0	351	341	0	-5.8%	19	2.5%	12	10.7%	28	2.4%	6	4.0	30	4.7	32
2006	7-9	6.9	7.4	292	328	+6	-6.9%	20	0.0%	16	3.1%	18	-3.8%	28	13.0	20	22.5	11
2007	4-12	8.1	6.3	259	414	+4	-26.5%	28	-15.5%	27	11.0%	28	0.0%	14	26.4	6	20.4	16
2008	11-5	9.7	8.7	391	325	-3	5.6%	16	12.9%	10	10.6%	25	3.3%	7	15.5	22	13.3	26

Strategic Tendencies

Run/Pass		Rank	Offense		Rank	Defense		Rank	Other		Rank
Runs, all plays	54%	2	3+ WR	45%	25	Rush 3	6.4%	12	2+ RB, Pct Runs	65%	9
Runs, first half	53%	1	4+ WR	13%	12	Rush 4	71.8%	4	1 RB/2 TE, Pct Runs	60%	5
Runs, first down	69%	1	2+ TE	35%	7	Rush 5	13.3%	28	1 RB/3+ WR, PctRuns	37%	3
Runs, second-long	48%	4	Single back	48%	23	Rush 6+	8.6%	14	Zone Blitz	2%	20
Runs, power sit.	78%	3	Play action	18%	15	Rush 7+	3.0%	5	Go for it on 4th	1.04	9
Runs, behind 2H	36%	10	Max protect	10%	7	Sacks by LB	6.1%	29	Offensive Pace	29.5	7
Pass, ahead 2H	34%	30	Outside pocket	18%	3	Sacks by DB	0.0%	30	Defensive Pace	29.9	3

Ch-ch-ch-changes: The 2007 Falcons ranked 27th in run/pass ratio on all plays and 28th in run/pass ratio on first downs. Last year they were second and first, respectively. ● Trends Unlikely to Continue Department: The Falcons threw only seven percent of passes to tight ends, 31st in the NFL. ● Think it is a good idea to big-blitz the rookie? Think again. The Falcons actually ranked seventh with 50.7% DVOA against six or more pass rushers. ● Atlanta had the second-worst defense in the league against draw plays, giving up 52.8% DVOA. Only Denver was worse. ● The Falcons also had a habit of falling for play-fakes, with the NFL's fifth highest gap between DVOA against passes/scrambles with a play fake (47.7% DVOA) and those without (7.2% DVOA). ● The Falcons improved from 30th to 11th in DVOA against sets with four or more wide receivers.

Passing

Player	DYAR	DVOA	Plays	NtYds	Avg	YAC	C%	TD	Int
Matt Ryan	1167	30.9%	455	3419	7.5	5.0	61.3%	16	11

Rushing

Player	DYAR	DVOA	Plays	Yds	Avg	TD	Fum	Suc
Michael Turner	203	4.1%	376	1699	4.5	17	3	48%
Jerious Norwood	57	7.1%	95	489	5.1	4	1	41%
Matt Ryan	-34	-30.0%	31	126	4.1	1	2	--
Jason Snelling	11	9.5%	15	62	4.1	0	0	47%
Harry Douglas	36	23.2%	12	69	5.8	1	0	--
Ovie Mughelli	2	-4.7%	5	16	3.2	0	0	80%

Receiving

Player	DYAR	DVOA	Plays	Ctch	Yds	Y/C	YAC	TD	C%
Roddy White	399	22.1%	148	88	1383	15.7	4.1	7	59%
Michael Jenkins	179	16.0%	81	50	777	15.5	3.4	3	62%
Harry Douglas	31	-2.2%	39	23	320	13.9	4.6	1	59%
Brian Finneran	-27	-22.0%	36	21	169	8.0	2.3	1	58%
Laurent Robinson*	21	36.8%	6	5	52	10.4	5.4	0	83%
Justin Peelle	25	7.9%	23	15	159	10.6	7.5	2	65%
Ben Hartsock	-12	-38.6%	6	3	26	8.7	4.7	0	50%
Tony Gonzalez	243	16.5%	155	96	1058	11.0	2.6	10	62%
Jerious Norwood	55	5.0%	54	36	338	9.4	8.5	2	67%
Jason Snelling	24	43.9%	11	8	89	11.1	10.8	0	73%
Ovie Mughelli	11	7.6%	10	8	57	7.1	5.3	0	80%
Michael Turner	2	-9.5%	9	6	41	6.8	5.2	0	67%

Offensive Line

Year	Yards	ALY	Rank	Power	Rank	10+ Yds	Rank	Stuff	Rank	Sacks	ASR	Rank	False	Cont.
2006	4.64	4.15	17	59%	23	23%	4	18%	11	47	10.5%	31	12	31
2007	4.04	3.42	32	62%	17	24%	5	26%	32	47	7.9%	24	27	26
2008	4.62	4.22	9	70%	11	23%	7	20%	24	17	3.6%	5	18	38

Year	LE	Rank	LT	Rank	Mid	Rank	RT	Rank	RE	Rank
2006	4.45	10	3.57	30	4.29	16	4.16	13	4.59	8
2007	3.36	26	3.63	28	3.24	32	3.07	32	4.32	11
2008	3.92	22	4.81	6	4.05	20	4.22	15	4.36	7

The most astonishing part of the Falcons revival in 2008 came up front. Atlanta improved in Adjusted Line Yards from dead last to ninth, while Adjusted Sack Rate leapt from 24th to fifth. Yes, the acquisition of a powerhouse runner helped, as did the precocious skills of the team's rookie quarterback. But the line was as big a reason as any for the reversal of fortune in the Georgia Dome. The new emphasis on straight-ahead blocking, rather than the stretch and cut scheme of the previous regime, seemed to have a energizing impact.

The decision to trade up and take Sam Baker in the first round of last year's draft was even more controversial than the decision to take Matt Ryan third overall. Baker started at left tackle opening day, but was plagued with injuries, including a concussion and hip and back woes. Todd Weiner stepped in and was very good, as the Falcons' ALY on runs behind left tackle jumped significantly compared to 2007. The Harvey Dahl-Todd McClure-Justin Blalock interior showed cohesion and consistency, but there is room for improvement, as the Falcons were below-average on runs up the middle and their runners were stuffed at the line 20 percent of the time. Tyson Clabo held down right tackle, and Atlanta's running to the right also improved over 2007. In case of injury, most of the Falcons' depth linemen have starting experience, including center Jeremy Newberry (ex-San Francisco/Oakland), guard Brett Romberg (ex-St. Louis), and tackle Will Svitek (ex-Kansas City).

Defensive Front Seven

Defensive Line	Age	Pos	Plays	TmPct	Overall Rk	Stop	Dfts	Stop%	Rk	AvYd	Pass Rush Rk	Sack	Hit	Hur	vs. Run Runs	St%	Yds	vs. Pass Pass	St%	Yds
Jonathan Babineaux	28	DT	39	4.9%	37	31	19	79%	26	0.6	4	3.5	8	10	30	77%	1.4	9	89%	-2.2
John Abraham	31	DE	38	4.8%	55	32	22	84%	16	-1.4	1	16.5	16	20	17	71%	2.7	21	95%	-4.7
Chauncey Davis	26	DE	38	4.8%	56	29	12	76%	48	1.7	40	4.0	0	6	30	77%	1.8	8	75%	1.1
Grady Jackson*	36	DT	29	3.9%	57	24	8	83%	11	0.6	5	2.0	0	2	26	81%	1.2	3	100%	-4.7
Jamaal Anderson	23	DE	29	3.9%	71	22	7	76%	51	2.2	62	2.0	3	8	23	74%	2.7	6	83%	0.2
Kindal Moorehead	31	DT	19	2.8%	--	14	6	74%	--	1.9	--	1.0	3	3	13	77%	1.1	6	67%	3.8

Linebackers	Age	Pos	Plays	TmPct	Overall Rk	Stop	Dfts	Stop%	AvYd	Pass Rush Sack	Hit	Hur	vs. Run Runs	St%	Rk	Yds	Rk	vs. Pass Tgts	Suc%	Rk	AdjYd	Rk
Keith Brooking*	34	ILB	106	13.5%	30	47	14	44%	6.2	0.0	5	1	52	58%	85	3.5	55	46	39%	77	8.1	80
Curtis Lofton	23	ILB	89	11.3%	53	54	13	61%	5.0	1.0	1	1	69	70%	25	3.9	75	15	67%	--	4.0	--
Michael Boley*	27	OLB	81	10.3%	66	41	14	51%	5.9	0.0	1	2	36	58%	82	4.4	95	44	57%	29	5.4	22
Coy Wire	31	OLB	21	2.7%	--	13	1	62%	3.6	0.0	0	0	10	60%	--	3.1	--	13	51%	--	4.7	--
Mike Peterson	33	ILB	84	12.0%	46	46	11	55%	4.8	1.0	2	3	64	66%	44	3.6	56	23	39%	76	6.8	55

Year	Yards	ALY	Rank	Power	Rank	10+ Yds	Rank	Stuff	Rank	Sack	ASR	Rank
2006	3.84	4.08	12	56%	6	12%	4	22%	5	38	7.9%	10
2007	4.40	4.44	28	62%	15	16%	16	17%	23	25	6.0%	21
2008	4.74	4.20	19	58%	5	22%	24	20%	9	34	6.9%	10

Year	LE	Rank	LT	Rank	Mid	Rank	RT	Rank	RE	Rank
2006	5.04	29	3.52	8	4.14	15	3.51	10	4.92	30
2007	4.97	27	4.72	25	4.38	27	3.90	14	4.87	28
2008	4.44	23	5.25	31	3.86	8	4.19	18	3.96	17

The good news: John Abraham was a terrorizing force off the edge: third in the NFL with 16.5 sacks, fourth with 16 quarterback hits, and sixth with 20 hurries. One charter noted his dominance by writing that "(Tampa Bay OT Donald) Penn tried to hold him at one point, but couldn't even pull that off." Abraham frequently flipped sides, and was unblockable from either direction.

The bad news: Atlanta was rather poor against the run. Opponents took advantage of Abraham's single-minded race to the quarterback and ran inside him. On the other side, 2007 first-rounder Jamaal Anderson has bust written all over him, but will get one more season to straighten things out. The team used its first-rounder this year on the tackle spot. Peria Jerry is "country strong," in the words of GM Thomas Dimitroff, and was excellent at one-gap penetration of lines at Ole Miss. He suffered a knee injury in minicamp; provided he recovers, Perry and Iowa alum Johnathan Babineaux will be expected to shore up the inside.

Atlanta finally cut ties with long-serving linebacker Keith Brooking and Michael Boley defected to New York, leaving middle man Curtis Lofton as the only returning starter. Lofton had a sturdy rookie campaign, and is the lone Falcon at the position with the speed to be effective in coverage. Coy Wire and Mike Peterson will flank Lofton. Peterson is aging but knows coach Mike Smith well from their time in Jacksonville, and is an upgrade over Brooking. Wire is a good tackler but lacks coverage ability. Third-year linebacker Stephen Nicolas will replace him on passing downs, or perhaps entirely, depending on his progress.

Defensive Secondary

Secondary	Age	Pos	Plays	Overall				vs. Run				vs. Pass										
				TmPct	Rk	Stop	Dfts	Yds	Rk	St%	Rk	Tgts	Tgt%	Rk	Dist	Suc%	Rk	AdjYd	Rk	Yds	PD	Int
Erik Coleman	27	SS	101	12.8%	8	22	10	10.5	73	22%	72	29	6.3%	47	15.3	45%	65	8.6	52	8.8	4	3
Lawyer Milloy*	36	SS	97	13.1%	5	32	7	6.6	36	38%	48	24	5.5%	58	10.5	51%	40	7.4	26	8.0	5	1
Chris Houston	24	CB	77	9.8%	26	29	13	9.0	61	33%	58	92	20.3%	25	11.9	54%	27	7.6	46	7.7	22	2
Domonique Foxworth*	26	CB	50	7.3%	62	22	7	7.4	51	56%	22	70	17.5%	49	10.9	62%	10	5.1	5	5.9	13	1
Brent Grimes	26	CB	37	6.3%	72	15	7	2.9	3	70%	5	53	15.4%	62	12.1	41%	76	8.2	59	8.2	7	1
Chevis Jackson	24	CB	36	4.6%	--	11	4	8.2	--	20%	--	37	8.1%	--	8.3	44%	--	6.5	--	6.8	6	1

Year	Pass D Rank	vs. #1 WR	Rk	vs. #2 WR	Rk	vs. Other WR	Rk	vs. TE	Rk	vs. RB	Rk
2006	23	35.5%	32	32.4%	31	-5.8%	16	1.2%	21	-37.4%	2
2007	27	-0.4%	14	31.4%	32	6.6%	25	27.2%	31	-5.3%	12
2008	18	3.0%	15	5.1%	20	-28.1%	7	25.1%	28	20.6%	29

Atlanta's best cover corner in 2008, Domonique Foxworth, signed a rich contract with Baltimore, leaving the Falcons young and vulnerable in the secondary. Even with Foxworth, the Falcons didn't fare well against the pass, but much of that is due to the poor coverage of the linebackers. The Falcons were 28th in DVOA against passes to enemy tight ends, and 29th against throws to running backs. Defense against passes to wide receivers was closer to average.

Nevertheless, the departure of Foxworth and veteran (clubhouse) Lawyer Milloy left depth issues in the secondary, so the Falcons used three draft picks to shore up the unit.

Second-rounder William Moore is expected to replace Milloy at strong safety; he was inconsistent as a senior at Missouri, but is a good hitter with ball skills. Free safety Erik Coleman isn't much against the run, and is about the only Falcon to tangle with Smith last season, but he looks like a starter by default.

Corner is wide open. Chris Houston will hold one starting spot — he's gradually improving his cover skills, but is small and ineffective against the run. The other spot could go to reserves Chevis Jackson or Brent Grimes, who started early in the season and showed he wasn't ready for prime time. Two rookies will press for playing time. Chris Owens from San Jose State is a good tackler, and William Middleton, another small school product (he was team MVP for Furman as a senior), is short but strong and fast. No matter who plays in the secondary, they are likely to deliver more turnovers than a year ago, when Atlanta defensive backs had only ten picks.

Special Teams

Year	DVOA	Rank	FG/XP	Rank	Net Kick	Rank	Kick Ret	Rank	Net Punt	Rank	Punt Ret	Rank	Hidden	Rank
2006	-3.8%	28	-14.6	32	12.4	4	-8.0	27	-11.1	30	-0.7	16	-3.8	21
2007	0.0%	14	-12.6	32	1.9	13	2.9	12	11.2	2	-3.3	20	-10.1	29
2008	3.3%	7	5.2	6	9.2	4	1.8	15	4.8	12	-1.6	19	6.3	5

After consecutive dead last rankings in placekicking, the Falcons ended the Morten Andersen social security program and brought in a great kicker of slightly newer vintage, Jason Elam. The result was nearly an 18-point improvement in value on field goals, up to sixth in the NFL. Michel Koenen kicked off well, but wasn't so good when it came to his primary duty, punting, In both areas, he benefited from outstanding coverage — both units were in the top ten in return points allowed compared to the NFL average. The returners were middle of the pack. Jerious Norwood proved more explosive from scrimmage than on kickoffs. Harry Douglas took over punt return duty from Adam Jennings, and was more effective, mainly thanks to a 61-yard touchdown return in Week 11.

There was also a hidden reason for Atlanta's better season: better luck when it came to opposing field-goal kickers. Kickers were 28-of-30 on field goals against Atlanta in 2007 (hitting all five opportunities from more than 48 yards away), but only 20-of-25 last year (with just one field goal more than 48 yards).

Coaching Staff

After the drama-filled reigns of Jim "I'd rather be in Seattle" Mora and Bobby "I'd rather be anywhere" Petrino, the simple professionalism of Mike Smith was a gale-force gust of fresh air. With schemes as basic as his name, Smith reintroduced power running and toughness to the team. Smith and offensive coordinator Mike Mularkey took a rookie quarterback, designed a system that didn't put him in many bad situations, emphasized caution, and watched him flourish. Paul Boudreau eliminated Alex Gibbs' cut-blocking system, and his line responded with career years.

Nevertheless, before the Falcons can start printing "NFC Champions" t-shirts with Tony Gonzalez's picture on the front, something has to be done about the defense. Coordinator Brian Van Gorder built tremendous defenses several miles to the east while at the University of Georgia, but he hasn't impressed in the pro ranks. Ironically, given the Petrino fiasco, BVG jumped to Steve Spurrier's staff after spending 2007 as Atlanta's linebacker coach, saying he always "wanted to be a college guy." One whole month later, he was back with the Falcons, with a promotion. Van Gorder's defenses are zone-heavy, and teaching responsibilities to an inexperienced secondary is his biggest challenge. Van Gorder will be under tremendous pressure to improve his youthful unit, lest it prevent the team from making the postseason.

Baltimore Ravens

Sustainability is a hot topic these days. Ecologists strive to attain a sustainable balance of resources and consumption. Economists study ways to achieve sustainable industrial and technological growth. And the Ravens are searching for sustainable success, particularly on offense, where the team has been mired in a recession for most of the last decade.

Thanks to coach John Harbaugh and coordinator Cam Cameron, the team appeared to make significant offensive strides last season. The Ravens now have a potential franchise quarterback in Joe Flacco. Cameron's retro-chic offense worked well enough to complement the team's typically devastating defense, bringing Baltimore within one game of the Super Bowl. But Cameron's groovy contraption wasn't built for long-term success. Despite the presence of Flacco and the return of the defensive old guard, the Ravens don't have the infrastructure necessary to build on last season's success, at least not in 2009.

The Ravens entered training camp in 2008 with Troy Smith and Kyle Boller competing for the starting quarterback job. Flacco, fresh from two seasons in a Division I-AA spread offense, was expected to watch and learn. Boller, a six-year veteran who flunked more starting opportunities than Spongebob flunked driving tests, injured his shoulder in training camp. Smith contracted tonsillitis, giving Flacco an opportunity to start the third exhibition game. Flacco's numbers weren't great in that game (18-of-37, 152 yards, one touchdown), but he wasn't substantially worse than Boller or Smith; Smith was just 8-of-17 with an interception in preseason action before getting sick. Harbaugh, recognizing that Boller and Smith weren't Montana and Young, decided to kick-start the rebuilding process by giving Flacco the starting job.

Harbaugh's decision could have been disastrous. Former coach Brian Billick was a compulsive quarterback juggler who yanked youngsters like Boller and Chris Redman in and out of the lineup. Billick never scaled down his offensive scheme to accommodate his quarterbacks, and the Ravens spent an otherwise successful decade waiting for their offense to catch up with their defense. Under Billick, the Ravens would have spent the season flip-flopping between Flacco and Smith, and neither would get a good opportunity to develop.

Harbaugh and Cameron had a better plan. They trimmed the playbook, emphasized the run, and created a mistake-averse offense that allowed their defense to win games. The new philosophy was obvious in the season opener, a 17-10 win against the Bengals. The Ravens ran 46 times and threw just 29 passes, with a 12-to-2 ratio as the Ravens nursed a seven-point lead in the fourth quarter. For big plays, Cameron called a Flacco bootleg and a Mark Clayton reverse that featured the 235-pound Flacco as a lead blocker. Both plays produced touchdowns. The

---

RAVENS SUMMARY

2008 Record: 11-5

Pythagorean Wins: 11.9 (2nd)

DVOA: 29.1% (3rd)

Offense: 4.3% (19th)

Defense: -24.5% (2nd)

Special Teams: 0.3% (16th)

Variance: 18.6% (21st)

2008: Defense is back in Baltimore, but Ravens just can't get past the rival Steelers.

2009: The defense should excel once again, with the offense giving back last year's gains.

2009 Mean Projection: 8.8 wins

On the Clock (0-3): 1%

Loserville (4-6): 14%

Mediocrity (7-8): 26%

Playoff Contender (9-10): 36%

Super Bowl Contender (11+): 22%

Projected Average Opponent: 4.1% (5th)

2009 Ravens Schedule

Week	Opp.	Week	Opp.	Week	Opp.
1	KC	7	BYE	13	at GB (Mon.)
2	at SD	8	DEN	14	DET
3	CLE	9	at CIN	15	CHI
4	at NE	10	at CLE (Mon.)	16	at PIT
5	CIN	11	IND	17	at OAK
6	at MIN	12	PIT		

Ravens defense was as good as ever, allowing just 154 net yards. Running, defense, and a little gadgetry: The Ravens had found a winning formula.

Harbaugh and Cameron tweaked that formula as the season went on. They didn't expand the passing game substantially; Flacco threw more than 30 passes in just three games, and he threw the same types of passes (like comebacks to Derrick Mason) over and over again. To keep the offense from becoming too predictable, Cameron mixed some 1970s tactics with wrinkles that he learned from his days coaching the Chargers and Dolphins, including:

THE FULLBACK DIVE: Fullback Le'Ron McClain made his debut as a rushing threat in the Bengals game, carrying the ball 19 times. Most of those carries came as a fourth-quarter clock killer, but later in the season, Cameron began lining McClain in front of Ray Rice or Willis McGahee and giving him the ball on old-fashioned "belly" plays. The fullback belly had all but disappeared from NFL playbooks in recent years: most teams use it as a third-and-inches play, if they use it at all. Cameron began calling it on first down or second-and-long, and he further expanded McClain's role by using him as a single-setback or tailback in a heavy formation. Opposing defenders had to adjust their keys and responsibilities to account for two running threats in the backfield, something many of them hadn't worried about since high school.

THE UNBALANCED LINE: Cameron tinkered with unbalanced lines in San Diego and Miami. By the end of last season, the Ravens were running five to ten plays per game from the formation. Tackles Jared Gaither and Willie Anderson lined up on the same side of the formation (usually the left), with Todd Heap aligned next to the guard on the other side. An unbalanced line changes the gap responsibilities of the defensive front seven, creating favorable blocking matchups (like Gaither against a 200-pound strong safety) for

the Ravens. Cameron called a few play-action passes from unbalanced formations, but he usually used it in conjunction with a two-back backfield to confuse the defense's gap reads and keys. Defenders knew the run was coming, but they didn't know who was running, where he was heading, and how many 320-pound blockers would be leading him.

THE WILDCAT: Cameron developed and installed a Wildcat package in November. In the Ravens' version of the scheme, Smith took the center snap, while Flacco either left the field or lined up as a running back or receiver. Smith threw a 43-yard touchdown pass to Flacco against the Raiders from the formation and had a handful of 7- to 8-yard runs from Weeks 8 to 13. In the short term, the Wildcat served its purpose: It gave defenses that weren't worried about a complex passing game something different to worry about.

THE BOMB: On the rare occasions when Flacco threw the ball, he threw it pretty far. Eight percent of the Ravens' passes traveled more than 30 yards in the air, a higher percentage than any other team but the Lions, who often threw deep in desperation. The bombs were often successful; the Ravens finished tied for eighth in the NFL with 11 pass plays of more than 40 yards, an impressive feat for the team that attempted the second fewest passes in the league.

With all of the fullback runs, punctuated by the occasional bomb, the Ravens offense often looked like something unearthed from a 1970s time capsule. The Ravens led the league in play-action passes (26 percent of all pass plays) and finished second in max-protect schemes (14 percent). Three-receiver sets were rare, especially after Demetrius Williams got hurt, and third-and-short was strictly a rushing down, with Cameron calling runs 85 percent of the time with one or two yards to go.

The wood paneling and lava lamps had the desired effect. The Ravens led the league in time of possession at 33:20 per game. The offense gave away just 21 turnovers, allowing the Ravens to finish third in the league in turnover differential. Cameron deflated the football while Ray Lewis, Terrell Suggs and Ed Reed provided plenty of scoring of their own in the form of fumble and interception returns. The result was a string of 41-13 and 36-7 wins against pretty good opponents.

As effective as Cameron's schemes were, they aren't

a long-term solution. The Ravens' Wildcat only had a four-week half life before it became a series of Troy Smith dives for no gain. Fullback belly plays have their place in an NFL offense, but if they were really a good way to move the ball, they wouldn't have disappeared circa 1985. Opposing defensive coordinators will adapt to the unbalanced line soon enough; if the Ravens try it against the Steelers this year, they may find James Harrison lined up against "right tackle" L.J. Smith, a matchup that will make Flacco's insurance agent cringe. The Ravens' offense is safe and methodical, but it is a few simple defensive adjustments away from becoming stagnant.

Cameron's job this year is to expand the offense while furthering Flacco's development. He must work quickly: Important weapons like Derrick Mason and Todd Heap are aging quickly, as are several members of the Reed-Lewis defensive core. Cameron went straight to work during the team's minicamps. McClain found himself back in a more traditional fullback role, blocking for halfbacks while taking relatively few handoffs. Cameron devoted extra reps to shotgun formations and the no-huddle offense. The Wildcat wrinkles and power-running concepts won't disappear completely, but Cameron's offense will look more like his Chargers scheme of three years ago and less like something Chuck Knox drew up for the Rams in 1977.

Cameron and Harbaugh are doing the right thing, but our projections are pessimistic about their chances for success. The team's lack of receiving firepower is a major problem. Mason is now 35 and played with a torn labrum that required offseason surgery. He may miss most of training camp. Williams is on the mend from an Achillies tendon injury. His leg was still wrapped when he practiced with the team in May. The Ravens didn't sign or draft any wide receivers until veteran Kelley Washington arrived in late May, and Washington is more of a kick-gunner than an offensive threat. New tight end L.J. Smith is a fumble-prone pass dropper who could end up as a third-stringer if Heap stays healthy and rookie Davon Drew develops quickly.

The offensive line is another area of concern. With the retirement of Willie Anderson, rookie Michael Oher will be expected to step right into a starting role. Left tackle Jared Gaither survived a year as Jonathan Ogden's successor but isn't an elite pass blocker. Matt Birk fills the void left by Jason Brown at center, but Birk is 33. There's ample depth, but the line projects to be adequate, not great. Pair an unexceptional line with an old and understaffed receiving corps, and you have a less-than-ideal supporting cast for a second-year quarterback. Cameron may have to pull more moon rocks from his goodie bag. When he does, opponents will be ready.

Even if the offense struggles, the Ravens can count on their defense. The team survived a late-winter scare when their top three linebackers — Lewis, Suggs, and Bart Scott — hit the free agent market simultaneously. The team tagged Suggs, and Lewis re-signed despite some tough talk about leaving Baltimore. From a personnel standpoint, the Ravens came out ahead on defense in the offseason. They lost Scott and ever-injured cornerback Chris McAlister, but they kept their big stars while signing solid cornerback Domonique Foxworth and drafting defensive end Paul Kruger. The biggest loss was defensive coordinator Rex Ryan, now the Jets head coach, but replacement Gregg Mattison is a veteran coach who is well-versed in the system. The defense won't produce six touchdowns like it did last year — that kind of production just doesn't carry over from year to year — but the Ravens should enjoy another year or two of defensive dominance before Lewis and Reed finally succumb to age and injuries.

In fact, the Ravens defense is actually projected to get better because it's likely to get healthier. The Ravens finished second in the NFL in Adjusted Games Lost by starters on defense last season, with McAlister, Dawan Landry, Kelly Gregg, and others missing a large part of the season. Assuming the Ravens' injury rate moves toward the mean, they'll be at closer to full strength in 2009 — a scary thought.

Overall, the 2009 Ravens will look frustratingly familiar to their fans. Their defense will dominate. Their offense will scuffle. Flacco may appear to take a step back as he learns to go through the depressing series of reads from Injured Mason to Inconsistent Mark Clayton to Injured Williams to Shaky Smith. There will be some 13-10 wins, some 13-10 losses, and their final record will depend on how far the Bengals and Browns managed to climb from their respective holes. The growing pains will be worthwhile if Harbaugh and Cameron can build something sustainable on offense. Ravens fans may once again head for the bathroom when their team has the ball so they don't miss the defense in action. Hopefully, this is the last year they'll have to do that.

Mike Tanier

2008 Ravens Stats by Week

Wk	vs.	W-L	PF	PA	YDF	YDA	TO	Total	Off	Def	ST
1	CIN	W	17	10	358	154	0	51%	10%	-44%	-3%
2	BYE										
3	CLE	W	28	10	273	169	+1	46%	2%	-47%	-2%
4	@PIT	L	20	23	243	237	0	54%	13%	-41%	0%
5	TEN	L	10	13	285	210	0	35%	5%	-44%	-13%
6	@IND	L	3	31	260	334	-5	-91%	-82%	14%	5%
7	@MIA	W	27	13	356	359	0	30%	28%	-2%	0%
8	OAK	W	29	10	375	234	0	37%	19%	-2%	15%
9	@CLE	W	37	27	429	274	+2	-14%	18%	6%	-26%
10	@HOU	W	41	13	328	355	+4	78%	22%	-44%	12%
11	@NYG	L	10	30	275	353	-1	-12%	-16%	-12%	-8%
12	PHI	W	36	7	248	206	+5	61%	10%	-69%	-18%
13	@CIN	W	34	3	451	155	+1	79%	19%	-53%	7%
14	WAS	W	24	10	281	254	+1	36%	-9%	-38%	7%
15	PIT	L	9	13	202	311	0	13%	-15%	-5%	23%
16	@DAL	W	33	24	388	327	+1	-6%	1%	6%	-1%
17	JAC	W	27	7	431	245	+4	60%	29%	-25%	6%
18	@MIA	W	27	9	286	276	+4	80%	21%	-49%	9%
19	@TEN	W	13	10	211	391	+3	25%	2%	-19%	4%
20	@PIT	L	14	23	198	275	-3	-12%	-28%	-21%	-5%

Trends and Splits

	Offense	Rank	Defense	Rank
Total DVOA	4.3%	19	-24.5%	2
Unadjusted VOA	4.5%	19	-25.8%	1
Weighted trend	4.0%	20	-21.4%	3
Variance	7.1%	16	12.1%	30
Average opponent	2.2%	26	-1.2%	5
Passing	11.3%	20	-23.2%	2
Rushing	8.8%	10	-26.2%	1
First down	-13.3%	27	-30.6%	1
Second down	9.5%	16	-20.3%	5
Third down	30.0%	7	-19.9%	6
First half	-4.9%	27	-30.7%	1
Second half	13.9%	12	-17.9%	4
Red Zone	1.9%	20	-50.2%	1
Late and close	22.4%	7	-25.2%	2

Five-Year Performance

Year	W-L	Pyth	Est W	PF	PA	TO	Total	Rk	Off	Rk	Def	Rk	ST	Rk	Off AGL	Rk	Def AGL	Rk
2004	9-7	9.6	10.0	317	268	+11	22.2%	8	-1.3%	16	-20.5%	2	3.0%	8	22.1	14	26.8	13
2005	6-10	6.9	7.3	265	299	-10	-1.7%	17	-13.7%	25	-11.6%	6	0.4%	14	22.5	11	28.9	6
2006	13-3	12.7	11.8	353	201	+17	28.8%	2	1.7%	15	-23.6%	1	3.5%	4	27.1	7	9.7	21
2007	5-11	5.0	6.9	275	384	-17	-3.9%	18	-12.7%	25	-8.7%	5	0.1%	13	26.2	7	32.4	7
2008	11-5	11.9	11.7	385	244	+13	29.1%	3	4.3%	19	-24.5%	2	0.3%	16	23.4	20	53.9	2

Strategic Tendencies

Run/Pass		Rank	Offense		Rank	Defense		Rank	Other		Rank
Runs, all plays	55%	1	3+ WR	34%	31	Rush 3	11.7%	5	2+ RB, Pct Runs	64%	12
Runs, first half	50%	5	4+ WR	8%	21	Rush 4	52.3%	29	1 RB/2 TE, Pct Runs	52%	17
Runs, first down	69%	2	2+ TE	24%	20	Rush 5	27.6%	5	1RB/3+WR, Pct Runs	37%	2
Runs, second-long	43%	8	Single back	38%	32	Rush 6+	8.4%	15	Zone Blitz	8%	7
Runs, power sit.	83%	1	Play action	26%	1	Rush 7+	2.2%	8	Go for it on 4th	1.34	3
Runs, behind 2H	38%	5	Max protect	14%	2	Sacks by LB	66.7%	3	Offensive Pace	29.4	6
Pass, ahead 2H	35%	28	Outside pocket	14%	11	Sacks by DB	13.6%	6	Defensive Pace	30.5	11

Even though the Ravens used play-action more than any other offense, they were one of only three offenses to gain fewer yards per play with play-action (5.9) than without (6.4). ● In 2007, only Green Bay ran less often in power situations; in 2008, no team ran more often. ● The Ravens had the second-lowest offensive DVOA with four or five wide receivers in the game (-42.1%), but an above-average DVOA when they lined up in formations with one, two, or three wide receivers. ● On defense, the Ravens were particularly strong against sets with just one wide receiver, as the DVOA gap between Baltimore (-61.5%) and number two Tampa Bay (-29.2%) was equal to the DVOA gap between Tampa Bay and 19th-ranked Buffalo. ● The Ravens hurried the other team's quarterback on a league leading 22 percent of pass plays after ranking 19th in 2007. ● Baltimore opponents only used play-action on 13 percent of pass plays. Only the Jets saw their opponents use play fakes less often. Good call by the opponents, as the Ravens had the league's best DVOA against play-action (-34.0%). This was the second straight year the Ravens ranked 31st in percentage of play-fakes against.

● Jim Harbaugh clearly didn't learn how to call fourth downs from his mentor Andy Reid. Reid has one of the lowest career Aggressive Index ratings and was dead last in 2008, while Harbaugh was third overall.

Passing

Player	DYAR	DVOA	Plays	NtYds	Avg	YAC	C%	TD	Int
Joe Flacco	384	2.4%	464	2786	6.0	5.3	60.4%	14	11
Troy Smith	62	184.2%	5	81	16.2	8.3	75.0%	1	0

Rushing

Player	DYAR	DVOA	Plays	Yds	Avg	TD	Fum	Suc
Le'Ron McClain	163	7.6%	232	907	3.9	10	3	51%
Willis McGahee	86	3.9%	170	671	3.9	7	2	46%
Ray Rice	25	-2.5%	108	462	4.3	0	1	42%
Joe Flacco	5	-9.0%	32	189	5.9	2	4	--
Lorenzo Neal*	1	-7.5%	12	25	2.1	0	0	50%
Mark Clayton	59	155.9%	6	81	13.5	1	0	--
Troy Smith	1	-10.0%	5	27	5.4	0	0	--

Receiving

Player	DYAR	DVOA	Plays	Ctch	Yds	Y/C	YAC	TD	C%
Derrick Mason	250	13.9%	121	81	1048	12.9	3.1	6	67%
Mark Clayton	32	-7.6%	82	41	695	17.0	4.2	3	50%
Demetrius Williams	-3	-14.6%	23	13	180	13.8	4.1	1	57%
Yamon Figurs	7	8.3%	5	1	43	43.0	2.0	1	20%
Todd Heap	49	4.2%	64	35	407	11.6	5.1	3	55%
Daniel Wilcox*	10	12.6%	7	5	19	3.8	1.2	2	71%
L.J. Smith	*-42*	*-16.7%*	*64*	*37*	*298*	*8.1*	*4.8*	*3*	*58%*
Ray Rice	81	25.8%	43	33	273	8.3	8.7	0	77%
Willis McGahee	-15	-22.0%	32	24	173	7.2	7.7	0	75%
Le'Ron McClain	-23	-28.0%	30	19	123	6.5	7.4	1	63%
Lorenzo Neal*	-36	-55.8%	15	7	35	5.0	7.9	0	47%

Offensive Line

Year	Yards	ALY	Rank	Power	Rank	10+ Yds	Rank	Stuff	Rank	Sacks	ASR	Rank	False	Cont.
2006	3.78	4.13	20	59%	24	14%	24	17%	7	17	3.7%	2	27	29
2007	4.02	3.77	27	68%	11	18%	14	18%	15	39	7.6%	22	23	29
2008	3.99	4.17	11	76%	3	16%	23	16%	8	33	6.8%	20	23	27

Year	LE	Rank	LT	Rank	Mid	Rank	RT	Rank	RE	Rank
2006	2.94	27	4.58	10	4.22	20	4.08	17	3.99	16
2007	4.81	5	4.03	21	3.63	31	4.22	15	2.89	32
2008	4.75	12	4.00	18	4.26	12	3.93	24	3.98	19

It's easy to keep sack totals low when you don't throw very often. It also helps to go max protect on 14 percent of all pass plays (second in the league) and to use play-action to slow the defense on 26 percent of all passes (first). This year, the Ravens must keep sack totals low while opening up the offense, and they must do it with several new faces on the line.

New center Matt Birk is a six-time Pro Bowler who hasn't missed a start in three years. He's much older than Jason Brown (who signed with the Rams), but his durability and experience are assets. He generally plays mistake-free football, with just four holding penalties and two blown blocks in the last two seasons. As a 33-year-old, Birk was allowed to skip some drills during the Ravens' May minicamp (players over 30 get extra rest), but Birk opted to participate anyway. "He was 29 today," joked Harbaugh.

Veteran Willie Anderson retired due to knee issues, leaving first-round pick Michael Oher, whose slums-to-riches story was the centerpiece of Michael Lewis' book *The Blind Side*, as the likely starter at right tackle. Lewis described Oher's learning disabilities in-depth, but Oher appeared to have a sizeable chunk of the playbook under his belt in May. The "learning disability" story may have been aggrandized to a degree: Oher played for multiple offensive coordinators at Ole Miss, but he always had the playbook digested in time to take the field.

Jared Gaither will start at left tackle unless Oher develops more quickly than expected. Gaither started 15 games last season and had some penalty problems — five holds, six false starts — but kept the quarterback clean. Ben Grubbs is developing into an excellent run blocker at left guard. With Marshall Yanda on the mend from a triad injury, Adam Terry may move inside to right guard. Terry also provides insurance at both tackle positions. Chris Chester, who started 11 games in Yanda's absence, is a valuable three-position sub who will become the most important person in Baltimore if Birk gets hurt.

Defensive Front Seven

Defensive Line	Age	Pos	Plays	TmPct	Overall Rk	Stop	Dfts	Stop%	Rk	AvYd	Rk	Pass Rush Sack	Hit	Hur	vs. Run Runs	St%	Yds	vs. Pass Pass	St%	Yds
Haloti Ngata	25	DE	61	8.3%	8	50	11	82%	22	1.8	47	1.0	10	10	47	85%	1.5	14	71%	2.8
Justin Bannan	30	DT	48	6.5%	15	34	7	71%	60	2.8	64	1.0	2	5	43	70%	3.1	5	80%	-0.2
Marques Douglas*	32	DE	35	4.8%	58	26	7	74%	55	1.8	48	0.0	0	1	33	76%	1.2	2	50%	11.5
Trevor Pryce	34	DE	28	3.8%	73	22	8	79%	34	0.8	16	4.5	12	16	19	74%	2.1	9	89%	-1.9

Linebackers	Age	Pos	Plays	TmPct	Overall Rk	Stop	Dfts	Stop%	AvYd	Pass Rush Sack	Hit	Hur	vs. Run Runs	St%	Rk	Yds	Rk	vs. Pass Tgts	Suc%	Rk	AdjYd	Rk
Ray Lewis	34	ILB	126	17.2%	10	70	27	56%	4.0	3.5	9	10	73	64%	51	3.4	48	46	52%	40	5.1	19
Bart Scott*	29	ILB	87	11.9%	48	59	17	68%	3.6	1.5	7	15	56	79%	9	2.7	18	33	54%	35	5.6	30
Terrell Suggs	27	OLB	78	10.6%	62	68	36	87%	0.3	8.0	11	20	49	88%	1	1.0	1	15	85%	--	3.3	--
Jarret Johnson	28	OLB	60	8.2%	82	46	20	77%	2.0	5.0	3	12	35	86%	3	2.3	6	13	51%	--	4.7	--

Year	Yards	ALY	Rank	Power	Rank	10+ Yds	Rank	Stuff	Rank	Sack	ASR	Rank
2006	3.26	3.37	2	56%	8	14%	9	21%	6	60	9.4%	1
2007	3.03	3.30	2	56%	8	12%	6	23%	4	32	6.9%	14
2008	3.32	3.15	1	64%	14	19%	18	24%	4	34	6.2%	16

Year	LE	Rank	LT	Rank	Mid	Rank	RT	Rank	RE	Rank
2006	2.72	4	2.99	2	3.74	2	3.46	8	2.23	1
2007	2.70	3	2.79	1	3.50	2	3.41	4	2.42	2
2008	3.29	6	3.54	7	3.09	1	2.97	3	3.09	9

Here are five year's worth of our individual defensive stats for Ray Lewis:

Year	Plays	Stops	Defeats	Stop Rate	TmPct	Rank (LB)
2004	155	92	26	59%	20.4%	4
2005	49	25	6	51%	16.9%	--
2006	111	68	28	61%	16.7%	15
2007	132	82	26	61%	19.2%	3
2008	126	70	27	56%	17.2%	10

What we have here is an old-fashioned career renaissance. Lewis' production has slipped from his early-decade heyday, but he bounced back from injury-plagued 2005 to produce a series of very solid, statistically similar seasons. Tackle stats are influenced by dozens of outside factors, but Lewis keeps putting up consistent numbers in the twilight of his career. He's not one of the ten best linebackers in the NFL right now, but he's still among the top 25, and he's probably the best ever once you account for his whole career.

Ironically, it was Lewis, not Terrell Suggs, who re-signed peacefully with the Ravens. Suggs told reporters in February that he was agreeable to a "hometown discount" to stay in Baltimore, while Lewis balked at the suggestion. The Ravens franchised Suggs, who didn't sign his tender offer and skipped May minicamp. The no-show is no big deal; coaches remained in contact with Suggs, who is expected to come to camp on time. Suggs remains a big-play generator, though there is a lot of penalty residue (three roughness fouls, three offside flags in 2008) to go with the sacks.

Bart Scott was the only free agent linebacker to leave Baltimore. Tavares Gooden, a second-year player from The U, is the favorite to replace him. Gooden recorded 100 tackles for the Hurricanes in 2007 but missed all of last season with a hip injury. He played with the first team at minicamp. Jameel McLean (2.5 sacks last year) will push Gooden.

There are few changes on the defensive line. Haloti Ngata has become one of the league's best gap-stuffing tackles. Kelly Gregg is back from knee surgery to replace Justin Bannan on the nose. Gregg and Trevor Pryce are old but still effective; Pryce recorded 16 hurries and 12 hits on quarterbacks last year. Second-round pick Paul Kruger will be groomed to eventually replace Pryce. Kruger is a true survivor: He lost his spleen and a kidney in an off-road trucking accident, then survived a vicious stabbing in January of 2008. The Utah product is undersized for a defensive end, but coaches are impressed with his intensity and motor. Bannan is still around to provide experience off the bench.

Defensive Secondary

Secondary	Age	Pos	Plays	Overall				vs. Run				vs. Pass										
				TmPct	Rk	Stop	Dfts	Yds	Rk	St%	Rk	Tgts	Tgt%	Rk	Dist	Suc%	Rk	AdjYd	Rk	Yds	PD	Int
Jim Leonhard*	27	SS	74	10.1%	38	25	7	8.2	64	44%	33	26	5.8%	52	7.8	52%	38	7.5	28	7.4	3	1
Ed Reed	31	FS	57	7.8%	62	28	18	6.8	40	39%	43	24	5.5%	59	16.1	62%	14	6.5	14	5.7	13	8
Corey Ivy*	32	CB	47	6.4%	67	23	14	6.3	38	44%	42	49	11.2%	76	11.3	49%	47	7.5	43	7.3	2	0
Fabian Washington	26	CB	46	8.4%	49	21	8	15.9	82	13%	78	66	20.0%	27	14.0	56%	21	7.7	48	7.4	14	1
Frank Walker	29	CB	44	6.4%	68	19	6	6.5	43	25%	75	55	13.5%	71	14.3	57%	18	6.5	30	5.8	9	1
Samari Rolle	33	CB	31	6.8%	66	14	7	8.5	58	33%	62	43	15.6%	61	10.7	64%	6	4.5	2	4.0	7	3
Chris McAlister*	32	CB	23	8.4%	--	11	6	6.3	--	33%	--	25	15.3%	--	12.7	54%	--	8.2	--	7.0	6	3
Domonique Foxworth	26	CB	50	7.3%	62	22	7	7.4	51	56%	22	70	17.5%	49	10.9	62%	10	5.1	5	5.9	13	1
Chris Carr	26	CB	27	3.3%	--	7	3	6.6	--	20%	--	39	8.3%	--	10.1	41%	--	6.9	--	6.6	5	1

Year	Pass D Rank	vs. #1 WR	Rk	vs. #2 WR	Rk	vs. Other WR	Rk	vs. TE	Rk	vs. RB	Rk
2006	2	-4.2%	11	-25.4%	3	-6.5%	14	-16.9%	6	-24.3%	7
2007	20	-11.7%	7	24.7%	30	-8.9%	16	6.8%	15	9.2%	26
2008	2	-15.2%	5	-26.4%	4	-14.9%	11	-33.0%	1	-7.5%	6

Ed Reed missed minicamp with a nerve impingement and was listed as "questionable" throughout the playoffs with a knee injury. The nerve injury is the type of lingering ailment that haunts a player for the rest of his career, but Reed routinely plays through pain and will shake off the effects once games start to matter. Dawan Landry landed on the IR after a spinal cord concussion last season. Landry spent the offseason strengthening his neck with team trainers, and he was practicing without restrictions in May. Landry can play close to the line or drop into deep coverage; his presence allows Reed to be even more of a freelancer.

Chris McAlister is gone after two injury-ruined seasons. Newcomer Domonique Foxworth registered impressive game charting statistics and finished second on the Falcons with 13 passes defensed.. Fabian Washington, a speedster acquired from the Raiders, started several games in McAlister's absence and is penciled in as the number-two cornerback. The team brought Samari Rolle back as an insurance policy; Rolle has been a step too slow for years, but he knows the scheme and can still guess right to produce an interception. Veteran Frank Walker was picked on by opponents whenever he came in for the nickel or dime packages, but his game charting statistics are surprisingly reasonable. Rookie Lardarius Webb out of Division I-AA Nicholls State is tiny (5-foot-9, 180 pounds) but has a rep as a big hitter and will battle for a slot role.

Special Teams

Year	DVOA	Rank	FG/XP	Rank	Net Kick	Rank	Kick Ret	Rank	Net Punt	Rank	Punt Ret	Rank	Hidden	Rank
2006	3.5%	4	9.0	2	4.6	12	3.6	8	5.3	10	-2.1	20	-4.8	23
2007	0.1%	13	0.2	18	-0.5	15	2.6	14	-6.1	26	4.3	8	-8.6	28
2008	0.3%	16	-2.1	22	-6.8	25	-7.4	27	20.9	1	-2.8	23	-15.7	30

Matt Stover started out in the Ravens/Browns organization in 1991. He played for Bill Belichick's Browns teams, kicking extra points after Bernie Kosar touchdowns. Last season, Stover ceded kickoff and long field goal duties to Steve Hauschka, and the team told Stover in March that they didn't plan to re-sign him. Stover's skills were diminishing — he hasn't kicked a 50-plus-yard field goal since 2006, and five 40-plus-yard field goals were his lowest total since 2001 — but he's still an accurate, reliable short-range kicker. The team may still call upon him if Hauschka and rookie Graham Gano don't deliver in camp. Hauschka was solid on kickoffs (65.9-yard average) and kicked a 54-yard field goal against the Texans last season. Gano, a rookie free agent from Florida State, was 24-of-26 last season and also has experience as a punter.

Yamon Figurs was an impressive return man as a rookie but fell off last year, averaging just 6.0 yards per punt return and calling for a fair catch on almost one-third of his attempts. Free agent Chris Carr is also a fair catch machine (20 in 52 attempts last season), but he's more effective on kickoffs than Figurs, and he's a more determined runner who will plow ahead for available yardage instead of dancing or running out of bounds. Rookie cornerback Lardarius Webb returned three interceptions for touchdowns in 2007 and both a kickoff and a punt for a touchdown in 2008, so he'll also get a look.

The team re-signed restricted free agent punter Sam Koch. Koch finished fifth in the NFL in net average, but once we adjust for weather and the field position of each punt, Koch had the most net value in the league (and was second in gross value behind Oakland's Shane Lechler). Koch pinned opponents inside the 20-yard line 34 times and recorded just nine touchbacks, excellent numbers for someone who often punted from around midfield. The coverage teams are strong and will get a boost from the acquisition of Kelley Washington, who served the Bengals and Patriots well as a kick gunner.

Coaching Staff

New defensive coordinator Greg Mattison is in his first year as a pro coordinator but has 38 years of coaching experience. Mattison isn't planning a major overhaul, and Ravens defenders are familiar with his coaching style. Ray Lewis compared Mattison to a grandfather: "Greg has been in the game for longer than when most of us were born. So just understanding that part of it gives him great credibility, really makes him who he is."

Offensive coordinator Cam Cameron wants the Ravens to get more creative and "reinvent themselves" this year, but he also stressed a keep-it-simple philosophy in a minicamp interview with the monthly magazine *Baltimore's Press Box*. "We started like we have for the last 25 years with '20 fullback belly' and we work from there to the stuff that we're going to do in the season." Last year, "20 fullback belly" *was* the stuff they did in the season, so Cameron is clearly looking to progress.

Quarterbacks coach Hue Jackson played a large role in Carson Palmer's development and deserves some credit for getting Joe Flacco ready to play. Jackson is a creative coach who designs unique drills — like making quarterbacks throw with their off hands — that improve focus and technique while keeping practices loose.

Buffalo Bills

Perhaps Bills fans knew that things were too good to be true in the early '90s. They knew — even as they watched a team with future Hall of Famers at quarterback, running back and wide receiver run a no-huddle offense that could put up 44 points in a blizzard — that there would be a reckoning. As they watched a team with the physical talent to win four consecutive AFC Championships and the mental fortitude to come storming back from a 32-point deficit in the playoffs with a backup quarterback at the helm, they suspected that they would have to pay the price sometime down the road. That divine retribution would not come in the form of a spectacular Matt Millen style 0-16 flameout but in the slow, grinding horror of watching a team in monochrome uniforms play mediocre and emotionless football year after year, a team that excelled at nothing, a team with no personality, presided over by a middling coach who would get the job despite an indifferent resume and would keep the job irrelevant of the results on the field.

In 2008, the Bills ranked 24th in offense and 25th in defense, a result that neatly encapsulates the Dick Jauron era. Under Jauron, the Bills have exhibited an improbably consistent mediocrity that goes well beyond their putting up three consecutive 7-9 seasons. During that run, Buffalo's unadjusted VOA, which does not take the quality of their opponents into account, barely moved, going from -8.1% to -9.2% to -7.6%. To anyone sitting in the stands, the team looked like they were

running in place. (Once the opposition is factored in, it becomes clear that after two thoroughly mediocre seasons, the Bills took a step backwards last year.)

The stagnancy was particularly pronounced on offense. While division rivals Miami, New England and New York received immediate boosts by adding players like Chad Pennington, Randy Moss and Brett Favre, the Bills simply churned out the same below-average fare over and over and over again. Miami's offensive DVOA jumped 25.6% when they put Pennington at quarterback; Randy Moss caused the Patriots' already potent offense to explode with a 30.3% jump; even Favre, whose one season in New York ended up in disappointment, still contributed to a 14.3% boost for the Jets. But neither personnel nor coaching changes managed to jump-start Buffalo's punchless attack. Between 2006 and 2008, the team swapped out J.P. Losman for Trent Edwards, replaced Willis McGahee with Marshawn Lynch, brought in veterans like Peerless Price and highly drafted rookies like James Hardy to complement Lee Evans and Josh Reed at receiver and replaced Steve Fairchild with Turk Schonert as offensive coordinator, but the net result was a flat line — Buffalo's offensive DVOA in 2006 was -8.7%; it crept up to -7.5% in 2007 and then inched up again to -6.2% in 2008.

Despite the negligible progress, offensive coordinator Turk Schonert thinks the offense is ready to break out, and in a nod to the great Bills teams of the 1990s

---

BILLS SUMMARY

2008 Record: 7-9

Pythagorean Wins: 7.8

DVOA: -8.4% (19th)

Offense: -5.3 (24th)

Defense: 9.3% (22nd)

Special Teams: 6.1% (1st)

Variance: 13.9% (11th)

2008: Zzzzzzzzzzz.

2009: T.O.! T.O. is in town! Things are gonna be diff... <clunk> ...zzzzzzzzzzz.

2009 Mean Projection: 5.3 wins

On the Clock (0-3): 19%

Loserville (4-6): 55%

Mediocrity (7-8): 18%

Playoff Contender (9-10): 7%

Super Bowl Contender (11+): 1%

Projected Average Opponent: -0.6% (21st)

2009 Bills Schedule

Week	Opp.	Week	Opp.	Week	Opp.
1	at NE (Mon.)	7	at CAR	13	NYJ (Thu.)
2	TB	8	HOU	14	at KC
3	NO	9	BYE	15	NE
4	at MIA	10	at TEN	16	at ATL
5	CLE	11	at JAC	17	IND
6	at NYJ	12	MIA		

he is dusting off the K-gun and installing a no-huddle attack. They may not be Jim Kelly, Thurman Thomas, and Andre Reed in their primes, but the Bills think they have a strong foundation in Edwards, Lynch and Evans, and they spent the offseason building up the talent to complement those players. The flashy acquisition is of course Terrell Owens, who signed a one-year, $6.5 million deal after being released by Dallas. No one could have guessed that the attention-hogging Owens would have considered taking his game to western New York, but there wasn't much demand for his services elsewhere. The theory is that adding a star receiver will stop opponents from rolling their coverage towards Evans, who only managed to score three touchdowns last year while fighting through double-teams on nearly every snap. Now Evans can run deep posts and go routes from the flanker position, loosening up the underneath coverage for Owens. T.O. will run most of the slants, drags, and outs, routes where he can use his physicality to rack up yardage after the catch. Josh Reed, miscast as a starter, will return to his natural position in the slot. Marshawn Lynch will add value on screens and as a safety outlet coming out of the backfield. The Bills will finally be able to dictate to defenses rather than having to take what the defense gives them.

The problem is that the offense only works if Terrell Owens is the T.O. of 2007 and not the aging player of 2008. Owens had his worst year as a pro last season, posting career lows in DVOA and DYAR, and catching only 35 percent of the passes intended for him on third downs. Owens had such difficulty getting away from press coverage that Dallas began putting him in motion or hiding him behind Patrick Crayton to keep cornerbacks from getting a clean shot at him. If Owens continues to have problems getting open or catching the ball once he is open, then Evans will get the same steady dose of combination coverages and the passing game will remain stuck in neutral.

Even if T.O. is no longer the elite player that he thinks he is, he will still help the Bills down in the red zone.

Owens caught six of his ten touchdowns inside the 20, which is one less than the combined output of Evans, Reed, Roscoe Parrish, James Hardy, and Steve Johnson, and he'll allow Turk Schonert to mix in more quick fades and corner routes, as well as more play-action calls. The other component to running successful play-action down near the goal line is making the defense respect the run option, and the team spent much of its energy overhauling an offensive line that was 24th in the league in power situations and that allowed defenses to stuff ballcarriers for zero or negative yardage on one out of every four carries. The Bills jettisoned the disappointing Derrick Dockery, got rid of both members of their platoon at center, traded away left tackle Jason Peters to Philadelphia for three draft picks, and went to town in free agency and the draft, adding new starters at every position along the interior line. Free agent Geoff Hangartner will man the center position, and the Bills used first- and second-round picks to add guard/center Eric Wood and guard Andre Levitre. Wood and Levitre were running with the first team in minicamps at right and left guard, respectively, and the Bills think that the upgrade in talent will offset the lack of continuity. With the combination of Marshawn Lynch and the highly underrated Fred Jackson, as well as newly acquired Dominic Rhodes, the Bills have the backs to take advantage of what could potentially be a stronger run-blocking unit.

Any gains in run blocking may be offset by difficulties in pass protection, however. Langston Walker will take over at left tackle, which at least makes good fiscal sense, as he is the highest-paid lineman on the team. At 6-foot-8 and 366 pounds, Walker is a fine run blocker, but he's no one's idea of a shutdown left tackle, and our game charters identified him as the weak link in the pass protection last year, which is saying something considering his company. The right tackle position is up in the air, with Brad Butler being the most likely option. That means that it is likely that the Bills will not have a single lineman playing in the same spot as in 2008. It all adds up to a unit that may not have the ability to hold up in protection long enough for Trent Edwards to make the no-huddle work. Edwards came into the league with a reputation for fragility, and he missed two games last year after taking a brutal hit from Arizona's Adrian Wilson; he's not likely to survive a full season if the Bills can't improve on their 8.1 percent Adjusted Sack Rate. Turk Schonert doesn't believe in sacrificing receiving options to protect the quarterback — last year only the Chiefs went to maximum protection less frequently — but with so many question marks up and down the offensive line, he may have to change his ways if he doesn't want to spend his December watching Ryan Fitzpatrick do his Frank Reich impersonation. So while overhauling the line was probably the right thing to do and will pay long-term dividends, there is a good chance it torpedoes any chance the Bills have at improving offensively in 2009.

The prospects on defense aren't much better. The Bills have done a nice job of stockpiling young talent on their defense under Dick Jauron, adding starters like Donte Whitner, Kyle Williams, Keith Ellison, Ko Simpson, Paul Posluszny and Leodis McKelvin, but it hasn't translated into a compelling product on the field. Indeed, last year the defense was, if anything, even more blandly symmetrical than the offense, ranking 24th against the pass and 23rd against the run. Things started off well enough, with good performances against the Seahawks and Jaguars, but a Week 5 beatdown at the hands of the Cardinals signaled the beginning of the end. In that game, defensive end Aaron Schobel re-injured his foot, and he would be out for the rest of the season. Without Schobel in the lineup the pass rush evaporated, and quarterbacks began picking the secondary apart. Three weeks later, Donte Whitner separated his shoulder, and while he would return to the lineup, he spent the last half of the year playing injured and flipping back and forth between strong and free safety. During an embarrassing 0-6 stretch against the AFC East, Buffalo's defensive DVOA averaged 15.2%, a number that would have been even higher had the final game against the Patriots not taken place amidst 55-mph winds that nearly knocked the goal posts down.

If things are going to improve in 2009, it means that the young talent on the roster will need to develop, because the team made only minor moves in free agency. Last year the Bills added two solid starters in Kavika Mitchell and Marcus Stroud, but this offseason the only move was signing Drayton Florence to replace Jabari Greer as the nickelback, which is a lateral move at best. Instead, the significant additions are returning players like Aaron Schobel and Donte Whitner, who will take the pressure off young players like Posluzsny, Ellison, and McKelvin, who often felt like they had to make something happen rather than simply concentrating on their assignments. Defensive coordinator Perry Fewell's preference is for light, fast players who can flow to the ball and make plays in zone coverage, and most of the roster fits the scheme

very well. If the Bills can put a pass rush together with just the front four, they can drop into coverage behind the rush and be effective. But that is a titanic "if." Aaron Schobel has to prove that he will have the same short area burst he had before the Lisfranc injury, and even if he does, his presence doesn't do much more than put the pass rush back on life support.

The Bills still have to generate pass rush from somewhere else, which is why they used the 11th overall selection on Penn State's Aaron Maybin. Maybin generated a lot of different opinions leading up to the draft. NFL Network analyst Mike Mayock (who we love) tabbed Maybin as a late-first round talent, citing concerns about his ability to stay on the field for three downs. "He had trouble against the run in college, let alone in the NFL. So the ability to set the edge is lacking. Even though I believe that he's an elite pass rusher, which is the most important thing, I don't think he's big enough yet or strong enough yet to do the other things." The bottom line is that Maybin only started one year at Penn State, where he played at 240 pounds, and he's not ready to play on run downs. Defensive coordinator Perry Fewell expected to draft a pass rush specialist, speculating at the combine, "He might not have to be a full-time starter, but if he can give us (help) in long-yardage situations or passing down situations to increase our pass rush, that will work for us. And then we can work him into being an every down player because football right now is so much situational. It's a situational game and sometimes you can pick a situational player." It's asking a lot of Maybin to come right in and produce as a rusher, but without a rush coming from somewhere, the defense is right back where it was last year.

And that, in short, is the problem. The expectation is that after the three straight 7-9 seasons, the Bills will take a step forward and compete for the AFC East title. But that was also the expectation last year, when the Bills raced out to a 5-1 start, only to revert to form over the second half of the season. Teams that reconfigure their entire offensive lines don't tend to morph into the 1999 Rams overnight, and teams that make no major additions to a mediocre defense don't generally see massive improvement. With a tougher schedule that features the NFC South and the AFC South, as well as two tilts against a Tom Brady-led Patriots team, it's doubtful that the Bills will improve enough to build significantly on their record. They look like a 7-9 team, which is to say this year at Orchard Park will look very familiar.

Sean McCormick

2008 Bills Stats by Week

Wk	vs.	W-L	PF	PA	YDF	YDA	TO	Total	Off	Def	ST
1	SEA	W	34	10	338	252	+2	47%	9%	-22%	16%
2	@JAC	W	20	16	285	243	0	36%	19%	-14%	3%
3	OAK	W	24	23	378	247	-2	-3%	14%	6%	-11%
4	@STL	W	31	14	277	380	+1	-17%	-14%	15%	11%
5	@ARI	L	17	41	287	373	-4	-65%	-33%	37%	4%
6	BYE										
7	SD	W	23	14	370	263	+3	68%	45%	-23%	-1%
8	@MIA	L	16	25	339	358	-3	-15%	-4%	11%	0%
9	NYJ	L	17	26	292	297	-2	-60%	-39%	18%	-4%
10	@NE	L	10	20	168	370	-1	-16%	-31%	6%	22%
11	CLE	L	27	29	334	337	-4	-15%	-18%	27%	30%
12	@KC	W	54	31	444	462	+5	-4%	16%	38%	17%
13	SF	L	3	10	350	195	0	-17%	-10%	-10%	-17%
14	MIA	L	3	16	163	295	-2	-66%	-63%	6%	3%
15	@NYJ	L	27	31	306	372	-2	-18%	-5%	33%	20%
16	@DEN	W	30	23	275	532	+2	10%	9%	15%	15%
17	NE	L	0	13	276	241	-1	-5%	-11%	-9%	-4%

Trends and Splits

	Offense	Rank	Defense	Rank
Total DVOA	-5.3%	24	9.3%	22
Unadjusted VOA	-0.7%	22	6.8%	20
Weighted trend	-9.4%	25	12.1%	25
Variance	7.0%	15	3.7%	4
Average opponent	2.9%	20	11.0%	32
Passing	-8.5%	27	17.3%	22
Rushing	5.8%	14	1.2%	21
First down	17.2%	3	12.5%	25
Second down	-34.5%	32	7.7%	17
Third down	-3.0%	22	5.5%	17
First half	-8.1%	28	16.5%	29
Second half	-2.1%	22	1.8%	14
Red Zone	-1.2%	24	-3.8%	14
Late and close	0.2%	22	7.6%	22

Five-Year Performance

Year	W-L	Pyth	Est W	PF	PA	TO	Total	Rk	Off	Rk	Def	Rk	ST	Rk	Off AGL	Rk	Def AGL	Rk
2004	9-7	11.0	11.6	395	284	+10	31.2%	3	-5.1%	21	-28.8%	1	7.5%	1	15.1	17	12.0	24
2005	5-11	5.2	5.5	271	367	+4	-20.0%	25	-19.4%	30	7.8%	26	7.2%	1	5.7	27	19.0	9
2006	7-9	7.7	7.9	300	311	-11	-2.7%	19	-6.7%	22	1.9%	15	5.9%	2	13.4	19	7.3	26
2007	7-9	4.9	8.3	252	354	+9	-5.8%	19	-8.9%	22	1.0%	18	4.2%	6	22.6	15	43.6	3
2008	7-9	7.8	6.9	336	342	-8	-8.4%	24	-5.3%	24	9.3%	22	6.1%	1	13.3	25	34.9	8

Strategic Tendencies

Run/Pass		Rank	Offense		Rank	Defense		Rank	Other		Rank
Runs, all plays	45%	11	3+ WR	54%	14	Rush 3	2.3%	28	2+ RB, Pct Runs	51%	28
Runs, first half	47%	10	4+ WR	12%	18	Rush 4	66.5%	14	1 RB/2 TE, Pct Runs	69%	1
Runs, first down	56%	6	2+ TE	30%	9	Rush 5	19.5%	20	1RB/3+WR, Pct Runs	30%	15
Runs, second-long	27%	31	Single back	62%	11	Rush 6+	11.7%	7	Zone Blitz	6%	11
Runs, power sit.	62%	24	Play action	12%	26	Rush 7+	0.9%	24	Go for it on 4th	1.08	8
Runs, behind 2H	36%	6	Max protect	5%	31	Sacks by LB	17.4%	16	Offensive Pace	32.4	27
Pass, ahead 2H	36%	27	Outside pocket	12%	14	Sacks by DB	19.6%	3	Defensive Pace	30.6	14

For the second straight season, Buffalo had the highest ratio of runs to passes when lining up with one running back and two tight ends, and one of the lowest ratios of runs to passes when lining up with two running backs. ● The Bills went from ranking second in frequency of max protect in 2007 to ranking second-to-last in frequency of max protect in 2008. This might be because they were rarely blitzed — the Bills faced the highest percentage of three-man rushes (12 percent) and a very low percentage of blitzes with six or more pass rushers (6.2 percent, 27th in NFL). ● Also possibly related: The Bills significantly cut down their use of the screen pass, barely throwing one per game after throwing the most of any team in 2007. ● Although the Bills ranked 24th in offensive DVOA, they only went three-and-out on 16.4 percent of drives, fifth in the NFL. However, Buffalo faced 15 third-and-10 situations and failed to convert on every single one. ● Buffalo had the worst defense in the AFC against play-action passes, and the biggest difference in the league between DVOA against play-action and DVOA without play-action. The Bills gave up 4.5 yards more per play when the opponent started with a play fake. ● The Bills' defense was far better when blitzing. They had 38.1% DVOA (31st) with four pass rushers, -12.7% DVOA (fourth) with five pass rushers, and -36.1% DVOA (sixth) with six or more pass rushers.

Passing

Player	DYAR	DVOA	Plays	NtYds	Avg	YAC	C%	TD	Int
Trent Edwards	278	-0.3%	400	2592	6.5	4.6	65.9%	11	10
J.P. Losman*	-321	-57.1%	116	465	4.0	4.3	63.0%	2	4
Ryan Fitzpatrick	-185	-18.0%	411	1762	4.3	3.6	59.7%	8	8

Rushing

Player	DYAR	DVOA	Plays	Yds	Avg	TD	Fum	Suc
Marshawn Lynch	77	-1.1%	250	1036	4.1	8	2	46%
Fred Jackson	91	7.0%	130	583	4.5	3	1	53%
Trent Edwards	28	8.0%	25	130	5.2	3	2	--
J.P. Losman*	33	58.4%	8	66	8.3	2	1	--
Xavier Omon	-17	-58.7%	6	5	0.8	0	0	17%
Ryan Fitzpatrick	88	21.7%	48	308	6.4	2	2	--
Terrell Owens	29	31.7%	7	33	4.7	0	0	--
Dominic Rhodes	25	-4.9%	152	538	3.5	6	0	49%

Receiving

Player	DYAR	DVOA	Plays	Ctch	Yds	Y/C	YAC	TD	C%
Lee Evans	191	11.2%	102	63	1025	16.3	4.0	3	62%
Josh Reed	123	7.5%	79	56	597	10.7	2.6	1	71%
Roscoe Parrish	-64	-30.1%	45	24	232	9.7	3.0	2	53%
James Hardy	-43	-38.6%	24	9	87	9.7	1.8	2	38%
Steve Johnson	44	24.5%	14	10	102	10.2	2.8	2	71%
Terrell Owens	75	-5.7%	139	69	1052	15.2	4.2	10	50%
Robert Royal*	-85	-30.4%	57	33	352	10.7	3.4	1	58%
Derek Schouman	11	0.6%	20	15	153	10.2	5.5	1	75%
Derek Fine	25	22.3%	12	10	94	9.4	2.9	1	83%
Marshawn Lynch	5	-12.5%	67	47	300	6.4	7.1	1	70%
Fred Jackson	67	12.4%	45	37	321	8.7	7.7	0	82%
Dominic Rhodes	54	2.2%	59	45	302	6.7	5.5	3	76%

Offensive Line

Year	Yards	ALY	Rank	Power	Rank	10+ Yds	Rank	Stuff	Rank	Sacks	ASR	Rank	False	Cont.
2006	3.74	3.88	26	69%	11	13%	26	19%	24	47	9.5%	29	18	31
2007	3.97	3.93	24	51%	28	16%	17	19%	18	26	5.4%	13	19	45
2008	4.21	4.12	13	62%	24	16%	21	18%	16	38	8.1%	25	15	30

Year	LE	Rank	LT	Rank	Mid	Rank	RT	Rank	RE	Rank
2006	4.48	9	4.24	16	3.69	30	3.83	28	3.35	27
2007	2.73	29	3.89	23	3.97	19	4.59	6	3.42	27
2008	5.68	2	4.16	15	3.76	25	4.69	2	4.20	10

You cannot be weak up the middle in the AFC East, not when you have to match up against massive nose tackles like Vince Wilfork and Kris Jenkins. Last season the Bills ranked just 24th in power situations despite having a very capable running back duo in Marshawn Lynch and Fred Jackson, and much of the offseason has been devoted to making it easier for the team to run the ball consistently between the guards. The makeover started in February when the team released the disappointing Derrick Dockery and signed Carolina's Geoff Hangartner to man the center position. Hangartner was primarily a backup in Carolina, but he played well when he was inserted in the starting lineup; he has the flexibility to play multiple spots on the line, but he'll be penciled in to man the middle. Flanking Hangartner will be a pair of rookies, second-rounder Andy Levitre and first-rounder Eric Wood. Wood was a bit of a surprise pick, but at least a few teams had him as the top-rated center in the class, and the four-year starter at Louisville has the size and strength that Turk Schonert is looking for. He'll start off at right guard as he acclimates to the pro game. Levitre played tackle for Oregon State, but at 6-foot-2 he has to move inside to be effective in the pros. Both rookies provide flexibility in that they have experience playing at multiple spots along the line, but the plan is to leave Levitre and Wood where they are and let them develop some consistency. Kirk Chambers will be the first option if either of the rookies struggles, but ideally he would act as the primary backup at both tackle and guard spots.

The interior line should be better, but it may not matter if the team cannot find the right answers at the tackle positions. Unable to come to a contract agreement with left tackle Jason Peters, the Bills sent him to Philadelphia in exchange for three picks, including the first-rounder that turned into Wood. Peters was inconsistent in 2008 and his Pro Bowl selection last season was a disgrace, but he was still a rare talent at the most important position on the line, and there is no clear replacement on the roster. For now, Langston Walker will slide over to man the left side, while Brad Butler kicks outside from right guard. Butler played 31 games at right tackle for Virginia, and it's a more natural fit for him. The Bills have shown interest in former Cincinnati tackle Levi Jones, but for now Chambers, Demetrius Bell, and Jonathan Scott provide the depth.

Defensive Front Seven

Defensive Line	Age	Pos	Plays	TmPct	Overall Rk	Stop	Dfts	Stop%	Rk	AvYd	Pass Rush Rk	Sack	Hit	Hur	vs. Run Runs	St%	Yds	vs. Pass Pass	St%	Yds
Ryan Denney	32	DE	64	8.1%	9	51	13	80%	28	1.7	41	3.5	3	6	52	77%	2.4	12	92%	-1.3
Kyle Williams	26	DT	55	7.0%	10	50	13	91%	1	1.4	13	1.5	5	8	48	92%	1.6	7	86%	0.0
Chris Kelsay	30	DE	52	6.6%	26	40	12	77%	43	1.4	31	2.5	7	9	37	81%	1.5	15	67%	1.0
Marcus Stroud	31	DT	52	6.6%	14	42	20	81%	17	1.6	19	2.5	4	8	40	78%	2.2	12	92%	-0.3
Spencer Johnson	28	DT	33	4.2%	52	27	5	82%	14	2.3	55	2.0	4	0	28	79%	3.1	5	100%	-2.2
Aaron Schobel	32	DE	20	8.1%	--	15	8	75%	--	1.4	--	1.0	5	6	17	76%	1.4	3	67%	1.7

Linebackers	Age	Pos	Plays	TmPct	Overall Rk	Stop	Dfts	Stop%	AvYd	Pass Rush Sack	Hit	Hur	vs. Run Runs	St%	Rk	Yds	Rk	vs. Pass Tgts	Suc%	Rk	AdjYd	Rk
Paul Posluszny	24	ILB	116	14.7%	21	63	14	54%	5.0	0.0	3	2	62	69%	27	2.9	24	37	53%	38	7.8	74
Kawika Mitchell	30	OLB	85	10.8%	59	38	16	45%	5.2	4.0	4	11	47	53%	97	3.5	52	31	36%	82	9.0	89
Keith Ellison	25	OLB	73	9.3%	73	36	4	49%	5.4	0.0	0	0	50	60%	74	4.4	92	18	48%	51	4.4	4
Pat Thomas	26	ILB	49	7.7%	86	26	8	53%	5.1	0.5	1	1	28	61%	66	3.3	45	17	39%	78	7.6	72

Year	Yards	ALY	Rank	Power	Rank	10+ Yds	Rank	Stuff	Rank	Sack	ASR	Rank
2006	4.83	4.69	29	69%	22	18%	24	15%	29	40	8.1%	6
2007	4.59	4.06	15	50%	2	21%	25	21%	7	26	4.7%	31
2008	4.09	3.80	7	65%	15	21%	23	20%	8	24	4.7%	28

Year	LE	Rank	LT	Rank	Mid	Rank	RT	Rank	RE	Rank
2006	5.27	30	5.02	28	4.74	30	4.12	17	4.08	17
2007	1.47	1	3.94	12	4.08	15	4.35	22	5.68	32
2008	4.15	18	4.40	19	3.73	6	3.46	6	3.02	8

Aaron Schobel gave new meaning to the term "most valuable player" last year. While he only recorded one sack on the season, the Bills as a team rang up ten sacks in the five games Schobel started. Once he went down, the defense only managed another 14 sacks the rest of the year. Schobel should be fully recovered from his Lisfranc injury, but that wasn't enough to make defensive coordinator Perry Fewell comfortable, so the team locked in on Penn State's Aaron Maybin with the 11th overall selection in the draft. Maybin had the quickest first step of any defender in the draft, and he produced at Penn State, notching 12 sacks and 20 tackles for a loss, but he is very raw as a prospect and cannot be expected to play on run downs until he bulks up. Chris Kelsay and Ryan Denney will continue to play just enough to make the team wish there was someone better to replace them, with second-year man Chris Ellis being the likeliest option. The inside is capably manned by Kyle Williams and Marcus Stroud, who helped make the Bills sixth-best in the league at stopping runs between the guards. Spencer Johnson provides the depth.

Paul Posluszny picked up where he left off in his truncated rookie season, ringing up 110 tackles (including 87 solo tackles) on his way to being named the team's defensive MVP. The man they call "Poz" improved his Stop Rate by ten percent over his rookie year, and his average tackle took place nearly a yard closer to the line of scrimmage. Kawika Mitchell was Fewell's blitzer of choice, and he responded by leading the team in sacks, hits and hurries. Keith Ellison returns as the third starter. Ellison is athletic but not very physical, and he needs to be protected by the defensive line in order to be effective. Ellison improved his coverage techniques and his route reading last year, and he developed into a surprisingly effective pass defender. John DiGiorgio provides depth at all three linebacker spots.

Defensive Secondary

Secondary	Age	Pos	Plays	TmPct	Rk	Stop	Dfts	Yds	Rk	St%	Rk	Tgts	Tgt%	Rk	Dist	Suc%	Rk	AdjYd	Rk	Yds	PD	Int
						Overall				**vs. Run**						**vs. Pass**						
Terrence McGee	29	CB	84	12.2%	9	32	10	14.5	78	35%	55	95	27.1%	1	14.0	44%	70	8.7	71	7.9	17	3
Bryan Scott	28	FS	67	8.5%	55	33	17	2.5	1	62%	6	22	5.5%	57	12.5	56%	25	7.7	37	8.0	1	0
Ko Simpson	26	FS	66	8.4%	58	14	4	7.7	51	22%	71	15	3.8%	75	13.5	45%	66	9.1	58	8.5	2	0
Donte Whitner	24	SS	62	9.7%	42	23	6	6.4	25	50%	16	21	6.5%	41	10.0	36%	76	10.3	68	10.1	0	0
Jabari Greer*	27	CB	43	8.7%	40	19	6	6.5	45	67%	9	44	17.7%	47	11.5	50%	45	6.1	20	5.9	7	2
Leodis McKelvin	24	CB	35	4.4%	81	12	6	10.1	69	38%	53	45	11.2%	77	10.5	44%	65	7.5	44	7.6	5	2
Reggie Corner	26	CB	23	3.9%	--	11	5	8.3	--	33%	--	29	9.7%	--	6.6	56%	--	5.9	--	5.5	4	0
Ashton Youboty	25	CB	22	8.9%	--	16	8	1.6	--	89%	--	19	14.9%	--	7.4	66%	--	5.2	--	4.8	1	0
Drayton Florence	29	CB	40	5.7%	74	14	4	5.6	28	64%	12	48	12.7%	74	15.6	48%	51	7.1	36	6.6	4	0

Year	Pass D Rank	vs. #1 WR	Rk	vs. #2 WR	Rk	vs. Other WR	Rk	vs. TE	Rk	vs. RB	Rk
2006	8	-25.6%	1	24.2%	29	-2.9%	19	-3.8%	16	0.8%	18
2007	17	-8.7%	9	23.9%	29	-15.2%	10	-13.1%	4	2.2%	22
2008	24	29.1%	30	-8.9%	10	-16.8%	9	-2.1%	13	16.0%	26

The secondary numbers have to be taken with a grain of salt, as a backfield of Lester Hayes, Deion Sanders, Ronnie Lott and Ed Reed would have had a hard time holding up with the kind of pass rush the Bills were bringing every week. That said, there is no getting around the fact that Terrence McGee had a tough time covering primary receivers. Opposing quarterbacks certainly noticed, which is why McGee was targeted more than any cornerback in football last season. McGee is miscast as a number one corner, but he's been soldiering on in that role since Nate Clements left for San Francisco. His relief is already on the roster in the form of second-year man Leodis McKelvin, who gave a glimpse of what he could do against Kansas City when he intercepted Tyler Thigpen twice, running one of those back for a touchdown. McKelvin is a superior athlete who has exceptional skills once he has the ball in his hands, but he had some trouble adjusting to the pro game after playing his college ball in the Sun Belt Conference at Troy. If he continues to develop, McKelvin will nail down the other starting spot, allowing the team to play Drayton Florence exclusively as the third corner. More likely, the two will end up platooning. Florence had a rough go of it in Jacksonville, getting benched between Week 5 and Week 13 and then getting released just 11 months after signing a six-year, $36 million contract. Florence comes cheaper these days — his deal with the Bills amounts to just $6 million over two years — and if he can regain his form from his San Diego days, he will be a cost-effective replacement for the departed Jabari Greer.

Donte Whitner was less effective last year than in 2007 after playing out of position at free safety, and with a separated shoulder to boot. Now that he's healthy, Whitner will go back to being the eighth defender in the box. Bryan Scott was a very pleasant surprise while filling in at both safety spots, and he will press the oft-injured Ko Simpson for playing time. Also in the mix is second-round pick Jairus Byrd, who will convert to safety after playing corner at Oregon. Byrd has the kind of ballhawking skills that have been missing at the back end, and if he shows enough in preseason, he has a very real chance at being the opening day starter alongside Whitner.

Special Teams

Year	DVOA	Rank	FG/XP	Rank	Net Kick	Rank	Kick Ret	Rank	Net Punt	Rank	Punt Ret	Rank	Hidden	Rank
2006	5.9%	2	8.7	4	-2.0	25	5.5	6	16.1	1	6.6	3	-2.2	16
2007	4.2%	6	5.9	4	-2.2	19	2.7	13	7.2	4	11.3	3	-2.0	19
2008	6.1%	1	-3.6	25	6.4	9	17.3	1	7.3	8	8.8	3	0.9	11

If there has been one area of consistent excellence under Dick Jauron, it would be the special teams unit, which finished the season as the best in the NFL for the third time in five seasons. Leodis McKelvin was a big hit in his first year as a kick return man. His 1,468 yards were second-best in the league behind Seattle's Josh Wilson, and his 28.2 yard average was third-best in the league. In the latter stages of the season, teams were squibbing balls to the up-men rather than risking a deep kick to McKelvin. Roscoe Parrish was equally effective in his role as a punt returner, and his 15.3 yards per return led the league. Brian Moorman only punted 58 times, the lowest total in his career, but he averaged a solid 44.1 yards per punt. Kicker Rian Lindell slipped a bit in November, when he missed four of his 13 field goal attempts as the Bills drifted out of contention, but he rebounded in December and is solid at the position.

Coaching Staff

Coaches never say that they are feeling the pressure, but it's hard to see how the Ivy League-educated Jauron could be unaware of the tenuousness of his position on the heels of his third consecutive 7-9 season. Jauron now has a career record of 57-76, with his only winning season coming in 2001 with the Bears. There was strong sentiment among the fan base to let the head coach go or at least to force him to make some changes, but the argument for continuity won the day, so Jauron was allowed to keep his staff intact. Jauron acknowledged the discontent in February, saying, "I understand their feelings because I'm a fan and I certainly have teams that I root for and the Buffalo Bills are at the top of the list, so when we don't win I'm not particularly happy either." (We're wondering which teams Jauron is rooting for *besides* the Bills.)

Offensive coordinator Turk Schonert is talking about returning the no-huddle attack to Buffalo in some sort of Retro Night tribute to the Jim Kelly-era Bills. Schonert wants to take advantage of Trent Edwards' tremendous accuracy to keep defenses on the field and unable to substitute. Schonert liked to run out of two tight-end sets, but he's likely to move towards more three-receiver looks as he tries to make the offense more uptempo. Perry Fewell prefers generating a pass rush with the front four, but he bowed to reality and started sending linebackers and defensive backs on blitzes when the linemen weren't creating pressure. Bills secondary players were responsible for nearly 20 percent of the team's sack total. Fewell lobbied hard for Aaron Maybin, but he will work the rookie in slowly, limiting him to third downs and long-yardage situations.

Carolina Panthers

The Carolina Panthers are making a daring wager, betting the 2009 season on … the 2008 Carolina Panthers. It appears that what the Panthers would like more than anything this year is another shot at last year; more specifically, another shot at the playoff debacle against the Arizona Cardinals. The Panthers are returning 21 of 22 starters, including the orchestrator of that fiasco, quarterback Jake Delhomme (who comes complete with a shiny new contract extension). Did the front office learn nothing from *Tommy Boy*? At their own peril, the arbiters of the Panthers destiny have chosen to ignore the Big Tom Callahan Rule of Football: "You're either growing or you're dying. There ain't no third direction." While the rule may have originally applied to auto parts, it works for football and dating, too. The 2009 season will determine if the team pays a price for ignoring the sage words uttered by that legendary John Fox look-a-like, Brian Dennehy.

Assuming that franchise-tagged superstar Julius Peppers can't force a trade, the starting lineup the Panthers field on opening day will be nearly identical to that of last season. Richard Marshall takes over the starting cornerback position of Ken Lucas, whose release was largely a salary-cap move, but that's not much of a change. Although Marshall did not start a game in 2008, he was a major contributor to the defense over the past three years as a nickelback, and he started 14 games between 2006 and 2007.

Targeting the status quo in today's NFL is a risky proposition, particularly in the NFC South. The standings seem to turn upside down each season. Since 2003, teams' average year-to-year correlation of wins is *negative* 0.49. Can Carolina succeed with the same lineup two years in a row?

There are only a handful of teams in recent years that entered a new year with a similarly consistent starting lineup. From 2004 through 2008, only 12 teams kept at least 20 starters from the previous season. Predictably, this approach is most often taken by good teams. Teams averaged 10.3 wins in seasons prior to returning 20-plus starters. On average, the teams won 9.7 games the following season, with six teams improving and six declining.

Of course, teams with double-digit wins are likely to decline whether they keep the same lineup or not; that's simple regression to the mean. Since 2004, teams with 10 or 11 wins that didn't return at least 20 starters won an average of 7.9 games the following year.

Despite the arguable presence of an "action bias" in which teams who don't make it to the Super Bowl feel compelled to "do something" in the offseason, there may be merit in keeping a winning team together for another run.

It would be difficult to blame head coach John Fox

PANTHERS SUMMARY

2008 Record: 12-4

Pythagorean Wins: 10.1 (9th)

DVOA: 19.0% (6th)

Offense: 18.0% (5th)

Defense: 1.5% (13th)

Special Teams: 2.5% (10th)

Variance: 19.6% (26th)

2008: Old-school running-and-defense model leads Carolina to division title.

2009: Panthers hold on 18 in a division where even the worst team might turn over blackjack when you least expect it.

2009 Mean Projection: 8.3 wins

On the Clock (0-3): 4%

Loserville (4-6): 20%

Mediocrity (7-8): 29%

Playoff Contender (9-10): 29%

Super Bowl Contender (11+): 19%

Projected Average Opponent: -6.6% (31st)

2009 Panthers Schedule

Week	Opp.	Week	Opp.	Week	Opp.
1	PHI	7	BUF	13	TB
2	at ATL	8	at ARI	14	at NE
3	at DAL (Mon.)	9	at NO	15	MIN
4	BYE	10	ATL	16	at NYG
5	WAS	11	MIA (Thu.)	17	NO
6	at TB	12	at NYJ		

and general manager Marty Hurney for wanting a "do-over" given how their 2008 season ended. The Panthers were the class of what might have been the best division in the NFL during the regular season. They looked like a team ready to do damage in January. Instead their quarterback stumbled his way to five interceptions and a fumble, cementing his plaque in the Hall of Fame of postseason implosions (probably somewhere in the Neil O'Donnell wing). If you enjoy the horror genre, feel free to check out any of the Delhomme low-light montages that Cardinals fans have been kind enough to post online. Each clip features the common themes of staring down receivers and double-clutching before throwing. If the same Delhomme shows up in 2009, the Panthers may regret their $20 million guaranteed investment in the only quarterback ever nicknamed "Bobby Boucher" by his teammates.

Then again, the usual salary cap rules get thrown out the window when we might be headed for an uncapped 2010 season. The Panthers needed to save money against the cap right away in order to re-sign left tackle Jordan Gross and to franchise Peppers, and renegotiating Delhomme's deal helped make those moves possible. The Panthers saved about $2.5 million under the 2009 cap by adding five years to Delhomme's existing deal. Under his previous deal, Delhomme would have counted $11.1 million against this year's cap, but he now counts approximately $8.6 million. Many fans are up in arms seeing a 34-year-old quarterback coming off of the worst game of his career get a new contract, but if the deal is essentially a two-year $20-million dollar deal, at least it won't cripple the franchise. The following years of the extension pay him $4.8 million in 2010, $5.8 million in 2011, $6.7 million in 2012, $7.7 million in 2013, and $8 million in 2014. Thus, if he somehow defies the odds, plays well and survives the first two years of the contract, it won't break the bank to keep him around. But what's the likelihood of that happening?

The Panthers brought in Rip Scherer from Cleveland as their new quarterback coach. In May minicamp, Scherer was introducing new drills in the hope of improving Delhomme's accuracy. Unfortunately, a fresh perspective may not be enough to address the major weakness in Delhomme's game. Fans looking for a rebound to 2007-level Jake should remember that his career-high 64 percent completion rate that season came against opponents who went on to post a combined .310 winning percentage. Delhomme's 59.4 completion percentage in 2008 was right on par with his career average of 59.7 percent. For his career, Delhomme averages nearly an interception per game, so last year's 17 picks in 17 games was hardly atypical.

The Panthers' much-needed help for wide receiver Steve Smith arrived via time machine in the form of Muhsin Muhammad. Muhammad returned to his early-decade Carolina form, but at 36 he is not a long-term solution. Dwayne Jarrett has another year to learn from Muhammad or the team will likely run out of patience. Despite entering his third season, Jarrett doesn't turn 23 until September, so the door isn't shut on his career yet. Similarly, young tight end Dante Rosario has the potential to be a receiving threat, but must be more consistent. Rosario hurt his push for playing time by leading the team with nine penalties over the course of the season.

Particularly as the season wore on, the passing game was merely a complement to what the Panthers did best: run the ball. Offensive coordinator Jeff Davidson didn't try to fool teams with three-wide sets. The Panthers lined up with a fullback or a second tight end and pounded the ball down opponents' throats. The strategic tendencies demonstrate a propensity to run the ball early, run the ball late, and run the ball often.

It may come as a surprise that the Panthers didn't lead the league in rushing DVOA, but that's only because the ground attack got off to a slow start. The passing game had success early in the year and was ranked seventh in the NFL through Week 9. Then the ground game took over, and the Panthers' revamped offensive line paired with running backs DeAngelo Williams and Jonathan Stewart to form a potent — and consistent — combination. After Week 6, Carolina put up 10 straight weeks of positive rushing DVOA, and the Panthers led the league with 39.9% rushing DVOA from Week 10 onward. They also had 66.1% rushing DVOA in the red zone, first in the league by a wide margin.

If the Panthers do plan on sending out the same

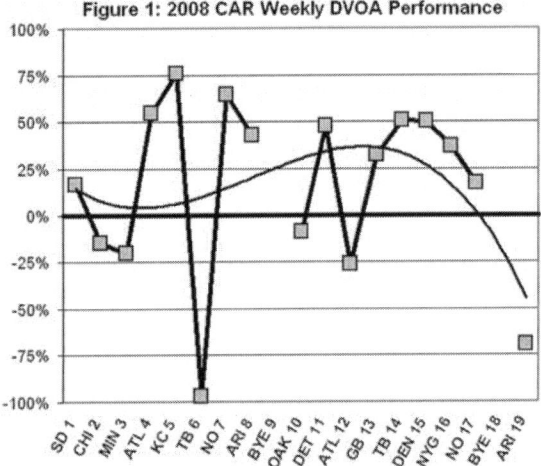

Figure 1: 2008 CAR Weekly DVOA Performance

starting lineup in 2008, they're going to need to figure out what went wrong with their defense at the
end of last season. The Panthers gave up an average
of 29.5 points and more than 389 yards per game
over the final seven weeks of the regular season,
and only one of their final six games had a negative
(i.e., good) defensive DVOA. The strength of the
defense was stopping the pass, and it is no coincidence that the two losses down the stretch were to
Atlanta and the New York Giants, teams that ran
the ball effectively. The inconsistency of the run
defense was most obvious against the Giants, as the
Panthers gave up 300 yards on the ground, including long, back-breaking runs to Brandon Jacobs and
Derrick Ward. The Panthers' run-stuffing defensive
tackle Ma'ake Kemoeatu missed the Giants game
with injury, demonstrating the importance of keeping blockers off of outstanding, but undersized,
middle linebacker Jon Beason.

One reason the Panthers struggled against the run was
lack of depth behind the defensive tackles, Kemoeatu
and Damione Lewis. Last year, rookie Nick Hayden
did not hold up well at the point of attack, so the hope
is that this year's third-round draft pick, Corey Irvin,
can contribute. Irvin joins the youth movement on
the line with the defensive ends of the future, Charles
Johnson and Everette Brown.

Ironically, while the players remain mostly the
same, the Panthers coaching staff has seen numerous
changes. A few assistants left for promotions, but a
few just seemed eager to get out of Carolina. Linebackers coach Ken Flajole left after six seasons with
the Panthers to become defensive coordinator of the
St. Louis Rams. Quarterbacks coach Mike McCoy,

who had spent nine seasons with the Panthers, was
hired as the Denver Broncos' offensive coordinator.
Defensive line coach Sal Sunseri left to be assistant
head coach and linebackers coach at Alabama after
seven seasons with the Panthers. But not everyone
left for a promotion. Defensive coordinator Mike
Trgovac joined the mass exodus of assistant coaches,
turning down a contract offer to remain in Carolina
and later accepting a position coach gig with the
Packers. Secondary coach Tim Lewis accepted the
same position with the Seattle Seahawks.

Hurney and Fox addressed the defensive coordinator
slot by hiring Ron Meeks, the former Colts defensive
coordinator. Meeks is not an aggressive coordinator; he
fears the blitz as if he's Belgian. His modus operandi
with the Colts was to sit back in the Tampa-2 and rush
with the front four only. Last year the Colts did not get
a single sack from a linebacker or defensive back. It's
unclear how this philosophy will mesh with that of Fox,
the former defensive coordinator with the Giants, who
will continue to take an active role on the defensive side
of the ball. The Panthers have played some two-deep
zone in the past, but they mixed in a lot of different coverages and schemes. For example, the Panthers ranked
fifth in the league in frequency of zone blitzes a year
ago, whereas the Colts ranked 31st.

If Meeks' track record is any indication, he may address the weaknesses in the run defense by asking
Chris Harris to put on his Bob Sanders wig and smack
some running backs in the mouth. Turns out, unbe-
knownst to the public, Harris finished out the 2008
season playing with a torn labrum in his shoulder.
Additionally, Beason suffered the same injury in the
October matchup with the Cardinals and continued to
play through it. Both Beason and Harris underwent
surgery during the offseason and should be back to
full strength in time for training camp. Thus the run
defense could be better than it was in the second half
of 2008 by virtue of the health of these two hitters.

If the 2009 Carolina Panthers hope to get their playoff "do-over," they need to buck the NFC South trend
of an annual standings reversal. The last NFC South
team to return 20-plus starters was Tampa Bay in 2006,
and the Bucs went from 11-5 in 2005 to 4-12 the following year. It seems unlikely that the Panthers will
suffer that same fate, especially since they have one
of the league's easiest projected schedules in 2009. So
are they growing or dying? This Carolina team is betting that they can grow via the status quo.

Mark Zajack

2008 Panthers Stats by Week

Wk	vs.	W-L	PF	PA	YDF	YDA	TO	Total	Off	Def	ST
1	@SD	W	26	24	388	316	0	17%	19%	8%	6%
2	CHI	W	20	17	216	256	+1	-15%	-16%	-8%	-8%
3	@MIN	L	10	20	204	305	-1	-21%	-20%	15%	15%
4	ATL	W	24	9	401	268	0	55%	44%	-22%	-11%
5	KC	W	34	0	441	127	+1	76%	0%	-69%	7%
6	@TB	L	3	27	282	315	-3	-97%	-27%	45%	-25%
7	NO	W	30	7	336	343	+2	64%	41%	-16%	7%
8	ARI	W	27	23	351	425	+1	43%	31%	-3%	9%
9	BYE										
10	@OAK	W	17	6	219	259	-1	-9%	-66%	-36%	21%
11	DET	W	31	22	366	316	+3	48%	45%	-6%	-3%
12	@ATL	L	28	45	408	392	+1	-27%	21%	31%	-16%
13	@GB	W	35	31	298	438	+1	33%	28%	14%	19%
14	TB	W	38	23	464	384	-2	50%	72%	22%	1%
15	DEN	W	30	10	400	279	+1	50%	22%	-22%	6%
16	@NYG	L	28	34	343	459	0	37%	46%	19%	10%
17	@NO	W	33	31	478	417	+2	17%	39%	28%	6%
18	BYE										
19	ARI	L	13	33	269	360	-5	-69%	-66%	10%	6%

Trends and Splits

	Offense	Rank	Defense	Rank
Total DVOA	18.0%	5	1.5%	13
Unadjusted VOA	17.2%	8	2.9%	15
Weighted trend	24.7%	2	5.7%	15
Variance	12.2%	28	5.0%	12
Average opponent	7.5%	5	7.0%	22
Passing	29.5%	9	-4.3%	8
Rushing	23.3%	2	8.7%	24
First down	14.3%	7	-3.2%	11
Second down	24.2%	5	4.1%	15
Third down	15.5%	15	5.8%	18
First half	14.5%	10	-0.7%	12
Second half	22.1%	5	3.5%	16
Red Zone	37.2%	2	3.7%	20
Late and close	28.5%	2	7.6%	23

Five-Year Performance

Year	W-L	Pyth	Est W	PF	PA	TO	Total	Rk	Off	Rk	Def	Rk	ST	Rk	Off AGL	Rk	Def AGL	Rk
2004	7-9	8.4	8.6	355	339	+12	2.7%	14	1.3%	13	-3.7%	13	-2.3%	24	31.5	8	10.6	26
2005	11-5	11.6	9.9	391	259	+16	18.6%	9	0.1%	14	-15.9%	2	2.5%	5	8.1	23	10.9	20
2006	8-8	6.9	7.9	270	305	-5	5.8%	14	-1.4%	17	-10.0%	4	-2.8%	24	26.8	8	23.6	10
2007	7-9	8.1	6.3	267	347	+1	-20.1%	26	-14.0%	26	1.2%	19	-4.9%	30	20.4	18	5.4	30
2008	12-4	10.1	10.1	414	329	+6	19.0%	6	18.0%	5	1.5%	13	2.5%	10	14.4	24	5.6	29

Strategic Tendencies

Run/Pass		Rank	Offense		Rank	Defense		Rank	Other		Rank
Runs, all plays	53%	3	3+ WR	31%	32	Rush 3	3.8%	21	2+ RB, Pct Runs	71%	2
Runs, first half	50%	4	4+ WR	8%	22	Rush 4	66.8%	12	1 RB/2 TE, Pct Runs	51%	19
Runs, first down	59%	5	2+ TE	38%	2	Rush 5	22.5%	16	1RB/3+WR, Pct Runs	18%	29
Runs, second-long	57%	1	Single back	45%	27	Rush 6+	6.9%	22	Zone Blitz	9%	5
Runs, power sit.	76%	4	Play action	23%	4	Rush 7+	1.0%	21	Go for it on 4th	0.74	29
Runs, behind 2H	35%	11	Max protect	6%	26	Sacks by LB	12.2%	21	Offensive Pace	31.1	16
Pass, ahead 2H	33%	31	Outside pocket	7%	26	Sacks by DB	8.1%	16	Defensive Pace	30.0	6

Even though the Panthers are clearly a run-first team, they tip their hand by almost never running when they go three-wide. This was the second straight season where they passed on more than 80 percent of downs with three or more receivers in the game. ● As in 2007, the Panthers ran more than any other team in second-and-long, but they were much better (4.9 yards per carry) than they were in 2007 (3.6 yards per carry). ● Carolina only ran 15 draw plays all season; only Cleveland and Houston ran fewer draws, and only Houston ran fewer draws as a percentage of all runs. ● The Panthers had 26.0% DVOA when opponents had only one wide receiver in the game, worst in the NFC. They were an above-average defense the rest of the time. ● A surprising fact: Excluding screen passes, where we typically do not list a defender, Carolina had the highest number of passes marked "uncovered."

Passing

Player	DYAR	DVOA	Plays	NtYds	Avg	YAC	C%	TD	Int
Jake Delhomme	828	18.0%	438	3204	7.3	5.0	59.6%	15	12

Rushing

Player	DYAR	DVOA	Plays	Yds	Avg	TD	Fum	Suc
DeAngelo Williams	385	28.3%	273	1515	5.5	18	0	47%
Jonathan Stewart	122	7.6%	184	838	4.6	10	2	45%
Brad Hoover	0	-9.0%	9	18	2.0	0	0	56%
Nick Goings*	-28	-98.9%	9	10	1.1	0	0	22%
Jake Delhomme	20	51.5%	6	34	5.7	2	0	--
Steve Smith	20	26.5%	5	40	8.0	0	0	--

Receiving

Player	DYAR	DVOA	Plays	Ctch	Yds	Y/C	YAC	TD	C%
Steve Smith	365	22.7%	129	78	1421	18.2	5.5	6	60%
Muhsin Muhammad	160	6.1%	107	65	923	14.2	4.9	5	61%
D.J. Hackett*	-20	-21.7%	28	13	190	14.6	6.1	0	46%
Dwayne Jarrett	1	-11.8%	19	10	119	11.9	2.9	0	53%
Jeff King	-7	-10.7%	34	21	195	9.3	3.8	1	62%
Dante Rosario	13	-0.9%	31	18	209	11.6	3.3	1	58%
DeAngelo Williams	-1	-14.5%	30	22	121	5.5	6.7	2	57%
Jonathan Stewart	-37	-49.5%	17	8	47	5.9	6.1	0	47%
Brad Hoover	-9	-27.1%	11	6	39	6.5	4.7	0	55%

Offensive Line

Year	Yards	ALY	Rank	Power	Rank	10+ Yds	Rank	Stuff	Rank	Sacks	ASR	Rank	False	Cont.
2006	3.98	3.95	24	50%	31	17%	12	18%	16	32	6.5%	16	19	36
2007	4.07	4.08	19	63%	16	14%	20	18%	17	33	6.4%	15	21	35
2008	5.01	4.26	8	79%	1	27%	1	19%	18	20	5.0%	9	32	25

Year	LE	Rank	LT	Rank	Mid	Rank	RT	Rank	RE	Rank
2006	4.57	6	4.23	18	4.05	22	4.38	8	2.38	32
2007	5.22	3	3.76	25	3.83	23	4.14	17	4.40	8
2008	4.14	19	4.08	17	4.26	11	4.60	4	4.19	11

With all the success of last season, it's easy to forget that the Panthers were not not happy with the offensive line after 2007. According to our game charting numbers, the Panthers were in the bottom half of the league that year with 20 blown blocks leading to sacks or intentional grounding. They cut that number in half in 2008. In the running game, the Panthers improved dramatically in Adjusted Line Yards and led the league in converting 79 percent of runs in power situations.

A key to the success was the shift from a zone-blocking scheme back to the old-school, hit-'em-in-the-mouth power blocking scheme of Panthers past. The other key, and it was a big one, was grabbing the 336-pound mauler Jeff Otah in the draft, enabling the Panthers to completely reshuffle their line. With Otah in place at right tackle, the Panthers had a new starter at every spot on the line in 2008. The left side of the line was a liability in 2007, with Travelle Wharton playing out of position at left tackle and Mike Wahle showing his age at left guard. In 2008, the Panthers shifted Wharton inside to his true position of guard and moved Jordan Gross from right tackle to left tackle. The same athleticism that allowed Wharton to play tackle makes him a devastating blocker when he pulls in the running game. And all Gross did was play at a Pro Bowl level. The Panthers particularly dominated in the run game when running right behind pulling left guard Wharton and Otah. With the emergence of Ryan Kalil at center, the Panthers didn't miss Justin Hartwig, who went to the Steelers in the offseason. Right guard was manned by Keydrick Vincent, who replaced the "troubled" Jeremy Bridges. Bridges is not nearly a good enough football player to make up for his annual off-the-field incidents. Vincent stepped up next to Otah, providing a potent combination in the run game.

Although every member of the line missed at least one game with various injuries, the depth was solid. In particular, Geoff Hangartner, a former starter at center, was able to fill in well for Kalil, who missed four games. The Panthers' loss of Hangartner to the Bills and Jeremy Bridges to the Redskins this offseason means depth will be a concern. The Panthers hope that fifth-round pick Duke Robinson from Oklahoma, who has experience at three positions, can step up if needed. If all five starters can stay healthy, this line will remain above-average in pass protection and could be the best run-blocking line in the league.

Defensive Front Seven

Defensive Line	Age	Pos	Plays	TmPct	Overall Rk	Stop	Dfts	Stop%	Rk	AvYd	Pass Rush Rk	Sack	Hit	Hur	vs. Run Runs	St%	Yds	vs. Pass Pass	St%	Yds
Julius Peppers	29	DE	54	6.5%	28	43	25	80%	29	0.0	7	14.5	10	24	31	71%	2.5	23	91%	-3.3
Damione Lewis	31	DT	46	5.9%	25	35	12	76%	42	1.9	33	3.5	1	6	37	70%	2.9	9	100%	-1.9
Tyler Brayton	30	DE	42	5.1%	47	27	9	64%	85	3.4	89	4.5	1	10	26	69%	3.7	16	56%	3.0
Ma'ake Kemoeatu	30	DT	38	5.2%	33	25	3	66%	68	3.1	70	0.0	0	0	33	70%	2.4	5	40%	7.6
Charles Johnson	23	DE	31	3.7%	74	28	14	90%	3	0.2	11	6.0	4	13	15	87%	2.9	16	94%	-2.3

Linebackers	Age	Pos	Plays	TmPct	Overall Rk	Stop	Dfts	Stop%	AvYd	Pass Rush Sack	Hit	Hur	vs. Run Runs	St%	Rk	Yds	Rk	vs. Pass Tgts	Suc%	Rk	AdjYd	Rk
Jon Beason	24	ILB	146	17.6%	7	75	16	51%	5.5	0.0	1	3	97	57%	87	4.4	90	43	51%	42	6.3	48
Thomas Davis	26	OLB	120	14.5%	24	64	30	53%	5.1	3.5	2	4	57	63%	55	4.5	96	47	62%	10	4.0	1
Na'il Diggs	31	OLB	50	6.0%	97	29	5	58%	4.9	1.0	2	1	38	63%	54	4.3	88	21	57%	24	6.7	54

Year	Yards	ALY	Rank	Power	Rank	10+ Yds	Rank	Stuff	Rank	Sack	ASR	Rank
2006	3.97	3.96	9	48%	2	16%	17	22%	4	41	8.1%	7
2007	3.85	3.90	9	53%	3	16%	14	21%	11	23	4.8%	29
2008	4.53	4.33	24	68%	20	19%	19	16%	26	37	7.4%	5

Year	LE	Rank	LT	Rank	Mid	Rank	RT	Rank	RE	Rank
2006	3.50	11	4.54	19	3.95	8	4.46	22	3.46	10
2007	2.20	2	3.97	13	4.16	18	3.45	5	4.75	26
2008	4.75	24	4.46	22	4.65	31	2.93	2	3.92	15

Factoring in the loss of defensive tackle Kris Jenkins to the Jets and defensive end Mike Rucker to retirement, the 2008 performance of the front seven was a pleasant surprise. Sure, Jenkins was an absolute monster for the Jets over the first half of the year, but veteran Damione Lewis, already entrenched in Carolina's defensive tackle rotation, stepped into Jenkins' starting role effectively. Lewis is certainly not the double-team swallowing run-stuffer that Jenkins is, but showed enough quickness and power as a pass-rusher to garner 3.5 sacks and at least five hurries for the second year in a row. The other starting tackle, Ma'ake Kemoeatu, did his job to keep blockers off of the linebackers. The Panthers got everything they could have hoped for out of Lewis and Kemo last season, but the lack of another tackle in heavy rotation will catch up to them this season with both players more than 30 years old. The Panthers hope that third-round draft pick Corey Irvin (Georgia) can be the third defensive tackle that they desperately need.

Julius Peppers was a monster in 2008. Peppers not only had 14.5 sacks (fifth in the NFL), but he had 24 hurries, third behind only Dwight Freeney (28) and Jared Allen (26). Oh, the wonders of a contract year. Peppers' resurgence from a career low 2.5 sacks in 2007 resulted in the Panthers hitting him with the franchise tag this offseason, in the hope of keeping him in a "contract year" for one more season. Oakland escapee Tyler Brayton started at the other defensive end in place of the retired Rucker, which gave the Panthers the luxury to bring 2007 third-rounder Charles Johnson along slowly. To say Johnson made the most of his limited snaps last year is an understatement. Of course, coming in on obvious passing downs opposite the automatic double-team of Julius Peppers can make for some favorable matchups. Nevertheless, Johnson showed the potential to be a cornerstone of the team's long-term plans at defensive end. If and when Peppers departs, the Panthers hope to replace him with 2009 second-round pick Everette Brown. The Panthers traded their 2010 first-round pick to move up and get the Florida State product, and a look at what Brown did for the Seminoles last year illustrates why; of Brown's 30 solo tackles in 13 games, 20 came behind the line of scrimmage, including 13 sacks. The young man gets upfield with alacrity.

The loss of Kris Jenkins was probably felt most by linebacker Jon Beason. Beason is everywhere on the field, a true sideline-to-sideline guy who has proven that, despite playing on the weak side in college, he's at home in the middle. While he still made a ridiculous number of plays, similar to 2007, those plays tended to be a little further downfield. It will be interesting to see if Beason's production changes with the arrival of new defensive coordinator Ron Meeks. Beason could see more deep middle pass coverage duty in a Carolina version of the Tampa-2, but that shouldn't be a problem for Beason with his speed and ball skills (three picks last year). After a brief experiment, starting his NFL career at safety, Thomas Davis has settled in at linebacker, where he covers like a defensive back, blitzes effectively, and hits people like they stole something. Na'il Diggs is the elder statesman of the crew, but his age didn't deter the team from extending his contract through 2014. The Panthers might try Dan Connor on the outside with his return from the ACL injury that cut short his rookie season. Connor was at Mike last year, but with Beason entrenched there, they may see what he can do elsewhere. Landon Johnson showed some flashes in Cincinnati, but he and James Anderson provide little more than special teams help and depth.

Defensive Secondary

Secondary	Age	Pos	Plays	TmPct	Rk	Stop	Dfts	Yds	Rk	St%	Rk	Tgts	Tgt%	Rk	Dist	Suc%	Rk	AdjYd	Rk	Yds	PD	Int
Chris Gamble	26	CB	110	13.3%	3	49	17	4.7	18	62%	16	99	22.3%	15	12.3	53%	32	5.8	11	6.3	18	3
Chris Harris	27	SS	72	8.7%	54	23	8	7.3	46	35%	53	25	5.6%	56	14.0	50%	46	7.6	31	7.7	3	1
Ken Lucas*	30	CB	70	8.5%	46	30	12	8.4	56	55%	24	84	18.9%	30	11.9	52%	36	8.0	55	8.5	12	2
Charles Godfrey	24	FS	64	7.7%	63	21	7	7.8	55	39%	45	32	7.1%	33	16.0	46%	59	7.9	41	9.1	4	1
Richard Marshall	25	CB	59	7.1%	64	25	13	4.4	12	67%	8	48	10.8%	78	9.2	50%	46	5.7	10	6.0	3	1

Header note: Overall | vs. Run | vs. Pass

Year	Pass D Rank	vs. #1 WR	Rk	vs. #2 WR	Rk	vs. Other WR	Rk	vs. TE	Rk	vs. RB	Rk
2006	9	-16.4%	6	7.3%	21	-17.0%	9	16.5%	29	-21.0%	9
2007	19	14.7%	24	1.3%	16	-12.6%	12	10.3%	22	-19.5%	5
2008	8	-5.1%	10	-0.2%	16	-2.5%	17	-13.0%	8	-13.7%	4

The light turned on for cornerback Chris Gamble last year, and he finally put all the pieces together to become the playmaker of the Carolina secondary. Gamble contributed as a solid tackler on the edge in the run game and complete cover corner. The solid play of Gamble and nickel corner Richard Marshall — combined with a dire cap situation — made the other 2008 starter, veteran Ken Lucas, expendable, and the Panthers released him after he refused a trade to Detroit. If Marshall can be as effective on the outside as he has been in the slot, he and Gamble could be among the top corner tandems in the league. Rookie second-round pick Sherrod Martin (Troy) will get a long look as the nickel corner; Martin played both corner and free safety in college and is known as both a ballhawk and a hitter, with four picks and 59 solo tackles as a senior. Vets C.J. Wilson and Dante Wesley are also in the mix for nickel and dime duties. Thanks to a good pass rush, active linebackers, and solid corners, strong safety Chris Harris and rookie free safety Charles Godfrey did not have to make a ton of plays and did their jobs without fanfare. Godfrey was quite the bargain as a third-round pick and looks to be the long-term answer at free safety. Add rookie Sherrod Martin to the foursome of Gamble, Marshall, Harris, and Godfrey, and new coordinator Ron Meeks could find himself drooling at the thought of running a Tampa-2 scheme with one of the better tackling secondaries in the league.

Special Teams

Year	DVOA	Rank	FG/XP	Rank	Net Kick	Rank	Kick Ret	Rank	Net Punt	Rank	Punt Ret	Rank	Hidden	Rank
2006	-2.8%	24	11.5	1	-1.8	23	-11.6	30	0.8	18	-15.3	32	-2.9	18
2007	-4.9%	30	2.1	12	-5.8	25	-12.4	30	-8.8	27	-4.0	21	1.5	14
2008	2.5%	10	6.6	4	17.3	1	-2.4	20	-10.5	29	4.0	5	-1.0	13

The Panthers were the only NFL team to employ a kickoff specialist in 2008, and it definitely paid off. Big-legged Brit Rhys Lloyd was the NFL leader in kickoff touchback percentage (34 percent) and helped the Panthers rank first in net kickoff value according to Football Outsiders analysis. Carolina's "other" kicker, John

Kasay, was no slouch himself; he missed only three field goals all year, two of those from 50 yards or more. As for punter Jason Baker, you may consider him a slouch. Independent of his coverage unit, Baker's punts lost 10.3 points worth of field position compared to an average NFL punter, second-worst in the NFL (ahead of only Kyle Larson of Cincinnati). His net average continued to decline and he was the first punter to have three punts blocked in a season since … Todd Sauerbrun for the 2003 Panthers. Are punters allergic to the air in Charlotte or something?

Journeyman returner Mark Jones returned both kickoffs and punts after Ryne Robinson tore his MCL and PCL in the preseason and missed the year. Jones put up close to league-average numbers, which was pretty good for a plan-B, but departed for Tennessee as a free agent. Robinson should be fully healthy this year, and the team would like to see him realize his potential and improve over his pedestrian 2007 numbers.

Coaching Staff

As quickly as the injury-marred 2007 season was forgotten, so were the rumblings about John Fox's job security. Fox has yet to go worse than 7-9 in seven years as Panthers head coach, and while this was the first time his team lost its first postseason game, the loss can hardly be chalked up to being out-coached. Under Fox, however, not all is stable on the coaching front. Fox saw the exodus of pretty much his entire defensive staff in the offseason. Defensive coordinator Mike Trgovac, with the team since 2002, turned down a contract extension to become the … wait, is this right? Defensive line coach with the Packers? A coach who turns down an extension to take a lower position elsewhere is certainly a rarity. He'll be replaced by former Indianapolis defensive coordinator Ron Meeks, who "resigned" once Jim Caldwell took over the Colts. Word is that Meeks was ushered to the door by the new regime, and it remains unclear how much of Meeks' scattered success in Indy was attributable to Tony Dungy. Don't expect him to have complete autonomy with Fox either. Exactly how the Tampa-2 principles espoused by Meeks will fit in with the man-to-man leanings of Fox remains a mystery, but Meeks does inherit a young defense with a lot of speed, which could make him look good.

Jeff Davidson wanted a mulligan after 2007, his first year at offensive coordinator. Installing a zone-blocking scheme and new offensive playbook while fielding four different quarterbacks over the course of the season made for a rocky debut. In 2008, he wisely ended his zone-blocking experiment, reverting to the power-run game of Carolina's past. The rest was division-winning history. Look for more of the same from the Panthers offense in 2009.

Chicago Bears

One of the amazing things about football is how teams can maintain an identity despite the natural rise, fall, and departure of all the people who were part of that identity. The New York Giants, for example: Despite the fact that Bill Parcells left nearly 20 years ago, the Giants are still built around a defense that excels at rushing the passer. Lawrence Taylor begat Jessie Armstead, who gave way to Michael Strahan, who was followed by Justin Tuck. The names change, but the philosophy and the results stay the same.

In Chicago, the identity is simpler: The defense does the work and the offense, at best, stays out of its way. The team has changed head coaches, general managers, offensive coordinators, and all of its personnel, but it hasn't really changed a thing. Chicago hasn't posted a positive offensive DVOA since 1995, resulting in a stretch of 13 years where the offense has failed to rank any higher than 18th in the league (Table 1). Only Detroit has managed to go as long as ten years without a positive offensive DVOA. Under GM Jerry Angelo, despite spending 62 percent of their draft value (according to the traditional NFL Draft Value Chart) on offensive players, Chicago has simply failed to develop an effective offense.

Enter one Jay Christopher Cutler to save the day. The only problem? He might not have come soon enough.

Outside of Cutler, the Bears organization is in a great deal of flux; while some parts of the team are past their prime, others are yet to reach it. Take the wideouts — Chicago's top five receivers heading into camp have a combined total of 145 career catches. Only 12 teams have had fewer career catches from their top five wideouts heading into a season in the DVOA era, and they averaged a passing DVOA of -19.9%; of those teams, only one — the 2008 Dolphins — had a positive DVOA. They'll get help from halfback Matt Forte, who led the team in receptions a year ago, and tight end Greg Olsen, who was second, but the team will need someone to emerge at wide receiver across from Devin Hester to be able to take advantage of Cutler's ability to stretch the field.

The offensive line, meanwhile, is full of veterans; the team will have three new starters on the line this year, including future Hall of Fame left tackle Orlando Pace, who hopes to extend his career past age 34; former Browns tackle Kevin Shaffer; and 2008 first-round pick Chris Williams, who will compete with Shaffer for the right tackle spot. Former Carolina utility lineman Frank Omiyale is likely ticketed for left guard, replacing the inconsistent Josh Beekman. While all this turnover is designed to bring more talent to a line that was overmatched at times a year ago, our research has shown that continuity plays an important role in offensive line success, and concerns about the health of Pace and Williams (who missed most of his rookie season with a herniated disc) are warranted. For Forte and

BEARS SUMMARY

2008 Record: 9-7

Pythagorean Wins: 8.7 (17th)

DVOA: 6.2% (15th)

Offense: -4.8% (23rd)

Defense: -6.8% (7th)

Special Teams: 4.2% (5th)

Variance: 9.7% (6th)

2008: Our kingdom for a quarterback.

2009: Well, if you'll take two first-round picks, that works too.

2009 Mean Projection: 10.5 wins

On the Clock (0-3): 0%

Loserville (4-6): 3%

Mediocrity (7-8): 12%

Playoff Contender (9-10): 36%

Super Bowl Contender (11+): 49%

Projected Average Opponent: -1.9% (24th)

2009 Bears Schedule

Week	Opp.	Week	Opp.	Week	Opp.
1	at GB	7	at CIN	13	STL
2	PIT	8	CLE	14	GB
3	at SEA	9	ARI	15	at BAL
4	DET	10	at SF (Thu.)	16	MIN (Mon.)
5	BYE	11	PHI	17	at DET
6	at ATL	12	at MIN		

Olsen to contribute in the passing game, the line will need to hold up and be effective in front of Cutler; otherwise, they'll be spending their time attempting to stand up blitzers, not making moves in the open field.

If the pieces around them fit as planned, Cutler, Forte, and Olsen should emerge as an elite trio. Forte was the glue that held the Bears' offense together a year ago, going straight from the second round into the starting lineup while handling rushing, receiving, and pass blocking with equal aplomb. Olsen, meanwhile, eliminated many of the mental mistakes and concentration issues that plagued his rookie year while showing off some of the softest hands in the league.

As for Cutler, there's not really a historical player to compare him to; quarterbacks who make the Pro Bowl in their third season just don't get traded very frequently. The only player in a remotely similar situation was Elvis Grbac, who made the Pro Bowl in his third season as a starter, but he was 30 and an unrestricted free agent. He only lasted a single year with the Ravens before being cut and retiring, which isn't about to happen with Cutler. We'll never be able to fully extricate a quarterback's performance from the performance of the players around him, and we know Cutler isn't able to bring Ryan Clady, Brandon Marshall, and Eddie Royal with him to the Windy City, but he is undoubtedly the closest thing to the elite quarterback that the Bears have sought for a generation. The last Bears quarterback to rank in the top ten in NFL passer rating was Erik Kramer in that 1995 campaign, 14 years ago; there have only been seven instances since the AFL-NFL merger of a team going that long without such a quarterback. The Bears have invested two first-round picks in the hopes that Cutler will end that streak.

If Cutler doesn't bring the Bears offense into the 21st century immediately, it might be too late to take advantage of Chicago's strong defense, which showed signs of slipping in 2008 despite being ranked seventh in the league for a second consecutive season. Simply put, Chicago couldn't rush the passer.

Lovie Smith, like other coaches from the Tampa-2 school of defense, relies on the defensive line to get pressure. Over the past three years, the Bears have gotten consistently effective pressure from their defensive tackles, driven by the ability of the mercurial Tommie Harris (Table 2). Since their Super Bowl run in 2006, though, the pressure provided by defensive ends Adewale Ogunleye, Alex Brown, and particularly Mark Anderson has dropped off. Anderson seemed like a future star three years ago, putting up 12 sacks as a rookie in a part-time role, but he wasn't able to adapt to life as a starter in 2007. Last year, Anderson moved back into his previous role, but he could only muster one sack.

Because of the lack of pressure, Smith and defensive coordinator Bob Babich were forced to frequently use what's known as a "mug" look, where the four down linemen are joined at the line of scrimmage by the linebackers and the strong safety. It can create confusion amongst pass protectors and allow the Bears to get a big blitz off very quickly or stuff all the gaps at the line of scrimmage. On the other hand, it forces the two cornerbacks and the free safety behind them to frequently go into a Cover-3, where each player is responsible for a third of the field and concerned primarily about ensuring that no receiver gets behind them, even if it means giving up chunks of yardage underneath.

As a result, the nature of how the Bears play defense changed altogether. Instead of rushing four and dropping players like Brian Urlacher and Lance Briggs into their familiar roles in pass coverage, the Bears became a team built around the big blitz (Table 3). Even when the Bears didn't deliver on it, they teased it with zone blitzes and players dropping off the line of scrimmage into assorted exotic coverage and pressure schemes that bore little resemblance to the Bears defense of the past several seasons.

Table 1: The Dexterity Of Suck
Chicago's Offensive DVOA, 1994-2008

Year	DVOA	Rank	Year	DVOA	Rank
1994	-2.5%	13	2002	-15.1%	27
1995	17.7%	5	2003	-20.3%	30
1996	-6.0%	21	2004	-36.5%	32
1997	-14.8%	26	2005	-16.8%	28
1998	-8.8%	19	2006	-4.2%	18
1999	-10.5%	21	2007	-20.4%	31
2000	-10.3%	23	2008	-4.3%	22

Table 2: Is A Pass Rush, Is Not A Pass Rush: Chicago Defense, 2006-2008

Year	Pass Att	DE Sacks	DT Sacks	LB/DB Sacks	Total Sacks	QB Hits per Pass
2006	581	25.5	10.5	4	40	14.8%
2007	541	18.5	9.5	12	40	13.6%
2008	622	12	10.5	4.5	27	12.4%

The solution, of course, is for the defensive line to get pressure. Without a significant outlay in free agency or a pick on Day One of the draft, though, Chicago's primary means of inducing change comes from new defensive line coach Rod Marinelli. Always the drill sergeant type in Detroit and Tampa Bay, where he worked alongside Smith previously, Marinelli will be entrusted with getting the most out of a defensive line that simply needs to play better in 2009. Specifically,

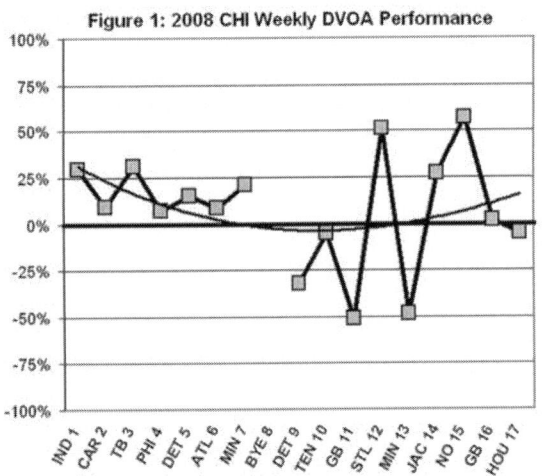

Figure 1: 2008 CHI Weekly DVOA Performance

that means Anderson; if he returns to his rookie form, the entire complexion of Chicago's defensive scheme changes for the better. It could also earn him a hefty contract, either in Chicago or elsewhere, as the former Alabama star is in the last year of his rookie deal.

Because the pass rush wasn't there last year, the secondary looked bad. Charles Tillman benefited from a league-high ten drops by receivers whom he was covering, while Nathan Vasher spent the year alternately injured and ineffective. Ironically, it was oft-injured free safety Mike Brown who stayed healthy, making it through 15 games for the first time in five seasons. Brown's release in the offseason opened up an opportunity at free safety for either Saints leftover Josh Bullocks or converted corner Zack Bowman, but whoever wins the job will need to develop the instincts and timing necessary to be a safety in Cover-2 (or Cover-3) quickly. When healthy, Brown was an excellent centerfielder who was rarely out of position; that helped the Bears limit opposing teams to a league-low average of 3.9 yards after the catch. While the Tampa-2 is designed to limit big plays, losing Brown might open up the Bears to a few more of them in 2009.

The Bears have two potentially championship-caliber cores of players. The veteran core is mostly defensive and has Briggs, Urlacher, Vasher, Tillman, Pace, and center Olin Kreutz, all of whom are 28 or older; the younger group has Cutler and Harris (both born on April 29, 1983) to go along with potentially elite players in Forte, Hester, Olsen, Anderson, and Williams, none of whom are older than 26. If everything goes right, Cutler will help the younger players step forward, Marinelli will light a spark underneath the pass rush, and the veteran group will maintain its elite level of play. If everything goes wrong, Smith's out of a job and the franchise starts over.

Our projection system leans towards the former, with strong defense and elite special teams propping up the performance of an average offense. Sound familiar? Bears fans won't complain if the same old story ends with another deep playoff run.

Bill Barnwell

Table 3: Tomorrow We Will Blitz Faster: Chicago Defense by Pass Rushers, 2007-2008

Rushers	4	5	6	7	Sacks	QB Hits per Pass
2007	71% (7)	22% (16)	6% (25)	1% (22)	40	13.6%
2008	61% (21)	25% (10)	14% (4)	5% (1)	27	12.4%
(NFL rank in parentheses)						

2008 Bears Stats by Week

Wk	vs.	W-L	PF	PA	YDF	YDA	TO	Total	Off	Def	ST
1	@IND	W	29	13	319	293	+1	30%	11%	-12%	7%
2	@CAR	L	17	20	256	216	-1	9%	-19%	-31%	-3%
3	TB	L	24	27	405	454	+2	31%	15%	-7%	8%
4	PHI	W	24	20	256	340	-2	7%	-20%	-14%	12%
5	@DET	W	34	7	425	185	+1	15%	-4%	-21%	-2%
6	@ATL	L	20	22	361	376	0	9%	16%	-4%	-11%
7	MIN	W	48	41	327	439	+4	21%	39%	22%	3%
8	BYE										
9	DET	W	27	23	320	333	+1	-33%	-18%	5%	-9%
10	TEN	L	14	21	243	304	0	-5%	10%	1%	-14%
11	@GB	L	3	37	234	427	0	-51%	-24%	34%	7%
12	@STL	W	27	3	334	207	+2	51%	-9%	-62%	-1%
13	@MIN	L	14	34	228	378	-2	-49%	-46%	9%	6%
14	JAC	W	23	10	296	278	0	27%	-15%	-30%	11%
15	NO	W	27	24	227	351	-1	57%	-11%	-39%	29%
16	GB	W	20	17	210	325	0	2%	-29%	-11%	20%
17	@HOU	L	24	31	294	455	0	-5%	18%	31%	8%

Trends and Splits

	Offense	Rank	Defense	Rank
Total DVOA	-4.8%	23	-6.8%	7
Unadjusted VOA	-6.7%	25	-7.2%	6
Weighted trend	-7.9%	23	-4.7%	7
Variance	4.8%	2	7.2%	24
Average opponent	4.8%	11	4.8%	15
Passing	4.6%	22	1.6%	10
Rushing	-4.3%	26	-17.6%	5
First down	-1.6%	22	-4.7%	9
Second down	-9.7%	24	4.0%	14
Third down	-2.9%	20	-26.5%	5
First half	5.3%	18	-2.8%	10
Second half	-14.3%	25	-10.2%	6
Red Zone	13.6%	10	-10.2%	11
Late and close	-15.9%	27	-10.5%	5

Five-Year Performance

Year	W-L	Pyth	Est W	PF	PA	TO	Total	Rk	Off	Rk	Def	Rk	ST	Rk	Off AGL	Rk	Def AGL	Rk
2004	5-11	4.8	4.4	231	331	-8	-27.1%	31	-36.1%	32	-7.2%	9	1.9%	11	32.6	7	32.8	7
2005	11-5	10.3	8.5	260	202	+6	0.8%	16	-18.1%	28	-21.5%	1	-2.6%	27	18.0	13	8.0	28
2006	13-3	12.4	10.8	427	255	+8	23.2%	6	-4.0%	18	-19.7%	2	7.6%	1	19.7	13	36.0	3
2007	7-9	7.6	7.5	334	348	-1	-5.8%	20	-21.3%	30	-6.0%	8	9.5%	1	18.4	23	50.3	2
2008	9-7	8.7	9.2	375	350	+5	6.2%	15	-4.8%	23	-6.8%	7	4.2%	5	14.4	23	19.3	18

Strategic Tendencies

Run/Pass		Rank	Offense		Rank	Defense		Rank	Other		Rank
Runs, all plays	43%	16	3+ WR	41%	26	Rush 3	1.1%	32	2+ RB, Pct Runs	64%	13
Runs, first half	44%	17	4+ WR	7%	26	Rush 4	60.5%	21	1 RB/2 TE, Pct Runs	35%	30
Runs, first down	48%	21	2+ TE	33%	8	Rush 5	24.7%	10	1RB/3+WR, Pct Runs	23%	23
Runs, second-long	39%	15	Single back	56%	17	Rush 6+	13.7%	4	Zone Blitz	7%	8
Runs, power sit.	69%	11	Play action	15%	20	Rush 7+	4.6%	1	Go for it on 4th	0.78	23
Runs, behind 2H	32%	17	Max protect	8%	20	Sacks by LB	5.6%	30	Offensive Pace	29.8	10
Pass, ahead 2H	47%	9	Outside pocket	7%	27	Sacks by DB	11.1%	9	Defensive Pace	30.2	8

Chicago had the league's worst fumble recovery rate on offense (nine out of 12 lost) but the league's best fumble recovery rate on defense (recovering seven of 10). ● Chicago had the league's third best offensive DVOA in the first quarter, but ranked 26th in the other three quarters combined. The Bears had a similar trend in 2007, although only in regards to the running game, because their passing game in 2007 was horrendous in every quarter. ● Chicago ranked 31st in offensive DVOA on passes thrown to the middle of the field. ● The Bears allowed a league-low 3.9 yards after catch, excelling both against passes behind the line of scrimmage (6.8, third) and passes beyond (3.2, first). ● Once again demonstrating the importance of the pass rush to Chicago's defense, the Bears ranked second in defensive DVOA when they hurried the quarterback, narrowly behind the Steelers.

Passing

Player	DYAR	DVOA	Plays	NtYds	Avg	YAC	C%	TD	Int
Kyle Orton*	334	-0.9%	495	2875	5.8	5.0	58.9%	18	12
Rex Grossman*	-70	-27.9%	65	249	3.8	3.2	52.4%	2	2
Jay Cutler	1380	22.0%	630	4530	7.2	4.7	62.9%	25	18

Rushing

Player	DYAR	DVOA	Plays	Yds	Avg	TD	Fum	Suc
Matt Forte	20	-7.1%	316	1239	3.9	8	1	43%
Kevin Jones	-28	-29.3%	34	109	3.2	0	0	29%
Adrian Peterson	17	13.7%	20	100	5.0	0	0	45%
Garrett Wolfe	-5	-17.3%	15	69	4.6	0	0	47%
Kyle Orton*	-3	-15.4%	15	54	3.6	3	2	--
Jason McKie	7	0.4%	11	26	2.4	2	0	55%
Devin Hester	44	131.6%	5	61	12.2	0	0	--
Rashied Davis	2	-29.2%	3	14	4.7	0	0	--
Rex Grossman*	12	24.7%	3	4	1.3	2	0	--
Jay Cutler	16	-4.0%	40	215	5.4	2	2	--

Receiving

Player	DYAR	DVOA	Plays	Ctch	Yds	Y/C	YAC	TD	C%
Devin Hester	23	-9.5%	92	52	667	12.8	3.8	3	57%
Rashied Davis	-23	-17.0%	67	35	445	12.7	4.3	2	52%
Brandon Lloyd*	26	-6.0%	49	26	364	14.0	2.3	2	53%
Marty Booker*	-122	-44.7%	49	14	211	15.1	7.2	2	29%
Greg Olsen	41	0.0%	82	54	574	10.6	4.6	5	66%
Desmond Clark	-108	-28.5%	73	41	367	9.0	4.2	1	72%
Michael Gaines	-22	-16.1%	36	23	260	11.3	3.8	1	64%
Matt Forte	201	33.1%	76	63	477	7.6	6.3	4	83%
Jason McKie	-9	-23.3%	15	11	64	5.8	5.9	1	73%
Adrian Peterson	-17	-43.8%	10	6	45	7.5	7.5	0	60%

Offensive Line

Year	Yards	ALY	Rank	Power	Rank	10+ Yds	Rank	Stuff	Rank	Sacks	ASR	Rank	False	Cont.
2006	4.07	4.42	7	71%	7	12%	27	15%	2	25	4.8%	6	21	42
2007	3.34	3.66	30	75%	3	9%	29	18%	13	43	7.1%	18	32	28
2008	3.89	3.94	25	63%	20	17%	16	18%	15	29	5.3%	11	22	48

Year	LE	Rank	LT	Rank	Mid	Rank	RT	Rank	RE	Rank
2006	3.61	21	4.66	8	4.76	1	4.03	20	4.26	13
2007	2.81	28	3.58	29	3.63	30	4.41	12	3.68	23
2008	2.77	28	4.08	16	4.17	15	3.92	25	3.78	22

As the Adjusted Line Yards figures clearly show, run blocking hasn't exactly been a strength for Chicago over the past couple seasons. The team drafted tackle Chris Williams last year in the hopes that he'd be able to start as a rookie, but Williams missed most of the year with a back injury and never really got on track. Instead, John Tait started at right tackle and backup John St. Clair moved to left tackle, where he was effective enough as a pass blocker to keep Kyle Orton upright for most of the year. Both have departed; Tait retired at the end of the season, while St. Clair signed with Cleveland in what amounted to a trade of tackles, as former Browns right tackle Kevin Shaffer signed with the Bears.

Shaffer is not the most prominent arrival on the offensive line, however; that title goes to Hall of Famer-to-be Orlando Pace. Pace was a cap casualty for the rebuilding Rams, but he signed a three-year, $15 million deal with the Bears just hours after the organization announced the Jay Cutler trade. Relying on Pace would be a foolhardy move, as he's missed 25 games over the last three seasons and contributed little as a run blocker last year; St. Louis was 28th in ALY on runs to left end, and 23rd on runs behind left tackle. Pencil him in for some decent pass blocking and eight starts, but don't expect much more. Pace's arrival may create a camp battle between Williams and Shaffer for the right tackle spot, but whoever loses that battle will get playing time in the likely event of a Pace injury. Chicago also added utility lineman Frank Omiyale from Carolina at the beginning of the free agent period; he'll be the starter at left guard, displacing Josh Beekman, who will be the utility guard and backup center behind veteran Olin Kreutz.

Defensive Front Seven

Defensive Line	Age	Pos	Plays	TmPct	Overall						Pass Rush				vs. Run			vs. Pass		
					Rk	Stop	Dfts	Stop%	Rk	AvYd	Rk	Sack	Hit	Hur	Runs	St%	Yds	Pass	St%	Yds
Adewale Ogunleye	32	DE	67	7.6%	13	53	26	79%	32	1.2	24	5.0	4	16	48	83%	1.6	19	68%	0.2
Alex Brown	30	DE	50	5.7%	42	44	24	88%	9	-0.7	5	6.0	11	11	37	84%	0.7	13	100%	-4.5
Tommie Harris	26	DT	36	4.7%	44	24	14	67%	67	1.4	15	5.0	5	7	29	62%	2.2	7	86%	-1.6
Dusty Dvoracek	28	DT	30	4.5%	46	24	8	80%	23	1.8	27	0.0	1	1	27	81%	1.7	3	67%	2.7
Israel Idonije	29	DE	29	3.3%	85	26	12	90%	4	0.4	13	3.5	5	3	15	80%	1.8	14	100%	-1.1
Marcus Harrison	25	DT	29	3.3%	65	22	5	76%	44	1.5	17	2.0	3	3	23	74%	2.0	6	83%	-0.7
Anthony Adams	29	DT	21	4.2%	51	15	3	71%	59	2.2	51	0.0	1	1	21	71%	2.2	0	0%	0.0
Mark Anderson	26	DE	20	2.3%	--	16	6	80%	--	1.7	--	1.0	4	6	17	76%	2.4	3	100%	-2.3

Linebackers	Age	Pos	Plays	TmPct	Overall					Pass Rush			vs. Run					vs. Pass				
					Rk	Stop	Dfts	Stop%	AvYd	Sack	Hit	Hur	Runs	St%	Rk	Yds	Rk	Tgts	Suc%	Rk	AdjYd	Rk
Lance Briggs	29	OLB	120	13.6%	29	80	34	67%	4.0	0.5	1	8	59	71%	20	2.9	25	44	59%	20	5.5	24
Brian Urlacher	31	ILB	102	11.6%	50	58	26	57%	4.9	0.0	3	7	50	66%	41	3.0	31	25	56%	31	4.7	11
Nick Roach	24	OLB	37	4.8%	--	20	3	54%	4.2	0.0	0	0	20	65%	--	1.7	--	10	67%	--	5.9	--
Pisa Tinoisamoa	28	OLB	100	12.8%	35	48	19	48%	5.2	3.0	2	2	61	54%	93	3.7	67	37	46%	59	8.2	81

Year	Yards	ALY	Rank	Power	Rank	10+ Yds	Rank	Stuff	Rank	Sack	ASR	Rank
2006	4.21	3.74	4	63%	15	22%	28	24%	2	40	6.6%	17
2007	4.55	3.84	5	57%	10	28%	32	23%	3	41	7.6%	5
2008	3.64	3.28	2	64%	11	23%	27	28%	1	28	5.0%	27

Year	LE	Rank	LT	Rank	Mid	Rank	RT	Rank	RE	Rank
2006	4.09	16	3.45	7	3.85	4	4.09	16	2.97	3
2007	4.79	26	3.33	2	3.79	5	3.83	9	3.87	13
2008	2.13	1	3.08	4	3.62	3	4.08	17	2.42	1

The Bears' front four is the unit that progress forgot. Little has changed in two years: Adewale Ogunleye is the veteran end who is effective, if not game-changing, against the run and the pass. Opposite him is Alex Brown, a serviceable end on a low salary who the Bears would prefer to replace with a superior player. In between are two-injury prone tackles. Tommie Harris is arguably the best defensive tackle in football when he's healthy, but we can't remember the last time he was. Dusty Dvoracek isn't as good or as healthy, having made it through only 13 games in his first three years because of injuries. Pass rush specialist Mark Anderson has simply failed to develop, with 12 sacks as a rookie in 2006 and just six since. The organization recognizes that the line needs some fresh blood, and spent their top pick on utility lineman Jarron Gilbert. At 6-foot-5 and 288 pounds, Gilbert will likely play both end and defensive tackle as part of a rotation with the two interior starters and backups Israel Idonije and Marcus Harrison. Even though Gilbert played mostly end at college, Jerry Angelo sees him as a potential pass-rush monster alongside Harris on the interior. Fourth-round pick Henry Melton was a 270-pound running back before Texas converted him to end as a senior; he's extremely raw, and will need some time to develop before the Bears hope to unleash him as a threat on the edge.

In 2007, Brian Urlacher was amongst the top ten in both Success Rate and Adjusted Pass Yards, but 80th in Run Stop Percentage and 88th in Run Yards, while Lance Briggs was amongst the top five in those two categories, but 68th in Success Rate and 58th in Adjusted Pass Yards. You can file that under "Weird Statistical Quirks," and this year, both players regressed some to the mean; in reality, Briggs is rightly regarded as an elite pass defender, while Urlacher excels in the running game. Pressing them both up to the line of scrimmage, while it created some confusion in the backfield, meant that Urlacher and Briggs' first step was often to backpedal away from the line of scrimmage, not to attack it. That plays away from their strengths.

On the strong side, Hunter Hillenmeyer lost his job after undergoing wrist surgery and never got it back; although Jamar Williams was expected to take the next open starting job at linebacker, the gig went instead to Nick Roach, who profiled as a superior run-stopper. After the Bears signed Pisa Tinoisamoa in the offseason, though, Williams and Roach might be competing with each other for a roster spot.

Defensive Secondary

Secondary	Age	Pos	Plays	TmPct	Rk	Stop	Dfts	Yds	Rk	St%	Rk	Tgts	Tgt%	Rk	Dist	Suc%	Rk	AdjYd	Rk	Yds	PD	Int
						Overall				vs. Run						vs. Pass						
Charles Tillman	28	CB	110	13.3%	2	41	15	11.7	74	37%	54	113	23.9%	3	10.6	44%	67	6.6	32	7.0	16	3
Kevin Payne	25	SS	96	10.9%	26	30	13	6.6	34	40%	39	37	7.4%	31	15.9	53%	31	9.1	57	8.9	7	4
Corey Graham	24	CB	89	10.1%	19	36	18	4.5	15	48%	34	69	13.6%	70	9.9	44%	68	6.9	34	7.3	7	1
Mike Brown*	31	FS	82	9.9%	39	32	13	4.9	12	47%	23	38	8.0%	23	11.8	53%	32	7.6	34	7.7	7	2
Danieal Manning	27	FS	31	4.0%	75	18	9	7.8	53	82%	1	24	5.5%	61	11.1	62%	12	8.0	44	8.3	2	1
Nathan Vasher	28	CB	30	6.8%	65	9	4	9.5	67	0%	81	58	22.9%	12	13.4	46%	57	7.8	50	7.9	8	1
Josh Bullocks	26	FS	41	5.1%	74	13	4	6.5	30	33%	58	17	3.7%	76	17.9	59%	22	8.6	51	8.4	6	1

Year	Pass D Rank	vs. #1 WR	Rk	vs. #2 WR	Rk	vs. Other WR	Rk	vs. TE	Rk	vs. RB	Rk
2006	1	-2.3%	13	-24.7%	4	-20.1%	8	-41.5%	1	-29.3%	4
2007	14	-26.3%	2	9.6%	21	-9.7%	15	5.4%	14	27.6%	31
2008	11	-2.1%	12	-14.4%	9	-2.1%	19	-25.8%	3	11.4%	24

As part of the scheme change that went on last year, the Bears spent more time in man coverage than they have in previous years. It was a bad move, most prominently featured in the Week 10 tilt against the Titans, when Kerry Collins pretty much moved the ball at will against the Chicago secondary. If the pass rush improves, the team should be able to return to more of their classic Tampa-2 stylings, which would benefit the secondary. Another thing that would help would be staying healthy: Starting corners Charles Tillman and Nathan Vasher missed a combined nine games, and nickelback Danieal Manning missed two more. Corey Graham did not impress, but he'll be the third corner by default. Trumaine McBride and 5-foot-9 rookie D.J. Moore will compete to be the dime corner, with the winner likely being whoever looks better on special teams.

Ironically, oft-injured free safety Mike Brown was the healthiest member of the secondary, but he was not retained after the year. He'll be replaced by former Saints safety Josh Bullocks, whose success rate belies a propensity for getting lost in coverage on deep routes. Zack Bowman slots in as Bullocks' backup; Bowman showed some promise in limited time at corner last year, and while he's still raw, the team's moving him to free safety in the hopes that he can win the job, not simply to provide depth. Craig Steltz will attempt to take the strong safety job away from Kevin Payne; Payne broke his arm as a rookie and then had surgery on his shoulder this past offseason, so if the Bears don't have a need for at least one injury-riddled safety in their lineup at all times, Steltz might be able to take over the job by merely staying on the field.

Special Teams

Year	DVOA	Rank	FG/XP	Rank	Net Kick	Rank	Kick Ret	Rank	Net Punt	Rank	Punt Ret	Rank	Hidden	Rank
2006	7.6%	1	8.8	3	18.9	1	3.4	9	2.0	16	11.7	2	11.0	3
2007	9.5%	1	6.5	3	6.0	8	14.9	4	10.6	3	18.0	1	33.0	1
2008	4.2%	5	4.2	10	-3.4	23	16.2	2	15.7	3	-8.3	29	19.6	2

The Bears missed the departed Brendon Ayanbedejo, who moved onto Baltimore and was their leader on kickoff coverage. While the aforementioned Jamar Williams is a capable replacement, he was replacing arguably the best special teams player in football, and it showed; Chicago's kick coverage went from second-best in the league in 2007 to below-average a year ago. Other guys off of the special teams unit that helped break holes open for Devin Hester are falling off, too; Idonije bulked up and is too large to play on special teams, while Adrian Peterson fell off as a gunner last year, with the lowlight being his Week 16 late hit that nearly cost Chicago their shot at a playoff spot.

The kickoff returns were still effective, though, thanks to new coverage guys like Williams and Garrett Wolfe, as well as the efforts of Danieal Manning, who was more than 20 points of field position better than Hester on kickoffs, and more than twice as valuable as any of Hester's previous years returning kicks. Hester, meanwhile, fell off a cliff on punt returns, going from being worth 20 points of field position above average in 2007 to nearly eight points below average in 2008.

Both kicker Robbie Gould and punter Brad Maynard are competent specialists with job security.

Coaching Staff

The most prominent change on the staff came in the form of the much-maligned Rod Marinelli, who takes over as the defensive line coach after a disastrous run as a head coach in Detroit. The move was played for comedy, but there are plenty of great assistant coaches and coordinators who simply weren't good head coaches, Dick LeBeau being the obvious example. Marinelli worked with Lovie Smith for five years in Tampa Bay when both were underneath Tony Dungy, so there's every reason to think that they should be able to work together and improve what has recently been a disappointing unit.

Despite calls to get rid of one or both coordinators, Smith chose to retain both offensive coordinator Ron Turner and defensive coordinator Bob Babich. Of the two, Turner would be the more obvious candidate to fall on his sword, as the Chicago offense has failed to post a DVOA better than -4.2% or finish higher in the league rankings than 18th during his four years as offensive coordinator. Then again, when he took over the offense, it was dead last in the NFL. So maybe mediocrity's actually an improvement. If the Bears don't make the play-offs this year, it would not be a total surprise to see Smith and his staff all depart the Windy City, with Mike Shanahan as the rumored replacement.

Cincinnati Bengals

In 2006, Cincinnati possessed a fearsome offense that featured a strong-armed passer, elite wide receivers, and a potent running game powered by one of the league's best lines. Just two seasons later, the offense was among the league's worst. Injuries, predictability, and the misfortune of playing in the same division with two fantastic defenses were among the factors.

The main culprit was the offensive line. The speed with which the unit dissolved was dizzying. The initial crack came when guard Eric Steinbach left for a big free agent contract in Cleveland. A key player bolting for a hated rival was bad enough. Worse, the team couldn't afford to pay Steinbach because of the money committed to tackles Willie Anderson and Levi Jones. The bookends promptly suffered injury after injury, to the point that Anderson was released before the season. Jones limped through much of last season before calling it a year, and now he too has been cut.

Combine that sequence with the retirement of center Rich Braham (perhaps the toughest Bengals player since Tim Krumrie) after 2006, and there's little wonder the team finished dead last in Adjusted Line Yards last season. Not to mention last in stuff percentage, second-to-last in yards gained on big runs, third-to-last in power situations, and third from the bottom with 25 blown blocks. The only unit to have a worse season was the Republican National Committee.

Cincinnati's drop in DVOA from 2007 to 2008 was a steep 26.1% (the slippage was foreshadowed by 2007's weighted DVOA). As Table 1 shows, 16 teams since 1999 have watched their total DVOA fall by at least 25%. The majority of them improved drastically in Year Three. At the top of the list sits the 2006 Jets, who used top picks on a tackle and center to spur their huge turnabout.

The Bengals followed a similar blueprint, spending the sixth overall pick on Andre Smith. The Alabama product squandered much of the good will from a dominant senior season with several questionable choices, starting by signing with an agent before the Sugar Bowl, rendering him ineligible to play. But if you were looking for a tackle to help reboot a running game, Smith would be the prototype — massive, nifty, and mean. The Bengals also drafted a center, Jonathan Luigs, in the fourth round. Of the Bengals' top nine linemen, only Bobbie Williams and Scott Kooistra are older than 27. Williams is a rock of a guard, strong and durable. The only games he's missed in the last three seasons were due to an appendectomy.

With no stability in front of him, Carson Palmer ran the official AMA gamut of injuries. During a preseason debacle against New Orleans, Palmer was blasted by former teammate Kevin Kaesviharn and suffered a broken nose. He sprained an ankle trying

---

BENGALS SUMMARY

2008 Record: 4-11-1

Pythagorean Wins: 3.2 (30th)

DVOA: -19.3% (26th)

Offense: -13.4% (28th)

Defense: 3.8% (16th)

Special Teams: -2.1% (26th)

Variance: 18.8% (22nd)

2008: Just as the defense attains respectability, the offense falls off a cliff.

2009: Holes on the offensive and defensive lines will not be filled by a healthy Carson Palmer.

2009 Mean Projection: 6.9 wins

On the Clock (0-3): 8%

Loserville (4-6): 36%

Mediocrity (7-8): 30%

Playoff Contender (9-10): 19%

Super Bowl Contender (11+): 7%

Projected Average Opponent: 2.2% (9th)

2009 Bengals Schedule

Week	Opp.	Week	Opp.	Week	Opp.
1	DEN	7	CHI	13	DET
2	at GB	8	BYE	14	at MIN
3	PIT	9	BAL	15	at SD
4	at CLE	10	at PIT	16	KC
5	at BAL	11	at OAK	17	at NYJ
6	HOU	12	CLE		

to elude the rush against Tennessee in Week 2, then had his right arm bent awkwardly the following week against the Giants. It turned out to be a partially torn ligament, one that at first appeared to require Tommy John replacement surgery.

Palmer opted for rest over surgery, and played effectively against Dallas after a week off. But the swelling and tenderness got worse, and Palmer was forced to sit the rest of the season, keeping his status shrouded in mystery. He refused to go under the knife, and made periodic cryptic comments about returning to the field, but with his team hopelessly out of the playoff chase, level headed thinking prevailed (for once) in Cincy.

The health of the franchise elbow will obviously be a determining factor in 2009. Palmer opened the team's minicamps by saying he was "one hundred percent." The optimist will point to Palmer's startling comeback from a devastating knee injury in the 2005 playoffs to throw for more than 4,000 yards in 2006. The pessimist will note that this new injury is to his throwing wing, his wide receiver weaponry is no longer state of the art, and the offensive line is hardly 2006 vintage.

Our projections lean toward the half-empty. It won't help that Palmer's most productive target has blown town for the west coast. T.J. Houshmandzadeh caught 294 passes over the past three seasons. His stellar play, fiery competitiveness and uniform-unfriendly name made Housh an iconic figure in Cincinnati. Raised in California and a college player at Oregon State, T.J. decided to complete the left coast trifecta, and signed with Seattle.

The Bengals signed a decent replacement, Laveranues Coles, whom KUBIAK likes to make up for about two-thirds of T.J.'s lost production. A far larger X factor is Chad Ochocinco Johnson, who separated a shoulder

during the preseason after one of the mouthiest summers the NFL has ever seen. Chad wanted desperately to be dealt, but the Bengals stood on principle and turned down the request, even when Washington reportedly dangled two first-rounders for the mercurial wideout. That nose the team cut off to spite its metaphorical face lay there all season, as Johnson sulked and went at half-speed.

It wasn't all on Chad. Once Palmer decided to shut it down, the Ryan Fitzpatrick Era dawned in Cincinnati. Like *Gigli*, it was painful to watch, and seemed to go on forever. Fitzpatrick preferred to cut and run at the earliest sniff of danger. This springbok-like behavior may have been fitting given the porous line, and he likely prevented an even worse Adjusted Sack Rate. But the constant scrambling wreaked havoc on the passing game. Defenses stopped worrying about deep and intermediate routes — Fitzpatrick seldom let them develop, and even if he did, he lacked the arm strength and accuracy to deliver. Deep threats Johnson and Chris Henry withered on the vine. Fitzpatrick has shuffled off to Buffalo, replaced by another mediocre passer of Celtic descent, J.T. O'Sullivan. Isn't anyone aware that the dominant European flavor in Cincinnati is German?

The running game in 2008 was even worse then the aerial attack, at least until the season's final month. Rudi Johnson succumbed to overuse and bad hamstrings, and was cut prior to opening Sunday. Chris Perry was finally healthy, and Bengals fans swiftly found themselves fondly recalling the days when he was on injured reserve. Perry didn't have the power to run inside or

Table 1: Biggest Offensive Drops in DVOA, 1999-2008

Team	Year	DVOA Prior Year	DVOA This Year	Change	DVOA Next Year	Change
NYJ	2005	22.1%	-21.5%	-43.6%	6.2%	27.7%
SEA	2006	27.4%	-10.0%	-37.5%	7.4%	17.5%
OAK	2003	24.2%	-11.3%	-35.5%	0.5%	11.7%
OAK	2006	-2.2%	-36.5%	-34.3%	-17.4%	19.1%
MIN	2005	18.4%	-15.3%	-33.7%	-17.3%	-2.0%
DEN	1999	30.8%	-2.3%	-33.1%	18.8%	21.1%
SF	1999	25.1%	-7.3%	-32.4%	17.8%	25.1%
DEN	2006	25.5%	-4.1%	-29.7%	10.3%	14.4%
NE	2008	45.2%	16.5%	-28.6%	--	--
STL	2002	18.2%	-8.2%	-26.4%	-9.5%	-1.3%
SF	2004	5.9%	-20.2%	-26.2%	-42.0%	-21.8%
CIN	2008	12.7%	-13.4%	-26.1%	--	--
KC	2007	7.3%	-18.2%	-25.4%	-4.6%	13.6%
STL	2007	3.3%	-22.0%	-25.3%	-24.0%	-2.0%
PHI	2005	16.0%	-9.1%	-25.1%	22.0%	31.1%
MIN	2001	17.9%	-7.1%	-25.0%	3.1%	10.1%

the speed to dart outside. And when he was tackled, he coughed it up. It wasn't until Cedric Benson was transported from the scrap heap to the starting eleven that the Bengals started to run it with any consistency. By that point, the team was 0-6, and the season was gone.

Benson was a pleasant surprise, given his rocky time in Chicago, on-field and off. He led the team in rushing, and contributed a pair of 100-yard efforts to close the season. Further confounding the critics, Benson has been a solid citizen and teammate in Cincinnati. That didn't mean that the team was sold on him, however. The Bengals searched high and wide for a replacement in the offseason, making a dedicated run at Derrick Ward, among others. In the end, they settled on Benson.

Ward may be superior, but Benson's size better fits the new direction the Bengals are taking. It is finally dawning on the Bengals and offensive coordinator Bob Bratkowski that they cannot compete in the AFC North without a little more smashmouth in the attack. Toward that end, the team made a rare player-for-player trade in May, sending seldom-used defensive tackle Orien Harris to St. Louis for fullback Brian Leonard. Leonard missed most of 2008 with a torn rotator cuff, but was deemed fit by the Rams before the deal. His versatility is attractive to a team that was forced to use converted tight end Daniel Coats at fullback last year.

The new tack toward a power game dovetails with the very quiet improvement of the Bengals' defense. New coordinator Mike Zimmer's schemes found ea-

ger disciples in Cincinnati, and the team responded with a strong season, especially against the run. From Week 10 on, the Bengals allowed opposing running backs a stingy 3.32 yards per carry.

Will that improvement carry over to 2009? As Table 2 shows, 13 defenses this decade have shown more improvement over the season's final eight weeks (including Dallas last season). Only three of the 12 got even better the following season.

(Bizarre aside — six different Bengals defenses appear in the top 28. There have been an awful lot of slow starts in Cincy, and many too-little, too-late improvements in the second half).

Cincinnati's personnel provides reason for optimism. Damato Peko emerged as more than just another swirling hairdo in 2008, leading the line in plays, while fellow Polynesian Jonathan Fanene put up good stats off the bench. Tank Johnson brings his arsenal to Bengal land, both in firearms and two-gap technique. He remains a steady run-stopper. Rookie Pat Sims played well when healthy.

The Bengals will field a pair of highly-drafted linebackers from USC, Keith Rivers and Rey Maualuga. The team is counting on Maualuga in particular to provide the sort of angry intensity Ray Lewis and James Harrison bring to Cincy's division rivals. Dhani Jones is more intellectual than intense, but he was surprisingly effective in 2008. If he can transfer some of his cover skills to Maualuga, who slipped in the draft on concerns he was a two-down player, the linebackers should be a strength.

What is seldom a strength in Cincinnati, at least since Coy Bacon retired, is pass rush. 2008 was no exception, as the Bengals managed only 17 sacks. Antwan Odom, who came over from Tennessee, wasn't the same player without Albert Haynesworth and Kyle Vanden Bosch drawing attention. He and Robert Geathers have talent, but struggled to stay on the field. The Bengals got highly talented but inconsistent Michael Johnson from Georgia Tech in the third round. The team desperately needs Johnson to help get heat on enemy quarterbacks.

Table 2: Biggest Second-Half Improvements in Run Defense, 2001-2008

Year	Team	DVOA Wks 1-9	Rank	DVOA Wks 10-17	Rank	Change	Run Def Full Year	Rank	DVOA Y+1	Rank
2002	SEA	25.8%	32	-10.2%	6	-36.0%	9.1%	29	-9.0%	14
2001	CIN	3.6%	23	-30.4%	1	-34.0%	-14.0%	9	0.4%	20
2008	DAL	8.9%	26	-20.8%	2	-29.7%	-3.7%	14	--	--
2001	JAC	3.9%	24	-25.3%	4	-29.2%	-10.7%	14	5.9%	27
2002	TEN	-3.0%	14	-31.1%	1	-28.1%	-15.6%	1	-7.7%	16
2003	GB	0.1%	23	-27.3%	2	-27.3%	-12.9%	9	2.4%	24
2003	SEA	3.9%	29	-22.6%	5	-26.5%	-9.0%	14	9.8%	30
2001	ARI	15.8%	31	-9.1%	13	-24.9%	2.7%	27	11.6%	31
2004	NYJ	-2.9%	18	-26.4%	2	-23.6%	-14.9%	5	6.6%	28
2005	NE	0.6%	22	-21.8%	3	-22.3%	-8.7%	15	-6.8%	10
2002	WAS	9.0%	27	-13.3%	2	-22.3%	-2.7%	16	4.7%	26
2004	NO	19.6%	31	-2.6%	17	-22.3%	8.5%	28	5.1%	26
2003	CHI	0.1%	22	-21.8%	6	-21.9%	-10.1%	11	-6.9%	12
2008	CIN	0.2%	18	-20.7%	3	-21.0%	-8.1%	8	--	--
2003	JAC	-6.8%	14	-27.4%	1	-20.6%	-16.7%	4	-8.6%	9

For the second straight season, the Bengals found defensive help off the street in midseason. In 2007 it was Jones; in 2008 it was safety Chris Crocker, who brought some veteran savvy to a young secondary. He and another reclamation project, Roy Williams, will join Chinedum Ndukwe to form a very physical group of safeties. All three are weak in coverage, however — look for opponents to attack with tight ends and running backs.

Corners Leon Hall and Johnathan Joseph are entering the magic years when good cornerbacks develop — clearly, an increase in pass rush would do wonders for their numbers. Both were first-round picks, and have shown that talent in flashes.

Whatever optimism exists among Bengals fans dissipates the instant the subject turns to management. Coach Marvin Lewis is liked but hardly respected. Owner Mike Brown draws most of the wrath. Between his mom-and-pop, 1940s vision of an NFL owner and his undying loyalty to troubled players, Cincinnati is a league punchline, unable to compete with the big boys. Come training camp, the Bengals will be the subject of HBO's *Hard Knocks* reality show. That should really help to swing perceptions of the franchise.

The frustration in Cincy has turned to action, at least on the part of the bloggers at WhoDey Revolution. The Web site dreamed up "Project Mayhem," one stage of which entailed erecting several billboards around the Queen City reading "Dear Bengals: Hire a G.M. Love, Your Fans." Fans activist and sedentary alike were even more outraged when the *Cincinnati Enquirer* revealed Brown has been giving himself "General Manager Bonuses" of several million dollars over the years. Not even the megabucks doled out to those financial wizards at A.I.G. who crashed the world economy engendered such fury.

Bengals fans are keenly aware of the clock ticking away on Palmer's career. Each failed season is another wasted year with an elite quarterback at the helm. While projected to finish out of the playoffs yet again, a wild card run isn't beyond comprehension. The striking power of 2006 is gone. If Cincy can compete successfully with defense and running, even Mike Brown might catch some slack.

Robert Weintraub

2008 Bengals Stats by Week

Wk	vs.	W-L	PF	PA	YDF	YDA	TO	Total	Off	Def	ST
1	@BAL	L	10	17	154	358	0	-43%	-37%	6%	0%
2	TEN	L	7	24	215	295	-1	-46%	-28%	3%	-14%
3	@NYG	L	23	26	347	406	0	-1%	10%	9%	-2%
4	CLE	L	12	20	211	261	-3	-67%	-65%	4%	2%
5	@DAL	L	22	31	269	373	0	11%	3%	5%	14%
6	@NYJ	L	14	26	171	252	+2	-29%	-28%	-8%	-10%
7	PIT	L	10	38	212	375	-1	-52%	4%	57%	1%
8	@HOU	L	6	35	253	384	-3	-104%	-31%	60%	-14%
9	JAC	W	21	19	312	282	-1	16%	11%	-15%	-9%
10	BYE										
11	PHI	T	13	13	282	391	+3	22%	-17%	-41%	-2%
12	@PIT	L	10	27	208	364	0	3%	29%	26%	0%
13	BAL	L	3	34	155	451	-1	-60%	-49%	15%	4%
14	@IND	L	3	35	252	334	-3	-72%	-49%	25%	2%
15	WAS	W	20	13	310	280	+2	23%	13%	-18%	-9%
16	@CLE	W	14	0	246	182	+3	40%	-9%	-55%	-6%
17	KC	W	16	6	329	220	+1	25%	9%	-9%	6%

Trends and Splits

	Offense	Rank	Defense	Rank
Total DVOA	-13.4%	28	3.8%	16
Unadjusted VOA	-17.3%	29	5.5%	16
Weighted trend	-10.7%	27	0.5%	11
Variance	7.5%	21	3.5%	3
Average opponent	4.7%	12	-4.1%	1
Passing	-9.4%	28	15.8%	21
Rushing	-10.6%	30	-8.1%	8
First down	-6.7%	23	-4.7%	10
Second down	-15.4%	29	11.5%	22
Third down	-21.5%	27	6.1%	19
First half	-4.1%	25	-3.1%	9
Second half	-24.4%	30	10.4%	24
Red Zone	5.0%	17	10.7%	22
Late and close	-20.4%	30	7.5%	21

Five-Year Performance

Year	W-L	Pyth	Est W	PF	PA	TO	Total	Rk	Off	Rk	Def	Rk	ST	Rk	Off AGL	Rk	Def AGL	Rk
2004	8-8	8.1	9.4	384	372	+4	13.2%	11	4.9%	11	-4.7%	11	3.7%	7	10.7	23	37.8	3
2005	11-5	9.7	10.3	421	350	+24	19.7%	8	21.9%	5	2.7%	23	0.4%	15	4.6	29	16.5	15
2006	8-8	9.1	8.6	373	331	+7	7.4%	11	15.1%	5	9.0%	26	1.3%	12	26.8	9	24.3	9
2007	7-9	7.9	8.5	380	385	+5	2.2%	14	12.7%	7	9.8%	27	-0.7%	20	20.8	17	24.4	12
2008	4-11-1	3.2	5.2	204	364	-2	-19.3%	26	-13.4%	28	3.8%	16	-2.1%	26	59.8	2	48.3	3

Strategic Tendencies

Run/Pass		Rank	Offense		Rank	Defense		Rank	Other		Rank
Runs, all plays	42%	20	3+ WR	63%	6	Rush 3	4.5%	19	2+ RB, Pct Runs	60%	20
Runs, first half	42%	21	4+ WR	12%	16	Rush 4	60.2%	23	1 RB/2 TE, Pct Runs	55%	11
Runs, first down	49%	19	2+ TE	15%	30	Rush 5	24.6%	11	1RB/3+WR, Pct Runs	23%	22
Runs, second-long	41%	10	Single back	56%	16	Rush 6+	10.7%	8	Zone Blitz	10%	2
Runs, power sit.	54%	29	Play action	9%	31	Rush 7+	1.5%	13	Go for it on 4th	1.02	10
Runs, behind 2H	32%	15	Max protect	6%	29	Sacks by LB	11.8%	22	Offensive Pace	32.8	30
Pass, ahead 2H	42%	16	Outside pocket	13%	12	Sacks by DB	26.5%	1	Defensive Pace	30.5	12

In a weird statistical quirk, this was the third straight year where Cincinnati ranked exactly sixth in the frequency of formations with three or more wideouts. It was also the fourth straight year where the Bengals ranked 30th or lower in using two-tight end sets. ● The Bengals were last in the league with an average of 3.8 yards after catch. ● Cincinnati never ran a draw play on third down, and only Pittsburgh and Detroit ran fewer screen passes on third-and-short. ● Even though the average offense runs play-action 17 percent of the time, the Bengals used play-action on less than 10 percent of plays for the second straight season. ● The Bengals' opponents presented a mirror image, leading the league by using play-action on 24 percent of pass plays. ● The Bengals zone-blitzed more often than any defense except for Philadelphia, and they also played much better defense when they did, with the league's biggest gap between DVOA when zone-blitzing (-50.6%) compared to all other plays (26.0%). ● Cincinnati led the league in percentage of sacks by defensive backs for the second straight year.

Passing

Player	DYAR	DVOA	Plays	NtYds	Avg	YAC	C%	TD	Int
Ryan Fitzpatrick*	-185	-18.0%	411	1762	4.3	3.6	59.7%	8	8
Carson Palmer	54	-5.0%	142	690	4.9	4.7	59.4%	3	4
Jordan Palmer	-70	-85.5%	14	30	2.1	4.1	58.3%	0	1
J.T. O'Sullivan	-414	-37.3%	257	1594	6.2	6.7	58.4%	8	11

Rushing

Player	DYAR	DVOA	Plays	Yds	Avg	TD	Fum	Suc
Cedric Benson	-35	-12.6%	214	747	3.5	2	2	40%
Chris Perry*	-137	-39.2%	103	267	2.6	2	5	29%
Ryan Fitzpatrick*	88	21.7%	48	308	6.4	2	2	--
Kenny Watson	11	12.5%	13	55	4.2	0	0	38%
James Johnson	2	-2.8%	9	29	3.2	0	0	33%
DeDe Dorsey	-5	-38.0%	5	8	1.6	0	0	20%
Andre Caldwell	30	69.0%	5	53	10.6	0	0	--
Carson Palmer	15	50.0%	5	38	7.6	0	0	--
J.T. O'Sullivan	20	9.1%	22	151	6.9	0	1	--

Receiving

Player	DYAR	DVOA	Plays	Ctch	Yds	Y/C	YAC	TD	C%
T.Houshmandzadeh*	163	2.5%	137	92	904	9.8	3.9	4	67%
Chad Johnson	91	-1.1%	97	53	540	10.2	1.7	4	52%
Chris Henry	10	-10.1%	46	19	220	11.6	1.0	3	41%
Antonio Chatman	-22	-21.7%	31	21	194	9.2	5.7	0	68%
Andre Caldwell	-27	-30.5%	19	11	78	7.1	4.2	0	58%
Glenn Holt*	-28	-42.5%	11	3	26	8.7	-0.3	1	27%
Laveranues Coles	143	2.0%	115	70	839	12.0	4.1	8	61%
Reggie Kelly	-55	-28.3%	42	31	207	6.7	3.0	1	74%
Ben Utecht	-62	-41.1%	28	16	123	7.7	2.8	0	57%
Daniel Coats	-48	-70.3%	10	2	19	9.5	5.0	0	20%
Chris Perry*	-77	-55.2%	35	21	76	3.6	4.1	0	60%
Cedric Benson	15	-2.8%	26	20	185	9.3	9.6	0	77%
Kenny Watson	-43	-94.0%	9	3	4	1.3	0.3	0	33%
James Johnson	7	1.6%	7	6	47	7.8	8.8	0	86%

Offensive Line

Year	Yards	ALY	Rank	Power	Rank	10+ Yds	Rank	Stuff	Rank	Sacks	ASR	Rank	False	Cont.
2006	3.97	4.38	9	72%	5	9%	29	19%	23	36	6.1%	13	25	26
2007	3.90	4.25	10	73%	5	10%	27	19%	20	17	3.2%	2	28	33
2008	3.22	3.31	32	56%	30	12%	31	24%	32	51	8.6%	27	14	37

Year	LE	Rank	LT	Rank	Mid	Rank	RT	Rank	RE	Rank
2006	4.11	15	4.39	13	4.29	17	5.23	1	3.85	18
2007	4.05	15	4.21	17	4.60	3	3.23	31	4.82	3
2008	1.45	32	3.28	29	3.66	28	3.23	30	3.35	25

This was perhaps the single worst unit in the entire NFL last season: dead last or close to it in Adjusted Line Yards, stuff rate, and power running, coupled with an inability to protect the dude with the thick wallet and his hands on the center's butt. The Bengals dropped from second to 27th in Adjusted Sack Rate and had 25 blown blocks that led to sacks or intentional grounding penalties, up from only ten in 2007. A season-ending injury to Carson Palmer and the hair-on-fire scrambling of Ryan Fitzpatrick were the telling sights.

Riddled by injury, players shuffled up and down the line with little to no cohesion from week to week. Beloved team leader (albeit oft-injured) Willie Anderson was cut on the eve of the season, only to start the AFC Championship game with Baltimore. Tackle Stacy Andrews, given the franchise tender before the season, clearly had a master plan at work — to be so awful, the Bengals would have no interest in re-signing him, and he would be free to go play with brother Shaun in Philly. Mission accomplished. On the other side, Levi Jones displayed all the mobility of the Roebling Bridge, and he too is finished in Chili City. At center, Eric Ghiaciuc was frequently overpowered by larger defensive tackles.

The 2009 line will be younger and inexperienced, but there is promise here. First-round choice Andre Smith had a catastrophic Combine, but was the best power blocker in college football at Alabama. If he shows any ability to pass block, he will be the left tackle from day one. If not, Smith will be on the right, while Anthony Collins, a promising second-year man whose insertion into the lineup late in the season helped steady the line a little, should be at left tackle. Rookie Jonathan Luigs, a two-time All-American at Arkansas, will get a shot at center, with Kyle Cook and Dan Santucci around if he isn't ready. The replacing of Ghiaciuc with anyone has to be considered addition by subtraction. Andrew Whitworth and Bobbie Williams are solid guards, when they get to play their natural positions — both were forced to play several spots last year (Whitworth, at least, is a pretty good tackle when he lines up there). Nate Livings, another emergency rookie starter last season, was impressive at guard as well. Scott Kooistra provides depth and several extra vowels.

Defensive Front Seven

Defensive Line	Age	Pos	Plays	TmPct	Overall					Pass Rush			vs. Run			vs. Pass		
					Rk	Stop	Dfts	Stop%	Rk	AvYd	Rk	Sack	Hit	Hur	Runs	St%	Yds	Pass	St%	Yds
Domata Peko	25	DT	68	8.2%	4	51	9	75%	50	2.5	59	0.5	3	5	58	76%	2.5	10	70%	2.7
Robert Geathers	26	DE	38	6.6%	24	28	10	74%	57	1.9	53	2.5	8	8	33	73%	2.4	5	80%	-1.0
Pat Sims	24	DT	35	6.1%	23	27	5	77%	37	2.3	54	1.0	5	2	33	76%	2.4	2	100%	0.5
John Thornton*	33	DT	32	4.1%	54	24	10	75%	46	2.0	36	3.0	5	4	22	68%	3.0	10	90%	-0.4
Jonathan Fanene	27	DE	31	3.7%	75	24	9	77%	36	2.0	54	0.0	4	2	29	79%	1.8	2	50%	5.0
Antwan Odom	28	DE	27	4.3%	64	18	6	67%	78	2.2	64	2.5	4	8	21	67%	2.1	6	67%	2.7
Frostee Rucker	26	DE	24	4.2%	66	20	7	83%	19	2.3	70	1.0	0	5	19	84%	1.8	5	80%	4.2
Tank Johnson*	28	DT	21	2.8%	72	17	6	81%	15	1.5	16	1.0	3	4	20	80%	1.9	1	100%	-6.0

Linebackers	Age	Pos	Plays	TmPct	Rk	Stop	Dfts	Stop%	AvYd	Sack	Hit	Hur	Runs	St%	Rk	Yds	Rk	Tgts	Suc%	Rk	AdjYd	Rk
						Overall				Pass Rush				vs. Run					vs. Pass			
Dhani Jones	31	ILB	121	14.5%	23	65	20	54%	4.3	0.0	2	2	71	62%	62	3.0	33	52	47%	55	5.7	34
Rashad Jeanty	26	OLB	88	10.6%	63	54	8	61%	4.1	0.5	2	0	71	68%	36	3.3	44	21	53%	36	5.6	29
Brandon Johnson	26	OLB	81	9.7%	69	44	19	54%	3.9	1.5	4	3	52	58%	84	2.6	14	30	51%	44	5.8	35
Keith Rivers	23	OLB	37	10.2%	--	26	4	70%	3.7	0.0	0	0	29	76%	--	3.2	--	5	94%	--	3.8	--

Year	Yards	ALY	Rank	Power	Rank	10+ Yds	Rank	Stuff	Rank	Sack	ASR	Rank
2006	4.03	4.16	16	56%	7	16%	18	18%	16	35	6.2%	22
2007	4.49	4.14	20	54%	5	23%	29	18%	20	22	3.8%	32
2008	3.85	4.16	16	64%	12	13%	6	18%	14	17	3.6%	31

Year	LE	Rank	LT	Rank	Mid	Rank	RT	Rank	RE	Rank
2006	3.38	8	4.44	17	4.57	26	3.50	9	3.45	9
2007	3.23	7	4.79	27	3.98	12	4.87	29	4.24	19
2008	5.08	30	3.95	11	4.49	26	3.96	14	2.54	2

Cincinnati suffered numerous injuries on defense last year, ranking third in the NFL in Adjusted Games Lost by defensive starters. The most notable injury — both on the field and in terms of leaguewide rules — was to linebacker Keith Rivers. The rookie was having a solid season when Hines Ward blasted him on a blindside crackback block, Ward"s helmet breaking Rivers' jaw and ending his year. Somehow, Ward wasn't penalized on the play, nor was he fined, but at the owners meeting, the "Hines Ward" rule was put into effect, making such hits on defenseless defenders illegal. Rivers' misfortune left more plays for Dhani Jones, one of the few defenders to suit up for all 16 games. Despite leading the Bengals in plays last year, Jones will likely have more time to study travel itineraries, thanks to the drafting of the ferocious Rey Maualuga from USC. Rashad Jeanty and Brandon Johnson provide youthful, quality depth at outside linebacker.

One Cincinnati defender who avoided the injury bug was tackle Domata Peko. Much was made of the Bengals' failure to acquire Shaun Rogers before the 2008 season, but the unheralded Peko was just as effective against the run — he had a higher Stop Rate and made his average run tackle after the same 2.5-yard gain as Rogers. Peko's emergence and the addition of space-eating rookie Pat Sims to the lineup in Week 6 helped the Bengals stuff the run in the second half of the season. The tackle rotation is even deeper in 2009 thanks to the addition of free agent Tank Johnson from Dallas and the return of 338-pound Jason Shirley, a 2008 fifth-rounder who only played three games in his rookie season. (In true Bengals fashion, both players carry significant character question marks.)

Alas, the improved run defense was outweighed by a total inability to put heat on the quarterback. The coaching staff clearly understood this problem, as the Bengals ran zone-blitzes more frequently than any defense other than Philadelphia and led the NFL in the percentage of sacks that came from defensive backs (26.5 percent). Antwan Odom signed for sizable dough to improve on Justin Smith's pass rush but flopped, only registering four quarterback hits — matching players such as Tampa Bay cornerback Ronde Barber and disappointing Jacksonville rookie Derrick Harvey. Opposite end Robert Geathers was somewhat more effective, although he was usually the player dropping into coverage when Cincinnati zone-blitzed. Like so many other Bengals defenders, Odom and Geathers lost significant time to injuries, a common thread that ran throughout the Bengals' season.

Defensive Secondary

Secondary	Age	Pos	Plays	Overall					vs. Run							vs. Pass								
				TmPct	Rk	Stop	Dfts	Yds	Rk	St%	Rk	Tgts	Tgt%	Rk	Dist	Suc%	Rk	AdjYd	Rk	Yds	PD	Int		
Leon Hall	24	CB	95	11.4%	11	41	15	5.0	20	47%	35	93	22.8%	13	13.3	41%	77	8.8	74	8.4	18	3		
Marvin White	25	FS	71	11.4%	23	26	4	7.4	47	43%	36	16	5.1%	65	12.1	68%	3	8.0	43	7.9	2	1		
Chinedum Ndukwe	24	SS	67	11.7%	18	26	8	4.6	11	47%	24	18	6.4%	43	12.1	50%	43	7.6	33	7.1	3	1		
Johnathan Joseph	25	CB	55	13.2%	4	25	5	6.4	39	55%	25	50	24.3%	2	12.6	44%	66	8.4	64	8.4	11	1		
Chris Crocker**	29	FS	46	6.3%	70	22	10	5.0	14	52%	14	23	6.4%	42	12.8	67%	6	7.1	19	7.2	5	1		
David Jones	23	CB	44	6.0%	73	15	6	10.7	72	11%	80	52	14.4%	63	10.6	40%	78	8.0	56	7.7	7	0		
Dexter Jackson*	32	SS	22	14.1%	--	3	0	9.0	--	8%	--	7	8.5%	--	9.7	33%	--	9.8	--	10.1	1	0		

*** Includes stats with both Miami and Cincinnati.*

Year	Pass D Rank	vs. #1 WR	Rk	vs. #2 WR	Rk	vs. Other WR	Rk	vs. TE	Rk	vs. RB	Rk
2006	28	12.1%	26	-15.3%	6	31.2%	30	-6.3%	13	23.2%	31
2007	30	20.8%	29	15.3%	24	-22.3%	8	9.9%	20	-9.4%	9
2008	21	18.8%	26	20.7%	25	4.2%	23	-28.6%	2	4.2%	17

Former first-rounders Leon Hall and Johnathan Joseph were expected to improve with a little experience. Our numbers don't show that they did, although given the lack of pass rush and the inept offense, that's not surprising. Joseph lost half his season to a foot injury. When he went out, Hall was switched over to cover top enemy wideouts — his yards in the air per attempt skyrocketed from 10.8 to 15.9 after Joseph's injury. Both Hall and Joseph have shown flashes, but whether either can develop into a corner worthy of a first-round pick is up in the air — and crucial to Cincinnati's improvement. David Jones is the nickel, and was poor when pressed into a starting role last year.

Free safety Chris Crocker was signed off the street at midseason after getting cut by Miami. He fit in perfectly with Mike Zimmer's system, and contributed seven solid games wearing stripes. The man he replaced at free safety, Marvin White, had an even higher success rate, 69 percent, before getting injured (this is a recording). Strong safety Chinedum Ndukwe provides above-average run support on the strong side but is iffy against the pass. So naturally, the Bengals opted to bring in Roy Williams, whose one notable quality in Dallas was an inability to cover. Zimmer coached Williams in Big D, though, and the team hopes the safety has a few big hits left in him.

Special Teams

Year	DVOA	Rank	FG/XP	Rank	Net Kick	Rank	Kick Ret	Rank	Net Punt	Rank	Punt Ret	Rank	Hidden	Rank
2006	1.3%	12	2.2	11	7.4	8	-8.0	28	9.7	5	-3.4	28	2.4	13
2007	-0.7%	20	4.6	8	-2.4	21	-1.8	20	1.6	13	-6.0	26	4.6	11
2008	-2.1%	26	2.2	12	-1.3	19	-1.2	18	-8.8	28	-3.3	24	2.7	10

Here's another area where Cincinnati struggled in 2008. Shayne Graham received the franchise tender, and is a generally reliable kicker, but is only average on kickoffs. Kyle Larson was the busiest (101 punts) and the worst (-12.2 points below average on gross punting value) punter in the league. He has been thanked for his service and discharged, replaced by fifth-round pick and local hero Kevin Huber, a local boy from McNicholas High School and the University of Cincinnati. Huber led Division I college football in net punting in 2007 and 2008.

Cincinnati's return teams are also in need of overhaul. Mediocre kick returner Glenn Holt has left for Minnesota. Antonio Chatman is still around, and hasn't impressed much in two seasons returning punts. Sixth-round pick Bernard Scott will get a chance at returning, provided he can stay out of trouble — even by Bengals standards, he's worrisome. Scott was arrested five times while attending four different colleges, finishing up at Abilene Christian. He led Division II in scoring and total yards per game while avoiding prison during his senior season.

Coaching Staff

For a while, Marvin Lewis was Cincinnati's Vince Lombardi, especially after leading the Bengals to their first playoff appearance in 15 years in 2005. Since then, Lewis is 19-28-1. In most NFL cities, that would have him polishing up his studio analyst resume tape — but this is Mike Brown Land, where patience is not only a virtue, it is a financial imperative. Lewis is under contract for two more seasons, and there is no reason to think he won't be on the sideline for both. The season-ending injury to Carson Palmer gave Lewis a pass in 2008, although the Bengals were impotent offensively even with the franchise quarterback behind center. Cincinnati was outscored by a whopping 152 points in the second half in 2008, which could be a function of the coaching staff's inability to make adjustments and counter the opponent's maneuvers. Even during the team's three-game win streak to close the season, the Bengals managed only two field goals after halftime.

Offensive coordinator Bob Bratkowski deserves much of the blame for the offensive drop-off. Yes, injuries played a role, but there was no system in place for competing with a backup quarterback. The Bengals often seemed unprepared to take the field, and they stuck to three-wide receiver sets even when they didn't have the proper personnel. Yet even after a 204-point season, Bratkowski still has a job. The position coach on the spot is Paul Alexander, whose offensive line was shambolic in 2008. Alexander played a key role in convincing Brown and Lewis to select Andre Smith with the sixth overall pick. A better line and an upright and healthy Palmer could lead to a quick turnaround. A repeat of last season could cost Alexander his job. On a brighter note, new defensive coordinator Mike Zimmer got his defense to play hard throughout the dismal season, and the improvement on that side of the ball was the highlight of the year in Cincy.

Cleveland Browns

In Cleveland, the new rebuilding plan looks a lot like the old rebuilding plan.

Four years ago, the Browns were reeling from the failures of the Butch Davis era, a time of front-office politicking, miscommunication, and missed opportunities. The organization was in disarray, and the team couldn't get traction after enjoying just one mildly successful season. Desperate to turn the corner, owner Randy Lerner hired a promising young executive from Baltimore (Phil Savage) and an offshoot from the Bill Belichick Family Tree (Romeo Crennel) as general manager and head coach of the Browns.

After four years of Savage and Crennel, the organization was once again in disarray, and the Browns were unable to get traction after just one mildly successful season. Under Savage, there was front-office politicking, poor communications (some involving e-mail) and plenty of missed opportunities. Once again desperate to find a workable front-office structure, Lerner hired another promising executive from Baltimore (George Kokinis) and another Belichick disciple (Eric Mangini) as his general manager and head coach.

Maybe things will be different this time.

Savage arrived in Cleveland in 2005 with an impressive resume. As Director of Player Personnel for the Ravens, he was Ozzie Newsome's right-hand man during the period in which they drafted players like Ray Lewis and Jonathan Ogden. The Butch Davis era in Cleveland was marked by organizational infighting, as Davis battled with holdovers from the Carmen Policy regime and filled his coaching staff with old boy network contacts from his University of Miami days. Savage was hired to bring professionalism to the front office while revamping the scouting department.

Savage's tenure didn't start smoothly. After the Browns finished 6-10 and dead last in scoring in his first season, Savage crossed swords with team president John Collins, a holdover from the Davis era. Lerner nearly fired Savage, but fans staged an e-mail campaign to save his job. The 2006 season was no better. Savage's top free agent selection, center LeCharles Bentley, suffered a freak injury on the first day of training camp and never played a single down for the Browns. Savage's drafts provided some exciting early-round prospects (Braylon Edwards, Kamerion Wimbley, D'Qwell Jackson), but no breakout superstars or late-round surprises, and the Browns record actually got worse. Crennel also came under fire, for subpar defenses (which finished 24th and 21st in the league in DVOA in 2005 and 2006), terrible, identity-free offenses, and an inability to control outspoken players (Kellen Winslow) and insubordinate assistants (Todd Grantham, who allegedly lobbied for Crennel's job at one point). After the 2006 season, both men needed a sudden turnaround to save their jobs and their reputations.

That turnaround came in 2007. Savage drafted left tackle Joe Thomas with the third overall pick, then jockeyed back into the first round to select Brady Quinn 22nd over-

BROWNS SUMMARY

2008 Record: 4-12

Pythagorean Wins: 4.4 (28th)

DVOA: -19.3% (27th)

Offense: -16.4% (29th)

Defense: 7.2% (17th)

Special Teams: 4.3% (4th)

Variance: 19.0% (24th)

2008: F**k you. Sincerely, Phil Savage.

2009: The Browns start their third straight rebuilding cycle with another trip to the Ozzie Newsome Cloning Vat.

2009 Mean Projection: 6.6 wins

On the Clock (0-3): 9%

Loserville (4-6): 40%

Mediocrity (7-8): 29%

Playoff Contender (9-10): 18%

Super Bowl Contender (11+): 4%

Projected Average Opponent: 3.4% (7th)

2009 Browns Schedule

Week	Opp.	Week	Opp.	Week	Opp.
1	MIN	7	GB	13	SD
2	at DEN	8	at CHI	14	PIT (Thu.)
3	at BAL	9	BYE	15	at KC
4	CIN	10	BAL (Mon.)	16	OAK
5	at BUF	11	at DET	17	JAC
6	at PIT	12	at CIN		

all. Thomas became an immediate star. Quinn held out of camp, but Derek Anderson emerged from a three-way battle as a credible starter. For a few weeks, Anderson was boffo, as were Edwards, Winslow, and other youngsters who finally lived up to their billing. The Browns scored 51 points in one game, 41 in another, and 33 in two more. Crennel's defenses were still mediocre (22nd in DVOA), but a suddenly explosive offense carried the Browns to a 10-6 record.

To the naked eye, the Browns were a team on the rise, but you didn't have to look too close to see the fissures. Their record was bolstered by wins over awful teams (Raiders, Dolphins, Rams) and by oddball victories: an 8-0 win over the Bills in a blizzard, a 33-30 win against the Ravens that featured a field goal bouncing off the base of the uprights. DVOA and Pythagoras saw the Browns as an 8.5-win team that was headed to a 6.5-win course adjustment in 2008.

Lerner, Savage and Crennel didn't see it that way. Crennel got a two-year contract extension after the 2007 season; Savage got an extension of his own in May of 2008. The team lost most all of their 2008 draft picks in various trades (including the one that allowed them to select Quinn), so Savage essentially sat out the draft, not making a selection until the fourth round. Savage and Crennel ignored the warning signs and stood pat, expecting the Browns to improve through a few veteran acquisitions, primarily defensive tackle Shaun Rogers and receiver Donte' Stallworth.

The stage was set for a systemic failure. Crennel and Savage were no longer on the same page. Crennel's staff had little use for Stallworth, a poor man's Edwards who didn't fit the team's need for a complementary possession receiver. Stallworth and Rogers brought two more malcontents onto a roster already groaning with them, and Stallworth never got on track after getting hurt during Week 1 warmups. Savage and Winslow traded accusations in the newspapers. In November, Savage dropped the f-bomb when responding to an angry fan's e-mail; the incident embarrassed the team and raised questions about Savage's judg-

ment. By December, both Anderson and Quinn were hurt, and the Browns were enduring weekly blowouts with Ken Dorsey and Bruce Gradkowski at quarterback.

Both Savage and Crennel were fired at season's end. Savage drew intense criticism, in part because of the flame mail (The GM responds to crank mail? *In season?*), but also because of his work habits. Savage, a road scout in Baltimore, only averaged about one day per week in his office. All of the road work created communication problems and limited his ability to meet roster needs during the season. Ultimately, there was plenty of blame to spread around. Savage didn't acquire enough talent, Crennel didn't develop the talent he got, and neither recognized the need to keep building once the team achieved a little success.

Enter Kokinis and Mangini. Kokinis began his career evaluating college players before moving to pro scouting in 2000. In recent years, he's worked as the Ravens' Director of Pro Personnel and one of their top contract negotiators. Kokinis fits the Ozzie Newsome mold better than Savage did: He's a work-from-the-office organizer and facilitator, unlike the road warrior Savage. He can't take credit for recent Ravens draft successes like Joe Flacco and Haloti Ngata, but he did get them signed and in camp on time, so he may be able to avoid headaches like the 2007 Brady Quinn holdout.

Mangini, like Kokinis, began his career with the old Browns (as a ball boy!). He later became a defensive assistant under Belichick before four up-and-down seasons with the Jets. His Jets legacy will forever be defined by the decision to insert newly-acquired Brett Favre into the lineup and live or die by the fading talents of a 39-year-old superstar who was learning the playbook on the installment plan.

Mangini is a defensive coach by reputation, but his offseason activities provide clues about what the Browns offense will look like. Brian Daboll arrived with Mangini to serve as offensive coordinator. Daboll was quarterbacks coach for the Jets for two seasons, meaning that he "coached" Favre and Chad Pennington, two guys who probably knew a thing or two before Daboll arrived. Before that, Daboll was a wide receivers coach for the Patriots. Daboll missed the Randy Moss pinball era in New England, but he was an assistant for some very prolific passing teams.

The Browns offense may mimic what the Jets did in 2008. If so, expect the team to abandon the run before the national anthem each week. The Jets were a good running team (fifth in DVOA, as opposed to 22nd in passing DVOA), but Mangini's staff treated runs like inconvenient obligations. The Jets ran on 56 percent of their first downs, but then ran just 41 percent of the time on all other downs, including just 31 percent of all third-and-short situations. It's as if Mangini's staff called a first-down handoff, shouted "Are you satisfied?" to the guys at the *New York Post* who demanded more Thomas Jones every week, then spread the field and ordered Favre to throw a short hitch, regardless of the situation.

With a coaching staff in place, Kokinis and Mangini began their roster overhaul by trading Winslow. The move improved team character but opened a major roster hole. Winslow was the team's best possession target, and the lack of capable receivers was exacerbated when Stallworth struck and killed a pedestrian while driving under the influence in March. Kokinis and Mangini even toyed with the idea of trading Edwards but thought better of it, in part because the market was flooded with headache receivers (Anquan Boldin, Plaxico Burress). They clearly wanted to remove all bad apples from the bushel, even if it meant another year of non-competition on offense.

The Browns then made headlines on draft day by trading down, down, and down some more. After a dizzying series of trades, the Browns roster looked very different. After trading down three times, the team selected center Alex Mack with the 21st pick overall. Extra picks brought needed depth at wide receiver (Brian Robiskie and Mohamad Massaquoi), linebacker (David Veikune and Kaluka Maiava), and elsewhere. Mangini and Kokinis further stocked the roster with ex-Jets: safety Abram Elam, defensive end Kenyon Coleman, and quarterback Brett Ratliff (the spoils of the Mark Sanchez trade), cornerback Hank Poteat, linebackers Eric Barton and David Bowens, and lineman C.J. Mosely (free agent signings). The new braintrust didn't fill every need — that would be impossible — but they erased a few mistakes from past eras while putting their own imprint on the roster.

The pieces are in place for a painful-but-productive rebuilding year. Quinn and Ratliff will battle for the quarterback job, with Anderson around to pick up the pieces if both crumble. Edwards provides a modicum of big-play credibility, Jerome Harrison and Josh Cribbs will provide a few highlights, and the offensive line will be stabilized by veteran free agents (including John St. Clair and Floyd Womack) while the team builds around a core of Thomas and Mack. Defensively, the transition from Crennel to Mangini won't be tumultuous: Both learned from the same sensei and run similar systems. There's little quality beyond D'Qwell Jackson, Elam, Wimbley, and cornerback Eric Wright, but there's enough quantity to produce a

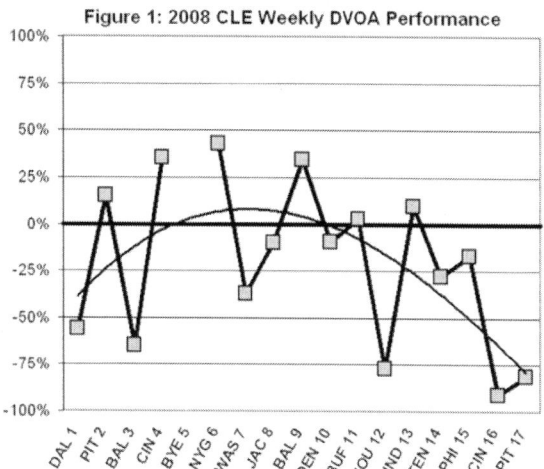

Figure 1: 2008 CLE Weekly DVOA Performance

middle-of-the-pack defense.

Mangini has proven capable of producing a winner after one year of rebuilding in the past, and Kokinis appears to be a worthy companion for the journey. The real test for the Browns braintrust comes in 2010 or 2011, after the team has settled on a quarterback, turned the corner, and climbed above .500. The Browns haven't had back-to-back winning seasons since Marty Schottenheimer and Bud Carson coached them in 1988 and 1989. The last two times the team bubbled over the .500 mark, in 2002 and 2007, they crashed to five- and four-win seasons the following year. Furthermore, Belichick disciples have been unable to sustain success in any of their coaching stops: Mangini, Crennel, and Charlie Weis at Notre Dame all faced quick collapses after very brief plateaus.

The last thing the Browns need is another slow climb to ten wins followed by a quick and devastating descent. The onus falls on Kokinis to keep the talent pipeline flowing the way Newsome does in Baltimore. He must maintain an aggressive approach to talent acquisition, even after the team achieves success, to avoid the complacency that set in for Mangini's Jets in 2007 and Crennel's Browns in 2008. He and Mangini must work in concert and avoid ego battles or communication gaps. Kokinis, not Mangini, is the most important person in the Browns organization, just as Savage was for four years and Butch Davis was for four years before that.

Ozzie Newsome left Cleveland with the rest of the old Browns in 1996. The new Browns have spent 13 years trying to find someone just like him. Kokinis could be the man. If not, Randy Lerner will tag another Ravens executive in four years, pair him with another Baby Belichick, and start over once more.

Mike Tanier

2008 Browns Stats by Week

Wk	vs.	W-L	PF	PA	YDF	YDA	TO	Total	Off	Def	ST
1	DAL	L	10	28	205	487	+1	-56%	-10%	52%	6%
2	PIT	L	6	10	208	281	-2	15%	-4%	1%	21%
3	@BAL	L	10	28	169	273	-1	-65%	-52%	9%	-4%
4	@CIN	W	20	12	261	211	+3	35%	-9%	-41%	3%
5	BYE										
6	NYG	W	35	14	454	373	+3	43%	48%	3%	-3%
7	@WAS	L	11	14	236	351	+1	-38%	-21%	16%	0%
8	@JAC	W	23	17	327	380	+1	-10%	-5%	14%	8%
9	BAL	L	27	37	274	429	-2	35%	19%	18%	34%
10	DEN	L	30	34	399	564	0	-10%	4%	32%	18%
11	@BUF	W	29	27	337	334	+4	3%	15%	-6%	-19%
12	HOU	L	6	16	240	383	-3	-77%	-87%	-9%	0%
13	IND	L	6	10	193	215	+1	10%	-15%	-24%	0%
14	@TEN	L	9	28	178	390	+2	-28%	-17%	8%	-3%
15	@PHI	L	10	30	196	418	+1	-17%	-34%	-16%	1%
16	CIN	L	0	14	182	246	-3	-91%	-81%	15%	5%
17	@PIT	L	0	31	126	369	-1	-81%	-42%	44%	5%

Trends and Splits

	Offense	Rank	Defense	Rank
Total DVOA	-16.4%	29	7.2%	17
Unadjusted VOA	-20.3%	30	8.6%	21
Weighted trend	-18.7%	29	6.1%	17
Variance	12.4%	29	5.5%	15
Average opponent	6.0%	8	-3.6%	2
Passing	-21.0%	31	11.7%	16
Rushing	0.3%	20	3.6%	23
First down	-12.3%	26	14.0%	26
Second down	-18.5%	31	0.1%	9
Third down	-20.4%	26	5.3%	15
First half	2.2%	20	8.7%	18
Second half	-34.0%	31	5.4%	18
Red Zone	-49.8%	31	-11.1%	10
Late and close	-19.7%	29	-1.4%	13

Five-Year Performance

Year	W-L	Pyth	Est W	PF	PA	TO	Total	Rk	Off	Rk	Def	Rk	ST	Rk	Off AGL	Rk	Def AGL	Rk
2004	4-12	4.9	5.5	276	390	-12	-19.6%	28	-13.2%	27	8.3%	23	1.9%	12	33.8	6	42.3	1
2005	6-10	5.6	6.3	232	301	-7	-16.6%	23	-13.5%	23	4.9%	24	1.8%	8	25.5	6	9.0	26
2006	4-12	4.4	4.8	238	356	-15	-16.1%	26	-15.5%	29	3.2%	19	2.6%	8	27.8	6	55.0	1
2007	10-6	8.5	8.9	402	382	-2	8.5%	12	8.5%	10	6.8%	21	6.9%	2	12.6	28	30.5	8
2008	4-12	4.4	6.1	232	350	+5	-19.3%	27	-16.4%	29	7.2%	17	4.3%	4	43.3	7	31.3	10

Strategic Tendencies

Run/Pass		Rank	Offense		Rank	Defense		Rank	Other		Rank
Runs, all plays	43%	15	3+ WR	47%	20	Rush 3	18.4%	2	2+ RB, Pct Runs	59%	21
Runs, first half	47%	9	4+ WR	12%	19	Rush 4	46.0%	31	1 RB/2 TE, Pct Runs	59%	9
Runs, first down	54%	12	2+ TE	22%	24	Rush 5	25.9%	7	1RB/3+WR, Pct Runs	20%	26
Runs, second-long	42%	9	Single back	51%	22	Rush 6+	9.7%	10	Zone Blitz	3%	17
Runs, power sit.	59%	26	Play action	18%	13	Rush 7+	1.5%	14	Go for it on 4th	0.72	31
Runs, behind 2H	36%	8	Max protect	8%	15	Sacks by LB	55.6%	7	Offensive Pace	30.4	12
Pass, ahead 2H	51%	4	Outside pocket	11%	20	Sacks by DB	8.3%	15	Defensive Pace	32.2	32

So much for the high-flying Browns aerial attack from two years ago; Cleveland ranked last in offensive DVOA with four or more wide receivers in the game (-48.0%). ● Cleveland ran the fewest draw plays of any team in the league. Less than three percent of runs were draws. Ten of Cleveland's 11 draw plays were run on first or second down. ● Cleveland had the worst offense in the league when opponents zone-blitzed, averaging just three yards per play with -116.6% DVOA. However, the Browns were actually very good against conventional big blitzes, with 22.5% DVOA against six or more pass rushers (11th in the league) compared to -29.8% DVOA against four pass rushers (dead last) and -6.5% DVOA against five pass rushers (26th). ● The Browns had an average defense against any formation with three or fewer wide receivers, but ranked 27th in defense against formations with four or five wide receivers. The defense showed a similar split in 2007, ranking 28th against formations with four or five wide receivers. ● As in 2007, the Browns defense faced very few screen passes to running backs, and although the sample size is small, their defense was excellent on these plays. We charted only 15 running back screens, and opponents gained an average of just 1.1 yards with no first downs and only two completions that gained more than 50 percent of needed yards. ● Stats in a similar vein: Cleveland ranked third in defensive DVOA against passes behind the line of scrimmage, but ranked 27th against passes thrown past the line of scrimmage. And Cleveland opponents threw only 16 percent of passes to running backs, the lowest percentage in the league.

Passing

Player	DYAR	DVOA	Plays	NtYds	Avg	YAC	C%	TD	Int
Derek Anderson	-15	-11.9%	302	1527	5.1	5.0	50.2%	9	8
Ken Dorsey	-242	-52.8%	99	349	3.5	3.4	47.3%	0	6
Brady Quinn	-68	-23.1%	90	509	5.7	5.3	50.6%	2	2
Bruce Gradkowski*	-234	-192.2%	25	8	0.3	3.3	33.3%	0	3

Rushing

Player	DYAR	DVOA	Plays	Yds	Avg	TD	Fum	Suc
Jamal Lewis	29	-6.0%	279	1002	3.6	4	1	40%
Jerome Harrison	79	52.7%	34	246	7.2	1	0	53%
Josh Cribbs	127	35.2%	29	167	5.8	1	0	--
Jason Wright*	16	8.2%	23	85	3.7	0	0	39%
Derek Anderson	-29	-41.1%	18	52	2.9	0	2	--
Lawrence Vickers	13	13.3%	10	31	3.1	0	0	70%
Brady Quinn	7	29.5%	3	23	7.7	0	0	--

Receiving

Player	DYAR	DVOA	Plays	Ctch	Yds	Y/C	YAC	TD	C%
Braylon Edwards	-45	-16.8%	138	55	873	15.9	4.0	4	40%
Donte' Stallworth	-91	-40.0%	45	17	170	10.0	5.1	2	38%
Syndric Steptoe	-81	-40.4%	41	19	182	9.6	2.9	1	46%
Josh Cribbs	-3	-17.4%	7	2	18	9.0	6.5	1	29%
Steve Sanders	-13	-42.4%	6	1	18	18.0	0.0	0	17%
Mike Furrey	-10	-16.7%	35	18	181	10.1	2.6	1	51%
David Patten	42	14.4%	20	11	162	14.7	4.0	1	55%
Kellen Winslow*	-23	-11.6%	83	43	428	10.0	2.8	3	52%
Steve Heiden	-13	-11.8%	42	23	249	10.8	5.1	0	55%
Darnell Dinkins*	-17	-32.8%	11	5	41	8.2	3.6	1	45%
Martin Rucker	-9	-29.7%	6	2	17	8.5	0.0	0	33%
Robert Royal	-85	-30.4%	57	33	352	10.7	3.4	1	58%
Jason Wright*	-17	-22.5%	37	22	155	7.0	5.5	2	59%
Jamal Lewis	31	4.6%	32	23	178	7.7	8.0	1	72%
Jerome Harrison	29	14.8%	18	12	116	9.7	9.3	1	67%
Lawrence Vickers	10	-2.3%	15	10	78	7.8	5.0	0	67%
Charles Ali	-25	-79.7%	6	4	13	3.3	3.3	0	67%

Offensive Line

Year	Yards	ALY	Rank	Power	Rank	10+ Yds	Rank	Stuff	Rank	Sacks	ASR	Rank	False	Cont.
2006	3.29	3.69	31	74%	3	7%	31	22%	31	54	9.2%	27	9	28
2007	4.46	4.60	2	64%	15	17%	15	14%	1	19	4.2%	5	26	38
2008	3.94	4.07	19	59%	27	15%	27	14%	5	24	4.4%	7	22	30

Year	LE	Rank	LT	Rank	Mid	Rank	RT	Rank	RE	Rank
2006	0.00	32	4.25	15	3.53	32	4.23	11	3.60	22
2007	6.03	1	5.10	3	4.35	7	4.70	4	4.92	2
2008	4.20	17	3.68	24	4.01	22	4.53	7	4.58	6

The Browns have had awful luck with centers. The team drafted Jeff Faine in the first round in 2003, but Faine lasted just three disappointing, injury-marred seasons. The team signed LeCharles Bentley to replace Faine in 2006. Bentley suffered a major injury during the first practice of training camp, setting an incredible chain of events into motion that involved six different potential starters, most of whom got hurt before the regular season started. (Faine, meanwhile, blossomed into a solid starter for the Saints and Buccaneers). The team acquired Hank Fraley as a stopgap, and Fraley stopped the gap for three full seasons.

Flabby and athletically limited even in his prime, Fraley will now give way to first-round pick Alex Mack. Mack is a smart decision maker with good weight room strength and athleticism, plus a bit of a mean streak. The knock on Mack is that he's a lunger who often winds up on the ground, so coaches will have to work on his technique. Fraley is still around but won't survive camp if Mack pans out.

After just two seasons, left tackle Joe Thomas has quickly earned access to the Perennial Pro Bowler VIP room. He suffered through a significant sophomore slump last year, blowing five blocks, drawing seven flags and contributing to the ugly run statistics you see above, but Pro Bowl voters have become infatuated with young tackles. Despite his shortcomings, Thomas is the Browns' top lineman and building block. Free agent

John St. Clair is the favorite to start at right tackle. St. Clair was awful early in his career with the Rams but had some productive seasons with the Bears. He blew six blocks at left tackle last season and will benefit from a transfer across the formation. Left guard Eric Steinbach is steady and dependable. Rex Hadnot will battle free agent Pork Chop Womack and all-purpose lineman Ryan Tucker at right guard. Tucker is trying to come back from a hip injury that sidelined him for most of 2008. Womack was the Seahawks' "extra lineman" for seven years before earning a starting job last year. Assuming he loses out to Hadnot or Tucker, he'll be a valuable bench player.

Defensive Front Seven

Defensive Line	Age	Pos	Plays	TmPct	Rk	Stop	Dfts	Stop%	Rk	AvYd	Rk	Sack	Hit	Hur	Runs	St%	Yds	Pass	St%	Yds
						Overall						Pass Rush			vs. Run			vs. Pass		
Shaun Rogers	30	DT	78	9.2%	1	57	17	73%	57	1.8	29	4.5	18	9	66	68%	2.5	12	100%	-2.3
Corey Williams	29	DE	54	6.4%	33	44	11	81%	23	2.5	75	0.5	1	7	46	78%	2.9	8	100%	0.3
Shaun Smith	28	DE	37	6.3%	35	24	4	65%	84	3.2	85	1.0	0	3	36	64%	3.5	1	100%	-7.0
Louis Leonard	25	DT	25	2.9%	68	11	2	44%	74	4.0	74	0.0	1	0	24	46%	3.6	1	0%	13.0
Santonio Thomas	28	DT	15	2.6%	--	13	2	87%	--	1.7	--	0.5	0	0	12	83%	2.3	3	100%	-1.0
Kenyon Coleman	30	DE	55	6.6%	25	43	6	78%	35	2.3	69	0.5	1	0	52	77%	2.7	3	100%	-3.7
C.J. Mosley	26	DT	19	2.3%	--	10	6	53%	--	3.1	--	1.5	1	4	13	38%	4.5	6	83%	0.2

Linebackers	Age	Pos	Plays	TmPct	Rk	Stop	Dfts	Stop%	AvYd	Sack	Hit	Hur	Runs	St%	Rk	Yds	Rk	Tgts	Suc%	Rk	AdjYd	Rk
						Overall				Pass Rush			vs. Run					vs. Pass				
D'Qwell Jackson	26	ILB	158	18.6%	2	84	26	53%	5.3	2.0	1	4	106	60%	68	4.4	91	33	42%	69	8.3	82
Andra Davis*	31	ILB	93	11.0%	57	53	11	57%	4.3	0.0	1	2	73	63%	56	3.5	51	17	42%	70	5.6	28
Kamerion Wimbley	26	OLB	66	7.8%	85	44	15	67%	3.8	4.0	6	11	49	69%	26	3.5	54	5	47%	--	7.3	--
Willie McGinest*	38	OLB	59	7.9%	83	43	13	73%	3.9	1.0	8	8	45	82%	5	3.0	30	13	43%	--	7.0	--
Leon Williams	26	ILB	38	5.1%	--	13	2	34%	7.1	0.0	0	1	22	50%	--	5.1	--	11	45%	--	6.6	--
Eric Barton	32	ILB	122	14.7%	22	63	8	52%	5.5	1.5	2	2	74	66%	39	3.4	47	34	41%	72	6.9	58
David Bowens	32	OLB	34	4.1%	--	19	9	56%	3.8	4.0	5	8	13	62%	--	3.4	--	8	27%	--	10.1	--

Year	Yards	ALY	Rank	Power	Rank	10+ Yds	Rank	Stuff	Rank	Sack	ASR	Rank
2006	4.73	4.64	27	58%	9	20%	26	15%	27	28	5.2%	30
2007	4.38	4.44	30	48%	1	15%	9	16%	26	28	4.8%	30
2008	4.68	4.71	32	58%	4	20%	20	14%	30	18	4.5%	30

Year	LE	Rank	LT	Rank	Mid	Rank	RT	Rank	RE	Rank
2006	4.87	26	4.95	27	4.54	23	4.43	21	5.44	32
2007	4.14	19	5.09	29	4.34	24	4.31	21	4.77	27
2008	5.44	31	4.72	27	4.61	30	4.54	26	4.83	27

Shaun Rogers remains one of the best two-down linemen in the NFL, and he had an effective season as a pass rusher and screen-stopper in 2008. He finished third in the league with 18 quarterback hits while tying for seventh with 23 knockdowns. He also remains a coach's headache. He missed the first week of OTAs after demanding a trade from the new Browns administration. Rogers eventually patched things up with Eric Mangini's staff, but a week of missed practice can have major ramifications for a player with Rogers' whistle-past-the-weight room conditioning. Rogers drew 11 penalties last year, five of them offsides or neutral zone infractions, a sign that he's trying to guess the snap to compensate for his declining quickness.

D'Qwell Jackson is the best of the other incumbent defenders. He can be a great all-purpose threat, but he spent much of 2008 making Little Dutch Boy tackles on a leaky defense. Jackson will get help from the riders on the Jets express. Eric Barton is an experienced, active linebacker well-versed in the system. Kenyon Coleman is a 295-pound two-gap end who can keep blockers off the linebackers. David Bowens is an end/linebacker tweener who can read screens and draws well while providing some pass-rush pop. C.J. Mosley adds depth and New York flavor to a line with enough bodies (including Shaun Smith and Robaire Smith) to overcome an injury or two.

Kamerion Wimbley was one of two veterans to give a presentation at the Browns rookie camp. (The other was Josh Cribbs, who also blows up the footballs and sells tickets.) The speaking engagement was a sign that Wimbley is still a part of the team's plans despite ever-shrinking big-play totals. Wimbley will be pushed by Alex Hall, who played well in limited action last year, and second-round rookie David Veikune. Veikune was born in Alaska but moved to Hawaii (smart move), played in three different college programs, and emerged as a prospect after recording 16 sacks in his last two seasons. He's a converted end, so it may take time for him to adjust at linebacker.

Defensive Secondary

Secondary	Age	Pos	Plays	TmPct	Rk	Stop	Dfts	Yds	Rk	St%	Rk	Tgts	Tgt%	Rk	Dist	Suc%	Rk	AdjYd	Rk	Yds	PD	Int
								Overall								**vs. Run**				**vs. Pass**		
Brandon McDonald	24	CB	90	10.6%	15	41	18	6.1	34	64%	13	86	23.2%	8	13.2	46%	56	8.7	73	8.6	16	5
Eric Wright	24	CB	78	9.2%	33	37	14	8.4	57	74%	4	82	22.1%	17	11.2	46%	60	7.9	53	7.8	13	3
Brodney Pool	25	FS	70	8.8%	53	24	15	7.9	58	37%	50	36	10.4%	4	11.2	50%	45	8.6	53	8.6	5	3
Sean Jones*	27	SS	60	9.4%	44	24	8	8.0	60	49%	18	15	5.2%	64	11.7	46%	62	9.1	56	9.5	4	4
Mike Adams	28	FS	43	5.8%	71	6	4	7.9	57	17%	75	16	4.8%	69	17.2	28%	78	13.1	76	12.7	2	2
Terry Cousin*	34	CB	29	3.4%	--	10	6	7.6	--	22%	--	30	8.1%	--	8.1	44%	--	7.9	--	7.8	2	1
Abram Elam	28	SS	63	7.6%	64	18	9	7.2	43	32%	61	21	4.4%	70	11.5	50%	48	10.3	67	10.1	4	1
Roderick Hood	28	CB	54	7.4%	60	23	5	15.2	81	17%	77	85	22.0%	18	12.6	45%	61	8.0	54	7.7	13	1
Corey Ivy	32	CB	47	6.4%	67	23	14	6.3	38	44%	42	49	11.2%	76	11.3	49%	47	7.5	43	7.3	2	0
Hank Poteat	32	CB	40	5.9%	--	16	6	7.6	--	63%	--	29	7.5%	--	6.0	50%	--	6.7	--	6.2	3	2

Year	Pass D Rank	vs. #1 WR	Rk	vs. #2 WR	Rk	vs. Other WR	Rk	vs. TE	Rk	vs. RB	Rk
2006	17	-15.7%	7	-4.2%	11	-2.5%	20	-25.1%	4	-16.1%	11
2007	23	1.0%	17	-16.2%	5	14.3%	28	19.5%	26	-8.7%	10
2008	17	-1.0%	14	49.5%	32	-30.8%	5	-10.2%	10	-4.1%	9

Abram Elam was the key to the draft-day Mark Sanchez-for-half-the-Jets-roster trade; Mangini reportedly wouldn't do the deal unless the strong safety was included. Elam is at his best near the line of scrimmage, and he's more physical than Sean Jones, now in Philadelphia. Free safety Brodney Pool is big, fast, consistent and durable, but he doesn't produce many big plays.

Third-year cornerback Eric Wright has become a reliable number-one corner. The Browns' dead-last ranking against number-two receivers can be laid at the feet of Brandon McDonald, who was relentlessly abused by opposing quarterbacks. He allowed six touchdowns, 39 first downs/touchdowns (fifth in NFL), and 1,219 passing yards (eighth). He did come around late in the year and started turning errant passes into turnovers (see his two interceptions against the Eagles), so he could still play a role. Roderick Hood joined the Browns after the Cardinals released him in a cap move. Hood is generally underrated and always comes out well in our game charting stats, but he also has a tendency to give up big plays (he tied for the league lead with eight touchdowns allowed) and he provides almost no value in run defense. He could challenge McDonald for the starting job, but will start camp as the nickelback. Veterans Corey Ivy and Hank Poteat will also vie for roles. Ivy is best suited to slot duty, and with 9.5 sacks in four years he can be very effective in the blitz package. Poteat followed Mangini from New England to the Jets to Cleveland, making him more of a binky than a potential starter.

One other player in the secondary mix is – no kidding – Josh Cribbs. Mangini taught Cribbs some defensive assignments in the offseason, and Cribbs could stick as a nickel defender when not playing slot receiver, Wildcat quarterback, kick returner, punt returner, and coverage specialist.

Special Teams

Year	DVOA	Rank	FG/XP	Rank	Net Kick	Rank	Kick Ret	Rank	Net Punt	Rank	Punt Ret	Rank	Hidden	Rank
2006	2.6%	8	-4.3	25	0.7	16	9.9	3	6.9	8	2.2	9	4.1	10
2007	6.9%	2	-1.1	22	6.6	5	31.2	1	-5.5	24	9.2	4	-3.8	21
2008	4.3%	4	1.8	15	-3.0	21	8.2	5	17.5	2	0.6	13	8.0	4

Kicking for an awful team can be a thankless job. Phil Dawson's official stats look low because the Browns only gave him 18 extra point opportunities. His percentages are a little low because Dawson was 3-of-6 from 50-plus yards, as Romeo Crennel kept sending him to bail out a stalled offense. This has been going on for years, with the Browns consistently ranking in the bottom five in points (2007 excluded) and Dawson doing his best to earn a paycheck on five extra points per month. Dawson, like the rest of his team, was shut out in the final weeks of 2009, but he's solid: Strong on kickoffs with the leg to hit some 50-yarders and the ability to work in bad weather.

On the flip side, punting for a bad team can be a blessing. Dave Zastudil had the best season of his seven-year career, posting highs in both gross and net average. Practice makes perfect: Zastudil punted at least five times in 11 different games. Zastudil was aided by solid coverage teams led by Browns Fetish Player Josh Cribbs. Cribbs has 59 total tackles in four seasons, making him one of the most prolific kick gunners in the business. He's also an excellent return man who didn't fumble at all in 2008 after losing the handle 12 times in his first three seasons.

Coaching Staff

Romeo Crennel and Eric Mangini both run exceptionally pure versions of the Bill Belichick-style 3-4 defense. Crennel's Browns finished second in the league in three-man rushes, but Mangini's Jets finished first, and Belichick's Patriots finished fourth. Mangini's 3-4 looks like a 3-4, with linebackers frequently playing off the line of scrimmage, as opposed to the Wade Philips 3-4 that looks like a 5-2. Mangini has had intermittent success with the scheme, which so far has only produced consistent results for Belichick. New coordinator Rob Ryan has a Patriots background (he was linebackers coach from 2000-2003, when Mangini was defensive backs coach) but his defenses in Oakland strayed from the pure Belichick model. He has tinkered with both 3-4 and 4-3 schemes (and even a 4-2-5 base scheme) and last year's Raiders were high in our rankings for both three-man (seventh) and four-man (eighth) rushes. Ryan shares Mangini's relative disinterest in blitzing, so expect a conservative approach this year.

Quarterbacks coach Carl Smith served in the same capacity for the Browns from 2001-2003. He spent four seasons as the Jaguars offensive coordinator, and was the USC quarterbacks coach for about four days in January before Eric Mangini hired him to return to Cleveland. Smith inherits a messy situation similar to the Tim Couch-Kelly Holcomb controversy the team endured during his first tenure. That turned into a no-win scenario; Smith must do a better job with Brady Quinn (or possibly Brett Ratliff) than he did with Couch.

Dallas Cowboys

"With nearly the entire starting lineup back, it seems absurd to suggest that the Cowboys might not be Super Bowl contenders again. The problem is that if the Dallas injury report ceases to be much smaller than the others in the league, the entire starting lineup won't be back. An injury to Romo, Owens, Adams, Ware, or Newman would turn the Cowboys overnight from a contender into a flawed team with a huge hole, and that's reflected in our pessimistic projection. It will take another season with an empty trainer's room for Dallas to live up to the standard of 2007."

— *Pro Football Prospectus 2008*, page 72

The 2008 Dallas Cowboys were defined by injury. Our statistics say that they were a team that experienced league-average health, ranking 15th in the league in Adjusted Games Lost for starters and 21st for AGL accrued by the entire roster. Those numbers, though, fail to take into account how dramatic an effect even that average amount of injuries had on a Dallas organization that was wholly unprepared to adjust and account for them. After all, the Cowboys had ranked among the top ten healthiest franchises in football every year from 2002 through 2007.

Ironically, last year's Cowboys missed the playoffs because they were built just like their hated rivals: the Daniel Snyder-era Washington Redskins.

The loss of quarterback Tony Romo had the most obvious impact. The broken pinky Romo suffered in overtime at the end of a Week 6 loss to Arizona led to ten quarters of Brad Johnson as the team's starting quarterback. Johnson, who had last been seen getting benched for Tarvaris Jackson at the end of the 2006 season, was not a good fit for the Dallas offense. Offensive coordinator Jason Gar-

rett's scheme involves spreading the field with multiple receivers downfield, relying on Romo to use his arm strength, improvisational ability, and knack for eluding the rush to pick up chunks of yardage. It's hard to think of a worse fit for Johnson, and it showed in his performance; among veteran quarterbacks with more than 80 dropbacks, only two backup quarterbacks in the past 15 years have had a passing DVOA so far below that of the team's starter (Table 1). Johnson's plodding brought an elite offense to its knees, yielding a loss to St. Louis and a 13-9 win against Tampa Bay where the margin of victory — Johnson's end-of-the-first-half touchdown pass to Roy Williams — came only after Buccaneers linebacker Cato June took an unsportsmanlike conduct penalty on a third-down play that would have otherwise ended the drive. Dallas averaged 24 points per game with Romo in the lineup and 13.6 when he was hurt.

Although it didn't receive the same level of attention or have the same visibility of impact, a groin injury suffered by cornerback Terence Newman had arguably an even greater impact on the Dallas defense. According to

COWBOYS SUMMARY

2008 Record: 9-7

Pythagorean Wins: 7.9 (19th)

DVOA: 4.4% (19th)

Offense: 6.7% (17th)

Defense: -0.6% (9th)

Special Teams: -2.8% (27th)

Variance: 29.1% (31st)

2008: They were dressed for success, but success never came.

2009: Have they paid enough dues to pay the rent?

2009 Mean Projection: 8.0 wins

On the Clock (0-3): 1%

Loserville (4-6): 25%

Mediocrity (7-8): 32%

Playoff Contender (9-10): 30%

Super Bowl Contender (11+): 12%

Projected Average Opponent: -2.1% (26th)

2009 Cowboys Schedule

Week	Opp.	Week	Opp.	Week	Opp.
1	at TB	7	ATL	13	at NYG
2	NYG	8	SEA	14	SD
3	CAR (Mon.)	9	at PHI	15	at NO (Sat.)
4	at DEN	10	at GB	16	at WAS
5	at KC	11	WAS	17	PHI
6	BYE	12	OAK (Thu.)		

Newman, the injury was suffered during the first week of training camp and was diagnosed by the Cowboys staff as torn scar tissue. The team held him out of the season opener, but upon his return, Newman struggled mightily. After he was torched by Santana Moss in a Week 4 loss, Newman's groin was reexamined to find a sports hernia, which kept him out for six weeks. Had the hernia been diagnosed in the first week of camp, Newman might have been able to avoid missing regular season action altogether. It's tantalizing to think what the effect would have been to the Cowboys, because upon his return, the Dallas pass defense took a huge step forward. From Weeks 1-9 (the weeks in which Newman was either hobbled or out following his surgery), the DVOA of the Cowboys pass defense was 12.7%, 24th in the league; after Newman returned following the Cowboys' Week 10 bye, the team's pass defense was the second-best in football, with a DVOA of -12.6%.

Soon, the issue of how the Cowboys were handling injuries came into question. After Marion Barber went down with a dislocated toe in Week 13, owner Jerry Jones called both Barber and the team's medical staff out when the mercurial back surprised Jones by not making the flight for the team's trip to Pittsburgh the next week. "He can play with that injured toe," Jones said. "He can play with the soreness and a combination of those things.

I see nothing that led us to believe he couldn't." Our injury database, meanwhile, shows that there hasn't been a single player in the 12 years of data we've compiled that was listed on the injury report with a dislocated toe and managed to avoid missing at least one game. Barber returned in Week 15 but was a shell of his healthy self and could only muster 15 yards on 13 carries over the final three weeks of the year.

While the Jones-as-Dear-Leader routine is nothing new (as chronicled in Jeff Pearlman's *Boys Will Be Boys*, covering the Cowboys dynasty of the '90s), his level of influence on the team's football operations is quickly reaching the point of concern. In order to get Garrett to spurn the advances of Baltimore and Miami a year ago, Jones gave his offensive coordinator a salary of $3 million per season and reportedly promised him the head coaching job once Jones saw fit to replace Wade Phillips. Suitably chastened, Phillips did what most people in a position of power and threatened with the loss of that power would do: He concentrated his authority and made himself more valuable. After the aforementioned poor performance of the Cowboys defense early in the year, Phillips took over the play-calling duties from defensive coordinator Brian Stewart, who was fired in the offseason and not replaced. While the Dallas defense improved after the switch, Phillips already had "final say" over each defensive play call, so there's reason to believe that he was already changing some of the calls even before Stewart's removal from the play-calling spot. Garrett also lost some of his luster following the Johnson fiasco, leading to speculation that Phillips would lose his job in the offseason and be replaced by a veteran head coach, not Garrett. In the end, everyone retained their jobs for another year.

Pearlman's book also (rather simplistically) pins the blame for the poor string of drafts the Cowboys had after the Jimmy Johnson era on Jones, with the responsibility for busts like Shante Carver and Sherman Williams falling on the owner. It's impossible to say who exactly is calling the shots in Dallas following the departure of Bill Parcells, but there's reason to be concerned that the same thing might be happening again. After a brilliant 2005 class

Table 1: The Worst Backup Quarterbacks in DVOA History (1994-2008)

Year	Team	Backup	DVOA	Starter	DVOA	Difference
2001	MIN	Spergon Wynn	-75.1%	Daunte Culpepper	0.8%	-75.9%
2005	PIT	Tommy Maddox	-34.2%	Ben Roethlisberger	35.1%	-69.3%
2008	DAL	Brad Johnson	-50.7%	Tony Romo	18.5%	-69.2%
1997	CHI	Rick Mirer	-68.9%	Erik Kramer	-0.6%	-68.3%
1994	TB	Trent Dilfer	-51.7%	Craig Erickson	10.3%	-62.0%
2002	CIN	Gus Frerotte	-55.3%	Jon Kitna	3.2%	-58.5%
1999	SF	Steve Stenstrom	-48.2%	Jeff Garcia	-1.3%	-46.9%
2003	ATL	Kurt Kittner	-57.3%	Doug Johnson	-11.0%	-46.3%
1996	OAK	Billy Joe Hobert	-43.7%	Jeff Hostetler	0.8%	-44.5%
2003	NYG	Jesse Palmer	-48.8%	Kerry Collins	-4.8%	-44.0%

Backups: Minimum 75 passes

yielded DeMarcus Ware, Marcus Spears, Marion Barber, and Chris Canty, Dallas has failed to impress on draft day. Of the 2006, 2007, and 2008 draft classes, only kicker Nick Folk and fullback Deon Anderson have made it into the starting lineup regularly. 2006 first-round pick Bobby Carpenter has been an absolute bust, while 2008 first-rounder Mike Jenkins was outplayed by fifth-round pick Orlando Scandrick. Mid-round picks like tackle James Marten, defensive end Jason Hatcher, tight end Anthony Fasano, and wide receiver Isaiah Stanback have failed to develop and ended up cut, traded, or buried deep on the bench, failing to provide the team with replacements for injured or aging starters. A poorly-reviewed performance in this year's draft doesn't engender much more hope.

It's those depth concerns that helped keep Dallas out of the playoffs a year ago, just like they have the Snyder-era stars-and-scrubs teams in Washington. When Jason Ferguson and Terry Glenn went down in 2007, they were replaced by able backups in Jay Ratliff (who then took another huge step forward and was the team's second-best defensive player in 2008) and Patrick Crayton, respectively. That wasn't the case a year ago, where the backups simply weren't up to snuff:

• Left guard Kyle Kosier only made it to three games, and replacements Montrae Holland and Cory Procter were a huge step backwards.

• Newman was replaced at first by Adam "Pacman" Jones, who wasn't up to a healthy Newman's standard even before he was suspended for off-field misbehavior; Jones gave way to Jenkins, whose inability to adapt to the speed and route-running abilities of pro receivers made him a liability.

• Strong safety Roy Williams missed virtually the entire season with a broken forearm, and backup Pat Watkins went down shortly thereafter with a stinger, yielding the safety job to third-stringer Keith Davis. While Davis is arguably better in coverage than Williams or Watkins, he pales in comparison as a run-stopper at the second level. While it's impossible to isolate the difference down to a lone player, Dallas allowed a higher percentage of rushing yards on long runs over 10 yards compared to the year before, most notably the 77- and 81-yard touchdown runs that closed out Texas Stadium in the Week 16 loss to Baltimore.

• Carpenter's failure to launch forced the team to sign aging middle linebacker Zach Thomas following the 2007 season. Thomas struggled to fit into the Cowboys scheme and was announcing his departure from the team as he walked off the field in Philadelphia. With no confidence in Carpenter or fellow draftee Kevin Burnett, who

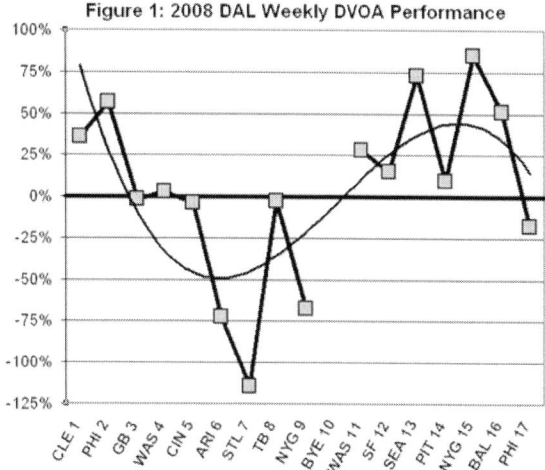

Figure 1: 2008 DAL Weekly DVOA Performance

was allowed to leave in free agency, Dallas went back into the free agent pool and came out with Keith Brooking, who hasn't played in a 3-4 scheme since 2003 and has serious issues in coverage.

The only position where a backup really emerged as a potentially successful starter was at halfback, where Tashard Choice filled in effectively for both Barber and Felix Jones.

Even if you believe that running backs are essentially fungible, it seems obvious that Garrett should find a role for Choice alongside Barber and Jones this year, in the interest of keeping all three of his backs fresh and healthy. It represents a larger organizational shift that the Cowboys offense will need to make. Gone are the days of Terrell Owens complaining about only getting 18 targets in a game; if everyone's healthy, the Cowboys offense could very well have all three of the aforementioned running backs, four wide receivers (Roy Williams, Crayton, Miles Austin, and Sam Hurd), and two tight ends (Jason Witten and Martellus Bennett) all expecting to see their fair share of touches on a weekly basis. Naturally, it's not likely that everyone will stay healthy; Williams has made it through a 16-game schedule only once in his five-year career, while Witten suffered through a separated shoulder, sprained ankle, and broken rib one year ago. Losing either of them — or Romo — would have a dramatic effect on the Dallas passing attack.

We can make the same sort of statement about virtually every Cowboys unit. If DeMarcus Ware or Newman gets hurt, the pass coverage goes down. If Leonard Davis goes down, the team will struggle to run the ball. If they lose Flozell Adams, they'll have a huge sieve at left tackle.

Although they're still vulnerable in those spots, Dallas did take at least a few steps forward in the offseason. Anthony Henry was sent to Detroit for Jon Kitna, who, at the very least, plays quarterback in the same way that Romo does. They've also replaced Roy Williams at safety with 26-year-old Gerald Sensabaugh, formerly of the Jaguars. The team gave Ken Hamlin the same sort of one-year "prove it" deal in 2006, and it worked out well for them. At the very least, Sen-sabaugh will be better in the Cowboys' Cover-4 than Williams was by the end of his tenure.

For the Cowboys to be an elite team in 2009, they'll need to have all their starters stay healthy or see a huge improvement in the performance of their backups from a year ago. Otherwise, forget about *Boys Will Be Boys*. The more apt title for a book about the 2008-2009 Cowboys may end up being *Boys Will Be 'Skins*.

Bill Barnwell

2008 Cowboys Stats by Week

Wk	vs.	W-L	PF	PA	YDF	YDA	TO	Total	Off	Def	ST
1	@CLE	W	28	10	487	205	-1	36%	54%	11%	-7%
2	PHI	W	41	37	380	337	-1	57%	58%	17%	16%
3	@GB	W	27	16	453	334	-1	-2%	6%	7%	-1%
4	WAS	L	24	26	344	381	-1	3%	35%	23%	-10%
5	CIN	W	31	22	373	269	0	-4%	16%	13%	-7%
6	@ARI	L	24	30	374	276	+2	-73%	-11%	15%	-47%
7	@STL	L	14	34	341	325	-4	-115%	-55%	51%	-8%
8	TB	W	13	9	172	262	+1	-3%	-3%	-1%	0%
9	@NYG	L	14	35	183	319	-1	-67%	-76%	-6%	3%
10	BYE										
11	@WAS	W	14	10	315	228	-1	28%	3%	-33%	-8%
12	SF	W	35	22	408	304	+1	15%	16%	2%	2%
13	SEA	W	34	9	447	322	+1	72%	52%	-8%	13%
14	@PIT	L	13	20	289	238	-3	10%	-13%	-34%	-12%
15	NYG	W	20	8	321	218	+2	85%	22%	-57%	7%
16	BAL	L	24	33	327	388	-1	51%	33%	-10%	7%
17	@PHI	L	6	44	298	303	-4	-18%	-23%	-1%	4%

Trends and Splits

	Offense	Rank	Defense	Rank
Total DVOA	6.7%	17	-0.6%	9
Unadjusted VOA	3.3%	21	-1.1%	9
Weighted trend	-0.6%	22	-9.0%	6
Variance	14.2%	31	5.8%	16
Average opponent	2.2%	25	-2.0%	4
Passing	15.8%	18	2.0%	12
Rushing	11.7%	7	-3.7%	14
First down	6.9%	13	-1.3%	14
Second down	-11.9%	25	-2.2%	8
Third down	35.9%	5	3.4%	13
First half	-0.4%	21	-7.5%	7
Second half	14.2%	11	7.3%	21
Red Zone	20.4%	7	-6.9%	12
Late and close	22.5%	6	4.5%	16

Five-Year Performance

Year	W-L	Pyth	Est W	PF	PA	TO	Total	Rk	Off	Rk	Def	Rk	ST	Rk	Off AGL	Rk	Def AGL	Rk
2004	6-10	5.1	6.6	293	405	-15	-14.6%	24	-9.0%	23	4.3%	20	4.4%	5	20.0	15	18.5	21
2005	9-7	8.5	8.2	325	208	-5	5.9%	13	1.1%	13	-5.5%	12	-0.7%	22	3.4	31	10.3	21
2006	9-7	9.8	8.6	425	350	+1	13.6%	9	13.0%	6	-0.9%	14	-0.2%	20	1.3	32	7.5	25
2007	13-3	11.0	10.8	455	325	+5	22.9%	4	17.4%	4	-5.8%	11	-0.4%	18	19.6	19	26.2	11
2008	9-7	7.9	8.3	362	365	-11	4.4%	19	6.7%	17	-0.6%	9	-2.8%	27	24.2	16	29.1	14

Strategic Tendencies

Run/Pass		Rank	Offense		Rank	Defense		Rank	Other		Rank
Runs, all plays	40%	26	3+ WR	48%	17	Rush 3	2.4%	26	2+ RB, Pct Runs	62%	15
Runs, first half	38%	28	4+ WR	5%	29	Rush 4	50.8%	30	1 RB/2 TE, Pct Runs	45%	24
Runs, first down	46%	25	2+ TE	30%	10	Rush 5	36.4%	1	1RB/3+WR, Pct Runs	18%	31
Runs, second-long	35%	21	Single back	60%	12	Rush 6+	10.5%	9	Zone Blitz	2%	23
Runs, power sit.	68%	14	Play action	12%	24	Rush 7+	1.4%	16	Go for it on 4th	0.89	17
Runs, behind 2H	29%	25	Max protect	6%	28	Sacks by LB	69.0%	2	Offensive Pace	31.1	17
Pass, ahead 2H	49%	7	Outside pocket	11%	21	Sacks by DB	6.9%	18	Defensive Pace	30.6	13

The Dallas offense needs to do something to fix its problem with starting games slowly:

Table 2: Somebody Please Wake Romo an Hour Earlier

Year	DVOA Q1	Rank	DVOA Q2-4	Rank
2006	-9.5%	23	18.9%	4
2007	-14.2%	25	27.1%	2
2008	-13.8%	25	13.7%	13

The Cowboys' use of play-action fakes dropped from 21 percent of plays (eighth in 2007) to 12 percent (24th in 2008). ● In 2007, the Cowboys ran an average number of draws but had the league's best DVOA on draws. Last year, 16 percent of all Dallas runs were draws (second to Arizona) but the Cowboys' DVOA on draws was only slightly above average (25.4% vs. NFL average of 17.4%). ● Dallas had the league's biggest gap between offense at home (27.8% DVOA, sixth) and offense on the road (-13.4% DVOA, 26th). ● The Dallas defense ranked seventh in the first half of games and 12th in the third quarter — but then collapsed to 27th in the fourth quarter. ● The Cowboys led the league allowing the fewest average yards after catch (6.5) on passes thrown behind the line of scrimmage. ● The Cowboys were much more likely to big-blitz once Wade Phillips took over the defensive play-calling from Brian Stewart. Dallas only sent six or more on 4.1 percent of pass plays in 2007 and 7.9 percent of pass plays through the first seven games of 2008. After Phillips started calling plays in Week 8, the Cowboys sent six or more on 13.0 percent of pass plays, which would have ranked fifth in the NFL for the entire season.

Passing

Player	DYAR	DVOA	Plays	NtYds	Avg	YAC	C%	TD	Int
Tony Romo	879	18.5%	475	3290	6.9	5.6	61.9%	26	14
Brad Johnson*	-207	-50.7%	88	364	4.1	4.8	52.6%	2	5
Brooks Bollinger*	-52	-55.2%	20	49	2.5	1.6	58.8%	1	1
Jon Kitna	-76	-19.9%	137	698	5.1	5.5	57.1%	5	5

Rushing

Player	DYAR	DVOA	Plays	Yds	Avg	TD	Fum	Suc
Marion Barber	43	-4.4%	238	885	3.7	7	3	41%
Tashard Choice	157	32.0%	93	471	5.1	2	1	45%
Felix Jones	118	81.8%	30	266	8.9	3	0	73%
Tony Romo	0	-12.2%	11	58	5.3	0	1	--
Terrell Owens*	29	31.7%	7	33	4.7	0	0	--
Jon Kitna	14	34.4%	5	34	6.8	0	0	--

Receiving

Player	DYAR	DVOA	Plays	Ctch	Yds	Y/C	YAC	TD	C%
Terrell Owens*	75	-5.7%	139	69	1052	15.2	4.2	10	50%
Roy Williams	-29	-17.1%	82	36	430	11.9	3.5	3	44%
Patrick Crayton	70	0.9%	69	39	551	14.1	5.4	4	57%
Miles Austin	106	48.7%	23	13	278	21.4	8.1	3	57%
Jason Witten	203	19.0%	120	81	952	11.8	4.1	5	68%
Martellus Bennett	112	59.0%	27	20	283	14.2	6.7	4	74%
Tony Curtis*	-40	-59.8%	12	8	37	4.6	2.9	0	67%
Marion Barber	56	4.3%	61	52	417	8.0	8.2	2	85%
Tashard Choice	29	3.9%	30	21	185	8.8	9.3	0	70%

Offensive Line

Year	Yards	ALY	Rank	Power	Rank	10+ Yds	Rank	Stuff	Rank	Sacks	ASR	Rank	False	Cont.
2006	4.21	4.36	10	63%	17	15%	20	19%	22	37	7.9%	23	25	48
2007	4.31	4.16	14	68%	12	20%	11	18%	14	25	4.5%	7	27	44
2008	4.48	4.10	14	68%	15	22%	8	18%	17	31	5.8%	13	24	31

Year	LE	Rank	LT	Rank	Mid	Rank	RT	Rank	RE	Rank
2006	3.51	22	5.46	1	4.25	19	4.02	22	4.76	7
2007	2.63	31	4.58	9	3.71	27	4.94	2	5.10	1
2008	5.12	4	3.65	27	4.12	17	4.60	3	3.03	29

The long and the short of it is that everyone simply played a little worse than he did in 2007, except for Kyle Kosier, whose broken foot held him to three games. He was replaced by Cory Proctor and Montrae Holland, nether of whom were up to even Kosier's standards of being an average guard. That had a knock-on effect on Andre Gurode, who struggled as a run blocker and was named to the Pro Bowl by sheer virtue of the fact that he'd been named to it the year before. In all fairness to Gurode, his shotgun snaps endangered Tony Romo's health slightly less than they did the year before.

The re-signing of a 33-year-old Flozell Adams to a six-year, $42 million deal before last season was met with some incredulity amongst some Cowboys fans. They saw Adams' absurd propensity for false starts — nine in each of the past two seasons, the most of any lineman over that two-year period — and assumed that they could do better. The only problem, unfortunately, is that the Cowboys haven't done better, with homegrown tackles like Doug Free, James Marten, and Pat McQuistan simply washing out. The team drafted Ball State tackle Robert Brewster in this year's third round, but without any sign that they can develop and deliver an offensive tackle, we're not inclined to think he'll have any impact. Adams' Pro Bowl nod, even as an injury replacement, was ridiculous; according to our game charters, he was one of the top ten tackles in blown blocks leading to sacks (with six) and the Cowboys declined significantly on runs behind left tackle.

The other two starters were the team's best. Right tackle Marc Colombo wasn't as good in pass protection as he was in 2007, but remained effective and — digging the knife in a little deeper to Bears fans — healthy. While left guard Leonard Davis wasn't the best interior lineman in the league as he (arguably) was in 2007, he was worthy of his Pro Bowl selection.

Defensive Front Seven

Defensive Line	Age	Pos	Plays	TmPct	Rk	Stop	Dfts	Stop%	Rk	AvYd	Rk	Sack	Hit	Hur	Runs	St%	Yds	Pass	St%	Yds
							Overall					Pass Rush			vs. Run			vs. Pass		
Jay Ratliff	28	DT	55	7.2%	5	48	21	87%	3	0.6	6	7.5	7	12	37	84%	1.9	18	94%	-1.9
Chris Canty*	27	DE	41	5.4%	45	29	8	71%	64	2.0	55	3.5	4	4	28	64%	2.8	13	85%	0.2
Marcus Spears	26	DE	37	4.8%	54	27	7	73%	59	2.6	78	1.0	5	3	33	73%	2.8	4	75%	0.8
Tank Johnson*	28	DT	21	2.8%	72	17	6	81%	15	1.5	16	1.0	3	4	20	80%	1.9	1	100%	-6.0
Stephen Bowen	25	DE	17	2.5%	--	11	2	65%	--	3.6	--	0.0	4	2	15	73%	3.1	2	0%	7.5
Jason Hatcher	27	DE	17	2.2%	--	13	3	76%	--	2.8	--	1.0	4	1	16	75%	3.4	1	100%	-8.0
Igor Olshansky	27	DE	28	3.2%	86	19	3	68%	74	3.4	87	1.5	2	3	26	65%	3.7	2	100%	-0.5

Linebackers	Age	Pos	Plays	TmPct	Rk	Stop	Dfts	Stop%	AvYd	Sack	Hit	Hur	Runs	St%	Rk	Yds	Rk	Tgts	Suc%	Rk	AdjYd	Rk
							Overall			Pass Rush			vs. Run					vs. Pass				
Bradie James	28	ILB	120	15.7%	18	68	23	57%	4.2	8.0	4	2	73	60%	70	3.9	74	35	41%	71	6.4	51
Zach Thomas*	36	ILB	97	12.7%	36	45	5	46%	5.0	1.0	1	4	66	55%	90	3.8	72	18	34%	85	6.9	60
DeMarcus Ware	27	OLB	86	11.3%	55	35	35	83%	0.6	20.0	13	16	53	81%	7	2.3	7	9	66%	--	5.2	--
Greg Ellis*	34	OLB	36	4.7%	--	20	12	56%	3.1	7.5	9	7	22	50%	--	4.0	--	4	44%	--	4.5	--
Anthony Spencer	25	OLB	28	4.9%	--	18	3	64%	2.7	1.5	1	4	23	70%	--	2.7	--	8	69%	--	3.7	--
Kevin Burnett*	27	ILB	27	3.5%	--	15	10	56%	5.1	2.0	1	3	5	20%	--	6.2	--	18	81%	1	4.3	3
Keith Brooking	34	ILB	106	13.5%	30	47	14	44%	6.2	0.0	5	1	52	58%	85	3.5	55	46	39%	77	8.1	80

Year	Yards	ALY	Rank	Power	Rank	10+ Yds	Rank	Stuff	Rank	Sack	ASR	Rank
2006	3.81	4.27	19	60%	10	11%	3	17%	25	34	7.3%	12
2007	4.01	3.87	8	67%	21	19%	22	21%	8	46	7.8%	4
2008	4.41	4.19	18	74%	26	23%	26	17%	20	59	9.9%	1

Year	LE	Rank	LT	Rank	Mid	Rank	RT	Rank	RE	Rank
2006	5.38	31	4.12	13	4.00	10	4.74	28	3.92	14
2007	2.89	5	3.73	9	3.99	13	4.06	18	4.10	16
2008	2.86	3	4.04	14	4.21	18	4.66	28	4.94	28

The ascension of Jay Ratliff to Pro Bowl nose tackle is nothing short of astounding. The 298-pound Ratliff is 30 pounds smaller than most NFL nose tackles, and as a seventh-round pick who only won the job when Jason Ferguson got hurt at the start of the 2007 season, the Cowboys would have been happy if he simply held serve. Instead, they got a nose tackle that seemed to live in the backfield, penetrating past hapless centers and guards to blow up play after play. Only 4-3 defensive tackle Kevin Willams had as many Defeats as Ratliff amongst interior linemen, and the latter's 7.5 sacks were as many as Patriots nose Vince Wilfork has had in his entire career. Ratliff's success has prompted the Cowboys to consider moving him to end, but without a nose tackle to replace him, it's hard to see how the move would make Dallas any better.

Outside of Ratliff and the superb DeMarcus Ware, who finished second in the league to Terrell Suggs in Defeats, there's wasn't a lot to write home about amongst the Dallas front seven. Ends Chris Canty and Marcus Spears were competent, but neither took a huge step forward; Canty departed in the offseason for the Giants, where he'll move to tackle. Despite the presence of prospects like Stephen Bowen and Jason Hatcher behind those guys, Dallas elected to bring in Igor Olshansky from San Diego, who should actually be a modest upgrade on Canty at a much cheaper price (four years, $18 million). Spears is in the final year of his deal, and unlikely to be re-signed after the year.

While middle linebacker Bradie James made noise about not making the Pro Bowl because of his sack total, he wasn't particularly effective against the running game or in pass coverage; in fact, James' most memorable moment in 2008 was being pancaked by Lorenzo Neal on the 82-yard touchdown run that turned the lights out at Texas Stadium. He was, however, better than Zach Thomas, who simply didn't adapt well to Wade Phillips' 3-4 scheme and had a season full of false steps and second guesses. Thomas departed after the season and was replaced by Keith Brooking, who was last seen chasing down ghosts in the Falcons' Wild Card game. Former first-round pick Bobby Carpenter lurks as the primary backup at both inside linebacker spots, with Matt Stewart and former Chargers special teams threat Carlos Polk as the other options. Greg Ellis also showed signs of age in his struggles with the running game, leading the team to replace him with another former first-round pick, Anthony Spencer. Spencer's still developing as a pass rusher, but has the athleticism to make plays as a run blitzer.

Defensive Secondary

Secondary	Age	Pos	Plays	TmPct	Rk	Overall Stop	Dfts	Yds	vs. Run Rk	St%	Rk	Tgts	Tgt%	Rk	vs. Pass Dist	Suc%	Rk	AdjYd	Rk	Yds	PD	Int
Ken Hamlin	28	FS	75	9.8%	41	13	4	10.7	75	23%	70	18	4.2%	72	15.1	49%	49	7.7	36	7.2	3	1
Anthony Henry*	33	CB	55	7.2%	63	17	6	7.3	50	25%	74	69	16.2%	56	11.9	43%	72	8.7	72	8.5	7	1
Terence Newman	31	CB	48	10.1%	20	22	11	5.3	23	57%	20	62	23.0%	11	13.6	40%	79	9.3	80	9.0	11	4
Adam Jones*	26	CB	37	8.6%	42	18	7	5.2	22	60%	18	51	21.2%	21	10.2	60%	12	6.4	28	6.0	9	0
Orlando Scandrick	23	CB	31	4.1%	82	14	9	17.5	83	50%	32	42	9.8%	80	8.6	61%	11	6.0	17	5.7	5	0
Keith Davis*	31	FS	25	3.3%	--	11	2	4.5	--	59%	--	11	2.5%	--	13.6	8%	--	16.5	--	15.9	0	0
Mike Jenkins	24	CB	23	3.4%	83	10	6	9.0	63	0%	81	40	10.6%	79	8.9	54%	26	6.6	31	6.2	5	1
Gerald Sensabaugh	26	SS	72	9.6%	43	26	9	6.6	35	43%	35	43	10.7%	2	12.8	53%	35	7.6	32	7.7	8	4

Year	Pass D Rank	vs. #1 WR	Rk	vs. #2 WR	Rk	vs. Other WR	Rk	vs. TE	Rk	vs. RB	Rk
2006	24	1.7%	14	1.7%	15	27.9%	29	-13.6%	8	6.6%	21
2007	8	5.2%	20	-26.4%	4	-14.2%	11	24.8%	30	5.0%	24
2008	10	4.4%	16	24.7%	26	-11.5%	12	19.5%	25	4.0%	15

After signing Terence Newman to a huge contract before the season, the organization hoped that he'd be the shutdown corner that his draft position and reputation purported him to be. Instead, they got a player who was really good for just under half the season. Before Newman had surgery on a sports hernia, opposing receivers went off: 14-of-16 for 175 yards and two touchdowns. One of the incomplete passes was a drop. Once he came back after Week 10, he was better: 24-of-46 for 334 yards with no touchdowns, four interceptions (one on a Hail Mary), and nine passes broken up. The Cowboys were paying for 16 games of that, but Newman has failed to start in 11 of the Cowboys' last 32 regular season games.

After the departures of Adam Jones and Anthony Henry, the opportunity to start opposite Newman will go to the winner of a camp battle between 2008 draft picks Mike Jenkins (first round) and Orlando Scandrick (fifth round). This sounds like a simple battle until you realize that Scandrick has outplayed Jenkins from the moment they both stepped on the field at organized team activities last summer. Scandrick was the significantly better player by our numbers, and that was reinforced on tape; Scandrick proved himself with solid coverage and earned more playing time as the year went along. Expect Jenkins to win the job at right corner and Scandrick to start in the slot, but Scandrick's probably the better player at the moment.

Replacing Roy Williams in the secondary will be Gerald Sensabaugh, signed to a one-year prove-it deal a la Ken Hamlin in 2006. Sensabaugh showed some promise as Jacksonville's strong safety, but was too inconsistent (and injury-prone) to justify a long-term deal from either the Jaguars or the Cowboys. He's best when he's close to the line of scrimmage, so expect to see a lot of Ken Hamlin in centerfield as the Cowboys play more Cover-1 than the quarters defense they often employed a year ago. Fifth-round pick DeAngelo Smith was a corner in college, but profiles as a free safety at the pro level; he'll be behind Pat Watkins, who can fill in at either safety spot with equal amounts of ineffectiveness.

Special Teams

Year	DVOA	Rank	FG/XP	Rank	Net Kick	Rank	Kick Ret	Rank	Net Punt	Rank	Punt Ret	Rank	Hidden	Rank
2006	-0.2%	20	-7.3	30	6.5	9	0.5	13	-2.8	22	1.8	11	-3.3	19
2007	-0.4%	18	2.6	11	-3.6	23	0.3	16	-0.6	19	-1.0	17	-6.8	24
2008	-2.8%	27	7.9	2	-7.1	27	-1.1	17	-7.4	27	-8.9	30	-8.5	25

The Cowboys decided to revamp their coverage units over the offseason, letting veterans like Keith Davis go and replacing them with draft picks like Jason Williams (third-round), Victor Butler (fourth-round), and the aforementioned Smith. The Cowboys' coverage units didn't stand out as particularly poor in our numbers — maybe slightly-below league average — so it seems like this might be a Jerry Jones pet peeve that the owner chose to indulge. The team will be forced to get away from its habit of using a four-man wedge after the NFL banned wedges of more than two players in the offseason.

Dallas also surprised everyone by drafting a kicker in the fifth round, USC's David Buehler. Buehler was a backup linebacker and running back at junior college before transferring to USC and becoming a full-time kicker, so he should be better on coverage than most kickers. Nick Folk didn't record a single touchback in 2008, so it's easy to envision Buehler making the squad as a kickoff specialist and superior coverage guy who eventually takes over the placekicking duties when Folk misses a few.

Punter Mat McBriar was off to an awful start before breaking his foot on the vicious blocked punt that ended the Cardinals game; replacement Sam Paulescu was better, but still below-average, so McBriar will be back in 2009.

Coaching Staff

Wade Phillips' job security has been the source of seemingly infinite discussion in Dallas, but last year's issues had less to do with Phillips' performance as a coach and more to do with injuries. Phillips heeded some of the early-season calls for his neck by doing what most head coaches do — taking more control. Phillips took over the play-calling duties from defensive coordinator Brian Stewart before the Week 8 tilt against Tampa Bay, and the resulting split was staggering: The Cowboys' defensive DVOA was 20.0% before that game, and -15.5% from that point on. Having a healthy Terence Newman helped, but it's obvious that Phillips' play-calling was at least part of the solution. Stewart was fired after the season and not replaced, so expect Phillips to run the defense again in 2009.

Offensive coordinator Jason Garrett took significant flak for the team's performance without Tony Romo in the lineup, as well as the nature of his play-calling vis-à-vis T.O., but he did a reasonably good job with the parts he had to work with at any given point of the season. Garrett has shown the ability to craft his team's playbook and game plan to the strengths of his players; the fact that Brad Johnson wasn't particularly good at anything doesn't change that. Garrett is still the handpicked successor to Wade Phillips, but Jerry Jones' hands have a way of finding new people to admire.

Denver Broncos

The 2008 season came to a very disappointing end for the Denver Broncos. They kicked away a three-game division lead by blowing their final three games, ending up 8-8 and out of the postseason by tiebreaker. But rarely have the clouds of failure come with such a blindingly bright silver lining.

The Broncos spent 2008 developing a dynamic young offense, with the emphasis on young. Quarterback Jay Cutler, just 25 years old, made his first Pro Bowl. His top three receivers — Brandon Marshall, Eddie Royal, and tight end Tony Scheffler — were also 25 or younger. The Broncos had practically stolen a franchise left tackle, Ryan Clady, with the 13th pick in the 2008 draft. The offensive line played so well that the Broncos were third in the league in yards per carry despite a cavalcade of injuries that eventually forced the team to give six different running backs at least one start. The Broncos were only 16th in the league in points scored, but ranked second in yards gained and first downs. They were also second in offensive DVOA, merely a tenth of a percentage point behind the rival Chargers.

But no matter how much the offense did to win games, the defense did more to lose them. The 2008 Denver Broncos had one of the worst defenses in NFL history — since 1994, the only team with a worse defensive DVOA was last year's Detroit Lions (Table 1). Pass rusher Elvis Dumervil had just five sacks; the rest of the defensive line was primarily made up of players who had been rejected by other teams. D.J. Williams has been the only starting-quality player at linebacker since a neck injury ended Al Wilson's career. Safeties Marlon McCree and Marquand Manuel looked old, and cornerback Champ Bailey — by far Denver's best defensive player — struggled with a groin injury for half the season. It didn't help that Denver also had terrible special teams units. The combination of bad defense and bad special teams meant that the Broncos offense was starting its average drive 74.2 yards away from the goal line — 1.5 yards further away than any other offense and more than four yards further than the NFL average (69.9).

Given the strengths and weaknesses of the Broncos at the end of 2008, the proper offseason strategy seemed fairly clear. The offense was fine and only likely to get better, although it needed depth at running back. The team needed to throw as many resources possible at the defense, both in free agency and the draft. The best bet would be to find young defenders who could develop alongside the offense, particularly young defensive backs who could learn from the veteran Bailey.

This is not the strategy that the Denver Broncos chose.

Denver owner Pat Bowlen began the offseason by firing head coach Mike Shanahan after 14 years with the franchise. Despite the Broncos' late-season col-

BRONCOS SUMMARY

2008 Record: 8-8

Pythagorean Wins: 6.2 (24th)

DVOA: -6.5% (17th)

Offense: 24.0% (2nd)

Defense: 24.7% (31st)

Special Teams: -5.8% (31st)

Variance: 21.8% (27th)

2008: An abysmal defense leads to a December collapse, and the end of the Mike Shanahan era in Denver.

2009: The new administration tears apart the successful offense, while the aging, dilapidated defense gets ... older?

2009 Mean Projection: 4.9 wins

On the Clock (0-3): 27%

Loserville (4-6): 51%

Mediocrity (7-8): 16%

Playoff Contender (9-10): 6%

Super Bowl Contender (11+): 1%

Projected Average Opponent: 7.8% (1st)

2009 Broncos Schedule

Week	Opp.	Week	Opp.	Week	Opp.
1	at CIN	7	BYE	13	at KC
2	CLE	8	at BAL	14	at IND
3	at OAK	9	PIT (Mon.)	15	OAK
4	DAL	10	at WAS	16	at PHI
5	NE	11	SD	17	KC
6	at SD (Mon.)	12	NYG (Thu.)		

lapse, the move was a bit shocking. The men were known to be close, and Shanahan still had three years and $20 million on his contract. Shanahan ran the entire organization, and his departure meant a major overhaul.

There are reasonable arguments both in favor of and against firing Shanahan. However, once Bowlen decided to make a change, the logical move was to find a young defensive mastermind to take over the team and fix the Broncos' glaring defensive problems. All the offense needed was a coordinator who ran something similar to the scheme that worked so well in 2008.

Denver interviewed a number of candidates from the defensive side, including two who got other head jobs, Steve Spagnuolo and Raheem Morris. New England offensive coordinator Josh McDaniels, however, knocked Bowlen's socks off with his plans to turn the Broncos into Patriots West. Bowlen hired McDaniels and gave him the keys to the kingdom. Bowlen fired Vice President of Football Operations Jim Goodman and his son, co-Assistant General Manager Jeff Goodman. The other co-Assistant G.M., Brian Xanders, was promoted and given the General Manager title, but it was clear that the 32-year-old McDaniels was now fully in charge.

McDaniels set to the task of re-making the Broncos in the image of the Bill Belichick Patriots. He hired

Mike Nolan to run a 3-4 defense, even though the Denver front seven didn't really fit a 3-4 alignment. (Of course, given how badly they played last year, it could be argued that they didn't really fit a 4-3 alignment either.) He signed familiar free agents, like running back LaMont Jordan, wide receiver Jabar Gaffney, and long-snapper Lonie Paxton. Then, although most people would find the idea of replacing Cutler ludicrous, he explored the possibility of bringing in a quarterback he had already had success with: New England backup Matt Cassel.

What came next was a soap opera of hurt feelings, closed-door meetings, missed text messages, and media sniping. The Broncos say they never really wanted to trade Cutler; other teams approached them, and they felt it was reasonable to at least listen to offers. They complain that once his ego was wounded, Cutler shut himself off from management and refused to answer calls or text messages from McDaniels or Bowlen. Cutler's side of the story is that McDaniels is a megalomaniac, who even during meetings called to smooth things out refused to tell Cutler that he was definitely Denver's quarterback for the long haul.

The truth is probably somewhere in the middle. New coaches like to send the message that nobody's job is safe, trying to keep their veteran players from getting complacent. However, if McDaniels thinks the only way to send this message is to repeatedly piss off his franchise quarterback, perhaps he needs to work on his interpersonal skills. After enough scandal to keep Peter King busy for six weeks, the McDaniels-Cutler relationship had reached Superfund toxicity levels, and the quarterback-hungry Bears came forward with an offer too good for Denver to refuse.

The Broncos got a pretty good haul when they traded Cutler, including two first-round picks and a quarterback (Kyle Orton) who could take over the starting role. (As a bonus, they sent Cutler to the NFC, where they will rarely have to face him.) Nevertheless, trading away a young Pro Bowl quarterback is simply unprecedented. Quarterbacks traded away in the past either had not yet established themselves or were already past their prime. Perhaps the closest comparison is the Colts dealing Jeff George to the Falcons after four seasons, but Cutler had more passing yards and touchdowns last year than George had in his final two seasons in Indianapolis combined. Looking at two-year similarity scores

Table 1: The Worst Defenses by DVOA, 1994-2008

Based on Usual Multi-Year Baseline			Normalized for Specific Season		
Year	Team	DVOA	Year	Team	Norm DVOA
2008	DET	29.2%	2000	MIN	26.9%
2008	DEN	24.7%	2008	DET	25.8%
2000	MIN	24.4%	1999	CLE	23.3%
2008	STL	23.4%	1996	ATL	22.7%
2004	MIN	23.0%	2004	MIN	22.5%
2004	SF	21.4%	1999	SF	21.5%
2002	ARI	20.1%	2005	HOU	21.4%
2005	HOU	19.9%	2008	DEN	21.3%
2002	DET	19.6%	2004	SF	20.9%
2008	HOU	17.9%	1998	CIN	20.6%

for Cutler, the first four names are Joe Montana, Peyton Manning, Brett Favre, and Tom Brady.

Kyle Orton will never be Jay Cutler, but he has recovered from his dismal rookie season to become a league-average quarterback. Given the quality of the receivers and offensive line, the most important need of the team was still a younger, rebuilt defense. Which is why so many of us were dumbfounded when the Broncos left players like Malcolm Jenkins and Brian Cushing on the board and used their first draft selection on Georgia running back Knowshon Moreno.

"I've learned the hard way that running backs are hard to come by," McDaniels told King after the draft. This quote begs the question: Has McDaniels been paying any attention to the offense of the team he just took over? Or his own offense in New England?

New England has spent one first-round pick on a running back this decade: Laurence Maroney, who has played well when healthy, but is generally considered a bust because he can't stay on the field. For the last two years, Maroney has shared time with Sammy Morris, a 30-year-old free agent who was originally a fifth-round pick. Morris has the higher rushing average of the two. Why devote draft value and cap space to a stud running back when your offense is so heavily based on the pass? When Josh McDaniels coordinated the best offense in NFL history two years ago, they had a double-digit lead (42 percent of plays) more often than they actually ran the ball (40 percent of plays, 19th in the NFL).

Denver, meanwhile, has been successfully plugging low-drafted (or undrafted) running backs into its zone blocking system and getting positive results since the days of vertical-striped brown socks. Take a look at four similar running backs and see if you can identify any of these numbers:

	G	Runs	RuYd	RuTD	Yd/At	Rec	RecYd	RecTD	Yd/Rec
Player A	15	249	1,216	12	4.88	37	364	1	9.8
Player B	16	268	1,282	9	4.78	50	377	1	7.5
Player C	15	251	1,228	9	4.89	43	260	1	6.0
Player TD	14	237	1,117	7	4.71	49	367	1	7.5

Player B and Player C are last year's phenomenal rookie running backs, Steve Slaton (B) and Chris Johnson (C). Player TD is, of course, Denver legend Terrell Davis in his rookie year of 1995. Who is Player A, who might be even better than these other three stars? Player A is the combined total for the top four running backs on the 2008 Denver Broncos: a 33-year-old veteran free agent (Michael Pittman), a seventh-round rookie converted fullback (Peyton Hillis), a second-year player nobody wanted to draft (Selvin Young), and some guy who was working at a cell phone stand in the mall (Tatum Bell).

Given what these guys did last year behind Denver's championship-quality offensive line, why on earth would a team with holes throughout its defense use the 12th overall selection on a running back? Even if Moreno matches last year's top rookie backs — even if he matches what the great Terrell Davis did in his first year — the Broncos have essentially gotten the exact same production they got a year ago out of four nobodies whose combined salary was probably less than what they'll give Moreno this season.

The Broncos did turn to defense after the Moreno pick, but even that involved some strange decisions. It's hard to argue with the selection of Tennessee defensive end Robert Ayers with the pick the Broncos got with the Cutler trade — he was one of the top pass rushers in the draft, a player with explosive speed and excellent hand moves who fills an important Denver need. But in the second round, the Broncos pulled a move even more stunning than the decision to draft Moreno. They traded their 2010 first-round pick to Seattle for the 37th overall pick, so they could take Wake Forest cornerback Alphonso Smith.

The point here is not to denigrate the talents of Smith; for all we know, he could be a Pro Bowl cornerback in the making. Yet here is another decision where McDaniels seems to have done things the opposite of the "Patriots Way." New England has kept the pipeline of top-rated young talent flowing into Foxboro by constantly dealing draft picks for higher-round picks the following year. A third-round pick in 2003 ended up a second-round pick in 2004, which was traded for Corey Dillon. The 28th overall pick in 2007 ended up the seventh overall pick in 2008 (plus a fourth-rounder, which was traded for Randy Moss). Two third-round picks this year were turned into two second-round picks for next year. If a team is willing to be patient and wait a year, there's a huge increase in value with no increase in risk.

Denver, on the other hand, is a team entering a major rebuilding period without next year's first-round pick (although they do still have Chicago's, from the Cutler trade). If the Broncos do fall apart — and when you deal away a franchise quarterback, there's a good chance of that happening — the pick they sent to Se-

Table 2: Oldest Starting Secondaries, 2000-2009

Year	Team	Mean Age Sec	Pass DVOA	Rank	Players
2009	DEN	32.3	--	--	Dawkins (36), Bailey (31), Goodman (31), Hill (31)
2007	DEN	32.0	11.5%	22	Lynch (36), Ferguson (33), Bly (30), Bailey (29)
2003	NO	31.8	0.0%	15	Carter (34), Ambrose (33), Bellamy (31), Jones (29)
2004	NO	31.8	17.8%	25	Ambrose (34), Bellamy (32), Thomas (31), Jones (30)
2000	CAR	31.3	-1.1%	14	Robinson (37), Davis (32), Evans (30), Minter (26)
2001	BAL	31.0	-14.0%	9	Woodson (36), Harris (32), Starks (27), McAlister (24)
2001	ATL	31.0	17.4%	27	Carter (32), Ambrose (31), Bradford (31), Buchanan (30)
2002	NE	30.5	-6.6%	9	Smith (37), Milloy (29), Jones (28), Law (28)
2004	DET	30.5	13.7%	23	Marion (34), Walker (34), Bly (27), Bryant (27)
2009	GB	30.5	--	--	Harris (35), Woodson (33), Bigby (28), Collins (26)
2002	PHI	30.3	-10.2%	5	Bishop (32), Vincent (31), Dawkins (29), Taylor (29)
2003	PIT	30.3	6.8%	20	Alexander (32), Washington (31), Logan (29), Scott (29)
2008	DEN	30.3	36.7%	31	Bly (31), McCree (31), Bailey (30), Abdullah (25)
2006	KC	30.3	5.5%	19	Law (32), Knight (31), Surtain (30), Wesley (28)

attle becomes hugely valuable. Yes, current rookie salaries mean the top picks in the NFL draft aren't as economically efficient as late-first and second-round picks. However, more star players still come from the first round of the draft than from later rounds, particularly at the quarterback position — you know, the most important position on the field and the one where Denver traded away its best young player.

At least the Smith pick gave Denver some desperately needed young secondary talent. Smith and fellow second-round draftee Darcel McBath will apprentice under a starting secondary that is simultaneously new and old — very, very old.

When the Broncos went to rebuild last year's secondary, they had to hit the free agent market because they had no young defensive backs in the organization. Obviously, you can't blame the Broncos for the fact that their most talented young cornerback of recent

vintage, Darrent Williams, was shockingly murdered after the 2006 season. However, you can blame them for not drafting any defensive backs in either 2006 or 2007, and for trading Domonique Foxworth to Atlanta for a seventh-round pick before Foxworth could reach his potential.

By definition, the free agent market is filled with veterans, but even by those standards the Broncos went with older players. They could have brought back Foxworth, who is 26, or gone after 28-year-old Bryant McFadden. Instead, they signed two 31-year-old ex-Dolphins, cornerback Andre' Goodman and safety Renaldo Hill. The final slot was filled by Denver's new éminence grise, longtime Philadelphia strong safety Brian Dawkins, who will be 36 this year.

Dawkins may be a future Hall of Famer, and safeties of his caliber have played into their late thirties (Rod Woodson and Aeneas Williams, to give two examples), but he has definitely been in decline over the past couple seasons. Furthermore, based on their projected opening day lineup, the Broncos will field the oldest secondary of any team since at least 2000 (Table 2), and one of the ten oldest defenses based on mean age. The other two secondaries where all four projected starters were at least 30 years old finished 25th and 27th in pass defense DVOA.

The front seven is a bit younger, but it is hard to pin down the age of the projected starting lineup when that lineup seems to change with each new article in the *Denver Post*. The Broncos have two good inside linebackers to anchor their 3-4 (D.J. Williams and free-agent signing Andra Davis) but they'll be surrounded by career backups, veterans with health issues, and young defensive ends who will have to play

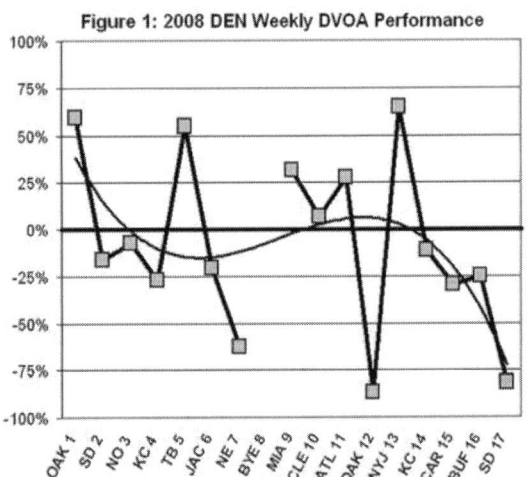

Figure 1: 2008 DEN Weekly DVOA Performance

out of position as outside linebackers.

You have to wonder how Denver fans will react if the Broncos have a true rebuilding season, completely out of playoff contention. Since 1991, the Broncos have won at least seven games every year except for 1999, when John Elway retired, Terrell Davis tore his ACL, and the Broncos went 6-10. If Steve Spagnuolo goes 5-11 in St. Louis, fans will see it as a first step. If Jim Schwartz goes 5-11 in Detroit, he may get a parade through downtown. If Josh McDaniels goes 5-11 with a team that was one win away from the playoffs last year — after an ego clash forced him to deal the fran-chise quarterback — it's hard to imagine that Denver fans will happily accept it.

Still, no matter what happens, it isn't like the Broncos have suddenly become the Bengals. Pat Bowlen remains one of the best owners in the NFL. There are a lot of smart people in the front office. Josh McDaniels has plenty of potential as a head coach, and while Mike Nolan may have failed in San Francisco, he has an excellent record as a defensive assistant. This is not the beginning of a decade-long winter of discontent. But in the short-term, it is not going to be pretty.

Aaron Schatz

2008 Broncos Stats by Week

Wk	vs.	W-L	PF	PA	YDF	YDA	TO	Total	Off	Def	ST
1	@OAK	W	41	14	441	307	+1	59%	74%	9%	-5%
2	SD	W	39	38	486	456	0	-16%	24%	21%	-19%
3	NO	W	34	32	369	502	-1	-7%	21%	29%	1%
4	@KC	L	19	33	446	370	-3	-27%	-3%	22%	-3%
5	TB	W	16	13	275	404	-5	54%	58%	15%	11%
6	JAC	L	17	24	323	416	-1	-21%	5%	30%	5%
7	@NE	L	7	41	275	404	-5	-62%	-20%	34%	-9%
8	BYE										
9	MIA	L	17	26	319	341	-2	32%	4%	-16%	12%
10	@CLE	W	34	30	564	399	0	7%	48%	30%	-12%
11	@ATL	W	24	20	332	364	+1	28%	24%	-1%	3%
12	OAK	L	10	31	319	318	-2	-87%	2%	54%	-36%
13	@NYJ	W	34	17	484	383	+1	65%	63%	-1%	1%
14	KC	W	24	17	425	260	-1	-12%	31%	29%	-13%
15	@CAR	L	10	30	279	400	-1	-30%	4%	29%	-4%
16	BUF	L	23	30	532	275	-2	-25%	31%	39%	-16%
17	@SD	L	21	52	406	491	-2	-82%	7%	76%	-13%

Trends and Splits

	Offense	Rank	Defense	Rank
Total DVOA	24.0%	2	24.7%	31
Unadjusted VOA	24.5%	2	24.8%	31
Weighted trend	21.5%	6	27.8%	32
Variance	6.9%	14	6.5%	21
Average opponent	4.5%	13	8.9%	27
Passing	30.1%	7	36.7%	31
Rushing	23.9%	1	13.3%	29
First down	14.0%	8	22.2%	30
Second down	36.9%	1	27.4%	30
Third down	23.0%	11	25.3%	27
First half	20.7%	3	13.7%	25
Second half	27.7%	2	35.6%	32
Red Zone	1.5%	21	23.2%	25
Late and close	17.8%	12	32.7%	32

Five-Year Performance

Year	W-L	Pyth	Est W	PF	PA	TO	Total	Rk	Off	Rk	Def	Rk	ST	Rk	Off AGL	Rk	Def AGL	Rk
2004	10-6	10.1	10.6	381	304	-9	24.4%	6	-3.6%	20	12.3%	25	1.3%	13	12.8	20	17.4	22
2005	13-3	11.7	11.7	395	258	+20	31.1%	2	25.5%	2	-8.5%	9	-2.9%	28	2.0	32	16.9	13
2006	9-7	8.4	7.0	319	305	0	-0.4%	15	-4.1%	20	-3.0%	12	0.7%	15	6.1	28	21.7	12
2007	7-9	5.7	7.3	320	409	+1	-1.1%	17	10.3%	8	7.0%	23	-4.4%	28	44.3	2	23.4	13
2008	8-8	6.2	7.0	370	448	-17	-6.5%	22	24.0%	2	24.7%	31	-5.8%	31	45.3	5	30.1	11

Strategic Tendencies

Run/Pass		Rank	Offense		Rank	Defense		Rank	Other		Rank
Runs, all plays	37%	31	3+ WR	66%	5	Rush 3	16.9%	3	2+ RB, Pct Runs	54%	26
Runs, first half	42%	24	4+ WR	14%	11	Rush 4	62.5%	19	1 RB/2 TE, Pct Runs	49%	20
Runs, first down	40%	32	2+ TE	25%	18	Rush 5	12.9%	29	1RB/3+WR, Pct Runs	30%	14
Runs, second-long	35%	23	Single back	72%	3	Rush 6+	7.7%	17	Zone Blitz	3%	18
Runs, power sit.	62%	23	Play action	19%	11	Rush 7+	1.7%	12	Go for it on 4th	0.72	30
Runs, behind 2H	26%	30	Max protect	11%	5	Sacks by LB	24.0%	11	Offensive Pace	29.0	3
Pass, ahead 2H	54%	2	Outside pocket	16%	7	Sacks by DB	4.0%	24	Defensive Pace	30.9	19

Denver lined up with three or more wideouts 50 percent more often than the year before, going from 28th in the league to fifth. ● Denver threw only 10 percent of passes to running backs; every other offense in the league was above 15 percent. ● Denver had 33.5% DVOA and 5.8 yards per carry on runs from single-back sets, compared to 2.8% DVOA and 3.4 yards per carry on runs with two backs. That was the largest yardage difference in the league, and the third largest DVOA difference. ● Maybe the 3-4 switch won't be so strange; Denver was the only 4-3 defense that rushed only three on more than eight percent of pass plays. ● Somewhat connected: Denver hurried the quarterback only nine percent of the time, the lowest figure in the league. ● Denver opponents used play-action on 23 percent of pass plays; only Cincinnati saw the play-fake more often. ● The Broncos had the league's worst DVOA against draws, giving up 7.7 yards per carry and 66.7% DVOA. ● Mike Shanahan was significantly less aggressive on fourth down than he had been in past seasons.

Passing

Player	DYAR	DVOA	Plays	NtYds	Avg	YAC	C%	TD	Int
Jay Cutler*	1380	22.0%	630	4530	7.2	4.7	62.9%	25	18
Kyle Orton	334	-0.9%	495	2875	5.8	5.0	58.9%	18	12

Rushing

Player	DYAR	DVOA	Plays	Yds	Avg	TD	Fum	Suc
Michael Pittman*	93	15.6%	76	320	4.2	4	0	57%
Peyton Hillis	151	41.0%	68	343	5.0	5	0	65%
Selvin Young*	40	9.4%	61	303	5.0	1	1	48%
Tatum Bell*	67	28.2%	44	249	5.7	2	0	48%
Jay Cutler*	16	-4.0%	40	215	5.4	2	2	--
Andre Hall*	2	-7.0%	35	152	4.3	0	2	54%
P.J. Pope*	52	57.7%	17	130	7.6	0	0	59%
Ryan Torain	21	21.6%	15	69	4.6	1	0	60%
Eddie Royal	36	21.1%	11	109	9.9	0	0	--
LaMont Jordan	113	22.2%	80	363	4.5	4	1	60%
Correll Buckhalter	69	11.0%	76	369	4.9	2	0	50%
Kyle Orton	-3	-15.4%	15	54	3.6	3	2	--

Receiving

Player	DYAR	DVOA	Plays	Ctch	Yds	Y/C	YAC	TD	C%
Brandon Marshall	85	-6.8%	181	104	1265	12.2	3.9	7	57%
Eddie Royal	115	-1.4%	129	91	980	10.8	3.8	5	71%
Brandon Stokley	47	-5.6%	85	49	525	10.7	3.4	4	58%
Darrell Jackson*	22	-0.1%	21	12	190	15.8	4.3	1	52%
Jabar Gaffney	42	-4.5%	65	38	468	12.3	3.1	2	58%
Tony Scheffler	123	22.1%	62	41	644	15.7	5.0	3	66%
Daniel Graham	48	6.7%	50	32	393	12.3	6.1	4	64%
Nate Jackson*	-17	-21.4%	17	11	84	7.6	3.2	1	65%
Peyton Hillis	82	55.7%	19	14	179	12.8	9.9	1	74%
Tatum Bell*	0	-13.2%	14	10	57	5.7	7.5	0	71%
Michael Pittman*	1	-12.2%	13	10	112	11.2	10.3	0	77%
Selvin Young*	-22	-60.2%	8	3	16	5.3	6.3	0	38%
Correll Buckhalter	153	62.1%	32	26	324	12.5	11.6	2	81%

Offensive Line

Year	Yards	ALY	Rank	Power	Rank	10+ Yds	Rank	Stuff	Rank	Sacks	ASR	Rank	False	Cont.
2006	4.44	4.14	18	63%	16	21%	7	17%	10	31	5.8%	9	17	33
2007	4.60	4.15	15	49%	32	23%	6	20%	23	32	5.9%	14	15	41
2008	4.96	4.78	1	70%	10	17%	17	14%	3	12	3.3%	4	11	48

Year	LE	Rank	LT	Rank	Mid	Rank	RT	Rank	RE	Rank
2006	2.55	30	3.96	23	4.55	6	4.36	10	3.41	24
2007	4.80	8	4.72	8	3.74	26	3.74	25	4.66	5
2008	5.84	1	4.89	5	4.51	5	4.31	11	5.20	2

The Denver offensive line had a phenomenal year in 2008, exhibiting superb blocking for both the run and the pass while ranking second behind New England in fewest false starts. Josh McDaniels has torn up the rest of the Denver roster, but smartly left the offensive line entirely intact: left tackle Ryan Clady, left guard Ben Hamilton, center Casey Weigmann, right guard Chris Kuper, and right tackle Ryan Harris will all return in 2009. Still, there are questions about this unit, starting with how their responsibilities and style will change in McDaniels' offense. Will they be as successful if McDaniels, as expected, uses less zone blocking than is traditional for the Broncos? Does the drafting of Knowshon Moreno make this a more run-heavy attack, or will they be as pass-heavy as the Broncos (and McDaniels' Patriots) were last year? And can Clady avoid the sophomore slump that hit other recent standout rookies at left tackle, such as Marcus McNeill and Joe Thomas? The Broncos also need to worry about depth: The same five linemen started all 16 games a year ago, and the backups have very little NFL experience except for former New England and Arizona tackle Brandon Gorin.

Defensive Front Seven

Defensive Line	Age	Pos	Plays	TmPct	Rk	Overall Stop	Dfts	Stop%	Rk	AvYd	Rk	Pass Rush Sack	Hit	Hur	vs. Run Runs	St%	Yds	vs. Pass Pass	St%	Yds
Ebenezer Ekuban*	33	DE	37	5.0%	50	24	8	65%	83	2.3	68	5.0	2	5	27	67%	3.0	10	60%	0.3
Marcus Thomas	23	DT	35	4.4%	47	26	2	74%	54	3.0	68	0.0	1	3	33	76%	2.9	2	50%	4.5
John Engelberger*	33	DE	30	4.1%	69	26	7	87%	11	1.7	44	1.0	0	5	27	89%	1.4	3	67%	4.0
Kenny Peterson	31	DE	25	3.2%	89	18	11	72%	61	2.4	74	3.0	7	3	19	68%	3.2	6	83%	0.0
Elvis Dumervil	25	DE	24	3.0%	90	19	10	79%	31	0.8	17	5.0	8	17	13	85%	2.4	11	73%	-1.0
Dewayne Robertson*	28	DT	22	3.0%	67	17	4	77%	36	1.4	14	1.5	2	1	20	75%	1.9	2	100%	-3.5
Ronald Fields	28	DT	19	2.3%	--	13	2	68%	--	3.0	--	0.0	1	0	18	72%	2.7	1	0%	9.0
Darrell Reid	27	DT	19	2.3%	--	16	5	84%	--	1.1	--	2.0	0	2	17	82%	1.9	2	100%	-6.0

Linebackers	Age	Pos	Plays	TmPct	Rk	Overall Stop	Dfts	Stop%	AvYd	Pass Rush Sack	Hit	Hur	vs. Run Runs	St%	Rk	Yds	Rk	vs. Pass Tgts	Suc%	Rk	AdjYd	Rk
Jamie Winborn	30	OLB	106	13.4%	31	64	15	60%	4.6	0.5	2	4	60	70%	24	3.5	53	36	49%	46	7.2	68
D.J. Williams	27	OLB	95	17.5%	8	53	19	56%	4.9	2.5	1	0	48	58%	80	4.1	80	38	48%	53	5.5	27
Nate Webster*	32	ILB	77	12.0%	45	48	11	62%	4.1	2.0	0	2	57	68%	33	2.9	26	22	59%	18	6.2	44
Wesley Woodyard	23	OLB	45	5.7%	--	21	9	47%	7.6	0.0	0	0	23	65%	--	5.1	--	13	41%	--	5.8	--
Boss Bailey*	30	OLB	39	13.2%	--	22	5	56%	5.7	0.0	1	0	13	77%	--	3.3	--	25	43%	65	8.9	88
Andra Davis	31	ILB	93	11.0%	57	53	11	57%	4.3	0.0	1	2	73	63%	56	3.5	51	17	42%	70	5.6	28

Year	Yards	ALY	Rank	Power	Rank	10+ Yds	Rank	Stuff	Rank	Sack	ASR	Rank
2006	4.18	4.36	22	76%	29	13%	5	17%	22	35	5.7%	27
2007	4.69	4.36	26	59%	12	21%	27	17%	24	33	6.1%	18
2008	5.12	4.26	22	63%	10	29%	32	17%	16	26	5.8%	19

Year	LE	Rank	LT	Rank	Mid	Rank	RT	Rank	RE	Rank
2006	4.95	27	4.54	20	4.34	18	4.04	14	3.65	12
2007	4.41	22	4.43	21	4.09	16	5.22	31	4.03	15
2008	3.82	12	4.48	23	4.41	24	4.52	25	3.74	14

Here's the weakest part of the team, and with the switch from 4-3 to 3-4, the unit with the most turmoil. The starting nose tackle will be Ronald Fields, a free agent signing who was a backup in San Francisco the last two years. Sure, Fields is supposed to be versatile, but an inability to crack the San Francisco defensive lineup isn't exactly a selling point. At defensive end will be some combination of two veteran holdovers, Marcus Thomas and Kenny Peterson, plus Ryan McBean, a 2007 fourth-round pick out of Oklahoma State who was cut by Pittsburgh after just one season and spent last year on Denver's practice squad. Last year's defensive ends are either gone (Ebenezer Ekuban, John Engelberger) or are being forced to outside linebacker by the move to a 3-4 scheme. Elvis Dumervil will probably start at right outside linebacker, and like Terrell Suggs in Mike Nolan's old Baltimore defense, he won't need to drop into coverage much. Denver's top two picks in the 2007 draft, Jarvis Moss and Tim Crowder, are also moving to outside linebacker, but word out of Denver says that the new administration isn't too fond of either player, with Xanders actually shopping Moss for a lowly seventh-round pick earlier this offseason. McDaniels and Nolan have their own new defensive end/outside linebacker, first-round pick Robert Ayers, and unlike Moss and Crowder he still has that fresh new-prospect smell. Some media reports have Ayers starting at outside linebacker, others at defensive end. The inside linebacker positions are a little more stable. D.J. Williams, who keeps getting jerked around from one linebacker position to another, is moving back inside again and playing 3-4 for the first time. He'll be joined by former Cleveland starter Andra Davis, signed in free agency.

Defensive Secondary

Secondary	Age	Pos	Plays	TmPct	Rk	Stop	Dfts	Yds	Rk	St%	Rk	Tgts	Tgt%	Rk	Dist	Suc%	Rk	AdjYd	Rk	Yds	PD	Int
						Overall			vs. Run								vs. Pass					
Marquand Manuel*	30	SS	84	10.6%	28	25	9	7.2	44	32%	62	39	9.2%	10	14.5	48%	52	9.9	63	10.0	4	0
Dre' Bly*	32	CB	70	8.9%	37	28	12	9.3	64	50%	28	91	21.7%	19	10.5	40%	80	8.6	69	8.5	9	2
Champ Bailey	31	CB	44	9.9%	--	18	7	11.2	--	39%	--	20	8.5%	--	11.0	45%	--	9.5	--	11.3	4	1
Josh Bell	25	CB	39	8.8%	39	14	5	2.4	1	75%	2	43	18.0%	42	14.5	46%	59	8.3	61	8.6	4	0
Karl Paymah*	27	CB	33	4.2%	--	8	6	10.3	--	25%	--	37	8.8%	--	9.7	43%	--	7.5	--	7.8	5	1
Marlon McCree*	32	FS	31	7.9%	--	8	4	9.3	--	35%	--	9	4.3%	--	13.8	20%	--	13.1	--	12.7	1	0
Josh Barrett	25	SS	21	7.1%	--	8	5	6.4	--	30%	--	12	7.6%	--	14.4	67%	--	5.4	--	5.5	3	1
Calvin Lowry	26	SS	20	3.7%	--	5	2	10.7	--	17%	--	4	1.4%	--	6.5	83%	--	3.1	--	3.8	1	0
Brian Dawkins	36	FS	81	10.3%	34	29	18	6.1	21	30%	66	33	7.4%	28	12.7	50%	47	8.8	54	8.9	5	1
Renaldo Hill	31	FS	79	10.2%	35	22	9	7.8	52	38%	47	38	7.6%	26	11.9	48%	54	8.2	48	8.2	4	3
Andre' Goodman	31	CB	57	7.4%	61	29	11	6.4	40	38%	51	92	18.6%	34	13.6	62%	8	6.3	22	6.4	21	5

Year	Pass D Rank	vs. #1 WR	Rk	vs. #2 WR	Rk	vs. Other WR	Rk	vs. TE	Rk	vs. RB	Rk
2006	10	-17.0%	5	-15.2%	7	-21.1%	5	2.1%	22	8.8%	23
2007	22	0.4%	15	-2.3%	14	6.6%	24	43.8%	32	-22.8%	3
2008	31	16.1%	24	25.2%	27	23.8%	30	31.9%	31	11.3%	23

The age of next year's Denver secondary is covered in the main essay, but let's talk about their individual talents. We're assuming that Champ Bailey still has his, despite last year's torn groin and the offseason surgery to repair torn elbow ligaments. Before he was hurt against the Patriots in Week 7, Bailey had much more Champ-like charting stats, allowing 5.7 yards per pass with a 64 percent Success Rate. He came back for the final two games in an attempt to halt Denver's slide out of playoff position, and boy, was it a mistake. During those two games we have him charted in coverage on six passes, all complete, all first downs, for an average of 18.2 yards.

Bailey's new partner at cornerback is Andre' Goodman, but it is hard not to think that last year's fabulous charting stats represented a career year at age 30. In 2007, Goodman had a 30 percent Success Rate as the Miami nickelback; in 2006 he ranked 15th in Success Rate but 65th in Yards per Pass, mixing generally good coverage with some monumental toastings. Other than the two starters, every other cornerback on the roster has one year of NFL experience or less. The nickelback will be second-rounder Alphonso Smith, a Wake Forest product who is short (5-foot-9) but has elite speed, instincts, and ball skills.

Veteran safeties Brian Dawkins and Renaldo Hill are certainly upgrades over Marlon McCree and Marquand Manuel, but again — there's nowhere to go but down for these guys. Dawkins' pass coverage has definitely fallen off with age, and too many of his run tackles last year came after first downs. Hill is now on his fourth team and has never been more than a league-average safety. Second-round pick Darcel McBath (Texas Tech) is a former cornerback who profiles as a free safety roaming centerfield; he's fast and reads quarterbacks well, but his smaller size (198 pounds) may make him a liability in run support and he has a habit of over-lunging and missing tackles.

Special Teams

Year	DVOA	Rank	FG/XP	Rank	Net Kick	Rank	Kick Ret	Rank	Net Punt	Rank	Punt Ret	Rank	Hidden	Rank
2006	0.7%	15	6.0	7	-0.1	20	-3.4	19	3.1	14	-1.7	17	-13.5	30
2007	-4.4%	28	1.9	13	-2.4	22	-14.7	31	-11.0	31	0.4	12	-8.4	27
2008	-5.8%	31	-12.2	32	-8.9	28	-7.3	26	-5.8	24	0.2	14	-7.6	24

Denver didn't just continue its secretly dismal record of special teams play in 2008; the Broncos took things to an all-new low, with the worst Broncos special teams in the 15 seasons for which we have play-by-play breakdown. The Broncos have ranked 20th or worse in special teams every year since 1999 with two exceptions: 2001 (ninth) and 2006 (15th). The word "secretly" shows why the Broncos never seem to worry about their poor special teams. Year after year of poor kickoffs and punts are masked by the effects of altitude, and this is compounded by the fact that the most visible part of special teams — field-goal kicking — happened to be the one area where the Broncos had a talented and reasonably consistent player.

Until last year, that is. With Jason Elam gone to Atlanta, Denver's placekicking value nosedived. Matt Prater seemed to have particular problems when the weather turned cold — he was 13-for-14 through Denver's Week 8 bye, but 12-for-20 in the final two months of the season. Prater was average on kickoffs, but the Broncos gave up 8.7 points worth of field position on returns, 30th ahead of only Arizona and Kansas City. Punt coverage was no better — Brett Kern was actually above average on gross punt value (3.1 points) but the Broncos gave up 6.9 points worth of returns, which ranked 28th. Denver's own returns were also mediocre, with an asterisk; rookie Eddie Royal was strong on kick returns but was so busy playing offense that he only returned about half the kickoffs. Rookie cornerback Alphonso Smith might share those responsibilities.

Does Josh McDaniels know there's a problem here? On one hand, Denver hired Mike Preifer as special teams coordinator, and his unit in Kansas City was subpar the past three years. Instead of signing an undrafted free agent to compete with Prater, they signed Tennessee punter Britton Colquitt (the "Eli Manning of punters") to compete with Kern, who wasn't a problem last season. On the other hand, Denver used a fourth-round pick on Notre Dame safety David Bruton, widely considered a special teams demon-in-the-making, and signed free agent Darrell Reid, who might have been the only strong special teams guy in Indianapolis.

Coaching Staff

Mike Nolan has been defensive coordinator for four different teams: the Giants from 1993-1996, the Redskins from 1997-1999, the Jets in 2000, and the Ravens from 2002-2004. Although his Redskins teams struggled (29th in defensive DVOA in 1998, 26th in 1999), his Jets team was sixth in defensive DVOA and his Ravens teams were all in the top four. Nolan stole his position coaches from around the division — Wayne Nunnely was coaching the San Diego defensive line, Don Martindale the Oakland linebackers. Nolan also brought Ed Donatell back to Denver as defensive backs coach; he held the same position a decade ago, and has the two Super Bowl rings to prove it.

Although you have to imagine that McDaniels is calling the plays and designing the offense, the official title of coordinator belongs to Mike McCoy, who was quarterbacks coach in Carolina the last two years. The two big holdovers from the Shanahan regime are the two men who have coached the successful Denver running game for the past decade: running back coach Bobby Turner and offensive line coach Rick Dennison.

Detroit Lions

The Lions weren't particularly good last year. You may have heard.

While they had the worst record in NFL history, they weren't the worst team. They had the second-worst DVOA of any team in the 15 seasons for which we've calculated DVOA, but they don't come close to the 2005 49ers, who won four games by a combined 15 points and lost the other 12 games by 204 (Table 1). Since the merger in 1970, there have been 32 teams whose Pythagorean winning percentage (as determined by their points scored and allowed) was below that of last year's Lions — including last year's Rams.

The variety of numbers needed to point out what the Lions did well last year, though, is a tribute to their futility. Their defense was ninth in the league in Adjusted Sack Rate. Their offensive line was 14th in the league on runs to right tackle, and fourth on runs to right end. They were the fifth-best team in the league when running the ball on third or fourth down. They also did solid work on special teams, with Jason Hanson leading the league in placekicking value and combining with the coverage units for the sixth-best kickoff performance in the league. It's just a shame they didn't get much practice.

It's also impractical to use the context of last year's team to discuss the 2009 Lions because 25 of the 53 players on the Week 1 roster a year ago aren't heading to Allen Park for training camp this year. Perhaps more importantly, the organizational culture that existed un-

der much-maligned general manager Matt Millen and coach Rod Marinelli has expired. Millen resigned during the season and Marinelli was fired in December, and while Martin Mayhew was hired from within to replace Millen, it is new head coach Jim Schwartz who has come to define the organization's identity.

While too easily labeled as the NFL's first "Moneyball" coach, Schwartz has a background in analytics and research that should appeal to readers of this tome. An economics major at Georgetown, Schwartz started off his career as a coaching assistant in Cleveland under Bill Belichick, where he conducted research on the year-to-year randomness of fumble recoveries that predated the existence of Football Outsiders (and our similar research) by a decade. Schwartz went on to become the defensive coordinator in Tennessee, where he rebuilt a defense that was taken apart by salary cap moves — twice. The Titans led the league in defensive DVOA in 2007 and were fifth a year ago.

Although Schwartz has consulted with us on projects in the past (as well as contributed a quote to the back cover of previous versions of this book), don't expect him to be quoting a player's DVOA when talking to the media. Schwartz isn't a mathematician who happens to be a football coach; he's a football coach who is comfortable using numbers, a film junkie who uses metrics to help make sense of what he sees on tape. Detroit fans won't get a coach who reduces players down to a number or a metric (nor should they), but one who knows when and how to

LIONS SUMMARY

2008 Record: 0-16

Pythagorean Wins: 2.8 (31st)

DVOA: -48.4% (30th)

Offense: -20.6% (30th)

Defense: 29.2% (32nd)

Special Teams: 1.4% (14th)

Variance: 19.3% (25th)

2008: The toughest, scrappiest 0-16 team you'll ever see concluded the Dark Ages of Detroit football.

2009: The Enlightenment arrives, but expecting a Dolphins or Falcons-esque revival is a little too much.

2009 Mean Projection: 5.8 wins

On the Clock (0-3): 16%

Loserville (4-6): 45%

Mediocrity (7-8): 24%

Playoff Contender (9-10): 12%

Super Bowl Contender (11+): 3%

Projected Average Opponent: 3.2% (8th)

2009 Lions Schedule

Week	Opp.	Week	Opp.	Week	Opp.
1	at NO	7	BYE	13	at CIN
2	MIN	8	STL	14	at BAL
3	WAS	9	at SEA	15	ARI
4	at CHI	10	at MIN	16	at SF
5	PIT	11	CLE	17	CHI
6	at GB	12	GB (Thu.)		

employ statistical analysis properly and effectively.

A good example is third down. Schwartz knows that a team's performance on third down has a disproportionate impact on their success relative to how they do on first and second down, so the Lions will spend more time in practice and film study breaking down both the plays they're likely to run on third down and likely to see the other team employ in those situations. He's aware that teams historically enjoy more success running the ball in third-and-short situations, so offensive coordinator Scott Linehan's play-calling will likely be tilted accordingly.

Schwartz's decision-making will be equally affected, though, by his experiences as a pro coach. As he initially struggled with rebuilding the Tennessee defense, Schwartz realized that all the scheming and analysis in the world was useless if it didn't fit the personnel he had in front of him. As a result, he began to construct his defenses with the primary goal of fitting the personnel he had in place. It seems like an odd thing to not take for granted, but one need only look at the defensive shift of the Chiefs this offseason to find a team that's attempting to make its players fit a desired scheme, not vice versa.

Last year, for example, Schwartz was blessed with a pair of elite pass rushers on the defensive line in Albert Haynesworth and Kyle Vanden Bosch, a group of linebackers who were excellent in coverage but weren't great blitzers, and a secondary that could do a little bit of everything. As a result, Tennessee rushed four 80.9 percent of the time, the second-highest percentage in the league, and played a lot of Cover-2. Only the Colts, another Cover-2 team, got fewer sacks than the Titans did from their linebackers.

Although long-time Chiefs coach Gunther Cunningham will be the defensive coordinator, Schwartz will obviously have a lot of say in what goes on in Detroit. The defense that he inherited and shaped this offseason is a polar opposite of what he had last year. The strength of the unit is at linebacker, where former Pro Bowler Julian Peterson and ex-Steelers middle linebacker Larry Foote were brought in to play alongside 2006 top-ten pick Ernie Sims. After playing in the Tampa-2 under Marinelli

for the first three years of his career, Sims will be expected to rush the passer and attack the line of scrimmage across from Peterson, while the stout Foote shores up the middle. With that group of linebackers joining promising pass-rushing end Clifford Avril, expect to see the Lions blitz five or six much more than frequently the Chiefs or the Titans did a year ago, throwing in some zone blitzes for good measure.

When Schwartz was interviewed after being hired, he mentioned that he wanted the Lions to be able to run the ball and stop the run. On the offensive side, his desire to build the team around an ability to run the ball would seemingly go against two different Football Outsiders precepts: In general, teams don't pass the ball frequently enough on first and second down, and they derive no benefit from "establishing the run" with carries early in the game. If that's what Schwartz means by being able to run the ball, he and Scott Linehan will oversee a very disappointing offense; what we believe Schwartz instead means is that he wants his team to be able to run the ball effectively in all situations, picking up chunks of yardage that push the Lions towards their next set of downs. Their success will weigh heavily on the performance of halfback Kevin Smith, who defied workload concerns and the general hindrances of playing for an 0-16 team to put together a relatively promising rookie season (-0.5% DVOA). Detroit has the makings of, at the very least, a competent offensive line, including center Dominic Raiola and tackles Jeff Backus and Gosder Cherilus. They'll receive help from first-round tight end Brandon Pettigrew, arguably the best blocking tight end to come out of college since Daniel Graham.

That desire to build around the running game, though, did not stop Detroit from taking Georgia quarterback Matthew Stafford with the first overall selection in the 2009 NFL Draft. After the successes of Matt Ryan and Joe Flacco a year ago, Stafford was said to be the franchise quarterback and face of the franchise the Lions desperately needed, with the right amount of leadership to go with a howitzer of an arm.

At Football Outsiders, we panned Stafford's selection at the top of the draft because of the findings of David

Table 1: Worst Teams of The DVOA Era

Year	Team	DVOA	Year	Team	DVOA
2005	SF	-56.6%	2003	ARI	-42.8%
2008	DET	-47.3%	2008	STL	-42.1%
2004	SF	-46.1%	2002	ARI	-41.9%
2000	ARI	-44.3%	1999	CLE	-41.7%
2000	CLE	-43.9%	2000	CIN	-41.7%

Table 2: Georgia QBs, First Three Seasons

Quarterback	Years	Cmp	Att	Cmp%	Yards	YPA
David Greene	2001-03	674	1141	59.1%	9020	7.91
Matthew Stafford	2006-08	564	987	57.1%	7731	7.83

Lewin and his Lewin Career Forecast, which discovered that completion percentage and games started were the only two indicators of any significance when attempting to project the NFL performance of college quarterbacks selected in the first two rounds. Stafford started 34 games in college, but only mustered a 57.1 completion percentage, placing him squarely alongside players like Patrick Ramsey, J.P. Losman, Shaun King, and for optimistic Lions fans, Ryan.

What's also worth noting in this case is that Stafford wasn't, by any means, a great quarterback in college. D.J. Shockley was the quarterback at Georgia the year before Stafford, but before him, David Greene was a four-year starter playing for the same coach as Stafford, Mark Richt, in the same scheme. Despite the fact that Greene was a third-round pick who was out of football by the end of the 2008 season, he managed to outperform Stafford when you compare the totals of each of their first three seasons at Georgia (Table 2). Greene went on to have a successful senior year, but Stafford came out as an undergraduate. It wouldn't be unprecedented for Stafford to succeed as a pro, but the numbers say that it's a risky proposition at best. If the Lions keep Stafford on the sidelines to start the season, veteran Daunte Culpepper and previous quarterback-of-the-future Drew Stanton will compete for the starting gig.

Whoever the Lions quarterback is will benefit from having the team's best player at wide receiver, Calvin "Megatron" Johnson, who emerged from an injury-riddled rookie season to take over games at times in 2008. In an offense that needed a hero, Johnson pulled off circus catches on a seemingly regular basis, and he certainly didn't benefit from having help around him. The Lions' passing DVOA was 9.1% on throws to Johnson and -16.4% on throws to everyone else; the resulting difference of 25.5% was the second-largest in football between a team's top receiver and his compadres, with only Carolina's Steve Smith standing out further. Factor in the difference between the running game of those two teams, and it's easy to suggest that Johnson was the most lonesome star in the league a year ago. Like Randy Moss, Johnson gives the Lions an opportunity to score on any pattern at any time against any coverage.

The Lions will win a game in 2009; likely, they'll win several. They don't profile as a team primed to enjoy a huge "miracle" season like Baltimore did a year ago, but the bar for success here isn't making the playoffs; it's merely looking like an organization that has some semblance of a clue. Whether this year's Lions win two, five, or eight games, the future is undoubtedly brighter in Detroit than it was one year ago.

Bill Barnwell

2008 Lions Stats by Week

Wk	vs.	W-L	PF	PA	YDF	YDA	TO	Total	Off	Def	ST
1	@ATL	L	21	34	316	474	-1	-74%	8%	82%	-1%
2	GB	L	25	48	311	447	-2	-39%	-12%	30%	3%
3	@SF	L	13	31	240	370	-2	-120%	-69%	52%	1%
4	BYE										
5	CHI	L	7	34	185	425	-1	-81%	-48%	37%	4%
6	@MIN	L	10	12	212	392	+2	7%	-14%	-16%	5%
7	@HOU	L	21	28	326	404	+1	-10%	2%	28%	16%
8	WAS	L	17	25	274	439	+1	-36%	-8%	13%	-16%
9	@CHI	L	23	27	333	320	-1	1%	2%	11%	10%
10	JAC	L	14	38	256	384	-1	-108%	-46%	49%	-13%
11	@CAR	L	22	31	316	366	-3	-43%	-12%	42%	11%
12	TB	L	20	38	207	252	0	-88%	-71%	1%	-15%
13	TEN	L	10	47	154	456	-2	-105%	-62%	32%	-10%
14	MIN	L	16	20	267	298	+2	-8%	-17%	-2%	7%
15	@IND	L	21	31	323	421	0	7%	11%	22%	18%
16	NO	L	7	42	255	532	-1	-85%	-21%	61%	-3%
17	@GB	L	21	31	316	484	-1	-22%	-1%	26%	5%

Trends and Splits

	Offense	Rank	Defense	Rank
Total DVOA	-20.6%	30	29.2%	32
Unadjusted VOA	-21.9%	31	30.4%	32
Weighted trend	-19.3%	30	24.8%	31
Variance	7.8%	22	5.4%	14
Average opponent	6.4%	7	0.5%	8
Passing	-16.7%	29	37.4%	32
Rushing	-13.4%	32	22.1%	31
First down	-18.2%	31	31.3%	32
Second down	-8.5%	23	26.4%	29
Third down	-43.5%	31	29.3%	31
First half	-19.9%	31	37.4%	32
Second half	-21.3%	29	19.6%	28
Red Zone	14.0%	9	36.9%	29
Late and close	-11.8%	25	13.1%	26

Five-Year Performance

Year	W-L	Pyth	Est W	PF	PA	TO	Total	Rk	Off	Rk	Def	Rk	ST	Rk	Off AGL	Rk	Def AGL	Rk
2004	6-10	6.4	7.7	296	350	+4	-9.0%	21	15.0%	10	-11.7%	5	-2.4%	25	24.6	12	7.8	30
2005	5-11	5.2	5.8	254	345	+1	-22.5%	27	-18.5%	29	-0.3%	19	-4.3%	32	7.3	25	29.8	5
2006	3-13	5.6	5.6	305	398	-9	-22.1%	31	-13.4%	28	11.4%	28	2.7%	6	12.5	23	14.9	14
2007	7-9	5.7	6.3	346	444	-1	-29.2%	30	-9.5%	24	16.7%	32	-3.0%	23	24.5	10	4.7	31
2008	0-16	2.8	2.3	268	517	-9	-48.4%	32	-20.6%	30	29.2%	32	1.4%	14	44.3	6	60.7	1

Strategic Tendencies

Run/Pass		Rank	Offense		Rank	Defense		Rank	Other		Rank
Runs, all plays	38%	28	3+ WR	46%	21	Rush 3	2.5%	25	2+ RB, Pct Runs	51%	27
Runs, first half	44%	18	4+ WR	13%	13	Rush 4	69.1%	10	1 RB/2 TE, Pct Runs	37%	28
Runs, first down	48%	20	2+ TE	22%	25	Rush 5	23.7%	13	1RB/3+WR, Pct Runs	17%	32
Runs, second-long	40%	12	Single back	43%	30	Rush 6+	4.7%	29	Zone Blitz	9%	3
Runs, power sit.	57%	28	Play action	12%	28	Rush 7+	1.0%	20	Go for it on 4th	0.93	15
Runs, behind 2H	31%	20	Max protect	9%	14	Sacks by LB	13.8%	19	Offensive Pace	32.5	28
Pass, ahead 2H	59%	1	Outside pocket	15%	8	Sacks by DB	3.4%	27	Defensive Pace	32.0	30

It's hard to run a ball-control offense when you are going 0-16. Although the Lions ranked 28th in situation-neutral pace, they were eighth in total pace (seconds per play). ● Don't make too much of the Lions' number-one rank in passing when ahead in the second half, because they weren't ahead in the second half very often. The Lions ran only 68 official plays with a second-half lead, and only nine with a second-half lead of more than a field goal. ● The Lions threw only nine percent of passes behind or at the line of scrimmage, the lowest percentage in the league. They threw only one screen pass on third-and-short (and it was a wide receiver screen). ● Detroit ranked 29th in DVOA on draw plays. ● Department of Blind Squirrels and Nuts: The Lions ranked eighth in DVOA with zero or one wide receiver in the formation. Green Bay was the only other team with a losing record that ranked in the top dozen of that category. ● Detroit faced four or more wide receivers on a league-low six percent of plays, although they had the league's worst DVOA against such formations. They also faced shotgun on a league-low 19 percent of plays, even though they ranked 30th in DVOA against shotgun and allowed a league-worst 9.0 yards per play.

Passing

Player	DYAR	DVOA	Plays	NtYds	Avg	YAC	C%	TD	Int
Dan Orlovsky*	198	0.3%	273	1552	5.7	4.4	56.5%	8	7
Jon Kitna*	-76	-19.9%	137	698	5.1	5.5	57.1%	5	5
Daunte Culpepper	-165	-32.0%	127	691	5.4	4.9	53.1%	4	6
Drew Stanton	-21	-27.6%	23	84	3.7	3.4	52.9%	1	0
Drew Henson*	-68	-304.8%	5	-4	-0.8	0.0	50.0%	0	0

Rushing

Player	DYAR	DVOA	Plays	Yds	Avg	TD	Fum	Suc
Kevin Smith	79	-0.5%	238	975	4.1	8	2	44%
Rudi Johnson*	-35	-21.3%	76	237	3.1	1	1	30%
Daunte Culpepper	-16	-34.5%	12	24	2.0	1	1	--
Jon Kitna*	14	34.4%	5	34	6.8	0	0	--
Aveion Cason	-2	-30.5%	4	7	1.8	0	0	0%
Dan Orlovsky	13	56.1%	4	30	7.5	0	0	--
Calvin Johnson	-28	-205.0%	3	-4	-1.3	0	1	--
Drew Stanton	0	-13.3%	3	20	6.7	0	0	--
Maurice Morris	38	-1.1%	132	577	4.4	0	1	45%

Receiving

Player	DYAR	DVOA	Plays	Ctch	Yds	Y/C	YAC	TD	C%
Calvin Johnson	256	9.1%	150	78	1331	17.1	6.3	13	52%
Shaun McDonald*	-55	-23.3%	66	35	339	9.7	1.9	2	53%
Mike Furrey*	-10	-16.7%	35	18	181	10.1	2.6	1	51%
John Standeford	-37	-26.6%	34	15	244	16.3	2.7	0	44%
Keary Colbert	-26	-25.2%	27	12	116	9.7	3.6	1	44%
Bryant Johnson	54	-3.7%	75	45	546	12.1	3.2	3	60%
Ronald Curry	-75	-33.0%	47	18	181	10.1	1.4	2	38%
Michael Gaines*	-22	-16.1%	36	23	260	11.3	3.8	1	64%
Casey FitzSimmons	-70	-44.1%	28	12	85	7.1	1.6	1	43%
John Owens*	-12	-20.7%	12	8	56	7.0	3.5	1	67%
Will Heller	-29	-69.0%	6	4	29	7.3	2.5	0	67%
Kevin Smith	15	-8.9%	54	39	286	7.3	6.8	1	72%
Rudi Johnson*	29	23.8%	14	12	88	7.3	6.6	1	86%
Jerome Felton	23	35.9%	9	9	53	5.9	4.4	0	100%
Moran Norris*	-13	-45.6%	7	4	16	4.0	2.0	0	57%
Maurice Morris	45	16.8%	27	19	136	7.2	6.3	2	70%
Terrelle Smith	-14	-46.9%	6	2	24	12.0	7.5	0	33%

Offensive Line

Year	Yards	ALY	Rank	Power	Rank	10+ Yds	Rank	Stuff	Rank	Sacks	ASR	Rank	False	Cont.
2006	3.62	3.59	32	37%	32	18%	11	25%	32	63	9.9%	30	33	22
2007	4.14	3.99	22	50%	29	20%	9	21%	25	54	8.3%	26	31	27
2008	3.81	3.47	31	71%	9	19%	12	24%	31	52	9.7%	32	22	21

Year	LE	Rank	LT	Rank	Mid	Rank	RT	Rank	RE	Rank
2006	3.51	23	3.89	25	3.73	29	4.08	18	2.84	30
2007	4.23	13	4.30	15	3.81	24	3.88	23	3.85	20
2008	2.14	31	3.84	22	2.83	32	4.23	12	4.65	4

Continuing our look at "Small Victories for the 2008 Detroit Lions," we congratulate left tackle Jeff Backus, who did not tie for the league lead in sacks allowed this year. Backus only allowed six, tied for sixth amongst all left tackles. Rookie right tackle Gosder Cherilus had four blown blocks leading to sacks, but he only started 13 games; former Broncos tackle George Foster started the other three and also ended up with four blown blocks. As former offensive coordinator Jim Colletto noted about Foster's level of play after benching him, "It's different than college." Gee, thanks Jim.

The interior of the line offered some respite. Ex-Cowboys backup Stephen Peterman showed enough promise in his two seasons as right guard to earn a five-year contract extension, but he has still a ways to go as a pass protector. While former Ravens starter Edwin Mulitalo was cut after the season, center Dominic Raiola was the line's best player, even with that Adjusted Line Yards figure for runs up the middle. The line's effectiveness when running for power, when combined with their struggles in getting stuffed, indicates that the problem was inconsistency, not necessarily talent. Damion Cook — he of the four-year gap between NFL games before last season — and project Manuel Ramirez will compete for the left guard spot. There's little depth behind them; the only linemen Detroit added in free agency were former Titans backup tackle Daniel Loper, who profiles as a guard at this level, and Redskins salary cap casualty Jon Jansen, who profiles as an "ESPN First Take" host at this age. Lydon Murtha, a seventh-round pick out of Nebraska, is huge (6-foot-7), but slow and can't stay on the field.

Defensive Front Seven

Defensive Line	Age	Pos	Plays	TmPct	Rk	Stop	Dfts	Stop%	Rk	AvYd	Rk	Sack	Hit	Hur	Runs	St%	Yds	Pass	St%	Yds
								Overall				Pass Rush			vs. Run			vs. Pass		
Dewayne White	30	DE	40	6.5%	27	27	13	68%	75	1.7	45	6.5	3	4	28	61%	3.3	12	83%	-1.8
Shaun Cody*	26	DT	39	4.8%	41	30	8	77%	39	1.6	20	0.0	3	4	35	74%	1.7	4	100%	0.8
Cory Redding*	29	DT	37	5.6%	29	25	14	68%	66	2.2	47	3.0	7	3	28	61%	3.4	9	89%	-1.4
Jared DeVries	33	DE	32	6.3%	37	27	7	84%	15	1.9	52	2.0	3	10	22	86%	2.0	10	80%	1.8
Chartric Darby	34	DT	31	4.0%	55	25	9	81%	18	1.7	25	1.5	1	1	27	81%	1.9	4	75%	0.8
Corey Smith*	30	DE	24	3.9%	72	20	14	83%	18	1.0	9	3.0	2	4	20	80%	1.2	4	100%	-5.5
Cliff Avril	23	DE	21	2.7%	--	15	12	71%	--	3.4	--	5.0	5	2	14	71%	5.3	7	71%	-0.3
Ikaika Alama-Francis	24	DE	21	3.2%	--	14	7	67%	--	1.9	--	1.0	0	2	13	85%	0.9	8	38%	3.5
Grady Jackson	36	DT	29	3.9%	57	24	8	83%	11	0.6	5	2.0	0	2	26	81%	1.2	3	100%	-4.7

Linebackers	Age	Pos	Plays	TmPct	Rk	Stop	Dfts	Stop%	AvYd	Sack	Hit	Hur	Runs	St%	Rk	Yds	Rk	Tgts	Suc%	Rk	AdjYd	Rk
					Overall					Pass Rush			vs. Run					vs. Pass				
Paris Lenon*	32	ILB	124	15.2%	20	63	16	51%	5.5	1.5	1	0	80	59%	78	3.7	62	30	60%	15	5.5	25
Ernie Sims	25	OLB	114	14.0%	27	51	19	45%	5.8	1.0	0	0	60	60%	73	4.3	89	44	44%	64	6.1	42
Ryan Nece*	30	OLB	61	7.5%	89	31	9	51%	5.0	1.5	0	0	39	56%	88	4.4	93	22	36%	83	6.8	56
Alex Lewis	28	OLB	21	3.7%	--	12	1	57%	4.8	0.0	0	0	18	67%	--	4.5	--	3	29%	--	35.3	--
Julian Peterson	31	OLB	90	10.5%	65	57	17	63%	4.3	5.0	4	13	52	65%	45	4.3	87	25	56%	33	5.5	26
Larry Foote	29	ILB	65	8.2%	81	48	10	74%	3.0	1.5	3	8	43	86%	2	2.4	12	20	40%	74	6.0	38

Year	Yards	ALY	Rank	Power	Rank	10+ Yds	Rank	Stuff	Rank	Sack	ASR	Rank
2006	4.23	4.43	23	71%	27	16%	15	16%	26	30	5.8%	24
2007	4.59	4.26	23	67%	22	21%	26	20%	16	37	6.3%	16
2008	5.38	4.57	29	72%	25	28%	31	19%	12	30	6.9%	11

Year	LE	Rank	LT	Rank	Mid	Rank	RT	Rank	RE	Rank
2006	3.79	14	5.52	32	4.53	22	3.97	12	4.40	21
2007	4.02	16	4.38	18	4.99	32	4.19	19	3.66	9
2008	4.09	14	5.07	30	5.01	32	3.86	12	4.34	23

Detroit's best positional grouping is at linebacker, where former first-round pick Ernie Sims toiled on the weak side a year ago. The Lions will move him and strongside backer Julian Peterson around to create confusion amongst the opposing offensive line, but unless Sims suddenly emerges as a great pass-rusher, opponents' collective reaction might be boredom. Sims has exactly three career sacks as a pro, and while Peterson had 10 sacks in each of his first two years in Seattle, he only had five a year ago. Detroit brought in Larry Foote on a one-year deal to man the middle; while it seems like a real coup to get a 29-year-old starting middle linebacker from the best defense in the league, Foote's played in the 3-4 his entire career, and the track record of Steelers linebackers heading elsewhere isn't great, so color us slightly skeptical. Jordan Dizon will be the primary backup; new defensive coordinator Gunther Cunningham said in May that he gets Dizon and Peterson confused when he sees the former on film, which is strange, because we didn't think it was appropriate for defensive coordinators to serve as player agents. Third-round pick DeAndre Levy also figures in the mix as a run-plugging outside linebacker.

The Lions' defensive line has, to put it nicely, a few question marks. The trade of Cory Redding left little on the interior, so the organization signed Grady Jackson to a one-year deal. Jackson's been remarkably healthy for a defensive lineman who turned 36 in January, perhaps owing to his late start in the league — Jackson didn't make it until he was 25. Chartric "Chuck" Darby starts at the other tackle spot, although it wouldn't be a surprise to see the promising Andre Fluellen take the job over at some point. Fluellen should interest Jim Schwartz in every way: A former converted end, he has excellent speed and agility on the interior, but struggles with motivation and consistency. It'll be up to the new coaching staff to get the most out of him.

The same sort of situation exists at end, where incumbents Jared DeVries and DeWayne White should be pushed out of jobs by young bucks Ikaika Alama-Francis and Clifford Avril. Avril was particularly impressive a year ago, standing out as arguably the best player on the worst defense in football at the end of the season. He's just a good situational pass rusher with some upside, but for a team that wasn't showing anything by the end of the year, Avril was the faintest glimmer of hope. He should be an integral part of the Lions' blitz packages.

Defensive Secondary

Secondary	Age	Pos	Plays	TmPct	Rk	Overall Stop	Dfts	vs. Run Yds	Rk	St%	Rk	Tgts	Tgt%	Rk	vs. Pass Dist	Suc%	Rk	AdjYd	Rk	Yds	PD	Int
Leigh Bodden*	28	CB	85	10.4%	16	22	11	10.8	73	12%	79	84	22.6%	14	13.4	38%	81	9.6	82	9.9	12	1
Travis Fisher*	30	CB	40	5.6%	--	14	2	6.8	--	50%	--	36	11.1%	--	10.7	42%	--	9.1	--	9.5	5	0
Brian Kelly*	33	CB	26	4.6%	--	8	2	5.8	--	50%	--	37	14.5%	--	12.5	34%	--	11.2	--	11.5	1	0
Daniel Bullocks	25	SS	94	11.5%	21	15	6	8.5	66	23%	68	18	4.9%	68	14.1	42%	70	12.5	74	12.6	1	0
Kalvin Pearson	31	SS	75	9.2%	50	34	13	6.5	32	57%	10	26	6.9%	38	11.9	57%	24	7.3	23	7.6	2	0
Dwight Smith*	31	FS	41	8.0%	59	14	3	10.0	71	40%	41	10	4.3%	71	9.3	35%	77	8.0	46	8.7	1	0
Phillip Buchanon	29	CB	58	7.7%	57	16	7	12.3	75	31%	64	72	18.5%	35	11.4	42%	74	7.3	38	7.8	6	2
Anthony Henry	33	CB	55	7.2%	63	17	6	7.3	50	25%	74	69	16.2%	56	11.9	43%	72	8.7	72	8.5	7	1

Year	Pass D Rank	vs. #1 WR	Rk	vs. #2 WR	Rk	vs. Other WR	Rk	vs. TE	Rk	vs. RB	Rk
2006	30	-22.2%	3	34.5%	32	31.9%	31	15.6%	28	8.3%	22
2007	31	15.0%	25	20.4%	26	0.6%	20	0.8%	9	36.4%	32
2008	32	41.3%	32	43.8%	31	22.3%	28	38.2%	32	-3.1%	10

Lions fans, did you despise last year's secondary? Good news: They're not coming back. The starting corners at the end of the season, Leigh Bodden and Travis Fisher, were both released in the offseason, as was strong safety Dwight Smith. Free safety Daniel Bullocks — the lone holdover — is likely moving to strong safety to mask his coverage issues.

The new guys all have the potential to be useful in their own different ways. The cream of the crop is rookie free safety Louis Delmas, chosen by the Lions with the first pick in the second round. While Delmas is undersized, he does everything you'd want a safety to do; he's great against the run, is effective against the pass even in man coverage, has great instincts and ball skills, is a huge hitter, and will be a defensive leader. When you read an article in *Sports Illustrated* in 2010 about the new Lions and their defensive swagger, Delmas will be the cover boy.

The primary cornerback should be Anthony Henry, acquired from the Cowboys in the Jon Kitna deal. Henry struggled last year and there was talk of moving him to free safety, but he's a serviceable corner, if an undersized one. Across from him will be Philip Buchanon, who had worn out his welcome in Tampa Bay and rode the shuttle up north without realizing that Rod Marinelli had left. Buchanon is an effective corner when he wants to be, but again, the coaching staff will have to massage the best out of him. The alternative would be former Titans dime corner Eric King, who came over with Schwartz in the offseason. King's a good contributor on coverage units, but he's not much more than a stopgap corner.

Special Teams

Year	DVOA	Rank	FG/XP	Rank	Net Kick	Rank	Kick Ret	Rank	Net Punt	Rank	Punt Ret	Rank	Hidden	Rank
2006	2.7%	6	7.7	6	5.9	10	-3.5	21	4.0	13	1.5	12	-6.8	24
2007	-3.0%	23	0.7	17	-15.8	30	-4.1	22	4.4	11	-2.6	19	9.7	7
2008	1.4%	14	10.7	1	7.7	6	-13.2	32	7.2	9	-4.4	27	-5.4	20

For all that Detroit had going against them last year, they did have very effective coverage units. Jason Hanson and Nick Harris were only about average on kickoffs and punts, respectively, but the coverage units were responsible for nearly eight points of field position on kickoffs and six on punts. If you want a scapegoat for Detroit having the worst kickoff returns in football, look at Brandon Middleton. He cost the Lions more than ten points of field position over 38 kicks, with Detroit's other return men combining for -3 points on 40 kicks. He fumbled three returns and muffed another. He had five returns of 15 yards or less, and 14 of less than 20 yards. He had exactly one return that went beyond 40 yards. He mercifully lost his job after fumbling in three consecutive weeks, and should not be allowed on an NFL field again without some sort of pass around his neck. Third-round pick Derrick Williams should step in immediately on kickoffs, with fifth-rounder Aaron Brown as the longshot, while either Williams or Buchanon will be the punt returner.

Hanson is a good kicker, but his season leading the league in field-goal value was a fluke. He missed only one kick all year and hit all eight of his attempts from 50-plus yards despite being 33-of-67 over the first 16 seasons of his career.

Coaching Staff

It's rare for a rookie head coach to have two coordinators with NFL head coaching experience, but that's exactly what Schwartz has in Scott Linehan (offense) and Gunther Cunningham (defense). Linehan will build the team around a power running approach while moving away from the zone blocking scheme that Detroit employed in 2008. Detroit's commitment to the run might surprise those readers who know Schwartz as perhaps the most Football Outsiders-friendly coach in the NFL; after all, our Web site was built on refuting the "run to win" premise. However, the idea that "establishing the run" is unnecessary sometimes obscures a broader, more obvious point: When a team can pick up first downs consistently and effectively, it doesn't matter how they get there. Expect to see a lot of Calvin Johnson getting down the field off of play-action.

As mentioned earlier, the 4-3 that the team runs under Cunningham will not be similar to the Tampa-2 scheme that Marinelli brought to town. The team will diversify its looks and the responsibilities of the defensive linemen, and even shift into something close to a 3-4 situationally. While Schwartz rarely blitzed in Tennessee, the presence of Albert Haynesworth and Kyle Vanden Bosch meant that he didn't have to; without those impact players on the line, Schwartz will pressure the quarterback with more aggressive blitz packages. The corners will play man coverage more frequently than Detroit's corners did a year ago, but these guys were all playing somewhere else, so they won't know any better.

Green Bay Packers

As we've discussed in numerous essays and articles in the past, some facets of football can and should be chalked up primarily to luck. Important things, too; things like fumble recovery rates and field goal accuracy of opponents, aspects of the game that can directly yield wins and losses, make careers, and cost people their jobs. It seems unfair and almost insulting to say that the efforts of 53 players and millions of dollars of investment can be subject to such randomness, but it's the truth.

Luck is the word that repeatedly comes up, for better or worse, when analyzing the 2008 Packers. It's extremely hard for a team to go 0-7 in games decided by four points or less; only two teams have done it in the past 25 years, and these two teams (the 1994 Panthers and the 2001 Titans) improved their record by a combined 11 games in the subsequent season. There's a 0.04 (virtually nonexistent) correlation between a team's performance in such close games from year-to-year, so this had nothing to do with some mantra about the Packers "knowing how to win." It was a mix of bad luck, bad play, and poor timing.

The Packers couldn't give away wins fast enough in close games. Standard-issue unlucky teams lose on last-second field goals, but the Packers were no ordinary team. They lost to the Titans when Rob Bironas got a second chance at a game-winning field goal

in overtime. Up three with time running out against Carolina, Green Bay let Steve Smith get open deep for a 54-yard pass play that set up a game-winning DeAngelo Williams plunge. They didn't even take other teams' largesse; when the Bears gave the Packers the ball inside their territory thanks to a kickoff penalty with three minutes left in a tied Week 16 game, Green Bay drove into field goal range and promptly had their shot at a game-winning field goal blocked. Needless to say, they lost in overtime. According to DVOA, Green Bay's defense was ninth-best in the league through the first three quarters of the game, but 25th in the fourth quarter.

The fact that the Packers were able to actually make it to six wins with such ineptitude at the end of games is pretty remarkable. Because of the underlying performance that drove the team to those six wins and those close losses, virtually every advanced metric you can name pegs last year's Packers team as far superior to your standard 6-10 fare. For one, DVOA says that the 2008 Packers were the best 6-10 team over the 15 seasons that constitute the "DVOA Era" (Table 1). Only one team that went 6-10 with a positive DVOA had a losing record the following season. Both our estimated wins metric and the Pythagorean projection derived from the Packers' points scored and against indicate a team that should have been closer to 9-7, not 6-10.

PACKERS SUMMARY

2008 Record: 6-10

Pythagorean Wins: 8.9 (15th)

DVOA: 10.6% (11th)

Offense: 12.3% (12th)

Defense: 1.4% (12th)

Special Teams: -0.3% (20th)

Variance: 13.6% (10th)

2008: Everything breaks bad and, amazingly, no one blames it on the departure of Brett Favre.

2009: The luck should even out, but the underlying performance won't be as strong.

2009 Mean Projection: 7.4 wins

On the Clock (0-3): 9%

Loserville (4-6): 29%

Mediocrity (7-8): 24%

Playoff Contender (9-10): 24%

Super Bowl Contender (11+): 14%

Projected Average Opponent: 1.6% (13th)

2009 Packers Schedule

Week	Opp.	Week	Opp.	Week	Opp.
1	CHI	7	at CLE	13	BAL (Mon.)
2	CIN	8	MIN	14	at CHI
3	at STL	9	at TB	15	at PIT
4	at MIN (Mon.)	10	DAL	16	SEA
5	BYE	11	SF	17	at ARI
6	DET	12	at DET (Thu.)		

While the Pythagorean projection system has been proven in the past to be a reliable indicator across multiple sports, it's literally a "dumb" projection system; while it has points scored and points against, it doesn't know the nature of how the points were scored. In this case, it doesn't factor in the one way in which the Packers were actually lucky — in a good way — in 2008: defensive points scored.

Through ten games last year, the Packers' defense had scored 42 points. It was a remarkable total: only eight teams since 1995 have recorded that many points in a whole season, let alone in ten games. Team members and journalists attributed the high total to the dangerous nature of the defensive backs, all of whom were capable of taking a turnover to the house at a moment's notice. In reality, it was a confluence of opportunity (high interception totals) and sheer luck.

The average defense from 1995 through 2007 contributed 16 points per season, by way of safeties and returns of either interceptions or fumbles. Remarkably, when we looked at the top 50 and the bottom 50 scoring defenses over the timeframe, the two subsets of teams scored just about an equal amount of points on defense in the season after (Table 2). Those top 50 teams saw their Pythagorean projection drop from 9.0 wins in the year when they scored all the defensive points to 7.9 in the following season. While DVOA

Table 1: Best 6-10 Teams of the DVOA Era

Year	Team	DVOA	DVOA Y+1	W-L Y+1
2008	GB	10.6%	--	--
1999	DEN	8.9%	18.8%	11-5
2003	NYJ	4.0%	27.5%	10-6
1997	DAL	3.7%	14.6%	10-6
2002	JAC	1.1%	1.3%	5-11
1999	PIT	1.1%	24.1%	9-7
2000	SF	0.3%	21.9%	12-4
2001	KC	-0.5%	25.4%	8-8
2006	MIA	-0.8%	-22.2%	1-15
1998	BAL	-0.9%	8.2%	8-8

accounts for the unlikelihood of the defensive points when projecting the 2009 Packers, neither Pythagoras nor the expectations of the fans and media do. It's very likely that this year's team won't make it to 419 points, and even more likely that the reason why won't have anything to do with the play of the offense.

The second-half collapse of the Packers defense led to the arrival of defensive coordinator Dom Capers, who spent last year as a positional coach in New England. As part of Capers' agreement when joining the team, Green Bay will move to a 3-4 defense in 2009, shifting star defensive end Aaron Kampman to outside linebacker in the process. It's impossible to say at this juncture whether the scheme change will be successful or not, but we can say with some authority that switching schemes is no panacea.

Since 1995, 30 teams have shifted out of the 3-4, 4-3, or Tampa-2 as their primary set and into one of the other two options. Those 30 teams had an average defensive DVOA of 1.2% in the season before their switch; in the season after, their DVOA improved to -0.3% (Table 3). However, that's not particularly impressive when we compare the group to a control set — teams that had a similar performance and didn't change schemes. For each team, we calculated the same values for any team that had a defensive DVOA within 1.5 percentage points, on either side, of the scheme-changing team the year before the switch. For example, the control group for the 2005 Jets and their 9.7% DVOA consisted of all teams with a defensive DVOA ranging from 8.2% to 11.2%.

In many cases, the shift in performance for the team changing scheme mirrored that of the control set; 24 of the 30 teams that changed scheme saw the difference in their defensive DVOA from year-to-year parrot that of the unchanged team. Seventeen of the 30 teams saw an improvement superior to that of the average improvement or decline of their comparable teams. However, if we look at teams that had a defensive DVOA between 2.7% and -0.7% — within 1.5 percentage points on either side of that 1.2% average figure we mentioned for the scheme-changing teams — the difference in performance between the average team that changes their scheme and the comparable team that doesn't is virtually negligible; three-tenths of a percentage point.

You'll also note a column in Table 3 that lists each subset's defensive DVOA in their first four games. Teams that switch schemes struggle over the first quarter of the season, with an average defensive DVOA worse than both their performance a year ago and their performance over the rest of the season. It makes sense that teams undergoing a change in scheme would struggle at first, as players miss assign-

Table 2: The Myth of the Scoring Defense

	Def Points	Year After	Difference	Points For	Year After	Difference
Top 50	35.0	14.8	-20.2	359.2	340.0	-19.2
Bottom 50	2.4	14.2	11.8	313.1	317.1	4.0

ments and spend more time thinking about what to do than actually just doing what they're supposed to do. The Packers play likely improved offenses in Chicago, Cincinnati, St. Louis, and Minnesota before their Week 5 bye. Expect the Packers to head into that bye with some questions being raised about their defensive play, and then expect them to come out of it an improved D.

The offense isn't undergoing as dramatic of a shift, but after the struggles of Ryan Grant on the ground in 2008, the team is moving away from the zone-blocking scheme they implemented several seasons ago and replacing it with man-on-man principles, which require larger blockers while allowing for more flexibility in the types of run plays and backs that can be employed. Unlike in previous seasons, when the team would seemingly rotate their three interior linemen around to different spots on the line every week depending upon who was healthy, the team has also made it a priority to assign players to specific spots and keep them there. This would be a much more reasonable statement if the Packers had, say, the offensive line of the Giants, but Green Bay's linemen are undersized and not particularly prone to being healthy. While the departure of right tackle Mark Tauscher will eliminate some of those health issues, he's also one of the team's better linemen when he's healthy, and the lack of an obvious replacement makes it likely that the team will have to experiment with multiple starters at that spot in 2009. It should also be noted that the running game was significantly better with fullback Korey Hall in the lineup; Hall should be around for all 16 games this season and may be joined by former LSU fullback Quinn Johnson in the team's "Full House" two-fullback set.

While the endless chatter before the campaign regarded quarterback Aaron Rodgers, he acquitted himself well in his first year as a starter. He was particularly impressive in the red zone, where his 44.8%

DVOA was third-best in the league (minimum: 50 attempts), behind only Peyton Manning and Chad Pennington. While his primary target outside the red zone was emerging star Greg Jennings, he successfully spread the ball out inside the 20 to receivers like Donald Lee (64.6% DVOA in the red zone), Donald Driver (34.5%), Jordy Nelson (48.3%), and Ryan Grant (100.3%). You often hear about quarterbacks developing a rapport with receivers (and Rodgers had done just that with Jennings), but Jennings and Driver work as well together as any two receivers in the league with regards to setting up their patterns and their cuts with similar depth and style. Nelson, meanwhile, could emerge as a key part of the offense as soon as this year; he has significant potential as a slot receiver and third-down threat for Rodgers, filling the same role that Steve Smith fills for the Giants.

Our projection for Green Bay is not as sanguine as it was a year ago, despite the ascension of Rodgers and the bad luck that befell Green Bay in 2008. The move to the 3-4 isn't a good short-term indicator of success, and while our system doesn't know it, Kampman is so frustrated by the switch that he has stopped talking to the media. The chances aren't good that Driver (age) and Jennings (injury) will make it through 32 games again. Both want new contracts. The offensive line is in disarray. The cornerbacks are old.

For Green Bay to return to the playoffs this year, an average amount of luck might not be enough.

Bill Barnwell

Table 3: Whither the Scheme Change?

	Defensive DVOA		
	Previous Year	First 4 Games	Full Season
Changed Schemes	1.2%	3.1%	-0.3%
Didn't Change Schemes	1.2%	0.9%	0.0%

2008 Packers Stats by Week

Wk	vs.	W-L	PF	PA	YDF	YDA	TO	Total	Off	Def	ST
1	MIN	W	24	19	317	355	+1	43%	42%	17%	18%
2	@DET	W	48	25	447	311	+2	-8%	-8%	-3%	-3%
3	DAL	L	16	27	334	453	+1	33%	20%	-9%	4%
4	@TB	L	21	30	181	327	-1	-44%	-51%	-16%	-10%
5	ATL	L	24	27	408	370	0	32%	41%	14%	4%
6	@SEA	W	27	17	313	177	+1	28%	0%	-23%	5%
7	IND	W	34	14	302	302	+2	67%	39%	-40%	-12%
8	BYE										
9	@TEN	L	16	19	390	347	-2	29%	24%	2%	7%
10	@MIN	L	27	28	361	184	+3	10%	-18%	-11%	16%
11	CHI	W	37	3	427	234	0	53%	49%	0%	3%
12	@NO	L	29	51	343	416	-2	-73%	-10%	47%	-15%
13	CAR	L	31	35	438	298	-1	8%	26%	14%	-4%
14	HOU	L	21	24	387	549	+3	13%	22%	12%	4%
15	@JAC	L	16	20	338	323	-1	-40%	-14%	30%	4%
16	@CHI	L	17	20	325	210	0	5%	13%	-22%	-29%
17	DET	W	31	21	484	316	+1	10%	20%	14%	4%

Trends and Splits

	Offense	Rank	Defense	Rank
Total DVOA	12.3%	12	1.4%	12
Unadjusted VOA	12.1%	9	2.7%	14
Weighted trend	13.1%	10	3.5%	13
Variance	7.4%	20	4.8%	8
Average opponent	3.6%	16	4.6%	14
Passing	28.8%	10	-8.2%	7
Rushing	4.3%	17	11.2%	28
First down	9.7%	11	-2.8%	12
Second down	-3.7%	22	0.6%	10
Third down	41.3%	2	10.0%	20
First half	20.0%	4	2.5%	15
Second half	4.1%	20	0.5%	11
Red Zone	25.7%	5	-1.3%	16
Late and close	8.6%	19	10.3%	25

Five-Year Performance

Year	W-L	Pyth	Est W	PF	PA	TO	Total	Rk	Off	Rk	Def	Rk	ST	Rk	Off AGL	Rk	Def AGL	Rk
2004	10-6	9.0	8.4	424	380	-14	2.9%	13	18.3%	6	16.4%	29	0.9%	14	14.9	18	9.1	28
2005	4-12	6.7	6.0	298	344	-24	-11.0%	21	-5.2%	16	2.0%	21	-3.8%	30	34.7	3	5.4	31
2006	8-8	6.2	7.7	301	366	0	-2.4%	18	-4.1%	19	-5.6%	11	-3.9%	29	22.8	11	10.3	20
2007	13-3	11.5	11.1	435	291	+4	19.9%	6	16.8%	5	-0.6%	16	2.5%	8	7.6	31	17.1	21
2008	6-10	8.9	8.9	419	380	+7	10.6%	11	12.3%	12	1.4%	12	-0.3%	20	12.5	27	37.2	7

Strategic Tendencies

Run/Pass		Rank	Offense		Rank	Defense		Rank	Other		Rank
Runs, all plays	42%	18	3+ WR	54%	13	Rush 3	1.4%	30	2+ RB, Pct Runs	64%	11
Runs, first half	43%	19	4+ WR	15%	7	Rush 4	75.8%	3	1 RB/2 TE, Pct Runs	41%	27
Runs, first down	51%	14	2+ TE	23%	22	Rush 5	15.6%	25	1RB/3+WR, Pct Runs	20%	27
Runs, second-long	39%	16	Single back	45%	25	Rush 6+	7.1%	20	Zone Blitz	2%	26
Runs, power sit.	65%	20	Play action	17%	17	Rush 7+	0.7%	26	Go for it on 4th	1.01	13
Runs, behind 2H	31%	21	Max protect	9%	10	Sacks by LB	18.5%	15	Offensive Pace	31.4	22
Pass, ahead 2H	45%	13	Outside pocket	18%	2	Sacks by DB	11.1%	9	Defensive Pace	30.7	15

We're not kidding about Ryan Grant missing fullback Korey Hall; the Packers had -14.9% rushing DVOA with one back in the formation but 0.9% DVOA with two or three backs, the second-largest gap behind Miami. 76 percent of Green Bay's running back carries came with at least two backs in the formation, the highest percentage in the league. ● Green Bay ranked third in DVOA on passes past the line of scrimmage, but 29th on passes thrown to receivers at or before the line of scrimmage. ● The Packers were 26th with just 4.4 average yards after catch after leading the NFL with an average of 5.7 yards after catch in 2007. ● Green Bay's defense had the best DVOA in the league against passes thrown to the middle of the field. ● The Packers are not falling for your play-action fake: They ranked second in DVOA against play-action (-33.1% DVOA) but 11th against passes and scrambles without a play fake (2.3% DVOA). ● Opposing running backs averaged 3.6 yards and -9.0% DVOA against the Packers when there were two backs in the formation, but a league-leading 5.6 yards and 27.3% DVOA in one-back sets. The Packers hope their new 3-4 helps the linebackers do a better job of containing the run when the offense spreads the field, but don't count on it — the team with the second-biggest gap was New England, whose 3-4 is similar to what Green Bay will run this year.

Passing

Player	DYAR	DVOA	Plays	NtYds	Avg	YAC	C%	TD	Int
Aaron Rodgers	932	14.8%	571	3807	6.7	4.4	64.5%	28	13
Matt Flynn	-15	-57.4%	5	6	1.2	1.5	40.0%	0	0

Rushing

Player	DYAR	DVOA	Plays	Yds	Avg	TD	Fum	Suc
Ryan Grant	-19	-10.1%	312	1204	3.9	4	4	46%
Brandon Jackson	62	25.3%	45	248	5.5	1	1	51%
Aaron Rodgers	73	16.3%	42	211	5.0	4	0	--
DeShawn Wynn	32	85.2%	8	110	13.8	1	0	63%
John Kuhn	1	-7.6%	8	10	1.3	1	0	63%

Receiving

Player	DYAR	DVOA	Plays	Ctch	Yds	Y/C	YAC	TD	C%
Greg Jennings	243	9.6%	140	80	1291	16.1	4.2	9	57%
Donald Driver	185	7.6%	116	74	1012	13.7	4.7	5	64%
Jordy Nelson	41	-2.6%	54	33	366	11.1	2.7	2	61%
James Jones	73	18.2%	30	20	274	13.7	3.1	1	67%
Ruvell Martin	6	-9.8%	26	15	149	9.9	2.9	1	58%
Donald Lee	26	1.0%	50	39	303	7.8	2.8	5	78%
Tory Humphrey	33	22.1%	16	11	162	14.7	7.6	0	69%
Jermichael Finley	-13	-21.8%	12	6	74	12.3	2.5	1	50%
Brandon Jackson	1	-13.2%	39	30	185	6.2	6.5	0	77%
Ryan Grant	16	1.1%	22	18	116	6.4	8.3	1	82%
Korey Hall	30	50.6%	7	7	38	5.4	2.9	1	100%
John Kuhn	21	34.5%	7	4	21	5.3	3.5	2	57%

Offensive Line

Year	Yards	ALY	Rank	Power	Rank	10+ Yds	Rank	Stuff	Rank	Sacks	ASR	Rank	False	Cont.
2006	4.11	4.16	16	63%	18	15%	19	18%	12	24	3.8%	3	22	30
2007	4.47	3.85	26	50%	30	27%	3	21%	24	19	3.2%	1	13	29
2008	4.25	4.09	17	74%	7	21%	9	20%	23	34	6.0%	14	16	30

Year	LE	Rank	LT	Rank	Mid	Rank	RT	Rank	RE	Rank
2006	4.58	5	4.73	7	3.90	26	4.10	16	3.36	26
2007	3.94	18	3.92	22	3.98	18	4.14	16	3.36	28
2008	4.97	7	4.30	12	4.25	13	3.57	28	3.18	28

Green Bay's Adjusted Line Yards figures are very interesting when you consider that they run outside of the guards 71 percent of the time, more than any team in football. That fits with the zone-blocking scheme that the Packers were running, but things are changing for the 2009 season. Green Bay will integrate man-blocking back into the offensive scheme this year, and it may affect who gets to play and where. The Packers have spent years rotating their young linemen in and out of different spots on the line, but the organization has decided that it wants stability.

To begin, right tackle Mark Tauscher is gone. Tauscher was worn down by wear-and-tear before tearing his ACL in Week 14 and going on IR. As of mid-June, he remained a free agent. There's a relative smorgasbord of guys with different red flags who could potentially replace him at right tackle, including Tony Moll (not particularly good, only 285 pounds), Breno Giacomini (extremely raw, one NFL game to his credit), T.J. Lang (fourth-round pick who doesn't really have the athleticism to play tackle and profiles as a guard at this level), and Jamon Meredith (fifth-round pick who has the athleticism, but simply wasn't a very good offensive lineman at South Carolina). Hold a gun to our head and we'll pick Moll, but it's going to be the weakest point of the line, especially when it comes to the man-blocking scheme.

Right guard will be manned by Josh Sitton, who impressed enough as a rookie to take over the position at the end of the year. Jason Spitz, who spent most of the year as the starter there, will compete with center Scott Wells for the job in the middle. Spitz is the more talented of the two, but struggles to stay healthy, meaning that he might win the job in camp and lose it during the season.

The left side of the line was a disappointment with regards to pass blocking a year ago, which may come into play. Left tackle Chad Clifton was about average with 5.5 sacks allowed, but left guard Daryn Colledge allowed 4.5 sacks, more than any regular left guard besides Alan Faneca (5.5). Colledge has been on the bubble for several years now, but the team simply hasn't found someone capable of replacing him on the interior; in the final year of his deal, they may opt to swap him out for third-year man Allen Barbre or the loser of the Spitz-Wells battle.

Defensive Front Seven

Defensive Line	Age	Pos	Plays	TmPct	Rk	Stop	Dfts	Stop%	Rk	AvYd	Rk	Sack	Hit	Hur	Runs	St%	Yds	Pass	St%	Yds
						Overall						Pass Rush			vs. Run			vs. Pass		
Aaron Kampman	30	DE	63	7.9%	11	46	14	73%	58	1.9	50	9.5	20	11	50	66%	3.4	13	100%	-4.2
Mike Montgomery	26	DE	58	8.3%	7	27	6	47%	93	2.8	83	2.5	3	2	53	42%	3.4	5	100%	-2.6
Ryan Pickett	30	DT	50	6.3%	19	38	5	76%	43	2.1	41	1.5	1	3	44	73%	2.6	6	100%	-1.3
Johnny Jolly	26	DT	50	6.3%	20	37	7	74%	55	2.6	62	0.0	3	4	47	74%	2.7	3	67%	1.3
Colin Cole*	29	DT	34	4.3%	50	26	10	76%	40	2.4	57	0.5	2	4	27	74%	2.7	7	86%	1.0

Linebackers	Age	Pos	Plays	TmPct	Rk	Stop	Dfts	Stop%	AvYd	Sack	Hit	Hur	Runs	St%	Rk	Yds	Rk	Tgts	Suc%	Rk	AdjYd	Rk
					Overall					Pass Rush			vs. Run					vs. Pass				
A.J. Hawk	25	OLB	87	10.9%	58	49	12	56%	5.8	3.0	1	3	58	60%	69	4.7	98	40	53%	39	6.5	53
Brady Poppinga	30	OLB	69	8.7%	79	40	10	58%	3.9	0.0	2	4	50	58%	83	3.3	43	18	58%	22	4.7	12
Brandon Chillar	27	OLB	67	9.6%	71	37	15	55%	5.7	1.0	4	4	24	54%	92	3.6	58	42	57%	28	6.0	40
Nick Barnett	28	ILB	51	11.4%	51	29	8	57%	4.2	0.0	0	3	36	64%	53	3.8	70	20	51%	43	6.0	39
Desmond Bishop	25	ILB	21	2.8%	--	11	6	52%	5.1	1.0	0	0	12	58%	--	3.1	--	11	38%	--	14.0	--

Year	Yards	ALY	Rank	Power	Rank	10+ Yds	Rank	Stuff	Rank	Sack	ASR	Rank
2006	4.17	4.43	24	53%	4	14%	7	14%	30	46	8.2%	5
2007	4.04	4.14	19	65%	18	15%	10	15%	29	36	6.0%	23
2008	4.56	4.45	27	74%	27	21%	21	13%	32	27	5.6%	21

Year	LE	Rank	LT	Rank	Mid	Rank	RT	Rank	RE	Rank
2006	4.55	23	4.80	25	4.60	27	3.53	11	4.24	19
2007	4.77	25	4.67	24	3.88	8	4.61	25	2.80	6
2008	4.83	25	3.37	6	4.41	25	5.09	30	4.59	25

Dom Capers' "offset" 3-4 defense is a one-gap scheme, meaning that the defensive linemen will each play off the edge of an offensive lineman and attack the gap directly in front of them, in between the two linemen. In a two-gap 3-4, the job of a defensive lineman is to occupy the gaps on either side of an offensive lineman. It's harder, and it doesn't really fit the skill set of the guys the Packers will have up front. The Packers were planning on starting Ryan Pickett in the all-important nose tackle spot, but after unexpectedly adding B.J. Raji in the draft, they can choose to shift either of the two to end. Raji is the more plausible candidate, as he's a better pass rusher than Pickett. Cullen Jenkins will definitely man one of the defensive line spots, with depth coming from the oft-injured Justin Harrell, a former first-round pick at defensive tackle, as well as promising end Michael Montgomery.

Behind them will be a set of potentially elite linebackers, each of whom has something to prove. The most prominent is left outside linebacker Aaron Kampman, who moves from end into a new role. He'll be tutored by Kevin Greene, who played that position for both the Steelers and the Panthers. Kampman was reportedly upset with the transition, feeling that he wouldn't be able to operate effectively in space as a pass defender. The right outside linebacker will likely be rookie Clay Matthews, Jr., who will need to adapt to the speed of the pro game after only one year as a starter at USC. If he can't handle the transition, Brady Poppinga will take his place.

On the interior, A.J. Hawk and Nick Barnett will swap roles. Hawk will play the "Buck" linebacker role as the strongside middle linebacker; that's the closest role in this defense to the traditional "Mike" (middle linebacker) role that Barnett played in the team's 4-3. In that role, Hawk will spend less time in man coverage and more time on run blitzes and rushing the passer, which the team thinks will play best to his strengths. Barnett will be the "Will" linebacker, who spends more time in pass coverage. Our statistics support the notion that Barnett's a better pass defender than Hawk, but either way, expect to see both Barnett and Hawk rush the passer more in 2009.

The nickel alignment, which Mike McCarthy expects to use on up to half of the defensive snaps, will be a 4-2-5 with two linemen over the guards and two linebackers with their hands in the dirt outside the tackles.

Defensive Secondary

Secondary	Age	Pos	Plays	TmPct	Rk	Stop	Dfts	Yds	Rk	St%	Rk	Tgts	Tgt%	Rk	Dist	Suc%	Rk	AdjYd	Rk	Yds	PD	Int
						Overall			vs. Run						vs. Pass							
Nick Collins	26	FS	83	10.4%	31	32	15	11.3	78	17%	76	42	9.4%	7	12.9	67%	5	7.1	21	8.0	12	7
Charles Woodson	33	CB	80	10.1%	21	42	21	7.7	53	48%	33	63	14.2%	65	10.8	64%	5	6.1	19	6.0	16	7
Tramon Williams	26	CB	67	8.4%	47	26	9	6.8	47	25%	73	82	18.6%	33	13.9	51%	41	7.7	47	8.1	14	5
Aaron Rouse	25	FS	50	7.2%	65	23	6	5.0	13	57%	8	16	4.2%	73	15.0	51%	41	6.6	16	6.8	3	2
Al Harris	35	CB	33	5.5%	76	16	4	5.4	25	43%	44	52	15.6%	60	17.9	66%	3	5.6	9	5.7	10	0
Atari Bigby	28	SS	23	6.6%	--	11	3	11.0	--	38%	--	14	7.3%	--	10.1	69%	--	9.0	--	9.3	2	1

Year	Pass D Rank	vs. #1 WR	Rk	vs. #2 WR	Rk	vs. Other WR	Rk	vs. TE	Rk	vs. RB	Rk
2006	5	-7.6%	10	-28.5%	2	-12.0%	11	-31.2%	3	14.7%	28
2007	16	-24.3%	3	-0.7%	15	25.4%	31	5.3%	13	-15.9%	6
2008	7	-23.2%	1	13.8%	23	-47.9%	3	-12.6%	9	1.5%	12

As part of the defensive switch, the responsibility for play calls, identifying and adjusting offensive shifts, and calling audibles goes to the safeties. That's a lot of responsibility to place on Nick Collins and Atari Bigby, and even more responsibility to place on their backups if Bigby or, in particular, Collins gets hurt. Injuries in the secondary created serious problems last year; Bigby and backup Aaron Rouse went down with early-season hamstring and knee injuries, respectively, leading to a start for the immortal Charlie Peprah. Rouse and Bigby came back, but when Bigby went down again in Week 13 with an ankle injury, the team replaced him with Charles Woodson and moved Tramon Williams into the starting lineup. The Packers allowed 408 yards in an absurd loss to the Texans before moving Woodson back to corner.

While Williams is a good athlete and has good ball skills, he falls for double moves like he picked the wrong play in Tecmo Bowl. He was pushed into the lineup when Al Harris tore his spleen and missed four games, and simply wasn't up to the task. He makes a fine nickel corner, but he's trouble if he has to be any more than that. Special teams stud Jarrett Bush is the dime corner, with the Packers matching an RFA offer sheet from the Titans to keep him in Wisconsin.

Special Teams

Year	DVOA	Rank	FG/XP	Rank	Net Kick	Rank	Kick Ret	Rank	Net Punt	Rank	Punt Ret	Rank	Hidden	Rank
2006	-3.9%	29	-5.9	29	3.4	14	-13.5	31	-4.9	23	-2.3	22	-14.4	31
2007	2.5%	8	1.1	16	7.1	4	-2.2	21	-3.7	22	12.3	2	-7.7	25
2008	-0.3%	20	-1.1	20	-1.6	20	-6.6	23	5.1	11	2.6	6	-1.4	16

Mason Crosby was just about average on kickoffs, but lost three points worth of field position thanks to poor coverage. On the other hand, the coverage units nearly kept Derrick Frost on the team; although Frost cost the team six points with his punts, the coverage units made up for it long enough that Frost lasted until December 1, when he was cut and replaced by Jeremy Kapinos. Kapinos was only average, but that still led to a marked improvement in the team's performance. All the Packers need now is a return man. Will Blackmon was subpar on kickoffs, but an effective punt returner. The team could choose to use Jordy Nelson as the primary kick returner if so inclined, but he was about as poor as Blackmon was, just on fewer kicks.

Coaching Staff

The arrival of Capers means the fourth defensive coordinator for Green Bay in five seasons; if Capers struggles, we're officially calling this the "Curse of Ed Donatell," after the defensive coordinator who was scapegoated for Freddie Mitchell's infamous catch on fourth-and-26. Capers brought in four new defensive coaches, including former All-Pro linebacker Kevin Greene, who will be tutoring Aaron Kampman as part of his duties. Offensive coordinator Joe Philbin is a holdover from before Mike McCarthy's arrival; although Philbin has the title and the commensurate salary, McCarthy calls the plays and dictates the offensive scheme. If the offense struggles for any reason, Philbin is an extremely plausible scapegoat.

Houston Texans

The Texans finished 8-8 last year, winning eight of their last 12 games. The organization thinks that a young offensive core and a few defensive tweaks have them in position to make a run at the playoffs. Optimistic Texans fans may be planning for their first-ever playoff appearance, but our projection system is raining on the parade with a mean projection of just 6.9 wins.

The fundamental problem for the Texans is that their 8-8 record last season overstates their proximity to the playoffs. A 9-7 team does sometimes make the playoffs. In last year's highly dispersed AFC, seven other teams were better than 8-8, and two other teams matched Houston's record. One of the few teams behind Houston was division rival Jacksonville — a team our projection system pegs for a huge rebound in 2009.

The Texans need more than a few lucky breaks to rise up into the playoffs in the uber-competitive AFC. For this team to separate itself from last year's 8-8 squad, it needs to make two fundamental changes. First, it needs to start protecting the ball on offense. Second, it needs to develop a competent run defense.

Offensively, the Texans last year moved the ball as well as almost any other team. They ranked third in the league in total yards, fifth in both yards per drive and yards per play. Yet they ranked only 11th in points per drive and 17th in overall points. The biggest culprit was a massive turnover problem. They were second in interceptions and seventh in fumbles lost. The Texans must hope that the solution is just for the people they have to play at a higher level, as their opening day lineup will be the same as their usual 2008 starting lineup.

The Texans have plenty of talent on the offensive side of the ball. Quarterback Matt Schaub has played at a high level during both of his seasons as a starter, no doubt helped by the incredible Andre Johnson. Where this team has really improved since head coach Gary Kubiak came on board is in its ability to run the ball. The Texans finally established continuity on their offensive line, with all five starters starting all 16 games last year. They found the perfect back for their system in Steve Slaton, and the rookie exploded for a franchise record 1,282 yards.

Still, this talent was on the team last year, and while the offense was good, it was not great. It is rare that a team moves the ball so well but turns it over so often. We have calculated drive stats dating back to 1998. During that time, only two teams have averaged more yards *and* more turnovers per drive, the 2001 Rams and the 2008 Broncos. The Rams fell apart the next season, declining from one of the great offenses in recent history to a below average offense. (The Broncos look poised for a similar decline after jettisoning Jay Cutler, but that's for a different chapter.)

Since so few teams have been as extreme as the Tex-

TEXANS SUMMARY

2008 Record: 8-8

Pythagorean Wins: 7.3 (21st)

DVOA: -6.8% (23rd)

Offense: 11.0% (14th)

Defense: 17.9% (29th)

Special Teams: 0.1% (17th)

Variance: 11.2% (8th)

2008: Generous Texans provide opponents with turnovers and huge running lanes.

2009: More of the same unless Schaub finally stays healthy and the defense gets its act together.

2009 Mean Projection: 6.9 wins

On the Clock (0-3): 4%

Loserville (4-6): 38%

Mediocrity (7-8): 36%

Playoff Contender (9-10): 18%

Super Bowl Contender (11+): 4%

Projected Average Opponent: 4.0% (6th)

2009 Texans Schedule

Week	Opp.	Week	Opp.	Week	Opp.
1	NYJ	7	SF	13	at JAC
2	at TEN	8	at BUF	14	SEA
3	JAC	9	at IND	15	at STL
4	OAK	10	BYE	16	at MIA
5	at ARI	11	TEN (Mon.)	17	NE
6	at CIN	12	IND		

ans, we needed to lower the threshold to find comparable teams. The Texans averaged 35.7 yards per drive and turned the ball over on 17.5 percent of their drives. Between 1998 and 2007, 14 teams averaged at least 31 yards per drive while turning the ball over at least 16 percent of the time (Table 1).

The overall group is not that predictive, as half the teams improved offensively the next season, while half regressed. Four teams had even more turnovers per drive the next season, and three of them predictably had a worse offensive DVOA (the exception being the Texans from 2007 to 2008). Six of the nine teams that lowered their turnovers per drive below 16 percent improved offensively the next season. Among the exceptions are teams that had massive quarterback problems, including the 2008 Bengals and the 2005 Rams, who often started Ryan Fitzpatrick and Jamie Martin, respectively.

Can the Texans get their turnover percentage below 16 percent? The answer seems to be most assuredly yes. Schaub threw ten interceptions in 380 attempts, a middle of the road number. Sage Rosenfels, his backup, threw ten in a mere 174 attempts. If Rosenfels had thrown interceptions at Schaub's rate, the Texans would have had five fewer turnovers. Their turnovers per drive would have decreased to 14.6 percent, which would have ranked 21st in the league.

Of course, the reason Rosenfels started five games is because Schaub has never been able to stay healthy, missing five games in each of his seasons as a starter. Needless to say, the easiest way for the Texans to improve is for Schaub to play all 16 games. If he is injured this year, he will be replaced by Dan Orlovsky. Orlovsky played adequately if not inspirationally for the Lions last season, and — most important for this exercise — threw eight interceptions in 255 attempts, a rate closer

to Schaub's than Rosenfels'.

So that's the good news: When explosive but high-turnover offenses cut their turnovers to a reasonable, if still high, rate, they generally improve the next season. The outlook for the defense is a bit more pessimistic. Last year's defense was abysmal (29th in DVOA), particularly against the run (30th in DVOA, 30th in Adjusted Line Yards). The Texans will have two different starting linebackers from Week 1 of last season, along with free agent defensive end Antonio Smith — but why should we expect that these minor tweaks will make a substantive difference when the franchise has failed for so long to acquire quality defenders?

The Texans' defensive problems stem from a franchise-long inability to acquire quality defenders deep into the draft. A cursory look at the roster sees that the Texans have three very good players in defensive end Mario Williams, linebacker DeMeco Ryans, and cornerback Dunta Robinson. All were taken in the first or second rounds, as were defensive tackles Travis Johnson and Amobi Okoye. Outside of the first two rounds, the Texans' ability to draft quality defenders is nearly non-existent (and it isn't perfect inside of the first two rounds, either: see "Babin, Jason").

Between 2002 and 2006, Houston selected defensive players with 16 draft picks from the third round on. Only cornerback DeMarcus Faggins is still on the Texans. This failure to draft well led to an unhealthy reliance on veteran free agents. Three of last year's four leading tacklers and five of the top ten came to the Texans as veteran free agents. The occasional acquisition of a free agent to fill a hole is a good thing,

Table 1: High Turnover Offenses that Moved the Ball

		That Season			Next Season			
Year	Team	Yds/DR	TO/DR	DVOA	Yds/DR	TO/DR	DVOA	DVOA Change
1999	MIN	31.3	0.19	13.4%	34.2	0.16	22.2%	+8.8%
2000	STL	38.7	0.17	31.7%	37.2	0.20	27.3%	-4.4%
2001	IND	31.6	0.19	6.7%	31.6	0.17	5.5%	-1.2%
2001	STL	37.2	0.21	27.3%	29.7	0.24	-3.7%	+31.0%
2002	IND	31.6	0.17	5.5%	34.7	0.11	17.1%	+11.6%
2002	PIT	31.4	0.17	6.1%	24.3	0.14	-9.1%	+15.2%
2002	MIN	31.9	0.20	8.5%	34.6	0.14	16.4%	+7.9%
2002	SEA	34.1	0.16	6.9%	31.4	0.14	13.6%	+6.7%
2002	BUF	31.8	0.16	-0.2%	23.7	0.18	-18.9%	+18.7%
2004	STL	32.9	0.21	0.8%	28.9	0.14	-3.6%	-4.4%
2006	PIT	33.2	0.19	5.2%	29.5	0.12	6.8%	+1.6%
2007	CIN	32.9	0.16	11.0%	21.7	0.09	-15.4%	-26.4%
2007	NO	32.1	0.16	10.1%	36.6	0.15	23.7%	+13.6%
2007	HOU	31.0	0.21	5.6%	35.7	0.22	11.4%	+5.8%

but relying on veteran free agents is a surefire way to overspend for mediocre production. Of the five defenders — safeties Eugene Wilson and Nick Ferguson, cornerback Jacques Reeves, and linebackers Kevin Bentley and Morlon Greenwood — only Wilson and Reeves were any good, and neither was a star.

The good news is that the Texans hired general manager Rick Smith after the 2006 draft, and the early results are promising. The 2007 draft brought cornerback Fred Bennett in the third round and linebacker Zach Diles in the seventh. The 2008 draft brought Xavier Adibi, projected to start as weakside linebacker, in the fourth round.

Still, Smith had further work to do on upgrading the defense. First, he cut some of the older players and attempted to revitalize with some youth. Then he added key pieces that should help the run defense. The biggest acquisition was Antonio Smith, an in-his-prime defensive end who plays the run well. The first two rounds of the draft brought defensive help with linebacker Brian Cushing in the first round and pass-rushing defensive end Connor Barwin in the second.

The other change was a decision to fire defensive coordinator Richard Smith (no relation) and much of the defensive staff. Smith's 29th-ranked defense last season was the best of his three-year tenure, but at the end of the day talent trumps coaching, and the Texans have always had bad defensive talent. They were the worst defense in DVOA the year before Smith arrived, and they have never ranked higher than 18th in their seven-year history.

New defensive coordinator Frank Bush has never been a defensive coordinator before. His style is therefore uncertain, but as someone who worked for Clancy Pendergast in Arizona, he likely will be more aggressive than Smith was last year. At the same time, he will still be running out many of the same players. The Texans have not solved their strong safety problem, as the aging Nick Ferguson remains in place. The underwhelming defensive tackle duo of Travis Johnson and Amobi Okoye also remains. Unless Bush can wave a magic wand, the team will still struggle defensively.

The one wild card is the presumptive full-time return of the real Dunta Robinson, who missed 10 games last year to injuries and never really looked like himself after returning. His return as a legitimate top cornerback allows the team to slide Fred Bennett to nickelback in hopes that he can return to his 2007 form after struggling through a major sophomore slump. With a better secondary, Bush can shift a safety into the box more often to stop the running attack.

Still, the Texans are basically the same team they were a year ago: slightly below average. They have no magic statistical indicator that portends success. Sure, a healthy Schaub will no doubt improve their production, and the run defense almost has to be a little better. The problem is that mediocre will just not be good enough in a division with three other playoff contenders and a conference loaded with talented teams. Until the defense can improve to league-average, the Texans will continue their recent run of mediocrity.

Ned Macey

2008 Texans Stats by Week

Wk	vs.	W-L	PF	PA	YDF	YDA	TO	Total	Off	Def	ST
1	@PIT	L	17	38	234	305	-2	-52%	-10%	36%	-6%
2	BYE										
3	@TEN	L	12	31	317	343	-1	-25%	-22%	6%	2%
4	@JAC	L	27	30	386	375	0	-18%	30%	42%	-5%
5	IND	L	27	31	391	314	-2	16%	20%	8%	4%
6	MIA	W	29	28	485	370	-3	25%	16%	11%	21%
7	DET	W	28	21	404	326	-1	-36%	15%	53%	2%
8	CIN	W	35	6	384	253	+3	64%	48%	1%	17%
9	@MIN	L	21	28	389	345	-2	-36%	-4%	26%	-6%
10	BAL	L	13	41	355	328	-4	-41%	-15%	30%	4%
11	@IND	L	27	33	356	474	-1	3%	25%	27%	6%
12	@CLE	W	16	6	383	240	+3	16%	-16%	-42%	-10%
13	JAC	W	30	17	326	388	+2	11%	16%	8%	3%
14	@GB	W	24	21	549	387	-3	-2%	27%	23%	-6%
15	TEN	W	13	12	375	281	+1	18%	9%	-14%	-5%
16	@OAK	L	16	27	324	362	0	-59%	-5%	37%	-17%
17	CHI	W	31	24	455	294	0	16%	51%	33%	-2%

Trends and Splits

	Offense	Rank	Defense	Rank
Total DVOA	11.0%	14	17.9%	29
Unadjusted VOA	7.1%	17	16.8%	28
Weighted trend	13.7%	9	16.4%	28
Variance	4.9%	3	6.9%	23
Average opponent	2.0%	28	-0.7%	6
Passing	28.2%	11	20.3%	24
Rushing	4.7%	16	15.5%	30
First down	12.1%	9	16.1%	27
Second down	6.2%	19	20.2%	28
Third down	16.5%	14	17.7%	23
First half	11.8%	13	13.0%	23
Second half	10.3%	16	22.6%	30
Red Zone	-15.6%	27	52.3%	32
Late and close	20.9%	9	31.7%	31

Five-Year Performance

Year	W-L	Pyth	Est W	PF	PA	TO	Total	Rk	Off	Rk	Def	Rk	ST	Rk	Off AGL	Rk	Def AGL	Rk
2004	7-9	7.1	7.6	309	339	+5	-6.2%	18	-0.5%	15	2.3%	18	-3.4%	28	5.7	29	5.4	32
2005	2-14	3.7	3.6	260	431	-8	-32.6%	31	-17.0%	27	19.9%	32	4.3%	3	8.7	22	9.3	25
2006	6-10	5.1	5.8	267	366	-3	-21.6%	30	-5.5%	21	14.0%	31	-2.1%	23	3.4	30	8.8	23
2007	8-8	7.9	7.7	379	384	-13	-6.3%	21	2.0%	15	14.2%	30	5.9%	3	24.2	13	26.4	10
2008	8-8	7.3	6.7	366	394	-10	-6.8%	23	11.0%	14	17.9%	29	0.1%	17	20.3	21	22.7	16

Strategic Tendencies

Run/Pass		Rank	Offense		Rank	Defense		Rank	Other		Rank
Runs, all plays	41%	23	3+ WR	36%	30	Rush 3	4.8%	18	2+ RB, Pct Runs	58%	23
Runs, first half	43%	20	4+ WR	6%	27	Rush 4	70.6%	7	1 RB/2 TE, Pct Runs	35%	29
Runs, first down	46%	28	2+ TE	30%	11	Rush 5	17.7%	23	1RB/3+WR, Pct Runs	24%	19
Runs, second-long	37%	20	Single back	45%	28	Rush 6+	6.9%	21	Zone Blitz	4%	15
Runs, power sit.	69%	10	Play action	22%	7	Rush 7+	1.9%	10	Go for it on 4th	1.20	7
Runs, behind 2H	30%	23	Max protect	8%	18	Sacks by LB	16.0%	18	Offensive Pace	32.9	31
Pass, ahead 2H	46%	12	Outside pocket	12%	17	Sacks by DB	4.0%	24	Defensive Pace	30.1	7

Houston used shotgun on only 11 percent of plays, the only AFC team to use shotgun formations less than 20 percent of the time. They led the league with 6.3 yards per play from non-shotgun formations, but ranked 29th with 4.8 yards per play from shotgun formations. Lest you think all Shanahans think alike, Kyle's dad used shotgun 48 percent of the time in Denver, fourth in the league. ● Houston used a tight end on a league-leading 95 percent of plays (tied with the Jets). ● Houston opponents only sent six or more on a big blitz 5.0 percent of the time, the lowest rate in the league. ● Matt Schaub completed 63 percent of his passes against five or more pass rushers, second in the league to Chad Pennington. ● Houston threw 36 percent of passes up the middle, the highest rate in the NFL, and only 30 percent of passes to the right, second lowest behind Tampa Bay. In 2007, the Texans ranked second in passes up the middle and last in passes to the right. This has nothing to do with the idiosyncrasies of the Houston official scorer, because the directional split of passes *against* Houston is unremarkable. ● Houston had a league-worst 32.2% DVOA on defense when the other team used fewer than two wide receivers. ● The Texans ranked 31st in pass defense DVOA when using the standard four pass rushers, but they ranked 10th with five pass rushers and second behind only Pittsburgh with six or more pass rushers.

Passing

Player	DYAR	DVOA	Plays	NtYds	Avg	YAC	C%	TD	Int
Matt Schaub	863	21.7%	407	2937	7.2	5.5	67.5%	15	10
Sage Rosenfels*	183	3.7%	184	1391	7.6	5.4	67.4%	6	10
Dan Orlovsky	198	0.3%	273	1552	5.7	4.4	56.5%	8	7
Rex Grossman	-70	-27.9%	65	249	3.8	3.2	52.4%	2	2

Rushing

Player	DYAR	DVOA	Plays	Yds	Avg	TD	Fum	Suc
Steve Slaton	166	5.8%	268	1285	4.8	9	2	44%
Ahman Green*	74	12.6%	74	294	4.0	3	0	55%
Ryan Moats	42	31.5%	26	94	3.6	1	0	50%
Matt Schaub	19	4.0%	21	76	3.6	2	2	--
Chris Taylor	-24	-55.7%	14	35	2.5	0	1	21%
Sage Rosenfels*	-27	-60.6%	9	38	4.2	0	1	--
Kevin Walter	23	62.7%	3	23	7.7	0	0	--

Receiving

Player	DYAR	DVOA	Plays	Ctch	Yds	Y/C	YAC	TD	C%
Andre Johnson	491	22.1%	171	115	1575	13.7	4.1	9	67%
Kevin Walter	225	16.8%	95	60	899	15.0	4.9	8	63%
David Anderson	59	13.1%	29	19	241	12.7	6.3	2	66%
Andre Davis	-1	-13.3%	28	13	213	16.4	4.8	0	46%
Jacoby Jones	27	54.9%	5	3	81	27.0	10.0	0	67%
Owen Daniels	173	18.2%	99	70	862	12.3	5.8	2	71%
Joel Dreessen	-31	-35.2%	17	11	76	6.9	3.5	0	65%
Steve Slaton	30	-3.8%	59	50	377	7.5	8.6	1	85%
Vonta Leach	11	-3.8%	18	12	103	8.6	5.9	0	67%
Ahman Green*	-31	-58.2%	14	11	32	2.9	5.8	0	79%
Ryan Moats	-10	-54.4%	5	3	14	4.7	5.0	0	60%

Offensive Line

Year	Yards	ALY	Rank	Power	Rank	10+ Yds	Rank	Stuff	Rank	Sacks	ASR	Rank	False	Cont.
2006	4.00	4.13	19	71%	8	14%	22	16%	3	43	9.3%	28	19	25
2007	3.91	4.30	8	69%	10	13%	22	15%	3	22	4.8%	10	23	37
2008	4.43	4.19	10	70%	13	24%	5	18%	14	32	6.1%	16	23	48

Year	LE	Rank	LT	Rank	Mid	Rank	RT	Rank	RE	Rank
2006	4.09	16	2.68	32	4.37	11	4.14	15	4.17	14
2007	4.85	4	4.43	12	4.17	12	4.63	5	4.07	15
2008	4.66	13	2.96	31	4.48	6	4.05	19	4.17	13

The Texans have finally developed a competent offensive line, and their resulting offensive success is quite clearly correlated. Gone are the days of quarterbacks spending games running for their lives. The Texans use aspects of the old Denver Broncos offense that Gary Kubiak brought with him, and the athletic linemen opened up numerous holes for Steve Slaton. Rookie left tackle Duane Brown stepped right into the starting lineup and flashed potential, but he also led the league with 10 blown blocks that led to sacks. On the other side, right tackle Eric Winston, a guy who dropped in the draft due to character issues, has proven to be an excellent find and a potential anchor for years to come. Import center Chris Myers from Denver knows the system but is limited physically and will likely step aside for third-round pick Antoine Caldwell (Alabama) in a couple of years. Caldwell could fight with Mike Brisiel at right guard as soon as this year, but Brisiel showed enough in his first year as a starter to get the first shot at playing time. Chester Pitts — a poor tackle on the awful Texans lines of earlier this decade — has molded himself into a surprisingly adept left guard, where his athleticism is often on display on running plays. One reason for caution is that no starter missed a game for injury last year, which hid the fact that the Texans have little to no proven depth.

Defensive Front Seven

Defensive Line	Age	Pos	Plays	TmPct	Rk	Stop	Dfts	Stop%	Rk	AvYd	Rk	Sack	Hit	Hur	Runs	St%	Yds	Pass	St%	Yds
								Overall				Pass Rush			vs. Run			vs. Pass		
Mario Williams	24	DE	53	7.3%	16	44	22	83%	20	0.3	12	12.0	15	22	36	78%	2.2	17	94%	-3.7
Anthony Weaver*	29	DE	46	6.3%	34	35	6	76%	50	3.4	88	0.0	0	4	41	78%	2.6	5	60%	9.4
Travis Johnson	27	DT	32	4.7%	43	25	3	78%	34	2.3	56	1.0	4	2	29	76%	2.7	3	100%	-1.0
Amobi Okoye	22	DT	23	3.6%	61	19	4	83%	13	1.8	30	1.0	2	14	19	84%	2.3	4	75%	-0.3
Jeff Zgonina	39	DT	19	2.6%	--	10	4	53%	--	3.9	--	0.0	0	1	18	56%	3.6	1	0%	9.0
Earl Cochran*	28	DE	18	5.0%	--	14	7	78%	--	1.8	--	2.0	0	1	12	75%	3.1	6	83%	-0.7
Tim Bulman	27	DT	17	2.7%	--	13	6	76%	--	2.4	--	4.0	8	4	12	67%	3.9	5	100%	-1.2
DelJuan Robinson	25	DT	15	2.1%	--	11	3	73%	--	2.2	--	0.0	0	2	13	77%	1.8	2	50%	5.0
Shaun Cody	26	DT	39	4.8%	41	30	8	77%	39	1.6	20	0.0	3	4	35	74%	1.7	4	100%	0.8
Antonio Smith	28	DE	37	4.7%	59	26	14	70%	70	1.8	46	3.5	10	4	29	72%	1.8	8	63%	1.9

Linebackers	Age	Pos	Plays	TmPct	Rk	Stop	Dfts	Stop%	AvYd	Sack	Hit	Hur	Runs	St%	Rk	Yds	Rk	Tgts	Suc%	Rk	AdjYd	Rk
								Overall		Pass Rush			vs. Run					vs. Pass				
DeMeco Ryans	25	ILB	113	15.6%	19	70	14	62%	4.6	1.0	3	5	79	62%	60	4.1	83	30	68%	5	4.9	17
Zach Diles	24	OLB	66	18.2%	5	34	9	52%	5.2	1.0	0	3	39	62%	63	4.2	86	25	32%	87	8.0	78
Morlon Greenwood*	31	OLB	43	6.3%	--	17	4	40%	5.5	0.0	0	0	30	40%	--	4.7	--	17	61%	13	4.4	7
Kevin Bentley	30	OLB	35	4.8%	--	20	5	57%	3.9	1.0	0	0	22	59%	--	4.0	--	10	54%	--	6.1	--
Xavier Adibi	25	OLB	33	10.4%	--	16	3	48%	4.8	0.0	1	1	17	71%	--	2.8	--	13	37%	--	8.3	--
Cato June	30	OLB	69	9.1%	76	40	15	58%	5.2	0.0	0	2	39	79%	8	3.2	38	38	56%	32	6.1	41
Buster Davis	26	ILB	23	7.3%	--	8	2	35%	5.0	0.0	0	0	15	33%	--	4.1	--	4	68%	--	6.1	--

Year	Yards	ALY	Rank	Power	Rank	10+ Yds	Rank	Stuff	Rank	Sack	ASR	Rank
2006	4.32	4.29	20	77%	30	15%	13	17%	21	28	5.8%	26
2007	4.33	4.32	25	76%	29	17%	18	16%	27	31	6.0%	22
2008	4.46	4.63	30	76%	29	13%	8	14%	29	25	5.4%	24

Year	LE	Rank	LT	Rank	Mid	Rank	RT	Rank	RE	Rank
2006	5.39	32	4.04	11	3.94	7	4.72	26	4.46	22
2007	4.47	24	4.73	26	4.36	26	3.64	7	4.24	18
2008	5.01	28	5.44	32	4.40	23	4.65	27	4.61	26

The Texans run defense was abysmal. Mario Williams, the best player in the front seven, is developing some bad habits and eschewing the run. Fellow first-rounder Amobi Okoye is still extremely young (22 years old), but he has yet to show any ability to command a double-team and makes few plays himself. The linebackers were a mess, with Morlon Greenwood past his expiration date, and Zach Diles specializing in making tackles six yards past the line of scrimmage. Xavier Adibi showed some promise at the weakside position. The big name, DeMeco Ryans, has failed to build on his outstanding rookie season. He struggles to fight off blocks and too often lets the play come to him.

The Texans have two valuable new pieces to strengthen the run defense. Defensive end Antonio Smith is a solid run defender (who will also improve the pass rush), and first-round pick Brian Cushing out of USC should be an upgrade at strongside linebacker. If nothing else, the Texans have depth at linebacker, adding veteran Cato June and returning the workmanlike Kevin Bentley. Their pass rush could also be improved by second-round pick Connor Barwin, who can play defensive end and push Smith inside in obvious passing situations. (Don't be surprised to see Barwin playing a little offense in goal-line packages; he was a tight end as a junior at the University of Cincinnati before switching to defensive end as a senior.)

Defensive Secondary

Secondary	Age	Pos	Plays	TmPct	Rk	Stop	Dfts	Yds	Rk	St%	Rk	Tgts	Tgt%	Rk	Dist	Suc%	Rk	AdjYd	Rk	Yds	PD	Int
Jacques Reeves	27	CB	69	9.5%	30	28	10	10.5	71	38%	50	99	23.3%	7	14.4	54%	28	8.0	57	7.6	18	4
Eugene Wilson	29	FS	69	12.7%	9	20	7	7.9	56	37%	49	23	7.1%	36	17.8	55%	27	9.1	55	9.0	6	2
Nick Ferguson	35	SS	54	8.5%	56	22	4	5.2	16	45%	30	20	5.2%	63	14.2	46%	61	9.5	62	8.9	1	0
Fred Bennett	25	CB	46	6.3%	69	14	5	3.9	8	44%	43	57	13.4%	72	12.6	46%	58	7.9	52	7.4	7	2
Dunta Robinson	27	CB	44	8.8%	38	17	8	6.5	44	30%	68	51	17.3%	50	9.7	44%	69	8.9	78	8.3	6	2
Brandon Harrison	25	SS	31	4.6%	--	10	2	7.5	--	40%	--	8	2.0%	--	8.7	39%	--	8.3	--	8.4	0	0
Will Demps*	30	FS	30	7.4%	--	9	3	6.3	--	35%	--	8	3.1%	--	14.4	13%	--	19.2	--	19.4	0	0
Demarcus Faggins*	30	CB	21	2.9%	--	8	5	5.6	--	40%	--	28	6.5%	--	8.7	41%	--	10.9	--	10.3	3	0

Year	Pass D Rank	vs. #1 WR	Rk	vs. #2 WR	Rk	vs. Other WR	Rk	vs. TE	Rk	vs. RB	Rk
2006	31	8.8%	23	-6.3%	10	26.2%	28	-0.9%	18	30.0%	32
2007	29	21.2%	30	-2.5%	13	4.5%	22	23.9%	28	-2.2%	16
2008	26	13.1%	22	-0.8%	14	32.0%	32	4.3%	18	16.0%	27

Both of Houston's corners are question marks: one due to health, the other to inconsistency. For the second consecutive season, franchise cornerback Dunta Robinson missed extensive time due to injuries. Robinson was never physically right all year, and his performance suffered as a result. Still, Robinson has exceptional cover skills and a track record of success. If he is fully healthy, he provides the Texans with an outstanding top cornerback. After 2007, we felt that the Texans would have an outstanding cornerback duo because rookie Fred Bennett dominated our charting statistics. By his second year, however, it was clear that teams had studied film and figured out what kind of receivers and routes they could use to attack Bennett. As a result, Bennett was terrible early on, and Gary Kubiak demoted him to nickelback after just three weeks, although Bennett did improve after that. The one cornerback who started all 16 games — and is likely to be starting alongside Robinson in 2009

— was free-agent pickup Jacques Reeves, a league-average player who is reasonable on short stuff but gives up too many big plays deep. The Texans increased their depth at the draft by using a fourth-round pick on New Mexico's Glover Quin, a physical corner who could excel in the slot, although some project him to eventually be a safety. They also added undersized but speedy cornerback Brice McCain out of Utah in the sixth round.

At safety, the Texans have made good use of former New England cornerback Eugene Wilson. Wilson plays it safe at times, but he is fundamentally sound in coverage. Nick Ferguson, on the other hand, was an unmitigated disaster, average as a run defender but consistently abused in coverage. The Texans failed to find an impact upgrade this offseason and will probably go with 2007 fifth-rounder Brandon Harrison as this year's starter. He's better in coverage but could not beat out Ferguson last season. The other possibilities including moving Quin to safety this season or hoping that seventh-round pick Troy Nolan out of Arizona State is ready to contribute as a rookie. The Quin move is obviously more intriguing, and if he shifts to safety in training camp, it is clear that the Texans realize they have a problem.

Special Teams

Year	DVOA	Rank	FG/XP	Rank	Net Kick	Rank	Kick Ret	Rank	Net Punt	Rank	Punt Ret	Rank	Hidden	Rank
2006	-2.1%	23	-0.6	17	-2.6	26	-6.1	26	-6.1	27	3.0	6	-8.7	26
2007	5.9%	3	4.9	7	8.6	1	21.2	2	0.9	16	-1.0	16	-1.4	16
2008	0.1%	17	0.6	17	6.8	8	-6.6	24	-6.6	26	6.3	4	-12.7	28

Overall, Houston special teams were average last year, but a few pieces are true assets. First, Kris Brown has a big leg for kickoffs and reasonable accuracy on field goals. Second, Jacoby Jones is an outstanding punt returner, breaking two for touchdowns and averaging an impressive 12.1 yards per return. The Texans did have a severe weakness in kick return blocking. Andre Davis got the bulk of the attempts before the Texans tinkered with Jones. Both struggled to gain consistent yardage. The Texans' biggest problem is at punter, where 40-year-old Matt Turk is approaching the end of the line. He's still reliable for directional kicking but no longer has the leg to get adequate hang time and distance when longer kicks are required. The Texans picked up undrafted free agent Justin Brantly out of Texas A&M, who has a big leg but may not have the consistency to punt in the NFL. He's supposed to be just a camp body, but the team would be wise to give him a real shot at the job.

Coaching Staff

Gary Kubiak has revolutionized the offense since coming on board as head coach in 2007. Matt Schaub has taken major steps forward, and Kubiak has turned the offensive line, which used to be the butt of jokes, into a strength. Of course, Kubiak needs to share credit with offensive coordinator Kyle Shanahan, who oversaw a big step forward in his first year on the job. Meanwhile, Alex Gibbs, now titled "assistant head coach/offense," is almost legendary for his ability to revamp an offensive line. On defense, the Texans fired Richard Smith and promoted Frank Bush. The long-time coach is getting his first chance to run a defense, with his previous coordinating experience being the 2001-03 Broncos special teams. Other than the basics of running a base 4-3, nobody is entirely certain what Bush's philosophy will be. He has worked under Larry Coyer and Clancy Pendergast, neither of whom is afraid to attack the quarterback. Needless to say, Bush has his work cut out for him taking over such a poor defense.

Indianapolis Colts

The 2008 Indianapolis Colts won at least 12 games for a record sixth straight season. The Colts have been the league's most stable team for a number of years, and, as of last year, little new could be said about them. The retirements of head coach Tony Dungy and offensive coordinator Tom Moore, however, leave the Colts as a test case for any number of questions about the value of coaches.

Dungy has an unparalleled record of consistency in the salary cap era. Between Tampa Bay and Indianapolis, Dungy coached an amazing 12 consecutive playoff teams. The one stain on this remarkable banner of consistency is that Dungy won "only" one Super Bowl. This achievement may have been celebrated rather than derided if not for the very inconvenient fact that Tampa Bay won their only Super Bowl the year after Dungy left.

Each new head coaching job is so unique that it is hard to make global statements. Our projection system can synthesize what normally happens, marking the Colts down slightly for its change in coordinators and lack of coaching continuity. Still, the range of possibilities calls for a more qualitative analysis. Are the Colts likely to repeat the 2002 Buccaneers Super Bowl championship in a post-Dungy era? Or are they more likely to descend into mediocrity like the post-Parcells 1991 New York Giants?

In last year's San Diego Chargers article, we noted that when very good teams change coaches, they generally remain very good teams. A look at the Colts roster makes it difficult to imagine that, barring an injury to Peyton Manning, the team will not win double-digit games again. Offensively, the Colts cut ties with long-time great Marvin Harrison. But Harrison missed most of 2007 and was a shell of his former self in 2008, and the Colts offense kept on ticking (second and fourth in DVOA the past two seasons). Other than Harrison, the entire starting lineup returns on both offense and defense.

Defensively, the Colts are the most talented they have been in recent memory. The past two years, the Colts' once-maligned defense has been an asset, not a detriment. It ranked tenth in DVOA last year and second in 2007. This year, the same players are there, along with massive supplements at defensive tackle. The second round of the draft brought Fili Moala (305 pounds), while Terrance Taylor (314 pounds) came in the fourth. Additionally, the Colts' best defensive tackle in 2007, Ed Johnson, returns to the team after he was released last season following an arrest for marijuana possession.

If Dungy and his whole coaching staff had returned, not only would the Colts' win total be easy to predict, but everyone would know exactly how they would play. The offense would be no-huddle with one primary receiver to each side and either two-tight end or three-receiver sets. The defense would predominately play Tampa-2, rarely blitz, and allow an enormous

---

COLTS SUMMARY

2008 Record: 12-4

Pythagorean Wins: 10.2 (8th)

DVOA: 15.3% (8th)

Offense: 17.2% (6th)

Defense: 0.1% (10th)

Special Teams: -1.8% (24th)

Variance: 18.0% (19th)

2008: 12 wins and an early playoff loss, a fitting end to the Dungy era.

2009: New staff + same Peyton Manning = same results.

2009 Mean Projection: 11.5 wins

On the Clock (0-3): 0%

Loserville (4-6): 0%

Mediocrity (7-8): 4%

Playoff Contender (9-10): 28%

Super Bowl Contender (11+): 68%

Projected Average Opponent: 0.9% (17th)

2009 Colts Schedule

Week	Opp.	Week	Opp.	Week	Opp.
1	JAC	7	at STL	13	TEN
2	at MIA (Mon.)	8	SF	14	DEN
3	at ARI	9	HOU	15	at JAC (Thu.)
4	SEA	10	NE	16	NYJ
5	at TEN	11	at BAL	17	at BUF
6	BYE	12	at HOU		

number of short completions.

Every number in our database that we use to project the Colts is based on this system that the Colts have run virtually unchanged since 2003. (While Dungy took over in 2002, the Colts switched to the no-huddle full time a year later). The offense is likely to remain schematically unchanged. The Colts are promoting wide receivers coach Clyde Christensen to replace Moore, and new head coach Jim Caldwell has been the quarterbacks coach the past few seasons. Moore and also-retired offensive line coach Howard Mudd will still be with the team as "consultants" and remain crucial parts of the offensive staff. Other than the noticeable absence of Harrison's number 88, the Colts offense will look like the same unit we have seen for the past half dozen years.

Defensively, however, the jury is most definitely out. After his elevation, Caldwell could have taken the safe route and kept defensive coordinator Ron Meeks. Instead, Meeks was let go, and Caldwell quickly settled on Larry Coyer as his replacement. In many ways, Coyer was an ideal fit for a team looking to bring incremental change to its defensive system. Coyer served as coordinator for Denver, running a traditional 4-3 defense that was marked by its aggressiveness. After he was fired from that job, he caught on as a defensive line coach in Tampa Bay, learning the intricacies of the Tampa-2 system that the Colts have run under Dungy.

Coyer takes over a defense that has developed into a reliable unit but one where run defense has always been an afterthought. The Colts under Dungy fluctuated between mediocre and abysmal on run defense, ranking 16th or worse every year but one. The struggles of the Colts' run defense are often ascribed to their undersized personnel, but the bigger issue is that Dungy wanted the base defense to be focused on defending the pass. In desperate times, most notably the 2006 playoffs, the Colts sacrificed pass rush to defend the run with some success. A focus on defending the run always imperiled the integrity of the zone defense and potentially allowed the dreaded big play.

To figure out Coyer's impact on the defense, we can look at two data sources. What sort of defenses did Coyer oversee as a coordinator, and what happened when Dungy left Tampa Bay? The recent decline of Denver's defense makes Coyer appear to be a real asset. He coordinated Denver's defenses from 2003 to 2006, during which time the defense ranked between fifth and 12th. Those four seasons represent four of the Denver defense's five highest rankings since 1997. Coyer's biggest weakness as a coordinator was his inability to control the Colts offense in the 2003 or 2004 playoffs. Now that weakness may be apparent every day in practice, but he can safely avoid defending Manning-to-Reggie Wayne on Sundays.

When Dungy left Tampa Bay, the Buccaneers retained defensive coordinator Monte Kiffin. Since Kiffin was a long-time associate of Dungy's, the theory was that the defense would remain elite and fundamentally the same. Dungy's influence is apparent in looking at Tampa Bay's DVOA before and after his departure. In Dungy's last four years in Tampa, his defenses ranked seventh, first, fourth, and second in DVOA. In 2002, the first year after his departure, Tampa Bay had -32.1% DVOA, the best defensive rating of the DVOA Era. (No other defense has been below -30% for a whole year.) The Buccaneers fell to third in the rankings in 2003, and have regressed from that dominant level to merely very good since 2004.

Other than the one-year spike in 2002, the other noticeable change in Tampa Bay after Dungy left is the improvement of the run defense. The Buccaneers from 1996 through 2001 never ranked higher than ninth in run defense. From 2002 through 2007, they never ranked lower than tenth. Coyer's run defenses in Denver were all above average, and twice ranked in the top 10.

We can reasonably predict that the Colts run defense will be better, but what we do not know is whether the Colts pass defense, freed from the shackles of a constant Tampa-2, will also improve. The 2002 Buccaneers were one of the great pass defenses of all-time, and the unit moved towards more man-to-man coverage. Obviously, that team had more talent than Indianapolis will have. Still, the possibility of a more diverse defense presents the possibility that the Colts can confuse opponents and force mistakes early in games. The Colts' system under Dungy excelled at protecting leads, but the Colts would have gained leads quicker if opponents were not able to methodically control the ball throughout the first half of games.

All of this is still effectively guesswork. The other possibility is that the Colts simply do not have the coverage corners to play anything but a safe Tampa-2. As Coyer tries to blitz more, teams will begin picking on the Colts for big plays. While the run defense improves, it comes at the expense of the pass rush, and teams will start connecting on deep passes on first down.

Whether the defense improves or regresses, the Colts are still likely playoff bound.

Despite ranking anywhere from third to 27th in defensive DVOA over the past six years, the Colts have always won 12 games because of their offense. The one final question left unanswered is whether the changing coaching staff can make the Colts more consistent winners in the playoffs.

Recent surprise runs by Carolina, Arizona, and the Giants have led to an increased understanding that the "best" team does not win every playoff game. The Colts themselves won the Super Bowl with their second lowest regular-season DVOA of the past six years. But even allowing for the occasional upset, the Colts' playoff record is extremely mediocre. During Dungy's tenure, the Colts went 7-6 in the playoffs, including home losses in 2005 and 2007.

Nonetheless, the Colts have been hesitant to make any wholesale changes to their approach. The Super Bowl in 2006 was a testament to the fact that staying the course sometimes helps, but the new coaching staff creates the possibility that the Colts could be more competitive in the playoffs.

The playoff failures have not always or even often been the fault of the defense.

In the Dungy era, the offense scored fewer than 20 points in six out of its 13 games. The Colts are 1-5 when scoring under 20 points and 6-1 when they score 20 or more points. In Peyton Manning's two playoff games before Dungy's arrival, the Colts scored fewer than 20 points and lost two close games.

Apart from the coaching change, the other potential change made with an eye towards the postseason is the drafting of running back Donald Brown in the first round. Brown will no doubt help in the regular season too, as the Colts had their worst rushing attack since 2002 last season. Still, the Colts are always planning for the playoffs, and their inability to consistently run the football in January has led to defeat on numerous occasions. Joseph Addai has totaled only 87 yards on a combined 29 carries in the Colts' last two playoff losses.

Addai was a first-round pick just three years ago, and his early success made him appear to be an excellent selection. He was a part-time back in college, and one knock on him was whether he would be able to withstand a large workload. The answer appears to be no. Addai was excellent as a rookie when he split carries with Dominic Rhodes, but he wore down in the second half of 2007 and was hampered by injuries throughout 2008.

Brown's presence can leave Addai fresher for the playoffs. In the 2006 playoffs, Addai averaged at least four yards per carry in three of the Colts' four wins, while Rhodes did in all four. If the Colts can get a consistent running attack in the playoffs, they can avoid the low scoring outputs that have sunk their Super Bowl aspirations too often in the past.

For all the talk of differences, the most likely outcome is that the product on the field is eerily similar to the teams of recent seasons. In most cases, talent dictates whether a team wins or loses. Most coaches understand that players need to be put in positions where they can excel. Since the Colts players are talented and have been specifically acquired for the schemes they have been running the past two years, it seems unlikely that much will change. Given the extraordinary run of success in the Dungy years, that's a very positive development for Colts fans.

Ned Macey

2008 Colts Stats by Week

Wk	vs.	W-L	PF	PA	YDF	YDA	TO	Total	Off	Def	ST
1	CHI	L	13	29	293	319	-1	-25%	4%	24%	-4%
2	@MIN	W	18	15	321	299	-1	0%	2%	-6%	-9%
3	JAC	L	21	23	325	403	-1	-17%	-5%	9%	-3%
4	BYE										
5	@HOU	W	31	27	314	391	+2	6%	10%	1%	-2%
6	BAL	W	31	3	334	260	+5	115%	44%	-58%	12%
7	@GB	L	14	34	302	302	-2	-50%	-28%	22%	-1%
8	@TEN	L	21	31	317	281	-2	35%	35%	2%	2%
9	NE	W	18	15	301	342	+2	24%	40%	17%	1%
10	@PIT	W	24	20	290	326	+3	62%	50%	-15%	-3%
11	HOU	W	33	27	474	356	+1	14%	28%	13%	0%
12	@SD	W	23	20	341	394	0	-5%	6%	17%	6%
13	@CLE	W	10	6	215	193	-1	-24%	-29%	-12%	-7%
14	CIN	W	35	3	334	252	+3	61%	35%	-31%	-5%
15	DET	W	31	21	421	323	0	-12%	19%	21%	-10%
16	@JAC	W	31	24	396	409	+1	29%	48%	14%	-6%
17	TEN	W	23	0	390	125	0	62%	28%	-37%	-2%
18	@SD	L	17	23	366	357	+2	15%	17%	-9%	-10%

Trends and Splits

	Offense	Rank	Defense	Rank
Total DVOA	17.2%	6	0.1%	10
Unadjusted VOA	18.3%	6	0.1%	11
Weighted trend	22.1%	5	-2.3%	8
Variance	6.2%	11	15.3%	32
Average opponent	3.1%	19	1.8%	12
Passing	41.8%	2	1.2%	9
Rushing	-6.5%	27	-1.0%	18
First down	-0.5%	21	3.3%	20
Second down	24.0%	6	2.5%	12
Third down	37.4%	4	-9.4%	8
First half	14.0%	11	4.3%	16
Second half	20.6%	8	-3.8%	7
Red Zone	12.8%	11	-13.9%	8
Late and close	20.9%	8	-10.1%	6

Five-Year Performance

Year	W-L	Pyth	Est W	PF	PA	TO	Total	Rk	Off	Rk	Def	Rk	ST	Rk	Off AGL	Rk	Def AGL	Rk
2004	12-4	11.5	12.0	522	351	+19	28.1%	4	33.2%	1	2.8%	19	-2.3%	23	11.1	22	30.1	9
2005	14-2	12.7	12.7	439	247	+12	33.6%	1	23.6%	3	-12.2%	5	-2.2%	25	7.8	24	16.2	16
2006	12-4	9.6	10.6	427	360	+7	17.3%	7	29.0%	1	8.8%	25	-2.9%	25	18.5	15	31.3	4
2007	13-3	12.5	12.4	450	262	+18	30.7%	2	24.3%	2	-12.3%	2	-5.9%	32	19.3	21	51.0	1
2008	12-4	10.2	10.5	377	298	+9	15.3%	8	17.2%	6	0.1%	10	-1.8%	24	31.8	12	39.6	6

Strategic Tendencies

Run/Pass		Rank	Offense		Rank	Defense		Rank	Other		Rank
Runs, all plays	37%	29	3+ WR	83%	1	Rush 3	5.3%	16	2+ RB, Pct Runs	46%	32
Runs, first half	35%	32	4+ WR	8%	23	Rush 4	84.8%	1	1 RB/2 TE, Pct Runs	62%	3
Runs, first down	46%	26	2+ TE	16%	29	Rush 5	7.8%	32	1RB/3+WR, Pct Runs	33%	6
Runs, second-long	30%	30	Single back	89%	1	Rush 6+	2.1%	32	Zone Blitz	0%	31
Runs, power sit.	64%	22	Play action	18%	14	Rush 7+	0.2%	30	Go for it on 4th	0.81	22
Runs, behind 2H	30%	22	Max protect	7%	22	Sacks by LB	0.0%	32	Offensive Pace	29.5	8
Pass, ahead 2H	46%	11	Outside pocket	4%	32	Sacks by DB	0.0%	30	Defensive Pace	32.0	31

We're not kidding when we say that the Indianapolis offensive scheme never changes. The Colts have led the league in the frequency of single-back sets for four straight years, but have also ranked 23rd or lower in usage of four or more wide receivers in all four years. ● The Colts only had two backs (including a tight end lined up at fullback) in the formation for 11 percent of their running back carries, by far the lowest percentage in the league. The next highest team (Pittsburgh) was at 28 percent, and the NFL average was 56 percent. ● When playing the Colts, teams chose to focus their defensive resources on receivers. Peyton Manning saw five or more rushers only 21 percent of the time, the lowest rate in the league. Only five percent of the time did the Indy line need to protect against six or more. Only Houston saw fewer big blitzes. ● Colts opponents used three or more wide receivers on only 39 percent of plays, the lowest rate in the league — fairly astonishing considering that those opponents were often playing from behind. ● Only 15 percent of passes against the Colts went over 15 yards through the air, the lowest percentage in the league. The Colts ranked 31st the year before, at 14 percent. ● The Colts were the first team in our database of individual defensive stats (which goes back to 1999) which had no sacks by either linebackers or defensive backs.

Passing

Player	DYAR	DVOA	Plays	NtYds	Avg	YAC	C%	TD	Int
Peyton Manning	1783	36.1%	572	3967	6.9	4.2	67.1%	27	11
Jim Sorgi	109	38.8%	30	178	5.9	5.5	73.3%	0	0

Rushing

Player	DYAR	DVOA	Plays	Yds	Avg	TD	Fum	Suc
Joseph Addai	49	-1.3%	155	544	3.5	5	1	48%
Dominic Rhodes*	25	-4.9%	152	538	3.5	6	0	49%
Chad Simpson	-15	-25.4%	15	43	2.9	1	1	60%
Lance Ball	17	20.0%	13	83	6.4	0	1	77%
Peyton Manning	-20	-35.2%	10	31	3.1	1	1	--
Najeh Davenport*	4	3.7%	8	26	3.3	0	0	63%

Receiving

Player	DYAR	DVOA	Plays	Ctch	Yds	Y/C	YAC	TD	C%
Reggie Wayne	332	19.1%	130	82	1128	13.8	3.6	7	63%
Marvin Harrison*	31	-9.2%	107	60	636	10.6	2.9	6	56%
Anthony Gonzalez	242	26.2%	79	57	664	11.6	3.1	5	72%
Dallas Clark	187	18.3%	107	77	848	11.0	4.7	6	72%
Gijon Robinson	4	-4.4%	24	19	166	8.7	5.4	0	79%
Tom Santi	2	-5.4%	13	10	64	6.4	4.3	1	77%
Jacob Tamme	-17	-54.1%	5	3	12	4.0	1.7	0	60%
Dominic Rhodes*	54	2.2%	59	45	302	6.7	5.5	3	76%
Joseph Addai	40	5.3%	39	25	206	8.2	6.5	2	64%

Offensive Line

Year	Yards	ALY	Rank	Power	Rank	10+ Yds	Rank	Stuff	Rank	Sacks	ASR	Rank	False	Cont.
2006	4.13	4.48	5	60%	22	10%	28	18%	13	15	3.4%	1	22	36
2007	4.03	4.46	4	78%	1	9%	31	15%	4	23	4.2%	6	20	34
2008	3.60	3.99	23	62%	21	9%	32	21%	27	14	2.8%	1	19	29

Year	LE	Rank	LT	Rank	Mid	Rank	RT	Rank	RE	Rank
2006	4.53	7	5.37	2	4.59	5	4.44	6	3.62	20
2007	3.67	23	5.84	2	4.57	5	4.07	19	4.43	7
2008	4.84	10	3.94	19	4.08	18	4.23	13	2.66	31

For the first time in years, this group was actually a weakness for the Colts. General personnel turnover and injuries exacted a toll on the offensive line throughout the year. The Colts got only 28 starts out of a possible 96 from linemen who started during their 2006 Super Bowl season. An offseason decision to keep guard Ryan Lilja instead of Jake Scott backfired when Lilja suffered a knee injury that cost him the season. Adding insult to injury (actually, injury to injury) was a banged up Jeff Saturday, who missed four games. Saturday is not the best center in football, but he is essential to the Colts because he is so in synch with Peyton Manning and able to adjust his fellow offensive linemen in the Colts' no-huddle. The injuries to Lilia and Saturday put a great deal of pressure on rookies Mike Pollak and Jamey Richard and were a big factor in the Colts' slow start to the season. The Colts had planned to let Saturday leave in free agency, but the final salary cap for 2009 was $4 million higher than expected, allowing them to re-sign him. The Colts were right to draft his eventual replacement in Richard, but the youngster's struggles last season (plus Manning's level of comfort) forced them to spend to retain the aging veteran.

Most troubling was the lack of development of Tony Ugoh. After a promising rookie year, Ugoh struggled to assert himself in the running game in his second season. His pass protection was still solid, but he may look better than he truly is because of Manning's ability to get rid of the ball quickly. Charlie Johnson settled in at left guard, where he is quick enough, but not really strong enough to deal with big defensive tackles. The final starter is Rian Diem, who continues to man right tackle with competence but not dominance.

Defensive Front Seven

Defensive Line	Age	Pos	Plays	TmPct	Rk	Stop	Dfts	Overall Stop%	Rk	AvYd	Rk	Pass Rush Sack	Hit	Hur	vs. Run Runs	St%	Yds	vs. Pass Pass	St%	Yds
Robert Mathis	28	DE	50	6.4%	32	40	24	80%	27	1.1	22	11.5	2	8	29	76%	3.1	21	86%	-1.7
Keyunta Dawson	23	DT	42	5.7%	27	22	2	52%	72	3.6	73	0.0	2	5	37	59%	3.1	5	0%	8.0
Eric Foster	24	DT	34	5.0%	35	24	4	71%	62	2.1	39	0.0	1	3	31	68%	2.1	3	100%	1.7
Josh Thomas*	28	DE	29	3.5%	82	22	4	76%	52	2.8	82	0.0	0	2	28	75%	2.9	1	100%	0.0
Raheem Brock	31	DT	28	3.3%	64	14	8	50%	73	3.0	67	3.5	7	8	19	47%	4.5	9	56%	-0.2
Dwight Freeney	29	DE	27	3.4%	83	23	14	85%	13	-1.0	3	10.5	13	28	16	75%	3.4	11	100%	-7.4
Darrell Reid*	27	DT	19	2.3%	--	16	5	84%	--	1.1	--	2.0	0	2	17	82%	1.9	2	100%	-6.0

Linebackers	Age	Pos	Plays	TmPct	Rk	Stop	Dfts	Overall Stop%	AvYd	Pass Rush Sack	Hit	Hur	vs. Run Runs	St%	Rk	Yds	Rk	vs. Pass Tgts	Suc%	Rk	AdjYd	Rk
Freddie Keiaho	27	OLB	104	14.2%	26	45	8	43%	5.9	0.0	2	1	66	58%	86	3.9	73	35	39%	79	7.2	66
Gary Brackett	29	ILB	100	15.9%	15	53	9	53%	5.6	0.0	1	1	67	69%	31	3.1	34	16	57%	26	7.2	67
Clint Session	24	OLB	90	10.7%	61	42	16	47%	4.6	0.0	0	1	65	54%	96	4.0	77	28	37%	81	7.0	62
Buster Davis*	26	ILB	23	7.3%	--	8	2	35%	5.0	0.0	0	0	15	33%	--	4.1	--	4	68%	--	6.1	--

Year	Yards	ALY	Rank	Power	Rank	10+ Yds	Rank	Stuff	Rank	Sack	ASR	Rank
2006	5.37	4.70	31	81%	32	23%	30	17%	24	25	6.2%	21
2007	3.80	3.92	11	71%	26	11%	4	20%	14	28	6.1%	19
2008	4.26	4.25	21	78%	30	18%	15	16%	23	30	5.5%	22

Year	LE	Rank	LT	Rank	Mid	Rank	RT	Rank	RE	Rank
2006	1.78	1	4.94	26	4.87	32	5.62	31	3.17	8
2007	3.78	14	3.38	3	4.04	14	4.68	27	3.27	7
2008	3.81	10	4.04	13	4.51	27	4.19	19	3.54	13

The Colts' defensive front has always been small, but perhaps never smaller than it was last year. The release of Ed Johnson after an early season drug arrest and the surprising preseason retirement of Quinn Pitcock suddenly left the Colts very shallow at defensive tackle. The result was a rotation of 2007 seventh-rounder Keyunta Dawson and two undrafted rookies, Eric Foster and Antonio Johnson (and to get Johnson, they had to sign him off the Tennessee practice squad). The undersized and overmanned group played hard but was generally outmatched. The Colts have responded by giving Johnson another chance and drafting a couple of big defensive tackles in Fili Moala (USC, second round) and Terrance Taylor (Michigan, fourth round). Moala in particular may be a draft steal; our friend Russ Lande at GM Jr. rated him as this year's second-best tackle prospect, ahead of first-rounders Peria Jerry and Evander Hood, because of his consistency and explosive closing burst. These players give the Colts the most defensive tackle depth they have had this decade. The increased size of the defensive linemen is a break from recent tradition, where the Colts continually employed sub-300 pound defensive tackles. The Colts now have three defensive tackles over 300 pounds for the first time since the team switched to the Tampa-2, although the presence of Foster and Raheem Brock presents them opportunity to go with undersized but speedy tackles when necessary.

Defensive ends Robert Mathis and Dwight Freeney continue to terrorize opposing quarterbacks. Mathis again got the lead in sacks, but Freeney's hurry and hit numbers show that he is the much more consistent pass rusher. Mathis, as a left defensive end, is forced to play the run more. While he makes more plays, his success rate is similar to Freeney's, and teams actually run more effectively behind their right tackle than their left tackle. This is true even though Mathis is replaced on run downs by the versatile Brock, who is technically the starter at end despite playing fewer snaps.

At linebacker, the Colts finally gave playing time to play-maker Clint Sessions, who is more likely to blow up plays than his outside counterpart Freddy Keiaho but also more likely to miss a tackle. Gary Brackett continues his outstanding career as a Tampa-2 inside linebacker, but it will be interesting to see how he fits into any adjustments made by new defensive coordinator Larry Coyer. The Colts also have linebacker depth with former starter Tyjuan Hagler and 2008 draftee Phillip Wheeler, who was slated to start before a lack of interest on the free agent market allowed Keiaho to return.

Defensive Secondary

Secondary	Age	Pos	Plays	TmPct	Rk	Stop	Dfts	Yds	Rk	St%	Rk	Tgts	Tgt%	Rk	Dist	Suc%	Rk	AdjYd	Rk	Yds	PD	Int
						Overall				vs. Run						vs. Pass						
Antoine Bethea	25	FS	104	12.4%	12	32	13	7.8	54	35%	52	29	7.1%	35	13.0	47%	57	7.3	22	7.5	5	2
Melvin Bullitt	24	SS	74	9.4%	45	33	15	4.2	7	52%	15	34	8.9%	12	9.1	44%	67	7.5	27	7.7	7	4
Tim Jennings	26	CB	70	8.4%	50	25	15	4.4	9	46%	39	64	15.8%	59	9.5	36%	82	8.9	76	8.5	8	2
Kelvin Hayden	26	CB	54	10.3%	18	27	11	5.0	21	50%	31	54	21.2%	20	10.0	56%	20	5.9	13	5.4	9	3
Marlin Jackson	26	CB	48	13.1%	--	21	10	3.7	--	56%	--	37	21.0%	--	6.9	42%	--	7.2	--	7.9	1	0
Bob Sanders	28	SS	41	13.0%	6	17	4	6.5	29	48%	21	12	7.9%	24	13.0	65%	8	5.1	6	4.9	2	1
Keiwan Ratliff*	28	CB	31	4.6%	--	12	6	7.3	--	33%	--	30	9.0%	--	9.8	43%	--	7.4	--	7.5	5	2

Year	Pass D Rank	vs. #1 WR	Rk	vs. #2 WR	Rk	vs. Other WR	Rk	vs. TE	Rk	vs. RB	Rk
2006	13	11.7%	25	15.1%	24	-13.8%	10	-8.4%	12	4.7%	20
2007	2	-21.3%	4	5.0%	17	-36.4%	2	-21.6%	2	4.4%	23
2008	14	21.6%	28	-15.8%	8	-10.7%	13	1.6%	14	8.4%	20

Quietly, the Colts have developed a very solid starting secondary. Bob Sanders gets all the headlines, but his body proved once again that it was too fragile to play with his ferocity. Injuries forced Sanders to miss ten games. He was replaced admirably by Mevlin Bullitt, who held his own in run support. On the outside, Kelvin Hayden really developed into a top-flight cornerback in his fourth year, earning a long-term contract. The big deal for Hayden may mean this is Marlin Jackson's last year. Jackson is less prone than Hayden to give up the big play through the air but more likely to give up the completion. Holding down the deep middle — often on his own given the Colts' need for a safety in the box — is Antoine Bethea, who provides consistency and very solid coverage ability.

The problem for the Colts is the lack of depth at cornerback. Tim Jennings was thrust into the starting lineup after a season-ending injury to Jackson last year, but is simply too small to play well consistently. After Jennings, the Colts were relying on cast-off Keiwan Ratliff, who left in the offseason. This year, the Colts will keep Jennings at the nickel position and try to break in third-round pick Jerraud Powers, an undersized but physical player out of Auburn.

Special Teams

Year	DVOA	Rank	FG/XP	Rank	Net Kick	Rank	Kick Ret	Rank	Net Punt	Rank	Punt Ret	Rank	Hidden	Rank
2006	-2.9%	25	4.8	8	-15.2	30	0.5	14	-9.7	29	2.5	8	10.0	4
2007	-5.9%	32	-12.4	31	-15.5	29	-4.7	23	-9.5	28	7.3	6	5.5	9
2008	-1.8%	24	-2.9	24	2.4	14	-9.0	29	9.0	7	-10.2	32	-4.7	19

Turns out you can count on three things in life: death, taxes, and miserable special teams for the Colts. They ranked 25th or worse for the fifth straight year. The Colts mercifully fired coordinator Russ Purnell and hired Ray Rychleski, which one assumes would have to improve the units. On the other hand, the Colts lost free agent Darrell Reid, the team's special teams captain and one of its few sure open-field tacklers. It is hard to imagine how bad the coverage teams would have been in the past few seasons without Reid, and Rychleski will have to completely revamp coverage teams to account for his loss. The Colts also bid farewell to long-time punter Hunter Smith and drafted Pat McAfee out of West Virginia to replace him. Adam Vinatieri had a quietly very solid season, as he fought off injuries that had limited his long-distance accuracy in recent years. He was also above average on kickoff distance, although the Colts' coverage team gave that value back and then some. The Colts' kick and punt return duties are in complete flux entering camp, with second-year wide receiver Pierre Garcon perhaps the most likely candidate for kick returns. The team has no obvious punt returner, and if it is not Garcon, the punt returner is likely not on the roster as of this writing.

Coaching Staff

Rarely has a team won 12 games and turned over this much of the coaching staff. Tony Dungy's decision to retire started a domino effect, as new head coach Jim Caldwell established his authority by dismissing defensive coordinator Ron Meeks and special teams coordinator Russ Purnell. The other coaches to depart were veteran offensive coordinator Tom Moore and offensive line coach Howard Mudd, who retired based on pending changes in the league's pension system. The replacements break into two camps. Caldwell, new offensive coordinator Clyde Christensen, and offensive line coach Pete Metzelaars were clear coaches-in-waiting who have been in the organization for a while. The offense is likely to remain the same, if only because of the continuity of players and Manning's admittedly large role in running his own offense. Meanwhile, Caldwell has put his own stamp on the team with the hiring of defensive coordinator Larry Coyer. The defense should be much more aggressive and much more dedicated to stopping the run. Despite the new larger defensive tackles, however, this team is still built around Tampa-2 personnel — so no matter what Caldwell or Coyer might want to do with the defense, the changes will not be too radical.

Jacksonville Jaguars

It wasn't supposed to be like this.

When the Jaguars' 2007 season ended with a near-miss divisional round loss to the Patriots, everything seemed to be in place for a deep playoff run in the following season. The team simply needed to put a few pieces together, figure out a way to beat the Colts, and hope for a few lucky breaks. Quarterback David Garrard was a rising star, the dynamic power running game featured Maurice Jones-Drew and Fred Taylor, the pass rush was ostensibly reinforced in the draft, and the front office took enough financial risks on free agents to show that the commitment was there. It looked pretty good, if you didn't look beneath the surface and see what several years of missteps had wrought. For every positive move the Jags had made, there was a negative pulling them backward. Every team will pay for their mistakes, and it just so happened that for the Jaguars, the bill came due all at once.

The downturn started early. In the season's first game, a 17-10 loss to the Titans, guards Vince Manuwai and Mo Williams were lost for the season. They joined starting center Brad Meester, who missed the first six games, on the sideline. Jacksonville had no answer for Tennessee's hyperactive front seven, and Fred Taylor led the team in rushing with only 18 yards. The Jags took advantage of inferior run defenses in wins over the Colts and Broncos, but a 3-3 start was revealed to be a mirage as the team went 2-8 down the stretch. No Jacksonville running back gained 100 yards or more after Maurice Jones-Drew's 125 in Week 6, and for a power-running team, that's a major problem. The ineffective play of tackles Khalif Barnes and Tony Pashos did not help the backups on the interior line, and rookie defensive ends Derrick Harvey and Quentin Groves failed to live up to expectations.

But there was no disaster like the receiving corps. No Jaguars receiver finished higher than 45th in DYAR. This was a scathing indictment of the team's personnel strategy over time. At any given time in 2008, you could see up to four pass-catchers drafted in the first round on the field, and not one produced in line with that designation. Reggie Williams, Matt Jones, Marcedes Lewis, and Troy Williamson all underperformed, and only Williamson was someone else's first-round mistake — Minnesota's, to be exact.

JAGUARS SUMMARY

2008 Record: 5-11

Pythagorean Wins: 6.2 (25th)

DVOA: 1.9% (20th)*

Offense: 12.6% (11th)

Defense: 10.2% (24th)

Special Teams: -0.5% (21st)

Variance: 8.1% (3rd)

2008: Playoff contendor bites the dust in a hail of injuries and questionable personnel choices.

2009: Rebound or rebuild?

2009 Mean Projection: 10.2 wins

On the Clock (0-3): 0%

Loserville (4-6): 3%

Mediocrity (7-8): 17%

Playoff Contender (9-10): 38%

Super Bowl Contender (11+): 42%

Projected Average Opponent: 1.4% (15th)

---

* This rating, and the optimistic forecast for Jacksonville, may seem odd to readers of our Web site who thought the Jaguars had a much lower rating at the end of 2008. As noted earlier in the book, our new, improved version of DVOA raised the rating for the 2008 Jaguars from -8.5% to 1.9%, the biggest jump of any team going back to 1995. For more on this issue, see the Statistical Toolbox.

2009 Jaguars Schedule

Week	Opp.	Week	Opp.	Week	Opp.
1	at IND	7	BYE	13	HOU
2	ARI	8	at TEN	14	MIA
3	at HOU	9	KC	15	IND (Thu.)
4	TEN	10	at NYJ	16	at NE
5	at SEA	11	BUF	17	at CLE
6	STL	12	at SF		

Any postseason review of the team's personnel moves indicated that changes needed to be made. Owner Wayne Weaver had a system in place where Vice President/Player Personnel James Harris, head coach Jack Del Rio, and Executive Director/College and Pro Personnel Gene Smith all had to agree on a transaction before it could happen. Paralysis by analysis? Too many cooks? Whatever the case, Harris resigned on December 23, leaving Smith with the first of two promotions — first to Harris' old position, then up again to General Manager on January 12. The consensus approach will come to an end, as Smith will be in charge of all personnel moves going forward.

The Harris drafts will not be fondly remembered. His first three picks in 2003 — Byron Leftwich, Rashean Mathis, and Vince Manuwai — were about as good as it ever got. He blew first-round picks on raw, toolsy receivers (Williams in 2004, Jones in 2005, tight end Lewis in 2006). He had entire draft classes that turned out to be washout lists due to a preference for pure athleticism over football sense, and in some cases, mere common sense.

But what really finished Harris was the combination of the 2008 draft and free agent class. The Jags inexplicably gave receiver Jerry Porter a six-year, $30 million contract. Porter caught 11 passes in 2008 and proved to be such a divisive influence (a well-documented tendency during his time in Oakland), that he was released after one season. Former San Diego cornerback Drayton Florence received $12 million in guarantees from the Jags, and responded by playing so badly that he was benched after four games.

The 2008 draft was a crapshoot, and Harris came up with snake eyes. The team traded up to pick Florida defensive end Derrick Harvey, who missed training camp in a holdout and took a while to get up to ramming speed. Then came the move to trade up in the second round and grab Auburn speed-rusher Quentin Groves. Those two picks cost the Jags several draft picks, and Harris was left holding the tab. Harvey

was a disappointment, and Groves didn't even make enough plays to be listed on the defensive tables later in the chapter. The errors were compounded when the Jaguars got very little from their late-round picks.

Past drafts also caught up to Harris. Williams and Jones spent more time in the police blotter than in the end zone. FO game charters credited Lewis with 10 dropped passes in 2008, an astonishing number for a tight end.

Though the new regime is denying it, the Jags look to be on a rebuilding track, with a number of longtime Jacksonville veterans leaving this offseason. Linebacker Mike Peterson landed in Atlanta after feuding with Del Rio, and end Paul Spicer, who combined with fellow veteran Reggie Hayward to out-produce the two rookies, signed with New Orleans. The February release of Fred Taylor was perhaps the most emotional decision Smith had to make — Taylor had been with the Jags since 1999 — and that move is as good any to launch a discussion of Jacksonville's future.

When Maurice Jones-Drew signed a four-year contract extension worth $17.5 million, he became the primary back in a system where he had never run for 200 carries. It's always been by committee for Pocket Hercules, and the rest of the crew is nothing but question marks. Chauncey Washington could be in the mix, as the front office seems to like his potential. Oft-injured fullback Greg Jones may get more carries. The sleeper candidate is Rashad Jennings, the Liberty University star taken in the seventh round. Something will have to be done — putting more than 300 carries on Jones-Drew's back is a risky proposition, not to mention what it would do to Garrard. In 2008, Jones-Drew was his quarterback's primary (who are we kidding — his only) safety valve in the short passing game.

Smith did get Garrard a few new weapons, starting with a new veteran partner who could produce great dividends. Like his new quarterback, ex-Rams receiver Torry Holt saw a severe production dropoff that was just as much about those around him. Quarterback Marc Bulger was benched for a time, and complementary targets were hard to find.

"I was in a situation and we all there in St. Louis were in a situation where there was no continuity," Holt said after he signed with the Jaguars. "We had some offensive line changes. Steven Jackson had missed some games so our running game kind of hurt us. Teams can roll and double and do things to kind of take me out of the ballgame … now my numbers drop and now people are saying I lost a step. Well maybe

I have. This will be my 11th season in the National Football League. Am I running the same way I did 10 years ago? Absolutely not, but I can still play and I can still play at a high level."

We like the potential productivity of the Garrard-Holt tandem, but that's in part because Garrard has so few weapons elsewhere. There are a number of statistical indicators pointing to a Jaguars revival. Jacksonville's Adjusted Games Lost for starters totaled 64.2, one of the top ten totals in the league. AGL including reserves was 158.4, which ranked fifth overall. The Jacksonville decline was rooted in bad front office decision-making as much as bad injury luck, but you don't need to look far back into history to see teams clear out a bad front office and make huge strides forward under new management. Two of last year's three turnaround teams — Miami and Atlanta — put the focus on new offensive stars and hoped that their defenses would pull their weight. (Baltimore already had a defense, of course; that was more a "Just Add Quarterback" situation.)

The Jags went with linemen in the first two rounds again, but offensive tackles Eugene Monroe from Virginia and Ebon Britton from Arizona have the potential for immediate impact. Since 2001, teams that spent at least 1200 points in standard draft value (per the Draft Value Chart) on offensive linemen improved in offensive DVOA by an average of 15 percent (for table, see St. Louis chapter). Monroe may be the best, most balanced offensive lineman in the 2009 class, and Britton comes to the NFL with a chip on his shoulder after being snubbed in the first round. "Every team that passed on me is gonna regret it for the rest of the history of that franchise," Britton said after the Jags took him 39th overall. "I've got my own agenda and that's first and foremost to take the Jacksonville Jaguars to the Super Bowl. Secondly, I'm gonna be the greatest offensive tackle to ever play this game." So the kids aren't lacking confidence. Veteran Tra Thomas will step in for the short term as the new linemen learn. Pashos is still with the team, but he's living on borrowed time.

If this team is going to turn it around, renewed success on both lines is the key. On offense, Garrard needs more time and Jones-Drew needs bigger and more consistent lanes. On defense, the underrated linebacker corps of Justin Durant, Daryl Smith, and Clint Ingram needs the front four to hold the point. The Jaguars are hoping that Manuwai and Williams can come back to full health and join the new tackles to solidify that offensive line. The front office was criticized in retrospect for trading Marcus Stroud to Buffalo for draft picks, but Stroud wasn't quite the rock he had once been, and the deal might have netted something if Harris' draft hadn't been so iffy. Rob Meier, who was a solid prospect going into the season, didn't match up in Stroud's place. Temple defensive tackle Terrance Knighton, who ran a 4.93 40 at his Pro Day, was added in the third round to bring extra strength to the interior line. Two new receivers came on board in the persons of Mike Thomas and Jarrett Dillard in the fourth and fifth rounds.

Two unfortunate tendencies from the Harris era may have continued, however. Jacksonville's habit of reaching for cornerbacks in the draft showed up when the team took William & Mary cornerback Derek Cox in the third round. Several different draft guides did not have Cox among the top 100 prospects at his position, but the Jags traded a second-round pick next year and a seventh-rounder in 2009 for the right to draft him. Then there's that tendency to take athletes without a position, like sixth-round tight end Zach Miller from Nebraska-Omaha. He's a converted option quarterback ... but at least he's not a first-rounder like Matt Jones was.

Years of mistakes can be painted over in a miracle season, and our projections favor a turnaround in Jacksonville. Smith must move forward as he tries to separate himself from the failures of the past collective. We're going to find out in 2009 whether the Jaguars' story ends with the line, "Meet the new boss, same as the old boss..."

Doug Farrar

2008 Jaguars Stats by Week

Wk	vs.	W-L	PF	PA	YDF	YDA	TO	Total	Off	Def	ST
1	@TEN	L	10	17	189	309	-1	8%	-24%	-26%	5%
2	BUF	L	16	20	243	285	0	-30%	-5%	28%	4%
3	@IND	W	23	21	403	325	+1	26%	22%	-1%	3%
4	HOU	W	30	27	375	386	0	25%	42%	28%	11%
5	PIT	L	21	26	213	415	+1	15%	35%	17%	-3%
6	@DEN	W	24	17	416	323	+1	25%	26%	-6%	-8%
7	BYE										
8	CLE	L	17	23	380	327	-1	-2%	21%	12%	-11%
9	@CIN	L	19	21	282	312	+1	-30%	-18%	30%	19%
10	@DET	W	38	14	384	256	+1	37%	25%	-5%	7%
11	TEN	L	14	24	257	344	0	-12%	1%	13%	1%
12	MIN	L	12	30	321	226	-4	7%	23%	-1%	-17%
13	@HOU	L	17	30	388	326	-2	-37%	-12%	13%	-13%
14	@CHI	L	10	23	278	296	0	-13%	-9%	5%	1%
15	GB	W	20	16	323	338	+1	61%	51%	-18%	-8%
16	IND	L	24	31	409	396	-1	-9%	30%	39%	0%
17	@BAL	L	7	27	245	431	-4	-35%	2%	37%	0%

Trends and Splits

	Offense	Rank	Defense	Rank
Total DVOA	12.6%	11	10.2%	24
Unadjusted VOA	11.3%	11	11.3%	24
Weighted trend	13.1%	11	11.2%	23
Variance	5.1%	4	4.2%	6
Average opponent	3.5%	17	1.6%	11
Passing	24.3%	12	26.4%	29
Rushing	7.2%	13	-6.4%	10
First down	5.7%	14	16.9%	28
Second down	12.2%	13	-9.8%	7
Third down	25.6%	9	28.0%	30
First half	14.9%	9	18.3%	30
Second half	10.5%	15	1.2%	13
Red Zone	4.3%	18	11.7%	23
Late and close	15.7%	13	-8.0%	8

Five-Year Performance

Year	W-L	Pyth	Est W	PF	PA	TO	Total	Rk	Off	Rk	Def	Rk	ST	Rk	Off AGL	Rk	Def AGL	Rk
2004	9-7	7.3	8.6	261	280	+6	3.3%	12	-2.5%	17	-6.2%	10	-0.4%	17	10.5	24	27.7	11
2005	12-4	10.7	10.3	361	269	+11	15.5%	11	4.4%	11	-10.5%	7	0.6%	13	13.7	19	17.9	10
2006	8-8	10.8	9.6	371	274	+1	23.7%	5	7.4%	10	-16.5%	3	-0.2%	19	12.3	25	40.3	2
2007	11-5	10.7	11.4	411	304	+9	23.7%	3	21.9%	3	-1.8%	15	0.0%	15	16.8	24	34.3	6
2008	5-11	6.2	8.9	302	367	-7	1.9%	20	12.6%	11	10.2%	24	-0.5%	21	48.8	4	15.4	22

Strategic Tendencies

Run/Pass		Rank	Offense		Rank	Defense		Rank	Other		Rank
Runs, all plays	42%	22	3+ WR	45%	23	Rush 3	2.8%	24	2+ RB, Pct Runs	57%	24
Runs, first half	48%	7	4+ WR	8%	25	Rush 4	65.6%	15	1 RB/2 TE, Pct Runs	55%	12
Runs, first down	45%	29	2+ TE	36%	6	Rush 5	19.1%	21	1RB/3+WR, Pct Runs	21%	25
Runs, second-long	40%	14	Single back	67%	8	Rush 6+	12.6%	5	Zone Blitz	3%	16
Runs, power sit.	68%	13	Play action	15%	18	Rush 7+	3.0%	6	Go for it on 4th	0.96	14
Runs, behind 2H	29%	24	Max protect	8%	17	Sacks by LB	19.0%	14	Offensive Pace	32.8	29
Pass, ahead 2H	46%	10	Outside pocket	16%	5	Sacks by DB	3.4%	27	Defensive Pace	31.9	29

For the second straight year, the Jaguars had one of the largest gaps between DVOA in shotgun (34.8%, seventh) and DVOA with the quarterback under center (4.0%, 14th). ● Jacksonville ran less than any other team from sets with three or more wide receivers, only 15.5 percent of plays. They were one of only two teams that never had a running back carry from a four-wide set (the Jets were the other). ● Game charters marked Jacksonville running only two wide receiver screens, the fewest in the NFL. ● Although the Jaguars ranked 24th in defensive DVOA, they stopped opponents three-and-out on 25.5 percent of drives, eighth in the league. ● The Jaguars may want to consider sending fewer big blitzes in 2009. Their defensive DVOA was 18th with five pass rushers (15.0%) but 28th with six or more pass rushers (53.0%). ● Jacksonville had the best DVOA against draw plays of any team that faced at least 20 draws (-47.4%). ● Betraying the weakness of their secondary depth, Jacksonville's defense got successively worse the more wide receivers were in the game for their opponent. However, they had the same problem in 2007 when they were 11-5.

Passing

Player	DYAR	DVOA	Plays	NtYds	Avg	YAC	C%	TD	Int
David Garrard	824	11.0%	581	3466	6.0	4.3	63.2%	15	10

Rushing

Player	DYAR	DVOA	Plays	Yds	Avg	TD	Fum	Suc
Maurice Jones-Drew	112	4.4%	197	826	4.2	12	4	46%
Fred Taylor*	-32	-14.3%	143	556	3.9	1	0	41%
David Garrard	80	9.6%	64	328	5.1	2	1	--
Chauncey Washington	-5	-36.0%	4	9	2.3	0	0	50%

Receiving

Player	DYAR	DVOA	Plays	Ctch	Yds	Y/C	YAC	TD	C%
Matt Jones*	102	-0.5%	107	65	761	11.7	3.0	2	61%
Dennis Northcutt	76	2.1%	68	44	545	12.4	2.5	2	65%
Reggie Williams*	41	-4.8%	63	38	371	9.8	2.0	4	60%
Mike Walker	38	3.7%	30	16	217	13.6	1.5	0	53%
Jerry Porter*	-13	-17.7%	29	11	181	16.5	2.8	1	38%
Troy Williamson	-33	-45.0%	13	5	30	6.0	0.8	1	38%
Torry Holt	12	-11.4%	119	64	796	12.4	2.3	4	54%
Marcedes Lewis	13	-4.6%	73	41	489	11.9	3.7	2	56%
Greg Estandia	3	-4.5%	15	10	113	11.3	3.1	0	67%
Richard Angulo	-10	-20.4%	11	8	63	7.9	3.0	0	73%
Maurice Jones-Drew	220	43.8%	75	62	568	9.2	9.1	2	83%
Fred Taylor*	-23	-32.2%	22	16	98	6.1	5.8	0	73%
Greg Jones	61	53.2%	16	13	116	8.9	7.3	1	81%

Offensive Line

Year	Yards	ALY	Rank	Power	Rank	10+ Yds	Rank	Stuff	Rank	Sacks	ASR	Rank	False	Cont.
2006	5.13	4.57	2	65%	14	23%	5	16%	5	30	7.0%	19	18	37
2007	4.81	4.09	18	61%	18	28%	2	23%	30	31	6.9%	17	19	30
2008	4.06	4.09	16	76%	6	17%	20	18%	13	42	7.9%	24	14	32

Year	LE	Rank	LT	Rank	Mid	Rank	RT	Rank	RE	Rank
2006	4.51	8	5.13	3	4.62	3	3.85	27	4.43	10
2007	4.81	6	3.67	26	4.07	15	5.01	1	3.24	31
2008	3.63	24	4.22	14	4.02	21	4.59	5	4.60	5

Jacksonville's problems started on the front lines in 2008, and nowhere was the disaster more evident than in this unit. A front five that was supposed to help the Jags contend for a Super Bowl berth fell apart in every way possible. Starting guards Vince Manuwai (knee) and Mo Williams (biceps) were lost for the year in the first game of the season. Center Brad Meester missed the first six games with his own biceps injury, and none of the replacements — predominantly Uche Nwaneri and Dennis Norman — could match the first-teamers. The tackles were healthy but didn't perform to expectations; left tackle Khalif Barnes led the team with six blown blocks, and right tackle Tony Pashos followed with 4.5, not to mention the four holding penalties he racked up in the Week 12 game against Minnesota. The decline in Jacksonville's pass protection was a primary factor in David Garrard's down year. The 2008 improvements shown in Power and Stuffed rankings have as much to do with Maurice Jones Drew's power as anything else.

Barnes signed with the Raiders in free agency; Pashos and Meester are still with the team, but Pashos plummeted down the depth chart after the Jags were done with free agency and the draft. Former Eagles tackle William "Tra" Thomas was signed as a short-term stopgap, and the team drafted Virginia's Eugene Monroe and Arizona's Eben Britton in the first two rounds. Monroe cleared the way for 16 of Virginia's total touchdowns in 2008. He has the quickness, strength, balance, and field awareness to develop into one of the greats over time. Britton has the athletic talent of a Joe Thomas and the discipline to have been penalized only four times in 2,461 offensive snaps through his collegiate career, according to his coaches' stats. He was also a Creative Writing major at Arizona, and he comes from a very diverse family. His journalist mom graduated from Columbia University and now runs a personal training business. His dad is a painter whose work has been shown in major galleries. His aunt coached Beyonce for her role in the Austin Powers *Goldmember* movie, and his grandmother, Estelle Parsons, won an Academy Award for her role as Blanche Barrow in *Bonnie and Clyde*. Unless Britton makes multiple Pro Bowls, he may be the black sheep of the family.

Defensive Front Seven

Defensive Line	Age	Pos	Plays	TmPct	Overall Rk	Stop	Dfts	Stop%	Rk	AvYd	Rk	Pass Rush Sack	Hit	Hur	vs. Run Runs	St%	Yds	vs. Pass Pass	St%	Yds
John Henderson	30	DT	46	7.0%	7	37	10	80%	20	1.8	32	2.0	2	2	38	76%	2.3	8	100%	-0.1
Paul Spicer*	34	DE	36	4.8%	57	32	9	89%	5	0.9	19	3.5	4	4	29	86%	1.7	7	100%	-2.4
Rob Meier	32	DT	30	4.3%	49	25	12	83%	8	0.7	8	2.0	3	3	27	81%	1.1	3	100%	-3.0
Reggie Hayward	30	DE	27	3.6%	79	26	20	96%	1	-1.3	2	4.5	7	6	17	94%	-0.2	10	100%	-3.1
Derrick Harvey	23	DE	20	2.7%	--	18	10	90%	--	0.1	--	3.5	4	5	11	82%	0.5	9	100%	-0.4
Tony McDaniel*	24	DT	19	4.1%	--	15	2	79%	--	2.2	--	0.5	1	1	15	80%	2.8	4	75%	0.0

Linebackers	Age	Pos	Plays	TmPct	Overall Rk	Stop	Dfts	Stop%	AvYd	Pass Rush Sack	Hit	Hur	vs. Run Runs	St%	Rk	Yds	Rk	vs. Pass Tgts	Suc%	Rk	AdjYd	Rk
Mike Peterson*	33	ILB	84	12.0%	46	46	11	55%	4.8	1.0	2	3	64	66%	44	3.6	56	23	39%	76	6.8	55
Justin Durant	23	OLB	74	11.3%	54	43	16	58%	4.8	0.0	1	2	40	70%	23	3.3	46	31	49%	47	6.9	61
Daryl Smith	27	OLB	73	11.1%	56	43	12	59%	5.0	2.5	1	6	40	65%	49	3.4	49	33	60%	14	6.3	47
Clint Ingram	26	OLB	32	4.3%	--	17	8	53%	4.7	2.0	3	0	23	61%	--	3.2	--	10	41%	--	6.8	--

Year	Yards	ALY	Rank	Power	Rank	10+ Yds	Rank	Stuff	Rank	Sack	ASR	Rank
2006	3.52	3.55	3	69%	25	15%	12	20%	11	35	7.2%	13
2007	4.20	4.26	24	57%	9	14%	7	19%	17	37	7.2%	10
2008	4.03	3.97	10	57%	3	18%	16	23%	6	29	6.3%	14

Year	LE	Rank	LT	Rank	Mid	Rank	RT	Rank	RE	Rank
2006	3.05	5	3.01	4	3.88	6	2.77	3	4.11	18
2007	4.00	15	4.42	20	4.36	25	4.69	28	3.86	12
2008	4.09	15	4.67	26	4.05	11	3.85	11	3.25	12

The Jags hope that the offensive linemen they took in the first two rounds this year are more effective than the top two defensive linemen they selected last year. First-round pick Derrick Harvey couldn't usurp veteran Reggie Hayward, and second-rounder Quentin Groves was just about invisible. Many defensive linemen improve in their second seasons as they get the hang of the more complicated and physically taxing pro game, and it isn't as if Harvey and Groves don't have talent. Harvey started to pick it up after a slow start that was exacerbated by a minicamp holdout, and he finished his rookie season with a two-sack performance against a Baltimore Ravens team that needed to win (and did) to secure a playoff spot. Groves was effective in fits and starts, but weight is his main problem — he can't keep it on. Playing as low as 251 pounds in his rookie year, Groves frequently disappeared against more powerful lines. Now, it's a matter of either bulking up or moving to linebacker. Veterans Reggie Hayward and Paul Spicer performed more consistently, if not spectacularly, but Spicer is now in New Orleans. Clearly, the kids will have to improve.

On the inside, tackles John Henderson and Rob Meier, who were supposed to anchor a great defense, both underperformed — Henderson missed time with an MCL injury, and Meier couldn't quite pick up the slack in the way that was expected after he led the NFL in Stop Rate in 2008. When Henderson missed a June OTAs with a shoulder injury, Jack Del Rio was not amused. "John has got a shoulder that, back when I played and even prior to that, I don't think anybody would have had to miss a snap for it," the former linebacker said on June 2. "I think it's a minor bruise of sorts." New GM Gene Smith likes what he has seen of third-round defensive tackle Terrance Knighton (Temple). At 6-foot-3 and 320 pounds, Knighton has impressive speed and looks like a nose tackle/three-technique hybrid.

Jacksonville is a bit more optimistic about its linebackers. Justin Durant, a superior athlete, will move inside to replace Mike Peterson, who landed in Jack Del Rio's doghouse and signed with the Falcons. Durant's speed is his primary asset, but like most fast, slightly undersized middlemen, he'll need the interior linemen to keep lanes open. Daryl Smith will play the weak side and Clint Ingram the strong side, but the Jags believe in the concept of interchangeable linebackers, so both outside men can perform with versatility. Last year, Ingram started the season as a fourth linebacker and moved up the depth chart as Smith replaced Peterson in the middle. He's more the straight-ahead run-stopper, while Smith's skill set is more balanced. Now that the roles are defined, this unit will be expected to push Jacksonville's defense forward as other moving parts are in flux.

Defensive Secondary

Secondary	Age	Pos	Plays	Overall TmPct	Rk	Stop	Dfts	vs. Run Yds	Rk	St%	Rk	vs. Pass Tgts	Tgt%	Rk	Dist	Suc%	Rk	AdjYd	Rk	Yds	PD	Int
Brian Williams	30	CB	92	12.3%	7	36	17	4.5	16	47%	38	82	20.5%	24	11.4	47%	52	9.8	83	9.9	9	2
Gerald Sensabaugh*	26	SS	72	9.6%	43	26	9	6.6	35	43%	35	43	10.7%	2	12.8	53%	35	7.6	32	7.7	8	4
Reggie Nelson	25	FS	56	9.2%	49	13	4	10.5	74	17%	77	20	6.2%	48	18.3	50%	44	13.2	77	13.2	4	2
Rashean Mathis	29	CB	49	8.7%	41	23	10	10.1	68	39%	48	58	19.3%	28	14.4	55%	24	7.5	42	7.1	8	4
Drayton Florence*	29	CB	40	5.7%	74	14	4	5.6	28	64%	12	48	12.7%	74	15.6	48%	51	7.1	36	6.6	4	0
Marlon McCree	32	FS	31	7.9%	--	8	4	9.3	--	35%	--	9	4.3%	--	13.8	20%	--	13.1	--	12.7	1	0

Year	Pass D Rank	vs. #1 WR	Rk	vs. #2 WR	Rk	vs. Other WR	Rk	vs. TE	Rk	vs. RB	Rk
2006	3	-7.7%	9	-38.1%	1	-32.3%	3	0.8%	20	-1.7%	17
2007	9	-7.6%	12	-36.0%	3	-4.6%	18	7.1%	16	-6.2%	11
2008	30	9.1%	21	2.6%	18	23.3%	29	26.6%	30	34.3%	32

And the hits just keep on coming — Jacksonville's secondary was quite the mess. The numbers above tell the on-field story, as the Jaguars declined against every type of receiver. Reggie Nelson, the supposed star at free safety, was a walking disaster in coverage. "He's been the culprit of some glaring mistakes," Jack Del Rio told the team's official site in December. "The eye violations (missed assignments) and (poor) tackling are parts of his game that need to come for him to go to the next level." Drayton Florence was benched after four games, a move that put safety Brian Williams at cornerback; Florence signed with the Bills in the offseason. Rashean Mathis was hampered by various leg injuries and was placed on injured reserve in early December. Mathis and Williams should be better as the team's starting cornerbacks this season. The starting safeties will be Nelson and Sean Considine, a free agent signing from Philadelphia who would probably be a backup in a better defensive backfield.

For depth, the Jags brought back veteran safety Marlon McCree, who was awful in Denver last year. They also have special teams standouts Brian Witherspoon and Scott Starks and third-round pick Derek Cox out of William & Mary. Cox may have a chip on his shoulder because several scouting services left him off their Top 100 lists at his position. He wasn't invited to the Combine, but a blistering Pro Day performance put him on Jacksonville's radar. It's a risky way to assess talent, given the divergent track speeds you'll see at different Pro Days, and an All-Colonial Athletic Association Second Team award isn't the kind of thing that perks the interest of most NFL personnel people.

Special Teams

Year	DVOA	Rank	FG/XP	Rank	Net Kick	Rank	Kick Ret	Rank	Net Punt	Rank	Punt Ret	Rank	Hidden	Rank
2006	-0.2%	19	1.4	12	12.9	2	8.1	5	-21.2	32	-2.5	23	12.1	2
2007	0.0%	15	-3.9	25	5.2	10	0.3	15	-1.9	20	0.0	14	-3.8	22
2008	-0.5%	21	-7.2	29	14.1	2	-7.7	28	-1.4	20	-0.6	16	-9.8	27

Buffalo special teams coach Bobby April, recognized by most as the best in the NFL, expressed his admiration for the work of cornerback Brian Witherspoon in the week leading up to Jacksonville's 20-16 loss to the Bills. "He's a gunner on punts, he's good on kickoff coverage and he returns kickoffs and punts really, really well," April told the *Buffalo News* about the Jags' fastest player. "That's a pretty good get for an (undrafted) free agent. But he's no free agent. He's a bona fide player." Witherspoon will go forward in his role as the team's primary return man.

What April's praise doesn't reconcile is that the Jaguars were mediocre in the return game, specifically on kick returns. However, Jacksonville had the best kickoff coverage in the NFL — returns against them were worth an estimated -13.95 points worth of field position below the league average. This jibes with "traditional" stats, as only the Steelers and Bills allowed fewer yards per kickoff return than Jacksonville's 19.9.

Good thing the coverage was so strong, because kicker Josh Scobee had an off year. It was the first season in his five-year career where he did not rank as one of the top kickers according to gross kickoff value, and he also had his lowest field-goal percentage since entering the NFL (76.0 percent). Like a lot of other players in Jacksonville, Scobee will likely rebound in 2009. Punter Steve Weatherford, who had recently been released by the Chiefs and Saints, replaced the injured Adam Podlesh in late November, and the two should battle for the job in 2009.

Coaching Staff

Del Rio was seen as one of the rising young coaches in the league as his team was expected to compete for an AFC championship in 2008, but now, he finds that the eyes are on him in a different way. Most likely, he'll respond by becoming more involved on the defensive side of things with new coordinator Mel Tucker. With a new voice up top in GM Gene Smith, and several new faces in personnel and scouting, Del Rio and his staff have something to prove. Nearly every unit disappointed, and if that doesn't change in 2009, the next purge could very well occur on Del Rio's level.

Offensive coordinator Dirk Koetter gets a bit of a free pass after all those injuries, but he'll be on the hook this season after the front office put so much effort into improving several offensive positions. Russ Purnell is Jacksonville's fourth special teams coordinator in seven years, but he's coached in the NFL since 1986 and has Super Bowl rings for his work with the Colts and Ravens. (Purnell and Del Rio worked together in Baltimore from 1999 through 2001.) Former Vikings head coach Mike Tice currently serves as Del Rio's assistant head coach and tight ends coach. He's an able lieutenant, though he needs to do something — stickum, hypnosis, aversion therapy — to stop Marcedes Lewis from dropping the ball all the time.

Kansas City Chiefs

When Herm Edwards took the Chiefs to the playoffs in 2006, few could see the downfall that followed his first year in Kansas City. In truth, that 9-7 season was a smoke-and-mirrors job, done with an aging team and primarily on the back of Larry Johnson, who became the poster child for Football Outsiders' arguments against running back overuse. A crumbling offensive line and an extremely unstable quarterback situation led to the disaster that was 2007, when the Chiefs lost their last nine games after starting out 4-3. Combine those nine losses with last year's franchise faceplant, and Kansas City's "youth movement" has suffered through a 2-23 run.

The 2008 draft was universally trumpeted as a coup for CEO Carl Peterson and Vice President of Player Personnel Bill Kuharich, but the first-year results were a mixed bag. LSU standout defensive tackle Glenn Dorsey had trouble adapting to his place in the Kansas City defense, but fellow first-round pick Branden Albert, who played guard at Virginia, slid out to left tackle and performed well. Cornerback Brandon Flowers looked like a second-round steal, and Texas running back Jamaal Charles averaged 5.3 yards per carry.

Still, one very good draft wasn't going to make up for so much personnel movement and franchise disappointment. Peterson ran the Chiefs for two decades, but had seen his deserved reputation as one of the most astute personnel men in the game take several hits in re-

cent years. Head men tend to pay with their jobs when teams are allowed to decline unchecked, and Peterson decided to jump before he was pushed, resigning in mid-December. Kuharich held on to his job through the draft, but he was fired in late April.

Former New England Vice President of Player Personnel Scott Pioli, who was hired January 13, was the most important offseason acquisition the Chiefs could make. Though Peterson had been bashed unmercifully in recent years, he was still the face of the franchise as much as any executive could be. Owner Clark Hunt had to strike gold and get a guy who would do for his Chiefs what Peterson had done for his father, Lamar Hunt, in the good times. Pioli's rep as a personnel man was just about unblemished, and other teams had been trying to hire him for years. As far back as 2005, it was only Pioli's refusal to take a great deal of Paul Allen's Microsoft money that put Tim Ruskell in Seattle.

After ten days of completely implausible "well, we're evaluating all current Chiefs personnel" talk, Pioli fired Edwards and began looking for a new head coach. The Chiefs needed a dynamic offensive mind and a leader who wouldn't accept marginal effort, and they found a man who fits both descriptions: Todd Haley, yet another alumnus of the Bill Parcells coaching clinic in Dallas but most recently offensive coordinator of the NFC Champion Cardinals. When defensive coordinator Gunther Cun-

CHIEFS SUMMARY

2008 Record: 2-14

Pythagorean Wins: 4.4 (29th)

DVOA: -27.8% (30th)

Offense: -4.6% (22nd)

Defense: 17.5% (28th)

Special Teams: -5.7% (30th)

Variance: 16.0% (15th)

2008: The Herm Era ends after a commitment to youth breeds unfortunate results.

2009: Will the new Chiefs fall into the same 3-4 trap as the Mangini Jets?

2009 Mean Projection: 6.7 wins

On the Clock (0-3): 14%

Loserville (4-6): 34%

Mediocrity (7-8): 24%

Playoff Contender (9-10): 20%

Super Bowl Contender (11+): 8%

Projected Average Opponent: 2.0% (12th)

2009 Chiefs Schedule

Week	Opp.	Week	Opp.	Week	Opp.
1	at BAL	7	SD	13	DEN
2	OAK	8	BYE	14	BUF
3	at PHI	9	at JAC	15	CLE
4	NYG	10	at OAK	16	at CIN
5	DAL	11	PIT	17	at DEN
6	at WAS	12	at SD		

ningham left to join Jim Schwartz's staff in Detroit, Pioli completed his mutant merger of Phoenix and Foxboro by snapping up Clancy Pendergast, who had lost a battle of office politics with Ken Whisenhunt. Much like the defenses that Pioli and Belichick built in New England, Pendergast's defenses are generally base 3-4 but sprinkle in creative formations and line schemes, overload blitzes, and different secondary looks. Until recently, that variety had been a reflection of Pendergast's desire to get the most from a roster low on talent. He's got better starters in Kansas City than he did when he was hired by the Cardinals in 2004, but there will still be rough spots early on.

With the coaching staff set, Pioli's next important move was to shore up a quarterback situation that had been iffy since Trent Green was heaving the ball around under Dick Vermeil's tutelage from 2001 through 2005. A year ago, injuries to Brodie Croyle and Damon Huard had left the Chiefs' starting job to former Minnesota seventh-round pick Tyler Thigpen. Instead of banking on Thigpen's development, Pioli acquired a familiar face — Matt Cassel, who had helped the Patriots to an 11-5 record in the wake of Tom Brady's season-ending knee injury. Cassel and veteran linebacker Mike Vrabel were acquired for the 34th overall draft pick in 2009. While Vrabel's primary function will be to help facilitate a defensive scheme transformation, Cassel's effect on the Chiefs could be galvanic — and surprisingly immediate.

The importance of fitting scheme to personnel cannot be overstated in a successful team reconstruction, and the Chiefs seem to have the right idea on offense. In Haley's Arizona system, Kurt Warner threw 412 of his 598 passes from the shotgun (68 percent). Cassel threw

Table 1: Todd and Matt's Shotgun Wedding

Team	DVOA Not Shotgun	DVOA Shotgun	Yd/Play Not Shotgun	Yd/Play Shotgun
ARI	3.0%	17.8%	5.1	6.9
KC	-15.7%	3.1%	4.1	5.9
NE	7.7%	25.4%	4.8	6.1
NFL Average	1.6%	12.8%	5.1	6.0

an even higher percentage of his passes from shotgun — 405 of 516 attempts, or 78.5 percent. Kansas City's running backs, receivers, and linemen will have little difficulty adapting to a heavy load of shotgun sets. Last year, looking for a way to help Thigpen succeed, Chiefs offensive coordinator Chan Gailey reached into his college bag of tricks and borrowed the pistol formation from the University of Nevada Wolfpack. The pistol is a sort of sawed-off shotgun in which the quarterback sets up in a shorter-than-usual dropback, and extra blockers facilitate power running more than in the traditional spread formations. Counting those pistol formations, Thigpen took the ball away from center on 359 of 420 pass attempts, an astonishing 85.5 percent. And like the Cardinals and the Patriots, the Chiefs were a much better offense from the shotgun/pistol in 2008 (Table 1).

The Chiefs will benefit from Cassel's growth in New England's offense in 2008, and there is the potential for a fairly effective offense, the lack of combustible targets notwithstanding. That's why the trade of future Hall of Famer Tony Gonzalez was a regrettable move, entrenched as it was in Gonzalez's desire to play for a winner again. The veteran tight end thrived in the pseudo-spread, which had him split out wide a large percentage of the time, and was the team's only consistent performer. Now, Cassel needs Dwayne Bowe to be Randy Moss while either Bears castoff Mark Bradley or ex-Seahawks slot receiver Bobby Engram turns into Wes Welker. That's a lot to ask. Second-year tight end Brad Cottam, another product of that 2008 draft, will be asked to step into the shoes of the best to ever play his position.

The bigger problem is on defense, where the Chiefs are joining the parade of Patriots-influenced teams switching to a 3-4 alignment. In 2008, the Chiefs provided pathetic levels of quarterback pressure without defensive end Jared Allen, who was traded to the Vikings for draft picks. In Minnesota, Allen put more heat on enemy quarterbacks than just about anyone in the NFL with a combined 75 hits, hurries and knockdowns. Tamba Hali was supposed to replace Allen but his breakout didn't happen; Hali was eventually moved back to the left side, while the Chiefs set the NFL record with only 10 sacks on the season. And by NFL record, we don't just mean for full seasons — the Chiefs broke the record of 11 sacks held by the 1982 Baltimore Colts, who only played *nine games*.

One year after he was taken fifth overall in the draft, Dorsey seems to be a man without a home on the line. He spent his rookie year as a square peg in a 4-3, failing to get consistent penetration as a three-technique tackle. Dorsey was considered a bust right away by some of Kansas City's more impatient journalists, but teammate and offensive guard Brian Waters told the *Kansas City Star* that the way the rookie was lined up wasn't working. "He has no chance in pass rush … I love it when a guy lines head-up," Waters said. The 3-4 has Dorsey moving to yet another position — or two, or three. He played nose tackle in minicamp, but now is projected to play defensive end. Who knows; perhaps he'll be a cornerback by Week 9.

Before the Chiefs go forward imposing a misfit scheme on current personnel, Pioli should look at the example set by former New England secondary coach Eric Mangini when he became the Jets' head coach before the 2006 season. Mangini and defensive coordinator Bob Sutton installed a 3-4 with personnel that posted unspectacular 4-3 performances under Herm Edwards the year before, and it just made things worse. The Jets dropped from 28th to dead last in run defense DVOA. The move negated any talent up front, and turned stud linebacker Jonathan Vilma into a third safety. Now, here come Pioli and Pendergast, looking to clamp an ill-fitting scheme on a defense — formerly coached by Herm Edwards again! — already moving in the wrong direction. The Chiefs ranked 28th in DVOA against the run in 2008; if that number doesn't improve, the new regime will have a lot to answer for. And Dorsey will have spent his first two years in different parts of the room, like a piano on moving day.

The 3-4 also may have taken the Chiefs out of the running for the 2009 draft's best player — Wake Forest linebacker Aaron Curry, who went to the Seahawks one pick after Kansas City chose third overall. Curry would have projected as an inside linebacker in a 3-4, and those types of players aren't drafted so early. Instead, the Chiefs went with LSU defensive lineman (yes, another one) Tyson Jackson. Jackson will join Dorsey at end in the 3-4, with Tank Tyler manning the nose.

Because this new Chiefs team is such a mixed bag, knowing what to expect is tough. We know that the AFC West is projected to be the Chargers and everybody else. Cassel and Haley will unquestionably drive an offensive upturn, and Jamaal Charles might be the surprise player here. Pendergast, however, could find himself alternating between 3-4 and 4-3 sets more than expected, running a hybrid scheme as he was known to do in Arizona. The correlations to the Mangini Jets are too close for comfort, and Pendergast has extensive experience with formation diversity and its positive effects on limited players.

Perhaps Pioli has thought about what his former college scouting director Thomas Dimitroff pulled off in Atlanta. Maybe Haley hopes that he can match the miracle performed by old friends Bill Parcells and Tony Sparano in Miami. The rest of us know that it is very unlikely that the 2009 Chiefs will be playoff contenders. The NFL may be used to one-year turnarounds, but if you want to build a Super Bowl champion instead of a surprise wild-card contender, you need to be decisively on the right track.

Doug Farrar

2008 Chiefs Stats by Week

Wk	vs.	W-L	PF	PA	YDF	YDA	TO	Total	Off	Def	ST
1	@NE	L	10	17	284	338	+1	-16%	-9%	6%	-1%
2	OAK	L	8	23	190	355	0	-78%	-53%	23%	-3%
3	@ATL	L	14	38	301	378	-2	-99%	-47%	37%	-15%
4	DEN	W	33	19	370	446	+3	8%	-1%	-8%	2%
5	@CAR	L	0	34	127	441	-1	-93%	-91%	-1%	-3%
6	BYE										
7	TEN	L	10	34	272	455	0	-77%	-19%	56%	-2%
8	@NYJ	L	24	28	330	420	+3	12%	30%	10%	-8%
9	TB	L	27	30	384	423	+3	-4%	38%	16%	-27%
10	@SD	L	19	20	339	400	+2	19%	22%	8%	6%
11	NO	L	20	30	330	369	0	-39%	-12%	18%	-9%
12	BUF	L	31	54	462	444	-5	-46%	7%	43%	-10%
13	@OAK	W	20	13	301	271	+1	-15%	-6%	10%	1%
14	@DEN	L	17	24	260	425	+1	-10%	5%	24%	9%
15	SD	L	21	22	277	394	+2	16%	23%	-15%	-22%
16	MIA	L	31	38	492	403	-2	-6%	39%	29%	-16%
17	@CIN	L	6	16	220	329	-1	-56%	-28%	29%	1%

Trends and Splits

	Offense	Rank	Defense	Rank
Total DVOA	-4.6%	22	17.5%	28
Unadjusted VOA	-1.0%	23	18.8%	29
Weighted trend	7.5%	17	19.1%	30
Variance	12.7%	30	4.0%	5
Average opponent	8.1%	2	7.7%	23
Passing	0.5%	23	24.6%	28
Rushing	-1.6%	22	10.5%	26
First down	-15.7%	30	21.1%	29
Second down	12.2%	14	7.6%	16
Third down	-9.2%	24	25.9%	28
First half	6.5%	15	13.3%	24
Second half	-15.6%	26	21.8%	29
Red Zone	4.1%	19	24.0%	26
Late and close	-15.4%	26	20.8%	29

Five-Year Performance

Year	W-L	Pyth	Est W	PF	PA	TO	Total	Rk	Off	Rk	Def	Rk	ST	Rk	Off AGL	Rk	Def AGL	Rk
2004	7-9	9.0	9.3	483	435	-6	15.2%	10	32.9%	2	17.1%	30	-0.5%	18	12.6	21	29.0	10
2005	10-6	10.0	11.1	403	325	+8	25.5%	5	22.2%	4	-5.1%	13	-1.9%	24	15.4	17	15.9	17
2006	9-7	8.5	8.4	331	315	+4	6.1%	13	7.3%	11	2.3%	16	1.2%	13	21.5	12	3.6	32
2007	4-12	4.5	5.1	226	335	-11	-18.9%	25	-18.2%	29	-2.5%	13	-3.3%	24	22.8	14	4.2	32
2008	2-14	4.4	4.5	291	440	+5	-27.8%	30	-4.6%	22	17.5%	28	-5.7%	30	30.4	13	16.9	20

Strategic Tendencies

Run/Pass		Rank	Offense		Rank	Defense		Rank	Other		Rank
Runs, all plays	39%	27	3+ WR	71%	2	Rush 3	3.3%	23	2+ RB, Pct Runs	59%	22
Runs, first half	39%	27	4+ WR	22%	3	Rush 4	71.1%	6	1 RB/2 TE, Pct Runs	60%	7
Runs, first down	47%	24	2+ TE	17%	28	Rush 5	16.0%	24	1RB/3+WR, Pct Runs	28%	16
Runs, second-long	30%	28	Single back	69%	6	Rush 6+	9.6%	11	Zone Blitz	2%	24
Runs, power sit.	64%	21	Play action	11%	30	Rush 7+	0.9%	25	Go for it on 4th	0.77	28
Runs, behind 2H	31%	19	Max protect	5%	32	Sacks by LB	20.0%	12	Offensive Pace	31.6	24
Pass, ahead 2H	42%	18	Outside pocket	16%	6	Sacks by DB	0.0%	30	Defensive Pace	30.8	17

Kansas City set an NFL record by using shotgun on 63 percent of offensive plays. Three teams used shotgun at least half the time last year: the Chiefs, the team whose offensive coordinator now coaches the Chiefs (Arizona, 50 percent), and the team whose quarterback was traded to the Chiefs (New England, 55 percent).　●　In 2007, the Chiefs were significantly better passing to the left side of the field compared to the right side. In 2008, things were reversed: the Chiefs ranked 31st in DVOA on passes to the left but seventh on passes to the right.　●　Tyler Thigpen benefited more than any quarterback from dropped interceptions, with nine.　●　Cincinnati and Arizona were the only offenses to use play-action less often than the Chiefs, while Cincinnati and Denver were the only defenses to face play-action more often than the Chiefs. 2008 was the second straight year the Chiefs ranked third in frequency of play-action by opponents.

Passing

Player	DYAR	DVOA	Plays	NtYds	Avg	YAC	C%	TD	Int
Tyler Thigpen	146	-6.2%	447	2500	5.6	4.5	55.3%	18	11
Damon Huard*	-228	-54.7%	90	414	4.6	4.0	62.5%	2	4
Brodie Croyle	21	-0.1%	30	141	4.7	4.9	69.0%	0	0
Quinn Gray*	70	109.7%	8	76	9.5	4.0	87.5%	1	0
Matt Cassel	*655*	*6.4%*	*565*	*3502*	*6.2*	*6.3*	*63.8%*	*21*	*11*

Rushing

Player	DYAR	DVOA	Plays	Yds	Avg	TD	Fum	Suc
Larry Johnson	-36	-12.7%	193	874	4.5	5	5	45%
Jamaal Charles	63	15.3%	67	361	5.4	0	1	54%
Tyler Thigpen	78	15.2%	56	386	6.9	3	2	--
Kolby Smith	-26	-24.5%	35	100	2.9	1	0	46%
Dantrell Savage	-7	-18.4%	15	53	3.5	0	0	47%
Matt Cassel	*82*	*15.8%*	*50*	*291*	*5.8*	*2*	*0*	*--*

Receiving

Player	DYAR	DVOA	Plays	Ctch	Yds	Y/C	YAC	TD	C%
Dwayne Bowe	29	-10.3%	157	86	1022	11.9	4.2	8	55%
Mark Bradley	-31	-18.9%	62	30	380	12.7	3.1	4	48%
Devard Darling	1	-12.1%	33	17	247	14.5	5.8	1	52%
Will Franklin*	-50	-53.1%	17	7	83	11.9	3.7	0	41%
Jeff Webb	-46	-52.9%	13	5	46	9.2	1.2	0	38%
Bobby Engram	*-32*	*-17.8%*	*80*	*47*	*489*	*10.4*	*3.6*	*0*	*59%*
Tony Gonzalez*	243	16.5%	155	96	1058	11.0	2.6	10	62%
Brad Cottam	-2	-10.2%	11	7	63	9.0	2.4	0	64%
Tony Curtis	*-40*	*-59.8%*	*12*	*8*	*37*	*4.6*	*2.9*	*0*	*67%*
Sean Ryan	*-12*	*-43.2%*	*5*	*3*	*15*	*5.0*	*4.3*	*0*	*60%*
Jamaal Charles	16	-6.2%	40	27	274	10.1	11.3	1	68%
Larry Johnson	-21	-37.6%	16	12	66	5.5	8.0	0	75%
Mike Cox	-49	-70.2%	13	8	19	2.4	2.6	0	62%
Kolby Smith	0	-14.3%	11	10	52	5.2	6.1	0	72%

Offensive Line

Year	Yards	ALY	Rank	Power	Rank	10+ Yds	Rank	Stuff	Rank	Sacks	ASR	Rank	False	Cont.
2006	4.34	4.17	15	74%	2	21%	8	18%	17	41	7.6%	21	17	28
2007	3.37	3.55	31	61%	20	12%	24	23%	29	55	9.1%	29	27	33
2008	4.46	3.72	29	58%	28	25%	3	22%	29	37	7.0%	21	13	29

Year	LE	Rank	LT	Rank	Mid	Rank	RT	Rank	RE	Rank
2006	3.46	24	4.50	12	4.50	8	2.49	32	4.59	9
2007	2.27	32	4.21	19	3.94	21	3.36	30	3.28	29
2008	4.22	16	4.29	13	3.55	30	3.15	31	4.15	15

Once upon a time, Kansas City had the best offensive line in the NFL. Then again, once upon a time, the Dow was over 14000. The Chiefs' stimulus package is named Branden Albert; like most first-round left tackles, the Virginia product showed both greatness and greenness as a rookie, and his skills will continue to develop in 2009. Nothing helps a young lineman like the chance to play next to a Pro Bowl veteran, and left guard Brian Waters is the true anchor of this offensive line. Center Rudy Niswanger is the weak link, a fourth-year undrafted free agent who sort of ended up as Kansas City's center by default. He needs to improve his run blocking, especially if the Chiefs want to get those tough yards in power situations, and he'll be pushed by free agent signing Eric Ghiaciuc, formerly of the Bengals. The Chiefs made no effort to re-sign right guard Adrian Jones, instead replacing him with ex-Chargers free agent Mike Goff. Right tackle Damion McIntosh completes the starting line. In Miami, he was always an underrated run blocker but subpar pass blocker; the Adjusted Line Yards numbers, as well as McIntosh's team-high six blown blocks, suggest that he struggled in both areas last year. His future replacement may be fifth-round pick Colin Brown, an impressively-sized (6-foot-7, 335 pounds) tackle prospect who suffered from inconsistency at the University of Missouri. Perhaps the best skill of the Kansas City line is doing the standing still; the Chiefs cut their false starts in half last year, and four of those 13 false starts came from backup tackle Herb Taylor, whose vision problem and inability to wear contacts force him to wear prescription sunglasses during games.

Defensive Front Seven

Defensive Line	Age	Pos	Plays	TmPct	Rk	Stop	Dfts	Stop%	Rk	AvYd	Rk	Sack	Hit	Hur	Runs	St%	Yds	Pass	St%	Yds
								Overall				Pass Rush			vs. Run			vs. Pass		
Tamba Hali	26	DE	57	7.2%	17	38	12	67%	79	3.6	90	3.0	5	15	43	70%	3.7	14	57%	3.1
Glenn Dorsey	24	DT	47	5.6%	30	39	8	83%	9	1.8	28	1.0	0	1	40	85%	1.5	7	71%	3.3
Turk McBride	24	DE	41	8.6%	6	29	10	71%	65	2.4	71	0.0	8	4	36	72%	1.7	5	60%	7.0
Tank Tyler	24	DT	41	4.9%	39	29	5	71%	61	2.6	61	0.0	6	5	39	72%	2.6	2	50%	4.0
Jason Babin*	29	DE	32	6.7%	22	22	5	69%	73	3.2	84	2.0	2	4	23	74%	3.0	9	56%	3.7
Alfonso Boone	33	DE	19	2.4%	--	16	5	84%	--	1.6	--	1.0	0	5	15	87%	1.9	4	75%	0.5

Linebackers	Age	Pos	Plays	TmPct	Rk	Stop	Dfts	Stop%	AvYd	Sack	Hit	Hur	Runs	St%	Rk	Yds	Rk	Tgts	Suc%	Rk	AdjYd	Rk
								Overall		Pass Rush			vs. Run					vs. Pass				
Derrick Johnson	27	OLB	89	12.0%	44	55	15	62%	3.8	1.5	0	3	53	66%	40	2.7	16	31	57%	30	4.9	15
Rocky Boiman*	29	OLB	69	11.9%	47	30	7	43%	5.6	0.0	0	1	38	53%	98	5.1	99	23	35%	84	6.2	45
Demorrio Williams	29	OLB	56	6.6%	94	31	8	55%	4.0	0.0	1	4	39	72%	19	2.4	11	24	42%	67	4.4	5
Pat Thomas*	26	ILB	49	7.7%	86	26	8	53%	5.1	0.5	1	1	28	61%	66	3.3	45	17	39%	78	7.6	72
Donnie Edwards*	36	OLB	34	9.2%	--	17	3	50%	5.3	0.0	0	0	22	68%	--	3.0	--	7	19%	--	8.9	--
Zach Thomas	36	ILB	97	12.7%	36	45	5	46%	5.0	1.0	1	4	66	55%	90	3.8	72	18	34%	85	6.9	60
Mike Vrabel	34	OLB	66	9.0%	78	47	15	71%	2.2	4.0	7	9	49	76%	12	1.9	3	18	63%	8	5.1	18

Year	Yards	ALY	Rank	Power	Rank	10+ Yds	Rank	Stuff	Rank	Sack	ASR	Rank
2006	4.15	4.13	15	63%	13	17%	22	22%	3	32	5.7%	28
2007	4.56	3.98	13	60%	14	22%	28	21%	10	37	7.9%	3
2008	5.16	4.44	26	81%	32	27%	30	14%	31	10	2.9%	32

Year	LE	Rank	LT	Rank	Mid	Rank	RT	Rank	RE	Rank
2006	4.37	19	4.02	10	3.82	3	4.78	29	4.85	29
2007	3.60	10	3.49	5	3.91	10	3.84	10	5.13	30
2008	5.02	29	4.23	17	4.37	22	4.86	29	3.94	16

At times this season, you may have trouble telling the difference between the Kansas City linebackers and an ad for Flomax. Sure, 36-year-old Donnie Edwards is gone, but 36-year-old Zach Thomas and 34-year-old Mike Vrabel have arrived to help spread the 3-4 gospel to Kansas City's younger defenders. Vrabel is still a quality player when it comes to stopping the run and rushing the quarterback but his pass coverage is lacking. (His charting stats are a bit misleading, as poor coverage by Vrabel often ends up as "Hole in Zone.") Thomas, on the other hand, just looked plain old in Dallas last year. His Stop Rate was poor, his pass coverage was poor, and he had just five Defeats, the second-lowest total for any linebacker with at least 50 plays. He also left Dallas because of his inability to fit into their 3-4 scheme, which makes one wonder why he decided to join a team that is switching to a 3-4 scheme.

Those two players will start alongside two players learning new positions. Derrick Johnson is the best defender on this team and there is unlikely to be a problem moving him from strong outside to strong inside. Also changing positions are Tamba Hali and Turk McBride, who will attempt to transition from 4-3 ends to 3-4 outside linebackers. McBride will definitely be a reserve, but Hali should earn a starting job. He won't have to worry so much about learning pass coverage skills, as he'll play the predominantly pass-rushing role known as "Predator" in Clancy Pendergast's defense (in the Parcells/Belichick 3-4, the same position is known as "Elephant"). When that outside linebacker isn't necessarily going after the quarterback, the Chiefs will rotate in ex-Falcons linebacker Demorrio Williams, who is quick but 20 to 30 pounds lighter than the usual 3-4 outside linebacker.

The starting linemen, as discussed earlier in the chapter, are probably going to be Tank Tyler at the nose with Glenn Dorsey and first-round pick Tyson Jackson on either side of him. The backup plan, in case Dorsey looks awful in the 3-4, is veteran Alfonso Boone, who is bigger and a better fit to play defensive end in the new scheme.

Defensive Secondary

Secondary	Age	Pos	Plays	TmPct	Rk	Stop	Dfts	Yds	Rk	St%	Rk	Tgts	Tgt%	Rk	Dist	Suc%	Rk	AdjYd	Rk	Yds	PD	Int
				Overall				vs. Run							vs. Pass							
Bernard Pollard	25	SS	99	11.7%	17	22	6	7.7	49	32%	63	28	6.4%	44	13.5	49%	50	7.8	38	8.4	4	1
Jarrad Page	25	FS	96	11.4%	24	36	17	8.0	59	41%	37	36	8.4%	15	15.7	53%	33	8.3	49	9.2	9	4
Brandon Flowers	23	CB	81	11.0%	13	35	16	7.6	52	47%	36	65	17.1%	51	9.0	58%	17	4.8	3	4.9	11	2
Brandon Carr	23	CB	79	9.3%	31	21	9	9.4	66	33%	56	79	18.3%	37	11.6	41%	75	8.3	60	9.0	7	2
Maurice Leggett	23	CB	39	6.2%	--	20	6	5.9	--	56%	--	36	11.0%	--	8.1	56%	--	6.9	--	7.1	6	1
Jon McGraw	30	FS	29	3.4%	--	7	1	10.9	--	23%	--	9	2.1%	--	14.4	60%	--	4.8	--	5.4	1	1

Year	Pass D Rank	vs. #1 WR	Rk	vs. #2 WR	Rk	vs. Other WR	Rk	vs. TE	Rk	vs. RB	Rk
2006	19	-19.3%	4	16.0%	25	42.0%	32	-15.5%	7	-3.7%	15
2007	10	14.3%	23	-3.7%	12	-33.0%	4	11.8%	23	-14.8%	7
2008	28	7.7%	19	-3.3%	12	-53.0%	1	15.7%	23	22.5%	30

Kansas City started two rookies named Brandon at cornerback last year, but our game charters found it really easy to tell which one was taken in the second round out of Virginia Tech (Flowers) and which one came in the fifth round out of Division II Grand Valley State (Carr). Still, although Carr may not be the future stud Flowers is, he should be able to hold on to his starting job and hopefully improve in 2009. Last year's nickelback, undrafted rookie Maurice Leggett, will get competition from veteran free agent signing Travis Daniels (ex-Dolphins and Browns) as well as third-round pick Donald Washington, a combine star who many observers feel came out of Ohio State too early (he wasn't even a starter in 2008). The safeties, Bernard Pollard and Jarrad Page, are basically average-level NFL starters. Both are strong tacklers who struggle if they have to cover tight ends man-to-man, but their ball skills in zone coverage are a big reason why the Chiefs have been so successful shutting down slot receivers over the past two years (Pollard, for example, knocked away two passes to Brandon Stokley late in last year's Week 4 upset over Denver). Page has ten interceptions as a pro, but four of them have come against the Raiders, which seems unfair somehow.

Special Teams

Year	DVOA	Rank	FG/XP	Rank	Net Kick	Rank	Kick Ret	Rank	Net Punt	Rank	Punt Ret	Rank	Hidden	Rank
2006	1.2%	13	-3.8	24	-3.2	27	-2.2	16	14.0	2	2.2	10	8.2	6
2007	-3.3%	24	-10.2	30	6.2	6	-14.9	32	5.9	8	-6.3	28	-15.9	31
2008	-5.7%	30	-8.4	30	-15.9	32	-6.8	25	0.7	19	-3.4	25	-15.7	31

Except for punter Dustin Colquitt, the Chiefs' special teams have been far from special over the past couple seasons — but like a lot of other things in Kansas City, special teams will be very different in 2009. Rookie kicker Connor Barth was a strong placekicker (10-for-12) but struggled on kickoffs. He'll have a training camp battle with this year's Mr. Irrelevant, South Carolina kicker Ryan Succop, who has a strong leg but has struggled with accuracy on field goals. No matter who wins the job, the coverage team has to get its act together; only Arizona allowed more value on kickoff returns. One player who should help improve the tackling is free agent linebacker Corey Mays, who Pioli knew from New England. Sixth-round wide receiver Quinten Lawrence from McNeese State has take-it-to-the-house speed and will probably handle both kick and punt returns, backed up by running back Dantrell Savage. Out of the cast of thousands who handled returns for the Chiefs in 2008, Savage was the best on kick returns and the worst on punt returns.

Coaching Staff

Without Herman Edwards around, who is going to tell these kids that you play to win the game? Todd Haley, that's who. In all sports, teams usually follow up a players' coach with a taskmaster and vice versa — and there aren't a lot of coaches who are "players coach-ier" than Edwards. Haley spent the early days laying down the law in Kansas City, but not in a way that is likely to backfire. If the new coach wants to send a signal to his players that nobody's job is guaranteed, waiving a fourth-round receiver who didn't do much as a rookie is a safer way to do it than playing "poke the ego" with your franchise quarterback.

Much like Jim Schwartz in Detroit, Haley has built a staff with experience that complements his youth. Chan Gailey is a holdover at offensive coordinator, but he should work well with Haley given that the Arizona and Kansas City offenses used similar spread strategies last season. Haley's Arizona partner, Clancy Pendergast, takes over the defense. The Chiefs will also employ two position coaches who were coordinators with other teams just a few months ago: Bill Muir (ex-Tampa Bay) will coach the offensive line while Gary Gibbs (ex-New Orleans) will coach the linebackers.

Miami Dolphins

It took two losses and a plane ride for the 2008 Miami Dolphins to find their identity. The Dolphins had a long flight home from Arizona after losing 31-10 to the Cardinals in Week 2. Chad Pennington completed 10 passes for 112 yards, Ronnie Brown led all Miami running backs with just 28 yards on the ground, and Anquan Boldin torched Miami's suspect secondary for three touchdowns. It was a bad start for a team trying to erase the memories of the 1-15 disaster of 2007. The old Dolphins of Cam Cameron and Randy Mueller would most likely have surrendered in the face of such a loss. The new Dolphins of Bill Parcells and Tony Sparano weren't giving in so easily.

On the flight back from Arizona, Sparano sat with quarterbacks coach David Lee, who had run a series of option plays at Arkansas in 2007 with Darren McFadden and Felix Jones. Called the "Wild Hog," the package consisted of various sets out of a single-wing base in which McFadden took shotgun snaps and either ran, handed off to Jones, or threw a pass. Sparano hoped that Lee, whom he had worked with in Dallas under Parcells, could implement these option plays and jump-start Miami's moribund offense.

"We knew when we rolled it out during the course of the New England week that you're taking a chance one way or the other," Sparano remembered at the 2009 Scouting Combine. "We also knew that, hey, this might be a two-play deal. We might go out there for

two plays and if it backfires or it doesn't give us the look that we wanted, maybe we don't see it anymore. It just so happened we started to get a couple of the pictures that we wanted to see, and we were able to go with it a little bit longer."

To say the least. With nothing to lose, the Dolphins ran the Wildcat plays in Week 3 against the New England Patriots, a team known for its intelligent defenders. The Patriots were overmatched from the word "go." Their front line was negated by overload blocking schemes, their linebackers were either outrun or out-thought, and the secondary was either biting on the spy look to running back Ronnie Brown, who played McFadden for the 'Fins, or lost in coverage on a counter option touchdown to tight end Anthony Fasano. At the same time, the Patriots were limited to 216 total yards and the formerly disappointing linebacker Joey Porter blew up with four of Miami's five sacks.

It's not often that a single game will so radically transform the fortunes of a team, but by decisively beating the defending AFC champions 38-13, the Dolphins got the first taste of what they could do — and the rest of the NFL got a taste of what was to come. After stumbling in losses to the Texans and Ravens to finish the first half of the season at 4-4, the Dolphins went on a 7-1 regular-season run and won the AFC East in one of the most shocking and completely enjoyable franchise comebacks in NFL history. The Miami season ended with a 27-9 Wild Card loss

DOLPHINS SUMMARY

2008 Record: 11-5

Pythagorean Wins: 8.8 (16th)

DVOA: 8.8% (14th)

Offense: 16.6% (7th)

Defense: 3.0% (15th)

Special Teams: -4.8% (29th)

Variance: 16.7% (16th)

2008: Wildcat!

2009: Somewhat less surprising Wildcat!

2009 Mean Projection: 6.4 wins

On the Clock (0-3): 8%

Loserville (4-6): 46%

Mediocrity (7-8): 29%

Playoff Contender (9-10): 15%

Super Bowl Contender (11+): 2%

Projected Average Opponent: 2.1% (10th)

2009 Dolphins Schedule

Week	Opp.	Week	Opp.	Week	Opp.
1	at ATL	7	NO	13	NE
2	IND (Mon.)	8	at NYJ	14	at JAC
3	at SD	9	at NE	15	at TEN
4	BUF	10	TB	16	HOU
5	NYJ (Mon.)	11	at CAR (Thu.)	17	PIT
6	BYE	12	at BUF		

to the Ravens, in which quarterback Chad Pennington threw lob after lob to the Baltimore defense, and the Wildcat was completely shut down.

For those who want more details, the Wildcat is detailed in a second essay later in the book. However, the Wildcat wasn't the only thing that put the 'Fins back on their feet. What else got Miami on the right track?

First, they fixed the three trap doors identified by Mike Tanier in *Pro Football Prospectus 2008* — the issues that had the franchise backsliding for a number of years. Hiring Parcells, who brought as many of his old Dallas compatriots as he possibly could, gave the front office a strong voice and set a clear path from top to bottom. The revolving door at quarterback ended in the short term with the signing of Chad Pennington, who was out in New York with the Brett Favre drama, and in the long term with the selection of Michigan's Chad Henne in the second round of the 2008 draft. And instead of spending draft picks for middling veterans, Parcells and general manager Jeff Ireland stuck to the plan, scoring early (first overall pick Jake Long) and later (small-school stud defensive end Kendall Langford).

And once they got on a roll, they stayed there. From Week 3 through the rest of the regular season, the offense posted negative DVOA in a game just twice. The defense was less consistent, but surprise players on both sides of the ball kept popping up and making plays. Langford, a third-round rookie out of Hampton, amassed sacks in his first two games. When Greg Camarillo was lost for the season with a November knee injury, the undrafted Davone Bess came out of nowhere for 30 catches in the last five regular-season games.

It was a miracle season, but what do the Dolphins do for an encore? There's a new name up top — real estate mogul Steve Ross bought an ownership share from Wayne Huizenga, completing a move that gives Ross 95 percent of the team and the stadium for ap-

proximately $1.1 billion. This immediately brought rumors of Parcells' departure to the surface — he's never going to work for another meddlesome owner under any circumstances — but Parcells stayed put. Ross seems to have less interest in the on-field action and more in the marketing of the Dolphins, long an attendance-challenged asset, to a city with infinite distractions and choices for the entertainment dollar. Even in the year of the great turnaround, the Dolphins finished 18th in average home attendance. According to ESPN.com, only the Lions sold a lower percentage of their seats.

Ross has hired Mike Dee of the Boston Red Sox to expand the brand, leading some to fear that should the new Dolphins win a Super Bowl in the next few years, the celebration will come to a halt so that Jimmy Fallon and Drew Barrymore can make out in a *Fever Pitch* sequel. Fear not, Dolphans — it's still a Parcells team, at least on the field.

In the draft, the Dolphins looked to address two primary issues — a secondary in which all four primary participants were on the wrong side of 30, and a kink in the Wildcat that allowed opposing safeties to cheat up and take the plays away (the Baltimore Ravens were especially adept at this in their two victories over Miami). Cornerbacks Vontae Davis of Illinois and Sean Smith of Utah were selected in the first two rounds, and West Virginia quarterback/running back/potential receiver Pat White was also selected in the second. Davis and Smith both have question marks and will most likely take time to fill in the defensive backfield, but White will get reps right away as Miami introduces new variants of trickeration. Rounds three and four brought receivers Brian Hartline and Patrick Turner, building up a group that was vulnerable when Greg Camarillo got hurt late in the season.

The Dolphins also looked to fill holes in free agency. Center Jake Grove (ex-Raiders) replaces Samson Satele on a line that finished 12th in Adjusted Line Yards overall, but 23rd up the middle. Cornerback Eric Green and safety Gibril Wilson should help the secondary in the short term. The front seven got two new names (well, one new and one old). Two-time Canadian Football League Defensive MVP Cameron Wake is a favorite of the coaching staff, and Parcells welcomed Jason Taylor back to the fold a year after trading him to the Redskins for the second-round pick used to draft Pat White.

As the defending AFC East champs, the Dolphins will have targets on their backs, and our research reveals that teams winning four or fewer games one season and ten or more the next drop an average of 2.7 games the following year (see table in Atlanta chapter). Miami also can't expect either their good health or their good turnover ratio to repeat in 2009. Miami had only 25.7 Adjusted Games Lost to injury in 2008, fourth-fewest in the NFL. Including reserves, Miami's AGL was 46.6, the best in the NFL. The Dolphins finished first in turnover ratio (+17), and our studies have shown that fumble luck is random. The Dolphins were +6 in fumbles, and Chad Pennington's regular-season interception rate was 1.5 percent, his lowest since 2002. The four picks in the playoff loss to the Ravens put him back on average ground.

On the plus side, Miami looks to have an offensive upswing based on our theory that teams with high DVOA on first and second down, but low on third down, will improve the following year. On offense, Miami finished fourth on first down, third on second down, and 21st on third down. And on the plus-plus side, Parcells has once again set up his team to succeed in the long term.

In the short-term, the Dolphins may be a disappointment. To repeat as division champions, they will have to overcome the strong likelihood that schedule strength, health, and fumble recovery luck will all revert to normal. They have to hope that Chad Pennington can have two straight healthy seasons for the first time in his career, or that Chad Henne (or, dare we say, White) is ready to fill his shoes. The young talent in the secondary has to grow up fast enough to handle the re-Brady'd Patriots, not to mention September opponents San Diego and Indianapolis. And the offensive braintrust has to figure out how to attack out-of-division teams like the Ravens, who destroyed Miami twice last season with intelligent, physical defense.

The Wildcat was the reaction to Miami's 0-2 start in 2008. If the Dolphins start slow in 2009, what else can they pull out of their bag of tricks?

Doug Farrar

2008 Dolphins Stats by Week

Wk	vs.	W-L	PF	PA	YDF	YDA	TO	Total	Off	Def	ST
1	NYJ	L	14	20	277	293	0	-28%	-10%	7%	-11%
2	@ARI	L	10	31	236	445	0	-71%	-37%	32%	-2%
3	@NE	W	38	13	461	215	+2	107%	70%	-49%	-13%
4	BYE										
5	SD	W	17	10	390	202	-1	62%	45%	-37%	-21%
6	@HOU	L	28	29	370	485	+3	8%	17%	-8%	-17%
7	BAL	L	13	27	359	356	0	22%	41%	17%	-2%
8	BUF	W	25	16	358	339	+3	28%	25%	-1%	2%
9	@DEN	W	26	17	341	319	+2	3%	-16%	-24%	-4%
10	SEA	W	21	19	361	298	-1	-16%	13%	24%	-6%
11	OAK	W	17	15	382	186	-1	-8%	31%	18%	-21%
12	NE	L	28	48	396	530	+1	-21%	33%	49%	-5%
13	@STL	W	16	12	327	278	+2	-8%	-13%	-2%	2%
14	@BUF	W	16	3	295	163	+2	50%	6%	-46%	-3%
15	SF	W	14	9	248	318	0	15%	24%	17%	8%
16	@KC	W	38	31	403	492	+2	6%	34%	39%	12%
17	@NYJ	W	24	17	319	331	+3	34%	12%	-24%	-2%
18	BAL	L	9	27	276	286	-4	-27%	-9%	15%	-4%

Trends and Splits

	Offense	Rank	Defense	Rank
Total DVOA	16.6%	7	3.0%	15
Unadjusted VOA	23.4%	3	-0.9%	10
Weighted trend	17.0%	8	7.4%	18
Variance	7.2%	17	6.6%	22
Average opponent	1.7%	30	10.4%	31
Passing	35.1%	6	5.7%	14
Rushing	8.4%	11	-0.6%	19
First down	17.2%	4	-5.5%	7
Second down	28.4%	3	16.5%	24
Third down	-2.9%	21	-1.6%	12
First half	18.8%	5	0.9%	14
Second half	14.5%	10	5.0%	17
Red Zone	46.5%	1	-21.9%	5
Late and close	13.4%	14	6.0%	17

Five-Year Performance

Year	W-L	Pyth	Est W	PF	PA	TO	Total	Rk	Off	Rk	Def	Rk	ST	Rk	Off AGL	Rk	Def AGL	Rk
2004	4-12	5.7	6.6	275	354	-17	-13.2%	22	-28.5%	31	-10.6%	7	4.7%	4	30.5	9	30.9	8
2005	9-7	8.0	8.8	318	317	+1	2.5%	15	-9.1%	18	-8.4%	10	3.2%	4	6.2	26	25.1	7
2006	6-10	7.2	7.2	260	283	+2	-0.8%	16	-9.4%	26	-9.3%	6	-0.7%	21	39.8	1	8.4	24
2007	1-15	3.8	4.2	267	437	-7	-22.2%	27	-5.3%	21	14.7%	31	-2.2%	22	24.4	11	37.8	4
2008	11-5	8.8	9.3	345	317	+17	8.8%	14	16.6%	7	3.0%	15	-4.8%	29	24.1	17	1.6	32

Strategic Tendencies

Run/Pass		Rank	Offense		Rank	Defense		Rank	Other		Rank
Runs, all plays	45%	10	3+ WR	45%	22	Rush 3	6.7%	11	2+ RB, Pct Runs	62%	14
Runs, first half	45%	13	4+ WR	11%	20	Rush 4	63.8%	16	1 RB/2 TE, Pct Runs	45%	25
Runs, first down	50%	15	2+ TE	36%	5	Rush 5	23.0%	14	1RB/3+WR, Pct Runs	25%	18
Runs, second-long	40%	12	Single back	42%	31	Rush 6+	6.6%	23	Zone Blitz	2%	25
Runs, power sit.	65%	18	Play action	21%	9	Rush 7+	1.0%	22	Go for it on 4th	0.86	18
Runs, behind 2H	25%	31	Max protect	18%	1	Sacks by LB	63.8%	5	Offensive Pace	33.7	32
Pass, ahead 2H	42%	19	Outside pocket	8%	24	Sacks by DB	12.5%	7	Defensive Pace	30.3	9

Chad Pennington led all quarterbacks (minimum 100 passes) with a 66 percent completion rate when facing five or more pass rushers. ● 63 percent of Miami's draw plays were run on first down, the highest rate of any team. Conversely, Miami only ran a draw play on third down once. ● Miami ranked fifth in DVOA on passes past the line of scrimmage, but 28th on passes thrown to receivers at or before the line of scrimmage. ● The Dolphins led the league in offensive DVOA in the red zone, but were just 12th if we limit the measurement to goal-to-go situations. ● Miami had the league's biggest gap between defense at home (-8.1% DVOA, fifth) and defense on the road (14.1% DVOA, 26th). ● Miami ranked ninth with -0.3% DVOA when sending the standard four pass rushers, but allowed 34.7% DVOA (26th) when rushing five and 33.9% DVOA (27th) when rushing six or more.

Passing

Player	DYAR	DVOA	Plays	NtYds	Avg	YAC	C%	TD	Int
Chad Pennington	1172	25.7%	501	3559	7.1	4.3	67.6%	19	7
Chad Henne	8	-2.3%	12	67	5.6	1.6	58.3%	0	0

Rushing

Player	DYAR	DVOA	Plays	Yds	Avg	TD	Fum	Suc
Ronnie Brown	127	5.1%	214	916	4.3	10	1	49%
Ricky Williams	31	-3.9%	160	663	4.1	4	4	48%
Lousaka Polite	36	18.3%	23	85	3.7	0	0	78%
Chad Pennington	32	36.8%	13	77	5.9	1	0	--
Patrick Cobbs	28	69.0%	12	88	7.3	1	0	33%
Ted Ginn	50	164.3%	5	73	14.6	2	0	--

Receiving

Player	DYAR	DVOA	Plays	Ctch	Yds	Y/C	YAC	TD	C%
Ted Ginn	19	-10.0%	93	56	791	14.1	3.1	2	60%
Greg Camarillo	64	-2.5%	83	55	613	11.1	3.0	2	66%
Davone Bess	80	1.3%	75	54	554	10.3	4.5	1	72%
Derek Hagan*	7	4.2%	6	3	51	17.0	2.3	0	50%
Brandon London	-5	-22.6%	6	3	30	10.0	0.3	0	50%
Ernest Wilford	-22	-54.6%	6	3	25	8.3	3.7	0	50%
Anthony Fasano	156	34.8%	53	34	454	13.4	4.1	7	64%
David Martin	131	37.3%	45	31	451	14.5	4.4	4	69%
Ronnie Brown	57	11.6%	43	33	254	7.7	5.6	0	51%
Ricky Williams	8	-9.6%	39	29	219	7.6	5.0	1	74%
Patrick Cobbs	110	53.5%	27	19	275	14.5	9.4	3	70%
Lousaka Polite	-8	-29.1%	8	6	24	4.0	4.3	0	75%

Offensive Line

Year	Yards	ALY	Rank	Power	Rank	10+ Yds	Rank	Stuff	Rank	Sacks	ASR	Rank	False	Cont.
2006	4.18	4.11	21	70%	9	19%	10	18%	20	41	7.1%	20	16	34
2007	4.22	4.01	21	70%	8	17%	16	19%	22	42	7.4%	20	19	41
2008	4.28	4.05	21	76%	5	17%	15	16%	9	26	5.7%	12	22	39

Year	LE	Rank	LT	Rank	Mid	Rank	RT	Rank	RE	Rank
2006	3.31	25	4.61	9	3.91	25	4.72	2	4.79	6
2007	3.81	20	4.98	4	3.77	25	3.73	26	4.59	6
2008	4.10	20	3.85	21	3.88	24	4.22	16	4.65	3

The most underrated aspect of Miami's success with odd formations was how well the offensive line worked in the various Wildcat sets. First overall pick Jake Long was the team's left tackle in all non-Wildcat plays, then slid to the right outside right tackle Vernon Carey when the Dolphins got tricky. The tackles are the no-doubt incumbents, and the team was impressed enough with Carey's work to sign him to a six-year contract in the offseason. Left guard Justin Smiley, acquired before the 2008 season, was great at pulling right in those formations. His job was to provide lanes for the power formations that had Ronnie Brown keeping the ball and heading up the middle. Smiley broke his left leg and tore ankle ligaments in the November 30 win over the Rams, and backup Andy Alleman finished the season. Center Samson Satele was solid when asked to pull and do things in space, but the Dolphins wanted more power and traded Satele to the Raiders for a sixth-round draft pick after signing ex-Oakland center Jake Grove to replace him. Grove and backup Al Johnson are better equipped to handle the 3-4 nose tackles in the AFC East that the Dolphins face twice a year, such as New England's Vince Wilfork and Kris Jenkins of the Jets.

Little-known fact: After Miami's 38-13 win over the Patriots in Week 3 (the debut of the Wildcat), all five O-line starters — Long, Smiley, Satele, right tackle Ikechuku Ndukwe, and Carey — were each nominated for the AFC Offensive Player of the Week Award. You don't see that every day. Ronnie Brown, the guy they blocked for, won the award after scoring five total touchdowns.

Defensive Front Seven

Defensive Line	Age	Pos	Plays	TmPct	Overall Rk	Stop	Dfts	Stop%	Rk	AvYd	Pass Rush Rk	Sack	Hit	Hur	vs. Run Runs	St%	Yds	vs. Pass Pass	St%	Yds
Vonnie Holliday*	34	DT	47	6.1%	24	38	12	81%	16	1.7	24	3.5	3	3	35	86%	1.7	12	67%	1.6
Kendall Langford	24	DE	34	4.4%	63	30	11	88%	7	1.2	23	2.0	0	4	29	86%	1.8	5	100%	-2.4
Randy Starks	26	DE	32	4.1%	67	26	10	81%	24	1.3	27	3.0	3	8	24	79%	2.0	8	88%	-0.8
Phillip Merling	24	DE	28	3.6%	78	16	5	57%	91	4.5	93	1.0	3	6	19	68%	3.7	9	33%	6.2
Jason Ferguson	35	DT	21	2.7%	73	16	5	76%	41	1.7	22	0.0	1	3	20	80%	1.1	1	0%	14.0
Jason Taylor	35	DE	35	5.8%	41	27	11	77%	40	1.4	32	3.5	1	7	19	63%	3.7	16	94%	-1.4
Tony McDaniel	24	DT	19	4.1%	--	15	2	79%	--	2.2	--	0.5	1	1	15	80%	2.8	4	75%	0.0

Linebackers	Age	Pos	Plays	TmPct	Overall Rk	Stop	Dfts	Stop%	AvYd	Pass Rush Sack	Hit	Hur	vs. Run Runs	St%	Rk	Yds	Rk	vs. Pass Tgts	Suc%	Rk	AdjYd	Rk
Channing Crowder	26	ILB	119	16.4%	13	57	17	48%	5.8	0.0	5	8	68	54%	91	4.0	78	53	51%	41	6.0	37
Akin Ayodele	30	ILB	78	10.1%	67	46	9	59%	3.8	0.0	0	2	53	60%	67	3.1	35	28	53%	37	7.8	75
Matt Roth	27	OLB	56	7.2%	90	40	14	71%	2.4	5.0	2	5	42	74%	15	2.7	19	11	54%	--	5.1	--
Joey Porter	32	OLB	47	6.1%	96	40	24	85%	-0.9	17.5	6	12	26	73%	18	2.3	8	5	76%	--	6.6	--

Year	Yards	ALY	Rank	Power	Rank	10+ Yds	Rank	Stuff	Rank	Sack	ASR	Rank
2006	3.55	3.82	6	66%	16	11%	2	18%	17	47	8.6%	4
2007	4.58	4.47	31	70%	24	18%	19	14%	30	30	7.3%	8
2008	4.06	4.11	14	69%	21	12%	4	19%	13	40	6.5%	13

Year	LE	Rank	LT	Rank	Mid	Rank	RT	Rank	RE	Rank
2006	3.62	12	4.40	16	4.00	9	3.20	5	2.98	5
2007	5.52	31	5.20	30	4.16	19	4.55	23	4.27	21
2008	3.64	9	3.80	8	4.29	19	4.30	23	3.13	11

Kendall Langford and Joey Porter were the surprises here, for vastly different reasons. Langford, a third-round rookie from Hampton, recorded a sack in his first two NFL games and consistently drew praise from his coaches for his play. In Miami's AFC East-clinching win over the Jets, he grabbed one of Brett Favre's three interceptions. Porter amassed 17.5 sacks in 2008 after totaling just 12.5 combined in the two years before. He finished second in the league in quarterback sacks, but first in jawing with opponents and even his own coaching staff when Tony Sparano tried to sub him out in a game against the Patriots in late November. Problem was, pass pressure outside of Porter was hard to find — nobody else was even in the neighborhood when it came to sacks, and only Matt Roth was in the same city. Matt Roth is transitioning smoothly from end to linebacker on the strong side, and had five sacks of his own.

To upgrade the rest of the pass rush, the Dolphins will look to two-time CFL Defensive Player of the year Cameron Wake and prodigal son Jason Taylor. Taylor butted heads with Bill Parcells and was dealt to the Redskins, but he missed Miami enough to come back a year later for a situational role. Wake left Penn State in 2005 with a reputation for a work ethic that didn't match his physical ability. Cut by the Giants in June of 2005, Wake signed with the B.C. Lions and got to work, putting up 39 sacks in two seasons. At least half the teams in the NFL were interested in welcoming him back to the U.S. this past offseason, and he worked out for eight different teams before signing a four-year contract with Miami that gave him more money ($4.9 million total) than any other CFL import in history. Wake is a straight-line pass rusher who can disrupt consistently if he isn't forced to sift through too many blockers.

The Dolphins will miss end Vonnie Holliday, but the 33-year-old would have counted for $5.75 million against the salary cap in 2009 and refused to take a pay cut. His release provides options for several defenders, most notably Philip Merling, who will be asked to step up in his second year. Tackle Jason Ferguson gave Bill Parcells everything expected when he came over from Dallas for a sixth-round draft pick before the 2009 season. Akin Ayodele and Channing Crowder comprise a solid middle unit behind Ferguson. Ayodele, another Dallas transplant, has long been an FO favorite — not a spectacular player, but one who gets the job done at a low cost. Crowder played well enough to receive a new three-year contract despite concerns about his knees.

Defensive Secondary

Secondary	Age	Pos	Plays	Overall				vs. Run				vs. Pass										
				TmPct	Rk	Stop	Dfts	Yds	Rk	St%	Rk	Tgts	Tgt%	Rk	Dist	Suc%	Rk	AdjYd	Rk	Yds	PD	Int
Yeremiah Bell	31	SS	130	16.8%	2	52	23	6.7	39	36%	51	69	14.0%	1	6.5	54%	28	6.0	8	6.1	9	0
Renaldo Hill*	31	FS	79	10.2%	35	22	9	7.8	52	38%	47	38	7.6%	26	11.9	48%	54	8.2	48	8.2	4	3
Will Allen	31	CB	65	8.4%	48	29	14	7.2	48	46%	40	90	18.3%	36	9.7	52%	35	7.8	49	7.6	18	3
Andre' Goodman*	31	CB	57	7.4%	61	29	11	6.4	40	38%	51	92	18.6%	34	13.6	62%	8	6.3	22	6.4	21	5
Tyrone Culver	25	CB	29	4.0%	--	10	5	5.9	--	29%	--	15	3.3%	--	12.3	52%	--	8.0	--	7.3	3	1
Jason Allen	26	FS	24	3.3%	78	6	4	11.0	77	0%	78	34	7.4%	30	14.5	48%	53	9.4	60	9.2	5	1
Gibril Wilson	28	SS	134	16.2%	3	62	17	4.6	10	55%	12	42	10.6%	3	12.5	53%	34	10.4	70	10.3	2	2
Eric Green	27	CB	37	5.8%	--	16	4	5.0	--	36%	--	37	11.0%	--	13.5	54%	--	9.4	--	9.4	6	1

Year	Pass D Rank	vs. #1 WR	Rk	vs. #2 WR	Rk	vs. Other WR	Rk	vs. TE	Rk	vs. RB	Rk
2006	12	7.8%	22	2.2%	17	9.0%	23	0.7%	19	-25.9%	5
2007	28	11.9%	22	21.6%	27	16.2%	30	0.8%	10	-3.9%	13
2008	12	-7.2%	9	36.7%	30	-22.2%	8	-14.2%	7	-24.8%	2

When you select two cornerbacks in the first two rounds of the draft, as the Dolphins did with Illinois' Vontae Davis and Utah's Sean Smith, you're speaking to an obvious need. Will Allen and Andre' Goodman had standout moments in 2008 — Goodman played particularly well down the stretch — but both players are reaching an age where the word "replacement" starts to get thrown around. The Dolphins saw enough in Allen to give a two-year extension worth $16.2 million with $10 million guaranteed, but they let Goodman head to Denver, where he signed a five-year, $25 million contract. Davis is the most physically gifted defensive back in the 2009 class, but like his brother Vernon, he has struggled to maximize his abilities. Playing in the same division with guys like Randy Moss and Terrell Owens, he's certainly in for an interesting education. Smith is a former receiver who can play sideline and slot. Both rookies will need time to develop, which is why the team signed Eric Green, formerly of the Cardinals, to a two-year, $6 million contract. Jones is a respected nickel-corner candidate who found his way back to Parcells from Dallas. The new acquisitions leave little room for 2006 first-round pick Jason Allen, who has spent his career switching between safety, cornerback, and all-purpose scapegoat.

One of the Dolphins safeties is destined to make fewer plays this year, because Miami has the two defensive backs who led the league in total defensive plays in 2008. Free agent acquisition Gibril Wilson spent last year cleaning up after the Oakland front seven, but he'll get to play more pass coverage as he shifts over to free safety in Miami. (He replaces Renaldo Hill, who joined Goodman in moving to Denver.) Strong safety Yeremiah Bell, who had 130 defensive plays to Wilson's 134, was re-signed to a four-year, $20 million contract.

Special Teams

Year	DVOA	Rank	FG/XP	Rank	Net Kick	Rank	Kick Ret	Rank	Net Punt	Rank	Punt Ret	Rank	Hidden	Rank
2006	-0.7%	21	-10.6	31	10.3	5	-4.3	23	2.3	15	-1.7	18	-4.0	22
2007	-2.2%	22	5.3	5	-18.5	32	-1.0	18	1.2	14	0.0	13	-7.9	26
2008	-4.8%	29	0.1	18	-9.2	30	-3.4	21	-13.7	30	-2.1	22	-3.1	18

The Dolphins cut kicker Jay Feely after rookie Dan Carpenter beat the veteran out in training camp — a pretty impressive feat, considering that Feely made 21 of 23 field goals in 2007 and was one of the few bright spots in that disastrous season. Carpenter made 21 of 25 in his inaugural campaign, and while he didn't quite match Feely's 85.7 percent field goal accuracy with the Jets, the Dolphins ranked fourth in the NFL in opponents' starting field position (their own 27.8-yard line, on average) after finishing 31st in 2007. Coverage was a problem — Miami was below league average in value allowed on punt and kickoff returns. Incumbent punter Brandon Fields put 24 of his punts inside the opposing 20-yard-line, tying him for tenth in the league, and his net value was positive at 1.81 points above average, but only Minnesota's Chris Kluwe and Washington's Durant Brooks had coverage teams allow a higher value to opposing returners than Miami (10.1 points of estimated field position). Patrick Cobbs added to his on-field contributions by outpacing incumbent Ted Ginn, Jr. in kickoff return value.

Coaching Staff

Between head coach Tony Sparano, quarterbacks coach David "Wildcat" Lee, and defensive coordinator Paul Pasqualoni (not to mention New Orleans' Sean Payton and Kansas City's Todd Haley), it's time to look at Bill Parcells' Dallas staff as yet another example of the Tuna's unmatched ability to identify and groom superior coaching talent. Sparano took over a team that was oh-for-regulation in 2007 and didn't lose hope when the team started 0-2. Instead, it was the coaching staff's inventiveness that gave a new swing to the playbook when they put together the Wildcat schemes on the flight home from a Week 2 loss in Arizona. Sparano possessed an expert hand with his players, knowing when to hug and when to slam the hammer down. And playing for one of the most demanding and respected forces in the league, he never seemed simply a Parcells puppet. This is a hungry staff with everything it takes to succeed — toughness, ingenuity, and the ability to communicate with players in ways that pay immediate dividends on the field. Offensive coordinator Dan Henning did well in his first season back with the Dolphins — he was the team's quarterbacks and receivers coach in 1979 and 1980. Henning belied his conservative reputation with the implementation of Lee's unique formations, and he's got a series of interesting challenges going forward as the Dolphins look to integrate those formations more organically into their offense — while at the same time preparing for the eventual shift in Chads from Pennington to Henne.

Minnesota Vikings

The Brad Childress-era Minnesota Vikings are doing their best to introduce the NFL to a word it bends over backwards trying to avoid: Despite.

When an NFL team wins the Super Bowl, everyone gets the credit, regardless of whether they were actually producing a positive contribution or not. You'll never read an article that talks about how the Ravens won Super Bowl XXXV *despite* the work of Trent Dilfer at quarterback; even though Dilfer had a -24.6% DVOA, the stories about those Ravens teams regard Dilfer as a game manager, a player who took what the defense gave him, even if it meant failing to get the ball downfield or pick up first downs on a regular basis. Dilfer's inadequacies weren't just glossed over; they were glorified!

Now, it's not fair of us to pick on Dilfer; there are examples of such players on every Super Bowl-winning team. (We're looking at you, Steelers interior offensive line.) Dilfer's the most prominent example, though, and the one most appropriate for the question we're going to discuss here: Can the Vikings win a championship despite Tarvaris Jackson?

One of the corollaries to this question, naturally, is whether Minnesota should have gone after Jay Cutler, Matt Cassel, or another quarterback this offseason, as opposed to acquiring Sage Rosenfels from the Texans. One person who believed that Minnesota was better off not committing serious resources to acquiring Cutler was, ironically, Trent Dilfer:

VIKINGS SUMMARY

2008 Record: 10-6

Pythagorean Wins: 9.2 (12th)

DVOA: 4.9% (18th)

Offense: -5.8% (25th)

Defense: -17.2% (4th)

Special Teams: -6.5% (32nd)

Variance: 12.1% (9th)

2008: We need to bench ~~Tarvaris Jackson~~ Gus Frerotte! Thank god we have ~~Gus Frerotte~~ Tarvaris Jackson!

2009: If they get StarCapped, it won't matter how many quarterbacks they collect.

2009 Mean Projection: 8.8 wins

On the Clock (0-3): 2%

Loserville (4-6): 12%

Mediocrity (7-8): 28%

Playoff Contender (9-10): 36%

Super Bowl Contender (11+): 23%

Projected Average Opponent: 1.1% (16th)

"What takes a quarterback to the next level is not arm strength or mobility or any of that stuff," Dilfer told the *Minneapolis Star-Tribune*. "It's the ability to play on critical downs. Manage third downs, or red zones or four-minute or two-minute situations.

"I think that Sage, Tarvaris, and Jay Cutler are all in the same boat in that sense. None have proven they can do it a high level consistently. I don't think because Cutler is a marquee name that he brings you any more quality in those situations."

Dilfer's statement requires some qualification. As mentioned in previous versions of this book, performance on third downs has a disproportionate effect, relative to other downs, on a team's success. As you've also read in the book in the past, it tends to regress to the mean from year-to-year, which is also true of quarterbacks as well. It's difficult to say that any of the three quarterbacks can be doing something at a high level "consistently" considering their relative inexperience as a starter.

Furthermore, while a quarterback has an impact when it comes to calling audibles in a team's "four-minute offense," the scheme they run when they're trying to kill clock in the fourth quarter, they don't throw the ball very often, so it's unfair to really provide passing statistics for that subset of the game.

To suggest that Cutler doesn't provide more quality in those situations, though, is at odds with the data (Table 1). While Cutler struggled in the red zone last year, he

2009 Vikings Schedule

Week	Opp.	Week	Opp.	Week	Opp.
1	at CLE	7	at PIT	13	at ARI
2	at DET	8	at GB	14	CIN
3	SF	9	BYE	15	at CAR
4	GB (Mon.)	10	DET	16	at CHI (Mon.)
5	at STL	11	SEA	17	NYG
6	BAL	12	CHI		

was fantastic inside of it the year before, and he was effective on third down in both seasons. Rosenfels was wildly erratic in a small sample, while Jackson was unimpressive in either season, outside of a bizarre split where he had a 26.3% DVOA on third down a year ago and a 3.0% DVOA on all other downs.

Furthermore, the idea that a quarterback needs to be particularly special in those situations to lead his team to a Super Bowl is untrue, and the example we can provide as an argument is, not coincidentally, Trent Dilfer. We mentioned that he had a -24.6% DVOA in 2000; when we look at the splits, he had a DVOA of -68.0% in the red zone and a -34.4% DVOA on third down. Among those situations, it was only in the two-minute game that he impressed, with a 25.9% DVOA. It wasn't just Dilfer, either; Ben Roethlisberger had a 2.2% DVOA a year ago, but that fell to -5.3% in the red zone and -31.3% on third down. Eli Manning was at -13.1% in 2007, and while he had a 5.9% DVOA in the red zone (thanks, Plaxico Burress!), he was at -20.7% on third down. Playing well in those situations is a good thing, of course, but by no means is it the signature of a Super Bowl quarterback.

What's particularly difficult about analyzing Jackson is the sheer fact that he hasn't done very much cumulatively; through three seasons, he has only 19 starts and 524 attempts. His supporters point to a steady rise in his statistics, but raising his completion percentage from 58.0 percent as a rookie to 59.1 percent in his third year isn't much of anything, especially when the

league completion rate has gone from 59.8 percent to 61.0 percent over the same two years. Using his rise in yards per attempt or touchdown-to-interception ratio a year ago is disingenuous, relying heavily on the effects of one freakish half against a Cardinals defense that was either confused, slumping, or bored and slacking off. Factor in Jackson's struggles against the Eagles in the NFC Wild Card game and his completion percentage on the season falls to a career-low 56.0 percent, while his yards per attempt fall back to 6.6, exactly the average he had the year before. A full season of Jackson or the newly-acquired Rosenfels will be an upgrade on the dire performance of Gus Frerotte a year ago, but there's plenty of evidence that either quarterback would need to be propped up by the rest of the team.

As for the gritty, gunslinging elephant in the room? Well, at the time of writing, Brett Favre's slow courtship by Minnesota had yet to reach a resolved conclusion. Truthfully, there's not a real difference; last year, Favre looked alternately injured and unconvincing against one of the easiest schedules a quarterback has had to face in the past 15 years, yielding a -2.2% DVOA. There's no reason to think that Favre would significantly improve the situation relative to Rosenfels, so even if the Vikings do sign him, their outlook wouldn't change dramatically.

Whoever the Vikings line up behind center will spend most of time handing off to Adrian Peterson, whose -0.3% DVOA (22nd in the league) indicates several things. First, it shows that DVOA will never be a perfect statistic; for all the value it has, it fails to understand how many defenders are keyed on stopping Peterson on each snap and the amount of work he has to go through to get the yardage he does. If someone suggests to you that Peterson's the 22nd-best halfback in football, they're simply wrong. The rating is also lower than you might expect because of a league-high nine fumbles. Peterson's player comment later in the book explains why that's not a huge worry for 2009. However, the low rating also indicates that Peterson isn't pushing his team towards first downs as frequently and reliably as he should. On first down, Peterson's Success Rate was below the league average; furthermore, he was stuffed for no gain or a loss of yardage on 20.4 percent of his first-down carries. Among backs with 100 carries on first down, only Larry Johnson, Marion Barber, Kevin Smith, Chris Johnson, and DeAngelo Williams were stuffed more frequently. That led to Minnesota having to face an

Table 1: Throwing In The Pinches

Quarterback	Year	Overall DVOA	Red Zone DVOA	3rd Down DVOA	Two-Minute DVOA
Jay Cutler	2007	19.4%	85.5%	33.4%	-9.2%
	2008	22.0%	-23.5%	20.8%	-0.4%
Sage Rosenfels	2007	24.3%	23.5%	78.4%	209.6%
	2008	3.7%	-36.6%	-9.6%	-118.6%
Tarvaris Jackson	2007	-5.3%	-25.8%	-25.0%	-171.8%
	2008	10.0%	-62.3%	26.3%	-86.1%
Average QB		4.3%	4.7%	5.9%	-13.5%

average of 8.11 yards to go on second down, the sixth-worst total in the league. The group of eight teams that averaged more than eight yards to go on second downs includes the Vikings, Steelers, and six teams that owned draft picks in the top eight of this year's draft (Table 2). On the flip side, though, the idea that Peterson is more likely to break a big gain than other backs is true; while the average back gains 15 or more yards on first down 4.8 percent of the time, Peterson picked up 15-plus on a full 8.0 percent of his first down carries, behind only Derrick Ward, Williams, and Mewelde Moore in that category.

When the Vikings brought in Bernard Berrian last offseason, the hope was that the threat of Berrian downfield in single coverage would prevent teams from pushing their safeties into the box. Berrian had a decent season (especially when you factor in the league-high six pass interference penalties he drew from opposing defensive backs), but it wasn't enough to prevent safeties from risking neutral zone infractions. Undeterred, the Vikings used their first-round pick this year on Florida wideout Percy Harvin, who profiles as a jack-of-all-trades type because of his usage patterns in Florida's offensive scheme. Harvin's a good athlete, and he may very well end up being a useful player out of the Wildcat, but the track record for SEC wide receivers and/or players taken out of gimmicky offensive schemes in the first round is the stuff of "worst pick" lists and talking head resumes. Harvin, who tested positive for marijuana at the Combine and missed the team's rookie minicamp with "dehydration" issues, will likely need to spend most of the season learning how to effectively run routes at the NFL level. The Vikings chose Harvin over Ole Miss tackle Michael Oher, who would have filled an obvious need for the team at right tackle and been able to contribute immediately; while these picks sometimes work out better than anyone could have hoped, it sure doesn't look like a good idea at this juncture.

The most pressing concern for Minnesota heading into 2009, though, is on the defensive side of the ball. There, tackles Kevin Williams and Pat Williams (no relation) are expected to be suspended for the first four games of the season after a lengthy court battle related to their use of StarCaps, a substance that would help prevent the detection of steroids in a player's system. While a discussion of the legalities and moral conduct of the issue is beyond the scope of this essay, losing the Williamses for four games would be a crushing blow to a defense that's built around their abilities in

Table 2: Second-And-Forever

Team	Avg. Yards To Go	Team	Avg. Yards To Go
SEA	8.38	MIN	8.11
STL	8.20	JAC	8.04
DET	8.18	CLE	8.03
OAK	8.13	DAL	7.99
PIT	8.12	WAS	7.94

the middle of the field. It's surprising that the issue of losing either of the Williamses hasn't come up earlier; despite the fact that Pat is 37 and Kevin plays virtually every down as the team's second-best pass rusher behind Jared Allen, each Williams has only missed a total of two regular season games in the four years they've spent playing together.

If the Williamses are forced to sit on the sidelines for the first four games of the year, it might not actually be such a terrible situation. The Vikes start the season off with a relatively forgiving slate of rushing attacks in Cleveland (20th in the league in rushing DVOA a year ago), Detroit (30th), San Francisco (27th), and Green Bay (19th). However, Minnesota certainly hasn't prepared for an extended departure from their star defensive tackles, as they didn't bring in a single fresh face at the position during the offseason.

In fact, the flow of players over the offseason as a whole was mostly out. The most prominent player the team brought in was Broncos nickelback Karl Paymah, while they lost leaders on both the offensive (center Matt Birk) and defensive (strong safety Darren Sharper) side of the ball. They'll expect to replace both starters with second-year players in John Sullivan and Tyrell Johnson, respectively; Johnson started seven games last year while free safety Madieu Williams was injured, but Sullivan has yet to start an NFL game and will have to show off the short-area ability of Birk in the blocking game while remembering all the line calls and adjusting protections on the fly.

Factoring in all these doubts, it's even harder to illustrate the concept of "despite" in Minnesota. With elite players sprinkled throughout the roster, it will depend upon stars like Peterson, Steve Hutchinson, Jared Allen, and Antoine Winfield to carry the weaker parts of the team to success. From the weakest parts of the roster, though? If they succeed and do win a Super Bowl, it won't mean that everyone actually is good, because the Vikings won't need good. They'll just need good enough.

Bill Barnwell

2008 Vikings Stats by Week

Wk	vs.	W-L	PF	PA	YDF	YDA	TO	Total	Off	Def	ST
1	@GB	L	19	24	355	317	-1	-9%	22%	11%	-20%
2	IND	L	15	18	299	321	+1	34%	-9%	-40%	4%
3	CAR	W	20	10	305	204	+1	25%	3%	-31%	-10%
4	@TEN	L	17	30	333	275	-3	-11%	-4%	1%	-6%
5	@NO	W	30	27	270	375	+4	-17%	-16%	-41%	-42%
6	DET	W	12	10	392	212	-2	-45%	-50%	-14%	-9%
7	@CHI	L	41	48	439	327	-4	-15%	30%	19%	-26%
8	BYE										
9	HOU	W	28	21	345	389	+2	30%	-1%	-25%	6%
10	GB	W	28	27	184	361	-3	-7%	-27%	-36%	-16%
11	@TB	L	13	19	210	363	-1	-31%	-13%	16%	-2%
12	@JAC	W	30	12	226	321	+4	7%	-16%	-19%	4%
13	CHI	W	34	14	378	228	+2	71%	17%	-57%	-3%
14	@DET	W	20	16	298	267	-2	-23%	-37%	-19%	-4%
15	@ARI	W	35	14	396	316	+1	78%	31%	-33%	14%
16	ATL	L	17	24	356	222	-4	-8%	-16%	-15%	-7%
17	NYG	W	20	19	349	364	-1	-12%	-18%	1%	7%
18	PHI	L	14	26	301	350	0	-9%	0%	-3%	-11%

Trends and Splits

	Offense	Rank	Defense	Rank
Total DVOA	-5.8%	25	-17.2%	4
Unadjusted VOA	-3.4%	24	-9.8%	5
Weighted trend	-8.5%	24	-16.5%	4
Variance	5.3%	7	11.8%	29
Average opponent	7.7%	3	6.5%	21
Passing	-1.6%	24	-15.9%	5
Rushing	-2.2%	23	-18.9%	4
First down	-7.0%	24	-5.5%	6
Second down	-14.1%	27	-25.1%	2
Third down	8.3%	16	-26.8%	3
First half	-3.6%	24	-18.0%	4
Second half	-7.9%	23	-16.2%	5
Red Zone	-19.7%	28	-43.1%	3
Late and close	-19.6%	28	-7.3%	9

Five-Year Performance

Year	W-L	Pyth	Est W	PF	PA	TO	Total	Rk	Off	Rk	Def	Rk	ST	Rk	Off AGL	Rk	Def AGL	Rk
2004	8-8	8.2	8.6	405	395	+1	-7.7%	20	18.4%	5	23.0%	32	-3.1%	27	43.4	2	8.0	29
2005	9-7	6.9	7.8	306	344	+5	-18.0%	24	-15.3%	26	2.1%	22	-0.6%	21	30.8	5	9.9	22
2006	6-10	6.6	7.9	282	327	+4	-10.9%	23	-17.3%	31	-10.0%	5	-3.6%	27	18.0	16	10.6	19
2007	8-8	9.5	8.9	365	311	+1	2.0%	15	0.1%	16	0.3%	17	2.1%	9	11.9	29	7.6	29
2008	10-6	9.2	8.3	379	333	-6	4.9%	18	-5.8%	25	-17.2%	4	-6.5%	32	10.0	29	24.0	15

Strategic Tendencies

Run/Pass		Rank	Offense		Rank	Defense		Rank	Other		Rank
Runs, all plays	50%	5	3+ WR	45%	24	Rush 3	1.2%	31	2+ RB, Pct Runs	66%	6
Runs, first half	52%	2	4+ WR	5%	30	Rush 4	66.7%	13	1 RB/2 TE, Pct Runs	53%	15
Runs, first down	61%	3	2+ TE	37%	3	Rush 5	25.0%	9	1RB/3+WR, Pct Runs	36%	4
Runs, second-long	47%	6	Single back	64%	10	Rush 6+	7.1%	19	Zone Blitz	7%	9
Runs, power sit.	79%	2	Play action	18%	16	Rush 7+	0.5%	29	Go for it on 4th	0.77	26
Runs, behind 2H	40%	2	Max protect	6%	30	Sacks by LB	20.0%	12	Offensive Pace	31.4	21
Pass, ahead 2H	40%	23	Outside pocket	12%	16	Sacks by DB	4.4%	23	Defensive Pace	30.8	18

Minnesota averaged a league-low 6.4 yards after catch on passes thrown behind or at the line of scrimmage. (So much for getting Adrian Peterson the ball in space.) On the other hand, the Vikings led the league by averaging five yards after catch on passes caught beyond the line of scrimmage. ● In 2007, the Vikings were the NFL's best team when running on second-and-long, with 55.6% DVOA and a mind-blowing 7.9 yards per carry. Last year, that declined to 5.1 yards per carry, not much above the league average of 4.7. Even worse was Minnesota's -19.8% DVOA in these situations, 28th in the NFL. The Vikings had four fumbles and lost yardage on one out of every ten runs on second-and-long. ● Minnesota ran on 33 percent of its plays with three or more wide receivers in the game, second only to Seattle. ● Only 19 percent of Minnesota passes were thrown to the middle of the field (29th in NFL) but 30 percent of their opponents' passes were thrown to the middle (second in the league, behind only Washington). ● Minnesota had the best defensive DVOA in the league against three-wide sets. ● The Vikings got the benefit of nine aborted snaps by their opponents, the highest total in the NFL.

Passing

Player	DYAR	DVOA	Plays	NtYds	Avg	YAC	C%	TD	Int
Gus Frerotte*	16	-10.4%	337	2134	6.3	5.3	59.3%	12	15
Tarvaris Jackson	219	10.0%	164	1052	6.4	5.4	59.9%	9	2
Sage Rosenfels	*183*	*3.7%*	*184*	*1391*	*7.6*	*5.4*	*67.4%*	*6*	*10*

Rushing

Player	DYAR	DVOA	Plays	Yds	Avg	TD	Fum	Suc
Adrian Peterson	121	-0.3%	363	1761	4.9	10	9	46%
Chester Taylor	28	-1.4%	101	399	4.0	4	0	43%
Tarvaris Jackson	-4	-15.2%	21	136	6.5	0	2	–
Gus Frerotte*	11	13.7%	7	19	2.7	1	0	–
Jeff Dugan	10	24.4%	4	7	1.8	0	0	100%
Bernard Berrian	19	66.7%	4	26	6.5	0	0	–
Sage Rosenfels	*-27*	*-60.6%*	*9*	*38*	*4.2*	*0*	*1*	*–*

Receiving

Player	DYAR	DVOA	Plays	Ctch	Yds	Y/C	YAC	TD	C%
Bernard Berrian	197	12.4%	95	48	964	20.1	6.4	8	51%
Bobby Wade	-21	-15.6%	89	53	645	12.2	4.4	2	60%
Sidney Rice	23	-3.8%	31	15	141	9.4	2.2	4	48%
Aundrae Allison	15	-4.5%	21	10	109	10.9	4.7	0	48%
Robert Ferguson*	-4	-23.1%	5	3	25	8.3	1.3	0	60%
Glenn Holt	*-28*	*-42.5%*	*11*	*3*	*26*	*8.7*	*-0.3*	*1*	*27%*
Visanthe Shiancoe	221	50.3%	59	42	596	14.2	4.3	8	71%
Jim Kleinsasser	4	-2.0%	13	6	92	15.3	7.0	0	46%
Garrett Mills	3	-3.0%	11	5	65	13.0	7.2	0	45%
Chester Taylor	104	25.4%	55	45	399	8.9	8.1	2	36%
Adrian Peterson	-70	-46.5%	39	21	125	6.0	5.9	0	60%
Naufahu Tahi	-76	-74.3%	21	16	37	2.3	2.4	0	76%

Offensive Line

Year	Yards	ALY	Rank	Power	Rank	10+ Yds	Rank	Stuff	Rank	Sacks	ASR	Rank	False	Cont.
2006	4.20	4.25	13	68%	12	16%	14	18%	18	43	7.7%	22	20	36
2007	5.44	4.18	13	76%	2	32%	1	22%	28	38	8.6%	28	21	42
2008	4.63	4.13	12	73%	8	25%	4	19%	21	43	8.9%	28	16	32

Year	LE	Rank	LT	Rank	Mid	Rank	RT	Rank	RE	Rank
2006	2.95	26	4.79	6	4.29	15	4.46	5	5.07	5
2007	4.64	9	4.17	20	4.27	9	4.04	21	3.45	26
2008	4.27	15	4.69	7	4.06	19	3.59	27	4.33	8

Right tackle remained the team's bugaboo in 2008, with Ryan Cook and Artis Hicks battling to see who could give the job away quicker. While Hicks is a utility lineman who's stretched at tackle and best at guard, Cook simply hasn't developed the consistency and technique needed to play regularly at this level. As a result, the Vikings used their second-round pick on Oklahoma tackle Phil Loadholt, who could step in immediately as the starter there. At 6-foot-8, 332 pounds, Loadholt's a massive human being, but he has the same technique issues that Cook has; it'll be on the coaching staff to develop him into the player Cook failed to become.

Center wasn't a problem in 2008, but it very well may be in 2009, as six-time Pro Bowler and Minnesota institution Matt Birk left for Baltimore on a three-year deal worth about $12 million. At those figures, it's pretty clear that the Vikings simply didn't think Birk was worth holding onto; Birk's no longer an excellent blocker, but he did handle all the line calls and managed to keep sack totals down despite having two very mediocre quarterbacks. Second-year man John Sullivan, a 2008 sixth-round selection out of Notre Dame, will take over in the middle.

The star-studded left side of the line remains the same, with Bryant McKinnie having an excellent year as a pass blocker; one blown block is a fantastic total for a left tackle, even though McKinnie missed four games. Steve Hutchinson allowed only two, but right guard Anthony Herrera tied for the league lead amongst guards with five sacks allowed. No one's expecting the right side of the line to be as good as the left side, but for the Vikings to take the next step forward, they'll have to be, at the very least, closer.

Defensive Front Seven

Defensive Line	Age	Pos	Plays	TmPct	Rk	Stop	Dfts	Stop%	Rk	AvYd	Rk	Sack	Hit	Hur	Runs	St%	Yds	Pass	St%	Yds
						Overall						Pass Rush			vs. Run			vs. Pass		
Kevin Williams	29	DT	63	8.3%	3	50	21	79%	27	0.8	9	8.5	9	20	44	77%	1.6	19	84%	-0.8
Ray Edwards	24	DE	56	7.9%	12	43	21	77%	44	1.4	28	5.0	14	14	40	78%	1.5	16	75%	0.9
Jared Allen	27	DE	53	7.0%	18	41	25	77%	37	-0.5	6	14.5	18	27	32	69%	1.7	21	90%	-3.7
Pat Williams	37	DT	46	7.0%	11	32	5	70%	64	2.2	45	1.0	2	2	38	68%	2.4	8	75%	1.1
Fred Evans	26	DT	16	2.1%	--	14	4	88%	--	1.8	--	0.0	2	2	16	88%	1.8	0	0%	0.0

Linebackers	Age	Pos	Plays	TmPct	Rk	Stop	Dfts	Stop%	AvYd	Sack	Hit	Hur	Runs	St%	Rk	Yds	Rk	Tgts	Suc%	Rk	AdjYd	Rk
					Overall					Pass Rush			vs. Run					vs. Pass				
Chad Greenway	26	OLB	119	15.7%	17	66	20	55%	5.1	5.0	3	5	62	63%	57	4.1	82	60	42%	68	8.4	83
Ben Leber	31	OLB	69	9.1%	75	39	12	57%	4.9	1.5	2	6	29	55%	89	3.7	68	39	58%	23	7.0	63
Napoleon Harris*	30	ILB	33	7.0%	--	19	6	58%	4.2	1.5	0	1	22	77%	--	1.8	--	5	21%	--	9.4	--
E.J. Henderson	29	ILB	27	14.3%	--	16	11	59%	5.1	1.0	2	0	14	79%	--	1.2	--	9	60%	--	5.8	--

Year	Yards	ALY	Rank	Power	Rank	10+ Yds	Rank	Stuff	Rank	Sack	ASR	Rank
2006	2.97	2.67	1	47%	1	23%	29	31%	1	30	5.0%	31
2007	3.23	3.26	1	54%	6	12%	5	25%	1	38	5.6%	28
2008	3.46	3.49	4	55%	2	16%	12	24%	5	45	9.0%	2

Year	LE	Rank	LT	Rank	Mid	Rank	RT	Rank	RE	Rank
2006	2.03	3	2.47	1	2.84	1	2.66	1	3.01	7
2007	2.74	4	4.13	15	2.82	1	4.04	16	4.35	22
2008	3.56	8	3.95	10	3.62	4	3.45	5	2.57	3

Adding Jared Allen had the desired effect; in addition to those 14.5 sacks, he finished second in the league in both quarterback hurries and hits. Allen wasn't even slowed by a separated shoulder and strained MCL, both of which he played through effectively. In addition to serving as an elite pass rusher, Allen also opened up opportunities for Kevin Williams, who had by far his best year as a pass rusher, although Ray Edwards wasn't particularly impressive across from Allen. You'd like to see more from a rusher who's in single coverage on literally every play.

As noted earlier in the chapter, both Kevin and Pat Williams were embroiled in the StarCaps scandal, which threatened to keep them out for four games apiece. After receiving an injunction preventing their suspension, Pat Williams promptly went down with a shoulder injury that kept him out of the final two games of the season and the playoff loss to the Eagles. It was the first start either of the Vikings' elite defensive tackles had missed since Kevin Williams went down for two games in 2005. It's remarkable that the players have remained so healthy up to this point, particularly the 37-year-old Pat Williams; it's a credit to the Vikings conditioning staff and their coaches for spotting them properly. There's precious little depth behind the Williamses, though, with former Rams washout Jimmy "Fredo" Williams and second-year project Letroy Guion the primary reserves.

E.J. Henderson's dislocated toes — yes, plural — may be most painful-sounding injury of the year, but it didn't have much of an effect on the Vikings defense, which actually performed slightly better without him (a difference in DVOA of -2.8%). The team went through David Herron and Vinny Ciurciu as Henderson's replacements before settling on journeyman Napoleon Harris, who was just about adequate. Herron will back Henderson up this year, with Ciurciu and Harris off to greener pastures. Sam linebacker Chad Greenway is a big hitter who still has some work to do taking on blockers and employing the right angles to ballcarriers, and Ben Leber got the sort of "He's here too!!" hype that you get when you're next to two extremely-hyped linebackers. Check out any columns from 2007 about Hunter Hillenmeyer if you don't know the type. Henderson's brother, Erin, will join Heath Farwell as the backups.

Defensive Secondary

Secondary	Age	Pos	Plays	TmPct	Rk	Stop	Dfts	Yds	Rk	St%	Rk	Tgts	Tgt%	Rk	Dist	Suc%	Rk	AdjYd	Rk	Yds	PD	Int
				Overall				vs. Run				vs. Pass										
Antoine Winfield	32	CB	101	13.4%	1	61	27	2.7	2	74%	3	78	17.9%	43	9.7	63%	7	5.9	16	6.0	12	2
Cedric Griffin	27	CB	97	12.8%	5	40	11	4.7	17	54%	26	102	23.5%	6	11.2	53%	33	7.6	45	7.8	8	1
Darren Sharper*	34	SS	71	9.4%	47	22	9	6.2	24	39%	42	33	7.5%	27	11.6	46%	58	10.3	69	10.9	5	1
Madieu Williams	28	FS	45	10.6%	30	15	6	10.4	72	33%	59	20	8.2%	17	12.8	64%	9	8.0	42	8.6	5	2
Tyrell Johnson	24	FS	26	3.4%	--	9	2	5.3	--	44%	--	14	3.1%	--	20.7	62%	--	6.5	--	7.3	3	1
Charles Gordon	25	CB	22	5.2%	--	11	7	0.5	--	100%	--	28	11.5%	--	12.2	51%	--	9.9	--	10.3	3	1
Karl Paymah	27	CB	33	4.2%	--	8	6	10.3	--	25%	--	37	8.8%	--	9.7	43%	--	7.5	--	7.8	5	1

Year	Pass D Rank	vs. #1 WR	Rk	vs. #2 WR	Rk	vs. Other WR	Rk	vs. TE	Rk	vs. RB	Rk
2006	16	16.7%	29	-13.1%	8	18.8%	26	10.7%	25	17.9%	29
2007	24	23.2%	31	17.5%	25	25.4%	32	-12.0%	5	1.8%	21
2008	5	-13.8%	7	-33.5%	2	-1.5%	20	18.0%	24	9.0%	22

Perhaps no one on the planet cared more about the Pro Bowl than Antoine Winfield, who was elated to make his first free trip to Hawaii after last season. His statistics match up with the perception of his performance; Winfield is not the type of corner that gets in a receiver's back pocket and doesn't allow him to breathe, but in much the same way as former Bills teammate Nate Clements, Winfield gives receivers a cushion and dares quarterbacks to throw at him. His phenomenal work in the running game is nothing new; he was just as good a year ago. Opposite him was Cedric Griffin, who continued his good year-bad year stretch with a solid enough season to earn a contract extension. You'd like to see more growth from a cornerback than Griffin has shown, but if he can be the player he was in 2008 for four years, he'll be one of the better second corners in the league. The organization was concerned about nickelback Charles Gordon after he suffered a gruesome broken ankle on punt return duty last year, so they signed former Broncos cornerback Karl Paymah and used a third-round pick on Georgia corner Asher Allen. Allen's an excellent cover corner and profiles as Winfield's long-term replacement.

Although 33-year-old strong safety Darren Sharper was effective against the run last year, the organization saw the writing on the wall for him and let him leave for New Orleans. The team will replace him with Tyrell Johnson, who played free safety for the first half of last season while free agent acquisition Madieu Williams was out with a neck injury. Although the Vikings play a lot of Cover-2, Johnson is better when attacking the line of scrimmage as opposed to making plays in centerfield. Williams is an effective cover safety when healthy, but playing so much zone prevents him from making a significant impact on the team's below-average performance against running backs and tight ends.

Special Teams

Year	DVOA	Rank	FG/XP	Rank	Net Kick	Rank	Kick Ret	Rank	Net Punt	Rank	Punt Ret	Rank	Hidden	Rank
2006	-3.6%	27	-3.4	23	-12.8	29	-2.6	17	-5.3	24	2.7	7	-3.8	20
2007	2.1%	9	5.2	6	5.1	11	6.3	7	0.9	15	-4.9	24	-12.0	30
2008	-6.5%	32	-0.5	19	-4.9	24	-4.4	22	-24.6	32	-3.8	26	5.2	7

Chris Kluwe made headlines in two ways last year. One was as a Grade-A dork, applying to join elite guilds on World of Warcraft message boards. No shame in that — he's got a lot of downtime, as he himself noted. The other side wasn't quite as fun; despite signing a contract extension during the 2007 season, Kluwe was nearly released after failing to place two punts to Reggie Bush out of bounds, resulting in 14 points and nearly costing the Vikings a victory.

He was on thin ice for the rest of the season, but truthfully, a good portion of the blame has to go to his punt coverage. Thanks in part to the Bush game, the Vikings had the second-worst punt coverage in the DVOA Era, giving up a total of 19.83 points of field position while allowing four touchdowns on the season. Number one? The 2002 Bengals, who gave up three scores, but also three more returns of ten or more yards than the Vikings did (Table 3).

Table 3: Worst Punt Coverage, 1994-2008

Team	Year	Return Pts+ vs.
CIN	2002	23.11
MIN	2008	19.83
LARM	1994	18.56
NYJ	2000	17.24
CHI	1997	16.71
ARI	2002	16.23
NO	1997	15.24
DET	2005	14.98
TEN	2002	14.95
MIN	1996	14.68

Strangely, the coverage on Ryan Longwell's kickoffs was above average and worth just about two points of field position. Maybe Kluwe should have hired a bunch of gold farmers to handle coverage.

Minnesota had four men return punts; only one, Bernard Berrian, was particularly good at it. Gordon was particularly terrible; he cost the team nearly seven points of field position on only 15 returns. The Vikings had eight different players return kicks, and while three of them were successful, they accounted for a total of 12 returns. New arrival Glenn Holt will likely be the primary kick returner, and as he cost Cincinnati 2.3 points of field position last year, he'll fit right in. Percy Harvin may also chip on returns, but he didn't return a single punt or kick during his three years at Florida, so while he's a great athlete, nobody knows if he'll be an effective return man.

Coaching Staff

A fair amount of Vikings fans spent this past offseason cleaning the Mike Tice stench off their pitchforks so they could go after Brad Childress. Minnesota might have made the playoffs, but their middling performance in a home loss to the Eagles did plenty to fuel the bloodlust. For better or worse, Childress' viability has become inextricably linked to that of Tarvaris Jackson — if Jackson plays like he did over the final few weeks of the regular season, Childress can expect a contract extension. Anything else, and he's probably in his final year with the team.

Defensive coordinator Leslie Frazier remains one of the hottest head coaching candidates in the league, and it has nothing to do with the Rooney Rule; his work on the defensive side of the ball made him the last man out in St. Louis' search for a coach, while John Harbaugh gave a media interview where he flat-out told the Broncos that Frazier was the best candidate for their vacancy. Having coached underneath Andy Reid, Marvin Lewis, and Tony Dungy, he certainly has the pedigree for the job. He may very well end up being Childress' replacement if he doesn't get a job elsewhere.

New England Patriots

We knew the 2008 season would be different 15 minutes in. Halfway through the first quarter in the season opener against the Kansas City Chiefs, Tom Brady threw deep to Randy Moss down the right sideline. Moss caught the ball 29 yards downfield and fumbled. The ball was recovered by Kansas City, but all eyes were back behind the line of scrimmage, where Brady was on the turf, screaming in pain. Backup Matt Cassel helped the team beat the Chiefs, 17-10, but Brady's health was all any Patriots fan cared about at that point. It was soon revealed that Brady had torn the ACL and MCL in his left knee, and he would be out for the season. Cassel, the former USC backup who had not started a game since high school, would replace him.

The Pats circled the wagons as expected, saying all the right things about Brady's ascent after Drew Bledsoe suffered a sheared blood vessel in his chest in 2001, but even Bill Belichick said that the two situations — and the two offenses — were like "apples and grapefruits." In 2001, Brady had nothing resembling the Randy Moss/Wes Welker combo. Cassel began the 2008 season with two decent games, running a spread-based offense with a heavy diet of shotgun checkdowns as opposed to Brady bombs. Then came the Week 3 loss to the Dolphins, where everything fell apart all at once. Linebacker Joey Porter sacked

Cassel four times, exposing weakness on the offensive line and Cassel's alarming lack of pocket presence, while Miami's Wildcat debut embarrassed a Pats defense that looked slow, underpowered, and out of position. It was Miami's first win in regulation since they beat the Pats, 21-0 on December 10, 2006, and it exposed a New England team with several flaws beyond Brady's absence.

Still, when we talk about myths and misperceptions, the notion that this was a team one knee injury away from total domination doesn't really ring true. Under Bill Belichick, the Patriots have survived catastrophic injuries to key players before, and 2008 was no different. Even with Brady out of the picture, New England was in the playoff hunt until the very end of the regular season. If the Patriots are going to meet our positive projections for 2009, four more myths must be debunked along the way.

PATRIOTS SUMMARY

2008 Record: 11-5

Pythagorean Wins: 10.6 (6th)

DVOA: 11.7% (9th)

Offense: 16.5% (8th)

Defense: 8.4% (21st)

Special Teams: 3.6% (6th)

Variance: 26.8% (30th)

2008: The follow-up to a historic season blows a gasket in the first game.

2009: Brady's back and you're gonna be in trouble; hey-la, hey-la, Tom Brady's back.

2009 Mean Projection: 11.4 wins

On the Clock (0-3): 0%

Loserville (4-6): 1%

Mediocrity (7-8): 5%

Playoff Contender (9-10): 27%

Super Bowl Contender (11+): 68%

Projected Average Opponent: -6.6% (32nd)

1. IT'S ALL ABOUT BRADY:

Brady's anticipation, pocket awareness, timing, and arm put him ahead of the pack, but once Cassel got the hang of things in the second half of the 2008 season, the offense really turned around. Cassel didn't share Brady's ability to connect with Randy Moss on deep bombs, but he did display a deft touch with fade routes, and he ran the offense better and better as he grew more aware of his surroundings. The most

2009 Patriots Schedule

Week	Opp.	Week	Opp.	Week	Opp.
1	BUF (Mon.)	7	vs. TB (U.K.)	13	at MIA
2	at NYJ	8	BYE	14	CAR
3	ATL	9	MIA	15	at BUF
4	BAL	10	at IND	16	JAC
5	at DEN	11	NYJ	17	at HOU
6	TEN	12	at NO (Mon.)		

important change was his ability to feel the pass rush and get rid of the ball under pressure instead of panicking: New England's Adjusted Sack Rate on offense dropped from 13.5 percent in the first six games to 5.7 percent over the final ten.

In the second half of the 2008 season, no offense was better than New England's. The DVOA totals may not have been as gaudy as they were in the first half of 2007, when the Pats ran through the rest of the NFL on Rookie Mode, but as we note below, that supremacy wasn't consistent even when Brady was healthy. This was a different offense than it had been under Brady — more yards after catch and fewer NFL Films highlights — but was actually more effective down the stretch than the Brady-led Pats had been in the last nine games (including postseason) of the 2008 season (Table 1). Belichick and offensive coordinator Josh McDaniels were smart enough to re-tool the offense so it would work for an inexperienced quarterback, and Cassel took the reins in admirable fashion.

By the Week 12 rematch with the Dolphins, Cassel was an entirely different quarterback. He had the fade and several quick passes in his arsenal, as well as an effective rollout pass and a new ability to fire the ball downfield under duress. In a 48-28 win, he threw for more than 400 yards for the second straight week, just the fifth quarterback to do that since the 1970 AFL-NFL merger. After that game, Moss put it succinctly: "Matt is getting in the comfort zone. He's playing some hellified ball."

Given half a season to pull it together in an offense that fit his strengths and kept his liabilities

Table 1: As the Patriots Turn

	Off DVOA	Def DVOA
Weeks 1-12, 2007	54.5%	-12.2%
Weeks 13-21, 2007	28.9%	1.5%
Weeks 1-9, 2008	1.1%	12.7%
Weeks 10-17, 2008	31.3%	4.6%

under control, Cassel produced like a playoff-caliber NFL quarterback. The real problem was on the defensive side.

2. THE AARP JOKES STILL APPLY TO THE DEFENSE: Several different factors combined to create an underperforming New England defense in 2008. The front seven was not adept at providing key stops, ranking dead last in stuffing opposing runners at the line, and the linebackers and defensive backs were far too vulnerable to passes over the middle. Pass pressure was spotty at best, which led to unfortunate coverage adventures on the back end. Veterans like Tedy Bruschi, Mike Vrabel, and Rodney Harrison were outdone by opposing offenses and their own mortality in ways they hadn't been before, and injuries forced the team to drag Junior Seau and Rosevelt Colvin off the street and into the starting lineup to replace Adalius Thomas and Thomas' replacement Pierre Woods, as well as other holes in the middle of the defense. Defensive Rookie of the Year Jerod Mayo really came on in the second half, showing a remarkable ability to put learning into action and benefit from any mistakes. He set a team record with 20 tackles against the Jets in November. Tackle opportunities are disproportionately high for inside linebackers, but Mayo's numbers indicate he's better than just the status quo.

Going forward, the defense is far more about youth and potential than it is about old guys hanging on because they're too smart to cut. Harrison and Vrabel are gone, although Bruschi is back because they need his ability to run the defense on the field. The draft brought cornerback Darius Butler and safety Patrick Chung into the mix, and both players have the talent to compete for major on-field time. Butler was the best cover corner in the 2009 draft class and Chung combines the kind of versatility Belichick loves with the experience of 51 college starts. Second-year cornerbacks Terrence Wheatley and Jonathan Wilhite will be obscured on the depth chart by free-agent acquisitions Shawn Springs and Leigh Bodden, but they add solid depth to what was a problem unit last year.

With Thomas healthy and Mayo benefiting from an NFL year under his belt, New England has two of the best every-down linebackers in the league at their physical peak. The front three of Ty Warren, Vince Wilfork, and Richard Seymour still doesn't have a member over the age of 29. The pieces are in place for New England's next defense, and there seems to be a bit less of the gritty overachiever element, and more pure talent with the potential to develop.

3. THE PATCHWORK RUNNING GAME DIDN'T WORK:
New England's running game was undersold because there were so many injuries, and so many backs contributed throughout the season. Filter out quarterback scrambles, and the Patriots ran 45 percent of the time. Only eight teams ran on a higher percentage of plays. In truth, the running game was the one consistently performing part of the team, ranking fifth in DVOA in the season's first half and third down the stretch. The committee was established when Laurence Maroney was placed on injured reserve in mid-October after playing in only three games. Morris and LaMont Jordan picked up the slack early in the season, until their own injuries put Kevin Faulk and BenJarvus Green-Ellis in the spotlight. Faulk and Morris were especially effective in the draws run out of New England's frequent shotgun sets, while both Jordan (who left for Denver in free agency) and Faulk ranked in the top ten for red zone DVOA among backs with at least 20 carries inside the 20. Maroney is coming back healthy, but he may have to fill out his reps as a returner if former Jacksonville star Fred Taylor has enough left in the tank to make this backfield competition even more interesting.

4. THERE'S NO WAY THEY CAN DO THIS AGAIN. RIGHT?
It depends on what "this" is. If you're expecting a return to 16-0 with Brady at the helm, remember that even in the second half of the 2007 season, the Patriots weren't that team anymore. Perhaps the more impressive team was the one that rebounded so decisively in the second half of the 2008 season despite abysmal injury luck — only the Bengals and Ravens had more injuries up and down the roster than the Patriots did. While New England's likely to be healthier in 2009, their division opponents are looking at a bit of regression the other way; the Jets had the healthiest starters in football, while Miami had the league's healthiest roster. The Bills were league-average. The Patriots also have the advantage of an extremely easy schedule for the second year in a row, although that's partly based on our poor projections for the rest of the AFC East.

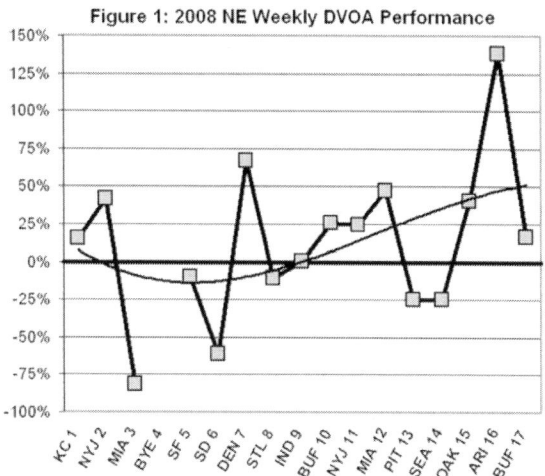

Figure 1: 2008 NE Weekly DVOA Performance

Brady's return to health is crucial for optimal success, but Cassel's performance last season didn't just put him in position to be the Chiefs' franchise quarterback. It also proved that the Patriots might be to quarterbacks what the Broncos are to running backs. It's just that Brady is Terrell Davis, and guys like Cassel — or current backups Matt Gutierrez and Kevin O'Connell — may be more at the Olandis Gary level. This is an offense built for quarterback success, and when you get a player of Brady's caliber, quarterback dominance. Scott Pioli, Belichick's longtime right-hand man, was the one who brought Cassel to Kansas City in his new role as the Chiefs' general manager. The loss of Pioli may be a hit to the team from a personnel perspective, but it shouldn't be a surprise; he's been weighing GM offers since at least early 2005.

In the end, the difference between just another Patriots team with double-digit wins and a Patriots team that can expect to compete for the Super Bowl has less to do with Brady's knee and more to do with a defense in flux. Last year's pass defense DVOA of 21.7% was the worst for New England since 2005, though improvements are expected with changes along the secondary. It is this, more than any other concern, which could keep the Patriots out of the elite in 2009. They will need Butler and Chung to play solidly in their first seasons — maybe not at Mayo's first-year level, but life has to be more difficult for the quarterbacks the Patriots face or it won't matter what Tom Brady does upon his return. If the Patriots want to cement their "Team of the Decade" status, defense will be the deciding factor.

Doug Farrar

2008 Patriots Stats by Week

Wk	vs.	W-L	PF	PA	YDF	YDA	TO	Total	Off	Def	ST
1	KC	W	17	10	338	284	-1	15%	6%	-5%	4%
2	@NYJ	W	19	10	260	256	+1	42%	19%	-11%	12%
3	MIA	L	13	38	215	461	-2	-82%	-41%	59%	19%
4	BYE										
5	@SF	W	30	21	377	199	+1	-10%	1%	13%	2%
6	@SD	L	10	30	299	404	0	-61%	-25%	24%	-12%
7	DEN	W	41	7	404	275	+5	67%	26%	-30%	11%
8	STL	W	23	16	348	361	-1	-11%	-1%	16%	7%
9	@IND	L	15	18	342	301	-2	0%	23%	29%	6%
10	BUF	W	20	10	370	168	+1	26%	24%	-18%	-16%
11	NYJ	L	31	34	511	375	0	24%	47%	5%	-18%
12	@MIA	W	48	28	530	396	-1	47%	59%	24%	13%
13	PIT	L	10	33	267	333	-4	-25%	-11%	5%	-8%
14	@SEA	W	24	21	344	339	+1	-25%	8%	49%	16%
15	@OAK	W	49	26	487	334	0	40%	62%	30%	8%
16	ARI	W	47	7	514	186	+2	138%	44%	-74%	20%
17	@BUF	W	13	0	241	276	+1	16%	11%	-7%	-1%

Trends and Splits

	Offense	Rank	Defense	Rank
Total DVOA	16.5%	8	8.4%	21
Unadjusted VOA	17.9%	7	5.7%	17
Weighted trend	24.2%	3	5.9%	16
Variance	8.2%	25	14.4%	31
Average opponent	2.4%	22	8.6%	25
Passing	18.5%	15	22.2%	26
Rushing	19.3%	4	-6.4%	9
First down	4.2%	16	1.1%	19
Second down	22.0%	9	8.3%	19
Third down	29.8%	8	21.0%	25
First half	20.7%	2	11.2%	21
Second half	12.2%	14	5.7%	19
Red Zone	6.6%	14	49.2%	31
Late and close	24.3%	5	-4.5%	10

Five-Year Performance

Year	W-L	Pyth	Est W	PF	PA	TO	Total	Rk	Off	Rk	Def	Rk	ST	Rk	Off AGL	Rk	Def AGL	Rk
2004	14-2	12.4	13.1	437	260	+9	35.9%	2	24.6%	3	-11.1%	6	0.2%	16	34.7	4	25.2	15
2005	10-6	9.1	8.9	379	338	-6	9.1%	12	16.8%	7	8.9%	27	1.1%	12	31.8	4	41.6	1
2006	12-4	12.2	11.0	385	237	+8	27.1%	4	15.1%	4	-9.3%	7	2.6%	7	12.8	21	27.3	7
2007	16-0	13.8	14.2	589	274	+16	53.1%	1	45.2%	1	-5.0%	12	3.0%	7	14.5	26	16.4	23
2008	11-5	10.6	9.6	410	309	+1	11.7%	9	16.5%	8	8.4%	21	3.6%	6	38.6	8	39.9	5

Strategic Tendencies

Run/Pass		Rank	Offense		Rank	Defense		Rank	Other		Rank
Runs, all plays	45%	9	3+ WR	70%	3	Rush 3	12.0%	4	2+ RB, Pct Runs	82%	1
Runs, first half	45%	12	4+ WR	14%	10	Rush 4	62.3%	20	1 RB/2 TE, Pct Runs	68%	2
Runs, first down	48%	22	2+ TE	26%	16	Rush 5	20.8%	17	1RB/3+WR, Pct Runs	33%	5
Runs, second-long	38%	18	Single back	71%	4	Rush 6+	4.8%	28	Zone Blitz	1%	29
Runs, power sit.	73%	5	Play action	13%	22	Rush 7+	0.6%	28	Go for it on 4th	1.28	4
Runs, behind 2H	29%	27	Max protect	8%	19	Sacks by LB	33.3%	9	Offensive Pace	29.2	5
Pass, ahead 2H	41%	20	Outside pocket	11%	19	Sacks by DB	11.7%	8	Defensive Pace	31.4	27

The biggest difference between Tom Brady and Matt Cassel? On short- and medium-length passes, New England's DVOA only dropped from first in 2007 to third in 2008. But on deep passes (16-plus yards through the air), they dropped from fifth in DVOA to 30th. Only Cincinnati and Seattle were worse. ● New England led the league with an average of 6.2 yards after catch. The Saints, who finished second, averaged just 5.6 yards after catch. ● The Patriots easily led the league in WR/TE screens, using this play 30 percent more often than any other team. They ranked third in DVOA among teams that ran more than ten WR/TE screens. ● The Patriots led the NFL with 67 draws, after ranking second in 2007 behind the Jets. Out of running backs with at least 80 carries, Kevin Faulk had the highest percentage of his runs as draw plays (36 percent). ● Perhaps showing the weakness of last year's secondary, the Patriots allowed 10.8% DVOA even when they hurried the quarterback. Only New Orleans and Detroit were worse. The Pats really got killed by allowing a league-high 7.3 yards after catch on passes where they hurried the quarterback. ● The Patriots benefited from opposing drops more than any other defense, as opponents dropped 8.1 percent of passes. ● New England's 47-7 destruction of Arizona during snowy Week 16 had a one-game DVOA of 138.3%, the second best one-game performance of any team during the DVOA Era. The only game that scored better was Philadelphia's 40-8 blowout of eventual Super Bowl champion San Francisco in Week 5 of 1994, with a DVOA of 141.0%.

Passing

Player	DYAR	DVOA	Plays	NtYds	Avg	YAC	C%	TD	Int
Matt Cassel*	655	6.4%	565	3502	6.2	6.3	63.8%	21	11
Tom Brady	13	4.3%	11	78	7.1	4.0	63.6%	0	0
Kevin O'Connell	-18	-51.4%	7	21	3.0	3.0	66.7%	0	0

Rushing

Player	DYAR	DVOA	Plays	Yds	Avg	TD	Fum	Suc
Sammy Morris	166	14.9%	156	728	4.7	7	1	49%
Kevin Faulk	178	46.5%	83	507	6.1	3	0	57%
LaMont Jordan*	113	22.2%	80	363	4.5	4	1	60%
BenJarvus Green-Ellis	55	6.7%	74	275	3.7	5	0	57%
Matt Cassel*	82	15.8%	50	291	5.8	2	0	--
Laurence Maroney	-2	-10.0%	28	93	3.3	0	0	54%
Heath Evans*	-11	-26.0%	11	23	2.1	0	0	55%
Fred Taylor	-32	-14.3%	143	556	3.9	1	0	41%

Receiving

Player	DYAR	DVOA	Plays	Ctch	Yds	Y/C	YAC	TD	C%
Wes Welker	188	3.5%	150	112	1165	10.4	6.6	3	75%
Randy Moss	134	0.5%	125	69	1011	14.7	5.0	11	55%
Jabar Gaffney*	42	-4.5%	65	38	468	12.3	3.1	2	58%
Sam Aiken	18	7.0%	11	8	101	12.6	10.0	0	73%
Greg Lewis	41	1.8%	35	19	247	13.0	2.7	2	54%
Joey Galloway	-55	-40.2%	28	13	138	10.6	3.5	0	46%
Benjamin Watson	-73	-29.5%	47	22	209	9.5	2.4	2	47%
David Thomas	-18	-22.6%	17	9	93	10.3	4.9	0	56%
Chris Baker	19	2.0%	30	21	194	9.2	2.6	0	70%
Alex Smith	42	8.9%	38	21	250	11.9	6.2	3	55%
Kevin Faulk	192	34.1%	74	58	486	8.4	8.2	3	78%
Sammy Morris	42	18.0%	24	17	161	9.5	9.2	0	71%
BenJarvus Green-Ellis	13	21.4%	6	3	37	12.3	11.7	0	50%
Fred Taylor	-23	-32.2%	22	16	98	6.1	5.8	0	73%

Offensive Line

Year	Yards	ALY	Rank	Power	Rank	10+ Yds	Rank	Stuff	Rank	Sacks	ASR	Rank	False	Cont.
2006	4.22	4.29	12	82%	1	16%	13	17%	8	29	5.7%	8	17	31
2007	4.25	4.63	1	70%	9	11%	26	16%	6	21	4.1%	4	20	25
2008	4.60	4.63	3	70%	12	16%	24	14%	1	48	8.5%	26	10	35

Year	LE	Rank	LT	Rank	Mid	Rank	RT	Rank	RE	Rank
2006	4.95	4	4.15	20	4.46	9	3.68	29	2.77	31
2007	4.45	11	4.88	5	4.61	2	4.58	7	4.37	9
2008	4.04	21	5.12	3	4.80	2	3.93	23	2.51	32

New England's line performed better than the sack numbers indicate; Matt Cassel's problems with pocket presence skewed the numbers, especially early on. Of Cassel's 47 sacks, 28 came in the season's first half. Still, the Patriots ranked third in the NFL in percentage of blown blocks — 25 in 582 pass plays equaled 4.3 percent, and only the Bengals and 49ers were worse. Left tackle Matt Light led the charge with seven. The running game stayed strong all season despite a host of injuries, especially when the platoon of backs ran behind Light, left guard Logan Mankins, and center Dan Koppen, who each started all 16 games. Things weren't so secure on the right side, and this has been a problem for the Patriots since at least the opening kickoff of Super Bowl XLII. Right guard Stephen Neal spent the first six games of the season on the Physically Unable to Perform list with a shoulder injury, and right tackle Nick Kaczur missed time because of a ankle injury. The line improved as Cassel got a sense of the pocket and people got healthy, and things should be on track with Tom Brady's return. The underrated running game will benefit once again from defenses forced to back into pass coverage.

The Pats re-signed Russ Hochstein to provide backup at multiple positions, and they took an interesting chance in the second round of the draft with Houston tackle Sebastian Vollmer. The 6-foot-8, 312-pound native of Germany came to America as a member of the European All-Stars at the 2004 Global Junior Championships in San Diego. Before that, he had helped his prep school team amass a 25-0 record. Houston beat out several other schools for Vollmer, who hopes to take the same Euro pipeline to success that Tennessee's Michael Roos did. Vollmer wasn't invited to the 2009 Combine, but he blew personnel people away at Houston's Pro Day when he ran a 5.12 40-yard dash. Vollmer can also play tight end, which fits into Bill Belichick's concept of positional versatility. Belichick may already be imagining Vollmer catching touchdowns from Tom Brady like a supersized Mike Vrabel. Who's going to cover a 6-foot-8 guy with a 37.5-inch vertical leap?

Defensive Front Seven

Defensive Line	Age	Pos	Plays	TmPct	Overall Rk	Stop	Dfts	Stop%	Rk	AvYd	Rk	Pass Rush Sack	Hit	Hur	vs. Run Runs	St%	Yds	vs. Pass Pass	St%	Yds
Vince Wilfork	28	DT	67	9.1%	2	56	11	84%	7	2.1	43	2.0	3	6	63	83%	2.4	4	100%	-2.5
Richard Seymour	30	DE	52	7.5%	15	47	16	90%	2	0.5	14	8.0	7	7	41	88%	2.1	11	100%	-5.3
Ty Warren	28	DE	41	6.8%	21	33	8	80%	25	2.2	61	2.0	2	6	39	79%	2.6	2	100%	-5.5
Jarvis Green	30	DE	29	4.5%	61	19	6	66%	81	1.9	51	2.0	3	11	23	65%	2.7	6	67%	-1.0
Mike Wright	27	DT	26	3.5%	63	15	5	58%	70	1.8	31	2.5	6	5	23	52%	3.3	3	100%	-9.3

Linebackers	Age	Pos	Plays	TmPct	Overall Rk	Stop	Dfts	Stop%	AvYd	Pass Rush Sack	Hit	Hur	vs. Run Runs	St%	Rk	Yds	Rk	vs. Pass Tgts	Suc%	Rk	AdjYd	Rk
Jerod Mayo	23	ILB	130	17.6%	6	55	12	42%	5.9	0.0	1	3	74	54%	94	4.1	79	38	59%	17	5.1	20
Tedy Bruschi	36	ILB	77	12.9%	34	48	5	62%	3.0	0.0	1	3	66	65%	47	2.7	17	5	43%	--	4.7	--
Mike Vrabel*	34	OLB	66	9.0%	78	47	15	71%	2.2	4.0	7	9	49	76%	12	1.9	3	18	63%	8	5.1	18
Adalius Thomas	32	OLB	36	8.7%	--	26	9	72%	1.6	5.0	3	4	20	80%	--	2.9	--	15	58%	--	5.6	--
Gary Guyton	24	ILB	28	4.1%	--	16	6	57%	5.4	0.0	1	4	17	65%	--	4.8	--	12	56%	--	5.1	--
Pierre Woods	27	OLB	27	4.9%	--	16	7	59%	4.9	1.0	2	2	15	73%	--	3.0	--	8	41%	--	5.9	--
Junior Seau*	40	ILB	21	11.4%	--	13	3	62%	3.4	0.0	0	1	17	76%	--	2.6	--	7	27%	--	14.6	--

Year	Yards	ALY	Rank	Power	Rank	10+ Yds	Rank	Stuff	Rank	Sack	ASR	Rank
2006	3.91	3.93	8	68%	21	17%	20	17%	20	44	7.9%	9
2007	4.40	4.11	18	68%	23	17%	17	18%	21	47	8.4%	2
2008	4.08	4.09	13	67%	18	17%	13	17%	19	31	6.0%	18

Year	LE	Rank	LT	Rank	Mid	Rank	RT	Rank	RE	Rank
2006	3.24	7	4.25	15	4.08	12	2.79	4	4.05	16
2007	4.12	17	4.16	17	4.16	20	4.67	26	2.63	4
2008	4.30	20	2.88	2	4.18	14	4.26	22	4.41	24

New England's pass defense ranked 31st in DVOA in the first half of the season, and that started up front. After an outstanding 2007, the Pats' pass rush regressed to the mean due to age and injury. End Richard Seymour led the team in sacks and was his normally dominant self, but Mike Vrabel's sack totals were a disappointment after 11 takedowns (and 15 hurries) in 2007. Adalius Thomas was supposed to provide elite production in several different areas, but he lost the second half of the season with a trip to the injured reserve list. Thomas' backup, Pierre Woods, also went on IR in mid-December.

The run defense was exposed — badly — in the Week 3 loss to the Dolphins. The Patriots' linebackers, always regarded as book-smart in a way that mitigated their age and subpar on-field speed, were exposed by Miami's multiple backfield formations. The older guys couldn't keep up with the changes in direction, and rookie Jerod Mayo got washed out over and over by pulling guard Justin Smiley. Bruschi's torn MCL put him out for the last three weeks of the season, but there's no question he'll be back in 2009 — the Pats will need his leadership with Vrabel gone to Kansas City. Bruschi was key to Mayo's development, getting the talented youngster in position to make plays, and Mayo was a quick learner. His 20 tackles against the Jets in Week 11 set a team record and put him on the path to a Defensive Rookie of the Year award. He'll become the linchpin of the linebacker corps along with a healthy Thomas. Woods is currently penciled in to the other starting outside linebacker spot, replacing Vrabel, but he will face competition in camp from last year's third-round pick Shawn Crable, a powerful tackler out of Michigan who essentially took a redshirt year in 2008, and this year's third-round pick Tyrone McKenzie, a versatile linebacker from South Florida who can play all over the field.

Prodigal son and pass-rush specialist Tully Banta-Cain returns from San Francisco and will show up on third downs.

When the season is over, the Patriots will need to decide what to do with stalwart nose tackle Vince Wilfork; his contract ends after this year and he's not happy about his salary. They drafted Boston College tackle Ron Brace in the second round in case they need an heir apparent.

Defensive Secondary

Secondary	Age	Pos	Plays	Overall TmPct	Rk	Stop	Dfts	vs. Run Yds	Rk	St%	Rk	vs. Pass Tgts	Tgt%	Rk	Dist	Suc%	Rk	AdjYd	Rk	Yds	PD	Int
Brandon Meriweather	25	FS	86	11.7%	20	24	12	6.4	26	31%	65	38	9.3%	9	13.9	50%	42	7.4	25	7.7	9	4
James Sanders	26	SS	67	10.4%	32	29	8	8.5	67	47%	25	20	5.6%	55	8.8	57%	23	10.1	66	9.9	4	1
Ellis Hobbs*	26	CB	57	7.7%	56	22	11	7.9	54	31%	65	74	18.0%	40	12.3	55%	25	8.5	67	8.7	11	3
Rodney Harrison*	37	SS	47	17.0%	1	21	6	6.7	37	57%	11	13	8.1%	20	4.9	45%	63	4.3	3	4.4	3	1
Deltha O'Neal*	32	CB	40	5.4%	77	13	6	9.0	62	33%	61	58	14.0%	67	12.1	51%	37	7.8	51	7.9	7	3
Lewis Sanders*	31	CB	26	5.6%	--	8	3	6.1	--	29%	--	15	5.7%	--	8.4	51%	--	6.6	--	6.3	1	0
Jonathan Wilhite	25	CB	25	3.4%	--	7	5	11.9	--	29%	--	37	9.0%	--	11.5	46%	--	8.3	--	7.9	1	1
Leigh Bodden	28	CB	85	10.4%	16	22	11	10.8	73	12%	79	84	22.6%	14	13.4	38%	81	9.6	82	9.9	12	1
Shawn Springs	34	CB	43	10.2%	--	16	5	5.9	--	38%	--	39	16.3%	--	10.7	47%	--	7.0	--	6.7	7	1

Year	Pass D Rank	vs. #1 WR	Rk	vs. #2 WR	Rk	vs. Other WR	Rk	vs. TE	Rk	vs. RB	Rk
2006	6	-3.7%	12	22.2%	28	-9.2%	13	-31.5%	2	13.9%	27
2007	5	1.1%	18	-7.4%	10	-8.7%	17	8.1%	19	0.1%	18
2008	27	6.1%	17	30.6%	28	-2.2%	18	2.2%	15	4.1%	16

The Patriots allowed 38 receptions of 20 or more yards, two more than their offense had. That's an indicator of a disappointing unit that never replaced Asante Samuel. Ellis Hobbs was the best of a bad group, but he fell off as the season went on. Deltha O'Neal incurred the wrath of our game charters (sample observation: "The fact that he was cut by the Bengals possibly could have been an indicator"). Hobbs was last seen complaining about his contract after he was traded to the Eagles for two fifth-round draft picks, and O'Neal was bad enough that reserve Jonathan Wilhite started down the stretch at left corner. Improvement will come in the form of second-round pick Darius Butler, the UConn product who attended Deion Sanders' "Prime U" school, impressed Bill Belichick at his Pro Day, and displayed the best coverage skills of any defensive back in the 2009 class. His abilities on special teams will provide extra value. The Pats also signed veteran Shawn Springs and former FO favorite Leigh Bodden. Bodden endured a disastrous season in Detroit a year after impressing in Cleveland. He's got good physicality at the line of scrimmage and excellent trail speed — he's just got to be used in the right scheme and circumstance. Springs was made redundant in Washington by DeAngelo Hall's questionable contract, but he still has enough in the tank to offer help in the right system.

First-round pick Patrick Chung replaces strong safety Rodney Harrison, who retired in June. Chung started 51 games for the Oregon Ducks and showed tremendous versatility at the rover position — playing corner and different safety/linebacker positions based on coverage needs. He'll be a great box safety in the NFL; the coverage skills are a bit less developed. Chung will rotate at safety with James Sanders and Brandon Meriweather, one of the many positions where the Patriots defense is getting younger and faster.

Special Teams

Year	DVOA	Rank	FG/XP	Rank	Net Kick	Rank	Kick Ret	Rank	Net Punt	Rank	Punt Ret	Rank	Hidden	Rank
2006	2.6%	7	-5.5	28	5.5	11	16.6	1	-5.9	25	4.9	4	3.7	11
2007	3.0%	7	-0.2	19	7.3	3	11.0	5	0.8	17	-1.1	18	1.7	13
2008	3.6%	6	7.5	3	-0.2	17	9.6	3	3.0	16	1.5	9	3.0	9

Eric Mangini stole special teams coach Brad Seely away to his Browns staff, so Bill Belichick brought in Scott O'Brien, who worked with Belichick in Cleveland years ago, to replace Seely. Ellis Hobbs may not be missed as a cornerback, but the Pats will need to replace his excellent kickoff returns. Several players will get a shot at replacing Hobbs, most notably receiver Sam Aiken and safety/receiver Matthew Slater (who fumbled twice on returns in 2008). Kelley Washington was little more than a coverage player in New England, but he'll get a shot to accentuate Baltimore's paper-thin receiver corps. Veteran long-snapper Lonie Paxton took his snow angels to Denver, where the Broncos signed him to a five-year contract. To replace him, the Pats made the rare move of drafting a long-snapper, Hawaii's Jake Ingram, near the end of the sixth round.

Kicker Stephen Gostkowski set a franchise record with 36 field goals, a good sign of the Brady-less offensive downturn, and he did it in only 40 attempts. He was 9-for-11 from 40 to 49 yards and a perfect 16-for-16 from 30 to 39. Gostkowski also had his usual strong year on kickoffs, and Chris Hanson was reasonable on punts, but the Patriots gave some of that value back with mediocre coverage teams.

Coaching Staff

Most head coaches would skip a beat after losing their offensive coordinator, secondary coach, and special teams coach (not to mention other support staff), but that's not Bill Belichick's modus operandi. Belichick goes through assistant coaches like Tony Soprano went through capos, and he's got a new set of challenges coming into the 2009 season. Nobody has the title of offensive coordinator now that Josh McDaniels is off bruising egos in the Rocky Mountains. 2009 will most likely be similar to 2005, when Belichick called the offensive plays while preparing McDaniels to take over for the departed Charlie Weis. This year's heir apparent is quarterbacks coach Bill O'Brien, a product of Football Outsiders University (a.k.a. Brown). Stability on the coaching staff comes from offensive line coach Dante Scarnecchia and defensive coordinator Dean Pees, who remain as trusted assistants.

The real question is how Belichick will do with personnel now that Scott Pioli has left to run the show in Kansas City. The two had worked together with nearly flawless results through the Patriots' dynasty years. Belichick has a two-pronged personnel unit going forward. First, there's Director of Player Personnel Nick Caserio, who looks to be the next graduate of Belichick U. To add experience to the mix, Belichick hired former Houston Oilers/Tennessee Titans general manager and ESPN.com contributor Floyd Reese. Belichick and Reese go way back, and Reese should provide valuable stability to a front office going through major transition.

New Orleans Saints

There's an old story about a *TV Guide* copy editor who saved time by publishing boilerplate episode capsules for certain shows. He used the same summary every week — "An alien force tries to take over the Enterprise" for *Star Trek*, or "Endora casts a spell to teach Darrin a lesson" for *Bewitched*. Usually, his boilerplate plot synopsis was so close to the real thing that no one noticed.

If that editor were still around, he could have published the same game summary for the 2008 Saints week after week, and no one would have caught on:

This week, the Saints spot their opponent an early lead thanks to mistakes and turnovers. Drew Brees then sparks a comeback, throwing dozens of passes to make the game close late in the fourth quarter. Unfortunately, the defense then gives up a long pass or commits a 40-yard interference penalty that sets up the game-winning score for the opponent.

How often would that summary have worked? Take a look at some of the Saints losses in 2008:

WEEK 2 VS. REDSKINS: The Saints spot the Redskins a 6-0 lead on two first quarter turnovers. Drew Brees sparks a comeback, throwing 32 passes to give the Saints a 24-15 lead in the fourth quarter. Unfortunately, the Saints defense allows two scores in less than three minutes, one set up by completions of 23, 17, and 25 yards, the other a 65-yard game-winning touchdown by Santana Moss.

WEEK 5 VS. VIKINGS: The Saints spot the Vikings a 17-10 lead on a blocked kick return touchdown and a Brees fumble. Brees sparks a comeback, throwing 46 passes to help the Saints to a 27-20 fourth quarter lead. Unfortunately, the Saints defense allows a 33-yard jump-ball touchdown to Bernard Berrian to tie the game. With less than two minutes to play, Berrian draws a 41-yard pass interference penalty against Kevin Kaesviharn to set up the Vikings' winning field goal.

WEEK 15 VS. THE BEARS: The Saints spot the Bears a 21-7 halftime lead, with one Bears touchdown coming on a game-opening kickoff return touchdown. Brees sparks a comeback, throwing 43 passes to give the Saints a 24-21 fourth-quarter lead. Unfortunately, the Bears tie the game in regulation. In overtime, Roman Harper commits a 38-yard pass interference foul against Devin Hester, setting up the Bears' winning field goal.

WEEK 17 VS. THE PANTHERS: The Saints spot the Panthers a 23-3 second quarter lead. One Panthers touchdown is set up by a Brees interception, the other comes on the return of a fumbled kickoff. Brees sparks a comeback, throwing 49 passes to help the Saints to a 31-30 fourth-quarter lead. With three minutes to play, Steve Smith catches a 39-yard pass that sets up the Panthers' game-winning field goal.

SAINTS SUMMARY

2008 Record: 8-8

Pythagorean Wins: 9.5 (11th)

DVOA: 9.9% (13th)

Offense: 21.1% (4th)

Defense: 10.7% (26th)

Special Teams: -0.6% (22nd)

Variance: 9.6% (5th)

2008: If the Saints were a movie, Jason Statham would star, and car batteries would be involved.

2009: Just because you *can* make the playoffs with a mediocre defense doesn't mean you should *try* to build a mediocre defense.

2009 Mean Projection: 7.8 wins

On the Clock (0-3): 5%

Loserville (4-6): 24%

Mediocrity (7-8): 31%

Playoff Contender (9-10): 27%

Super Bowl Contender (11+): 14%

Projected Average Opponent: -6.0% (29th)

2009 Saints Schedule

Week	Opp.	Week	Opp.	Week	Opp.
1	DET	7	at MIA	13	at WAS
2	at PHI	8	ATL (Mon.)	14	at ATL
3	at BUF	9	CAR	15	DAL (Sat.)
4	NYJ	10	at STL	16	TB
5	BYE	11	at TB	17	at CAR
6	NYG	12	NE (Mon.)		

It was that kind of year for the Saints. On offense, they were the Bourbon Street Bombers, the Greatest Show on the Bayou. Their passing game wasn't the NFL's best (the Chargers and Colts topped them in DVOA), but it was the most prolific, and arguably the most exciting. Brees picked defenses apart with his surgical passing, leading the league in Pass Accuracy[1] for the second straight year. Sean Payton baffled opponents, calling stack formations, middle screens, and play-action seamers like Urban Meyer on a Starbucks binge. The Saints used the pass as a long handoff, throwing 123 passes at or behind the line of scrimmage, most in the league by 18 passes. They also used the pass as a long pass, throwing 33 bombs, more than any team but the Lions. They threw the ball early, threw it often, and threw it well.

But the passing game was all they had. The Saints' running game ranked ninth in DVOA by season's end, but most of their production came when Pierre Thomas took over the featured role late in the year. Their defense was penalty-prone and big-play generous. Their special teams were adventurous, their kicking and coverage units as reliable as the entertainment on open mic night. Every Saints game was a thrill ride of cliffhangers and false endings; unfortunately, the bad guys too often won in the end.

The Saints know they have a problem. Their passing game will be as good as ever this season, maybe better if Marques Colston and Reggie Bush stay healthy for 16 games. All they have to do is fix everything else. Payton and general manager Mickey Loomis made major changes in the offseason. They signed several new defenders, drafted others, grabbed a punter in the fifth round of the draft and invited some ex-Pro Bowl defenders out of retirement. There was a lot of motion at 5800 Airline Drive, but much of it seemed wasted. Of all the new faces, only one is

likely to make a major difference: new defensive coordinator Gregg Williams.

Williams' arrival signals a change of emphasis for the Saints defense. He's a go-for-broke blitzer whose Redskins defenses led the league in six- and seven-man rushes in 2007. He didn't send the wolves quite as often with the Jaguars in 2008, but his defense still ranked fifth when it came to sending six or more pass rushers. Williams' stated goal this season is too "create havoc," and defenders welcomed the new philosophy during spring minicamps.

Williams replaces Gary Gibbs, whose read-and-react scheme was supposed to be risk-averse but was too safe for its own good. Gibbs' defenses generated little pass rush, putting far too much pressure on a secondary filled with old injured guys (Mike McKenzie), free agent mistakes (Jason David), and former substitute teachers who had no business being in the NFL (Kaesviharn). The Saints produced just 28 sacks and 15 interceptions last year, tiny totals for a team that engaged in weekly 40-pass shootouts. Gibbs' defense failed to harass quarterbacks like Matt Ryan (no sacks in two meetings), Jake Delhomme (two sacks and no turnovers in two meetings) or Gus Frerotte (one sack for zero yards, no interceptions), quarterbacks who could have been rattled into mistakes if they took a few more hits. With Williams calling the blitzes, rookies and journeymen won't feel as safe in the pocket.

Unfortunately, Williams may not have the personnel he needs to fully implement his scheme. The Saints entered the offseason in cap trouble, forcing them to clip coupons on the free agent market. Their seven-defender free agent haul looks impressive until you filter out the old players (Darren Sharper, Rod Coleman), the bit players (Anthony Hargrove, Anthony Waters) and the old bit players (Paul Spicer, Pierson Prioleau). The Saints also had just one pick in the first three rounds of the draft. They made a great choice (Ohio State cornerback Malcolm Jenkins), but they needed more help.

Jenkins and former Bills cornerback Jabari Greer were the team's best offseason roster additions. They'll join Sharper, incumbent safety Roman Harper, and second-year cornerback Tracy Porter in a rebuilt secondary that will play a lot of man coverage in Williams' system. Greer, a pesky, undersized defender, is no superstar, and Sharper is too old and slow to depend

---

[1]*Pass Accuracy is defined as the percentage of passes not marked by our charters as overthrown, underthrown, thrown ahead, thrown behind, or thrown out of bounds. For more information including 2008 leaders, see Appendix.*

upon in man coverage, but they represent an upgrade because their names aren't David or Kaesviharn.

The rest of the new Saints defenders represent another season on the treadmill. The team played Free Agent Defender Bingo in 2006 (linebackers Scott Fujita and Anthony Simmons, safety Bryan Scott, tackle Hollis Thomas), 2007 (David, Kaesviharn, linebacker Brian Simmons) and last year (defensive end Bobby McCray, linebacker Dan Morgan, cornerbacks Randall Gay and Aaron Glenn). Their defense has become a halfway house for middle-tier veterans and guys with one foot on the field and one in the pension office. A few of the acquisitions (notably middle linebacker Jonathan Vilma, who arrived in a trade) have played well, but the Saints defense is littered with former free agent mistakes. Instead of building around a young core, the Saints keep choking on free agent fodder. That makes the dual comeback attempts of Dan Morgan and Rod Coleman particularly disturbing. Both are last-resort longshots (in fact, Morgan retired again in early June), but the Saints still waste vital practice reps on reclamation projects when they should concentrate on younger players.

The Saints also had significant special teams problems last year, finishing 22nd in special teams DVOA. They had the highest special teams variance in the league, which will happen when you change kickers and punters the way Lauren Conrad changes outfits. When Bush was returning punts for touchdowns or Payton found a kicker-punter combo that worked, the Saints special teams were good. When Bush was hurt or the Specialists-of-the-Month couldn't cut it, they were awful. The only consistency came from the coverage units, which were bad all year long.

By season's end, Payton had stopped worrying and learned to love kicker Garrett Hartley and punter Glenn Pakulak. Payton is very high on Hartley, the third kicker the Saints employed in 2008. There were plenty of veterans like John Carney and Matt Stover on the free agent market, but Payton passed on them, perhaps figuring that one will be available when a fit of pique overcomes him in late August. Pakulak has no such job security; the Saints traded up in the fifth round to select SMU punter Thomas Morstead. Whoever wins the job can move into Steve Weatherford's old condo, paying rent on a weekly basis.

The Saints' running game was also a problem in the first half of last season, and they averaged 3.8 or fewer yards per rush in 10 of their first 12 games. Like the kicking game, the running game sorted itself out at the end of the year. Thomas took over the starting role in Week 11 and averaged 5.7 yards per carry over the final six games. With Thomas getting 15 carries per game, the Saints no longer had to wait for Deuce McAllister to get healthy or for Reggie Bush to stop tiptoeing around the backfield. Thomas and Bush combined for 182 yards on 26 carries against the Falcons in Week 14, a sign that Bush can be more effective as a change-up than as a 15-carry regular. The Saints don't need a 30-carry workhorse in the backfield, but they do need the basics, like effective goal-line rushing. Thomas, with six touchdowns and one first down in 10 carries inside the five, could fill that need.

Our projection calls for another season of 33-30 gunfights and 8-8 mediocrity, but you don't have to strain your eyes to see the Saints as a 12-win team. Not everything has to break right: Williams' system could breathe life into the defense, or the new secondary could be better than advertised, or a full year starting Thomas could push the offense past the tipping point and into 2007 Patriots territory. A few minor adjustments could turn last year's formulaic cliffhanger losses into victories. It's just as likely, though, that the Saints sputter through another year of lapses in the secondary and frustrating special teams.

The Saints are bipolar, and they'll stay that way as long as the passing game is great and everything else is mired in a perpetual rebuild. They're a fun team to watch every week, but fans will start tuning out if they don't tweak the formula.

Mike Tanier

2008 Saints Stats by Week

Wk	vs.	W-L	PF	PA	YDF	YDA	TO	Total	Off	Def	ST
1	TB	W	24	20	337	352	0	-5%	21%	19%	-7%
2	@WAS	L	24	29	250	455	-2	-28%	-19%	31%	22%
3	@DEN	L	32	34	502	369	-1	4%	31%	8%	-19%
4	SF	W	31	17	467	312	+1	-2%	5%	-2%	-9%
5	MIN	L	27	30	375	270	-4	22%	-15%	0%	36%
6	OAK	W	34	3	441	226	+2	43%	45%	-7%	-10%
7	@CAR	L	7	30	343	336	-2	-14%	7%	16%	-5%
8	SD	W	37	32	409	451	+2	24%	57%	28%	-5%
9	BYE										
10	@ATL	L	20	34	521	361	-3	-41%	-5%	31%	-5%
11	@KC	W	30	20	369	330	0	37%	27%	0%	10%
12	GB	W	51	29	416	343	+2	65%	56%	0%	9%
13	@TB	L	20	23	332	254	-2	0%	0%	-9%	-9%
14	ATL	W	29	25	414	414	+1	45%	48%	15%	12%
15	@CHI	L	24	27	351	227	+1	-35%	-4%	3%	-28%
16	@DET	W	42	7	532	255	+1	38%	40%	7%	6%
17	CAR	L	31	33	417	478	-2	3%	46%	35%	-8%

Trends and Splits

	Offense	Rank	Defense	Rank
Total DVOA	21.1%	4	10.7%	26
Unadjusted VOA	20.5%	5	10.0%	23
Weighted trend	25.9%	1	10.0%	21
Variance	6.7%	13	4.9%	11
Average opponent	4.3%	14	6.0%	20
Passing	37.9%	3	17.8%	23
Rushing	9.1%	9	2.8%	22
First down	9.1%	12	-0.7%	15
Second down	23.0%	7	19.0%	27
Third down	41.1%	3	18.1%	24
First half	18.7%	6	15.6%	27
Second half	24.0%	4	5.9%	20
Red Zone	21.8%	6	-5.5%	13
Late and close	27.6%	3	9.1%	24

Five-Year Performance

Year	W-L	Pyth	Est W	PF	PA	TO	Total	Rk	Off	Rk	Def	Rk	ST	Rk	Off AGL	Rk	Def AGL	Rk
2004	8-8	6.6	6.1	348	405	+7	-19.5%	27	-11.9%	26	13.3%	27	5.7%	3	9.2	25	10.7	25
2005	3-13	3.6	5.4	235	398	-24	-22.5%	28	-13.5%	24	7.3%	25	-1.8%	23	24.9	8	14.6	18
2006	10-6	10.3	9.1	413	322	-4	6.6%	12	10.5%	8	4.6%	22	0.7%	14	30.6	4	14.6	15
2007	7-9	7.8	7.6	379	388	-7	-9.0%	22	7.9%	11	13.3%	29	-3.6%	25	21.4	16	13.7	25
2008	8-8	9.5	9.5	463	393	-4	9.9%	13	21.1%	4	10.7%	26	-0.6%	22	24.0	18	33.4	9

Strategic Tendencies

Run/Pass		Rank	Offense		Rank	Defense		Rank	Other		Rank
Runs, all plays	37%	30	3+ WR	49%	16	Rush 3	5.4%	15	2+ RB, Pct Runs	55%	25
Runs, first half	36%	30	4+ WR	12%	17	Rush 4	69.8%	9	1 RB/2 TE, Pct Runs	32%	31
Runs, first down	41%	31	2+ TE	26%	15	Rush 5	15.6%	26	1RB/3+WR, Pct Runs	23%	21
Runs, second-long	30%	29	Single back	52%	20	Rush 6+	9.2%	12	Zone Blitz	4%	13
Runs, power sit.	66%	17	Play action	22%	6	Rush 7+	1.2%	19	Go for it on 4th	1.02	12
Runs, behind 2H	29%	26	Max protect	6%	23	Sacks by LB	10.7%	24	Offensive Pace	30.2	11
Pass, ahead 2H	50%	5	Outside pocket	6%	28	Sacks by DB	8.9%	14	Defensive Pace	29.4	2

The Saints had the league's largest gap between DVOA in Shotgun (51.9%, first) and DVOA from standard formations (9.8%, ninth). ● New Orleans had the league's highest DVOA on screen passes, with seven touchdowns and eight more first downs on 33 running back screens. Given that statistic, it's no wonder the Saints led the league in percentage of passes thrown behind or at the line of scrimmage for the second straight year. ● Saints opponents threw 31 percent of their passes to number-one receivers, the most in the league. They also threw only 16 percent of passes to running backs (31st) and 16 percent to tight ends (28th). ● When hurries don't help: The Saints allowed a league-high 36.8% DVOA and 6.6 yards per pass when they hurried the quarterback. ● Saints opponents threw a league-high 42 percent of passes to the left side of the field — but the Saints actually had a better DVOA against passes to the left (20.6%, sixth) than against passes to the middle (65.4%, 21st) or right (49.3%, 26th).

Passing

Player	DYAR	DVOA	Plays	NtYds	Avg	YAC	C%	TD	Int
Drew Brees	1921	33.9%	647	4962	7.7	5.6	65.8%	34	16

Rushing

Player	DYAR	DVOA	Plays	Yds	Avg	TD	Fum	Suc
Pierre Thomas	161	16.9%	129	625	4.8	9	1	62%
Deuce McAllister*	86	9.6%	106	418	3.9	5	0	59%
Reggie Bush	-2	-9.0%	106	404	3.8	2	2	45%
Mike Bell	2	-4.5%	13	42	3.2	1	0	38%
Mike Karney*	16	15.8%	8	10	1.3	2	0	75%
Aaron Stecker*	5	7.9%	8	43	5.4	0	0	25%
Drew Brees	-7	-24.0%	8	34	4.3	0	1	--
Devery Henderson	10	1.7%	4	33	8.3	0	0	--
Heath Evans	-11	-26.0%	11	23	2.1	0	0	55%

Receiving

Player	DYAR	DVOA	Plays	Ctch	Yds	Y/C	YAC	TD	C%
Lance Moore	232	12.7%	120	79	930	11.8	3.7	11	66%
Marques Colston	111	2.8%	88	47	760	16.2	4.9	5	53%
Devery Henderson	215	36.5%	56	32	793	24.8	8.6	4	57%
Robert Meachem	114	64.0%	20	12	289	24.1	5.1	3	60%
David Patten*	42	14.4%	20	11	162	14.7	4.0	1	55%
Jeremy Shockey	11	-5.0%	72	50	481	9.6	4.2	0	69%
Billy Miller	150	28.8%	62	45	579	12.9	4.2	1	73%
Mark Campbell*	41	25.1%	16	12	121	10.1	5.8	2	75%
Sean Ryan*	-12	-43.2%	5	3	15	5.0	4.3	0	60%
Darnell Dinkins	-17	-32.8%	11	5	41	8.2	3.6	1	45%
Reggie Bush	118	15.3%	72	52	440	8.5	7.5	4	72%
Pierre Thomas	136	40.2%	41	31	284	9.2	9.7	3	76%
Deuce McAllister*	41	16.0%	23	18	128	7.1	8.8	1	78%
Aaron Stecker*	16	8.8%	12	9	52	5.8	4.8	1	75%
Mike Karney*	-31	-57.3%	12	9	18	2.0	2.6	0	75%

Offensive Line

Year	Yards	ALY	Rank	Power	Rank	10+ Yds	Rank	Stuff	Rank	Sacks	ASR	Rank	False	Cont.
2006	3.99	4.29	11	54%	30	13%	25	18%	14	23	4.3%	4	23	37
2007	3.86	4.36	7	66%	13	9%	30	18%	10	16	3.5%	3	17	32
2008	4.17	4.37	6	64%	18	15%	26	15%	7	13	2.9%	2	20	28

Year	LE	Rank	LT	Rank	Mid	Rank	RT	Rank	RE	Rank
2006	4.26	13	4.06	21	4.45	10	3.88	25	4.38	11
2007	3.96	17	3.42	30	4.96	1	3.96	22	3.75	22
2008	4.53	14	5.17	2	4.45	8	4.31	10	3.20	27

Judged by the sack totals, the Saints have the best offensive line in the NFL, but Drew Brees has a lot to do with those totals. He has a quick release and is one of the best decision-makers in the league, so he usually gets rid of the ball before trouble arrives. The Saints' scheme, built around three-step drops, screens, and short passes, also keeps sack totals low. Even if you remove the Brees influence, however, the Saints still have a strong line, featuring excellent continuity and a very good pair of guards.

Right guard Jahri Evans, the team's best lineman, signed a one-year tender offer and may get a long-term deal before the start of the season. Evans is the Saints' best run blocker, and he excels at cutting down defensive tackles on short passes, giving Brees an open throwing lane in the middle of the field. When the Saints announce their All-Time Players with Glasses Team, Evans and Willie Roaf will block for Chuck Muncie. Left guard Karl Nicks is a converted defensive lineman who was dogged by character issues at Nebraska but hasn't had any recent problems. He's a 345-pound piledriver with surprising mobility who played well as a rookie. Center Jonathan Goodwin replaced Jeff Faine last season after Faine signed with the Buccaneers. Goodwin and Brees bobbled a few early-season exchanges, but Goodwin's play was solid overall. Free agent signing Nick Leckey had starting experience in Arizona and St. Louis and should push Goodwin.

Left tackle Jammal Brown made the Pro Bowl because he was the left tackle on a team that allowed only 16 sacks, not because he earned the honor personally. Brown committed eight holding penalties and had rough outings against top pass rushers like Julius Peppers. Jon Stinchcomb will be back at right tackle after signing a five-year contract in the offseason. Stinchcomb is not very mobile and can be beaten to the inside, but he's a good run blocker who plays within himself. There's little depth at tackle, so while neither Brown nor Stinchcomb is an elite player, losing either would be disastrous.

Defensive Front Seven

Defensive Line	Age	Pos	Plays	TmPct	Rk	Stop	Dfts	Stop%	Rk	AvYd	Rk	Sack	Hit	Hur	Runs	St%	Yds	Pass	St%	Yds
								Overall				Pass Rush			vs. Run			vs. Pass		
Will Smith	28	DE	61	7.5%	14	41	12	67%	77	2.2	65	3.5	8	8	52	67%	2.4	9	67%	1.4
Kendrick Clancy	31	DT	37	5.2%	34	26	8	70%	63	2.2	44	2.0	2	4	29	69%	2.3	8	75%	1.5
Sedrick Ellis	24	DT	36	5.5%	31	26	12	72%	58	1.7	21	4.0	3	9	27	63%	2.8	9	100%	-1.8
Charles Grant	31	DE	35	8.7%	5	27	8	77%	41	2.0	56	3.0	5	15	30	73%	3.0	5	100%	-4.0
Bobby McCray	28	DE	26	3.2%	87	23	10	88%	6	0.9	20	6.0	7	12	17	94%	1.2	9	78%	0.4
Paul Spicer	34	DE	36	4.8%	57	32	9	89%	5	0.9	19	3.5	4	4	29	86%	1.7	7	100%	-2.4

Linebackers	Age	Pos	Plays	TmPct	Rk	Stop	Dfts	Stop%	AvYd	Sack	Hit	Hur	Runs	St%	Rk	Yds	Rk	Tgts	Suc%	Rk	AdjYd	Rk
								Overall		Pass Rush			vs. Run					vs. Pass				
Jonathan Vilma	27	ILB	138	17.1%	11	79	20	57%	4.8	1.0	3	5	96	63%	59	3.8	71	45	59%	21	5.7	33
Scott Shanle	30	OLB	92	11.4%	52	54	11	59%	4.3	2.0	1	0	45	67%	38	2.8	22	45	63%	9	4.7	10
Scott Fujita	30	OLB	83	11.7%	49	45	7	54%	4.6	0.0	0	3	57	65%	50	3.4	50	13	58%	--	4.4	--

Year	Yards	ALY	Rank	Power	Rank	10+ Yds	Rank	Stuff	Rank	Sack	ASR	Rank
2006	4.59	4.16	17	48%	3	23%	31	19%	13	38	7.9%	8
2007	3.99	4.09	16	62%	16	15%	11	17%	25	32	5.6%	27
2008	4.15	4.21	20	80%	31	14%	10	17%	15	28	5.1%	25

Year	LE	Rank	LT	Rank	Mid	Rank	RT	Rank	RE	Rank
2006	4.49	22	4.75	24	4.11	13	3.46	7	3.95	15
2007	5.35	29	4.12	14	3.88	9	3.49	6	4.66	25
2008	4.42	22	4.25	18	4.18	15	4.26	21	4.01	18

Gregg Williams told the *New Orleans Times-Picayune* that he plans to throw the kitchen sink at opposing offenses. "We are going to have multiple, and I mean multiple, defensive looks and packages," he said. "I can tell you today that people won't say the Saints will be a base 4-3 or 3-4 defense. We will look different every single week and maybe even every different defensive series. We may be running six defensive backs out there, maybe four linebackers, who knows?"

No matter what package Williams uses, Jonathan Vilma will be right in the middle of things. Vilma was the Saints best defender last year, and the team rewarded him with a five-year contract in February. Vilma played poorly in Eric Mangini's 3-4 scheme in New York, but Williams' 3-4 wrinkle will look more like something the Steelers or Chargers use than Mangini's base 3-4 alignment.

Vilma is flanked by a rogues gallery of second-tier free agent acquisitions from years past. Scott Fujita is an adequate stack-and-shed linebacker who can be useful as a pass rusher. Scott Shanle is a space defender who is acceptable in pass coverage. Neither is a big-play threat, and the Saints have little depth behind them. Dan Morgan attempted a comeback but retired in June. Mark Simoneau is still on the roster despite missing all of last season with a back injury. If the Saints opt not to fill their bench with animated sarcophagi, they may give a role to second-year pro Jo-Lonn Dunbar. Unfortunately, fourth-round rookie Stanley Arnoux got hurt in minicamp and will miss the 2009 season.

Charles Grant has spent the last four seasons proving that his 10.5-sack campaign in 2004 was a fluke. He was healthy for just eight games last season, and he faces a possible four-game suspension in the StarCaps scandal. Right end Will Smith was also implicated in the scandal, so the Saints may start the season with Bobby McCray and Paul Spicer as their starting ends. McCray had two-sack games against the Raiders and Bucs last year but was otherwise invisible as a pass rush specialist. Spicer is a role player who learned Williams' system in Jacksonville last year. When available, Smith can still be an effective pass rusher, but he bore the brunt of constant double-teams last year.

Rookie tackle Sedrick Ellis showed signs of life late last season, notching two sacks in the final three games and making more appearances on the stat sheet. He'll start beside Kendrick Clancy, yet another diffident journeyman defender from the Saints' vast collection. Rod Coleman, who hasn't played since a boating accident in 2007, signed with the Saints to provide tackle depth and to make Morgan's aborted comeback seem less ridiculous.

Defensive Secondary

Secondary	Age	Pos	Plays	Overall				vs. Run				vs. Pass										
				TmPct	Rk	Stop	Dfts	Yds	Rk	St%	Rk	Tgts	Tgt%	Rk	Dist	Suc%	Rk	AdjYd	Rk	Yds	PD	Int
Roman Harper	27	SS	89	11.7%	15	29	12	6.7	38	33%	60	29	6.7%	40	21.6	45%	64	12.8	75	13.3	7	0
Randall Gay	27	CB	68	9.6%	29	27	14	8.6	59	32%	63	73	18.1%	39	11.3	48%	49	6.3	25	6.5	16	0
Kevin Kaesviharn*	33	SS	65	11.7%	19	15	5	7.3	45	41%	38	19	5.8%	53	17.5	40%	72	10.0	65	11.0	2	2
Usama Young	24	CB	41	5.4%	78	16	8	8.7	60	29%	71	43	9.8%	81	11.7	51%	38	5.4	6	5.7	8	2
Josh Bullocks*	26	FS	41	5.1%	74	13	4	6.5	30	33%	58	17	3.7%	76	17.9	59%	22	8.6	51	8.4	6	1
Jason David	27	CB	33	4.7%	80	15	9	6.0	32	67%	10	56	13.8%	69	15.7	53%	31	8.5	65	8.5	10	5
Tracy Porter	23	CB	30	11.9%	--	11	8	9.6	--	40%	--	39	27.1%	--	11.9	48%	--	7.6	--	8.0	3	1
Mike McKenzie*	33	CB	25	7.1%	--	13	5	2.9	--	78%	--	27	13.4%	--	16.2	50%	--	7.6	--	8.3	2	1
Jabari Greer	27	CB	43	8.7%	40	19	6	6.5	45	67%	9	44	17.7%	47	11.5	50%	45	6.1	20	5.9	7	2
Darren Sharper	34	SS	71	9.4%	47	22	9	6.2	24	39%	42	33	7.5%	27	11.6	46%	58	10.3	69	10.9	5	1

Year	Pass D Rank	vs. #1 WR	Rk	vs. #2 WR	Rk	vs. Other WR	Rk	vs. TE	Rk	vs. RB	Rk
2006	21	27.8%	31	8.0%	22	-37.9%	2	-12.3%	10	-34.0%	3
2007	32	59.2%	32	-10.6%	8	12.5%	27	15.9%	25	9.6%	27
2008	22	23.5%	29	-30.7%	3	-0.7%	21	7.4%	20	7.5%	19

Saints opponents completed just 56.8 percent of their passes, the seventh lowest percentage in the NFL. It's what they did with those completions that mattered. The Saints allowed 53 pass plays of more than 20 yards, the third highest total in the league, and opponents averaged 12.4 yards per catch, the fifth highest figure in the league.

When they weren't allowing long gains, Saints defensive backs were committing pass interference. Roman Harper was the worst offender, with three interference flags for 83 yards to go with two defensive holds. Jason David committed three interference fouls that gave opponents 61 yards, while Kevin Kaesviharn added a 41-yard interference penalty. Harper and Kaesviharn also committed one unnecessary roughness foul each. Total it up, and the three defenders combined for 251 yards of penalty yardage.

Kaesviharn is gone, as are Mike McKenzie and Josh Bullocks, neither of whom could stay healthy. Harper retained his starting job at strong safety despite an off year; he's a big hitter who will spend more time in the box in defensive coordinator Gregg Williams' scheme. Free agent addition Darren Sharper has lost several steps and gets by on experience, so he will have to be protected by the system. Williams may slide rookie cornerback Malcolm Jenkins to free safety in some packages, allowing Sharper to blitz or work underneath zones.

Jenkins played cornerback with the first-team defense in May minicamp and appears slated to start. He may be a step too slow to cover Steve Smith-types, but the Saints have plenty of options at cornerback: Tracy Porter, Jabari Greer, Randall Gay, and possibly David. Porter, a second-round pick last year, won a starting job in training camp but injured his wrist while jumping to defend a pass against the Vikings. (Bernard Berrian caught the pass for a game-tying touchdown; the play typifies the Saints' 2008 season). Greer, signed away from Buffalo, missed the last six weeks of 2008 with a knee injury. He's a tiny-but-tough defender with a knack for stopping the run. Gay had the most passes defensed of any defender who failed to record an interception last season. David, a solid Cover-2 defender in his days with the Colts, has been awful since coming to New Orleans, but the Saints have a habit of keeping their free agent mistakes around forever and ever.

Special Teams

Year	DVOA	Rank	FG/XP	Rank	Net Kick	Rank	Kick Ret	Rank	Net Punt	Rank	Punt Ret	Rank	Hidden	Rank
2006	0.7%	14	2.7	10	0.4	18	-3.3	18	6.3	9	-1.9	19	12.8	1
2007	-3.6%	25	-5.3	27	-1.7	18	-7.5	27	-2.3	21	-4.3	23	-3.3	20
2008	-0.6%	22	-5.3	28	-7.0	26	1.3	16	-3.8	22	11.4	2	-2.7	17

Morten Andersen earned selection into the Saints Hall of Fame in early May. The team was probably tempted to offer him a contract instead. Garrett Hartley enters camp as the team's kicker after going 13-for-13 on field goals and booming nine touchbacks in eight games. Sean Payton said in April that Hartley "will kick in this league for a long time," meaning that Payton will probably cut him in October. Hartley made his share of big kicks in four seasons at Oklahoma, but he missed five extra points his senior season, a sign that he is capable of mental and mechanical lapses. The Saints didn't bring in any competition or insurance for Hartley; they are either super-confident or they think Andersen's bust will be able to suit up.

Rookie punter Thomas Morstead is known for his hang time. He grossed just 41.8 yards per punt in his final year at SMU, but he gives the coverage units ample time to get downfield. Morstead's a big guy (6-foot-4, 225 pounds) who can deliver a hit if a returner slips past the coverage. Glenn Pakulak averaged 47.7 yards on 24 late-season punts and will push Morstead.

Reggie Bush is one of the game's most dangerous punt returners. Pierre Thomas handled kickoffs well last season; if his role in the offense increases, Courtney Roby may take over return duties. Several new arrivals will help beef up the special teams units, including free agents Heath Evans, Anthony Waters, and Pierson Prioleau.

Coaching Staff

Sean Payton stands at the vanguard of the Neo-Parcells Offensive Coaches, a group that also includes Tony Sparano and Jason Garrett and will spin off a few others as assistants like Doug Marrone earn head coaching jobs. These new-era coaches run very different systems, but all are open to radical ideas and share a willingness to overturn conventional wisdom. Think of them as guys "empowered" by the Tuna's imprimatur; since they worked for Parcells, they get a few years of free benefit of the doubt when they install the Wildcat or empty the backfield on third-and-inches. All are running quarterback-friendly offenses that have the league's copycats spending extra hours in the film room. Payton is the maverick of the group, a mad scientist who isn't afraid to tinker with stack formations and elaborate counter plays. Even if he never gets the Saints defense to catch up to its offense, he may be remembered as another Don Coryell or Jack Pardee.

Marrone, the Saints' offensive coordinator last year, left the team to become the head coach of Syracuse with two games left in the regular season. Payton didn't bother replacing him until the offseason. Pete Carmichel is now the nominal coordinator, though Payton calls all of the plays and makes most of the important decisions. Carmichel has been Drew Brees' quarterbacks coach since both were with the Chargers, so he provides a valuable sounding board/buffer zone between the quarterback and the head coach.

Several defensive assistants were retained from the Gary Gibbs staff, including linebackers coach Joe Vitt and secondary coach Dennis Allen. New defensive line coach Bill Johnson spent last season doing the same job for the Broncos. This isn't exactly a dream staff; if you wanted to create the worst possible defense last year, you could have started by pairing the Broncos' defensive line with the Saints' secondary. Gregg Williams may have to coach up his coaches while he coaches up his players.

New York Giants

An important concept to remember when it comes to any sort of statistical or trend analysis is that correlation does not necessarily mean causation. Taken on the most literal level, it's painfully obvious. The fact that you spilled some mustard on your pants at lunch and then got a promotion later in the day does not mean that you should be liberally dousing yourself with Gulden's regularly. It gets trickier, though, when you notice results that would reasonably follow from an event. If that promotion came the day after you wore your suit to the office for the first time in a year, well, you might start dressing up for work every day.

With that idea in mind, we present the 2008 New York Giants. Before Plaxico Burress shot himself in the leg on an ill-fated night in November, the team was 10-1; afterwards, they went 2-4, including a playoff loss at home against the archrival Eagles. The correlation of the incident to the team's downswing in performance yielded a simple narrative: The Giants offense wasn't as good without Plaxico Burress, and it turned them into a totally different team.

That narrative is simply untrue.

The Giants' passing offense actually improved with Burress out of the lineup (Table 1). That analysis includes the Week 12 game against the Cardinals, in which Burress came out in the first quarter with a hamstring injury and didn't return, as well as the NFC Divisional Round loss to the Eagles. Burress was also suspended for the Week 5 game against the Seahawks; if you include this 44-6 victory, the Burress-free passing game looks even more impressive. The running game declined some without the threat of Burress stretching the field to concern opposing safeties, but it wasn't enough to drag the offense down; the team's offensive DVOA was 20.6% with Burress in the lineup and 27.8% over the eight games he wasn't around.

Although the Giants scored 27.5 points per game with Burress in the lineup and 23.8 when he was sidelined (including the Cardinals and Seahawks games), they played a harder slate of defenses. The average defensive DVOA of the teams that faced them when they had Burress was -2.1%; without Burress, the average team they faced had a -5.9% defensive DVOA.

Instead, what drove the Giants' demise was the defense. Unless you want to pin the blame on Antonio Pierce's extracurricular issues related to the Burress incident, Burress had nothing to do with the decline. Instead, it was a regression in the team's sack rate that correlated well with the team's dip in performance, culminating in the playoff game versus the Eagles in which — despite playing behind an offensive line missing multiple starters — Donovan McNabb was not sacked once (although a hurry led to an intentional grounding penalty in the end zone). While Justin Tuck had 8.5

GIANTS SUMMARY

2008 Record: 12-4

Pythagorean Wins: 11.3 (4th)

DVOA: 27.0% (4th)

Offense: 23.7% (3rd)

Defense: -1.5% (8th)

Special Teams: 1.8% (11th)

Variance: 17.9% (18th)

2008: Great first half of the season with a fade down the stretch giving way to a disappointing opening playoff loss. Are you 2005 or 2006 in disguise?

2009: Our favorites to win the division, as long as the offensive line stays intact.

2009 Mean Projection: 10.0 wins

On the Clock (0-3): 1%

Loserville (4-6): 8%

Mediocrity (7-8): 18%

Playoff Contender (9-10): 31%

Super Bowl Contender (11+): 42%

Projected Average Opponent: -2.9% (28th)

2009 Giants Schedule

Week	Opp.	Week	Opp.	Week	Opp.
1	WAS	7	ARI	13	DAL
2	at DAL	8	at PHI	14	PHI
3	at TB	9	SD	15	at WAS (Mon.)
4	at KC	10	BYE	16	CAR
5	OAK	11	ATL	17	at MIN
6	at NO	12	at DEN (Thu.)		

sacks over the first ten games of the season and a respectable 3.5 more in the final seven games of the year (from Arizona on), everyone else disappeared. Mathias Kiwanuka had 8.5 sacks by the Cardinals game and 1.5 after. Fred Robbins, Dave Tollefson, and Barry Cofield combined for 11 sacks before the trip to Glendale and all of one sack afterwards.

It's impossible to pinpoint the exact cause of the precipitous drop. The preseason loss of Osi Umenyiora to a torn lateral meniscus undoubtedly stretched the team, forcing them to move Kiwanuka back to defensive end on what appears to be a permanent basis. Robbins was the only rotation player to miss a game of any consequence, so there wasn't a dramatic shift in the team's injury rate. There's no sign that the scheme of newly-departed defensive coordinator Steve Spagnuolo stagnated or was "figured out" by opposing offenses, either.

The working theory of the Giants organization is simpler: The front seven got tired. Although they knew that getting Umenyiora back would help assuage some depth issues, general manager Jerry Reese went shopping in free agency and came back with linebacker Michael Boley and defensive tackles Rocky Bernard and Chris Canty. Canty is the most interesting signing of the three; a defensive end in Dallas' 3-4 scheme, Canty will move to defensive tackle for the Giants and play there on most downs. All in all, the team should be able to rotate as many as four starting-caliber defenders at both end and tackle, while Boley and second-round pick Clint Sintim project as the new starters at outside linebacker. New defensive coordinator Bill Sheridan hopes to get more of a pass rush from those spots than a year ago, when starters Gerris Wilkinson and Danny Clark combined for zero sacks.

Table 1: Sweat Pants ≠ Holster:
Giants' DVOA With and Without Plaxico Burress

	Weeks	Off Pass	Off Run	Defense	Def Sack Rate
w/ Plaxico	1-4, 6-11	29.5%	21.1%	-6.5%	9.4%
w/o Plaxico	5, 12-19	36.1%	18.7%	0.4%	5.5%
w/o Plaxico, SEA excluded	12-19	29.9%	11.3%	2.6%	5.3%

Sheridan's ascension to the role following Spagnuolo's departure for St. Louis will come with some changes. Spagnuolo's blitz-happy scheme relied on a combination of speed and deception; a typical play, for example, might involve lining up Kiwanuka and Tuck on the same side of the field, only to have them drop back while the overload blitz came from the other side. Perhaps owing to the increased depth allowed him by the free agent acquisitions, Sheridan has said that he will move away from the Jim Johnson-influenced subterfuge and employ simpler blitz schemes, relying on fresher players to get past tired blockers.

On one hand, you can see how the move would make sense. Dropping Tuck or Umenyiora into coverage prevents them from doing what they do best — rush the passer — as frequently as possible. When the Giants ran zone blitzes a year ago, they were significantly worse than the average NFL team (Table 2). They were most successful when they rushed four and dropped seven into coverage. When Spagnuolo got on the head coaching radar by holding the Patriots to 14 points in the Giants' Super Bowl XLII win, he didn't devise some brilliant blitz scheme to throw Tom Brady and company off track. He simply rushed four on most plays and dropped his linebackers into hook zones that interfered with the routes of the Patriots' underneath receivers. Expect Sheridan to employ more of that approach in 2009, with fewer big-blitzes or blitzes out of the secondary.

It's that secondary which may end up being the concern of the defense. While Corey Webster built on his 2007 playoff performance and had a huge 2008 campaign, the rest of the secondary was unimpressive. Aaron Ross looked lost for most of the year, taking too many false steps and failing to make tackles downfield. Nickel corner Terrell Thomas looked very good as a rookie, and might end up taking Ross' job if the former Texas star continues to struggle, but the Giants would be much better off if Ross could hold up in coverage and Thomas could stay in the nickel. There's also uncertainty at safety, where 2008 first-round pick Kenny Phillips takes over at strong safety from James Butler, with no depth behind either him or free starter Michael Johnson. The organization's failure to address depth issues before the sixth round of this year's draft — the team signed only mediocre Texans safety C.C. Brown in free agency — could very well come back to bite them if Webster or Phillips goes down with an injury.

The place where New York has impressively managed to avoid injury for two years running is on the offensive line. No starter has missed a regular-season game for two seasons. (We say "New York" and not "the Giants" because it's also true of the Jets over the past two years.) It's a remarkable accomplishment, considering that no other team has seen its starting five linemen make it through two consecutive seasons without missing a single start since 2003. In 2002 and 2003, both the Chiefs and the Vikings managed to pull off the feat; neither made it to three years, although the Chiefs' starters only missed a single game in 2004; the Vikings' linemen missed 18 games in each of 2004 and 2005.

For the Giants, the basis of their team's strength is in the combination of the offensive line with fullback Madison Hedgecock, so losing even one player for any period of time would be a huge problem. When Kareem McKenzie struggled with a back injury last year and had to come out for periodic extended breathers in the middle of games, he was replaced by utility lineman Kevin Boothe, who proceeded to nearly get Eli Manning killed. The team has only Boothe and second-round pick William Beatty for recognizable backups, so an injury to a key player like right guard Chris Snee or center Shaun O'Hara could be disastrous for the offense.

Even more disastrous, of course, would be the loss of Eli Manning. The once-embattled quarterback had his best season as a pro in 2008, improving his completion percentage and yards per attempt while cutting his interceptions in half, although it's worth noting that his six dropped interceptions were tied for third-most in the league. Manning still has accuracy issues — his rating of 80.9 percent on our accuracy index (see Appendix) was below the league average of 82.6 percent, and 26th amongst quarterbacks who threw at last 100 passes, but he has improved his accuracy on crossing routes and short out patterns. He saw a huge leap in his performance on third down, thanks to the great early-season performance of second-year receiver Steve Smith, but Smith regressed at the end of the year; he had 14 conversions on third down through Week 12, but only three afterwards. Although the offense as a whole didn't skip a beat without Burress, it's very possible that Smith's performance was affected; much like Wes Welker and Randy Moss in New England, Burress' ability to occupy the safety from the moment the ball is snapped prevents the safety from biting on the underneath route and making Smith pay

Table 2: Giants Defense by Type of Pass Rush

Rushers	Giants		Rest Of NFL	
	YPA	Success Rate	YPA	Success Rate
3	8.4	38%	6.5	57%
4	5.4	60%	6.2	55%
5	7.2	57%	6.3	55%
6	5.6	59%	5.4	60%
7	4.9	50%	5.1	64%
Zone Blitz	7.9	50%	5.9	58%

when he decides to go over the middle.

We'll likely find out whether that was the case in 2009, because after the Giants released Burress and decided not to acquire either Braylon Edwards or Anquan Boldin, they spent two draft picks on receivers who are unlikely to reproduce Burress' production. First-round pick Hakeem Nicks (North Carolina) is a good route-runner who likely profiles as the replacement for Amani Toomer on the other side of the field, while third-rounder Ramses Barden (Cal Poly) has the height (6-foot-6) but not many of the same skills that Burress had; namely, running effective routes and catching the ball. Instead, the team will likely employ Domenik Hixon as the primary "X" receiver once more; Hixon had a 6.5% DVOA when he was starting in Burress' role (as opposed to Burress' 4.9% DVOA), with a superior catch rate and yardage per catch total. In other words, he played better, prominent drop against Philly aside.

The brook is also bubbling with talent at running back, where the departure of Derrick Ward in free agency should open up a spot for either Danny Ware or Ahmad Bradshaw. Bradshaw had a bit of a lost season in 2008, thanks in part to spending a chunk of his offseason in jail. Although he's a talented runner, the Giants would like to have the backup to Brandon Jacobs be someone who can pass block, and Bradshaw isn't that guy. Ware, a coaches' favorite, could very well emerge as the primary backup and become a fantasy sleeper thanks to Jacobs' annual injury.

Reese has built a powerhouse team around two often-dominant lines and a very good quarterback. In the long run, it will be keeping those cornerstones healthy and intact that will determine the success of this team, not the presence of one wide receiver. As long as the offensive line doesn't fall apart and the pass rush doesn't totally collapse under Sheridan, the Giants are the favorites in the NFC East, if not the NFC as a whole.

Bill Barnwell

2008 Giants Stats by Week

Wk	vs.	W-L	PF	PA	YDF	YDA	TO	Total	Off	Def	ST
1	WAS	W	16	7	354	209	-1	22%	12%	-12%	-2%
2	@STL	W	41	13	441	201	+1	62%	39%	-10%	12%
3	CIN	W	26	23	406	347	0	10%	35%	25%	0%
4	BYE										
5	SEA	W	44	6	523	187	+1	91%	75%	-19%	-3%
6	@CLE	L	14	35	373	454	-3	-64%	23%	89%	2%
7	SF	W	29	17	273	253	+3	25%	-5%	-32%	-2%
8	@PIT	W	21	14	282	249	+4	63%	-1%	-52%	12%
9	DAL	W	35	14	319	183	+1	97%	16%	-84%	-3%
10	@PHI	W	36	31	401	300	0	32%	29%	19%	22%
11	BAL	W	30	10	353	275	+1	56%	37%	-22%	-3%
12	@ARI	W	37	29	321	371	+2	24%	23%	12%	13%
13	@WAS	W	23	7	404	320	+1	7%	10%	2%	-2%
14	PHI	L	14	20	211	331	0	-1%	15%	8%	-8%
15	@DAL	L	8	20	218	321	-2	-37%	-29%	15%	7%
16	CAR	W	34	28	459	343	0	13%	43%	19%	-11%
17	@MIN	L	19	20	364	349	+1	48%	43%	-10%	-5%
18	BYE										
19	PHI	L	11	23	307	276	-1	22%	-2%	-28%	-3%

Trends and Splits

	Offense	Rank	Defense	Rank
Total DVOA	23.7%	3	-1.5%	8
Unadjusted VOA	22.9%	4	-1.2%	8
Weighted trend	20.7%	7	-0.4%	10
Variance	5.7%	9	4.8%	9
Average opponent	0.6%	31	-2.3%	3
Passing	35.7%	5	1.9%	11
Rushing	20.7%	3	-5.6%	12
First down	21.2%	1	-16.3%	4
Second down	20.5%	11	8.1%	18
Third down	34.4%	6	12.5%	22
First half	21.7%	1	-2.2%	11
Second half	26.2%	3	-0.8%	9
Red Zone	17.8%	8	-0.7%	17
Late and close	30.0%	1	7.3%	20

Five-Year Performance

Year	W-L	Pyth	Est W	PF	PA	TO	Total	Rk	Off	Rk	Def	Rk	ST	Rk	Off AGL	Rk	Def AGL	Rk
2004	6-10	6.7	6.4	303	347	+4	-15.5%	25	-10.3%	25	5.8%	22	0.7%	15	8.6	26	41.9	2
2005	11-5	10.7	10.4	422	314	+12	17.4%	10	8.9%	9	-4.1%	14	4.4%	2	5.5	28	30.2	4
2006	8-8	7.8	9.0	355	362	0	14.3%	8	12.8%	7	-1.1%	13	0.4%	16	16.4	17	31.0	5
2007	10-6	8.6	8.0	373	351	-9	1.1%	16	-0.3%	18	-2.1%	14	-0.7%	19	13.8	27	14.5	24
2008	12-4	11.3	11.4	427	294	+9	27.0%	4	23.7%	3	-1.5%	8	1.8%	11	6.2	32	29.6	13

Strategic Tendencies

Run/Pass		Rank	Offense		Rank	Defense		Rank	Other		Rank
Runs, all plays	48%	7	3+ WR	48%	18	Rush 3	1.6%	29	2+ RB, Pct Runs	68%	4
Runs, first half	45%	14	4+ WR	13%	14	Rush 4	63.5%	18	1 RB/2 TE, Pct Runs	59%	8
Runs, first down	55%	10	2+ TE	23%	21	Rush 5	18.9%	22	1RB/3+WR, Pct Runs	28%	17
Runs, second-long	50%	2	Single back	54%	18	Rush 6+	15.9%	2	Zone Blitz	6%	10
Runs, power sit.	71%	7	Play action	15%	19	Rush 7+	3.9%	3	Go for it on 4th	0.77	27
Runs, behind 2H	44%	1	Max protect	9%	13	Sacks by LB	8.3%	27	Offensive Pace	31.7	26
Pass, ahead 2H	43%	15	Outside pocket	7%	25	Sacks by DB	4.8%	22	Defensive Pace	31.2	24

Could Madison Hedgecock not be the blocker that people think he is? Big Blue had the league's second biggest difference between runs from single-back sets (40.9% DVOA, 6.7 yards per carry) and runs from two-back sets (8.8% DVOA, 4.4 yards per carry). The only team with a bigger difference was division rival Philadelphia, a team famous for spurning the fullback position in recent years. ● Opponents blitzed Eli Manning with at least five pass rushers on 41 percent of pass plays, the highest rate in the league — and they did it because it works. The Giants had a league-leading 62.9% DVOA when opponents rushed four, but 5.6% DVOA (24th) when opponents rushed five and -10.9% DVOA (22nd) when opponents rushed six or more. ● On the defensive side of the ball, the Giants' use of the big blitz (six or more pass rushers) over the past three seasons has gone from 3.1 percent of passes (30th in the NFL) to 10.6 percent of passes (10th) to 15.9 percent of passes (second). ● The Giants gave up only 2.8 yards per carry on draw plays, and ranked fourth in defensive DVOA. ● The Giants had the league's best fumble recovery rate on offense (recovering 11 of 14) but the league's worst fumble recovery rate on defense (recovering only five of 17). ● Despite New York's excellent running game, Tom Coughlin has actually become less aggressive on fourth down over time. For his career, Coughlin ranks 36 out of 95 coaches (1994-2008) with an Aggressiveness Index of 1.075. However, Coughlin has not had AI above 1.0 (league average) since he started coaching the Giants five years ago, and last year he had the lowest AI of his career.

Passing

Player	DYAR	DVOA	Plays	NtYds	Avg	YAC	C%	TD	Int
Eli Manning	1032	19.7%	515	3182	6.2	4.1	60.6%	21	9
David Carr	128	138.4%	14	137	9.8	2.9	75.0%	2	0

Rushing

Player	DYAR	DVOA	Plays	Yds	Avg	TD	Fum	Suc
Brandon Jacobs	300	22.4%	219	1090	5.0	15	3	51%
Derrick Ward*	265	25.8%	182	1027	5.6	2	2	51%
Ahmad Bradshaw	20	-1.4%	67	356	5.3	1	2	49%
Eli Manning	14	17.2%	7	26	3.7	1	0	--
David Carr	3	25.0%	3	15	5.0	0	0	--

Receiving

Player	DYAR	DVOA	Plays	Ctch	Yds	Y/C	YAC	TD	C%
Amani Toomer*	77	-2.3%	88	48	580	12.1	2.8	5	55%
Steve Smith	88	1.0%	82	57	577	10.1	3.4	3	62%
Domenik Hixon	142	11.5%	73	43	596	13.9	3.3	2	59%
Plaxico Burress*	94	4.9%	66	35	454	13.0	1.9	5	53%
Sinorice Moss	67	46.0%	15	12	153	12.8	2.0	2	80%
Mario Manningham	8	0.3%	6	4	26	6.5	5.5	0	67%
Derek Hagan	*7*	*4.2%*	*6*	*3*	*51*	*17.0*	*2.3*	*0*	*50%*
Kevin Boss	84	14.8%	55	33	384	11.6	4.8	6	60%
Darcy Johnson	28	48.9%	6	4	46	11.5	0.5	2	67%
Derrick Ward*	107	24.0%	55	41	384	9.4	10.0	0	75%
Madison Hedgecock	-3	-16.4%	15	8	52	6.5	5.9	1	53%
Brandon Jacobs	-21	-42.6%	12	6	36	6.0	4.5	0	50%
Ahmad Bradshaw	25	93.3%	6	5	42	8.4	10.2	1	83%

Offensive Line

Year	Yards	ALY	Rank	Power	Rank	10+ Yds	Rank	Stuff	Rank	Sacks	ASR	Rank	False	Cont.
2006	4.99	4.49	4	71%	6	19%	9	19%	25	25	5.4%	7	22	30
2007	4.79	4.48	3	70%	7	20%	8	17%	9	28	5.0%	11	14	48
2008	5.28	4.62	4	62%	23	25%	2	17%	10	28	5.0%	10	12	48

Year	LE	Rank	LT	Rank	Mid	Rank	RT	Rank	RE	Rank
2006	5.18	3	3.60	29	4.32	13	4.56	4	5.23	2
2007	4.80	7	4.21	18	4.50	6	4.35	14	4.81	4
2008	5.02	5	5.17	1	4.84	1	4.04	20	3.72	24

It's interesting to compare how our numbers match up with perception; although conventional wisdom — and most people's eyes — had the Giants as the best run-blocking line in recent memory, our numbers list Denver as the best set of run blockers in football. That's reinforced by their Power numbers. Wouldn't the best run-blocking line in football be able to get a yard when they need it? In reality, we suspect that the Giants were actually the best line when it comes to the ground game in 2008, but that the difference between them and the rest of the league was overstated.

The Giants' run game involves lots of pulling guards and patience on sweeps, traps, and counter plays, although the team does not hesitate to pull either left tackle David Diehl or center Shaun O'Hara. (Right tackle Kareem McKenzie goes for a jaunt less frequently.) Right guard Chris Snee is the star, a mauler who can effectively block anyone on the field at any level. O'Hara's superb at chipping defensive tackles and then occupying a linebacker, thereby preventing them from getting over to the edge before the back makes his cut and heads up the field. You'll note that the team was far better running to the left side than they were to the right; that's the difference in ability between Snee (pulling to the left) and left guard Rich Seubert (pulling to the right). Seubert was better in 2007, and he'd still be a starting guard on a fair amount of NFL teams, but he remains the line's weakest link.

The starters were very good in pass protection. Diehl went from tying for the league lead with 11 sacks allowed in 2007 to five last year, only slightly above-average for a left tackle. He still struggles to play with leverage against pass rushers on the outside, though; overcompensating for his lack of speed, he gets out of his base easily and can be pushed back to the quarterback.

We say "the starters" because of the performance of one Kevin Boothe. Taking over for a banged-up McKenzie over the course of the season, Boothe allowed four sacks despite seeing, perhaps, one-tenth of the snaps that McKenzie played. Boothe's struggles are a sign of what may very well happen when someone on the offensive line does suffer an injury. Perhaps with Boothe's struggles in mind, the Giants spent the 60th overall pick on UConn tackle William Beatty, who profiles as the long-term replacement for McKenzie at right tackle. At 6-foot-5, Guy Whimper returns as the other backup tackle after missing all of 2008 with a broken foot; with the departure of backup center/guard Grey Ruegamer, Whimper or Boothe could also see time at guard if either Seubert or Snee go down.

Defensive Front Seven

Defensive Line	Age	Pos	Plays	TmPct	Rk	Stop	Dfts	Stop%	Overall Rk	AvYd	Rk	Pass Rush Sack	Hit	Hur	vs. Run Runs	St%	Yds	vs. Pass Pass	St%	Yds
Justin Tuck	26	DE	67	9.0%	3	59	28	88%	8	0.1	10	12.0	10	19	47	87%	1.6	20	90%	-3.5
Mathias Kiwanuka	26	DE	52	7.0%	20	43	19	83%	21	1.6	38	8.0	10	13	37	86%	1.9	15	73%	0.9
Barry Cofield	25	DT	45	6.4%	17	34	7	76%	45	2.2	48	2.5	2	1	37	73%	3.1	8	88%	-2.1
Fred Robbins	32	DT	38	5.8%	26	34	17	89%	2	-0.3	1	5.5	2	9	27	89%	0.3	11	91%	-1.7
Renaldo Wynn*	35	DE	24	3.2%	88	17	8	71%	62	1.5	36	2.0	0	5	20	75%	1.4	4	50%	1.8
Jay Alford	26	DT	15	2.0%	--	12	5	80%	--	1.1	--	2.5	2	3	9	89%	1.9	6	67%	0.0
Rocky Bernard	30	DT	56	7.0%	9	36	11	64%	69	3.2	71	4.0	6	7	43	63%	3.3	13	69%	2.5
Chris Canty	27	DE	41	5.4%	45	29	8	71%	64	2.0	55	3.5	4	4	28	64%	2.8	13	85%	0.2

Linebackers	Age	Pos	Plays	TmPct	Rk	Stop	Dfts	Stop%	Overall AvYd	Pass Rush Sack	Hit	Hur	vs. Run Runs	St%	Rk	Yds	Rk	vs. Pass Tgts	Suc%	Rk	AdjYd	Rk
Antonio Pierce	31	ILB	96	13.7%	28	48	18	50%	6.2	1.5	0	5	50	66%	42	3.6	60	44	33%	86	8.7	87
Danny Clark	32	OLB	67	9.0%	77	44	7	66%	3.0	0.0	1	3	57	70%	22	2.6	13	9	39%	--	5.1	--
Chase Blackburn	26	ILB	43	5.8%	--	26	8	60%	4.8	1.0	1	1	29	69%	--	2.5	--	11	50%	--	9.3	--
Bryan Kehl	25	OLB	32	4.3%	--	17	4	53%	4.5	1.0	0	1	26	46%	--	5.1	--	5	99%	--	1.4	--
Michael Boley	27	OLB	81	10.3%	66	41	14	51%	5.9	0.0	1	2	36	58%	82	4.4	95	44	57%	29	5.4	22

Year	Yards	ALY	Rank	Power	Rank	10+ Yds	Rank	Stuff	Rank	Sack	ASR	Rank
2006	3.73	3.77	5	70%	26	17%	19	21%	7	32	6.3%	19
2007	4.01	3.76	3	63%	17	20%	23	22%	6	53	8.8%	1
2008	3.71	3.33	3	58%	6	22%	25	24%	3	42	7.2%	7

Year	LE	Rank	LT	Rank	Mid	Rank	RT	Rank	RE	Rank
2006	3.49	10	2.99	3	4.17	16	2.73	2	4.75	27
2007	2.90	6	4.60	22	3.63	3	3.35	2	4.40	23
2008	3.15	4	3.32	5	3.27	2	3.97	15	3.12	10

By making so many additions to what was an already fearsome front seven, the Giants give themselves all kinds of redundancies and fallback plans.

At defensive end, Osi Umenyiora returns from a lost year, thanks a torn lateral meniscus suffered in the war of attrition that is the yearly Giants-Jets exhibition game. (For those who don't remember, Jason Sehorn suffered a career-changing knee injury in the same game years earlier.) Umenyiora will start on the right side, with Justin Tuck on the left side. Having given up on converting Mathias Kiwanuka into a linebacker, the team will liberally rotate Kiwanuka in for Umenyiora and Tuck to keep all three fresh; it'll dampen the tackle and sack totals for the starters in IDP leagues, but might keep them healthy and productive for all 16 games. The same sort of rotation will exist on the interior; expect free-agent acquisitions Chris Canty and Rocky Bernard to start, but the team will rotate Jay Alford, Barry Cofield, and Fred Robbins in and out virtually every down. Robbins tired badly down the stretch last year, with all 5.5 of his sacks coming by Week 7.

Middle linebacker Antonio Pierce is the heart and soul of the defense, and while he's still an effective run blitzer, he struggled mightily in coverage last year. He is sometimes victimized solely because he's the one guy left in a hook zone when the blitz doesn't get there, but even that doesn't explain away how poor his performance was. Among qualifying linebackers, only James Farrior allowed more than the 5.8 yards after catch averaged on throws with Pierce in coverage. Pierce will have new bookends around him that might help this year, though; the weakside starter will be former Atlanta linebacker Michael Boley. Boley fell out of favor with the new regime in Atlanta because of his struggles against the run, and even lost his job at the end of the season, but the Giants recognize that Boley is an explosive athlete capable of rushing the passer (although he didn't show it last year) and being an effective pass defender both in zone and against tight ends in man coverage. Although we don't often use the term in football, he'll make for a nice platoon with second-year linebacker Bryan Kehl, who isn't much of a pass rusher, but does a good job of plugging up holes in the running game.

The strongside linebacker will be second-round pick Clint Sintim, assuming that he picks up the playbook and the speed of the game at the level the Giants expect him to. 2008 starter Danny Clark, thrust into the position after Kiwanuka was moved to end, was inconsistent and limited athletically; in a front seven built on quickness and the ability to rush the passer, Sintim's a better bet. The Virginia product had 11 sacks as a senior, so he can get to the quarterback, but he's not particularly experienced in coverage and might not have the skill set to play on the outside. Don't be surprised if he eventually replaces Pierce at middle linebacker, but for now, he gives the team yet another pass rusher. Sintim will be backed up by Gerris Wilkinson and special teams demon Zak DeOssie.

Defensive Secondary

Secondary	Age	Pos	Plays	TmPct	Overall Rk	Stop	Dfts	Yds	vs. Run Rk	St%	Rk	Tgts	Tgt%	vs. Pass Rk	Dist	Suc%	Rk	AdjYd	Rk	Yds	PD	Int
Corey Webster	27	CB	74	9.9%	22	40	17	5.8	30	47%	37	69	16.5%	52	11.1	62%	9	5.4	7	5.0	25	3
James Butler*	27	FS	71	10.1%	37	28	9	6.4	28	44%	32	25	6.4%	45	10.4	66%	7	7.5	30	7.6	4	3
Michael Johnson	25	SS	69	9.2%	48	34	15	3.0	2	68%	3	35	8.2%	16	8.0	47%	55	7.1	20	7.1	4	2
Kenny Phillips	23	FS	67	9.0%	51	27	16	6.4	27	48%	19	29	6.8%	39	13.5	61%	15	7.5	29	7.1	3	1
Aaron Ross	26	CB	60	8.6%	43	23	11	4.4	11	50%	30	88	22.3%	16	10.9	48%	50	8.9	77	8.5	9	3
Kevin Dockery	25	CB	45	7.4%	58	22	12	3.9	7	63%	15	43	12.6%	75	12.6	58%	16	6.3	24	5.6	8	1
Terrell Thomas	25	CB	34	6.1%	--	15	8	3.7	--	70%	--	23	7.2%	--	10.7	59%	--	7.1	--	7.9	4	1

Year	Pass D Rank	vs. #1 WR	Rk	vs. #2 WR	Rk	vs. Other WR	Rk	vs. TE	Rk	vs. RB	Rk
2006	18	-9.9%	8	-1.4%	12	6.0%	22	20.1%	31	-1.9%	16
2007	15	9.2%	21	-15.2%	6	-22.4%	7	24.8%	29	12.0%	29
2008	9	-16.1%	3	6.4%	21	-15.8%	10	8.9%	21	30.3%	31

After we devoted a whole section of the Giants chapter in last year's book to the myth that Corey Webster took a huge step forward in the playoffs, well, Corey Webster went ahead and took a huge step forward during the 2008 regular season. Only a year removed from being a healthy scratch during parts of the 2007 campaign, Webster looked like a stud cornerback on film in 2008, combining his athleticism with significantly improved awareness and footwork to stick to opposing wideouts. Webster led the league by breaking up an impressive 32.1 percent of the passes thrown at him, and he even became a better tackler and willing run defender on the edge. On this form, his five-year, $43.5 million dollar contract extension was well deserved.

Across from him, though, was disappointment: Aaron Ross was expected to be a competent corner as soon as he stepped on to an NFL field after starring at Texas, and while he was acceptable in 2007, teams avoiding Webster enjoyed plenty of success going after Ross in 2008. He was lucky to be the beneficiary of six drops, or his numbers would have looked even worse. Ross struggled to get proper jams at the line, and then when receivers caught the ball, he had tackling issues. Ross will get another season to prove that 2008 was just an off year, but if he struggles early, his replacement may very well be the promising Terrell Thomas, who'd be high on our

Top 25 Prospects list if he had been the first third-round pick of the 2008 draft instead of the final second-round pick. In addition to being an excellent player on coverage units, Thomas was superb as the team's slot corner, taking the job away from Kevin Dockery and Sam Madison by Week 8. Madison was released in the offseason and might retire, while Dockery will be back for the final year of his rookie deal as the dime corner.

The only other change in the secondary is at strong safety, where James Butler followed Steve Spagnuolo to St. Louis. The Giants will likely move Michael Johnson, who started at free safety last year, to that spot. That opens up free safety for 2008 first-round pick Kenny Phillips, who impressed in limited duty last year. Johnson isn't great in coverage and works best as a blitzer and run defender close to the line of scrimmage, so he's likely a better fit at strong safety. Phillips will need to hold the fort deep when the blitz doesn't get there. The Giants imported C.C. Brown from Houston to back both safeties up; it is in the best interests of Giants fans everywhere that he does not make it onto the field.

Special Teams

Year	DVOA	Rank	FG/XP	Rank	Net Kick	Rank	Kick Ret	Rank	Net Punt	Rank	Punt Ret	Rank	Hidden	Rank
2006	0.4%	16	0.8	13	3.1	15	-10.5	29	11.3	3	-2.3	21	-1.3	15
2007	-0.7%	19	-2.9	24	-5.8	24	3.5	10	5.5	10	-4.3	22	5.3	10
2008	1.8%	11	3.7	11	-11.3	31	4.4	9	11.7	5	2.0	8	0.4	12

When Lawrence Tynes went down with a knee injury in camp, the team brought in John Carney as his replacement. Carney proceeded to start the year by kicking 12 consecutive field goals, giving him the job for good and limiting Tynes to kickoff duties when he was able to get on the active roster. It wasn't the right play; as good as Carney was on field goals, he had no leg strength. The 44-year-old only attempted one field goal beyond 50 yards, and he was the worst kickoff man in football; coincidentally, he was not retained by the team. Somehow, this combination added up to a Pro Bowl trip. Punter Jeff Feagles made the Pro Bowl at 42, thanks to his ability to avoid returns of any sort by accurately angling his punts or simply kicking them out of bounds. He'll be back for another year.

The coverage units are run by DeOssie, who was added to the Pro Bowl roster by the coaches in only his second season. He's joined on an above-average coverage unit by Thomas and backup middle linebacker Chase Blackburn. The team used a four-man wedge last year, so that will change. Domenik Hixon was competent when he returned punts, but he's probably off those duties if he's going to start at wide receiver, leaving a hole at the position. Ahmad Bradshaw was unimpressive and inconsistent as a kick returner, but with the Giants arguably needing to justify his roster spot, expect him to be the primary man on kickoff returns in 2009.

Coaching Staff

The departure of Spagnuolo to St. Louis resulted in the promotion of Bill Sheridan from linebackers coach to defensive coordinator. It will be Sheridan's first time as the defensive coordinator at any level. Sheridan has said that he will retain Spagnuolo's scheme, but drop his pass rushers — specifically Tuck — into pass coverage less frequently, with the idea that they're better off going after the quarterback more often. That should create more opportunities for pressure, but also eliminate some of the confusion that Spagnuolo's defense thrived upon.

Offensively, Kevin Gilbride took some heat for his play-calling against the Eagles in the Divisional round loss, but the problem was less with the scheme and more with the execution. Gilbride has had a habit of wearing out his welcome, though, so it wouldn't a surprise to see the blame fall on him if the offense gets off to a slow start. Head coach Tom Coughlin appears to have moved on from his old drill instructor style of coaching permanently, but again, it'll be interesting to see what happens if the team does struggle at the start of the year.

New York Jets

Woody Johnson has made it clear that so long as he is the owner, the Jets will always have a dynamic coach and a big time quarterback. In 2006, when Eric Mangini was making guest appearances on *The Sopranos* and Chad Pennington was winning Comeback Player of the Year, it seemed like Johnson was all set. The 2006 Jets weren't a very good team; they ranked 17th in DVOA and made the playoffs primarily because of a soft schedule, but that didn't make the team's collapse the following season any less of a shock to Johnson. Suddenly, Pennington's limited arm strength was on full display and Mangini's smoke and mirrors stopped fooling opponents.

With the prospect of another season of Pennington looming large in 2008, the team went on a spending spree in free agency and then capped it with the biggest move of all, plucking Brett Favre away from the Packers. Just like that, the Jets became one of the headline draws in the league. Favre was ragged out of the gate, but he threw in enough gunslinger moments to keep the media happy, and the other big-ticket additions like Alan Faneca, Calvin Pace, and Kris Jenkins performed as advertised. Expectations reached a fever pitch in Week 12, when the Jets followed up a dramatic overtime victory in New England with a resounding beatdown of previously unbeaten Tennessee. The Jets were in first place at 8-3, and the city was abuzz with talk of an all-New York Super Bowl.

That's when the wheels came off. The Jets went 1-4 down the stretch, letting the AFC East lead slip away from them. Favre threw two touchdowns and eight interceptions in December, while completing only 56.8 percent of his passes and looking visibly out of control of his ball placement. By the time the Jets squared off against Chad Pennington and Miami in the season's final week, they were out of contention for the division title and needed help just to qualify as a wild card. The team gave an uninspired effort highlighted by the final three interceptions of Favre's career (at least for now), and a few hours later Eric Mangini was fired, despite Woody Johnson's public assurance that no decision would be made in the heat of the moment.

Had the Jets come to their 9-7 record in a different manner, there is little question that Mangini would still be the coach. But after the 8-3 start, the expectations got out of hand. The reality is that the Jets were never the elite team that the media made them out to be. They were capable of great performances, and their 47-3 demolition of St. Louis resulted in one of the highest single-game DVOA ratings put up by any team this season. With the exception of the St. Louis game, however, the whole season exhibited the same up-and-down pattern (Figure 1). The Jets didn't play well against inferior competition in many of their early season wins; the primary difference in December was that they were playing poorly and losing instead of squeaking by. Even at the height of their fortunes, the Jets' DVOA

JETS SUMMARY

2008 Record: 9-7

Pythagorean Wins: 9.2 (13th)

DVOA: 5.4% (17th)

Offense: 5.1% (18th)

Defense: 2.5% (14th)

Special Teams: 2.8% (8th)

Variance: 15.7% (14th)

2008: Favre Favre Favre Favre Favre ... splat.

2009: Rex Ryan, Bart Scott, and a rookie quarterback, but they're not turning into last year's Ravens.

2009 Mean Projection: 6.2 wins

On the Clock (0-3): 11%

Loserville (4-6): 45%

Mediocrity (7-8): 26%

Playoff Contender (9-10): 15%

Super Bowl Contender (11+): 3%

Projected Average Opponent: -2.0% (25th)

2009 Jets Schedule

Week	Opp.	Week	Opp.	Week	Opp.
1	at HOU	7	at OAK	13	at BUF (Thu.)
2	NE	8	MIA	14	at TB
3	TEN	9	BYE	15	ATL
4	at NO	10	JAC	16	at IND
5	at MIA (Mon.)	11	at NE	17	CIN
6	BUF	12	CAR		

was never higher than 13.2%, good for tenth in the league. At that same time, the Giants were sitting on a DVOA of 41.5%; the Jets were closer to 27th-ranked Oakland than they were to their supposed crosstown (well, cross-stadium) Super Bowl opponents.

To replace Mangini, Woody Johnson and general manager Mike Tannenbaum turned to Baltimore Ravens defensive coordinator Rex Ryan. The Ravens defensive coordinator job has become a glamour position in much the same way that the 49ers offensive coordinator position used to be, and Ryan is the third coach in the last ten years to use it as a springboard to a head coaching job. Ryan comes across as both personable and confident in his interactions with the media, but he's stepping into a pressure cooker, because the weight of last year's expectations still hangs heavy over the club. The sputtering finish was largely blamed on a broken-down Favre, as well as a timid Mangini, who was not willing to intervene even as the hired gun took the team down with interception after interception. With Favre gone and a more aggressive and attacking defense in place, the Jets should challenge for the division title. That is the expectation. The reality is that this is a team that is likely to struggle,

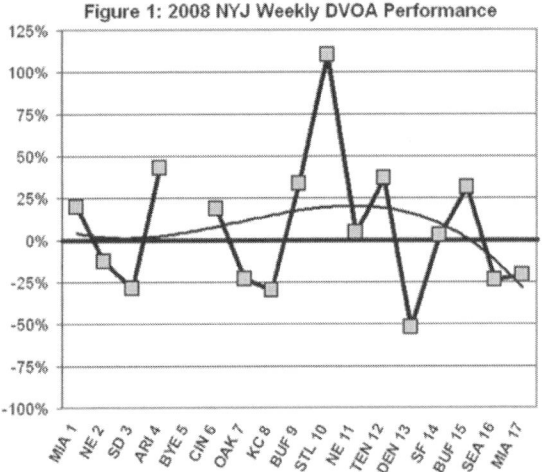

Figure 1: 2008 NYJ Weekly DVOA Performance

particularly on the offensive side of the ball, and is more likely to take several steps back than it is to leap forward into championship contention.

Hopefully the team works to its strengths and creates a solid offensive identity that allows the young talent to develop. With no Favre to placate, coordinator Brian Schottenheimer can stick to pounding the run with AFC rushing leader Thomas Jones, the explosive Leon Washington, and rookie battering ram Shonn Greene. In rookie Mark Sanchez, Schottenheimer has a quarterback with an outstanding play-action fake and terrific accuracy on the move, a guy who is perfectly suited to running an offense built around misdirection to generate downfield passing opportunities. If David Clowney can be the vertical target that he showed signs of being in the preseason, and if Dustin Keller builds on his impressive rookie season and becomes a matchup nightmare who can both stretch the seams and be a reliable safety valve on third downs, and if Jerricho Cotchery can hold his own as a number-one receiver and provide a target outside the hashes, then the offense could work. The offense might not have the explosiveness it flashed at times with Favre at the helm, but it would make sense from a game-planning perspective.

That's a lot of ifs. The biggest if is Sanchez, who arrives in New York with good looks, charm, and a lot of physical ability, but not much starting experience. The two biggest predictors of future NFL success for top quarterback prospects are games started in college and career completion percentage, in that order. No quarterback taken in the first round in the last twelve years has started as few games as Sanchez. The list of first-round quarterbacks who have started 25 games or fewer in college includes major busts like Akili Smith, Jim Druckenmiller, Tim Couch, Ryan Leaf and Alex Smith. Sanchez may well develop into the franchise quarterback everyone expects him to become. USC's absurd roster depth was the reason for his lack of experience, rather than any talent deficiency on the part of Sanchez, and even our own quarterback projection guru Dave Lewin considered him the top quarterback in the draft. Still, we are talking about a guy who started for only one season in college now having to adjust to the pro game while succeeding one of the most legendary quarterbacks in NFL history and playing in the media capital of the world. The Jets have Kellen Clemens, who is entering his fourth year in the offense, and they could certainly start the season with him while allowing their prize rookie to develop slowly, but Rex Ryan doesn't seem inclined to follow that model.

For years, Jets fans watched Chad Pennington dink and dunk his way down the field and assumed that Pennington's arm was a wet blanket smothering the offense. Get rid of him and Brian Schottenheimer's offense would stop nibbling at defenses and start eating up big chunks of yardage with downfield throws. As it turns out, the lack of a vertical offense is by design, and plugging in a big-armed quarterback did nothing to change it. The Jets' average pass on first down went 7.9 yards through the air, 29th in the league. On third-and-short, of the Jets didn't take their chances with big plays down the field; their average pass went 5.5 yards in the air, 24th in the league. Favre ran the Pennington offense in New York, while Pennington successfully ran a more vertical offense in Miami.

That's not to say that Favre did not improve the Jets offense; it's just that the improvement came primarily in the running game. While Favre tested defenses deep far less than people realized, coordinators continued to call their defenses as if they expected him to start chucking the ball deep to Donald Driver any moment, and they kept their safeties back accordingly. With only seven defenders to block, the average yards per carry for Jets backs exploded. Defenses are unlikely to show the same level of respect to Mark Sanchez, so that dominant ground game may not be there as a crutch while Sanchez learns the ropes.

While Sanchez's inexperience is a major reason why the Jets offense will probably be worse this year, it isn't the only one. Fans don't normally consider the impact that strength of schedule has on a team's performance, and they are even less likely to consider the role that health plays, but both played very much in New York's favor in 2008. Our research has shown that offensive injuries have a much more dramatic impact on a team's performance than defensive injuries, and last year the Jets had one of the healthiest groups of offensive starters in the league. It's unlikely that the team will remain injury-free for two straight seasons, and with little to no depth at wide receiver, tight end, or along the offensive line, any injury has the potential to seriously derail the offense. It's debatable whether the Jets can put together a functional offense with Jerricho Cotchery as the number-one wideout or Dustin Keller as the true primary pass catcher, but it's a given that they won't if those players miss any significant time. No matter who plays, the schedule is much less favorable, with the weak sister West divisions replaced by the AFC and NFC South.

Any struggles on offense will likely be overlooked if the defense plays like Ryan's championship-caliber unit in Baltimore. Ryan has brought in three former Ravens to help install his defense — Marques Douglas, Jim Leonhard, and Bart Scott — but the Jets think they have most of the pieces in place already. Indeed, one of the reasons Ryan was hired was because he promised to make use of the talent that was at hand. Ryan's scheme doesn't exactly overlap Mangini's — Ryan is famed for his aggressiveness, while Mangini rushed three and dropped eight more than any coach in the league — but they require similar kinds of athletes. After spending three seasons and a great deal of money turning over a roster designed by Herm Edwards to play a Tampa-2 scheme, the Jets weren't about to bring in a coach whose scheme called for another overhaul.

Much of the expectation of defensive improvement is based not on the new personnel but on the addition of Ryan himself, whose defenses ranked among the top five in DVOA in three of his four seasons as coordinator. Since 1996, there have been 33 coaching changes where teams hired a coach with a defensive background; in 20 of those cases, the team's defensive DVOA improved the following season. But there is a catch. In eight of those cases, teams were promoting from within, and as it turns out, it's a spectacularly effective practice. In seven of the eight instances where a team promoted either their defensive coordinator or their linebackers coach to head coach, the defense improved. Hiring from outside was more problematic. The Jets defensive performance declined with the hires of Eric Mangini and Herm Edwards, despite their reputations as defensive gurus. Ravens coordinators have had modest success in their first season with their new teams; Marvin Lewis brought down the Bengals' defensive DVOA by just 2.3% in Cincinnati, and Mike Nolan nudged the 49ers defensive DVOA from 21.4% in 2004 down to 15.8% in 2005, although it ranked 31st both seasons.

A six-percent improvement won't turn the Jets defense into an elite unit, but Rex Ryan is inheriting a team with a great deal more talent than the teams Lewis and Nolan inherited. The Jets have a dominant nose tackle in Kris Jenkins; an excellent cadre of linebackers in Calvin Pace, Bart Scott, David Harris, and Bryan Thomas; and Pro Bowl-quality defensive backs in corner Darrelle Revis and safety Kerry Rhodes.

They don't have any natural pass rushers, however, and they run into trouble when teams spread them out and isolate their second and third corners. The Jets addressed the coverage deficiencies by replacing safety Abram Elam with the rangier Jim Leonhard, and by trading for Lito Sheppard, who has experience making plays in a pressure man scheme. The other half of the equation is to amp up the pass rush. Ryan loves to blitz, and his packages figure to be more creative than Bob Sutton's, but ideally the pass rush would come from Vernon Gholston, whose rookie season was embarrassingly unproductive. Rightly or wrongly, much of the blame for Gholston's lack of development fell on Mangini and his staff, and the sixth overall selec-

tion in 2008 will get a clean slate with Ryan. If Gholston can come close to being the pass rushing terror he was at Ohio State, it will go a long way towards solidifying the defense.

With Rex Ryan and Mark Sanchez, it is very possible that Woody Johnson has hit on his prize combination of a dynamic coach and a big-time quarterback. But it's unlikely that they will perform to those expectations this year. In a league where rookie quarterbacks and rookie head coaches figured prominently in the playoffs just a year ago, and with the bitterness of last season's collapse still fresh in New York, neither Ryan nor Sanchez figures to have much of a honeymoon.

Sean McCormick

2008 Jets Stats by Week

Wk	vs.	W-L	PF	PA	YDF	YDA	TO	Total	Off	Def	ST
1	@MIA	W	20	14	293	277	0	19%	-2%	-33%	-11%
2	NE	L	10	19	256	260	-1	-13%	-7%	-6%	-12%
3	@SD	L	29	48	308	357	-3	-29%	-24%	30%	26%
4	ARI	W	56	35	373	468	+6	43%	38%	-10%	-5%
5	BYE										
6	CIN	W	26	14	252	171	-2	19%	-11%	-14%	16%
7	@OAK	L	13	16	418	344	-3	-23%	-10%	13%	-1%
8	KC	W	28	24	420	330	-3	-30%	-1%	29%	0%
9	@BUF	W	26	17	297	292	-2	33%	15%	-24%	-6%
10	STL	W	47	3	373	200	+5	110%	32%	-62%	17%
11	@NE	W	34	31	375	511	0	4%	11%	35%	28%
12	@TEN	W	34	13	409	281	-1	37%	43%	10%	4%
13	DEN	L	17	34	383	484	-1	-52%	-27%	35%	10%
14	@SF	L	14	24	182	375	+1	3%	13%	9%	-2%
15	BUF	W	31	27	372	306	+2	31%	37%	0%	-5%
16	@SEA	L	3	13	265	295	0	-24%	-15%	7%	-2%
17	MIA	L	17	24	286	276	+4	-21%	-15%	-1%	-8%

Trends and Splits

	Offense	Rank	Defense	Rank
Total DVOA	5.1%	18	2.5%	14
Unadjusted VOA	11.2%	12	0.3%	12
Weighted trend	7.7%	15	4.8%	14
Variance	5.2%	6	2.7%	2
Average opponent	2.0%	29	9.8%	30
Passing	6.3%	21	12.6%	18
Rushing	15.0%	5	-10.7%	7
First down	2.6%	18	-5.5%	5
Second down	22.5%	8	18.2%	26
Third down	-18.8%	25	-6.5%	9
First half	4.7%	19	-7.3%	8
Second half	5.4%	18	13.0%	26
Red Zone	5.5%	16	-12.0%	9
Late and close	4.7%	20	-2.0%	12

Five-Year Performance

Year	W-L	Pyth	Est W	PF	PA	TO	Total	Rk	Off	Rk	Def	Rk	ST	Rk	Off AGL	Rk	Def AGL	Rk
2004	10-6	10.2	11.3	333	261	+17	27.5%	5	22.1%	4	-3.1%	14	2.3%	9	6.9	28	23.3	18
2005	4-12	4.5	5.2	240	355	-6	-21.1%	26	-21.5%	31	-0.4%	18	0.0%	18	57.7	1	16.9	14
2006	10-6	8.7	7.7	316	295	0	-1.2%	17	6.2%	12	10.6%	27	3.2%	5	7.6	26	4.2	31
2007	4-12	5.4	5.0	268	355	-4	-16.7%	24	-9.0%	23	9.1%	26	1.4%	10	19.6	20	18.5	19
2008	9-7	9.2	9.0	405	356	-1	5.4%	17	5.1%	18	2.5%	14	2.8%	8	7.3	31	10.5	28

Strategic Tendencies

Run/Pass		Rank	Offense		Rank	Defense		Rank	Other		Rank
Runs, all plays	42%	19	3+ WR	48%	19	Rush 3	24.1%	1	2+ RB, Pct Runs	65%	10
Runs, first half	42%	22	4+ WR	15%	6	Rush 4	44.8%	32	1 RB/2 TE, Pct Runs	60%	6
Runs, first down	56%	7	2+ TE	23%	23	Rush 5	25.1%	8	1RB/3+WR, Pct Runs	22%	24
Runs, second-long	31%	27	Single back	45%	26	Rush 6+	6.0%	24	Zone Blitz	2%	19
Runs, power sit.	44%	32	Play action	14%	21	Rush 7+	1.3%	17	Go for it on 4th	1.41	2
Runs, behind 2H	26%	29	Max protect	7%	21	Sacks by LB	47.5%	8	Offensive Pace	31.3	19
Pass, ahead 2H	45%	14	Outside pocket	5%	31	Sacks by DB	16.3%	5	Defensive Pace	31.3	25

The Jets used a tight end on a league-leading 95 percent of plays (tied with Houston). ● The Jets threw more screen passes on third-and-short than any offense except the Cardinals. Three-quarters of these were wide receiver screens. ● The Jets ran only 16 percent of the time when they had three or more wide receivers in the game, second to Jacksonville, and never ran from a four-wide set. ● The Jets' defense was much better against conventional formations (-11.4% DVOA, 4.4 yards per play) than shotgun formations (28.1% DVOA, 6.6 yards per play) — a massive change compared to the year before. In 2007 the Jets had the league's worst defense against conventional formations and ranked second in defense against the shotgun. ● The defense's Adjusted Sack Rate on first down was twice as high as it was on second or third down. ● The Jets big-blitzed (six or more pass rushers) less than half as often as they did in 2007. ● The Jets had the league's top DVOA against draw plays, with an asterisk — we only charted eight draws against them, and every other defense faced at least 20 draws. ● The Jets ranked sixth in defensive DVOA in the first quarter, 12th in the second quarter, and 24th in both the third and fourth quarters.

Passing

Player	DYAR	DVOA	Plays	NtYds	Avg	YAC	C%	TD	Int
Brett Favre*	334	-2.2%	560	3353	6.0	4.9	66.3%	22	21
Kellen Clemens	-44	-127.4%	5	26	5.2	3.3	60.0%	0	1

Rushing

Player	DYAR	DVOA	Plays	Yds	Avg	TD	Fum	Suc
Thomas Jones	252	11.9%	290	1312	4.5	13	2	54%
Leon Washington	95	23.8%	76	448	5.9	6	1	51%
Brad Smith	62	43.1%	12	113	9.4	0	1	--
Brett Favre*	-42	-71.3%	12	41	3.4	1	3	--
Tony Richardson	31	59.3%	10	65	6.5	0	0	70%
Jesse Chatman*	-9	-61.3%	5	8	1.6	0	0	40%

Receiving

Player	DYAR	DVOA	Plays	Ctch	Yds	Y/C	YAC	TD	C%
Laveranues Coles*	143	2.0%	115	70	839	12.0	4.1	8	61%
Jerricho Cotchery	98	-1.6%	111	71	858	12.1	4.7	6	64%
Chansi Stuckey	131	24.0%	45	32	359	11.2	5.6	4	71%
Brad Smith	-59	-53.8%	19	12	71	5.9	4.2	0	63%
Dustin Keller	55	2.3%	78	48	535	11.1	3.5	3	62%
Chris Baker*	19	2.0%	30	21	194	9.2	2.6	0	70%
Bubba Franks	-34	-51.1%	12	6	47	7.8	4.2	0	50%
Leon Washington	77	10.2%	61	47	357	7.6	7.6	2	77%
Thomas Jones	71	12.7%	42	36	207	5.8	6.5	3	86%
Tony Richardson	-43	-91.5%	7	1	4	4.0	3.0	0	14%

Offensive Line

Year	Yards	ALY	Rank	Power	Rank	10+ Yds	Rank	Stuff	Rank	Sacks	ASR	Rank	False	Cont.
2006	3.40	3.88	25	56%	27	8%	30	21%	27	34	6.7%	17	19	42
2007	3.88	3.94	23	50%	31	12%	25	18%	11	53	9.3%	30	11	44
2008	4.81	4.72	2	61%	25	20%	10	14%	4	30	6.5%	19	20	48

Year	LE	Rank	LT	Rank	Mid	Rank	RT	Rank	RE	Rank
2006	2.73	29	4.50	11	3.87	27	4.69	3	3.60	21
2007	3.42	25	3.02	32	4.08	14	4.13	18	3.92	19
2008	5.16	3	2.83	32	4.75	3	4.97	1	5.31	1

A year ago, the line was in turmoil. Mike Tannenbaum and Eric Mangini handed out $65.5 million, including $32 million in guaranteed money, to free agents Alan Faneca and Damien Woody in an attempt to fix a sieve-like line that could neither keep its quarterbacks healthy nor push defenders off the line of scrimmage. It was an expensive way to go about things, but it worked, and now the Jets will bring back the same five starters.

Alan Faneca was the prize free agent in last year's class, and he turned in an excellent performance at left guard that resulted in his eighth Pro Bowl selection. Faneca allowed left tackle D'Brickashaw Ferguson and center Nick Mangold to concentrate on their own assignments instead of worrying about rushers blowing through the A gap, so he effectively elevated the play at three different line spots. Ferguson was considered a major disappointment early in his career, and though he has improved, our game charters indicate that he does have problems with bull rushers who can get into his chest. The Titans lined up Albert Haynesworth at defensive end on several occasions, and Haynesworth plowed right through Ferguson. Because of his somewhat narrow build, Ferguson has trouble driving defenders backwards. The Jets were worst in the league at runs behind left tackle, and they only attempted it on eight percent of their total rushes. That doesn't mean that Ferguson is hopeless; he can be an effective positional blocker, and he's one of the few tackles to have the agility to easily get out into space on screen plays. Mangold had another superlative year, and he's starting to warrant serious consideration as the league's best center. He used to have problems when lined up directly across from massive nose tackles, but he has gotten stronger and now consistently wins at the point of attack no matter who is in front of him.

The right side of the line was dominant when asked to clear running lanes. Damien Woody, who came into the league as a center, has now settled in on the outside. Woody is the mirror opposite of Ferguson -- a thumper in the run game who struggles to handle edge rushers when asked to hold up in pass protection. It's certainly not unusual to have a tackle set with differing skill sets, but few teams have so extreme a disparity. While the Jets were the league's worst when running behind Ferguson, they had the best Adjusted Line Yards in the league running off right tackle. Brandon Moore is the only starter whose job was in jeopardy, as he was briefly released while the team flirted with Steelers guard Chris Kemoeatu. In the end, Kemoeatu re-signed with Pittsburgh and the Jets gave Moore a shiny new contract, a bit of flip-flopping that cost the team $3 million in guaranteed money. Matt Slauson, who played for offensive line coach Bill Callahan at Nebraska, was drafted in the sixth round to provide depth, along with two veteran holdovers, center/guard Rob Turner and tackle Wayne Turner.

Defensive Front Seven

Defensive Line	Age	Pos	Plays	TmPct	Overall Rk	Stop	Dfts	Stop%	Rk	AvYd	Rk	Pass Rush Sack	Hit	Hur	vs. Run Runs	St%	Yds	vs. Pass Pass	St%	Yds
Shaun Ellis	32	DE	58	7.0%	19	41	11	71%	66	2.1	59	8.0	2	12	44	70%	3.0	14	71%	-0.8
Kenyon Coleman*	30	DE	55	6.6%	25	43	6	78%	35	2.3	69	0.5	1	1	52	77%	2.7	3	100%	-3.7
Kris Jenkins	30	DT	54	6.5%	16	42	16	78%	35	1.1	11	3.5	5	4	44	80%	1.4	10	70%	-0.3
Mike Devito	25	DE	24	2.9%	91	18	4	75%	54	2.2	63	0.5	1	4	21	76%	2.1	3	67%	2.7
Sione Pouha	30	DT	24	2.9%	70	18	1	75%	51	3.0	69	0.5	0	0	18	83%	2.1	6	50%	6.0
C.J. Mosley*	26	DT	19	2.3%	--	10	6	53%	--	3.1	--	1.5	1	4	13	38%	4.5	6	83%	0.2
Marques Douglas	32	DE	35	4.8%	58	26	7	74%	55	1.8	48	0.0	0	1	33	76%	1.2	2	50%	11.5
Howard Green	30	DT	20	2.9%	71	15	3	75%	48	2.3	52	1.0	0	1	18	78%	2.4	2	50%	1.0

Linebackers	Age	Pos	Plays	TmPct	Overall Rk	Stop	Dfts	Stop%	AvYd	Pass Rush Sack	Hit	Hur	vs. Run Runs	St%	Rk	Yds	Rk	vs. Pass Tgts	Suc%	Rk	AdjYd	Rk
Eric Barton*	32	ILB	122	14.7%	22	63	8	52%	5.5	1.5	2	2	74	66%	39	3.4	47	34	41%	72	6.9	58
Calvin Pace	29	OLB	81	9.8%	68	47	21	58%	3.9	7.0	4	18	44	59%	77	3.3	41	28	45%	62	8.5	84
David Harris	25	ILB	76	13.3%	32	41	9	54%	5.3	1.0	1	3	46	61%	65	3.9	76	37	48%	50	6.9	59
Bryan Thomas	30	OLB	59	7.1%	91	43	17	73%	2.5	5.5	1	7	41	78%	10	2.8	21	13	51%	--	5.9	--
David Bowens*	32	OLB	34	4.1%	--	19	9	56%	3.8	4.0	5	8	13	62%	--	3.4	--	8	27%	--	10.1	--
Bart Scott	29	ILB	87	11.9%	48	59	17	68%	3.6	1.5	7	15	56	79%	9	2.7	18	33	54%	35	5.6	30

Year	Yards	ALY	Rank	Power	Rank	10+ Yds	Rank	Stuff	Rank	Sack	ASR	Rank
2006	4.65	4.93	32	67%	18	14%	8	10%	32	35	6.4%	18
2007	4.32	4.85	32	78%	30	9%	2	11%	32	29	6.6%	15
2008	3.66	3.94	9	68%	19	13%	5	16%	24	41	6.8%	12

Year	LE	Rank	LT	Rank	Mid	Rank	RT	Rank	RE	Rank
2006	4.96	28	5.21	30	4.57	25	5.64	32	4.52	23
2007	5.09	28	5.32	31	4.50	30	5.25	32	4.91	29
2008	4.11	16	4.42	21	3.92	9	4.22	20	2.83	5

Kris Jenkins was an absolute beast in his first season in New York, and the run defense fell off markedly late in the year when Jenkins suffered a herniated disk in his back. (Gang Green allowed 3.34 Adjusted Line Yards per carry before Week 13, but 4.42 ALY from Week 13 on.) While Jenkins was healthy, he was a one-man wrecking crew, stonewalling blockers and taking down running backs at the line of scrimmage, not to mention collapsing pockets and sacking quarterbacks. Jenkins' performance in Buffalo was one of the most dominant displays by any interior lineman all year; he sacked Trent Edwards twice, hurried Edwards into throwing an interception that Abram Elam returned for a touchdown, and stuffed Fred Jackson on a fourth-and-1. Jenkins will be joined up front by nine-year veteran Shaun Ellis, whose renaissance as a pass rusher coincided neatly with the arrival of Jenkins, and Marques Douglas, who Rex Ryan brought in from Baltimore to replace the departed Kenyon Coleman. It's a line with a lot of experience or with a lot of age, depending on your point of view. Mike Devito, Sione Pouha, and Howard Green figure in as rotational players.

The Jets have a stable of king-sized outside linebackers with elite athleticism in Calvin Pace, Bryan Thomas, and Vernon Gholston, and they should allow Ryan to mix and match defensive fronts and send pass rushers from anywhere and everywhere. That of course assumes that Gholston will develop into something more than this decade's Mike Mamula. Actually, that's being unfair to Mamula — Gholston signed late, was stonewalled by third-string tackles in the preseason, and played himself completely out of the defensive rotation by December. Rex Ryan has compared Gholston's potential to that of Terrell Suggs, but barring a truly incredible leap, Gholston is unlikely to see more than spot duty behind Pace and Thomas. The inside linebackers are outstanding now that David Harris is teaming with free agent prize Bart Scott. Ryan and defensive coordinator Mike Pettine never had any doubt that they wanted Scott to quarterback the defense, and they showed up on his doorstep 15 minutes after the start of free agency and flew him to New York in a private jet. It's debatable if any inside linebacker is worth $48 million, but Scott has eye-popping numbers and represents a massive upgrade over Eric Barton. Backup Marques Murrell is the younger brother of former Jet running back Adrian Murrell. Unlike a certain first-round pick, he flashed natural pass rushing ability in preseason, so while he won't crack the starting lineup, he may be in line for an increased role this fall.

Defensive Secondary

Secondary	Age	Pos	Plays	TmPct	Rk	Stop	Dfts	Yds	Rk	St%	Rk	Tgts	Tgt%	Rk	Dist	Suc%	Rk	AdjYd	Rk	Yds	PD	Int
			Overall					**vs. Run**				**vs. Pass**										
Kerry Rhodes	27	FS	89	10.7%	27	29	14	6.2	23	45%	29	36	7.4%	29	11.3	53%	37	6.3	10	6.7	6	2
Dwight Lowery	24	CB	80	9.6%	28	37	19	5.4	26	67%	7	91	18.9%	32	10.9	44%	63	7.4	40	7.4	16	1
Darrelle Revis	24	CB	74	8.9%	36	35	16	8.3	55	58%	19	77	16.1%	58	10.3	53%	29	6.3	23	5.9	13	5
Abram Elam*	28	SS	63	7.6%	64	18	9	7.2	43	32%	61	21	4.4%	70	11.5	50%	48	10.3	67	10.1	4	1
Hank Poteat*	32	CB	40	5.9%	--	16	6	7.6	--	63%	--	29	7.5%	--	6.0	50%	--	6.7	--	6.2	3	2
Eric Smith	26	FS	30	6.4%	--	9	3	8.5	--	29%	--	9	3.3%	--	13.8	48%	--	3.7	--	4.3	4	1
Drew Coleman	27	CB	26	5.6%	--	14	8	6.7	--	100%	--	26	9.6%	--	7.5	48%	--	8.2	--	8.0	6	0
David Barrett*	32	FS	22	3.9%	76	13	4	3.7	3	71%	2	20	5.9%	51	11.9	59%	19	6.9	18	6.7	3	1
Ty Law*	35	CB	21	5.8%	--	5	2	10.3	--	0%	--	25	11.7%	--	9.2	40%	--	9.4	--	9.4	3	0
Jim Leonhard	27	SS	74	10.1%	38	25	7	8.2	64	44%	33	26	5.8%	52	7.8	52%	38	7.5	28	7.4	3	1
Donald Strickland	29	CB	36	5.0%	--	21	8	4.1	--	75%	--	34	8.8%	--	5.5	48%	--	6.6	--	6.4	5	0
Lito Sheppard	28	CB	24	3.0%	--	12	6	0.0	--	0%	--	37	8.4%	--	9.5	48%	--	9.7	--	9.5	5	1

Year	Pass D Rank	vs. #1 WR	Rk	vs. #2 WR	Rk	vs. Other WR	Rk	vs. TE	Rk	vs. RB	Rk
2006	20	2.8%	17	6.1%	18	5.8%	21	-11.9%	11	2.3%	19
2007	18	20.8%	28	-8.5%	9	-12.2%	13	7.4%	17	16.6%	30
2008	16	-5.1%	11	-1.6%	13	7.9%	25	25.2%	29	8.7%	21

Darrelle Revis is the cornerstone piece that the rest of the secondary will be built around. Revis has all the qualities of a shutdown cornerback, though he sometimes gets overwhelmed by big, physical receivers. He led the team with five interceptions, including game-enders against Miami and Buffalo, and he was effective coming off the corner as a blitzer. Offenses quickly recognized that the best way to attack the Jets was to spread them out and isolate their second and third corners in coverage, so the team traded for disgruntled Eagles corner Lito Sheppard. Sheppard has been brutally inconsistent over the past four years — our game charting numbers had him as one of the league's best corners in 2006 but one of the worst in 2005, 2007, and 2008. Still, has experience as a playmaker in a pressure defense and might be helped by a change of scenery. Dwight Lowery had a fairly typical rookie season; quarterbacks threw at him a lot, and he alternated between making plays and getting his lunch money taken. In the second Patriots-Jets game, Matt Cassel spent the entire second half throwing to whoever Lowery happened to be covering and rolled up 400 yards of passing offense — after that, Lowery saw his playing time decrease in favor of a rickety Ty Law. Lowery did a great job in run support, however, and showed enough in coverage to give the team hope that he'll develop. He'll compete with Sheppard for a starting role, but even if Lowery loses, it would make sense to let him play on the outside against three-receiver sets and let Sheppard cover the quick-twitch slot receivers. Drew Coleman and former Green Bay first-rounder Ahmad Carroll are also in the mix.

The safeties look solid on paper. Jim Leonhard has more range than the departed Abram Elam, and he should allow Kerry Rhodes to play more in the box. Leonhard followed up a terrible season in Buffalo with an excellent one in Baltimore, but it remains to be seen if he had a breakout year or if he looked better than he really is due to the outstanding players around him. He's also a little small for a starting safety at 5-foot-8, 185 pounds, and every hard tackle brings Eric Smith that much closer to the starting lineup. Rhodes' had a quiet season last year, with little in the way of impact plays, but he was steady, as his Success Rate on passes improved by ten percent over 2007.

Special Teams

Year	DVOA	Rank	FG/XP	Rank	Net Kick	Rank	Kick Ret	Rank	Net Punt	Rank	Punt Ret	Rank	Hidden	Rank
2006	3.2%	5	0.4	15	-1.1	21	14.3	2	7.9	7	-2.6	24	6.7	9
2007	1.4%	10	-2.7	23	-6.7	27	17.4	3	0.5	18	-0.2	15	-0.4	15
2008	2.8%	8	-3.7	26	7.4	7	9.0	4	1.9	17	2.1	7	-6.6	21

Thanks to Mike Westhoff, the Jets routinely have one of the better special teams units in the league, and last year was no exception. Westhoff knows what he's looking for in a return man, and from Santana Moss to Justin Miller to Leon Washington, he has consistently found players who give coverage teams fits. Washington was the AFC Pro Bowl kick returner, averaging more than 25 yards per return. Washington also returned punts, but he's off the punt return team this season so he can concentrate on offense. Replacing him will be Jim Leonhard, who handled the job capably for the Ravens. Kicker Jay Feely was signed when Mike Nugent hurt himself, but he kicked so well that he held onto the job even after Nugent was ready to come back. Nugent never delivered on the expectations that came with being a second-round pick, and his surprising lack of leg strength was most evident on kickoffs, where he only managed 12 touchbacks in his time with the Jets; Feely, who was undrafted when he came out of Michigan in 1999, recorded seven touchbacks in 2008 alone. Punting was a problem last season, and the fact that the team is bringing back Reggie Hodges to compete with rookie T.J. Conley (Idaho) can't leave anyone brimming with confidence that the problem has been solved.

Coaching Staff

In many ways, Rex Ryan is the polar opposite of Eric Mangini. His responses during press conferences and interviews are candid and frequently humorous. He comes from a famous football family with a New York connection; his father, Buddy, made his reputation while working on Weeb Ewbank's staff. Rather than being a wunderkind who shot up through the ranks, Ryan was an established coordinator who was passed over for several head coaching jobs, including the one in Baltimore, before finally getting his shot with the Jets. Still, what made Ryan a more attractive candidate than Steve Spagnuolo or Jim Schwartz was the similarities his scheme shared with Mangini's. Ryan has run a classic 3-4, as well as his 46 hybrid, and his scheme is a close enough fit that he'll be able to utilize the expensive personnel that general manager Mike Tannenbaum spent the last two seasons acquiring.

Offensive coordinator Brian Schottenheimer was considered for the head coaching job, and the team thinks he has a bright future despite the December flameout; one of the preconditions the Jets management placed on Ryan was that he agree to retain Schottenheimer as offensive coordinator. Schottenheimer likes to use a lot of motion and gimmickry, which went over very well in 2006 but hasn't been as effective since then. Mike Pettine, who is the defensive coordinator (at least in name), came over with Ryan from Baltimore, where he was the outside linebackers coach for four seasons. His primary job is to spend a lot of time with Vernon Gholston, who in Year Two is already a reclamation project. Mike Westhoff returns for his ninth season as special teams coach.

Oakland Raiders

In coverage of the recent financial crisis, you may have read about the dangers of insolvent institutions being propped up by government support. When Japan went into recession in the mid-1990s, a number of banks kept draining government bailout funds but were too weak to lend money and help the economy recover. Instead, they made a series of pointless high-stakes gambles, desperately trying to resurrect their past status as solvent financial institutions. These institutions came to be known as "zombie banks."

In much the same way, the Oakland Raiders are a "zombie franchise."

If the NFL were a European soccer league, the Raiders would be relegated by now, playing in the third division against the Pacifica Islanders and Portland Monarchs. They were only propped up this long by the efforts of former head coach Jon Gruden and quarterback Rich Gannon, who led an early-2000s renaissance that peaked with an appearance in Super Bowl XXXVII. The bubble burst two years after Gruden departed for Tampa Bay, and since then the Raiders have six straight seasons finishing 5-11 or worse. They've had five head coaches since Gruden and five different quarterbacks on top of the depth chart since Gannon. Despite the churn and turnover, they make the same mistakes every offseason, signing veteran free agents to exorbitant contracts above market rate, overdrafting players because of their ob-

session with speed, and cornering the market on wide receivers with knee problems. The Raiders have become so predictable that even their surprising decisions on draft day fit neatly into the historical pattern of "surprising Raiders decisions."

And always, there is the never-ending soap opera. There were rumors that owner Al Davis would fire wunderkind head coach Lane Kiffin before the 2008 season even started. Davis blamed Kiffin for underachieving talent; Kiffin pointed out that there wasn't much talent to begin with. Kiffin said that Davis wouldn't talk to him, while Davis asserted that he spoke to Kiffin regularly. The axe finally fell four weeks in, when Davis held a bizarre press conference where he called out Kiffin as "a professional liar." The head job went to offensive line coach Tom Cable, whose prior head coaching record consisted of four seasons at the University of Idaho, where he went 11-35 and lost five games to Division I-AA teams. Even that didn't end the soap opera; by the end of the season, Cable and Kiffin were sniping at each other in the press over Kiffin stealing away Raiders assistants for his new staff at the University of Tennessee.

Cable may have won more games than Kiffin, but basically it was the same-old, same-old. Including 2007, the Raiders had a -24.9% DVOA under Kiffin and a -25.4% DVOA under Cable. Occasionally the

---

RAIDERS SUMMARY

2008 Record: 5-11

Pythagorean Wins: 4.6 (27th)

DVOA: -23.3% (29th)

Offense: -21.3% (31st)

Defense: 7.8% (19th)

Special Teams: 5.8% (2nd)

Variance: 32.3% (32nd)

2008: Inconsistent Raiders struggle to score with the pass and stop the run.

2009: For the good of the game, it is time to ask Al Davis to step aside and find new ownership.

2009 Mean Projection: 6.0 wins

On the Clock (0-3): 13%

Loserville (4-6): 46%

Mediocrity (7-8): 25%

Playoff Contender (9-10): 14%

Super Bowl Contender (11+): 2%

Projected Average Opponent: 2.0% (11th)

2009 Raiders Schedule

Week	Opp.	Week	Opp.	Week	Opp.
1	SD (Mon.)	7	NYJ	13	at PIT
2	at KC	8	at SD	14	WAS
3	DEN	9	BYE	15	at DEN
4	at HOU	10	KC	16	at CLE
5	at NYG	11	CIN	17	BAL
6	PHI	12	at DAL (Thu.)		

Raiders would put all the pieces together, particularly when they ended the year with surprising upsets of Houston and Tampa Bay, but there's a difference between ending on a high note and just plain inconsistency. The Raiders were the league's least consistent team last year, ranking last in offensive variance and 30th in defensive variance.

The other big story from Oakland's 2008 offseason, besides the Davis-Kiffin soap opera, was the signing of some ridiculous veteran contracts. This offseason was highlighted by the un-doing of most of those contracts, whether the veterans in question flopped or not. Kwame Harris, the Human Hold? Adios. Justin Griffith, Kalimba Edwards, see you later. Gibril Wilson played well at strong safety, but the Raiders needed salary cap space. Javon Walker kept his roster spot with a massive contract restructuring. Tommy Kelly stuck around because, even though he's absurdly overpaid, the Raiders aren't going to do better.

The Raiders followed up their great veteran purge with a head-scratching 2009 draft. Oakland was in desperate need of a number-one wide receiver and saw Michael Crabtree, the consensus best receiver in the draft, drop into their laps at number seven. Instead, they chose Darrius Heyward-Bey out of Maryland, a size/speed prospect who ran a sub-4.4 40-yard dash at the combine but had only 51 receptions in 2007 and 42 in 2008, less than half of what Crabtree had at Texas Tech.

The problem is not that Heyward-Bey won't be a successful NFL receiver; he certainly has the raw talent to make an impact. The problem is that the Raiders didn't get proper value for their pick. They could have traded down to a team that wanted Crabtree, gained extra picks, and Heyward-Bey would almost assuredly have been there later in the first round — where he would also have demanded a smaller rookie contract. The lack of value from the Heyward-Bey pick was nothing compared to their second-round pick, safety Michael Mitchell, a player who every independent draft analyst had going in the sixth round or later. (To be fair to the Raiders, a report in the *Chicago Tribune* stated that the Bears were planning on choosing Mitchell two picks later, although this was later contradicted by a report in the *Chicago Sun-Times* which said the Bears were waiting to take Mitchell with one of their two fourth-round picks.)

Finally, a team whose biggest problem on defense has been stopping the run spent three later-round picks on pass rushers without taking a defensive tackle or standard-sized linebacker. Sure, Mitchell is supposed to help them stop the run, but the Raiders' problem has been stopping the run in the front seven, not stopping the run with a strong safety. Last year, strong safety Wilson made 87 run plays (tackles or assists), a total 50 percent higher than any other safety in the league. It's the highest total for any defensive back in our individual stats database, which currently goes back to 1999. The Raiders didn't need to replace Wilson, they needed to replace the guys in front of him.

No matter how controversial the Heyward-Bey selection was, the Raiders are not going to sink or swim on the strength of this year's first-round pick. They are going to sink or swim on the strength of their first-round pick from two years ago: quarterback JaMarcus Russell. Unlike this year's picks, the Russell selection didn't upset conventional wisdom, but so far Russell is having the same developmental problems that have plagued so many other Oakland youngsters.

According to our DYAR stats, only two quarterbacks with at least 300 pass attempts had more negative value than Russell in 2008. It was his second straight season below replacement level, and while the Raiders would like to believe that Russell has plenty of room for growth, two years of negative DYAR has been a remarkably accurate indicator of which young quarterbacks will wash out of the league.

Thirty-five quarterbacks drafted between 1995 and 2007 threw at least 50 passes in each of their first two NFL seasons, and a dozen of those quarterbacks had negative DYAR (i.e., below replacement level) in both seasons (Table 1). Is there reason to believe that Russell can become the first successful quarterback off this list? Sure, but nothing we might say about Russell wouldn't also have been said about a number of these other players. Russell has tremendous arm strength, but that was also a signature trait for players like Kyle Boller and Quincy Carter. We want to expect that a first overall pick will develop, no matter how slowly, but Tim Couch and Alex Smith also went first overall,

Table 1: QBs Below Replacement Level In First Two Seasons

Player	Team	Year 1	Att Y1	DYAR Y1	Year 2	Att Y2	DYAR Y2
Kyle Boller	BAL	2003	224	-289	2004	464	-118
Quincy Carter	DAL	2001	176	-105	2002	221	-13
Tim Couch	CLE	1999	399	-683	2000	215	-96
Charlie Frye	CLE	2005	164	-94	2006	392	-215
Rex Grossman	CHI	2003	72	-53	2004	84	-6
Joey Harrington	DET	2002	430	-272	2003	554	-436
Danny Kanell	NYG	1996	70	-195	1997	325	-87
Mike McMahon	DET	2001	115	-96	2002	147	-196
JaMarcus Russell	OAK	2007	66	-144	2008	402	-188
Akili Smith	CIN	1999	153	-432	2000	267	-30
Alex Smith	SF	2005	165	-880	2006	442	-125
Danny Wuerffel	NO	1997	113	-275	1998	144	-272
Spergon Wynn	CLE/MIN	2000	54	-21	2001	98	-422

and Joey Harrington and Akili Smith both went in the top three. Russell's not responsible for the mess surrounding the Oakland franchise — but then again, it isn't like Joey Harrington had any control over Matt Millen's constantly blown draft picks.

This cloud does have a silver lining, if we look at Russell's second season in two halves. Russell suffered from knee and ankle injuries during the second half of the season, but improved his performance anyway. Russell completed 49 percent of his passes through Week 9, then 62 percent of his passes the rest of the way. He averaged -44 DYAR over his first eight starts, but 24 DYAR for his last seven. If that second-half improvement carries over into 2009, perhaps Russell can avoid the following in the footsteps of other first overall busts like Couch, Smith, and David Carr.

Cable has publicly accused Russell of needing a better work ethic, and it is obvious from looking at him that he has problems controlling his weight. To push their young quarterback, the Raiders signed Jeff Garcia as a veteran backup. Jeff Garcia is not a guy who you bring in when you want to have a shiny, happy locker room, and it didn't take him long to start pushing Russell through the power of the press. When Russell struggled with his accuracy at OTAs, Garcia gave a radio interview to Chris Myers, stating that "with what I bring as a player, from a competitive nature … if that gives us a better chance to win football games, then that decision is going to have to be left up to the coach and hopefully he can make the right decision for the team."

If Russell does get benched for Garcia sometime this season, it will continue the distressing pattern of Raiders first-round picks getting replaced when they can't make it as starters in year three. Fabian Washington,

Tyler Brayton, Napoleon Harris, and Michael Huff were all benched partway through their third seasons. Philip Buchanon was traded away after three years. Robert Gallery didn't get benched, but he did get switched over to the less-important guard position. The one exception is Nnamdi Asomugha, because no matter what rules hold as the Oakland organization grows more and more pathetic, Nnamdi Asomugha is always the exception. He's also the exception to Oakland's habit of handing out questionable contracts. When the Raiders gave Nnamdi Asomugha the biggest contract ever given to a defensive player in the NFL, nobody questioned the move.

Asomugha is not the only successful part of this Raiders team. The running game last year was not as productive in 2008 as it had been the year before, but it is poised for a rebound in 2009. The Raiders have a strong stable of backs in Justin Fargas, Michael Bush, and 2008 first-round pick Darren McFadden, whose underwhelming rookie year was in large part caused by a case of turf toe. Cable's zone-blocking scheme was successful two years ago, and should be successful again this year, especially with developing youngster Mario Henderson and former Jaguars left tackle Khalif Barnes replacing the horrendous Kwame Harris and the aging Cornell Green. If Russell clicks with speedsters like Heyward-Bey and Johnnie Lee Higgins, that will stretch the defense and free things up even more for the running backs to gain yardage. "After all," thinks Al Davis, "that's how it worked in 1976 and 1983."

Which is the problem, of course. Like a zombie bank taking ridiculous risks as it desperately tries to regain its solvency, the Raiders have been flailing around making the same mistakes over and over again as they try to recapture the magic of the '70s. Everything is about speed. The receivers can run fast but can't catch. The defensive linemen are fast enough to harass the quarterback, but rarely bring him down. The linebackers do well covering passes but have trouble sifting through trash to stop the run. The offensive line is agile enough to excel at zone-blocking but not strong enough to stop opposing pass rushers. And every single year, the flags fly, with the Raiders continually ranking near the top of the league in penalties.

This team is not hopeless. If Russell finally starts to

match his potential — or the Raiders pull him for Garcia early — and the defense stays relatively injury-free, this team could find itself 8-8 or even 9-7. But unless that improvement is driven by a dramatic leap forward by Russell, it won't represent a step towards annual contention. And if the front office stays in the same rut making the same weird offseason decisions, even improvement from Russell won't turn this into a winning franchise.

Aaron Schatz

2008 Raiders Stats by Week

Wk	vs.	W-L	PF	PA	YDF	YDA	TO	Total	Off	Def	ST
1	DEN	L	14	41	307	441	-1	-91%	-45%	54%	9%
2	@KC	W	23	8	355	190	0	52%	-3%	-45%	11%
3	@BUF	L	23	24	247	378	+2	-7%	-6%	10%	9%
4	SD	L	18	28	323	295	0	-7%	-27%	-18%	1%
5	BYE										
6	@NO	L	3	34	226	441	-2	-87%	-48%	40%	0%
7	NYJ	W	16	13	344	418	+3	-10%	-13%	1%	4%
8	@BAL	L	10	29	234	375	0	-21%	5%	16%	-9%
9	ATL	L	0	24	77	453	-1	-136%	-128%	17%	9%
10	CAR	L	6	17	259	219	+1	-12%	-66%	-78%	-24%
11	@MIA	L	15	17	186	382	+1	-14%	-26%	13%	25%
12	@DEN	W	31	10	318	319	+2	66%	30%	-10%	26%
13	KC	L	13	20	271	301	-1	-44%	-26%	20%	3%
14	@SD	L	7	34	163	372	-3	-69%	-64%	25%	19%
15	NE	L	26	49	334	487	0	-77%	-13%	49%	-15%
16	HOU	W	27	16	362	324	0	51%	4%	-26%	21%
17	@TB	W	31	24	337	380	0	14%	31%	27%	10%

Trends and Splits

	Offense	Rank	Defense	Rank
Total DVOA	-21.3%	31	7.8%	19
Unadjusted VOA	-16.1%	28	13.3%	26
Weighted trend	-20.0%	31	8.2%	19
Variance	15.8%	32	4.8%	10
Average opponent	11.1%	1	9.3%	29
Passing	-17.7%	30	4.2%	13
Rushing	-11.0%	31	10.7%	27
First down	-9.2%	25	0.1%	16
Second down	-13.4%	26	3.5%	13
Third down	-51.2%	32	27.3%	29
First half	-32.4%	32	5.5%	17
Second half	-10.9%	24	10.3%	23
Red Zone	-30.2%	29	31.8%	28
Late and close	1.1%	21	6.2%	18

Five-Year Performance

Year	W-L	Pyth	Est W	PF	PA	TO	Total	Rk	Off	Rk	Def	Rk	ST	Rk	Off AGL	Rk	Def AGL	Rk
2004	5-11	5.1	6.2	320	442	-17	-14.3%	23	0.5%	14	13.3%	26	-1.5%	22	24.6	13	19.6	19
2005	4-12	5.5	7.4	290	383	-4	-6.4%	20	-2.2%	15	0.7%	20	-3.5%	29	16.3	14	33.3	2
2006	2-14	2.7	3.9	168	332	-23	-31.4%	32	-36.5%	32	-8.1%	8	-3.0%	26	25.3	10	4.5	30
2007	4-12	4.9	4.1	283	398	-11	-28.8%	29	-17.4%	28	6.8%	22	-4.6%	29	25.1	9	18.2	20
2008	5-11	4.6	5.0	263	388	+1	-23.3%	29	-21.3%	31	7.8%	19	5.8%	2	35.8	10	18.4	19

Strategic Tendencies

Run/Pass		Rank	Offense		Rank	Defense		Rank	Other		Rank
Runs, all plays	49%	6	3+ WR	38%	28	Rush 3	8.3%	7	2+ RB, Pct Runs	60%	19
Runs, first half	51%	3	4+ WR	2%	32	Rush 4	70.2%	8	1 RB/2 TE, Pct Runs	52%	16
Runs, first down	56%	9	2+ TE	24%	19	Rush 5	12.8%	30	1RB/3+WR, Pct Runs	31%	10
Runs, second-long	48%	5	Single back	44%	29	Rush 6+	8.7%	13	Zone Blitz	1%	28
Runs, power sit.	69%	12	Play action	25%	3	Rush 7+	1.7%	11	Go for it on 4th	1.61	1
Runs, behind 2H	36%	9	Max protect	10%	6	Sacks by LB	6.3%	28	Offensive Pace	31.3	20
Pass, ahead 2H	24%	32	Outside pocket	15%	9	Sacks by DB	6.3%	20	Defensive Pace	31.5	28

The Aggressiveness Index (i.e. go for it on fourth) rating above is for Tom Cable only, and it requires a little explanation. Overall, Cable only "went for it" on three out of 24 fourth downs (excluding second-half catch-up situations). However, he ends up with a very high AI rating because those three happened to be very unusual situations: fourth-and-3, fourth-and-6, and fourth-and-10. ● The Raiders need to run play-action as often as possible. They ranked third in play-action frequency last year, but that still wasn't enough, because they were so much better when they used a play-fake. With play-action, the Raiders had a 37.9% DVOA, 12th in the league; without play-action, they had -39.3% DVOA, worst in the league. ● JaMarcus Russell connected on just 37 percent of passes when facing five or more pass rushers, the worst completion percentage in the league (minimum 100 passes). ● The Raiders' offense had an Adjusted Sack Rate of 14.5 percent on third down, more than twice as high as their Adjusted Sack Rate on first or second down. Even worse, the Raiders fumbled on 10 of these 25 sacks. ● Looking for evidence that the Raiders linebackers have trouble sifting through trash to make tackles? For two straight seasons, the Raiders have been significantly better against runs from one-back sets as opposed to two-back sets. Last year they allowed 4.5 yards per carry and -2.6% DVOA with one back, 5.0 yards per carry and 14.2% DVOA with two backs.

Passing

Player	DYAR	DVOA	Plays	NtYds	Avg	YAC	C%	TD	Int
JaMarcus Russell	-122	-16.0%	402	2313	5.8	5.3	54.1%	13	8
Andrew Walter	-213	-77.8%	53	163	3.1	6.4	45.8%	0	3
Marques Tuiasosopo*	-87	-288.0%	5	-22	-4.4	0.0	50.0%	0	0
Jeff Garcia	569	10.9%	395	2591	6.6	4.9	65.9%	12	6
Bruce Gradkowski	-234	-192.2%	25	8	0.3	3.3	33.3%	0	3

Rushing

Player	DYAR	DVOA	Plays	Yds	Avg	TD	Fum	Suc
Justin Fargas	-77	-17.3%	219	841	3.8	1	4	42%
Darren McFadden	-2	-8.9%	113	500	4.4	4	3	38%
Michael Bush	17	-3.9%	95	421	4.4	3	1	41%
JaMarcus Russell	31	18.6%	15	129	8.6	1	1	--
Johnnie Lee Higgins	25	146.7%	3	34	11.3	0	0	--
Andrew Walter	-4	-38.0%	3	19	6.3	0	0	--
Jeff Garcia	20	-1.0%	30	143	4.8	1	2	--
Gary Russell	13	-0.5%	28	77	2.8	3	0	57%
Lorenzo Neal	1	-7.5%	12	25	2.1	0	0	50%

Receiving

Player	DYAR	DVOA	Plays	Ctch	Yds	Y/C	YAC	TD	C%
Ronald Curry*	-75	-33.0%	47	18	181	10.1	1.4	2	38%
Ashley Lelie*	-91	-38.0%	45	11	197	17.9	2.2	2	24%
Johnnie Lee Higgins	29	-3.6%	42	22	366	16.6	9.1	4	52%
Javon Walker	4	-11.0%	32	15	196	13.1	2.1	1	47%
Chaz Schilens	2	-11.8%	32	15	226	15.1	2.8	2	47%
Zach Miller	92	9.2%	86	56	778	13.9	4.4	1	65%
Tony Stewart	1	-6.1%	15	11	81	7.4	2.4	0	73%
Darren McFadden	107	33.3%	39	30	285	9.5	9.8	0	77%
Michael Bush	35	7.6%	30	19	162	8.5	8.3	0	63%
Justin Fargas	-8	-25.9%	15	10	52	5.2	5.9	0	67%
Justin Griffith*	40	34.6%	13	9	85	9.4	5.2	1	69%
Luke Lawton	-8	-26.2%	11	6	30	5.0	5.0	0	55%
Lorenzo Neal	-36	-55.8%	15	7	35	5.0	7.9	0	47%

Offensive Line

Year	Yards	ALY	Rank	Power	Rank	10+ Yds	Rank	Stuff	Rank	Sacks	ASR	Rank	False	Cont.
2006	3.74	3.81	29	58%	25	15%	18	22%	29	72	12.3%	32	28	26
2007	4.20	4.10	16	55%	25	16%	18	19%	21	41	8.6%	27	38	34
2008	4.15	3.92	26	62%	22	17%	14	19%	19	39	9.4%	30	30	29

Year	LE	Rank	LT	Rank	Mid	Rank	RT	Rank	RE	Rank
2006	4.33	12	3.70	28	3.85	28	4.37	9	3.06	28
2007	3.65	24	4.45	11	3.95	20	4.38	13	4.14	14
2008	4.98	6	4.54	9	3.55	29	4.36	8	2.97	30

Oakland's linemen took a step back after their run-blocking improvement of 2007. Perhaps they were distracted when their position coach had to take over the whole team. Robert Gallery and Cooper Carlisle remain at guard this season, but the center and tackles will be new. Miami signed away Oakland center Jake Grove in free agency, so the Raiders sent a sixth-rounder to the Dolphins for the player Grove will replace, Samson Satele. This is a great example of adding value by trading for a player who fits your scheme better than he fits the scheme on his current team; Satele is not a strong enough blocker for Miami's power-running attack, but his agility fits in with Oakland's zone-blocking scheme. The tackles will be free agent signing Khalif Barnes, formerly of Jacksonville, and 2007 third-rounder Mario Henderson, although it is a bit unsure which one will play on which side. The Raiders are very high on Henderson, who moved into the starting lineup last December after two years of preparation. His particular strengths include proper technique with his hands, moving his feet laterally, and — unique perhaps for an Oakland lineman — avoiding penalties. (In proper flag-happy Oakland tradition, the Raiders managed fewer false starts than the year before *and still ranked second in the NFL*.) Barnes has been absurdly inconsistent during his NFL career, but remember, it has only been one year since he was the anchor of an excellent offensive line for a team that went 11-5. The Raiders also signed Erik Pears from Denver, giving them another backup with starting experience in a similar zone blocking scheme. As for last year's starting tackles, Cornell Green remains for depth, while infamous YouTube block-blowing celebrity Kwame Harris has been mercifully put out to pasture.

Defensive Front Seven

Defensive Line	Age	Pos	Plays	TmPct	Overall Rk	Stop	Dfts	Stop%	Rk	AvYd	Rk	Pass Rush Sack	Hit	Hur	vs. Run Runs	St%	Yds	vs. Pass Pass	St%	Yds
Tommy Kelly	29	DT	58	7.0%	8	46	11	79%	29	2.8	65	4.5	6	13	50	78%	3.6	8	88%	-2.1
Jay Richardson	25	DE	53	6.4%	31	37	8	70%	72	2.6	77	3.0	1	6	47	66%	3.2	6	100%	-2.7
Kalimba Edwards*	30	DE	47	6.5%	29	31	14	66%	80	2.7	80	5.0	3	11	39	64%	3.4	8	75%	-0.4
Gerard Warren	31	DT	41	5.0%	36	34	13	83%	10	1.0	10	4.0	2	5	35	83%	1.9	6	83%	-4.0
Terdell Sands	30	DT	31	3.7%	58	27	6	87%	4	1.7	23	2.0	2	3	26	88%	2.0	5	80%	0.0
Derrick Burgess	31	DE	26	5.0%	48	22	9	85%	14	0.7	15	3.5	5	18	19	84%	1.9	7	86%	-2.6
Trevor Scott	25	DE	15	1.8%	--	9	7	60%	--	1.5	--	5.0	1	4	8	50%	4.0	7	71%	-1.4

Linebackers	Age	Pos	Plays	TmPct	Overall Rk	Stop	Dfts	Stop%	AvYd	Pass Rush Sack	Hit	Hur	vs. Run Runs	St%	Rk	Yds	Rk	vs. Pass Tgts	Suc%	Rk	AdjYd	Rk
Kirk Morrison	27	ILB	137	16.5%	12	81	18	59%	5.1	1.0	1	0	94	70%	21	3.2	40	37	43%	66	8.5	85
Thomas Howard	26	OLB	101	12.2%	43	60	23	59%	5.4	1.0	2	3	62	61%	64	4.6	97	42	72%	4	4.6	8
Ricky Brown	26	OLB	38	10.5%	--	16	2	42%	6.2	0.0	0	1	26	50%	--	4.3	--	13	34%	--	7.9	--
Greg Ellis	34	OLB	36	4.7%	--	20	12	56%	3.1	7.5	9	7	22	50%	--	4.0	--	4	44%	--	4.5	--

Year	Yards	ALY	Rank	Power	Rank	10+ Yds	Rank	Stuff	Rank	Sack	ASR	Rank
2006	4.06	4.03	11	61%	11	16%	16	20%	10	34	7.5%	11
2007	5.06	4.36	27	72%	27	25%	31	18%	22	27	5.8%	24
2008	4.65	4.46	28	75%	28	18%	14	15%	27	32	7.3%	6

Year	LE	Rank	LT	Rank	Mid	Rank	RT	Rank	RE	Rank
2006	3.86	15	3.31	5	4.06	11	4.56	23	4.56	25
2007	4.42	23	5.02	28	4.38	28	3.85	11	4.25	20
2008	3.81	11	4.09	15	4.37	21	5.19	31	5.36	30

The Raiders' run defense collapsed in 2007, and last year's attempts to reverse that collapse didn't work. Big-money Tommy Kelly moved from defensive end to tackle, but failed to provide a stout wall in the middle. His average run tackle came after a gain of 3.6 yards, the highest figure for any defensive tackle who made at least 20 running plays. The Raiders signed pass-rushing end Kalimba Edwards away from Detroit, and he stopped the run, well, like a pass-rushing end. Meanwhile, last-chance veterans like Ed Hartwell and Greg Spires never even made it out of training camp. Edwards and the other Oakland linemen did manage to get to the other team's quarterback fairly often, although getting near the quarterback doesn't mean taking him down — game charters marked the Raiders with a hurry on 16 percent of pass plays, fifth in the NFL, but they were a dismal 30th in Adjusted Sack Rate. The Raiders were also one of just five defenses to allow a positive DVOA even when they managed to hurry the quarterback.

Continuing the theme, both outside linebackers, Thomas Howard and Ricky Brown, are better pass defenders than they are run defenders. According to scouts, the same is true about middle linebacker Kirk Morrison, but his stats tell the opposite story. Morrison had an off year in coverage (after ranking in the top ten linebackers in both Success Rate and Adjusted Yards per Pass in 2007) while putting up reasonable numbers against the run. Only 11 linebackers were involved in a higher percentage of their team's run tackles. Unfortunately, we have no count of opportunities and the subjective evidence says that Morrison whiffs as often as he makes the play — charters probably noted Morrison missing a tackle more than any other defender in the NFL last year.

Jay Richardson will step in to the starting lineup after Edwards was cut, and they have played around with the idea of moving Brown to the middle to back up Morrison and replacing him with reserve Jon Alston, a 2006 third-rounder originally drafted by St. Louis. Oakland did use three picks this year on players for the front seven, but those players include a very raw pass-rushing end (third-rounder Matt Shaughnessy of Wisconsin) and two DE/OLB tweeners (Slade Norris of Oregon State in the fourth, Stryker Sulak of Missouri in the sixth) who would fit better on a team that played a 3-4. (Odd, since they are now the only 4-3 team in their division.) If the Raiders actually want to try improving their run defense, you may see undrafted free agent Frantz Joseph from Florida Atlantic, who finished second in Division I-A in tackles per game.

(Right before we went to press, the Raiders signed Dallas cap casualty Greg Ellis, who would move to defensive end in the Oakland 4-3. He's still an effective player, but brings Oakland yet another defender whose game is about taking down the quarterback, not defending the run.)

Defensive Secondary

Secondary	Age	Pos	Plays	TmPct	Rk	Stop	Dfts	vs. Run Yds	Rk	St%	Rk	Tgts	Tgt%	Rk	Dist	Suc%	Rk	AdjYd	Rk	Yds	PD	Int
Gibril Wilson*	28	SS	134	16.2%	3	62	17	4.6	10	55%	12	42	10.6%	3	12.5	53%	34	10.4	70	10.3	2	2
Hiram Eugene	29	FS	54	6.5%	68	12	1	9.5	70	23%	69	8	1.9%	78	16.7	37%	75	7.9	40	8.9	1	0
Nnamdi Asomugha	28	CB	49	6.3%	71	25	8	4.5	14	40%	46	32	8.6%	83	11.0	58%	14	5.9	15	6.2	7	1
Chris Johnson	30	CB	44	5.7%	75	22	12	13.8	77	25%	76	61	16.5%	53	14.3	67%	2	5.5	8	6.2	10	3
Michael Huff	26	SS	29	3.5%	77	10	4	8.2	63	40%	40	24	6.1%	49	10.8	55%	26	8.5	50	8.5	4	0
Rashad Baker*	27	FS	28	5.4%	--	14	7	6.2	--	62%	--	8	3.1%	--	21.0	68%	--	6.7	--	7.3	4	3
Stanford Routt	26	CB	23	3.0%	--	9	5	18.8	--	25%	--	32	8.6%	--	12.8	54%	--	6.8	--	6.8	6	0
Keith Davis	31	FS	25	3.3%	--	11	2	4.5	--	59%	--	11	2.5%	--	13.6	8%	--	16.5	--	15.9	0	0

Year	Pass D Rank	vs. #1 WR	Rk	vs. #2 WR	Rk	vs. Other WR	Rk	vs. TE	Rk	vs. RB	Rk
2006	4	-23.6%	2	28.6%	30	-20.2%	7	-2.8%	17	-18.9%	10
2007	13	-32.3%	1	28.9%	31	5.0%	23	-10.4%	7	7.6%	25
2008	13	-19.6%	2	31.0%	29	-0.4%	22	-16.6%	5	3.8%	14

Archie Manning. Lee Roy Selmon. Buck Williams. Ernie Banks. Steve Carlton in the early Phillies years. On the historic list of great players trapped on bad teams, the name Nnamdi Asomugha will take a prime position. Asomugha is the best cornerback in the league; with Champ Bailey getting older and struggling with injury last year, there isn't even a question anymore. No, he wasn't in the top ten for Success Rate or Adjusted Yards per Pass, but does it matter when he completely shuts down one side of the field? We charted Asomugha in coverage on 32 passes, which tied for 96th in the NFL despite the fact that Asomugha started 15 games. Only 20 percent of passes against Oakland were categorized as "short left," with every other defense at 24 percent or higher. When Asomugha did allow a reception, receivers averaged just 0.7 yards after catch, making him the only cornerback with more than 15 charted passes to average less than a yard after catch.

DeAngelo Hall was just miserable across from Asomugha, but veteran Chris Johnson played very well after the Raiders cut Hall at midseason. The Raiders signed him to a four-year, $11.3 million contract in the offseason, but you have to wonder if the Raiders are going to get the player they got in 2008. Johnson is a 30-year-old veteran who bounced around to four different teams after Green Bay took him with a seventh-round pick in 2003, and he had one career start before last season. That half-season performance screams "fluke." Stanford Routt is a reasonable nickelback, but would be stretched if inserted into the starting lineup. Behind those three are Justin Miller, picked up after the Jets waived him last year, and John Bowie, who has only played two games in the two seasons since he became famous as the player chosen with the pick acquired in the Randy Moss trade.

The Raiders made Gibril Wilson the third-highest paid safety in the NFL before last season, then cut him in February to make salary cap space. The remaining safeties have a lot of promise but also a lot to prove. Hiram Eugene is best when playing deep centerfield. Tyvon Branch is a hard-hitter who excelled on special teams last season. Michael Huff probably has one more year to prove he wasn't a draft bust, but even he may not have as much to prove as second-rounder Michael Mitchell, the guy nobody except the Raiders had in the top 100 on their draft board. Our friend Russ Lande did get to Mitchell in his 2009 draft guide, calling him "the type of safety you sign as a free agent if you need a backup safety who can contribute as a short-yardage run support safety and on special teams, but not good enough in coverage to get regular playing time on defense." That may be a problem as the Raiders plan to alternate safeties at strong and free instead of having defined roles.

Special Teams

Year	DVOA	Rank	FG/XP	Rank	Net Kick	Rank	Kick Ret	Rank	Net Punt	Rank	Punt Ret	Rank	Hidden	Rank
2006	-3.0%	26	-0.6	18	-15.9	31	9.8	4	-8.1	28	-3.0	26	2.2	14
2007	-4.6%	29	2.9	10	0.8	14	-7.6	29	-5.8	25	-17.2	32	13.2	3
2008	5.8%	2	1.9	14	-0.8	18	3.6	13	13.9	4	15.2	1	16.2	3

Here's something that went right for the Raiders in 2008, as Oakland had the fourth-highest improvement in special teams DVOA since 1994, and the highest since 2000 (Table 2). The biggest turnaround was from Johnnie Lee Higgins. In 2007, his punt returns were worth -8.8 points, with two muffed punts, two fumbles, and lost yardage on three of 20 returns. In 2008, he was worth a league-high 15.2 points, with three touchdowns and no fumbles. Higgins wasn't that great on kick returns, but Justin Miller was after he signed with Oakland at midseason. Shane Lechler was fabulous as always, and the coverage team further limited opponents by stripping the ball three times and allowing only four returns longer than 20 yards. Sebastian Janikowski was mediocre on field goals and kickoffs. Unfortunately for Oakland, special teams are so inconsistent that the Raiders could easily go back to being below-average in 2009, like five of the teams on Table 2. One player to watch is Tyvon Branch — the rookie safety from Connecticut was a big part of the improved punt coverage, but he may not be on special teams if he moves into the starting lineup to replace Gibril Wilson.

Table 2: Largest Year-to-Year Special Teams Improvement, 1994-2008

Team	Year	ST DVOA Prev Year	ST DVOA	Change	ST DVOA Next Year
SEA	1998	-9.8%	3.3%	13.1%	3.4%
NYJ	1997	-6.8%	5.6%	12.4%	-0.9%
CHI	1998	-8.2%	2.4%	10.7%	-2.3%
OAK	2008	-4.6%	5.8%	10.3%	--
CHI	2006	-2.6%	7.6%	10.2%	9.5%
NO	2002	0.7%	10.0%	9.3%	-1.2%
CIN	2003	-8.1%	1.2%	9.2%	3.7%
BUF	2004	-1.7%	7.5%	9.2%	7.2%
KC	1997	-3.2%	5.9%	9.1%	-1.6%
WAS	2003	-6.7%	2.2%	8.9%	-3.9%

Coaching Staff

Tom Cable's main qualities as head coach of the Oakland Raiders are loyalty to Al Davis and a willingness to be head coach of the Oakland Raiders. This is a job that numerous young coaching candidates haven't even wanted to interview for in recent years. Cable's first year as the non-interim coach brings a heavy amount of turnover to the assistant ranks. The Raiders technically won't have an offensive coordinator; Cable will call plays and handle the running game strategy while Ted Tollner will be "passing game coordinator." Tollner was quarterbacks coach in San Francisco last year; before that he was offensive coordinator under Steve Mariucci in both Detroit and San Francisco. Also on staff is former Jets coordinator Paul Hackett, who as quarterbacks coach is responsible for developing JaMarcus Russell.

Longtime defensive coordinator Rex Ryan decided there was a limit to how often Al Davis could pass him up for the top job, so he took Eric Mangini's invitation to come to Cleveland. Former Seahawks coordinator John Marshall will probably bring some significant changes to Oakland's defensive strategy. The Seahawks blitzed much more often than the Raiders, sending five pass rushers nearly twice as often and ranking fourth in zone blitzes compared to just 28th for Oakland. In the secondary, Seattle primarily played a Cover-2 zone, which seems like a bad fit for a team that stars Nnamdi Asomugha. Marshall does have a history of adapting his zone when he feels he has a top cornerback, however, and in the second half of both 2007 and 2008 he let Marcus Trufant play more man-on-man against the other team's top receiver.

Brian Schneider, the architect of last year's special teams turnaround, left Oakland to take the same position at USC. Only in Oakland would a successful coordinator happily make a lateral move to a college program. He'll be replaced by John Fassel, son of Jim, who has been a special teams assistant in Oakland and Baltimore.

Philadelphia Eagles

Ninety-point-nine percent.

Those are the odds that this essay would be totally different. Those are the odds, heading into Week 17, that the Eagles needed to overcome to make the playoffs. Using the log5 methodology (as seen in last year's Giants essay) and each team's Pythagorean win percentage, the Eagles needed to beat the Cowboys (60.2 percent chance of occurring), while the Raiders beat the Buccaneers (19.7 percent chance, without factoring in the game's 1 p.m. EST start in Tampa or the absence of Nnamdi Asomugha) and either the Texans beat the Bears (41.9 percent) or the Giants beat the Vikings (34.8 percent, without including the fact that the Giants played substitutes for a good portion of the game). The likelihood of all those things happening is 9.1 percent.

Of course, the Raiders shocked the Buccaneers and the Bears lost to the Texans in the 1 p.m. set of games, giving the Eagles a clear path to a playoff berth by beating the Cowboys. What was more shocking than anything, though, was how Philly beat their hated rivals. After a season where everything seemed to go against them, the breaks finally went the Eagles' way. A team whose luck saw opponents successfully convert their first 18 field goals (including four from 50-plus yards) somehow managed to force and recover fumbles inside their own 30 on back-to-back drives and return them both for touchdowns, breaking open a game that ended up serving as a 44-6 coronation party for the team's ultimately unsuccessful playoff run.

And yet, had simply one result not gone the Eagles' way in Week 17, this essay would be totally different. There's every reason to believe that Andy Reid, Donovan McNabb, or both would've been sent packing out of Philly following a topsy-turvy year that saw Reid's play-calling (through offensive coordinator Marty Morninhweg) and McNabb's inconsistent play become the subject of relentless questioning, even by the exorbitant standards of Philadelphia talk radio. They owe their jobs not just to their own performance in Week 17 and the playoffs, but to the Week 17 performances of Michael Bush and Andre Johnson. Had they gone on to win the Super Bowl, you would have read stories about the Eagles peaking at the right time or having unwavering belief in themselves, and it would be nonsense. They got lucky.

That's not to say that the Eagles weren't a good team, though; by DVOA, they ranked as the best team in football, a position they held or were close to for a good portion of the season. Through dominant wins over Pittsburgh, Atlanta, and Arizona, they were the only team in the league to have three games with a DVOA of 70% or better.

Why did they need the better part of a miracle to make the playoffs, then? The primary complaint of most Philadelphia observers was that the team simply couldn't run the ball in short-yardage situations, a proxy to the long-standing calls for Andy Reid to run the ball more frequently. The issues in short-

---

EAGLES SUMMARY

2008 Record: 9-6-1

Pythagorean Wins: 11.3 (5th)

DVOA: 33.5% (1st)

Offense: 11.7% (13th)

Defense: -20.3% (3rd)

Special Teams: 1.6% (13th)

Variance: 15.1% (12th)

2008: The most exhausting football team we ever knew.

2009: The mean projection's below ten wins, thanks to turnover on the offensive line and an expected rise to injuries on defense.

2009 Mean Projection: 9.3 wins

On the Clock (0-3): 0%

Loserville (4-6): 8%

Mediocrity (7-8): 23%

Playoff Contender (9-10): 41%

Super Bowl Contender (11+): 27%

Projected Average Opponent: 0.9% (18th)

2009 Eagles Schedule

Week	Opp.	Week	Opp.	Week	Opp.
1	at CAR	7	at WAS (Mon.)	13	at ATL
2	NO	8	NYG	14	at NYG
3	KC	9	DAL	15	SF
4	BYE	10	at SD	16	DEN
5	TB	11	at CHI	17	at DAL
6	at OAK	12	WAS		

yardage were real in 2008, as highlighted by the team's failure to punch the ball in from the one-yard line in a crushing loss to Chicago, but it hasn't been a long-standing trend. Philadelphia's actually been amongst the top ten in runs inside the opposition's five-yard line since Andy Reid's arrival, which rests concerns about their short-yardage capabilities on the absence of a real fullback (alleviated some by the arrival of Kyle Eckel halfway through the season and then the signing of Leonard Weaver this offseason) and Shawn Andrews, the team's best lineman (who returns to the starting lineup this year after missing virtually the entire 2008 season). In addition, the team was hesitant to use McNabb in short-yardage situations early in the year because of concerns that he might get injured; as the year went on, they started to use him more frequently on sneaks, and he picked up first downs or touchdowns on five of his seven yard-to-go opportunities over the final ten weeks of the regular season.

As a Web site whose first article exposed the mythology of "establishing the run," we tend to see Reid's pass-happy ways in a more sanguine light. Looking at the team's situational play-calling on a down-by-down basis, Philly passes the ball about five percent more frequently than the league-average team does (Table 1). This helps yield better-than-average success rates on all downs, even while the team gains fewer yards on first down than the league average. This makes sense when you consider the scheme Philly runs, a short passing game that's designed to put the team in manageable situations and pick up first downs. If anything, the Eagles should have thrown the ball more on third down; their success rate passing the ball in those situations was superior to the average team, while their running game was below-average.

If we break down our play-calling analysis even further, there are situational opportunities for the Eagles to exploit. Take first down, for example, where the Eagles ran 14 screens to their running backs; they gained 8.1 yards per attempt and had a success rate of 64 percent, superior to the league averages of 5.9 yards per attempt with a 50 success rate. On the flip side, they only gained 3.5 yards on first down draws, when the league average was 5.1 yards per attempt.

On second-and-short (three yards or less), they probably pass too frequently. Despite the obvious ability of a pass play to create opportunities downfield for big gains, Philadelphia could only muster a 46 percent success rate and 4.3 yards per attempt on passing plays; meanwhile, they had a 63 percent success rate and 4.1 yards per attempt when running the ball. The league average in the situation is 3.7 yards on run plays and 6.0 yards on pass plays.

On third down, their 6.4 average yards to go were the fifth-fewest in the league, which led to a higher success rate. In third-and-short — the situation in which they purportedly struggled a year ago — their 59 percent success rate was exactly league-average, although they averaged only 3.4 yards per play as opposed to the league average of 4.3. When they ran the ball, they succeeded 61 percent of the time, below the league average of 68 percent, but it was a 28-carry sample. Their success rate running in that situation was 24th in the league, but below them were teams like Arizona (28th), Indianapolis (30th), and Pittsburgh (dead last). You can still be a championship-caliber team, even if you aren't great at converting in third-and-short.

As for McNabb's inconsistency? His lowest ebb — his performance in Weeks 11 and 12 that led to his second-half benching in the latter game, a 36-7 drubbing by the Ravens — was bad, but it wasn't exactly unprecedented. His DVOA in the two games was -56.0% and -72.6%, respectively; in 2008 alone, an even worse stretch was put on by Ben Roethlisberger, who had back-to-back games with a DVOA of -96.3% (Week 10 against the Giants) and then -70.3% (Week 11 against the Redskins, a game he eventually came out of with a shoulder injury). In reality, McNabb had a season where he

Table 1: Eagles Play-calling, Success vs. League Average

	Down	Pct Pass	Suc Rate Pass	YPA Pass	Pct Run	Suc Rate Run	YPA Run	Suc Rate Tot	YPA Tot
NFL	1	48.5%	48%	6.6	51.5%	36%	4.3	42%	5.5
	2	53.8%	47%	6.2	46.2%	45%	4.4	46%	5.3
	3	75.6%	36%	5.5	24.4%	53%	4.6	40%	5.3
Eagles	1	53.0%	48%	5.9	47.0%	37%	4.2	43%	5.1
	2	58.2%	47%	6.4	41.8%	49%	4.7	48%	5.7
	3	78.5%	41%	6.6	21.5%	46%	2.7	42%	5.8

was relatively effective, just one pockmarked by two awful games (Table 2). He didn't bounce back, or redouble his efforts, or anything really notable over the final few weeks of the season; he just went back to playing at about the same level he'd established before his six awful quarters. There was no reason to think that he was finished and/or needed to be replaced.

The real factor that drove the Eagles' playoff run was on the other side of the ball, where the team's run defense became the league's best in the second half of the season. Led by consecutive first-round picks Mike Patterson (2005) and Brodrick Bunkley (2006), the Eagles were able to get by with a set of relative no-name linebackers in Stewart Bradley, Akeem Jordan, and Chris Gocong. One of our biggest concerns about the Eagles in 2009, in fact, is driven by how successful that front seven was a year ago. Other than backup defensive end Victor Abiamiri, not a single member of the rotation at either defensive line or linebacker missed a single game a year ago, something that's extremely unlikely to recur. That health even extended to the secondary, where the four starters combined for a total of 63 starts, with only Asante Samuel missing even a single game due to injury. That's also not likely to recur in 2009.

(The Eagles already have injury issues on the other side of the ball, where halfback Brian Westbrook suffered a high ankle sprain over the summer that should keep him out until the regular season and nag him thereafter.)

One player who certainly won't be suiting up in that secondary is longtime Eagles safety Brian Dawkins, who acrimoniously departed for Denver after Philadelphia failed to offer him a contract this offseason. Dawkins has undoubtedly lost a step — his reserve spot in the Pro Bowl can be chalked up either to tenure or opponents mistaking him for Quintin Mikell — but he did play a large role on this team in terms of leadership. Dawkins joins offensive tackles Tra Thomas and Jon Runyan as elder Eagles who have been shipped off, and while the Eagles replaced Thomas and Runyan with Jason Peters and Stacy Andrews, respectively, there's no guarantee that this generation of players will enjoy the success that the Dawkins-Thomas-Runyan troika did. Furthermore, our research indicates that the best offensive lines are the ones that experience continuity, so while Philadelphia has added superior talent with their free agent acquisitions, it may take a season for that talent to gel into a superior line.

Those three players were part of a five-man group that has been with Reid since his first playoff team in

Table 2: A Passing Aberration

Weeks	McNabb DVOA	Rank
1-10	37.9%	4
11-12	-57.7%	30
13-17	33.1%	7

2000; the only two left now are kicker David Akers and McNabb, which brings the question of McNabb's future with the team squarely into focus. In all likelihood, had the Eagles not hit their one-in-ten lottery ticket in Week 17, McNabb would also have departed in the offseason, with Kevin Kolb taking over. That move fits the quiet rebuild that the Eagles have undergone since the 2004 run to the Super Bowl. The core of this Eagles' team isn't the 32-year-old McNabb; it's guys like Peters, DeSean Jackson, Trent Cole, Bunkley, and Patterson, all of whom are 27 or younger and were acquired after the Super Bowl trip.

The team responded to McNabb's 2008 season by restructuring his deal to give him more guaranteed cash, but notably, they chose not to extend the deal past 2010. While the Miracle of Week 17 may have engendered goodwill and saved McNabb from potentially being released, it wasn't a reason to build around McNabb for the next several years. The organization has not hesitated to let go of "essential" players like Terrell Owens, Hugh Douglas, Jeremiah Trotter, and Dawkins. Unless Donovan McNabb can deliver a championship in either of the next two seasons, his days in Philadelphia are likely numbered. And the odds against him doing that are higher than ninety point nine percent.

Bill Barnwell

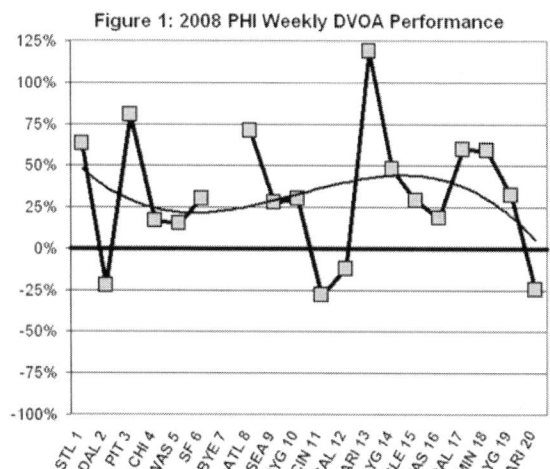

Figure 1: 2008 PHI Weekly DVOA Performance

2008 Eagles Stats by Week

Wk	vs.	W-L	PF	PA	YDF	YDA	TO	Total	Off	Def	ST
1	STL	W	38	3	522	166	0	63%	41%	-10%	12%
2	@DAL	L	37	41	337	380	+1	-22%	19%	29%	-13%
3	PIT	W	15	6	260	179	0	81%	13%	-57%	10%
4	@CHI	L	20	24	340	256	+2	16%	0%	-28%	-11%
5	WAS	L	17	23	254	388	0	15%	18%	17%	14%
6	@SF	W	40	26	383	306	+2	30%	22%	-10%	-2%
7	BYE										
8	ATL	W	27	14	432	335	+2	71%	39%	-32%	0%
9	@SEA	W	26	7	419	233	-1	28%	5%	-10%	13%
10	NYG	L	31	36	300	401	0	30%	33%	-14%	-16%
11	@CIN	T	13	13	391	282	-3	-28%	-40%	-23%	-10%
12	@BAL	L	7	36	206	248	-5	-12%	-43%	-14%	17%
13	ARI	W	48	20	437	260	+3	119%	65%	-45%	9%
14	@NYG	W	20	14	331	211	0	48%	21%	-34%	-7%
15	CLE	W	30	10	418	196	-1	29%	-10%	-31%	8%
16	@WAS	L	3	10	275	249	-1	18%	-2%	-23%	-2%
17	DAL	W	44	6	303	298	+4	60%	10%	-43%	7%
18	@MIN	W	26	14	350	301	0	59%	29%	-12%	19%
19	@NYG	W	23	11	276	307	+1	32%	-16%	-44%	4%
20	@ARI	L	25	32	454	369	-2	-25%	18%	37%	-6%

Trends and Splits

	Offense	Rank	Defense	Rank
Total DVOA	11.7%	13	-20.3%	3
Unadjusted VOA	10.7%	13	-20.1%	3
Weighted trend	7.8%	14	-24.7%	2
Variance	7.8%	23	8.3%	25
Average opponent	2.3%	23	1.2%	10
Passing	21.3%	14	-20.6%	3
Rushing	7.6%	12	-19.8%	3
First down	4.0%	17	-23.6%	3
Second down	13.2%	12	-12.1%	6
Third down	24.5%	10	-26.6%	4
First half	18.3%	7	-21.5%	3
Second half	4.8%	19	-19.0%	3
Red Zone	-0.8%	22	-20.5%	7
Late and close	-8.4%	23	-18.7%	4

Five-Year Performance

Year	W-L	Pyth	Est W	PF	PA	TO	Total	Rk	Off	Rk	Def	Rk	ST	Rk	Off AGL	Rk	Def AGL	Rk
2004	13-3	11.5	11.4	386	260	+6	23.2%	7	16.0%	9	-1.4%	16	5.9%	2	26.2	11	25.7	14
2005	6-10	5.9	7.4	310	388	-7	-2.8%	18	-9.1%	19	-6.3%	11	0.0%	17	43.0	2	12.3	19
2006	10-6	9.8	11.6	398	328	+5	27.2%	3	22.0%	3	-7.1%	9	-1.9%	22	13.6	18	21.3	13
2007	8-8	9.1	9.6	336	300	-8	13.7%	10	13.1%	6	-5.9%	9	-5.4%	31	15.4	25	23.2	14
2008	9-6-1	11.3	11.7	416	289	+3	33.5%	1	11.7%	13	-20.3%	3	1.6%	13	35.5	11	3.5	31

Strategic Tendencies

Run/Pass		Rank	Offense		Rank	Defense		Rank	Other		Rank
Runs, all plays	40%	25	3+ WR	58%	11	Rush 3	3.8%	22	2+ RB, Pct Runs	51%	29
Runs, first half	37%	29	4+ WR	15%	5	Rush 4	59.1%	24	1 RB/2 TE, Pct Runs	46%	22
Runs, first down	47%	23	2+ TE	19%	26	Rush 5	20.4%	18	1RB/3+WR, Pct Runs	32%	8
Runs, second-long	37%	19	Single back	60%	13	Rush 6+	16.8%	1	Zone Blitz	13%	1
Runs, power sit.	54%	30	Play action	25%	2	Rush 7+	4.5%	2	Go for it on 4th	0.61	32
Runs, behind 2H	32%	14	Max protect	10%	8	Sacks by LB	11.5%	23	Offensive Pace	29.6	9
Pass, ahead 2H	48%	8	Outside pocket	11%	18	Sacks by DB	16.7%	4	Defensive Pace	31.2	21

Jim Johnson knows when to send the house, and when to send pass rushers the quarterback won't expect. The Eagles not only led the league in zone blitzes but also in DVOA on zone blitzes, allowing -70.0% DVOA and 3.4 yards per play compared to -9.9% DVOA and 5.6 yards per play on other passes/scrambles. The Eagles also led the league in defensive DVOA with five or more pass rushers and ranked fourth in DVOA sending six or more pass rushers. ● Philadelphia opponents threw only 19 percent of passes to number-one receivers, the lowest percentage in the league. ● The Eagles ranked fourth in DVOA against passes to the left and third in DVOA against passes to the right, but only 17th in DVOA against passes to the middle of the field. ● On offense, the Eagles had the league's biggest difference in rushing DVOA depending on how many running backs were in the formation. With one back, they averaged 5.0 yards per carry with 29.1% DVOA; with two backs, they averaged 3.2 yards per carry with -13.1% DVOA. ● Philadelphia ranked 31st in DVOA with fewer than two wide receivers in the game, ahead of only St. Louis — but the Eagles ranked fourth in DVOA with three wideouts and fifth in DVOA with four or more wideouts.

Passing

Player	DYAR	DVOA	Plays	NtYds	Avg	YAC	C%	TD	Int
Donovan McNabb	1048	15.6%	594	3816	6.4	5.0	61.2%	24	11
Kevin Kolb	-139	-75.7%	34	144	4.2	3.6	50.0%	0	4

Rushing

Player	DYAR	DVOA	Plays	Yds	Avg	TD	Fum	Suc
Brian Westbrook	151	6.9%	233	936	4.0	9	1	48%
Correll Buckhalter*	69	11.0%	76	369	4.9	2	0	50%
Donovan McNabb	-38	-31.3%	34	151	4.4	2	3	--
Kyle Eckel	-2	-10.2%	24	79	3.3	0	0	58%
Lorenzo Booker	-12	-24.7%	20	53	2.7	0	0	40%
DeSean Jackson	70	50.5%	17	96	5.6	1	0	--
Tony Hunt*	5	7.9%	4	9	2.3	1	0	75%
Kevin Kolb	-9	-67.3%	3	12	4.0	0	0	--
Leonard Weaver	-1	-9.0%	30	130	4.3	0	1	47%

Receiving

Player	DYAR	DVOA	Plays	Ctch	Yds	Y/C	YAC	TD	C%
DeSean Jackson	40	-8.3%	120	62	912	14.7	4.1	3	52%
Kevin Curtis	-19	-16.5%	63	33	390	11.8	2.7	2	52%
Jason Avant	51	-0.7%	57	32	377	11.8	2.4	2	56%
Hank Baskett	89	8.6%	51	33	439	13.3	4.6	3	65%
Greg Lewis*	41	1.8%	35	19	247	13.0	2.7	2	54%
Reggie Brown	33	-0.9%	35	18	252	14.0	3.8	2	51%
L.J. Smith*	-42	-16.7%	64	37	298	8.1	4.8	3	58%
Brent Celek	77	21.9%	38	27	318	11.8	6.1	1	71%
Brian Westbrook	59	0.2%	73	54	400	7.4	7.0	5	74%
Correll Buckhalter*	153	62.1%	32	26	324	12.5	11.6	2	81%
Lorenzo Booker	-34	-75.1%	10	6	11	1.8	3.2	0	60%
Dan Klecko	5	-3.5%	8	6	36	6.0	4.2	0	75%
Tony Hunt*	2	-8.1%	6	6	42	7.0	4.3	0	100%
Leonard Weaver	45	15.6%	32	20	222	11.1	10.0	2	63%

Offensive Line

Year	Yards	ALY	Rank	Power	Rank	10+ Yds	Rank	Stuff	Rank	Sacks	ASR	Rank	False	Cont.
2006	4.68	4.54	3	62%	21	16%	17	16%	4	28	6.0%	12	26	48
2007	4.73	4.46	5	74%	4	19%	12	19%	19	49	7.6%	21	14	31
2008	4.05	4.06	20	55%	31	17%	19	19%	22	23	4.2%	6	13	30

Year	LE	Rank	LT	Rank	Mid	Rank	RT	Rank	RE	Rank
2006	4.43	11	4.23	17	4.61	4	4.17	12	5.21	3
2007	5.26	2	5.93	1	4.14	13	4.45	10	3.60	25
2008	3.43	25	3.10	30	4.45	7	4.36	9	3.76	23

The arrival of Jason Peters and Stacy Andrews, along with the return of Shawn Andrews, should give the Eagles supreme flexibility and depth along the offensive line. After spending nine years knowing that Tra Thomas and Jon Runyan were the starting tackles, Philly has multiple options at both spots. Peters is almost guaranteed the left tackle job, but if he struggles, shows up out of shape, or gets injured, they could employ left guard Todd Herremans there. On the right side, the team could start either of the Andrews brothers at tackle, with the other one inside at guard.

Herremans will compete with Max Jean-Gilles for the second season in a row for the left guard spot; Herremans won the job in camp a year ago, but received a demerit after missing a team meeting and was benched as a result. Had Jean-Gilles not been filling in for the injured Andrews at right guard, he very well might have lost his spot for good. Jean-Gilles broke his leg in Week 13 and was replaced rather admirably by backup center Nick Cole; if Jamaal Jackson struggles for consistency again, it's entirely possible that Cole could win the center job.

If it were up to us, we'd go with Peters (who allowed only two sacks in 2007, an impressive total for a left tackle), Jean-Gilles at left guard, Jackson at center, Stacy Andrews at right guard, and Shawn Andrews at right tackle. You want to have your best players in the most difficult spots, and the Eagles' two most talented linemen are Peters and the younger Andrews.

Defensive Front Seven

Defensive Line	Age	Pos	Plays	TmPct	Rk	Stop	Dfts	Overall Stop%	Rk	AvYd	Rk	Pass Rush Sack	Hit	Hur	vs. Run Runs	St%	Yds	vs. Pass Pass	St%	Yds
Trent Cole	27	DE	77	9.7%	1	59	29	77%	45	1.3	26	9.0	12	23	61	74%	1.9	16	88%	-1.2
Juqua Parker	31	DE	50	6.3%	36	40	14	80%	26	0.9	21	5.0	3	14	33	73%	1.8	17	94%	-0.8
Brodrick Bunkley	26	DT	49	6.2%	21	34	4	69%	65	2.6	60	2.0	1	1	41	68%	2.6	8	75%	2.8
Mike Patterson	26	DT	43	5.4%	32	32	4	74%	53	2.7	63	0.5	1	3	38	79%	2.5	5	40%	4.4
Darren Howard	33	DE	29	3.7%	76	25	20	86%	12	-0.9	4	10.0	6	4	13	69%	2.4	16	100%	-3.6

Linebackers	Age	Pos	Plays	TmPct	Rk	Stop	Dfts	Overall Stop%	AvYd	Pass Rush Sack	Hit	Hur	vs. Run Runs	St%	Rk	Yds	Rk	vs. Pass Tgts	Suc%	Rk	AdjYd	Rk
Stewart Bradley	25	ILB	113	14.3%	25	67	26	59%	4.8	1.0	4	4	69	65%	46	3.7	66	38	49%	49	7.6	73
Omar Gaither	25	OLB	60	7.6%	88	39	15	65%	3.9	2.5	0	5	31	74%	14	2.8	20	25	57%	27	6.2	46
Chris Gocong	26	OLB	53	6.7%	92	39	14	74%	2.7	2.0	1	1	34	74%	16	2.8	23	28	63%	7	4.9	16
Akeem Jordan	24	OLB	44	5.6%	--	25	8	57%	5.3	0.0	0	0	27	70%	--	3.0	--	14	47%	--	5.2	--

Year	Yards	ALY	Rank	Power	Rank	10+ Yds	Rank	Stuff	Rank	Sack	ASR	Rank
2006	4.28	4.33	21	53%	5	13%	6	20%	9	40	9.3%	2
2007	3.89	3.94	12	59%	11	18%	20	23%	2	37	7.4%	6
2008	3.60	3.70	6	61%	9	15%	11	22%	7	48	8.4%	4

Year	LE	Rank	LT	Rank	Mid	Rank	RT	Rank	RE	Rank
2006	4.14	18	5.16	29	4.47	21	4.73	27	2.99	6
2007	3.77	13	3.53	6	4.16	21	3.87	13	4.01	14
2008	3.24	5	3.04	3	4.21	17	4.31	24	3.02	7

The ascension of the defensive tackle combination of Mike Patterson and Brodrick Bunkley from promising to elite came over the second half of the season; from Week 9 on, Philly had the best run defense in football by a decent margin (-24.7% DVOA versus second-place Cincinnati's -19.7% DVOA). While that has something to do with the maturing of the linebackers behind them, Bunkley and Patterson did a fantastic job of keeping offensive linemen away from the second level. They're not dramatic, penetrating one-gap tackles who accrue tons of defeats, but simply a pair of players who teams struggle to account for on every play. Behind them will be top 2007 pick Trevor Laws, who barely played in his rookie year because of the play of the guys in front of him.

One of the effects of the tackles' performance was to give the defensive ends freedom to get in the backfield and make plays. While Trent Cole only had nine sacks, he led the league in plays made by an end, stops (tied with Justin Tuck), defeats, and was fourth in the league in hurries. Behind him, the team got consistent contribution from Darren Howard and Chris Clemons in part-time roles, although Juqua Parker was no great shakes as the starting end opposite Cole. The organization is hoping that Victor Abiamiri is the long-term solution at left end, but he has spent most of his young career recovering from various injuries; he started last year with a broken wrist and ended it with a Lisfranc sprain of his foot. If he stays healthy — admittedly, a big if — his ascension up the depth chart could come quickly.

Omar Gaither was the team's most prominent linebacker entering the season, and when his move to the weak side was made permanent in training camp, he was expected to produce as a playmaker and coverage linebacker. Instead, he was benched after Week 11 for his struggles on screen passes and spent the rest of the year on special teams. (If you're the conspiracy type, rumors also have it that the organization benched him for refusing to sign a contract extension.) He'll get a chance to compete with Akeem Jordan for the job again this year; Jordan can't rush the passer, but he's better than Gaither at sifting through trash and getting to the ballcarrier or receiver. Middle linebacker Stewart Bradley was about what we expected last year; he's effective against the run and a sure tackler, but he still has a ways to go in coverage. Strongside backer Chris Gocong is probably the unit's best player, although it's strange that the same guy who registered 42 sacks at Cal Poly isn't used more as a pass rusher. Depth at linebacker is a problem, as the only real linebacker of any note behind the starters will be the loser of the Jordan/Gaither battle. Everyone else is either a special teams player or a developmental prospect.

Defensive Secondary

Secondary	Age	Pos	Plays	Overall TmPct	Rk	Stop	Dfts	vs. Run Yds	Rk	St%	Rk	Tgts	Tgt%	Rk	Dist	Suc%	Rk	vs. Pass AdjYd	Rk	Yds	PD	Int
Quintin Mikell	29	SS	94	11.9%	14	47	20	4.2	8	54%	13	31	7.1%	34	11.5	59%	21	8.1	47	8.1	8	3
Brian Dawkins*	36	FS	81	10.3%	34	29	18	6.1	21	30%	66	33	7.4%	28	12.7	50%	47	8.8	54	8.9	5	1
Sheldon Brown	30	CB	62	7.8%	54	31	16	7.2	49	50%	29	57	12.9%	73	11.1	69%	1	5.1	4	4.6	14	1
Asante Samuel	28	CB	60	8.1%	53	29	11	12.4	76	0%	81	73	17.8%	46	10.7	56%	22	6.5	29	5.8	24	4
Joselio Hanson	28	CB	36	4.6%	--	17	8	8.0	--	60%	--	39	8.8%	--	8.6	66%	--	5.7	--	5.7	4	1
Lito Sheppard*	28	CB	24	3.0%	--	12	6	0.0	--	0%	--	37	8.4%	--	9.5	48%	--	9.7	--	9.5	5	1
Sean Jones	27	SS	60	9.4%	44	24	8	8.0	60	49%	18	15	5.2%	64	11.7	46%	62	9.1	56	9.5	4	4
Ellis Hobbs	26	CB	57	7.7%	56	22	11	7.9	54	31%	65	74	18.0%	40	12.3	55%	25	8.5	67	8.7	11	3
Rashad Baker	27	FS	28	5.4%	--	14	7	6.2	--	62%	--	8	3.1%	--	21.0	68%	--	6.7	--	7.3	4	3

Year	Pass D Rank	vs. #1 WR	Rk	vs. #2 WR	Rk	vs. Other WR	Rk	vs. TE	Rk	vs. RB	Rk
2006	7	2.0%	15	18.9%	26	-29.7%	4	-5.9%	14	-6.2%	14
2007	11	-10.1%	8	6.9%	19	2.0%	21	-10.9%	6	1.7%	20
2008	3	-1.4%	13	-26.2%	5	-51.1%	2	6.9%	19	7.4%	18

The loss of Brian Dawkins will undoubtedly have an emotional impact on the team, but in between the lines, Dawkins was a shell of his former self. He was still a decent safety with the same preternatural ability to rip the ball out (most prominently seen during the Week 17 game against Dallas), but he missed more tackles than ever before and was several steps slow in both man and zone coverage. Former Browns safety Sean Jones and backup Quintin Demps will compete in camp to replace Dawkins; Jones is the more talented player, and better against the run, but Demps is the superior centerfielder and is signed for three more years, while Jones is locked up on a one-year deal. That level of cost certainty for a starting safety goes a long way within the organization. Quintin Mikell will be the other safety; it was easy to write his excellent performance in 2007 off as a bit of a fluke, but Mikell was arguably even better last year, and it was certainly he — not Dawkins — who deserved a trip to Hawaii. Mikell should be the next player the Eagles lock up to a long-term contract.

Philly also arguably enjoyed the best pair of starting cornerbacks in the league. Asante Samuel broke up 31.2 percent of the passes in his direction, a percentage surpassed only by Corey Webster amongst starting corners, while Sheldon Brown served as the more consistent and conservative defender. Both were extremely effective and should remain so in 2009, although Brown could potentially hold out in an attempt to get a new deal. The Eagles floated him as part of a package to acquire Anquan Boldin, so they're not opposed to the idea of trading him. Lito Sheppard was expected to be the nickelback, but was terrible in limited usage and lost his job to Joselio Hanson, who played well enough to earn a five-year, $21 million contract to remain with the team. He'll be competing with Ellis Hobbs, who was acquired from the Patriots for two fifth-round picks; Hobbs is injury-prone and lacks the size to play consistently on the edge, but could be very effective as a nickel or dime corner in the slot. No team in the league has more quality or depth at corner, one through four, than Philly.

Special Teams

Year	DVOA	Rank	FG/XP	Rank	Net Kick	Rank	Kick Ret	Rank	Net Punt	Rank	Punt Ret	Rank	Hidden	Rank
2006	-1.9%	22	-5.1	27	7.9	7	-5.4	25	-6.0	26	-2.7	25	-15.2	32
2007	-5.4%	31	-4.1	26	-2.4	20	-7.1	26	-10.3	30	-7.5	30	10.8	6
2008	1.6%	13	-1.8	21	3.5	13	4.3	10	3.4	15	0.1	15	-12.7	29

The Eagles essay in last year's book noted the correlation between the team's success and the years in which their coverage units were effective, and 2008 helped reinforce that in a strange way. Philadelphia's coverage on punt returns was relatively average all season, but their work defending against kick returns took a huge step forward when they signed Tracy White after the Packers released him on October 7. At that point, the Eagles had allowed 4.6 points worth of field position on returns through five weeks, one of the worst totals in the league; after White entered the lineup in Week 7, their kick coverage was actually worth 3.4 points over the remainder of the season. While that's not entirely attributable to White, there's no doubt that he had a huge impact. The Howard product will lead the way again on special teams in 2009. Quintin Demps was a very good kick returner, but if he becomes the starting safety, the Eagles may very well take him off return duties. DeSean Jackson was just about average returning punts.

David Akers is no longer the best kicker in football, but undoubtedly buoyed by shaving his mustache, he was about average on both scoring plays and kickoffs in 2008. Saverio Rocca had an inconsistent season that added up to adequacy; he could be pushed by undrafted free agent Ken Parrish, who averaged just over 40 yards a punt in his career at Division II East Stroudsburg in Pennsylvania.

Coaching Staff

The most pressing issue regarding the staff involves defensive coordinator Jim Johnson, who was diagnosed with melanoma at the end of the season after it formed a tumor in his spine. Johnson is still coaching, but will likely be more hands-off than he was in previous seasons. If Johnson is unable to coach, he'd likely be replaced by secondary coach Sean McDermott. Former special teams coordinator Rory Segrest, whose lack of experience was covered in these pages a year ago, has moved to defensive line coach; he'll be replaced by Ted Daisher, formerly of the Browns.

As for Reid and the offense, well, there's not much to say that hasn't been covered by a million Philly sports talk radio hosts and guests already. Although it's become a cottage industry to attempt to do so, it's impossible to extricate Philadelphia's success over the last decade from Reid's performance and vice versa. As long-time readers of FO know, we're not sympathetic to the "establish the run" crowd, so Reid's offensive philosophy plays well with us. With that being said, there comes a point for every coach — even the great ones — where change is necessary. Veterans who have heard the same speeches for years tune out, while the organization struggles to identify its weaknesses and adapt philosophies and game plans that worked at the beginning of their tenure to the current league. Philadelphia is one of the smartest franchises in football, and Reid is one of the game's best coaches, but had the Buccaneers beat the Raiders in Week 17, that's what would be on Reid's tombstone right now. He got a reprieve because the team made it to the NFC Championship game once it had the opportunity, but going forward, it will be up to Reid to prove that he's still ahead of the curve.

Pittsburgh Steelers

The Steelers are the NFL's master vintners. They're a family-run company that does business the old fashioned way. While their competitors cut corners, the Steelers produce their product using time-honored methods. Because of their commitment to organizational stability, fiscal sanity, careful player development, and long-range planning, the Steelers produce a consistently excellent product. Once in a while, they create a masterpiece.

The Steelers Method is the "right" way to build a football team, in the same way that growing grapes on French hillsides and stomping them with bare feet is the right way to make wine. Every football franchise — every sports franchise, for that manner — pays lip service to the virtues of the Steelers Method: frugality, building through the draft, fostering continuity from the owner's box to the coaching staff. But very few organizations practice those virtues. The Steelers manage to succeed using business tactics that date back to the era before free agency, and they've remained successful for almost a generation. The Steelers have had 13 winning seasons, reached the playoffs 12 times, won two Super Bowls, and lost another, with four seasons of 12-4 or better — all in the last 17 years. It's an amazing record, though it's eclipsed by the team's other period of dominance in the 1970s.

The Steelers 2008 roster shows the hallmarks of a vintner's craftsmanship. Twenty-four of the Steelers'

top 30 regulars last year spent their entire career with the team. (We're including fullback Carey Davis, who played one game for the Falcons in 2004 but joined the Steelers in 2006). Six of those players were first-round picks, but seven joined the team as undrafted free agents, and seven others were drafted in the fourth round or later. Among the players who came from this "free talent pool" of street free agents and late-round picks: the Defensive Player of the Year (James Harrison), the team's featured running back (Willie Parker), three of their starting offensive linemen (Chris Kemoeatu, Willie Colon, Darnell Stapleton), plus a kicker, a fullback, and three of the top five players in the defensive line rotation.

All of that low-cost talent is the key to the Steelers Method. The Steelers draft very well, but so do the Ravens, Patriots, and many other teams. The Steelers gain an edge by developing bench talent better than any other team in the league. The Steelers' bench is truly a stepping stone to the starting lineup, as illustrated by the development of players like Harrison (one year on the practice squad, four as a situational player), Kemoeatu (two seasons on the bench), and defensive end Brett Keisel (three years on the bench), among others. While Ben Roethlisberger had one of the greatest rookie seasons in history, most Steelers rookies spend at least a year as apprentices before earning starting jobs. The nine career Steelers who started on defense last year (not including James Farrior and Ryan Clark,

STEELERS SUMMARY

2008 Record: 12-4

Pythagorean Wins: 11.8 (3rd)

DVOA: 29.6% (2nd)

Offense: 3.7% (21st)

Defense: -26.9% (1st)

Special Teams: -1.1% (23rd)

Variance: 10.8% (7th)

2008: Great defense, 12 wins, Super Bowl champions ... typical Steelers.

2009: Danny Boy heads for Eire, but the salary cap pipes won't call for the Steelers for at least another year.

2009 Mean Projection: 9.6 wins

On the Clock (0-3): 1%

Loserville (4-6): 10%

Mediocrity (7-8): 20%

Playoff Contender (9-10): 33%

Super Bowl Contender (11+): 37%

Projected Average Opponent: 0.4% (20th)

2009 Steelers Schedule

Week	Opp.	Week	Opp.	Week	Opp.
1	TEN (Thu.)	7	MIN	13	OAK
2	at CHI	8	BYE	14	at CLE (Thu.)
3	at CIN	9	at DEN (Mon.)	15	GB
4	SD	10	CIN	16	BAL
5	at DET	11	at KC	17	at MIA
6	CLE	12	at BAL		

whose careers started elsewhere) averaged 2.0 seasons on the bench before cracking the lineup, and only Casey Hampton earned a starting job as a rookie.

The Steelers Method works because success begets success — they usually don't have to rush rookies into the starting lineup — but also because of outstanding organizational continuity. The Steelers changed head coaches in 2006, but they haven't changed paradigms since Bill Cowher became head coach in 1992. Mike Tomlin's hire two seasons ago was a smooth power transfer. Tomlin retained several members of Cowher's staff, and several of those coaches are still on the team three years later. General Manager Kevin Colbert has held the post since 2000, and there hasn't been a hint of front office feuding since he replaced Tom Donahoe. The Rooneys are among the most trusted, beloved owners in sports: They get involved without meddling, and they lead effectively by delegating to their executives and coaches.

Top-down stability allows the Steelers to implement long-range plans. The Steelers can acquire second-day draft picks, develop them slowly, then fit them into the lineup knowing that there won't be any major regime changes during the players' development cycle. The team's talent pipeline works most efficiently at linebacker. The Steelers have been executing variations on the same 3-4 scheme since before Cowher took over and has been pulling All-Pros off the conveyor belt through three presidential administrations. They draft linebackers in the second or third round (that's when they picked LaMarr Woodley, Kendrell Bell, Joey Porter, Jason Gildon, Chad Brown, and Levon Kirkland), inculcate them into the system for a few years, then turn them loose on opposing quarterbacks. They know just what type of linebacker they want (Harrison, Porter, Lawrence Timmons, and others were defensive ends in college), and each defender comes of age just when his predecessor has gotten too old or expensive. The Steelers do the same thing at other positions, with varying degrees of success. Not

every unit is superlative every year, but they rarely have a crisis and they always have a plan.

The 2008 world champions were the greatest triumph of the Steelers Method. That doesn't mean that they were a great Steelers team. The 2008 Steelers were no better than the 2005 Super Bowl winners, and they weren't as good as the 2004 team that went 15-1 but lost in the playoffs. They weren't that much better than the 2007, 2002, or 2001 teams. The 2008 team lost to most of the top contenders they played in the regular season (the Eagles, Colts, Giants and Titans), and battled toe-to-toe to beat second-tier contenders like the Chargers (an 11-10 win), Ravens (two wins by a combined seven points) and Cowboys (a 20-13 win on a last-minute interception return touchdown). The 2008 Steelers had a poor offensive line and unreliable running game, and they suffered through major injuries to important players like Hampton, Parker, defensive end Aaron Smith and left tackle Marvel Smith.

The 2008 Steelers were deeply flawed, but they won the Super Bowl because of their method. They won because their player acquisition system always provides enough talent to keep them within range of double-digit wins. They won because their bench is always deep enough to absorb an injury or two. They won because their offensive and defensive schemes are always fully implemented and understood by players who had the time to learn them. In a year with lots of good teams but no great ones, these are the things that decide who wins the title. Last year's Steelers were just another Steelers team: That's praise for the organization, not an insult to the reigning champs.

The Steelers Method is so effective that it cannot be derailed by minor mishaps. A bad draft or a spate of major injuries can slow the Steelers, but it cannot kill them, and the team is likely to bounce back from the odd 6-10 season stronger than ever thanks to a high draft pick (see 2004). The only forces strong enough to plunge the Steelers into a losing cycle would be a change of ownership or a salary cap cataclysm. The Steelers came frighteningly close to experiencing both this offseason.

Soon after Roger Goodell became commissioner, he ordered the Rooney family to divest itself from its New York and Florida gambling interests or sell the team. That led to a split among the various Rooney siblings; older brothers Dan and Art Junior (Steelers chairman and president, respectively) wanted to maintain control of the team, while younger brothers Timothy, Patrick, and John wanted to keep the family's profitable horse and dog tracks. Dan and Art Junior didn't have the capital to buy their brothers out, leading to a variety of financial machinations that made Hyman Roth's scheme from *The Godfather: Part II* look like an ATM withdrawal. The team was suddenly one Internet billionaire away from trading all its draft picks and engaging in bidding wars with the Redskins for the services of overrated veterans.

Luckily, Dan and Art Junior were able to assemble a group of investors, led by former Steelers receiver John Stallworth, to buy out the other brothers. The sale was an extension of the Steelers Method. The brothers refused to leverage the franchise and go into deep debt to maintain their ownership stake. The transaction was handled with minimal rancor, considering the hundreds of millions of dollars involved. And in an absurd case of building through the draft, the Steelers selected a player in the fourth round of the 1974 draft and developed him into a co-owner. Once the ownership situation stabilized, Dan Rooney left the team to become Ambassador to Ireland. With Art Junior still around and the front office intact, Danny Boy's eyes will still be smiling as he watches his team from the Emerald Isle.

The Steelers also found themselves atypically close to the salary cap in the offseason. The team entered free agency with a salary cap of only $127.2 million because of $800,000 in overages from the previous year. Roethlisberger alone ate up over $13 million of that space. After the team splurged on Harrison's extension and franchised Max Starks, they had to make some significant moves — releasing Larry Foote, restructuring Hines Ward and others — to clear $5.7 million, enough to sign their rookies with precious little to spare.

The Steelers' cap problems were overblown by several media outlets. The team's cap grew tight after signing important players like Harrison, Starks, and Kemoeatu, not before. Foote was a solid player, but replacement Timmons is already on the roster, and one cut does not a cap crisis make. The team's cap crunch looks worse for 2010, except that A) there might not be a cap and B) several of the players slated to become free agents probably won't be resigned. Parker's contract ends this year, but the Steelers will just replace him with Rashard Mendenhall, last year's first-round pick. Hampton is a great player, but the Steelers always let old defenders walk (plus, market demand for Hampton may be dampened by the presence of Vince Wilfork, a similar but younger 3-4 nose tackle, in the same free agent class). The team can easily free up money by restruc-

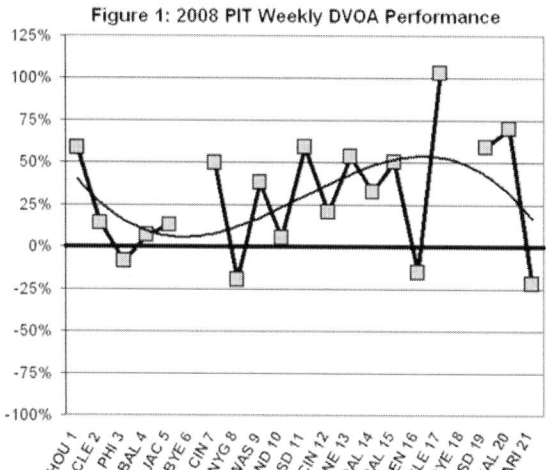

Figure 1: 2008 PIT Weekly DVOA Performance

turing Roethlisberger (whose cap number actually goes down slightly in 2010), by giving up on Starks, or by jiggling some other deals. The Steelers, long the most financially conservative team in the NFL, are starting to do the things other teams do: spending huge money on Harrison, risking future dead money by extending Big Ben's contract, and so on. These aren't canonical Steelers Method tactics, but the team is still a long way from getting into major cap trouble.

Eventually, something will kill the Steelers: an uncapped year, major on-field rules changes (like those that stopped the 1970s Steelers), Mike Tomlin's appointment as ambassador to Luxembourg. None of these things will happen in 2009. There has been minimal roster turnover, the team's core is young, and players like Timmons and Mendenhall are poised to make an impact. The Steelers will win another 10 to 12 games this year, giving them another puncher's chance at the Super Bowl. With the ownership situation settled and Tomlin entrenched, the Steelers could keep this up indefinitely.

Ten years from now, Peyton Manning will be on his last legs, the Patriots dynasty of the 2000s will be the stuff of NFL Films documentaries, Brett Favre will be in the Hall of Fame (possibly chained to a wall), guys like Chad Johnson and Plaxico Burress will be distant memories, and thousands of players will have reached the NFL, played through brief careers of varying significance, and retired. But chances are someone will be writing a season preview about the Steelers, dissecting their 12-6 season in 2018, raving about their linebackers, and marveling at Tomlin's longevity. Some things, like fine wine and Steelers football, never go out of style.

Mike Tanier

2008 Steelers Stats by Week

Wk	vs.	W-L	PF	PA	YDF	YDA	TO	Total	Off	Def	ST
1	HOU	W	38	17	305	234	+2	58%	23%	-31%	4%
2	@CLE	W	10	6	281	208	+2	14%	1%	-14%	-1%
3	@PHI	L	6	15	179	260	0	-9%	-40%	-27%	4%
4	BAL	W	23	20	237	243	0	7%	-19%	-21%	4%
5	@JAC	W	26	21	415	213	-1	13%	1%	-11%	1%
6	BYE										
7	@CIN	W	38	10	375	212	+1	50%	46%	-6%	-2%
8	NYG	L	14	21	249	282	-4	-20%	-54%	-43%	-9%
9	@WAS	W	23	6	224	221	+1	38%	-3%	-46%	-5%
10	IND	L	20	24	326	290	-3	5%	-2%	0%	7%
11	SD	W	11	10	410	218	+2	59%	24%	-44%	-9%
12	CIN	W	27	10	364	208	0	21%	34%	7%	-6%
13	@NE	W	33	10	333	267	+4	54%	7%	-47%	0%
14	DAL	W	20	13	238	289	+3	33%	-32%	-53%	11%
15	@BAL	W	13	9	311	202	0	50%	19%	-42%	-11%
16	@TEN	L	14	31	374	322	-4	-15%	-3%	8%	-5%
17	CLE	W	31	0	369	126	+1	103%	38%	-67%	-2%
18	BYE										
19	SD	W	35	24	342	290	+2	59%	27%	-19%	13%
20	BAL	W	23	14	275	198	+3	-12%	-28%	-21%	-5%
21	ARI	W	27	23	292	407	+1	-22%	11%	33%	1%

Trends and Splits

	Offense	Rank	Defense	Rank
Total DVOA	3.7%	21	-26.9%	1
Unadjusted VOA	3.6%	20	-24.7%	2
Weighted trend	7.7%	16	-28.9%	1
Variance	8.0%	24	10.3%	28
Average opponent	4.9%	10	-0.5%	7
Passing	12.9%	19	-31.0%	1
Rushing	5.8%	15	-21.7%	2
First down	5.1%	15	-25.8%	2
Second down	20.9%	10	-20.4%	4
Third down	-23.8%	28	-37.6%	1
First half	-10.0%	29	-26.0%	2
Second half	18.4%	9	-27.8%	1
Red Zone	8.6%	13	-50.0%	2
Late and close	12.4%	16	-22.1%	3

Five-Year Performance

Year	W-L	Pyth	Est W	PF	PA	TO	Total	Rk	Off	Rk	Def	Rk	ST	Rk	Off AGL	Rk	Def AGL	Rk
2004	15-1	11.5	12.1	372	251	+11	38.1%	1	17.4%	8	-18.5%	3	2.2%	10	13.7	19	24.3	16
2005	11-5	11.6	11.6	398	258	+7	27.9%	4	10.8%	8	-15.6%	3	1.5%	10	15.5	16	9.9	23
2006	8-8	9.1	8.5	353	315	-8	10.9%	10	8.1%	9	-7.0%	10	-4.1%	30	12.6	22	14.0	17
2007	10-6	11.4	9.3	393	269	+3	20.0%	5	9.6%	9	-11.8%	3	-1.4%	21	9.1	30	19.7	17
2008	12-4	11.8	11.4	347	223	+4	29.6%	2	3.7%	21	-26.9%	1	-1.1%	23	37.6	9	16.5	21

Strategic Tendencies

Run/Pass		Rank	Offense		Rank	Defense		Rank	Other		Rank
Runs, all plays	44%	14	3+ WR	59%	10	Rush 3	8.7%	6	2+ RB, Pct Runs	70%	3
Runs, first half	41%	26	4+ WR	14%	9	Rush 4	57.8%	25	1 RB/2 TE, Pct Runs	62%	4
Runs, first down	56%	8	2+ TE	37%	4	Rush 5	30.8%	2	1RB/3+WR, Pct Runs	32%	9
Runs, second-long	35%	22	Single back	74%	2	Rush 6+	2.7%	31	Zone Blitz	5%	12
Runs, power sit.	57%	27	Play action	12%	27	Rush 7+	0.2%	31	Go for it on 4th	0.81	21
Runs, behind 2H	32%	16	Max protect	6%	27	Sacks by LB	75.5%	1	Offensive Pace	30.9	14
Pass, ahead 2H	39%	24	Outside pocket	12%	15	Sacks by DB	2.0%	29	Defensive Pace	29.9	4

Think you might get somewhere by blitzing Ben Roethlisberger? Steelers' opponents sent six or more on a big blitz 15 percent of the time, the highest rate in the league — and while Roethlisberger is known for his ability to make seemingly-impossible plays under pressure, he apparently doesn't do it as often as you might expect, because the Steelers ranked 28th with -36.2% DVOA when facing a big blitz. (Roethlisberger also saw smaller blitzes, with five pass rushers on 39 percent of pass plays, second only to Eli Manning.) ● Oh Kreider Where Art Thou? Pittsburgh had two backs in the formation for only 28 percent of running back carries, the second-lowest percentage in the league and half the NFL average. ● Pittsburgh's offense ranked 29th in DVOA for the first half of games, ninth in DVOA for the second half. ● Pittsburgh is the only team that never ran a screen play on third down. ● As in 2007, the Steelers were significantly much more efficient when they went three-wide (21.1% DVOA) or four-wide

(29.1% DVOA) instead of using the conventional two wide receivers (-7.4% DVOA). ● Pittsburgh's defensive DVOA was just league average against formations with only one wide receiver — but it was the league's best or near the top in pretty much any other category. The Steelers ranked first against standard formations with two wideouts, second against three-wide formations, and first against four-wide formations. They were first when sending four pass rushers, sixth when sending five, and first again when sending six or more. They were first without play-action and fourth with play-action. They were first when they hurried the quarterback. They were first against passes to the left and second against passes to the right, although just 11th against passes up the middle.

Passing

Player	DYAR	DVOA	Plays	NtYds	Avg	YAC	C%	TD	Int
Ben Roethlisberger	288	-2.2%	518	3110	6.0	4.5	60.6%	17	13
Byron Leftwich*	175	66.0%	38	281	7.4	4.9	60.0%	2	0

Rushing

Player	DYAR	DVOA	Plays	Yds	Avg	TD	Fum	Suc
Willie Parker	46	-2.9%	209	789	3.8	5	0	41%
Mewelde Moore	139	14.3%	140	588	4.2	5	0	51%
Gary Russell*	13	-0.5%	28	77	2.8	3	0	57%
Ben Roethlisberger	-2	-13.6%	23	110	4.8	2	2	--
Rashard Mendenhall	-8	-20.8%	19	58	3.1	0	0	26%
Carey Davis	1	-5.4%	12	35	2.9	0	0	17%
Nate Washington*	14	23.1%	5	18	3.6	0	0	--

Receiving

Player	DYAR	DVOA	Plays	Ctch	Yds	Y/C	YAC	TD	C%
Hines Ward	294	16.9%	125	82	1047	12.8	4.9	8	66%
Santonio Holmes	39	-8.2%	114	55	821	14.9	3.7	6	48%
Nate Washington*	70	-0.8%	78	40	631	15.8	3.3	3	51%
Limas Sweed	-24	-46.7%	10	6	64	10.7	2.7	0	60%
Shaun McDonald	-55	-23.3%	66	35	339	9.7	1.9	2	53%
Heath Miller	116	20.8%	66	48	514	10.7	4.8	3	73%
Matt Spaeth	-14	-15.2%	26	17	136	8.0	4.4	0	65%
Mewelde Moore	56	4.6%	53	40	320	8.0	5.9	1	75%
Willie Parker	-34	-72.9%	11	4	15	3.8	6.5	0	36%
Carey Davis	-22	-67.7%	6	5	27	5.4	4.2	0	57%

Offensive Line

Year	Yards	ALY	Rank	Power	Rank	10+ Yds	Rank	Stuff	Rank	Sacks	ASR	Rank	False	Cont.
2006	4.38	4.04	22	63%	19	24%	3	18%	15	49	8.0%	25	16	28
2007	4.21	4.05	20	60%	21	19%	13	18%	12	47	10.1%	31	14	38
2008	3.79	3.95	24	64%	19	15%	28	22%	30	50	9.2%	29	20	39

Year	LE	Rank	LT	Rank	Mid	Rank	RT	Rank	RE	Rank
2006	3.97	19	3.84	27	4.31	14	3.56	31	3.91	17
2007	4.53	10	4.52	10	3.70	28	4.42	11	4.15	13
2008	4.84	9	4.69	8	3.91	23	3.15	32	4.05	16

The Steelers will always allow too many sacks as long as Ben Roethlisberger is their quarterback. Big Ben holds the ball too long and rarely checks down, resulting in lots of sacks that are either incomplete passes or short completions for other quarterbacks. His habits also inspire our game charters to pose philosophical questions, like "Why does Roethlisberger pump fake when there is a defender wrapped around his ankles?"

Still, Big Ben can only shoulder so much blame. The Steelers offensive line often had communication problems last year, which allowed blitzers to get into the backfield unchecked. Right tackle Willie Colon was beaten regularly and needed constant help from backs and tight ends. The Steelers' Sack Rate improved last year, particularly on early downs — Roethlisberger was sacked just 22 times on 325 first- and second-down attempts last season as opposed to 30 times on 271 early-down attempts in 2007, and 27 times on 315 early down attempts in 2006 — but it was still far too high.

The Steelers were also flagged for 20 false start penalties, with Colon (six) and Chris Keomatu (five) as the biggest offenders. Both players were re-signed in the offseason, but Colon only received a one-year contract, an indication that while the team values continuity, they watched the same film we watched. Second-round pick Kraig Urbik is the likely successor to Colon. Urbik started his Wisconsin career at right tackle before spending three seasons at right guard. He has the size (6-foot-6, 328 pounds) and mobility to grow into a starter at right tackle.

Left tackle Max Starks played the 2008 season under a one-year contract as a transition player, earning $6.9 million. The Steelers franchised Starks this year, guaranteeing him $8.45 million. Starks signed the offer and didn't make any immediate demands for a long-term deal. "I'm blessed to be in this position," Starks said in late May, no doubt aware that he's the most overpaid player on the roster.

Center Justin Hartwig arrived from Carolina last year to play 16 games of nearly mistake-free football. Hartwig, 30, should start for another season or two. Sixth-round pick A.Q. Shipley will be groomed as Hartwig's replacement. One of the funniest moments from NFL Network's draft coverage came when Mike Mayock (a little loopy after 13 hours on television) began touting Shipley like the second coming of Mike Webster, ranting about how Shipley "chews on defenders' ankles." Mayock was referring to the Rose Bowl, in which Shipley kept scrapping after the whistle with USC tackle Fili Moala, despite the fact that Penn State was getting clobbered. Shipley is definitely a guy who finishes his blocks, but we're not sure if he has ever actually chewed on anyone.

Defensive Front Seven

Defensive Line	Age	Pos	Plays	TmPct	Overall					Pass Rush			vs. Run			vs. Pass		
					Rk	Stop	Dfts	Stop%	Rk	AvYd	Rk	Sack	Hit	Hur	Runs	St%	Yds	Pass	St%	Yds
Aaron Smith	33	DE	63	8.0%	10	55	17	87%	10	0.9	18	5.5	4	5	46	87%	1.7	17	88%	-1.1
Travis Kirschke	35	DE	44	5.6%	43	31	5	70%	67	2.2	60	2.0	5	2	38	71%	2.5	6	67%	0.2
Brett Keisel	31	DE	43	8.7%	4	34	12	79%	33	2.3	67	1.0	0	1	34	88%	1.5	9	44%	5.3
Casey Hampton	32	DT	23	3.6%	62	18	3	78%	32	2.2	50	1.0	0	0	20	80%	2.5	3	67%	0.3
Nick Eason	29	DE	18	2.4%	--	13	6	72%	--	0.4	--	1.5	0	3	12	58%	2.3	6	100%	-3.5
Chris Hoke	33	DT	16	2.0%	--	12	3	75%	--	1.6	--	0.5	1	3	12	75%	1.8	4	75%	1.0

Linebackers	Age	Pos	Plays	TmPct	Overall				Pass Rush				vs. Run					vs. Pass			
					Rk	Stop	Dfts	Stop%	AvYd	Sack	Hit	Hur	Runs	St%	Rk	Yds	Rk	Tgts	Suc%	Rk	AdjYd	Rk
James Farrior	34	ILB	138	17.5%	9	93	27	67%	3.6	3.5	3	7	85	75%	13	2.6	15	44	47%	54	7.2	69
James Harrison	31	OLB	92	12.5%	38	68	29	74%	1.8	16.0	8	17	52	83%	4	2.3	5	16	62%	11	4.4	6
Larry Foote*	29	ILB	65	8.2%	81	48	10	74%	3.0	1.5	3	8	43	86%	2	2.4	12	20	40%	74	6.0	38
LaMarr Woodley	24	OLB	62	8.4%	80	43	26	69%	2.5	11.5	7	14	34	68%	35	3.6	61	18	60%	16	5.8	36
Lawrence Timmons	23	OLB	60	7.6%	87	30	17	50%	5.5	5.0	8	11	26	54%	95	3.7	64	24	64%	6	6.1	43

Year	Yards	ALY	Rank	Power	Rank	10+ Yds	Rank	Stuff	Rank	Sack	ASR	Rank
2006	3.31	3.84	7	63%	14	10%	1	19%	14	39	6.9%	15
2007	3.84	3.85	6	55%	7	16%	13	20%	12	36	7.2%	11
2008	3.41	3.81	8	53%	1	9%	1	17%	18	51	8.7%	3

Year	LE	Rank	LT	Rank	Mid	Rank	RT	Rank	RE	Rank
2006	1.97	2	4.71	21	3.86	5	4.03	13	4.54	24
2007	5.61	32	3.55	7	4.11	17	3.35	3	2.32	1
2008	4.35	21	4.83	29	3.63	5	3.95	13	2.86	6

The Steelers' top four linebackers recorded 36 sacks, tying for the highest total in team history since the sack became an official sack in 1982. Here are the top five sack seasons by Steelers linebackers (only top four linebackers included):

Table 2: Steelers' Line-Sackers

Year	Sacks	Linebackers
2008	36	James Harrison, Lawrence Timmons, LaMar Woodley, James Farrior
1994	36	Kevin Greene, Greg Lloyd, Chad Brown, Levon Kirkland
2001	32	Jason Gildon, Kendrell Bell, Joey Porter, Earl Holmes
2002	30	Joey Porter, Jason Gildon, Clark Haggans, Rodney Bailey
1996	26.5	Chad Brown, Jason Gildon, Levon Kirland, Carlos Emmons

This year's corps could be even stronger than last year's. Lawrence Timmons, an often-used situational player last year, will replace Larry Foote, who was released. Timmons has finished his two-year apprenticeship on the bench and appears ready to make the big step forward that both Woodley and Harrison made after learning the craft from the sidelines. With Timmons in the starting lineup, Leslie Frazier and Arnold Harrison are the favorites to see action as extra linebackers in the team's "11 Angry Men" fronts.

The top five contributors to the defensive line rotation are over 30, so top draft pick Evander Hood will have to make a contribution right away. Hood would be a square peg in many systems because he lacks great initial quickness and doesn't have the size or power to play defensive tackle in a 4-3. In Pittsburgh, he's likely to slide into Aaron Smith's role as the pass rushing left end. Smith is still effective in his role, and Travis Kirschke did an excellent job off the bench when Smith and Brett Keisel got hurt last season. Keisel missed time with calf and knee injuries, but his experience is a major asset: He's the defender who read Eli Manning's lips in the huddle and used the information to stuff a Brandon Jacobs run at the goal line in Week 7 against the Giants.

Only the Steelers can keep an All-Pro defensive tackle *and* his backup around for eight years. Casey Hampton still plays at a high level, in part because the team isn't afraid to use Chris Hoke for about 20 snaps per game. The team's "11 Angry Men" packages also keep players fresh: Only one or two linemen play in those sets, so the 30-something 300-pounders can count on some extra rest in third-and-long situations.

Defensive Secondary

Secondary	Age	Pos	Plays	TmPct	Rk	Stop	Dfts	Yds	Rk	St%	Rk	Tgts	Tgt%	Rk	Dist	Suc%	Rk	AdjYd	Rk	Yds	PD	Int
						Overall			vs. Run						vs. Pass							
Troy Polamalu	28	SS	90	11.4%	22	52	25	4.5	9	65%	4	46	10.0%	5	12.5	67%	4	4.6	4	4.2	14	7
Ryan Clark	30	FS	89	12.9%	7	27	9	6.1	22	35%	56	33	8.2%	18	15.2	64%	10	6.4	13	5.8	4	1
Ike Taylor	29	CB	77	9.8%	25	30	12	5.9	31	29%	69	87	18.9%	31	12.5	50%	43	7.5	41	7.3	14	1
Bryant McFadden*	28	CB	48	9.7%	27	25	10	6.0	33	80%	1	51	17.6%	48	9.4	51%	39	6.4	26	5.7	9	2
William Gay	24	CB	39	4.9%	79	19	6	10.1	70	38%	52	42	9.0%	82	10.0	66%	4	4.5	1	3.3	8	1
Deshea Townsend	34	CB	28	4.7%	--	17	8	4.8	--	50%	--	37	10.6%	--	7.5	59%	--	6.8	--	6.8	9	2
Keiwan Ratliff	28	CB	31	4.6%	--	12	6	7.3	--	33%	--	30	9.0%	--	9.8	43%	--	7.4	--	7.5	5	2

Year	Pass D Rank	vs. #1 WR	Rk	vs. #2 WR	Rk	vs. Other WR	Rk	vs. TE	Rk	vs. RB	Rk
2006	14	18.3%	30	20.5%	27	-42.6%	1	8.8%	24	-40.5%	1
2007	7	-8.5%	10	8.0%	20	-33.7%	3	8.0%	18	-30.4%	1
2008	1	-14.4%	6	2.9%	19	-40.4%	4	-14.6%	6	-26.6%	1

Troy Polamalu led all safeties in Defeats. He tied Brian Scott of the Bills for the league lead in Run Defeats and finished tied for second behind Yeremiah Bell in Pass Defeats (Bell had 15; Nick Collins and Eric Weddle also had 14). Polamalu's Stop Rate of 58 percent was the highest in the league for a safety with more than 50 plays; besides Polamalu, only Adrian Wilson of the Cardinals and Quentin Mikell of the Eagles cracked the 50 percent mark. Defensive statistics are highly circumstance-driven, and safeties who play close to the line like Polamalu get a huge boost when Stops and Defeats are tabulated. Still, the statistics confirm what just about everyone knows: Polamalu is the best safety in the NFL.

Ike Taylor isn't the ideal number-one cornerback, but he's a good system fit who keeps plays in front of him. The Steelers play a lot of Cover-3 in the secondary, and Taylor has the thankless task of dropping into a deep zone, then rushing up to make tackles on the rare occasions when the opposing quarterback has time to throw a complete pass.

Cornerback Bryan McFadden signed with the Cardinals, but the Steelers are loaded with potential replacements. William Gay played well in spot starts last season. His lone interception was a big one: He picked off a pass in the end zone to secure a 13-9 win against the Ravens in Week 15. Deshea Townsend, who has been with the Steelers since 1998, also had a heroic interception last year: His 26-yard return of an errant Tony Romo pass gave the Steelers a 20-13 win against the Cowboys in Week 14. Keiwan Ratliff, a former first-round pick by the Bengals who never panned out, offers depth as a dime back.

Free safety Ryan Clark is forced to play the deep middle in Cover-3 situations, so most of his tackles are clean-up jobs after completed passes. Third-round pick Keenan Lewis played cornerback at Oregon State but has the size (6-foot-1, 208 pounds) to play free safety. He's not a big hitter, but he's a smart, quick defender who could thrive in deep zone coverage.

Special Teams

Year	DVOA	Rank	FG/XP	Rank	Net Kick	Rank	Kick Ret	Rank	Net Punt	Rank	Punt Ret	Rank	Hidden	Rank
2006	-4.1%	30	-4.4	26	-9.9	28	-5.0	24	0.5	19	-5.4	30	-2.5	17
2007	-1.4%	21	6.9	2	-7.6	28	0.3	17	3.1	12	-10.8	31	4.5	12
2008	-1.1%	23	0.9	16	8.1	5	-10.3	30	4.4	13	-9.4	31	-7.3	22

On a team with few holes, the most interesting camp battle could occur at punt returner. Santonio Holmes was the team's top return man last year, but he may be too valuable on offense to risk in the role. Shaun McDonald returned punts for the Lions and Rams, but his career average is just 6.3 yards. Mewelde Moore has the right skill set, but he called for 12 fair catches against just six returns last season. Rookie Mike Wallace returned kickoffs at Oregon State but hasn't returned a punt since high school. Fellow rookie Keenan Lewis and second-year receiver Limas Sweed could also see looks as punt returners. Moore and Wallace will probably handle kickoffs. The Steelers haven't had a truly dangerous return man since Antwaan Randle El left and are hoping a playmaker emerges.

Jeff Reed is excellent on kickoffs (19 touchbacks in two seasons) and a dependable placekicker. The kick and punt coverage teams are also very good and often populated by regulars like Ike Taylor, James Harrison, and Lawrence Timmons. The team re-signed Keyaron Fox as a special teams specialist; Fox had 21 coverage tackles last season.

Dan Sepulveda is expected to return from the ACL injury that sidelined him all of last season. Sepulveda, who engaged in light practice at May minicamp, became a fan favorite in 2007 because of his booming punts, linebacker-caliber tackles against return men, and the occasional pass on a fake punt. The team signed Dirk Johnson, who punted in 12 games for the Cardinals but was released in December, as Sepulveda insurance.

There's a position battle brewing at long snapper. Greg Warren was the team's snapper for three seasons before tearing an ACL in October. Warren was still working his way back in May minicamp, so the team signed rookie free agent Mark Estermyer from Pitt. "I want to go out there every day and snap my butt off," Estermyer told the *Beaver County Times*, giving the world one unintentionally hilarious image.

Coaching Staff

The Steelers led the league in running plays and first-down runs in 2007. Last year, Bruce Arians opened the playbook a little wider, calling four percent fewer runs on first down and nine percent fewer runs on second-and-long. The increased passing probably reflected Arians' confidence in the team's ability to avoid sacks: Two years ago, he was afraid that a second-and-10 pass would lead to third-and-18. Arians remains a guru of the single-back set, and the Steelers use a variety of trips and bunch formations. Arians loves to run from bunch formations, allowing Heath Miller and hard-blocking receivers like Hines Ward to crack linebackers and safeties on the second level.

Most of Bill Cowher's defensive assistants stayed with the team when Mike Tomlin took over in 2007, and they are still on the staff: Just another way the Steelers maintain continuity and quality. Defensive coordinator Dick LeBeau is the perfect sounding board and consigliore for Mike Tomlin: a 70-year-old coach who was with the Steelers in the mid-1990s and was one of the innovators of the zone blitz. Line coach John Mitchell and linebackers coach Keith Butler are also holdovers who know how to mold players to fit the system.

St. Louis Rams

In the NFL, every season brings surprises. Perennial losers make the playoffs, powerhouses suddenly fall apart, "buzz teams" that are expected to improve don't, and old, declining teams become rejuvenated. Every offseason, commentators sift through the evidence, trying to figure out which team will go from a losing season to a surprise playoff run. But not every team that goes from loser to winner qualifies as a "surprise team."

If Seattle or Jacksonville returns to the playoffs in 2009, does either squad really qualify as a "surprise team?" Seattle won five straight AFC West titles until Arizona broke the streak last year. Jacksonville was considered a leading Super Bowl contender just 12 months ago and made the postseason in both 2006 and 2007. A rebound from either team doesn't really qualify as a surprise.

If Chicago wins the NFC North, is it the "surprise team?" Not really. The Chicago defense and special teams have been strong for years, and they just traded for a Pro Bowl quarterback. Plenty of experts will pick the Bears as a playoff team this year. If they go 10-6, it won't be a surprise.

Now, the St. Louis Rams? Here's a team with a miserable 5-27 record over the past two seasons. Although they snuck into the 2004 playoffs at 8-8, they have not had a winning record since 2003. That's three straight seasons of mediocrity followed

by two of futility. Last year's Rams lost every way possible. They had embarrassing losses, like when they were outscored a combined 88-16 by the two New York teams. They had frustrating losses, including back-to-back home losses to the other two awful NFC West teams by a combined four points. They had only two games with DVOA over 0% (Figure 1), and one of them came when the Dallas Cowboys were playing Brad Johnson at quarterback, which technically counts as a "Senior League" game. A winning season from the 2009 St. Louis Rams would be quite a surprise.

Well, surprise: It may happen. And not in the "any team can turn it around in the NFL when you least expect it" way. It may happen in the "clear numerical trends supporting the thesis" way.

A surprise playoff run would certainly be a satisfying start to the new era of Rams football. The team cleaned house this offseason, from the front office to the locker room. (The change will even extend to the owner's box soon, since the Rams are being put up for sale by the estate of their late owner, Georgia Frontiere.) General manager Jay Zygmunt resigned and was replaced by Billy Devaney, who had been hired as the vice president of pro personnel just a year earlier. Devaney hired Kevin Demoff away from Tampa Bay as Director of Football Operations; Demoff was in

RAMS SUMMARY

2008 Record: 2-14

Pythagorean Wins: 2.6 (32nd)

DVOA: -47.5% (31st)

Offense: -24.0% (32nd)

Defense: 23.4% (30th)

Special Teams: -0.2% (18th)

Variance: 23.1% (29th)

2008: After another injury-wracked season, the Rams clean house.

2009: There's a reasonable chance for a "miracle season" here. Really.

2009 Mean Projection: 8.2 wins

On the Clock (0-3): 7%

Loserville (4-6): 22%

Mediocrity (7-8): 23%

Playoff Contender (9-10): 27%

Super Bowl Contender (11+): 21%

Projected Average Opponent: 1.5% (14th)

2009 Rams Schedule

Week	Opp.	Week	Opp.	Week	Opp.
1	at SEA	7	IND	13	at CHI
2	at WAS	8	at DET	14	at TEN
3	GB	9	BYE	15	HOU
4	at SF	10	NO	16	at ARI
5	MIN	11	ARI	17	SF
6	at JAC	12	SEA		

charge of the cap for one of the most economically efficient teams in the league. Head coach Scott Linehan was fired in the middle of last season after losing the locker room, and interim coach Jim Haslett was not kept on. Devaney created a definitive break from the era of the "Greatest Show on Turf" by hiring a coach with a defensive background instead of an offensive one: Giants defensive coordinator Steve Spagnuolo.

Then, Devaney made an even more definitive break with the past by releasing veteran left tackle Orlando Pace and wide receiver Torry Holt within a week of each other. Pace had been with the Rams for a dozen seasons, Holt for ten. Both are likely to eventually make the Hall of Fame, but each player has seen his effectiveness sapped by age and injury (Pace more than Holt). The departure of these two future Hall of Famers means that defensive end Leonard Little is the only player left who took the field when the Rams lost to the Patriots in Super Bowl XXXVI (Marc Bulger was also on that team, but as the third-string emergency quarterback).

Despite the departures of Holt and Pace, our pro-

jection system believes that the Rams offense will improve, going from the league's worst ranking to the middle of the pack, if not higher. Here's why:

The Rams drafted Jason Smith second overall. Teams that use a lot of draft value (based on the classic "draft value chart") on offensive linemen improve on offense the following season. Correlation does not equal causation — the 2002 Bills improved because they traded for Drew Bledsoe, not because they drafted Mike Williams fourth overall — but the numbers are pretty stunning. From 2001-2008, a dozen teams used at least 1,200 "draft value points" on offensive linemen during the first four rounds of the draft (Table 1). All 12 teams improved on offense the following season, by an average of 15 percentage points of DVOA. Of course, nearly all of these offenses were below average the year before, but they weren't necessarily bottom of the barrel. Four of the five teams that spent at least 2,000 "value points" on offensive linemen improved by more than 20 percentage points of DVOA, and all five of these teams had offensive DVOA above 0.0% that season.

The Rams lost a lot of games to injury last season. St. Louis finished third in Adjusted Games Lost by offensive starters, behind Seattle and Cincinnati. Steven Jackson, the Rams' best player, was in and out of the lineup with a strained thigh. Three starting skill players — receiver Drew Bennett, fullback Brian Leonard, and tight end Randy McMichael — missed most of the year with injuries. Guard Jacob

Table 1: Teams with 1200+ Draft Value in Offensive Linemen, 2001-2009

Team	Year	OL Draft Value	OFF DVOA	OFF DVOA Prev Yr	Change	Players (Picks)
MIA	2008	3074	16.6%	-5.3%	21.9%	Jake Long (1), Shawn Murphy (110)
OAK	2004	2950	0.5%	-11.3%	11.7%	Robert Gallery (2), Jake Grove (45)
ARI	2001	2500	2.7%	-21.0%	23.6%	Leonard Davis (2)
NYJ	2006	2440	6.2%	-21.5%	27.7%	D'Brickashaw Ferguson (4), Nick Mangold (29)
CLE	2007	2100	8.5%	-15.5%	24.0%	Joe Thomas (3)
CAR	2003	1800	-7.0%	-23.2%	16.2%	Jordan Gross (8), Bruce Nelson (50)
BUF	2002	1800	2.9%	-7.2%	10.1%	Mike Williams (4)
ARI	2007	1700	-2.7%	-8.8%	6.1%	Levi Brown (5)
MIN	2002	1540	3.1%	-7.1%	10.1%	Bryant McKinnie (7), Ed Ta'amu (132)
CIN	2002	1300	-2.4%	-14.1%	11.6%	Levi Jones (10)
DET	2001	1300	-14.3%	-17.7%	3.4%	Jeff Backus (18), Dominic Raiola (50)
DEN	2008	1278	24.0%	10.3%	13.7%	Ryan Clady (12), Kory Lichtensteiger (108)
STL	2009	2500	--	-24.0%	--	Jason Smith (2)
JAC	2009	1900	--	12.6%	--	Eugene Monroe (8), Eben Britton (39)
CIN	2009	1682	--	-13.4%	--	Andre Smith (6), Jonathan Luigs (106)

Table 2: Worst Red Zone Passing, 2000-2008

Team	Year	Red Zone Pass DVOA	Off DVOA	Off DVOA Y+1	Change
CHI	2004	-142.8%	-36.1%	-18.1%	18.1%
ARI	2000	-114.1%	-21.0%	2.7%	23.6%
HOU	2002	-113.9%	-41.4%	-16.4%	24.9%
STL	2008	-110.5%	-24.0%	--	--
BUF	2003	-103.5%	-18.2%	-5.1%	13.1%
OAK	2006	-94.8%	-36.5%	-17.4%	19.1%
ATL	2001	-86.4%	-13.8%	3.5%	17.3%
DAL	2003	-82.6%	-8.9%	-3.6%	5.3%
DAL	2002	-80.4%	-22.4%	-8.9%	13.5%
CIN	2001	-79.8%	-14.1%	-2.4%	11.6%
BAL	2000	-74.3%	-9.5%	-10.1%	-0.7%
GB	2006	-73.7%	-4.1%	16.8%	20.9%

Bell had a strained hamstring, and Pace was a walking pile of aches and pains.

As we've mentioned several times in the book, teams with a high number of injuries have a good chance of improvement the next year. From 2001-2008, 34 teams had at least 30 AGL for offensive starters, and these teams improved on offense the next year by an average of 3.8% DVOA. Now, it's true that the Rams have lost a lot of games to injury for two straight years. They ranked number one in offensive AGL in 2007. Perhaps they are just brittle. But if we look at teams with the most offensive AGL over two years instead of one, the trends are the same. Teams that averaged 30 AGL from offensive starters over a two-year period improved on offense by an average of 3.7% DVOA in the third season. Even if there was something about those old Rams that left them predisposed to injury, half of last year's starters are on other teams now, so they should be healthier one way or another.

The Rams were abysmal running in the red zone. St. Louis ranked 31st in the NFL with -37.8% DVOA on running plays in the red zone. This is a stat that tends to regress to the mean from year to year. From 2000-2007, 20 teams had red-zone rushing DVOA below -30%. The following season, these teams improved on offense by an average of 4.2% DVOA.

Of course, just like with injury rates, just because a stat tends to regress to the mean doesn't mean that it always does so. As bad as the Rams were in the red zone last year, they were even worse in 2007, when their red zone rushing DVOA of -86.9% was the worst of any team from 2000-2008. Is Steven Jack-

son just a terrible goal-line running back? We doubt it. In fact, the Rams' red zone rushing DVOA in 2006 was positive, 11.1%. In addition, as with injury rates, the rebound trend is just as strong for teams that have been poor for two years instead of one. The ten teams from 1999-2007 that had two straight years of red zone rushing DVOA below -20% improved their overall offensive DVOA in the third season by 7.9%, although the median improvement was just 3.0%. Looking at teams with two straight years of red zone rushing DVOA below -15%, we get more teams that improved by small amounts — with 17 qualifying teams, the average improvement was 7.8% and the median improvement was 6.3%.

As bad as their running game was near the goal line, the passing game was even worse. The Rams' passing DVOA in the red zone last season was an execrable -110.5%, the fourth worst figure of any team this decade. Marc Bulger was 13-for-30, averaging just 2.4 yards per pass with four touchdowns and an interception. Trent Green was a complete disaster: 1-for-8 with no touchdowns, two interceptions, and a sack. Include a four-yard Defensive Pass Interference call against Dwight Lowery of the Jets, and Green gained zero net yards per pass in the red zone.

No quarterback could be this bad in the red zone year after year and keep his job, and poor red zone passing is a massive indicator of offensive improvement. The four other teams since 2000 with DVOA below -100% each improved on offense the next year by at least 13 percentage points of DVOA (Table 2). Twenty-one teams since 2000 had passing DVOA below -60% in the red zone; 19 of these teams improved on offense the next year, while the other two (the 2001 Ravens and 2003 Lions) dropped by less than one percentage point of DVOA. The average change for these 21 teams was 13.7% DVOA.

The St. Louis offense recovered only five of 17 fumbles in 2008. Since fumble recovery is essentially random, the Rams' offense could fumble the same number of times in 2009 and we would expect four fewer turnovers.

The indicators why the Rams' defense may improve to league-average are not quite as strong; since defense is by nature more variable from year

Table 3: High and Low Standard Deviations from 2009 Win Projections

Team	Mean Wins	StDev	Team	Mean Wins	StDev
STL	8.2	2.76	HOU	6.9	1.98
GB	7.4	2.76	JAC	10.2	1.95
CAR	8.3	2.64	SD	12.5	1.95
ARI	5.6	2.62	NE	11.4	1.91
NYG	10.0	2.62	BUF	5.3	1.89
PIT	9.6	2.61			

to year than offense is, a good amount of the projection is based on every defense simply regressing to the mean each year. However, there is at least one strong statistical indicator pointing to a Rams improvement on defense as well. Like taking an offensive lineman high, drafting front seven players over a two-year span often leads to a significant defensive improvement. Over the past two drafts, the Rams have spent 3,138 "draft value points" on front seven players in the first four rounds, including last year's choice of defensive end Chris Long second overall and this year's second-round selection of Ohio State middle linebacker James Laurinaitis. Since 2001, a dozen teams have spent more than 3,000 "draft value points" on front seven players over a two-year span; seven improved their defensive DVOA, four by more than 10 percentage points. Subjectively, there is reason to believe that young talent in the front seven means even more to the Rams than to other teams trying to turn things around, because of the hire of Spagnuolo. The hope in St. Louis is that his defensive schemes can turn players like Long and Adam Carriker into a top rush

like the one Spagnuolo won a Super Bowl with in New York.

All of this optimism does need to be tempered by the presence of some substantial holes on the St. Louis roster. The secondary, for example, is a significant weakness. Although Oshiomogho Atogwe and free agent addition James Butler give St. Louis a good pair of safeties, the Rams have only one cornerback, Ron Bartell, whose past performance has reached the level of even an average NFL starter. There's very little depth at linebacker, especially after Chris Draft was forced into the starting lineup by the May decision to release last year's leading tackler, Pisa Tinoisamoa.

The Rams' wide receiver corps is also filled with question marks. Going into training camp, the top three receivers on the depth chart are Donnie Avery, Keenan Burton, and Laurent Robinson, who combined have just four years of NFL experience and 108 receptions. Toss in Derek Stanley and rookie Brooks Foster, and the top five receivers have just 114 receptions. As we pointed out in the chapter on the Chicago Bears, teams with very little career experience from their wide receivers have generally had very poor passing games. Many of these teams struggled because their quarterbacks were as green as their wideouts; that's not a problem for the Rams, but it will be if Bulger is hurt and the Rams have to depend on Kyle Boller or Brock Berlin.

Put it all together, and the Rams have very little depth anywhere except the lines. If they go through a spate of injuries anything like what they've seen the last two seasons, they're going to get keelhauled by the rest of the league. Again.

In our simulation that produces the win projections at the start of the chapter, the Rams have a higher standard deviation than any other team (Table 3). Even with all these positive indicators, their mean projection calls for just eight wins. And just because the Rams are virtually guaranteed to improve doesn't mean they're guaranteed to improve by much. Both the offense and defense could get a little better, and the Rams would still end up 5-11.

But the seeds for the "miracle season" are here. It's more likely to happen in St. Louis than it is to happen in Oakland, or San Francisco, or Buffalo. For the first time in a while, Rams fans have actual reason for hope. Maybe it won't pay off, but at least that's something.

Aaron Schatz

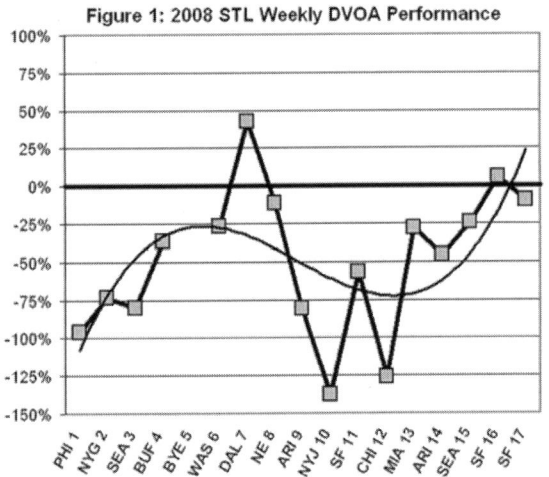

Figure 1: 2008 STL Weekly DVOA Performance

2008 Rams Stats by Week

Wk	vs.	W-L	PF	PA	YDF	YDA	TO	Total	Off	Def	ST
1	@PHI	L	3	38	166	522	0	-96%	-35%	57%	-4%
2	NYG	L	13	41	201	441	-1	-73%	-32%	41%	0%
3	@SEA	L	13	37	240	407	-1	-80%	-45%	46%	11%
4	BUF	L	14	31	380	277	-1	-36%	-10%	13%	-13%
5	BYE										
6	@WAS	W	19	17	200	368	+2	-27%	-35%	8%	17%
7	DAL	W	34	14	325	341	+4	43%	27%	-19%	-3%
8	@NE	L	16	23	361	348	+1	-11%	-8%	-1%	-4%
9	ARI	L	13	34	231	510	-3	-81%	-46%	44%	9%
10	@NYJ	L	3	47	200	373	-5	-137%	-79%	55%	-4%
11	@SF	L	16	35	406	334	-1	-57%	-13%	31%	-13%
12	CHI	L	3	27	207	334	-2	-126%	-94%	29%	-4%
13	MIA	L	12	16	278	327	-2	-28%	-25%	6%	3%
14	@ARI	L	10	34	308	335	-2	-46%	-23%	21%	-2%
15	SEA	L	20	23	342	333	0	-25%	-13%	20%	8%
16	SF	L	16	17	343	273	+3	5%	-13%	-17%	2%
17	@ATL	L	27	31	408	417	+3	-10%	16%	20%	-6%

Trends and Splits

	Offense	Rank	Defense	Rank
Total DVOA	-24.0%	32	23.4%	30
Unadjusted VOA	-24.5%	32	21.3%	30
Weighted trend	-22.8%	32	18.0%	29
Variance	9.3%	27	6.2%	19
Average opponent	4.1%	15	5.0%	16
Passing	-26.1%	32	23.7%	27
Rushing	-10.4%	29	23.0%	32
First down	-27.1%	32	25.8%	31
Second down	-15.4%	30	31.2%	31
Third down	-31.4%	30	4.1%	14
First half	-13.3%	30	23.8%	31
Second half	-35.0%	32	22.8%	31
Red Zone	-70.2%	32	44.1%	30
Late and close	-38.8%	32	28.9%	30

Five-Year Performance

Year	W-L	Pyth	Est W	PF	PA	TO	Total	Rk	Off	Rk	Def	Rk	ST	Rk	Off AGL	Rk	Def AGL	Rk
2004	8-8	6.1	5.6	319	392	-24	-26.5%	30	-3.2%	19	15.8%	28	-7.5%	32	27.1	10	19.0	20
2005	6-10	6.4	5.1	363	429	-10	-25.5%	30	-9.6%	21	12.0%	29	-3.9%	31	24.8	9	6.6	29
2006	8-8	7.6	7.4	367	381	+14	-13.8%	25	3.3%	14	12.7%	30	-4.4%	31	3.3	31	5.0	29
2007	3-13	3.7	3.7	263	438	-10	-34.9%	32	-22.0%	31	9.1%	25	-3.9%	27	52.4	1	27.4	9
2008	2-14	2.6	2.0	232	465	-5	-47.5%	31	-24.0%	32	23.4%	30	-0.2%	18	50.3	3	29.9	12

Strategic Tendencies

Run/Pass		Rank	Offense		Rank	Defense		Rank	Other		Rank
Runs, all plays	42%	21	3+ WR	60%	9	Rush 3	4.1%	20	2+ RB, Pct Runs	49%	31
Runs, first half	47%	8	4+ WR	20%	4	Rush 4	60.2%	22	1 RB/2 TE, Pct Runs	56%	10
Runs, first down	49%	17	2+ TE	27%	14	Rush 5	28.4%	4	1RB/3+WR, Pct Runs	32%	7
Runs, second-long	38%	17	Single back	70%	5	Rush 6+	7.3%	18	Zone Blitz	2%	22
Runs, power sit.	65%	19	Play action	12%	25	Rush 7+	1.2%	18	Go for it on 4th	1.23	6
Runs, behind 2H	32%	18	Max protect	12%	4	Sacks by LB	13.3%	20	Offensive Pace	30.5	13
Pass, ahead 2H	50%	6	Outside pocket	5%	30	Sacks by DB	20.0%	2	Defensive Pace	30.4	10

St. Louis threw to the right side of the field more often than any other team (52 percent of passes) and threw to the middle the least often (14 percent). The same pattern existed on defense, where Rams opponents led the league in frequency throwing right (48 percent) and were last in frequency throwing to the middle (16 percent). This doesn't seem to be an issue with the St. Louis scorer, because when you combine the Rams offense and defense, the percentage of passes marked as "middle" was roughly the same at home and on the road. This becomes even more interesting when you see that Rams opponents didn't take advantage of the middle of the field even though the Rams had *by far* the worst pass defense against passes up the middle: 137.2% DVOA, when only one other team (Buffalo) was above 75%. The average pass against the middle of the Rams defense gained 11.9 yards, with no other defense above 10 — and the average pass marked "deep middle" gained 21.2 yards with no other defense above 18. ● St. Louis had the worst defense in the league against play-action passes, giving up 4.6 yards more per pass when the opponent used a play fake. ● The St. Louis defense ranked 30th in Adjusted Sack Rate on first down, but 11th on second down and third on third down. ● Rams opponents ran on 39 percent of their plays out of three-wide sets, the highest figure in the league. ● Note that the "go for it on fourth" rating above is for Jim Haslett only.

Passing

Player	DYAR	DVOA	Plays	NtYds	Avg	YAC	C%	TD	Int
Marc Bulger	-259	-19.8%	485	2550	5.3	4.9	57.1%	11	12
Trent Green*	-204	-52.9%	79	471	6.0	5.9	52.8%	0	6

Rushing

Player	DYAR	DVOA	Plays	Yds	Avg	TD	Fum	Suc
Steven Jackson	66	-2.5%	253	1047	4.1	7	5	46%
Antonio Pittman	12	-4.9%	79	296	3.7	0	0	44%
Kenneth Darby	9	-1.9%	32	140	4.4	0	1	41%
Travis Minor	-11	-30.3%	13	29	2.2	0	0	23%
Donnie Avery	33	32.8%	9	59	6.6	1	0	--
Marc Bulger	8	8.8%	7	50	7.1	0	0	--
Dante Hall	4	-25.2%	4	9	2.3	0	0	--
Keenan Burton	0	-40.1%	3	8	2.7	0	0	--
Mike Karney	16	15.8%	8	10	1.3	2	0	75%

Receiving

Player	DYAR	DVOA	Plays	Ctch	Yds	Y/C	YAC	TD	C%
Torry Holt*	12	-11.4%	119	64	796	12.4	2.3	4	54%
Donnie Avery	-32	-16.5%	104	54	684	12.7	3.8	4	52%
Dane Looker	-67	-31.9%	47	23	271	11.8	2.4	2	49%
Keenan Burton	-30	-26.7%	29	13	172	13.2	4.4	1	45%
Dante Hall	9	-5.6%	18	12	105	8.8	1.2	1	67%
Derek Stanley	-15	-29.3%	12	6	119	19.8	10.5	1	50%
Laurent Robinson	21	36.8%	6	5	52	10.4	5.4	0	83%
Randy McMichael	6	-2.2%	21	11	139	12.6	6.0	1	52%
Joe Klopfenstein	-41	-41.0%	19	11	124	11.3	3.1	0	58%
Daniel Fells	10	6.2%	11	7	81	11.6	5.6	0	64%
Anthony Becht*	-31	-48.7%	11	6	39	6.5	3.2	0	55%
Steven Jackson	46	0.2%	62	40	379	9.5	9.4	1	65%
Antonio Pittman	4	-11.4%	27	18	137	7.6	8.7	0	67%
Kenneth Darby	75	43.6%	21	19	183	9.6	10.1	0	90%
Travis Minor	9	13.0%	6	5	35	7.0	6.6	0	83%
Dan Kreider*	-19	-96.8%	5	0	0	0.0	0.0	0	0%
Mike Karney	-31	-57.3%	12	9	18	2.0	2.6	0	75%

Offensive Line

Year	Yards	ALY	Rank	Power	Rank	10+ Yds	Rank	Stuff	Rank	Sacks	ASR	Rank	False	Cont.
2006	4.36	4.41	8	63%	20	16%	15	18%	19	49	7.9%	24	41	27
2007	3.98	3.72	28	54%	26	22%	7	21%	27	48	8.1%	25	29	17
2008	3.99	3.73	28	66%	16	16%	22	19%	20	45	7.8%	23	28	25

Year	LE	Rank	LT	Rank	Mid	Rank	RT	Rank	RE	Rank
2006	2.43	31	4.27	14	4.67	2	4.03	21	5.20	4
2007	2.73	30	3.13	31	4.01	17	3.66	27	4.06	16
2008	2.58	29	3.68	25	3.76	26	4.58	6	3.29	26

It's rare that a team can cut a seven-time Pro Bowl left tackle and actually upgrade their offensive line, but the Rams were wise to part ways with Orlando Pace, whose seemingly endless stream of injuries limited his effectiveness and destroyed any and all attempts at line continuity. Then, general manager Billy Devaney did the smart thing by using the second overall pick on Baylor tackle Jason Smith. During May minicamps, the Rams used Smith at right tackle and started Alex "The Human Penalty" Barron on the left side. It's not entirely clear why the Rams are hesitant to start Smith at left tackle — Jake Long, Joe Thomas, and Ryan Clady all made a smooth transition to the professional ranks, and there's no obvious reason why Smith wouldn't follow the same path.

Smith isn't the only big new addition; the Rams also secured the services of former Ravens center Jason Brown, the top offensive lineman available in free agency. Brown is strong, smart, and battle-tested after lining up opposite Kelly Gregg, Trevor Pryce and Haloti Ngata in practice every day for the past four years. Brown also provides some much needed veteran leadership for a unit that often plays with a certain immaturity. That would be our cue to mention right guard Richie Incognito, whose existence seems dedicated to defying his last name through acts of embarrassing petulance. Jacob Bell occupies the other guard spot. The Rams do have good depth on the line — rookie tackle Phillip Trautwein (Florida) was one of the best players left in the undrafted free agent pool, while all those injuries in recent years have given backups like Mark Setterstrom and Adam Goldberg starting experience.

Defensive Front Seven

Defensive Line	Age	Pos	Plays	TmPct	Rk	Stop	Dfts	Overall Stop%	Rk	AvYd	Rk	Pass Rush Sack	Hit	Hur	vs. Run Runs	St%	Yds	vs. Pass Pass	St%	Yds
Victor Adeyanju	26	DE	47	6.0%	39	30	11	64%	87	2.7	79	2.0	2	3	42	64%	2.7	5	60%	2.4
James Hall	32	DE	43	5.5%	44	29	12	67%	76	1.7	39	6.5	4	5	35	60%	3.5	8	100%	-6.5
Chris Long	24	DE	39	5.0%	49	31	13	79%	30	1.5	37	4.0	6	3	33	79%	2.3	6	83%	-3.2
Clifton Ryan	25	DT	32	4.1%	53	25	7	78%	33	2.2	46	0.0	1	3	30	77%	2.4	2	100%	-0.5
La'Roi Glover*	35	DT	31	4.0%	56	25	6	81%	19	2.3	53	0.5	6	2	27	81%	2.6	4	75%	0.0
Adam Carriker	25	DT	23	3.1%	66	20	4	87%	5	2.1	42	0.0	3	2	23	87%	2.1	0	0%	0.0
Leonard Little	35	DE	18	2.6%	--	16	12	89%	--	-0.6	--	6.0	5	13	10	80%	2.1	8	100%	-3.9

Linebackers	Age	Pos	Plays	TmPct	Rk	Stop	Dfts	Overall Stop%	AvYd	Pass Rush Sack	Hit	Hur	vs. Run Runs	St%	Rk	Yds	Rk	vs. Pass Tgts	Suc%	Rk	AdjYd	Rk
Pisa Tinoisamoa*	28	OLB	100	12.8%	35	48	19	48%	5.2	3.0	2	2	61	54%	93	3.7	67	37	46%	59	8.2	81
Will Witherspoon	29	ILB	75	9.6%	70	37	7	49%	5.7	1.0	2	2	45	60%	72	4.2	84	27	47%	56	7.6	71
Quinton Culberson	23	OLB	45	5.8%	--	26	7	58%	4.6	0.0	0	1	32	59%	--	4.0	--	12	81%	--	3.7	--
Chris Draft	33	OLB	30	5.1%	--	17	4	57%	5.3	0.0	1	3	21	62%	--	3.1	--	11	74%	--	3.3	--

Year	Yards	ALY	Rank	Power	Rank	10+ Yds	Rank	Stuff	Rank	Sack	ASR	Rank
2006	4.94	4.66	28	67%	20	21%	27	13%	31	34	6.6%	16
2007	4.34	4.18	21	54%	4	21%	24	21%	9	31	6.2%	17
2008	5.23	4.65	31	66%	17	24%	29	17%	21	30	6.2%	15

Year	LE	Rank	LT	Rank	Mid	Rank	RT	Rank	RE	Rank
2006	4.85	24	4.72	23	4.84	31	4.38	20	3.55	11
2007	3.65	11	4.15	16	4.28	23	3.86	12	5.13	31
2008	5.74	32	3.89	9	4.36	20	5.20	32	5.28	29

While Spagnuolo's attention will be spread thin as a rookie coach, he undoubtedly will want to focus on developing the team's previous two first-round picks, tackle Adam Carriker and end Chris Long. Carriker has struggled though an uneven two seasons, with his versatility actually creating more problems than it was worth; the team couldn't decide where to line him up and kept changing his responsibilities as a result. While Spagnuolo's fond of moving his players around, he's intending to keep Carriker at the left defensive tackle spot, where his responsibility will primarily be to penetrate through his gap and rush the passer. Clifton Ryan is the favorite to start at the nose.

Long showed flashes while starting all 16 games last year, and while he only had four sacks, it's far too early to suggest that he's anything resembling a disappointment. Remember, Mario Williams only had 4.5 sacks as a rookie in 2006. He remains a very promising two-way prospect at end. Leonard Little starts across from him; the only reason why he wasn't released along with Holt and Pace was because the team will actually save $5 million in cap space by having him play as opposed to cutting him. The failure of Victor Adeyanju to develop also figured into that decision; Adeyanju will return on a one-year deal this season before likely departing.

After the previous management signed Will Witherspoon away from Carolina and moved him into the middle, the new braintrust is moving him to the weak side in the hopes that he'll make more plays. That also opens up a spot for second-round pick James Laurinaitis, who made his name playing in the middle for Ohio State. The idea is to put Witherspoon in a place where he can rush the passer and attack the line of scrimmage, but it's also a move defined by Laurinaitis' limitations; while he's a sure tackler and has excellent instincts, his athleticism is questionable at this level. The team unexpectedly cut Pisa Tinoisamoa in May after discovering that he wasn't stout enough to handle strong-side backer; Chris Draft is the likely starter, but don't be surprised if the Rams go shopping during training camp cutdowns for a better player.

Defensive Secondary

Secondary	Age	Pos	Plays	TmPct	Rk	Stop	Dfts	Yds	Rk	St%	Rk	Tgts	Tgt%	Rk	Dist	Suc%	Rk	AdjYd	Rk	Yds	PD	Int
				Overall				vs. Run				vs. Pass										
O.J. Atogwe	29	FS	87	11.2%	25	21	13	10.8	76	20%	74	24	6.0%	50	18.7	38%	73	10.7	71	10.6	5	5
Ronald Bartell	27	CB	77	9.9%	23	32	9	14.5	79	30%	66	95	23.5%	5	12.1	57%	19	5.9	14	5.9	19	3
Jason Craft*	33	CB	66	9.0%	34	27	13	6.4	42	39%	47	53	14.1%	66	7.9	47%	53	8.6	68	8.4	6	1
Corey Chavous*	33	SS	61	7.8%	60	21	7	5.7	20	35%	54	22	5.5%	60	14.5	46%	60	14.8	78	14.6	1	0
Fakhir Brown*	32	CB	54	8.5%	44	18	8	9.4	65	29%	70	68	20.8%	22	12.9	43%	71	8.8	75	8.6	12	1
Tye Hill	27	CB	22	11.3%	--	6	0	4.5	--	50%	--	19	18.9%	--	15.2	30%	--	14.9	--	14.3	1	0
James Butler	27	FS	71	10.1%	37	28	9	6.4	28	44%	32	25	6.4%	45	10.4	66%	7	7.5	30	7.6	4	3

Year	Pass D Rank	vs. #1 WR	Rk	vs. #2 WR	Rk	vs. Other WR	Rk	vs. TE	Rk	vs. RB	Rk
2006	25	10.8%	24	6.6%	20	-20.8%	6	8.4%	23	-7.4%	13
2007	25	19.1%	27	12.5%	22	-23.6%	6	1.2%	11	-3.2%	14
2008	25	7.2%	18	7.3%	22	25.5%	31	2.8%	16	-0.8%	11

First, the good news: The Rams have one very good safety — Oshiomogho Atogwe, arguably the Rams' best player last year — and one entirely serviceable one (strong safety James Butler, who Spagnuolo brought over from New York). Now that most casual fans are aware of the skills of a certain hard-to-spell cornerback who plays in Oakland, Atogwe has taken on the mantle of "NFL's most underrated defensive back of Nigerian descent." For extra bonus points, he's also Canadian, raised in Windsor, Ontario. Perhaps that is why he had such an un-NFL-star-like reaction of gratitude after the Rams stuck the franchise tag on him: "It's a blessing to come out here and play. And to be thought of as one of the top five at my position is an honor. I relish this."

Now, the bad news: The Rams have one decent cornerback (Ron Bartell, who significantly improved his charting stats last year) and one giant question mark as to who will be playing alongside him. It has been three years since the Rams took Tye Hill 15th overall, but it is increasingly obvious that not only is the oft-injured Hill never going to be a lockdown corner, but he's barely serviceable in nickel packages. The remaining options on the roster are equally terrifying: Jonathan Wade is really just a backup, and rookie Bradley Fletcher (the third-round draft pick out of Iowa) is better suited to play safety in the NFL. They also have 2008 fourth-round pick Justin King, who missed his entire rookie season with a torn ligament in his big toe.

Special Teams

Year	DVOA	Rank	FG/XP	Rank	Net Kick	Rank	Kick Ret	Rank	Net Punt	Rank	Punt Ret	Rank	Hidden	Rank
2006	-4.4%	31	3.9	9	-16.0	32	-13.7	32	0.0	20	-0.1	14	-11.5	28
2007	-3.9%	27	-5.3	28	-18.4	31	-7.6	28	6.1	7	2.5	11	-17.9	32
2008	-0.2%	18	5.1	7	2.3	15	-10.9	31	4.2	14	-1.8	20	-16.6	32

Sometimes, average is good. Sure, the Rams' special teams only ranked 18th in total DVOA, but compared to the team's rank on total defense (30th) and total offense (32nd), that's not so bad. The improvement is largely attributable to kicker Josh Brown, who delivered a 10-point positive swing in the kicking game. In the return game, injuries to Dante Hall eventually resulted in his being replaced by Derek Stanley, who was average in 25 returns (we mean that literally: his returns were worth -0.01 points of field position). Hall went unsigned, so Stanley should return kicks and punts again this year. Donnie Jones returns as the punter; he gets very good distance on his punts, but often outkicks his coverage units.

The Rams have also been victimized by the "hidden" factors that affect special teams play and are out of their control. Like what? Well, opposing field goal kickers were 31-of-32 against them last year. Nick Folk missed a 46-yarder in Week 7. That's it. They've also been getting annihilated on kickoffs; after you throw out squibs and onside kicks, the average kickoff against the Rams went 68.3 yards in both 2007 and 2008. That's the highest figure in the league both years, higher even than Denver.

Coaching Staff

Two years ago, Steve Spagnuolo turned down an offer to become head coach for the Redskins, one of the NFL's most storied franchises — albeit one owned by the NFL's version of George Steinbrenner circa 1985 — to remain the highest paid defensive coordinator in the league. So why in the world would he leave one year later to become head coach of the hapless Rams? The answer was partially revealed during the draft after the Rams used their second-, third- and fourth-round picks to select defensive players. Between those selections and the first-round picks the Rams invested in their defensive line the two years prior, Spagnuolo clearly believes he can work the same magic that he did in New York. It's also clear that he has a good working relationship with general manager Bill Devaney — after the draft, Devaney joked that Spagnuolo used some "stealth moves" to take over the Rams' draft board — and is consulted on all roster moves that Devaney makes.

Spagnuolo has hired 19 new coaches (!) but here we'll focus on the two coordinators. Former Carolina Panthers linebackers coach Ken Flajole (believe it or not, it's pronounced to rhyme with "a-hole") will serve as defensive coordinator, though obviously Spagnuolo will be heavily involved in scheming as well. Flajole plans to have the Rams' underwhelming cornerbacks press wide receivers at the line more frequently, relying upon the more talented safeties to provide coverage help deep. Flajole is also considered an expert on coaxing great play out of mediocre linebackers, a theory which will be put to the test this year.

On offense, Spagnuolo hired former Eagles quarterback coach Pat Shurmur as his coordinator. Befitting someone from the Bill Walsh-Andy Reid coaching tree, Shurmur is installing a version of the West Coast Offense similar to what we've seen in Philadelphia since, well, forever. It's a good fit for quarterback Marc Bulger, whose accuracy is better than his arm strength, and the emphasis on short, quick passes should reduce the number of times an Alex Barron miscue leads to Bulger getting pile-driven into the artificial turf. Steven Jackson will play the Brian Westbrook role in this offense, which should make more than a few fantasy football owners very, very happy.

San Diego Chargers

The San Diego Chargers are the prohibitive favorites to win Super Bowl XLIV. Our 2009 statistical projection for the Chargers is so off the charts that it may endanger the boundaries of reality.

In the six years that Football Outsiders has been doing preseason team projections, only one team has had a projection this impressive: the 2007 New England Patriots. In fact, this year's Chargers enter the season looking even stronger than the Patriots did two years ago. The 2007 Patriots averaged 33.5% DVOA and 12.1 wins in our 10,000 preseason simulations. This Chargers team averages 40.3% DVOA and 12.5 wins in the preseason simulations. If they meet their average projection, they'll have the fourth-best DVOA of any team since 1994.

How can a team coming off an 8-8 season have such outsized expectations? Start with the fact that the 2008 Chargers didn't play anything like an 8-8 team. They would have been 9-7 if not for Ed Hochuli's blown fumble call against Denver in Week 2, but that's not the only issue. The Chargers outscored opponents by a total of 92 points. They lost four games by a field goal or less, and they had no losses by more than nine points. The Pythagorean formula gives them 10.2 wins. Our "estimated wins" formula, based on DVOA in specifically important situations, gives them 10.6 wins.

The Chargers were extraordinarily strong in one

CHARGERS SUMMARY

2008 Record: 8-8

Pythagorean Wins: 10.2 (7th)

DVOA: 17.5% (7th)

Offense: 24.1% (1st)

Defense: 8.3% (20th)

Special Teams: 1.7% (12th)

Variance: 17.2% (17th)

2008: Disappointing Chargers still slip into playoffs after Denver implodes.

2009: Ridiculous Numbers vs. the Power of Norvalicious.

2009 Mean Projection: 12.5 wins

On the Clock (0-3): 0%

Loserville (4-6): 0%

Mediocrity (7-8): 1%

Playoff Contender (9-10): 12%

Super Bowl Contender (11+): 87%

Projected Average Opponent: -2.9% (27th)

area: pass offense, where they had the best DVOA in the league. They were mediocre in every other area, and that includes the things that you need to do in order to salt away games late: running the ball and playing defense. In four of their eight losses, the Chargers let their opponents march down the field for the winning score in the final two minutes. That doesn't even count Week 10 against Kansas City, when the Chargers let the Chiefs go down the field in the final two minutes to make the score 20-19, but the Chiefs chose to go for two and didn't make it.

However, mediocre does not mean "poor," and there was really no area on the field where the 2008 Chargers had an outright weakness. Even the problem that garnered the most press attention, the decline of former MVP LaDainian Tomlinson, was not as bad as it appeared on the surface. Tomlinson's average of 3.8 yards per carry spurred questions about whether he had hit the career wall at age 29. But while Tomlinson definitely was not the same player he had been in past years, he wasn't quite as bad as that yards per carry average suggests. His biggest problem was the lack of breakaway runs — he had only seven runs of 15 or more yards, compared to 26 such runs in 2007. On the other hand, Tomlinson had an excellent 67 percent Success Rate on third and fourth down.

Some of the struggles can be blamed on injuries

2009 Chargers Schedule

Week	Opp.	Week	Opp.	Week	Opp.
1	at OAK (Mon.)	7	at KC	13	at CLE
2	BAL	8	OAK	14	at DAL
3	MIA	9	at NYG	15	CIN
4	at PIT	10	PHI	16	at TEN (Fri.)
5	BYE	11	at DEN	17	WAS
6	DEN (Mon.)	12	KC		

— Tomlinson played for much of the year with turf toe, then tore a groin tendon right before the playoffs — but given all the aches and pains he's had the last couple years, it's safe to say that Tomlinson will have to deal with nagging injuries the rest of his career. While he will no longer be transcendent, he's probably not finished either. One good sign is that he continued to be useful as a receiver in 2008. The end of a good running back's career is often foreshadowed by a big drop in receptions one or two years prior, but Tomlinson has had between 50 and 60 receptions for five straight years. Tomlinson restructured his contract this offseason in order to remain in San Diego, which in turn allowed the Chargers to retain his change-of-pace partner, Darren Sproles, with an expensive one-year contract.

The media was so busy talking about whether or not Tomlinson was toast that nobody mentioned just how robust the Chargers' passing game was. Name a passing split, and the Chargers were among the best teams in the league. They had the highest DVOA on passes behind the line of scrimmage, the highest DVOA on passes of 1 to 15 yards, and the highest DVOA on deep passes of 16-plus yards. They ranked first on passes to the right or center of the field and sixth on passes to the left side. They ranked first in DVOA with play-action and second in DVOA without play-action, first in passing DVOA with Rivers under center and fourth with him in shotgun. Among quarterbacks with at least 100 passes, Rivers ranked first in DVOA on passes to wide receivers, second on passes to running backs, and — wait, this can't be right — 17th on passes to tight ends?

Actually, that is right. The Chargers had the best passing game in the league despite an off year from their best receiver. Thanks in part to slow recovery from offseason foot surgery as well as a hip stinger, Antonio Gates had his first season under

900 yards since 2003. He ranked 13th among tight ends in DVOA, the lowest ranking of his career. The healthier, better Gates is strong reason to believe that San Diego's offense will remain one of the league's best.

The defense isn't going to reach the same heights as the offense, but we're projecting significant improvement in 2009. The reasoning starts with the good ol' Plexiglass Principle, the idea that teams which decline tend to improve the following year, and vice versa. The Chargers ranked sixth in defensive DVOA in 2007, including third in pass defense.

The main reason the defense struggled in 2008 was health, which then becomes another reason to expect a rebound. Based on Adjusted Games Lost by starters, the San Diego defense actually had average health in 2008. However, what matters is not just how many injuries there were, but who was injured. The trends regarding health are a little more complicated than "teams with more injuries tend to bounce back the following year." On defense, Adjusted Games Lost by linebackers have a much stronger correlation with improving defense than Adjusted Games Lost by defensive linemen. The Chargers had 18.3 AGL from starting linebackers, leading the NFL, but just 1.4 AGL from starting defensive linemen. The linebacker who racked up the majority of those Adjusted Games Lost happened to be the team's best defensive player, Shawne Merriman, and defenses that add (or return) a player with double-digit sacks tend to improve. And all of these statistical measures of injury don't even account for the fact that cor-

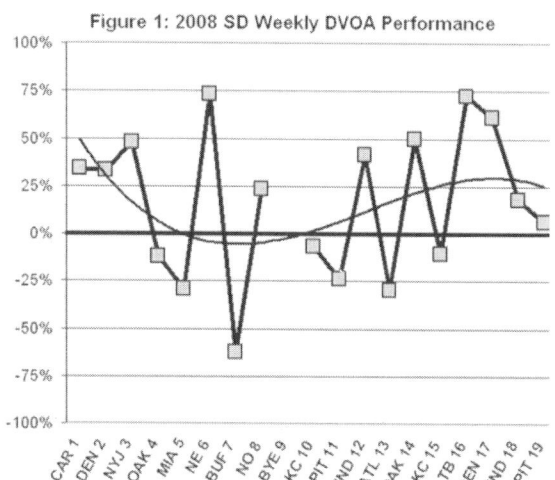

Figure 1: 2008 SD Weekly DVOA Performance

Table 1: Effect of Short-Yardage Runs on Defensive DVOA, 2000-2008

OL Power	Avg. Def DVOA	Avg. Def DVOA Next Year	Avg. Change
>70%	1.0%	-0.8%	-1.9%
65-70%	-2.4%	-1.5%	0.8%
60-65%	-3.0%	-1.9%	1.1%
<60%	-0.3%	2.1%	2.4%

nerback Antonio Cromartie played the entire year with a fractured hip, and is bound to be better now that he's had time to heal.

Despite our best efforts to separate offense and defense with our DVOA ratings, the two units do interact. For example, teams that are strong in short-yardage situations tend to see their defenses improve (Table 1). Although their running game was mediocre overall, the Chargers were one of the best short-yardage running teams in the league last year, with a 78 percent Success Rate in power situations.

Another interesting trend that runs in San Diego's favor: Defenses whose opponents tend to milk the clock improve the following season. From 2000-2007, there were 32 defenses whose opponents averaged more than 2:50 in time of possession per drive. The following year, these defenses improved by an average of -4.7% DVOA (Table 2).

But wait, there's more. The average age of San Diego's projected starting front seven is 28.0, and the average age of the projected starting secondary is 27.9. This defense is right smack in the middle of its prime, with a balanced mix of younger players and veterans.

In total, the package is awfully impressive. A powerful offense and a talented defense almost guaranteed to improve. We haven't even mentioned the consistently good special teams or the schedule, one of the league's ten easiest (according to average DVOA of opponent). Between the sidelines, it seems like a Chargers championship is inevitable. On the sidelines, however, stands the Force of Evitability.

Table 2: Effect of Opposing Time of Possession on Defensive DVOA, 2000-2008

Average Opponent Drive	Avg. Def DVOA	Avg. Def DVOA Next Year	Avg. Change
Over 2:50	9.9%	5.1%	-4.7%
2:40-2:50	3.3%	1.7%	-1.6%
2:30-2:40	-2.7%	-2.2%	0.5%
Under 2:30	-9.0%	-2.7%	6.3%

His name is Norv Turner.

Two years ago, in *Pro Football Prospectus 2007*, we looked at Turner's poor historical record. He was one of only eight coaches who had a career losing record and still fell short of their teams' Pythagorean projection by at least one half-win every 16 games. He also ranked as one of history's worst coaches when it came to holding fourth-quarter leads.

Despite two postseason appearances, Turner's historical record of underperformance hasn't really changed. Both of his Chargers teams fell short of their Pythagorean projection, making it nine years out of 11 where Turner's teams have won fewer games than you would expect given their points scored and allowed. You read the rundown of fourth-quarter losses earlier in the chapter, so you know that problem hasn't gone away either.

It's not strong enough to say that Turner is on the hot seat this season; it's more like the biblical burning bush, blazing continuously since Turner took the San Diego job two years ago. Sportswriters started penning "fire Norv" columns when the Chargers started 1-3 in 2007. When Turner fired defensive coordinator Ted Cottrell halfway through last season, many observers thought he was trying to deflect the blame for San Diego's 4-5 start. Off and on for two years, players like Shawne Merriman have been complaining to the press that teammates aren't trying hard enough. Turner's former players like Jerry Rice and Warren Sapp have called him out in the press as incompetent. Certainly, some of his current players share that opinion.

No matter how good this team plays during the regular season, it only takes one bad game to get knocked out of the playoffs. The Chargers can go 14-2 or 15-1, but there may still come a battle of the minds where Turner has to out-coach Bill Belichick, or Mike Tomlin, or Jeff Fisher. No matter how much talent this team has, it's tough to put your money on the Chargers when that time comes.

During the regular season, however, this team looks like it is going to be a juggernaut. Essentially, they're combining the 2008 Chargers offense with the 2007 Chargers defense, and that combination creates the best team in the National Football League. What happens when that team is coached by Norv Turner? Tune in this January to find out.

Aaron Schatz

2008 Chargers Stats by Week

Wk	vs.	W-L	PF	PA	YDF	YDA	TO	Total	Off	Def	ST
1	CAR	L	24	26	316	388	0	34%	36%	5%	3%
2	@DEN	L	38	39	456	486	0	33%	24%	10%	20%
3	NYJ	W	48	29	357	308	+3	48%	55%	-14%	-21%
4	@OAK	W	28	18	295	323	0	-12%	-8%	-3%	-8%
5	@MIA	L	10	17	202	390	+1	-29%	-13%	31%	14%
6	NE	W	30	10	404	299	0	73%	49%	-24%	0%
7	@BUF	L	14	23	263	370	-3	-62%	-3%	57%	-3%
8	@NO	L	32	37	451	409	-2	24%	40%	26%	10%
9	BYE										
10	KC	W	20	19	400	339	-2	-7%	16%	29%	6%
11	@PIT	L	10	11	218	410	-2	-24%	-5%	21%	2%
12	IND	L	20	23	394	341	0	41%	33%	-9%	0%
13	ATL	L	16	22	201	348	+3	-30%	-26%	-7%	-11%
14	OAK	W	34	7	372	163	+3	50%	21%	-43%	-15%
15	@KC	W	22	21	394	277	-2	-11%	-2%	26%	17%
16	@TB	W	41	24	370	342	+3	72%	75%	7%	4%
17	DEN	W	52	21	491	406	+2	61%	66%	16%	11%
18	IND	W	23	17	357	366	-2	15%	17%	-9%	-10%
19	@PIT	L	24	35	290	342	-2	6%	39%	28%	-4%

Trends and Splits

	Offense	Rank	Defense	Rank
Total DVOA	24.1%	1	8.3%	20
Unadjusted VOA	26.8%	1	9.4%	22
Weighted trend	24.0%	4	8.9%	20
Variance	9.1%	26	5.3%	13
Average opponent	6.6%	6	7.9%	24
Passing	54.9%	1	14.4%	19
Rushing	4.0%	18	-0.2%	20
First down	12.0%	10	9.3%	24
Second down	25.2%	4	9.2%	20
Third down	45.0%	1	5.4%	16
First half	15.0%	8	15.7%	28
Second half	32.6%	1	0.6%	12
Red Zone	29.1%	4	-20.7%	6
Late and close	20.1%	10	-2.2%	11

Five-Year Performance

Year	W-L	Pyth	Est W	PF	PA	TO	Total	Rk	Off	Rk	Def	Rk	ST	Rk	Off AGL	Rk	Def AGL	Rk
2004	12-4	11.2	10.7	446	313	+15	19.1%	9	18.2%	7	-3.9%	12	-3.0%	26	15.3	16	6.0	31
2005	9-7	10.7	10.9	418	312	-8	23.4%	6	20.8%	6	-2.5%	16	0.1%	16	13.9	18	20.5	8
2006	14-2	12.1	12.0	492	303	+13	29.1%	1	27.0%	2	2.4%	17	4.4%	3	7.3	27	28.1	6
2007	11-5	11.3	9.6	412	284	+24	18.4%	7	5.8%	14	-8.2%	6	4.3%	5	24.4	12	12.9	26
2008	8-8	10.2	10.6	439	347	+4	17.5%	7	24.1%	1	8.3%	20	1.7%	12	12.4	28	22.2	17

Strategic Tendencies

Run/Pass		Rank	Offense		Rank	Defense		Rank	Other		Rank
Runs, all plays	45%	12	3+ WR	37%	29	Rush 3	4.9%	17	2+ RB, Pct Runs	60%	18
Runs, first half	45%	16	4+ WR	6%	28	Rush 4	63.7%	17	1 RB/2 TE, Pct Runs	43%	26
Runs, first down	55%	11	2+ TE	30%	12	Rush 5	27.0%	6	1RB/3+WR, Pct Runs	18%	30
Runs, second-long	33%	25	Single back	46%	24	Rush 6+	4.4%	30	Zone Blitz	0%	32
Runs, power sit.	67%	16	Play action	20%	10	Rush 7+	0.2%	32	Go for it on 4th	0.89	16
Runs, behind 2H	36%	7	Max protect	9%	11	Sacks by LB	64.8%	4	Offensive Pace	31.5	23
Pass, ahead 2H	35%	29	Outside pocket	9%	23	Sacks by DB	3.7%	26	Defensive Pace	30.7	16

If the Chargers are any indication, fourth-quarter performance is not a skill that a team maintains from year to year. The Chargers' offense led the league in fourth-quarter DVOA in 2006, was 30th in 2007, and then led the league again last year. ● San Diego ranked first in offensive DVOA when using play-action — a major difference from 2007, when they ranked 30th in DVOA with play-action. ● For the second straight year, San Diego threw a lower percentage of passes to wide receivers than any other team. Only four percent of passes went to slot receivers (not including Antonio Gates lined up in the slot). ● San Diego led the league in defensive DVOA against passes behind the line of scrimmage, but ranked 23rd against passes thrown past the line of scrimmage. ● San Diego's opponents used shotgun on 44 percent of plays and three or more wide receivers on 64 percent of plays. Both figures led the league. ● San Diego opponents only dropped 3.3 percent of passes, tied with Seattle for the lowest rate in the NFL. ● The Chargers ranked 31st in the percentage of pass plays where they hurried the quarterback, ahead of only the Broncos.

Passing

Player	DYAR	DVOA	Plays	NtYds	Avg	YAC	C%	TD	Int
Philip Rivers	1522	35.6%	510	3993	7.8	5.5	65.5%	34	11

Rushing

Player	DYAR	DVOA	Plays	Yds	Avg	TD	Fum	Suc
LaDainian Tomlinson	88	-1.3%	292	1110	3.8	11	0	45%
Darren Sproles	64	17.8%	61	330	5.4	1	0	49%
Philip Rivers	3	-9.8%	21	89	4.2	0	2	--
Jacob Hester	-6	-14.9%	19	95	5.0	1	1	47%
Mike Tolbert	-15	-28.7%	13	37	2.8	0	0	54%
Vincent Jackson	47	180.8%	4	69	17.3	0	0	--
Michael Bennett	*-26*	*-83.2%*	*7*	*12*	*1.7*	*0*	*0*	*57%*

Receiving

Player	DYAR	DVOA	Plays	Ctch	Yds	Y/C	YAC	TD	C%
Vincent Jackson	369	32.9%	100	59	1098	18.6	3.3	7	59%
Chris Chambers	64	0.3%	64	33	462	14.0	1.8	5	52%
Malcom Floyd	200	58.9%	37	27	465	17.2	1.7	4	73%
Legedu Naanee	8	-3.3%	11	8	64	8.0	3.3	0	73%
Buster Davis	15	14.2%	7	4	59	14.8	8.8	0	57%
Antonio Gates	140	15.5%	92	60	704	11.7	3.7	9	65%
Brandon Manumaleuna	27	13.9%	19	15	127	8.5	4.2	2	79%
LaDainian Tomlinson	52	-1.5%	77	52	415	8.0	8.7	1	68%
Darren Sproles	171	73.1%	34	29	348	12.0	12.2	5	85%
Mike Tolbert	82	72.0%	15	13	171	13.2	11.8	1	87%
Jacob Hester	49	44.6%	13	12	91	7.6	7.5	1	92%

Offensive Line

Year	Yards	ALY	Rank	Power	Rank	10+ Yds	Rank	Stuff	Rank	Sacks	ASR	Rank	False	Cont.
2006	5.38	4.74	1	73%	4	29%	1	13%	1	28	6.4%	15	18	39
2007	4.52	3.93	25	61%	19	26%	4	21%	26	24	4.7%	8	18	30
2008	4.08	4.08	18	78%	2	17%	18	15%	6	25	6.1%	17	16	33

Year	LE	Rank	LT	Rank	Mid	Rank	RT	Rank	RE	Rank
2006	5.75	2	5.03	4	4.29	18	4.40	7	5.59	1
2007	4.31	12	3.64	27	3.90	22	3.55	29	4.34	10
2008	3.19	26	3.82	23	4.34	10	4.17	17	4.18	12

For the second straight year, the Chargers' offensive line was functional but unspectacular. Improved blocking in short-yardage situations was offset by a decline in pass blocking, and the clear weak point was right tackle Jeromey Clary. In his first year as a starter, game charters marked him with eight blown blocks, tied for second in the NFL and more than every other San Diego player combined. He also led the team with five false starts. Left tackle Marcus McNeill and center Nick Hardwick were solid after returning from early-season injuries (bulging discs in the neck for McNeill, a severe foot sprain for Hardwick). McNeill did have neck surgery in February, and while the team insists he'll be fine in time for the season, a setback would mean mediocre veteran L.J. Shelton protecting Philip Rivers' blind side. Kris Dielman continues to be one of the league's better left guards, but right guard Mike Goff was not retained and signed with Kansas City in free agency. Goff will either be replaced by veteran Kynan Forney or third-round pick Louis Vasquez out of Texas Tech. Forney is known as a strong run blocker; he signed in San Diego after Atlanta cut him last August, but never made it into a game because the starting guards stayed healthy. Vasquez is strong and aggressive but may lack the agility and speed to become a strong pulling guard or block well on screen passes.

Defensive Front Seven

Defensive Line	Age	Pos	Overall									Pass Rush				vs. Run			vs. Pass		
			Plays	TmPct	Rk	Stop	Dfts	Stop%	Rk	AvYd	Rk	Sack	Hit	Hur	Runs	St%	Yds	Pass	St%	Yds
Jamal Williams	33	DT	59	6.8%	12	47	13	80%	25	1.5	18	1.5	0	2	49	82%	1.5	10	70%	1.4
Luis Castillo	26	DE	40	4.9%	51	28	8	70%	71	2.5	76	1.5	2	7	35	66%	2.8	5	100%	0.4
Igor Olshansky*	27	DE	28	3.2%	86	19	3	68%	74	3.4	87	1.5	2	3	26	65%	3.7	2	100%	-0.5
Ryon Bingham	28	DT	25	2.9%	69	14	4	56%	71	3.4	72	1.5	1	3	20	50%	3.4	5	80%	3.4
Jacques Cesaire	29	DE	24	2.8%	92	17	5	71%	63	2.1	58	2.0	2	6	20	65%	3.0	4	100%	-2.5

Linebackers	Age	Pos	Overall							Pass Rush			vs. Run					vs. Pass				
			Plays	TmPct	Rk	Stop	Dfts	Stop%	AvYd	Sack	Hit	Hur	Runs	St%	Rk	Yds	Rk	Tgts	Suc%	Rk	AdjYd	Rk
Stephen Cooper	30	ILB	105	16.2%	14	50	20	48%	5.6	1.5	0	2	50	62%	61	3.3	42	34	38%	80	7.1	65
Shaun Phillips	28	OLB	79	9.2%	74	51	22	65%	3.0	8.5	5	16	43	67%	37	2.9	27	20	57%	25	6.5	52
Matt Wilhelm	28	ILB	52	6.0%	98	18	5	35%	6.8	0.0	1	4	19	68%	32	2.3	10	29	31%	89	8.1	79
Tim Dobbins	27	ILB	49	5.7%	99	24	6	49%	5.0	0.0	0	0	25	60%	71	3.0	28	20	45%	61	7.0	64
Jyles Tucker	25	OLB	37	5.3%	--	24	11	65%	2.4	5.0	1	7	20	60%	--	3.5	--	5	60%	--	4.7	--
Marques Harris*	28	OLB	22	2.7%	--	13	4	59%	3.1	2.5	3	9	15	53%	--	4.4	--	3	40%	--	6.4	--
Kevin Burnett	27	ILB	27	3.5%	--	15	10	56%	5.1	2.0	1	3	5	20%	--	6.2	--	18	81%	1	4.3	3

Year	Yards	ALY	Rank	Power	Rank	10+ Yds	Rank	Stuff	Rank	Sack	ASR	Rank
2006	4.05	4.10	13	78%	31	15%	11	17%	19	61	9.1%	3
2007	4.25	4.44	29	65%	19	16%	12	16%	28	42	7.0%	13
2008	4.13	4.44	25	61%	8	11%	3	15%	28	28	5.6%	20

Year	LE	Rank	LT	Rank	Mid	Rank	RT	Rank	RE	Rank
2006	4.39	20	4.12	14	4.17	17	4.26	18	2.97	4
2007	5.37	30	5.93	32	4.25	22	3.77	8	3.82	11
2008	4.86	26	4.75	28	4.10	12	3.61	7	5.91	32

In San Diego, defensive success is predicated on two things: Jamal Williams clogging up the middle, and everybody else getting to the quarterback. Williams held up his part of the bargain, but with Shawne Merriman out for the season, the pass rush was a problem. The Chargers expect a reversal of fortune this year thanks to the return of Merriman and the arrival of first-round pick Larry English, a DE/OLB tweener out of Northern Illinois. English gives the Chargers the freedom to rotate outside linebackers and keep them fresh, but he's also insurance in case Merriman has a setback with his knee or Shaun Phillips has further legal trouble. (Hitting quarterbacks is good; hitting hotel security guards, not so much.) Even with Merriman back, the Chargers have to figure out how to annoy the quarterback when they don't take him down — for the second straight season, San Diego's defense ranked 31st in hurries per pass play.

San Diego also used a fourth-round pick north of the border, grabbing Vaughn Martin out of Western Ontario with a move that would have made avowed small school specialist and long-time Chargers general manager Bobby Beathard proud. He'll move from tackle to end and compete with Ryon Bingham to replace right defensive end Igor Olshansky, who signed with Dallas in free agency. Both players could help improve the run defense, as Adjusted Line Yards show that has been the weaker side against the run for a few years now. Stephen Cooper holds down one inside linebacker spot as the man with the helmet radio, but the other spot is up in the air. Last year, Matt Wilhelm was benched for Tim Dobbins at midseason. Wilhelm is supposed to be better in coverage while Dobbins is better against the run, although they're not far from each other in any of our stats. Ex-Cowboys free agent Kevin Burnett has better pass coverage stats than either, and could beat them both out for the starting spot in camp.

Defensive Secondary

Secondary	Age	Pos	Plays	TmPct	Rk	Stop	Dfts	Yds	Rk	St%	Rk	Tgts	Tgt%	Rk	Dist	Suc%	Rk	AdjYd	Rk	Yds	PD	Int
Eric Weddle	24	FS	130	15.1%	4	38	15	8.1	61	21%	73	54	10.0%	6	8.0	54%	29	6.2	9	6.2	5	1
Quentin Jammer	30	CB	104	12.1%	10	45	16	6.7	46	38%	49	98	18.1%	38	10.7	51%	42	6.2	21	6.2	19	2
Antonio Cromartie	25	CB	73	8.5%	45	23	6	6.3	37	30%	67	98	18.0%	41	8.8	42%	73	8.3	63	8.1	10	2
Clinton Hart	32	SS	71	9.4%	46	31	10	5.2	17	45%	31	41	8.6%	13	14.4	54%	30	9.3	59	9.8	6	0
Antoine Cason	23	CB	67	7.8%	55	31	18	6.2	36	44%	41	75	13.9%	68	6.4	55%	23	5.8	12	5.7	9	2
Steve Gregory	26	CB	36	4.4%	--	10	3	5.9	--	33%	--	19	3.6%	--	11.6	47%	--	6.2	--	6.8	4	0

Year	Pass D Rank	vs. #1 WR	Rk	vs. #2 WR	Rk	vs. Other WR	Rk	vs. TE	Rk	vs. RB	Rk
2006	11	12.4%	27	-0.4%	13	-5.8%	17	-13.4%	9	12.4%	26
2007	3	-8.2%	11	-73.9%	1	14.6%	29	9.9%	21	-11.8%	8
2008	20	17.0%	25	-22.8%	6	-6.8%	14	21.1%	27	-10.5%	5

San Diego's pass defense had two big problems last season: the decline of the pass rush, and the decline of Antonio Cromartie, who truly learned the meaning of the words "sophomore slump." Cromartie dropped in every statistic, particularly interceptions (from a league-leading ten to just two). The lovefest was over among our game charters; if their comments weren't criticizing Cromartie because he fell for a double move, they were criticizing him for giving too much cushion — and apparently, a simple slant route worked against him pretty much without fail. Cromartie also had 11 penalties, second in the NFL among defensive players. Astonishingly, Cromartie revealed after the season that he played the entire year with a fractured hip suffered in Week 1. It's hard to tell how much to blame the hip for Cromartie's poor 2008, and how much to blame the fact that his athletic ability still surpasses his knowledge and technique. A strong rebound performance from Cromartie is the biggest difference between the Chargers matching our exorbitant statistical projection and the Chargers stumbling into the playoffs simply because they play in a bad division. The other cornerbacks were fine — Quentin Jammer had basically the same slightly above-average season he had in 2007, and rookie first-round pick Antoine Cason was swell as the nickelback. Fifth-round pick Brandon Hughes (Oregon State) brings depth. Eric Weddle had an excellent first year as the starting free safety, providing the requisite strong coverage, hard hits, and field smarts. Clinton Hart was a bit iffy at strong safety and will compete for his job with converted cornerback Steve Gregory and sixth-round pick Kevin Ellison, a USC product with size, good instincts, and an excellent closing burst who may eventually have to switch to linebacker because of his lack of open-field speed.

Special Teams

Year	DVOA	Rank	FG/XP	Rank	Net Kick	Rank	Kick Ret	Rank	Net Punt	Rank	Punt Ret	Rank	Hidden	Rank
2006	4.4%	3	7.8	5	8.4	6	2.4	10	10.8	4	-3.4	27	-12.4	29
2007	4.3%	5	1.6	14	7.3	2	6.2	8	6.8	5	3.4	9	13.9	2
2008	1.7%	12	-2.4	23	-3.3	22	6.7	7	10.1	6	-1.1	18	-1.4	15

Mike Scifres had one of the most dominating games by a punter in playoff history, pinning the Colts inside their own 10 on five of six punts in San Diego's wild card victory. Scifres has consistently excellent hang time, although he didn't dominate quite like that for the whole season. Nate Kaeding was below average on both field goals and kickoffs, but a rebound is likely considering that he was one of the better kickers in the league in 2006 and 2007. Darren Sproles had another excellent year on kick returns, although he was just average on punt returns. Special teams is a unit that sees a lot of turnover in most organizations, but if Sproles had not broken his ankle in the 2006 preseason, the Chargers would be using the same three specialists for the fifth straight year.

Coaching Staff

The big coaching news in San Diego came at midseason, when the Chargers fired defensive coordinator Ted Cottrell and replaced him with linebackers coach (and former Chicago defensive coordinator) Ron Rivera. Some writers felt Turner simply jettisoned Cottrell because he needed to find a scapegoat for San Diego's 3-5 start. On the surface, it looks like the defense improved after Rivera took over — the Chargers allowed nearly a touchdown less per game after Week 9. However, that change is primarily due to the way luck and schedule split. The average Chargers opponent over the first eight games had 9.3% offensive DVOA. After the bye week, the average opponent had 3.9% offensive DVOA. Before the bye, San Diego forced eight fumbles and recovered three; after the bye, they forced four fumbles and recovered all of them. Control for these issues, and we see San Diego's defense didn't really change — the Chargers ranked 19th on defense before Week 9, 18th afterwards. Clarence Shelmon still holds the title of offensive coordinator, although it is more accurate to say he coaches the running game while Turner handles the passing game and play-calling. Rob Chudzinski returns to the coaching staff after two years as the offensive coordinator in Cleveland; he holds the titles of tight ends coach and assistant head coach.

San Francisco 49ers

The San Francisco 49ers, as currently devised, are an obscure football team. They haven't had a winning record past Week 3 in five years. Over that same time frame, they've failed to score 40 points in a game even once. They play in a division that the other 28 teams look forward to seeing on the schedule, and they haven't won it since 2002. Their highlights are buried as the final segment on national recap shows. Agents use them as an organization to bid up their clients, only to take the player elsewhere or accept an offer after the Niners have blown away the market. For most football fans, the modern-day 49ers have only two important functions: to ensure that every team plays 16 games and to allow Frank Gore to accrue fantasy points.

That they are merely obscure and not downright awful should be cause for celebration; the difference between the Matt Millen-era Lions and the Scot McCloughan-era Niners is context and luck. San Francisco is coming off of the third-worst four-year stretch of any team in the 15-year history of DVOA, a gory stat made worse by the knowledge that the 2004-2007 Niners occupy the worst slot. (The 2000-2003 Cardinals are second.) San Francisco's record is inflated — if that term can even be used — thanks to a weak schedule and a 9-5 record in games decided by three points or less; they actually have accrued fewer Pythagorean wins than the Lions since the arrival of McCloughan and deposed head coach Mike Nolan in the spring of 2005 (Table 1). This is not a team a few bounces away from being a contender; it is one that is a few bounces away from serving as the argument for an NFL second division, if only to have a place for the 49ers and Raiders to be relegated to.

We could rehash the number one overall selection of Alex Smith four years ago, but that's not the organization's worst pick. Smith was the most appealing option in a weak draft, much the same as Matt Stafford was for Detroit this year. Where the organization truly failed was in 2006; despite owning two picks in what will likely go down as the best first round of the decade, they turned up two borderline starters on a bad team.

No team had ever selected a tight end higher than the 49ers did Vernon Davis (sixth overall), and there was a reason why. In all our research related to the draft, tight end has invariably been one of the easiest positions at which to find a very good player. Tight ends selected on Day Two start more games over the course of their career than any other position; over the past 30 years, meanwhile, the average tight end making it to his first Pro Bowl has done so from a later draft position than players at any other position (Table 2).

If Davis just ended up being a very good tight end, it would still be subpar value from the sixth overall pick, but he hasn't even developed into that. Davis' skill set entering into his fourth season boils down to being a poor man's Jim Kleinsasser. Davis was supposed to be

49ERS SUMMARY

2008 Record: 7-9

Pythagorean Wins: 6.9 (23rd)

DVOA: -13.9% (25th)

Offense: -11.3% (27th)

Defense: 7.3% (18th)

Special Teams: 4.6% (3rd)

Variance: 7.4% (2nd)

2008: Our drill sergeant with no head coaching experience has come to save the franchise from the regime of ... the drill sergeant with no head coaching experience we hired in 2005!

2009: At least the Raiders are *entertainingly* bad.

2009 Mean Projection: 5.7 wins

On the Clock (0-3): 15%

Loserville (4-6): 51%

Mediocrity (7-8): 22%

Playoff Contender (9-10): 10%

Super Bowl Contender (11+): 2%

Projected Average Opponent: 4.7% (4th)

a terrifying downfield threat against linebackers and safeties thanks to his 4.38 40-yard dash; instead, his NFL average of 11.0 yards per catch puts him behind such noted speed demons as Brent Celek and Desmond Clark. On the bright side, he is just as muscular as when the Niners fell in love with him.

Manny Lawson, the 22nd overall pick, missed most of his second season with a torn ACL, but over three years he has just 5.5 sacks in 32 games. That's not what a team desperate for a pass rusher was hoping for. When the team went to a nickel package as their defensive base set last year, Lawson went to the bench, a sign of his lack of development. Even if we pretend that those 32 games only came over two seasons, there's not a lot of hope for Lawson; of the last 32 linebackers to be drafted in the first round and produce fewer than six sacks in their first two years, only two — LaVar Arrington and Jamir Miller — have produced a ten-sack season afterwards.

The organization has been left wanting by their Day Two picks as well. A rebuilding team, through the confluence of luck and opportunity, needs to be able to find a few diamonds in the rough in the later rounds of the draft to provide their (hopefully successful) earlier picks with some support. Take Tennessee, which rebuilt around the same time that San Francisco did. Even though Adam Jones and Vince Young have been disappointments, the team's success in finding and nurturing players like Cortland Finnegan and David Stewart has allowed them to use precious resources and salary cap space elsewhere. San Francisco will only start one player on Opening Day that they found after the second round under McCloughan: linebacker Parys Haralson, who only has his starting job because free agent acquisition Tully Banta-Cain showed up to last year's training camp out of shape.

San Francisco will probably start undrafted free agent Shaun Hill at quarterback, a player who the team signed after the Vikings cast him off in 2005. Much has been made of Hill's 7-3 record as the 49ers starter, but it is misguided enthusiasm. Two of his wins came against last year's 2-14 Rams. Two more came against teams with nothing to play for, including the 2007 Buccaneers, who were actively resting all their players. That leaves Hill with a win over the Bengals in 2007 and victories over the Bills and Jets last year, in which the team scored a combined 54 points. Color us impressed. The team attempted to sign Kurt Warner in the offseason, only for Warner to march their deal back to Arizona and use it to prove that he'd take less money to stay in the

Table 1: Niners vs. Lions

Year	San Francisco		Detroit	
	Wins	Pyth. Wins	Wins	Pyth. Wins
2005	4	3.2	5	5.2
2006	7	5.1	3	5.6
2007	5	3.7	7	5.7
2008	7	6.9	0	2.8
Totals	23	18.9	15	19.3

desert. That left Hill to fight with Smith in yet another quarterback battle. Insert your own joke here.

That impending struggle to find the least mediocre quarterback drives home another point about the team's struggle to find success. Often, stories about teams not having an "identity" or "having to find themselves" are simply stories to fill vast inches of column space. In this case, though, San Francisco really has failed to develop any sort of coherent identity as a team, and it's hurt them when it comes to player acquisition and long-term planning. Are they a 3-4 team or a 4-3 team? Nolan tried to maneuver them into a 3-4 over the course of his tenure, but by the time he was fired last year, he still had the team alternating between 4-3 and 3-4 fronts, with free agent acquisition Justin Smith playing both as a down lineman and an outside linebacker. After Nolan was let go, defensive coordinator Greg Manusky played the 3-4 as his base package more consistently, resulting in increased playing time for Haralson and Lawson on the outside, but at the expense of Smith playing out of position as an undersized 3-4 end.

Their offense has undergone the same sort of confusion. The departure of Norv Turner to Oakland before the 2007 season left the team without an effective offensive coordinator or a qualified candidate willing to take the position on, resulting in the disastrous tenure of Jim Hostler. His departure led to the desperate hiring of Mike Martz, who attempted to implement his pass-happy scheme with approximately one-quarter of the personnel needed to pull it off.

Table 2: First-Time Pro Bowlers

Pos	Avg. Draft Rd	Pos	Avg. Draft Rd
QB	2.7	T	1.6
RB	2.2	DE	2.5
FB	2.7	DT	2.1
WR	2.7	LB	2.6
TE	3.0	CB	2.0
C	2.5	S	2.7
G	3.0		

2009 49ers Schedule

Week	Opp.	Week	Opp.	Week	Opp.
1	at ARI	7	at HOU	13	at SEA
2	SEA	8	at IND	14	ARI (Mon.)
3	at MIN	9	TEN	15	at PHI
4	STL	10	CHI (Thu.)	16	DET
5	ATL	11	at GB	17	at STL
6	BYE	12	JAC		

After Mike Singletary became head coach in October, Martz lost the battle of the third estate; according to the media, Singletary tamed Martz, bringing the offense back to a run-oriented base. However, that conventional wisdom doesn't actually fit reality. The team passed the ball on 53 percent of first downs when Nolan was head coach, with that figure rising to 55 percent after Singletary took over in Week 8. Instead of shifting to a ball-control approach, the team went five-wide more frequently, enjoying far more success in that set than they had over the first seven games of the season. Of course, that may also have something to do with the presence of J.T. O'Sullivan as the starting quarterback; the player Martz brought in to start had 22 turnovers — 11 interceptions and 11 fumbles — in eight starts, while he was sacked on an astounding 12.7 percent of his dropbacks.

The team fired Martz and will introduce Jimmy Raye as the team's latest offensive coordinator this year. Raye will implement a ball-control scheme built around Gore and a developing offensive line led by left tackle Joe Staley, who the team signed to a seven-year extension in the offseason after only two years as a pro. We're skeptical of Raye's ability. In nine seasons as an NFL offensive coordinator, Raye's teams have finished in the bottom third of the league in scoring five times; he's only had an above-average offense at one of his five stops, that being the 1998-2000 Chiefs. Raye also noted this offseason that Frank Gore has "the capability to carry the ball 25 times [per game]." That is always a good sign that your offensive coordinator is talking nonsense; 25 carries a game would add up to 400 on the season, a figure that Gore will meet if — and only if — the 49ers go 16-0.

The 49ers are depending on two fresh faces to get them out of their decade-long rut. The first is Singletary, who was almost universally considered to be a great selection when the 49ers picked him to replace Nolan. When he benched Davis following a personal foul penalty, he was raised to deity status. Singletary even had the expected effect on team discipline, as the 49ers went from accumulating 8.9 penalties a game under Nolan in 2008 to 6.1 with Singletary running the locker room.

The jury's still out on Singletary as a coach, though. We don't have a meaningful sample to analyze things like his clock management or usage patterns yet, and while he's won in the court of public opinion so far, there's no obvious indicator screaming that Singletary's going to be a great coach. The team went 5-4 at him with the helm, but a lot of the same issues we brought up with Hill's record earlier come up with Singletary; furthermore, the team recovered 20 of the 31 fumbles that hit the turf while Singletary was coach, and that's luck, not will.

The other man carrying this team's hopes upon his shoulders is Michael Crabtree, who fell to the 49ers with the tenth overall pick despite being, arguably, the best offensive player in the draft. Research later in this book backs up the optimism about Crabtree's potential, but even if he fulfills that potential, Crabtree is the team's only real threat in the passing game — barring a huge step forward from Josh Morgan or Brandon Jones, or a huge step backwards (in time) from Isaac Bruce. Furthermore, very few rookie receivers go straight from college to superstardom. Even Calvin Johnson and Larry Fitzgerald, the most obviously similar players to Crabtree, each had fewer than 800 receiving yards in their first seasons.

And so, we believe, the obscurity will continue. Our projection of another year of mediocrity comes because of a crippling lack of progress over the last four seasons in locating, nurturing, and properly implementing talent up and down the roster. We've barely mentioned the stars of the team in this essay — players like Gore, Patrick Willis, and Nate Clements — because, truthfully, they don't matter in this sort of situation. They could be the best players in the league at their respective positions and it wouldn't be enough to overcome the mediocrity that permeates the majority of the roster.

The result is another year spent in the shadows for an organization that's made it a habit.

Bill Barnwell

Table 3: Passing Game Under Nolan, Singletary

	Nolan			Singletary		
Blockers	% Frequency	YPA	Success Rate	% Frequency	YPA	Success Rate
5	41%	5.7	35%	48%	6.6	46%
6	39%	6.3	45%	38%	5.3	48%
7	16%	6.9	30%	14%	6.0	45%
All		6.1	39%		6.0	47%

2008 49ers Stats by Week

Wk	vs.	W-L	PF	PA	YDF	YDA	TO	Total	Off	Def	ST
1	ARI	L	13	23	291	285	-5	-14%	-19%	1%	6%
2	@SEA	W	33	30	365	351	+2	-31%	-20%	3%	-9%
3	DET	W	31	13	370	240	+2	51%	26%	-26%	0%
4	@NO	L	17	31	312	467	-1	-17%	-24%	4%	12%
5	NE	L	21	30	199	377	-1	16%	-3%	-10%	9%
6	PHI	L	26	40	306	383	-2	-25%	-13%	17%	5%
7	@NYG	L	17	29	253	273	-3	-37%	-54%	-20%	-3%
8	SEA	L	13	34	388	261	-2	-52%	-28%	31%	7%
9	BYE										
10	@ARI	L	24	29	336	374	-3	-15%	-26%	22%	34%
11	STL	W	35	16	334	406	+1	-2%	6%	23%	15%
12	@DAL	L	22	35	304	408	-1	-34%	-4%	28%	-2%
13	@BUF	W	10	3	195	350	0	-35%	-35%	3%	3%
14	NYJ	W	24	14	375	182	-1	-14%	0%	14%	0%
15	@MIA	L	9	14	318	248	0	-17%	13%	21%	-9%
16	@STL	W	17	16	273	343	-3	-49%	-43%	12%	7%
17	WAS	W	27	24	359	268	0	24%	21%	-1%	3%

Trends and Splits

	Offense	Rank	Defense	Rank
Total DVOA	-11.3%	27	7.3%	18
Unadjusted VOA	-6.8%	26	6.1%	18
Weighted trend	-11.4%	28	13.0%	26
Variance	5.1%	5	4.3%	7
Average opponent	3.4%	18	9.2%	28
Passing	-8.2%	26	15.7%	20
Rushing	-2.8%	24	-2.4%	17
First down	-13.5%	28	0.1%	17
Second down	-15.1%	28	12.7%	23
Third down	0.0%	19	11.2%	21
First half	-4.2%	26	13.7%	26
Second half	-18.8%	28	0.3%	10
Red Zone	-33.2%	30	0.1%	18
Late and close	-21.2%	31	-8.7%	7

Five-Year Performance

Year	W-L	Pyth	Est W	PF	PA	TO	Total	Rk	Off	Rk	Def	Rk	ST	Rk	Off AGL	Rk	Def AGL	Rk
2004	2-14	3.4	2.3	259	452	-19	-42.5%	32	-20.2%	29	21.4%	31	-0.9%	19	34.1	5	33.9	6
2005	4-12	3.2	1.6	239	428	-9	-56.4%	32	-42.0%	32	15.8%	31	1.4%	11	25.4	7	32.6	3
2006	7-9	5.1	6.2	298	412	-5	-19.3%	27	-7.5%	23	11.8%	29	0.0%	18	19.4	14	6.2	28
2007	5-11	3.7	4.0	219	364	-12	-34.2%	31	-31.3%	32	7.4%	24	4.5%	4	31.8	5	19.5	18
2008	7-9	6.9	6.9	339	381	-17	-13.9%	25	-11.3%	27	7.3%	18	4.6%	3	24.9	15	5.4	30

Strategic Tendencies

Run/Pass		Rank	Offense		Rank	Defense		Rank	Other		Rank
Runs, all plays	40%	24	3+ WR	61%	7	Rush 3	5.5%	14	2+ RB, Pct Runs	61%	17
Runs, first half	42%	23	4+ WR	24%	2	Rush 4	68.9%	11	1 RB/2 TE, Pct Runs	45%	23
Runs, first down	46%	27	2+ TE	25%	17	Rush 5	20.2%	19	1RB/3+WR, Pct Runs	30%	13
Runs, second-long	34%	24	Single back	67%	9	Rush 6+	5.4%	26	Zone Blitz	4%	14
Runs, power sit.	60%	25	Play action	11%	29	Rush 7+	1.4%	15	Go for it on 4th	0.85	19
Runs, behind 2H	28%	28	Max protect	13%	3	Sacks by LB	56.7%	6	Offensive Pace	31.6	25
Pass, ahead 2H	41%	21	Outside pocket	17%	4	Sacks by DB	10.0%	13	Defensive Pace	29.0	1

W.hile shotgun rates around the league went up from 27 percent to 32 percent, San Francisco's rate of using shotgun actually dropped by more than half, from 33 percent in 2007 to 15 percent in 2008. Yet the 49ers were actually much better in shotgun (20.3% DVOA, 7.7 yards per play) than in standard formations (-15.8% DVOA, 4.9 yards per play). That's the second-highest DVOA gap in the league, and the largest gap in yards per play. ● San Francisco's offensive DVOA ranked 30th with one wide receiver in the game and 32nd with two wide receivers, but was league average with three or more wide receivers. ● We charted San Francisco and Washington with the most tight end screens, 13 apiece. No other team was in double digits. ● 49ers opponents threw 25 percent of passes to their running backs, the highest rate in the league — even though San Francisco had a top 10 defense against passes to running backs. Only 13 percent of passes against San Francisco went to tight ends, the lowest rate in the league. ● San Francisco opponents used four or more wide receivers on 22 percent of plays, the highest rate in the league. ● Note that the "go for it on fourth" rating above is for Mike Singletary only.

Passing

Player	DYAR	DVOA	Plays	NtYds	Avg	YAC	C%	TD	Int
Shaun Hill	180	-2.4%	313	1912	6.1	4.4	63.7%	13	8
J.T. O'Sullivan*	-414	-37.3%	257	1594	6.2	6.7	58.4%	8	11
Damon Huard	*-228*	*-54.7%*	*90*	*414*	*4.6*	*4.0*	*62.5%*	*2*	*4*

Receiving

Player	DYAR	DVOA	Plays	Ctch	Yds	Y/C	YAC	TD	C%
Isaac Bruce	159	6.0%	108	61	835	13.7	3.0	7	56%
Bryant Johnson*	54	-3.7%	75	45	546	12.1	3.2	3	60%
Josh Morgan	-12	-16.3%	43	20	319	16.0	4.3	3	47%
Arnaz Battle	75	11.0%	42	24	318	13.3	5.5	2	57%
Jason Hill	72	9.5%	40	30	317	10.6	3.8	2	75%
Dominique Zeigler	10	4.8%	8	5	97	19.4	8.0	0	63%
Brandon Jones	*75*	*3.2%*	*62*	*41*	*449*	*11.0*	*2.5*	*1*	*66%*
Vernon Davis	-54	-24.6%	49	31	358	11.5	8.0	2	63%
Delanie Walker	7	-1.1%	16	10	155	15.5	10.8	1	63%
Frank Gore	62	2.5%	66	43	373	8.7	7.7	2	65%
Michael Robinson	85	54.9%	20	17	202	11.9	7.6	0	85%
DeShaun Foster*	35	12.8%	20	16	133	8.3	5.3	1	80%
Zak Keasey	-21	-81.4%	5	3	25	8.3	6.0	0	60%
Moran Norris	*-13*	*-45.6%*	*7*	*4*	*16*	*4.0*	*2.0*	*0*	*57%*

Rushing

Player	DYAR	DVOA	Plays	Yds	Avg	TD	Fum	Suc
Frank Gore	69	-1.7%	240	1038	4.3	6	6	47%
DeShaun Foster*	-78	-31.9%	76	238	3.1	1	2	43%
J.T. O'Sullivan*	20	9.1%	22	151	6.9	0	1	--
Michael Robinson	-23	-32.3%	19	50	2.6	0	1	53%
Shaun Hill	38	24.5%	17	117	6.9	2	1	--

Offensive Line

Year	Yards	ALY	Rank	Power	Rank	10+ Yds	Rank	Stuff	Rank	Sacks	ASR	Rank	False	Cont.
2006	4.99	4.42	6	55%	28	26%	2	17%	6	35	6.8%	18	20	26
2007	4.31	4.19	12	57%	24	15%	19	15%	5	55	10.3%	32	26	45
2008	3.96	4.28	7	52%	32	13%	30	17%	11	55	9.4%	31	24	26

Year	LE	Rank	LT	Rank	Mid	Rank	RT	Rank	RE	Rank
2006	5.90	1	4.17	19	4.36	12	3.99	23	4.29	12
2007	3.25	27	4.30	16	4.19	11	4.46	9	4.01	17
2008	4.90	8	3.94	20	4.53	4	3.53	29	3.86	21

The downside of Al Davis's dementia leading to Michael Crabtree's availability is that, for the second year in a row, the 49ers failed to address their needs at tackle in the draft. They did sign former Steelers left tackle Marvel Smith in free agency, with plans of starting him on the right side of the line, but Smith is 30 and has played in only 17 games over the past two years due to recurring back problems. Suffice to say, he's not a long-term solution. Smith's signing also means that Joe Staley will play left tackle again this year. Staley is undoubtedly the 49ers' most talented lineman, and he can handle the responsibilities of protecting Shaun Hill's (or Alex Smith's) blindside, but he's also an extraordinarily aggressive player who's "mauler" mentality is far better suited for the right side, clearing open lanes for Frank Gore (note that Gore's production has dropped significantly in the two years that Staley has manned the left side).

As for the interior of the line, the 49ers got (relatively) younger over the course of 2008 after the aged Barry Sims was gently put out to pasture. Rookie Chilo Rachal will start at right guard, David Bass (who recovered nicely from a torn pectoral in the offseason) will play left, and veteran center Eric Heitmann will return in the middle. All of these players are perfectly adequate — which is not say that any are outstanding — but if any of them get hurt, the 49ers could be forced to play a very unpleasant game of O-Line Shuffleboard. San Francisco did sign Alex Boone, an undrafted free agent from Ohio State, who is big (6-foot-8, 312 pounds), talented (two-time All Big-Ten selection), and thirsty: After attending a Super Bowl party this year, Boone was arrested for going on a "drunken tirade" in Orange County, jumping on top of cars, yanking a tow-truck cable (?), and breaking a window before finally being brought down by Taser. This comes three years after Boone was arrested for DUI, at which time he admitted he was drinking 30 to 40 beers *per night*. Wade Boggs might have found a new friend.

Defensive Front Seven

Defensive Line	Age	Pos	Plays	TmPct	Overall Rk	Stop	Dfts	Stop%	Rk	AvYd	Pass Rush Rk	Sack	Hit	Hur	vs. Run Runs	St%	Yds	vs. Pass Pass	St%	Yds
Justin Smith	30	DE	76	9.3%	2	58	18	76%	49	1.9	49	7.0	11	15	60	70%	2.7	16	100%	-1.4
Aubrayo Franklin	29	DT	47	5.7%	28	35	9	74%	52	1.9	34	1.0	2	1	43	72%	2.2	4	100%	-1.0
Isaac Sopoaga	28	DT	40	4.9%	38	30	5	75%	49	2.4	58	1.0	1	2	37	76%	2.8	3	67%	-1.7
Ray McDonald	24	DE	31	4.0%	70	16	6	52%	92	4.3	92	1.0	2	9	23	39%	5.2	8	88%	1.6
Ronald Fields*	28	DT	19	2.3%	--	13	2	68%	--	3.0	--	0.0	1	0	18	72%	2.7	1	0%	9.0
Demetric Evans	*30*	*DE*	*35*	*4.7%*	*60*	*26*	*13*	*74%*	*56*	*2.4*	*73*	*3.5*	*3*	*7*	*26*	*69%*	*3.2*	*9*	*89%*	*0.2*

Linebackers	Age	Pos	Plays	TmPct	Overall Rk	Stop	Dfts	Stop%	AvYd	Pass Rush Sack	Hit	Hur	vs. Run Runs	St%	Rk	Yds	Rk	vs. Pass Tgts	Suc%	Rk	AdjYd	Rk
Patrick Willis	24	ILB	151	18.4%	4	77	24	51%	5.4	1.0	2	2	86	59%	76	4.4	94	45	76%	2	4.1	2
Takeo Spikes	33	OLB	102	12.4%	39	55	11	54%	4.8	1.0	3	3	67	63%	58	4.2	85	35	46%	58	5.7	32
Manny Lawson	25	OLB	46	6.4%	95	29	9	63%	3.3	3.0	0	2	27	78%	11	1.8	2	14	51%	--	4.4	--
Parys Haralson	25	OLB	39	4.8%	--	27	19	69%	2.0	8.0	1	14	19	58%	--	3.5	--	8	62%	--	3.8	--
Marques Harris	*28*	*OLB*	*22*	*2.7%*	*--*	*13*	*4*	*59%*	*3.1*	*2.5*	*3*	*9*	*15*	*53%*	*--*	*4.4*	*--*	*3*	*40%*	*--*	*6.4*	*--*

Year	Yards	ALY	Rank	Power	Rank	10+ Yds	Rank	Stuff	Rank	Sack	ASR	Rank
2006	4.33	4.55	26	67%	19	15%	10	17%	23	34	6.2%	20
2007	3.88	4.06	14	70%	25	14%	8	20%	15	31	5.7%	25
2008	3.89	4.03	12	70%	22	14%	9	17%	17	30	5.0%	26

Year	LE	Rank	LT	Rank	Mid	Rank	RT	Rank	RE	Rank
2006	4.10	17	4.07	12	4.72	29	4.59	24	4.77	28
2007	3.71	12	3.90	11	4.39	29	4.04	17	2.73	5
2008	3.36	7	4.63	25	3.96	10	4.03	16	4.24	21

Under Mike Nolan, the 49ers ran a hybrid defensive scheme that toggled between a 3-4 and a 4-3. No longer. Under defensive coordinator Greg Manusky (who was hired by Nolan but kept on by Singletary) the 49ers are now firmly in the 3-4 camp. End Justin Smith is by far their most effective and reliable player on the defensive line, and he proved to be worth every penny of his $45 million contract. In the dedicated 3-4, Smith will no longer be forced to drop back in pass coverage, and instead he can concentrate on rushing the quarterback's blind side. At 285 pounds, though, he's undersized for a 3-4 end, so there may be some issues with wear and tear as the season goes along. The rest of the line will be filled by a rotation of veterans Isaac Sopoaga and Aubrayo Franklin and 2007 first-round pick Kentwan Balmer. Balmer had significant question marks coming out of college, and as a rookie he struggled to shed blockers and had trouble staying on the active roster. Nonetheless, Manusky seems committed to getting Balmer into the starting lineup, and claims he's "right on track to becoming a fine football player." Backups include Demetric Evans, Ray McDonald (who's coming off reconstructive knee surgery), and rookie Ricky Jean-Francois (a seventh-round developmental project out of LSU).

The conventional wisdom holds that inside linebacker Patrick Willis slipped a little last year after his phenomenal rookie campaign, but the reality is that Willis played at about the same level, and only the expectations have changed. Such is the price of success. After getting involved in whopping 180 plays in 2007, which ranked him second overall in the league, he slipped to 151 last year — which ranked him fourth. Much like fellow NFC West denizen Lofa Tatupu, Willis also chafed at the responsibility of wearing the "green dot" helmet last year.

As for the outside linebackers, Manusky is on record as stating that Parys Haralson and Manny Lawson will see lots of playing time this year, and both may rotate to a defensive end position on third downs when San Francisco goes to a 4-2-5 or 4-1-6 defense. Lawson has gained 15 pounds thus far in the offseason and will have increased pass-rushing responsibilities this year. The other project is outside linebacker Ahmad Brooks, the talented underachiever who is in dire need of Singletary the Motivator's personal attention. When he reads the play correctly (which is not all that often), Brooks can certainly "bring the wood," so his development would provide the 49ers with valuable depth. Third-rounder Scott McKillop (Pitt) is a high-instinct, low-athleticism middle linebacker; the upside would be Zach Thomas or Tedy Bruschi, but the reality is more like H.B. Blades.

Defensive Secondary

Secondary	Age	Pos	Plays	TmPct	Rk	Stop	Dfts	Yds	Rk	St%	Rk	Tgts	Tgt%	Rk	Dist	Suc%	Rk	AdjYd	Rk	Yds	PD	Int
								Overall							**vs. Run**				**vs. Pass**			
Michael Lewis	29	SS	102	12.4%	11	43	20	5.2	18	47%	26	42	9.4%	8	12.2	49%	51	8.0	45	8.0	5	0
Nate Clements	30	CB	71	9.2%	32	32	16	5.3	24	41%	45	85	20.6%	23	11.8	53%	30	7.1	37	6.8	10	2
Walt Harris	35	CB	67	8.2%	51	33	13	3.2	4	60%	17	72	16.2%	55	11.7	44%	64	8.0	58	7.9	14	3
Mark Roman	32	SS	58	7.1%	66	22	7	6.9	41	46%	27	35	7.8%	25	13.9	42%	69	11.1	72	11.1	1	0
Donald Strickland*	29	CB	36	5.0%	--	21	8	4.1	--	75%	--	34	8.8%	--	5.5	48%	--	6.6	--	6.4	5	0
Dre' Bly	32	CB	70	8.9%	37	28	12	9.3	64	50%	28	91	21.7%	19	10.5	40%	80	8.6	69	8.5	9	2

Year	Pass D Rank	vs. #1 WR	Rk	vs. #2 WR	Rk	vs. Other WR	Rk	vs. TE	Rk	vs. RB	Rk
2006	27	3.0%	18	-10.2%	9	-4.6%	18	36.4%	32	18.5%	30
2007	26	0.7%	16	14.2%	23	-0.6%	19	23.2%	27	-2.5%	15
2008	19	8.1%	20	0.8%	17	8.2%	26	3.3%	17	-4.4%	8

The 49ers headed into 2009 with every intention of starting cornerback Walt Harris again, but he tore his ACL in May and will be out for the season. As a result, the 49ers will start Tarell Brown, the third-year cornerback out of Texas, on the right side. His 2008 charting stats are poor (30 percent Success Rate, 8.0 adjusted yards per pass) but the sample size is small (15 passes). Defensive coordinator Greg Manusky prefers Brown to the 49ers' 2008 third-round pick, Reggie Smith, who was going to be moved to safety, although Harris's injury may change those plans. (The 49ers also signed veteran Dre' Bly in late May, and he may start over both Brown and Smith.) Nate Clements should continue his solid play on the left side of the field, but he will hit 30 this year and the decline may start sooner than the 49ers would like; such are the consequences of building the secondary through free agency rather than the draft.

As for the safeties, here's a statistical glitch in the matrix: Last year, Michael Lewis was involved in 12.4 percent of the 49ers' plays on defense, precisely the same number as 2007, and he ranked 11th in the league both years. Lewis is reliable, but the same cannot be said for 32-year-old free safety Mark Roman, who spent most of 2008 wandering around the backfield aimlessly. Roman is being benched in favor of Dashon Goldson, the 2007 fourth-round pick out of Washington. Goldson has good "ballhawking" skills, for lack of a better description, but he has struggled with injuries throughout his brief career — whether he can survive a full 16-game season remains an open question.

Special Teams

Year	DVOA	Rank	FG/XP	Rank	Net Kick	Rank	Kick Ret	Rank	Net Punt	Rank	Punt Ret	Rank	Hidden	Rank
2006	0.0%	18	-0.3	16	-1.4	22	0.3	15	1.8	17	-0.5	15	-10.7	27
2007	4.5%	4	4.6	9	2.1	12	-1.5	19	18.1	1	3.3	10	-5.1	23
2008	4.6%	3	4.4	8	9.6	3	6.0	8	5.6	10	1.4	10	-1.0	14

The 49ers have been excellent on special teams for the past couple seasons. Last year's biggest surprise was the strong performance turned in by kick returner Allen Rossum, who proved that he remains one of the fastest players in the NFL at age 33. Last year Rossum's returns were worth 7.8 points of field position on kickoffs and 5.2 points of field position on punts, compared to average returns. The combined total was sixth among all returners, higher than Joshua Cribbs, Darren Sproles, or Leon Washington. Andy Lee turned in another great season, although he may have been eclipsed by Oakland's Shane Lechler for the prestigious title of NFL's Best Punter. Fortunately, Blue Bottle isn't a prohibited substance. Joe Nedney has played three consecutive full seasons, so he appears to be finally over whatever bad karma made him the most injured kicker in football early in the decade.

Coaching Staff

Mike Singletary's impromptu decision to play "Pants-Off Dance-Off" in his first week as interim head coach last year did not augur well for his prospects of becoming a permanent fixture in San Francisco. But after two quick losses, the 49ers quickly steadied themselves under Singletary's guidance, and with five victories in their final seven games, 49ers owner Jed "Boy Wonder" York — he's younger than some of the players on his payroll — rewarded him with a new four-year, $10 million contract.

Before the 'Niners faithful get too excited about Samurai Mike, however, there are some reasons to remain cautious about the coaching staff he's assembled. "New" offensive coordinator Jimmy Raye II has been bouncing around the NFL for a long time, but as mentioned in the chapter, it's not entirely clear why. Conventional wisdom suggests Raye tends to favor the run over the pass, but given the stockpile of young talent the 49ers' have amassed at wide receiver, Raye contends that the offense will be balanced. "At this point, I don't see it as run-oriented or pass-oriented," Raye told reporters in May. "What we are doing is installing both run and pass equally." Like we said: balanced.

On other side of the ball, Singletary decided to keep Greg Manusky on as defensive coordinator, despite Manusky being a Mike Nolan hire. A member of the Marty Schottenheimer coaching tree, Manusky is considered a rising star in the coaching world, and he's firmly entrenched in the 3-4 defensive camp — there may be many hybrids driving around San Francisco, but the 49ers defense should not be included among them.

Seattle Seahawks

2008 was a bad season to be an offensive player in the NFL. The Jaguars watched their offensive line fall apart in the first game of the year. The Broncos were pulling running backs out of the mall and tossing them into the starting lineup. Yet when it comes to offensive injuries, those teams couldn't even touch the Seattle Seahawks. Which is a good thing, because the slightest touch would probably have broken another Seattle wide receiver.

We use Adjusted Games Lost to track how badly each team was hurt by injury in any given season, then break it down by offense and defense. We currently have this data going back to 1996, and no offense during that span can touch the 2008 Seahawks, whose starters had 66.3 AGL. No other team has more than 60 AGL from offensive starters; last year's Bengals come close at 59.8. More than half the teams in that time span came in under 20. Seattle stands well ahead of the curve here.

With most of those players returning to health in 2009, a return to the playoffs is very likely. The Seahawks are the only NFC team that reached the divisional round of the playoffs every year from 2003 to 2007, and many of the players from those teams remain on the roster. However, that also means those players have put on a lot of years. If Seattle misses out on the postseason this year, it may be time to blow up the roster and start over.

The wide receiver injuries started before the season

even began, with neither starter Deion Branch nor slot receiver Bobby Engram available at the start of the year. Branch played just one game in the first half of the season. Engram missed all of September. Then in the season opener, Nate Burleson tore his ACL and was out for the year. Logan Payne tore his MCL a week later, and was also out for the year. Billy McMullen and Michael Bumpus were signed off the street in Week 3, and both were lost for the season by Week 6.

At quarterback, Matt Hasselbeck missed five games between October and November, then missed all of December.

The situation at offensive line was more stable, but ended in even greater havoc. Sean Locklear missed September with a knee injury. Guard Rob Sims tore his pec in the season opener and, like Burleson, was lost for the year. Things stabilized until mid-November, but then a Seahawks offensive lineman suffered a season-ending injury four times in five weeks. The Seahawks played their last two games of the season with the entire first-string offensive line on injured reserve.

When the season was over, the Seahawks had by far the league's highest Adjusted Games Lost by wide receivers, and were a narrow second to Jacksonville for injuries at offensive line. Only three offensive players had started 12 or more games: Koren Robinson (signed off the street in October), Floyd Womack (supposedly a backup at guard and tackle), and left

2009 Seahawks Schedule

Week	Opp.	Week	Opp.	Week	Opp.
1	STL	7	BYE	13	SF
2	at SF	8	at DAL	14	at HOU
3	CHI	9	DET	15	TB
4	at IND	10	at ARI	16	at GB
5	JAC	11	at MIN	17	TEN
6	ARI	12	at STL		

tackle Walter Jones.

Which of these injuries will linger over to 2009? Branch, Burleson, Jones, and left guard Mike Wahle were held out of April drills with various ailments. Matt Hasselbeck is now 34 years old with a history of back troubles, although he has not missed a game in an odd-numbered year since 2001. (In Hasselbeck's attic, there's a painting of Chad Pennington that has a separated shoulder in odd-numbered years.) Jones, 35, has missed at least one game in three of the past four seasons, and just had microfracture surgery on his knee. Branch is the most likely player to miss part of 2009. The seven-year pro has only once played all 16 games in a season, and again this year there are questions whether he will be ready for training camp.

The defense was much healthier than the offense last season, suffering only one significant injury, but it was a big one: End Patrick Kerney played his last game in Week 8 against San Francisco. After elbow surgery, Kerney was also held out of spring drills, and is expected to miss the start of this year's training camp.

Not satisfied to sit back and hope for improved health, Seattle made some major acquisitions over the offseason. Most newsworthy was the free agent signing of wide receiver T.J. Houshmandzadeh from Cincinnati. Though the massively-monikered wideout has been a good possession receiver, leading the league in catches in 2007, he has also been limited to short routes; at least 39 percent of his targets in the past three years have come within 5 yards of the line of scrimmage; last year that number soared to 50 percent. Since Burleson is a somewhat better deep threat than Branch, the plan is to start Burleson and Houshmandzadeh, then move Housh into the slot when Branch comes on the field for third downs. That trio, along with second-year tight end John Carlson (whose rookie campaign was one of the very few bright spots at Qwest Field), would make for an impressive set of pass catchers, complementing each other's styles nicely.

Among other new Seahawks, the most notable come on defense. Tackles Colin Cole and Cory Redding were brought in to shore up the run defense, and cornerback Ken Lucas may be the top corner on his new/old team. All those pale, however, compared to the new defensive star in Seattle: former Wake Forest linebacker Aaron Curry, taken fourth overall in last April's draft. The Butkus Award winner and consensus top collegiate player available, Curry will start from day one at weakside linebacker, and is expected to excel in pass rushing, pass coverage, and run defense.

Overseeing all this change will be new coach Jim Mora, who has been the team's defensive backs coach for the past two seasons. The Seahawks ranked 12th in pass coverage in his first season with the club, but sank to 30th last year. One of Mora's first moves upon being promoted to head coach was to hire Greg Knapp as offensive coordinator. Knapp spent the past two years running Oakland's offense after doing the same in Atlanta for three years under Mora. Those offenses were at 0.0% or worse in DVOA in four out of five seasons. Perhaps Knapp will do a better job with the offense now that he has an experienced, veteran

Table 1: Ouch! You're Breaking My Heart! Most Offensive Adjusted Games Lost, 2004-2007

Team	Year	Off. AGL	W-L	Off. DVOA	Next Yr W-L	Next Yr Off. DVOA	Change
NYJ	2005	57.7	4-12	-21.5%	10-6	6.2%	27.7%
STL	2007	52.4	3-13	-22.0%	2-14	-24.0%	-2.0%
TB	2004	48.2	5-11	-6.1%	11-5	-6.4%	-0.3%
DEN	2007	44.3	7-9	10.3%	8-8	24.0%	13.7%
MIN	2004	43.4	8-8	18.4%	9-7	-15.3%	-33.7%
PHI	2005	43.0	6-10	-9.1%	10-6	22.0%	31.1%
TB	2007	42.0	9-7	6.1%	9-7	4.0%	-2.1%
MIA	2006	39.8	6-10	-9.4%	1-15	-5.3%	4.1%
TEN	2004	37.0	5-11	-2.8%	4-12	-9.5%	-6.7%
WAS	2007	36.6	9-7	-0.2%	8-8	13.1%	13.3%
AVERAGE			6.2-9.8	-3.6%	7.2-8.8	0.9%	4.5%

pocket quarterback — who, by the way, loves dogs.

With all the turnover on both sides of the ball, there were some areas that simply couldn't be addressed. The top running backs are still the mediocre Julius Jones and the one-dimensional T.J. Duckett; the safeties are still Deon Grant and the Human Highlight Reel For Opposing Teams, Brian Russell.

Seattle should score more points in 2009 with just average injury luck. The ten most injured offenses from 2004 to 2007 averaged 6.2 wins and a -3.6% offensive DVOA; the next year, those numbers jumped to 7.2 wins and 0.9% DVOA. Four of those offenses jumped at least 10% in DVOA, most notably the 2005-06 Eagles, who went from -9.1% to 31.1%. However, success is not guaranteed. Half of those offenses actually declined the following season. The 2004-05 Vikings completely collapsed, falling from 18.4% to -15.3%.

If that happens to Seattle this season, then expect a complete overhaul in 2010, and the last links to the 2005 Super Bowl team to be cut. Hasselbeck and Jones, the best Seahawks ever at their positions, will almost certainly be gone. With no star quarterback or running back to build around, the offense could be directionless. Aside from the linebackers, most of the best players on either side of the ball will be north of 30, and any of those players could be replaced.

The good news for Seattle fans is that improvement could come quickly the following season. In addition to their own first-round pick next April, the Seahawks will also have Denver's first-round choice, swapped for a second-rounder this year. If we're right about Denver, then a Seattle collapse would mean a pair of top-ten draft picks in 2010. And as Thomas Dimitroff has shown in Atlanta, it is possible to find a starting quarterback and left tackle in the same draft.

That's all worst-case scenario, though. More likely, Seattle will regain its division crown and host another playoff game this year. With the uncertainty that would come with a second losing season, this will be a crucial campaign for the Seahawks. It could be playoffs or bust.

Vince Verhei

2008 Seahawks Stats by Week

Wk	vs.	W-L	PF	PA	YDF	YDA	TO	Total	Off	Def	ST
1	@BUF	L	10	34	252	338	-2	-104%	-57%	25%	-22%
2	SF	L	30	33	351	365	-2	-15%	-4%	16%	5%
3	STL	W	37	13	407	240	+1	30%	28%	-4%	-2%
4	BYE										
5	@NYG	L	6	44	187	523	-1	-87%	-26%	62%	2%
6	GB	L	17	27	177	313	-1	-36%	-35%	5%	3%
7	@TB	L	10	20	176	402	-1	-1%	-6%	15%	20%
8	@SF	W	34	13	261	388	+2	20%	18%	1%	3%
9	PHI	L	7	26	233	419	+1	-1%	2%	1%	-2%
10	@MIA	L	19	21	298	361	+1	0%	3%	11%	8%
11	ARI	L	20	26	196	458	-1	-49%	-54%	5%	10%
12	WAS	L	17	20	228	386	-1	-9%	-12%	7%	9%
13	@DAL	L	9	34	322	447	-1	-82%	-25%	58%	1%
14	NE	L	21	24	339	344	-1	37%	44%	3%	-4%
15	@STL	W	23	20	333	342	0	-30%	-9%	25%	4%
16	NYJ	W	13	3	295	265	0	16%	-4%	-8%	12%
17	@ARI	L	21	34	330	457	-1	-59%	-24%	34%	-1%

Trends and Splits

	Offense	Rank	Defense	Rank
Total DVOA	-9.7%	26	14.9%	27
Unadjusted VOA	-9.0%	27	14.3%	27
Weighted trend	-9.5%	26	13.3%	27
Variance	7.2%	18	2.1%	1
Average opponent	2.8%	21	5.2%	17
Passing	-3.7%	25	29.3%	30
Rushing	-3.4%	25	-2.7%	16
First down	-15.1%	29	9.1%	23
Second down	7.3%	18	17.2%	25
Third down	-26.5%	29	22.0%	26
First half	-2.3%	23	11.6%	22
Second half	-17.0%	27	18.8%	27
Red Zone	-8.8%	26	0.8%	19
Late and close	-11.6%	24	13.9%	27

Five-Year Performance

Year	W-L	Pyth	Est W	PF	PA	TO	Total	Rk	Off	Rk	Def	Rk	ST	Rk	Off AGL	Rk	Def AGL	Rk
2004	9-7	7.9	7.6	371	373	+8	-2.9%	16	4.1%	12	5.7%	21	-1.3%	20	7.3	27	23.5	17
2005	13-3	12.3	11.7	452	271	+10	29.7%	3	27.4%	1	-2.9%	15	-0.6%	20	11.8	20	17.1	12
2006	9-7	7.8	6.3	335	341	-8	-12.9%	24	-10.0%	27	5.5%	23	2.6%	9	31.1	3	6.7	27
2007	10-6	10.7	9.1	393	291	+10	14.2%	9	7.4%	12	-5.9%	10	0.9%	11	18.9	22	21.9	15
2008	4-12	5.4	5.6	294	392	-7	-21.9%	28	-9.7%	26	14.9%	27	2.6%	9	66.3	1	12.7	27

Strategic Tendencies

Run/Pass		Rank	Offense		Rank	Defense		Rank	Other		Rank
Runs, all plays	45%	13	3+ WR	60%	8	Rush 3	7.3%	9	2+ RB, Pct Runs	51%	30
Runs, first half	45%	11	4+ WR	14%	8	Rush 4	56.9%	26	1 RB/2 TE, Pct Runs	55%	12
Runs, first down	49%	18	2+ TE	12%	32	Rush 5	24.1%	12	1RB/3+WR, Pct Runs	37%	1
Runs, second-long	40%	11	Single back	52%	21	Rush 6+	11.7%	6	Zone Blitz	9%	4
Runs, power sit.	70%	8	Play action	23%	5	Rush 7+	2.4%	7	Go for it on 4th	0.77	25
Runs, behind 2H	39%	4	Max protect	8%	16	Sacks by LB	17.1%	17	Offensive Pace	26.9	1
Pass, ahead 2H	42%	17	Outside pocket	19%	1	Sacks by DB	5.7%	21	Defensive Pace	31.2	23

Mike Holmgren finally agreed to use shotgun formations over the last couple years, but that didn't mean he wanted to use them much. The 2008 Seahawks used shotgun six percent of the time, the only team last year below ten percent. The Seahawks were awful in the shotgun (-64.5% DVOA) but that comes with a small sample size asterisk. In fact, the year before, with similar small sample size, they had been fabulous in the shotgun (50.0% DVOA).   ● For the third straight year, the Seahawks threw more than half their passes to the right side of the field. (They led the league in 2006 and 2007, but ranked second behind St. Louis in 2008.)   ● Seneca Wallace was the only quarterback in the league (minimum 100 passes) who didn't throw an interception on a play with five or more pass rushers.   ● Seattle ran 36 percent of the time when they had three or more wide receivers in the game, the highest rate in the league.   ● Seattle only benefitted from opponents dropping 3.3 percent of passes, tied with San Diego for the lowest rate in the NFL.   ● What 12th Man? Seattle's defense was much better on the road (3.2% DVOA, 19th) than it was at home (27.5% DVOA, 30th).

Passing

Player	DYAR	DVOA	Plays	NtYds	Avg	YAC	C%	TD	Int
Seneca Wallace	295	7.3%	258	1482	5.7	5.0	58.8%	11	3
Matt Hasselbeck	-334	-34.2%	230	1116	4.9	4.0	52.4%	5	10
Charlie Frye*	-58	-46.3%	26	64	2.5	3.5	52.2%	2	2

Rushing

Player	DYAR	DVOA	Plays	Yds	Avg	TD	Fum	Suc
Julius Jones	-9	-10.1%	158	697	4.4	2	4	39%
Maurice Morris*	38	-1.1%	132	577	4.4	0	1	45%
T.J. Duckett	56	7.2%	62	172	2.8	8	0	56%
Leonard Weaver*	-1	-9.0%	30	130	4.3	0	1	47%
Seneca Wallace	8	1.3%	12	81	6.8	0	0	--
Matt Hasselbeck	28	46.2%	11	69	6.3	0	0	--
Owen Schmitt	2	6.0%	5	21	4.2	0	0	20%

Receiving

Player	DYAR	DVOA	Plays	Ctch	Yds	Y/C	YAC	TD	C%
Bobby Engram*	-32	-17.8%	80	47	489	10.4	3.6	0	59%
Deion Branch	-7	-14.2%	59	30	412	13.7	5.0	4	51%
Koren Robinson*	7	-11.2%	58	31	400	12.9	3.7	2	53%
Courtney Taylor	-67	-46.7%	25	9	98	10.9	4.0	0	36%
Billy McMullen	-32	-35.2%	18	7	124	17.7	2.7	1	39%
Nate Burleson	20	14.4%	9	5	60	12.0	1.4	1	56%
Michael Bumpus	12	4.1%	8	5	48	9.6	5.0	1	63%
Jordan Kent	-44	-99.8%	7	0	0	0.0	0.0	0	0%
T.J. Houshmandzadeh	163	2.5%	137	92	904	9.8	3.9	4	67%
John Carlson	144	19.2%	80	55	627	11.4	4.0	5	69%
Will Heller*	-29	-69.0%	6	4	29	7.3	2.5	0	67%
John Owens	-12	-20.7%	12	8	56	7.0	3.5	1	67%
Leonard Weaver*	45	15.6%	32	20	222	11.1	10.0	2	63%
Maurice Morris*	45	16.8%	27	19	136	7.2	6.3	2	70%
Julius Jones	-56	-53.1%	25	14	66	4.7	6.4	0	67%
Owen Schmitt	3	-7.0%	8	6	29	4.8	2.0	0	75%
Justin Griffith	40	34.6%	13	9	85	9.4	5.2	1	69%

Offensive Line

Year	Yards	ALY	Rank	Power	Rank	10+ Yds	Rank	Stuff	Rank	Sacks	ASR	Rank	False	Cont.
2006	3.70	3.75	30	70%	10	14%	23	20%	26	49	8.8%	26	25	32
2007	3.92	3.69	29	52%	27	20%	10	25%	31	37	7.1%	19	17	34
2008	4.13	3.82	27	76%	4	20%	11	20%	25	36	7.0%	22	24	29

Year	LE	Rank	LT	Rank	Mid	Rank	RT	Rank	RE	Rank
2006	4.18	14	3.95	24	3.61	31	3.88	24	2.94	29
2007	3.91	19	3.80	24	3.65	29	3.80	24	3.27	30
2008	2.88	27	4.37	10	3.70	27	3.96	22	4.15	14

This unit was hit by injury nearly as hard by injuries as Seattle's wide receiver corps. The intended starting five — Walter Jones, Mike Wahle, Chris Spencer, Rob Sims, and Sean Locklear — never saw the field together, and by season's end all were on the IR. Floyd Womack ended up starting 14 games at guard and tackle, the most of any Seattle blocker — and then signed with Cleveland in free agency.

Interestingly, for all the carnage along the line, there was not a significant decline in performance between the starters and their backups. Stats like Rushing DVOA, ALY, and yards per carry were consistent all year long. In some ways the blocking actually peaked in the final four games. The only real dropoff the end of the year was in big plays; the running game offered no home-run threat over the last quarter of the season. The pass blocking actually improved over that same quarter. This is all an indictment of the first string as much as it is a compliment to the second sting.

Table 2: Seattle Offensive Line Throughout 2008

Weeks	Run DVOA	Yd/At	ALY	10+	Stuff	ASR
Wk 1-5	7.1%	4.66	4.09	22%	16%	7.4%
Wk 6-9	-12.1%	3.88	3.06	25%	25%	7.0%
Wk 10-13	-6.0%	4.40	3.75	24%	22%	9.2%
Wk 14-17	-5.9%	4.14	4.18	11%	18%	4.0%

The most worrisome long-term injuries were to Jones and Wahle, who missed spring drills recovering from respective knee and shoulder injuries. If healthy, they'll both be starting, along with Locklear. The center and right guard positions are less clear. Spencer, a first-round draftee in 2005, has failed to live up to expectations. He's in the final year of his contract and is playing for his job. Sims tore his pectoral muscle off the bone in last year's season opener in Buffalo and missed the rest of the season. He has only one full season as a starter under his belt. The two players most likely to take their jobs are Ray Willis, a tackle who started three games at guard last year, and second-round draft pick Max Unger, who played tackle and center at Oregon. Unger looks like the long-term answer at center, but head coach Jim Mora and offensive coordinator Greg Knapp seem reluctant to trust a rookie to play center in their offense, which places extra weight on the snapper to call correct blocking assignments. Spencer has struggled with that exact task over his career, so we'll see how the coaches feel come September. Further depth is provided by Steve Vallos, who started the final five games at center, and Mansfield Wrotto, who started four games at guard.

Mora and Knapp rely heavily on zone blocking, which will be a dramatic shift for a unit that has emphasized size over speed. The smallest prominent Seahawks lineman is the 304-pound Wahle. By comparison, the Denver Broncos, the league's most prominent zone-blocking team, started four players smaller than that last year.

Defensive Front Seven

Defensive Line	Age	Pos	Plays	TmPct	Overall Rk	Stop	Dfts	Stop%	Rk	AvYd	Pass Rush Rk	Sack	Hit	Hur	vs. Run Runs	St%	Yds	vs. Pass Pass	St%	Yds
Rocky Bernard*	30	DT	56	7.0%	9	36	11	64%	69	3.2	71	4.0	6	7	43	63%	3.3	13	69%	2.5
Darryl Tapp	25	DE	53	6.2%	38	41	13	77%	38	2.4	72	5.5	7	13	43	79%	3.0	10	70%	-0.4
Brandon Mebane	24	DT	39	4.6%	45	30	13	77%	38	0.5	3	5.5	13	5	30	77%	1.1	9	78%	-1.6
Lawrence Jackson	24	DE	29	3.4%	84	18	4	62%	88	4.0	91	2.0	2	4	23	70%	3.6	6	33%	5.5
Patrick Kerney	33	DE	24	6.4%	30	18	8	75%	53	1.4	30	5.0	3	9	13	69%	2.6	11	82%	-0.1
Craig Terrill	29	DT	20	2.3%	74	17	7	85%	7	1.2	12	2.0	3	5	18	83%	2.1	2	100%	-6.5
Howard Green*	30	DT	20	2.9%	71	15	3	75%	48	2.3	52	1.0	0	1	18	78%	2.4	2	50%	1.0
Baraka Atkins	25	DE	17	3.5%	--	11	5	65%	--	2.2	--	2.0	3	3	14	64%	2.4	3	67%	1.3
Cory Redding	29	DT	37	5.6%	29	25	14	68%	66	2.2	47	3.0	7	3	28	61%	3.4	9	89%	-1.4
Colin Cole	29	DT	34	4.3%	50	26	10	76%	40	2.4	57	0.5	2	4	27	74%	2.7	7	86%	1.0

Linebackers	Age	Pos	Plays	TmPct	Overall Rk	Stop	Dfts	Stop%	AvYd	Pass Rush Sack	Hit	Hur	vs. Run Runs	St%	Rk	Yds	Rk	vs. Pass Tgts	Suc%	Rk	AdjYd	Rk
Lofa Tatupu	27	ILB	98	12.2%	42	58	14	59%	5.7	0.0	4	8	60	73%	17	3.6	57	29	45%	60	8.0	77
Julian Peterson*	31	OLB	90	10.5%	65	57	17	63%	4.3	5.0	4	13	52	65%	45	4.3	87	25	56%	33	5.5	26
Leroy Hill	27	OLB	84	13.1%	33	52	16	62%	4.3	1.0	1	1	44	82%	6	2.1	4	32	48%	52	5.4	23
D.D. Lewis	30	ILB	38	5.1%	--	20	6	53%	5.7	0.0	0	0	21	86%	--	1.3	--	16	31%	88	7.4	70

Year	Yards	ALY	Rank	Power	Rank	10+ Yds	Rank	Stuff	Rank	Sack	ASR	Rank
2006	4.73	3.98	10	69%	23	29%	32	21%	8	41	7.2%	14
2007	4.11	3.77	4	60%	13	24%	30	22%	5	45	7.3%	7
2008	4.18	4.16	17	70%	23	19%	17	19%	10	35	6.0%	17

Year	LE	Rank	LT	Rank	Mid	Rank	RT	Rank	RE	Rank
2006	3.73	13	4.72	22	4.12	14	3.34	6	2.85	2
2007	4.33	20	3.75	10	3.81	6	3.90	15	2.44	3
2008	4.12	17	4.41	20	4.20	16	3.82	9	4.13	20

The loss of Patrick Kerney in Week 8 started a domino effect that had far-reaching effects on the Seahawks defense. On the surface, their pass rush dropped by almost a sack per game without Kerney, but that's misleading. They feasted on a lot of bad offensive lines in the first half of the season, especially San Francisco, which surrendered 13 sacks to Seattle in two games. When Kerney was injured, the Seahawks' Adjusted Sack Rate fell from 6.4 percent to 5.8 percent. However, without opponent adjustments, the dropoff looks much more severe, 8.1 percent to 5.6 percent. Still, the loss of their only superior individual pass rusher forced Seattle to use more blitzes, and zone blitzes in particular. While all that blitzing helped to get pressure on opposing passers, it also opened holes in the running game; the Seahawks' DVOA against the run was -8.7% in the first half of the season, but 3.9% in the second half. Seattle is counting on a healthy season from Kerney, as well as development of 2007 first-round pick Laurence Jackson, who disappointed in his rookie campaign. Jackson was benched in Week 6, although he was back in the starting lineup after Kerney was hurt. Backing up both will be Darryl Tapp, who had seven sacks as a full-time starter in 2007.

With three-year starter Rocky Bernard leaving for the Giants in free agency, the Seahawks brought in a pair of tackles, trading for Detroit's Cory Redding and signing Colin Cole from Green Bay. The 330-pound Cole will team with the 314-pound Brandon Mebane to form an intimidating duo, with Redding coming off the bench on passing downs. The Seahawks have also been trying Redding at end.

Seattle's linebackers, already the strength of the team, may be even better in 2009, and will certainly be younger. Fourth-overall pick Aaron Curry is eight years younger than last year's starter, Julian Peterson, who was dealt to Detroit for Redding. Curry should immediately improve Seattle's coverage of opposing running backs, which has ranked near the bottom of the league for two years in a row. Leroy Hill, one of the league's top run defenders, signed a contract extension over the offseason that will keep him in Seattle through at least

2014. The previously consistent Lofa Tatupu had a relatively bad year in 2008, giving up big plays in both the run and the pass. He should benefit from the improvement in the defensive line. The best linebacker on the bench is D.D. Lewis, who started 12 games for Seattle's Super Bowl team of 2005.

Defensive Secondary

						Overall				vs. Run					vs. Pass								
Secondary	Age	Pos	Plays	TmPct	Rk	Stop	Dfts	Yds	Rk	St%	Rk	Tgts	Tgt%	Rk	Dist	Suc%	Rk	AdjYd	Rk	Yds	PD	Int
Josh Wilson	24	CB	84	9.8%	24	30	10	6.4	41	50%	27	84	17.9%	44	12.3	47%	54	8.5	66	8.6	10	4
Deon Grant	30	FS	84	9.8%	40	30	11	8.1	62	35%	55	38	8.0%	21	14.2	60%	18	7.3	24	7.3	10	2
Marcus Trufant	29	CB	77	9.0%	35	27	8	6.1	35	33%	57	89	19.0%	29	13.2	47%	55	8.3	62	8.4	11	1
Brian Russell	31	FS	72	8.4%	57	19	8	9.1	68	31%	64	23	4.9%	67	15.5	43%	68	7.6	35	7.8	2	0
Kelly Jennings	27	CB	54	6.3%	70	22	9	15.0	80	33%	60	76	16.3%	54	12.0	48%	48	9.4	81	9.6	11	0
Jordan Babineaux	27	SS	48	6.4%	69	19	8	5.1	15	46%	28	26	6.4%	46	6.5	60%	17	6.3	11	6.7	3	1
Ken Lucas	*30*	*CB*	*70*	*8.5%*	*46*	*30*	*12*	*8.4*	*56*	*55%*	*24*	*84*	*18.9%*	*30*	*11.9*	*52%*	*36*	*8.0*	*55*	*8.5*	*12*	*2*

Year	Pass D Rank	vs. #1 WR	Rk	vs. #2 WR	Rk	vs. Other WR	Rk	vs. TE	Rk	vs. RB	Rk
2006	22	4.9%	19	-24.2%	5	16.7%	25	11.5%	27	-25.1%	6
2007	12	-13.8%	6	6.0%	18	9.2%	26	13.9%	24	-23.5%	2
2008	29	40.2%	31	15.0%	24	-5.4%	15	20.2%	26	14.3%	25

The return of Ken Lucas to the Pacific Northwest should boost Seattle's defense considerably. The duo of Josh Wilson and, especially, Kelly Jennings proved woefully inadequate last season. Jennings, Seattle's first-round pick in 2006, performed so poorly against both run and pass last year that he now finds himself looking up at Kevin Hobbs, an undrafted player with 20 career games, on the depth chart. Lucas brings experience and, more importantly, size to the backfield — at 6 feet and 205 pounds, he's the biggest corner on the team. Wilson moves to the nickel, and should fare better against slot receivers than he did against starters. Marcus Trufant's charting numbers were poor last season, but expect a performance this year more like his 2007 campaign, when he was top 30 in both Success Rate and Adjusted Yards per Pass.

In the past four seasons, Deon Grant has ranked 58th, 64th, first, and 55th among safeties in Run Stop Rate. Whatever happened in 2007 that made him such a terror, don't expect it to return. He improved somewhat in pass coverage last season, but it's hard to argue that Grant has lived up to the $30 million contract he signed in 2007, which allegedly included the highest signing bonus for a safety to that point in league history. And then there's Brian Russell, one of the worst starting players in the NFL. He brings nothing to the table as far as run support. He creates virtually no turnovers, collecting just one interception over the past two seasons despite starting every game. And while his individual coverage numbers look all right, consider that the Seahawks' defense posted a 131.2% DVOA against deep passes last season, worse than any team save Detroit. Frankly, it's hard to find anything he does well. C.J. Wallace and Jordan Babineaux sit on the bench behind these two, which should say everything you need to know about them. The safety position has been an afterthought in Seattle for years now. Of these four players, only Grant was drafted — and that was by Jacksonville.

Special Teams

Year	DVOA	Rank	FG/XP	Rank	Net Kick	Rank	Kick Ret	Rank	Net Punt	Rank	Punt Ret	Rank	Hidden	Rank
2006	2.6%	9	0.6	14	4.0	13	1.8	11	8.6	6	0.4	13	6.8	8
2007	0.9%	11	1.5	15	-1.7	17	6.8	6	-9.6	29	8.6	5	-1.9	18
2008	2.6%	9	4.4	9	5.8	10	4.0	11	0.7	18	0.6	12	-9.7	26

For those who have any doubts that kickoff value is more consistent than field-goal value, let us tell you the story of Olindo Mare. Last year, Mare led the NFL in gross kickoff value, 8.7 points of estimated field position better than an average kicker. It was the fourth time in six years that Mare has led the league, and the other two years he was third (2004) and fifth (2007). Over that same period, Mare's weather-adjusted field-goal values have gone like this: -5.6, -0.5, 0.9, -10.6, -5.7, and 4.4. Over the past two years alone, his field-goal percentage jumped from 59 percent to 89 percent.

Punter Ryan Plackemeier was cut after he followed a calamitous 2007 with a poor performance in the season opener against Buffalo. He was replaced by Jon Ryan, who was a vast improvement. Both Mare and Ryan will be back this season. In the return game, Josh Wilson fell from stellar to good, and was outperformed by rookie Justin Forsett on a per-return basis. Forsett also proved adequate as a punt returner. If he can handle the lion's share of returns, it would allow Wilson to concentrate on defensive play.

Coaching Staff

Jim Mora's first head coaching stint in Atlanta started with a run to the 2004 NFC Championship game, but then flamed out with back-to-back non-playoff seasons. That hot-then-cold pattern showed itself in each individual season, as Mora's Falcons always finished worse in Weighted DVOA than in Total DVOA. The offense concocted by Greg Knapp was known for I-formations, zone blocking, plenty of runs, and a heavy use of play-action passing. It will be a major transition for Seattle, home to Mike Holmgren's timing-based passing attack for the past decade, but the Seahawks got a head start by increasing their use of play-action from league-average to fifth overall last season.

The defense will rest in the hands of first-time coordinator Casey Bradley, formerly linebackers coach in Tampa Bay. Bradley learned the finer points of the Tampa-2 defense from Monte Kiffin, but Mora is a defensive-minded coach, and his teams in Atlanta usually brought a lot of pressure. An aggressive attack might also be the best way to let Leroy Hill and Aaron Curry make plays. It will be interesting to see how the two styles mesh.

Tampa Bay Buccaneers

You read all the way to the end of the Bucs Coaching Staff comments in our 2008 book, right? If you didn't, you missed a little tip about an assistant coach on the rise by the name of Raheem Morris. We said he would soon be considered for a head job somewhere in the league. Little did we dream it would be right there in Tampa, thanks to a strange turn of events that saw the team collapse, the defensive coordinator channel Rodney Dangerfield in *Back To School*, and the head coach go from 9-3 to *Monday Night Football* in a few short months.

The madness began, as it often does, in Oakland. The sickness in Al Davis Land affected the Bucs. Lane Kiffin's firing and subsequent hiring at the University of Tennessee resulted in Lane's father, longtime Tampa Bay defensive coordinator Monte Kiffin, joining his son as a Vol. While that might earn Monte a few Father of the Year votes, his timing left something to be desired. The Bucs were 9-3 and cruising toward a playoff spot at the time. Kiffin obviously thought the team could handle his divided loyalties, but was proven dead wrong. While their defensive coordinator's heart and mind were clearly on Rocky Top, the Bucs defense seemed totally lost once their mentor turned his attention elsewhere.

The last four games of the season were a disaster for the Bucs' once-proud D, especially against the run. The Panthers humbled them on *Monday Night Football*, putting up 299 rushing yards. Atlanta beat them in overtime at the Georgia Dome, as Michael Turner waltzed down the field to set up the winning field goal. Then, the Bucs cratered in home losses to AFC West squads San Diego and Oakland. The Raiders game was particularly galling, and not just because of the irony of Tampa Bay's fate being determined by Oakland yet again. Just when it seemed they might back into the playoffs, the Bucs allowed 17 fourth-quarter points to the punchless Silver-and-Black (non-)attack. The losses cost the Bucs a wild card spot, setting the stage for what followed.

The poor play on defense was the undersea earthquake that resulted in a tsunami of a staff shakeup. Before the start of 2008, head coach Jon Gruden and general manager Bruce Allen were re-signed to extensions through the 2011 season. When the season ended and no immediate move was made, it appeared the pair would survive for 2009. But quietly, the Glazer family had turned their attention away from Manchester United's chase for the Premier League title. They took a closer look at the Bucs' failure to make the playoffs in four of the last six seasons, a run of mediocre drafts, and the inability to choose and develop a franchise quarterback, and decided enough was enough. Chucky and Allen were canned. Gruden said he felt "blindsided" by the move, but recovered nicely, setting the NFL Network and ESPN against one another in a bidding war for his services. *Monday Night Football* won out, and Gruden will spend 2009 analyzing games while making odd faces and secretly pondering where he wants to coach next.

BUCCANEERS SUMMARY

2008 Record: 9-7

Pythagorean Wins: 9.0 (14th)

DVOA: 11.1% (10th)

Offense: 4.0% (20th)

Defense: -7.3% (6th)

Special Teams: -0.3% (19th)

Variance: 15.3% (13th)

2008: Defensive collapse leads to mass firings, on field and off.

2009: Rebuilding the Pirate Ship, gangplank by gangplank.

2009 Mean Projection: 7.2 wins

On the Clock (0-3): 8%

Loserville (4-6): 30%

Mediocrity (7-8): 29%

Playoff Contender (9-10): 24%

Super Bowl Contender (11+): 8%

Projected Average Opponent: -6.3% (30th)

2009 Buccaneers Schedule

Week	Opp.	Week	Opp.	Week	Opp.
1	DAL	7	vs. NE (U.K.)	13	at CAR
2	at BUF	8	BYE	14	NYJ
3	NYG	9	GB	15	at SEA
4	at WAS	10	at MIA	16	at NO
5	at PHI	11	NO	17	ATL
6	CAR	12	at ATL		

Allen was replaced by Tampa Bay's pro personnel director Mark Dominik, but attention centered on the Morris hire. The Bucs clearly hope he will provide a bit of Mike Tomlin South, a young, hungry, brainy assistant who relates to the players but won't hesitate to chew their asses out when called upon to do so. Given the warm surroundings, we probably won't find out whether Morris wears a long leather coat as stylishly as Tomlin. Given the level of talent Gruden left behind, we aren't going to see anything close to Pittsburgh's success the last two seasons either.

Season tickets at the Pirate Ship were available for the first time in recent memory this offseason, and the first draft choice of the Raheem Regime didn't exactly get those phones ringing off the hook. The Bucs traded up two slots to select Kansas State quarterback Josh Freeman. It goes without saying that his development will be a shorthand referendum on Morris' tenure as coach. It takes some guts to tie your fortune to a young quarterback as an opening gambit. It paid off elsewhere in the NFC South for Mike Smith and Atlanta, and Morris is close to Freeman, having been defensive coordinator at K-State while Freeman was there. Some scouts see the sack-shedding, ad-libbing game of Ben Roethlisberger in the massive Freeman. Others see Big Ben's penchant for throwing interceptions. If Freeman has anywhere near the success Roethlisberger has had, Tampa fans will forget they ever criticized the pick.

Inconsistency in name and numbers defined the Bucs quarterback situation the last few years under Gruden. Chucky was forever collecting another warm body the coach believed he could mold into another Rich Gannon or Brad Johnson. The "all-comers" approach to choosing a quarterback continues into the Morris era. In addition to Freeman, four others were in the mix during the spring. Luke McCown, Josh Johnson, Byron Leftwich, and Brian Griese were all on hand for a competition Morris described confusingly as "One bone, five dogs, best man wins." Wait — is this Bucs Cam on the NFL Network, or are they bringing *Manimal* out of mothballs? Whoever emerges with the bone, he is projected to be more dog than efficient quarterback.

Not a man jack among these mediocrities is passer enough to build a decent statline without prime assistance from the rest of the offense. The Bucs made three moves in the offseason to give the winner of the quarterback derby a fighting chance First, wide receiver Antonio Bryant was re-signed. Bryant has had multiple issues on multiple teams, and missed all of 2007 after a DUI, failed drug test, and lawsuit against the NFL. Amazingly, he responded with a 2008 that was not only incident-free but worthy of a number-one receiver contract. Bryant was top ten in DYAR and made several highlight film type grabs. He was franchised, and signed the tender in late-February.

A day later, the Bucs dealt a couple of draft choices to Cleveland for another disgruntled but talented pass catcher, tight end Kellen Winslow, Jr. Assuming he can pull a Bryant and avoid trouble (not to mention staph infections), Winslow should be a prolific player — our projections have fourth among all tight ends in yardage, and second in yards per catch. Even if he falls short of that lofty status, he should be a huge upgrade over Jerramy Stevens, who provides as much drama and far more drops. Winslow's position coach, Alfredo Roberts, also made the move from Cleveland to Tampa in the offseason.

Finally, about a week after landing Winslow, the Bucs signed free agent running back Derrick Ward. The Giants slasher was the best back available, and Tampa Bay beat out several teams for his services. The question remains — how much of his success is attributable to New York's potent offensive line? KUBIAK

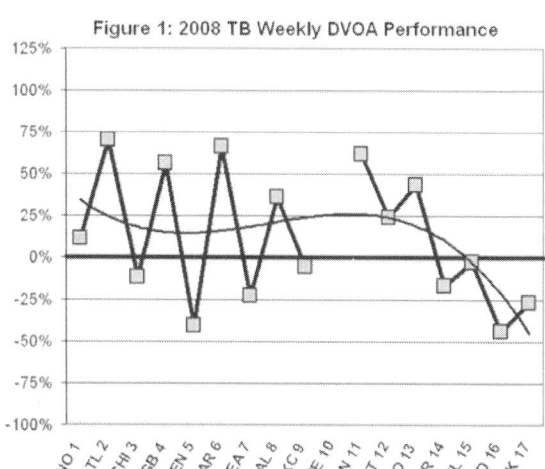

Figure 1: 2008 TB Weekly DVOA Performance

thinks Ward's production level will fall off hugely from a 2008 in which he was fourth in the NFL in DYAR. While Ward and Earnest Graham (who is coming off a knee injury) potentially offer a good 1-2 combo, much will depend on Tampa Bay's line improving over a poor effort a season ago. Tampa Bay's athletic but smallish offensive line is switching from a power- to a zone-blocking scheme in 2009. The Bucs can improve their running game if the new approach, combined with some fanny kicking by new line coach Pete Mangurian, gets better play out of tackles Donald Penn and Jeremy Trueblood. The explosive Ward, who is particularly effective at identifying and hitting the hole, should be the primary beneficiary of the new approach.

It's a whole new day on the defensive side of the ball as well. The eponymous Tampa-2 zone that Kiffin and Tony Dungy turned into one of the most widely-copied schemes in the league is out. With it go Derrick Brooks, Cato June, and Jovan Hoye, three starters geared toward the Tampa-2 style. It will be strange to see the Bucs lining up without Brooks on the weak side; it isn't overstating matters to say he might be the best Cover-2 linebacker ever to suit up.

Jim Bates is the new defensive coordinator, and he'll have to incorporate several new players into his system. All eyes will be on Jermaine Phillips, who moves from safety to the Will linebacker spot manned so capably by Brooks over the years. On the opposite flank, Angelo Crowell, who missed 2008 with a knee injury, comes to town from Buffalo. Barrett Ruud returns to man the middle. Speed isn't as crucial as positioning in the Bates defense, so the offseason will be critical for the outside linebackers to learn the scheme and be ready for opening day.

The Bucs will be featuring space-eating tackles after years of knifers, and Roy Miller was selected out of Texas in the second round to man the gaps. On the end, Gaines Adams appears on the verge of a breakout season as a pass rusher. Our game charters noted plenty of promise ("an absolutely outlandish first step … just inhuman … a lovely inside swim move … a pretty spin move"). The technique certainly seems to be there; now Adams needs to find some consistency. The same goes for Stylez G. (formerly Greg) White. White played more like Michael J. Fox than Teen Wolf in 2008, but if he regains his 2007 form, the Bucs have an outstanding rotation, including steady Jimmy Wilkerson.

The NFC South has established a reputation as a division where the unexpected is the norm. Certainly, the mass upheaval in coaches and personnel make Tampa Bay an unknown quantity. Atlanta went to war with a rookie general manager, head coach, and quarterback a year ago, and went 11-5 and made the playoffs. The happy talk from Tampa maintains that Freeman is meant to sit and watch as a rookie while one of the other from the crowded quarterback stable holds down the fort. More than likely, however, Freeman will be called upon at some point, depending on his development. The pieces are otherwise in place for the team to be competitive. What the Bucs get from the coaches and quarterbacks will decide if 2009 is a write-off or a successful season featuring a team rebuilt on the fly.

Robert Weintraub

2008 Buccaneers Stats by Week

Wk	vs.	W-L	PF	PA	YDF	YDA	TO	Total	Off	Def	ST
1	@NO	L	20	24	352	438	0	11%	11%	7%	7%
2	ATL	W	24	9	311	234	+1	70%	4%	-65%	1%
3	@CHI	W	27	24	454	407	-2	-12%	3%	10%	-5%
4	GB	W	30	21	327	181	+1	56%	-23%	-78%	1%
5	@DEN	L	13	16	307	333	0	-41%	-17%	15%	-8%
6	CAR	W	27	3	315	282	+3	66%	27%	-39%	0%
7	SEA	W	20	10	402	176	+1	-23%	4%	-6%	-34%
8	@DAL	L	9	13	262	172	-1	36%	4%	-29%	2%
9	@KC	W	30	27	423	384	-3	-6%	2%	35%	28%
10	BYE										
11	MIN	W	19	13	363	210	+1	62%	47%	-13%	2%
12	@DET	W	38	20	252	207	0	24%	-26%	-40%	11%
13	NO	W	23	20	254	332	+2	43%	-10%	-39%	14%
14	@CAR	L	23	38	384	464	+2	-17%	34%	40%	-10%
15	@ATL	L	10	13	325	373	+2	-3%	-19%	-27%	-10%
16	SD	L	24	41	342	370	-3	-44%	3%	45%	-2%
17	OAK	L	24	31	380	337	0	-27%	21%	47%	-1%

Trends and Splits

	Offense	Rank	Defense	Rank
Total DVOA	4.0%	20	-7.3%	6
Unadjusted VOA	4.9%	18	-4.8%	7
Weighted trend	6.8%	18	-1.4%	9
Variance	4.3%	1	6.0%	18
Average opponent	7.5%	4	8.8%	26
Passing	16.2%	17	-10.5%	6
Rushing	-1.5%	21	-3.9%	13
First down	15.7%	5	3.9%	21
Second down	-1.9%	21	-25.1%	1
Third down	-7.7%	23	-1.6%	11
First half	6.0%	17	-11.2%	6
Second half	2.5%	21	-2.7%	8
Red Zone	-1.1%	23	15.2%	24
Late and close	8.8%	18	2.9%	14

Five-Year Performance

Year	W-L	Pyth	Est W	PF	PA	TO	Total	Rk	Off	Rk	Def	Rk	ST	Rk	Off AGL	Rk	Def AGL	Rk
2004	5-11	7.9	7.9	301	304	-9	-2.1%	15	-6.1%	22	-7.6%	8	-3.6%	29	48.2	1	13.8	23
2005	11-5	8.9	8.1	300	274	+7	3.2%	14	-6.4%	17	-9.9%	8	-0.2%	19	15.7	15	6.5	30
2006	4-12	3.6	5.1	211	353	-12	-20.0%	29	-15.6%	30	4.6%	21	0.1%	17	30.0	5	26.6	8
2007	9-7	10.0	10.1	334	270	+15	17.1%	8	6.1%	13	-10.8%	4	0.2%	12	42.0	3	12.6	27
2008	9-7	9.0	9.0	361	323	+4	11.1%	10	4.0%	20	-7.3%	6	-0.3%	19	27.6	14	15.2	23

Strategic Tendencies

Run/Pass		Rank	Offense		Rank	Defense		Rank	Other		Rank
Runs, all plays	43%	17	3+ WR	50%	15	Rush 3	7.7%	8	2+ RB, Pct Runs	65%	8
Runs, first half	41%	25	4+ WR	8%	24	Rush 4	71.3%	5	1 RB/2 TE, Pct Runs	30%	32
Runs, first down	53%	13	2+ TE	28%	13	Rush 5	15.5%	27	1RB/3+WR, Pct Runs	23%	20
Runs, second-long	31%	26	Single back	54%	19	Rush 6+	5.6%	25	Zone Blitz	8%	6
Runs, power sit.	70%	9	Play action	13%	23	Rush 7+	1.0%	23	Go for it on 4th	0.84	20
Runs, behind 2H	33%	12	Max protect	6%	25	Sacks by LB	10.3%	26	Offensive Pace	31.3	18
Pass, ahead 2H	37%	25	Outside pocket	12%	13	Sacks by DB	10.3%	12	Defensive Pace	31.0	20

Last year, Tampa Bay's favorite stat was the quarterback hurry. The defense had the NFL's third best DVOA when it hurried the opposing quarterback, behind only Pittsburgh and Chicago. Meanwhile, Jeff Garcia had a league-leading 70.7% DVOA when hurried. He gained 7.8 yards per play when we marked a hurry, more than a yard better than any other quarterback. ● How much better was Antonio Bryant compared to the other Bucs receivers? Tampa Bay threw the league's highest percentage of passes to the left side of the field, and ranked eighth in DVOA on passes to the left. They threw the league's lowest percentage of passes to the right side of the field, and ranked 31st in DVOA on passes to the right. ● Although Tampa Bay ranked just 23rd with -1.1% DVOA in the red zone, they were third in the league with 42.1% DVOA if we look only at goal-to-go situations. ● The Bucs may not have run often in second-and-long, but they were the best team in the league when they did, with 39.4% DVOA and 6.2 yards per carry. ● Tampa Bay's defense was far better against shotgun formations than against standard formations, to an extent unmatched by any other team. They allowed 1.2% DVOA and 5.5 yards per play against non-shotgun formations, but -34.7% DVOA and 4.7 yards per play against shotgun formations.

Passing

Player	DYAR	DVOA	Plays	NtYds	Avg	YAC	C%	TD	Int
Jeff Garcia*	569	10.9%	395	2591	6.6	4.9	65.9%	12	6
Brian Griese	-14	-12.3%	193	1028	5.3	4.0	60.4%	5	7
Byron Leftwich	*175*	*66.0%*	*38*	*281*	*7.4*	*4.9*	*60.0%*	*2*	*0*

Rushing

Player	DYAR	DVOA	Plays	Yds	Avg	TD	Fum	Suc
Warrick Dunn*	41	-2.9%	186	786	4.2	2	0	46%
Earnest Graham	1	-8.5%	132	563	4.3	4	2	48%
Cadillac Williams	7	-6.2%	63	233	3.7	4	1	51%
Jeff Garcia*	20	-1.0%	30	143	4.8	1	2	--
Clifton Smith	-1	-11.1%	8	40	5.0	0	1	75%
B.J. Askew	25	39.3%	7	14	2.0	2	0	86%
Michael Bennett*	-26	-83.2%	7	12	1.7	0	0	57%
Derrick Ward	*265*	*25.8%*	*182*	*1027*	*5.6*	*2*	*2*	*51%*

Receiving

Player	DYAR	DVOA	Plays	Ctch	Yds	Y/C	YAC	TD	C%
Antonio Bryant	284	13.3%	138	83	1253	15.1	4.4	7	60%
Michael Clayton	18	-8.8%	61	38	484	12.7	5.1	1	50%
Ike Hilliard*	147	19.5%	58	47	424	9.0	2.6	5	81%
Joey Galloway*	-55	-40.2%	28	13	138	10.6	3.5	0	46%
Maurice Stovall	-38	-85.8%	7	3	25	8.3	0.7	0	43%
Jeremy Stevens	-9	-9.6%	59	36	397	11.0	3.8	2	61%
Alex Smith*	42	8.9%	38	21	250	11.9	6.2	3	55%
John Gilmore	24	9.2%	21	15	147	9.8	5.8	1	71%
Kellen Winslow	*-23*	*-11.6%*	*83*	*43*	*428*	*10.0*	*2.8*	*3*	*52%*
Warrick Dunn*	39	-3.7%	68	47	330	7.0	6.0	1	69%
Earnest Graham	24	-1.1%	33	23	174	7.6	5.4	0	70%
B.J. Askew	-5	-18.8%	18	13	66	5.1	5.6	0	72%
Cadillac Williams	10	13.3%	7	7	43	6.1	5.9	0	100%
Jameel Cook	5	5.0%	5	3	24	8.0	5.7	0	60%
Clifton Smith	-17	-71.8%	5	4	24	6.0	1.5	0	80%
Derrick Ward	*107*	*24.0%*	*55*	*41*	*384*	*9.4*	*10.0*	*0*	*75%*

Offensive Line

Year	Yards	ALY	Rank	Power	Rank	10+ Yds	Rank	Stuff	Rank	Sacks	ASR	Rank	False	Cont.
2006	3.67	3.83	27	64%	15	14%	21	22%	30	33	5.9%	10	22	28
2007	4.10	4.42	6	59%	23	13%	21	16%	7	36	7.9%	23	22	42
2008	4.09	4.04	22	65%	17	18%	13	17%	12	32	6.3%	18	17	35

Year	LE	Rank	LT	Rank	Mid	Rank	RT	Rank	RE	Rank
2006	2.94	28	4.02	22	3.99	23	4.07	19	4.10	15
2007	3.99	16	4.30	14	4.58	4	4.56	8	4.00	18
2008	2.16	30	3.54	28	4.35	9	3.91	26	3.90	20

Jeff Jagodzinski has installed a zone blocking system in Tampa, and it should fit the nimble athletes the Bucs have. Last season, the Bucs O-line was poor, falling 16 spots in Adjusted Line Yards. That was partially because they tended to eschew zone plays just when they seemed to build some rhythm. Tackles Donald Penn and Jeremy Trueblood were the weaker links. Penn didn't adhere himself to his new coaches when he sat out the first minicamp in a dispute over his tender. He signed a one-year deal soon afterward, but expect the Bucs to start looking around for a replacement. Second-year man Jeremy Zuttah could be that player, although his skill set is better suited to guard.

Center Jeff Faine played up to his huge contract in 2008, and will be expected to quarterback the new schemes being instituted. Guards Davin Joseph and Arron Sears were high draft choices, and played that way. Joseph made the Pro Bowl, and Sears wasn't far behind. They are athletic enough to adapt to the new zone system, and not having to pull so much might help extend their careers. (Maybe not in Sears' case — he missed voluntary camp with "personal issues" that reportedly were concussion-related. At the same time, he appeared in fine fettle at a football camp in Alabama, so perhaps the concerns are overstated.) The Bucs also spent a fifth-round pick on Xavier Fulton from Illinois, who had a strong combine and is a convert from defensive end.

Defensive Front Seven

Defensive Line	Age	Pos	Plays	TmPct	Rk	Stop	Dfts	Stop%	Rk	AvYd	Rk	Sack	Hit	Hur	Runs	St%	Yds	Pass	St%	Yds
						Overall						Pass Rush			vs. Run			vs. Pass		
Kevin Carter*	36	DE	51	6.7%	23	39	10	76%	46	1.7	43	4.0	5	12	42	74%	2.4	9	89%	-1.4
Gaines Adams	26	DE	44	5.8%	40	34	14	77%	39	1.4	34	6.5	12	14	26	65%	3.3	18	94%	-1.4
Chris Hovan	31	DT	44	6.2%	22	33	6	75%	47	2.0	38	1.0	4	5	40	75%	2.3	4	75%	-1.0
Jovan Haye*	27	DT	34	4.8%	40	25	4	74%	56	2.0	37	0.0	1	2	32	72%	2.1	2	100%	0.0
Stylez G. White	30	DE	31	4.1%	68	26	14	84%	17	1.2	25	5.0	10	5	19	79%	2.8	12	92%	-1.3
Jimmy Wilkerson	28	DE	23	3.0%	--	21	10	91%	--	0.0	--	5.0	6	4	14	86%	2.6	9	100%	-3.9
Ryan Sims	29	DT	18	2.5%	--	16	4	89%	--	0.8	--	1.5	3	3	14	86%	2.0	4	100%	-3.5

Linebackers	Age	Pos	Plays	TmPct	Rk	Stop	Dfts	Stop%	AvYd	Sack	Hit	Hur	Runs	St%	Rk	Yds	Rk	Tgts	Suc%	Rk	AdjYd	Rk
						Overall				Pass Rush			vs. Run					vs. Pass				
Barrett Ruud	26	ILB	142	18.7%	1	75	24	53%	5.2	3.0	2	1	96	58%	81	4.1	81	25	61%	12	4.8	14
Derrick Brooks*	36	OLB	80	10.6%	64	54	15	68%	3.9	0.0	0	1	55	69%	29	3.0	32	28	54%	34	4.7	13
Cato June*	30	OLB	69	9.1%	76	40	15	58%	5.2	0.0	0	2	39	79%	8	3.2	38	38	56%	32	6.1	41

Year	Yards	ALY	Rank	Power	Rank	10+ Yds	Rank	Stuff	Rank	Sack	ASR	Rank
2006	3.92	4.12	14	74%	28	15%	14	19%	15	25	5.5%	29
2007	3.88	4.24	22	73%	28	11%	3	14%	31	33	7.0%	12
2008	4.52	4.03	11	66%	16	23%	28	16%	25	29	7.1%	8

Year	LE	Rank	LT	Rank	Mid	Rank	RT	Rank	RE	Rank
2006	3.48	9	3.34	6	4.38	19	4.97	30	3.80	13
2007	4.12	18	3.60	8	4.55	31	4.59	24	3.30	8
2008	3.83	13	4.56	24	4.15	13	3.83	10	2.73	4

Seeing the Bucs line up on Sundays this season without Derrick Brooks at weakside linebacker will be like watching *60 Minutes* without seeing Mike Wallace — the show goes on, but it just won't be the same. Converted safety Jermaine Phillips has the unenviable role of filling Brooks' sizable cleats. Phillips is a good hitter and plays well against the run; he was a top ten safety in Stop Rate. A less traumatic change at linebacker involves swapping Cato June out for Angelo Crowell. The former Buffalo Bills starter missed all of 2008 with a knee injury, and he spent most of 2007 cleaning up after successful pass completions. Tampa Bay's linebackers were excellent in coverage last year, blanketing enemy backs and tight ends, but that could fall off with Crowell and Phillips on the wings. Barrett Ruud is the holdover in the middle, and he was in on more of his team's plays than any defender in the NFL last year.

The front four are the opposite of the linebackers — strong outside, in transition inside. Tackle Ryan Sims didn't get much playing time in 2008, but that should change under Bates. Stamina is a concern with Sims, however. He tends to disappear later in games and has been injury-prone, but is talented enough to keep getting chances. Chris Hovan is still on the roster, but at 296 pounds is lighter than the new regime prefers. The Bucs went after widebody Roy Miller of Texas in the third round, and he'll see plenty of action in Bates' system, as will second-year man Dre Moore. Defensive end Gaines Adams had a strong 2008, and Jimmy Wilkerson is steady on the other side. Stylez G. White spent a little too much time sorting through his list of new names (second choice — Rembrandt Q. Einstein) and fell off from his outstanding 2007. He'll get some push from rookie Kyle Moore (fourth round, USC) as situational rush end this season.

Defensive Secondary

Secondary	Age	Pos	Plays	Overall TmPct	Rk	Stop	Dfts	vs. Run Yds	Rk	St%	Rk	Tgts	vs. Pass Tgt%	Rk	Dist	Suc%	Rk	AdjYd	Rk	Yds	PD	Int
Ronde Barber	34	CB	85	11.2%	12	44	20	3.5	5	63%	14	79	20.2%	26	9.2	45%	62	9.2	79	9.7	12	4
Jermaine Phillips	30	SS	65	12.5%	10	29	10	4.0	5	57%	9	23	8.4%	14	13.0	37%	74	11.4	73	11.9	4	3
Tanard Jackson	24	FS	59	7.8%	61	24	8	7.1	42	47%	22	20	5.0%	66	17.4	63%	11	6.7	17	7.2	4	1
Phillip Buchanon*	29	CB	58	7.7%	57	16	7	12.3	75	31%	64	72	18.5%	35	11.4	42%	74	7.3	38	7.8	6	2
Sabby Piscitelli	26	SS	50	7.0%	67	17	9	9.1	69	28%	67	21	5.6%	54	14.8	53%	36	4.8	5	4.9	6	2
Aqib Talib	24	CB	29	4.1%	--	15	8	5.2	--	33%	--	32	8.6%	--	13.4	58%	--	5.5	--	6.2	8	4

Year	Pass D Rank	vs. #1 WR	Rk	vs. #2 WR	Rk	vs. Other WR	Rk	vs. TE	Rk	vs. RB	Rk
2006	29	5.9%	20	6.5%	19	-9.3%	12	11.4%	26	-10.4%	12
2007	4	-20.0%	5	-13.6%	7	-11.7%	14	3.7%	12	0.9%	19
2008	6	15.5%	23	-49.7%	1	6.1%	24	-18.7%	4	-24.2%	3

Tampa Bay ranked sixth in pass defense DVOA, but that had less to do with the secondary and more to do with a quality pass rush and quality coverage by the linebackers. The secondary primarily played Cover-4 in 2008, and it led to some strange splits — first and third wideouts had a field day against the Bucs, but they completely shut down number-two receivers. Some examples: Donald Driver was 1-for-5 for eight yards in Week 4, Shaun McDonald was 2-for-8 for 21 yards in Week 12, and Michael Jenkins held without a catch on seven passes in Week 2. Take out Muhsin Muhammad, and number-two receivers averaged less than 25 yards per game against the Bucs.

With the Tampa-2 now the Somewhere-Other-Than-Tampa-2, many fans wondered why cornerback Ronde Barber wasn't let go as part of the grand rebuilding plan. The 34-year-old was typically strong against the run in 2008, but his game charting stats were even lower than his mediocre 2007 numbers. Barber is smart, and Morris (the secondary coach last season, remember) feels he is veteran enough to adapt while mentoring the youngsters around him. One of those is Aqib Talib, a 2008 first-round pick who looks ready to step into a starting role this season. The Bucs are also quite high on Elbert Mack, who will see the field plenty. Just 23, the speedy if small corner is yet another product of the excellent defensive finishing school in Troy, Alabama. If Mack even approximates the production of fellow alums Leodis McKelvin, DeMarcus Ware, and Osi Umenyiora, the Bucs will have a sturdy replacement for Barber.

The Bucs are set at free safety with Tanard Jackson. He's a stopper in the passing game, and only 24. The strong safety job is Sabby Piscatelli's to lose. Sabatino was born in Boca, not Bologna, so he loves the pigskin and not the calcio. He was OK in five starts last year, but should improve with more field time — he lost almost all of his 2007 rookie season to a broken foot. Will Allen provides depth. He is athletic but lacks instinctive ability and misses too many tackles to be a starter.

Special Teams

Year	DVOA	Rank	FG/XP	Rank	Net Kick	Rank	Kick Ret	Rank	Net Punt	Rank	Punt Ret	Rank	Hidden	Rank
2006	0.1%	17	-1.6	20	12.7	3	-3.4	20	-1.5	21	-5.6	31	7.0	7
2007	0.2%	12	-0.3	20	-1.3	16	3.2	11	5.7	9	-6.1	27	-1.4	17
2008	-0.3%	19	-4.8	27	4.5	12	2.9	14	-5.4	23	1.4	11	5.5	6

Mike Nugent is a cautionary tale against using a high draft pick on a kicker, but that's no big deal in Tampa — they're not the ones who blew the pick. Nugent missed almost the entire 2008 season with a torn hamstring, and now he's just another free agent kicker who will spend his career bouncing between teams. What's important to Tampa Bay is that incumbent Matt Bryant was clearly slipping — he may have set a franchise record with 131 points, but his placekicking dropped to 27th in our ratings and his kickoff distance was even poorer than it was in 2007. Nugent has the bigger leg, both in kickoff distance and in long field goals.

Bryant's three-year-old son died last September, and the day after burying him, Bryant booted three field goals in a nine-point win over Green Bay. It was a feat every bit as "heroic" and "brave" as those Brett Favre gets feted for on a regular basis. Not only was there very little fanfare, but the team brought in someone to take his job less that a year later. Such is the status of kickers in the NFL.

The Bucs' kick coverage was outstanding — filter out Bryant's weak kicks, and only the Jaguars did a better job of stopping returns. The punt coverage fell off after a strong 2007, though punter Josh Bidwell was slightly above average. Clifton Smith came off the practice squad in midseason to revive the moribund return teams. Mission accomplished, to put it mildly. Smith combined for 15.3 return points, second in the NFL behind Daniel Manning, and wound up in the Pro Bowl. It was one of the more unlikely success stories of 2008. Smith will need to string together a couple more seasons of that kind of productivity to approach the return impact of his idol, Deion Sanders.

Coaching Staff

One quality Raheem Morris appears to share with Mike Tomlin, with whom he will be inevitably compared, is the decisiveness to go his own way. Both men came through the ranks as Cover-2 zone disciples under Monte Kiffin. But just as Tomlin was secure enough to stick with the winning zone blitz schemes fashioned by Dick LeBeau, Morris has eschewed the comfort of what he knows for a new defense, bringing in Jim Bates from defense-challenged Denver as the new defensive coordinator. Bates prefers mammoth tackles, linebackers who split wide and force the play to the interior, and press coverage in the secondary. He'll have to be given some time to alter the personnel to fit his scheme.

On the other hand, fans sick to death of Jon Gruden's dink-and-dunk attack will likely welcome whatever new offensive coordinator Jeff Jagodzinski has to offer. J-Jag had an eventful road to Tampa. After two successful years at Boston College, the coach got the itch to return to the NFL (he spent eight years in the NFL as an offensive assistant in various cities). Jagodzinski had his eye on the open Jets gig, but B.C.'s athletic director had other ideas. He let his coach know that he would be canned if he so much as interviewed in New York. Jagodzinski took the interview, lost his college job, and didn't get the Jets post, either. Seems like a bad week, but Jagodzinski landed on his feet in Tampa, and will be considered for the next round of open head coach slots.

Tennessee Titans

For years, the Tennessee Titans wandered through the desert of salary cap purgatory. The plan was to rebuild the team around dynamic young quarterback Vince Young and a stout defense, and it worked — somewhat. Young now looks like a flop, but the defense has kept its side of the bargain and then some, primarily thanks to impenetrable tackle Albert Haynesworth. By 2007, Haynesworth had developed into arguably the most irreplaceable defensive player in the league, and the Titans had become a playoff team.

Last year, the slow build hit warp speed, as the Titans started the year 10-0 and ended up as the number-one seed in the powerful AFC. Unfortunately, the season ended with a close playoff loss to Baltimore, followed by Haynesworth hitting the open market — and leaving Nashville for Daniel Snyder's big bucks in Washington.

Haynesworth is a singular player who forced opposing teams to account for him. The Titans actually have a reasonable stable of young replacements for him, but they won't attract the constant double-teams that let the rest of Tennessee's defensive linemen feast on one-on-one blocking. Though the tackles Haynesworth leaves behind are young, most of the other starting defenders are aging and generally past their prime. The Tennessee defense will continue its slide from dominant in 2007 to very good in 2008 to above average in 2009. That leaves the Titans in an awkward position, relying on their offense to get them back to the playoffs.

The irony of Haynesworth's departure is that the Titans may be the most successful team in the NFL when it comes to acquiring defensive contributors on the free agent market. Kyle Vanden Bosch, Jevon Kearse, David Thornton, Nick Harper, and Chris Hope all arrived through veteran free agency. All started last season, and all except Kearse played at a high level. But Hope is the only one of those five players under 30, and even he will turn 29 this season. The only way to make up for the loss of Haynesworth is for the other Titans defenders to improve — but add in stalwart linebacker Keith Bulluck, age 32, and more than half the Titans defense is at an age where nearly all players are declining. The Titans are about to start feeling the downside of shopping on the veteran free agent market just as their best homegrown player leaves via that market.

The full impact of losing Haynesworth is difficult to calculate because players of his quality have rarely changed teams in recent years. This decade, only five defenders have changed teams the year after they made first or second team AP All-Pro: Jeremiah Trotter, Champ Bailey, Adalius Thomas, Asante Samuel, and Jared Allen. Two of those players were actually traded away for sizable returns. None of those players was a defensive tackle.

The results for the teams who let their star defenders leave are generally negative. Four of the five teams

TITANS SUMMARY

2008 Record: 13-3

Pythagorean Wins: 12.1 (1st)

DVOA: 26.9% (5th)

Offense: 9.0% (16th)

Defense: -16.6% (5th)

Special Teams: 1.3% (15th)

Variance: 9.6% (4th)

2008: Kerry Collins plus a stout defense equal the league's best record.

2009: Kerry Collins plus a not-as-stout defense equal a fringe playoff contendor.

2009 Mean Projection: 9.3 wins

On the Clock (0-3): 1%

Loserville (4-6): 12%

Mediocrity (7-8): 22%

Playoff Contender (9-10): 34%

Super Bowl Contender (11+): 30%

Projected Average Opponent: 6.6% (2nd)

2009 Titans Schedule

Week	Opp.	Week	Opp.	Week	Opp.
1	at PIT (Thu.)	7	BYE	13	at IND
2	HOU	8	JAC	14	STL
3	at NYJ	9	at SF	15	MIA
4	at JAC	10	BUF	16	SD (Fri.)
5	IND	11	at HOU (Mon.)	17	at SEA
6	at NE	12	ARI		

who lost players saw defensive DVOA rise (i.e. get worse) by at least 7.7%. The only exception was Washington, which substantially improved after the departure of Champ Bailey. Washington made multiple changes, but most importantly, they added the almost-equally excellent Shawn Springs to replace Bailey. (Seattle's defense, meanwhile, was 7.1% DVOA worse after Springs' departure.)

Obviously, a sample size of five is not going to lead to a statistically significant result. Too many factors are in play to describe a team's performance. The wholesale youth movement in Kansas City last season would have sunk that defense even if they had not traded Allen. Plus, all these defenses were above average with their All-Pro player, so simple regression to the mean predicts a decline.

Still, the Titans have made no outside moves to bolster the defense in Haynesworth's absence. The Titans are promoting second-year man Jason Jones, who was downright fearsome in limited time last year, including a 3.5-sack game against the Steelers when Haynesworth was injured. They also drafted Sen'Derrick Marks in the draft's second round; the Auburn product is extremely raw but fills Tennessee's quota of pointless apostrophes. Even if Marks takes a while to develop, the Titans will not be weak at defensive tackle, but these players cannot replicate Haynesworth's enormous production.

One final loss for the defense is long-term defensive coordinator Jim Schwartz, who left to be the head coach of the Lions. Schwartz was replaced from within, so the scheme should remain the same, but the departure of one of the game's most intelligent coordinators is yet another factor pointing towards a defensive regression.

To return to the playoffs, the Titans offense will have to pick up the slack. This is both easier and more difficult than it appears. The conventional view is that the Titans have no offensive talent, that they do not have the ability to improve with the same squad. Last year,

however, the Titans offense was surprisingly effective, ranking 14th in DVOA with a very respectable 8.8%. The season proved that the Titans do possess some offensive talent.

The downside is that the Titans already are a productive offense. Improvement here is not merely a matter of achieving basic competence, but instead, requires the much more difficult step of moving from good to great. Skeptics have to wonder how a team that seemed to milk so much out of limited talent could improve even more.

The key to the Titans' offensive revival was the Week 1 injury to Vince Young. The supposed face of the franchise had been offensive Rookie of the Year in 2007 and had led the Titans to the playoffs in 2008. The problem was that he had stagnated and failed to put in the effort required, both on and off the field, to take his game to the next level. His unquestionable athletic ability and flashes of brilliance led to the Titans trying to develop an offense to suit Young rather than using the other 10 players on the field to the best of their abilities.

When Young went down, Kerry Collins was ready. Collins has been a success at numerous points throughout his career and combines intelligent decisions with prototypical size and arm strength. Collins has never been great, but he is competent and, more to the point for Tennessee, capable of minimizing mistakes while running a conventional offense.

Still, Collins has his limitations. He does not move well in the pocket, and while he takes few sacks, he is forced to throw the ball away too often. His turnover problems in the playoffs were more a result of playing the opportunistic Ravens, but Collins has never been the most efficient quarterback with the ball. Collins is also no spring chicken at age 37, which means both that he is likely to get worse and that he is not a long-term solution at quarterback. The continuing presence of Young on the roster will always create tension, and if the Titans and/or Collins struggle early, Jeff Fisher will feel pressure to switch back to Young.

More important than the concerns about Collins is the dearth of quality receivers on the roster. The team somehow functioned with Justin Gage, Justin McCareins, and Brandon Jones as their top three receivers last season. McCareins was let go, and Jones left in free agency, but the replacements — Nate Washington and first-round pick Kenny Britt — are not exactly Randy Moss and Larry Fitzgerald. Washington is a deep threat who has never started in the NFL, and Britt is a big, but raw, rookie receiver. The Titans are under a constant handicap because none of their receivers force opposing defenses to double-team them.

The result of that is, on most plays, eight men in the box. The Titans' very good offensive line was still able to open up enough holes for the dynamic Chris Johnson to break some long runs, while Johnson's much bigger partner LenDale White has mastered the effective three-yard gain. The two could do more, but the ability of opposing teams to constantly defend the run prevents what should be an excellent running game from truly dominating.

If the Titans do reach a higher level of offense, most of the credit should go to the offensive line. The group was as physical as any in the NFL, combining bruising run blocking with sufficient pass protection to allow Collins to avoid sacks. The line's most noted player, Kevin Mawae, is a bit long in the

tooth at 38, but the rest of the line is in its prime. Still, the Titans were lucky last year to avoid the injury bug. Starting offensive linemen only missed one game, when Mawae sat out the meaningless season-ending contest with the Colts. If the offensive line suffers injuries, the Titans offense would likely cease to be effective.

The good news is that even our most pessimistic projections see the Titans on the fringes of the playoffs. The bad news is that, despite their relatively recent return to prominence, the Titans' window is exceedingly narrow. Collins and too many core defenders are getting old, and the Titans will be hard-pressed to avoid another rebuilding period. As such, if the Titans want to make a serious run at a Super Bowl, there is no time like the present. The offense had better be ready to lead them there.

Ned Macey

2008 Titans Stats by Week

Wk	vs.	W-L	PF	PA	YDF	YDA	TO	Total	Off	Def	ST
1	JAC	W	17	10	309	189	+1	5%	-27%	-51%	-19%
2	@CIN	W	24	7	295	215	+1	34%	10%	-34%	-10%
3	HOU	W	31	12	343	317	+1	44%	-2%	-45%	1%
4	MIN	W	30	17	275	333	+3	56%	33%	-13%	9%
5	@BAL	W	13	10	210	285	0	15%	-11%	-13%	13%
6	BYE										
7	@KC	W	34	10	455	272	0	48%	50%	2%	-1%
8	IND	W	31	21	281	317	+2	28%	13%	-10%	4%
9	GB	W	19	16	347	390	+2	17%	15%	-9%	-7%
10	@CHI	W	21	14	304	243	0	19%	12%	-5%	2%
11	@JAC	W	24	14	344	257	0	43%	15%	-21%	7%
12	NYJ	L	13	34	281	409	+1	3%	24%	21%	0%
13	@DET	W	47	10	456	154	+2	81%	-6%	-68%	20%
14	CLE	W	28	9	390	178	-2	22%	11%	-14%	-2%
15	@HOU	L	12	13	281	375	-1	-9%	-28%	-10%	9%
16	PIT	W	31	14	322	374	+4	77%	51%	-28%	-1%
17	@IND	L	0	23	125	390	0	-39%	-33%	4%	-2%
18	BYE										
19	BAL	L	10	13	391	211	-3	32%	12%	-23%	-4%

Trends and Splits

	Offense	Rank	Defense	Rank
Total DVOA	9.0%	16	-16.6%	5
Unadjusted VOA	10.3%	14	-14.9%	4
Weighted trend	10.8%	13	-10.4%	5
Variance	6.4%	12	9.1%	26
Average opponent	2.2%	24	4.5%	13
Passing	17.4%	16	-19.3%	4
Rushing	10.5%	8	-12.9%	6
First down	2.4%	19	-2.2%	13
Second down	11.1%	15	-21.5%	3
Third down	17.8%	13	-33.0%	2
First half	9.4%	14	-11.7%	5
Second half	8.6%	17	-21.8%	2
Red Zone	34.8%	3	-33.9%	4
Late and close	13.3%	15	-27.7%	1

Five-Year Performance

Year	W-L	Pyth	Est W	PF	PA	TO	Total	Rk	Off	Rk	Def	Rk	ST	Rk	Off AGL	Rk	Def AGL	Rk
2004	5-11	5.8	5.4	344	439	-1	-17.8%	26	-2.8%	18	11.3%	24	-3.8%	30	37.0	3	37.1	4
2005	4-12	4.9	5.3	299	421	-6	-23.2%	29	-9.5%	20	15.7%	30	2.0%	7	21.3	12	8.6	27
2006	8-8	6.0	6.8	324	400	+2	-9.6%	22	-8.2%	24	3.9%	20	2.5%	10	34.2	2	9.0	22
2007	10-6	8.1	9.2	301	297	0	9.5%	11	-3.4%	20	-13.3%	1	-0.4%	17	4.7	32	10.3	28
2008	13-3	12.1	11.6	375	234	+14	26.9%	5	9.0%	16	-16.6%	5	1.3%	15	9.0	30	14.4	24

Strategic Tendencies

Run/Pass		Rank	Offense		Rank	Defense		Rank	Other		Rank
Runs, all plays	51%	4	3+ WR	39%	27	Rush 3	2.4%	27	2+ RB, Pct Runs	67%	5
Runs, first half	48%	6	4+ WR	2%	31	Rush 4	80.9%	2	1 RB/2 TE, Pct Runs	51%	18
Runs, first down	61%	4	2+ TE	39%	1	Rush 5	11.6%	31	1RB/3+WR, Pct Runs	30%	12
Runs, second-long	44%	7	Single back	59%	14	Rush 6+	5.2%	27	Zone Blitz	1%	27
Runs, power sit.	72%	6	Play action	18%	12	Rush 7+	0.6%	27	Go for it on 4th	1.02	11
Runs, behind 2H	33%	13	Max protect	10%	9	Sacks by LB	3.4%	31	Offensive Pace	28.7	2
Pass, ahead 2H	37%	26	Outside pocket	11%	22	Sacks by DB	6.8%	19	Defensive Pace	31.2	22

Although the Titans were not a less run-oriented offense with Kerry Collins behind center, they did become a much faster offense. Tennessee's situation-neutral pace went from 26th in the NFL in 2007 to second overall in 2008. ● Collins was also much better at play-action fakes, and the Titans improved from 22nd in DVOA on play-action to eighth. ● Even though Titans opponents were passing in an attempt to come from behind in nearly every game, they only used four or more wide receivers on seven percent of plays, the second-lowest rate in the league. ● The Titans allowed -0.4% DVOA on deep passes (16-plus yards in the air), the only defense with a negative DVOA on such passes. ● Tennessee ranked fourth in defensive DVOA when hurrying the quarterback, but their percentage of hurries per pass play dropped from third in the league in 2007 to 17th in 2008.

Passing

Player	DYAR	DVOA	Plays	NtYds	Avg	YAC	C%	TD	Int
Kerry Collins	738	15.3%	430	2712	6.3	4.9	58.6%	12	7
Vince Young	-150	-69.7%	40	219	5.5	7.4	61.1%	1	2

Rushing

Player	DYAR	DVOA	Plays	Yds	Avg	TD	Fum	Suc
Chris Johnson	175	9.2%	251	1228	4.9	9	1	44%
LenDale White	144	7.5%	200	774	3.9	15	0	54%
Quinton Ganther	19	45.6%	9	61	6.8	0	0	67%
Ahmard Hall	-1	-9.9%	8	22	2.8	0	1	63%
Kerry Collins	11	10.4%	8	61	7.6	0	0	--
Vince Young	-1	-17.4%	6	29	4.8	0	0	--
Nate Washington	14	23.1%	5	18	3.6	0	0	--

Receiving

Player	DYAR	DVOA	Plays	Ctch	Yds	Y/C	YAC	TD	C%
Justin Gage	116	6.7%	74	34	651	19.1	5.3	6	46%
Justin McCareins*	-108	-31.5%	73	31	416	13.4	3.0	0	42%
Brandon Jones*	75	3.2%	62	41	449	11.0	2.5	1	66%
Lavelle Hawkins	-4	-16.9%	12	7	68	9.7	2.9	0	58%
Nate Washington	70	-0.8%	78	40	631	15.8	3.3	3	51%
Bo Scaife	39	-0.4%	84	58	561	9.7	6.1	2	69%
Alge Crumpler	-4	-8.7%	41	24	257	10.7	5.3	1	59%
Chris Johnson	-20	-19.8%	62	43	260	6.0	6.0	1	52%
Ahmard Hall	36	14.5%	18	13	138	10.6	10.5	2	72%
LenDale White	-43	-90.3%	10	5	16	3.2	3.0	0	50%
Quinton Ganther	14	25.3%	6	6	43	7.2	7.7	0	100%

Offensive Line

Year	Yards	ALY	Rank	Power	Rank	10+ Yds	Rank	Stuff	Rank	Sacks	ASR	Rank	False	Cont.
2006	4.29	3.83	28	67%	13	22%	6	17%	9	29	6.0%	11	16	34
2007	3.90	4.22	11	71%	6	12%	23	16%	8	30	6.6%	16	15	38
2008	4.45	4.10	15	61%	26	24%	6	22%	28	12	3.2%	3	16	45

Year	LE	Rank	LT	Rank	Mid	Rank	RT	Rank	RE	Rank
2006	3.77	20	3.25	31	3.96	24	4.16	14	3.53	23
2007	3.71	22	4.87	6	4.34	8	3.60	28	3.77	21
2008	3.86	23	4.35	11	4.13	16	4.04	21	4.01	18

How do you have an above average offense when all your skill position players (except for Chris Johnson) are average or worse? Simple: You build one of the game's toughest and most physical offensive lines. Our game charters marked the Titans with only seven blown blocks, tied for the lowest total in the league, and only three of them were by the starting linemen. The group is anchored by standout left tackle Michael Roos, arguably the best run-blocking left tackle in football today. Center Kevin Mawae plays the role of cagey veteran, but he still is surprisingly agile for his age (38 this season). His Pro Bowl selection may have been largely reputation but was not ridiculous. Mawae had new starting guards on each side of him last season, one a free agent (Jake Scott on the right, signed from the Colts) and one an internal development project (Eugene Amano on the left, a 2004 seventh-round pick). Amano was surprisingly effective, while Scott was solid but a bit of a disappointment considering his pedigree and sizable contract. The unsung star of the team is David Stewart, a mammoth right tackle who has quietly become one of the most consistent players at his position. All told, this group is filled with above-average players who together form one of the league's elite lines. Its pedestrian ALY stats are primarily a function of opposing teams' constant barrage of eight-man fronts (although Chris Johnson's penchant for dancing in the backfield is another factor). As with all teams where the offensive line remained healthy, the reserves are an untested group. An injury here, particularly to either tackle, could be devastating. First in line to replace a tackle might be rookie Troy Kropog, a raw fourth-round pick out of Tulane. In the interior of the line, first crack may go to Leroy Harris, a 2007 fourth-round pick out of North Carolina.

Defensive Front Seven

Defensive Line	Age	Pos	Plays	TmPct	Rk	Overall Stop	Dfts	Stop%	Rk	AvYd	Pass Rush Rk	Sack	Hit	Hur	vs. Run Runs	St%	Yds	vs. Pass Pass	St%	Yds
Tony Brown	29	DT	53	6.8%	13	42	19	79%	30	0.7	7	4.0	11	10	37	76%	1.3	16	88%	-0.6
Albert Haynesworth*	28	DT	51	7.0%	6	41	19	80%	21	0.2	2	8.5	14	8	38	76%	1.5	13	92%	-3.5
Jevon Kearse	33	DE	37	4.5%	62	26	15	70%	69	1.7	42	3.5	8	10	24	67%	2.5	13	77%	0.2
Jason Jones	23	DE	33	4.9%	52	20	11	61%	90	2.8	81	5.0	3	1	19	42%	4.5	14	86%	0.4
Dave Ball	27	DE	27	3.5%	81	19	6	70%	68	1.4	33	4.5	9	8	21	62%	3.3	6	100%	-5.2
Jacob Ford	26	DE	26	3.6%	80	20	11	77%	42	0.0	8	7.0	6	6	17	65%	2.5	9	100%	-4.8
Kyle Vanden Bosch	31	DE	22	4.2%	65	16	9	73%	60	2.0	57	4.5	14	7	13	69%	3.0	9	78%	0.7
Kevin Vickerson	26	DT	15	4.1%	--	12	5	80%	--	0.8	--	1.5	2	0	10	90%	1.3	5	60%	-0.2
Jovan Haye	27	DT	34	4.8%	40	25	4	74%	56	2.0	37	0.0	1	2	32	72%	2.1	2	100%	0.0

Linebackers	Age	Pos	Plays	TmPct	Rk	Overall Stop	Dfts	Stop%	AvYd	Pass Rush Sack	Hit	Hur	vs. Run Runs	St%	Rk	Yds	Rk	vs. Pass Tgts	Suc%	Rk	AdjYd	Rk
Keith Bulluck	32	OLB	104	12.5%	37	50	16	48%	4.9	0.5	0	1	60	58%	79	3.2	37	40	45%	63	6.3	50
David Thornton	31	OLB	84	10.8%	60	52	19	62%	4.2	0.0	2	3	39	69%	28	2.3	9	53	50%	45	6.3	49
Stephen Tulloch	24	ILB	79	9.5%	72	47	12	59%	4.5	1.0	0	1	50	68%	34	3.2	36	18	59%	19	5.3	21
Ryan Fowler	27	ILB	25	3.0%	--	14	5	56%	5.6	0.0	0	0	16	63%	--	2.4	--	5	58%	--	3.7	--

Year	Yards	ALY	Rank	Power	Rank	10+ Yds	Rank	Stuff	Rank	Sack	ASR	Rank
2006	4.47	4.48	25	69%	24	18%	25	17%	18	26	5.8%	25
2007	4.11	3.86	7	78%	31	18%	21	20%	13	40	7.2%	9
2008	3.81	3.62	5	64%	13	21%	22	25%	2	44	7.1%	9

Year	LE	Rank	LT	Rank	Mid	Rank	RT	Rank	RE	Rank
2006	4.85	25	3.97	9	4.41	20	4.08	15	5.19	31
2007	3.27	8	4.42	19	3.93	11	2.90	1	4.42	24
2008	2.52	2	2.69	1	3.85	7	3.32	4	5.39	31

Albert Haynesworth may have been the best defensive tackle in football the past two seasons, so to think his loss will not be felt is an enormous mistake. His replacement, His replacement, Jason Jones showed promise and will likely be an above-average tackle (although he played primarily at end as a rookie). Unfortunately, the other players on the line are probably not as good as they appeared while playing with Haynesworth. Tony Brown made a number of great plays last year, and his overall stat line is similar to Haynesworth's. Brown, however, often had only a guard to beat, while Haynesworth occupied the other guard and the center. This year, Brown will be the marked man and no longer free to wreak havoc. The Titans hope that second-round pick

Sen'Derrick Marks will help provide a valuable third man in a talented, if no longer dominant, defensive tackle rotation. He has a strong build but tends to tire easily and may have come out of Auburn too early.

As noted earlier in the chapter, the Titans have serious age problems at defensive end. Jevon Kearse occasionally flashed the form that made him a dominant player in his first go-round with the Titans, but he did not make a consistent impact and is not likely to improve at age 33. Jacob Ford is already the better pass rusher and will likely earn at least half the snaps even if Kearse retains the meaningless title of "starter." On the other side, Kyle Vanden Bosch's production lagged last season. A groin injury limited him to only ten games last season and hampered him even when he was on the field. As a result, he only amassed 4.5 sacks, his lowest total since arriving in Tennessee. Vanden Bosch is too often referred to as a high-energy guy who succeeds only on effort. Like all great pass-rushing defensive ends, he had an explosive first step. Vanden Bosch is now on the wrong side of 30. As he loses a half-step either through age or injury, he suddenly becomes just another pass rusher. The Titans hope that the diminished output was merely the result of the groin injury that should be healed by this season.

The linebackers are a solid unit with no real weaknesses. Keith Bulluck is entering the savvy veteran stage of his career, where his intelligence allows him to compensate for declining physical skills. David Thornton is very good in coverage and a strong enough run defender to be a very-good-but-not-quite-Pro Bowl level of player. Stephen Tulloch was inconsistent in his first year as a starter, but he flashes enough big play ability that the Titans have to be encouraged about his long-term potential. Depth is a bit of a problem, particularly with the aging Bulluck. The Titans have to hope that fourth-round pick Gerald McRath (Southern Miss) is ready immediately if Bulluck or Thornton goes down to injury.

Defensive Secondary

Secondary	Age	Pos	Plays	TmPct	Rk	Stop	Dfts	Yds	Rk	St%	Rk	Tgts	Tgt%	Rk	Dist	Suc%	Rk	AdjYd	Rk	Yds	PD	Int
									vs. Run				**vs. Pass**									
Cortland Finnegan	25	CB	86	10.4%	17	40	24	3.6	6	65%	11	76	16.1%	57	13.5	51%	40	7.3	39	7.5	18	5
Chris Hope	29	SS	86	10.4%	33	33	16	6.5	31	44%	34	35	7.3%	32	13.6	62%	13	5.8	7	5.9	7	4
Nick Harper	35	CB	85	12.6%	6	42	19	4.8	19	56%	21	91	23.8%	4	12.1	60%	13	6.1	18	6.0	11	2
Michael Griffin	24	FS	74	8.9%	52	32	13	5.5	19	38%	46	43	9.0%	11	14.1	61%	16	6.5	15	6.4	10	7
Vincent Fuller	27	FS	45	5.4%	72	15	11	7.7	50	50%	17	33	7.0%	37	9.2	47%	56	7.8	39	7.6	3	0
Chris Carr*	26	CB	27	3.3%	--	7	3	6.6	--	20%	--	39	8.3%	--	10.1	41%	--	6.9	--	6.6	5	1
Demarcus Faggins	30	CB	21	2.9%	--	8	5	5.6	--	40%	--	28	6.5%	--	8.7	41%	--	10.9	--	10.3	3	0

Year	Pass D Rank	vs. #1 WR	Rk	vs. #2 WR	Rk	vs. Other WR	Rk	vs. TE	Rk	vs. RB	Rk
2006	15	7.6%	21	1.9%	16	-6.2%	15	-24.0%	5	11.5%	25
2007	1	-4.0%	13	-5.3%	11	-36.5%	1	-21.7%	1	-20.9%	4
2008	4	-15.5%	4	-16.0%	7	-30.2%	6	-8.8%	11	-7.4%	7

The Titans have become primarily a zone team, which has led to the continued productivity of the now ancient Nick Harper. Harper seemed an odd addition when he came to the Titans in 2006, but in year three (at age 34), he had simply outstanding charting numbers, ranking in the top 20 in both Adjusted Yards per Pass and Success Rate. How was it that Cortland Finnegan, with far inferior stats, was the Pro Bowler instead? It turns out that sometimes Pro Bowl voters do know a thing or two. Harper basically plays a short zone on every play with a safety over the top. He is a sure tackler who prevents big gains, but dozens of cornerbacks could perform similarly if so sheltered by the scheme. The Titans are much more likely to let Finnegan cover an opposing receiver one-on-one. Sometimes the results are discouraging (Andre Johnson destroyed the Titans with 208 yards in Week 16), but Finnegan's coverage ability gives Michael Griffin more freedom to freelance. Griffin really came into his own last season, finally at home as a safety. He still makes the occasional mistake and too often seems to be playing on instinct, but he's developing into the next great ball-hawking safety. Griffin's boom-or-bust style fits nicely opposite the extremely steady Chris Hope. Hope appears to always be where he is supposed to be, and while he lacks Griffin's athleticism, his pass defense is equally strong.

The Titans' major problem in the secondary is a lack of depth. Their skilled safeties allowed for good numbers against opposing slot receivers and tight ends, but reserve cornerbacks Vincent Fuller and Chris Carr both struggled when pressed into action either as nickelbacks or as injury replacements for Harper. Rookie third-round pick Ryan Mouton should compete for playing time here, and the Titans have never been shy about playing young cornerbacks. The Hawaii product has strong instincts and ball skills but may find that his lack of size (5-foot-9, 187 pounds) is a problem against bigger, stronger receivers.

Special Teams

Year	DVOA	Rank	FG/XP	Rank	Net Kick	Rank	Kick Ret	Rank	Net Punt	Rank	Punt Ret	Rank	Hidden	Rank
2006	2.5%	10	-1.4	19	-1.9	24	1.2	12	4.2	12	12.4	1	8.8	5
2007	-0.4%	17	8.7	1	5.9	9	-6.7	25	-4.4	23	-5.7	25	13.0	4
2008	1.3%	15	6.6	5	1.4	16	3.7	12	-2.4	21	-1.8	21	20.4	1

Rob Bironas has developed into one of the elite placekickers in the NFL. He has been outstanding as a placekicker the past two seasons, but his strong leg means he should provide value on kickoffs even when he inevitably has an inconsistent year on field goals. The Titans are not as fortunate at punter, where Craig Hentrich has now struggled for two consecutive seasons. It seems unlikely that the Titans punter since 1998 will be better at age 38. With Chris Carr now in Baltimore, kick and punt returns will be handled by free agent veteran Mark Jones, who was league-average with Carolina a year ago. The Titans' top gunner is Donnie Nickey, a long-time special teams stalwart who still excels on both punt and kick coverage.

Good luck on special teams contributed to Tennessee's 13-3 record a year ago, but the Titans can't expect opposing kickers to only hit 67 percent of their field goals again in 2009.

Coaching Staff

The past two seasons have put Jeff Fisher back into the conversation about the league's best coaches. These repeat playoff performers have been prototypical Fisher teams. They play hard-nosed defense and run the ball incessantly. The Titans have ranked in the top half of NFL passing attempts in only two of Fisher's 14 full seasons as a head coach. The return of offensive coordinator Mike Heimerdinger paid dividends for the Titans, who posted their first above-average offense since 2003.

Long time defensive coordinator Jim Schwartz left for the thankless task of coaching the Lions. The Titans valued continuity and promoted defensive backs coach Chuck Cecil. Cecil worked for Schwartz throughout his eight-year run as defensive coordinator, and Cecil's work with the defensive backs the past two seasons has been exemplary. The Titans' general strategy will likely remain similar, although Cecil may be forced to blitz more often than Schwartz out of necessity due to the departure of Haynesworth.

Washington Redskins

After the first eight games of the 2008 season, the Washington Redskins had a 6-2 record, and all was right with the world. Jason Campbell threw zero interceptions in 230 attempts and completed two-thirds of his passes. Clinton Portis rushed for 944 yards on 187 carries, leading the league. The Redskins became the first team in NFL history to go through their first five games without a turnover of any kind. Rookie safety Chris Horton, a seventh-round pick, was the NFC Defensive Rookie of the Month for September. Washington beat the eventual NFC champion Arizona Cardinals, as well as division rivals the Cowboys and Eagles. New head coach Jim Zorn was being talked about in the same breathless tones as fellow first-year saviors Mike Smith in Atlanta and Tony Sparano in Miami.

After the second eight-game stretch of the 2008 season, the Redskins had an 8-8 record, and everything had fallen apart. Campbell threw more interceptions (six) than touchdowns (five) with a completion rate below 60 percent. Portis rushed for 543 yards on 155 carries, and he dropped from 5.0 yards per carry in the first half of the season to 3.5 in the second half. Zorn's name had lost just about all of its luster, and Campbell would soon discover that the team was desperate to replace him.

The Redskins ranked third in Offensive DVOA through their Week 10 bye, ninth in passing, second in rushing. In the final seven games, Washington's

---

REDSKINS SUMMARY

2008 Record: 8-8

Pythagorean Wins: 7.0 (22nd)

DVOA: 10.4% (12th)

Offense: 13.1% (9th)

Defense: 0.8% (11th)

Special Teams: -2.0% (25th)

Variance: 6.9% (1st)

2008: The West Coast came to Washington, and it worked for half a season.

2009: Just a minor threat, but Washington fans are used to that.

2009 Mean Projection: 7.8 wins

On the Clock (0-3): 3%

Loserville (4-6): 25%

Mediocrity (7-8): 31%

Playoff Contender (9-10): 30%

Super Bowl Contender (11+): 11%

Projected Average Opponent: -0.8% (22nd)

---

passing game ranked 20th in DVOA, the running game 18th.

So, what happened? Campbell was definitely checking down more down the stretch, even in down-and-distance situations that demanded more — his Yards per Attempt plummeted from 7.6 to 5.4. However, his receivers didn't do him any favors. More and more, teams facing the Redskins were able to focus on Santana Moss because the other pass-catchers weren't bringing anything to the table. Portis, who was on an MVP pace early on, picked up a number of minor injuries as the season (and his workload) progressed — he was on pace for 374 carries halfway through the season and finished with 342. The Redskins finished second in the NFL in Adjusted Line Yards in Weeks 1-9 (4.72), and dropped to 26th in the second half (3.95), a drop that mirrored Portis' own numbers. Injuries affected the team, especially the torn triceps that ended left tackle Chris Samuels' season in December, but Washington suffered only 51 percent of their Adjusted Games lost in Weeks 11-17, and the league average was 58 percent. The problems ran deeper.

Few of the Redskins' acquisitions made much of a difference. Washington drafted three receivers in the second round — wideouts Devin Thomas and Malcolm Kelly, as well as tight end Fred Davis — and got a total of 20 catches and 163 yards for their trouble. (The three players combined for a miserable catch

2009 Redskins Schedule

Week	Opp.	Week	Opp.	Week	Opp.
1	at NYG	7	PHI (Mon.)	13	NO
2	STL	8	BYE	14	at OAK
3	at DET	9	at ATL	15	NYG (Mon.)
4	TB	10	DEN	16	DAL
5	at CAR	11	at DAL	17	at SD
6	KC	12	at PHI		

rate of 42 percent.) Long-time Dolphins sackmaster Jason Taylor, acquired from Miami for a second-round draft pick after end Philip Daniels blew out his knee in training camp, missed time with a calf injury in September, lost his 133-game starting streak and his job to Demetric Evans early in the season, and is now back in Miami. Cornerback DeAngelo Hall, having poisoned the Falcons locker room and turned the non-Nnamdi Asomugha side of Oakland's secondary into a dream for enemy quarterbacks, was signed in November. Hall provided playmaking ability, but he got his reps ahead of Carlos Rogers, who was playing at a Pro Bowl clip in the season's first half.

The disappointment was palatable. The Redskins have been known as big spenders and underachievers throughout the Daniel Snyder era, and the trend has been to go back to the well whenever things don't work out. Snyder and Executive Vice President Vinny Cerrato did this with a vengeance in the offseason. While veterans like Samuels, Antwaan Randle El, and Andre Carter were re-structuring their contracts to free up cap space, and the release of veteran cornerback Shawn Springs freed up $6 million more, Snyder and Cerrato were wining and dining dominant free agent defensive tackle Albert Haynesworth. They eventually signed Haynesworth to a seven-year, $100 million contract with $41 million guaranteed, and may have had a deal in place before free agency even began, depending on how much weight you put behind the speculation of Haynesworth's former team in Tennessee. The size of the deal is understandable — Haynesworth will completely change the face of a front four that amassed only 19 sacks in 2008.

Less defensible was the six-year, $55 million deal given to Hall after only half a season of efficient work. Hall was a disaster in Oakland, and though his raw talent is undeniable, he's not generally known as the kind of player open to the kind of heavy coaching it would take to make him an elite NFL corner. If opposing quarterbacks focus on Hall and throw away from

Carlos Rogers as they threw towards Hall and away from Asomugha in Oakland, this could be yet another high-priced free agent deal the Redskins regret.

After ostensibly improving their defense, Snyder and Cerrato moved on to their non-existent quarterback problem. The second-half offensive malaise left the team noncommittal when it came to a contract extension for Campbell. As the soap opera between Jay Cutler and the Denver Broncos unraveled, it was revealed that the Redskins were involved in any number of deals that ended with Cutler landing in D.C. When the Bears made a better offer, Snyder and Cerrato turned their attention to USC quarterback Mark Sanchez, but the Jets had the draft picks to move up and take Sanchez where Washington didn't. The front office has done all the standard backtracking after whiffing on two new quarterback options, but Campbell's now in a contract year. He may find that playing for a ticket out is an even better incentive than staying put for more years and more money. 2009 will be the second for Campbell in Zorn's West Coast Offense, and anyone who thinks the system is something a quarterback can pick up in one season should go back and review early tapes of Brett Favre or Matt Hasselbeck.

One thing the Redskins should investigate is Campbell's excellence in the shotgun formation. In recent years, Football Outsiders has published all sorts of data showing that passing offenses are more efficient out of the shotgun. Last year, 155 of Campbell's 506 passing attempts came from the shotgun, and the Redskins' passing DVOA jumped from 9.1% to 35.6% when Campbell backed up from under center. It would also be nice if Campbell had more than one starting-quality wideout, and an offensive line without question marks just about everywhere.

If the Redskins don't improve on last season, one could easily imagine Snyder writing off the remainder of Jim Zorn's contract and going after one of the many big-name ex-coaches cooling their heels in hiatus as the rest of the NFL trends toward younger or less-experienced coaches and more nimble front offices. Those who know Snyder's affection for the big-splash move have already speculated that Mike Shanahan or Mike Holmgren wouldn't mind the kind of contract Snyder might pay to put butts in the seats. Even Hall of Fame coaches would have trouble creating a Super Bowl champion out of the current roster, and the long-time philosophy of building from the big names down simply doesn't work.

The overriding problem that will affect on-field suc-

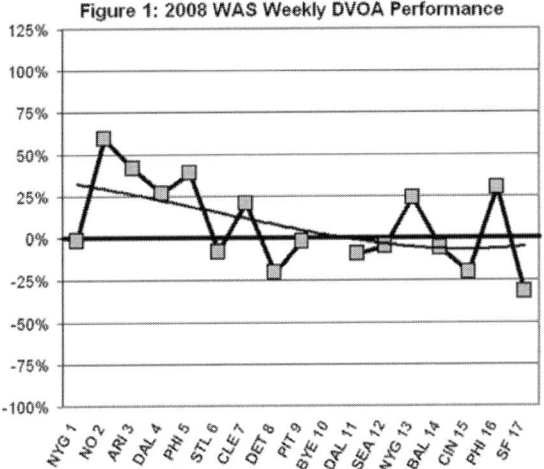

Figure 1: 2008 WAS Weekly DVOA Performance

cess has been the same through the Snyder/Cerrato era: inefficient free agency hauls and poor or nonexistent drafts have left two personnel holes for every one that is filled. The second-round pick the 'Skins used on Taylor was the one they needed to acquire Cutler. In a draft with few elite players and a great deal of under-the-radar talent, losing that second-round pick also kept the Redskins from acquiring one of any number of players who could have helped right away. 2009 first-round pick Brian Orakpo is a dynamic player, but word is that he'll alternate between defensive end and outside linebacker — they need him to replace Taylor as a pass rusher and Marcus Washington as a strong-side run-stopper because Taylor was a miss and they dawdled on replacing Washington.

It was a good move to bring back guard Derrick Dockery after Buffalo cut him for cap space, but then the Redskins made their own cap cut in veteran right tackle Jon Jansen. The options to replace Jansen are questionable, and if Samuels' return hits any snags, the Redskins' tackle depth will be seriously stretched. If their 2008 crew of drafted receivers doesn't show major improvement, the Redskins should be taken to task for missing out entirely on the best class of offensive line talent in NFL history. As we show in the Offensive Line section of Washington's unit comments, any time without Samuels is time in which the offense falls apart again.

Our projections have the Redskins at the top of the NFL's also-rans, and at the bottom of a very competitive NFC East. The crazy-quilt offense is expected to improve in the second year of Zorn's tutelage, but for that to happen, the starters will have to defy age and the kids will have to seriously improve. Campbell's improved command of the playbook won't matter if he's running for his life all the time. Portis and Moss, his two most effective weapons, are aging; Ladell Betts is a good change-of-pace for Portis but couldn't be the entire running game on his own, and the talent behind Moss has been extremely disappointing. A league-average defense last year should improve with Haynesworth alone, if we assume that playing Orakpo in two different positions doesn't lead to the kind of adjustment issues frequently seen from first-year defensive linemen. We also have to assume that Hall, no longer playing for a contract, won't revert back to the player who poisoned locker rooms and provided effective coverage less than half the time in previous locations.

The Redskins' blueprint for success hasn't worked to date, and it's not one that's been effective through NFL history. Teams that treat the offseason like a fantasy football draft, and only dip a toe in the water for the real draft occasionally, will find themselves behind the eight-ball every year as those teams drafting wisely shoot ahead of them in the value sweepstakes.

This isn't news to most NFL observers and participants, but the Redskins haven't received the memo yet. They didn't before the 2008 draft, when they tried to trade first- and third-round picks to Cincinnati for Chad Johnson, even as Cerrato was bragging that the team was turning over a new leaf and focusing on the draft from here on out. Cerrato hasn't seen any more of that memo since his first run in D.C., before Marty Schottenheimer fired him, when he brought Bruce Smith, Deion Sanders, Irving Fryar, and Mark Carrier to the team and got very little for his trouble. The Redskins haven't seen that memo in the decade Daniel Snyder has owned the team, which is why they've had higher player payrolls than any other franchise since 1999 and have a 76-84 regular-season record, and three playoff berths, to show for it. Facing a brutal division, and a changing league, the Redskins could get worse before they get better if a sea change in thinking isn't around the corner.

Doug Farrar

2008 Redskins Stats by Week

Wk	vs.	W-L	PF	PA	YDF	YDA	TO	Total	Off	Def	ST
1	@NYG	L	7	16	209	354	+1	-2%	-4%	-2%	0%
2	NO	W	29	24	455	250	+2	59%	50%	-41%	-31%
3	ARI	W	24	17	323	313	+2	42%	44%	2%	0%
4	@DAL	W	26	24	381	344	+1	27%	34%	19%	12%
5	@PHI	W	23	17	388	254	0	39%	55%	8%	-8%
6	STL	L	17	19	368	200	-2	-8%	-7%	-9%	-9%
7	CLE	W	14	11	351	236	-1	20%	21%	-8%	-9%
8	@DET	W	25	17	439	274	-1	-21%	-8%	31%	19%
9	PIT	L	6	23	221	224	-1	-2%	-1%	-9%	-9%
10	BYE										
11	DAL	L	10	14	228	315	+1	-9%	-16%	-7%	0%
12	@SEA	W	20	17	386	228	+1	-5%	14%	6%	-13%
13	NYG	L	7	23	320	404	-1	24%	19%	-11%	-7%
14	@BAL	L	10	24	254	281	-1	-6%	-17%	-18%	-8%
15	@CIN	L	13	20	280	310	-2	-21%	-11%	30%	20%
16	PHI	W	10	3	249	275	+1	30%	10%	-11%	9%
17	@SF	L	24	27	268	359	0	-32%	6%	38%	0%

Trends and Splits

	Offense	Rank	Defense	Rank
Total DVOA	13.1%	9	0.8%	11
Unadjusted VOA	9.3%	16	0.8%	13
Weighted trend	3.2%	21	3.2%	12
Variance	5.5%	8	6.4%	20
Average opponent	2.2%	27	0.8%	9
Passing	23.5%	13	6.1%	15
Rushing	12.3%	6	-5.7%	11
First down	1.4%	20	7.5%	22
Second down	31.0%	2	1.8%	11
Third down	6.3%	17	-12.3%	7
First half	6.3%	16	-0.6%	13
Second half	21.1%	7	2.0%	15
Red Zone	6.5%	15	24.8%	27
Late and close	24.9%	4	4.3%	15

Five-Year Performance

Year	W-L	Pyth	Est W	PF	PA	TO	Total	Rk	Off	Rk	Def	Rk	ST	Rk	Off AGL	Rk	Def AGL	Rk
2004	6-10	7.1	6.8	240	265	-1	-6.5%	19	-17.5%	28	-14.8%	4	-3.9%	31	4.3	31	36.9	5
2005	10-6	9.9	10.4	359	293	+1	22.3%	7	6.8%	10	-14.0%	4	1.5%	9	11.2	21	9.6	24
2006	5-11	6.1	6.8	307	376	-5	-8.3%	21	4.9%	13	14.9%	32	1.7%	11	12.4	24	10.6	18
2007	9-7	8.7	8.3	334	310	-5	6.2%	13	-0.2%	17	-6.7%	7	-0.3%	16	36.6	4	16.8	22
2008	8-8	7.0	8.9	265	296	0	10.4%	12	13.1%	9	0.8%	11	-2.0%	25	12.6	26	42.5	4

Strategic Tendencies

Run/Pass		Rank	Offense		Rank	Defense		Rank	Other		Rank
Runs, all plays	46%	8	3+ WR	56%	12	Rush 3	6.9%	10	2+ RB, Pct Runs	65%	7
Runs, first half	45%	15	4+ WR	13%	15	Rush 4	55.8%	28	1 RB/2 TE, Pct Runs	53%	14
Runs, first down	50%	16	2+ TE	19%	27	Rush 5	22.9%	15	1RB/3+WR, Pct Runs	31%	11
Runs, second-long	48%	3	Single back	58%	15	Rush 6+	14.4%	3	Zone Blitz	2%	21
Runs, power sit.	67%	15	Play action	22%	8	Rush 7+	3.7%	4	Go for it on 4th	0.78	24
Runs, behind 2H	39%	3	Max protect	9%	12	Sacks by LB	10.4%	25	Offensive Pace	31.0	15
Pass, ahead 2H	40%	22	Outside pocket	15%	10	Sacks by DB	10.4%	11	Defensive Pace	30.0	5

Zone-blitzing the Redskins may not be the wisest move. Washington faced more zone blitzes than any other offense — 7.1 percent of pass plays — and shredded those blitzes with 89.1% DVOA, the best in the NFC. The numbers look even better if you take out division rival Philadelphia. In the other 14 games, Jason Campbell was 20-of-29 against zone blitzes, averaging 10.0 yards per play (including a five-yard scramble on third-and-2) with only one sack and no turnovers. ● Washington was the only team to run a draw play on fourth down all season, against Philadelphia in Week 5. Clinton Portis gained the first down and iced a 23-17 win by running a draw from fourth-and-1 with 2:48 left. ● Washington tied San Francisco with the most tight end screens, 13 apiece. No other team was in double digits. ● Washington's defense forced a three-and-out on 32.7 percent of drives, tops in the league. ● Washington received the benefit of more dropped passes than any other defense (42) and ranked second in drops per pass behind New England. ● Washington was second in percentage of passes to the middle of the field on offense, and first on defense, but this is related to a quirk of the FedEx Field official scorer. Combining the Washington offense and defense, 45 percent of passes under 16 yards were marked as "middle." No other stadium was above 35 percent.

Passing

Player	DYAR	DVOA	Plays	NtYds	Avg	YAC	C%	TD	Int
Jason Campbell	655	8.3%	542	3006	5.5	5.3	62.6%	13	5

Rushing

Player	DYAR	DVOA	Plays	Yds	Avg	TD	Fum	Suc
Clinton Portis	285	11.7%	342	1487	4.3	9	3	48%
Ladell Betts	7	-6.1%	61	206	3.4	1	1	48%
Jason Campbell	88	44.2%	31	273	8.8	1	0	--
Shaun Alexander*	-20	-62.7%	11	24	2.2	0	0	27%
Mike Sellers	-26	-87.4%	6	24	4.0	0	1	33%
Rock Cartwright	-5	-35.7%	5	14	2.8	0	0	40%
Devin Thomas	45	300.6%	3	53	17.7	1	0	--

Receiving

Player	DYAR	DVOA	Plays	Ctch	Yds	Y/C	YAC	TD	C%
Santana Moss	73	-6.0%	138	79	1044	13.2	5.5	6	57%
Antwaan Randle El	96	1.4%	87	53	593	11.2	3.7	4	61%
Devin Thomas	-33	-28.4%	27	15	120	8.0	2.7	0	56%
James Thrash*	-50	-43.8%	22	9	81	9.0	2.2	1	41%
Malcolm Kelly	-41	-62.2%	11	3	18	6.0	1.7	0	27%
Chris Cooley	105	7.6%	111	83	849	10.2	5.7	1	75%
Todd Yoder	1	-5.9%	10	8	50	6.3	2.3	1	80%
Fred Davis	-31	-53.1%	10	3	27	9.0	4.7	0	30%
Clinton Portis	54	15.3%	36	28	218	7.8	8.9	0	78%
Ladell Betts	19	-1.4%	35	22	200	9.1	8.2	0	63%
Mike Sellers	21	9.0%	15	12	98	8.2	5.1	1	80%

Offensive Line

Year	Yards	ALY	Rank	Power	Rank	10+ Yds	Rank	Stuff	Rank	Sacks	ASR	Rank	False	Cont.
2006	4.41	4.22	14	55%	29	16%	16	19%	21	19	4.4%	5	26	42
2007	3.73	4.09	17	60%	22	10%	28	18%	16	29	5.1%	12	24	24
2008	4.13	4.41	5	69%	14	13%	29	14%	2	38	6.0%	15	18	29

Year	LE	Rank	LT	Rank	Mid	Rank	RT	Rank	RE	Rank
2006	4.00	18	4.93	5	4.50	7	3.87	26	3.84	19
2007	4.07	14	4.82	7	4.06	16	4.06	20	3.68	24
2008	4.77	11	5.04	4	4.17	14	4.07	18	4.02	17

Washington's power, particularly in the first half of the season, came when running to the left, with left tackle Chris Samuels and fullback Mike Sellers blocking the edge, and left guard Pete Kendall and center Casey Rabach maintaining the middle. Samuels played through knee injuries at a Pro Bowl level until he went down in Week 14 with a torn triceps and was placed on injured reserve. He'll be back with a restructured contract, and the Redskins had better hope that what Samuels himself has referred to as a "long, hard road" to recovery doesn't hit any snags — Washington posted their three worst offensive DVOA totals in Week 8 (when Samuels was inactive with that balky knee) and Weeks 15 and 17, when he was gone for the year.

Table 1: With and Without Chris Samuels

Weeks	RB Yards	ALY	Power
Weeks 1-7	4.78	4.86	86%
Weeks 8-13	4.09	4.20	67%
Weeks 14-17	2.92	3.74	50%

Kendall, the only member of that line to start all 16 games in both 2007 and 2008, may not be back at all this season — the Redskins signed Derrick Dockery to a five-year, $26.5 million contract after Dockery was cut by the Bills. Dockery was, of course, a third-round pick by the Redskins in 2003, and left for Buffalo before the 2007 to become the highest-paid guard in an inflated market. Right tackle Jon Jansen struggled especially in pass protection and was released in late May. The Redskins preferred to let Jansen go, allowing the $6 million in guaranteed money left on his contract to accelerate to the team's 2009 salary cap. However, only backup-level talent is available to replace him. Jansen was quickly signed by the Lions, and the Redskins opened a competition at right tackle between ex-Panther Jeremy Bridges, youngster Stephon Heyer, and former Bills first-round washout Mike Williams. Problem is, Bridges has more than a passing familiarity with the police blotter, Heyer hasn't been much better than Jansen, and Williams is trying to work his way back to 380 pounds after spending some time in the "Over 400" club. Most have Heyer as the favorite to replace Jansen, but Williams and Dockery are very close — that could prove to be a tiebreaker.

The problem with this line is that the Redskins haven't drafted to rebuild — they missed out on all the elite linemen of the last two draft classes, selecting only Northern Iowa guard Chad Rinehart in the third round in 2008. Washington's betting a lot on an aging group to stay healthy, and journeymen to suddenly improve. Judging from the second half of the 2008 season, things could fall apart quickly if those bets are lost.

Defensive Front Seven

Defensive Line	Age	Pos	Plays	TmPct	Overall Rk	Stop	Dfts	Stop%	Rk	AvYd	Rk	Pass Rush Sack	Hit	Hur	vs. Run Runs	St%	Yds	vs. Pass Pass	St%	Yds
Andre Carter	30	DE	38	5.1%	46	29	11	76%	47	1.4	29	4.0	13	13	30	73%	2.3	8	88%	-2.3
Jason Taylor*	35	DE	35	5.8%	41	27	11	77%	40	1.4	32	3.5	1	7	19	63%	3.7	16	94%	-1.4
Demetric Evans*	30	DE	35	4.7%	60	26	13	74%	56	2.4	73	3.5	3	7	26	69%	3.2	9	89%	0.2
Kedric Golston	26	DT	29	4.8%	42	24	4	83%	12	2.2	49	2.0	3	3	24	83%	2.3	5	80%	2.0
Cornelius Griffin	33	DT	29	4.4%	48	23	7	79%	28	2.0	35	1.0	4	4	26	77%	2.3	3	100%	-1.0
Anthony Montgomery	25	DT	24	3.7%	60	19	4	79%	31	2.9	66	2.0	2	4	20	80%	3.6	4	75%	-0.3
Lorenzo Alexander	26	DT	19	2.7%	--	16	4	84%	--	1.2	--	2.0	3	3	15	80%	2.3	4	100%	-2.8
Albert Haynesworth	*28*	*DT*	*51*	*7.0%*	*6*	*41*	*19*	*80%*	*21*	*0.2*	*2*	*8.5*	*14*	*8*	*38*	*76%*	*1.5*	*13*	*92%*	*-3.5*
Renaldo Wynn	*35*	*DE*	*24*	*3.2%*	*88*	*17*	*8*	*71%*	*62*	*1.5*	*36*	*2.0*	*0*	*5*	*20*	*75%*	*1.4*	*4*	*50%*	*1.8*

Linebackers	Age	Pos	Plays	TmPct	Overall Rk	Stop	Dfts	Stop%	AvYd	Pass Rush Sack	Hit	Hur	vs. Run Runs	St%	Rk	Yds	Rk	vs. Pass Tgts	Suc%	Rk	AdjYd	Rk
London Fletcher	34	ILB	138	18.4%	3	73	19	53%	5.0	0.5	2	5	92	60%	75	3.7	69	32	74%	3	4.6	9
Rocky McIntosh	27	OLB	92	12.3%	41	47	14	51%	4.3	2.0	2	0	60	50%	99	3.7	65	25	49%	48	5.7	31
H.B. Blades	24	ILB	50	6.7%	93	30	6	60%	5.0	0.0	0	0	36	64%	52	3.7	63	9	49%	--	9.0	--
Marcus Washington*	32	OLB	45	9.6%	--	23	5	51%	5.0	0.0	1	2	32	59%	--	3.7	--	14	59%	--	5.1	--

Year	Yards	ALY	Rank	Power	Rank	10+ Yds	Rank	Stuff	Rank	Sack	ASR	Rank
2006	4.71	4.70	30	62%	12	18%	23	15%	28	19	4.6%	32
2007	3.67	4.09	17	65%	20	8%	1	18%	19	33	5.7%	26
2008	3.97	4.30	23	61%	7	11%	2	19%	11	24	4.7%	29

Year	LE	Rank	LT	Rank	Mid	Rank	RT	Rank	RE	Rank
2006	4.45	21	5.34	31	4.55	24	4.70	25	4.61	26
2007	4.34	21	4.64	23	3.76	4	4.22	20	4.14	17
2008	4.28	19	4.19	16	4.53	28	3.78	8	4.33	22

The Redskins gave up a great deal for Albert Haynesworth, signing him to a seven-year, $100 million deal that includes $41 million guaranteed (and bring the tampering issue to the forefront in the bargain), but there's absolutely no doubt that he's worth it when healthy. Haynesworth is the rarest of all defensive tackles, equally adept at occupying blockers (up to three consistently) and blowing past those constant double-teams to terrorize quarterbacks. First-round draft pick Brian Orakpo from Texas will benefit greatly from Mr. Haynesworth's acumen. Orakpo had 11.5 sacks and 17 tackles for loss in 2008, and he's expected to be the second part of an upgrade to a Washington line that amassed only 19 sacks in 2008. Veteran Andre Carter has maybe one more season in Washington, and tackle Cornelius Griffin will fill out the front four. Everything depends on Haynesworth, but he's got the talent to avoid Jason Taylor's square-peg season. Taylor cost the 'Skins a second-round draft pick and didn't do much in return, getting cut in March so that Washington wouldn't be tied up with his $8 million salary in 2009.

Those looking for evidence that London Fletcher has slowed a step at age 34 may have to wait awhile. The underrated captain teams with Rocky McIntosh to make plays just about everywhere. The question mark is on the strong side. Marcus Washington was released, and one of the things the Redskins liked about Orakpo was that he could play linebacker in certain sets. Watch out for fifth-round pick Cody Glenn, a converted running back from Nebraska with a world of talent and an equal amount of baggage. The real reason for his four-game suspension at the end of the 2008 season is unknown — the original story, that he was suspended for selling tickets, turned out not to be true.

Defensive Secondary

Secondary	Age	Pos	Plays	TmPct	Rk	Stop	Dfts	Yds	Rk	St%	Rk	Tgts	Tgt%	Rk	Dist	Suc%	Rk	AdjYd	Rk	Yds	PD	Int
								vs. Run				**vs. Pass**										
DeAngelo Hall**	26	CB	95	12.2%	8	35	15	5.5	27	27%	72	85	23.1%	10	13.2	50%	44	7.0	35	6.9	17	5
Carlos Rogers	28	CB	80	10.7%	14	43	19	4.5	13	55%	23	97	23.2%	9	12.6	58%	15	6.4	27	5.8	24	2
Chris Horton	25	SS	77	11.7%	16	35	13	3.8	4	59%	7	20	5.3%	62	10.7	51%	39	9.5	61	8.9	5	3
LaRon Landry	24	SS	76	10.1%	36	28	10	8.3	65	39%	44	17	3.9%	74	16.4	72%	2	3.3	1	2.6	7	2
Fred Smoot	30	CB	61	8.1%	52	23	12	4.4	10	69%	6	60	14.3%	64	11.2	35%	83	8.7	70	8.6	7	1
Shawn Springs*	34	CB	43	10.2%	--	16	5	5.9	--	38%	--	39	16.3%	--	10.7	47%	--	7.0	--	6.7	7	1
Mike Green	33	SS	20	5.3%	--	13	3	2.9	--	79%	--	3	1.2%	--	8.8	53%	--	5.2	--	5.2	0	0

**Includes stats with both Oakland and Washington.

Year	Pass D Rank	vs. #1 WR	Rk	vs. #2 WR	Rk	vs. Other WR	Rk	vs. TE	Rk	vs. RB	Rk
2006	32	2.5%	16	9.1%	23	15.0%	24	18.6%	30	-24.0%	8
2007	6	3.6%	19	-39.0%	2	-29.4%	5	-3.9%	8	9.8%	28
2008	15	-11.2%	8	-4.7%	11	-3.9%	16	-5.2%	12	17.1%	28

Cornerback DeAngelo Hall was a flat-out disaster in Oakland, lasting only half a season after the Falcons got sick of him. But the Redskins liked enough of what they saw in half a season after picking him up off the scrapheap to give him a six-year contract with $23 million guaranteed. The difference between Hall's play in Oakland and Washington was substantial, but it may not have been quite as large as you think. Here are Hall's pass coverage stats split between the two teams, along with where Hall would rank if we only counted his play from that half of the season:

Table 2: A Tale of Two DeAngelos

Team	Weeks	Tgts	Dist	Suc%	Rk	APaYd	Rk	PaYd	PD	Int
OAK	1-9	58	13.0	48%	51	7.9	53	8.2	11	3
WAS	11-17	29	13.1	58%	14	4.9	4	4.0	6	2

Notice the difference between Adjusted Yards per Pass and regular Yards per Pass? In Oakland, Hall had to defend against some of the best quarterbacks in the league, including Jay Cutler, Drew Brees, Philip Rivers, and Matt Ryan. Hall's four starts for Washington came against Joe Flacco, Ryan Fitzpatrick, Donovan McNabb, and Shaun Hill. Alert readers will remember former Redskins cornerback Walt Harris' "career year" for the 49ers in 2006. Harris grabbed eight interceptions in that year — including two from Raiders backup Marques Tuiasosopo, two from Seahawks backup Seneca Wallace, one from Jake Plummer (on his way out in Denver), and one from Cutler (embryonic version). Moral of the story: When defensive backs enjoy massive spikes in performance, look at the quarterbacks.

The Redskins benched Carlos Rogers to move Hall into the starting lineup opposite Shawn Springs, but Springs is now in New England's Veteran Placement Program. That puts Rogers, whose $602,000 base salary more than doubled due to escalator clauses, back into the starting lineup. Rogers will be eligible for free agency after the 2009 season and since the Redskins reportedly thought about dangling him in a trade over the draft weekend, we expect 2009 to be his last year in the District. His eventual replacement may be third-round pick Kevin Barnes (Maryland), most famous for delivering a YouTube hit on Cal running back Jahvid Best that caused Best to vomit right on the field. Of course, there's danger in that physical style — Barnes suffered season-ending shoulder and collarbone injuries halfway through the 2008 season after colliding with Wake Forest receiver D.J. "I'm Anquan's Brother" Boldin.

Washington's young safety duo looks solid going forward. LaRon Landry is still developing, and the Redskins hope he can play as well against the rest of the NFL as he does against the Seahawks. Of his four career interceptions, three have come against Matt Hasselbeck (including two in the 2007 Wild Card game). The Redskins like his range at free safety. Horton came out of nowhere as a seventh-round pick out of UCLA and really impressed. He lacks Troy Polamalu's versatility, but he has that same kamikaze style. He's a perfect fit for the box defender — a small linebacker, really — that the Redskins prefer from their strong safety. Horton's ascent knocked Reed Doughty to the bench, but Doughty's still around in case of injury.

Special Teams

Year	DVOA	Rank	FG/XP	Rank	Net Punt	Rank	Punt Ret	Rank	Net Kick	Rank	Kick Ret	Rank	Hidden	Rank
2006	1.7%	11	-2.9	22	0.0	19	5.1	7	4.4	11	3.7	5	3.0	12
2007	-0.3%	16	-1.1	21	-6.0	26	6.1	9	6.1	6	-7.0	29	11.9	5
2008	-2.0%	25	-9.4	31	5.7	11	7.7	6	-15.3	31	-0.6	17	-7.4	23

Shaun Suisham received a low tender of $1.01 million as a restricted free agent after a connecting on a career-low 72 percent of his field goals last season. He also struggled on kickoffs; Washington's positive value in our net kickoff ratings is solely due to quality coverage that prevented big returns. Nevertheless, Suisham should be able to survive a camp battle with Dave Rayner, who was on the roster of five different teams over the last two years. Ryan Plackemeier was waived after finishing 37th in net average at 33.8 yards per punt. Zac Atterberry, who lost a battle to Plackemeier last season, is the short-term plan to replace him.

FO favorite Rock Cartwright had another excellent return season, tenth in individual kickoff value according to Football Outsiders metrics. Cartwright was Washington's only consistently productive special-teamer — Antwaan Randle El did almost nothing on punt returns, although Santana Moss took one of his six returns for a touchdown. With all the unproductive young receivers on this roster, you'd think someone would be able to take that job. Linebacker Khary Campbell and fullback Mike Sellers tied for the team lead with 16 solo special teams tackles apiece.

Coaching Staff

Jim Zorn was one of three first-year head coaches with no background as an offensive or defensive coordinator who posted at least a .500 record in 2008. But unlike Baltimore's John Harbaugh and Tony Sparano at Miami, Zorn didn't lead his team to a better record than the year before. The Redskins started out 6-2 before their freefall, and Zorn's future will most likely be tied to the success of Jason Campbell in Year Two. If things don't improve, Dan Snyder could very easily overpay one of the many future Hall-of-Fame coaches currently on hiatus.

Zorn and offensive coordinator Sherman Smith follow the pattern established by Mike Holmgren, Zorn's mentor in Seattle — Zorn calls the plays on offense, and Smith provides support. Defensive coordinator Greg Blache is a talented, eminently quotable coach who will be expected to take the Redskins' defense to the top with all the offseason money spent on Albert Haynesworth and DeAngelo Hall. The man with the biggest challenge is offensive line coach Joe Bugel — he's one of the real legends among position coaches, but his line is a house of cards going into the new season. Keep an eye on defensive backs coach Jerry Gray when head coaching vacancies come up in the future — Gray has excelled with a young Washington secondary over the last four years after five seasons as Buffalo's defensive coordinator. He also made four straight Pro Bowls from 1986 through 1989 as a cornerback for the Rams.

Quarterbacks

The 2008 NFL season was defined by quarterback health. Of the top five quarterbacks by DYAR from 2007, four had their seasons dramatically affected by injury. Tom Brady missed virtually the entire season with a torn ACL. Peyton Manning spent the first half of the season recovering from his own knee issues on the field. Brett Favre played through a painful torn biceps tendon that cost him velocity and accuracy, while the four games Tony Romo missed with a broken finger likely cost the Cowboys a playoff spot.

With only Drew Brees remaining healthy enough to keep his spot amongst the top five, a young new crop of quarterbacks ascended to the top of our statistical tables. While Manning finished second in the league in DYAR for the second consecutive season, Brees took the crown as the NFL leader with 1,920. Kurt Warner isn't anyone's idea of youthful, but Philip Rivers and Jay Cutler also forced their way into the reckoning with impressive steps forward. Below the top five, other young quarterbacks like Aaron Rodgers, Matt Ryan, and Matt Cassel had excellent seasons.

In general, it was a banner year for passing. The league-wide DVOA for quarterbacks was 5.5%, a significant increase over 3.3% in 2007. (In case you are wondering, the average for a given season is not zero because the baseline we use to compare plays for DVOA is made up of multiple years worth of data; the average for the whole period is zero.) Teams experimented with previously gimmicky offenses, as the Dolphins used the Wildcat to early success and the Chiefs, somewhat less notably, used the Pistol offense made famous by the Nevada Wolfpack. We live in exciting offensive times, and as teams take advantage of hyper-aggressive defenses and specialized personnel sets, expect offensive sets to become even wackier in 2009.

In this section of the book, we give the last three years' worth of numbers for the top two quarterbacks on each team's depth chart as well as other quarterbacks who played significant time in 2008 or may be important in 2009. Each quarterback also gets a projection from our KUBIAK fantasy football projection system, based on a complicated regression analysis that takes into account numerous variables including projected role, performance over the past two years, performance on third down vs. all downs, experience of the projected offensive line, historical comparables, collegiate stats, height, age, and strength of schedule.

It is difficult to accurately project statistics for a 162-game baseball season, but it is exponentially more difficult to accurately project statistics for a 16-game football season because of the small size of the data samples involved. With that in mind, we ask that you consider the listed projections not as a prediction of exact numbers, but the mean of a range of possible performances. What's important is not so much the exact number of yards and touchdowns we project, but whether or not we're projecting a given player to improve or decline. Along those same lines, rookie projections will not be as accurate as veteran projections due to lack of data.

Our quarterback projections look a bit different than our projections for the other skill positions. At running back and wide receiver, second-stringers see plenty of action, but, at quarterback, either a player starts or he does not start. We recognize that, when a starting quarterback gets injured in Week 8, you don't want to grab your *Football Outsiders Almanac* to find out if his backup is any good only to find that we've projected that the guy will throw 12 passes this year. Therefore, like we did last year, we have projected all quarterbacks to start all 16 games. If, say, Tom Brady goes down in November, you can look up Kevin O'Connell, divide the stats by 16, and get an idea of what we think each player will do in an average week. There is one exception: Pat White of the Miami Dolphins, who will get playing time all year long in the Wildcat and is projected with passes, runs, and receptions.

Each player's projection also includes **Risk**, our measure of the likelihood a given player will fall short of his listed KUBIAK projection for any reason. This has caused a bit of confusion since we introduced the Risk variable a couple of years ago, so let us restate: Risk is about more than just injury risk. Like the main KUBIAK projection, the Risk projection includes a number of different variables, but the most important are a) health; b) age; c) for quarterbacks, the likelihood the player will lose the starting job; and d) for other positions, how much of a player's KUBIAK projection is based on a subjective interpretation of his expected playing time.

This year's Risk variable is a bit different than in past seasons. Risk now comes in four colors: Red, Yellow, Green, and Blue. In the past, the majority of players were marked Red, because football projections are inherently risky; unfortunately, this meant that we couldn't draw attention to the players who were *abnormally* risky. Therefore, the default rating is now Green instead of Red. Players who have higher than normal risk are marked Yellow, and players with the highest risk are marked Red. In addition, players with the strongest chance to match or even surpass their projections are marked Blue. Most players marked Blue will be backups with low projections, but a handful are starters or situational players who can be considered slightly better breakout candidates.

HOW TO READ THE QUARTERBACK STATISTICS TABLE

The first line contains biographical data — each player's name, height, weight, college, draft position, birth date, and age. Height and weight are the best data we could find; weight, of course, can fluctuate during the offseason (hello, JaMarcus Russell). Age is very simple, the number of years between the player's birth year and 2009, but birthdate is provided if you want to figure out exact age.

Draft position gives draft year and round, with the overall pick number with which the player was taken in parentheses. In the sample table, it says that Jay Cutler was chosen in the 2006 draft in the first round with the 11th overall pick. Undrafted free agents are listed as "FA" with the year they came into the league, even if they were only in training camp or on a practice squad.

To the far right of the first line is the player's **Risk** for fantasy football in 2009.

Next, we give the last three years of player stats. The majority of these statistics are passing numbers, though the final five columns on the right are the quarterback's rushing statistics.

The first few columns after the year and team the player played for are standard numbers: games (**G**), pass attempts (**Att**), pass completions (**Cmp**), completion percentage (**C%**), passing yards (**Yds**), passing touchdowns (**TD**), and interceptions (**INT**). These numbers are official NFL totals and therefore include plays we leave out of our own metrics, such as clock-stopping spikes, and omit plays we include in our metrics, such as sacks and aborted snaps. Note that the games total includes all games the player appeared in, not just games started, which is why a backup quarterback who holds on field goals will often be listed with 16 games played.

The next column is fumbles (**FUM**), which adds together all fumbles by this player, whether turned over to the defense or recovered by the offense (explained in the essay "Pregame Show"). Even though this fumble total is listed among the passing numbers, it includes all fumbles, including those on sacks, aborted snaps, and rushing attempts. By listing fumbles and interceptions next to one another we hope to give a general idea of how many total turnovers the player was responsible for.

Next comes Adjusted Sack Rate (**ASR**). This is the same statistic you'll find in the team chapters, only here it is specific to the individual quarterback. It represents sacks and intentional groundings per pass play (total pass plays = pass attempts + sacks) adjusted based on down, distance, and strength of schedule. NFL average Adjusted Sack Rate has been dropping in recent seasons, from 6.9 percent in 2006 to 6.5 percent in 2007 and 6.2 percent last year.

The next two columns are Net Yards per Pass (**NY/P**), a standard stat but a particularly good one, and the player's rank (**Rk**) in Net Yards per Pass for that season. Consider the inclusion of this number our tribute to the godfather of football stats, Bud Goode. It consists of passing yards minus yards lost on sacks, divided by total pass plays.

The five columns remaining in passing stats give our advanced metrics: **DVOA** (Defense-Adjusted Value Over Average), **DYAR** (Defense-Adjusted Yards Above Replacement), and **YAR** (Yards Above Replacement), along with the player's rank in both DVOA and DYAR. These

Quarterback Statistics Sample

Jay Cutler   Height: 6-4   Weight: 225   College: Vanderbilt   Draft: 2006/1 (11)   Born: 29-Apr-1983   Age: 26   Risk: Green

Year	Team	G	Att	Comp	C%	Yds	TD	INT	FUM	ASR	NY/P	Rk	DVOA	Rk	DYAR	Rk	YAR	Runs	Yds	TD	DVOA	DYAR
2006	DEN	5	137	81	59.1%	1001	9	5	5	7.8%	6.7	13	-12.7%	33	-15	33	68	12	18	0	-159.0%	-65
2007	DEN	16	467	297	63.6%	3497	20	14	7	5.5%	6.8	12	19.4%	11	973	8	809	44	205	1	9.3%	38
2008	DEN	16	616	384	62.3%	4526	25	18	3	2.3%	7.2	7	22.0%	7	1380	5	1503	57	200	2	-4.0%	16
2009	CHI		493	301	61.2%	3409	20	12	9		5.9		3.0%					63	190	3	-5.5%	

| 2008: | 43% Short | 36% Mid | 14% Deep | 7% Bomb | YAC: 4.7 (26) | 2007: | 45% Short | 37% Mid | 12% Deep | 6% Bomb | YAC: 5.2 (9) |

metrics compare each quarterback's passing performance to league-average or replacement-level baselines based on the game situations that quarterback faced. DVOA and DYAR are also adjusted based on the opposing defense. The methods used to compute these numbers are described in detail in the "Statistical Toolbox" introduction in the front of the book. The important distinctions between them are:

• DVOA is a rate statistic, while DYAR is a cumulative statistic. Thus, a higher DVOA means more value per pass play, while a higher DYAR means more aggregate value over the entire season.

• Because DYAR is defense-adjusted and YAR is not, a player whose DYAR is higher than his YAR faced a harder-than-average schedule. A player whose DYAR is lower than his YAR faced an easier-than-average schedule.

To qualify for a ranking in Net Yards per Pass, passing DVOA, and passing DYAR in a given season, a quarterback must have had 100 pass plays in that season. There are 41 quarterbacks ranked for 2008, 51 quarterbacks for 2007, and 45 ranked for 2006.

The final five columns contain rushing statistics, starting with **Runs**, rushing yards (**Yds**), and rushing touchdowns (**TD**). Once again, these are official NFL totals and include kneeldowns, which means you get to enjoy statistics such as Jake Delhomme running 20 times for 21 yards. The final two columns give **DYAR** and **DVOA** for quarterback rushing, which are calculated separately from passing. Rankings for these statistics, as well as numbers that are not adjusted for defense (YAR and VOA) can be found on our Web site, FootballOutsiders.com.

The italicized row of statistics for the 2009 season is our 2009 KUBIAK projection, as detailed above. Again, in the interest of producing meaningful statistics, all quarterbacks are projected to start a full 16-game season, regardless of the likelihood of them actually doing so (except for Pat White).

The final line represents data from the Football Outsiders game charting project. First, we break down charted passes based on distance: **Short** (5 yards or less), **Mid** (6 to 15 yards), **Deep** (16 to 25 yards), and **Bomb** (26 or more yards). These numbers are based on distance in the air only and include both complete and incomplete passes. Passes thrown away or tipped at the line are not included, nor are passes on which the quarterback's arm was hit by a defender while in motion. We also give Yards after Catch (YAC) and with the Rank in parentheses for the 41 quarterbacks who qualify.

A number of third- and fourth-string quarterbacks are briefly discussed at the end of the chapter in a section we call "Going Deep."

Top 20 QB by Passing DYAR (Total Value), 2008

Rank	Player	Team	DYAR
1	Drew Brees	NO	1921
2	Peyton Manning	IND	1783
3	Philip Rivers	SD	1522
4	Kurt Warner	ARI	1404
5	Jay Cutler	DEN	1380
6	Chad Pennington	MIA	1172
7	Matt Ryan	ATL	1167
8	Donovan McNabb	PHI	1048
9	Eli Manning	NYG	1032
10	Aaron Rodgers	GB	932
11	Tony Romo	DAL	879
12	Matt Schaub	HOU	863
13	Jake Delhomme	CAR	828
14	David Garrard	JAC	824
15	Kerry Collins	TEN	738
16	Jason Campbell	WAS	655
17	Matt Cassel	NE	655
18	Jeff Garcia	TB	569
19	Joe Flacco	BAL	384
20	Brett Favre	NYJ	334

Top 20 QB by Passing DVOA (Value per Pass), 2008

Rank	Player	Team	DVOA
1	Peyton Manning	IND	36.1%
2	Philip Rivers	SD	35.6%
3	Drew Brees	NO	33.9%
4	Matt Ryan	ATL	30.9%
5	Chad Pennington	MIA	25.7%
6	Kurt Warner	ARI	22.4%
7	Jay Cutler	DEN	22.0%
8	Matt Schaub	HOU	21.7%
9	Eli Manning	NYG	19.7%
10	Tony Romo	DAL	18.5%
11	Jake Delhomme	CAR	18.0%
12	Donovan McNabb	PHI	15.6%
13	Kerry Collins	TEN	15.3%
14	Aaron Rodgers	GB	14.8%
15	David Garrard	JAC	11.0%
16	Jeff Garcia	TB	10.9%
17	Tarvaris Jackson	MIN	10.0%
18	Jason Campbell	WAS	8.3%
19	Seneca Wallace	SEA	7.3%
20	Matt Cassel	NE	6.4%

Derek Anderson
Height: 6-6　Weight: 239　College: Oregon State　　Draft: 2005/6 (213)　Born: 15-Jun-1983　Age: 26　Risk: Yellow

Year	Team	G	Att	Comp	C%	Yds	TD	INT	FUM	ASR	NY/P	Rk	DVOA	Rk	DYAR	Rk	YAR	Runs	Yds	TD	DVOA	DYAR
2006	CLE	5	117	66	56.4%	793	5	8	1	6.0%	6.3	24	-22.8%	39	-94	34	-120	4	47	0	34.4%	7
2007	CLE	16	527	298	56.5%	3787	29	19	4	3.5%	7.0	9	12.3%	15	797	10	888	32	70	3	34.2%	50
2008	CLE	10	283	142	50.2%	1615	9	8	8	4.7%	5.1	36	-11.9%	32	-15	33	-140	25	55	0	-41.1%	-29
2009	CLE		471	255	54.1%	3122	16	22	11		5.7		-19.8%					10	37	0	21.0%	

2008:	50% Short	32% Mid	14% Deep	5% Bomb	YAC: 5.0 (20)	2007:	43% Short	36% Mid	17% Deep	4% Bomb YAC: 5.0 (17)

We're really looking at a three-game wonder here. Anderson had three excellent games in the first half of 2007: September 16th against the Bengals, October 14th against the Dolphins, and October 21st against the Rams. He completed 56 of 83 passes (67 percent) for 821 yards, 11 touchdowns, and one interception in those three games, which were against some of the league's worst defenses. Those games account for more than a quarter of Anderson's career touchdowns and add 1.3 points to his career completion percentage of 54.6. If you strike those games from his record, Anderson's 2007 season doesn't look much different from 2006 and 2008. It's not entirely fair or reasonable to just erase those games – they really happened, and Anderson may have games like that again – but it makes sense to brand Anderson as a low-completion percentage, low-TD/INT ratio passer who at his best is capable of a brief hot flash. That's the kind of quarterback you plant on the bench, not the kind who competes for a starting job.

Kyle Boller
Height: 6-3　Weight: 220　College: California　　Draft: 2003/1 (19)　Born: 17-Jun-1981　Age: 28　Risk: Blue

Year	Team	G	Att	Comp	C%	Yds	TD	INT	FUM	ASR	NY/P	Rk	DVOA	Rk	DYAR	Rk	YAR	Runs	Yds	TD	DVOA	DYAR
2006	BAL	5	55	33	60.0%	485	5	2	2	5.1%	8.3	--	19.9%	--	118	--	95	22	34	0	-40.4%	-16
2007	BAL	12	275	168	61.1%	1743	9	10	6	8.6%	5.3	38	-11.6%	33	-10	33	1	19	89	0	13.1%	25
2009	STL		404	252	62.3%	2342	12	19	6		5.2		-30.6%					30	88	1	-26.5%	

2007:	44% Short	32% Mid	16% Deep	8% Bomb	YAC: 3.3 (51)

Boller missed the 2008 season with a shoulder injury, and no one outside his immediate family noticed he was gone. The Rams signed him as a veteran backup, not as an heir apparent: He was the team's Plan B when they couldn't sign Gus Frerotte. Former Ravens center Jason Brown said this about Boller in early April: "I love him to death, but you see what getting hit one too many times early in your career can do to you. He became gun shy … If there was a flash of anything, something, it might have been far to the edge, he was like (flinching). And he started to scramble. You have to have the faith in your offensive line to where you say, 'Hey, I know these guys are going to give me the seconds that I need in order to get this ball off.'" Brown, like Boller, is now in St. Louis, so their dysfunctional relationship ("I love you but you won't let me block for you!") can continue.

Todd Bouman
Height: 6-2　Weight: 229　College: St. Cloud State　　Draft: 1997/FA　Born: 1-Aug-1972　Age: 37　Risk: Red

Year	Team	G	Att	Comp	C%	Yds	TD	INT	FUM	ASR	NY/P	Rk	DVOA	Rk	DYAR	Rk	YAR	Runs	Yds	TD	DVOA	DYAR
2005	NO	16	122	68	55.7%	722	2	7	4	5.9%	5.1	36	-36.6%	44	-222	39	--	8	15	0	-42.7%	-12
2009	JAC		427	246	57.7%	3029	10	13	10		6.2		-4.9%					33	38	0	-6.0%	

Yes, that line really says "2005," because that's the last time Bouman saw game action. Since then he's bounced from Green Bay to Jacksonville to St. Louis to Baltimore and back to Jacksonville. The surprise release of Cleo Lemon makes him the top backup to David Garrard, and we did say just a page or two ago that we would provide projections for two quarterbacks per team. By the way, last year was the first time in his seven-year career that Garrard played more than 12 games. Uh-oh.

Tom Brady

Height: 6-4　Weight: 220　College: Michigan　　　Draft: 2000/6 (199)　Born: 3-Aug-1977　Age: 32　Risk: Green

Year	Team	G	Att	Comp	C%	Yds	TD	INT	FUM	ASR	NY/P	Rk	DVOA	Rk	DYAR	Rk	YAR	Runs	Yds	TD	DVOA	DYAR
2006	NE	16	516	319	61.8%	3529	24	12	13	5.2%	6.5	17	17.4%	8	1009	5	953	49	102	0	4.4%	25
2007	NE	16	578	398	68.9%	4806	50	8	4	4.1%	7.8	1	56.9%	1	2788	1	2698	37	98	2	3.7%	25
2008	NE	1	11	7	63.6%	76	0	0	0	1.2%	7.1	--	4.3%	--	13	--	23	0	0	0	--	--
2009	NE		512	340	66.4%	4040	34	9	7		7.4		39.1%					33	68	1	17.5%	
2008:	60% Short		20% Mid		10% Deep		10% Bomb		YAC: 4.0 (--)			2007:	52% Short		29% Mid		11% Deep		7% Bomb YAC: 5.1 (14)			

Despite missing most of the 2008 due to the Knee that Roared, Brady's lost year was anything but boring. He watched Matt Cassel make a mint with his offense, married Gisele, had a new player safety rule named after him, flipped his kayak in the Charles River, and participated in New England's OTAs without limitation. We do want to address Brady's battle with post-surgical infection, if only to say that it's barely worth addressing. Yes, it's a serious medical concern not just for Brady, but anyone that faces surgery, even in the best and most conscientious of hospitals. No, despite a lot of hyper reporting, he was never really in any danger of missing the 2009 season. It's virtually the same thing that happened to Peyton Manning, but the Indianapolis media isn't quite as breathless and any paparazzi plying their trade in Indy would find themselves getting dragged over to the Bean Lot after dark. Brady had an infection in his knee; it was detected, handled, and ... Brady continued on with what seems to be a normal, effective recovery from ACL reconstruction. He would rather it not have happened, but any change in the timeline of his recovery was so minor that it's moot. Don't expect the crazy numbers of 2007, but there's no reason to think that a healthy Tom Brady won't have the Patriots competing for another Super Bowl win. Tip your cap to Kerlan-Jobe next time you see Brady throw a touchdown pass.

Drew Brees

Height: 6-0　Weight: 221　College: Purdue　　　Draft: 2001/2 (32)　Born: 15-Jan-1979　Age: 30　Risk: Green

Year	Team	G	Att	Comp	C%	Yds	TD	INT	FUM	ASR	NY/P	Rk	DVOA	Rk	DYAR	Rk	YAR	Runs	Yds	TD	DVOA	DYAR
2006	NO	16	554	356	64.3%	4418	26	11	5	3.7%	7.8	3	25.1%	2	1386	2	1458	42	32	0	-72.4%	-51
2007	NO	16	652	440	67.5%	4423	28	18	9	3.6%	6.5	16	17.0%	12	1287	5	1193	23	52	1	14.2%	23
2008	NO	16	635	413	65.0%	5069	34	17	5	2.5%	7.8	1	33.9%	3	1921	1	1799	22	-1	0	-24.0%	-7
2009	NO		593	366	61.7%	4248	33	11	7		6.6		29.0%					24	50	0	1.4%	
2008:	51% Short		29% Mid		13% Deep		7% Bomb		YAC: 5.6 (3)			2007:	55% Short		29% Mid		10% Deep		5% Bomb YAC: 4.7 (23)			

Brees threw 123 passes to intended receivers behind or at the line of scrimmage. This made up 21 percent of his passes, the highest total and percentage in the league. Brees completed 101 of those passes, but these ultra-short passes only accounted for a small portion of Brees' videogame-worthy production. The average team completes about 64 passes behind the line of scrimmage, and Brees' production still looks amazing even if you take away 40 short completions. Brees' numbers on passes longer than 21 yards through the air is much more remarkable: He completed 29 of 63 (46 percent). The average NFL team completes about 17.5 long passes per year, with a completion rate around 34 percent. Write off 40 of Brees' screens as glorified handoffs if you want, but Brees still completed about a dozen more long passes than the average NFL starter. That's the engine that drives the Saints offense, and it's why Brees is so much more than the big league version of a college spread-option passer.

Marc Bulger

Height: 6-3　Weight: 215　College: West Virginia　　　Draft: 2000/6 (168)　Born: 5-Apr-1977　Age: 32　Risk: Green

Year	Team	G	Att	Comp	C%	Yds	TD	INT	FUM	ASR	NY/P	Rk	DVOA	Rk	DYAR	Rk	YAR	Runs	Yds	TD	DVOA	DYAR
2006	STL	16	588	370	62.9%	4301	24	8	8	8.0%	6.8	11	16.6%	11	1142	4	1274	18	44	0	12.4%	12
2007	STL	12	378	221	58.5%	2392	11	15	5	9.4%	5.2	41	-16.5%	40	-142	42	-81	9	13	0	78.6%	9
2008	STL	15	440	251	57.0%	2720	11	13	5	7.9%	5.2	35	-19.8%	36	-259	38	-149	14	41	0	8.8%	8
2009	STL		479	290	60.6%	3211	16	13	4		6.0		-0.3%					22	56	1	5.7%	
2008:	47% Short		33% Mid		12% Deep		8% Bomb		YAC: 4.9 (23)			2007:	43% Short		34% Mid		17% Deep		6% Bomb YAC: 3.7 (46)			

First, the good news: New general manager Billy Devaney made it a priority to upgrade the Rams' offensive line this offseason, signing center Jason Brown from the Ravens and using the second overall pick on Baylor left tackle Jason Smith. Given that Bulger has spent most of the past two seasons pasted to the turf and/or battling the resulting injuries, solving the protection problems should help improve a passing offense that ranked 31st in the league in DVOA. On the other hand, the Rams receiving corps consists of second-year wide receiver Donnie Avery and a bunch of unknowns who have less than 25 career catches — *combined*. Add to that Bulger's wildly inconsistent play last year — interim head coach Jim Haslett benched him in mid-November after the Rams fell behind the Jets by 40 points at the half — and there are more than a few Rams fans who were hoping that their team would select USC's Mark Sanchez. Devaney is systematically focused on making the Rams younger at every position, so this is a make-or-break year for Bulger's future in St. Louis.

Jason Campbell

Height: 6-4   Weight: 223   College: Auburn   Draft: 2005/1 (25)   Born: 31-Dec-1981   Age: 27   Risk: Red

Year	Team	G	Att	Comp	C%	Yds	TD	INT	FUM	ASR	NY/P	Rk	DVOA	Rk	DYAR	Rk	YAR	Runs	Yds	TD	DVOA	DYAR
2006	WAS	7	207	110	53.1%	1297	10	6	4	3.3%	6.0	32	-0.7%	17	140	21	159	24	107	0	23.0%	29
2007	WAS	13	417	250	60.0%	2700	12	11	11	4.7%	6.0	25	4.4%	22	432	17	344	36	185	1	-12.3%	0
2008	WAS	16	506	315	62.3%	3245	13	6	6	7.1%	5.5	32	8.3%	18	655	16	582	47	258	1	44.2%	88
2009	WAS		510	322	63.1%	3182	12	12	10		5.4		-5.7%					63	246	2	6.1%	

| 2008: | 56% Short | 31% Mid | 9% Deep | 5% Bomb | YAC: 5.3 (11) | 2007: | 49% Short | 30% Mid | 13% Deep | 9% Bomb YAC: 4.7 (24) |

Will Jason Campbell ever catch a break? He has played in seven different offensive systems through his college and pro careers. When veteran Todd Collins reunited with offensive coordinator Al Saunders from their Kansas City days (ah, sweet continuity) and played combustively down the stretch in 2007, many wondered if it wasn't time to give Collins the starting job. That was followed by a 2008 season that started with great praise and fizzled at the end. Then, the Jay Cutler trade rumors and the notion that the Redskins were interested in Mark Sanchez. Yes, he dunked down too often on third down (4.95 Yards Per Attempt in third-and-3 to -7, and 5.86 YPA on third-and-8 to -10), but none of his rookie receivers showed much at all. And for all the talk about Campbell's second-half decline in 2008, it's worth noting that the entire offense fell apart — the Redskins' passing DVOA went from ninth to 20th, but the rushing DVOA also dropped from second to 18th. Campbell's got the tools to succeed, especially in the West Coast Offense Jim Zorn runs. He just may not have the receivers.

David Carr

Height: 6-3   Weight: 223   College: Fresno State   Draft: 2002/1 (1)   Born: 21-Jul-1979   Age: 30   Risk: Blue

Year	Team	G	Att	Comp	C%	Yds	TD	INT	FUM	ASR	NY/P	Rk	DVOA	Rk	DYAR	Rk	YAR	Runs	Yds	TD	DVOA	DYAR
2006	HOU	16	442	302	68.3%	2767	11	12	14	9.6%	5.7	39	-8.6%	28	81	26	-50	54	193	2	-3.0%	20
2007	CAR	6	136	73	53.7%	635	3	5	1	8.7%	3.8	51	-29.1%	47	-171	44	-221	17	59	0	-9.9%	2
2008	NYG	3	12	9	75.0%	115	2	0	0	7.1%	8.7	--	138.4%	--	128	--	113	8	10	0	25.0%	3
2009	NYG		455	237	52.0%	2152	14	24	12		4.3		-57.6%					82	287	2	18.9%	

| 2008: | 42% Short | 25% Mid | 33% Deep | 0% Bomb | YAC: 2.9 (--) | 2007: | 52% Short | 27% Mid | 10% Deep | 10% Bomb YAC: 3.9 (44) |

Carr mopped up during the second half of the Week 17 game against the Vikings and looked passable, although he did take his one requisite "Terrifying Sack That David Carr Never Sees Coming" for the half. Retained by the Giants, Carr will continue to play the role of scapegoat-in-waiting if Eli Manning goes down.

Matt Cassel

Height: 6-4   Weight: 232   College: USC   Draft: 2005/7 (230)   Born: 17-May-1982   Age: 27   Risk: Green

Year	Team	G	Att	Comp	C%	Yds	TD	INT	FUM	ASR	NY/P	Rk	DVOA	Rk	DYAR	Rk	YAR	Runs	Yds	TD	DVOA	DYAR
2006	NE	6	8	5	62.5%	32	0	0	1	27.2%	1.4	--	-90.4%	--	-52	--	-49	2	4	0	20.1%	3
2007	NE	6	7	4	57.1%	38	0	1	0	1.2%	5.4	--	-80.6%	--	-35	--	-35	4	12	1	274.3%	15
2008	NE	16	516	327	63.4%	3693	21	11	7	8.7%	6.2	17	6.4%	20	655	17	781	73	270	2	15.8%	82
2009	KC		501	299	59.6%	3277	20	14	15		5.9		3.6%					40	132	3	-1.1%	

| 2008: | 52% Short | 32% Mid | 10% Deep | 6% Bomb | YAC: 6.3 (2) | 2007: | 71% Short | 29% Mid | 0% Deep | 0% Bomb YAC: 4.0 (--) |

Cassel's ascent after Tom Brady's knee injury came from a few factors beyond the young quarterback himself.

The Patriots had a shotgun-heavy, short-and-long passing game set up for the former seventh-round pick from USC. The shotgun sets, which comprised 405 of his 516 pass attempts, gave Cassel a clean pocket and time enough to scan the field and hit his targets. What looks good for him in Kansas City is that new head coach Todd Haley made his bones drawing up game plans for Kurt Warner last year, and those game plans featured 69 percent shotgun sets. The fumbles and sack rate are reasons for concern, and he doesn't have the same quality of targets in K.C., but Cassel should avoid the major schematic transitions some quarterbacks face when working with new teams. The Patriots also rose from 25th in passing DVOA in the season's first half to third in the final eight games, a solid indicator that Cassel's getting the hang of the pro game.

Kellen Clemens   Height: 6-2 Weight: 215 College: Oregon   Draft: 2006/2 (49)   Born: 6-Jun-1983   Age: 26 Risk: Green

Year	Team	G	Att	Comp	C%	Yds	TD	INT	FUM	ASR	NY/P	Rk	DVOA	Rk	DYAR	Rk	YAR	Runs	Yds	TD	DVOA	DYAR
2006	NYJ	2	1	0	0.0%	0	0	0	1	79.2%	-5.4	--	-251.5%	--	-80	--	-85	2	10	0	-23.4%	-1
2007	NYJ	10	250	130	52.0%	1529	5	10	6	9.6%	5.1	42	-18.9%	42	-136	41	-183	27	111	1	-1.0%	16
2008	NYJ	2	5	3	60.0%	26	0	1	0	1.5%	5.2	--	-127.4%	--	-44	--	-41	3	-3	0	--	--
2009	NYJ		437	284	64.9%	2857	12	13	16		5.6		-12.7%					80	277	2	-3.1%	
2008:	40% Short		40% Mid		20% Deep		0% Bomb		YAC: 3.3 (--)			2007:	43% Short		35% Mid		14% Deep		7% Bomb YAC: 5.1 (15)				

It's make-or-break time for Clemens, who was touted by Ron Jaworski and Merril Hoge as a better prospect than Vince Young or Matt Leinart back when that wasn't supposed to be a backhanded compliment. Clemens hasn't shown much to this point beyond a propensity for throwing interceptions. The best scenario for Clemens is that he follows in the footsteps of Drew Brees, another undersized second-round pick who struggled early on but put it all together just as the organization was ready to pull the plug on him. The worst-case scenario is that he doesn't make the final roster.

Kerry Collins   Height: 6-5 Weight: 240 College: Penn State   Draft: 1995/1 (5)   Born: 30-Dec-1972   Age: 36 Risk: Green

Year	Team	G	Att	Comp	C%	Yds	TD	INT	FUM	ASR	NY/P	Rk	DVOA	Rk	DYAR	Rk	YAR	Runs	Yds	TD	DVOA	DYAR
2006	TEN	4	90	42	46.7%	549	1	6	0	4.0%	5.9	--	-45.8%	--	-205	--	-201	0	0	0	--	--
2007	TEN	6	82	50	61.0%	531	0	0	1	6.2%	5.7	--	15.3%	--	148	--	170	3	-3	0	--	--
2008	TEN	16	415	242	58.3%	2676	12	7	5	2.2%	6.2	16	15.3%	13	738	15	715	25	49	0	10.4%	11
2009	TEN		455	271	59.5%	2986	13	11	6		5.9		3.8%					25	49	0	19.9%	
2008:	48% Short		28% Mid		15% Deep		9% Bomb		YAC: 4.9 (25)			2007:	54% Short		25% Mid		11% Deep		11% Bomb YAC: 4.3 (--)				

When Vince Young got hurt in Week 1, Collins was not necessarily anything more than a temporary stopgap. He played so efficiently, however, that Jeff Fisher's decision to keep Collins the starter was met with no controversy. Collins has always been a good, but not great quarterback, and even at his advanced age, his arm is strong enough to keep defenses honest. He bought into his role as "game manager" and made the plays necessary for the Titans to win a number of low-scoring affairs. Despite the impressive numbers, Collins' success with limited wide receivers stems from the attention other teams pay to the running game. Collins tried to take advantage of this by throwing deep on first down (average pass length 10.2 yards, a yard more than the NFL average). The low completion percentage on those deep first-down passes held Collins' DVOA down but kept defenses honest.

Todd Collins   Height: 6-4 Weight: 219 College: Michigan   Draft: 1995/2 (45)   Born: 5-Nov-1971   Age: 38 Risk: Red

Year	Team	G	Att	Comp	C%	Yds	TD	INT	FUM	ASR	NY/P	Rk	DVOA	Rk	DYAR	Rk	YAR	Runs	Yds	TD	DVOA	DYAR
2007	WAS	4	105	67	63.8%	888	5	0	4	5.8%	7.6	2	31.6%	4	311	20	288	8	1	0	19.4%	4
2009	WAS		462	266	57.6%	2750	12	14	12		4.9		-22.8%					22	70	1	-12.0%	
2007:	50% Short		28% Mid		15% Deep		7% Bomb		YAC: 5.4 (6)														

Sometimes, it's who you know. Todd Collins hit the jackpot when he got to run the Al Saunders offense that he knew well from their Kansas City days together. He struggled more in Jim Zorn's West Coast offense, and may lose the backup spot to Colt Brennan.

Brodie Croyle   Height: 6-3   Weight: 205   College: Alabama   Draft: 2006/3 (85)   Born: 6-Feb-1983   Age: 26   Risk: Red

Year	Team	G	Att	Comp	C%	Yds	TD	INT	FUM	ASR	NY/P	Rk	DVOA	Rk	DYAR	Rk	YAR	Runs	Yds	TD	DVOA	DYAR
2006	KC	2	7	3	42.9%	23	0	2	1	12.8%	1.6	--	-139.5%	--	-70	--	-71	3	-3	0	--	--
2007	KC	9	224	127	56.7%	1227	6	6	6	7.5%	4.7	47	-18.5%	41	-112	40	-164	7	18	0	-38.5%	-7
2008	KC	2	29	20	69.0%	151	0	0	0	3.2%	4.7	--	-0.1%	--	21	--	19	0	0	0	--	--
2009	KC		440	215	48.8%	3010	19	23	11		6.2		-23.6%					43	152	0	-8.0%	

2008:	57% Short	32% Mid	11% Deep	0% Bomb	YAC: 4.9 (--)	2007:	50% Short	33% Mid	11% Deep	6% Bomb YAC: 4.1 (37)

Perhaps Brodie Croyle would have developed into a good NFL quarterback, but at this point he's had so many injuries that we'll never know. He played most of his sophomore year at Alabama with a separated shoulder, and tore his ACL as a junior. His NFL record includes back and hand injuries in 2007, then a separated shoulder that knocked him out late in the first game of 2008 against the Patriots. (Given what else happened in that game, this was probably the all-time winner for "quarterback injury ignored on highlight shows.") He returned to start Week 7 against Tennessee, but tore his MCL and was done for the year. While Croyle was gone, he dropped to third on the depth chart. Let's see if he can make it through the season without tripping on his clipboard and breaking his arm.

Daunte Culpepper   Height: 6-4   Weight: 264   College: UCF   Draft: 1999/1 (11)   Born: 28-Jan-1977   Age: 32   Risk: Green

Year	Team	G	Att	Comp	C%	Yds	TD	INT	FUM	ASR	NY/P	Rk	DVOA	Rk	DYAR	Rk	YAR	Runs	Yds	TD	DVOA	DYAR
2006	MIA	4	134	81	60.4%	929	2	3	3	14.1%	5.9	35	-23.1%	40	-109	37	-77	10	20	1	-8.1%	2
2007	OAK	7	186	108	58.1%	1331	5	5	6	10.4%	5.9	31	-4.9%	27	77	27	-4	20	40	3	-11.9%	0
2008	DET	5	115	60	52.2%	786	4	6	5	10.8%	5.4	33	-32.0%	38	-165	36	-274	12	25	1	-34.5%	-16
2009	DET		461	271	58.8%	3442	15	16	10		6.2		-3.1%					31	102	1	-24.2%	

2008:	42% Short	40% Mid	7% Deep	11% Bomb	YAC: 4.9 (24)	2007:	49% Short	30% Mid	13% Deep	8% Bomb YAC: 5.0 (16)

Culpepper's ascension from street free agent to Lions starting quarterback in the matter of a week was puzzling. Did it mean that the Lions playbook took three days to master, or did Culpepper just read the first ten pages, only to decide that it was boring and that he should head to the campus bookstore for the Cliff Notes? Either way, Culpepper looked downright bizarre playing the part of a supersized Jeff Garcia, trying to duck underneath rushers and maneuver around the pocket long enough to launch bomb after bomb at Calvin Johnson. He'll keep the seat warm until Matt Stafford's ready or he falls off the seat and has to go on IR.

Jay Cutler   Height: 6-4   Weight: 225   College: Vanderbilt   Draft: 2006/1 (11)   Born: 29-Apr-1983   Age: 26   Risk: Green

Year	Team	G	Att	Comp	C%	Yds	TD	INT	FUM	ASR	NY/P	Rk	DVOA	Rk	DYAR	Rk	YAR	Runs	Yds	TD	DVOA	DYAR
2006	DEN	5	137	81	59.1%	1001	9	5	5	7.8%	6.7	13	-12.7%	33	-15	33	68	12	18	0	-159.0%	-65
2007	DEN	16	467	297	63.6%	3497	20	14	7	5.5%	6.8	12	19.4%	11	973	8	809	44	205	1	9.3%	38
2008	DEN	16	616	384	62.3%	4526	25	18	3	2.3%	7.2	7	22.0%	7	1380	5	1503	57	200	2	-4.0%	16
2009	CHI		493	301	61.2%	3409	20	12	9		5.9		3.0%					63	190	3	-5.5%	

2008:	43% Short	36% Mid	14% Deep	7% Bomb	YAC: 4.7 (26)	2007:	45% Short	37% Mid	12% Deep	6% Bomb YAC: 5.2 (9)

One of the absurd arguments presented against Cutler's value this offseason was the fact that Cutler threw 11 picks on third down last year. It makes for a snappy quote, but it's a measure of what happened, not what's going to. Cutler threw picks on 7.4 percent of his third down attempts, more than any other qualifying quarterback; a year ago, though, that figure was 2.1 percent, the seventh-best total in the league. The can't-handle-the-heat quarterback who was most likely to throw a pick when his team desperately needed a first down? Peyton Manning, with nine in 137 attempts (6.6 percent). The chief offender in 2006 was Ben Roethlisberger. It's a statistical fluke that has no bearing on Cutler's future or his value. There are holes in Cutler's game just like there are holes in any quarterback's game, but there's no statistical smoking gun that points to a fundamental flaw. The Bears paid for an elite quarterback and they're getting one.

Jake Delhomme

Height: 6-2 Weight: 205 College: Louisiana-Lafayette   Draft: 1998/FA   Born: 10-Jan-1975 Age: 34 Risk: Green

Year	Team	G	Att	Comp	C%	Yds	TD	INT	FUM	ASR	NY/P	Rk	DVOA	Rk	DYAR	Rk	YAR	Runs	Yds	TD	DVOA	DYAR
2006	CAR	13	431	263	61.0%	2805	17	11	6	5.8%	6.1	28	-0.9%	18	303	18	416	18	12	0	9.0%	4
2007	CAR	3	86	55	64.0%	624	8	1	1	6.6%	6.5	--	17.7%	--	176	--	249	6	26	0	-4.9%	2
2008	CAR	16	414	246	59.4%	3288	15	12	4	4.7%	7.3	6	18.0%	11	828	13	817	20	21	2	51.5%	20
2009	CAR		410	218	53.2%	2682	14	12	8		5.5		-19.4%					29	68	1	-16.9%	

2008:	39% Short	38% Mid	13% Deep	9% Bomb	YAC: 5.0 (19)	2007:	49% Short	36% Mid	6% Deep	9% Bomb	YAC: 5.7 (--)

Delhomme started every game for the Panthers in 2008, which worked out relatively well until the six-turnover playoff stinker against the Cardinals. If you can bear to watch the lowlights of the game, generously uploaded to Youtube by Cards fans, they reveal Delhomme staring down his receiver, double-clutching, or patting the ball before all five interceptions, and the sack in which he was stripped. Where did this come from after Delhomme's solid season? Reeking of 20-20 hindsmell, of course, there were two regular season hiccups: a 3-INT turdwich in Tampa and a 4-INT turdwich royale with cheese in Oakland. The Panthers, desperate to save money under the cap this year, hope a contract extension with $20 million in guaranteed money will somehow wash the stink away. They did not bring in any new competition for Delhomme, but I'm sure Panthers fans will be closely watching a newly healthy Matt Moore and last year's backup, Josh McCown, in the preseason. On a positive note, and surprisingly for a team that thrives on a power running game, Delhomme's shotgun DVOA was fourth among quarterbacks with at least 50 shotgun throws, behind only Brees, Peyton Manning, and Eli Manning(!).

Dennis Dixon

Height: 6-4 Weight: 205 College: Oregon   Draft: 2008/5 (156) Born: 11-Jan-1985 Age: 24 Risk: Yellow

Year	Team	G	Att	Comp	C%	Yds	TD	INT	FUM	ASR	NY/P	Rk	DVOA	Rk	DYAR	Rk	YAR	Runs	Yds	TD	DVOA	DYAR
2009	PIT		422	269	63.8%	3199	21	12	10		5.8		6.9%					93	467	1	-3.9%	

Dixon completed a three-yard pass to Hines Ward and knelt twice at the end of the Steelers' 31-0 rout of Cleveland in the season finale. It was more than the team expected of Dixon, whom they drafted in the fifth round as a long-range project. Dixon did provide some preseason highlights, including a 47-yard touchdown run, and the team thinks enough of his practice work that they let Byron Leftwich leave. Dixon should beat out Charlie Batch as Roethlisberger's main backup and could be a spark plug off the bench if pressed into duty.

Ken Dorsey

Height: 6-4 Weight: 205 College: Miami   Draft: 2003/7 (241) Born: 22-Apr-1981 Age: 28 Risk: N/A

Year	Team	G	Att	Comp	C%	Yds	TD	INT	FUM	ASR	NY/P	Rk	DVOA	Rk	DYAR	Rk	YAR	Runs	Yds	TD	DVOA	DYAR
2008	CLE	4	91	43	47.3%	370	0	7	2	4.6%	3.4	--	-52.8%	--	-242	--	-343	2	0	0	--	--

2008:	59% Short	25% Mid	6% Deep	10% Bomb	YAC: 3.4 (--)

When you have a rep as a smart signal caller and you spend three years on the bench, you're supposed to be ready to turn in a passable performance in the event of a quarterback emergency. Dorsey wasn't. He entered the lineup at the end of the Colts game on November 30 and his play deteriorated on an attempt-by-attempt basis. By the time he suffered a concussion and bruised ribs against the Bengals a month later, it was clear he wasn't providing anything a random rookie couldn't offer. Dorsey's career is likely over; after last December, there's no reason to see any more.

Trent Edwards

Height: 6-4 Weight: 231 College: Stanford   Draft: 2007/3 (92) Born: 30-Oct-1983 Age: 26 Risk: Yellow

Year	Team	G	Att	Comp	C%	Yds	TD	INT	FUM	ASR	NY/P	Rk	DVOA	Rk	DYAR	Rk	YAR	Runs	Yds	TD	DVOA	DYAR
2007	BUF	10	269	151	56.1%	1630	7	8	4	4.1%	5.5	35	-7.8%	30	58	31	42	14	49	0	11.3%	12
2008	BUF	14	374	245	65.5%	2699	11	10	9	6.3%	6.5	14	-0.3%	24	278	24	476	37	117	3	8.0%	28
2009	BUF		478	295	61.7%	3221	16	16	13		5.7		-19.5%					62	253	2	-1.3%	

2008:	50% Short	34% Mid	11% Deep	5% Bomb	YAC: 4.6 (28)	2007:	53% Short	31% Mid	9% Deep	7% Bomb	YAC: 5.4 (5)

The knocks on Edwards coming out of Stanford were that he struggled to elevate the play when surrounded by underwhelming talent and that he had durability issues. Edwards upped his completion percentage significantly from his rookie year, but it translated into a DVOA that hovered just below average, thanks to one of the easiest schedules in NFL history. As for the durability issues, well, he missed two games with a groin injury and was knocked out early in Arizona. He also struggled to play well early in games. He threw only one touchdown to five interceptions in the opening quarter, and his completion percentage was 60 percent, as compared to 67 percent in quarters two through four. His poor KUBIAK projection, like our overall projection for the Bills, is based in large part on the inexperienced offensive line.

Brett Favre

Height: 6-2 Weight: 225 College: Southern Mississippi   Draft: 1991/2 (33)   Born: 10-Oct-1969 Age: 40 Risk: Red

Year	Team	G	Att	Comp	C%	Yds	TD	INT	FUM	ASR	NY/P	Rk	DVOA	Rk	DYAR	Rk	YAR	Runs	Yds	TD	DVOA	DYAR
2006	GB	16	613	343	56.0%	3885	18	18	7	3.5%	6.1	26	-1.2%	19	408	14	479	23	29	1	-55.4%	-24
2007	GB	16	535	356	66.5%	4155	28	15	8	2.7%	7.5	3	28.0%	5	1437	3	1457	29	12	0	-43.4%	-15
2008	NYJ	16	522	343	65.7%	3472	22	22	10	5.9%	6.0	23	-2.2%	26	334	20	559	21	43	1	-71.3%	-42
2009	MIN?		509	337	66.2%	3558	25	18	5		6.6		13.2%					18	26	1	-20.9%	

2008:	52% Short	31% Mid	10% Deep	7% Bomb	YAC: 4.9 (21)	2007:	54% Short	30% Mid	8% Deep	8% Bomb	YAC: 5.7 (1)

They work as rangers at golf courses, drivers at auto auctions, ride operators at amusement parks and crossing guards at elementary schools. They are former engineers, insurance salesmen, and teachers who retired, grew bored quickly with their leisure, then rejoined the workforce, usually for reasons more emotional than financial. Most drove their spouses and children crazy for a year or two before returning to work. None of them realized that they would miss the rat race until they left it.

Favre can't substitute teach or wrangle geese with his dog at the county park. He'd make a terrible coach and an unlistenable announcer. There are only so many charity golf tournaments he can attend. He embraces retirement then fears it, accepts his declining skills then tries to deny them, just like millions of other professionals facing the ends of their careers. But instead of driving his family crazy, he drives America crazy, aided by a Favre-obsessed sports media that ignores a dozen hockey games to cover one text message to Brad Childress.

Favre will play this year, or he won't. If he plays, he'll be worse than the Favre of Old but better than Tarvaris Jackson. If he retires, his name will surface after every quarterback's ACL tear, and we'll probably do this dance again in 2010. Favre deserves to go out on his own terms; we just wish he would decide what those terms are before he makes his 4,000th retirement announcement.

Ryan Fitzpatrick

Height: 6-2 Weight: 221 College: Harvard   Draft: 2005/7 (250) Born: 24-Nov-1982 Age: 27 Risk: Red

Year	Team	G	Att	Comp	C%	Yds	TD	INT	FUM	ASR	NY/P	Rk	DVOA	Rk	DYAR	Rk	YAR	Runs	Yds	TD	DVOA	DYAR
2008	CIN	12	372	221	59.4%	1905	8	9	10	9.4%	4.2	40	-18.0%	35	-185	37	-327	60	304	2	21.7%	88
2009	BUF		420	270	64.4%	2568	16	13	16		5.5		-18.9%					62	250	3	4.6%	

2008:	49% Short	36% Mid	9% Deep	6% Bomb	YAC: 3.6 (41)

Cambridge, Massachusetts, suffered two blows in 2008. Out Of Town News, the world's greatest newsstand, closed up shop after more than half a century in Harvard Square. And Crimson alum Ryan Fitzpatrick was forced to play quarterback for a dozen games in Cincinnati. While he was predictably grim as a passer, Fitz's propensity to take off and run at the slightest provocation was actually beneficial given the ineptitude of the Bengals' pass blocking. His scrambles were often the team's main offensive weapon. His excellence on first down (5.4% DVOA, compared to DVOA below -30% on other downs) was likely a result of defenses surprised by seeing the ball in the air, rather than under Fitzpatrick's arm. Cincy made little attempt to retain Runnin' Ryan, and Fitzpatrick signed with Buffalo to back up Trent Edwards. Should he be forced into the starting role on Lake Erie, the contrast won't be as great as it was with Carson Palmer.

Joe Flacco
Height: 6-7   Weight: 236   College: Delaware   Draft: 2008/1 (18)   Born: 16-Jan-1985   Age: 24   Risk: Green

Year	Team	G	Att	Comp	C%	Yds	TD	INT	FUM	ASR	NY/P	Rk	DVOA	Rk	DYAR	Rk	YAR	Runs	Yds	TD	DVOA	DYAR
2008	BAL	16	428	257	60.0%	2971	14	12	11	7.0%	6.0	22	2.4%	22	384	19	282	52	180	0	-9.0%	5
2009	BAL		500	291	58.1%	3026	15	10	15		5.2		-8.9%					37	167	1	18.9%	

2008:	45% Short	36% Mid	10% Deep	9% Bomb	YAC: 5.3 (13)

The Ravens got an unscheduled bye in Week 2 of last season when Hurricane Ike forced the cancellation of their game against the Texans. Flacco, in his second week as an NFL starter, returned home to South Jersey and had a Sunday lunch at a sports pub near his hometown. He entered the dining area, which was crowded with football fans watching dozens of high-def televisions and following their bets/fantasy teams on their cell phones. None of these devoted fans noticed or recognized the NFL starter in their midst; one or two said something to the effect of "check out that tall dude out over there." The only person who acknowledged Flacco was his former math teacher, who is also an Internet football writer of limited notoriety. Flacco and the teacher smiled and waved and went about their business.

It was an odd scene. It tells us a lot about Flacco, a talented young man so unassuming that he's barely a celebrity in the suburb where he grew up. It also casts an ironic light on contemporary fandom. We're digitally connected to games across the continent and emotionally connected to teams we follow on an minute-by-minute basis, but we're so personally disconnected that we don't recognize the players we root for when they are eating lunch next to us. Everyone knows who Joe Flacco is now; it seems strange that just a few months ago, he could go unrecognized among his own neighbors.

Matt Flynn
Height: 6-2   Weight: 228   College: LSU   Draft: 2008/7 (209)   Born: 20-Jun-1985   Age: 24   Risk: Green

Year	Team	G	Att	Comp	C%	Yds	TD	INT	FUM	ASR	NY/P	Rk	DVOA	Rk	DYAR	Rk	YAR	Runs	Yds	TD	DVOA	DYAR
2008	GB	4	5	2	40.0%	6	0	0	1	-0.1%	1.2	--	-57.4%	--	-15	--	-25	4	4	0	-47.3%	-3
2009	GB		448	263	58.7%	2373	24	18	4		5.2		-19.4%					17	46	1	13.8%	

2008:	60% Short	40% Mid	0% Deep	0% Bomb	YAC: 1.5 (--)

JaMarcus Russell's backup at LSU, Flynn beat out Brian Brohm for the backup job behind Aaron Rodgers with a strong preseason, including a 100.2 passer rating. Fortunately, Brohm isn't upset about it; the two are still best buds on MySpace. Flynn is a dangerous backup quarterback: Exciting and athletic enough to make you think he's capable of more, his lack of arm strength and inconsistent mechanics likely preclude him from having much of a shot at the pro level. Then again, you might have said the same thing about Matt Cassel heading into 2008.

Josh Freeman
Height: 6-6   Weight: 250   College: Kansas State   Draft: 2009/1 (17)   Born: 13-Jan-1988   Age: 21   Risk: Yellow

Year	Team	G	Att	Comp	C%	Yds	TD	INT	FUM	ASR	NY/P	Rk	DVOA	Rk	DYAR	Rk	YAR	Runs	Yds	TD	DVOA	DYAR
2009	TB		489	240	49.0%	3003	19	20	7		5.7		-23.7%					38	270	1	-18.2%	

After selecting him in the first round, new Bucs coach Raheem Morris admitted that he was "married" to the player he first saw when he was Kansas State's defensive coordinator and Freeman its starting quarterback. Will it be Paul Newman and JoAnne Woodward or Britney and K-Fed? Morris' blushing bride is a bit of a jumble; when he has time to step into a pass, Freeman's got prototypical arm strength and above-average accuracy. If the conditions aren't ideal, though, Freeman's fundamentals disappear and he short-arms the ball. Playing with a middling offense in Kansas State, Freeman was expected to do it all and often tried to, yielding both good (team leader) and bad (forces passes) tendencies. The Lewin Career Forecast sees a 59.1 percent completion percentage and 32 career starts and suggests adequacy.

Gus Frerotte

Height: 6-3 Weight: 225 College: Tulsa   Draft: 1994/7 (197) Born: 3-Jul-1971 Age: 38 Risk: N/A

Year	Team	G	Att	Comp	C%	Yds	TD	INT	FUM	ASR	NY/P	Rk	DVOA	Rk	DYAR	Rk	YAR	Runs	Yds	TD	DVOA	DYAR
2006	STL	1	3	1	33.3%	27	0	0	--	--	--	--	--	--	--	--	--	0	0	0	--	--
2007	STL	8	167	94	56.3%	1014	7	12	2	6.2%	5.4	36	-26.2%	45	-175	45	-141	6	3	0	--	--
2008	MIN	11	301	178	59.1%	2157	12	15	4	8.7%	6.1	21	-10.4%	31	16	31	25	19	7	1	--	--

2008:	47% Short	35% Mid	12% Deep	7% Bomb	YAC: 5.3 (10)	2007:	39% Short	40% Mid	14% Deep	7% Bomb	YAC: 3.6 (48)

Frerotte came in for a deposed Tarvaris Jackson in Week 3 under the guise that his presence would provide adjectives more commonly related to anti-inch ointment. His calming, soothing presence led Antoine Winfield to recover a fumble and return it for a touchdown, giving the Vikings a much-needed win. Unfortunately, his interception rate was three times that of Jackson's, which made it hard to play off that game manager look. Frerotte fractured his back just before losing his job, and wasn't re-signed in the offseason. He may need to look in that mirror and utter Kimbo Slice's famous parting words: "I'm done, Gus."

Jeff Garcia

Height: 6-1 Weight: 195 College: San Jose State   Draft: 1999/FA Born: 24-Feb-1970 Age: 39 Risk: Red

Year	Team	G	Att	Comp	C%	Yds	TD	INT	FUM	ASR	NY/P	Rk	DVOA	Rk	DYAR	Rk	YAR	Runs	Yds	TD	DVOA	DYAR
2006	PHI	8	188	116	61.7%	1309	10	2	6	4.2%	6.8	12	17.4%	9	359	17	365	25	87	0	6.2%	17
2007	TB	13	327	209	63.9%	2440	13	4	3	6.2%	6.9	10	19.5%	10	691	13	746	35	116	1	1.0%	17
2008	TB	12	346	244	70.5%	2712	12	6	7	6.5%	6.6	13	10.9%	16	569	18	673	35	148	1	-1.0%	20
2009	OAK		482	301	62.6%	3184	16	10	15		5.8		-1.2%					40	155	2	-24.5%	

2008:	58% Short	26% Mid	8% Deep	8% Bomb	YAC: 4.9 (22)	2007:	53% Short	29% Mid	10% Deep	8% Bomb	YAC: 5.5 (3)

Stretching back to his days as a Calgary Stampeder, Garcia has moved up the depth chart with alacrity. Would anyone be surprised if he was at the helm of the Silver and Black by midseason? Sure, he's pushing 40, but he completed more than 70 percent of his passes last year, had a decent DVOA, and fought his way out of Jon Gruden's doghouse to get back to his usual starting role. You'd think being married to a former Playmate of the Year would mellow a guy, but Garcia still plays angry. Watch your back, JaMarcus.

David Garrard

Height: 6-1 Weight: 238 College: East Carolina   Draft: 2002/4 (108) Born: 14-Feb-1978 Age: 31 Risk: Yellow

Year	Team	G	Att	Comp	C%	Yds	TD	INT	FUM	ASR	NY/P	Rk	DVOA	Rk	DYAR	Rk	YAR	Runs	Yds	TD	DVOA	DYAR
2006	JAC	11	241	145	60.2%	1735	10	9	6	8.3%	6.6	15	-4.8%	24	107	23	108	47	250	0	17.0%	56
2007	JAC	12	325	208	64.0%	2509	18	3	7	6.9%	7.0	8	37.4%	3	1088	7	986	49	185	1	13.3%	58
2008	JAC	16	535	335	62.6%	3620	15	13	7	7.6%	5.9	26	11.0%	15	824	14	734	73	322	2	9.6%	80
2009	JAC		462	297	64.2%	3290	19	11	9		6.4		14.9%					77	305	3	4.2%	

2008:	41% Short	38% Mid	15% Deep	6% Bomb	YAC: 4.3 (36)	2007:	39% Short	40% Mid	15% Deep	6% Bomb	YAC: 4.6 (25)

The concept of "quarterback wins" has always been a ridiculous one, because of the disproportionate credit/blame it places on the signal-caller in the ultimate team sport. In 2008, David Garrard lost his two starting guards in the first game of the regular season, didn't have his starting center for the first six games, and had nothing remotely resembling a reliable receiver. When you're bailing out all the time and looking for indifferent, injured, or suspended targets, it's tough to be successful. Jacksonville receivers dropped 34 passes last year, twice as many as they did the year before. Garrard ranked first in quarterback knockdowns with 110, and was second behind Kurt Warner with 73 quarterback hits. He was also in the top five for passes thrown away due to pressure. In short, last year's disaster was less his fault than you might think. He'll play better in 2009 thanks to the team's new offensive linemen and the purging of its least effective receivers (i.e., almost all of them).

Quinn Gray

Height: 6-3   Weight: 246   College: Florida A&M   Draft: 2002/FA   Born: 21-May-1979   Age: 30   Risk: N/A

Year	Team	G	Att	Comp	C%	Yds	TD	INT	FUM	ASR	NY/P	Rk	DVOA	Rk	DYAR	Rk	YAR	Runs	Yds	TD	DVOA	DYAR
2006	JAC	2	22	13	59.1%	166	0	0	0	4.7%	7.0	--	26.5%	--	50	--	60	2	26	2	206.8%	29
2007	JAC	8	144	80	55.6%	986	10	5	2	6.8%	6.0	26	20.9%	8	301	21	312	19	57	0	22.2%	20
2008	KC	1	8	7	87.5%	76	1	0	0	1.3%	9.5	--	109.7%	--	70	--	76	1	27	0	166.6%	11

2008:	88% Short	0% Mid	13% Deep	0% Bomb	YAC: 4.0 (--)	2007:	36% Short	36% Mid	20% Deep	7% Bomb	YAC: 4.4 (34)

The former Jacksonville backup bounced around from Houston to Indianapolis to Kansas City last season, with his only action coming late in a blowout loss to Buffalo. He's put up phenomenal DVOA ratings in limited duty over the past three years, but when you look closer, you see that his best performances come in Week 17 or mop-up duty late in blowouts. He's a free agent again and will likely bounce to whichever team sees its backup go down in a preseason game.

Trent Green

Height: 6-3   Weight: 217   College: Indiana   Draft: 1993/8 (222)   Born: 9-Jul-1970   Age: 39   Risk: N/A

Year	Team	G	Att	Comp	C%	Yds	TD	INT	FUM	ASR	NY/P	Rk	DVOA	Rk	DYAR	Rk	YAR	Runs	Yds	TD	DVOA	DYAR
2006	KC	8	198	121	61.1%	1342	7	9	4	9.6%	6.1	27	-2.5%	22	121	22	-15	19	59	0	-8.2%	2
2007	MIA	5	141	85	60.3%	987	5	7	2	5.5%	6.5	15	7.8%	19	174	22	123	7	32	0	-34.7%	-7
2008	STL	3	72	38	52.8%	525	0	6	0	7.9%	6.0	--	-52.9%	--	-204	--	-181	3	4	0	75.4%	6

2008:	44% Short	29% Mid	18% Deep	9% Bomb	YAC: 5.9 (--)	2007:	46% Short	35% Mid	17% Deep	2% Bomb	YAC: 5.4 (7)

It's unfortunate that Green ended his career with one of its worst performances — a four-interception, -151 DYAR performance against the Bears in Week 12 — because he was quite the quarterback when he was healthy. He didn't accrue the sort of lengthy career numbers you'd expect from a great quarterback because he didn't become an NFL regular until 28, the result of spending five years tiptoeing around the fringes of the league. Imagine if Charlie Whitehurst emerged as an effective starting quarterback in 2010 and had a late peak that got him into two Pro Bowls. That's Trent Green's career. He's another reminder that after all the draft chatter and scoutspeak, there are probably a half-dozen Greens or Kurt Warners or James Harrisons out there who never got the chance.

Brian Griese

Height: 6-3   Weight: 215   College: Michigan   Draft: 1998/3 (91)   Born: 18-Mar-1975   Age: 34   Risk: Red

Year	Team	G	Att	Comp	C%	Yds	TD	INT	FUM	ASR	NY/P	Rk	DVOA	Rk	DYAR	Rk	YAR	Runs	Yds	TD	DVOA	DYAR
2006	CHI	6	32	18	56.3%	220	1	2	2	7.6%	6.2	--	-52.3%	--	-84	--	-87	6	-5	0	-254.9%	-12
2007	CHI	7	262	161	61.5%	1803	10	12	5	6.1%	6.2	21	-15.0%	37	-67	37	40	13	28	0	-3.7%	4
2008	TB	5	184	110	59.8%	1073	5	7	1	5.3%	5.3	34	-12.3%	33	-14	32	-19	5	-1	0	24.3%	3
2009	TB		498	295	59.2%	3135	19	20	12		5.7		-14.5%					27	41	0	4.7%	

2008:	55% Short	30% Mid	11% Deep	4% Bomb	YAC: 4 (40)	2007:	52% Short	28% Mid	14% Deep	5% Bomb	YAC: 5.6 (2)

Somehow, Griese won eight of ten games he started in Tampa. The high winning percentage wasn't enough to save his job; Tampa tried to deal him before the draft, but couldn't find any takers. Strangely, they didn't release him afterwards, or in May, or in June. Is he still on the team as you are reading this? What on earth are they waiting for? Griese is much better from the shotgun, with a 17.5% DVOA in the shotgun and a -43.0% DVOA under center last season, so he'd be a great fit as a backup for someone like New England.

Rex Grossman

Height: 6-1   Weight: 222   College: Florida   Draft: 2003/1 (22)   Born: 23-Aug-1980   Age: 29   Risk: Yellow

Year	Team	G	Att	Comp	C%	Yds	TD	INT	FUM	ASR	NY/P	Rk	DVOA	Rk	DYAR	Rk	YAR	Runs	Yds	TD	DVOA	DYAR
2006	CHI	16	480	262	54.6%	3193	23	20	7	4.3%	6.4	21	-9.3%	29	60	29	212	24	2	0	15.4%	9
2007	CHI	8	225	122	54.2%	1411	4	7	5	8.9%	4.9	44	-21.8%	43	-167	43	-262	14	27	0	-28.2%	-7
2008	CHI	3	62	32	51.6%	257	2	2	0	3.1%	3.8	--	-27.9%	--	-70	--	-94	3	4	2	24.7%	12
2009	HOU		421	206	48.8%	2697	15	20	5		5.7		-22.8%					16	46	0	-7.7%	

2008:	47% Short	33% Mid	13% Deep	7% Bomb	YAC: 3.2 (--)	2007:	45% Short	30% Mid	18% Deep	8% Bomb	YAC: 4.6 (26)

In a case of poor timing, Grossman's only start in 2008 came against the Titans and their elite pass defense; if Kyle Orton had just gotten hurt a week earlier, Grossman would have had the chance to start against the lowly Lions. Instead, Grossman was terrible against Tennessee and had a freaky-bad performance (8-of-18 for 58 yards) in relief of Orton against Detroit. Grossman was not re-signed in the offseason and stumbled into Houston; at least he can show Dan Orlovsky where the back of the end zone is.

Caleb Hanie   Height: 6-2   Weight: 225   College: Colorado State   Draft: 2008/FA   Born: 11-Sep-1985   Age: 24   Risk: Green

Year	Team	G	Att	Comp	C%	Yds	TD	INT	FUM	ASR	NY/P	Rk	DVOA	Rk	DYAR	Rk	YAR	Runs	Yds	TD	DVOA	DYAR
2009	CHI		422	234	55.5%	2408	17	16	8		4.7		-24.2%					50	176	1	11.0%	

See? When we said at least two quarterbacks per team, we weren't kidding around. A Mel Kiper favorite (the Golden Hairdo said Hanie had "the second strongest arm in the draft after Joe Flacco"), Hanie was the Bears' third quarterback last year after signing as an undrafted free agent out of Colorado State. We'll be shocked if the Bears don't sign some sort of veteran backup before the season starts.

Joey Harrington   Height: 6-4   Weight: 220   College: Oregon   Draft: 2002/1 (3)   Born: 21-Oct-1978   Age: 31   Risk: Blue

Year	Team	G	Att	Comp	C%	Yds	TD	INT	FUM	ASR	NY/P	Rk	DVOA	Rk	DYAR	Rk	YAR	Runs	Yds	TD	DVOA	DYAR
2006	MIA	11	388	223	57.5%	2236	12	15	5	4.3%	5.5	42	-14.9%	34	-98	35	-241	19	24	0	-33.6%	-19
2007	ATL	12	348	215	61.8%	2215	7	8	1	8.7%	5.3	39	-5.8%	29	123	25	142	14	33	0	-12.4%	0
2009	NO		497	298	59.9%	2751	19	15	12		4.8		-14.3%					28	84	1	20.4%	

2007:	56% Short	31% Mid	8% Deep	5% Bomb	YAC: 5.2 (10)

The Saints re-signed Harrington in March; he'll battle Mark Brunell for the number-two job behind Drew Brees. Whoever loses the battle becomes arguably the best third-string quarterback in the NFL, which is a true booby prize when you play for a team whose starter hasn't missed a game since 2004.

Matt Hasselbeck   Height: 6-4   Weight: 233   College: Boston College   Draft: 1998/6 (187)   Born: 25-Sep-1975   Age: 34   Risk: Green

Year	Team	G	Att	Comp	C%	Yds	TD	INT	FUM	ASR	NY/P	Rk	DVOA	Rk	DYAR	Rk	YAR	Runs	Yds	TD	DVOA	DYAR
2006	SEA	12	371	210	56.6%	2442	18	15	3	8.4%	6.0	31	-10.2%	31	23	30	118	18	110	0	38.6%	33
2007	SEA	16	562	352	62.6%	3966	28	12	6	6.9%	6.4	17	12.8%	14	938	9	1167	39	89	0	-11.1%	1
2008	SEA	7	209	109	52.2%	1216	5	10	1	9.0%	4.8	38	-34.2%	39	-334	40	-262	11	69	0	46.2%	28
2009	SEA		508	334	65.8%	3857	20	9	6		7.0		25.4%					36	91	0	-0.4%	

2008:	39% Short	39% Mid	17% Deep	5% Bomb	YAC: 4 (39)	2007:	48% Short	32% Mid	14% Deep	6% Bomb YAC: 4.7 (22)

Hasselbeck's injuries, age, and salary were all high enough this spring that the Seahawks were rumored to be pursuing quarterbacks Matthew Stafford or Mark Sanchez in the draft. Hasselbeck bristled at these suggestions. "I mean, you could do that, that's your prerogative," Hasselbeck said of such a possibility. "It won't change anything I do. I'm getting ready to play football this year. I am going to play football this year. I'm not concerned at all (about my back)." Since the Seahawks didn't draft a passer early (they did take Rutgers signal-caller Mike Teel in the sixth round) and made no effort to bring in a veteran quarterback, it's clear they're not concerned about Hasselbeck's back either. He had no issues at a predraft minicamp under new coach Jim Mora, but that could change when the pads go on and the hits are for real. KUBIAK loves that NFC West schedule and sees a huge rebound.

Chad Henne   Height: 6-2 Weight: 225 College: Michigan   Draft: 2008/2 (57)   Born: 2-Jul-1985   Age: 24 Risk: Green

Year	Team	G	Att	Comp	C%	Yds	TD	INT	FUM	ASR	NY/P	Rk	DVOA	Rk	DYAR	Rk	YAR	Runs	Yds	TD	DVOA	DYAR
2008	MIA	1	12	7	58.3%	67	0	0	0	0.7%	5.6	--	-2.3%	--	8	--	17	0	0	0	--	--
2009	MIA		455	280	61.5%	3360	17	13	8		6.2		5.5%					15	61	0	13.1%	
2008:	50% Short	40% Mid		10% Deep		0% Bomb	YAC: 1.6 (--)															

Henne struggled through injuries through his Michigan career, but still managed 47 starts and one of the greatest freshman seasons any quarterback has ever enjoyed. In mop-up duty for Chad Pennington, he displayed the attributes needed for any budding NFL starter. He'll get a little less bench time this season, and the Dolphins' starting quarterback job is probably his to lose in 2010 or if Pennington can't stay healthy in 2009. When you hear rumblings that Pat White is in the mix for the second spot, don't believe them — Henne has been targeted as the future quarterback of the Dolphins.

Shaun Hill   Height: 6-3 Weight: 235 College: Maryland   Draft: 2002/FA   Born: 9-Jan-1980   Age: 29 Risk: Yellow

Year	Team	G	Att	Comp	C%	Yds	TD	INT	FUM	ASR	NY/P	Rk	DVOA	Rk	DYAR	Rk	YAR	Runs	Yds	TD	DVOA	DYAR
2007	SF	3	79	54	68.4%	501	5	1	2	9.7%	5.7	--	6.0%	--	101	--	129	12	14	1	8.1%	6
2008	SF	9	288	181	62.8%	2046	13	8	8	7.7%	6.2	18	-2.4%	28	180	28	306	24	115	2	24.5%	38
2009	SF		494	280	56.7%	3032	19	18	13		5.3		-18.2%					39	167	0	-1.7%	
2008:	50% Short	28% Mid		17% Deep		5% Bomb	YAC: 4.4 (33)				2007:	66% Short	28% Mid		5% Deep		0% Bomb	YAC: 4.6 (--)				

It took two months for the 49ers to put an end to the J.T. O'Sullivan experiment, and thus for the second straight year, Shaun Hill found himself thrust into the starting job almost by accident. He was successful enough to retain the job for 2009, but there are signs that he's riding a bit of luck. His third down DVOA of 8.5% doesn't match his performance on first down (-3.8%) or second down (-9.7%). If that regresses back to league average — and there's no reason to think that it won't — Hill looks worse. He might want to consider inviting Michael Crabtree over for board games and drills every night to try and establish a rapport with him.

Damon Huard   Height: 6-3 Weight: 215 College: Washington   Draft: 1997/FA   Born: 9-Jul-1973   Age: 36 Risk: Red

Year	Team	G	Att	Comp	C%	Yds	TD	INT	FUM	ASR	NY/P	Rk	DVOA	Rk	DYAR	Rk	YAR	Runs	Yds	TD	DVOA	DYAR
2006	KC	10	244	148	60.7%	1878	11	1	6	5.7%	7.2	7	24.3%	3	584	12	655	9	9	0	-175.4%	-30
2007	KC	11	332	206	62.0%	2257	11	13	6	9.9%	5.6	33	-11.8%	34	-14	34	8	9	-1	0	-86.7%	-13
2008	KC	5	81	50	61.7%	477	2	4	3	9.7%	4.7	--	-54.7%	--	-228	--	-217	4	13	0	174.4%	7
2009	SF		424	266	62.8%	2802	11	16	14		5.4		-18.1%					1	1	0	-43.1%	
2008:	47% Short	32% Mid		11% Deep		9% Bomb	YAC: 4.0 (--)				2007:	43% Short	34% Mid		17% Deep		7% Bomb	YAC: 4.5 (29)				

The Huard brothers are the Bizarro Mannings: three brothers — Damon, Brock, and Luke — who eached played quarterback for their strong, God-fearing father, Mike Huard of Puyallup High School. Like Peyton and Eli, Damon and Brock both had successful college careers. Unlike Peyton and Eli, Damon and Brock never managed to hold onto a starting job in the NFL. And then's there Luke Huard, who struggled at North Carolina with injuries and coaching changes, never played in the pros, and now is an assistant coach at Illinois State. (Somewhere in an office in downtown Manhattan, Cooper Manning is nodding.) In any event, Damon may serve as the 49ers' third quarterback this year if he can beat out Ball State's Nate Davis. If not, he may start preparing for his new coaching career.

Tarvaris Jackson
Height: 6-2   Weight: 225   College: Alabama State   Draft: 2006/2 (64)   Born: 21-Apr-1983   Age: 26   Risk: Yellow

Year	Team	G	Att	Comp	C%	Yds	TD	INT	FUM	ASR	NY/P	Rk	DVOA	Rk	DYAR	Rk	YAR	Runs	Yds	TD	DVOA	DYAR
2006	MIN	4	81	47	58.0%	475	2	4	1	8.8%	5.5	--	-52.7%	--	-238	--	-236	15	77	1	-3.7%	6
2007	MIN	12	294	171	58.2%	1911	9	12	5	6.5%	6.0	23	-5.8%	28	105	26	156	54	260	3	25.4%	80
2008	MIN	7	149	88	59.1%	1056	9	2	5	8.8%	6.1	20	10.0%	17	219	25	211	26	139	0	-15.2%	-4
2009	MIN		460	271	58.8%	3128	21	13	5		6.1		0.6%					70	292	4	21.8%	

| 2008: | 39% Short | 41% Mid | 10% Deep | 10% Bomb | YAC: 5.4 (9) | 2007: | 45% Short | 37% Mid | 9% Deep | 10% Bomb YAC: 4.9 (19) |

Which Tarvaris Jackson do you want to believe in? The one who had a 23.5% DVOA over the final four games of the regular season, including a four-touchdown game against the Cardinals? If you give him credit for Arizona's blown coverages and a decent game against a Giants team that had nothing to play for, you can probably squint hard enough to see a young Jake Plummer there. Even if you want to aspire to that level, Jackson's just not that guy. His performance in a small sample at the end of the year was thanks to those friendly scenarios and a huge third-down split (26.3% DVOA on third and fourth down, 3.0% otherwise) that is totally out of line with his prior splits. If you want to believe that it's a new skill, you've probably been on the bandwagon all along. However, no matter how well he plays, the quality of his offensive line and running game will drag his numbers upwards, and his rushing value makes him a viable fantasy football asset.

Brad Johnson
Height: 6-5   Weight: 226   College: Florida State   Draft: 1992/9 (227)   Born: 13-Sep-1968   Age: 41   Risk: N/A

Year	Team	G	Att	Comp	C%	Yds	TD	INT	FUM	ASR	NY/P	Rk	DVOA	Rk	DYAR	Rk	YAR	Runs	Yds	TD	DVOA	DYAR
2006	MIN	15	439	270	61.5%	2750	9	15	9	6.7%	5.9	37	-17.8%	36	-202	41	-186	29	82	1	-4.6%	9
2007	DAL	16	11	7	63.6%	79	0	0	0	8.8%	5.8	--	-13.8%	--	-2	--	-7	5	-5	0	-105.6%	-7
2008	DAL	3	78	41	52.6%	427	2	5	1	9.0%	4.3	--	-50.7%	--	-207	--	-232	2	-1	0	--	--

| 2008: | 47% Short | 34% Mid | 10% Deep | 10% Bomb | YAC: 4.8 (--) | 2007: | 64% Short | 18% Mid | 9% Deep | 9% Bomb YAC: 7.6 (--) |

It wasn't that Johnson had lost a step by 2008; he'd lost all his steps, leaving him unable to sidestep the rush and fearful of holding onto the ball for too long. That eliminated passing windows, leaving Johnson to dink, dunk, and pray. While such a contest holds a significant amount of potential as a VH1 reality show for former punt, pass, and kick competitors, Johnson's probably finished.

Jon Kitna
Height: 6-2   Weight: 220   College: Central Washington   Draft: 1997/FA   Born: 21-Sep-1972   Age: 37   Risk: Green

Year	Team	G	Att	Comp	C%	Yds	TD	INT	FUM	ASR	NY/P	Rk	DVOA	Rk	DYAR	Rk	YAR	Runs	Yds	TD	DVOA	DYAR
2006	DET	16	596	372	62.4%	4208	21	22	9	9.9%	6.4	18	-2.3%	21	370	15	295	34	156	2	-9.2%	4
2007	DET	16	561	355	63.3%	4068	18	20	12	8.2%	6.1	22	-1.2%	23	390	18	293	25	63	0	-31.7%	-15
2008	DET	4	120	68	56.7%	758	5	5	3	11.3%	5.0	37	-19.9%	37	-76	34	-119	6	34	0	34.4%	14
2009	DAL		395	251	63.7%	3099	21	12	12		6.6		6.5%					26	69	0	22.7%	

| 2008: | 44% Short | 36% Mid | 12% Deep | 8% Bomb | YAC: 5.5 (5) | 2007: | 43% Short | 33% Mid | 19% Deep | 6% Bomb YAC: 4.3 (35) |

Kitna's time in Detroit ended after he suffered a minor back injury and was unceremoniously dumped on IR. Although teams often cut their veterans later in the season after making this sort of roster move, Kitna was granted no such favor by the Detroit braintrust. Dealt to Dallas for Anthony Henry, he's the ideal backup for Tony Romo: A mobile quarterback with improvisational skills.

Kevin Kolb
Height: 6-3   Weight: 218   College: Houston   Draft: 2007/2 (36)   Born: 24-Aug-1984   Age: 25   Risk: Green

Year	Team	G	Att	Comp	C%	Yds	TD	INT	FUM	ASR	NY/P	Rk	DVOA	Rk	DYAR	Rk	YAR	Runs	Yds	TD	DVOA	DYAR
2008	PHI	6	34	17	50.0%	144	0	4	0	0.3%	4.2	--	-75.7%	--	-139	--	-175	13	2	0	-67.3%	-9
2009	PHI		444	281	63.4%	3100	18	17	7		6.1		-13.7%					42	115	1	-8.6%	

| 2008: | 39% Short | 48% Mid | 10% Deep | 3% Bomb | YAC: 3.6 (--) |

Kolb got his first chance at playing time in perhaps the worst scenario possible: thrust into action against an elite defense with no notice. Unsurprisingly, he did not impress, although his -59.3% DVOA in the Ravens game was slightly better than McNabb's -72.6%. Being as that was Kolb's only significant action of the campaign, there's very little evidence that Kolb's status is any different than it was at this time last year. He's still in line to get the first crack at the Eagles' starting job after McNabb, with no real idea of when that will be.

Byron Leftwich　　Height: 6-5　Weight: 245　College: Marshall　　　　Draft: 2003/1 (7)　　Born: 14-Jan-1980　Age: 29　Risk: Yellow

Year	Team	G	Att	Comp	C%	Yds	TD	INT	FUM	ASR	NY/P	Rk	DVOA	Rk	DYAR	Rk	YAR	Runs	Yds	TD	DVOA	DYAR
2006	JAC	6	183	108	59.0%	1159	7	5	5	5.6%	6.0	29	-10.1%	30	13	31	138	25	41	2	-12.3%	0
2007	ATL	3	58	32	55.2%	279	1	2	6	9.4%	3.8	--	-65.0%	--	-215	--	-218	6	7	0	-137.7%	-37
2008	PIT	5	36	21	58.3%	303	2	0	0	7.2%	7.4	--	66.0%	--	175	--	170	4	7	1	662.7%	16
2009	TB		518	312	60.1%	3499	12	15	9		5.6		-13.0%					45	205	3	20.6%	

2008:	18% Short	65% Mid	12% Deep	6% Bomb	YAC: 4.9 (--)	2007:	50% Short	30% Mid	12% Deep	8% Bomb	YAC: 3.8 (--)

Leftwich signed a two-year deal with the Bucs for one of two reasons. Either: a) the Bucs wanted a better veteran quarterback than Luke McCown on the roster to mentor Josh Freeman (most sane people's opinion); or b) the Bucs wanted to create a smokescreen to make other teams think they wouldn't draft Freeman, making it easier for the team to trade up and select him (Freeman's tinfoil hat opinion). Leftwich played well enough in relief efforts against the Redskins and Browns to earn a new contract, but he's now three full seasons removed from his last full-time starting gig, and his shortcomings are well-known. He may be finding his niche as the next Trent Dilfer.

Matt Leinart　　Height: 6-5　Weight: 225　College: USC　　　　Draft: 2006/1 (10)　　Born: 11-May-1983　Age: 26　Risk: Green

Year	Team	G	Att	Comp	C%	Yds	TD	INT	FUM	ASR	NY/P	Rk	DVOA	Rk	DYAR	Rk	YAR	Runs	Yds	TD	DVOA	DYAR
2006	ARI	12	377	214	56.8%	2547	11	12	9	5.7%	6.4	19	-1.2%	20	246	19	215	22	49	2	4.7%	13
2007	ARI	5	112	60	53.6%	647	2	4	1	3.5%	5.4	37	-3.3%	25	58	30	72	11	42	0	1.0%	8
2008	ARI	4	29	15	51.7%	264	1	1	2	6.8%	8.0	--	-23.9%	--	-26	--	-20	4	5	0	63.7%	5
2009	ARI		547	321	58.6%	3473	19	17	14		5.5		-12.0%					46	199	2	16.1%	

2008:	23% Short	54% Mid	8% Deep	15% Bomb	YAC: 6.5 (--)	2007:	43% Short	39% Mid	10% Deep	9% Bomb	YAC: 4.3 (36)

Meet the one guy in Arizona who was probably disappointed to see the Cardinals re-sign Kurt Warner. That move sent Leinart back to the bench, where he has resided since his not-half-bad rookie season of 2006. Although Leinart had just seen the keys to the Cardinals offense yanked out of his hands, he assured Kent Somers of the *Arizona Republic* that he would not ask for a trade. Instead, he'll collect his reported $1.11 million 2009 salary and be content to play in preseason and blowout games, all while spending the coldest part of the year in sunny Phoenix. You know what? Maybe he wasn't disappointed when Warner came back.

Cleo Lemon　　Height: 6-2　Weight: 215　College: Arkansas State　　　　Draft: 2001/ FA　　Born: 16-Aug-1979　Age: 30　Risk: N/A

Year	Team	G	Att	Comp	C%	Yds	TD	INT	FUM	ASR	NY/P	Rk	DVOA	Rk	DYAR	Rk	YAR	Runs	Yds	TD	DVOA	DYAR
2006	MIA	4	68	38	55.9%	412	2	1	2	7.7%	6.0	--	4.9%	--	73	--	69	3	7	0	-19.2%	-1
2007	MIA	9	309	173	56.0%	1773	6	6	7	7.8%	4.9	45	-15.5%	38	-91	39	-71	31	102	4	24.5%	62
2008	JAC	1	2	0	0.0%	0	0	0	0	0.0%	0.0	--	-130.0%	--	-17	--	-13	2	-3	0	--	--

2008:	100% Short	0% Mid	0% Deep	0% Bomb	YAC: 4.9 (--)	2007:	49% Short	31% Mid	13% Deep	7% Bomb	YAC: 4.8 (21)

Lemon is best known as the primary quarterback for the Dolphins during the 1-15 season in 2007, but it wasn't as if his performance tipped the scales on a disastrous year. He signed a three-year, $8.1 million contract with the Jags before the 2008 season, which was right about the time the Jags started doing crazy things like giving a $30 million contact to Jerry Porter. Now, both players are ex-Jaguars; Jacksonville waived Lemon in June even though that leaves Todd Bouman as their top backup.

J.P. Losman

Height: 6-2 Weight: 217 College: Tulane Draft: 2004/1 (22) Born: 12-Mar-1981 Age: 28 Risk: N/A

Year	Team	G	Att	Comp	C%	Yds	TD	INT	FUM	ASR	NY/P	Rk	DVOA	Rk	DYAR	Rk	YAR	Runs	Yds	TD	DVOA	DYAR
2006	BUF	16	429	268	62.5%	3051	19	14	10	9.5%	6.3	22	-8.3%	27	85	25	12	38	140	1	-25.7%	-24
2007	BUF	8	175	111	63.4%	1204	4	6	2	7.3%	5.9	30	-8.9%	32	26	32	25	20	110	0	-10.7%	1
2008	BUF	5	104	63	60.6%	584	2	5	6	13.8%	4.1	41	-57.1%	41	-321	39	-293	12	70	2	58.4%	33

2008:	49% Short	41% Mid	4% Deep	6% Bomb	YAC: 4.3 (35)	2007:	52% Short	27% Mid	12% Deep	9% Bomb YAC: 5.2 (12)

Losman's last meaningful snap as in a Buffalo uniform was a microcosm of everything that went wrong during his tenure with the Bills. He executed a play fake that fooled no one, drifted off to his right, and never felt the backside pressure coming from Jets' safety Abram Elam. Rather than throw the ball away or take a sack that would have safeguarded a win, Losman tried to make something happen, and by fumbling he snatched defeat from the jaws of victory. Losman is mobile and throws a terrific deep ball, but his game management skills have barely advanced from his rookie season. He's a sack or a turnover waiting to happen. He may be in training camp for some team, but rumors have him playing for Jim Fassel's Las Vegas franchise in the new minor league UFL.

Eli Manning

Height: 6-4 Weight: 218 College: Mississippi Draft: 2004/1 (1) Born: 3-Jan-1981 Age: 28 Risk: Blue

Year	Team	G	Att	Comp	C%	Yds	TD	INT	FUM	ASR	NY/P	Rk	DVOA	Rk	DYAR	Rk	YAR	Runs	Yds	TD	DVOA	DYAR
2006	NYG	16	522	301	57.7%	3244	24	18	10	5.5%	5.9	36	3.9%	16	519	13	475	25	21	0	-38.8%	-17
2007	NYG	16	529	297	56.1%	3336	23	20	11	5.1%	5.6	32	-13.1%	35	-70	38	-60	29	69	1	-0.9%	11
2008	NYG	16	479	289	60.3%	3238	21	10	5	5.6%	6.1	19	19.7%	9	1032	9	942	20	10	1	17.2%	14
2009	NYG		502	306	60.9%	3356	21	13	7		6.1		11.2%					21	37	1	10.3%	

2008:	42% Short	38% Mid	12% Deep	8% Bomb	YAC: 4.1 (38)	2007:	46% Short	32% Mid	15% Deep	7% Bomb YAC: 4.4 (32)

Manning broke out by improving his accuracy on underneath throws, improving his completion percentage by four percentage points and cutting his interception ratio nearly in half. The bad news is that it's hard to hold onto these improvements; of the 18 quarterbacks who experienced similar "breakouts" in the past 30 years, 11 saw their completion percentage and interception ratio both regress in the subsequent season. Only two of the quarterbacks improved in both categories in the subsequent season: Doug Williams and Eli's brother, Peyton.

Eli's improvements came from more consistent footwork and the nature of his throws; with passes that previously went to Plaxico Burress and Jeremy Shockey heading towards the surer-handed Steve Smith and Kevin Boss, Manning was more likely to be bailed out if a throw was slightly off. While Manning led the league in passes dropped in 2008, he fell to 12th in 2009; meanwhile, he was tied for third in the league in dropped interceptions. Manning also had an absurd third-down split, putting up a DVOA of 48.8% on third down and 9.5% on the other downs. The evidence available points to Manning regressing some in 2009; expect something between his 2005-2007 level of performance and the guy who excelled for most of 2008.

Peyton Manning

Height: 6-5 Weight: 230 College: Tennessee Draft: 1998/1 (1) Born: 24-Mar-1976 Age: 33 Risk: Green

Year	Team	G	Att	Comp	C%	Yds	TD	INT	FUM	ASR	NY/P	Rk	DVOA	Rk	DYAR	Rk	YAR	Runs	Yds	TD	DVOA	DYAR
2006	IND	16	557	362	65.0%	4397	31	9	3	3.3%	7.8	4	51.0%	1	2308	1	2287	23	36	4	48.2%	42
2007	IND	16	515	337	65.4%	4040	31	14	7	4.2%	7.3	5	40.6%	2	1845	2	1679	20	-5	3	17.3%	16
2008	IND	16	555	371	66.8%	4002	27	12	1	2.8%	6.9	11	36.1%	1	1783	2	1780	20	21	2	-35.2%	-20
2009	IND		526	348	66.2%	4045	31	10	4		7.5		40.9%					21	37	1	-14.2%	

2008:	51% Short	30% Mid	10% Deep	9% Bomb	YAC: 4.2 (37)	2007:	45% Short	34% Mid	12% Deep	9% Bomb YAC: 4.5 (31)

An infection from offseason knee injury made Manning look decidedly human through the season's first seven games. At that point he had ten touchdowns and nine interceptions, and the Colts were 3-4. Manning then became Manning again, leading a 9-0 finish with 17 touchdowns and three interceptions, thanks in part to an impossibly weak schedule. Still, Manning lacked faith in either his own ability to evade the rush or his patchwork offensive line, and he was too content to take underneath routes. The good news was that his sacks stayed at their usual low level despite poor pass protection, but he completed the fewest 20-plus-yard passes of his career. With Marvin Harrison gone, and safeties cheating to Reggie Wayne's side, Manning will need to work on developing new options for big plays down the field. He remains the safest play in fantasy football for what seems like the tenth straight year.

Josh McCown   Height: 6-4   Weight: 212   College: Sam Houston State   Draft: 2002/3 (81)   Born: 4-Jul-1979   Age: 30   Risk: Green

Year	Team	G	Att	Comp	C%	Yds	TD	INT	FUM	ASR	NY/P	Rk	DVOA	Rk	DYAR	Rk	YAR	Runs	Yds	TD	DVOA	DYAR
2007	OAK	9	190	111	58.4%	1151	10	11	11	6.9%	5.2	40	-29.1%	48	-239	48	-169	29	143	0	-11.4%	1
2009	CAR		357	213	59.7%	2097	7	12	11		4.7		-32.7%					39	75	1	-0.5%	

2007:	50% Short	26% Mid	12% Deep	11% Bomb	YAC: 4.9 (20)

McCown signed with Miami last year, but became expendable after the Dolphins acquired Chad Pennington in the 2008 preseason. He signed with Carolina but never threw a pass, which may have been cathartic after accruing two careers worth of punishment in his stints with the Cardinals, Raiders, and Lions. McCown's only action in Carolina was four kneeldowns to end two of the Panthers' wins. How unfamiliar must that have been? Considering he had 39 fumbles in 46 career games prior to 2008, we think it's nice that McCown was trusted to carry out that duty. Job well done. Despite McCown's experience, he may lose his backup job to Matt Moore, who the Panthers like as their quarterback of the future.

Luke McCown   Height: 6-3   Weight: 208   College: Louisiana Tech   Draft: 2004/4 (106)   Born: 12-Jul-1981   Age: 28   Risk: Yellow

Year	Team	G	Att	Comp	C%	Yds	TD	INT	FUM	ASR	NY/P	Rk	DVOA	Rk	DYAR	Rk	YAR	Runs	Yds	TD	DVOA	DYAR
2007	TB	5	139	94	67.6%	1009	5	3	3	11.0%	6.0	27	-13.9%	36	-28	35	97	12	117	0	86.7%	52
2008	TB	2	1	0	0.0%	0	0	0	0	0.0%	0.0	--	0.0%	--	0	--	--	3	15	0	178.9%	2
2009	TB		479	306	63.8%	2976	16	12	12		5.4		-6.4%					53	284	1	-22.6%	

2007:	61% Short	22% Mid	14% Deep	4% Bomb	YAC: 5.3 (8)

McCown has stuck around the fringes of a starting opportunity for years now; occasionally, a player who gets talked up like this turns into Jake Delhomme. More frequently, though, perpetually-hyped backup quarterbacks end up looking like J.T. O'Sullivan when they finally get their chance. McCown was expected to get that chance after re-signing in Tampa, but the Bucs followed that move by signing Byron Leftwich and drafting Josh Freeman in the first round.

Donovan McNabb   Height: 6-2   Weight: 226   College: Syracuse   Draft: 1999/1 (2)   Born: 25-Jan-1976   Age: 33   Risk: Green

Year	Team	G	Att	Comp	C%	Yds	TD	INT	FUM	ASR	NY/P	Rk	DVOA	Rk	DYAR	Rk	YAR	Runs	Yds	TD	DVOA	DYAR
2006	PHI	10	316	180	57.0%	2647	18	6	4	7.2%	8.0	2	18.8%	6	660	9	751	32	212	3	58.9%	95
2007	PHI	14	473	291	61.5%	3324	19	7	7	8.5%	6.0	24	8.2%	18	658	14	666	50	236	0	2.3%	28
2008	PHI	16	571	345	60.4%	3916	23	11	7	4.5%	6.4	15	15.6%	12	1048	8	1079	39	147	2	-31.3%	-38
2009	PHI		502	316	62.9%	3761	21	8	11		6.7		25.0%					50	174	2	9.9%	

2008:	48% Short	32% Mid	14% Deep	6% Bomb	YAC: 5.0 (17)	2007:	49% Short	33% Mid	12% Deep	6% Bomb	YAC: 5.2 (11)

Donovan McNabb defies all labels. He's no longer the mobile quarterback of his youth, but he's recovered enough from his injuries to be a plus in the running game. He's accurate enough to play quarterback in a West Coast offense, but his erratic mechanics yield stretches of extreme wildness (he led the league with 14 incompletes where our game charters marked the defender as "Hole in Zone"). He's capable of looking like an All-Pro and a scared rookie in the same game, but his seasonal numbers are remarkably consistent from year to year. He was great on third down a year ago after being far below his average on first and second down in each of the previous three seasons. He's the franchise quarterback who needs an extension weeks after he's the over-the-hill quarterback who needs to be released.

What is McNabb at this point, then, besides the human manifestation of variance and arguments against small sample size? The operative word is capable. On any given play, McNabb is capable of being the best quarterback in the NFL. He's going to go through peaks and valleys, but over the course of an entire year, he's going to be good enough to give the Eagles a chance to go to the Super Bowl. In a less tolerant organization, though, McNabb would likely be gone after being affixed to the bench following his demotion at halftime against the Ravens. Had Rex Ryan dialed back the pressure and Kevin Kolb had a great day, McNabb might never have found his way back to the Philly starting job. If his next valley is that low, he might not make it back up.

Kevin O'Connell

Height: 6-6 Weight: 228 College: San Diego State   Draft: 2008/3 (94) Born: 25-May-1985 Age: 24 Risk: Yellow

Year	Team	G	Att	Comp	C%	Yds	TD	INT	FUM	ASR	NY/P	Rk	DVOA	Rk	DYAR	Rk	YAR	Runs	Yds	TD	DVOA	DYAR
2008	NE	2	6	4	66.7%	23	0	0	0	13.9%	3.0	--	-51.4%	--	-18	--	-17	3	-6	0	--	--
2009	NE		464	295	63.6%	3430	24	11	5		7.0		20.4%					35	86	2	-15.4%	

2008:	50% Short	50% Mid	0% Deep	0% Bomb	YAC: 3.0 (--)

One of the reasons the Pats felt comfortable trading Matt Cassel was their confidence in O'Connell's development. He's got the right pedigree for a New England "where the hell did this guy come from?" quarterback: an under-the-radar college prospect with workable mechanics. He'll fight it out with Matt Gutierrez for the spot behind Tom Brady, though he probably has the inside track at this point. At San Diego State, O'Connell received tutelage from Aztecs head coach and former NFL quarterback Chuck Long, led his team in rushing and passing in 2007, and was the only quarterback invited to the 2008 Scouting Combine who wasn't listed as a pro prospect at his position before the season. Conventional wisdom says he'll need serious development to do anything at the NFL level, but isn't what what we all said about Matt Cassel?

Dan Orlovsky

Height: 6-4 Weight: 238 College: Connecticut   Draft: 2005/5 (145) Born: 18-Aug-1983 Age: 26 Risk: Green

Year	Team	G	Att	Comp	C%	Yds	TD	INT	FUM	ASR	NY/P	Rk	DVOA	Rk	DYAR	Rk	YAR	Runs	Yds	TD	DVOA	DYAR
2008	DET	10	255	143	56.1%	1616	8	8	3	5.5%	5.7	29	0.3%	23	198	26	157	7	29	0	56.1%	13
2009	HOU		439	250	56.9%	2838	13	15	11		5.5		-12.7%					32	98	1	-27.9%	

2008:	44% Short	31% Mid	14% Deep	11% Bomb	YAC: 4.4 (32)

Orlovsky became a symbol of the Lions' ineptitude when he unknowingly waggled out of the end zone during his first start, resulting in a safety and a lifetime lowlight for the young quarterback. He actually played pretty well outside of his gaffe, becoming the only one of Detroit's five quarterbacks to record a positive DVOA on the season. He left Detroit after the year and made his way to Houston, where he'll be the primary backup to a very injury-prone quarterback. He could surprise if — or when — given the chance.

Kyle Orton

Height: 6-4 Weight: 226 College: Purdue   Draft: 2005/4 (106) Born: 14-Nov-1982 Age: 27 Risk: Green

Year	Team	G	Att	Comp	C%	Yds	TD	INT	FUM	ASR	NY/P	Rk	DVOA	Rk	DYAR	Rk	YAR	Runs	Yds	TD	DVOA	DYAR
2007	CHI	3	80	43	53.8%	478	3	2	2	4.0%	5.7	--	-25.0%	--	-72	--	-6	5	-1	0	-30.3%	-3
2008	CHI	15	465	272	58.5%	2972	18	12	6	5.9%	5.7	27	-0.9%	25	334	21	323	24	39	3	-15.4%	-3
2009	DEN		581	361	62.2%	3473	17	15	13		5.2		-6.6%					16	38	0	-5.9%	

2008:	52% Short	26% Mid	16% Deep	6% Bomb	YAC: 5.0 (16)	2007:	51% Short	35% Mid	7% Deep	7% Bomb	YAC: 6.6 (--)

For all the missteps Josh McDaniels may have taken this offseason, acquiring Orton in the Jay Cutler deal may prove to be a masterstroke. Orton was en route to an excellent year before hurting his ankle and coming back too early; he had a DVOA of 18.5% before the injury and -22.9% afterwards. It's admittedly difficult to reconcile Orton's pre-2008 persona with the performance level of a franchise quarterback, but ask yourself this: How would Orton be perceived had he not been rushed into action as a rookie? He'd be an emerging star, not a punchline with half a good season to his name. Credit goes to McDaniels and Brian Xanders for judging the player for what he is, not what he once was.

J.T. O'Sullivan
Height: 6-2 Weight: 220 College: UC Davis   Draft: 2002/6 (186) Born: 25-Aug-1979 Age: 30 Risk: Yellow

Year	Team	G	Att	Comp	C%	Yds	TD	INT	FUM	ASR	NY/P	Rk	DVOA	Rk	DYAR	Rk	YAR	Runs	Yds	TD	DVOA	DYAR
2007	DET	4	26	13	50.0%	148	1	2	1	10.2%	4.5	--	-21.5%	--	-18	--	0	4	-10	0	-255.8%	-33
2008	DET	9	220	128	58.2%	1678	8	11	11	12.8%	6.0	24	-37.3%	40	-414	41	-292	30	145	0	9.1%	20
2009	CIN		409	259	63.3%	2553	14	16	13		5.1		-22.7%					42	87	1	-7.5%	

2008:	45% Short	27% Mid	21% Deep	7% Bomb	YAC: 6.7 (1)	2007:	46% Short	33% Mid	4% Deep	17% Bomb	YAC: 6.2 (--)

Despite ranking dead last in DYAR for quarterbacks with more than 100 passing attempts last year, O'Sullivan still received $128,164 under the NFL's "performance pay" system. It's probably safe to assume he hasn't been a vocal critic of Wall Street bonuses, either. He was mercifully released by San Francisco in the offseason, and found his way to Cincinnati, where he'll serve as the primary backup to Carson Palmer as the latter returns from his elbow injury. If the Bengals ever actually need to use O'Sullivan to do more than hold a clipboard, they'll wish they'd invested more on their backup quarterback spot. They didn't learn from last year?

Carson Palmer
Height: 6-5 Weight: 230 College: USC   Draft: 2003/1 (1) Born: 27-Dec-1979 Age: 29 Risk: Red

Year	Team	G	Att	Comp	C%	Yds	TD	INT	FUM	ASR	NY/P	Rk	DVOA	Rk	DYAR	Rk	YAR	Runs	Yds	TD	DVOA	DYAR
2006	CIN	16	520	324	62.3%	4035	28	13	16	6.1%	7.3	6	21.7%	4	1189	3	1007	26	37	0	-9.3%	2
2007	CIN	16	575	373	64.9%	4131	26	20	8	3.2%	6.8	11	20.1%	9	1215	6	1204	24	10	0	-17.8%	-3
2008	CIN	4	129	75	58.1%	731	3	4	2	7.9%	4.8	39	-5.0%	29	54	30	-56	6	38	0	50.0%	15
2009	CIN		506	306	60.5%	3554	22	12	8		6.3		12.2%					14	45	0	24.4%	

2008:	45% Short	41% Mid	11% Deep	2% Bomb	YAC: 4.7 (27)	2007:	45% Short	32% Mid	16% Deep	7% Bomb	YAC: 4.1 (38)

Palmer's decision to avoid surgery on his right elbow will be closely watched, and open to 20/20 hindsight if the franchise quarterback has to miss time because of it in 2009. Palmer has shown Borg-like regenerative ability before, rehabbing a nuked knee over a single offseason in 2006. As Will Carroll says, it's better to not cut than to cut, and Palmer declared his elbow fully healed in April, so let's assume he's ready to play. The Bengals offensive line had more holes than a whiffle ball last year, and the unit's ability to protect Palmer will determine whether Cincinnati will waste another year of his career. Palmer's first-down passing splits were atrocious, as defenses could easily stop the run while still doubling Cincy's receivers. He was much more effective out of the shotgun, which may have resulted from the lack of reps with his top receivers in the offseason hurting his timing (T.J. and the Ocho sat out, Chris Henry was suspended). Palmer and his wife welcomed twins to the world in January, so regardless of the strength of his elbow, his mind is probably mush.

Chad Pennington
Height: 6-3 Weight: 225 College: Marshall   Draft: 2000/1 (18) Born: 26-Jun-1976 Age: 33 Risk: Red

Year	Team	G	Att	Comp	C%	Yds	TD	INT	FUM	ASR	NY/P	Rk	DVOA	Rk	DYAR	Rk	YAR	Runs	Yds	TD	DVOA	DYAR
2006	NYJ	16	485	313	64.5%	3352	17	16	6	5.9%	6.7	14	10.4%	13	740	7	595	35	109	0	4.6%	23
2007	NYJ	9	260	179	68.8%	1765	10	9	3	9.1%	5.6	34	-3.6%	26	141	24	77	20	32	1	-30.3%	-21
2008	MIA	16	476	321	67.4%	3653	19	7	3	5.0%	7.1	10	25.7%	5	1172	6	1399	30	62	1	36.8%	32
2009	MIA		492	321	65.2%	3576	22	14	7		6.6		15.3%					29	105	1	-7.7%	

2008:	47% Short	35% Mid	14% Deep	5% Bomb	YAC: 4.3 (34)	2007:	52% Short	30% Mid	12% Deep	5% Bomb	YAC: 3.6 (47)

Bill Parcells knew what he was doing with he selected Pennington with the 18th pick in the 2000 draft — this is the quintessential Tuna quarterback. A professional through and through who knows that his role is just as transitory as the whims of the Godfather, Pennington led the Dolphins back from the abyss in 2008 with an efficiency required from his anonymous receiver corps and a willingness to fit in that included lining up wide in various Wildcat formations. This year, he'll get a little heat from the two quarterbacks Parcells has taken in the second round of the last two drafts — Chad Henne and Pat White — and he will likely move on to another team in 2010. Still, although he's about five chapters down in Miami's unbelievable comeback story, none of it could have happened without him.

Brady Quinn   Height: 6-4   Weight: 232   College: Notre Dame   Draft: 2007/1 (22)   Born: 27-Oct-1984   Age: 25   Risk: Yellow

Year	Team	G	Att	Comp	C%	Yds	TD	INT	FUM	ASR	NY/P	Rk	DVOA	Rk	DYAR	Rk	YAR	Runs	Yds	TD	DVOA	DYAR
2007	CLE	1	8	3	37.5%	45	0	0	0	1.6%	5.6	--	3.2%	--	7	--	8	0	0	0	--	--
2008	CLE	3	89	45	50.6%	518	2	2	0	1.1%	5.7	--	-23.1%	--	-68	--	26	5	21	0	29.5%	7
2009	CLE		486	288	59.3%	3411	15	16	14		6.1		-0.4%					30	135	0	-5.0%	

2008:	48% Short	36% Mid	10% Deep	6% Bomb	YAC: 5.3 (--)	2007:	14% Short	86% Mid	0% Deep	0% Bomb	YAC: 6.0 (--)

Three games aren't a lot to gauge a player's potential on. Quinn looked very solid in a Thursday night loss to the Broncos, then played poorly in a game and a half against the Bills and Texans before breaking a finger. His performances and raw stats were bad enough to worry Browns fans but good enough to prompt offseason trade interest from the Jets and Broncos (whose new coach is a collector of such curios). Quinn should enter camp as the Browns starter, but Brett Ratliff arrived in the draft day trade, and Ratliff has a way of making August his own. Many of our indicators, starting with the Lewin Career Forecast, are positive for Quinn. We don't have an indicator for the fickle heart of a coach looking to put his stamp on a team.

Patrick Ramsey   Height: 6-2   Weight: 218   College: Tulane   Draft: 2002/1 (32)   Born: 14-Feb-1979   Age: 30   Risk: Red

Year	Team	G	Att	Comp	C%	Yds	TD	INT	FUM	ASR	NY/P	Rk	DVOA	Rk	DYAR	Rk	YAR	Runs	Yds	TD	DVOA	DYAR
2007	DEN	2	48	29	60.4%	262	1	1	1	6.4%	4.9	--	-24.5%	--	-44	--	14	2	6	0	19.3%	5
2008	DEN	1	3	2	66.7%	19	0	0	1	26.1%	3.3	--	-111.5%	--	-26	--	-26	0	0	0	--	--
2009	TEN		425	224	52.8%	2372	8	12	6		4.7		-23.4%					35	84	0	34.8%	

2008:	100% Short	0% Mid	0% Deep	0% Bomb	YAC: 5.0 (--)	2007:	59% Short	30% Mid	9% Deep	2% Bomb	YAC: 2.9 (--)

What is Patrick Ramsey's role in Tennessee? On the surface, it seems the Titans signed Ramsey specifically to give Vince Young's ego a swift kick in the ass. During camp, you'll hear so much about Ramsey pushing Young that you may begin to assume they are a two-man bobsled team. And yet, Ramsey worked well with Mike Heimerdinger in Denver two years ago, and his style is much more similar to that of Kerry Collins. If Collins goes down in the middle of the game, which makes more sense: Trying to take advantage of an unprepared defense with the scrambling Young, or using a quarterback like Ramsey who can steadily execute the original game plan?

Chris Redman   Height: 6-3   Weight: 223   College: Louisville   Draft: 2000/3 (75)   Born: 7-Jul-1977   Age: 32   Risk: Blue

Year	Team	G	Att	Comp	C%	Yds	TD	INT	FUM	ASR	NY/P	Rk	DVOA	Rk	DYAR	Rk	YAR	Runs	Yds	TD	DVOA	DYAR
2007	ATL	7	149	89	59.7%	1079	10	5	3	5.7%	6.5	14	5.5%	21	163	23	221	8	16	0	-79.7%	-20
2009	ATL		387	230	59.5%	2366	12	13	12		5.2		-15.3%					26	62	1	0.4%	

2007:	48% Short	34% Mid	11% Deep	7% Bomb	YAC: 5.4 (4)

Redman may have been the only person in the state of Georgia who was sorry to see Bobby Petrino go. The Louisville grad had signed with the Austin Wranglers of the Arena League when Petrino brought him to Atlanta. 2007 was a General Sherman-level disaster for the Falcons, but Redman showed flashes of decency in four starts, with an NFC Player of the Week nod after he dropped four touchdown passes on the Seahawks. But then his rabbi blew town for Arkansas, Matt Ryan was drafted, and Redman returned to the bench. He didn't play a down in 2008, and will only get action in case of a Ryan injury. If he can shake off the rust, Redman should provide decent short-term relief. Otherwise, that 2007 call from Petrino still let Redman spend two years collecting sizable paychecks to watch Ryan play. There are worse jobs.

Philip Rivers

Height: 6-4   Weight: 226   College: North Carolina State   Draft: 2004/1 (4)   Born: 8-Dec-1981   Age: 28 Risk: Green

Year	Team	G	Att	Comp	C%	Yds	TD	INT	FUM	ASR	NY/P	Rk	DVOA	Rk	DYAR	Rk	YAR	Runs	Yds	TD	DVOA	DYAR
2006	SD	16	460	284	61.7%	3388	22	9	7	6.2%	7.0	9	17.9%	7	904	6	943	48	49	0	-41.7%	-45
2007	SD	16	460	277	60.2%	3152	21	15	11	4.4%	6.2	20	6.9%	20	551	16	450	29	33	1	-23.6%	-12
2008	SD	16	478	312	65.3%	4009	34	11	8	5.4%	7.7	2	35.6%	2	1522	3	1621	31	84	0	-9.8%	3
2009	SD		468	309	66.0%	3724	31	10	5		7.5		41.8%					25	48	1	-11.2%	

| 2008: | 47% Short | 29% Mid | 16% Deep | 8% Bomb | YAC: 5.5 (6) | 2007: | 48% Short | 29% Mid | 16% Deep | 8% Bomb YAC: 4.6 (27) |

The patron saint of the Lewin Career Forecast had a year to remember in 2008, ranking among or at the top of the league in virtually every metric. Even more impressively, there are no indicators that Rivers' sublime performance was buoyed by flukiness; in fact, it's downright eerie how consistently good Rivers was. He was just as good on second down (46.5% DVOA) as he was on third down (47.7%). He was great both in the shotgun (30.7%) and out of it (38.9%), and he matched his standard level of performance when inside the red zone (35.2%). Remember that he did it all on a healing torn ACL, and it's shocking that Rivers didn't make more noise in the MVP race. If the Chargers live up to our projections in 2009, Rivers will certainly be in the reckoning.

Aaron Rodgers

Height: 6-2   Weight: 223   College: California   Draft: 2005/1 (24)   Born: 2-Dec-1983   Age: 26 Risk: Green

Year	Team	G	Att	Comp	C%	Yds	TD	INT	FUM	ASR	NY/P	Rk	DVOA	Rk	DYAR	Rk	YAR	Runs	Yds	TD	DVOA	DYAR
2006	GB	2	15	6	40.0%	46	0	0	1	15.4%	1.9	--	-59.4%	--	-54	--	-68	2	11	0	25.6%	3
2007	GB	2	28	20	71.4%	218	1	0	0	9.2%	6.5	--	31.7%	--	84	--	68	7	29	0	27.8%	10
2008	GB	16	536	341	63.6%	4038	28	13	9	6.4%	6.8	12	14.8%	14	932	10	966	56	207	4	16.3%	73
2009	GB		505	295	58.4%	3696	24	13	13		6.3		8.6%					48	173	3	-8.0%	

| 2008: | 46% Short | 32% Mid | 14% Deep | 8% Bomb | YAC: 4.4 (31) | 2007: | 58% Short | 35% Mid | 4% Deep | 4% Bomb YAC: 6.3 (--) |

Rodgers laid the Favre controversy to rest quickly with a string of good games to start the season; by the time the Packers' bye week rolled around in Week 8, Rodgers was signing a six-year, $65 million contract extension. His success was driven by extraordinary performance on third down (35.3% DVOA, as opposed to 19.2% on first down and -7.7% on second down), almost exclusively on passes to Greg Jennings and James Jones, each of whom had the same sort of split. Don't be surprised if you see a slight downtick in Rodgers' cumulative numbers because he doesn't stay on the field as frequently as he did a year ago.

Ben Roethlisberger

Height: 6-4   Weight: 242   College: Miami (Ohio)   Draft: 2004/1 (11)   Born: 2-Mar-1981   Age: 28 Risk: Green

Year	Team	G	Att	Comp	C%	Yds	TD	INT	FUM	ASR	NY/P	Rk	DVOA	Rk	DYAR	Rk	YAR	Runs	Yds	TD	DVOA	DYAR
2006	PIT	15	469	280	59.7%	3513	18	23	5	8.4%	7.0	10	8.0%	15	616	11	428	32	98	2	-1.9%	15
2007	PIT	15	404	264	65.3%	3154	32	11	9	10.7%	6.3	19	15.7%	13	748	11	855	35	204	2	24.6%	65
2008	PIT	16	469	281	59.9%	3301	17	15	14	9.4%	5.9	25	-2.2%	27	288	23	228	34	102	1	-13.6%	-2
2009	PIT		473	297	62.8%	3639	25	12	9		6.8		20.0%					29	87	1	14.3%	

| 2008: | 41% Short | 39% Mid | 14% Deep | 7% Bomb | YAC: 4.5 (29) | 2007: | 36% Short | 40% Mid | 18% Deep | 6% Bomb YAC: 4.0 (43) |

Big Ben's 2008 season was statistically very similar to his 2006 season. His 2007 season was also similar, except for the touchdown total: Roethlisberger threw 23 red zone touchdowns that year, in contrast to 11 each in 2006 and 2008. What you see is what you get at this point: excellent durability, a relatively low completion percentage coupled with high yards per attempt, a too-high sack total in the mid-40s, and a touchdown-to-interception ratio below what you'd like from an elite quarterback. If the KUBIAK projection system is right, Roethlisberger may solve that touchdown-to-interception problem this year (with some help from a significantly easier out-of-division schedule). If KUBIAK is wrong, and 2007 was an aberration, then Roethlisberger's lack of development is a problem. If his production slips by a few percentage points, he'll be a below-average quarterback, and while his durability remains a major asset, he won't be able to play through concussions and cracked ribs forever. Roethlisberger may be the kind of quarterback who ages suddenly and falls out of the lineup soon after his 30th birthday. Luckily for him, he has two Super Bowl rings, so his legacy is safe.

Tony Romo
Height: 6-2 Weight: 227 College: Eastern Illinois Draft: 2003/FA Born: 21-Apr-1980 Age: 29 Risk: Yellow

Year	Team	G	Att	Comp	C%	Yds	TD	INT	FUM	ASR	NY/P	Rk	DVOA	Rk	DYAR	Rk	YAR	Runs	Yds	TD	DVOA	DYAR
2006	DAL	16	337	220	65.3%	2903	19	13	9	6.6%	8.2	1	18.9%	5	696	8	821	34	102	0	0.1%	14
2007	DAL	16	520	335	64.4%	4211	36	19	9	4.4%	7.4	4	25.5%	6	1295	4	1349	31	129	2	12.4%	28
2008	DAL	13	450	276	61.3%	3448	26	14	10	5.1%	7.1	8	18.5%	10	879	11	732	28	41	0	-12.2%	0
2009	DAL		492	303	61.6%	3666	25	12	10		6.5		18.8%					38	96	1	24.7%	

2008: 44% Short 36% Mid 12% Deep 8% Bomb YAC: 5.6 (4) 2007: 40% Short 42% Mid 12% Deep 7% Bomb YAC: 5.0 (18)

Romo has shown the rare ability to consistently raise his level of play on third down; in each of his three seasons as a starter, his DVOA on third down has far surpassed that of first and second down. It comes down to Romo's propensity for keeping plays alive and improvising with his receivers while remaining accurate outside the pocket. The solution, defensive coordinators? Blitz more. Romo's success rate goes down as the defense sends more rushers; on plays where the defense sent three, Romo's success rate in 2008 was 56 percent; that dropped steadily with each rusher added, all the way down to a success rate of 33 percent when teams rushed seven. Romo might be able to slip past one would-be sack artist on every down, but he can't get past three or four.

Sage Rosenfels
Height: 6-4 Weight: 218 College: Iowa State Draft: 2001/4 (109) Born: 6-Mar-1978 Age: 31 Risk: Yellow

Year	Team	G	Att	Comp	C%	Yds	TD	INT	FUM	ASR	NY/P	Rk	DVOA	Rk	DYAR	Rk	YAR	Runs	Yds	TD	DVOA	DYAR
2006	HOU	4	39	27	69.2%	265	3	1	0	4.3%	6.9	--	47.3%	--	158	--	156	4	5	0	-49.2%	-5
2007	HOU	9	240	154	64.2%	1684	15	12	4	2.6%	6.7	13	24.3%	7	599	15	373	21	51	1	41.5%	30
2008	HOU	6	174	116	66.7%	1431	6	10	4	5.4%	7.6	3	3.7%	21	183	27	140	11	37	0	-60.6%	-27
2009	MIN		469	303	64.6%	2968	19	12	5		5.6		-1.3%					22	26	0	-14.1%	

2008: 47% Short 35% Mid 14% Deep 4% Bomb YAC: 5.4 (8) 2007: 46% Short 35% Mid 13% Deep 7% Bomb YAC: 3.8 (45)

Rosenfels is in that uncomfortable place where he is a great backup quarterback, but a team is in trouble if he is the starter. His completion percentage and yards per attempt were actually a little better than Matt Schaub's, but Rosenfels threw interceptions twice as frequently. His meltdown against the Colts in Week 11, where he single-handedly gave the game away with three fourth-quarter turnovers, was extreme but emblematic of Rosenfels' inability to protect the ball. If Brett Favre doesn't show up, Minnesota will have a difficult decision between Rosenfels and Jackson. Each one probably ranks somewhere between the 25th and 35th best quarterbacks in the world, but as a starter for a playoff contender, that is a liability more often than not.

JaMarcus Russell
Height: 6-6 Weight: 265 College: LSU Draft: 2007/1 (1) Born: 9-Aug-1985 Age: 24 Risk: Red

Year	Team	G	Att	Comp	C%	Yds	TD	INT	FUM	ASR	NY/P	Rk	DVOA	Rk	DYAR	Rk	YAR	Runs	Yds	TD	DVOA	DYAR
2007	OAK	4	66	36	54.5%	373	2	4	5	8.9%	4.7	--	-42.7%	--	-144	--	-208	5	4	0	-36.2%	-3
2008	OAK	15	368	198	53.8%	2423	13	8	12	8.0%	5.6	30	-16.0%	34	-122	35	-4	17	127	1	18.6%	31
2009	OAK		488	265	54.3%	3235	14	9	9		5.7		-6.7%					38	139	2	-23.4%	

2008: 42% Short 32% Mid 19% Deep 7% Bomb YAC: 5.3 (12) 2007: 53% Short 29% Mid 10% Deep 8% Bomb YAC: 4.3 (--)

So it turns out that when you take a player whose natural talent surpasses his command of the fundamentals, and you put him on a franchise that's a complete circus, things don't turn out well. Who knew? The Oakland chapter goes in depth on the poor outlook for quarterbacks who post negative DYAR in their first two seasons. If you are looking to buy Russell a 24th birthday present, may we suggest a Jeff Garcia voodoo doll?

Matt Ryan
Height: 6-5 Weight: 224 College: Boston College Draft: 2008/1 (3) Born: 17-May-1985 Age: 24 Risk: Green

Year	Team	G	Att	Comp	C%	Yds	TD	INT	FUM	ASR	NY/P	Rk	DVOA	Rk	DYAR	Rk	YAR	Runs	Yds	TD	DVOA	DYAR
2008	ATL	16	434	265	61.1%	3440	16	11	5	3.5%	7.4	4	30.9%	4	1167	7	1030	55	104	1	-30.0%	-34
2009	ATL		470	280	59.5%	3184	21	11	12		6.1		13.7%					47	247	2	26.2%	

2008: 42% Short 36% Mid 13% Deep 8% Bomb YAC: 5 (18)

Ryan dwarfed fellow rookie Joe Flacco's stats (nearly 800 more DYAR, for example), in case there was any question about the Rookie of the Year voting after the postseason. Atlanta's potent running attack was enough threat to allow Ryan to be far and away the best quarterback on first down (not counting tiny sample All-Pros Byron Leftwich and David Carr), with a DVOA of 52.1% and almost half of his DYAR. Ryan wowed the Falcons staff in pre-draft interviews with preternatural understanding of their offense, and gets a good bit of credit for Atlanta's vast improvement in Adjusted Sack Rate; he showed excellent ball skills and speedy decision-making that belied his experience. Along with the addition of Tony Gonzalez, that could help Ryan avoid the sophomore slump that the KUBIAK system is predicting.

Mark Sanchez   Height: 6-3   Weight: 225   College: USC   Draft: 2009/1 (5)   Born: 11-Nov-1986   Age: 23   Risk: Green

Year	Team	G	Att	Comp	C%	Yds	TD	INT	FUM	ASR	NY/P	Rk	DVOA	Rk	DYAR	Rk	YAR	Runs	Yds	TD	DVOA	DYAR
2009	NYJ		458	254	55.6%	2981	13	16	7		6.0		-28.7%					23	84	1	-21.4%	

Midway through Sanchez's private workout with the Jets, coach Rex Ryan turned to general manager Mike Tannenbaum and said, "This is our guy. Let's go get him." The Jets did just that, so now the questions are, 1) Is Sanchez worth the price the team paid? and 2) When will he be ready to start? Judging from the effusive praise of analysts like the NFL Network's Mike Mayock and Mike Lombardi, the answers are: "Yes, and sooner than you think." Sanchez doesn't have Matthew Stafford's arm, and he has less starting experience than any first-round pick in recent memory, but he has great footwork, a mean play-action fake, and the ability to throw accurately while on the move. With Ryan's commitment to running the football, Sanchez's skill set fits the offense better than any other quarterback on the roster. It's because of that fit, and not because of his star quality, that Sanchez will likely be the opening day starter — but it's because of that lack of experience that his KUBIAK projection is so poor.

Matt Schaub   Height: 6-5   Weight: 237   College: Virginia   Draft: 2004/3 (90)   Born: 25-Jun-1981   Age: 28   Risk: Yellow

Year	Team	G	Att	Comp	C%	Yds	TD	INT	FUM	ASR	NY/P	Rk	DVOA	Rk	DYAR	Rk	YAR	Runs	Yds	TD	DVOA	DYAR
2006	ATL	16	27	18	66.7%	208	1	2	0	6.3%	7.4	--	47.2%	--	95	--	74	7	21	0	27.6%	8
2007	HOU	11	289	192	66.4%	2241	9	9	8	6.6%	7.1	6	8.2%	17	381	19	377	17	52	0	-8.2%	3
2008	HOU	11	380	251	66.1%	3043	15	10	10	6.7%	7.3	5	21.7%	8	863	12	672	31	68	2	4.0%	19
2009	HOU		511	322	63.1%	3633	19	11	11		6.3		12.1%					45	147	1	-13.1%	

2008:	50% Short	35% Mid	10% Deep	5% Bomb	YAC: 5.5 (7)	2007:	45% Short	38% Mid	10% Deep	7% Bomb	YAC: 4.0 (41)

Has a star quietly developed in Houston? Schaub's only real problem the past two years is staying on the field. He's missed five games in each of his two seasons as a full-time starter. He has been better on a per play basis than Eli Manning, for one, each of the past two seasons. Other than injuries, Schaub's one weakness is in the shotgun. Only JaMarcus Russell threw more passes from the shotgun while declining as much between regular and shotgun snaps.

Chris Simms   Height: 6-4   Weight: 220   College: Texas   Draft: 2003/3 (97)   Born: 29-Aug-1980   Age: 29   Risk: Yellow

Year	Team	G	Att	Comp	C%	Yds	TD	INT	FUM	ASR	NY/P	Rk	DVOA	Rk	DYAR	Rk	YAR	Runs	Yds	TD	DVOA	DYAR
2006	TB	3	106	58	54.7%	585	1	7	1	2.5%	5.3	43	-32.5%	44	-154	39	-215	4	7	1	58.8%	10
2008	TEN	1	2	1	50.0%	7	0	0	0	33.1%	-1.0	--	-78.0%	--	-14	--	-14	0	0	0	--	--
2009	DEN		577	383	66.3%	3386	15	16	17		5.2		-3.1%					30	52	0	-0.4%	

2008:	0% Short	50% Mid	0% Deep	50% Bomb	YAC: 1.0 (--)

Simms made it all the way back from a spleenectomy that ruined his 2006 season and cost him 2007, and he parlayed his good health into a free agent contract with Denver. Simms has a legitimate shot at playing time, competing with Kyle Orton to play with a quality collection of skill players. Orton is certainly the favorite for the job, but Simms' 2005 season, his last healthy one, is nearly as good as Orton's year last year. In truth, both quarterbacks are good enough to put pressure on the starter if they are backups, but not good enough to avoid leaving the door open for the other one. Nobody should be surprised if both start some games for Denver this season.

Alex Smith
Height: 6-4 Weight: 212 College: Utah Draft: 2005/1 (1) Born: 7-May-1984 Age: 25 Risk: Green

Year	Team	G	Att	Comp	C%	Yds	TD	INT	FUM	ASR	NY/P	Rk	DVOA	Rk	DYAR	Rk	YAR	Runs	Yds	TD	DVOA	DYAR
2006	SF	16	442	257	58.1%	2890	16	16	10	6.9%	6.1	25	-15.3%	35	-126	38	-119	44	147	2	-10.5%	3
2007	SF	7	193	94	48.7%	914	2	4	10	8.8%	3.8	50	-49.4%	49	-507	50	-429	13	89	0	35.6%	24
2009	SF		470	281	59.9%	2879	17	9	15		5.1		-9.5%					25	127	0	26.6%	

2007:	45% Short	32% Mid	12% Deep	10% Bomb	YAC: 3.4 (50)

For a guy who scored so high on the Wonderlic, it's hard to understand why Smith was so eager to restructure his contract to stay in San Francisco, where he'll almost certainly end up playing second-string to Shaun Hill. It's equally hard to figure out why Smith would ask Hill to be a groomsman at his wedding — did he want to compete with Hill for his fiance's attention too? The 49ers have promised him the opportunity to compete for a starting job, but Smith no longer has the protection or support of the front office or the coaching staff, and now he's getting paid like a backup.

Troy Smith
Height: 6-0 Weight: 225 College: Ohio State Draft: 2007/5 (174) Born: 20-Jul-1984 Age: 25 Risk: Green

Year	Team	G	Att	Comp	C%	Yds	TD	INT	FUM	ASR	NY/P	Rk	DVOA	Rk	DYAR	Rk	YAR	Runs	Yds	TD	DVOA	DYAR
2007	BAL	4	76	40	52.6%	452	2	0	5	4.5%	5.4	--	5.2%	--	85	--	41	12	54	1	17.5%	15
2008	BAL	5	4	3	75.0%	82	1	0	0	19.4%	16.2	--	184.2%	--	62	--	66	9	24	0	-10.0%	1
2009	BAL		453	284	62.8%	2558	13	11	7		5.0		-13.7%					65	305	1	43.4%	

2008:	0% Short	50% Mid	25% Deep	25% Bomb	YAC: 8.3 (--)	2007:	34% Short	45% Mid	15% Deep	6% Bomb	YAC: 4.3 (--)

In an October radio interview, Terrell Suggs said he thought Smith, not Joe Flacco, should be the Ravens starting quarterback, stating that Smith was "the better man for the job." Suggs later clarified/waffled/backpedaled, saying that the pair should split time. The comments could have sparked an ugly controversy, but they didn't because: A) the Ravens went on to win four straight games with Flacco as the starter, and B) everyone knows Suggs spends so much time with his foot in his mouth that his podiatrist had to marry his dentist.

All of Smith's 2008 action came in Wildcat packages: He ran some quarterback draws and played pitch-and-catch with Flacco for a few gadget big plays. The Wildcat disappeared as Flacco grew more comfortable and defenses figured out that Smith wasn't going to throw very often. Smith has the skills to be more than a gadget guy, but despite Suggs' endorsement, his career potential maxes out at the "peppery spark plug off the bench" level.

Jim Sorgi
Height: 6-3 Weight: 194 College: Wisconsin Draft: 2004/6 (193) Born: 3-Dec-1980 Age: 29 Risk: Blue

Year	Team	G	Att	Comp	C%	Yds	TD	INT	FUM	ASR	NY/P	Rk	DVOA	Rk	DYAR	Rk	YAR	Runs	Yds	TD	DVOA	DYAR
2007	IND	4	36	18	50.0%	132	1	0	2	4.7%	3.1	--	-1.9%	--	21	--	-8	6	-4	0	-1.9%	1
2008	IND	1	30	22	73.3%	178	0	0	0	0.5%	5.9	--	38.8%	--	109	--	62	5	8	0	75.2%	6
2009	IND		447	288	64.3%	2769	13	13	6		5.7		-1.8%					54	139	1	-27.1%	

2008:	79% Short	11% Mid	7% Deep	4% Bomb	YAC: 5.5 (--)	2007:	73% Short	15% Mid	9% Deep	3% Bomb	YAC: 4.2 (--)

A year ago, many people would have considered Sorgi a better quarterback than Matt Cassel. Now, Cassel has a contract with $36 million in guaranteed money, while Sorgi remains a Week 17 star earning $1 million. Sorgi's in the last year of his contract, and the drafting of Curtis Painter could make this his last year as Manning's caddy.

Matthew Stafford   Height: 6-3 Weight: 237 College: Georgia   Draft: 2009/1 (1)   Born: 7-Feb-1988   Age: 21 Risk: Yellow

Year	Team	G	Att	Comp	C%	Yds	TD	INT	FUM	ASR	NY/P	Rk	DVOA	Rk	DYAR	Rk	YAR	Runs	Yds	TD	DVOA	DYAR
2009	DET		487	246	50.6%	2882	16	18	7		5.6		-27.2%					42	244	2	39.6%	

In lieu of rehashing the Stafford debate again, let's review what Stafford needs to work on before he'll be ready to contribute as an NFL quarterback. Everyone knows about the arm, and no one doubts his ability to digest the playbook. Those are positives. The biggest issue with Stafford is his footwork; to use a term that might not fit all that well, he gets lazy at times. That results in the occasional sailed throw that gets picked off and looks bad. Donovan McNabb does the same thing, though, so it's not exactly a deal-breaker. He's agile, so he can escape the pocket when he needs to, but he fails to set himself when he's going to throw on the run and is inaccurate. That's fixable. Unlike most college quarterbacks, who struggle with their accuracy on the deep out, Stafford's problem is his ability to consistently throw underneath crossing patterns, and his propensity to give away play locations with sloppy screens. Those are also both footwork-related problems. If Daunte Culpepper can stay healthy, the Lions would prefer to have Stafford on the sidelines in 2009, adjusting to the speed of the game in practice and improving his footwork by working with quarterback coach Jeff Horton.

Tyler Thigpen   Height: 6-3 Weight: 220 College: Coastal Carolina   Draft: 2007/7 (217) Born: 14-Apr-1984   Age: 25 Risk: Green

Year	Team	G	Att	Comp	C%	Yds	TD	INT	FUM	ASR	NY/P	Rk	DVOA	Rk	DYAR	Rk	YAR	Runs	Yds	TD	DVOA	DYAR
2007	KC	1	6	2	33.3%	41	0	1	0	13.4%	4.6	--	-80.5%	--	-29	--	-38	0	0	0	--	--
2008	KC	14	420	230	54.8%	2608	18	12	4	6.2%	5.5	31	-6.2%	30	146	29	219	62	386	3	15.2%	78
2009	KC		457	229	50.2%	2897	18	17	12		5.5		-14.8%					57	294	2	3.1%	

| 2008: | 45% Short | 37% Mid | 9% Deep | 9% Bomb | YAC: 4.5 (30) | 2007: | 14% Short | 57% Mid | 14% Deep | 14% Bomb YAC: 14.0 (--) |

When you consider both his lack of experience and the quality of the Chiefs' offensive line, Thigpen's season showed promise. But it was far from a definitive statement that said this was the quarterback the Chiefs should build around for the future. He makes a good backup for Matt Cassel, because they have similar skills (getting into rhythm with the short pass, scrambling under pressure) except for Thigpen's inferior accuracy. If Thigpen does have to start again, the Chiefs will need to figure out why he faltered so much at the end of games. His 2008 stats show a clear, dramatic trend where he played very well in the first quarter, was mediocre in the second and third quarters, and then struggled to complete even short passes in the fourth quarter.

Tyler Thigpen by Quarter

	Comp	Att	Yds	C%	Yd/At	TD	INT	DVOA
1st Quarter	56	90	633	62%	7.0	5	1	25.1%
2nd Quarter	59	113	794	52%	7.0	8	5	-6.6%
3rd Quarter	53	93	557	57%	6.0	1	2	-10.5%
4th Quarter	62	120	626	52%	5.2	4	4	-25.2%

Billy Volek   Height: 6-2 Weight: 214 College: Fresno State   Draft: 2000/FA   Born: 28-Apr-1976   Age: 33 Risk: Green

Year	Team	G	Att	Comp	C%	Yds	TD	INT	FUM	ASR	NY/P	Rk	DVOA	Rk	DYAR	Rk	YAR	Runs	Yds	TD	DVOA	DYAR
2006	SD	1	2	1	50.0%	4	0	0	3	33.1%	-0.7	--	-136.1%	--	-26	--	-23	3	-3	0	--	--
2007	SD	5	10	3	30.0%	6	0	1	2	16.0%	-0.1	--	-167.3%	--	-121	--	-128	11	-7	0	-362.4%	-14
2009	SD		380	244	64.3%	2729	24	11	7		6.6		18.5%					5	12	0	29.8%	

| 2007: | 67% Short | 22% Mid | 0% Deep | 11% Bomb | YAC: 1.7 (--) |

Although Philip Rivers was coming off of reconstructive knee surgery last offseason, his recovery went well enough to keep Volek off the field in 2008. Yes, Volek earned $3,754,800 last year to live in San Diego and hold a clipboard every Sunday. If you read that statement and managed to avoid envy, well, you're a better person than we are.

Seneca Wallace
Height: 5-11   Weight: 196   College: Iowa State   Draft: 2003/4 (110)   Born: 6-Aug-1980   Age: 29   Risk: Green

Year	Team	G	Att	Comp	C%	Yds	TD	INT	FUM	ASR	NY/P	Rk	DVOA	Rk	DYAR	Rk	YAR	Runs	Yds	TD	DVOA	DYAR
2006	SEA	9	141	82	58.2%	927	8	7	6	9.3%	6.0	30	-28.3%	42	-165	40	-130	12	122	0	30.3%	21
2007	SEA	10	28	19	67.9%	215	2	1	1	10.9%	6.5	--	-14.6%	--	-7	--	7	4	17	0	27.5%	8
2008	SEA	10	242	141	58.3%	1532	11	3	4	5.6%	5.7	28	7.3%	19	295	22	286	16	78	0	1.3%	8
2009	SEA		421	249	59.3%	2852	18	14	7		6.3		2.0%					22	71	1	16.0%	

2008:	45% Short	39% Mid	10% Deep	6% Bomb	YAC: 5 (15)	2007:	54% Short	35% Mid	12% Deep	0% Bomb	YAC: 6.1 (--)

Wallace saw more action in 2008 than ever before, and he showed remarkable adequacy, especially given the injury woes Seattle suffered at wide receiver and along the offensive line. His greatest strength was his ability to avoid turnovers; only Jason Campbell threw for a lower interception rate, and he did it with a greater reliance on short passes. Wallace's reward for such success? A return to the bench and a position as one of the better backup passers in the league. Wallace may never get a chance to develop as a starting quarterback. He'll be 29 years old by the time the season starts, and that ship has sailed.

Andrew Walter
Height: 6-5   Weight: 234   College: Arizona State   Draft: 2005/3 (69)   Born: 11-May-1982   Age: 27   Risk: Green

Year	Team	G	Att	Comp	C%	Yds	TD	INT	FUM	ASR	NY/P	Rk	DVOA	Rk	DYAR	Rk	YAR	Runs	Yds	TD	DVOA	DYAR
2006	OAK	12	276	147	53.3%	1677	3	13	13	13.6%	5.1	44	-45.6%	46	-658	46	-619	14	30	0	-101.5%	-42
2007	OAK	1	8	5	62.5%	38	0	0	0	-0.4%	4.8	--	-11.5%	--	0	--	1	0	0	0	--	--
2008	OAK	2	49	22	44.9%	204	0	3	1	9.5%	3.1	--	-77.8%	--	-213	--	-232	5	19	0	-38.0%	-4
2009	OAK		464	282	60.8%	3098	15	14	13		5.4		-16.4%					38	166	1	-31.0%	

2008:	64% Short	20% Mid	11% Deep	5% Bomb	YAC: 6.4 (--)	2007:	63% Short	25% Mid	0% Deep	13% Bomb	YAC: 5.0 (--)

The Raiders expected to nurture the strong-armed Walter as their quarterback of the future when they took him in the third round of the 2005 draft. Even though he didn't get on the field as a rookie, they had enough confidence in him to pass on Matt Leinart with the seventh pick in 2006, which they used instead on Texas safety Michael Huff. Unfortunately, it turned out Walter did not possess superpowers which would allow him to bypass Oakland's complete lack of pass protection, so the Raiders used the first overall pick in 2007 to take an even stronger-armed quarterback, JaMarcus Russell. Last year, Leinart couldn't break into the Arizona lineup, Huff was benched, Russell was a disappointment, and when knee tendinitis forced Russell out of the lineup at midseason, the Panthers used Walter as a chew toy. This whole chain of events hasn't worked out well for anyone involved, has it?

Kurt Warner
Height: 6-2   Weight: 220   College: Northern Iowa   Draft: 1998/FA   Born: 22-Jun-1971   Age: 38   Risk: Red

Year	Team	G	Att	Comp	C%	Yds	TD	INT	FUM	ASR	NY/P	Rk	DVOA	Rk	DYAR	Rk	YAR	Runs	Yds	TD	DVOA	DYAR
2006	ARI	7	168	108	64.3%	1377	6	5	8	7.4%	7.5	5	-4.7%	23	74	27	154	13	3	0	-63.8%	-16
2007	ARI	14	451	281	62.3%	3417	27	17	9	5.2%	7.0	7	11.3%	16	699	12	878	17	15	1	-113.6%	-37
2008	ARI	16	598	401	67.1%	4583	30	14	11	5.0%	7.1	9	22.4%	6	1404	4	1446	18	-2	0	-63.1%	-12
2009	ARI		568	362	63.7%	4036	25	14	19		6.2		11.5%					12	15	0	-6.2%	

2008:	49% Short	35% Mid	10% Deep	6% Bomb	YAC: 5.1 (14)	2007:	41% Short	39% Mid	14% Deep	5% Bomb	YAC: 4.5 (30)

Warner's Super Bowl record is a microcosm of his entire career, an erratic collection of highs and lows. He holds the three highest passing-yardage games in Super Bowl history, and he's the only quarterback to twice lead Super Bowl comebacks, only to see his defense give the lead away each time. On the other hand, his team fell behind in the first place in part because Warner had thrown an interception that was returned for a touchdown. His entire career has been similarly filled with impossible peaks and plummeting valleys. A move to San Francisco just months after a shocking Super Bowl run would have ensured further intrigue, but after a dalliance with the 49ers, Warner re-signed with Arizona for two years and $19 million in guaranteed money. He still makes mistakes under a heavy pass rush; he ranked sixth in interceptions, fourth in fumbles last season. Still, this offense is built around his quick release and accuracy on short-range darts, and if the team is to return to the playoffs, they'll need Warner to excel once again.

Pat White Height: 6-1 Weight: 192 College: West Virginia Draft: 2009/2 (44) Born: 25-Feb-1986 Age: 23 Risk: Yellow

Year	Team	G	Att	Comp	C%	Yds	TD	INT	FUM	ASR	NY/P	Rk	DVOA	Rk	DYAR	Rk	YAR	Runs	Yds	TD	DVOA	DYAR
2009	MIA		25	17	69.5%	212	1	1	2		7.5		4.9%					40	208	3	7.3%	

White has the opportunity to legitimize the Wildcat. What the Dolphins did last year with the formation was exciting, and it was fun to watch copycats spring up around the league, but White was drafted specifically to run this offense because he's got a skill set that Ronnie Brown, Josh Cribbs, and most of the other Wildcat "quarterbacks" lack. White is a better passer than any other Cat, including Troy Smith, who ran some plays from the formation last year. He's also the right decision maker for the offense: a guy who knows how to read the defense on an option handoff or throw the ball away on an option pass. And of course, the guy can run. If White has a breakthrough rookie season, the Wildcat will cease to be a fad, and teams will draft White/Smith/Seneca Wallace types precisely for the role. If he flops, he'll likely take the Wildcat with him, and we'll go back to calling guys like him "Slash" players. Our projection for White also includes 17 receptions for 201 yards and a touchdown.

Vince Young Height: 6-5 Weight: 233 College: Texas Draft: 2006/1 (3) Born: 18-May-1983 Age: 26 Risk: Blue

Year	Team	G	Att	Comp	C%	Yds	TD	INT	FUM	ASR	NY/P	Rk	DVOA	Rk	DYAR	Rk	YAR	Runs	Yds	TD	DVOA	DYAR
2006	TEN	15	357	184	51.5%	2199	12	13	6	6.5%	5.8	38	-6.9%	25	99	24	9	83	552	7	3.1%	58
2007	TEN	15	382	238	62.3%	2546	9	17	8	6.7%	5.9	29	-8.4%	31	74	28	58	93	395	3	-9.7%	9
2008	TEN	3	36	22	61.1%	219	1	2	2	7.8%	5.2	--	-69.7%	--	-150	--	-121	8	27	0	-17.4%	-1
2009	TEN		438	252	57.5%	2544	9	13	9		4.7		-30.6%					95	422	2	15.7%	

| 2008: | 63% Short | 14% Mid | 9% Deep | 14% Bomb | YAC: 7.4 (--) | 2007: | 45% Short | 34% Mid | 12% Deep | 8% Bomb | YAC: 4.6 (28) |

From rookie of the year to playoff quarterback to the bench. Last season was a disappointment for Young, as his failure to develop led to his benching, which was emotionally devastating for someone who has always been great. Young was fairly impressive as a rookie, but he has failed to improve at all since then; the Titans' efforts to tailor their offense for Young held the team back. Young still has all the tools necessary to become a very good NFL quarterback. The question is whether his struggles lead him to work harder on improving his accuracy and his ability to read defenses — or whether his struggles lead him to spend more time complaining to the press.

GOING DEEP

Erik Ainge, NYJ: Ainge had a rough initiation into the NFL. He struggled mightily in training camp, was placed on IR with a foot injury, and still managed to get a four-game suspension for anabolic steroids. Ainge has excellent size, but he needs to get stronger, and he's carrying around a rented Chad Pennington arm. Any shot he had at getting consideration as a starter went out the window with the arrival of Mark Sanchez.

Brett Basanez, CHI: Basanez spent most of 2006 and all of 2008 on Carolina's practice squad, and missed all of 2007 with a wrist injury. The Northwestern product has come home to Chicago to compete with Caleb Hanie for the right to hold Jay Cutler's blood glucose meter.

Charlie Batch, PIT: Has now reached the Jason Garrett stage of his career: Batch is the third-stringer behind Ben Roethlisberger and an ever-changing backup. This year, Dennis Dixon is expected to supplant Batch, just as Byron Leftwich did last year. There are worse ways to ride out a recession. (2007 stats: 17-for-36, 232 yards, 2 TD, 3 INT, 0.5% DVOA, 28 DYAR.)

John Beck, BAL: The former BYU standout was a favorite of ex-Dolphins coach Cam Cameron when he was drafted in the second round by Miami in 2007. He got lost in the Parcells switch — buried behind Chad Henne — and signed with the Ravens (offensive coordinator: Cam Cameron) after Miami released him. He'll fight for a backup spot behind Joe Flacco in a friendly offense. (2007 stats: 60-for-107, 559 yards, 1 TD, 3 INT, -51.7% DVOA, -303 DYAR.)

Brock Berlin, STL: The only reason Berlin is in the book is because he was lucky enough to catch on with the Rams, who have a need for a third-string quarterback because of repeated injuries to Marc Bulger. Unfortunately, they also have a need for a new third-string quarterback because of repeated injuries to Brock Berlin. (2008 stats: 17-for-28, 153 yards, 0 TD, 1 INT, -22.6% DVOA, -19 DYAR.)

Todd Boeckman, JAC: A big, relatively immobile pocket passer, Boeckman was solid in 2007, completing 64 percent of his passes for 2,379 yards, 25 touchdowns, and 14 interceptions and leading Ohio State to the BCS Championship Game. In 2008, he split time with star freshman Terrelle Pryor and threw only 93 passes with five touchdowns and two interceptions. Far from evasive, Boeckman is only as good as the offensive line protecting him, but he has a strong, accurate arm if given time to throw.

Brooks Bollinger, FA: Good ol' Wee Brooks Bollinger looked good compared to Brad Johnson; once Johnson was benched, though, Bollinger threw an interception on his first pass. Bollinger finished the game, but didn't attempt another pass till Week 17. Bollinger was a free agent at press time and may end up in the new UFL. (2008 stats: 10-for-17, 71 yards, 1 TD, 1 INT, -55.2% DVOA, -52 DYAR.)

Rhett Bomar, NYG: The Giants' fifth-round pick started for Oklahoma as a freshman, but transferred to Sam Houston State after being dismissed from the Sooners for multiple infractions. He's mobile and has a huge arm, but will force throws and has a chip on his shoulder. In other words, he's a great Madden quarterback.

John David Booty, MIN: The USC product had a terrible rookie preseason and was lucky to make the roster; his shot at keeping the roster spot depends on how long he can distract Brad Childress with shiny things.

Tom Brandstater, DEN: At 6-foot-5, 220 pounds, Denver's sixth-round pick has long been considered a pro prospect because of his measurables, but after a breakout 2007 season, his peripheral numbers fell in 2008 due to a tougher slate. However, Fresno State's Passing S&P+ ranking (explained in the college football section of the book) went up, from 36th in 2007 to 34th in 2008. For his career, Brandstater completed 59 percent of his passes for 47 touchdowns and 32 interceptions.

Colt Brennan, WAS: Brennan enjoyed one of those greased-up statistical collegiate careers as a shotgun quarterback in June Jones' Hawaii system. The initial professional transition was about as expected, but there is room for encouragement. The transition from the college spread to the West Coast Offense isn't a pass length issue, which is fortunate for Brennan, as he doesn't have the arm, or the feel for play-action, that made former shotgun quarterback Joe Flacco so successful early on.

Brian Brohm, GB: Brohm was expected to serve as Aaron Rodgers' primary backup, but after putting up a 45.2 quarterback rating in the preseason, he fell behind Matt Flynn and was the team's third quarterback. Now that Aaron Rodgers has emerged as the long-term starter, Brohm's going to need a lot of things to go right to get a shot at a starting job. He may end up as the Lewin Career Forecast's biggest misfire.

Hunter Cantwell, CAR: Brohm's backup and eventual replacement at Louisville, Cantwell performed significantly worse in his lone year as the starter than Brohm did in the senior year that knocked him out of the first round. Because he's 6-foot-5, though, Cantwell caught on with the Panthers as an undrafted free agent. Carolina plays against Jason Campbell this year, so maybe they signed him for a scout team drill where Cantwell meanders aimlessly in the pocket and takes sacks.

Nate Davis, SF: The 49ers' fifth-round pick was athletic enough to run for 10 touchdowns in three years at Ball State, and his 64 percent completion rate last year helped the Cardinals start 12-0. His draft stock slid for two reasons. First, his hands: In BSU's two 2008 losses, Davis fumbled eight times. Second, concerns about his learning disability. "I don't think that in football I have a learning disability," said Davis after the draft, "It's just during school." To be honest, all that book learnin' hasn't exactly done wonders for Alex Smith's career.

A.J. Feeley, PHI: Usurped for the backup job by Kevin Kolb, Feeley did not get on the field in 2008. He need not concern himself with such frivolities, though; now that there's another women's professional soccer league in America, fiancee Heather Mitts can feed the family.

Charlie Frye, OAK: Frye spent the offseason working out with Kent State quarterback Julian Edelman, helping him make the transition to wide receiver. Edelman was drafted in the seventh round by the Patriots. Maybe Frye will one day be able to say that he helped make Edelman a success. That would be a much nicer legacy than Frye's touchdown-to-interception ratio of 16-to-25, or his career average of just 9.8 yards per completion. Signed by Oakland in June, because you can never have too many fourth-string quarterbacks.

Bruce Gradkowski, OAK: Gradkowski's name is Polish for "Spergon Wynn." He quarterbacked the Browns in two shutout losses at the end of last season; his longest completion spanned 12 yards, his second-longest five yards, and the 18 yards he lost in sacks ate up most of the 26 yards for which he passed on 21 attempts. To be fair, it wasn't a true indicator of Gradkowski's talents (he was signed one week before he entered the lineup), but any momentum he built up during a workmanlike starting stint in 2006 is long gone. (2008 stats: 7-for-21, 26 yards, 0 TD, 3 INT, -192.2% DVOA, -234 DYAR.)

Matt Gutierrez, NE: Gutierrez actually looked much stronger than Matt Cassel in the preseason, leading to some surprise when Cassel beat him out. Chalk that one up as Patriots front office 1, WEEI callers 0. Gutierrez is a big, mobile guy who will benefit from a system that is starting to look for quarterbacks like what Denver's offense is for running backs.

Gibran Hamdan, BUF: Hamdan was twice allocated to NFL Europa while a member of the Seattle Seahawks. The first time was in 2005, when he beat out Kurt Kittner, only to break his collarbone four games into the season. The Seahawks tried again in 2006, and Hamdan promptly broke his ankle in the seventh game. Should Trent Edwards and Ryan Fitzpatrick both miss time due to injury, history suggests that Hamdan would be joining them in short order.

Graham Harrell, CLE: A lob-and-catch spread quarterback at Texas Tech, Harrell put up silly numbers, including 10,816 yards, 93 touchdowns, and a completion rate over 70 percent in his final two seasons. Harrell's stats are pumped up by thousands of yards worth of tunnel screens, and he went undrafted despite good size and an adequate arm. The Browns brought him to camp to further confuse their quarterback situation; he's probably a camp arm, but Harrell could get his name added to the mix with a few good practices.

Drew Henson, FA: Yet another data point in the argument that players who can't decide between baseball and football at the professional level tend to wash out, Henson made his way to the Lions thanks to the presence of quarterback coach Scot Loeffler, who worked with Henson at Michigan. He threw two passes and took three sacks. Both Loeffler and Henson departed after the season, but Loeffler's the one with the job.

Josh Johnson, TB: For a spell in the offseason, Johnson appeared to be the untested, rawboned quarterback named Josh who would be handed the keys to the Bucs attack. In a selection heavily influenced by a great combine workout, the Bucs took Johnson in the fifth round of the 2008 draft. The coaches like his arm and size — they just like Josh Freeman's more.

Stephen McGee, DAL: This fourth-rounder is only the second quarterback the Cowboys have drafted in the past 18 years; as a strong-armed quarterback without much in the way of accuracy, he's not likely to even match the impact of the other one selected, Quincy Carter.

Matt Moore, CAR: After breaking his leg in the Panthers final preseason contest, Moore was inactive for most of the year. His injury prompted the Panthers to trade with Miami for Josh McCown to hold the clipboard. Despite his current third-string status on the depth chart, don't count out Moore as Carolina's quarterback of the future. His route to the NFL includes winning his first start as a true freshman for UCLA, transferring to Oregon State, getting drafted by the Los Angeles Angels, and being mentioned as a favorite sleeper pick of NFL Films' Greg Cosell during the 2005 draft. Harkening back to 2007, the Panthers went 2-1 in Moore's three starts to end the season, and he was named the NFL's Offensive Rookie of the Month in December. The Panthers may cash in on Moore's potential if Delhomme is on a short leash this year, which he already is with many fans. (2007 stats: 63-for-111, 730 yards, 3 TD, 5 INT, -2.8% DVOA, 66 DYAR.)

Keith Null, STL: A tall, strong-armed Division II quarterback whose quarterback coach at West Texas A&M was Ryan Leaf. That's gotta be worth a sixth-round pick, right?

Curtis Painter, IND: The Colts threw a bone to their fans by taking the hometown boy in the sixth round of this year's draft, and he'll compete with Jim Sorgi for the right to put up big fantasy numbers in Week 17. Throughout his career at Purdue, Painter tended to rack up big numbers against bad defenses and do little against good ones. As a junior in 2007, he completed 63 percent of his passes for 3,846 yards, 29 touchdowns and 11 interceptions — but Purdue ranked only 65th in our college metric "Passing S&P+," which takes into account the quality of opposing defense.

Jordan Palmer, CIN: Little bro was mistaken for Carson and mobbed by fans at the 2003 draft, when the elder Palmer was the first overall pick. It remains Jordan's signature NFL moment. (2008 stats: 7-for-12, 41 yards, 0 TD, 2 INT, -85.5% DVOA, -70 DYAR.)

Brett Ratliff, CLE: Eric Mangini liked Brett Ratliff so much that he insisted on including Ratliff as part of the package for Mark Sanchez. Ratliff played very well in the 2008 preseason, where he posted a quarterback rating of 122.6 and threw four touchdowns. He spent two years at Butte College, where he succeeded Aaron Rodgers, before finishing up his college career at Utah. He has good size and an above average arm, and while he may not be the starting quarterback in 2009, a Brady Quinn flop would put him in play for the job in 2010.

D.J. Shockley, ATL: If Shockley didn't tear his ACL in the 2007 preseason, it's almost certain he would have had some starts under his belt by now. In a different universe, Shockley impresses enough that season, and is popular enough from his time as a Georgia Bulldog, that the Falcons decide to select Glenn Dorsey instead of Matt Ryan in the 2008 draft. No amount of residual goodwill from Shockley's Dawg days (or Terrapin Pale Ale, the glorious microbrew bottled in Athens) is enough to convince any Falcons fan that outcome would have been better for the franchise.

Paul Smith, JAC: Smith shattered the school records at Tulsa, although it isn't like the Golden Hurricane had a long and prolific football history. He's a scrappy leader type who moves well in the pocket but is a bit undersized (6-foot-1) with arm strength somewhere between Troy Smith and Charlie Frye. Smith spent last year on the Jaguars practice squad and will compete with Todd Boeckman for the right to wonder why Todd Bouman is still in the league.

Drew Stanton, DET: Stanton got 17 passes to prove that he wasn't Detroit's quarterback of the future; now, sandwiched between Daunte Culpepper and Matthew Stafford, he's not likely to see the field and will have to hope that someone remembers his college days when he becomes a free agent in 2011. He took six sacks, which translates to 156 over a full season. (2008 stats: 9-for-17, 119 yards, 1 TD, 0 INT, -27.6% DVOA, -21 DYAR.)

Mike Teel, SEA: Teel was a nice "local boy makes good" story through most of his first two years as Rutgers starting quarterback, RU's best two-year span since 1978-79. When the Scarlet Knights fell on hard times early in 2008, he was the fall guy. He was temporarily benched as RU started 1-5, but he turned it on during their seven-game win streak to end the season. Teel is a fiery leader whose overall stats suggest steady improvement and belie his streakiness.

Marques Tuiasosopo, FA: Tui returned to the Raiders after a year in exile (a.k.a. New Jersey), but spent the whole season as the third quarterback, with more sacks (two) than complete passes (one). At age 30, you have to figure his NFL career is done.

Charlie Whitehurst, SD: The knock on Whitehurst has always been his inability to handle pressure and maintain his presence in the pocket. He was sacked five times in 58 dropbacks last preseason. Granted, he was playing behind the second-team line, but he was also up against second-team pass rushers. He's a free agent after the season, but no one would have wanted the first half of Matt Cassel's 2008, and that's what Whitehurst appears to be.

John Parker Wilson, ATL: Wilson played for three different offensive coordinators at Alabama, and by 2008 he was playing in a scaled-down system with simplified reads because every player in the program was suffering mental whiplash. Wilson played well in the new scheme and has a rep as a smart player and leader, but he's athletically limited, and of course he's now trapped behind Matt Ryan. He's a poor man's Jason Campbell and has the skills to be a useful backup.

Andre' Woodson, NYG: Woodson still has that great arm, but efforts to change his mechanics and speed up his delivery while improving his accuracy haven't taken. With the existing coaching staff sour on him, Woodson's likely to lose his roster spot to Rhett Bomar in training camp.

Anthony Wright, FA: Wright spent all of 2008 on IR with a neck injury suffered in the preseason. If he's not retiring, his attempt to go underground has been incredibly successful.

Running Backs

Every season, the first pick in most fantasy drafts will be the best running back in football. Usually, there's a national consensus about which one or two players should be considered with the first pick, but in 2009, the race will be wide open.

Adrian Peterson might be the favorite, but there are enough questions about his durability and relative lack of touchdowns to make a healthy amount of fantasy owners go elsewhere. Maurice Jones-Drew has the touchdowns and the pedigree in a smaller sample, but is unproven as a feature back. Matt Forte was a workhorse as a rookie and will get the touches needed to accrue massive yardage totals, but he'll need to score more as well. Steven Jackson's been hurt in each of the last two seasons. DeAngelo Williams had only had one big year and will split carries with Jonathan Stewart. Michael Turner was overworked a year ago.

It goes on. Even the players normally depended on as first-round backs have issues. LaDainian Tomlinson struggled with injuries and is sharing the workload with Darren Sproles. Fred Taylor looked painfully slow in Jacksonville and was cut; he now plays in a pass-happy attack in New England. Frank Gore has had health issues, not to mention "how often is San Francisco near the goal line?" issues. Brian Westbrook's already out for the preseason. There are very few safe bets in this year's crop of running backs.

That's reflected by KUBIAK, which projects 11 backs to be above 200 fantasy points in a standard league, with another eight backs in the range between 179 and 191 points. Of course, in a situation where your team's fantasy success might come down to taking the right one of those players, chance favors the prepared mind. So read up on this year's running backs, combine that research with training camp notes, and figure out who fits your league's scoring system best. (Remember: The relative value of Peterson compared to Jones-Drew and Forte changes dramatically in a "points per reception" league.)

In the following section we give the last three years' statistics as well as a 2009 KUBIAK projection for every running back who played a significant role in 2008, or is expected to play a significant role in 2009.

How to Read the Running Back Statistics Table

The first line contains biographical data — each player's name, height, weight, college, draft position, birth date, and age. Height and weight are the best data we could find; weight, of course, can fluctuate during the offseason. **Age** is very simple, the number of years between the player's birth year and 2009, but birth date is provided if you want to figure out exact age.

Draft position gives draft year and round, with the overall pick number with which the player was taken in parentheses. In the sample table, it says that Clinton Portis was chosen in the 2002 draft in the second round with the 51st overall pick. Undrafted free agents are listed as "FA" with the year they came into the league, even if they were only in training camp or on a practice squad.

To the far right of the first line is the player's **Risk** for fantasy football in 2009. The changes made to the Risk variable this year are explained fully in the introduction to quarterbacks. The standard is for players to be marked Green. Players with higher than normal risk are marked Yellow, and players with the highest risk are marked Red. Players who are most likely to match or surpass our forecast — primarily second-stringers with low projections — are marked Blue.

Next we give the last three years of player stats. The first number is games played (**G**). This is the official NFL total and may include games in which a player appeared on special teams, but did not carry the ball or catch a pass. The next four columns are familiar: **Runs**, rushing yards (**Yds**), yards per rush (**Yd/R**) and rushing touchdowns (**TD**).

The entry for fumbles (**FUM**) includes all fumbles by this running back, no matter whether they were recovered by the offense or defense. Holding onto the ball is an identifiable skill; fumbling it so that your own offense can recover it is not. (For more on this issue, see the essay "Pregame Show" in the front of the book.) This entry combines fumbles on both carries and receptions.

The next five columns give our advanced metrics for rushing: **DVOA** (Defense-Adjusted Value Over Average), **DYAR** (Defense-Adjusted Yards Above Replacement), and **YAR** (Yards Above Replacement), along with the player's rank (**Rk**) in both DVOA and DYAR. These metrics compare every carry by the running back to a league-average baseline based on the game situations in which that running back carried the ball. DVOA and DYAR are also adjusted based on the opposing defense. The methods used to compute these numbers are described in detail in the "Statistical Toolbox" introduction in the front of the book. The important distinctions between them are:

• DVOA is a rate statistic, while DYAR is a cumulative statistic. Thus, a higher DVOA means more value per play, while a higher DYAR means more aggregate value over the entire season.

• Because DYAR is defense-adjusted and YAR is not, a player whose DYAR is higher than his YAR faced a harder-than-average schedule. A player whose DYAR is lower than his YAR faced an easier-than-average schedule.

To qualify for ranking in rushing DVOA and DYAR, a running back must have had 100 carries in that season. There are 49 running backs ranked for 2008, 49 for 2007, and 47 backs for 2006.

The final rushing statistic is Success Rate (**Suc%**). This number represents running back consistency, measured by successful running plays divided by total running plays. (The definition for success is explained in the "Statistical Toolbox" introduction in the front of the book.) A player with high DVOA and a low Success Rate mixes long runs with plays on which he was stuffed at or behind the line of scrimmage. A player with low DVOA and a high Success Rate generally gets the yards needed, but rarely gets more. The league-average Success Rate in 2008 was 48 percent. Success Rate is not adjusted for the defenses a player faced.

The ten columns to the right of Success Rate give

data for each running back as a pass receiver. Receptions (**Rec**) counts passes caught, while Passes (**Pass**) counts total passes thrown to this player, complete or incomplete. The next four columns list receiving yards (**Yds**), Catch Rate (**C%**), yards per catch (**Yd/C**), and receiving touchdowns (**TD**).

Our research has shown that receivers bear some responsibility for incomplete passes, even though only their catches are tracked in official statistics. Catch Rate represents receptions divided by all intended passes for this running back. The average NFL running back caught 73 percent of passes in 2008.

Finally we have receiving DVOA and DYAR, which are entirely separate from rushing DVOA and DYAR. To qualify for ranking in receiving DVOA and DYAR, a running back must have 25 passes thrown to him in that season. There are 52 running backs ranked for 2008, 57 for 2007, and 54 for 2006. Numbers without opponent adjustment (YAR, and VOA) can be found on our Web site, FootballOutsiders.com.

The italicized row of statistics for the 2009 season is our 2009 KUBIAK projection based on a complicated regression analysis that takes into account numerous variables including projected role, performance over the past two years, projected team offense and defense, historical comparables, height, age, experience of the offensive line, and strength of schedule.

For rookie running backs, we'll also be mentioning a new metric: Points Over Expected (**POE**), which analyzes the output of college football running backs by comparing the expected EqPts value of every carry for a given ball-carrier (based on the quality of the rushing defense against which he's running) to the actual output. A positive POE indicates an above-average runner, with an average runner accruing exactly 0 POE. For more details on EqPts, see the college football section of this book.

It is difficult to accurately project statistics for a 162-game baseball season, but it is exponentially more difficult to accurately project statistics for a 16-game football season. Consider the listed pro-

Running Back Statistics Sample

Clinton Portis   Height: 5-11 Weight: 212 College: Miami   Draft: 2002/2 (51) Born: 1-Sep-1981 Age: 28 Risk: Green

Year	Team	G	Runs	Yds	Yd/R	TD	FUM	DVOA	Rk	DYAR	Rk	YAR	Suc%	Rec	Pass	Yds	C%	Yd/C	TD	DVOA	Rk	DYAR	Rk
2006	WAS	8	127	523	4.1	7	0	11.6%	8	111	19	86	44%	17	26	170	65%	10.0	0	7.0%	26	36	32
2007	WAS	16	325	1262	3.9	11	6	-3.0%	30	75	26	47	46%	47	58	389	81%	8.3	0	15.5%	18	97	10
2008	WAS	16	342	1487	4.3	9	3	11.7%	8	285	3	233	48%	28	36	218	78%	7.8	0	15.3%	15	54	23
2009	*WAS*		*282*	*1218*	*4.3*	*7*	*2*	*3.3%*						*21*	*30*	*144*	*70%*	*6.9*	*0*	*13.6%*			

jections not as a prediction of exact numbers, but the mean of a range of possible performances. What's important is less the exact number of yards we project, and more which players are projected to improve or decline. Actual performance will vary from our projection less for veteran starters and more for rookies and third-stringers, for whom we must base our projections on much smaller career statistical samples. Touchdown numbers will vary more than yardage numbers.

The main section for running backs is followed by a table with statistics for fullbacks, along with comments. Finally, in a section we call "Going Deep," we briefly discuss lower-round rookies, free-agent veterans, and practice-squad players who may play a role during the 2009 season or beyond.

Top 20 RB by Rushing DYAR (Total Value), 2008

Rank	Player	Team	DYAR
1	DeAngelo Williams	CAR	385
2	Brandon Jacobs	NYG	300
3	Clinton Portis	WAS	285
4	Derrick Ward	NYG	265
5	Thomas Jones	NYJ	252
6	Michael Turner	ATL	203
7	Chris Johnson	TEN	175
8	Sammy Morris	NE	166
9	Steve Slaton	HOU	166
10	Le'Ron McClain	BAL	163
11	Pierre Thomas	NO	161
12	Brian Westbrook	PHI	151
13	LenDale White	TEN	144
14	Mewelde Moore	PIT	139
15	Ronnie Brown	MIA	127
16	Jonathan Stewart	CAR	122
17	Adrian Peterson	MIN	121
18	Maurice Jones-Drew	JAC	112
19	Fred Jackson	BUF	91
20	LaDainian Tomlinson	SD	88

Top 20 RB by Rushing DVOA (Value per Rush), 2008

Rank	Player	Team	DVOA
1	DeAngelo Williams	CAR	28.3%
2	Derrick Ward	NYG	25.8%
3	Brandon Jacobs	NYG	22.4%
4	Pierre Thomas	NO	16.9%
5	Sammy Morris	NE	14.9%
6	Mewelde Moore	PIT	14.3%
7	Thomas Jones	NYJ	11.9%
8	Clinton Portis	WAS	11.7%
9	Deuce McAllister	NO	9.6%
10	Chris Johnson	TEN	9.2%
11	Le'Ron McClain	BAL	7.6%
12	Jonathan Stewart	CAR	7.6%
13	LenDale White	TEN	7.5%
14	Fred Jackson	BUF	7.0%
15	Brian Westbrook	PHI	6.9%
16	Steve Slaton	HOU	5.8%
17	Ronnie Brown	MIA	5.1%
18	Maurice Jones-Drew	JAC	4.4%
19	Michael Turner	ATL	4.1%
20	Willis McGahee	BAL	3.9%

Top 10 RB by Receiving DYAR (Total Value), 2008

Rank	Player	Team	DYAR
1	Maurice Jones-Drew	JAC	220
2	Matt Forte	CHI	201
3	Kevin Faulk	NE	192
4	Darren Sproles	SD	171
5	Correll Buckhalter	PHI	153
6	Pierre Thomas	NO	136
7	Reggie Bush	NO	118
8	Patrick Cobbs	MIA	110
9	Derrick Ward	NYG	107
10	Darren McFadden	OAK	107

Top 10 RB by Receiving DVOA (Value per Pass), 2008

Rank	Player	Team	DVOA
1	Darren Sproles	SD	73.1%
2	Correll Buckhalter	PHI	62.1%
3	Patrick Cobbs	MIA	53.5%
4	Maurice Jones-Drew	JAC	43.8%
5	Pierre Thomas	NO	40.2%
6	Kevin Faulk	NE	34.1%
7	Darren McFadden	OAK	33.3%
8	Matt Forte	CHI	33.1%
9	Ray Rice	BAL	25.8%
10	Chester Taylor	MIN	25.4%

Joseph Addai

Height: 6-0   Weight: 205   College: LSU   Draft: 2006/1 (30)   Born: 3-May-1983   Age: 26   Risk: Green

Year	Team	G	Runs	Yds	Yd/R	TD	FUM	DVOA	Rk	DYAR	Rk	YAR	Suc%	Rec	Pass	Yds	C%	Yd/C	TD	DVOA	Rk	DYAR	Rk
2006	IND	16	226	1081	4.8	7	2	18.4%	5	276	4	286	62%	40	50	325	69%	8.1	1	-2.1%	35	38	30
2007	IND	15	261	1072	4.1	12	0	11.1%	16	222	5	257	54%	41	49	364	84%	8.9	3	43.5%	3	150	3
2008	IND	12	155	544	3.5	5	1	-1.3%	26	49	27	44	48%	25	39	206	64%	8.2	2	5.3%	22	40	29
2009	IND		175	687	3.9	4	2	-3.8%						37	54	276	69%	7.5	1	5.1%			

Through one and a half seasons of his career, Addai had won a Super Bowl and looked destined for stardom. After gaining 100 yards in four of his first seven games as the primary back in 2007, Addai has done so only twice in his past 24 games. In playoff losses to San Diego the past two seasons, Addai has totaled 87 yards on 29 carries. Last year's problems are easily ascribed to a lingering shoulder injury. His days as a first-round fantasy selection are over for now, as he'll split carries with first-round pick Donald Brown.

Shaun Alexander

Height: 5-11   Weight: 225   College: Alabama   Draft: 2000/1 (19)   Born: 30-Aug-1977   Age: 32   Risk: N/A

Year	Team	G	Runs	Yds	Yd/R	TD	FUM	DVOA	Rk	DYAR	Rk	YAR	Suc%	Rec	Pass	Yds	C%	Yd/C	TD	DVOA	Rk	DYAR	Rk
2006	SEA	10	252	896	3.6	7	5	-13.8%	44	-53	45	-37	43%	12	16	48	81%	4.0	0	-16.7%	--	-3	--
2007	SEA	13	207	716	3.5	4	2	-17.3%	46	-74	48	-91	38%	14	25	76	56%	5.4	1	-36.4%	58	-30	54
2008	WAS	4	11	24	2.2	0	0	-62.7%	--	-20	--	-15	27%	1	1	9	100%	9.0	0	83.4%	--	5	--

In 2005, he was the NFL MVP. Two years later, he was an injury-plagued disappointment who was essentially replaced by Julius Jones. After an 11-carry season in 2008, Alexander's just trying to catch on. "I think that if a team gave me a shot, I think that they would be so pleased," he told Bay Area radio station KNBR in May. "They would feel like they got a ticket to have somebody that could play really, really well for nothing. I think that would shock a lot of people." It would indeed, since he's lost most of the burst and acceleration that made him special once upon a time. Heavily reliant on a great offensive line even at his best, Alexander may find that it's time to hang it up.

Marion Barber

Height: 5-11   Weight: 218   College: Minnesota   Draft: 2005/4 (109)   Born: 10-Jun-1983   Age: 26   Risk: Green

Year	Team	G	Runs	Yds	Yd/R	TD	FUM	DVOA	Rk	DYAR	Rk	YAR	Suc%	Rec	Pass	Yds	C%	Yd/C	TD	DVOA	Rk	DYAR	Rk
2006	DAL	16	135	654	4.8	14	0	30.5%	1	257	6	250	56%	23	32	196	63%	8.5	2	-18.0%	49	-8	50
2007	DAL	16	204	975	4.8	10	1	18.0%	5	233	3	203	49%	44	55	282	82%	6.4	2	-12.5%	40	4	39
2008	DAL	15	238	885	3.7	7	3	-4.4%	35	43	30	31	41%	52	61	417	85%	8.0	2	4.3%	26	56	20
2009	DAL		217	883	4.1	8	2	0.9%						52	67	468	78%	9.0	2	13.7%			

Barber's cumulative statistics exaggerate the decline in his level of performance during his first year as the Cowboys' featured runner. Barber was afflicted by injuries twice over the course of the year that grossly affected the context he was playing in. First, Tony Romo's broken finger brought upon the plague of Brad Johnson and allowed teams to stuff the box with nine men on most downs; for those three games, the Dallas offense consisted of handing Barber the ball and seeing him spin and juke tacklers for gains of two or three yards that should have been losses of four or five. Romo's return helped, but in Week 13, Barber dislocated his pinkie toe and never really recovered, coming back for 15 yards on 13 carries over the final three weeks of the year. Barber's DVOA when healthy and with Romo in the lineup was -1.3%; with Romo out or after dislocating his toe, it was -14.9%. Even accounting for the time spent with Johnson, pro-rating his healthy stats to 16 games yields totals of just under 1,200 yards and 10 touchdowns. He'll always be an injury risk thanks to his bruising style, but when he's healthy, Barber is arguably the best offensive weapon Dallas has.

Mike Bell

Height: 6-1   Weight: 218   College: Arizona   Draft: 2006/FA   Born: 23-Apr-1983   Age: 26   Risk: Red

Year	Team	G	Runs	Yds	Yd/R	TD	FUM	DVOA	Rk	DYAR	Rk	YAR	Suc%	Rec	Pass	Yds	C%	Yd/C	TD	DVOA	Rk	DYAR	Rk
2006	DEN	15	157	677	4.3	8	1	2.3%	21	77	24	108	51%	20	27	158	67%	7.9	0	8.6%	23	37	31
2007	DEN	5	6	3	0.5	0	1	-110.1%	--	-24	--	-22	33%	1	1	7	100%	7.0	0	76.8%	--	4	--
2008	NO	4	13	42	3.2	1	0	-4.5%	--	2	--	9	38%	1	2	14	50%	14.0	0	113.5%	--	10	--
2009	NO		44	153	3.5	1	2	-4.1%						6	7	57	86%	9.5	1	9.9%			

Bell looked good in very limited action as the Saints' No. 3 back last season. Now three years removed from a brief stint as the Broncos' featured back and two years removed from an aborted switch to fullback, Bell is no longer a serious prospect, but he's the only experienced back on the Saints roster after Reggie Bush and Pierre Thomas. His size and ability to play a little fullback make him a valuable bench player.

Tatum Bell

Height: 5-11   Weight: 213   College: Oklahoma State   Draft: 2004/2 (41)   Born: 2-Mar-1981   Age: 28   Risk: N/A

Year	Team	G	Runs	Yds	Yd/R	TD	FUM	DVOA	Rk	DYAR	Rk	YAR	Suc%	Rec	Pass	Yds	C%	Yd/C	TD	DVOA	Rk	DYAR	Rk
2006	DEN	13	233	1025	4.4	2	3	-4.3%	31	36	30	52	41%	24	31	115	87%	4.8	0	-16.9%	48	-6	48
2007	DET	5	44	182	4.1	1	1	-5.5%	--	6	--	5	50%	14	21	63	67%	4.5	0	-46.4%	--	-35	--
2008	DEN	7	44	249	5.7	2	0	28.2%	--	67	--	76	48%	10	14	57	71%	5.7	0	-13.2%	--	0	--

Bell allegedly stole Rudi Johnson's luggage last September after Johnson replaced Bell on the Lions roster. Under the circumstances, Bell wasn't the best player to retain on a roster flooded with baggage-toting new arrivals at running back. Bell reportedly had an airport luggage carousel installed in the Broncos clubhouse to efficiently transport carry-ons and overnight bags to his secret workshop. He was seen walking around team headquarters wearing an "LaMont" lapel pin, a 2004 NFC Championship ring, and underwear clearly stenciled with "J.J., don't forget to change! Oma." When we called Bell to confirm the rumors, the voicemail said, "Hey, this is Knowshon. Leave a message." The reporter we sent to personally investigate the story cannot find his laptop. Bell's late-season numbers weren't bad, but Josh McDaniels didn't sign half the free-agent runners in America because he had confidence in Bell's abilities.

Michael Bennett

Height: 5-9   Weight: 209   College: Wisconsin   Draft: 2001/1 (27)   Born: 13-Aug-1978   Age: 31   Risk: Red

Year	Team	G	Runs	Yds	Yd/R	TD	FUM	DVOA	Rk	DYAR	Rk	YAR	Suc%	Rec	Pass	Yds	C%	Yd/C	TD	DVOA	Rk	DYAR	Rk
2006	KC	11	36	200	5.6	0	1	19.2%	--	36	--	34	56%	9	12	77	83%	8.6	0	51.1%	--	52	--
2007	KC/TB	14	61	241	4.0	1	0	-5.1%	--	9	--	2	41%	15	22	101	68%	6.7	1	-30.7%	--	-18	--
2008	TB	5	7	12	1.7	0	0	-83.2%	--	-26	--	-21	57%	1	1	2	100%	2.0	0	-56.8%	--	-3	--
2009	SD		40	195	4.9	2	2	45.4%						8	10	79	80%	9.9	0	-3.7%			

Reportedly claimed by the Chargers on waivers specifically to keep him away from the Broncos, Bennett saw little action behind the combination of LaDainian Tomlinson and Darren Sproles. As a back with great straight-line speed but limited vision and agility, it's difficult to craft a role for Bennett in San Diego's running back rotation that doesn't interfere with the reps that are already earmarked for the guys ahead of him. The only way he'll see significant time is if someone gets hurt.

Cedric Benson

Height: 5-10   Weight: 215   College: Texas   Draft: 2005/1 (4)   Born: 28-Dec-1982   Age: 26   Risk: Green

Year	Team	G	Runs	Yds	Yd/R	TD	FUM	DVOA	Rk	DYAR	Rk	YAR	Suc%	Rec	Pass	Yds	C%	Yd/C	TD	DVOA	Rk	DYAR	Rk
2006	CHI	15	157	647	4.1	6	0	7.9%	14	104	20	122	47%	8	10	54	78%	6.8	0	17.9%	--	18	--
2007	CHI	11	196	674	3.4	4	4	-17.0%	45	-67	44	-57	40%	17	27	123	63%	7.2	0	-20.6%	48	-10	45
2008	CIN	12	214	747	3.5	2	2	-12.6%	44	-35	45	-70	40%	20	26	185	77%	9.3	0	-2.9%	35	15	39
2009	CIN		227	839	3.7	3	3	-6.3%						41	55	318	75%	7.7	2	36.3%			

Benson was seemingly ticketed for Bustville alongside fellow Texas Longhorns Mike Williams and Johnny "Lam" Jones. He was bounced out of Chicago after BWI (boating while intoxicated) and resisting arrest charges (later dropped). Benson's unlikely redemption came at Paul Brown Stadium, where all manner of reprobates are granted asylum. Like that of his team, Benson's strong finish is likely a mirage — he put up his two best games against the Browns (171 yards) and Chiefs (111 and a score), while scarcely denting the Ravens or Steelers defenses. Still, in a season when the Cincy rushing attack finished dead last in DVOA, Benson's toughness and ability to hold on to the damn ball made him look like Corey Dillon circa 2000. After failing to land Derrick Ward, the Bengals hastily re-signed Benson to a two-year deal. He'll be the starter by default, and likely a below-average one.

Ladell Betts   Height: 5-11 Weight: 223 College: Iowa   Draft: 2002/2 (56)   Born: 27-Aug-1979   Age: 30   Risk: Red

Year	Team	G	Runs	Yds	Yd/R	TD	FUM	DVOA	Rk	DYAR	Rk	YAR	Suc%	Rec	Pass	Yds	C%	Yd/C	TD	DVOA	Rk	DYAR	Rk
2006	WAS	16	245	1154	4.7	4	4	11.6%	9	194	11	178	46%	53	64	445	69%	8.4	1	11.6%	19	107	11
2007	WAS	16	93	335	3.6	1	1	-13.9%	--	-21	--	-21	45%	21	32	174	66%	8.3	1	-6.3%	32	14	34
2008	WAS	13	61	206	3.4	1	1	-6.1%	--	7	--	-13	48%	22	35	200	63%	9.1	0	-1.4%	33	19	36
2009	WAS		139	649	4.7	6	2	9.7%						19	34	184	56%	9.7	1	-19.0%			

Someone's got to take the load off of Clinton Portis' shoulders, and Jim Zorn might look to Betts to do the job. He got more touches late in the season as Portis picked up various small injuries, and reports from 2009 OTAs indicate that he's been a standout. Betts is a good receiver out of the backfield, which helps a team with few complementary passing options outside of Santana Moss and Chris Cooley when Portis is off the field, and he's decent enough in all areas for backup duty. Jim Zorn needs to learn the lesson that his mentor Mike Holmgren didn't with Shaun Alexander: You keep your marquee back alive with judicious use of your complementary backs. In that regard, Betts may be the key to Clinton Portis' future.

Lorenzo Booker   Height: 5-10 Weight: 191 College: Florida State   Draft: 2007/3 (71)   Born: 14-Jun-1984   Age: 25   Risk: Red

Year	Team	G	Runs	Yds	Yd/R	TD	FUM	DVOA	Rk	DYAR	Rk	YAR	Suc%	Rec	Pass	Yds	C%	Yd/C	TD	DVOA	Rk	DYAR	Rk
2007	MIA	7	28	125	4.5	0	0	16.3%	--	34	--	29	54%	28	36	237	78%	8.5	0	26.7%	9	85	12
2008	PHI	10	20	53	2.7	0	0	-24.7%	--	-12	--	-16	40%	6	10	11	60%	1.8	0	-75.2%	--	-34	--
2009	PHI		23	106	4.6	1	1	17.0%						20	29	193	69%	9.7	2	9.4%			

The Eagles traded a fourth-round pick for Booker during the weekend of the 2008 draft after failing to trade up and pick him the year before. He was expected to serve as the poor man's Brian Westbrook when Correll Buckhalter was unable to, but once the Eagles finally acquired him, they were disappointed with what they saw. Booker was inactive for six of the final eight games of the season, and did not show the same explosiveness that he did as a college back. It's worth noting that although he certainly has great acceleration, he had an unimpressive Speed Score of 96.5 coming out of the Combine, indicating that his athleticism might not play at the NFL level. He'll get one more chance to emerge this year, but with LeSean McCoy in the mix, he's likely the third back at best.

Ahmad Bradshaw   Height: 5-10 Weight: 198 College: Marshall   Draft: 2007/7 (250)   Born: 19-Mar-1986   Age: 23   Risk: Red

Year	Team	G	Runs	Yds	Yd/R	TD	FUM	DVOA	Rk	DYAR	Rk	YAR	Suc%	Rec	Pass	Yds	C%	Yd/C	TD	DVOA	Rk	DYAR	Rk
2007	NYG	12	23	190	8.3	1	0	50.5%	--	59	--	45	61%	2	5	12	40%	6.0	0	-62.6%	--	-14	--
2008	NYG	15	67	355	5.3	1	2	-1.4%	--	20	--	-2	49%	5	6	42	83%	8.4	1	93.3%	--	25	--
2009	NYG		35	173	5.0	1	2	-8.9%						16	26	106	62%	6.6	1	-9.4%			

Bradshaw spent parts of August 2008 and February 2009 in jail after violating his probation, and although he had decent raw statistics, DVOA shows that his effectiveness as a runner was nowhere near that of Brandon Jacobs or Derrick Ward. His jailtime over the summer limited his ability to work on his pass blocking and receiving in training camp, and he's made little progress on this front since joining the league. Although it seems logical that his role will expand with the departure of Ward to Tampa Bay, expect Danny Ware to pick up most of Ward's carries, and if Andre Brown impresses, Bradshaw could very quickly be traded or released.

Andre Brown
Height: 6-0   Weight: 224 College: North Carolina State   Draft: 2009/4 (129) Born: 15-Dec-1986 Age: 22 Risk: Blue

Year	Team	G	Runs	Yds	Yd/R	TD	FUM	DVOA	Rk	DYAR	Rk	YAR	Suc%	Rec	Pass	Yds	C%	Yd/C	TD	DVOA	Rk	DYAR	Rk
2009	NYG		42	207	4.9	3	0	23.1%						6	8	59	75%	9.8	0	17.8%			

Brown had the best Speed Score (110.2) of any back in this year's class; it's no surprise that the Giants selected him, as they also drafted Brandon Jacobs, possessor of the best Speed Score in the ten years we've developed the metric for (123.5). Even better, he's not just a good athlete; he's a good receiver out of the backfield and is a stout pass blocker, so his game is NFL-ready. As a stout runner on the interior, expect him to do a lot of the work between the tackles at first while Danny Ware handles the sweeps that Derrick Ward used to run. He has the same injury issues that all the Giants backs seem to have, so he probably won't end up as a 300-carry back, but spotted properly, he'll be very good.

Chris Brown
Height: 6-3   Weight: 219 College: Colorado   Draft: 2003/3 (93) Born: 17-Apr-1981 Age: 28 Risk: Red

Year	Team	G	Runs	Yds	Yd/R	TD	FUM	DVOA	Rk	DYAR	Rk	YAR	Suc%	Rec	Pass	Yds	C%	Yd/C	TD	DVOA	Rk	DYAR	Rk
2006	TEN	5	41	156	3.8	0	1	-17.5%	--	-15	--	-8	41%	2	9	4	22%	2.0	0	-82.8%	--	-45	--
2007	TEN	12	102	462	4.5	5	1	13.8%	10	100	22	113	57%	19	21	128	90%	6.7	0	13.9%	--	32	--
2009	HOU		24	76	3.2	1	1	-3.4%						8	11	80	73%	9.9	0	-22.3%			

Brown usually gets hurt sometime in October, but last year he avoided the autumn rush and hit the PUP list in August with a herniated disk. Brown was cleared to play in March but was limited in OTAs. He and Ryan Moats are battling for the number-two job behind Steve Slaton, with Brown getting a look as a short-yardage back. Brown may be able to stay healthy on a three-carry-per week workload, but the Titans grew weary of deactivating Brown every Columbus Day, and the Texans will probably feel the same way soon.

Donald Brown
Height: 5-10 Weight: 210 College: Connecticut   Draft: 2009/1 (27) Born: 11-Apr-1987 Age: 22 Risk: Yellow

Year	Team	G	Runs	Yds	Yd/R	TD	FUM	DVOA	Rk	DYAR	Rk	YAR	Suc%	Rec	Pass	Yds	C%	Yd/C	TD	DVOA	Rk	DYAR	Rk
2009	IND		147	623	4.3	5	3	2.1%						42	62	349	68%	8.3	0	-6.8%			

Solid in his first two seasons, Brown exploded in 2008, averaging 5.7 yards per carry over 28.2 carries per game. That yielded 27.3 Points Over Expected (POE), the 12th-best figure in the nation. Like most rookies, Brown needs to work on his pass blocking; playing for the Colts, though, it's impossible to get reps unless you've leveled up your pass blocking attribute five or six times. That could lead to an arbitrage opportunity in fantasy, where Joseph Addai sees the bulk of the action for the first half of the season before Brown eats away at his carries over the second half.

Ronnie Brown
Height: 6-0   Weight: 232 College: Auburn   Draft: 2005/1 (2) Born: 12-Dec-1981 Age: 27 Risk: Green

Year	Team	G	Runs	Yds	Yd/R	TD	FUM	DVOA	Rk	DYAR	Rk	YAR	Suc%	Rec	Pass	Yds	C%	Yd/C	TD	DVOA	Rk	DYAR	Rk
2006	MIA	13	241	1008	4.2	5	4	-8.3%	35	3	34	41	46%	33	38	276	63%	8.4	0	2.4%	30	40	28
2007	MIA	7	119	602	5.1	4	0	21.2%	2	156	11	194	51%	39	46	389	85%	10.0	1	52.0%	1	160	2
2008	MIA	16	214	916	4.3	10	1	5.1%	17	127	15	132	49%	33	43	254	77%	7.7	0	11.6%	19	57	19
2009	MIA		238	1131	4.8	7	4	1.6%						38	46	260	83%	6.8	1	12.4%			

Brown was the pointman in Miami's Wildcat, taking the snaps and making the reads that determined Steeler, Power, and Counter. Now that Pat White may take some of those snaps to freeze opposing safeties, Brown could see more carries in a traditional role after playing the committee with Ricky Williams in 2008. Draft-day trade rumors were likely bunk — the Dolphins know how pivotal Brown is to their offense. 2009 will be his contract year, his offseason conditioning regimen has been outstanding by all accounts, and consistent health seems to be the only thing standing between Brown and a great season.

Correll Buckhalter

Height: 6-0   Weight: 222 College: Nebraska   Draft: 2001/4 (121) Born: 6-Oct-1978   Age: 31 Risk: Red

Year	Team	G	Runs	Yds	Yd/R	TD	FUM	DVOA	Rk	DYAR	Rk	YAR	Suc%	Rec	Pass	Yds	C%	Yd/C	TD	DVOA	Rk	DYAR	Rk
2006	PHI	16	83	345	4.2	2	1	5.2%	--	49	--	41	58%	24	28	256	71%	10.7	1	26.6%	5	70	19
2007	PHI	14	62	313	5.0	4	0	21.9%	--	81	--	78	48%	12	21	87	57%	7.3	0	-8.6%	--	6	--
2008	PHI	14	76	369	4.9	2	0	11.0%	--	69	--	55	50%	26	32	324	81%	12.5	2	62.1%	2	153	5
2009	DEN		56	235	4.2	1	3	-20.0%						35	44	253	80%	7.2	1	0.0%			

Philly was spoiled by Buckhalter, a player who mirrored Brian Westbrook so well that the team didn't have to change their offense whatsoever when bringing in their backup. That's not to say that Buckhalter is as good as Westbrook — he does everything the first-stringer does at around 85 to 90 percent — but having a backup in the same vein as your starter is preferable to a Tony Romo/Brad Johnson sort of situation. Buckhalter's now stayed relatively healthy for three consecutive seasons, missing only four games over that timespan, and the Broncos were convinced enough to give him a four-year, $10 million deal. The only problem is that they drafted Knowshon Moreno, a similar, superior player, two months after they signed Buckhalter and J.J. Arrington. Although Josh McDaniels will rotate his backs frequently, there's probably not going to be enough of an opportunity for Buckhalter to justify his contract, and he could very easily be Motown Philly back again in 2010.

Michael Bush

Height: 6-2   Weight: 242 College: Louisville   Draft: 2007/4 (100) Born: 16-Jun-1984   Age: 25 Risk: Green

Year	Team	G	Runs	Yds	Yd/R	TD	FUM	DVOA	Rk	DYAR	Rk	YAR	Suc%	Rec	Pass	Yds	C%	Yd/C	TD	DVOA	Rk	DYAR	Rk
2008	OAK	15	95	421	4.4	3	1	-3.9%	--	17	--	20	41%	19	30	162	63%	8.5	0	7.5%	21	35	31
2009	OAK		60	250	4.2	1	3	-26.8%						18	23	141	78%	7.9	0	3.5%			

After spending the better part of two years making it back from a broken leg, Bush finally got onto the field and showed flashes of brilliance as the power back in the team's rotation. Eagles fans owe him a beer or two after his 177-yard, two-touchdown performance against the Buccaneers in Week 17 that helped propel Philly into the playoffs. There was talk of trading Bush or moving him to fullback this year with Oren O'Neal injured, but the signing of Lorenzo Neal leaves him to play what the Raiders hope will be the Brandon Jacobs role in their three-headed running back rotation.

Reggie Bush

Height: 6-0   Weight: 200 College: USC   Draft: 2006/1 (2)   Born: 2-Mar-1985   Age: 24 Risk: Yellow

Year	Team	G	Runs	Yds	Yd/R	TD	FUM	DVOA	Rk	DYAR	Rk	YAR	Suc%	Rec	Pass	Yds	C%	Yd/C	TD	DVOA	Rk	DYAR	Rk
2006	NO	16	155	565	3.6	6	2	-2.4%	27	38	28	8	44%	88	122	742	68%	8.4	2	22.4%	8	272	1
2007	NO	12	157	581	3.7	4	7	-19.4%	48	-72	47	-69	46%	73	98	417	74%	5.7	2	-9.6%	36	25	32
2008	NO	10	106	404	3.8	2	2	-9.0%	41	-2	41	8	45%	52	72	440	72%	8.5	4	15.3%	16	118	7
2009	NO		113	493	4.4	3	6	-5.8%						82	111	714	74%	8.7	3	-4.9%			

Two knee injuries may have scared Bush straight. His attendance at OTAs was in the "near 100-percent range" according to reports, and he's talking the good talk about doing whatever it takes to stay healthy and finally emerge as a true featured back. It's not too late for Bush to "get it." He's only 24 and could have a long, productive career if he stays healthy and learns to hit holes instead of dancing in the backfield. There's also a good chance that he'll never be a true 20-carry featured back; he may simply max out as the world's most talented third-down back and punt returner. That makes him a severe disappointment as a former second pick overall but a very useful player in a multidimensional offense. The Saints didn't pursue another back in the offseason, so they have faith in Bush and Pierre Thomas. We just don't know yet if the ticket should read Bush-Thomas or Thomas-Bush.

Jamaal Charles

Height: 5-11   Weight: 200 College: Texas   Draft: 2008/3 (73)   Born: 27-Dec-1986 Age: 22 Risk: Green

Year	Team	G	Runs	Yds	Yd/R	TD	FUM	DVOA	Rk	DYAR	Rk	YAR	Suc%	Rec	Pass	Yds	C%	Yd/C	TD	DVOA	Rk	DYAR	Rk
2008	KC	16	67	357	5.3	0	1	15.3%	--	63	--	66	54%	27	40	272	68%	10.1	1	-6.2%	38	16	37
2009	KC		144	605	4.2	3	2	-2.9%						31	41	214	76%	6.9	0	-3.8%			

Jamaal Charles is a very fast runner who patiently looks for running lanes rather than lowering his shoulder and pushing the pile. That makes him an excellent fit for both the "pistol" style attack Kansas City ran last year and the shotgun-spread attack Todd Haley ran in Arizona. As with most smaller running backs, there are questions about whether Charles could handle a starter's workload, but Haley isn't going to have his starting running back carry the ball 25 times a game anyway. His fantasy sleeper value may depend on how allergic Larry Johnson's ego is to the word "committee."

Tashard Choice
Height: 5-11 Weight: 215 College: Georgia Tech　　Draft: 2008/4 (122) Born: 20-Nov-1984 Age: 25 Risk: Green

Year	Team	G	Runs	Yds	Yd/R	TD	FUM	DVOA	Rk	DYAR	Rk	YAR	Suc%	Rec	Pass	Yds	C%	Yd/C	TD	DVOA	Rk	DYAR	Rk
2008	DAL	16	92	472	5.1	2	1	32.0%	--	157	--	105	45%	21	30	185	70%	8.8	0	3.9%	27	29	34
2009	DAL		71	331	4.7	2	3	5.5%						25	33	225	76%	9.0	1	20.9%			

Choice was a Speed Score favorite (104.9, well above-average for a fourth-round pick) who didn't figure to get much playing time as a rookie behind Barber and Felix Jones. Once both went down with injuries, Choice showed off quick feet and a pleasantly surprising mix of skills. Some of the credit has to go to the offensive line, but Choice's versatility and production-for-salary would make him an asset for any team in the league. With Barber and Jones back in the lineup, Choice will probably have to wait again for someone to get hurt. Not trading him at the peak of his value — this offseason — was a misstep.

Patrick Cobbs
Height: 5-8 Weight: 210 College: North Texas　　Draft: 2006/FA　　Born: 31-Jan-1983 Age: 26 Risk: Green

Year	Team	G	Runs	Yds	Yd/R	TD	FUM	DVOA	Rk	DYAR	Rk	YAR	Suc%	Rec	Pass	Yds	C%	Yd/C	TD	DVOA	Rk	DYAR	Rk
2007	MIA	14	15	47	3.1	1	0	7.8%	--	10	--	10	47%	2	6	20	50%	10.0	0	-15.5%	--	-1	--
2008	MIA	16	12	88	7.3	1	0	69.0%	--	28	--	30	33%	19	27	275	70%	14.5	2	53.5%	3	110	8
2009	MIA		32	151	4.7	1	2	18.0%						11	20	109	55%	9.9	0	12.3%			

Cobbs is a do-everything guy who received a two-year contract extension after the 2008 season. His highlight was the two-touchdown receiving day against the Texans, one of which came on a neat little option razzle-dazzle, but he also excelled in third down and red zone situations, and helped out in the return game. This is the kind of unheralded contributor you find in bulk on championship teams, and he'll continue to see many roles in Miami.

Glen Coffee
Height: 6-1 Weight: 200 College: Alabama　　Draft: 2009/3 (74) Born: 1-May-1987 Age: 22 Risk: Green

Year	Team	G	Runs	Yds	Yd/R	TD	FUM	DVOA	Rk	DYAR	Rk	YAR	Suc%	Rec	Pass	Yds	C%	Yd/C	TD	DVOA	Rk	DYAR	Rk
2009	SF		60	296	4.9	2	1	-3.1%						16	19	141	84%	8.8	0	15.2%			

Two years after a 2006 knee injury forced him to redshirt, Coffee had a terrific junior season season for Alabama, posting 1,383 yards rushing and 11 total touchdowns. He produced 25.2 POE, placing him 15th in the country, but only posted a Speed Score of 95.0 at the Combine. Drafted by the 49ers, Coffee does everything Frank Gore does, only not quite as well, so he's more a backup than a third-down or goal line specialist.

Kenneth Darby
Height: 5-10 Weight: 211 College: Alabama　　Draft: 2007/7 (246) Born: 26-Dec-1982 Age: 26 Risk: Red

Year	Team	G	Runs	Yds	Yd/R	TD	FUM	DVOA	Rk	DYAR	Rk	YAR	Suc%	Rec	Pass	Yds	C%	Yd/C	TD	DVOA	Rk	DYAR	Rk
2007	TB	1	2	9	4.5	0	0	25.9%	--	4	--	3	50%	2	3	16	67%	8.0	0	-6.2%	--	2	--
2008	STL	10	32	140	4.4	0	1	-1.9%	--	9	--	4	41%	19	21	183	90%	9.6	0	43.5%	--	75	--
2009	STL		101	459	4.6	4	4	5.3%						29	39	274	74%	9.5	1	-9.3%			

Drafted in the seventh round of the 2007 draft by the Tampa Bay Buccaneers but cut before the 2008 season started, the former Alabama tailback signed on with the Rams, seeming destined to spend the year on the practice squad. Instead, the Rams' coaching staff seemed to warm to him as the year progressed, and Darby eventually supplanted Travis Minor and Antonio Pittman as the backup to Steven Jackson. He only got the chance to return five kicks, but Darby managed the most of those opportunities by averaging 26.8 yards on the return, five yards better than Dante Hall's average. In fantasy football, he may be little more than a handcuff to S-Jack, but in real life Darby is a very useful player on the Rams roster.

James Davis

Height: 5-11   Weight: 215   College: Clemson   Draft: 2009/6 (195)   Born: 1-Jan-1986   Age: 23   Risk: Yellow

Year	Team	G	Runs	Yds	Yd/R	TD	FUM	DVOA	Rk	DYAR	Rk	YAR	Suc%	Rec	Pass	Yds	C%	Yd/C	TD	DVOA	Rk	DYAR	Rk
2009	CLE		41	158	3.8	0	1	-7.7%						9	13	76	69%	8.4	0	-3.7%			

Behind a shaky offensive line on a team in tumult, Davis saw his averages fall across the board his senior year, averaging just 4.4 yards per carry and posting just two 100-yard games (he had five in 2007). His 6.7 POE ranked only 73rd in the nation. Once a star recruit from Georgia, Davis overcame quite a few injuries in his time at Clemson and could be an injury risk in the pros. He also could see more rookie carries than other low-round draft picks if our projection for Jamal Lewis is correct.

T.J. Duckett

Height: 6-0   Weight: 254   College: Michigan State   Draft: 2002/1 (18)   Born: 17-Feb-1981   Age: 28   Risk: Green

Year	Team	G	Runs	Yds	Yd/R	TD	FUM	DVOA	Rk	DYAR	Rk	YAR	Suc%	Rec	Pass	Yds	C%	Yd/C	TD	DVOA	Rk	DYAR	Rk
2006	WAS	11	38	132	3.5	2	1	-18.3%	--	-16	--	-22	37%	2	2	16	50%	8.0	0	-171.3%	--	-18	--
2007	DET	12	65	335	5.2	3	1	12.2%	--	56	--	59	38%	4	7	54	57%	13.5	0	47.8%	--	26	--
2008	SEA	16	62	172	2.8	8	0	7.2%	--	56	--	79	56%	0	1	0	0%	0.0	0	-80.5%	--	-3	--
2009	SEA		151	727	4.8	4	3	-8.0%						5	7	45	71%	9.0	0	6.5%			

Duckett is good at taking the ball and running as hard as he can in a straight line between the guards, and bad at everything else. He has had seven seasons now to prove otherwise and come up short. He averaged 4.1 yards up the middle last season, 2.3 yards to either side. It's not that he has no speed — he has 17 20-yard runs in 717 career carries, similar to Marion Barber's 19 in 715 — but that he has no moves or cutting ability of any kind at all. Defenders will take Duckett down or be trampled, but they will never, ever miss him. On a per-carry basis, he's probably the best goal-line back in football; he's scored 34 touchdowns inside the five when an average back would've been expected to score 25.6.

Warrick Dunn

Height: 5-9   Weight: 180   College: Florida State   Draft: 1997/1 (12)   Born: 5-Jan-1975   Age: 34   Risk: N/A

Year	Team	G	Runs	Yds	Yd/R	TD	FUM	DVOA	Rk	DYAR	Rk	YAR	Suc%	Rec	Pass	Yds	C%	Yd/C	TD	DVOA	Rk	DYAR	Rk
2006	ATL	16	286	1140	4.0	4	1	-2.9%	28	66	25	-1	39%	22	27	170	74%	7.7	1	21.4%	10	53	25
2007	ATL	16	227	720	3.2	4	2	-20.0%	49	-108	49	-124	37%	37	59	238	63%	6.4	0	-29.6%	54	-48	57
2008	TB	15	186	786	4.2	2	0	-2.9%	32	41	31	66	46%	47	68	330	69%	7.0	0	-3.7%	36	39	30

Dunn's long career is probably over, which means the league has lost one of its best citizens and a perennial Walter Payton Award candidate. Now 34, Dunn no longer can summon the burst and lower body power that enabled him to play 13 seasons despite weighing less than 200 pounds. His (likely) last season was a decent one, at least, especially on first and second downs. His 20 carries on third and fourth down went for a -41.4% DVOA. The other 166 totes were much more effective.

Justin Fargas

Height: 6-1   Weight: 220   College: USC   Draft: 2003/3 (96)   Born: 25-Jan-1980   Age: 29   Risk: Red

Year	Team	G	Runs	Yds	Yd/R	TD	FUM	DVOA	Rk	DYAR	Rk	YAR	Suc%	Rec	Pass	Yds	C%	Yd/C	TD	DVOA	Rk	DYAR	Rk
2006	OAK	16	178	659	3.7	1	1	-12.0%	42	-24	40	-6	40%	13	21	91	67%	7.0	0	19.2%	--	49	--
2007	OAK	14	222	1009	4.5	4	3	1.6%	24	92	24	99	46%	23	32	188	72%	8.2	0	21.8%	11	57	20
2008	OAK	14	218	853	3.9	1	4	-17.3%	47	-77	47	-46	42%	10	15	52	67%	5.2	0	-25.9%	--	-8	--
2009	OAK		150	693	4.6	5	3	7.5%						10	13	84	77%	8.4	1	28.5%			

With JaMarcus Russell struggling and Darren McFadden hobbled, the Raiders offense at points last year essentially boiled down to handing the ball off to Fargas and hoping he'd make something happen. The man we call "Snuggly Bear" is a useful back who would look like a star for a team like the Giants or the Ravens, but he's not Barry Sanders. His -6.9% DVOA on first down is closer to his real level of play than his overall DVOA.

Fargas was involved in an unsavory incident in the offseason, making an appearance in a web video by Oakland rapper Yukmouth — "The Human Torch" — promoting what appeared to be the second annual Smoke-A-Thon. Until Roger Goodell starts making rounds on International Boulevard, Fargas should avoid suspension.

Kevin Faulk   Height: 5-8   Weight: 202   College: LSU   Draft: 1999/2 (46)   Born: 5-Jun-1976   Age: 33   Risk: Green

Year	Team	G	Runs	Yds	Yd/R	TD	FUM	DVOA	Rk	DYAR	Rk	YAR	Suc%	Rec	Pass	Yds	C%	Yd/C	TD	DVOA	Rk	DYAR	Rk
2006	NE	15	25	123	4.9	1	0	19.7%	--	28	--	27	44%	43	56	356	59%	8.3	2	-1.4%	33	47	26
2007	NE	16	62	265	4.3	0	0	15.2%	--	63	--	62	56%	47	59	383	80%	8.1	1	31.0%	8	146	4
2008	NE	15	83	507	6.1	3	0	46.5%	--	178	--	193	57%	58	74	486	78%	8.4	3	34.1%	6	192	3
2009	NE		61	288	4.7	2	3	30.1%						44	58	464	76%	10.5	2	24.0%			

Once again, Faulk was New England's jack-of-all-trades. He helped an anonymous running back rotation as a safety net in the passing game, a productive back in the red zone, and with the occasional return. His carries diminished in the season's second half as the Patriots rifled through different options. Faulk and Sammy Morris were the only successful backs when the Patriots ran their favorite draw play, and with defenses adjusting to the Brady aerial attack again, there should be plenty of opportunities to run the draw in 2009.

Justin Forsett   Height: 5-8   Weight: 190   College: California   Draft: 2008/7 (233)   Born: 14-Oct-1985   Age: 24   Risk: Green

Year	Team	G	Runs	Yds	Yd/R	TD	FUM	DVOA	Rk	DYAR	Rk	YAR	Suc%	Rec	Pass	Yds	C%	Yd/C	TD	DVOA	Rk	DYAR	Rk
2009	SEA		35	163	4.6	0	2	36.8%						11	17	102	65%	9.3	1	11.8%			

Forsett thrilled Seattle fans with an explosive preseason game against Chicago, then was released before the season began. Indianapolis signed him, but released him three games into the year, and he ended up back in Seattle. Forsett has good quickness and agility, but bad hands, struggling with fumbles and as a receiver.

Matt Forte   Height: 6-2   Weight: 222   College: Tulane   Draft: 2008/2 (44)   Born: 10-Dec-1985   Age: 23   Risk: Red

Year	Team	G	Runs	Yds	Yd/R	TD	FUM	DVOA	Rk	DYAR	Rk	YAR	Suc%	Rec	Pass	Yds	C%	Yd/C	TD	DVOA	Rk	DYAR	Rk
2008	CHI	16	316	1238	3.9	8	1	-7.1%	38	20	38	53	43%	63	76	477	83%	7.6	4	33.1%	8	201	2
2009	CHI		322	1272	4.0	14	3	8.4%						68	91	417	75%	6.1	2	30.1%			

It's rare to see a rookie back as assured as Forte, who had the starting job fall into his lap after Cedric Benson's summer indiscretions and made it his own. From Week 1, Forte ran, received, and blocked like a veteran back; only Frank Gore had a higher percentage of his team's touches. He was more dependable than most veteran backs that get the moniker, as he didn't register a single blown block and had no fumble issues to speak of. The one negative was that he wore down quickly following 73 carries in the first three weeks, but he was used more judiciously by Lovie Smith thereafter and averaged 4.3 yards per carry after the Week 8 bye. He lacks the top-end speed needed to be an elite back, but he has everything else you'd want. The best compliment we can give Forte? The closest skill set we can think of to his is Emmitt Smith's. Forte is that special of a player.

DeShaun Foster   Height: 6-0   Weight: 222   College: UCLA   Draft: 2002/2 (34)   Born: 10-Jan-1980   Age: 29   Risk: N/A

Year	Team	G	Runs	Yds	Yd/R	TD	FUM	DVOA	Rk	DYAR	Rk	YAR	Suc%	Rec	Pass	Yds	C%	Yd/C	TD	DVOA	Rk	DYAR	Rk
2006	CAR	14	227	897	4.0	3	3	-2.0%	26	63	26	14	45%	32	46	159	69%	5.0	0	-5.1%	38	23	40
2007	CAR	16	247	876	3.5	3	5	-15.8%	44	-72	46	-60	43%	25	36	182	69%	7.3	1	-24.3%	50	-22	50
2008	SF	16	76	234	3.1	1	2	-31.9%	--	-78	--	-65	43%	16	20	133	80%	8.3	1	12.9%	--	35	--

And here's to you, DeShaun Foster
We loved to mock you more than you will know (Whoa, whoa, whoa)
God bless you please, DeShaun Foster
Heaven holds a place for your low DVOA
(Hey, hey, hey ... hey, hey, hey)

We'd like to know a little bit about you for our files
We'd like to help you learn to help yourself
Look around you, all you see are unsympathetic eyes
Stroll around the ground
Until you fall down

Where have you gone, DeShaun Foster
The Arena League turns its lonely eyes to you (Woo, woo, woo)
What's that you say, Mike Tanier?
DeShaun has left us and gone away
(Hey, hey, hey ... hey, hey, hey)

Frank Gore
Height: 5-9   Weight: 217   College: Miami   Draft: 2005/3 (65)   Born: 14-May-1983   Age: 26   Risk: Green

Year	Team	G	Runs	Yds	Yd/R	TD	FUM	DVOA	Rk	DYAR	Rk	YAR	Suc%	Rec	Pass	Yds	C%	Yd/C	TD	DVOA	Rk	DYAR	Rk
2006	SF	16	312	1695	5.4	8	5	10.1%	12	242	8	261	47%	61	86	485	62%	8.0	1	10.5%	20	132	8
2007	SF	15	260	1102	4.2	5	3	4.3%	21	130	14	79	42%	53	69	436	77%	8.2	1	14.3%	19	110	7
2008	SF	14	240	1036	4.3	6	6	-1.7%	29	69	25	72	47%	43	66	373	65%	8.7	2	2.4%	28	62	17
2009	SF		246	1129	4.6	7	3	18.3%						45	61	356	74%	7.9	2	39.2%			

Although everyone thinks of Norv Turner as a quarterback guru, it's worth noting that Gore's production has declined significantly in the two years since he left to coach the Chargers. Tackle Joe Staley's move from the right to the left side might have something to do with it too. Gore's touchdown totals should improve under new 49ers offensive coordinator Jimmy Raye, who plans to rely on Gore in the red zone despite Gore's historical struggle with holding onto the ball in that area. Don't worry about Gore losing too many touches to third-round pick Glen Coffee, either — he is still the feature back in this offense.

Earnest Graham
Height: 5-9   Weight: 225   College: Florida   Draft: 2004/ (FA)   Born: 15-Jan-1980   Age: 29   Risk: Red

Year	Team	G	Runs	Yds	Yd/R	TD	FUM	DVOA	Rk	DYAR	Rk	YAR	Suc%	Rec	Pass	Yds	C%	Yd/C	TD	DVOA	Rk	DYAR	Rk
2006	TB	16	11	59	5.4	0	0	56.5%	--	26	--	27	45%	1	4	4	75%	4.0	0	58.5%	--	14	--
2007	TB	15	222	898	4.0	10	0	8.4%	18	162	9	175	50%	49	69	324	71%	6.6	0	-16.5%	42	-10	46
2008	TB	10	132	563	4.3	4	2	-8.5%	39	1	39	25	48%	23	33	174	70%	7.6	0	-1.1%	32	24	35
2009	TB		81	401	4.9	5	2	21.1%						18	25	165	72%	9.2	0	-17.7%			

It's hard not to pull for undrafted players, particularly those who have had the impact that Graham has. Then again, seventh-round picks elicit much the same reaction, and that's where Derrick Ward, Graham's replacement as Bucs bellcow back, was selected. Graham managed exactly one adjusted yard over replacement in an injury-hit '08. Graham was woeful in the red zone, but his Success Rate was actually slightly higher than Ward's.

Ryan Grant
Height: 6-1   Weight: 224   College: Notre Dame   Draft: 2005/ FA   Born: 9-Dec-1982   Age: 26   Risk: Red

Year	Team	G	Runs	Yds	Yd/R	TD	FUM	DVOA	Rk	DYAR	Rk	YAR	Suc%	Rec	Pass	Yds	C%	Yd/C	TD	DVOA	Rk	DYAR	Rk
2007	GB	15	188	956	5.1	8	1	10.6%	17	149	12	139	47%	30	37	145	81%	4.8	0	-31.7%	56	-38	56
2008	GB	16	312	1203	3.9	4	4	-10.1%	42	-19	43	-21	46%	18	22	116	82%	6.4	1	1.1%	--	16	--
2009	GB		270	1014	3.8	9	3	3.2%						18	25	139	72%	7.7	0	3.1%			

What happened? Well, for one, his fullback got hurt. Korey Hall missed five games in 2009; in those contests, Grant averaged 2.98 yards per carry and had a DVOA of -26.9%. In the other 11 games, Grant averaged 4.22 yards per carry and his DVOA was -3.2%. He struggled in short yardage, converting only 15 of his 25 attempts with a yard to go (the average back converts 71 percent of those carries), and he had a -15.8% DVOA in the red zone (league average was -0.6%), which explains why his touchdown total was so low. Teams challenged Aaron Rodgers to throw early in the season by pushing their safeties up to the line of scrimmage to stop Grant.

Does all that mean that Grant's sophomore slump was an aberration? Maybe, maybe not. Freely available (well, sixth-round pick-valued) talent like Grant are freely available for a reason; they need to be in the right situation to succeed, and the difference between them succeeding and struggling can be as slim as the loss of a fullback or a right tackle (Mark Tauscher), or the presence of an extra safety in the box. The Packers might have expected more when they signed him to a four-year deal after the 2007 season, but when you go searching around in the bargain bin and find something you like, you're not necessarily supposed to commit serious coin to it.

Ahman Green

Height: 6-0   Weight: 218   College: Nebraska   Draft: 1998/3 (76)   Born: 16-Feb-1977   Age: 32   Risk: N/A

Year	Team	G	Runs	Yds	Yd/R	TD	FUM	DVOA	Rk	DYAR	Rk	YAR	Suc%	Rec	Pass	Yds	C%	Yd/C	TD	DVOA	Rk	DYAR	Rk
2006	GB	14	266	1059	4.0	5	2	2.4%	20	116	16	85	43%	46	63	373	70%	8.1	1	-6.2%	40	24	37
2007	HOU	6	70	260	3.7	2	0	3.2%	--	33	--	37	41%	14	18	123	78%	8.8	0	-9.7%	--	4	--
2008	HOU	8	74	294	4.0	3	0	12.6%	--	74	--	76	55%	11	14	32	79%	2.9	0	-58.1%	--	-31	--

A running back can hit the end of the road through ineffectiveness or injury. Green was relatively effective when he was on the field last year, but he just could not stay healthy for the second consecutive year. He battled groin and hamstring injuries before his knee knocked him out for the season. He still wants to play, but at this point, no team's taken the plunge on a broken-down model. If this is the end, however, Green still has had an outstanding career. He has six 1,000-yard seasons, was the feature back in some very good Green Bay rushing offenses, and earned a place among the top 30 in career rushing yards.

Shonn Greene

Height: 5-11   Weight: 235   College: Iowa   Draft: 2009/3 (65)   Born: 21-Aug-1985   Age: 24   Risk: Red

Year	Team	G	Runs	Yds	Yd/R	TD	FUM	DVOA	Rk	DYAR	Rk	YAR	Suc%	Rec	Pass	Yds	C%	Yd/C	TD	DVOA	Rk	DYAR	Rk
2009	NYJ		73	299	4.1	4	4	-16.7%						22	27	127	81%	5.8	0	-31.9%			

The knock on Greene is that he doesn't have the speed to get to the corner in the NFL. That's probably true, but he was the most physical inside runner in the draft, and with Leon Washington on the roster, Greene won't be asked to run off tackle very often. Instead, he's here to improve the Jets' 61 percent Success Rate in power situations by slamming his 235 pounds straight up the gut. Considering the fact that Rex Ryan's Ravens team built their running game around fullback Le'Ron McClain last season, it seems likely that Greene will get his share of touches in New York's three-headed running back committee.

BenJarvus Green-Ellis

Height: 5-11   Weight: 220   College: Mississippi   Draft: 2008/FA   Born: 2-Jul-1985   Age: 24   Risk: Red

Year	Team	G	Runs	Yds	Yd/R	TD	FUM	DVOA	Rk	DYAR	Rk	YAR	Suc%	Rec	Pass	Yds	C%	Yd/C	TD	DVOA	Rk	DYAR	Rk
2008	NE	9	74	275	3.7	5	0	6.7%	--	55	--	66	57%	3	6	37	50%	12.3	0	21.4%	--	13	--
2009	NE		36	115	3.2	0	2	-20.3%						5	6	36	83%	7.2	1	21.0%			

His name may sound like a law firm, leading to the "Boston Legal" nickname, but Green-Ellis' function was as an injury replacement in 2008, scoring touchdowns in five of six games in the middle of the season when other backs were hurt. Now that the depth chart has righted itself and Fred Taylor is added to mix, Green-Ellis will find it difficult to stick and stay. Green-Ellis appeared in nine games last season, and as an undrafted free agent, his practice squad eligibility has been exhausted.

Andre Hall

Height: 5-10 Weight: 205 College: USF   Draft: 2006/FA   Born: 20-Aug-1982 Age: 27 Risk: N/A

Year	Team	G	Runs	Yds	Yd/R	TD	FUM	DVOA	Rk	DYAR	Rk	YAR	Suc%	Rec	Pass	Yds	C%	Yd/C	TD	DVOA	Rk	DYAR	Rk
2007	DEN	10	44	216	4.9	2	1	-4.9%	--	7	--	-10	39%	2	2	69	100%	34.5	0	161.0%	--	23	--
2008	DEN	8	35	144	4.1	0	2	-7.0%	--	2	--	3	54%	3	3	25	100%	8.3	0	68.7%	--	18	--

It takes a nation of millions to play running back for the Denver Broncos. Hall is different from the others because a) he never started a game and b) he's an accomplished kick returner, which means that his chances of getting picked up by another team are probably higher than those of Selvin Young or P.J. Pope. Like the other Denver backs, he missed a significant part of the season with an injury, in his case a broken hand.

Jerome Harrison

Height: 5-10 Weight: 200 College: Washington State   Draft: 2006/5 (145) Born: 26-Feb-1983 Age: 26 Risk: Red

Year	Team	G	Runs	Yds	Yd/R	TD	FUM	DVOA	Rk	DYAR	Rk	YAR	Suc%	Rec	Pass	Yds	C%	Yd/C	TD	DVOA	Rk	DYAR	Rk
2006	CLE	10	20	60	3.0	0	1	-46.2%	--	-26	--	-29	30%	9	14	47	79%	5.2	0	-12.7%	--	1	--
2007	CLE	8	23	142	6.2	0	0	40.4%	--	45	--	52	74%	2	2	19	100%	9.5	0	96.3%	--	8	--
2008	CLE	15	34	246	7.2	1	0	52.7%	--	79	--	76	53%	12	18	116	67%	9.7	1	14.7%	--	29	--
2009	CLE		162	793	4.9	6	5	8.0%						44	64	397	69%	9.0	1	8.9%			

Harrison has been extremely productive from a per-touch standpoint for two years, yet he has never carried the ball more than eight times in a game. That's a little silly, particularly on a team that routinely gave Jamal Lewis 20 touches per game so he could grind out 66 yards. Harrison is small, but lots of 5-foot-9 running backs thrive in a 12- to 15-carry, four- to five-catch role. The new Browns staff may use Harrison the way they used Leon Washington in New York last season: as a passing down back in an offense where second-and-4 is considered a passing down. Harrison deserves the expanded role. If we're right about Jamal Lewis collapsing, he'll get it.

Jacob Hester

Height: 5-11 Weight: 230 College: LSU   Draft: 2008/3 (69)   Born: 8-May-1985 Age: 24 Risk: Green

Year	Team	G	Runs	Yds	Yd/R	TD	FUM	DVOA	Rk	DYAR	Rk	YAR	Suc%	Rec	Pass	Yds	C%	Yd/C	TD	DVOA	Rk	DYAR	Rk
2008	SD	16	19	95	5.0	1	1	-14.9%	--	-6	--	2	47%	12	13	91	92%	7.6	1	44.6%	--	49	--
2009	SD		37	110	3.0	2	2	17.9%						6	6	63	100%	10.5	0	23.5%			

San Diego hoped to use Hester in the Mike Alstott role that he filled in his final year at LSU, but Hester simply wasn't effective as a halfback, lost his carries to Darren Sproles, and had been converted to fullback by the end of the year. It's hard to see how he'd make his way back into that role in 2009, so expect him to compete with Mike Tolbert for the fullback job and serve as a member of the coverage units.

Tim Hightower

Height: 6-0 Weight: 226 College: Richmond   Draft: 2008/5 (149) Born: 23-May-1986 Age: 23 Risk: Yellow

Year	Team	G	Runs	Yds	Yd/R	TD	FUM	DVOA	Rk	DYAR	Rk	YAR	Suc%	Rec	Pass	Yds	C%	Yd/C	TD	DVOA	Rk	DYAR	Rk
2008	ARI	16	143	399	2.8	10	1	-20.5%	48	-79	48	-60	37%	34	50	237	68%	7.0	0	-10.2%	41	10	40
2009	ARI		105	291	2.8	1	3	-15.5%						42	57	370	74%	8.8	1	22.5%			

Hightower became the 13th rookie since 1960 to get at least 100 carries and average fewer than 3.0 yards per rush. There are plenty of busts on that list, but also some shockingly good names, like Jim Nance, Floyd Little, and Ricky Bell, so there's no need to give up on Hightower despite his slow start. He'll start the season ahead of Beanie Wells, the Cardinals' first-round draft choice. At 6-foot-1 and 237 pounds, Wells is slightly larger than Hightower; he should be a similar, but superior, player. Hightower should still be the back on third-and-long, where he makes an effective outlet receiver.

Peyton Hillis

Height: 6-1   Weight: 240   College: Arkansas   Draft: 2008/7 (227)   Born: 21-Jan-1986   Age: 23   Risk: Red

Year	Team	G	Runs	Yds	Yd/R	TD	FUM	DVOA	Rk	DYAR	Rk	YAR	Suc%	Rec	Pass	Yds	C%	Yd/C	TD	DVOA	Rk	DYAR	Rk
2008	DEN	12	68	343	5.0	5	0	41.0%	--	151	--	156	65%	14	19	179	74%	12.8	1	55.9%	--	82	--
2009	DEN		24	89	3.7	0	1	-19.9%						19	23	195	83%	10.3	0	-9.7%			

What kind of odds would you have gotten if you had bet before last season that Denver's leading rusher would be their seventh-round rookie fullback? That pretty much tells you what kind of year it was in Denver, at least on the offensive side of the ball. Like all the other backs who went through Denver last year, Hillis got a chance to start a couple games, played well, and then suffered a season-ending injury (in his case, a torn hamstring). With the arrival of Knowshon Moreno, Correll Buckhalter, LaMont Jordan, and so forth, Hillis isn't going to get any starts at halfback this year, but Josh McDaniels will probably use him as a fullback/halfback hybrid, or what Heath Evans was in New England.

Brandon Jackson

Height: 5-10   Weight: 210   College: Nebraska   Draft: 2007/2 (63)   Born: 2-Oct-1985   Age: 24   Risk: Green

Year	Team	G	Runs	Yds	Yd/R	TD	FUM	DVOA	Rk	DYAR	Rk	YAR	Suc%	Rec	Pass	Yds	C%	Yd/C	TD	DVOA	Rk	DYAR	Rk
2007	GB	11	75	267	3.6	1	0	-9.4%	--	-3	--	-12	44%	16	22	130	73%	8.1	0	-3.7%	--	12	--
2008	GB	13	45	248	5.5	1	1	25.3%	--	62	--	65	51%	30	39	185	77%	6.2	0	-13.2%	44	1	44
2009	GB		108	461	4.3	1	3	16.8%						18	26	180	69%	10.0	0	-12.5%			

Jackson was supposed to be in a partial timeshare with Ryan Grant, but even when Grant struggled, the Packers hesitated to give Jackson more work. It's because Jackson simply hasn't picked up pass blocking. Green Bay cut Vernand Morency in August hoping that Jackson would be good enough to get by, but his struggles forced the Packers to give Kregg Lumpkin and DeShawn Wynn more playing time and tire Grant out further with pass protection duties on plays where he'd otherwise be taking a play off. 2009 will be his final chance to figure things out before he loses his job.

Fred Jackson

Height: 6-1   Weight: 215   College: Coe   Draft: 2007/FA   Born: 20-Feb-1981   Age: 28   Risk: Red

Year	Team	G	Runs	Yds	Yd/R	TD	FUM	DVOA	Rk	DYAR	Rk	YAR	Suc%	Rec	Pass	Yds	C%	Yd/C	TD	DVOA	Rk	DYAR	Rk
2007	BUF	8	58	300	5.2	0	0	19.7%	--	64	--	68	47%	22	29	190	72%	8.6	0	9.2%	23	34	27
2008	BUF	16	130	571	4.4	3	1	7.0%	14	91	19	94	53%	37	45	317	82%	8.6	0	12.4%	18	67	16
2009	BUF		141	622	4.4	3	3	-7.0%						53	80	330	66%	6.2	1	-41.8%			

The most effective running back on the Bills last year was not Marshawn Lynch; it was Fred Jackson. Jackson had the fifth-best Success Rate in football in 2008, and his DYAR and DVOA rankings led the team. The former Sioux City Bandit and Rhein Fire star logged 81 of his 130 carries in November and December, as offensive coordinator Turk Schonert moved in the direction of a two-back platoon. Jackson should fend off Dominic Rhodes and open the season as the nominal starter while Lynch serves his suspension.

Steven Jackson

Height: 6-2   Weight: 231   College: Oregon State   Draft: 2004/1 (24)   Born: 22-Jul-1983   Age: 26   Risk: Yellow

Year	Team	G	Runs	Yds	Yd/R	TD	FUM	DVOA	Rk	DYAR	Rk	YAR	Suc%	Rec	Pass	Yds	C%	Yd/C	TD	DVOA	Rk	DYAR	Rk
2006	STL	16	346	1528	4.4	13	2	8.0%	13	243	7	238	48%	90	110	806	63%	9.0	3	7.4%	25	151	2
2007	STL	12	237	1002	4.2	5	4	-7.4%	36	11	36	-5	43%	38	52	271	73%	7.1	1	-15.3%	41	-4	41
2008	STL	12	253	1042	4.1	7	5	-2.5%	31	66	26	45	46%	40	62	379	65%	9.5	1	0.2%	31	46	26
2009	STL		265	1298	4.9	11	2	20.7%						48	64	389	75%	8.1	2	23.3%			

In Week 13, after the Rams lost to the Dolphins 16-12, interim coach Jim Haslett said that Steven Jackson received only one carry in the fourth quarter because Jackson was, quote, gassed. "No I wasn't gassed," Jackson responded. "It wasn't my conditioning. I wish he'd stop saying that." In a related story, Haslett is now the new head coach of the United Football League's Orlando franchise. Jackson fought through a frustrating thigh injury last year but was fully recovered by the end of the season. With the upgrades to the Rams' offensive line — and new head coach Steve Spagnulo's stated intention of emphasizing the run — Jackson's poised for a monster statistical year.

Brandon Jacobs   Height: 6-4   Weight: 256   College: Southern Illinois   Draft: 2005/4 (110)   Born: 6-Jul-1982   Age: 27   Risk: Green

Year	Team	G	Runs	Yds	Yd/R	TD	FUM	DVOA	Rk	DYAR	Rk	YAR	Suc%	Rec	Pass	Yds	C%	Yd/C	TD	DVOA	Rk	DYAR	Rk
2006	NYG	15	96	423	4.4	9	2	16.4%	--	125	--	115	58%	11	14	149	57%	13.5	0	7.1%	--	22	--
2007	NYG	11	202	1009	5.0	4	4	18.3%	4	220	6	249	57%	23	38	174	61%	7.6	2	-21.5%	49	-16	49
2008	NYG	13	219	1089	5.0	15	3	22.4%	3	300	2	247	51%	6	12	36	50%	6.0	0	-42.6%	--	-21	--
2009	NYG		292	1417	4.9	10	4	14.0%						10	17	48	59%	4.8	0	-60.0%			

It's pretty clear what Jacobs is at this point in his career. He's not going to play in all 16 games, he's not a great receiver (dropping four of the 12 passes thrown to you usually means about that much), and the coaching staff has to spot him and rest him regularly. For that package, though, you get one of the best pure running backs in the league, and arguably the best back in football between the tackles. He's dominant near the goal line, scoring 12 touchdowns inside the 5 last year when an average back, in the same situations, would have been expected to score 9.4. He's improved dramatically as a pass blocker, registering nary a blown block last year even as the Giants ran more three- and four-wideout sets. Giving running backs long-term deals is usually a fool's errand, but the four-year, $25 million deal the Giants gave Jacobs is an absolute bargain.

Edgerrin James   Height: 6-0   Weight: 214   College: Miami   Draft: 1999/1 (4)   Born: 1-Aug-1978   Age: 31   Risk: N/A

Year	Team	G	Runs	Yds	Yd/R	TD	FUM	DVOA	Rk	DYAR	Rk	YAR	Suc%	Rec	Pass	Yds	C%	Yd/C	TD	DVOA	Rk	DYAR	Rk
2006	ARI	16	337	1159	3.4	6	3	-10.6%	39	-29	43	15	45%	38	60	217	60%	5.7	0	-7.8%	42	20	41
2007	ARI	16	324	1222	3.8	7	4	-1.0%	27	101	21	74	46%	24	39	204	64%	8.5	0	-11.2%	38	6	38
2008	ARI	13	133	514	3.9	3	1	0.0%	21	46	29	39	44%	12	18	85	67%	7.1	0	-12.6%	--	1	--

It has been a year of tragedy and triumph for Edge. When he was benched at the start of the 2008 season, he asked for his release. The team refused, and when all was said and done he was starting again, this time in the Super Bowl. Then in April, Andia Denise Wilson, James' long-time girlfriend and the mother of his four children, passed away due to leukemia at the age of 30. One day after her funeral, James was inducted into the University of Miami Sports Hall of Fame. At the end of the month, the Cardinals drafted Beanie Wells, and finally released James. So, now what? He's still productive, and there should be demand for a back with this kind of experience, but there's a lot of wear on these tires. At age 30, James is already eighth all time in career carries; one more 300-carry season would vault him into fifth place. James could bounce around a lot the next few years; teams will sign him as long as he's productive, but nobody's going to give him a long-term deal.

Rashad Jennings   Height: 6-1   Weight: 232   College: Liberty   Draft: 2009/7 (250)   Born: 26-Mar-1985   Age: 24   Risk: Green

Year	Team	G	Runs	Yds	Yd/R	TD	FUM	DVOA	Rk	DYAR	Rk	YAR	Suc%	Rec	Pass	Yds	C%	Yd/C	TD	DVOA	Rk	DYAR	Rk
2009	JAC		44	187	4.2	0	1	23.7%						9	10	66	90%	7.4	1	-4.0%			

Jennings started his college career at University of Pittsburgh, but transferred to Liberty because of family health problems. He rushed for 1,000 yards three times at Liberty, then impressed scouts at Senior Bowl practices. Jennings is a good interior runner with adequate speed (Speed Score: 99.7) who will fight for extra yardage, and he has some receiving skills. He looks like a seventh-round steal who could emerge as the top change-up back to Maurice Jones-Drew.

Chris Johnson

Height: 5-11 Weight: 197 College: East Carolina   Draft: 2008/1 (24) Born: 23-Sep-1985 Age: 24 Risk: Yellow

Year	Team	G	Runs	Yds	Yd/R	TD	FUM	DVOA	Rk	DYAR	Rk	YAR	Suc%	Rec	Pass	Yds	C%	Yd/C	TD	DVOA	Rk	DYAR	Rk
2008	TEN	15	251	1228	4.9	9	1	9.2%	10	175	7	165	44%	43	62	260	69%	6.0	1	-19.8%	46	-20	48
2009	TEN		268	1225	4.6	8	4	7.2%						37	49	304	76%	8.2	1	-7.6%			

He was just the medicine the Titans' staid offense needed, providing big play potential every time he touched the ball, but his injury in the playoff loss to Baltimore proved to be the Titans' undoing. Johnson managed an impressive nine touchdowns, but most were on long runs. He should continue to lose goal-line carries to Len-Dale White — who is much better in short-yardage situations — and breaking that many long touchdown runs seems unlikely. The one area where Johnson could improve is as a receiver, where his shiftiness should be an asset, but he needs to better understand the timing of the passing offense.

Larry Johnson

Height: 6-1 Weight: 230 College: Penn State   Draft: 2003/1 (27) Born: 19-Nov-1979 Age: 30 Risk: Red

Year	Team	G	Runs	Yds	Yd/R	TD	FUM	DVOA	Rk	DYAR	Rk	YAR	Suc%	Rec	Pass	Yds	C%	Yd/C	TD	DVOA	Rk	DYAR	Rk
2006	KC	16	416	1789	4.3	17	2	6.5%	15	257	5	266	45%	41	67	410	67%	10.0	2	17.5%	12	135	7
2007	KC	8	158	559	3.5	3	1	-14.0%	43	-35	42	-41	41%	30	42	186	71%	6.2	1	-19.1%	46	-12	47
2008	KC	12	193	874	4.5	5	5	-12.7%	45	-36	46	-4	45%	12	16	74	75%	6.2	0	-37.6%	--	-21	--
2009	KC		214	946	4.4	10	4	14.1%						19	23	83	83%	4.4	0	-13.0%			

Johnson may have lost half of 2007 to the Curse of 370, but his 2008 season was the bigger mess. He rang up his fourth arrest for assault after allegedly spitting a drink in a woman's face at a Kansas City nightclub, and was suspended by the Chiefs for one game and the league for another. On the field, the Chiefs' transition to a spread-shotgun attack meant more playing time for Jamaal Charles and less for Johnson. By the end of the year, he was telling the press, "The city is tired of me, and the organization and I have run our course together. It's time to move on for me." The arrival of Scott Pioli and Todd Haley probably didn't make him feel better, because he's still a pound-the-rock guy living in a spread-the-field world. The Chiefs may still try to deal Johnson during the preseason, but you have to wonder what a team will give up for a running back with a monster contract and very little tread left on his tires. Sure, he averaged 4.5 yards per carry last year, but that was inflated by a schedule of bad run defenses; DVOA says he wasn't much better than the year before.

Felix Jones

Height: 6-0 Weight: 200 College: Arkansas   Draft: 2008/1 (22) Born: 8-May-1987 Age: 22 Risk: Yellow

Year	Team	G	Runs	Yds	Yd/R	TD	FUM	DVOA	Rk	DYAR	Rk	YAR	Suc%	Rec	Pass	Yds	C%	Yd/C	TD	DVOA	Rk	DYAR	Rk
2008	DAL	6	30	266	8.9	3	0	81.8%	--	118	--	119	73%	2	2	10	100%	5.0	0	6.2%	--	2	--
2009	DAL		151	732	4.9	5	4	15.4%						52	69	556	75%	10.7	1	49.0%			

Players who look like athletic freaks of nature in college rarely show the same level of sheer athletic dominance at the next level. Jones is an exception. It's hard to make more of an impact with 48 touches than Jones did; he led the league in rushing DVOA for guys with more than 10 carries, was the fifth-best kickoff return man in the league on a per-kickoff basis (minimum: 10 returns), and was arguably the most dynamic player on a team full of skill position stars before suffering a series of injuries that kept him out for the final ten games of the season.

So why are we still skeptical of Jones' potential impact at the pro level? Mainly, it's because there are a lot of things Jones can't do that good running backs have to do. He's not a good receiver. He's an ineffectual blocker. He can beat anyone to the corner, but he doesn't show the patience in his cuts — yet — needed to be consistently effective. It was telling that Jason Garrett didn't further integrate Jones into the lineup as the season went along, and to be quite honest, it's really hard to be more successful in such a limited role than Jones was this year. For Jones to be valuable enough to justify his selection as a first-round pick, he'll need to improve in the other areas of the game enough for the Cowboys to feel comfortable increasing his role and his reps.

Greg Jones

Height: 6-1   Weight: 250   College: Florida State   Draft: 2004/2 (55)   Born: 4-Apr-1981   Age: 28   Risk: Red

Year	Team	G	Runs	Yds	Yd/R	TD	FUM	DVOA	Rk	DYAR	Rk	YAR	Suc%	Rec	Pass	Yds	C%	Yd/C	TD	DVOA	Rk	DYAR	Rk
2007	JAC	16	42	119	2.8	2	0	-6.3%	--	4	--	10	48%	11	19	99	58%	9.0	2	11.4%	--	33	--
2008	JAC	12	2	13	6.5	0	0	3.3%	--	1	--	1	50%	13	16	116	81%	8.9	1	53.2%	--	61	--
2009	JAC		40	156	3.9	4	2	33.5%						6	7	66	86%	11.0	0	-15.5%			

Jones' workload may have been spartan in 2008, but that's about to change. Jack Del Rio has said that he wants to see Jones carry the ball more, as opposed to just blocking, and he's a good bet to get some crucial short-yardage work when Pocket Hercules needs a rest from all those runs up the middle.

Julius Jones

Height: 5-10   Weight: 211   College: Notre Dame   Draft: 2004/2 (43)   Born: 14-Aug-1981   Age: 28   Risk: Yellow

Year	Team	G	Runs	Yds	Yd/R	TD	FUM	DVOA	Rk	DYAR	Rk	YAR	Suc%	Rec	Pass	Yds	C%	Yd/C	TD	DVOA	Rk	DYAR	Rk
2006	DAL	16	267	1084	4.1	4	1	2.0%	22	112	18	95	45%	9	15	142	53%	15.8	0	28.7%	--	38	--
2007	DAL	16	164	588	3.6	2	0	-6.7%	35	12	35	9	37%	23	26	203	88%	8.8	0	38.3%	4	75	14
2008	SEA	15	158	698	4.4	2	4	-10.1%	43	-9	42	-1	39%	14	25	66	56%	4.7	0	-53.1%	51	-56	50
2009	SEA		232	1023	4.4	11	1	15.0%						31	43	219	72%	7.1	3	17.8%			

Jones thought that signing with Seattle meant he would be the star of the show, with no Marion Barber looking over his shoulder. Instead, Maurice Morris opened the season as the starter, and Jones came in off the bench. Morris was injured in that first game, and in the next two weeks, Jones put up 127 yards against the 49ers and 140 against the Rams. However, he struggled with fumbles, and was pulled in and out of the lineup; he had only six carries in the season's final four games. He told the *Seattle Times* he's excited about the team's new zone-blocking scheme: "Downhill and off to the races. That definitely fits my style of running a little bit better." The Seahawks are likely to run the ball more often under new coach Jim Mora, and Jones will get the bulk of the carries.

Kevin Jones

Height: 5-11   Weight: 221   College: Virginia Tech   Draft: 2004/1 (30)   Born: 21-Aug-1982   Age: 27   Risk: Green

Year	Team	G	Runs	Yds	Yd/R	TD	FUM	DVOA	Rk	DYAR	Rk	YAR	Suc%	Rec	Pass	Yds	C%	Yd/C	TD	DVOA	Rk	DYAR	Rk
2006	DET	12	181	689	3.8	6	4	-22.1%	46	-109	47	-86	40%	61	78	520	74%	8.5	2	17.2%	14	147	4
2007	DET	13	153	581	3.8	8	2	-2.7%	28	40	31	20	47%	32	44	197	73%	6.2	0	-12.3%	39	4	40
2008	CHI	11	34	109	3.2	0	0	-29.3%	--	-28	--	-19	29%	2	2	5	100%	2.5	0	-86.0%	--	-8	--
2009	CHI		50	236	4.7	2	2	2.6%						7	9	64	78%	9.1	0	-20.5%			

When you watch Jones play, it's incredibly difficult to figure out how he's not a star. He's got the ideal combination of size and speed, excellent agility, soft hands, and is a willing pass blocker. The answer is consistency and health, neither of which are traits Jones possesses with any sort of regularity. He's still essentially the same raw talent that he was coming out of college, something he can thank those injuries and the crack Detroit coaching staff for. He's the sort of player who could put everything together in the right situation and have a 1,400-yard season, but thanks to the vagaries of chance, he's more likely to be out of the league.

Thomas Jones

Height: 5-10   Weight: 220   College: Virginia   Draft: 2000/1 (7)   Born: 19-Aug-1978   Age: 31   Risk: Green

Year	Team	G	Runs	Yds	Yd/R	TD	FUM	DVOA	Rk	DYAR	Rk	YAR	Suc%	Rec	Pass	Yds	C%	Yd/C	TD	DVOA	Rk	DYAR	Rk
2006	CHI	16	296	1210	4.1	6	1	3.2%	19	147	14	146	48%	36	47	154	72%	4.3	0	-21.4%	52	-23	53
2007	NYJ	16	310	1119	3.6	1	2	-11.3%	40	-36	43	-43	43%	28	34	217	82%	7.8	1	34.4%	5	80	13
2008	NYJ	16	290	1312	4.5	13	2	11.9%	7	252	5	262	54%	36	42	207	86%	5.8	2	12.7%	17	71	15
2009	NYJ		219	904	4.1	8	2	-11.8%						25	31	157	81%	6.3	1	17.8%			

All it took was a revamping of the offensive line, but Jones rebounded from his one-touchdown 2007 campaign to lead the AFC in rushing in 2008. Most importantly, Jones went from inept to lethal in goal-line situations, as he scored on 13 of his 18 touches inside the five-yard line. Despite the impressive numbers, the 30-year-old

Jones is not an irreplaceable part, and when he started posturing for a new contract in the offseason, management let him know as much by drafting Shonn Greene and making noise about getting Leon Washington more involved in the offense.

Maurice Jones-Drew
Height: 5-8 Weight: 205 College: UCLA Draft: 2006/2 (60) Born: 23-Mar-1985 Age: 24 Risk: Red

Year	Team	G	Runs	Yds	Yd/R	TD	FUM	DVOA	Rk	DYAR	Rk	YAR	Suc%	Rec	Pass	Yds	C%	Yd/C	TD	DVOA	Rk	DYAR	Rk
2006	JAC	16	166	941	5.7	13	1	22.0%	4	217	10	263	51%	46	62	436	66%	9.5	2	16.7%	15	126	9
2007	JAC	15	167	768	4.6	9	1	2.1%	23	81	25	96	46%	40	55	407	73%	10.2	0	32.0%	7	142	5
2008	JAC	16	197	824	4.2	12	4	4.4%	18	112	18	107	46%	62	75	565	83%	9.1	2	43.8%	4	220	1
2009	JAC		303	1421	4.7	14	2	13.3%						55	69	457	80%	8.3	3	28.1%			

Jones-Drew's new $31 million contract, $17.5 million of which is guaranteed, makes him the face of the franchise and places an equal burden on the shoulders of Pocket Hercules and his quarterback. Backs that average 10 to 12 carries per game don't get money like this, no matter how good they are, so the big question going forward is what effect an increased workload will have on him. Of special concern will be Jones-Drew's ability to be a scoring threat at the same rate with that increased responsibility — in 2008, he had the highest red zone Success Rate of any back with more than 20 carries inside the 20, and only Carolina's Jonathan Stewart had a higher red zone DVOA. More carries, an improved line, and defenses forced to account for a better group of Jacksonville receivers all point the way for Jones-Drew's ascent to the upper tier of his position. Your eyes do not deceive you: Jones-Drew, not Adrian Peterson, has the best KUBIAK projection of any running back.

LaMont Jordan
Height: 5-10 Weight: 230 College: Maryland Draft: 2001/2 (49) Born: 11-Nov-1978 Age: 31 Risk: Red

Year	Team	G	Runs	Yds	Yd/R	TD	FUM	DVOA	Rk	DYAR	Rk	YAR	Suc%	Rec	Pass	Yds	C%	Yd/C	TD	DVOA	Rk	DYAR	Rk
2006	OAK	10	114	434	3.8	2	0	-8.2%	34	2	35	-4	34%	10	16	74	63%	7.4	0	-43.2%	--	-29	--
2007	OAK	12	144	549	3.8	3	1	-14.0%	42	-32	41	-8	37%	28	34	247	82%	8.8	0	19.7%	13	65	17
2008	NE	8	80	363	4.5	4	1	22.2%	--	113	--	104	60%	0	0	0	--	0.0	0	--	--	--	--
2009	DEN		49	171	3.5	1	2	-17.4%						14	17	96	82%	6.9	0	0.0%			

Jordan started punching the clock for the Patriots late in the season; his 40 carries combined in the season's last two games matched the 40 he had the rest of the season after missing several games with a calf injury. He led the Patriots' crazy-quilt running back rotation in red zone DVOA, DVOA on third and fourth down, and overall Success Rate. Now in Denver, he could be a valuable addition to a Josh McDaniels offense that will reportedly feature less of Denver's traditional zone blocking and more of a standard run-blocking scheme.

Jamal Lewis
Height: 5-11 Weight: 245 College: Tennessee Draft: 2000/1 (5) Born: 29-Aug-1979 Age: 30 Risk: Green

Year	Team	G	Runs	Yds	Yd/R	TD	FUM	DVOA	Rk	DYAR	Rk	YAR	Suc%	Rec	Pass	Yds	C%	Yd/C	TD	DVOA	Rk	DYAR	Rk
2006	BAL	16	314	1132	3.6	9	4	-9.6%	38	-13	38	-5	42%	18	26	115	62%	6.4	0	-18.1%	50	-7	49
2007	CLE	15	298	1304	4.4	9	4	1.5%	25	125	15	88	45%	30	39	248	77%	8.3	2	33.3%	6	99	8
2008	CLE	16	279	1002	3.6	4	1	-6.0%	37	29	34	-50	40%	23	32	178	72%	7.7	0	4.6%	24	31	32
2009	CLE		150	488	3.3	5	2	0.9%						22	32	180	69%	8.2	1	13.2%			

Jamal Lewis' total carries by gain:

Yards	Carries	Yards	Carries
Losses/no gain	40	8-10 yards	13
1-2 yards	95	11-20 yards	17
3-4 yards	73	21-30 yards	1
5-7 yards	40		

This is the very definition of plodding. About 44 percent of all rushing plays are stopped for a gain of two yards are less; Lewis' average last season was 48.4 percent. That wouldn't be a major problem if Lewis pushed a few 11- to 20-yard runs into the 21- to 30-yard category, or maybe the 30-plus category, which Lewis failed to crack. With no big play capability, Lewis has become a plowhorse, and while this sort of back is usually effective on the goal line, Lewis contributed four touchdowns on 18 carries inside the five last year, when the average back would've scored 8.14 times. Couple that with Lewis' minor knee surgery in April and his 30th birthday party in August, and you have a recipe for a massive production tailspin. The new Browns brass still thinks of Lewis as a featured back. They are part of a shrinking minority.

Marshawn Lynch
Height: 5-11   Weight: 215   College: California   Draft: 2007/1 (12)   Born: 22-Apr-1986   Age: 23   Risk: Green

Year	Team	G	Runs	Yds	Yd/R	TD	FUM	DVOA	Rk	DYAR	Rk	YAR	Suc%	Rec	Pass	Yds	C%	Yd/C	TD	DVOA	Rk	DYAR	Rk
2007	BUF	13	280	1115	4.0	7	1	-5.0%	33	42	29	50	45%	18	26	184	69%	10.2	0	14.1%	20	41	24
2008	BUF	15	250	1036	4.1	8	2	-1.1%	25	77	24	105	46%	47	67	300	70%	6.4	1	-12.5%	43	5	42
2009	BUF		167	655	3.9	3	2	-14.0%						32	42	224	76%	7.0	1	-21.7%			

Lynch was named as an alternate to the Pro Bowl, but like Willis McGahee before him, his raw yardage numbers look better than his DVOA or DYAR. Lynch, like the rest of the Buffalo offense, really struggled on second down, generating a DVOA of –20.9% on his 68 carries. He also had his problems inside the five-yard line, where Lynch carried the ball 12 times and only came away with three touchdowns. It wasn't all Lynch's fault — Buffalo's offensive line was terrible in power situations all season. On the other hand, getting caught driving around Oakland with a concealed firearm is most certainly his fault, and with this being Roger Goodell's "No Felony or Misdemeanor-Related Fun League," Lynch will be spending the first three games of the season on the sidelines serving his suspension.

Laurence Maroney
Height: 5-11   Weight: 205   College: Minnesota   Draft: 2006/1 (21)   Born: 5-Feb-1985   Age: 24   Risk: Yellow

Year	Team	G	Runs	Yds	Yd/R	TD	FUM	DVOA	Rk	DYAR	Rk	YAR	Suc%	Rec	Pass	Yds	C%	Yd/C	TD	DVOA	Rk	DYAR	Rk
2006	NE	14	175	745	4.3	6	1	-4.5%	32	31	31	58	46%	22	30	194	70%	8.8	1	23.1%	7	78	17
2007	NE	13	185	835	4.5	6	0	16.7%	6	199	7	207	58%	4	8	116	50%	29.0	0	87.5%	--	42	--
2008	NE	3	28	93	3.3	0	0	-10.0%	--	-2	--	-4	54%	0	0	0	--	0.0	0	--	--	--	--
2009	NE		134	539	4.0	4	3	-2.2%						8	13	75	62%	9.3	0	3.7%			

Maroney struggled through the season until a shoulder injury ended his year in October. In May, he revealed that he actually played through the 2008 season with a broken bone in the shoulder. "I feel like it still shows my toughness and my dedication to the team and how much I really want to contribute," he told the *Boston Globe*. The Fred Taylor signing indicated that the Pats aren't counting on Maroney to be a feature back in 2009, but he'll get one more chance to impress.

Deuce McAllister
Height: 6-1   Weight: 232   College: Mississippi   Draft: 2001/1 (23)   Born: 27-Dec-1978   Age: 30   Risk: N/A

Year	Team	G	Runs	Yds	Yd/R	TD	FUM	DVOA	Rk	DYAR	Rk	YAR	Suc%	Rec	Pass	Yds	C%	Yd/C	TD	DVOA	Rk	DYAR	Rk
2006	NO	15	244	1057	4.3	10	2	11.4%	10	221	9	190	54%	30	36	198	75%	6.6	0	25.6%	6	95	14
2007	NO	3	24	92	3.8	0	1	-21.1%	--	-12	--	-14	42%	4	5	15	80%	3.8	0	-26.5%	--	-4	--
2008	NO	13	107	418	3.9	5	0	9.6%	9	86	22	107	59%	18	23	128	78%	7.1	1	16.0%	--	41	--

McAllister spent 2008 in the nether-region between "injured" and "healthy." He missed two of the first three games of the season while recovering from his second ACL surgery in three years. He rushed 20 times against the Niners in Week 4, but after that his health status started changing on an hour-by-hour basis. Sometimes he got 18 carries, sometimes none, and it was impossible to determine his availability until after pregame warm-ups. McAllister had more knee surgery in the offseason, then began working to improve his hip and ankle strength: His doctors believe that early-career ankle injuries caused a cascading effect that led to his knee problems. McAllister still wants to play, and he's still a useful situational back if he can stay somewhat healthy. He earns the coveted role of First Player Called When a Featured Back Gets Hurt in Camp for 2009.

Le'Ron McClain
Height: 6-0   Weight: 256   College: Alabama   Draft: 2007/4 (137)   Born: 27-Dec-1984   Age: 24   Risk: Green

Year	Team	G	Runs	Yds	Yd/R	TD	FUM	DVOA	Rk	DYAR	Rk	YAR	Suc%	Rec	Pass	Yds	C%	Yd/C	TD	DVOA	Rk	DYAR	Rk
2007	BAL	16	8	18	2.3	0	0	-29.3%	--	-7	--	-6	25%	9	13	55	69%	6.1	1	-33.0%	--	-15	--
2008	BAL	16	232	902	3.9	10	3	7.6%	11	163	10	97	51%	19	30	123	63%	6.5	1	-28.0%	49	-23	49
2009	BAL		50	210	4.2	4	2	-9.1%						22	29	163	76%	7.4	1	23.0%			

Most of McClain's early-season carries came as a fourth quarter battering ram. In the first 12 weeks of the season, he had just 14 first-quarter carries, three of them in short-yardage situations. By the end of the season, McClain was being used as something just short of a featured back: He had 31 first-quarter carries in the final four games, the kind of workload the starter in a typical committee backfield might expect. McClain averaged just 3.17 yards per rush in those late-season, first-quarter carries, a clear sign of the Peter Principle at work. McClain was very good as a short-yardage player, clock-eater, and change-up runner from the fullback position, but his lack of receiving chops and big play ability make him a liability as a 20-carry workhorse. Harbaugh and Cameron will scale back his role as they open up the offense, but they shouldn't abandon the fullback belly play completely: Three or four of them per game can still be very effective.

LeSean McCoy
Height: 5-11   Weight: 210   College: Pittsburgh   Draft: 2009/2 (53)   Born: 12-Jul-1988   Age: 21   Risk: Yellow

Year	Team	G	Runs	Yds	Yd/R	TD	FUM	DVOA	Rk	DYAR	Rk	YAR	Suc%	Rec	Pass	Yds	C%	Yd/C	TD	DVOA	Rk	DYAR	Rk
2009	PHI		122	594	4.9	5	3	9.4%						27	32	213	84%	7.9	0	18.2%			

Within 48 hours of the draft, we'd read in three different articles that McCoy was a Brian Westbrook clone, a good complement to Westbrook, and a player who didn't fit the Eagles scheme whatsoever. What is he, really? Well, from what we've seen, he's a shifty back with great acceleration and good instincts for knowing where and how to hit the hole. He's got the tools to be a great receiver, but doesn't have a ton of experience. Sounds good so far, right? Well, the bad news is that he can't pass block and he has serious fumble issues, so he won't be getting any playing time until he solves both those problems. He did play at Milford Academy, so as expected, he's quiet and eager to please.

Darren McFadden
Height: 6-2   Weight: 210   College: Arkansas   Draft: 2008/1 (4)   Born: 27-Aug-1987   Age: 22   Risk: Yellow

Year	Team	G	Runs	Yds	Yd/R	TD	FUM	DVOA	Rk	DYAR	Rk	YAR	Suc%	Rec	Pass	Yds	C%	Yd/C	TD	DVOA	Rk	DYAR	Rk
2008	OAK	13	113	499	4.4	4	3	-8.9%	40	-2	40	26	38%	29	39	285	77%	9.8	0	33.3%	7	107	10
2009	OAK		171	813	4.8	3	4	4.7%						47	63	395	75%	8.4	1	10.2%			

A mean case of turf toe cost McFadden the better part of six weeks, limiting his explosiveness. It also kept the man who made the "Wildcat" famous on the sidelines while it became a staple of NFL offenses. His effectiveness as a receiver was a good sign that he'll eventually become the all-around back that he was sold as coming out of school, and when you factor in the debilitating nature of turf toe injuries (look at Warrick Dunn's 2001 or LaDainian Tomlinson's 2008 if you have questions), McFadden's still on pace to be a star. It would help if he got the ball in better situations; 23 percent of his carries came on second-and-8 or more, the fifth-highest percentage in the league for backs with more than 50 carries.

Willis McGahee

Height: 6-0   Weight: 228 College: Miami   Draft: 2003/1 (23)   Born: 20-Oct-1981   Age: 28 Risk: Yellow

Year	Team	G	Runs	Yds	Yd/R	TD	FUM	DVOA	Rk	DYAR	Rk	YAR	Suc%	Rec	Pass	Yds	C%	Yd/C	TD	DVOA	Rk	DYAR	Rk
2006	BUF	14	259	990	3.8	6	4	-3.3%	29	57	27	29	45%	18	28	156	61%	8.7	0	-23.6%	53	-16	52
2007	BAL	15	294	1207	4.1	7	4	-8.2%	38	5	38	57	42%	43	49	231	88%	5.4	1	-2.8%	30	29	30
2008	BAL	13	170	671	3.9	7	2	3.9%	20	86	21	91	46%	24	32	173	75%	7.2	0	-22.0%	47	-15	46
2009	BAL		131	504	3.8	4	4	-29.9%						20	29	160	69%	8.0	0	-22.3%			

McGahee's success in the red zone (DVOA of 25.4% and a 56 percent Success Rate on 34 carries) saved an otherwise awful season. McGahee lost carries to Le'Ron McClain and Ray Rice as the season wore on, and he didn't do much with the carries he did get. McGahee was a solid citizen in offseason workouts, a sign that he knows that his stock is falling and that his next contract (he's in the final year of a three-year deal) will be his last. Despite a 2007 effort to force-feed McGahee into the passing game, he provides little value as a receiver. McGahee's saving grace in Baltimore is that McClain is a pure interior runner and Rice is a pure scatback, making McGahee the team's only all-purpose threat. That kept him from being a June cap casualty, but it won't net him more than 12 to 15 touches per game this year.

Rashard Mendenhall

Height: 5-11 Weight: 210 College: Illinois   Draft: 2008/1 (23)   Born: 19-Jun-1987   Age: 22 Risk: Red

Year	Team	G	Runs	Yds	Yd/R	TD	FUM	DVOA	Rk	DYAR	Rk	YAR	Suc%	Rec	Pass	Yds	C%	Yd/C	TD	DVOA	Rk	DYAR	Rk
2008	PIT	4	19	58	3.1	0	0	-20.8%	--	-8	--	-10	26%	2	3	17	67%	8.5	0	24.7%	--	5	--
2009	PIT		157	716	4.6	5	2	19.1%						49	56	382	88%	7.8	2	-36.2%			

Mendenhall had a strong 2008 preseason — 54 carries, 224 yards — and was working his way into the Steelers rotation when he suffered a season-ending shoulder injury against the Ravens in his first NFL start. Before that game, Mendenhall text-messaged Ray Rice and predicted a big game; Rice showed the message to teammates to get them fired up. It would have been great bulletin board material if you could staple a text message to a bulletin board. Mendenhall is a big back who should fill a major short-yardage need if he's ready to go in 2009. He'll be fine, unless he leaves some trash-talk on Chris Johnson's Facebook before the season opener.

Ryan Moats

Height: 5-8   Weight: 210 College: Louisiana Tech   Draft: 2005/3 (77)   Born: 17-Dec-1982   Age: 26 Risk: Green

Year	Team	G	Runs	Yds	Yd/R	TD	FUM	DVOA	Rk	DYAR	Rk	YAR	Suc%	Rec	Pass	Yds	C%	Yd/C	TD	DVOA	Rk	DYAR	Rk
2006	PHI	8	22	69	3.1	0	0	-11.7%	--	-3	--	-2	45%	0	1	0	0%	0.0	0	0.0%	--	0	--
2008	HOU	9	26	94	3.6	1	0	31.5%	--	42	--	30	50%	3	5	14	60%	4.7	0	-54.4%	--	-10	--
2009	HOU		33	128	3.9	0	2	8.4%						8	14	79	57%	9.9	0	0.5%			

Most of Moats' production (such as it was) came in at garbage time: three carries in a 35-6 win over the Bengals, seven more in a 41-13 loss to the Ravens, 12 carries for 34 yards in the meaningless season finale against the Bears. Moats is a tough low-center-of-gravity runner who hasn't seen much action since 2005, when he was the runner of desperation for the Eagles at the end of the Owens Implosion season. He's a poor receiver and an awful decision maker who often lines up in the wrong position, if not the wrong stadium. Gary Kubiak called Moats and Chris Brown his "2-a and 2-b" backs behind Steve Slaton. That means Moats could play a major role in 2009, though it is likely that Kubiak is hoping for backs 1-b through 1-z to emerge.

Mewelde Moore

Height: 5-11 Weight: 209 College: Tulane   Draft: 2004/4 (119) Born: 24-Jul-1982   Age: 27 Risk: Yellow

Year	Team	G	Runs	Yds	Yd/R	TD	FUM	DVOA	Rk	DYAR	Rk	YAR	Suc%	Rec	Pass	Yds	C%	Yd/C	TD	DVOA	Rk	DYAR	Rk
2006	MIN	16	24	131	5.5	0	0	40.3%	--	32	--	28	33%	46	62	468	69%	10.2	1	13.4%	18	111	10
2007	MIN	12	20	113	5.7	0	1	31.5%	--	25	--	27	50%	6	8	48	75%	8.0	0	-7.6%	--	2	--
2008	PIT	16	140	588	4.2	5	0	14.3%	6	139	14	105	51%	40	53	320	75%	8.0	1	4.6%	25	55	21
2009	PIT		76	307	4.0	2	2	-12.0%						28	41	254	68%	9.1	1	14.6%			

The Steelers threw just 75 passes to running backs last year; only the Panthers and Broncos targeted their backs for fewer throws. Moore was the target of 53 of those passes, and DVOA says he did a serviceable job with them. The low target totals are partly a matter of scheme and partly the result of Ben Roethlisberger's unwillingness to check down when he's in danger. At any rate, Moore is a backfield receiver for a team that doesn't use backfield receivers much. Not a great career move. Moore got a desperation trial as a short-yardage back last year with mixed results. He scored just three touchdowns in 11 goal-to-go carries, but his red zone DVOA was 21.8%, with a Success Rate of 64 percent on 41 carries. The moral of the story: Moore can slice and dice for yardage from the 20-yard line to the five-yard line, but then its time to bring in a bigger gun.

Knowshon Moreno
Height: 5-11 Weight: 207 College: Georgia   Draft: 2009/1 (12) Born: 16-Jul-1987 Age: 22 Risk: Red

Year	Team	G	Runs	Yds	Yd/R	TD	FUM	DVOA	Rk	DYAR	Rk	YAR	Suc%	Rec	Pass	Yds	C%	Yd/C	TD	DVOA	Rk	DYAR	Rk
2009	DEN		225	1025	4.6	10	2	5.7%						39	48	303	81%	7.8	0	15.9%			

Moreno's one of the more fascinating players to come out of this year's draft. At Georgia, he was a jack-of-all-trades back who helped save Matthew Stafford's bacon on more than one occasion — producing a 30.6 POE that was eighth-best in the country — but it was Stafford who went first overall because of his tools. Moreno doesn't have great measurables, and a 96.9 Speed Score pegs him to be a bust, but Moreno's exactly the sort of player that Speed Score struggles with: an agile back who can catch passes and pass block. The hope is that he ends up somewhere between Brian Westbrook and Emmitt Smith, two players who Speed Score whiffed on.

Maurice Morris
Height: 5-11 Weight: 202 College: Oregon   Draft: 2002/2 (54) Born: 1-Dec-1979 Age: 30 Risk: Red

Year	Team	G	Runs	Yds	Yd/R	TD	FUM	DVOA	Rk	DYAR	Rk	YAR	Suc%	Rec	Pass	Yds	C%	Yd/C	TD	DVOA	Rk	DYAR	Rk
2006	SEA	16	161	604	3.8	0	1	-11.3%	40	-17	39	-23	39%	11	20	46	55%	4.2	0	-45.9%	--	-38	--
2007	SEA	14	140	628	4.5	4	2	0.7%	26	57	28	45	51%	23	32	213	72%	9.3	1	17.1%	15	55	21
2008	SEA	13	132	574	4.3	0	1	-1.1%	24	38	32	25	45%	19	27	136	70%	7.2	2	16.8%	13	45	28
2009	DET		88	527	6.0	1	1	18.5%						9	13	90	69%	10.0	0	-30.0%			

Morris will come in to spell Kevin Smith and limit his carries, but expect to see Smith back in the game on third downs. He was tremendous there, posting a DVOA of 33% in his rookie season. Morris, meanwhile, is close to average overall, but has never been higher than -18% on third downs in his career, and has often been far worse than that. Morris will be 30 in December, so expecting him to be anything more than a boom-or-bust change of pace is unrealistic.

Sammy Morris
Height: 6-0 Weight: 218 College: Texas Tech   Draft: 2000/5 (156) Born: 23-Mar-1977 Age: 32 Risk: Green

Year	Team	G	Runs	Yds	Yd/R	TD	FUM	DVOA	Rk	DYAR	Rk	YAR	Suc%	Rec	Pass	Yds	C%	Yd/C	TD	DVOA	Rk	DYAR	Rk
2006	MIA	12	92	400	4.3	1	2	-20.0%	--	-46	--	-21	42%	21	35	162	63%	7.7	0	-24.6%	54	-24	54
2007	NE	6	85	384	4.5	3	0	15.3%	--	92	--	97	54%	6	8	35	75%	5.8	0	-20.2%	--	-3	--
2008	NE	13	156	727	4.7	7	1	14.9%	5	166	8	154	49%	17	24	161	71%	9.5	0	18.1%	--	42	--
2009	NE		76	307	4.0	1	2	-14.9%						18	24	159	75%	8.8	1	22.5%			

The most productive of New England's grab bag of running backs in 2008 according to our numbers, Morris often alternated carries with LaMont Jordan and put up 100-plus-yard games against the punching bag defenses of Denver and Oakland. He'll have competition for first-down carries from Fred Taylor this year, but should get enough time to make an impact again.

Jerious Norwood
Height: 6-0 Weight: 204 College: Mississippi State   Draft: 2006/3 (79) Born: 23-Jul-1983 Age: 26 Risk: Green

Year	Team	G	Runs	Yds	Yd/R	TD	FUM	DVOA	Rk	DYAR	Rk	YAR	Suc%	Rec	Pass	Yds	C%	Yd/C	TD	DVOA	Rk	DYAR	Rk
2006	ATL	14	99	633	6.4	2	0	35.1%	--	170	--	150	53%	12	15	102	67%	8.5	0	-7.5%	--	5	--
2007	ATL	15	103	613	6.0	1	0	24.5%	1	133	13	126	48%	28	39	277	72%	9.9	0	21.6%	12	73	15
2008	ATL	16	95	489	5.1	4	1	7.1%	--	57	--	72	41%	36	54	338	67%	9.4	2	5.0%	23	55	22
2009	ATL		117	547	4.7	1	1	3.2%						41	52	385	79%	9.4	1	22.0%			

Last year we questioned why Atlanta would sign Michael Turner when it had a smaller-sample star with better prospects on the roster. Norwood did have another productive season, although not nearly as strong as the previous two. Turner's heavy workload has to be reduced, with Norwood the beneficiary. Norwood also continues to be an effective weapon in the passing game. So long as the extra carries don't hinder Norwood's explosiveness (and Turner avoids the Curse of 370), Atlanta should have a frightening thunder/lightning combo in 2009.

Willie Parker

Height: 5-10　Weight: 209　College: North Carolina　　Draft: 2004/FA　　Born: 11-Nov-1980　Age: 29　Risk: Red

Year	Team	G	Runs	Yds	Yd/R	TD	FUM	DVOA	Rk	DYAR	Rk	YAR	Suc%	Rec	Pass	Yds	C%	Yd/C	TD	DVOA	Rk	DYAR	Rk
2006	PIT	16	337	1494	4.4	13	6	3.3%	18	165	13	133	45%	31	42	222	67%	7.2	3	-4.5%	37	23	39
2007	PIT	15	321	1316	4.1	2	4	-10.8%	39	-27	39	-13	42%	23	31	164	74%	7.1	0	2.9%	27	28	31
2008	PIT	11	210	791	3.8	5	0	-2.9%	33	46	28	41	41%	3	11	13	36%	4.3	0	-72.9%	--	-34	--
2009	PIT		211	704	3.3	9	1	-4.2%						14	19	88	74%	6.3	1	6.6%			

A strong postseason (70-246-2) overshadowed a disappointing season that was interrupted twice by knee and shoulder injuries. Parker's best games were the first two of the season: 53 carries, 241 yards, and three touchdowns against the Texans and Browns. By December, Parker went through a three-game 45-103-0 stretch that forced the Steelers to add Gary Russell to the rushing rotation. Parker is a poor receiver for a little back, but he's a gifted slasher who is worth 10 to 15 carries per game in a committee backfield.

Cedric Peerman

Height: 5-10　Weight: 216　College: Virginia　　Draft: 2009/6 (185)　Born: 10-Oct-1986　Age: 23　Risk: Green

Year	Team	G	Runs	Yds	Yd/R	TD	FUM	DVOA	Rk	DYAR	Rk	YAR	Suc%	Rec	Pass	Yds	C%	Yd/C	TD	DVOA	Rk	DYAR	Rk
2009	BAL		29	141	4.9	0	2	14.7%						19	21	151	90%	7.9	0	5.3%			

The Ravens drafted several high-character players this year, including Paul Kruger, the defensive end who spent two years on Mormon mission, and Peerman, an ordained deacon who grew up on a tobacco plantation. They may just be trying to counterbalance the Bengals in the AFC North. Peerman played behind the great Eugene Monroe-Brandon Albert lines at Virginia but never put up big numbers, in part because he was often injured. Despite the lack of production, he's a decent prospect as an all-purpose back, a good receiver who rarely fumbles despite tiny 7⅞-inch hands. Peerman is tied with Giants draftee Andre Brown for this year's highest Speed Score (110.2).

Chris Perry

Height: 6-0　Weight: 224　College: Michigan　　Draft: 2004/1 (26)　Born: 27-Dec-1981　Age: 27　Risk: N/A

Year	Team	G	Runs	Yds	Yd/R	TD	FUM	DVOA	Rk	DYAR	Rk	YAR	Suc%	Rec	Pass	Yds	C%	Yd/C	TD	DVOA	Rk	DYAR	Rk
2006	CIN	6	10	57	5.7	0	0	27.5%	--	16	--	14	60%	9	11	42	82%	4.7	0	-20.8%	--	-4	--
2008	CIN	13	104	269	2.6	2	5	-39.2%	49	-137	49	-176	29%	20	35	71	60%	3.6	0	-55.2%	52	-77	52

The Bengals have never had much luck with highly touted backs from the Big Ten (see Griffin, Archie or Carter, Ki-Jana), and Perry is another failure. Five fumbles in five weeks, including one in the fourth quarter in Dallas just when it seemed the winless Bengals were poised for an upset, ended Perry's big shot after several frustrating years of injury-wrecked seasons. Since 1994, only one running back with at least 100 carries had a lower rushing DVOA than Perry did last year: Lamar Smith with the 1998 Saints. Perry also had the third lowest combined rushing and receiving DYAR in history, behind Smith again, this time with the 2001 Dolphins, and Jonathan Wells with the 2002 Texans. Reports have him playing for the Orlando franchise in the new UFL.

Adrian Peterson
Height: 6-2   Weight: 217   College: Oklahoma   Draft: 2007/1 (7)   Born: 21-Mar-1985   Age: 24   Risk: Red

Year	Team	G	Runs	Yds	Yd/R	TD	FUM	DVOA	Rk	DYAR	Rk	YAR	Suc%	Rec	Pass	Yds	C%	Yd/C	TD	DVOA	Rk	DYAR	Rk
2007	MIN	14	238	1341	5.6	12	5	16.4%	7	228	4	232	45%	19	29	268	69%	14.1	1	43.6%	2	97	9
2008	MIN	16	363	1760	4.8	10	9	-0.3%	22	121	17	172	46%	21	39	125	54%	6.0	0	-46.5%	50	-70	51
2009	MIN		373	1837	4.9	12	7	5.1%						23	27	189	85%	8.2	1	5.9%			

The acquisition of Bernard Berrian was supposed to move safeties away from the line of scrimmage and give Peterson a better shot at gaining consistent yardage, but while his raw numbers went up thanks to 125 additional carries, his yards per carry and his FO metrics took a nosedive. No one doubts that he's capable of doing special things any time he has the ball in his hands, but if you're really an elite back, you need to be pushing your team consistently towards first downs. Peterson's DVOA on first down was 2.6%, exactly the league average; he gained five or more yards 45 percent of the time, while other halfbacks did so at a 47 percent clip.

The other thing perceived to be holding Peterson back are his fumble issues, but that shouldn't be a problem going forward. Peterson fumbled once every 40 rushes or so, the 27th-highest ratio out of the 197 instances of a back carrying the ball 300 times. In the subsequent year, every back who fumbled more than once every 45 rushes fumbled, on average, once every 98.3 attempts, better than the league average of once every 89.9 attempts. That's a list that includes Eric Dickerson, Walter Payton, Earl Campbell, and Tony Dorsett. In other words, assuming he makes adjustments, Peterson should be fine.

Antonio Pittman
Height: 5-11   Weight: 207   College: Ohio State   Draft: 2007/4 (107)   Born: 9-Dec-1985   Age: 23   Risk: Green

Year	Team	G	Runs	Yds	Yd/R	TD	FUM	DVOA	Rk	DYAR	Rk	YAR	Suc%	Rec	Pass	Yds	C%	Yd/C	TD	DVOA	Rk	DYAR	Rk
2007	STL	11	38	139	3.7	0	0	-8.7%	--	0	--	-6	34%	3	9	15	33%	5.0	0	-86.8%	--	-39	--
2008	STL	12	79	296	3.7	0	0	-4.9%	--	12	--	-6	44%	18	27	132	67%	7.3	0	-11.4%	42	4	43
2009	STL		73	355	4.9	4	2	-18.3%						8	12	71	67%	8.8	0	-6.9%			

He looked good in racking up 178 of his 296 rushing yards last year in just two games against the 49ers and Patriots, but the NFL plays 16 games (for now), so Pittman appears to have lost his job as Steven Jackson's backup to the unheralded Kenneth Darby. Skipping a Saturday walkthrough after his 23rd birthday party the night before probably wasn't the best decision he's ever made.

Michael Pittman
Height: 6-0   Weight: 228   College: Fresno State   Draft: 1998/4 (95)   Born: 14-Aug-1975   Age: 34   Risk: N/A

Year	Team	G	Runs	Yds	Yd/R	TD	FUM	DVOA	Rk	DYAR	Rk	YAR	Suc%	Rec	Pass	Yds	C%	Yd/C	TD	DVOA	Rk	DYAR	Rk
2006	TB	16	50	245	4.9	1	1	8.8%	--	32	--	32	39%	47	77	405	58%	8.6	0	-5.3%	39	42	27
2007	TB	10	68	286	4.2	0	0	-4.6%	--	10	--	8	44%	26	39	191	67%	7.3	0	-24.4%	51	-24	51
2008	DEN	8	76	320	4.2	4	0	15.6%	--	93	--	88	57%	10	13	112	77%	11.2	0	-12.2%	--	1	--

Pittman was actually supposed to be Denver's fullback at one point in training camp, but with all the injuries he was returned to halfback, where he inevitably suffered his own season-ending injury (a lingering neck stinger). Pittman's receiving numbers have been down the last couple years, and his rushing numbers in 2008 were likely the product of the quality Denver blocking, but that won't stop some team from bringing him in for training camp.

Clinton Portis
Height: 5-11   Weight: 212   College: Miami   Draft: 2002/2 (51)   Born: 1-Sep-1981   Age: 28   Risk: Green

Year	Team	G	Runs	Yds	Yd/R	TD	FUM	DVOA	Rk	DYAR	Rk	YAR	Suc%	Rec	Pass	Yds	C%	Yd/C	TD	DVOA	Rk	DYAR	Rk
2006	WAS	8	127	523	4.1	7	0	11.6%	8	111	19	86	44%	17	26	170	65%	10.0	0	7.0%	26	36	32
2007	WAS	16	325	1262	3.9	11	6	-3.0%	30	75	26	47	46%	47	58	389	81%	8.3	0	15.5%	18	97	10
2008	WAS	16	342	1487	4.3	9	3	11.7%	8	285	3	233	48%	28	36	218	78%	7.8	0	15.3%	15	54	23
2009	WAS		282	1218	4.3	7	2	3.3%						21	30	144	70%	6.9	0	13.6%			

Portis does not like minicamp, and he's put together what he believes is solid medical evidence that organized team activities are bad ideas in the current climate. "It's too soon to be back," he told the Associated Press in early May. "Bad weather. Swine flu going around. This water could have some Swine flu in it, then all of us would be dead. In Mexico, they canceled all sporting events. They need to do that in the U.S." His interesting sense of humor aside, Portis posted his best season in years despite a sub-elite passing attack and an iffy offensive line. Redskins coach Jim Zorn learned how to drive a running back into the ground from Mike Holmgren, and the workload was disconcerting early in the year. But Portis is still The Man in this offense — he is a devastating pass blocker, his 28.9% red zone DVOA was among the best for backs with enough carries to make a difference, and he posted positive DVOA on every down. The challenge for the Redskins will be to build enough of an offense around him and avoid working him into the ground.

Dominic Rhodes
Height: 5-9   Weight: 203 College: Midwestern State   Draft: 2001/ (FA)   Born: 17-Jan-1979   Age: 30 Risk: Red

Year	Team	G	Runs	Yds	Yd/R	TD	FUM	DVOA	Rk	DYAR	Rk	YAR	Suc%	Rec	Pass	Yds	C%	Yd/C	TD	DVOA	Rk	DYAR	Rk
2006	IND	16	187	641	3.4	5	2	-9.1%	37	-4	37	3	49%	36	47	251	55%	7.0	0	-11.6%	45	7	44
2007	OAK	10	75	302	4.0	1	1	-2.0%	--	21	--	38	51%	11	18	70	61%	6.4	0	-36.8%	--	-21	--
2008	IND	15	152	538	3.5	6	0	-4.9%	36	25	37	19	49%	45	59	302	76%	6.7	3	2.2%	29	54	24
2009	BUF		63	323	5.1	1	3	-8.6%						21	30	198	70%	9.4	0	-0.2%			

They say you can never go home again, and Rhodes is one more example. After an aborted one-year stay in Oakland, Rhodes came back to the Colts to again share carries with Joseph Addai. Unlike the 2006 season, Addai was not clearly the superior player, but the problem is that Rhodes was no better; Addai had just gotten worse. The Colts decided the reunion would be a one-year engagement, and Rhodes signed a deal with Buffalo in the offseason to be a temporary fill-in for the suspended Marshawn Lynch.

Ray Rice
Height: 5-8   Weight: 199 College: Rutgers   Draft: 2008/2 (55)   Born: 22-Jan-1987   Age: 22 Risk: Red

Year	Team	G	Runs	Yds	Yd/R	TD	FUM	DVOA	Rk	DYAR	Rk	YAR	Suc%	Rec	Pass	Yds	C%	Yd/C	TD	DVOA	Rk	DYAR	Rk
2008	BAL	13	107	454	4.2	0	1	-2.5%	30	25	36	18	42%	33	43	273	77%	8.3	0	25.8%	9	81	13
2009	BAL		171	715	4.2	6	4	3.6%						33	54	253	61%	7.7	2	-31.1%			

Rice demonstrated some big play ability and had one excellent game (154 yards against the Browns on November 2nd) before missing the last three games of the year and most of the playoffs with a shin injury. Rice spent the offseason working on his blocking and receiving, and he could easily carve out a 20-touch role in the offense if he rounds out his game. Durability will always be a concern for the diminutive Rice, but he fits well as the big-play threat in a three-headed backfield — and based on what we saw in OTAs, he'll be the lead back in the Baltimore committee this year.

Michael Robinson
Height: 6-2   Weight: 217 College: Penn State   Draft: 2006/4 (100) Born: 6-Feb-1983   Age: 26 Risk: Red

Year	Team	G	Runs	Yds	Yd/R	TD	FUM	DVOA	Rk	DYAR	Rk	YAR	Suc%	Rec	Pass	Yds	C%	Yd/C	TD	DVOA	Rk	DYAR	Rk
2006	SF	16	38	116	3.1	2	0	-29.5%	--	-41	--	-36	34%	9	12	47	50%	5.2	0	-28.9%	--	-12	--
2007	SF	15	26	121	4.7	0	1	-27.4%	--	-20	--	-13	38%	11	13	73	85%	6.6	0	28.1%	--	26	--
2008	SF	16	19	50	2.6	0	1	-32.3%	--	-23	--	-19	53%	17	20	202	85%	11.9	0	54.9%	--	85	--
2009	SF		49	179	3.6	1	2	-28.3%						25	29	226	86%	9.0	0	2.2%			

Michael Robinson scored two touchdowns against the Eagles in Week 3 of his rookie year, kicking off a fantasy football waiver wire stampede. He has not scored a single touchdown in the NFL since. Last year, he was a forgotten man after Mike Singletary took over as head coach — which seems odd, since he's an ex-quarterback and 2008 was the Year of the Wildcat. The drafting of Glen Coffee does not augur well for his playing time.

Gary Russell

Height: 5-10   Weight: 229   College: Minnesota   Draft: 2007/FA   Born: 8-Sept-1986   Age: 23   Risk: Red

Year	Team	G	Runs	Yds	Yd/R	TD	FUM	DVOA	Rk	DYAR	Rk	YAR	Suc%	Rec	Pass	Yds	C%	Yd/C	TD	DVOA	Rk	DYAR	Rk
2007	PIT	3	7	21	3.0	0	0	10.7%	--	6	--	-1	43%	0	0	0	--	0.0	0	--	--	--	--
2008	PIT	12	28	77	2.8	3	0	-0.5%	--	13	--	11	57%	1	2	-2	50%	-2.0	0	-139.5%	--	-13	--
2009	OAK		15	45	3.0	1	2	-4.4%						2	3	11	67%	5.5	0	0.0%			

Fifteen of Russell's 28 carries came in the red zone, which is why his DVOA was average despite an awful 2.8 yards per carry. The Steelers used him mostly as a goal-line runner, a role he filled with a four-yard loss and a one-yard touchdown in the Super Bowl. This offseason, the Steelers waived him, the Bengals signed him, the Bengals waived him two weeks later, and then the Raiders signed him. So his family is unsure what color scheme to wear to games; they just know it should include black. Russell is an adequate roster back who can return kicks and play special teams, but it's hard to imagine he'll get even goal-line vulture work behind Oakland's three superior backs.

Dantrell Savage

Height: 5-8   Weight: 187   College: Oklahoma State   Draft: 2008/ ()   Born: 15-Feb-1985   Age: 24   Risk: Red

Year	Team	G	Runs	Yds	Yd/R	TD	FUM	DVOA	Rk	DYAR	Rk	YAR	Suc%	Rec	Pass	Yds	C%	Yd/C	TD	DVOA	Rk	DYAR	Rk
2008	KC	8	15	53	3.5	0	0	-18.4%	--	-7	--	-2	47%	2	2	0	100%	0.0	0	-120.6%	--	-14	--
2009	KC		36	183	5.0	0	2	3.1%						4	5	32	80%	8.1	0	-13.3%			

The Chiefs currently have a mess of running backs behind Jamaal Charles and Larry Johnson, but when the roster shakes out, Savage has two advantages over his competitors. First, he's a reasonably good kickoff return man. Second, he's a very different type of back, nearly 40 pounds lighter than Kolby Smith, Jackie Battle, or Javarris Williams. Alas, it is hard for him to play the "small and shifty third-down back" role because he's not really that shifty and he struggles in pass protection.

Bernard Scott

Height: 5-10   Weight: 200   College: Abilene Christian   Draft: 2009/6 (209)   Born: 10-Feb-1984   Age: 25   Risk: Yellow

Year	Team	G	Runs	Yds	Yd/R	TD	FUM	DVOA	Rk	DYAR	Rk	YAR	Suc%	Rec	Pass	Yds	C%	Yd/C	TD	DVOA	Rk	DYAR	Rk
2009	CIN		38	178	4.7	0	1	38.8%						20	24	190	83%	9.5	2	-37.1%			

Let's see … five arrests, left Southeastern Oklahoma State after his redshirt year, kicked off the University of Central Arkansas team for hitting a coach, then led Division II in all-purpose yards at Abilene Christian. Of course Bernard Scott ended up with the Cincinnati Bengals! He's a one-cut runner who has good vision to find the hole and then attacks it with a quick burst, and he's a deep fantasy sleeper because there's always a chance that the Cedric Benson comeback will hit a pothole.

Steve Slaton

Height: 5-9   Weight: 197   College: West Virginia   Draft: 2008/3 (89)   Born: 4-Jan-1986   Age: 23   Risk: Yellow

Year	Team	G	Runs	Yds	Yd/R	TD	FUM	DVOA	Rk	DYAR	Rk	YAR	Suc%	Rec	Pass	Yds	C%	Yd/C	TD	DVOA	Rk	DYAR	Rk
2008	HOU	16	268	1282	4.8	9	2	5.8%	16	166	9	148	44%	50	59	377	85%	7.5	1	-3.9%	37	30	33
2009	HOU		285	1214	4.3	8	3	5.9%						55	75	405	73%	7.4	3	4.4%			

Slaton was the 11th running back taken in the 2008 draft, but he arguably had the best rookie season. Slaton excelled in Gary Kubiak's one-cut running back system, and he showed both big play ability and a knack for gaining consistently positive yardage. The massive deficiency in Slaton's game is near the goal line, and the Texans probably need a consistent short-yardage back to pair with him; He scored four touchdowns inside the five last year when the average back would've converted 7.9 times. He angered Kubiak (the coach) with his occasional lapses in concentration as a rookie, something not reflected in KUBIAK (the projection system).

Kevin Smith

Height: 6-1　Weight: 217　College: Central Florida　Draft: 2008/3 (64)　Born: 17-Dec-1986　Age: 22　Risk: Red

Year	Team	G	Runs	Yds	Yd/R	TD	FUM	DVOA	Rk	DYAR	Rk	YAR	Suc%	Rec	Pass	Yds	C%	Yd/C	TD	DVOA	Rk	DYAR	Rk
2008	DET	16	238	976	4.1	8	2	-0.5%	23	79	23	90	44%	39	54	286	72%	7.3	0	-8.9%	39	15	38
2009	DET		254	1064	4.2	9	2	10.4%						30	45	200	67%	6.7	0	1.8%			

Despite his college workload, Smith stayed healthy and played remarkably well considering the team and the situation that surrounded him. If 238 carries seems like too few for a back that started 12 games, well, you're right; the Lions simply didn't get ahead frequently enough to be in situations where Smith would have the chance to run the clock out. Only 31 of his carries came when the Lions were in possession of a lead of any sort. He should see 30 to 40 more carries in 2009 just by virtue of the Lions winning a few games. As a solid blocker and receiver out of the backfield, he also doesn't need to come out on third downs. If he can stay healthy, he could end up surprising people as an effective fantasy RB2.

Kolby Smith

Height: 5-11　Weight: 220　College: Louisville　Draft: 2007/5 (148)　Born: 15-Dec-1984　Age: 24　Risk: Red

Year	Team	G	Runs	Yds	Yd/R	TD	FUM	DVOA	Rk	DYAR	Rk	YAR	Suc%	Rec	Pass	Yds	C%	Yd/C	TD	DVOA	Rk	DYAR	Rk
2007	KC	16	112	407	3.6	2	0	-3.4%	31	25	34	53	49%	22	29	148	76%	6.7	0	-9.0%	--	7	--
2008	KC	7	35	100	2.9	1	0	-24.5%	--	-26	--	-32	46%	10	11	52	91%	5.2	0	-14.3%	--	0	--
2009	KC		45	203	4.5	2	2	1.3%						18	24	168	75%	9.3	1	-8.7%			

It was Smith, not Jamaal Charles, who drew starting duties when Larry Johnson was suspended at midseason, but he struggled for two games and tore his ACL in the third. He missed May minicamps because he wasn't ready to get on the field yet, but if he's healthy by the time the season starts, Todd Haley will find a way to use him. Although Smith doesn't have the straight-ahead speed to be a starting back, his mix of size and quickness would fit well in a hybrid fullback/halfback role similar to Heath Evans or Greg Jones.

Jason Snelling

Height: 5-11　Weight: 230　College: Virginia　Draft: 2007/7 (244)　Born: 29-Dec-1983　Age: 25　Risk: Red

Year	Team	G	Runs	Yds	Yd/R	TD	FUM	DVOA	Rk	DYAR	Rk	YAR	Suc%	Rec	Pass	Yds	C%	Yd/C	TD	DVOA	Rk	DYAR	Rk
2007	ATL	7	13	43	3.3	1	0	3.0%	--	9	--	10	54%	0	0	0	--	0.0	0	--	--	--	--
2008	ATL	16	15	62	4.1	0	0	9.5%	--	11	--	9	47%	8	11	89	73%	11.1	0	43.9%	--	24	--
2009	ATL		56	173	3.1	1	3	-19.0%						17	20	146	85%	8.6	1	5.6%			

On a different team, Snelling might get a shot to be Michael Turner, instead of watching from the sideline, kinda sorta hoping the real thing gets banged up. Snelling put 88 yards on the Ravens in the preseason last year, is a powerful inside runner, and the team likes his receiving ability. He was busted for driving without insurance in April, an ironic charge given that insurance is exactly what he provides for the Birds.

Darren Sproles

Height: 5-6　Weight: 181　College: Kansas State　Draft: 2005/4 (130)　Born: 20-Jun-1983　Age: 26　Risk: Yellow

Year	Team	G	Runs	Yds	Yd/R	TD	FUM	DVOA	Rk	DYAR	Rk	YAR	Suc%	Rec	Pass	Yds	C%	Yd/C	TD	DVOA	Rk	DYAR	Rk
2007	SD	15	37	164	4.4	2	0	0.9%	--	13	--	18	41%	10	12	31	83%	3.1	0	-46.9%	--	-21	--
2008	SD	16	61	330	5.4	1	0	17.8%	--	64	--	82	49%	29	34	342	85%	11.8	5	73.1%	1	171	4
2009	SD		158	690	4.4	4	1	-3.3%						38	55	387	69%	10.2	2	34.6%			

It's become almost impossible to figure out what the diminutive star can be. The book on Sproles was always that he was a talented player, but too small to stay healthy and effective at the NFL level. Four years into his career, although he's yet to carry the ball more than 61 times in a season, he's suffered one traumatic injury — a broken ankle that cost him the 2006 season — and otherwise stayed healthy, missing two games over the other three seasons.

The problem is that there's simply not a comparable player to Sproles in NFL history. There's no running back of his size who ever enjoyed sustained success at the pro level. Players like Dino Hall and Sylvester

Stamps were good in small doses, but never got more than 30 carries or so; Dave Meggett had an inch and ten pounds on Sproles and was a better receiver than Sproles is. San Diego re-signed him partly for PR reasons after losing Michael Turner the year before, but also to just try and get another year to figure out what he can be.

Aaron Stecker
Height: 5-10   Weight: 213   College: Western Illinois   Draft: 2000/FA   Born: 13-Nov-1975   Age: 34   Risk: N/A

Year	Team	G	Runs	Yds	Yd/R	TD	FUM	DVOA	Rk	DYAR	Rk	YAR	Suc%	Rec	Pass	Yds	C%	Yd/C	TD	DVOA	Rk	DYAR	Rk
2006	NO	12	4	11	2.8	0	0	10.2%	--	3	--	2	25%	19	28	190	79%	10.0	0	2.5%	29	31	34
2007	NO	16	115	448	3.9	5	1	4.1%	22	64	27	64	50%	36	43	211	86%	5.9	0	5.0%	26	49	23
2008	NO	6	8	43	5.4	0	0	7.9%	--	5	--	7	25%	9	12	52	75%	5.8	1	8.8%	--	16	--

Stecker is now 34 and coming off a season-ending hamstring injury. He still has minimal value as an all-purpose sub who can run, catch, return, and cover kicks, but there are younger players who can fill those roles.

Jonathan Stewart
Height: 5-11   Weight: 235   College: Oregon   Draft: 2008/1 (13)   Born: 21-Mar-1987   Age: 22   Risk: Red

Year	Team	G	Runs	Yds	Yd/R	TD	FUM	DVOA	Rk	DYAR	Rk	YAR	Suc%	Rec	Pass	Yds	C%	Yd/C	TD	DVOA	Rk	DYAR	Rk
2008	CAR	16	184	836	4.5	10	2	7.6%	12	122	16	149	45%	8	17	47	47%	5.9	0	-49.4%	--	-37	--
2009	CAR		186	975	5.2	10	3	23.7%						12	14	59	86%	4.9	0	-15.0%			

Carolina fans didn't have to wait long to see the potential of their first pick in the 2008 draft. In his Bank of America Stadium preseason debut, Stewart ripped off a 50-yard touchdown on his way to 10 carries for 100 yards. It was all downhill running from there, as Stewart kept the chains moving with a 60 percent Success Rate on third and fourth down. A ridiculous 48% DVOA in the red zone paired with a 64 percent red zone Success Rate on 28 carries put him in a class with teammate DeAngelo Williams and only two other cartoon-ishly unstoppable red-zone studs: Brandon "The Juggernaut" Jacobs and Maurice "Mighty Mouse" Jones-Drew. Thunder, Thunder, Thunder, Thunder-cats, Ho! Thundercats are on the move, thundercats are loose …

Frank Summers
Height: 5-9   Weight: 241   College: UNLV   Draft: 2009/5 (169)   Born: 6-Sep-1985   Age: 24   Risk: Green

Year	Team	G	Runs	Yds	Yd/R	TD	FUM	DVOA	Rk	DYAR	Rk	YAR	Suc%	Rec	Pass	Yds	C%	Yd/C	TD	DVOA	Rk	DYAR	Rk
2009	PIT		31	100	3.3	4	0	41.8%						9	10	75	90%	8.3	1	40.0%			

Summers is an insurance policy in case Rashard Mendenhall flops as a short-yardage runner. Frank the Tank is 5-foot-9, 241 pounds, with a center of gravity shoved halfway down a tectonic plate. That makes him a solid short-yardage prospect, and Summers also has some receiving chops and a special teams mentality. "I love special teams," Summers told reporters after the draft. "It's a time for me to really hit somebody without carrying the ball, just to run 60 or 50 yards downfield like a crazy man." Talk like that makes Bill Cowher want to come out of retirement.

Chester Taylor
Height: 5-11   Weight: 213   College: Toledo   Draft: 2002/6 (207)   Born: 22-Sep-1979   Age: 30   Risk: Blue

Year	Team	G	Runs	Yds	Yd/R	TD	FUM	DVOA	Rk	DYAR	Rk	YAR	Suc%	Rec	Pass	Yds	C%	Yd/C	TD	DVOA	Rk	DYAR	Rk
2006	MIN	15	303	1216	4.0	6	4	-7.8%	33	10	33	5	46%	42	51	288	70%	6.9	0	17.3%	13	103	12
2007	MIN	14	157	844	5.4	7	5	8.0%	20	101	20	98	46%	29	43	281	67%	9.7	0	15.7%	17	64	18
2008	MIN	16	101	399	4.0	4	0	-1.4%	28	28	35	37	43%	45	55	399	82%	8.9	2	25.4%	10	104	11
2009	MIN		54	266	4.9	1	3	-10.7%						32	51	315	63%	9.9	1	-4.9%			

It was a relatively pedestrian year for Taylor in all ways except one: Taylor's DVOA as a receiver on third down was an astounding 69.3%, and the 111 DYAR he earned there was nearly double that of any other back. He picked up 11 first downs or touchdowns on his 31 targets, including a 47-yard touchdown against the Packers in Week 10 that ended up being a key play in a 28-27 victory. It was a fluky performance — Taylor's DVOA as a third-down receiver has never been anything close to that high before — but a useful one for a team that needed any help they could get in the passing game. Taylor's always been overqualified to be a backup; if Adrian Peterson gets hurt, the dropoff between him and Taylor in effectiveness wouldn't be as significant as most people think.

Fred Taylor   Height: 6-1   Weight: 234 College: Florida   Draft: 1998/1 (9)   Born: 27-Jan-1976   Age: 33   Risk: Green

Year	Team	G	Runs	Yds	Yd/R	TD	FUM	DVOA	Rk	DYAR	Rk	YAR	Suc%	Rec	Pass	Yds	C%	Yd/C	TD	DVOA	Rk	DYAR	Rk
2006	JAC	15	231	1146	5.0	5	2	11.1%	11	172	12	192	44%	23	28	242	68%	10.5	1	3.6%	28	32	33
2007	JAC	15	223	1202	5.4	5	2	11.1%	15	171	8	165	45%	9	14	58	64%	6.4	0	-18.3%	--	-3	--
2008	JAC	13	143	556	3.9	1	0	-14.3%	46	-32	44	-24	41%	16	22	98	73%	6.1	0	-32.2%	--	-23	--
2009	NE		160	679	4.2	3	3	-0.9%						7	10	58	70%	8.3	0	35.8%			

After a 10-year career in which he became the most popular and beloved player in franchise history, Taylor left the Jags over what was first termed a contract dispute — the team wanted to unload some or all of his $6 million cap hit for 2009. Signing with the Patriots, Taylor will compete for time with Laurence Maroney and a barrel full of backups for a situational role. In 2008, Taylor's third-down and red zone numbers were unimpressive, so expect the Patriots to go elsewhere when they really need to move the chains.

Pierre Thomas   Height: 5-11   Weight: 210 College: Illinois   Draft: 2007/FA   Born: 18-Dec-1984   Age: 24   Risk: Red

Year	Team	G	Runs	Yds	Yd/R	TD	FUM	DVOA	Rk	DYAR	Rk	YAR	Suc%	Rec	Pass	Yds	C%	Yd/C	TD	DVOA	Rk	DYAR	Rk
2007	NO	12	52	252	4.8	1	0	33.5%	--	87	--	78	60%	17	23	151	83%	8.9	1	25.5%	--	53	--
2008	NO	15	129	625	4.8	9	1	16.9%	4	161	11	190	62%	31	41	284	76%	9.2	3	40.2%	5	136	6
2009	NO		196	882	4.5	8	6	-6.0%						63	84	428	75%	6.8	2	-15.6%			

Thomas rushed 99 times for 501 yards and six touchdowns in his final seven games. There was some pre-draft talk about the Saints drafting Beanie Wells or some other power runner, but they didn't really need one. Thomas is effective in the red zone (DVOA of 35.4% on 24 carries) and as a goal-to-go runner (six touchdowns in 10 attempts). He's also a solid all-purpose runner and a good enough receiver to post higher receiving DVOA and DYAR than Reggie Bush. The KUBIAK projection gives Thomas all of his own carries, most of Deuce McAllister's, and a few of Bush's. He can do a lot with that many touches, but he won't get many more in the pass-crazy Saints offense.

LaDainian Tomlinson   Height: 5-10   Weight: 221 College: TCU   Draft: 2001/1 (5)   Born: 23-Jun-1979   Age: 30   Risk: Green

Year	Team	G	Runs	Yds	Yd/R	TD	FUM	DVOA	Rk	DYAR	Rk	YAR	Suc%	Rec	Pass	Yds	C%	Yd/C	TD	DVOA	Rk	DYAR	Rk
2006	SD	16	348	1815	5.2	28	2	23.4%	3	453	1	498	49%	56	80	508	69%	9.1	3	13.9%	17	139	6
2007	SD	16	315	1474	4.7	15	0	13.6%	11	287	2	288	45%	60	86	475	70%	7.9	3	10.6%	22	113	6
2008	SD	16	292	1110	3.8	11	0	-1.3%	27	88	20	107	45%	52	77	426	68%	8.2	1	-1.4%	34	52	25
2009	SD		233	893	3.8	13	1	5.1%						59	81	513	73%	8.7	1	23.5%			

The iconic image of an injured, sullen, and embarrassed Tomlinson on the sidelines during the 2007 playoffs seemed to carry on with him through the 2008 campaign. A toe injury slowed him during the year, and a torn groin muscle limited him to five carries in the playoffs. The knock that was Tomlinson lost a step, which is true — he went from 13 carries of more than 20 yards or more in 2007 to six a year ago. His offensive line didn't play as well, either, but it wasn't like Tomlinson was getting stuffed; while 15 percent of his carries in 2008 failed to go for positive yardage, that figure was at 21 percent in 2007.

Much like the case with teammate Darren Sproles, it's difficult to tell what's left with Tomlinson; history is littered with 30-year-old running backs, even great ones, for whom past performance had absolutely no relevance to future performance. Tomlinson hasn't been overworked since his 372-carry season in 2002, but the cumulative effect of being so successful may be adding up for him. Only Emmitt Smith, Edgerrin James, Barry Sanders, Jerome Bettis, and Walter Payton had more carries before the age of 30 than Tomlinson's 2,657. None of the five won a rushing title after the age of 29. Tomlinson may still be a useful player, but the MVP candidate in the Chargers backfield from here on out is Philip Rivers, not LT.

Ryan Torain

Height: 6-1   Weight: 222   College: Arizona State   Draft: 2008/5 (139)   Born: 10-Aug-1986   Age: 23   Risk: Red

Year	Team	G	Runs	Yds	Yd/R	TD	FUM	DVOA	Rk	DYAR	Rk	YAR	Suc%	Rec	Pass	Yds	C%	Yd/C	TD	DVOA	Rk	DYAR	Rk
2008	DEN	2	15	69	4.6	1	0	21.6%	--	21	--	26	60%	0	0	0	--	0.0	0	--	--	--	--
2009	DEN		37	118	3.2	0	2	-31.5%						33	35	287	94%	8.7	1	-7.6%			

They were handing out so many running back injuries in Denver last year that rookie Ryan Torain got two: a broken elbow in training camp that cost him the first month of the season, and then a torn left ACL in his second game back, Week 10 at Cleveland. Torain wasn't far enough along in his rehab to participate in any minicamps, and at this point he's fallen to fifth or sixth on the Denver depth chart. It wouldn't be a surprise to see him cut in late August, and given how much Mike Shanahan liked him, it wouldn't be a surprise to see him sign either this year in Houston — he's a larger, shoulder-lowering interior runner who would partner well with Steve Slaton — or next year with whichever team hires Shanahan to be its head coach.

Michael Turner

Height: 5-10   Weight: 237   College: Northern Illinois   Draft: 2004/5 (154)   Born: 13-Feb-1982   Age: 27   Risk: Red

Year	Team	G	Runs	Yds	Yd/R	TD	FUM	DVOA	Rk	DYAR	Rk	YAR	Suc%	Rec	Pass	Yds	C%	Yd/C	TD	DVOA	Rk	DYAR	Rk
2006	SD	13	80	502	6.3	2	0	34.7%	--	142	--	137	55%	3	3	47	67%	15.7	0	79.0%	--	21	--
2007	SD	16	71	316	4.5	1	1	-27.4%	--	-52	--	-41	28%	4	7	16	57%	4.0	0	-60.5%	--	-19	--
2008	ATL	16	376	1699	4.5	17	3	4.1%	19	203	6	259	48%	6	9	41	67%	6.8	0	-9.5%	--	2	--
2009	ATL		291	1183	4.1	10	4	-14.6%						10	13	82	77%	8.2	0	5.0%			

Boy, we really blew this one last year, didn't we? Turner's 2008 projection may have been the worst in the four-year history of KUBIAK: 215 carries, 807 yards, and only two touchdowns. Whoops. We had a player with very little track record. We knew that receiving numbers are often more important than rushing numbers for projecting a running back's future value. We expected that Matt Ryan would struggle like most rookie quarterbacks, that the Atlanta offensive line would be as poor as it was in 2007, and that Turner wouldn't be able to rack up clock-killing carries on a losing team. It ended up being a perfect storm of perfectly reasonable but — in this case — incorrect assumptions. The appropriate mea culpa would be to announce that we've learned our lesson, giving Turner a spectacular projection for 2009. Except … we just can't do that for a back facing the Curse of 370, on a team that is likely to regress after last year's surprising wild card run. As Neil Young once sang, "I've been wrong before, and I'll be there again. I don't have any answers, my friend."

Derrick Ward

Height: 5-11   Weight: 233   College: Ottawa (Kansas)   Draft: 2004/7 (235)   Born: 30-Aug-1980   Age: 29   Risk: Green

Year	Team	G	Runs	Yds	Yd/R	TD	FUM	DVOA	Rk	DYAR	Rk	YAR	Suc%	Rec	Pass	Yds	C%	Yd/C	TD	DVOA	Rk	DYAR	Rk
2007	NYG	8	125	602	4.8	3	2	13.0%	13	112	18	108	46%	26	40	179	65%	6.9	1	-20.3%	47	-14	48
2008	NYG	16	182	1025	5.6	2	2	25.8%	2	265	4	214	51%	41	55	384	75%	9.4	0	24.0%	11	107	9
2009	TB		197	815	4.1	7	3	-4.7%						31	48	204	65%	6.6	0	-15.1%			

After leaving a slight mark on the 2007 Giants before breaking his leg, Ward emerged as the ideal complement to Jacobs' brute force approach and led the league in yards per carry. What makes Ward so effective is his patience; he was brilliant on the Giants' tosses, sweeps, and counters because he was great at reading his blocks and picking the right gap to run through. Most impressively, he's gone from being a total non-entity in the passing game in college — literally, he caught seven passes over six years at two schools — to being a very effective part of a good NFL passing attack, albeit primarily on screens. Ward left for Tampa Bay in the offseason; with their implementation of the Alex Gibbs zone-blocking scheme underway, Ward's success depends on his health and the play of the line in front of him.

Danny Ware

Height: 6-0   Weight: 225 College: Georgia   Draft: 2007/FA   Born: 18-Feb-1985 Age: 24 Risk: Green

Year	Team	G	Runs	Yds	Yd/R	TD	FUM	DVOA	Rk	DYAR	Rk	YAR	Suc%	Rec	Pass	Yds	C%	Yd/C	TD	DVOA	Rk	DYAR	Rk
2008	NYG	6	2	15	7.5	0	0	62.0%	--	8	--	8	100%	0	0	0	--	0.0	0	--	--	--	--
2009	NYG		70	301	4.3	3	1	-0.8%						13	15	82	87%	6.3	0	-37.5%			

An extremely deep sleeper, Ware's had a tricky path to get here: He lost his job at Georgia to Kregg Lumpkin, left too early as a result, went undrafted, and bounced around Tennessee and both New York teams before sticking with the Giants. Despite his inexperience, he's highly-regarded within the organization and could steal Ahmad Bradshaw's roster spot with a good camp. If you're looking for someone to grab in the last round of your fantasy draft as an all-or-nothing pick, Ware's that guy.

Chauncey Washington

Height: 6-0   Weight: 211 College: USC   Draft: 2008/7 (213) Born: 29-Apr-1985 Age: 24 Risk: Green

Year	Team	G	Runs	Yds	Yd/R	TD	FUM	DVOA	Rk	DYAR	Rk	YAR	Suc%	Rec	Pass	Yds	C%	Yd/C	TD	DVOA	Rk	DYAR	Rk
2008	JAC	6	4	9	2.3	0	0	36.0%	--	-5	--	-5	50%	1	1	9	100%	9.0	0	69.1%	--	7	--
2009	JAC		51	227	4.5	2	2	34.2%						21	25	154	84%	7.3	2	-15.3%			

Here's a guy to keep an eye on, now that Fred Taylor's gone and Pocket Hercules is the main man in Jacksonville. Washington has an intriguing combination of size and speed (4.52), and he goes into the season as Maurice Jones-Drew's primary backup (though seventh-round pick Rashad Jennings could be a steal and take some of those carries). Washington's used to living under the radar after lagging behind LenDale White and Reggie Bush at USC, but his powerful style fits the Jags' running game to a "T."

Leon Washington

Height: 5-9   Weight: 199 College: Florida State   Draft: 2006/4 (117) Born: 29-Aug-1982 Age: 27 Risk: Yellow

Year	Team	G	Runs	Yds	Yd/R	TD	FUM	DVOA	Rk	DYAR	Rk	YAR	Suc%	Rec	Pass	Yds	C%	Yd/C	TD	DVOA	Rk	DYAR	Rk
2006	NYJ	16	151	650	4.3	4	1	14.0%	7	133	15	129	49%	25	31	270	55%	10.8	0	17.9%	11	66	22
2007	NYJ	16	71	353	5.0	3	1	2.3%	--	30	--	37	37%	36	51	213	71%	5.9	0	-10.4%	37	10	36
2008	NYJ	16	76	448	5.9	6	1	23.8%	--	95	--	98	51%	47	61	355	77%	7.6	2	9.3%	20	75	14
2009	NYJ		60	288	4.8	1	1	-26.0%						44	67	325	66%	7.4	1	11.0%			

Leon Washington is Reggie Bush without the oversized contract and the racy *GQ* photo spreads with Kim Kardashian. Washington averaged six yards a carry and scored three touchdowns in the fourth quarter, where he was used as the change-of-pace back to overwhelm defenses already tired from a steady diet of Thomas Jones. Washington is one of the league's elite return men, but he's being taken off punt return duty, which suggests the team envisions giving him a greater role in the offense. He'll be Mark Sanchez's safety valve on third downs.

Kenny Watson

Height: 5-11   Weight: 220 College: Penn State   Draft: 2001/ (FA)   Born: 13-Mar-1978 Age: 31 Risk: Red

Year	Team	G	Runs	Yds	Yd/R	TD	FUM	DVOA	Rk	DYAR	Rk	YAR	Suc%	Rec	Pass	Yds	C%	Yd/C	TD	DVOA	Rk	DYAR	Rk
2006	CIN	16	25	138	5.5	1	0	35.4%	--	41	--	42	52%	23	32	213	73%	9.3	0	31.7%	4	86	15
2007	CIN	16	178	763	4.3	7	2	13.0%	12	162	10	178	56%	52	67	374	78%	7.2	0	-4.7%	31	32	28
2008	CIN	10	13	55	4.2	0	0	12.5%	--	11	--	3	38%	3	9	4	33%	1.3	0	-94.0%	--	-43	--
2009	CIN		96	431	4.5	1	0	9.6%						10	14	73	71%	7.3	0	-30.0%			

The Bengals like Watson as a third-down back, to the point where he might as well carry a sign reading, "I'm getting the ball!" on his way to the huddle — but his Success Rate was exactly 0 percent running on third and fourth down, and he posted a depressing -99.2% DVOA as a third-down receiver. Breaking it up occasionally helped, as Watson ran for a 75 percent Success Rate on first-down carries. In retrospect, he should have gotten the starting gig over Chris Perry last season. Now, it's probably too late for Watson to make much impact, in Cincy or elsewhere. Then again, if the Cedric Benson comeback fails and the coaches go looking for a replacement, we know they'll find Watson in the locker room, whereas Bernard Scott might be in police custody.

Leonard Weaver

Height: 6-0 Weight: 251 College: Carson-Newman Draft: 2005/FA Born: 23-Sep-1982 Age: 27 Risk: Red

Year	Team	G	Runs	Yds	Yd/R	TD	FUM	DVOA	Rk	DYAR	Rk	YAR	Suc%	Rec	Pass	Yds	C%	Yd/C	TD	DVOA	Rk	DYAR	Rk
2007	SEA	16	33	146	4.4	1	0	16.0%	--	40	--	39	61%	39	52	313	75%	8.0	0	17.4%	14	87	11
2008	SEA	14	30	130	4.3	0	1	-9.0%	--	-1	--	-1	47%	20	32	222	63%	11.1	2	15.6%	14	45	27
2009	PHI		36	154	4.2	2	2	24.1%						40	55	359	73%	9.0	1	0.9%			

Weaver seems like a perfect fit for the Eagles. He'll help them as a short-yardage blocker; Seattle was fourth in power-situation rushing last season. He'll help them as a rusher; he played better than his DVOA last season, which was ruined by one fumble. And he'll help them as a receiver, where he has been highly ranked among backs for two years in a row. He even has big-play ability; witness his 43- and 62-yard touchdown receptions against San Francisco. Eagles fans and Donovan McNabb may both fall in love with this guy.

Chris Wells

Height: 6-1 Weight: 237 College: Ohio State Draft: 2009/1 (31) Born: 7-Aug-1988 Age: 21 Risk: Yellow

Year	Team	G	Runs	Yds	Yd/R	TD	FUM	DVOA	Rk	DYAR	Rk	YAR	Suc%	Rec	Pass	Yds	C%	Yd/C	TD	DVOA	Rk	DYAR	Rk
2009	ARI		187	627	3.4	7	3	-21.4%						17	20	149	85%	8.7	2	34.3%			

Beanie was a big-time recruit from Akron who immediately produced for Ohio State's consecutive national title runners-up. He produced at least 5.5 yards per carry all three seasons at OSU and appeared pretty durable until missing three games in 2008 to a toe injury. Wells seems like the perfect runner for the Arizona offense, a bruising back that should provide a power complement to the finesse of the aerial show. Wells was very consistent in college, with at least 100 yards in 17 of his final 22 games, though he only produced 8.7 POE (No. 53 in the country) in 2008. His Speed Score of 105.9 was below average for a first-round runner, but the Cardinals got him at the very end of the round, and they couldn't ask for a better fit for their team: His size/speed combination is comparable to Larry Johnson. He will probably play behind Tim Hightower at first, but should be starting by midseason. Note that his projection is extremely poor because KUBIAK projects rookies primarily on team variables, and the Arizona running game has been lousy for years now.

Brian Westbrook

Height: 5-8 Weight: 203 College: Villanova Draft: 2002/3 (91) Born: 2-Sep-1979 Age: 30 Risk: Red

Year	Team	G	Runs	Yds	Yd/R	TD	FUM	DVOA	Rk	DYAR	Rk	YAR	Suc%	Rec	Pass	Yds	C%	Yd/C	TD	DVOA	Rk	DYAR	Rk
2006	PHI	15	240	1217	5.1	7	1	23.9%	2	314	2	299	48%	77	109	699	66%	9.1	4	5.2%	27	147	5
2007	PHI	15	278	1333	4.8	7	0	19.9%	3	334	1	318	53%	90	120	771	75%	8.6	5	12.6%	21	190	1
2008	PHI	14	233	936	4.0	9	1	6.9%	15	151	12	130	48%	54	73	402	74%	7.4	5	0.2%	30	59	18
2009	PHI		205	904	4.4	6	1	4.8%						66	84	562	79%	8.5	4	24.1%			

No, the statistical indicators aren't pretty. Westbrook played hurt for virtually the entire season, starting with an ankle injury, following that with a broken rib that caused him to miss his standard two games, and finishing up with knee swelling that reduced him to a shell of his former self by the time the playoffs rolled around. Simply put, there's not enough cartilage left in Westbrook's knee; the result is bone scraping on bone, causing the swelling that Westbrook experienced. About the only option the Eagles would have left would be Synvisc injections, the same treatment Randy Johnson uses to keep his knees lubricated. That's Westbrook's last resort, and honestly, it's not that far away from coming into play.

Offseason arthroscopic surgery on his knee was supposed to alleviate some of the problems, but Westbrook promptly sprained his ankle at the end of May and is expected to miss the entire preseason. He'll turn 30 before his next regular season game, he's yet to even make it through a single NFL season without missing at least one game, and that is likely thanks to careful workload management by a franchise smart enough to understand how to properly deploy their best player. For all the vitriol spewed at Andy Reid for not running the ball more frequently, it might be the runs Reid didn't order that allow Westbrook to play for an extra season or avoid a traumatic injury. The hope is that his ankle injury doesn't cascade to a major knee injury, because if it does, Westbrook's career is likely over.

LenDale White

Height: 6-2   Weight: 235   College: USC   Draft: 2006/2 (45)   Born: 20-Dec-1984   Age: 24   Risk: Yellow

Year	Team	G	Runs	Yds	Yd/R	TD	FUM	DVOA	Rk	DYAR	Rk	YAR	Suc%	Rec	Pass	Yds	C%	Yd/C	TD	DVOA	Rk	DYAR	Rk
2006	TEN	13	61	244	4.0	0	1	-2.3%	--	15	--	21	35%	14	20	60	60%	4.3	0	-13.9%	--	0	--
2007	TEN	16	303	1110	3.7	7	5	-6.5%	34	26	33	61	46%	20	31	114	65%	5.7	0	-17.5%	44	-6	43
2008	TEN	16	200	773	3.9	15	0	7.5%	13	144	13	155	54%	5	10	16	50%	3.2	0	-90.3%	--	-43	--
2009	TEN		201	875	4.4	13	3	14.5%						6	9	36	67%	5.9	1	-43.2%			

White had about as productive a season as someone with 773 yards who averaged fewer than four yards per carry can have. White's big body always manages to push forward, and he is very good in short-yardage situations. White is not just a goal-line vulture, as he finds holes well enough to make successful runs in first-and-10 situations. Most impressive for White, however, are the zero fumbles. He fumbled five times in 2007, so whether this was good luck or improved awareness could make the difference between whether White is a decent player or a real asset.

Cadillac Williams

Height: 5-11   Weight: 217   College: Auburn   Draft: 2005/1 (5)   Born: 21-Apr-1982   Age: 27   Risk: Red

Year	Team	G	Runs	Yds	Yd/R	TD	FUM	DVOA	Rk	DYAR	Rk	YAR	Suc%	Rec	Pass	Yds	C%	Yd/C	TD	DVOA	Rk	DYAR	Rk
2006	TB	14	225	798	3.5	1	3	-11.8%	41	-28	42	-69	39%	30	44	196	75%	6.5	0	10.0%	21	68	20
2007	TB	4	54	208	3.9	3	1	10.6%	--	44	--	32	52%	3	5	17	60%	5.7	0	-108.4%	--	-24	--
2008	TB	6	63	233	3.7	4	1	-6.2%	--	7	--	39	51%	7	7	43	100%	6.1	0	13.3%	--	10	--
2009	TB		43	185	4.3	1	2	-0.2%						5	9	39	56%	7.7	0	-16.6%			

Winner of the Maud Muller Award for "what might have been," Cadillac worked all the way back from a devastating knee injury to his patellar tendon, rocked four touchdowns on just 63 carries, and then promptly tore the patellar in his other knee. The Caddy will be parked at the very least until midseason, and may be released.

DeAngelo Williams

Height: 5-10   Weight: 217   College: Memphis   Draft: 2006/1 (27)   Born: 25-Apr-1983   Age: 26   Risk: Green

Year	Team	G	Runs	Yds	Yd/R	TD	FUM	DVOA	Rk	DYAR	Rk	YAR	Suc%	Rec	Pass	Yds	C%	Yd/C	TD	DVOA	Rk	DYAR	Rk
2006	CAR	13	121	501	4.1	1	1	-1.5%	25	36	29	30	47%	33	36	313	86%	9.5	1	48.9%	1	148	3
2007	CAR	16	144	717	5.0	4	0	11.9%	14	104	19	109	41%	23	38	175	63%	7.6	1	-25.9%	52	-25	52
2008	CAR	16	273	1515	5.5	18	0	28.3%	1	385	1	442	47%	22	30	121	73%	5.5	2	-14.5%	45	-1	45
2009	CAR		225	1121	5.0	11	3	11.6%						19	24	114	79%	6.0	0	-12.5%			

It's hard to believe that DeAngelo Williams had started exactly 2 games in 2 years prior to 2008. We never understood why he only carried the ball nine times per game behind DeShaun Foster in 2006 and 2007 (and we still don't). In 2007 he ranked 19th in DYAR and averaged five yards per carry. When finally given the bulk of the carries in 2008, all Williams did was lead all running backs in DYAR and get better as he put more miles on his tires. He averaged 3.7 yards per carry in September, 4.9 in October, 5.9 in November, and 7.0 in December. At this rate, he should score every time he touches the ball by 2012 (100 years earlier than predicted by Rush on "2112").

Ricky Williams

Height: 5-10 Weight: 228 College: Texas   Draft: 1999/1 (5)   Born: 21-May-1977 Age: 32 Risk: Blue

Year	Team	G	Runs	Yds	Yd/R	TD	FUM	DVOA	Rk	DYAR	Rk	YAR	Suc%	Rec	Pass	Yds	C%	Yd/C	TD	DVOA	Rk	DYAR	Rk
2007	MIA	1	6	15	2.5	0	1	-66.7%	--	-16	--	-16	50%	0	0	0	--	0.0	0	--	--	--	--
2008	MIA	16	160	659	4.1	4	4	-3.9%	34	31	33	36	48%	29	39	219	74%	7.6	1	-9.6%	40	8	41
2009	MIA		125	524	4.2	2	3	2.1%						15	23	151	65%	10.1	0	22.1%			

Where does Williams fit in Miami's offensive going forward? His abysmal numbers on third and fourth down (-75.2% DVOA) and in the red zone (-21.1% DVOA, the only Miami back with a negative red zone DVOA) would seem to indicate a reduced role, though he did look good as the sweeper in the Wildcat. He's said that he wants to play two more years and then retire, leading to the termination of one of the more interesting NFL careers. Williams is set to make $3.4 million for the Dolphins in a contract year, so that second season may come elsewhere.

Jason Wright

Height: 5-10 Weight: 210 College: Northwestern   Draft: 2004/FA   Born: 12-Jul-1982   Age: 27 Risk: Red

Year	Team	G	Runs	Yds	Yd/R	TD	FUM	DVOA	Rk	DYAR	Rk	YAR	Suc%	Rec	Pass	Yds	C%	Yd/C	TD	DVOA	Rk	DYAR	Rk
2006	CLE	13	62	189	3.0	0	1	-18.0%	--	-23	--	-51	40%	6	11	82	64%	13.7	0	-1.8%	--	8	--
2007	CLE	16	60	277	4.6	1	1	5.6%	--	37	--	50	50%	24	37	233	65%	9.7	0	16.5%	16	63	19
2008	CLE	15	23	85	3.7	0	0	8.2%	--	16	--	10	39%	22	37	156	59%	7.1	1	-22.5%	48	-17	47
2009	ARI		33	99	3.0	2	2	8.1%						19	22	201	86%	10.6	0	3.2%			

Wright's production tailed off sharply last year. It appeared that the coaches couldn't figure out roles for him and Jerome Harrison: Wright went through a five-game stretch where he got one carry per game, as if it was a contractual obligation. Now in Arizona, his reasonable blocking and receiving skills make him a good complement to Beanie Wells and Tim Hightower.

DeShawn Wynn

Height: 5-10 Weight: 232 College: Florida   Draft: 2007/7 (228) Born: 9-Oct-1983   Age: 26 Risk: Green

Year	Team	G	Runs	Yds	Yd/R	TD	FUM	DVOA	Rk	DYAR	Rk	YAR	Suc%	Rec	Pass	Yds	C%	Yd/C	TD	DVOA	Rk	DYAR	Rk
2007	GB	7	50	203	4.1	4	0	13.4%	--	45	--	29	36%	9	14	73	64%	8.1	0	11.4%	--	18	--
2008	GB	5	8	110	13.8	1	1	85.2%	--	32	--	35	63%	3	3	30	100%	10.0	0	-109.9%	--	-14	--
2009	GB		35	171	4.8	1	2	26.8%						9	12	96	75%	10.7	0	-7.4%			

Wynn was cut in training camp and spent two months on the practice squad before being added to the active roster; his 73-yard touchdown run against the Lions in Week 17 should serve as the highlight of his professional career. In case you are wondering, that low receiving DVOA comes because he fumbled on one of his three receptions. Wynn will probably beat out Kregg Lumpkin for a roster spot, but this team uses multiple fullbacks more than they use a third halfback.

Selvin Young

Height: 5-11 Weight: 207 College: Texas   Draft: 2007/ FA   Born: 1-Oct-1983   Age: 26 Risk: N/A

Year	Team	G	Runs	Yds	Yd/R	TD	FUM	DVOA	Rk	DYAR	Rk	YAR	Suc%	Rec	Pass	Yds	C%	Yd/C	TD	DVOA	Rk	DYAR	Rk
2007	DEN	15	140	729	5.2	1	1	8.4%	19	92	23	82	43%	35	43	231	81%	6.6	0	-7.6%	33	14	33
2008	DEN	8	61	303	5.0	1	1	9.4%	--	40	--	47	48%	3	8	16	38%	5.3	0	-60.2%	--	-22	--

Young was the first float in the Broncos' 2008 parade of running backs, starting the first five games of the season before a groin injury took him out for a month and a half. When he returned in December, he suffered a herniated disc in his neck, and that ended up costing him his career in Denver. Since doctors wouldn't clear him to play, the Broncos waived him in April. Young hopes the injury will heal on its own without surgery, which could have him ready to play in September and ready to sign with whatever team has a cascade of running back injuries in 2009.

GOING DEEP

J.J. Arrington, FA: Just as it seemed like Arrington's chance at a career had disappeared, the benching of Edgerrin James and the struggles of Tim Hightower gave him the opening he needed to become a part of the team's rotation as a scatback. He used the opportunity to sign a four-year, $10 million contract with Denver in the offseason, only to be cut after failing his physical at OTAs. He will likely miss the 2009 season after microfracture surgery. (2008 stats: 30 carries for 188 yards, 1 TD, 31.2% DVOA, 44 DYAR; 30-for-40 on passes, 254 yards, 1 TD, 23.3% DVOA, 81 DYAR.)

Lance Ball, IND: At 5-foot-9, Bell has prototypical Colts size, so it's no surprise that he ended up on their practice squad after he failed to catch on with the Rams as a rookie free agent last year. He made it onto the active roster for a meaningless Week 17 game against the Titans and had 83 yards on 13 carries (20.0% DVOA, 0 DYAR). That translates to about eight Week 1-16 yards, which is why he'll probably be back on the practice squad in 2009 after the team used their first-round pick on Donald Brown.

Jackie Battle, KC: Battle is an undrafted practice-squadder out of the University of Houston who snuck onto the roster late in 2007, then again last year when Larry Johnson was suspended at midseason. He had no carries last year and is sixth on the depth chart at running back, so it will take a Denver-like cascade of injuries for him to matter in 2009.

Aaron Brown, DET: The Lions' sixth-round pick was suspended for virtually his entire senior season of high school after a graffiti-gone-bad incident designed to "…intimidate the incoming freshmen." As a senior at TCU, he was suspended three games for violating school policy. He says that he's learned his lesson, but you would think he might have done that after high school. He's a good receiver out of the backfield who probably won't stick.

Brian Calhoun, FA: Calhoun suffered a quad injury in training camp and missed the entire season. He's only been healthy enough to play in 11 games over his first three seasons, he never showed much in those 11 games to begin with, and the new Detroit coaching staff had no motivation to justify his selection by the previous braintrust.

Aveion Cason, DET: Cason was placed on IR before the season and then waived by the Lions on September 4, only to sign with them in November and appear in five games. He's a replacement-level return man who offers little offensively.

Jesse Chatman, FA: Chatman's season failed to launch after he was suspended in the preseason for the presence of a diuretic in his system. He came back for three games, but was placed on injured reserve with a knee injury suffered on special teams at the end of October. Released after the season, Chatman's attracted no attention and appears to be an ex-NFL running back at this point.

Alonzo Coleman, DAL: Wade Phillips can do this player comment for us. "He didn't play as well in preseason as we would have liked and that probably held him back some, and he hasn't played a lot of special teams."

Najeh Davenport, FA: Davenport always plays well when he is on the field, but for whatever reason three teams have decided not to give him consistent carries. The Colts used him mostly as a kick returner but released him before the playoffs. He has yet to catch on, and it seems he could still help a team as a second, or certainly third, running back. (2008 stats: 8 carries for 26 yards, 3.7% DVOA, 4 DYAR.)

Clifton Dawson, HOU: The Colts organization handed the ball off to seven players in 2008, but Dawson wasn't one of them. He was released after the season and caught on with Houston, where he'll hope to stick on special teams.

Herb Donaldson, NO: An undrafted rookie from Western Illinois, Donaldson rushed for 1,784 yards and 21 touchdowns as a senior — including 157 yards and two touchdowns against Arkansas. He's a poor fit for the Saints' offense because he's a low center-of-gravity power runner with average speed and little receiving ability, but he gets high marks for toughness, so he could stick on special teams.

DeDe Dorsey, CIN: A severely strained hammy shelved the pride of Broken Arrow, Oklahoma, after only four games in 2008. Dorsey has made some big plays in his limited participation (183 yards on only 21 carries in 2007), and is Cincinnati's lone speed back, so he should return as a situational player in 2009.

Reuben Droughns, FA: Droughns lined up strictly on special teams in 2008. He left the Giants after the season and is now a free agent, his career probably finished.

Kyle Eckel, PHI: For a team starved for lead blocking, Eckel was a godsend. In reality, he's the girl who's really a six but looks like she's an eight because she's surrounded by threes and fours. Leonard Weaver will take over the role as the starting fullback, but Eckel will still see time as the up back on run plays and as a special teamer. (2008 stats: 24 carries for 79 yards, -10.2% DVOA, -2 DYAR.)

Allen Ervin, DET: The former Lambuth star, who led all NAIA backs with nearly 1,300 rushing yards and 14 touchdowns, trained for the combine and the draft in 2008 while working nights at GNC. That wasn't enough to get drafted, and he was cut by the Lions in June, but he did land on the Lions practice squad in November. He's quick for a back in the 225-pound range, but needs to make huge strides as a pass blocker if he wants to get on the field.

Heath Evans, NO: The Saints signed Evans to replace Mike Karney (now with the Rams) because they needed a more versatile fullback. Karney is a traditional lead blocker, while Evans is more of a hybrid with some value as a single setback (123 carries for 453 yards in four years with the Patriots) and an all-purpose special teamer (24 career tackles). Evans won't play much, but he'll appear in a few of Sean Payton's 94,000 personnel packages. (2008 stats: 11 carries for 23 yards, -26.0% DVOA, -11 DYAR.)

Arian Foster, HOU: Tennessee's starting halfback was a first-team preseason All-American, but struggled with knee issues and ended up running for only 570 yards and one touchdown as a senior. He went undrafted and caught on with the Texans, whose coaches have fallen for him as a receiver out of the backfield. If he can stay in one piece, he could be a sleeper as the Texans' change-of-pace back.

Quinton Ganther, TEN: The third running back on a team that uses two. He beat out Chris Henry for that job last season, but now he will also have to beat out Javon Ringer. Even if Ringer becomes the presumptive third back, Ganther could be LenDale White's backup if the big guy gets injured. (2008 stats: 9 carries for 61 yards, 45.6% DVOA, 19 DYAR; 6-for-6 on passes, 25.3% DVOA, 14 DYAR.)

Nick Goings, FA: Nick Goings made $1.6 million dollars last season, $275,000 more than DeAngelo Williams. Goings had nine carries for 10 yards and a DVOA of -98.9%, 127.2 percentage points lower than that of DeAngelo Williams. Nick Goings was released in February. Raise your hand if you are surprised.

Mike Goodson, CAR: Despite being known for explosive speed, Goodson only produced a 97.9 Speed Score and, considering expectations, had a rather disappointing three seasons at Texas A&M. A solid receiving threat, Goodson caught 90 passes for 7 touchdowns in his career, but his rushing production went down each season, from 847 yards (6.7 per carry) in 2006, to 711 (4.6) in 2007, to 408 (4.3) in 2008. His 0.2 POE (130rd in the country) shows that he was extremely average carrying the ball.

Mike Hart, IND: An impressive preseason got the slow-footed college star a job as the Colts' third back, but he tore his ACL on his third career touch. The Colts liked him, so if he's close to 100 percent, he can make the team, but odds are the knee will still bother him, and he'll have to look elsewhere, probably outside the NFL.

Chris Henry, TEN: When we wrote in *PFP 2008* that Henry wouldn't get too many carries, we still didn't mean "one." Henry was one of the top five overdrafts of the decade, and it isn't 20/20 hindsight; even back in 2007, nobody was quite sure why the Titans used a second-round pick on him. His place on the team is in jeopardy with the addition of Javon Ringer. (2007 stats: 31 carries for 119 yards, 2 TD, -13.5% DVOA, -6 DYAR.)

Maurice Hicks, FA: Hicks hasn't posted an above-average performance on kick returns in any of the previous three seasons, so it's no surprise that the Vikings cut him in February. The shelf life of 31-year-old kick returners without jobs is relatively short, so if he doesn't have a contract by the time you read this, he's probably finished.

P.J. Hill, NO: If Pierre Thomas cannot handle short-yardage duties, Hill could get a look. The 230-pounder was an effective interior runner at Wisconsin, and he scored 42 touchdowns to go with 3,966 yards in three seasons. The downside: Hill is a poor receiver, and a 2005 left tibia injury has become a chronic problem that limits his production.

Tony Hunt, FA: Hunt was released on October 14 and didn't catch on anywhere; his inability to pass block or contribute to special teams left him totally useless in Philly … and everywhere else, really. It's not easy to find a team that wants a third running back who doesn't play on third or fourth down.

Gartrell Johnson, SD: As a bruising Day Two pick from a mid-level school (Colorado State), it's pretty clear who Johnson will attempt to replace in San Diego: Michael Turner. The big difference? Turner profiled as a supreme athlete, with a Speed Score of 116.6; Johnson had the worst Speed Score of any back selected in this year's draft, a woeful 89.0.

Ian Johnson, MIN: Boise State's most famous crochet artist went undrafted after disappointing scouts with his performance in the week leading up to the East/West Game. He ran the second-fastest 40 time at the Combine (4.46, which also gives him the third highest Speed Score at 107.2) but apparently that didn't change any minds. Johnson can catch the ball and has reasonable pass-blocking skills, so if he can impress Minnesota coaches he could end up a third-down back and backup to Adrian Peterson when Chester Taylor's contract ends after this season.

Rudi Johnson, FA: Johnson was cut in camp by the Bengals and he signed with the Lions; he took Tatum Bell's roster spot, and Bell promptly stole Johnson's luggage. Johnson struggled through a knee injury for most of the year, and insulted the organization on the way out. Surprisingly, he was not re-signed. Johnson was never a great athlete, so the step he lost may have been the only one that made him a worthwhile use of a roster spot. (2008 stats: 76 carries for 237 yards, 1 TD, -21.3% DVOA, -35 DYAR; 12-for-14 on passes, 88 yards, 1 TD, 23.8% DVOA, 29 DYAR.)

Jamall Lee, CAR: Lee played at Bishop's College in Quebec and ran the fastest 40-yard dash time — in the low 4.3 range — at the Canadian Football League combine. Obviously, we don't know anything about the conditions of the field at the CFL combine, but Lee is 225 pounds, so that would work out to an impressive Speed Score around 125.

Brian Leonard, CIN: Heading into 2008, the Rams believed that Leonard had fully recovered from offseason surgery to both shoulders. He lasted all of month before going back on injured reserve with, you guessed it, another shoulder injury. As a result, and only two years after drafting him, the Rams traded Leonard to the Bengals for defensive tackle Orien Harris. The Bengals will use Leonard much like the Seahawks used Leonard Weaver, i.e., as a pass-catching fullback with relatively minimal blocking responsibilities (for a fullback). (2007 stats: 86 carries for 303 yards, -5.1% DVOA, 12 DYAR; 30-for-39 on passes, -7.7% DVOA, 13 DYAR.)

Kregg Lumpkin, GB: The undrafted Georgia product beat out Vernand Morency and Noah Herron for the third running back spot in training camp and emerged as a competent all-around back, if not necessarily one with serious breakout potential. The rap on him has always been his health, and after tearing his ACL his sophomore year and suffering knee and hand injuries as a senior, Lumpkin only made it through two games before suffering a pulled hamstring that ended his season. He's a useful player if he's healthy, but depending on him for any sort of serious workload is foolish.

Travis Minor, FA: He's old and serves no particularly useful function on special teams. Minor is one of those guys who comes into the league, bounces around for seven or eight years making more money than most teachers will in a lifetime, and then retires to a career in insurance sales. (2008 stats: 13 carries for 29 yards, -30.3% DVOA, -11 DYAR.)

Chris Ogbonnaya, STL: As much of a receiving threat as anything else — last year he had 74 carries and 46 receptions — the Houston product was a steadying force for Texas in 2008. He is a high-character pick who has experience at both running back and wide receiver. He was more versatile than productive, posting just a combined 6.74 POE in 121 touches rushing and receiving.

Xavier Omon, BUF: A 2008 sixth-rounder, Omon was a four-time All-Mid-America Intercollegiate Athletics Association selection while toting the rock for Northwest Missouri State, and was the first college football player to run for at least 1,500 yards in four straight seasons. How that translates into the NFL is anyone's guess, but Omon, who has already survived two of his brothers, has the kind of story everyone wants to see end well. (2008 stats: 6 carries for 5 yards, -58.7% DVOA, -17 DYAR.)

Jalen Parmele, BAL: Parmele spent most of last season on the Dolphins practice squad. The Ravens signed him in late December and gave him two carries in the season finale, one for 31 yards and one for a loss of four. Parmele rushed for more than 1,000 yards twice at Toledo, and his 111.2 Speed Score was the highest of any non-first round back in the 2008 draft. He's a thick power runner with poor receiving skills, battling for a back-of-the-bench position and hoping that Willis McGahee talks his way out of Baltimore.

Alvin Pearman, JAC: Pearman was featured as a return man during his first two years with the Jaguars. He then lost his job to LaBrandon Toefield and was traded to the Seahawks for a draft pick. A solid start in Seattle ended with a Week 4 ACL injury. Jacksonville welcomed him back after Fred Taylor's season-ending thumb injury in December of 2008, and Pearman scored on the one touch he got — a 23-yard pass. He might stick as the team looks to shape a rotation around Maurice Jones-Drew.

Adrian Peterson, CHI: "The Other" Adrian Peterson nearly cost Chicago a shot at a playoff spot when his late hit on a kickoff in Week 16 set up the opposing Packers on the Bears' 35-yard line. A blocked field goal saved the Bears' bacon, but marginal players who make conspicuous errors have a way of losing their roster spots. (2008 stats: 20 carries for 100 yards, 13.7% DVOA, 17 DYAR.)

P.J. Pope, DEN: Pope spent two and a half years bouncing around practice squads until Denver's epidemic of running back injuries finally got him some NFL carries and even an NFL start, Week 16 against Buffalo. Naturally, he suffered a season-ending hamstring tear after five carries and 42 yards. The new Broncos administration doesn't expect to need a seventh-string running back again this year, and waived him after the season. (2008 stats: 17 carries, 130 yards, 57.7% DVOA, 52 DYAR.)

Javon Ringer, TEN: Undersized (5-foot-9, 202 pounds) and not particularly fast (91.6 Speed Score — he doesn't seem to have regained all of the speed he had before his 2005 knee injury), Ringer's biggest strength by far was his ability at Michigan State to take a beating game after game. He carried 390 times in 13 games in 2008 and 843 times in his career (plus 96 receptions), but he only managed better than five yards per carry in a game three times last year. His numbers were distinctly average in 2008 (-0.3 POE, 137rd in the country), but if durability is a skill, he displayed it last year.

Mike Sellers, WAS: Sellers held out of OTAs, unhappy with the four-year, $4-million contract he signed in 2007. The one-time tight end reached the Pro Bowl as a fullback, but he's: a) a fullback; b) 33 years old; c) playing in a system that won't give 26 carries and 17 catches like he earned in 2008. Sellers wisely returned to practice in June, wiser with the knowledge that he's an old and very replaceable cog in the machine. (2008 stats: -87.4% rushing DVOA, -26 DYAR; 9.0% receiving DVOA, 21 DYAR)

Chad Simpson, IND: He lost the battle with Mike Hart for the third running back job, but an injury to Hart opened the door for a roster spot. Simpson did little in his limited opportunities and will battle to make the roster this season. (2008 stats: 15 carries for 43 yards, 1 TD, -25.4% DVOA, -15 DYAR.)

Clifton Smith, TB: From undrafted free agent to practice squadder to the Pro Bowl in one season — not bad. Smith became the first Buc to ever return a punt and a kickoff for touchdowns in the same season, and he only dressed for nine games. He's probably too valuable on special teams to risk playing at running back, especially when the Bucs have Earnest Graham and Cadillac Williams to backup Derrick Ward. (2008 stats: 8 carries for 40 yards, -11.1% DVOA, -1 DYAR.)

Olaniyi Sobomehin, NO: On his only NFL carry, Sobomehin coughed the ball up at the goal line against the Niners and injured his shoulder on the play. It was probably his Moonlight Graham moment.

LaRod Stephens-Howling, ARI: LeSean McCoy's backup at Pittsburgh was taken as a potential kick returner by the Cardinals in the seventh round; he got compared to Darren Sproles because of his 5-foot-7, 180-pound frame, and because no one else in NFL history has succeeded while being that small.

Chris Taylor, HOU: A big physical back who could be adequate in short-yardage situations. He lacks the speed to play on a regular basis. (2008 stats: 14 carries for 35 yards, -55.7% DVOA, 24 DYAR.)

Darius Walker, DEN: Walker bounced around the practice squads of the Texans and the Rams last year without appearing in a game. He signed to be Denver's 23rd-string running back, which is a sign of what little interest there was in him around the league.

Javarris Williams, KC: A seventh-round pick of the Chiefs, Williams put up a 105.9 Speed Score that was the fourth-best amongst this year's crop of rookie backs. He'll battle Kolby Smith to be the third-string back — if he's willing to play dirty, one or two shots to Smith's surgically reconstructed knee might do the trick.

Garrett Wolfe, CHI: Wolfe was primarily a special teams gunner before tearing his hamstring in Week 14 and missing the rest of the season. The Bears are promising to give him more time as a change of pace to Forte, but his inability to pass block cancels out the benefit they might get from his receiving abilities. The Bears would love for him to be Leon Washington, but he's going to end up being closer to Travis Jervey. You can decide if that's worth aspiring to. (2008 stats: 13 carries for 69 yards, -17.3% DVOA, -5 DYAR.)

Wide Receivers

Who's the best receiver in the NFL? Well, it depends on who — and when — you ask.

During the 2008 playoffs, it was impossible to give any answer but "Larry Fitzgerald." In four games (including three against top-eight pass defenses) plus the Pro Bowl, Fitzgerald put up what amounted to a good season for some wide receivers: 35 catches for 627 yards and nine touchdowns. Furthermore, the numbers don't do his performance justice; Fitzgerald's catches came leaping over defenders, running through tackles, and on the edges of fingertips. He was spectacular. It was the most dominant performance, arguably, in postseason history.

As for the regular season? Well, our numbers give the prize to Andre Johnson of the Texans, who had seven games of 10 catches or more in 2008. While he didn't compile the highlight reel that Fitzgerald did, his fourth-down catch against Miami in Week 6 to keep the Texans' final drive alive and eventually help them win their first game of the year was our pick for the best catch of the 2008 season. On top of that, Johnson put up superior cumulative numbers to Fitzgerald without having an All-Pro quarterback or a top talent playing across from him at wide receiver. Fitzgerald did it in the playoffs, but Johnson didn't have that option because of the quality of team around him.

Our answer? It's a cop-out. Fitzgerald is 1A, and Johnson is 1B. We get equally afraid when our favorite team faces them, and when they're not, we get equally excited when the ball goes up in either of their directions. We're blessed to watch them both play.

In the following section we give the last three years worth of statistics, as well as a 2009 projection, for every receiver who played a significant role in 2008, or is expected to play a significant role in 2009.

How to Read the Receiver Statistics Table

The first line contains biographical data — each player's name, height, weight, college, draft position, birth date, and age. Height and weight are the best data we could find; weight, of course, can fluctuate during the offseason. **Age** is very simple, the number of years between the player's birth year and 2009, but birth date is provided if you want to figure out exact age.

Draft position gives draft year and round, with the overall pick number with which the player was taken in parentheses. In the sample table, it says that Roddy White was chosen in the 2005 draft in the first round with the 27th overall pick. Undrafted free agents are listed as "FA" with the year they came into the league, even if they were only in training camp or on a practice squad.

To the far right of the first line is the player's **Risk** for fantasy football in 2009. The changes made to the Risk variable this year are explained fully in the introduction to quarterbacks. The standard is for players to be marked Green. Players with higher than normal risk are marked Yellow, and players with the highest risk are marked Red. Players who are most likely to match or surpass our forecast — primarily second-stringers with low projections — are marked Blue. (You will notice that there are significantly fewer "Green" players at wide receiver when compared to other positions. That's not specific to the position, it just happens to be the outcome of the 2009 projections.)

Next we give the last three years of player stats. Note that rushing stats are not included for receivers, but that any receiver with at least three carries last year will have his 2008 rushing stats appear in his team's chapter, and some receivers are listed with small rushing projections to go with their receiving projections in Appendix A at the end of the book.

On in the receiver table, the first column after the year and team for which that receiver played that year is games played (**G**). This is the official NFL total and may include games in which a player appeared on special teams, but did not play wide receiver. Receptions (**Rec**) counts passes caught, while Passes (**Pass**) counts passes thrown to this player, complete or incomplete. The next four columns list receiving yards (**Yds**), catch rate (**C%**), yards per catch (**Yd/C**), and receiving touchdowns (**TD**).

Catch rate, or receptions divided by total passes, is

an attempt to rectify a major problem in conventional statistics, which lay the blame for incomplete passes entirely on quarterbacks. Historical study shows that receivers definitely have an impact on whether a ball is complete or incomplete. We're still working to break down the degree to which the responsibility for an incomplete is shared by the quarterback and receiver, but it is clearly closer to 50-50 than it is to the 100-0 currently reflected in NFL stats. Wide receivers that are used in longer pass patterns will generally catch a lower percentage of passes. The average NFL wide receiver caught 57 percent of the passes thrown to him in 2008, 58 percent of the passes in 2007, and 56 percent in 2006; for tight ends, those same figures were 64 percent in 2008, 65 percent in 2007, and 62 percent in 2006.

(Note: Incomplete pass does not mean dropped pass; dropped passes are not specified in publicly available play-by-play, and, while we have the data from game charting, it is not yet merged into our other statistics.)

Next comes Yards After Catch (**YAC**), based on information from the game charting project, and rank (**Rk**) in Yards After Catch. That is followed by five columns with our advanced metrics for receiving: **DVOA** (Defense-Adjusted Value Over Average), **DYAR** (Defense-Adjusted Yards Above Replacement), and **YAR** (Yards Above Replacement), along with the player's rank in both DVOA and DYAR. These metrics compare every pass intended for a receiver and the results of that pass to a league-average baseline based on the game situations in which passes were thrown to that receiver. DVOA and DYAR are also adjusted based on the opposing defense. The methods used to compute these numbers are described in detail in the "Statistical Toolbox" introduction in the front of the book. The important distinctions between them are:

• DVOA is a rate statistic, while DYAR is a cumulative statistic. Thus, a higher DVOA means more value per pass play, while a higher DYAR means more aggregate value over the entire season.

• Because DYAR is defense-adjusted and YAR is not, a player whose DYAR is higher than his YAR faced a harder-than-average schedule. A player whose DYAR is lower than his YAR faced an easier-than-average schedule.

To qualify for ranking in YAC, receiving DVOA, or receiving DYAR, a wide receiver must have had 50 passes thrown to him in that season. We ranked 79 wideouts in 2008, 86 in 2007, and 83 in 2006. Tight ends qualify with 25 targets in a given season; we ranked 43 tight ends in 2008 and 2006, with 44 in 2007.

The final four columns break down pass length based on the Football Outsiders charting project. The categories are **Short** (5 yards or less), **Mid** (6 to 15 yards), **Deep** (16 to 25 yards), and **Bomb** (26 or more yards). These numbers are based on distance in the air only and include both complete and incomplete passes.

The italicized row of statistics for the 2009 season is our 2009 KUBIAK projection based on a complicated regression analysis that takes into account numerous variables including projected role, performance over the past two years, projected team offense and defense, projected quarterback statistics, historical comparables, height, age, and strength of schedule.

It is difficult to accurately project statistics for a 162-game baseball season, but it is exponentially more difficult to accurately project statistics for a 16-game football season. Consider the listed projections not as a prediction of exact numbers, but as the mean of a range of possible performances. What's important is less the exact number of yards we project, and more which players are projected to improve or decline. Actual performance will vary from our projection less for veteran starters and more for rookies and third-stringers, for whom we must base our projections on much smaller career statistical samples. Touchdown numbers will vary more than yardage numbers.

A few low-round rookies, guys listed at seventh on the depth chart, and players who are listed as wide

Wide Receiver Statistics Sample

Roddy White   Height: 6-1   Weight: 201   College: UAB   Draft: 2005/1 (27)   Born: 2-Nov-1981   Age: 28   Risk: Green

Year	Team	G	Rec	Pass	Yds	C%	Yd/C	TD	YAC	Rk	DVOA	Rk	DYAR	Rk	YAR	Short	Mid	Deep	Bomb
2006	ATL	16	30	64	506	47%	16.9	0	2.2	78	-12.6%	65	0	65	6	15%	45%	13%	27%
2007	ATL	16	83	137	1202	61%	14.5	6	5.5	7	1.3%	45	149	29	167	34%	41%	16%	10%
2008	ATL	16	88	148	1382	59%	15.7	7	4.1	33	22.1%	6	399	3	361	27%	45%	17%	12%
2009	*ATL*		*84*	*156*	*1183*	*54%*	*14.1*	*8*			*11.0%*								

receivers but really only play special teams are briefly discussed at the end of the chapter in a section we call "Going Deep."

Two notes regarding our advanced metrics: We cannot yet fully separate the performance of a receiver from the performance of his quarterback. Be aware that one will affect the other. In addition, these statistics measure only passes thrown to a receiver, not performance on plays when he is not thrown the ball, such as blocking and drawing double-teams.

Top 20 WR by DYAR (Total Value), 2008

Rank	Player	Team	DYAR
1	Andre Johnson	HOU	493
2	Larry Fitzgerald	ARI	402
3	Roddy White	ATL	399
4	Vincent Jackson	SD	369
5	Steve Smith	CAR	365
6	Reggie Wayne	IND	332
7	Hines Ward	PIT	289
8	Antonio Bryant	TB	284
9	Anquan Boldin	ARI	269
10	Calvin Johnson	DET	256
11	Derrick Mason	BAL	249
12	Greg Jennings	GB	243
13	Anthony Gonzalez	IND	242
14	Steve Breaston	ARI	239
15	Lance Moore	NO	232
16	Kevin Walter	HOU	225
17	Devery Henderson	NO	215
18	Bernard Berrian	MIN	198
19	Lee Evans	BUF	191
20	Wes Welker	NE	187

Top 20 WR by DVOA (Value per Pass), 2008

Rank	Player	Team	DVOA
1	Devery Henderson	NO	36.5%
2	Vincent Jackson	SD	32.9%
3	Anthony Gonzalez	IND	26.3%
4	Steve Smith	CAR	22.7%
5	Andre Johnson	HOU	22.4%
6	Roddy White	ATL	22.1%
7	Larry Fitzgerald	ARI	19.8%
8	Ike Hilliard	TB	19.5%
9	Reggie Wayne	IND	19.2%
10	Kevin Walter	HOU	16.8%
11	Hines Ward	PIT	16.2%
12	Michael Jenkins	ATL	16.0%
13	Steve Breaston	ARI	14.1%
14	Anquan Boldin	ARI	13.9%
15	Derrick Mason	BAL	13.9%
16	Antonio Bryant	TB	13.3%
17	Lance Moore	NO	12.6%
18	Bernard Berrian	MIN	12.4%
19	Domenik Hixon	NYG	11.5%
20	Lee Evans	BUF	11.2%

Top 10 TE by DYAR (Total Value), 2008

Rank	Player	Team	DYAR
1	Tony Gonzalez	KC	243
2	Visanthe Shiancoe	MIN	220
3	Jason Witten	DAL	203
4	Dallas Clark	IND	188
5	Owen Daniels	HOU	183
6	Anthony Fasano	MIA	156
7	Billy Miller	NO	150
8	John Carlson	SEA	143
9	Antonio Gates	SD	140
10	David Martin	MIA	131

Top 10 TE by DVOA (Value per Play), 2008

Rank	Player	Team	DVOA
1	Martellus Bennett	DAL	58.8%
2	Visanthe Shiancoe	MIN	50.0%
3	David Martin	MIA	37.3%
4	Anthony Fasano	MIA	34.8%
5	Billy Miller	NO	28.8%
6	Tony Scheffler	DEN	22.2%
7	Heath Miller	PIT	22.1%
8	Brent Celek	PHI	21.9%
9	Owen Daniels	HOU	19.3%
10	John Carlson	SEA	19.1%

Aundrae Allison

Height: 6-1   Weight: 192   College: East Carolina   Draft: 2007/5 (146)   Born: 25-Jun-1984   Age: 25   Risk: Green

Year	Team	G	Rec	Pass	Yds	C%	Yd/C	TD	YAC	Rk	DVOA	Rk	DYAR	Rk	YAR	Short	Mid	Deep	Bomb
2007	MIN	11	8	18	122	44%	15.3	0	6.0	--	-35.6%	--	-32	--	-35	19%	50%	13%	19%
2008	MIN	15	10	21	109	48%	10.9	0	4.7	--	-4.4%	--	15	--	21	32%	41%	14%	14%
2009	MIN		15	28	200	54%	13.3	1			-8.7%								

Despite being fantastic on kick returns in 2007, Allison was taken off that beat and replaced by Chester Taylor and Maurice Hicks, both of whom were below-average. That left Allison as a gunner without much of a defined role in the offense; at one point, he had a stretch of nine targets with one catch, one interception, and seven incomplete passes to his credit. The Vikings should restore him to return duties and not worry about finding a place for him in the offense; with Berrian and Percy Harvin in the lineup, there's no spot for Allison there, anyway.

David Anderson

Height: 5-11   Weight: 195   College: Colorado State   Draft: 2006/7 (251)   Born: 28-Jul-1983   Age: 26   Risk: Yellow

Year	Team	G	Rec	Pass	Yds	C%	Yd/C	TD	YAC	Rk	DVOA	Rk	DYAR	Rk	YAR	Short	Mid	Deep	Bomb
2006	HOU	9	1	1	27	100%	27.0	0	22	--	179.2%	--	13	--	12	100%	0%	0%	0%
2007	HOU	8	12	17	131	71%	10.9	1	1.8	--	19.7%	--	44	--	42	40%	47%	13%	0%
2008	HOU	16	19	29	241	66%	12.7	2	6.3	--	13.1%	--	59	--	52	44%	52%	4%	0%
2009	HOU		37	57	486	65%	13.1	2			4.0%								

Undersized and shifty, Anderson fits into the Wes Welker/Antwaan Randle El class of slot receivers; he's slowly increased his playing time each year to the point where he now enters the season as the Texans' third receiver. He has limited upside, and the Texans' lack of receiver depth is belied by the number of snaps he will play. As he showed on YouTube over the offseason, his Ron Jaworski impersonation opens up a second career for him if he can't make it in the National Football League.

Miles Austin

Height: 6-3   Weight: 219   College: Monmouth (NJ)   Draft: 2006/FA   Born: 30-Jun-1984   Age: 25   Risk: Red

Year	Team	G	Rec	Pass	Yds	C%	Yd/C	TD	YAC	Rk	DVOA	Rk	DYAR	Rk	YAR	Short	Mid	Deep	Bomb
2007	DAL	16	5	10	76	50%	15.2	0	8.6	--	33.8%	--	43	--	37	25%	33%	17%	25%
2008	DAL	12	13	23	278	57%	21.4	3	7.7	--	48.7%	--	106	--	99	26%	35%	13%	26%
2009	DAL		41	73	687	56%	16.8	4			6.6%								

Austin's great numbers look similar to those Patrick Crayton put up as a part-timer player in 2006, but they're totally different receivers. While Crayton's a slot guy who works underneath, Austin's a bona fide deep threat who uses his deceptive speed and 6-foot-2 frame to work past defensive backs, and he's excellent at tracking the deep ball — he didn't drop a single pass last year. It's tempting to suggest that he benefited from being left alone in coverage, but he wasn't marked as "Uncovered" once all season, and caught passes against Asante Samuel, Corey Webster, Carlos Rogers, and Dominique Rodgers-Cromartie. His raw numbers would look better had he not missed time with a sprained ACL last year. The Cowboys noticed his performance, since they're moving him into the starting lineup and leaving Patrick Crayton in the slot, even though Crayton was the starter before the Roy Williams trade. Go get him; he won't be the third-best receiver in football, but he could very well end up having a season that looks like Alvin Harper authored it.

Jason Avant

Height: 6-1   Weight: 210   College: Michigan   Draft: 2006/4 (109)   Born: 20-Apr-1983   Age: 26   Risk: Blue

Year	Team	G	Rec	Pass	Yds	C%	Yd/C	TD	YAC	Rk	DVOA	Rk	DYAR	Rk	YAR	Short	Mid	Deep	Bomb
2006	PHI	8	7	15	68	47%	9.7	1	3.7	--	-36.8%	--	-25	--	-22	50%	17%	17%	17%
2007	PHI	15	23	33	267	70%	11.6	2	2.3	--	20.1%	--	85	--	74	26%	55%	16%	3%
2008	PHI	15	32	57	377	56%	11.8	2	2.4	72	-0.6%	43	51	54	43	31%	39%	24%	6%
2009	PHI		14	23	142	61%	10.1	1			-8.7%								

Avant was a reliable receiver on third down, with a 14.6% DVOA and 58 percent catch rate. However, unlike the other Eagles' receivers, Avant isn't a threat to do much after he catches the ball. He's strictly a slot receiver, with only one pass target where the Eagles had just two wide receivers on the field. The arrival of Jeremy Maclin doesn't directly threaten his role or his roster spot, but if Maclin develops quickly, he could take Kevin Curtis' spot in the starting lineup, which would force Curtis into the slot and put Avant on the bench.

Donnie Avery

Height: 5-11 Weight: 186 College: Houston   Draft: 2008/2 (33) Born: 12-Jun-1984 Age: 25 Risk: Red

Year	Team	G	Rec	Pass	Yds	C%	Yd/C	TD	YAC	Rk	DVOA	Rk	DYAR	Rk	YAR	Short	Mid	Deep	Bomb
2008	STL	15	53	104	674	52%	12.7	3	3.8	41	-16.5%	71	-32	75	-7	34%	30%	17%	18%
2009	STL		79	118	1081	67%	13.7	10			20.9%								

Avery was a surprise choice at the beginning of the second round a year ago, and while the Rams won't be earning any medals for their player acquisitions over the past few seasons, Avery appears to be one unpopular pick that they hit on. He didn't settle into the lineup until Week 8, when he burned the Patriots for 163 yards in the first three quarters. Before that game, he'd averaged fewer than five targets per game; afterwards, he was right around eight. He works best as a deep threat with a possession receiver to play off of; on third down over that second-half period, where receivers need to run more precise routes and defenders know where players are likely to end up, Avery was 6-of-16 for 40 yards.

To meet our projections for him this year and emerge as an excellent all-around receiver, Avery will need to improve his intermediate game. The good news is that this sort of player often does; think about guys like Lee Evans and Greg Jennings, who started their careers out as bomb targets and then filled in the rest of their game. Avery should see the same sort of progression.

Hank Baskett

Height: 6-4 Weight: 215 College: New Mexico   Draft: 2006/FA Born: 4-Sep-1982 Age: 27 Risk: Green

Year	Team	G	Rec	Pass	Yds	C%	Yd/C	TD	YAC	Rk	DVOA	Rk	DYAR	Rk	YAR	Short	Mid	Deep	Bomb
2006	PHI	16	22	43	464	51%	21.1	2	4.9	--	12.9%	--	83	--	85	21%	29%	24%	26%
2007	PHI	16	16	22	142	73%	8.9	1	2.4	--	-2.7%	--	16	--	6	43%	48%	10%	0%
2008	PHI	15	33	51	440	65%	13.3	3	4.6	21	8.6%	23	89	39	84	32%	48%	16%	4%
2009	PHI		29	44	256	66%	8.8	1			7.5%								

It was cute to read headlines about Kendra Wilkinson getting married to an "Eagles star" or an "Eagles ace," only to realize that they were talking about a fourth receiver whose best skill is his height. Baskett started off the year with a 90-yard touchdown catch on his first pass, and had eight receptions for 83 yards when the Eagles beat Pittsburgh in Week 3, but he lost a lot of his reps when Kevin Curtis made his return.

Arnaz Battle

Height: 6-1 Weight: 217 College: Notre Dame   Draft: 2003/6 (197) Born: 22-Feb-1980 Age: 29 Risk: Green

Year	Team	G	Rec	Pass	Yds	C%	Yd/C	TD	YAC	Rk	DVOA	Rk	DYAR	Rk	YAR	Short	Mid	Deep	Bomb
2006	SF	16	59	86	686	70%	11.6	3	4.1	29	3.3%	42	106	44	122	46%	37%	11%	6%
2007	SF	16	50	104	600	48%	12.0	5	3.1	57	-31.3%	83	-151	86	-122	36%	43%	13%	8%
2008	SF	9	24	42	318	57%	13.3	0	5.5	--	11.0%	--	75	--	97	29%	48%	17%	7%
2009	SF		34	52	335	65%	9.9	1			-7.5%								

He's a great downfield blocker and fearless going over the middle, but he's also 29 years old and coming off an injury-plagued season that saw his yardage numbers plummet from 2007 (although his DVOA actually improved dramatically). Battle still has a role to play on this team, just not a very big one. As the test case for injections of Synvisc (the same treatment Randy Johnson used to extend his career), Battle's primary function may end up being as a medical comp for Brian Westbrook.

Drew Bennett

Height: 6-5   Weight: 206   College: UCLA   Draft: 2000/FA   Born: 26-Aug-1978   Age: 31   Risk: N/A

Year	Team	G	Rec	Pass	Yds	C%	Yd/C	TD	YAC	Rk	DVOA	Rk	DYAR	Rk	YAR	Short	Mid	Deep	Bomb
2006	TEN	16	46	97	737	47%	16.0	3	2.7	65	-7.9%	58	36	59	25	12%	45%	27%	16%
2007	STL	14	33	73	375	45%	11.4	3	2.8	70	-24.4%	77	-68	77	-70	21%	49%	21%	8%
2008	STL	1	1	1	4	100%	4.0	0	0.0	--	-52.7%	--	-3	--	-3	100%	0%	0%	0%

In two years with the Rams, Bennett made $13 million. As you can see from the numbers above, the Rams didn't exactly get the return on their investment they hoped for. They saved only $50,000 on the salary cap by cutting Bennett, a sign of what little value he had in the STL. It's pretty clear that Bennett's monster numbers in 2004 (1,247 yards receiving and 11 touchdowns) make him eligible for the Germane Crowell-Peerless Price Six-Sigma Statistical Oddities club for wide receivers.

Earl Bennett

Height: 6-0   Weight: 209   College: Vanderbilt   Draft: 2008/3 (70)   Born: 23-Mar-1987   Age: 22   Risk: Red

Year	Team	G	Rec	Pass	Yds	C%	Yd/C	TD	YAC	Rk	DVOA	Rk	DYAR	Rk	YAR	Short	Mid	Deep	Bomb
2009	CHI		49	78	663	63%	13.5	6			15.6%								

Bennett didn't even get on the field as a rookie, but he could have a very big role in a Bears offense that requires a possession receiver who can go over the middle. That fits Bennett's skill set perfectly: He's tough, has good hands, and is an excellent route-runner, great at selling his moves and accelerating out of cuts without wasting motion. He has experience playing with Jay Cutler, who was his teammate at Vanderbilt and threw passes to Bennett during the latter's Pro Day. A role (and numbers) similar to the Giants' version of Steve Smith in 2008 would not be an unreasonable assumption for Bennett's 2009.

Bernard Berrian

Height: 6-1   Weight: 183   College: Fresno State   Draft: 2004/3 (78)   Born: 27-Dec-1980   Age: 28   Risk: Yellow

Year	Team	G	Rec	Pass	Yds	C%	Yd/C	TD	YAC	Rk	DVOA	Rk	DYAR	Rk	YAR	Short	Mid	Deep	Bomb
2006	CHI	15	51	102	775	50%	15.2	6	4.1	32	-8.2%	59	36	58	54	26%	33%	13%	28%
2007	CHI	16	71	128	951	55%	13.4	5	3.5	46	-7.3%	64	54	59	68	26%	41%	20%	12%
2008	MIN	16	48	95	964	51%	20.1	7	6.4	3	12.4%	18	198	18	220	16%	45%	14%	24%
2009	MIN		46	92	762	50%	16.6	9			12.9%								

Add six receptions and 127 receiving yards to those totals, derived from the pass interference penalties Berrian drew; he led the league in both categories, a legitimate skill that Berrian first exhibited during his time in Chicago. In addition to his speed, Berrian's brilliant at setting up those defensive backs stuck chasing him with subtle moves while the ball's in the air to create space for himself, something he famously showed off against New Orleans in the 2006 NFC Championship Game. He'd benefit from playing with a better quarterback; 29 percent of the throws to Berrian were marked as being incomplete due to the quarterback's fault (throw was out of bounds, overthrown, underthrown, thrown ahead, or thrown behind), while the league average is only 14 percent. The Vikings paid him to make Tarvaris Jackson better, and he did; he just can't make Jackson what the Vikings want him to be.

Davone Bess

Height: 5-10   Weight: 195   College: Hawaii   Draft: 2008/FA   Born: 13-Sep-1985   Age: 24   Risk: Yellow

Year	Team	G	Rec	Pass	Yds	C%	Yd/C	TD	YAC	Rk	DVOA	Rk	DYAR	Rk	YAR	Short	Mid	Deep	Bomb
2008	MIA	16	54	75	554	72%	10.3	1	4.5	22	1.3%	38	81	43	91	50%	34%	14%	3%
2009	MIA		50	74	601	68%	12.0	4			14.6%								

Bess was on the "sleeper" list of more than one draft analyst, but he may have been discounted by the spread offense stigma. When Greg Camarillo went down with a knee injury in November, Bess stepped up and caught 30 of his 54 receptions in Miami's last five regular-season games. He's a good bet to start 2009 in the slot, but could find his way back into the starting lineup depending on Camarillo's health.

Anquan Boldin

Height: 6-1   Weight: 218   College: Florida State   Draft: 2003/2 (54)   Born: 3-Oct-1980   Age: 29   Risk: Yellow

Year	Team	G	Rec	Pass	Yds	C%	Yd/C	TD	YAC	Rk	DVOA	Rk	DYAR	Rk	YAR	Short	Mid	Deep	Bomb
2006	ARI	16	83	152	1203	55%	14.5	4	4.5	21	-0.2%	47	146	31	146	25%	48%	15%	12%
2007	ARI	12	71	100	853	71%	12.0	9	5.3	10	16.3%	17	229	17	237	46%	35%	14%	5%
2008	ARI	12	89	126	1038	71%	11.7	11	6.1	5	13.9%	14	269	9	248	47%	42%	7%	3%
2009	ARI		90	144	1112	63%	12.4	7			-3.1%								

Boldin excels everywhere on the field, but especially in the red zone, where he is perhaps the NFL's preeminent scoring threat. Over the last four seasons, he has posted red zone DVOAs ranging from a high of 70.5% in 2007 to a "low" of 31.2% in 2006. For all the notoriety teammate Larry Fitzgerald gets as a red zone weapon, Boldin has outperformed him in that area every season, usually by a wide margin. That's what Boldin brings to the table. What he does not bring to the table is any kind of big-play threat. He ranked eighth in catches and 16th in yards, but just 39th in catches of 20 or more yards. So he won't be stretching defenses to open running room, and he won't necessarily command double-coverage, because he's unlikely to deliver a knockout blow. Worse, while Boldin deserves respect for missing only two games after Jets safety Eric Smith basically imploded his face, the fact remains that Boldin has been brittle over his career, missing four or more games three times in his six seasons. That's probably why he remains with Arizona — nobody wants to trade for a receiver who is likely to be hurt again.

Marty Booker

Height: 6-0   Weight: 212   College: Louisiana-Monroe   Draft: 1999/3 (78)   Born: 31-Jul-1976   Age: 33   Risk: N/A

Year	Team	G	Rec	Pass	Yds	C%	Yd/C	TD	YAC	Rk	DVOA	Rk	DYAR	Rk	YAR	Short	Mid	Deep	Bomb
2006	MIA	14	55	90	747	61%	13.6	6	4.9	15	12.8%	19	178	21	176	32%	45%	17%	6%
2007	MIA	15	50	105	556	48%	11.1	1	2.6	75	-27.2%	79	-121	84	-114	34%	35%	26%	5%
2008	CHI	13	14	49	211	29%	15.1	2	7.2	--	-44.8%	--	-122	--	-127	30%	30%	32%	9%

Conventional wisdom says that losing a step of speed means you can't go deep anymore, but in reality things are a lot more complicated. Losing a step means that you can't get separation from a defender, making it easy for him to cover you if you do decide to run that go route. It's easier for defenders to keep up with double moves, and that's the easiest way for a receiver to get open deep, so that's unavailable. Some of your intermediate patterns go out the window; since defensive backs aren't worried about you running past them, they don't bother giving you a cushion, which makes it a lot harder to run a curl. Without that quick-twitch turn of the hips, quarterbacks are reticent to throw the out, and since you don't get any faster when you're running the in, safeties and corners playing zone can jump your routes far easier than they could with a faster player. Essentially, you're down to running slants and crossing patterns, which is a good way to get injured.

You can probably tell that we're suggesting Booker lost that step. More so than the statistics above, consider this: Booker had 12 of the 49 passes thrown to him defensed (24.5 percent). On average, 8.7 percent of passes league-wide are defensed. Booker's a free agent, and although he might want to continue his career, any team interested in signing him is fighting a losing battle.

Dwayne Bowe

Height: 6-3   Weight: 212   College: LSU   Draft: 2007/1 (23)   Born: 21-Sep-1984   Age: 25   Risk: Yellow

Year	Team	G	Rec	Pass	Yds	C%	Yd/C	TD	YAC	Rk	DVOA	Rk	DYAR	Rk	YAR	Short	Mid	Deep	Bomb
2007	KC	16	70	118	995	59%	14.2	5	5.2	12	10.1%	26	208	20	226	29%	39%	19%	13%
2008	KC	16	86	157	1022	55%	11.9	7	4.1	30	-10.3%	66	29	63	53	44%	32%	14%	10%
2009	KC		84	142	1194	59%	14.2	10			15.5%								

Bowe has settled in nicely as Kansas City's top receiver, and he'll continue to fly a little bit under the radar until the Chiefs are fully rebuilt. Looking at similarity scores for other receivers entering their third seasons, we get a list that includes Andre Johnson, Marques Colston, Marvin Harrison, Keyshawn Johnson, and Joey Galloway.

Mark Bradley

Height: 6-1   Weight: 201   College: Oklahoma   Draft: 2005/2 (39)   Born: 29-Jan-1982   Age: 27   Risk: Red

Year	Team	G	Rec	Pass	Yds	C%	Yd/C	TD	YAC	Rk	DVOA	Rk	DYAR	Rk	YAR	Short	Mid	Deep	Bomb
2006	CHI	10	14	23	282	61%	20.1	3	6.2	--	32.8%	--	79	--	85	33%	33%	10%	24%
2007	CHI	15	6	17	71	35%	11.8	1	3.3	--	-45.2%	--	-45	--	-33	33%	28%	17%	22%
2008	CHI/KC	12	30	63	380	48%	12.7	3	3.1	56	-20.0%	77	-37	76	-45	43%	30%	8%	19%
2009	KC		52	100	705	52%	13.6	5			-0.9%								

The easy comment would be that the Bears got tired of waiting for Bradley to get healthy, but actually, Bradley was healthy for the entire 2007 season and the beginning of 2008, and in 17 games the Bears threw him a grand total of 18 passes, of which he caught only six. So the Bears apparently just got tired of waiting for Bradley, period. Kansas City picked him up when the Bears waived him after two games, and plugged him into the starting lineup for the second half of the year. He was basically a replacement-level receiver, but that's not bad for a guy who joined a team midyear, and he still has some potential. One interesting wrinkle is that the Chiefs decided the better way to use his speed was to pick up yards after catching short passes rather than sending him deep a lot. As you can see from that 2008 YAC figure, it didn't quite work at first, but things might be different with Matt Cassel under center — consider the ridiculous YAC the Patriots put up a year ago.

Deion Branch

Height: 5-9   Weight: 193   College: Louisville   Draft: 2002/2 (65)   Born: 18-Jul-1979   Age: 30   Risk: Green

Year	Team	G	Rec	Pass	Yds	C%	Yd/C	TD	YAC	Rk	DVOA	Rk	DYAR	Rk	YAR	Short	Mid	Deep	Bomb
2006	SEA	14	53	101	725	52%	13.7	4	3.5	45	-2.3%	51	81	51	85	11%	60%	22%	7%
2007	SEA	11	49	85	661	58%	13.5	4	4.2	29	1.6%	44	96	50	106	41%	33%	16%	10%
2008	SEA	8	30	59	412	51%	13.7	4	5.0	12	-14.1%	69	-7	69	17	29%	45%	11%	15%
2009	SEA		43	72	571	60%	13.3	2			7.7%								

In 2005, Branch's last season in New England, his red zone DVOA was 82.2%. In three seasons in Seattle, it has been no higher than -11.0%. So not only is Branch always hurt, but when he does make it onto the field, he hasn't played particularly well. After yet another knee surgery, Branch did not participate in a predraft April minicamp, and may not be able to practice until June. When asked if he could depend on Branch, Seattle offensive coordinator Greg Knapp replied "I don't know yet … I haven't worked with [him] on the field yet." It's a bad sign when that's the strongest endorsement your coach can offer. When he is playing this fall, Branch will be in a new role. No longer the top receiver, he will come off the bench when the Seahawks go three-wide and run intermediate routes while T.J. Houshmandzadeh handles the short stuff and Nate Burleson goes deep.

Steve Breaston

Height: 6-0   Weight: 193   College: Michigan   Draft: 2007/5 (142)   Born: 20-Aug-1983   Age: 26   Risk: Yellow

Year	Team	G	Rec	Pass	Yds	C%	Yd/C	TD	YAC	Rk	DVOA	Rk	DYAR	Rk	YAR	Short	Mid	Deep	Bomb
2007	ARI	16	8	14	92	57%	11.5	0	4.6	--	-19.4%	--	-8	--	-9	29%	50%	14%	7%
2008	ARI	16	77	113	1006	68%	13.1	3	3.0	60	14.1%	13	239	14	222	31%	42%	15%	12%
2009	ARI		57	89	781	64%	13.7	4			7.0%								

In the four games Anquan Boldin missed last season, Breaston caught 21 passes for 276 yards, and the Cardinals went 3-1. That's not to say that he's a part you can swap in if Boldin gets hurt or traded; they have different skill sets. He's not the fierce downfield blocker that Boldin is, nor does he have the hands that Boldin does, but he's a better downfield receiver thanks to far superior speed. Breaston had six catches on passes that went 25 yards or more in the air; Boldin also has six … over the past *three* years. If the team loses Boldin and Breaston becomes the full-time starter, the result will be a change in the offense: Larry Fitzgerald will run shorter routes, Breaston will try to play the Boldin role, or the team will have to find a new slot receiver to replace Boldin. Sean Morey, anyone?

Kenny Britt Height: 6-4 Weight: 215 College: Rutgers Draft: 2009/1 (30) Born: 19-Sep-1988 Age: 21 Risk: Yellow

Year	Team	G	Rec	Pass	Yds	C%	Yd/C	TD	YAC	Rk	DVOA	Rk	DYAR	Rk	YAR	Short	Mid	Deep	Bomb
2009	TEN		49	82	560	60%	11.4	4			-11.2%								

One of Greg Schiano's marquee recruits, Britt is a prototypical NFL receiver, combining strength and above-average speed. He caught 178 passes and 17 touchdowns in three seasons in Piscataway, serving as Mike Teel's go-to guy in 2007 and 2008. Tennessee's first-round pick will combine with Nate Washington to form a new set of Titans receivers; while Washington will serve as the downfield guy, Britt will serve as a possession receiver and target over the middle. To be successful in that role, he'll need to get better at breaking press coverage at the line of scrimmage.

Reggie Brown Height: 6-1 Weight: 197 College: Georgia Draft: 2005/2 (35) Born: 13-Jan-1981 Age: 28 Risk: Blue

Year	Team	G	Rec	Pass	Yds	C%	Yd/C	TD	YAC	Rk	DVOA	Rk	DYAR	Rk	YAR	Short	Mid	Deep	Bomb
2006	PHI	16	46	92	816	50%	17.7	8	4.0	37	10.9%	21	174	22	165	24%	38%	19%	20%
2007	PHI	16	61	111	780	55%	12.8	4	2.8	69	-7.4%	65	46	61	31	29%	44%	20%	7%
2008	PHI	10	18	35	252	51%	14.0	1	3.8	--	-0.8%	--	33	--	21	27%	48%	15%	9%
2009	PHI		11	23	192	48%	17.5	2			-12.1%								

When you're an Eagles receiver who doesn't participate on special teams, you need to be really effective in the passing game to make Andy Reid happy. Brown started the year on the sidelines with a strained hamstring, came back and had three targets in three weeks, then suffered a groin injury and never got back into the flow of things. With Brown's contract harboring a $9 million signing bonus and the Eagles far under the cap this year, it would make sense for them to cut him this offseason and eat the cap hit while they know they can.

Isaac Bruce Height: 6-0 Weight: 188 College: Memphis Draft: 1994/2 (33) Born: 10-Nov-1972 Age: 37 Risk: Green

Year	Team	G	Rec	Pass	Yds	C%	Yd/C	TD	YAC	Rk	DVOA	Rk	DYAR	Rk	YAR	Short	Mid	Deep	Bomb
2006	STL	16	74	126	1098	59%	14.8	3	3.6	43	10.3%	22	234	11	229	27%	34%	26%	13%
2007	STL	14	55	101	733	54%	13.3	4	2.5	76	0.8%	49	109	45	97	18%	47%	26%	10%
2008	SF	16	61	108	835	56%	13.7	7	3.0	61	6.0%	29	159	25	194	25%	39%	29%	7%
2009	SF		31	63	411	49%	13.3	2			-15.1%								

Bruce did exactly what was asked of him last year, providing the 49ers with a reliable target on intermediate passing routes and steady veteran leadership. He also appears to have great rapport with quarterback Shaun Hill. After briefly contemplating retirement, Bruce returns to play the same role again this year, but be forewarned: with Michael Crabtree and San Francisco's stable of other youngsters at wide receiver, Bruce's numbers may drop significantly.

Antonio Bryant Height: 6-1 Weight: 192 College: Pittsburgh Draft: 2002/2 (63) Born: 9-Mar-1981 Age: 28 Risk: Yellow

Year	Team	G	Rec	Pass	Yds	C%	Yd/C	TD	YAC	Rk	DVOA	Rk	DYAR	Rk	YAR	Short	Mid	Deep	Bomb
2006	SF	14	40	91	733	44%	18.3	3	4.1	33	-11.6%	62	8	62	17	15%	32%	33%	19%
2008	TB	16	83	138	1248	60%	15.0	7	4.4	23	13.3%	16	284	8	277	33%	38%	13%	16%
2009	TB		75	132	974	57%	13.0	7			6.5%								

From the fringes returned Bryant, who has managed to make three comebacks by the age of 28. After nearly being blackballed by the league following a 2007 lawsuit to take a positive drug test off his record, Bryant was given a chance by the Buccaneers and emerged as the top receiver for a team that desperately needed one. He also won plenty of fantasy owners their leagues with 435 yards and four touchdowns over the traditional play-off rounds, Weeks 14 through 16. Noting his propensity for disappearing (sometimes literally), the Bucs were wisely loathe to offer Bryant a long-term deal and tagged him with the Franchise designation; KUBIAK doesn't know about Bryant's makeup issues and projects a slight regression, but Bryant could be a Pro Bowl receiver or not catch a single pass in 2009, and we wouldn't be surprised by either.

Nate Burleson   Height: 6-0   Weight: 192 College: Nevada   Draft: 2003/3 (71)   Born: 19-Aug-1981 Age: 28 Risk: Green

Year	Team	G	Rec	Pass	Yds	C%	Yd/C	TD	YAC	Rk	DVOA	Rk	DYAR	Rk	YAR	Short	Mid	Deep	Bomb
2006	SEA	16	18	37	192	49%	10.7	2	2.0	--	-16.2%	--	-10	--	-16	27%	39%	21%	12%
2007	SEA	16	50	95	694	53%	13.9	9	3.9	35	1.2%	46	107	46	139	23%	41%	26%	11%
2008	SEA	1	5	9	60	56%	12.0	1	1.4	--	14.4%	--	20	--	21	22%	56%	22%	0%
2009	SEA		63	103	896	61%	14.2	6			18.0%								

Burleson tore his ACL in the season opener against Buffalo. Eight months later, he was still recovering from surgery and wearing a brace on his knee, practicing running routes but not participating in 7-on-7 drills at an April minicamp. He was hopeful, but not certain, that he would be ready in time for training camp. When healthy, Burleson is not just Seattle's top deep threat, but also their best kick returner.

Plaxico Burress   Height: 6-5   Weight: 226 College: Michigan State   Draft: 2000/1 (8)   Born: 12-Aug-1977 Age: 32 Risk: N/A

Year	Team	G	Rec	Pass	Yds	C%	Yd/C	TD	YAC	Rk	DVOA	Rk	DYAR	Rk	YAR	Short	Mid	Deep	Bomb
2006	NYG	15	63	121	988	52%	15.7	10	3.6	42	1.9%	45	140	34	124	25%	36%	23%	16%
2007	NYG	16	70	141	1025	50%	14.6	12	4.0	34	-0.5%	51	139	32	114	24%	37%	21%	18%
2008	NYG	10	35	66	454	53%	13.0	4	1.8	78	4.9%	30	94	37	98	19%	48%	19%	14%

You're probably familiar with the Burress story, but in case you missed last year: Contract extension. Missed meeting. Suspension. Hamstring injury. Painful lesson that sweat pants are not a holster. Suspension. IR. Release. When he made it onto the field, he was having a typical Plaxico Burress season.

Everyone's been afraid to touch Burress because of the pending criminal case that could put him in jail for a minimum of three years, thanks to Burress' refusal to cop a plea. For a player who turns 32 right around the time this book is released, a three-year sentence would pretty much end his career as a starting receiver. Even if Burress only misses part of this year and is able to return in full for the 2010 campaign, he'll never see a contract resembling the five-year, $35 million extension he signed last year.

Keenan Burton   Height: 6-1   Weight: 200 College: Kentucky   Draft: 2008/4 (128)   Born: 13-Oct-1985 Age: 24 Risk: Red

Year	Team	G	Rec	Pass	Yds	C%	Yd/C	TD	YAC	Rk	DVOA	Rk	DYAR	Rk	YAR	Short	Mid	Deep	Bomb
2008	STL	13	13	29	172	45%	13.2	1	4.4	--	-26.6%	--	-30	--	-26	30%	37%	26%	7%
2009	STL		32	58	431	55%	13.5	2			-2.9%								

Looking for a deep sleeper in your fantasy draft this year? Burton runs excellent routes, isn't afraid to go across the middle, has great hops (he had the highest vertical leap at the 2007 NFL Combine), and loves to study film (he played quarterback in high school). With Donnie Avery occupying most (if not all) of the defensive backs' attention this year, the Rams will need someone to emerge as Bulger's possession-receiver safety blanket, and Burton is the most likely candidate.

Deon Butler   Height: 5-10 Weight: 168 College: Penn State   Draft: 2009/3 (91)   Born: 4-Jan-1986 Age: 23 Risk: Red

Year	Team	G	Rec	Pass	Yds	C%	Yd/C	TD	YAC	Rk	DVOA	Rk	DYAR	Rk	YAR	Short	Mid	Deep	Bomb
2009	SEA		19	35	248	55%	12.9	1			-19.4%								

Butler broke Bobby Engram's career receptions record at Penn State, and he'll replace Engram as a slot man in Seattle's overhauled receiver rotation. From his first minicamp, Butler impressed with his ability to run tight routes and get open downfield. Butler's 4.38 speed is what sets him apart from the average small slot guy, and should Deion Branch miss any more time due to injury, Butler could be just as valuable split wide. One quality Butler definitely shares with Engram is an ability to move the chains — 38 of his 47 receptions in 2008 were for first downs.

Andre Caldwell
Height: 6-1   Weight: 200 College: Florida   Draft: 2008/3 (97)   Born: 15-Apr-1985 Age: 24 Risk: Red

Year	Team	G	Rec	Pass	Yds	C%	Yd/C	TD	YAC	Rk	DVOA	Rk	DYAR	Rk	YAR	Short	Mid	Deep	Bomb
2008	CIN	7	11	19	78	58%	7.1	0	3.5	--	-30.5%	--	-27	--	-36	50%	44%	6%	0%
2009	CIN		34	53	355	65%	10.4	3			4.0%								

Caldwell's rookie year had some promise, despite foot injuries that took away more than half his season. He was serviceable as a kick returner, and had 83 total yards in the final game of the year. 49 of those were on four runs, which could provide a clue to how Caldwell may be used in 2009.

Greg Camarillo
Height: 6-1   Weight: 190 College: Stanford   Draft: 2006/FA   Born: 18-Apr-1982 Age: 27 Risk: Yellow

Year	Team	G	Rec	Pass	Yds	C%	Yd/C	TD	YAC	Rk	DVOA	Rk	DYAR	Rk	YAR	Short	Mid	Deep	Bomb
2007	MIA	15	8	10	160	80%	20.0	2	8.4	--	82.0%	--	72	--	76	20%	50%	30%	0%
2008	MIA	11	55	83	613	66%	11.1	2	3.0	62	-2.5%	50	64	51	96	37%	43%	16%	4%
2009	MIA		53	82	695	65%	13.1	3			16.5%								

In 2007, Camarillo jumped into the spotlight as the guy whose overtime touchdown catch prevented the Dolphins from posting the first 0-16 single-season record in NFL history. The new administration in Miami found more uses for him, seeing the advantages to a reliably consistent receiver in a rotation without a lot of experience. When he went down for the season in late November with a torn ACL, his 55 catches ranked 14th in the league. In his absence, Davone Bess emerged as a reliable replacement, and the team selected three wide receivers in the first four rounds of the draft. Camarillo's likely to begin the year as the starter across from Ted Ginn, but there's no guarantee he'll end it that way.

Chris Chambers
Height: 5-11 Weight: 210 College: Wisconsin   Draft: 2001/2 (52)   Born: 12-Aug-1978 Age: 31 Risk: Green

Year	Team	G	Rec	Pass	Yds	C%	Yd/C	TD	YAC	Rk	DVOA	Rk	DYAR	Rk	YAR	Short	Mid	Deep	Bomb
2006	MIA	16	59	153	677	39%	11.5	4	3.2	51	-37.3%	83	-300	84	-314	31%	31%	24%	14%
2007	MIA/SD	16	66	129	970	51%	14.7	4	2.3	78	-4.2%	58	84	55	81	18%	45%	28%	10%
2008	SD	14	33	64	462	52%	14.0	5	1.8	77	0.2%	42	64	52	71	22%	43%	23%	12%
2009	SD		44	75	606	59%	13.8	5			13.4%								

Even we have to give respect where respect is due: Chambers started off the year on a downright freaky tip, scoring touchdowns on four of his first six receptions. Through five games, he had five touchdowns on 11 catches for a DVOA of 26.0%. He went down in Week 5 with a sprained ankle, though, and when he came back a few weeks later, he was the same old Chris Chambers the rest of the way, failing to catch a touchdown pass and putting up a DVOA of -17.3%. If he returns to catching a touchdown pass every other reception, he'll be incredibly valuable. Otherwise, he'll be Chris Chambers.

Antonio Chatman
Height: 5-9   Weight: 177 College: Cincinnati   Draft: 2003/FA   Born: 12-Feb-1979 Age: 30 Risk: Red

Year	Team	G	Rec	Pass	Yds	C%	Yd/C	TD	YAC	Rk	DVOA	Rk	DYAR	Rk	YAR	Short	Mid	Deep	Bomb
2006	CIN	3	3	5	22	60%	7.3	0	3.7	--	-15.3%	--	-1	--	-4	40%	20%	20%	20%
2007	CIN	13	19	29	149	66%	7.8	1	3.5	--	-12.4%	--	1	--	6	48%	34%	17%	0%
2008	CIN	10	21	31	194	68%	9.2	0	5.5	--	-21.8%	--	-22	--	-21	47%	37%	3%	13%
2009	CIN		23	35	248	66%	10.8	1			-17.1%								

Chatman caught 15 passes in three games started by Carson Palmer. When Ryan Fitzpatrick took over, Chatman disappeared from the offense, mainly because Fitz preferred taking off and running to going through his route progressions. Then, Chatman nearly had his head ripped off by a Quintin Mikell "tackle" and was done for the season. Assuming he can still turn his neck to look for the ball, Chatman will have to outduel Andre Caldwell for the slot receiver position.

Mark Clayton

Height: 5-10 Weight: 193 College: Oklahoma   Draft: 2005/1 (22) Born: 2-Jul-1982   Age: 27 Risk: Green

Year	Team	G	Rec	Pass	Yds	C%	Yd/C	TD	YAC	Rk	DVOA	Rk	DYAR	Rk	YAR	Short	Mid	Deep	Bomb
2006	BAL	16	67	112	939	60%	14.0	5	5.3	6	2.1%	44	129	36	130	37%	44%	9%	10%
2007	BAL	16	48	89	531	54%	11.1	0	2.2	81	-18.4%	75	-41	75	-27	25%	53%	16%	6%
2008	BAL	16	41	82	695	50%	17.0	3	4.2	28	-7.5%	59	32	61	38	25%	43%	12%	21%
2009	BAL		43	78	493	55%	11.5	2			-7.3%								

Befallen by injury in 2007, Clayton looked like he'd forgotten to heal over the offseason; he caught just 13 passes in the first seven games, but then came alive with 28-597-3 in the final nine, including catches for 47, 48, 53, and 70 yards. A number-two receiver who catches about three passes per game and a bomb every other week works for this offense, especially since Clayton provides some trick-play capability (he threw a touchdown pass and ran 42 yards for a touchdown in the season opener). If Clayton's production slips a little, he becomes a drain on the Ravens offense, as his injury-limited playoff production (six catches in three games) demonstrates.

Michael Clayton

Height: 6-3 Weight: 197 College: LSU   Draft: 2004/1 (15) Born: 13-Oct-1982 Age: 27 Risk: Yellow

Year	Team	G	Rec	Pass	Yds	C%	Yd/C	TD	YAC	Rk	DVOA	Rk	DYAR	Rk	YAR	Short	Mid	Deep	Bomb
2006	TB	12	33	65	356	51%	10.8	1	3.2	50	-19.7%	74	-36	74	-30	33%	48%	15%	5%
2007	TB	14	22	40	301	55%	13.7	0	5.7	--	-14.1%	--	-5	--	-3	42%	31%	19%	8%
2008	TB	15	38	61	484	62%	12.7	1	5.1	10	-8.8%	62	19	66	14	60%	28%	9%	4%
2009	TB		48	84	655	57%	13.6	3			-5.9%								

The perpetually disappointing Clayton was deactivated for the opener in New Orleans after running afoul of Jon Gruden. He stayed bitter throughout the season, and a free agent move seemed imminent. But the new regime in Tampa won him over, and Clayton re-signed. Clayton had some moments catching short passes and breaking tackles — he was tenth in the league in YAC. But his catch rate is low, and Bucs fans wince at the all-too-frequent drops. He'll be the second receiver by default, but needs to show his new boss that he has something more to offer than loyalty.

David Clowney

Height: 6-0 Weight: 188 College: Virginia Tech   Draft: 2007/5 (157) Born: 8-Jul-1985   Age: 24 Risk: Red

Year	Team	G	Rec	Pass	Yds	C%	Yd/C	TD	YAC	Rk	DVOA	Rk	DYAR	Rk	YAR	Short	Mid	Deep	Bomb
2008	NYJ	2	1	2	26	50%	26.0	0	5.0	--	15.9%	--	5	--	6	0%	0%	50%	50%
2009	NYJ		27	50	407	54%	15.0	4			-8.6%								

Clowney lit up the league in the preseason, gaining 222 yards and scoring two touchdowns on deep bombs from Brett Ratliff, but he injured his collarbone and didn't see regular season action until Week 15 against Buffalo. Clowney has blazing deep speed, which makes him unique among Jets receivers, and he'll be given every chance to win a starting spot.

Laveranues Coles

Height: 5-11 Weight: 193 College: Florida State   Draft: 2000/3 (78) Born: 29-Dec-1977 Age: 31 Risk: Green

Year	Team	G	Rec	Pass	Yds	C%	Yd/C	TD	YAC	Rk	DVOA	Rk	DYAR	Rk	YAR	Short	Mid	Deep	Bomb
2006	NYJ	16	91	151	1098	60%	12.1	6	3.2	49	-0.9%	49	144	32	124	35%	43%	14%	9%
2007	NYJ	12	55	89	646	62%	11.7	6	2.6	73	5.6%	36	129	39	135	37%	35%	17%	12%
2008	NYJ	16	70	115	850	61%	12.1	7	4.1	29	2.0%	36	144	27	161	30%	44%	15%	10%
2009	CIN		59	110	753	54%	12.8	4			-9.0%								

Coles is coming in to replace the departed T.J. Houshmandzadeh, and in fact, the two receivers had very similar performances last year. Despite his reputation as a speedster, Coles has never been much of a vertical receiver. Instead, he's a high-effort player who excels at hitches and comeback routes and who can take a hit and hold onto the football. He still has a big day or two in him, like when he caught eight balls for 105 yards and three touchdowns against the Cardinals last year, but at this point in his career, Coles is a complementary receiver, not a primary target.

Austin Collie

Height: 6-1 Weight: 200 College: BYU   Draft: 2009/4 (127) Born: 1-Jan-1985 Age: 24 Risk: Red

Year	Team	G	Rec	Pass	Yds	C%	Yd/C	TD	YAC	Rk	DVOA	Rk	DYAR	Rk	YAR	Short	Mid	Deep	Bomb
2009	IND		26	40	334	66%	12.7	1			8.2%								

An underrated playmaker for BYU, Collie caught 109 passes in two seasons sandwiching a two-year mission in 2005-06, then caught 106 for 1,538 yards and 15 touchdowns as a junior in 2008. He racked up 100-plus yards in each of his final 11 games in a Cougar uniform. He is not overly strong or fast for the NFL level, but his great route-running and fearlessness make him a perfect candidate to take over Anthony Gonzalez's slot position as Gonzalez moves into the starting lineup. He'll have to beat out Pierre Garcon for the role.

Marques Colston

Height: 6-4 Weight: 212 College: Hofstra   Draft: 2006/7 (252) Born: 5-Jun-1983 Age: 26 Risk: Red

Year	Team	G	Rec	Pass	Yds	C%	Yd/C	TD	YAC	Rk	DVOA	Rk	DYAR	Rk	YAR	Short	Mid	Deep	Bomb
2006	NO	14	70	115	1038	61%	14.8	8	5.2	8	14.0%	17	250	9	260	33%	44%	17%	6%
2007	NO	16	98	144	1202	68%	12.3	11	4.1	30	17.1%	14	354	5	341	43%	43%	10%	4%
2008	NO	11	47	88	760	53%	16.2	5	4.9	14	2.8%	33	111	33	110	29%	44%	20%	7%
2009	NO		85	141	1261	60%	14.8	11			19.5%								

Colston had 22 catches for 306 yards and four touchdowns in his final three games, a sign that he was back to his regular role as the Saints' top possession target after a season where he struggled with thumb and knee injuries. He's one of the best in-traffic receivers in the league, specializing in quick slants, shallow drags, and zone-breaker routes out of the Saints' stack formations. The Saints never really had Colston and Reggie Bush healthy last year. Put them on the field with Lance Moore and Devery Henderson and opponents might as well get the kickoff return team ready. Of course, that assumes that Colston can stay on the field; he had microfracture surgery on his knee in January, and while the team has played it off as a minor surgery, the term still gives us pause.

Jerricho Cotchery

Height: 6-0 Weight: 199 College: North Carolina State Draft: 2004/4 (108) Born: 16-Jun-1982 Age: 27 Risk: Yellow

Year	Team	G	Rec	Pass	Yds	C%	Yd/C	TD	YAC	Rk	DVOA	Rk	DYAR	Rk	YAR	Short	Mid	Deep	Bomb
2006	NYJ	16	82	125	961	66%	11.7	6	4.3	25	7.7%	33	212	16	198	40%	42%	17%	1%
2007	NYJ	15	82	127	1130	65%	13.8	2	4.9	16	11.3%	21	238	14	221	38%	39%	15%	8%
2008	NYJ	16	71	111	858	64%	12.1	5	4.7	20	-1.5%	48	99	34	124	40%	34%	12%	14%
2009	NYJ		68	130	930	52%	13.7	7			-1.1%								

Cotchery is coming off an unimpressive season and is now being asked to fill the role of a number-one receiver on a team with no clear second option. He averaged only nine yards a reception when the Jets went to a three-receiver look, six yards less than his average with the team's base personnel. Cotchery can beat a jam and makes catches in traffic, and he needs to because he doesn't get a lot of separation. If he can concentrate on running short and intermediate routes, Cotchery should be Mark Sanchez's first look on most passing plays.

Michael Crabtree

Height: 6-3   Weight: 214   College: Texas Tech   Draft: 2009/1 (10)   Born: 14-Sep-1987   Age: 22   Risk: Red

Year	Team	G	Rec	Pass	Yds	C%	Yd/C	TD	YAC	Rk	DVOA	Rk	DYAR	Rk	YAR	Short	Mid	Deep	Bomb
2009	SF		70	110	928	63%	13.3	7			13.4%								

How long do you think it took 49ers general manager Scot McLoughlan to decide to take Crabtree with the 10th overall pick? Fifteen seconds? Five? Crabtree's stock slipped on draft day due to irrational fears that he's a closet "diva" — in reality, the kid just likes nice clothes — and concerns over his minor foot injury, but the fact is that he's the most talented skill position player to come out of this draft. He instantly becomes San Francisco's number-one wide receiver, but before everyone gets too excited, remember that Calvin Johnson had "only" 756 yards and four touchdowns in his rookie season.

Patrick Crayton

Height: 6-1   Weight: 205   College: NW Oklahoma State   Draft: 2004/7 (216)   Born: 7-Apr-1979   Age: 30   Risk: Green

Year	Team	G	Rec	Pass	Yds	C%	Yd/C	TD	YAC	Rk	DVOA	Rk	DYAR	Rk	YAR	Short	Mid	Deep	Bomb
2006	DAL	16	36	48	516	75%	14.3	4	5.8	--	36.2%	--	187	--	197	31%	46%	18%	5%
2007	DAL	15	50	81	697	62%	13.9	7	5.7	5	19.5%	12	205	21	186	29%	48%	11%	13%
2008	DAL	16	39	69	550	57%	14.1	4	5.2	9	0.9%	40	70	50	71	28%	55%	11%	6%
2009	DAL		36	70	584	51%	16.2	2			-7.6%								

Among the more ludicrous moments of the 2008 Cowboys season was seeing the Dallas offense try to create space for 6-foot-3, 224-pound Terrell Owens by motioning him directly behind 6-foot-1, 205-pound Patrick Crayton in the slot, forcing Crayton to absorb the pressure at the line while allowing Owens a clean break.

  Despite a 15.0% DVOA over the first six weeks of the season, the Cowboys decided Crayton was solely a slot receiver, leading to the Roy Williams trade and Crayton's return to the role he was so effective in previously. He didn't play as well there, with his DVOA falling to -10.0% for the rest of the season. He remains a valuable cog in the offense as a third-down receiver who finds holes in zones; he had a DVOA of 25.2% on third down versus -16.1% on first down and -8.2% on second down. He'll play out of the slot this year, although he's capable of doing more.

Josh Cribbs

Height: 6-1   Weight: 192   College: Kent State   Draft: 2005/FA   Born: 9-Jun-1983   Age: 26   Risk: Yellow

Year	Team	G	Rec	Pass	Yds	C%	Yd/C	TD	YAC	Rk	DVOA	Rk	DYAR	Rk	YAR	Short	Mid	Deep	Bomb
2006	CLE	16	10	15	91	67%	9.1	0	4.9	--	-37.9%	--	-28	--	-29	33%	60%	7%	0%
2007	CLE	16	3	6	37	67%	12.3	0	9.5	--	-32.7%	--	-10	--	-7	67%	17%	17%	0%
2008	CLE	15	2	7	18	29%	9.0	1	6.5	--	-17.4%	--	-3	--	-7	57%	14%	14%	14%
2009	CLE		14	25	238	56%	17.0	1			-9.7%								

The Browns called their Wildcat formation the "Flash" last year, naming it after Cribbs' Kent State alma mater. Cribbs spent a lot of December in the Flash, and most of his 29 carries came when Ken Dorsey and Bruce Gradkowski were the Browns' quarterbacks and it made sense to get experimental. Eric Mangini compared Cribbs to Jerricho Cotchery in the offseason, which is good news for Cribbs, who shouldn't be pigeonholed as a trick-play machine. Cribbs will get a long look as a traditional receiver this year, and he remains one of the best all-purpose special teamers in the NFL. (Note: Cribbs' projection also includes 16 carries for 155 yards.)

Ronald Curry

Height: 6-2   Weight: 220   College: North Carolina   Draft: 2002/FA   Born: 28-May-1979   Age: 30   Risk: Red

Year	Team	G	Rec	Pass	Yds	C%	Yd/C	TD	YAC	Rk	DVOA	Rk	DYAR	Rk	YAR	Short	Mid	Deep	Bomb
2006	OAK	16	62	89	727	70%	11.7	1	3.1	53	7.3%	35	136	35	157	32%	54%	10%	4%
2007	OAK	16	55	97	717	57%	13.0	4	4.0	31	0.9%	48	105	48	102	39%	34%	14%	13%
2008	OAK	13	19	47	181	38%	9.5	2	1.4	--	-33.0%	--	-75	--	-79	20%	53%	18%	8%
2009	DET		53	89	639	60%	12.1	2			-2.1%								

Every player goes through slumps now and then, but slumping when the team fires the head coach is not particularly good timing. Although Curry had been Oakland's most efficient receiver in 2006 and 2007, Tom Cable benched him at midseason for rookie Chaz Schilens. The collapse in catch rate wasn't all Curry's fault, despite an early-season case of the dropsies. The Raiders used him on longer routes, and JaMarcus Russell had trouble getting him the ball in stride. Curry had very few yards after catch, and a disproportionate number of his incomplete passes were marked by our game charters as "Thrown Ahead." He should fit in well as Detroit's slot receiver, although he isn't exactly going to enjoy an upgrade in the quarterback accuracy department.

Kevin Curtis

Height: 5-11   Weight: 186   College: Utah State   Draft: 2003/3 (74)   Born: 17-Jul-1978   Age: 31   Risk: Yellow

Year	Team	G	Rec	Pass	Yds	C%	Yd/C	TD	YAC	Rk	DVOA	Rk	DYAR	Rk	YAR	Short	Mid	Deep	Bomb
2006	STL	16	40	57	479	70%	12.0	4	2.9	59	24.8%	5	169	26	160	53%	21%	17%	9%
2007	PHI	16	77	135	1110	57%	14.4	6	4.6	22	5.1%	37	194	22	186	28%	36%	22%	13%
2008	PHI	9	33	63	390	52%	11.8	2	2.7	67	-16.5%	72	-19	70	-13	24%	56%	10%	10%
2009	PHI		49	86	710	57%	14.5	4			-0.3%								

Curtis missed the first six weeks after having surgery on a sports hernia, and it took him a few weeks after that to get into form. Throw in a late-season concussion and calf injuries, and it was a wasted year for the former Rams receiver. That's an issue that occasionally comes up with players who are signed and brought into expanded roles; a player like Curtis, who operated out of the slot and didn't play on every down, was less likely to get injured in his part-time role than as a primary receiver for the Iggles. Philly overpaid for Curtis after they failed to get Wes Welker from Miami, and now that they've added Jeremy Maclin and DeSean Jackson, Curtis' skill set isn't as necessary as it once was. When you consider that Maclin was already lining up at split end in rookie minicamp and that Curtis' salary nearly doubles next year, don't be surprised if 2009 is Curtis' final year with the team.

Devard Darling

Height: 6-1   Weight: 213   College: Washington State   Draft: 2004/3 (82)   Born: 16-Apr-1982   Age: 27   Risk: Green

Year	Team	G	Rec	Pass	Yds	C%	Yd/C	TD	YAC	Rk	DVOA	Rk	DYAR	Rk	YAR	Short	Mid	Deep	Bomb
2007	BAL	16	18	39	326	46%	18.1	3	4.4	--	4.3%	--	53	--	59	19%	32%	32%	16%
2008	KC	16	17	33	247	52%	14.5	1	5.6	--	-12.1%	--	1	--	-5	33%	39%	6%	21%
2009	KC		14	28	206	50%	14.7	1			-16.5%								

It's been five years now, so we can probably stop saying Darling has "great upside" and just call him what he is: a fourth receiver whose job is to go deep on third-and-long and occasionally catch slip-screens in the spread offense.

Andre Davis

Height: 6-1   Weight: 195   College: Virginia Tech   Draft: 2002/2 (47)   Born: 12-Jun-1979   Age: 30   Risk: Green

Year	Team	G	Rec	Pass	Yds	C%	Yd/C	TD	YAC	Rk	DVOA	Rk	DYAR	Rk	YAR	Short	Mid	Deep	Bomb
2006	BUF	16	2	7	13	29%	6.5	0	5.0	--	-70.4%	--	-28	--	-31	40%	20%	20%	20%
2007	HOU	14	33	63	583	52%	17.7	3	3.1	60	2.6%	42	76	57	80	25%	43%	17%	15%
2008	HOU	12	13	28	213	46%	16.4	0	4.8	--	-13.2%	--	-1	--	1	21%	36%	14%	29%
2009	HOU		17	37	281	46%	16.5	2			-20.6%								

The life of a speed receiver is short. Davis made enough big plays over the years to be an asset as a third receiver. Those days are numbered, as Davis is 30 years old and no longer the burner he once was. The weak

Houston receiving corps gives him a chance to stick around for another year or two, but the gas light has turned on as his NFL career heads toward empty.

Chris Davis

Height: 5-10 Weight: 182 College: Florida State   Draft: 2007/4 (128) Born: 23-Jan-1984 Age: 25 Risk: Red

Year	Team	G	Rec	Pass	Yds	C%	Yd/C	TD	YAC	Rk	DVOA	Rk	DYAR	Rk	YAR	Short	Mid	Deep	Bomb
2007	TEN	12	5	9	38	56%	7.6	0	5.0	--	-83.3%	--	-49	--	-45	63%	38%	0%	0%
2008	TEN	5	2	3	31	67%	15.5	0	6.5	--	34.9%	--	12	--	12	33%	67%	0%	0%
2009	TEN		20	34	240	59%	12.0	1			-12.2%								

Davis, the Titans' fourth-round pick in 2007, has caught just seven career passes and is yet to start a game. He'd be considered a major disappointment if 2007 third-round pick Paul Williams wasn't considerably worse. Davis bulked up in the offseason, and Kerry Collins praised his improvement during minicamp. If it comes down to Davis vs. Williams, Davis will win, but the Titans probably don't need either of them now that Kenny Britt and Nate Washington are on the team.

Craig Davis

Height: 6-1 Weight: 203 College: LSU   Draft: 2007/1 (30) Born: 5-Oct-1985 Age: 24 Risk: Blue

Year	Team	G	Rec	Pass	Yds	C%	Yd/C	TD	YAC	Rk	DVOA	Rk	DYAR	Rk	YAR	Short	Mid	Deep	Bomb
2007	SD	14	20	34	188	59%	9.4	1	3.7	--	-0.7%	--	33	--	32	44%	41%	13%	3%
2008	SD	4	4	7	59	57%	14.8	0	8.8	--	14.2%	--	15	--	17	57%	43%	0%	0%
2009	SD		17	32	222	53%	13.1	0			-23.3%								

"Buster" has made virtually no impact on the Chargers after being taken in the first round of the 2007 draft. He missed most of last season with a groin injury, and hasn't ingratiated himself to the coaching staff with his efforts. Fourth wide receivers who don't play special teams tend to do that. Davis will need to compete with Malcom Floyd for the third receiver spot in camp; if he doesn't make it, he could very well be out of a job, the latest SEC wideout bust. We think he has a shot to contribute, but he'll have to stay healthy.

Rashied Davis

Height: 5-9 Weight: 180 College: San Jose State   Draft: 2005/FA Born: 24-Jul-1979 Age: 30 Risk: Yellow

Year	Team	G	Rec	Pass	Yds	C%	Yd/C	TD	YAC	Rk	DVOA	Rk	DYAR	Rk	YAR	Short	Mid	Deep	Bomb
2006	CHI	16	22	56	303	39%	13.8	2	2.9	60	-21.3%	78	-37	75	-43	30%	39%	20%	11%
2007	CHI	16	17	31	165	55%	9.7	0	3.3	--	-24.6%	--	-27	--	-31	57%	20%	20%	3%
2008	CHI	16	35	67	445	52%	12.7	2	4.3	25	-17.0%	74	-23	72	-9	42%	29%	23%	6%
2009	CHI		31	48	406	65%	13.1	2			-16.0%								

Davis had 161 yards in two games against the Lions, and 284 yards in the other 12 games combined. See, picking on the Lions isn't only fun — it can be profitable too! Davis lost playing time as the season went along, recording almost as many catches (eight) as drops (five) over the final eight weeks of the season. He lost his job to Earl Bennett in the offseason and will become the Bears' slot receiver, assuming he makes the team.

Early Doucet

Height: 6-0 Weight: 212 College: LSU   Draft: 2008/3 (81) Born: 28-Oct-1985 Age: 24 Risk: Yellow

Year	Team	G	Rec	Pass	Yds	C%	Yd/C	TD	YAC	Rk	DVOA	Rk	DYAR	Rk	YAR	Short	Mid	Deep	Bomb
2008	ARI	7	14	17	90	82%	6.4	0	3.8	--	-4.4%	--	12	--	12	65%	29%	6%	0%
2009	ARI		41	61	485	67%	11.8	2			6.1%								

Poor Early Doucet. He spent most of his time in LSU playing behind Craig Davis and Dwayne Bowe, then moved on to the NFL, only to be drafted by the team with the league's deepest wide receiving corps. Maybe he can hang out with Matt Leinart on the sidelines and they can talk about how talented their teammates are. Doucet's best chance to play in 2009 would be to beat out Jerheme Urban for the fourth receiver spot. The Cardinals would love to see that happen.

Harry Douglas   Height: 5-11   Weight: 176   College: Louisville   Draft: 2008/3 (84)   Born: 16-Sep-1984   Age: 25   Risk: Yellow

Year	Team	G	Rec	Pass	Yds	C%	Yd/C	TD	YAC	Rk	DVOA	Rk	DYAR	Rk	YAR	Short	Mid	Deep	Bomb
2008	ATL	16	23	39	320	59%	13.9	1	4.6	--	-2.3%	--	30	--	18	45%	29%	18%	8%
2009	ATL		32	54	437	59%	13.7	6			21.5%								

Douglas was a nice surprise as a rookie slot receiver, especially as a blocker, getting every ounce out of his 171 pounds. Douglas was scrappy from the start, throwing a training camp punch at veteran Lawyer Milloy. Perhaps he was a little too eager — he wore down noticeably down the stretch, snaring only five catches in the last five games (including playoffs). An excellent athlete (he turned down a chance to play hoops for Rick Pitino at Louisville), the local favorite is an explosive threat on end-arounds and as a punt returner, scoring both ways in 2008. The plethora of offensive talent in the huddle will probably hold down Douglas' numbers, but he will benefit from the added space that Tony Gonzalez's presence will create inside.

Donald Driver   Height: 6-0   Weight: 188   College: Alcorn State   Draft: 1999/7 (213)   Born: 2-Feb-1975   Age: 34   Risk: Yellow

Year	Team	G	Rec	Pass	Yds	C%	Yd/C	TD	YAC	Rk	DVOA	Rk	DYAR	Rk	YAR	Short	Mid	Deep	Bomb
2006	GB	16	92	172	1295	53%	14.1	8	5.6	3	-4.4%	55	111	43	109	33%	36%	19%	12%
2007	GB	15	82	122	1048	67%	12.8	2	4.8	17	10.0%	27	221	18	222	40%	44%	8%	8%
2008	GB	16	74	115	1012	64%	13.7	5	4.7	18	7.9%	25	187	21	185	44%	33%	14%	9%
2009	GB		72	127	1018	57%	14.1	8			10.3%								

Driver gave way to Greg Jennings as the primary receiver last year, with 117 targets to Jennings' 141. He was the better receiver on first down, averaging 11.7 yards per attempt to Jennings' 8.6; on the other two downs, though, Jennings was far superior. Interestingly, most teams kept their primary cornerback on Driver; he was shadowed by Terence Newman, Marcus Trufant, and Antoine Winfield, while Jennings drew the secondary corners. Driver has remained remarkably healthy, missing only five games in the last nine years, but that could be a problem. When you miss time with a knee injury, for example, although your knee obviously is in bad shape, you also get a chance to heal the other parts of your body that are banged up if not particularly injured. Driver's developed a streak of health, which is good, but the wear-and-tear without any rest might end up shortening his career, which would be bad.

Braylon Edwards   Height: 6-3   Weight: 211   College: Michigan   Draft: 2005/1 (3)   Born: 21-Feb-1983   Age: 26   Risk: Yellow

Year	Team	G	Rec	Pass	Yds	C%	Yd/C	TD	YAC	Rk	DVOA	Rk	DYAR	Rk	YAR	Short	Mid	Deep	Bomb
2006	CLE	16	61	125	884	49%	14.5	6	5.5	5	-10.2%	61	25	61	36	25%	45%	17%	13%
2007	CLE	16	80	153	1289	52%	16.1	16	4.0	32	3.3%	40	189	24	212	31%	32%	30%	7%
2008	CLE	16	55	138	873	40%	15.9	3	3.8	36	-16.8%	73	-45	77	-86	31%	33%	21%	15%
2009	CLE		59	115	948	51%	16.1	8			8.8%								

The same criticisms we raised of Derek Anderson in his player comment also apply to Edwards, who showed signs of becoming an elite receiver in 2007 thanks to big games against the Bengals, Patriots, Rams, and Cardinals. Last year, he led the league in dropped passes and was markedly inconsistent, with as many games below 20 yards (three) as he did over 100 yards. The problem is with his deployment and the players around him. When he had Joe Jurevicius and Kellen Winslow across the field from him in 2006, Edwards was a threat to go deep on every play; the resulting cushion provided him by corners opened up opportunities for him underneath to serve as an effective receiver, as well as ample opportunities to actually go long and use his frame to beat up on opposing corners and safeties. When the Browns swapped out Jurevicius for Donte' Stallworth a year later, they brought in a poor man's Edwards — an oft-injured speed merchant. Since Stallworth's game revolves around deeper patterns, if Edwards wanted to go deep, he had to head past Stallworth — you can see the change in his percentages in the table above. With Stallworth out of the picture, Edwards should benefit from playing alongside Brian Robiskie, who should occupy more attention underneath and allow Edwards to run more patterns in the 15- to 20-yard range. In a contract year, he should be somewhere between his 2007 and 2008 campaigns.

Bobby Engram

Height: 5-10   Weight: 188   College: Penn State   Draft: 1996/2 (52)   Born: 7-Jan-1973   Age: 36   Risk: Red

Year	Team	G	Rec	Pass	Yds	C%	Yd/C	TD	YAC	Rk	DVOA	Rk	DYAR	Rk	YAR	Short	Mid	Deep	Bomb
2006	SEA	7	24	36	290	67%	12.1	1	2.8	--	14.3%	--	71	--	76	29%	46%	21%	4%
2007	SEA	16	94	134	1147	70%	12.2	6	3.9	37	12.7%	19	268	10	293	34%	45%	16%	4%
2008	SEA	13	47	80	489	59%	10.4	0	3.6	46	-17.9%	76	-32	74	-39	41%	40%	14%	5%
2009	KC		44	66	600	67%	13.6	2			9.6%								

The batteries finally ran out on Seattle's never-ending third down machine. Engram's third-down DVOA went from 37.4% in 2006 to 0.1% in 2007 and then to -27.5% last year. He'll try to revive his career with Kansas City, but at the age of 36, it's probably the end of the road for one of the original FO binkies.

Lee Evans

Height: 5-10   Weight: 197   College: Wisconsin   Draft: 2004/1 (13)   Born: 11-Mar-1981   Age: 28   Risk: Yellow

Year	Team	G	Rec	Pass	Yds	C%	Yd/C	TD	YAC	Rk	DVOA	Rk	DYAR	Rk	YAR	Short	Mid	Deep	Bomb
2006	BUF	16	82	137	1292	60%	15.8	8	4.6	18	22.7%	7	378	3	357	21%	45%	16%	18%
2007	BUF	16	55	113	849	49%	15.4	5	3.5	48	-10.2%	71	21	68	26	25%	41%	17%	17%
2008	BUF	16	63	102	1017	62%	16.1	3	4.0	34	11.2%	20	191	19	213	22%	50%	13%	14%
2009	BUF		66	125	1006	53%	15.2	7			2.8%								

Evans is one of the elite deep threats in the league, and stat lines like his two catches for 100 yards against the Cardinals or his four catches for 102 yards against the Seahawks reflect as much. Evans was deadly on third downs, where he caught 76 percent of the balls thrown his way and put up a DVOA of 35.1%. The Bills rewarded Evans with a four-year extension in October and with a big-name, big-ego receiver to draw coverage away in March. Evans will play flanker and should continue to be Trent Edwards' primary option, but shhhhhh … don't tell Terrell Owens that.

Brian Finneran

Height: 6-5   Weight: 210   College: Villanova   Draft: 1999/FA   Born: 31-Jan-1976   Age: 33   Risk: Red

Year	Team	G	Rec	Pass	Yds	C%	Yd/C	TD	YAC	Rk	DVOA	Rk	DYAR	Rk	YAR	Short	Mid	Deep	Bomb
2008	ATL	16	21	36	169	58%	8.0	1	2.3	--	-22.0%	--	-27	--	-38	29%	57%	14%	0%
2009	ATL		13	22	150	59%	11.5	1			-20.2%								

The fact that the affable Finneran played at all, following two seasons lost to knee injuries, was a nice story. But his height and smarts once again made him a third-down threat (16 receptions, 14 of which moved the chains). By rights, he should be transitioning into a radio career — he has made weekly appearances on local sports stations for years — but he deserves another year in the league, and, by golly, he'll get one.

Larry Fitzgerald

Height: 6-2   Weight: 223   College: Pittsburgh   Draft: 2004/1 (3)   Born: 31-Aug-1983   Age: 26   Risk: Green

Year	Team	G	Rec	Pass	Yds	C%	Yd/C	TD	YAC	Rk	DVOA	Rk	DYAR	Rk	YAR	Short	Mid	Deep	Bomb
2006	ARI	13	69	111	946	62%	13.7	6	2.6	67	18.5%	9	271	8	290	29%	38%	26%	7%
2007	ARI	15	100	167	1409	60%	14.1	10	2.7	72	9.1%	28	291	8	301	23%	48%	18%	11%
2008	ARI	16	96	154	1431	62%	14.9	12	4.7	19	19.8%	7	402	2	414	34%	41%	16%	9%
2009	ARI		100	170	1285	59%	12.9	11			12.6%								

Fitzgerald's ridiculous postseason (30 catches, 546 yards, and 7 touchdowns) moved him from Fantasy Football Star On A Bad Team to Household Name Who Can Beat You By Himself. Thanks to the early start to his career, he may be the only player with a shot to break Jerry Rice's records. (He's 226 catches and 2,400 yards ahead of where Rice was at the same age.) He's a perennial elite receiver and a reasonable answer to the question of "Who's the best overall player in the NFL?" But it's time to blow up one myth about him once and forever: He's not a particularly dominant red zone threat. His red zone DVOA last season was just 6.1%; teammates Anquan Boldin, Steve Breaston, and Jerheme Urban were all in the 40s and 50s. And it's not just last year; only once has Fitzgerald's DVOA in the red zone topped 10%. He's good inside the 20, but Arizona has better options. Remember that the next time he fails to catch a jump ball on a fade pattern.

Malcom Floyd

Height: 6-5 Weight: 225 College: Wyoming Draft: 2004/FA Born: 8-Sep-1981 Age: 28 Risk: Yellow

Year	Team	G	Rec	Pass	Yds	C%	Yd/C	TD	YAC	Rk	DVOA	Rk	DYAR	Rk	YAR	Short	Mid	Deep	Bomb
2006	SD	12	15	32	210	47%	14.0	3	3.1	--	-6.3%	--	16	--	21	27%	40%	10%	23%
2007	SD	6	7	13	97	54%	13.9	0	1.3	--	-5.6%	--	7	--	10	31%	15%	46%	8%
2008	SD	13	27	37	465	73%	17.2	4	1.7	--	58.9%	--	200	--	203	26%	14%	49%	11%
2009	SD		38	57	504	67%	13.3	4			8.2%								

When Buster Davis went down with his groin injury, it gave Floyd a chance to show what he can do, and as a 6-foot-5 receiver situated in the slot, he became a valuable part of the team's three-wideout and red zone sets. He also made it back from a Week 15 collapsed lung in time for the playoffs, earning him the same sort of plaudits Philip Rivers got for playing through a torn ACL in the 2007 playoffs. Floyd would benefit from playing on a team where he can be the designated tall guy, but with Vincent Jackson and Antonio Gates around, he's surrounded by giants. This will be his final year with the team.

Mike Furrey

Height: 6-0 Weight: 185 College: Northern Iowa Draft: 2003/FA Born: 12-May-1977 Age: 32 Risk: Red

Year	Team	G	Rec	Pass	Yds	C%	Yd/C	TD	YAC	Rk	DVOA	Rk	DYAR	Rk	YAR	Short	Mid	Deep	Bomb
2006	DET	16	98	146	1086	67%	11.1	6	3.1	54	8.0%	29	225	13	213	36%	43%	19%	2%
2007	DET	16	61	91	664	67%	10.9	1	3.0	62	6.4%	34	135	35	131	45%	29%	22%	3%
2008	DET	9	18	35	181	51%	10.1	0	2.6	--	-16.7%	--	-10	--	-22	41%	38%	19%	3%
2009	CLE		24	40	387	60%	16.1	2			-5.3%								

As expected, Furrey was a poor fit outside of the Mike Martz pass-happy scheme the Lions ran in 2006 and 2007, struggling before suffering a season-ending concussion in Week 10. Lacking the secondary skills and route-running ability you want in most receivers, Furrey was quietly released after the season and caught on with Cleveland, where he'll compete against Brian Robiskie to be the team's possession receiver across from Braylon Edwards.

Jabar Gaffney

Height: 6-1 Weight: 193 College: Florida Draft: 2002/2 (33) Born: 1-Dec-1980 Age: 29 Risk: Red

Year	Team	G	Rec	Pass	Yds	C%	Yd/C	TD	YAC	Rk	DVOA	Rk	DYAR	Rk	YAR	Short	Mid	Deep	Bomb
2006	NE	10	11	20	142	55%	12.9	1	2.2	--	7.8%	--	33	--	24	41%	18%	18%	24%
2007	NE	16	36	50	449	72%	12.5	5	3.3	53	22.5%	10	144	31	135	51%	32%	9%	9%
2008	NE	16	38	65	468	58%	12.3	2	3.1	54	-4.5%	53	42	56	54	33%	40%	19%	9%
2009	DEN		27	45	265	60%	9.8	1			9.1%								

We've spent the offseason debating whether Eddie Royal or Brandon Stokley will be playing the "Wes Welker" role as Josh McDaniels brings his offensive scheme to Denver, but it seems safe to say that Jabar Gaffney will be playing the "Jabar Gaffney" role. Gaffney has no upside, but he certainly has his uses, particularly on third down; there, Gaffney was 16-of-22 with 12 first downs and a touchdown.

Justin Gage

Height: 6-4 Weight: 208 College: Missouri Draft: 2003/5 (143) Born: 25-Jan-1981 Age: 28 Risk: Red

Year	Team	G	Rec	Pass	Yds	C%	Yd/C	TD	YAC	Rk	DVOA	Rk	DYAR	Rk	YAR	Short	Mid	Deep	Bomb
2006	CHI	8	4	8	68	50%	17.0	0	4.0	--	-42.4%	--	-19	--	-21	25%	38%	13%	25%
2007	TEN	16	55	85	750	65%	13.6	2	4.3	26	15.0%	18	192	23	200	26%	41%	16%	17%
2008	TEN	12	34	74	651	46%	19.1	6	5.3	8	6.7%	27	116	31	134	16%	36%	26%	22%
2009	TEN		56	88	756	64%	13.5	7			11.7%								

Three years ago, we considered Gage one of the worst receivers in football. Now he is the number-one receiver on a team that had the best record in the AFC. The Titans decided last year that Gage was best used as a way to stretch the opposing defense. His catch rate was abysmal, and he did very little once teams became aware of his deep ability. The acquisition of Nate Washington complicates matters, as Washington does what Gage did last year, only arguably better. The Titans could return Gage to his 2007 role, but teams had taken away Gage's underneath stuff early last season. The past two seasons are probably the best of Gage's career, but he could settle in as a decent third option, as Tennessee continues to upgrade its receiving corps.

Joey Galloway   Height: 5-11 Weight: 197 College: Ohio State   Draft: 1995/1 (8)   Born: 20-Nov-1971 Age: 38 Risk: Green

Year	Team	G	Rec	Pass	Yds	C%	Yd/C	TD	YAC	Rk	DVOA	Rk	DYAR	Rk	YAR	Short	Mid	Deep	Bomb
2006	TB	16	62	141	1057	44%	17.0	7	4.7	16	-12.2%	63	5	63	31	20%	37%	25%	17%
2007	TB	15	57	98	1014	58%	17.8	6	6.6	3	17.1%	13	235	15	250	27%	39%	18%	16%
2008	TB	9	13	28	138	46%	10.6	0	3.5	--	-40.2%	--	-55	--	-58	41%	33%	7%	19%
2009	NE		44	71	720	62%	16.4	3			2.7%								

Despite age and injuries, both Pittsburgh and New England went hard after the speedy Galloway, with the champs losing out to the Pats. KUBIAK loves the idea of Tom Brady chucking deep ones to him, and it isn't hard to conjure the image of Galloway streaking down the sideline in Foxboro multiple times in 2009.

Pierre Garcon   Height: 6-0   Weight: 210 College: Mount Union   Draft: 2008/6 (205) Born: 8-Aug-1985   Age: 24 Risk: Red

Year	Team	G	Rec	Pass	Yds	C%	Yd/C	TD	YAC	Rk	DVOA	Rk	DYAR	Rk	YAR	Short	Mid	Deep	Bomb
2008	IND	14	4	4	23	100%	5.8	0	2.5	--	20.2%	--	11	--	5	100%	0%	0%	0%
2009	IND		37	56	553	66%	14.9	6			36.4%								

He's become an organizational favorite, with both Bill Polian and Jim Caldwell showering him with praise over the offseason. That makes him favorite to be the Colts' slot receiver now that Anthony Gonzalez is becoming a starter, which in turn makes him a viable late-round pick in deep fantasy leagues. Garcon became the first player from Mount Union to be drafted in 60 years, and his 14 games played last year as a special teamer marks the record for Mount Union players, surpassing the 13 games played by Corl Zimmerman of the 1927-29 Dayton Triangles. We're always inclined to appreciate small school players anyway, but the fact that Garcon's official Web site is trying to make money as an Amazon affiliate for video games is glorious. Imagine Albert Haynesworth doing that.

Ted Ginn   Height: 5-11 Weight: 178 College: Ohio State   Draft: 2007/1 (9)   Born: 12-Apr-1985 Age: 24 Risk: Yellow

Year	Team	G	Rec	Pass	Yds	C%	Yd/C	TD	YAC	Rk	DVOA	Rk	DYAR	Rk	YAR	Short	Mid	Deep	Bomb
2007	MIA	16	34	71	420	48%	12.4	2	5.1	13	-25.8%	78	-71	79	-67	40%	33%	11%	16%
2008	MIA	16	56	93	790	60%	14.1	2	3.1	55	-10.0%	65	19	65	47	26%	43%	21%	10%
2009	MIA		66	102	930	65%	14.1	8			20.4%								

Comforted by the soft bias of low expectations, Ginn improved just enough in his second season to highlight the gap between potential and production. The routes are still iffy (though better) and he still gets taken out by physical coverage. At some point, the Dolphins will need more from Ginn, the famed Parcells needle will emerge, and we'll see whether Ginn can find a way to make himself an every-play threat. KUBIAK is optimistic and sees a third-year breakout.

Anthony Gonzalez Height: 6-0   Weight: 193 College: Ohio State   Draft: 2007/1 (32) Born: 18-Sep-1984 Age: 25 Risk: Yellow

Year	Team	G	Rec	Pass	Yds	C%	Yd/C	TD	YAC	Rk	DVOA	Rk	DYAR	Rk	YAR	Short	Mid	Deep	Bomb
2007	IND	13	37	51	576	73%	15.6	3	5.4	9	43.7%	1	240	13	237	30%	45%	13%	11%
2008	IND	16	57	79	664	72%	11.6	4	3.1	58	26.3%	3	242	13	219	36%	47%	13%	4%
2009	IND		74	115	1183	64%	16.0	9			21.8%								

On a per-play basis, Gonzalez has been outstanding through his first two seasons. The question is whether that translates as he becomes a starter on the outside and sees starting corners on a regular basis. Last year's playoff game is instructive, as Gonzalez dominated the first half, torching nickelback Antoine Cason for 6 catches and 97 yards. The Chargers adjusted with help for Cason in the second half, and Gonzalez was shut out. Still, the Colts have enough weapons that Gonzalez should get his one-on-one opportunities, and Manning will find him when he does. Gonzalez has the upside to put up 1,200 yards and 10 touchdowns this season.

D.J. Hackett Height: 6-2   Weight: 199 College: Colorado   Draft: 2004/5 (157) Born: 31-Jul-1981   Age: 28 Risk: N/A

Year	Team	G	Rec	Pass	Yds	C%	Yd/C	TD	YAC	Rk	DVOA	Rk	DYAR	Rk	YAR	Short	Mid	Deep	Bomb
2006	SEA	14	45	66	610	68%	13.6	4	4.2	27	31.1%	2	215	14	223	28%	56%	12%	4%
2007	SEA	6	32	47	384	68%	12.0	3	4.3	--	13.1%	--	100	--	100	40%	46%	15%	0%
2008	CAR	9	13	28	181	46%	13.9	0	6.1	--	-21.6%	--	-19	--	-21	33%	41%	22%	4%

It's easy to forget that Hackett was a Week 1 starter for the Carolina Panthers last year. In fact, it's not really worth remembering. He only got the start because Steve Smith attacked Ken Lucas's face with extreme prejudice. D.J. was kind enough to get injured upon Smith's return, to the surprise of no one. Hackett ended his reign as an annual DVOA-tease when, upon his return, he engaged in an epic battle with Dwayne Jarrett for the third receiver position, which somehow they both appeared to lose. Carolina cut their ties with Hackett in February. As for Hackett's chances of catching on with another team, it was reported in March that the Redskins were not interested in Hackett. That's probably good luck. Expect Hackett to sign somewhere by training camp.

Dante Hall Height: 5-8   Weight: 187 College: Texas A&M   Draft: 2000/5 (153) Born: 1-Sep-1978   Age: 31 Risk: N/A

Year	Team	G	Rec	Pass	Yds	C%	Yd/C	TD	YAC	Rk	DVOA	Rk	DYAR	Rk	YAR	Short	Mid	Deep	Bomb
2006	KC	15	26	40	204	65%	7.8	2	2.8	--	-3.8%	--	28	--	24	46%	30%	24%	0%
2007	STL	7	5	12	27	42%	5.4	0	3.6	--	-55.3%	--	-37	--	-38	42%	42%	8%	8%
2008	STL	8	12	18	105	67%	8.8	0	1.2	--	-5.5%	--	9	--	11	35%	53%	12%	0%

From the blurb on Amazon.com for *Dante Hall: X Factor*: "X-citing. X-traordinary. X-cellent. Whatever adjective can be dreamed up, it cannot compare to the 2003 dream season Dante Hall enjoyed for the Kansas City Chiefs. From an appearance on the *The Late Show with David Letterman* to etching his name into the NFL record books, Dante 'The X-Factor' Hall turned the NFL into his own personal playground and helped the Chiefs get back to the postseason for the first time since 1998." As of May 2009, only one copy of *X-Factor* is left in stock, so, you know, order now. Hall is a free agent.

James Hardy Height: 6-6   Weight: 220 College: Indiana   Draft: 2008/2 (41)   Born: 24-Dec-1985 Age: 23 Risk: Green

Year	Team	G	Rec	Pass	Yds	C%	Yd/C	TD	YAC	Rk	DVOA	Rk	DYAR	Rk	YAR	Short	Mid	Deep	Bomb
2008	BUF	14	9	24	87	38%	9.7	2	1.8	--	-38.6%	--	-43	--	-31	22%	52%	17%	9%
2009	BUF		14	22	147	63%	10.6	0			-9.9%								

Hardy was drafted to be a red zone target for a team that had all kinds of trouble throwing touchdowns inside the 20, and the 6-foot-6 former Hoosier did pull in a pair of touchdowns; unfortunately, it was the only place on the field where Hardy did much of anything, as he struggled to get off the line and to catch the ball when it was thrown to him. Hardy tore his ACL in Week 15, which makes him a candidate for the PUP list; the arrival of Terrell Owens gives the team no reason to rush him back.

Marvin Harrison

Height: 6-0   Weight: 175   College: Syracuse   Draft: 1996/1 (19)   Born: 25-Aug-1972   Age: 37   Risk: N/A

Year	Team	G	Rec	Pass	Yds	C%	Yd/C	TD	YAC	Rk	DVOA	Rk	DYAR	Rk	YAR	Short	Mid	Deep	Bomb
2006	IND	16	95	148	1366	64%	14.4	12	2.8	63	30.3%	4	510	1	488	25%	42%	18%	14%
2007	IND	5	20	32	247	63%	12.4	1	2.0	--	3.5%	--	43	--	36	28%	47%	6%	19%
2008	IND	15	60	107	636	56%	10.6	5	2.9	64	-9.1%	63	31	62	24	38%	31%	11%	20%

The end came extremely quickly for Harrison. Two years after leading the league in DYAR, he is likely to retire, as a knee injury has sapped him of the speed he needs to be effective. Last season, Harrison was a shell of himself, averaging a measly 10.6 yards per reception. Merely two years ago, it looked like Harrison would retire as the second most prolific receiver in history. While he will likely remain second in receptions, he retires fourth in receiving yards and fifth in touchdowns, with Terrell Owens and Randy Moss likely to pass him in yards. Harrison does retire as the all-time leader in DYAR, a stat we have dating back to 1994. Moss and Owens are about 300 DYAR behind him, so Moss will likely catch him, and Owens conceivably could. Ranking Harrison historically is something probably best done when contemporaries like Owens, Moss, and Isaac Bruce have finished their careers. Postseason struggles and playing most of his career with Peyton Manning undermine any claim Harrison has of being the second greatest modern receiver behind Jerry Rice. Still, his eight-year run of dominance from 1999-2006 is unmatched by anything besides Rice's 1989-1996. Those great seasons break into two categories: 1999-2002 and 2003-2006. Before 2003, the Colts did not have a great second receiving option. During those four years, Harrison averaged a ridiculous 117 catches per season. His 143 receptions in 2002 are 20 more than any other receiver has ever caught in a season. Starting in 2003, Harrison and Reggie Wayne became co-number one receivers, and Marvin's conventional numbers dropped, but he still twice ranked in the top five in DYAR and never below 14th. This consistent excellence is a rare treat in the NFL, and Harrison will rightly be celebrated in Canton as soon as he is eligible.

Percy Harvin

Height: 5-11   Weight: 195   College: Florida   Draft: 2009/1 (22)   Born: 28-May-1988   Age: 21   Risk: Yellow

Year	Team	G	Rec	Pass	Yds	C%	Yd/C	TD	YAC	Rk	DVOA	Rk	DYAR	Rk	YAR	Short	Mid	Deep	Bomb
2009	MIN		44	63	457	70%	10.4	2			13.0%								

A full list of SEC wide receivers chosen in the first round of the draft this decade: Dwayne Bowe, Robert Meachem, Buster Davis, Troy Williamson, Matt Jones, Michael Clayton, Donte' Stallworth, Travis Taylor. Is that really a list of players you'd be happy spending first-rounders on? Harvin's got good hands and he's great after the catch, we know. He'll be a useful weapon on quick hitches and the Vikings will likely use him in the Wildcat and on reverses, sure. But wouldn't you want to spend what may be your last first-round pick as a head coach on someone whose skill set isn't mirrored by the receiver across from him? Wouldn't you want a receiver who can separate from defensive backs and run better routes than Harvin can? And — perhaps most importantly — wouldn't you want to avoid drafting a guy who failed a test for weed that he knew about in advance? We certainly can't guarantee that Harvin will fail at the NFL level; he showed off too much talent at Florida to do so. But as far as red flags go? He raises more than any other first-round pick. As one of two receivers we expect to get more than 10 carries (the other is Josh Cribbs), Harvin's projection includes 37 carries for 181 yards and a touchdown.

Lavelle Hawkins

Height: 5-11   Weight: 187   College: California   Draft: 2008/4 (126)   Born: 12-Jul-1986   Age: 23   Risk: Red

Year	Team	G	Rec	Pass	Yds	C%	Yd/C	TD	YAC	Rk	DVOA	Rk	DYAR	Rk	YAR	Short	Mid	Deep	Bomb
2008	TEN	13	7	12	68	58%	9.7	0	2.9	--	-16.9%	--	-4	--	-4	45%	36%	18%	0%
2009	TEN		11	17	111	64%	10.3	1			-16.5%								

The Titans have a bad habit of drafting receivers in the middle rounds, giving them absolutely no role in the offense for a few years, then releasing them so the team can sign guys like Justin Gage and Nate Washington. Hawkins, Paul Williams, Chris Davis, Courtney Roby, Roydell Williams, Brandon Jones (who had a role but did nothing with it) — they start to run together after a while. Hawkins has a small chance to break the cycle because he's just a sophomore, showed a little progress last year, and is getting tips from cornerback Cortland Finnegan on how to improve his technique. Even if he emerges from the Gage/Williams/Davis slag heap, he'll be fourth-string receiver on a team that doesn't even use three wide receivers very much.

Devery Henderson
Height: 5-11 Weight: 191 College: LSU   Draft: 2004/2 (50) Born: 26-Mar-1982 Age: 27 Risk: Red

Year	Team	G	Rec	Pass	Yds	C%	Yd/C	TD	YAC	Rk	DVOA	Rk	DYAR	Rk	YAR	Short	Mid	Deep	Bomb
2006	NO	13	32	54	745	59%	23.3	5	4.9	13	40.7%	1	228	12	248	17%	37%	17%	28%
2007	NO	16	20	43	409	47%	20.5	3	3.8	--	9.7%	--	78	--	66	14%	36%	26%	24%
2008	NO	16	32	56	793	57%	24.8	3	8.3	1	36.5%	1	215	17	207	22%	29%	20%	29%
2009	NO		35	64	706	55%	20.2	4			14.8%								

Henderson on third downs last year: 12-of-15, 307 yards, one 81-yard touchdown, and a DVOA of 114.7%. Receivers usually don't put up consistent stat lines like Henderson's: reception totals in the 20s or 30s, yard-per-catch averages in the low 20s. Typically, a 32-catch, 700-yard season is a sign that a third wideout caught a few flukey 75-yard touchdowns. The next year, he either inherits a 70-catch role (with his yards per catch dropping sharply) or crashes back to typical third-wideout numbers. Henderson is a legitimate 20-plus-yards-per-catch target like the kind that roamed the earth in the 1960s and 1970s. The Saints were satisfied enough with his performance to sign him to a four-year contract in March. Henderson will remain a third or fourth receiver, but he'll appear on at least a half dozen highlight reels.

Chris Henry
Height: 6-4 Weight: 197 College: West Virginia   Draft: 2005/3 (83) Born: 17-May-1983 Age: 26 Risk: Yellow

Year	Team	G	Rec	Pass	Yds	C%	Yd/C	TD	YAC	Rk	DVOA	Rk	DYAR	Rk	YAR	Short	Mid	Deep	Bomb
2006	CIN	13	36	75	605	48%	16.8	9	4.0	34	8.4%	28	124	38	127	11%	54%	15%	20%
2007	CIN	8	21	38	343	55%	16.3	2	3.0	--	6.0%	--	56	--	65	21%	37%	13%	29%
2008	CIN	12	19	46	220	41%	11.6	2	1.0	--	-10.1%	--	10	--	-20	24%	38%	20%	18%
2009	CIN		37	73	511	51%	13.8	4			-4.0%								

In July, Marvin Lewis puffed out his chest and declared that the Bengals "had no interest" in bringing back the talented but troubled Henry. Less than a month later, with several of his receivers hobbled, Lewis meekly announced that Henry would return to Cincy. It was a capitulation that neatly encapsulated Lewis' time as head coach, with expedience valued over principle. After serving a four-game suspension, Henry was back in the lineup. Unfortunately, the speed and size that make him a dangerous deep threat was wasted with Ryan Fitzpatrick as his quarterback — FitzPopgun couldn't reach most of Henry's routes with two throws. While Henry may never live down getting arrested while wearing his own jersey in 2006, he did keep his nose clean last season, thus letting Pacman Jones take the lead in the "West Virginia Alumni Knucklehead Derby."

Devin Hester
Height: 5-11 Weight: 185 College: Miami   Draft: 2006/2 (57) Born: 4-Nov-1982 Age: 27 Risk: Yellow

Year	Team	G	Rec	Pass	Yds	C%	Yd/C	TD	YAC	Rk	DVOA	Rk	DYAR	Rk	YAR	Short	Mid	Deep	Bomb
2007	CHI	16	20	39	299	51%	15.0	2	6.4	--	-21.5%	--	-28	--	-27	36%	39%	6%	19%
2008	CHI	15	51	92	665	57%	13.0	3	3.8	38	-9.6%	64	23	64	26	33%	28%	24%	15%
2009	CHI		62	111	858	56%	13.8	5			2.7%								

Hester confounded the critics (ourselves included) by doing what he'd failed to accomplish at Miami: He became a successful wide receiver. While he got by through the first few weeks on sheer athleticism and a scheme that didn't require him to do too much, he became a significantly better route runner as the season went along.

Hester had a 6.4% DVOA before the Week 9 bye and fell to -18.1% afterwards, but that drop has more to do with the struggles of Kyle Orton than Hester's performance. He'll never have great hands, so expecting him to turn into a star is asking for a little much, and he'd be better served as a second receiver than as a team's primary threat, but Hester should continue to take steps forward this year and could make the Pro Bowl — as a receiver — if everything goes right. Note that the numbers above don't include the 83 yards he gained on pass interference penalties, including 77 yards on two penalties against the Saints in Week 15.

Darrius Heyward-Bey   Height: 6-3   Weight: 206 College: Maryland   Draft: 2009/1 (7)   Born: 26-Feb-1987   Age: 22   Risk: Yellow

Year	Team	G	Rec	Pass	Yds	C%	Yd/C	TD	YAC	Rk	DVOA	Rk	DYAR	Rk	YAR	Short	Mid	Deep	Bomb
2009	OAK		29	63	461	46%	16.0	3			-25.5%								

It isn't Heyward-Bey's fault that he's become a punchline for the diseased decision-making process in Oakland. Had he been selected by the Titans with the 30th overall pick, for example, the jokes about Heyward-Bey failing to even make first-team All-ACC would be replaced by talk of his gamebreaking speed and the holes he'll create for the running game. Instead, because of a mix of senility and hubris, Heyward-Bey has to fight the battle of an entire franchise as opposed to simply getting on with the already-difficult task of becoming an NFL wide receiver. As a rookie, he's not likely to produce a high catch total, but his speed will actually keep safeties honest and open up lanes for Darren McFadden and company in the running game.

Johnnie Lee Higgins   Height: 5-11 Weight: 186 College: UTEP   Draft: 2007/3 (99)   Born: 8-Sep-1983   Age: 26   Risk: Yellow

Year	Team	G	Rec	Pass	Yds	C%	Yd/C	TD	YAC	Rk	DVOA	Rk	DYAR	Rk	YAR	Short	Mid	Deep	Bomb
2007	OAK	16	6	8	47	75%	7.8	0	0.3	--	-19.7%	--	-4	--	-4	38%	38%	13%	13%
2008	OAK	16	22	42	366	52%	16.6	4	9.1	--	-3.7%	--	29	--	36	31%	31%	24%	14%
2009	OAK		43	74	633	58%	14.7	2			-7.4%								

Higgins had a phenomenal sophomore year as a return man, leading the league with 15.2 points worth of field position on punt returns. With Javon Walker and Drew Carter sidelined, and Ronald Curry in the doghouse, he also emerged as the Raiders' number-one receiver. Heyward-Bey will probably knock Higgins out of the starting lineup, since the Raiders will want Chaz Schilens in for his blocking skills on early downs, but Higgins will get plenty of looks from the slot. It's not like the Raiders are going to be running out a lot of leads with two-tight end sets late in games.

Jason Hill   Height: 6-1   Weight: 204 College: Washington State   Draft: 2007/3 (76)   Born: 20-Feb-1985   Age: 24   Risk: Blue

Year	Team	G	Rec	Pass	Yds	C%	Yd/C	TD	YAC	Rk	DVOA	Rk	DYAR	Rk	YAR	Short	Mid	Deep	Bomb
2007	SF	5	1	2	6	50%	6.0	0	0.0	--	-68.8%	--	-9	--	-8	50%	50%	0%	0%
2008	SF	16	30	40	317	75%	10.6	2	3.8	--	9.5%	--	72	--	82	50%	38%	8%	5%
2009	SF		19	31	176	61%	9.3	0			-11.2%								

Hill will, uh, battle Arnaz Battle in training camp to see who becomes the 49ers' starting slot receiver. Hill posted virtually all of his catches after Mike Singletary took over as head coach, and he appears to work well with Shaun Hill (maybe it's a last-name thing?), so he would appear to have the inside track for a starting job. But could the 49ers really rely on a rookie (Crabtree) and two second-year players (Hill and Josh Morgan) as their starting receiving corps?

Ike Hilliard   Height: 5-11 Weight: 210 College: Florida   Draft: 1997/1 (7)   Born: 5-Apr-1976   Age: 33   Risk: N/A

Year	Team	G	Rec	Pass	Yds	C%	Yd/C	TD	YAC	Rk	DVOA	Rk	DYAR	Rk	YAR	Short	Mid	Deep	Bomb
2006	TB	16	34	55	339	62%	10.0	2	4.0	35	-16.9%	71	-18	70	-2	49%	44%	7%	0%
2007	TB	15	62	86	722	72%	11.6	1	5.0	14	5.8%	35	122	42	134	51%	37%	8%	4%
2008	TB	16	47	58	424	81%	9.0	4	2.6	69	19.5%	8	147	26	156	48%	46%	4%	2%

Hilliard was unsigned at press time, but the 33-year-old still has some game left, based on his tremendous 81 percent catch rate and positive DVOA. A team like the 2008 Browns that lacked a possession receiver could use Hilliard's effective mix of reliable hands and underappreciated route-running. We're looking at you, Jaguars.

Domenik Hixon   Height: 6-2   Weight: 200   College: Akron   Draft: 2006/4 (130)   Born: 8-Oct-1984   Age: 25   Risk: Red

Year	Team	G	Rec	Pass	Yds	C%	Yd/C	TD	YAC	Rk	DVOA	Rk	DYAR	Rk	YAR	Short	Mid	Deep	Bomb
2007	DEN/NYG	12	1	1	5	100%	5.0	0	1.0	--	-39.9%	--	-2	--	-1	100%	0%	0%	0%
2008	NYG	16	43	73	596	59%	13.9	2	3.3	52	11.5%	19	142	28	112	21%	51%	12%	16%
2009	NYG		81	129	1051	63%	13.0	9			14.4%								

As we explained in the Giants chapter, the team wasn't any worse with Hixon as their primary receiver than they were with Plaxico Burress. The Giants extract the most out of Hixon by limiting his responsibilities and reps, allowing them to get a fresh player in the game capable of working at all levels of the field. He's not a great route-runner, but he has good agility and forces cornerbacks to honor deeper patterns, and he's willing to go over the middle. He's not quite the blocker Burress was, but very few receivers are. As for his hands, everyone remembers the famous drop against the Eagles 51 yards downfield, but it was one of only two drops he had all season, a great total for a player who was thrown the ball, on average, 14 yards away from the line of scrimmage. At $530,000, Hixon is a bargain for one more year, but don't expect the Giants to re-sign him in what will be the final year of his deal.

Santonio Holmes   Height: 5-11   Weight: 190   College: Ohio State   Draft: 2006/1 (25)   Born: 3-Mar-1984   Age: 25   Risk: Red

Year	Team	G	Rec	Pass	Yds	C%	Yd/C	TD	YAC	Rk	DVOA	Rk	DYAR	Rk	YAR	Short	Mid	Deep	Bomb
2006	PIT	16	49	86	824	57%	16.8	2	5.1	10	17.5%	12	212	17	210	21%	60%	11%	8%
2007	PIT	13	52	85	942	61%	18.1	8	4.9	15	26.3%	6	260	11	274	16%	42%	22%	19%
2008	PIT	15	55	114	821	48%	14.9	5	3.8	39	-8.1%	60	40	60	25	22%	48%	20%	9%
2009	PIT		71	128	1104	55%	15.5	7			18.0%								

Holmes' Super Bowl MVP performance turned him into a temporary celebrity in the offseason: his talk-show tour ran the gamut from Jay Leno to Regis & Kelly. If Holmes plays his cards right, he could parlay his "Steelers Wide Receiver with a Great Super Bowl Highlight Reel" success into other outlets. He could reach the Hall of Fame, become a sideline reporter, maybe make an unsuccessful run at the Pennsylvania Governor's chair. By April, Holmes was done playing footsie with the Joy Behars of the world and back at Steelers OTAs. He was saying all the right things: "You got to climb the mountain again. You're already at the top, but it start's a new season, therefore you've got to climb it again and reach the top again," he told reporters in April. Good cliché choice, Santonio: You had a great game, but you aren't a great receiver yet, and the Steelers need you to climb up and reach your potential as a true number-one wideout. KUBIAK's annual Santonio Holmes breakout projection is becoming a bit of a tradition around here.

Torry Holt   Height: 6-0   Weight: 190   College: North Carolina State   Draft: 1999/1 (6)   Born: 5-Jun-1976   Age: 33   Risk: Yellow

Year	Team	G	Rec	Pass	Yds	C%	Yd/C	TD	YAC	Rk	DVOA	Rk	DYAR	Rk	YAR	Short	Mid	Deep	Bomb
2006	STL	16	93	179	1188	52%	12.8	10	3.0	57	-4.2%	54	121	39	147	25%	38%	22%	15%
2007	STL	16	93	149	1189	62%	12.8	7	2.2	80	7.8%	31	243	12	245	26%	42%	23%	9%
2008	STL	16	64	119	796	54%	12.4	3	2.3	74	-11.4%	68	12	67	14	26%	54%	10%	10%
2009	JAC		81	126	1119	64%	13.8	7			11.9%								

When the 2008 season ended, the Rams were one of the oldest teams in the league. By the time the draft rolled around, they'd become one of the youngest after general manager Billy Devaney went on a merciless cutting spree. The biggest casualty, of course, was Torry Holt, who posted his worst receiving totals since his rookie campaign ten years ago. Although some of the blame may be pinned on an increasingly ineffective Marc Bulger, who played most of last year wondering if he was going to be paralyzed, the reality is that Holt's production has been steadily declining for six seasons. He's suffered a lot of wear-and-tear on his body, too — in his first press conference after joining the Jaguars, Holt demonstrated his stomach-churning ability to bend one of his fingers sideways at a 90-degree angle. "This is what I got out of the game, crooked fingers," Holt said. "In '07, I think it was against the Steelers, I popped it out and it didn't pop back in." Despite the decline, his KUBIAK projection is huge because he is far and away the best and most experienced receiver on an offense whose opponents will be devoting most of their resources to stopping the run.

T.J. Houshmandzadeh   Height: 6-1   Weight: 197   College: Oregon State   Draft: 2001/7 (204)   Born: 26-Sep-1977   Age: 32   Risk: Green

Year	Team	G	Rec	Pass	Yds	C%	Yd/C	TD	YAC	Rk	DVOA	Rk	DYAR	Rk	YAR	Short	Mid	Deep	Bomb
2006	CIN	14	90	132	1081	68%	12.0	9	3.5	47	16.6%	15	310	5	291	39%	39%	17%	5%
2007	CIN	16	112	170	1143	66%	10.2	12	3.1	58	4.8%	38	234	16	223	40%	39%	15%	6%
2008	CIN	15	92	137	904	67%	9.8	4	3.8	40	2.4%	34	163	23	118	50%	41%	8%	1%
2009	SEA		87	128	1004	68%	11.5	9			23.6%								

Housh's departure to Seattle ends the Touraj Era in Cincinnati, one that saw him work his way from seventh-round afterthought to become one of the most productive and popular Bengals ever. The operative term is "work." On a team defined by selfishness and a lack of character, T.J. was a practice animal and a ferocious competitor on Sundays. He battled defensive backs off the line of scrimmage, referees for not calling the obvious interference and holding penalties that were inflicted upon him, even Carson Palmer when he dared look elsewhere. Even with Chad Johnson on the other side, T.J. caught 294 balls in the last three seasons, so the yapping and his precision routes clearly paid off. Now 32, what little speed T.J. once had is gone; 91 percent of his passes were short or middle distance. Without adjusting for opponent, his YAR ranked 33rd; after adjustments, his DYAR ranked 23rd, 10 spots higher, so replacing four annual clashes with Baltimore and Pittsburgh with St. Louis and San Francisco will likely offset a decline in 2009. Provided the West Coast doesn't mellow that intensity, Housh should be Seattle's top receiver for the next year or two.

Juaquin Iglesias   Height: 6-0   Weight: 204   College: Oklahoma   Draft: 2009/3 (39)   Born: 22-Aug-1987   Age: 22   Risk: Red

Year	Team	G	Rec	Pass	Yds	C%	Yd/C	TD	YAC	Rk	DVOA	Rk	DYAR	Rk	YAR	Short	Mid	Deep	Bomb
2009	CHI		23	36	311	64%	13.6	2			5.0%								

For the second year in a row, the Bears chose a possession receiver in the third round; while Earl Bennett didn't make a single catch a year ago, Iglesias should be able to step in and play a role in the Chicago offense from Day One. A slot receiver who runs good routes, he'll be competing with Rashied Davis, a player who the organization isn't particularly fond of to begin with. Iglesias was also very effective going over the middle at Oklahoma, a role that will likely come in handy. Expect Iglesias to contribute on third downs at first, but if Bennett struggles, he could advance quickly.

Darrell Jackson   Height: 6-0   Weight: 201   College: Florida   Draft: 2000/3 (80)   Born: 6-Dec-1978   Age: 31   Risk: N/A

Year	Team	G	Rec	Pass	Yds	C%	Yd/C	TD	YAC	Rk	DVOA	Rk	DYAR	Rk	YAR	Short	Mid	Deep	Bomb
2006	SEA	13	63	112	956	56%	15.2	10	4.0	38	9.4%	25	190	19	190	24%	46%	17%	13%
2007	SF	15	46	104	497	44%	10.8	3	1.9	84	-27.8%	80	-126	85	-112	28%	39%	20%	13%
2008	DEN	12	12	21	190	57%	15.8	1	4.3	--	0.0%	--	22	--	21	50%	25%	15%	10%

His career sure collapsed quickly, didn't it? Jackson actually started for the Broncos on opening day, but had only two games all season with more than one reception, and the Broncos made no effort to re-sign him when his one-year contract ended. The list of players with similar three-year career spans is fairly interesting; number one is former Seahawk and Viking Sam McCullum, but the list also includes Marty Booker (also over the past three years) and the final three seasons of Antonio Freeman, Sean Dawkins, and Cris Collinsworth. Bet you never knew that Collinsworth was done by age 30, did you?

DeSean Jackson

Height: 6-0   Weight: 178   College: California   Draft: 2008/2 (49)   Born: 1-Dec-1986   Age: 23   Risk: Red

Year	Team	G	Rec	Pass	Yds	C%	Yd/C	TD	YAC	Rk	DVOA	Rk	DYAR	Rk	YAR	Short	Mid	Deep	Bomb
2008	PHI	16	62	120	912	52%	14.7	2	4.1	32	-8.3%	61	41	57	43	32%	32%	22%	14%
2009	PHI		63	120	1006	53%	16.0	7			-14.1%								

Outside of the infamous premature spike that nearly cost the Eagles a touchdown, Jackson had a solid rookie year as the team's primary receiver and even as part of the running game, although it felt like a trick Reid went to one too many times early in the season. One thing Jackson needs to work on is disguising his cuts and his routes; just under 16 percent of the passes thrown to him were defensed, far worse than the 4.5 percent averaged by the rest of the team. If Jackson can improve his consistency — he had four games where he had fewer than three catches and 21 yards — and work on the little things, he should take another step forward and emerge as one of the most promising young receivers in the league.

Dexter Jackson

Height: 5-10   Weight: 182   College: Appalachian State   Draft: 2008/2 (58)   Born: 5-Aug-1986   Age: 23   Risk: Yellow

Year	Team	G	Rec	Pass	Yds	C%	Yd/C	TD	YAC	Rk	DVOA	Rk	DYAR	Rk	YAR	Short	Mid	Deep	Bomb
2009	TB		23	41	357	56%	15.5	1			-14.4%								

Jackson has already been on the cover of *Sports Illustrated* (memorializing Appalachian State's shocking upset over Michigan in 2007). He's not likely to repeat that feat in the pros. He didn't catch a pass his rookie season, and Jon Gruden admitted the Bucs reached when they chose Jackson in the second round. His lofty draft status means he'll get his chances, but Tampa Bay picked another wideout, Sammie Stroughter, this year. That either urges Jackson forward, or means a trip back to Decatur, Georgia, and his post-football life.

Vincent Jackson

Height: 6-5   Weight: 241   College: Northern Colorado   Draft: 2005/2 (61)   Born: 14-Jan-1983   Age: 26   Risk: Green

Year	Team	G	Rec	Pass	Yds	C%	Yd/C	TD	YAC	Rk	DVOA	Rk	DYAR	Rk	YAR	Short	Mid	Deep	Bomb
2006	SD	16	27	56	453	48%	16.8	6	3.0	56	3.0%	43	67	55	71	24%	33%	13%	30%
2007	SD	16	41	81	623	51%	15.2	3	2.7	71	-2.6%	56	63	58	59	22%	36%	22%	21%
2008	SD	16	59	100	1098	59%	18.6	7	3.3	50	32.9%	2	369	4	387	14%	39%	27%	21%
2009	SD		68	124	1040	55%	15.3	10			17.5%								

We mentioned in last year's book that Jackson's performance in the 2007 playoffs (12 catches, 207 yards) might establish a new level of performance for him in the 2008 season. He wasn't quite that good, but he had a season straight out of Alvin Harper's peak as a dynamic downfield receiver who was capable of breaking open a game at any time. Jackson's stat line was something out of the '60s or '70s; of the 116 guys who have averaged more than 18 yards a catch in a season where they caught 50 passes or more, 98 of them occurred outside of the DVOA Era (1994-2008). The guys who have done it since then are a mix of stars (Randy Moss, Henry Ellard, Terry Glenn), second bananas (Jake Reed, Derrick Alexander), and flashes in the pan (Albert Connell, Ashley Lelie, Michael Westbrook). Of those players, the most accurate comparison might be Alexander, who spent the prime of his career as the second option on a team with an elite tight end.

Dwayne Jarrett

Height: 6-4   Weight: 219   College: USC   Draft: 2007/2 (45)   Born: 11-Sep-1986   Age: 23   Risk: Red

Year	Team	G	Rec	Pass	Yds	C%	Yd/C	TD	YAC	Rk	DVOA	Rk	DYAR	Rk	YAR	Short	Mid	Deep	Bomb
2007	CAR	7	6	13	73	46%	12.2	0	0.2	--	-49.3%	--	-34	--	-29	33%	25%	33%	8%
2008	CAR	9	10	19	119	53%	11.9	0	2.9	--	-11.8%	--	1	--	9	25%	63%	13%	0%
2009	CAR		33	60	379	55%	11.5	3			-2.3%								

D.J. Hackett's departure as a cap casualty means, "Congratulations Mr. Jarrett, the third receiver job in Carolina is yours." It's the least they can do for his 16 catches in 16 career games, right? Of course, coming out of

USC as "the guy most likely to be Mike Williams," that might count as overachieving. Plodding upfield with his 6-foot-4 frame and career 1.9 YAC, the Panthers are praying Jarrett can be their Muhsin Muhammad of the future. If Jarrett learns how to use his size, this could be a breakout year. Heck, he's still only 23.

Michael Jenkins

Height: 6-4   Weight: 217 College: Ohio State   Draft: 2004/1 (29)   Born: 18-Jun-1982 Age: 27 Risk: Yellow

Year	Team	G	Rec	Pass	Yds	C%	Yd/C	TD	YAC	Rk	DVOA	Rk	DYAR	Rk	YAR	Short	Mid	Deep	Bomb
2006	ATL	16	39	83	436	47%	11.2	7	2.5	69	-18.1%	73	-35	73	-34	27%	42%	19%	11%
2007	ATL	15	53	85	532	62%	10.0	4	3.5	47	0.6%	50	86	54	98	51%	43%	3%	4%
2008	ATL	16	50	81	777	62%	15.5	3	3.4	48	16.0%	12	180	22	174	24%	41%	20%	15%
2009	ATL		48	89	684	54%	14.2	3			-6.9%								

From the moment he caught Matt Ryan's first career pass and turned it into a 62-yard touchdown, Jenkins was off to a career year. Atlanta's run threat helped Jenkins immensely, as his 141 DYAR and 57.2% DVOA on first down demonstrates. His numbers should decline, but not drastically. More importantly, Jenkins has embraced his role as the number-two option. Hopefully, that maturity isn't ephemeral.

Greg Jennings

Height: 5-11   Weight: 192 College: Western Michigan   Draft: 2006/2 (52)   Born: 21-Sep-1983 Age: 26 Risk: Yellow

Year	Team	G	Rec	Pass	Yds	C%	Yd/C	TD	YAC	Rk	DVOA	Rk	DYAR	Rk	YAR	Short	Mid	Deep	Bomb
2006	GB	14	45	105	632	43%	14.0	3	7.0	1	-24.4%	81	-99	82	-82	33%	37%	13%	17%
2007	GB	13	53	84	920	63%	17.4	12	7.7	1	31.0%	2	299	7	284	39%	35%	8%	18%
2008	GB	16	80	140	1292	57%	16.2	9	4.2	27	9.6%	21	243	12	256	22%	43%	23%	12%
2009	GB		81	162	1245	50%	15.4	10			8.7%								

Jennings proved that his record level of improvement in 2007 was no fluke, as he "regressed" into one of the most promising young wide receivers in football. He was one of only six receivers in the league to score five or more touchdowns of 20 yards or more, an indicator of his ability on double moves and deeper patterns. Despite averaging 14.4 yards in the air for each catch, he still managed a far above average 4.1 yards per catch, profiling him as similar last year to Steve Smith (Carolina), Lee Evans, and Randy Moss. Not bad company. About the only complaint fantasy owners had about Jennings are that his touchdowns fell from 12 in 13 games to 9 in 16; you can chalk that up to his red zone DVOA going from a fluky-high 81.7% in 2007 to an average 6.3%. Jennings enters 2009 in the final year of his four-year, $2.85 million rookie contract that's been one of the biggest bargains in football; assuming he doesn't suffer a Javon Walker-style contract year injury, he should expect to make that much in four *games* of his next deal.

Andre Johnson

Height: 6-2   Weight: 221 College: Miami   Draft: 2003/1 (3)   Born: 11-Jul-1981   Age: 28 Risk: Green

Year	Team	G	Rec	Pass	Yds	C%	Yd/C	TD	YAC	Rk	DVOA	Rk	DYAR	Rk	YAR	Short	Mid	Deep	Bomb
2006	HOU	16	103	164	1147	63%	11.1	5	4.2	26	-0.4%	48	161	28	139	44%	31%	14%	12%
2007	HOU	9	60	86	851	70%	14.2	8	4.2	28	29.7%	3	287	9	273	27%	45%	15%	13%
2008	HOU	16	115	170	1575	68%	13.7	8	4.1	31	22.4%	5	493	1	465	32%	44%	19%	5%
2009	HOU		93	147	1336	63%	14.4	11			17.3%								

Andre Johnson must have spent the postseason banging his head against the wall as Larry Fitzgerald took over the role of "consensus best receiver in football." Can't we wait until Andre Johnson gets his shot at the playoffs before we make this decision? Johnson not only led the league in DYAR, but he attracted enough attention to make the pedestrian Kevin Walter a real asset. He is a complete receiver: adept at gaining yards after the catch and fighting for first downs, but fast enough to get deep on any cornerback. The only limitation on his fantasy value is a relatively low eight touchdowns, tied for his career high. Fitzgerald may have had 12 touchdowns, but Johnson actually had the higher red-zone DVOA, so a lack of ability near the goal line is not the problem. His teammates are.

Bryant Johnson

Height: 6-2   Weight: 214   College: Penn State   Draft: 2003/1 (17)   Born: 7-Mar-1981   Age: 28   Risk: Red

Year	Team	G	Rec	Pass	Yds	C%	Yd/C	TD	YAC	Rk	DVOA	Rk	DYAR	Rk	YAR	Short	Mid	Deep	Bomb
2006	ARI	16	40	74	740	54%	18.5	4	6.0	2	17.9%	11	172	24	168	30%	38%	20%	12%
2007	ARI	16	46	88	528	52%	11.5	2	1.8	87	-10.2%	70	17	70	12	26%	55%	12%	7%
2008	SF	16	45	75	546	60%	12.1	3	3.2	53	-3.6%	52	54	53	76	41%	36%	19%	4%
2009	DET		45	78	595	58%	13.2	4			3.1%								

In *PFP 2008*, we wrote that Johnson's production while a member of the Cardinals was "steady" and that he "would catch about 45 passes, usually with very little big-play sizzle." Last year, Johnson caught exactly 45 passes, with very little big-play sizzle. Any guesses as to what he'll do for the Lions this year?

Calvin Johnson

Height: 6-5   Weight: 239   College: Georgia Tech   Draft: 2007/1 (2)   Born: 25-Sep-1985   Age: 24   Risk: Yellow

Year	Team	G	Rec	Pass	Yds	C%	Yd/C	TD	YAC	Rk	DVOA	Rk	DYAR	Rk	YAR	Short	Mid	Deep	Bomb
2007	DET	15	48	93	756	52%	15.8	4	3.4	51	-0.6%	52	87	52	79	21%	31%	36%	11%
2008	DET	16	78	150	1331	52%	17.1	12	6.3	4	9.1%	22	256	10	227	33%	35%	14%	19%
2009	DET		69	141	1092	49%	15.8	12			-1.2%								

It's hard to imagine an elite receiver surrounded by less than Johnson was last year. Even the early Andre Johnson had Domanick Williams to work with in the backfield. "Megatron" caught passes from five different quarterbacks in 2009, something Andre Johnson or Larry Fitzgerald never had to go through. Among the three quarterbacks who threw to him more than three times, he was best with Daunte Culpepper (18.7% DVOA), which bodes well for a 2009 that will likely involve Culpepper as the starter for part of the campaign. Johnson had a 56.3% DVOA in the red zone, and no other Lions receiver had a red zone DVOA better than 8.8% — despite the fact that the defense was probably keyed specifically to stop Johnson on every passing play remotely near the goal line. That's just sheer physical dominance. Once the Lions start placing pieces around him, the debate between the two Johnsons and Fitzgerald for the title of best receiver in football is going to be epic.

Steve Johnson

Height: 6-2   Weight: 200   College: Kentucky   Draft: 2008/7 (224)   Born: 22-Jul-1986   Age: 23   Risk: Red

Year	Team	G	Rec	Pass	Yds	C%	Yd/C	TD	YAC	Rk	DVOA	Rk	DYAR	Rk	YAR	Short	Mid	Deep	Bomb
2008	BUF	11	10	14	102	71%	10.2	2	2.8	--	24.5%	--	44	--	55	54%	38%	8%	0%
2009	BUF		18	33	260	55%	14.4	2			-12.7%								

It was Johnson who was the best Bills rookie receiver last year. The Bills drafted 6-foot-6 James Hardy to be their unstoppable target inside the 20, but Johnson matched him in touchdowns and, more importantly, was actually productive with his limited opportunities outside the red zone. Johnson has good size and the coaching staff really likes him, so he has a chance to beat out Roscoe Parrish as the fourth receiver.

Brandon Jones

Height: 6-1   Weight: 208   College: Oklahoma   Draft: 2005/3 (96)   Born: 6-Oct-1982   Age: 27   Risk: Green

Year	Team	G	Rec	Pass	Yds	C%	Yd/C	TD	YAC	Rk	DVOA	Rk	DYAR	Rk	YAR	Short	Mid	Deep	Bomb
2006	TEN	16	27	54	384	50%	14.2	4	2.5	70	13.8%	18	114	42	113	20%	42%	18%	20%
2007	TEN	9	21	34	248	62%	11.8	2	3.2	--	-3.6%	--	25	--	19	29%	43%	14%	14%
2008	TEN	16	41	62	449	66%	11.0	1	2.5	70	3.2%	32	75	47	75	30%	48%	15%	8%
2009	SF		21	36	184	58%	8.8	1			-2.3%								

The 2005 draftee took four years to finally establish himself as a regular contributor, and as a reward for his one good season, he received a five-year, $16 million contract from San Francisco. Yay, money! Jones has good speed and good hands, but he does not get consistent separation. The drafting of Michael Crabtree immediately pushes him back into a role as a third receiver, and Josh Morgan could push him back to fourth.

James Jones

Height: 6-1   Weight: 207 College: San Jose State   Draft: 2007/3 (78)   Born: 31-Mar-1984 Age: 25 Risk: Green

Year	Team	G	Rec	Pass	Yds	C%	Yd/C	TD	YAC	Rk	DVOA	Rk	DYAR	Rk	YAR	Short	Mid	Deep	Bomb
2007	GB	16	47	80	676	59%	14.4	2	4.7	18	-10.1%	69	16	72	18	38%	39%	15%	8%
2008	GB	10	20	30	274	67%	13.7	1	3.1	--	18.2%	--	73	--	92	34%	48%	3%	14%
2009	GB		21	38	297	55%	14.2	1			-10.5%								

Whether it's fair or not, marginal players often lose their jobs because of injuries. Jones was no exception; a sprained knee cost him time at the beginning of the year and opened up opportunities for Jordy Nelson and Ruvell Martin. When he came back for good after Week 10 (even though he was suffering from a "squished nerve," which sounds like something you definitely wouldn't want to happen to your nerve), he was strictly a downfield receiver. Jones will be the fourth wide receiver this year, but if Greg Jennings can't stay healthy, Jones would be the one to step in and take his place. That's a role in which he'd have significant fantasy value.

Matt Jones

Height: 6-6   Weight: 242 College: Arkansas   Draft: 2005/1 (21)   Born: 22-Apr-1983 Age: 26 Risk: N/A

Year	Team	G	Rec	Pass	Yds	C%	Yd/C	TD	YAC	Rk	DVOA	Rk	DYAR	Rk	YAR	Short	Mid	Deep	Bomb
2006	JAC	14	41	76	643	54%	15.7	4	4.4	22	-4.6%	56	49	57	86	22%	41%	22%	14%
2007	JAC	12	24	50	317	48%	13.2	4	3.5	50	-7.8%	66	19	69	18	27%	41%	20%	12%
2008	JAC	12	65	108	761	60%	11.7	2	3.0	59	-1.4%	46	96	36	127	18%	54%	19%	8%

Jones might be Exhibit A in the case against former Jacksonville general manager James Harris. He was the Jags' most efficient receiver in 2008 — which is a bit like being the best musician in Warrant — but he also spent far too much time on the wrong side of the law. Jones' three-game suspension, the result of a felony cocaine possession bust, derailed his season at the end. He would later follow up with a probation violation, at which point the Jags had seen enough. On- and off-field concerns have kept Jones from catching on with another team, but you have to wonder if another Arkansas alum with the same last name — fella named Jerry in Dallas — might not take a shot. Whatever happens, Jones climbs to the top of the "Workout Warrior" cautionary tale list.

Malcolm Kelly

Height: 6-4   Weight: 218 College: Oklahoma   Draft: 2008/2 (51)   Born: 30-Dec-1986 Age: 22 Risk: Red

Year	Team	G	Rec	Pass	Yds	C%	Yd/C	TD	YAC	Rk	DVOA	Rk	DYAR	Rk	YAR	Short	Mid	Deep	Bomb
2008	WAS	5	3	11	18	27%	6.0	0	1.7	--	-62.1%	--	-41	--	-43	38%	25%	13%	25%
2009	WAS		14	29	177	49%	12.3	1			-28.0%								

For years, fans and media have been lambasting the Redskins for trading their draft picks for middling and/ or elderly veterans. Perhaps we owe the Redskins an apology. Kelly showed up in less than optimal shape, struggled through injury, and missed spring minicamp with a knee problem. At 6-foot-4, he should at least be a dynamite option towards the goal line, but at the moment, his height just means that the bell desk needs to stock up on extra-long sheets inside Jim Zorn's doghouse. His path to a steady spot on the active roster involves becoming a willing participant on special teams and catching 50 extra passes a day after practice.

Ashley Lelie

Height: 6-3   Weight: 200 College: Hawaii   Draft: 2002/1 (19)   Born: 16-Feb-1980 Age: 29 Risk: Red

Year	Team	G	Rec	Pass	Yds	C%	Yd/C	TD	YAC	Rk	DVOA	Rk	DYAR	Rk	YAR	Short	Mid	Deep	Bomb
2006	ATL	15	28	68	430	41%	15.4	1	2.3	77	-17.9%	72	-28	72	-32	12%	42%	20%	26%
2007	SF	15	10	26	115	38%	11.5	0	1.3	--	-52.9%	--	-82	--	-74	27%	27%	23%	23%
2008	OAK	13	11	45	197	24%	17.9	2	2.2	--	-38.0%	--	-91	--	-91	21%	38%	24%	17%

Lowest catch rates by WR with at least 25 pass targets, 1994-2008:

Player	Year	Team	Rec	Pass	RecYd	RecTD	C%
Reche Caldwell	2003	SD	8	34	80	0	24%
Ashley Lelie	2008	OAK	11	45	197	2	24%
Bryan Gilmore	2006	SF	8	31	150	1	26%
Marty Booker	2008	CHI	14	49	211	2	29%
Todd Pinkston	2000	PHI	10	34	181	0	29%
Kevin Lee	1995	NE	8	27	107	0	30%
Michael Westbrook	2002	CIN	8	26	94	2	31%
Darren Chiaverini	2001	DAL	10	32	107	2	31%
Ernie Mills	1997	CAR	11	35	127	1	31%
David Patten	1999	NYG	9	28	115	0	32%

So just in case Al Davis was wondering, you need more than just speed to be a successful NFL receiver. Lelie is currently unsigned.

Greg Lewis
Height: 6-0   Weight: 180 College: Illinois   Draft: 2003/FA   Born: 12-Feb-1980 Age: 29 Risk: Blue

Year	Team	G	Rec	Pass	Yds	C%	Yd/C	TD	YAC	Rk	DVOA	Rk	DYAR	Rk	YAR	Short	Mid	Deep	Bomb
2006	PHI	16	24	37	348	65%	14.5	2	3.3	--	16.8%	--	81	--	95	15%	59%	7%	19%
2007	PHI	15	13	23	265	57%	20.4	3	4.0	--	31.7%	--	85	--	91	18%	32%	18%	32%
2008	PHI	16	19	35	247	54%	13.0	1	2.7	--	1.8%	--	41	--	45	19%	50%	16%	16%
2009	NE		14	22	174	64%	12.4	2			-7.4%								

Lewis is the reason young Eagles shouldn't be complaining about their second contracts; given a new six-year deal in his second season after signing with the team as an unrestricted free agent, Lewis simply failed to develop any further as a receiver. Lewis will play out the final year of that deal as a depth receiver and special teams gunner in New England.

Brandon Lloyd
Height: 6-0   Weight: 184 College: Illinois   Draft: 2003/4 (124) Born: 5-Jul-1981   Age: 28 Risk: Green

Year	Team	G	Rec	Pass	Yds	C%	Yd/C	TD	YAC	Rk	DVOA	Rk	DYAR	Rk	YAR	Short	Mid	Deep	Bomb
2006	WAS	15	23	58	365	41%	15.9	0	2.5	68	-22.2%	79	-42	77	-38	17%	46%	12%	25%
2007	WAS	8	2	11	14	18%	7.0	0	8.0	--	-85.3%	--	-59	--	-54	25%	13%	25%	38%
2008	CHI	11	26	49	364	53%	14.0	2	2.3	--	-6.0%	--	26	--	37	13%	49%	24%	13%
2009	DEN		21	40	260	53%	12.4	2			-19.4%								

Lloyd caught 13 passes for 216 yards in the first three games of the season, leading to the inevitable stories about how Lloyd was comfortable at home in Illinois and had a special rapport with Kyle Orton and his former employers had all missed on him. Then he tore his PCL in Week 4, missed the next five games, and didn't get his job back until Week 15, at which point he finished the season with seven catches for 71 yards over the final three games. It's not that he has bad hands, since he only dropped one pass last year; it's that Lloyd simply hasn't developed. The book on him coming out of school was that he ran poor routes and had no interest in selling himself out over the middle, and he still doesn't. He used his height and his build to catch passes at Illinois, but hasn't put the effort in to really learn the nuances of the position and grow as a player. Denver signed him in June when Brandon Marshall started demanding a trade.

Dane Looker
Height: 6-0   Weight: 194 College: Washington   Draft: 2000/FA   Born: 5-Apr-1976   Age: 33 Risk: N/A

Year	Team	G	Rec	Pass	Yds	C%	Yd/C	TD	YAC	Rk	DVOA	Rk	DYAR	Rk	YAR	Short	Mid	Deep	Bomb
2007	STL	13	6	14	38	43%	6.3	0	1.8	--	-42.9%	--	-34	--	-39	43%	50%	7%	0%
2008	STL	13	23	47	271	49%	11.8	2	2.4	--	-31.8%	--	-67	--	-55	28%	39%	24%	9%

On September 28, 2008, Looker suffered a concussion while playing against the Bills. A few days later, his career — to say nothing of his life — seemed in jeopardy after a CAT scan revealed a brain "abnormality." After a few tense days, however, his doctors determined that he was in no danger and Looker returned to play the rest of the season. His DVOA may be horrible, but no one should question Dane Looker's fortitude. Currently a free agent.

Jeremy Maclin

Height: 6-1   Weight: 200   College: Missouri   Draft: 2009/1 (19)   Born: 26-Aug-1988   Age: 21   Risk: Red

Year	Team	G	Rec	Pass	Yds	C%	Yd/C	TD	YAC	Rk	DVOA	Rk	DYAR	Rk	YAR	Short	Mid	Deep	Bomb
2009	PHI		42	77	546	54%	13.2	3			-12.0%								

Philadelphia was pleasantly surprised to see Maclin still on the board at 19, and traded up two picks to get him. While most draft-day observers were surprised when Philadelphia went for a potential DeSean Jackson clone rather than tight end Brandon Pettigrew, the Eagles had a much higher grade on Maclin, who they see as the number-one wideout they were supposed to be shopping for this offseason. Maclin's an intelligent player with both elite athleticism and an excellent work ethic, so he's not Freddie Mitchell or Percy Harvin. His biggest issue at this point is route-running, but the coaching staff obviously feels it's a weakness they can coach up. Expect Maclin to be a part-time receiver and return specialist this year before emerging as the Eagles' best receiver by 2011, assuming that he can stay healthy.

Mario Manningham

Height: 6-0   Weight: 181   College: Michigan   Draft: 2008/3 (95)   Born: 25-May-1986   Age: 23   Risk: Yellow

Year	Team	G	Rec	Pass	Yds	C%	Yd/C	TD	YAC	Rk	DVOA	Rk	DYAR	Rk	YAR	Short	Mid	Deep	Bomb
2008	NYG	7	4	6	26	67%	6.5	0	5.5	--	0.3%	--	8	--	4	71%	14%	14%	0%
2009	NYG		16	32	245	50%	15.3	1			-13.8%								

Of Manningham's six targets, three were on screen passes and two were quick slants thrown by David Carr in Week 17. Despite the issues with Burress and the team's need for a downfield threat, Manningham made little impact as a rookie. He wasn't an effective receiver over the middle or in the short-to-intermediate game at Michigan, and he can't block, limiting his chances in the Giants offense. In his sophomore season, he'll need to make progress on those things and hope that Ramses Barden doesn't usurp his playing time.

Brandon Marshall

Height: 6-4   Weight: 230   College: UCF   Draft: 2006/4 (119)   Born: 23-Mar-1984   Age: 25   Risk: Yellow

Year	Team	G	Rec	Pass	Yds	C%	Yd/C	TD	YAC	Rk	DVOA	Rk	DYAR	Rk	YAR	Short	Mid	Deep	Bomb
2006	DEN	15	20	37	309	54%	15.5	2	5.5	--	-8.0%	--	14	--	19	23%	48%	19%	10%
2007	DEN	16	102	170	1325	60%	13.0	7	5.2	11	-1.6%	54	148	30	157	39%	40%	13%	8%
2008	DEN	15	104	181	1265	57%	12.2	6	3.9	35	-6.7%	58	85	42	105	32%	40%	16%	12%
2009	DEN		86	135	1024	63%	12.0	10			4.9%								

Marshall's goal before the season was 140 receptions, even after he was suspended for the season opener by Roger Goodell. He started off with an 18-catch performance in the Hochuli Game against San Diego, but settled into a six-catch-per-game average after that, despite leading the league in targets. He drifted in and out of games at times, with Loser League-style performances of 25 yards against Tampa Bay, 27 yards against Miami, 48 yards against Buffalo, and 55 yards against San Diego in the season finale. Despite his massive frame, Marshall put up a -25.1% DVOA in the red zone, and after three games with a touchdown to start the season, he only scored in two of the remaining 12 games (against Kansas City and Cleveland, not exactly shutdown defenses). A March arrest for disorderly conduct following a fight with his fiance is yet another sign of his lack of maturity; he remains one of the league's best young receivers, but there are a lot of things that need to change for him to get rid of the "young" qualifier.

Ruvell Martin

Height: 6-4   Weight: 217   College: Saginaw Valley State   Draft: 2006/FA   Born: 10-Aug-1982 Age: 27 Risk: Red

Year	Team	G	Rec	Pass	Yds	C%	Yd/C	TD	YAC	Rk	DVOA	Rk	DYAR	Rk	YAR	Short	Mid	Deep	Bomb
2006	GB	13	21	43	358	49%	17.0	1	3.2	--	6.6%	--	65	--	52	25%	50%	18%	7%
2007	GB	15	16	28	242	57%	15.1	4	3.8	--	22.1%	--	87	--	95	20%	37%	13%	30%
2008	GB	13	15	26	149	58%	9.9	1	2.9	--	-9.8%	--	6	--	7	42%	50%	4%	4%
2009	GB		23	37	253	62%	11.0	1			-10.0%								

Martin is essentially the same player he was in 2006. He's a guy who fills a role — he's not going to hurt the team, but he doesn't have any upside either.

Derrick Mason

Height: 5-10   Weight: 190 College: Michigan State   Draft: 1997/4 (98)   Born: 17-Jan-1974 Age: 35 Risk: Green

Year	Team	G	Rec	Pass	Yds	C%	Yd/C	TD	YAC	Rk	DVOA	Rk	DYAR	Rk	YAR	Short	Mid	Deep	Bomb
2006	BAL	16	68	112	750	61%	11.0	2	2.1	79	-3.7%	53	79	54	84	30%	53%	10%	7%
2007	BAL	16	103	164	1087	63%	10.6	5	2.9	68	-6.0%	60	88	51	89	43%	40%	14%	3%
2008	BAL	16	80	121	1037	67%	13.0	5	3.1	57	13.9%	15	249	11	241	20%	54%	15%	10%
2009	BAL		85	143	1022	59%	12.0	8			10.9%								

The all-time reception leaders among wide receivers listed under six feet in height: Steve Largent (819), Henry Ellard (814), Derrick Mason (790), Charlie Joiner (750), Gary Clark (699). Largent and Ellard were 5-foot-11, so Mason will become the shortest player ever to catch 800 passes sometime in September, and he'll become history's most productive pass-catching Smurf by Halloween.

Mason's counting stats were down and his FO metrics were up last year, but really he had the same season he's been having since 2001: He caught lots of short passes, did a great job on third downs (DVOA of 41.5% on 36 throws), and proved remarkably durable for a tiny 33-year-old. Mason gritted his way through a dislocated shoulder over the second half of the season and the playoffs; offseason surgery didn't restore the shoulder back to 100 percent, so it might be something to watch out for in training camp and during the preseason.

Mohamed Massaquoi

Height: 6-2   Weight: 200 College: Georgia   Draft: 2009/2 (50)   Born: 24-Nov-1986 Age: 23 Risk: Red

Year	Team	G	Rec	Pass	Yds	C%	Yd/C	TD	YAC	Rk	DVOA	Rk	DYAR	Rk	YAR	Short	Mid	Deep	Bomb
2009	CLE		21	35	198	61%	9.3	1			-9.1%								

Both Massoquoi and fellow rookie Brian Robiskie are big receivers with good blocking skills. From a strategic standpoint, their presence should allow offensive coordinator Brian Daboll to run the ball out of three- and four-wideout sets. Jerome Harrison could take a pitch and run to the right behind a trips-right formation. Robiskie and Massaquoi can neutralize their cornerbacks/nickelbacks, Braylon Edwards can take his defender deep, and Robert Royal can stay the hell out of everyone's way. Instant long gain for Harrison. Or, Massaquoi and Robiskie can block for Josh Cribbs on a tunnel screen. The point is that neither rookie will have great numbers in 2009, because the overall offense they are playing for will be bad. That doesn't mean they cannot contribute. Massaquoi, in particular, has a rep as a try-hard competitor who lacks ideal speed and drops too many passes, so he will have to sell himself as a complementary player.

Justin McCareins

Height: 6-2   Weight: 215 College: Northern Illinois   Draft: 2001/4 (124) Born: 11-Dec-1978 Age: 30 Risk: N/A

Year	Team	G	Rec	Pass	Yds	C%	Yd/C	TD	YAC	Rk	DVOA	Rk	DYAR	Rk	YAR	Short	Mid	Deep	Bomb
2006	NYJ	16	23	39	347	59%	15.1	1	4.4	--	9.6%	--	74	--	66	24%	29%	18%	29%
2007	NYJ	16	19	46	232	41%	12.2	0	2.0	--	-24.0%	--	-44	--	-67	18%	56%	18%	9%
2008	TEN	14	30	73	412	42%	13.7	0	3.0	63	-31.5%	79	-108	79	-110	21%	27%	30%	21%

McCareins had a good year in Tennessee in 2003 before mostly disappointing the Jets from 2004 through 2007. So much for the triumphant return: Apparently Tennessee is not some sort of magic land for McCareins. The

Titans' other top two receivers, Justin Gage and Brandon Jones, had above-average DVOAs, while McCareins had comfortably the worst DVOA of any receiver targeted at least 50 times. He is unsigned at this time, and he will struggle to make a team if one does eventually come calling.

Shaun McDonald
Height: 5-10 Weight: 183 College: Arizona State   Draft: 2003/4 (106) Born: 13-Jun-1981 Age: 28 Risk: Blue

Year	Team	G	Rec	Pass	Yds	C%	Yd/C	TD	YAC	Rk	DVOA	Rk	DYAR	Rk	YAR	Short	Mid	Deep	Bomb
2006	STL	16	13	19	136	68%	10.5	1	1.2	--	-17.0%	--	-6	--	-4	44%	33%	11%	11%
2007	DET	16	79	126	943	63%	11.9	6	3.2	55	-1.8%	55	106	47	102	31%	47%	15%	8%
2008	DET	12	35	66	332	53%	9.5	1	1.9	76	-23.4%	78	-55	78	-64	22%	57%	12%	9%
2009	PIT		9	16	132	56%	14.6	1			-13.6%								

Another Martz-era addition that failed to cope with the new order, McDonald was a Loser League stud in 2008, with eight games of six points or less. He "peaked" with a game that sadly pulled the penalty, because it was one of the great lines of the Lions season: 0 receptions on 6 targets for -7 yards. Yes, 0 receptions for -7 yards, thanks to a lateral on the game's final play that McDonald fumbled away. He went down with an ankle injury in Week 13 and missed the rest of the season, and although he signed with the Steelers after the draft, there's no obvious roster spot for him to take.

Robert Meachem
Height: 6-2 Weight: 214 College: Tennessee   Draft: 2007/1 (27) Born: 28-Sep-1984 Age: 25 Risk: Red

Year	Team	G	Rec	Pass	Yds	C%	Yd/C	TD	YAC	Rk	DVOA	Rk	DYAR	Rk	YAR	Short	Mid	Deep	Bomb
2008	NO	14	12	20	289	60%	24.1	3	5.1	--	63.9%	--	113	--	110	10%	43%	19%	29%
2009	NO		16	50	304	32%	19.0	1			-33.2%								

The 2007 first-rounder finally got on the field, and only caught 12 passes, but that included receptions of 71, 54, and 47 yards. He also had a 21-yard catch and a 20-yard run. Meachem fits best as a designated deep threat and cocky loudmouth, but in New Orleans, those roles are filled by Devery Henderson and Jeremy Shockey, respectively. The Saints offense accommodates redundancy and duplication of duties (count their tight ends if you have an hour), so Meachem could stay on the roster as a burner in four-wideout sets. He would be wise not to test Sean Payton's patience.

Lance Moore
Height: 5-9 Weight: 177 College: Toledo   Draft: 2006/FA Born: 31-Aug-1983 Age: 26 Risk: Green

Year	Team	G	Rec	Pass	Yds	C%	Yd/C	TD	YAC	Rk	DVOA	Rk	DYAR	Rk	YAR	Short	Mid	Deep	Bomb
2006	NO	4	1	3	10	33%	10.0	0	7.0	--	-33.2%	--	-5	--	-8	100%	0%	0%	0%
2007	NO	16	32	50	302	64%	9.4	2	1.8	86	6.7%	33	77	56	61	33%	41%	16%	10%
2008	NO	16	79	120	928	66%	11.7	10	3.6	45	12.6%	17	232	15	196	39%	40%	15%	6%
2009	NO		54	92	715	59%	13.2	4			8.6%								

Moore injured his shoulder while weightlifting in April. He's expected back for the start of training camp, but the injury could put him behind the eight-ball on a roster teeming with good receivers. Moore became the Saints' go-to receiver when Marques Colston got hurt and looked like Derrick Mason Junior, catching lots of hitches in traffic and using his quickness to stay alive in the middle of the field. (He was the target on 25 percent of the Saints' third-down passes, one of the highest figures in the NFL.) Moore is entering a contract year; if he gets lost in the shuffle and puts up so-so numbers, he could be a discount free agent to watch in 2010.

Josh Morgan
Height: 6-0 Weight: 219 College: Virginia Tech   Draft: 2008/6 (174) Born: 20-Jun-1985 Age: 24 Risk: Red

Year	Team	G	Rec	Pass	Yds	C%	Yd/C	TD	YAC	Rk	DVOA	Rk	DYAR	Rk	YAR	Short	Mid	Deep	Bomb
2008	SF	12	20	43	319	47%	16.0	3	4.3	--	-16.3%	--	-12	--	-1	28%	31%	28%	13%
2009	SF		43	75	475	57%	11.0	3			18.0%								

Morgan managed to generate plenty of buzz by catching nine passes for 182 yards in the first two games of the 2008 preseason. Then he caught a staph infection after playing in the Oakland Coliseum, dropped 15 pounds, and struggled to remain in the starting lineup. Morgan has all the tools (size, speed, hands) to succeed in the NFL, and early reports from April minicamps suggest he's got the coaching staff (to say nothing of local beat reporters) excited again. The dilemma for the 49ers coaching staff is that Morgan possesses essentially the same skill set as Michael Crabtree. This is what coaching staffs refer to as a "happy problem," and there haven't been a lot of those in San Francisco recently.

Randy Moss

Height: 6-4   Weight: 200 College: Marshall   Draft: 1998/1 (21)   Born: 13-Feb-1977 Age: 32 Risk: Yellow

Year	Team	G	Rec	Pass	Yds	C%	Yd/C	TD	YAC	Rk	DVOA	Rk	DYAR	Rk	YAR	Short	Mid	Deep	Bomb
2006	OAK	13	42	97	553	43%	13.2	3	2.4	73	-19.9%	75	-52	79	-56	12%	48%	19%	20%
2007	NE	16	98	160	1493	61%	15.2	23	3.3	52	29.3%	4	569	1	562	27%	41%	18%	14%
2008	NE	16	69	125	1008	55%	14.6	11	5.0	11	0.5%	41	134	29	134	25%	43%	14%	18%
2009	NE		95	150	1391	63%	14.6	13			20.4%								

It wasn't quite the pitch-and-catch he enjoyed with Tom Brady — Matt Cassel wasn't as consistent with the 9-routes that might put Moss in the Hall of Fame someday — and the numbers told that story. Still, Moss is yet another example of a former malcontent who finds inner peace in the Patriots locker room. In March, he agreed to a restructuring of his contract to help the Patriots sign Fred Taylor and Chris Baker. While Matt Cassel got better as the season went along, that improvement didn't come on deep passes to Moss. Cassel completed two of his first three passes to Moss that went 30 yards or more in the air; the pair went 1-for-23 on such passes the rest of the way, and that doesn't even include plays where Moss was open and Cassel didn't see him or checked down. Brady and Moss were 10-of-20 on those passes in 2007, so expect a few more deep touchdowns for number 81 in 2009.

Santana Moss

Height: 5-10 Weight: 185 College: Miami   Draft: 2001/1 (16)   Born: 1-Jun-1979   Age: 30 Risk: Green

Year	Team	G	Rec	Pass	Yds	C%	Yd/C	TD	YAC	Rk	DVOA	Rk	DYAR	Rk	YAR	Short	Mid	Deep	Bomb
2006	WAS	14	55	100	790	54%	14.4	6	4.6	20	-4.9%	57	60	56	76	35%	35%	17%	14%
2007	WAS	14	61	115	808	53%	13.2	3	3.1	59	-9.8%	68	26	67	10	40%	30%	16%	15%
2008	WAS	16	79	138	1044	57%	13.2	6	5.5	6	-6.0%	57	73	48	96	44%	34%	11%	12%
2009	WAS		74	126	873	59%	11.8	6			5.2%								

Few Redskins players showed the effects of the team's Jekyll-and-Hyde offensive production more than Moss. He started out with 42 receptions for 658 yards and five touchdowns in the first half of the season, and fell to 37 catches for 386 yards and one score in the final eight games. Like Chris Cooley, Moss suffered from the inability of the receivers around him to provide relief as complementary options. In the offseason, he was one of many Redskins players asked to restructure his contract. His responsibility in the offense, however, will not diminish at all.

Sinorice Moss

Height: 5-8   Weight: 185 College: Miami   Draft: 2006/2 (44)   Born: 28-Dec-1983 Age: 25 Risk: Green

Year	Team	G	Rec	Pass	Yds	C%	Yd/C	TD	YAC	Rk	DVOA	Rk	DYAR	Rk	YAR	Short	Mid	Deep	Bomb
2006	NYG	6	5	11	25	45%	5.0	0	4.6	--	-61.2%	--	-45	--	-47	88%	0%	0%	13%
2007	NYG	13	21	37	225	57%	10.7	0	3.4	--	-26.2%	--	-39	--	-47	36%	48%	9%	6%
2008	NYG	10	12	15	153	80%	12.8	2	2.0	--	46.0%	--	67	--	67	29%	43%	21%	7%
2009	NYG		18	28	203	64%	11.3	1			-11.9%								

Moss was effective in limited doses last year, but he simply hasn't taken the steps forward that the Giants expected when they drafted him in 2006. Maybe the fact that he had 63 catches in four seasons at Miami should have been a sign. He's an athlete who's failed to turn his tools into skills, and he doesn't contribute enough as a return man to eke out a living there. In the final year of his deal, he'll have to beat out special teams dynamo and Giants legend David Tyree for a roster spot by being a far superior receiver; if he really had that talent, though, he would have shown it by now.

Muhsin Muhammad

Height: 6-2   Weight: 217 College: Michigan State   Draft: 1996/2 (43)   Born: 5-May-1973   Age: 36 Risk: Green

Year	Team	G	Rec	Pass	Yds	C%	Yd/C	TD	YAC	Rk	DVOA	Rk	DYAR	Rk	YAR	Short	Mid	Deep	Bomb
2006	CHI	16	60	117	863	51%	14.4	5	2.8	64	-2.7%	52	91	47	94	20%	41%	29%	9%
2007	CHI	16	40	81	570	49%	14.3	3	4.7	20	-6.2%	61	41	63	46	23%	48%	21%	8%
2008	CAR	16	65	107	923	61%	14.2	5	4.9	15	6.1%	28	160	24	154	29%	54%	11%	7%
2009	CAR		45	88	572	51%	12.7	2			-11.5%								

As much as we're sure Muhsin missed the company of Sexy Rexy and Neck Beard, he was a far more successful receiver upon his return to Carolina. Funny how your catch rate can go up by 10 percent when you have a quarterback with decent accuracy. That's a good thing, because Muhammed isn't exactly getting a lot of separation. By running good routes and boxing out defensive backs, he's giving the Panthers a reasonable option when coverage is rolled to Steve Smith. In particular, Muhsin was highly effective on first down, with a 27.5% DVOA, compared to -23.8% on third and fourth down.

Legedu Naanee

Height: 6-2   Weight: 225 College: Boise State   Draft: 2007/5 (172) Born: 16-Sep-1983 Age: 26 Risk: Blue

Year	Team	G	Rec	Pass	Yds	C%	Yd/C	TD	YAC	Rk	DVOA	Rk	DYAR	Rk	YAR	Short	Mid	Deep	Bomb
2007	SD	13	8	13	69	62%	8.6	0	6.6	--	-28.7%	--	-16	--	-12	46%	38%	8%	8%
2008	SD	16	8	11	64	73%	8.0	0	3.3	--	-3.3%	--	8	--	9	70%	10%	20%	0%
2009	SD		15	22	132	68%	8.8	1			-6.6%								

If you could pull off any stat line ad nauseum in the NFL, catching eight passes for about 65 yards each year would not be the line you would choose. For most wide receivers, it would be a one-way ticket to the CFL, but Naanee's versatility and ability to handle everything from wide receiver to H-Back allows him to hold on to a roster spot.

Jordy Nelson

Height: 6-3   Weight: 217 College: Kansas State   Draft: 2008/2 (36)   Born: 31-May-1985 Age: 24 Risk: Red

Year	Team	G	Rec	Pass	Yds	C%	Yd/C	TD	YAC	Rk	DVOA	Rk	DYAR	Rk	YAR	Short	Mid	Deep	Bomb
2008	GB	16	33	54	366	61%	11.1	2	2.7	66	-2.6%	51	41	58	44	22%	51%	16%	12%
2009	GB		33	55	439	60%	13.3	4			6.2%								

As a rookie, Nelson showed serious promise as a slot receiver and put up solid advanced numbers (compare him to Greg Jennings' -24.4% DVOA and 43 percent catch rate if you really want to see a bad rookie receiver). Although it's easy to compare him to other white guys, the closest comp to the player Nelson will grow up to be is Joe Jurevicius; a tall possession receiver who's deadly within 12 yards of the line of scrimmage. He's great at disguising his routes and using his speed to blow past linebackers or his size to overwhelm defensive backs. Like most young receivers, he needs to work on his blocking and some other minor issues, but if the Packers' passing game is among the top two or three in the league next year, Nelson's improvement will be the primary reason why.

Hakeem Nicks

Height: 6-2   Weight: 210 College: North Carolina   Draft: 2009/1 (29)   Born: 14-Jan-1988 Age: 21 Risk: Red

Year	Team	G	Rec	Pass	Yds	C%	Yd/C	TD	YAC	Rk	DVOA	Rk	DYAR	Rk	YAR	Short	Mid	Deep	Bomb
2009	NYG		47	85	664	55%	14.2	3			-14.0%								

Nicks likens himself to Anquan Boldin, and it's a reasonable comparison. Nicks isn't one to blow you away with speed; he's a technician who focuses on every little step and movement he makes to gain the upper hand on defensive backs. He uses his hands effectively at the line of scrimmage to break press coverage, and then sets up defensive backs with excellent route-running. You can just see Eli Manning practicing 20 back-shoulder throws a day to him. Nicks was used frequently on slants at UNC, so he's not afraid to go over the middle. While it's been suggested that he'll take over Plaxico Burress' role in the offense, his skill set and usage patterns at school make it much more likely that he'll be on the other side of the field, replacing the departed Amani Toomer, with Domenik Hixon remaining as the split end.

Dennis Northcutt

Height: 5-11   Weight: 175   College: Arizona   Draft: 2000/2 (32)   Born: 22-Dec-1977   Age: 31   Risk: Yellow

Year	Team	G	Rec	Pass	Yds	C%	Yd/C	TD	YAC	Rk	DVOA	Rk	DYAR	Rk	YAR	Short	Mid	Deep	Bomb
2006	CLE	13	22	45	228	49%	10.4	0	4.5	--	-30.6%	--	-64	--	-60	46%	32%	5%	16%
2007	JAC	15	44	73	601	60%	13.7	4	2.9	66	11.3%	22	133	37	120	24%	50%	20%	6%
2008	JAC	14	44	68	545	65%	12.4	2	2.4	73	2.1%	35	76	45	72	26%	52%	14%	8%
2009	DET		26	43	370	60%	14.2	1			-3.4%								

The good news: Northcutt showed up for 18 catches in the last three games of Jacksonville's weird, wild season. The bad news: He had been conducting an invisibility seminar before then. He's got the potential to make a difference in a receiver rotation that's Torry Holt and Everybody Else at this point, but by June there were rumors that the Jaguars had soured on Northcutt and were looking to deal him.

Chad Ochocinco

Height: 6-1   Weight: 192   College: Oregon State   Draft: 2001/2 (36)   Born: 9-Jan-1978   Age: 31   Risk: Yellow

Year	Team	G	Rec	Pass	Yds	C%	Yd/C	TD	YAC	Rk	DVOA	Rk	DYAR	Rk	YAR	Short	Mid	Deep	Bomb
2006	CIN	16	87	152	1369	57%	15.7	7	3.6	41	17.0%	13	361	4	337	18%	47%	19%	16%
2007	CIN	16	93	161	1440	58%	15.5	8	3.2	56	10.7%	24	303	6	291	19%	44%	26%	11%
2008	CIN	13	53	97	540	55%	10.2	4	1.7	79	-1.2%	45	90	38	53	13%	64%	15%	8%
2009	CIN		75	135	1046	56%	13.9	10			13.7%								

Between March and August of 2008, the Artist Formerly Known as Chad Johnson received almost daily media attention, single-handedly keeping the NFL Network on the air during the excruciatingly long months between Brett Favre's retirement and Brett Favre's un-retirement. But come the fall, the name "Ocho Cinco" was barely ever mentioned. The Chad's execution of the Rosenhaus Trade Forcing Master Plan was as maladroit as Cincinnati's offensive execution. A shoulder injury sustained in preseason hampered him all year, and once Carson Palmer went down, Ochocinco checked out mentally. His trade value has plummeted, and his uncanny body control and exceptional speed have slipped with time and punishment. Chad is a good candidate for a late-career rejuvenation with a good team, a la Randy Moss, but his decline in Cincinnati is likely to accelerate — although without T.J. Houshmandzdeh to share passes, his raw totals may not.

Terrell Owens

Height: 6-3   Weight: 226   College: Tenn.-Chattanooga   Draft: 1996/3 (89)   Born: 7-Dec-1973   Age: 36   Risk: Yellow

Year	Team	G	Rec	Pass	Yds	C%	Yd/C	TD	YAC	Rk	DVOA	Rk	DYAR	Rk	YAR	Short	Mid	Deep	Bomb
2006	DAL	16	85	152	1180	56%	13.9	13	4.0	36	10.2%	23	274	7	284	34%	28%	23%	15%
2007	DAL	15	81	141	1355	57%	16.7	15	4.3	25	28.2%	5	448	3	435	25%	43%	19%	13%
2008	DAL	16	69	139	1052	50%	15.2	10	4.2	26	-5.7%	56	75	46	57	24%	45%	15%	16%
2009	BUF		66	130	935	51%	14.2	7			-10.2%								

With the best interests of you the reader in mind, we'd like to keep this one brief, since you've probably heard a lot about Terrell Owens at this point. There have been 15 receivers over the age of 32 that cracked the league's top ten in DYAR and then fell out in a subsequent season. Only one of those 15 receivers was able to make it back into the top ten, and his name is Jerry Rice. For all that Terrell Owens is, he's not Jerry Rice.

The biggest problem for Owens is that he wasn't able to break man coverage at the line, something that wouldn't have been a problem several years ago. The Cowboys alleviated that to an extent by sending Owens in motion on a regular basis and lining him up next to or behind Patrick Crayton in the slot, which did work: Owens averaged 9.4 yards per attempt and had a 50 percent Success Rate in three-wide receiver sets, as opposed to 5.0 yards per attempt and a 35 percent success rate with only two wide receivers on the field. Moving to Buffalo, he won't have to face the other team's best cornerback, and he'll only be expected to work underneath and work in single coverage. He should rebound some, but the T.O. that mattered — the one who teams had to gameplan around — is gone. No matter what he says.

Roscoe Parrish

Height: 5-9　Weight: 168　College: Miami　　　Draft: 2005/2 (55)　Born: 16-Jul-1982　Age: 27　Risk: Green

Year	Team	G	Rec	Pass	Yds	C%	Yd/C	TD	YAC	Rk	DVOA	Rk	DYAR	Rk	YAR	Short	Mid	Deep	Bomb
2006	BUF	16	23	40	320	58%	13.9	2	6.5	--	-16.8%	--	-13	--	-22	44%	28%	8%	20%
2007	BUF	16	35	58	352	60%	10.1	1	3.6	44	-13.4%	73	-3	73	-21	45%	35%	5%	15%
2008	BUF	13	24	45	232	53%	9.7	1	3.0	--	-30.1%	--	-64	--	-45	40%	40%	14%	5%
2009	BUF		15	25	183	60%	12.2	1			-13.9%								

Parrish was shopped around in the offseason but there were no takers, so he'll return to Buffalo's big tent at wide receiver — the team currently had nine receivers on the roster going in to training camp — and try to convince Turk Schonert that he has a role to play on offense. Parrish was dreadful on third downs last year, and despite having better speed, he's unlikely to challenge Josh Reed for slot duty. Strictly a situational player.

David Patten

Height: 5-10　Weight: 190　College: Western Carolina　　　Draft: 1997/FA　Born: 19-Aug-1974　Age: 35　Risk: Yellow

Year	Team	G	Rec	Pass	Yds	C%	Yd/C	TD	YAC	Rk	DVOA	Rk	DYAR	Rk	YAR	Short	Mid	Deep	Bomb
2006	WAS	5	1	4	25	25%	25.0	0	0.0	--	-25.5%	--	-4	--	-6	50%	0%	50%	0%
2007	NO	16	54	88	792	61%	14.7	3	4.6	21	6.9%	32	138	33	133	30%	37%	19%	14%
2008	NO	5	11	20	162	55%	14.7	1	4.0	--	14.4%	--	42	--	36	16%	37%	26%	21%
2009	CLE		22	39	327	56%	14.9	1			-5.4%								

Patten's career looked pretty dead after he caught just one pass for the 2006 Redskins, but then he came out of nowhere to become the number-two receiver for the Saints in 2007. Last year, he went back to the nowhere from whence he came, losing his job to Lance Moore when he was out with an early-season groin injury and ending up inactive most of the time even after he got healthy. Eric Mangini knows him from their Patriots days, so he'll serve as an insurance policy in case youngsters like Brian Robskie and Mohamed Massaquoi can't adapt to the NFL.

Jerry Porter

Height: 6-2　Weight: 220　College: West Virginia　　　Draft: 2000/2 (47)　Born: 14-Jul-1978　Age: 31　Risk: N/A

Year	Team	G	Rec	Pass	Yds	C%	Yd/C	TD	YAC	Rk	DVOA	Rk	DYAR	Rk	YAR	Short	Mid	Deep	Bomb
2006	OAK	4	1	4	19	25%	19.0	0	0.0	--	-24.3%	--	-3	--	-3	0%	50%	25%	25%
2007	OAK	16	44	102	705	43%	16.0	6	4.3	27	-10.5%	72	17	71	16	20%	38%	22%	20%
2008	JAC	10	11	30	181	37%	16.5	1	2.8	--	-21.1%	--	-22	--	-25	24%	45%	24%	7%

If you need any indication that the Great Jacksonville Receiver Disaster of 2008 was less about bad luck and more about horrid personnel decisions, we need look no further then Porter, who landed in Art Shell's doghouse in Oakland after reportedly expressing concern that champagne was no longer allowed in the locker room. Porter also couldn't understand why Al Davis would take offense when he parked in Davis' personal parking space, and why people reacted negatively when he was seen cheering and pumping his fist when his own quarterback, Aaron Brooks, was sacked for the seventh time in a game against the Chargers. The Jaguars then gave this man a seven-year, $30 million contract with $10 million guaranteed. He alternated between injury and complete ineffectiveness before being placed on injured reserve in mid-December. After 11 catches — yes, nearly $1 million per catch — Porter was unceremoniously released. Sometimes, you get what you deserve.

Antwaan Randle El

Height: 5-10　Weight: 186　College: Indiana　　　Draft: 2002/2 (62)　Born: 17-Aug-1979　Age: 30　Risk: Green

Year	Team	G	Rec	Pass	Yds	C%	Yd/C	TD	YAC	Rk	DVOA	Rk	DYAR	Rk	YAR	Short	Mid	Deep	Bomb
2006	WAS	16	32	63	351	51%	11.0	3	2.5	71	-20.9%	77	-42	76	-37	40%	23%	23%	15%
2007	WAS	15	51	77	728	66%	14.3	1	3.6	43	16.9%	15	179	27	183	29%	45%	15%	10%
2008	WAS	16	53	87	593	61%	11.2	4	3.7	43	1.3%	37	96	35	78	35%	53%	9%	4%
2009	WAS		50	85	638	59%	12.8	2			8.7%								

Randle El's production — starting with his yards per catch — fell to earth after a hot 2007. The Redskins hope that second-year men Devin Thomas and Malcolm Kelly will compete for the starting job, but their question marks, and Randle El's willingness to restructure his contract, could put him in a featured role by default. He's also a valued member of the Eastern Motors team, giving him a level of credibility in D.C. approaching that of bands on Dischord and Ben's Chili Bowl.

Josh Reed

Height: 5-10 Weight: 208 College: LSU   Draft: 2002/2 (36) Born: 1-May-1980 Age: 29 Risk: Green

Year	Team	G	Rec	Pass	Yds	C%	Yd/C	TD	YAC	Rk	DVOA	Rk	DYAR	Rk	YAR	Short	Mid	Deep	Bomb
2006	BUF	13	34	48	410	71%	12.1	2	4.3	--	10.4%	--	81	--	83	51%	32%	12%	5%
2007	BUF	15	51	87	578	59%	11.3	0	4.0	33	-6.9%	63	39	64	35	44%	40%	16%	0%
2008	BUF	13	56	79	597	71%	10.7	1	2.6	68	7.5%	26	123	30	148	32%	51%	13%	4%
2009	BUF		20	33	213	61%	10.6	1			-9.2%								

Last year the Bills drafted James Hardy; this year, they signed Terrell Owens. If Josh Reed thinks that his employer is trying to replace him, he's right. Reed has been miscast as a starting receiver, but he's a much better third option than Roscoe Parrish. If Reed can catch 70 percent of the balls that come his way and continue to be a reliable option on third downs, he'll have a significant role in the offense.

Sidney Rice

Height: 6-4 Weight: 200 College: South Carolina   Draft: 2007/2 (44) Born: 1-Sep-1986 Age: 23 Risk: Red

Year	Team	G	Rec	Pass	Yds	C%	Yd/C	TD	YAC	Rk	DVOA	Rk	DYAR	Rk	YAR	Short	Mid	Deep	Bomb
2007	MIN	13	31	53	396	58%	12.8	4	3.0	63	11.1%	23	98	49	87	29%	48%	6%	17%
2008	MIN	13	15	31	141	48%	9.4	4	2.2	--	-3.8%	--	24	--	26	26%	55%	13%	6%
2009	MIN		43	84	481	51%	11.2	3			-9.3%								

Rice was in the ideal situation to succeed — across from a speedy deep threat on a team that needed a possession receiver — but his knee failed to cooperate, and by the time he came back, Bobby Wade was entrenched as the starter. When Rice did play, though, his down splits were remarkable; despite a -58.9% DVOA on first down and an even worse -94.7% DVOA on second down, he was a stud on third down with a 37.7% DVOA. He caught 12 of the 16 passes thrown to him on third down, picking up eight first downs and three touchdowns in the process. If he's healthy in the preseason and you play in a PPR league, make sure he's the second Minnesota wideout you target in your fantasy draft, not Percy Harvin.

Koren Robinson

Height: 6-1 Weight: 205 College: North Carolina State Draft: 2001/1 (9)   Born: 19-Mar-1980 Age: 29 Risk: N/A

Year	Team	G	Rec	Pass	Yds	C%	Yd/C	TD	YAC	Rk	DVOA	Rk	DYAR	Rk	YAR	Short	Mid	Deep	Bomb
2006	GB	4	7	16	89	44%	12.7	0	2.7	--	-19.3%	34	-8	32	2	19%	38%	31%	13%
2007	GB	9	21	34	241	62%	11.5	1	5.7	--	-16.4%	36	-10	38	4	45%	42%	9%	3%
2008	SEA	12	31	58	400	53%	12.9	2	3.7	42	-11.2%	67	7	68	1	27%	43%	21%	9%

When T.J. Houshmandzadeh arrived in Seattle for an introductory press conference, he held up a jersey bearing number 84. This was Koren Robinson's jersey number, and it was a signal to the press and to Robinson that his presence was no longer required in the Emerald City. Though Robinson has apparently come to grips with his battles with alcoholism, *Pro Football Weekly* reported in January that a degenerative knee condition will end his career.

Laurent Robinson

Height: 6-2 Weight: 199 College: Illinois State   Draft: 2007/3 (75) Born: 20-May-1985 Age: 24 Risk: Yellow

Year	Team	G	Rec	Pass	Yds	C%	Yd/C	TD	YAC	Rk	DVOA	Rk	DYAR	Rk	YAR	Short	Mid	Deep	Bomb
2007	ATL	15	37	74	437	50%	11.8	1	3.5	45	-29.3%	81	-97	81	-84	32%	35%	17%	15%
2008	ATL	6	5	6	52	83%	10.4	0	5.4	--	36.8%	--	21	--	18	67%	33%	0%	0%
2009	STL		47	82	593	57%	12.6	3			-0.2%								

The change in regimes in the ATL didn't help Robinson, who suffered through a lost season and was unloaded to receiver-desperate St. Louis. The issue here is injury; Robinson has had hamstring problems in 2007 and 2008, and threw in a knee strain last year to boot. When he's on the field, he's a useful downfield receiver who's still learning the craft and has some upside. Robinson will have to beat out Keenan Burton for the starting job across from Donnie Avery, but more importantly, he'll have to beat away those repeated hamstring injuries.

Ryne Robinson

Height: 5-9   Weight: 179 College: Miami (OH)   Draft: 2007/4 (118) Born: 4-Nov-1984   Age: 25 Risk: Green

Year	Team	G	Rec	Pass	Yds	C%	Yd/C	TD	YAC	Rk	DVOA	Rk	DYAR	Rk	YAR	Short	Mid	Deep	Bomb
2007	CAR	16	4	8	35	50%	8.8	0	4.3	--	-36.7%	--	-15	--	-14	50%	50%	0%	0%
2009	CAR		10	18	124	53%	13.0	0			-20.2%								

An MCL injury cost him all of 2008, but Robinson should be back as the Panthers' primary returner on both punts and kickoffs in 2009. His return numbers in 2007 were relatively pedestrian, but he gets the job back by default after journeyman returner Mark Jones left in free agency for the Titans. Because the Panthers are so weak at receiver, Robinson will even have the opportunity to compete for a role in the offense. Back in the 2007 draft, Robinson was known for leading the country in punt return yardage and touchdowns, but some scouts also complimented his route running. He caught 91 balls as a senior at Miami (Ohio) from a quarterback that was not Ben Roethlisberger.

Brian Robiskie

Height: 6-3   Weight: 199 College: Ohio State   Draft: 2009/2 (36) Born: 3-Dec-1987   Age: 22 Risk: Red

Year	Team	G	Rec	Pass	Yds	C%	Yd/C	TD	YAC	Rk	DVOA	Rk	DYAR	Rk	YAR	Short	Mid	Deep	Bomb
2009	CLE		63	103	657	61%	10.5	4			3.9%								

The son of Terry Robiskie, a former Raiders and Dolphins receiver and a long-time NFL coach, Robiskie posted fine numbers at Ohio State in 2007 (55 catches, 935 yards, 11 touchdowns) before falling off a bit as a senior (42-535-8), largely because the Buckeyes became infatuated with fleet-footed Terrelle Pryor at quarterback. Robiskie is a pure possession receiver with a good reputation as a zone-breaker and blocker, and Donte' Stallworth's legal troubles basically hand him a starting role opposite Braylon Edwards.

Eddie Royal

Height: 5-10 Weight: 184 College: Virginia Tech   Draft: 2008/2 (42) Born: 21-May-1986 Age: 23 Risk: Green

Year	Team	G	Rec	Pass	Yds	C%	Yd/C	TD	YAC	Rk	DVOA	Rk	DYAR	Rk	YAR	Short	Mid	Deep	Bomb
2008	DEN	15	91	129	980	71%	10.8	5	3.8	37	-1.4%	47	115	32	120	45%	35%	12%	9%
2009	DEN		65	98	745	66%	11.5	4			1.2%								

Among wide receivers with 100 targets, Royal's catch rate of 71 percent was second only to … Wes Welker, whose role in the Patriots' offensive scheme Royal may be expected to emulate under Josh McDaniels. Royal's catch rate was even more impressive when you consider that his passes were caught an average of 9.8 yards away from the line of scrimmage, while Welker's were only 4.9 yards away. Royal was also effective on both kick and punt returns; each of Denver's eight other kick returners and two other punt returners cost the team field position, but Royal was above-average on both fronts. From here, he looks less like Welker and more like Anquan Boldin without the blocking, which is still pretty nifty.

Chaz Schilens

Height: 6-4   Weight: 208 College: San Diego State   Draft: 2008/7 (226) Born: 7-Nov-1985   Age: 24 Risk: Red

Year	Team	G	Rec	Pass	Yds	C%	Yd/C	TD	YAC	Rk	DVOA	Rk	DYAR	Rk	YAR	Short	Mid	Deep	Bomb
2008	OAK	16	15	32	226	47%	15.1	2	2.8	--	-11.8%	--	2	--	2	28%	31%	28%	14%
2009	OAK		56	89	538	63%	9.6	4			7.6%								

If the Raiders are going to run a Broncos-influenced offense, they'll need their own version of Rod Smith: a smaller-school wide receiver with superb blocking skills. The good news is that they think they have that guy in Schilens, with the added benefit of size (Smith was four inches shorter). The bad news is that Schilens has not yet proven that his Rod Smith skills include Rod Smith hands and a Rod Smith catch rate. Jerry McDonald of the *Contra Costa Times* made a good point in an offseason column; While many people will compare Darrius Heyward-Bey to Michael Crabtree because of the decision the Raiders made on draft day, it is Schilens who will really play the same role in the Raiders offense that Crabtree plays for the 49ers.

Jerome Simpson

Height: 6-2   Weight: 190   College: Coastal Carolina   Draft: 2008/2 (46)   Born: 4-Feb-1986   Age: 23   Risk: Yellow

Year	Team	G	Rec	Pass	Yds	C%	Yd/C	TD	YAC	Rk	DVOA	Rk	DYAR	Rk	YAR	Short	Mid	Deep	Bomb
2008	CIN	6	1	3	2	33%	2.0	0	3.0	--	-46.2%	--	-12	--	-14	25%	75%	0%	0%
2009	CIN		26	45	339	58%	13.1	2			1.3%								

Cincinnati's reputation for finding and developing wide receivers owes a great deal to Hue Jackson, the position coach when Chad Johnson and T.J. Houshmandzadeh rose to prominence. Simpson needed some of Hue's magic, but unfortunately, Jackson was tutoring Joe Flacco in Baltimore. Simpson's measurables are nice, but the Division I-AA product (he caught Tyler Thigpen's passes at Coastal Carolina) has struggled to master NFL route-running. Marvin Lewis admitted in the offseason that the staff "failed" Simpson last year, so he'll get another chance to prove worthy of that second-round pick.

Brad Smith

Height: 6-2   Weight: 210   College: Missouri   Draft: 2006/4 (103)   Born: 12-Dec-1983   Age: 25   Risk: Red

Year	Team	G	Rec	Pass	Yds	C%	Yd/C	TD	YAC	Rk	DVOA	Rk	DYAR	Rk	YAR	Short	Mid	Deep	Bomb
2006	NYJ	16	9	14	61	64%	6.8	0	4.1	--	-24.3%	--	-13	--	-18	58%	42%	0%	0%
2007	NYJ	16	32	67	325	48%	10.2	2	3.8	39	-23.7%	76	-56	76	-81	39%	32%	21%	8%
2008	NYJ	15	12	19	64	63%	5.3	0	4.2	--	-53.8%	--	-59	--	-54	63%	32%	5%	0%
2009	NYJ		39	73	460	53%	11.8	2			-8.7%								

Smith was a four-year starter at quarterback for Missouri and was only the second player in Division-I history to pass for 2,000 yards and rush for 1,000 yards in the same season, but all that athletic talent hasn't quite translated to the pro level, and many of offensive coordinator Brian Schottenheimer's exotic play calls designed to make Smith into a triple threat seem much ado about nothing. Sometimes Smith will flash, as he did against Oakland (four catches for 29 yards plus four runs for 59 yards), but most of Smith's stat lines barely registered. He probably has one more year to develop into a solid receiving option.

Steve Smith

Height: 5-9   Weight: 179   College: Utah   Draft: 2001/3 (74)   Born: 12-May-1979   Age: 30   Risk: Green

Year	Team	G	Rec	Pass	Yds	C%	Yd/C	TD	YAC	Rk	DVOA	Rk	DYAR	Rk	YAR	Short	Mid	Deep	Bomb
2006	CAR	14	83	139	1166	60%	14.0	8	5.2	7	6.7%	36	213	15	215	34%	30%	21%	15%
2007	CAR	15	87	148	1002	58%	11.5	7	5.5	8	-8.6%	67	47	60	51	43%	34%	11%	12%
2008	CAR	14	78	129	1421	60%	18.2	6	5.5	7	22.7%	4	365	5	391	26%	37%	18%	20%
2009	CAR		74	142	1057	52%	14.3	9			7.4%								

Don't ask why Steve has daughters named Boston and Peyton. Don't ask whether his internship at Morgan Stanley last summer sent the economy into a downward spiral. Don't ask what Ken Lucas said. Just ask what Steve Smith can do when reunited with Jake Delhomme and Muhsin Muhammad. What if I told you there was a top-five wide-out who could put up 42.0% DVOA and 7.3 yards after catch in the red zone, all while rocking a "Papa Smurf" tattoo? Is that something you might be interested in?

Steve Smith   Height: 6-0   Weight: 197 College: USC   Draft: 2007/2 (51) Born: 6-May-1985 Age: 24 Risk: Yellow

Year	Team	G	Rec	Pass	Yds	C%	Yd/C	TD	YAC	Rk	DVOA	Rk	DYAR	Rk	YAR	Short	Mid	Deep	Bomb
2007	NYG	5	8	14	63	57%	7.9	0	2.5	--	-15.9%	--	-4	--	-14	31%	46%	0%	23%
2008	NYG	16	57	82	574	70%	10.1	1	2.5	71	1.0%	39	88	40	89	38%	46%	10%	6%
2009	NYG		74	111	800	67%	10.8	4			9.6%								

There were times last year where Smith looked like the heir apparent to Bobby Engram as the NFL's Third Down Machine, which makes it surprising that he only ended up with a 5.1% DVOA on the penultimate down. He converted for a first down or a touchdown on 53 percent of his third-down chances, while the rest of the Giants were at 44 percent and the league average was 40 percent. The reason why his DVOA isn't higher is his inability to do much after he catches the ball. The average receiver gained 15 yards per third-down catch, but Smith only gained 11. Over the course of 40 or 50 catches a season, that adds up. Smith also had five completions on third down that came up a yard short of the sticks; granted, the Giants are better than most teams at converting with one yard to go, but DVOA doesn't link those two plays together, nor should it. Smith will need to improve after the catch and run more precise routes to go from being a good third-down target to an elite one. Although he's been billed as the starting flanker in place of the departed Amani Toomer, don't be surprised if Hakeem Nicks takes that spot over the course of the season and Smith moves back into the slot.

Donte' Stallworth   Height: 6-0   Weight: 197 College: Tennessee   Draft: 2002/1 (13) Born: 10-Nov-1980 Age: 29 Risk: N/A

Year	Team	G	Rec	Pass	Yds	C%	Yd/C	TD	YAC	Rk	DVOA	Rk	DYAR	Rk	YAR	Short	Mid	Deep	Bomb
2006	PHI	12	38	78	725	49%	19.1	5	5.6	4	8.0%	30	127	37	134	19%	37%	29%	15%
2007	NE	16	46	74	697	62%	15.2	3	6.8	2	12.2%	20	150	28	146	42%	34%	8%	15%
2008	CLE	11	17	45	170	38%	10.0	1	5.1	--	-40.0%	53	-91	63	-101	49%	33%	5%	13%

Even before Stallworth was involved in a DUI auto accident that killed a pedestrian, the Browns were probably writing him out of their plans. The team had already traded Kellen Winslow, a sign that they were aggressively dumping bad apples from the bushel. Stallworth's yards-per-catch are in a three-year tailspin, making him a big-play receiver who no longer makes big plays. While Stallworth's bad behavior didn't get a lot of pre-accident ink, his four-year, four-team travelogue says a lot about his overall character. We've probably seen the last of Stallworth, who once had the talent to be a true number-one receiver, but squandered one too many opportunities and couldn't stay healthy.

John Standeford   Height: 6-4   Weight: 206 College: Purdue   Draft: 2004/FA Born: 15-Apr-1982 Age: 27 Risk: Red

Year	Team	G	Rec	Pass	Yds	C%	Yd/C	TD	YAC	Rk	DVOA	Rk	DYAR	Rk	YAR	Short	Mid	Deep	Bomb
2008	DET	9	15	33	244	45%	16.3	0	2.7	--	-24.3%	--	-30	--	-45	18%	39%	21%	21%
2009	DET		24	45	264	53%	11.0	1			-12.7%								

The Lions had Megatron at one receiver position. On the other side, they started with Thundercracker before resorting to Frenzy, then Rumble, and finally Laserbeak. Forced into the starting lineup after Shaun McDonald and Mike Furrey went on IR, Standeford ended up being part of our favorite Lions play of the season. On second-and-1 from the Vikings 30, the Lions lined up in the I-Formation and ran play-action. Not a bad idea, of course — sell the play fake, try and hit Calvin Johnson going to the end zone, right? Nope — Lions offensive coordinator Jim Colletto kept Johnson in to pass block on the play so he could send Standeford out on a pattern. Remember, readers: These are the professionals.

Syndric Steptoe

Height: 5-9   Weight: 194   College: Arizona   Draft: 2007/7 (234)   Born: 6-Dec-1984   Age: 25   Risk: Yellow

Year	Team	G	Rec	Pass	Yds	C%	Yd/C	TD	YAC	Rk	DVOA	Rk	DYAR	Rk	YAR	Short	Mid	Deep	Bomb
2008	CLE	16	19	41	182	46%	9.6	0	2.9	--	-40.4%	--	-81	--	-97	44%	47%	9%	0%
2009	CLE		16	25	203	64%	12.7	1			-3.5%								

Take away a 53-yard reception against the Jaguars, and Steptoe averaged just 7.2 yards per catch and 3.2 yards per target. Steptoe was the Browns' third receiver for most of the year and actually finished fourth on the team in receiving yards despite almost transcendently awful numbers for several stretches. For example, Steptoe caught six passes for 31 yards in five games in November, catching at least one pass in each game. The Browns drafted two rookie receivers and signed two others as free agents, so Steptoe can probably be consigned to the bulging "What were they thinking?" file for the 2008 Browns.

Brandon Stokley

Height: 5-11   Weight: 197   College: Louisiana-Lafayette   Draft: 1999/4 (105)   Born: 23-Jun-1976   Age: 33   Risk: Red

Year	Team	G	Rec	Pass	Yds	C%	Yd/C	TD	YAC	Rk	DVOA	Rk	DYAR	Rk	YAR	Short	Mid	Deep	Bomb
2006	IND	4	8	11	85	73%	10.6	1	3.6	--	34.1%	--	38	--	39	25%	42%	17%	17%
2007	DEN	13	40	71	635	56%	15.9	5	3.0	64	25.2%	8	216	19	207	14%	55%	20%	11%
2008	DEN	15	49	85	528	58%	10.8	3	3.4	49	-5.7%	55	47	55	66	34%	55%	8%	4%
2009	DEN		33	54	410	61%	12.3	1			10.3%								

On one hand, Brandon Stokley last year continued to do what he does best: play slot receiver. Only three of the 85 passes to Stokley came without three or more receivers on the field. On the other hand, Stokley wasn't running the same deep routes down the seam that he ran in years past. He had the same catch rate, but on easier passes — in fact, Stokley's catch rate was the same on short throws (within five yards of the line of scrimmage) as it was on medium and deep throws. He's supposed to play the Wes Welker role in the Josh McDaniels offense, but that ain't gonna fly if he's only catching three out of every five passes.

Maurice Stovall

Height: 6-5   Weight: 222   College: Notre Dame   Draft: 2006/3 (90)   Born: 21-Feb-1985   Age: 24   Risk: Red

Year	Team	G	Rec	Pass	Yds	C%	Yd/C	TD	YAC	Rk	DVOA	Rk	DYAR	Rk	YAR	Short	Mid	Deep	Bomb
2006	TB	9	7	13	102	54%	14.6	0	3.5	--	-6.7%	--	6	--	6	30%	50%	20%	0%
2007	TB	15	10	13	86	77%	8.6	1	2.3	--	8.4%	--	21	--	21	38%	54%	0%	8%
2008	TB	5	3	7	25	43%	8.3	0	0.7	--	-85.8%	--	-38	--	-35	14%	71%	14%	0%
2009	TB		16	28	125	57%	7.8	1			4.5%								

The deeply religious Stovall makes the job easy for his coaches, and his willingness to serve as a gunner will always earn him a roster spot, but it would be nice if some more receiving skills came with that 6-foot-5 frame. At the moment, he can't even beat Michael Clayton out for the "Designated Tall Guy" spot in the Tampa Bay starting lineup. He missed most of last year with a hamstring injury, but should be 100 percent for 2009.

Chansi Stuckey

Height: 5-11   Weight: 197   College: Clemson   Draft: 2007/7 (235)   Born: 4-Oct-1983   Age: 26   Risk: Yellow

Year	Team	G	Rec	Pass	Yds	C%	Yd/C	TD	YAC	Rk	DVOA	Rk	DYAR	Rk	YAR	Short	Mid	Deep	Bomb
2008	NYJ	15	32	45	359	71%	11.2	3	5.6	--	24.1%	--	131	--	137	55%	33%	10%	2%
2009	NYJ		43	69	511	62%	11.9	2			-5.1%								

Stuckey missed his whole rookie year with a broken foot, but made an immediate impression as a sophomore, hauling in Brett Favre's fourth-down desperation heave against Miami for what proved to be the decisive touchdown in Week 1. But as the season went along, Stuckey seemed to get lost in the shuffle, losing out on playing time to tight end Dustin Keller. Even so, Stuckey finished second in DYAR among receivers who caught fewer than 50 passes behind San Diego's Malcom Floyd, and his DVOA was by far the best on the team. Ideally,

Stuckey would be a third receiver, but with no established option behind Jerricho Cotchery, he may be called upon to play in base sets.

Limas Sweed
Height: 6-4   Weight: 212 College: Texas   Draft: 2008/2 (53)   Born: 25-Dec-1984 Age: 24 Risk: Red

Year	Team	G	Rec	Pass	Yds	C%	Yd/C	TD	YAC	Rk	DVOA	Rk	DYAR	Rk	YAR	Short	Mid	Deep	Bomb
2008	PIT	11	6	10	64	60%	10.7	0	2.7	--	-46.2%	--	-24	--	-21	30%	40%	20%	10%
2009	PIT		29	60	470	49%	16.0	4			6.7%								

Sweed is best known as the guy who dropped a 50-yard bomb before halftime of the AFC Championship game against the Ravens. Sweed was wide-open for an easy touchdown. After he dropped the ball, he sulked on the field, forcing the Steelers to use a precious timeout in a still-close game. Sweed made a clutch third-down catch later in the game, and he spent the offseason putting in extra practice time in an effort to claim Nate Washington's third-wideout role. The team signed Shaun McDonald after the draft, but Sweed still has an inside track on the role: His size makes him a better prospect as a blocker, and he's a better deep threat than McDonald.

Devin Thomas
Height: 6-2   Weight: 215 College: Michigan State   Draft: 2008/2 (34)   Born: 15-Nov-1986 Age: 23 Risk: Red

Year	Team	G	Rec	Pass	Yds	C%	Yd/C	TD	YAC	Rk	DVOA	Rk	DYAR	Rk	YAR	Short	Mid	Deep	Bomb
2008	WAS	16	15	27	120	56%	8.0	0	2.7	--	-28.4%	--	-33	--	-45	46%	42%	13%	0%
2009	WAS		35	54	361	65%	10.3	1			8.6%								

Arguably the top receiver prospect in the 2008 draft class, Thomas was a huge disappointment for the Redskins. Jim Zorn said that the team was "spoon-feeding" Thomas the playbook, while his iffy route running limited him to bubble screens and quick hitches for most of the season; he wasn't even thrown a deep pass until Week 13. It's worth noting that Thomas barely saw the field until his junior year of college, so it's no surprise that he's unrefined and struggles to adjust to a new level of competition quickly. At the moment, he is a receiver who works much better on paper than he does on — or in — practice. Missing the first few days of OTAs in March wasn't a good sign.

Amani Toomer
Height: 6-3   Weight: 208 College: Michigan   Draft: 1996/2 (34)   Born: 8-Sep-1974   Age: 35 Risk: N/A

Year	Team	G	Rec	Pass	Yds	C%	Yd/C	TD	YAC	Rk	DVOA	Rk	DYAR	Rk	YAR	Short	Mid	Deep	Bomb
2006	NYG	8	32	50	360	64%	11.3	3	1.4	83	7.4%	34	79	53	88	26%	46%	17%	11%
2007	NYG	16	59	104	760	57%	12.9	3	3.5	49	3.2%	41	133	36	120	32%	42%	22%	4%
2008	NYG	16	48	88	580	55%	12.1	4	2.8	65	-2.3%	49	77	44	63	27%	45%	18%	9%

A Giants lifer, Toomer spent his final year with the team as an adequate starter, although his rate of passes defensed (greater than 11 percent), his low yards after catch figure, and the decrease in his catch rate indicate a player who's struggling more and more to gain separation from opposing defensive backs. The one place he was effective was in the red zone; there, his 8.7% DVOA was the best amongst Giants players who were thrown more than two passes. Toomer criticized the organization after the offseason, claiming that they'd let Kurt Warner, Kerry Collins, and Ike Hilliard leave before they were done as players. If Toomer wants to eke out a veteran existence in the same way that Hilliard has, he'll need to be on the right team at the right time. At the time of writing, no one had even been rumored to be showing interest in Toomer, so he might have 31 more organizations to criticize shortly.

Jerheme Urban
Height: 6-3   Weight: 212 College: Trinity International   Draft: 2003/FA   Born: 26-Nov-1980 Age: 29 Risk: Green

Year	Team	G	Rec	Pass	Yds	C%	Yd/C	TD	YAC	Rk	DVOA	Rk	DYAR	Rk	YAR	Short	Mid	Deep	Bomb
2007	ARI	10	22	38	329	58%	15.0	2	3.7	--	22.4%	--	101	--	92	20%	43%	29%	9%
2008	ARI	16	34	51	448	67%	13.2	4	4.7	17	8.5%	24	88	41	89	32%	47%	15%	6%
2009	ARI		21	37	259	57%	12.3	1			-12.4%								

Urban played exceptionally well last year as Arizona's fourth receiver, which is proof that virtually anyone could have excelled as Arizona's fourth receiver. Urban is the definition of "replacement level." He was replaced in Seattle, he was replaced in Dallas, and the Cardinals are hoping that Early Doucet will replace him sooner rather than later in Arizona.

Bobby Wade
Height: 5-10   Weight: 193   College: Arizona   Draft: 2003/5 (139)   Born: 25-Feb-1981   Age: 28   Risk: Yellow

Year	Team	G	Rec	Pass	Yds	C%	Yd/C	TD	YAC	Rk	DVOA	Rk	DYAR	Rk	YAR	Short	Mid	Deep	Bomb
2006	TEN	16	33	58	461	57%	14.0	2	5.0	11	5.8%	38	81	52	76	40%	20%	32%	8%
2007	MIN	16	54	83	647	65%	12.0	3	3.0	65	8.1%	30	131	38	132	43%	43%	9%	6%
2008	MIN	16	53	89	645	60%	12.2	2	4.4	24	-15.6%	70	-21	71	-3	40%	48%	8%	3%
2009	MIN		49	87	517	56%	10.5	2			-5.6%								

Wade is your standard Chili's or Applebee's; he's mediocre wide receiver comfort food. As far as possession receivers go, Wade's probably one of the worst starters in the league. He's too small to block on the outside and struggles to seal the edge, costing Adrian Peterson some yards when he tries to bounce plays out wide. He drops one pass for every six he catches, doesn't go deep (with an average catch eight yards away from the line of scrimmage), isn't good on third down, and is a subpar punt returner. He's steady and works hard, so teams know what they're going to get with Wade … but why'd you want that in your starting lineup, we don't know.

Javon Walker
Height: 6-3   Weight: 220   College: Florida State   Draft: 2002/1 (20)   Born: 14-Oct-1978   Age: 31   Risk: Red

Year	Team	G	Rec	Pass	Yds	C%	Yd/C	TD	YAC	Rk	DVOA	Rk	DYAR	Rk	YAR	Short	Mid	Deep	Bomb
2006	DEN	16	69	126	1084	55%	15.7	8	5.0	12	8.0%	31	207	18	214	29%	40%	14%	18%
2007	DEN	8	26	50	287	52%	11.0	0	4.5	24	-30.7%	82	-68	78	-49	34%	53%	9%	4%
2008	OAK	8	15	32	196	47%	13.1	1	2.1	--	-11.0%	--	4	--	-8	21%	52%	24%	3%
2009	OAK		15	35	190	43%	12.7	1			-25.5%								

Walker's career now lies at the bottom of a gorge, having gone careening off the cliff two years ago. The awesome 2006 comeback from a torn ACL is a distant memory after two years of chronic knee and ankle injuries. He had further knee surgery in April without even telling the Raiders about it until May. Walker will go down as one of the worst veteran signings in NFL history, but at least the Raiders were able to convince him to restructure his six-year, $55 million contract he signed in 2008. Walker agreed to ditch a $5 million roster bonus and lower his annual salary in return for having that salary guaranteed in 2009-2010. Even that guarantee might not keep him around; he's the fourth or fifth receiver right now, and it isn't like a 31-year-old with a gimpy knee is going to play special teams for you.

Mike Walker
Height: 6-2   Weight: 209   College: Central Florida   Draft: 2007/3 (79)   Born: 11-Nov-1984   Age: 25   Risk: Red

Year	Team	G	Rec	Pass	Yds	C%	Yd/C	TD	YAC	Rk	DVOA	Rk	DYAR	Rk	YAR	Short	Mid	Deep	Bomb
2008	JAC	9	16	30	217	53%	13.6	0	1.5	--	3.7%	--	38	--	18	10%	52%	28%	10%
2009	JAC		39	64	503	61%	12.9	2			4.3%								

For two straight training camps, Walker has blown away the Jacksonville brass with excellent hands, crisp route-running, and a positive work ethic — and then suffered knee injuries. This year, he's penciled into the starting lineup, and when you combine Walker's inexperience and injury history with our extremely optimistic projection for the Jacksonville offense, you get a massive risk-reward candidate for fantasy players. The Jaguars' other new starting wideout, Torry Holt, is a Mike Walker believer; after his arrival in Jacksonville, he told reporters "I was telling Mike Walker the other day, if we can keep him healthy, he has to think and train in the Pro Bowl level." Is that above or below the mezzanine?

Mike Wallace

Height: 6-0   Weight: 199 College: Mississippi   Draft: 2009/3 (84)   Born: 1-Aug-1986   Age: 23 Risk: Red

Year	Team	G	Rec	Pass	Yds	C%	Yd/C	TD	YAC	Rk	DVOA	Rk	DYAR	Rk	YAR	Short	Mid	Deep	Bomb
2009	PIT		21	35	269	61%	12.7	1			1.7%								

Wallace is a good match for the Steelers, who needed a deep slot option to replace Nate Washington and a return man to replace everyone who has held that role this decade. Wallace only caught 101 passes in his final three seasons at Ole Miss, but he made them count, averaging 18.9 yards per catch and scoring 15 touchdowns. He caught an 88-yard pass against Louisiana-Monroe in 2008, a 77-yarder against Florida in 2007, a 72-yarder against Mississippi State in 2008, and a 68-yarder against Missouri in 2007. All that and Andy Rooney, tonight on *60 Minutes*.

Kevin Walter

Height: 6-3   Weight: 221 College: Eastern Michigan   Draft: 2003/7 (255) Born: 4-Aug-1981   Age: 28 Risk: Yellow

Year	Team	G	Rec	Pass	Yds	C%	Yd/C	TD	YAC	Rk	DVOA	Rk	DYAR	Rk	YAR	Short	Mid	Deep	Bomb
2006	HOU	16	17	21	160	81%	9.4	0	2.7	--	2.7%	--	25	--	27	38%	52%	0%	10%
2007	HOU	16	65	106	800	61%	12.3	4	2.6	74	9.1%	29	184	25	182	27%	50%	12%	12%
2008	HOU	16	60	95	899	63%	15.0	8	4.9	16	16.8%	10	225	16	229	33%	44%	17%	6%
2009	HOU		65	108	819	60%	12.6	5			2.9%								

In one of the odder individual performances of the season, Kevin Walter suddenly became a deep threat. The deep outside opposite the dominant Andre Johnson is an obvious defensive weak spot, but Walter was an unlikely player to take advantage. After never averaging more than 12.3 yards per reception, Walter averaged 15. In his first five years, Walter caught 11 passes that gained 20 yards and 2 that gained 40 or more. Last year, he caught 15 that gained 20 or more and four that gained 40 or more. Maybe it was a new level of performance, but Walter screams regression to the mean.

Hines Ward

Height: 6-0   Weight: 205 College: Georgia   Draft: 1998/3 (92)   Born: 8-Mar-1976   Age: 33 Risk: Yellow

Year	Team	G	Rec	Pass	Yds	C%	Yd/C	TD	YAC	Rk	DVOA	Rk	DYAR	Rk	YAR	Short	Mid	Deep	Bomb
2006	PIT	14	74	127	975	59%	13.2	6	4.6	19	4.3%	40	171	25	145	29%	44%	20%	7%
2007	PIT	13	71	113	732	64%	10.3	7	3.1	61	2.0%	43	127	40	146	30%	50%	19%	2%
2008	PIT	16	81	126	1043	65%	12.9	7	5.0	13	16.2%	11	289	7	294	33%	48%	14%	6%
2009	PIT		91	144	1127	63%	12.4	8			9.3%								

What a remarkable, consistent season for a 32-year-old who appeared to be entering the decline phase of his career after 2007. Ward posted five-year highs in receptions and yards. He had a positive DVOA on first, second, and third downs (27.6%, 4.6%, and 8.3%) and in the red zone (10.7% on a team-high 21 targets). He caught four or more passes in 11 games. His blocking remains so outstanding that the Steelers frequently run sweeps to Ward's side of the field, counting on him to crack safeties and linebackers. Santonio Holmes has finally emerged as the true number-one receiver in Pittsburgh, but Ward is such a natural possession receiver that he should be able to slide into a 50-catch niche and stay there for a few years.

Nate Washington

Height: 6-1   Weight: 185 College: Tiffin   Draft: 2005/FA   Born: 28-Aug-1983 Age: 26 Risk: Yellow

Year	Team	G	Rec	Pass	Yds	C%	Yd/C	TD	YAC	Rk	DVOA	Rk	DYAR	Rk	YAR	Short	Mid	Deep	Bomb
2006	PIT	16	35	69	624	51%	17.8	4	3.1	55	16.9%	14	151	29	143	22%	38%	22%	18%
2007	PIT	16	29	56	450	52%	15.5	5	2.5	77	16.5%	16	124	41	133	9%	44%	26%	20%
2008	PIT	16	40	78	631	51%	15.8	3	3.3	51	-0.8%	44	70	49	51	11%	49%	21%	19%
2009	TEN		38	64	588	59%	15.5	2			1.2%								

Washington spent three years as the Steelers' third receiver and one of their favorite deep threats. He caught four passes of 40 or more yards last season, and his consistently low catch rates are partly the result of all the deep passes he had to chase. Now in Tennessee, he'll fill a 1B or 2A role opposite veteran Justin Gage. Eventually, the Titans want to start Washington and rookie Kenny Britt, with Washington as the deep receiver and Britt the possession guy — but it may take a year for Britt to develop, and Washington doesn't have the skills or resume of a true number-one receiver. The Titans have a habit of Peter Principle promotions at wide receiver since Derrick Mason left, and Washington looks like another good role player who is about to be miscast.

Reggie Wayne

Height: 6-0　Weight: 203　College: Miami　　Draft: 2001/1 (30)　Born: 17-Nov-1978　Age: 31　Risk: Green

Year	Team	G	Rec	Pass	Yds	C%	Yd/C	TD	YAC	Rk	DVOA	Rk	DYAR	Rk	YAR	Short	Mid	Deep	Bomb
2006	IND	16	86	137	1310	63%	15.2	9	2.3	76	30.9%	3	469	2	440	21%	46%	19%	14%
2007	IND	16	104	156	1510	67%	14.5	10	3.8	40	23.1%	9	450	2	440	32%	35%	18%	14%
2008	IND	16	82	130	1145	63%	14.0	6	3.6	44	19.2%	9	332	6	327	33%	38%	13%	17%
2009	IND		92	143	1153	64%	12.5	10			16.0%								

Wayne was considered Marvin Harrison's understudy for so long that even as Wayne became the better player, people always assumed he was young. In fact, Wayne turns 31 this season and probably is on the downside of his career. Wayne was dominant in 2007 when Harrison was not on the field, but numerous attempts to revitalize Harrison last year led to fewer balls being fed to Wayne. Still, Wayne remains one of the very best receivers in football, and he still is plenty good to put up monstrous numbers as Manning feels less pressure to keep another receiver happy.

Wes Welker

Height: 5-9　Weight: 190　College: Texas Tech　　Draft: 2004/FA　Born: 1-May-1981　Age: 28　Risk: Yellow

Year	Team	G	Rec	Pass	Yds	C%	Yd/C	TD	YAC	Rk	DVOA	Rk	DYAR	Rk	YAR	Short	Mid	Deep	Bomb
2006	MIA	16	67	100	687	67%	10.3	1	4.1	30	-1.1%	50	86	49	85	53%	34%	8%	5%
2007	NE	16	112	145	1175	77%	10.5	8	5.7	6	21.3%	11	383	4	354	65%	29%	6%	0%
2008	NE	16	111	150	1165	75%	10.5	3	6.6	2	3.4%	31	187	20	195	63%	30%	6%	1%
2009	NE		107	152	1113	70%	10.4	8			27.2%								

With New England's offense morphing into a YAC machine after Tom Brady's knee injury, Welker became the pointman. He led the NFL with 744 total yards after catch, and his ability to take the quick slant and convert it into yardage will make him Brady's security blanket once again. He's also great at splitting little combo routes with Randy Moss — the Pats know how to take advantage of the challenges that the duo brings to any secondary.

Roddy White

Height: 6-1　Weight: 201　College: UAB　　Draft: 2005/1 (27)　Born: 2-Nov-1981　Age: 28　Risk: Green

Year	Team	G	Rec	Pass	Yds	C%	Yd/C	TD	YAC	Rk	DVOA	Rk	DYAR	Rk	YAR	Short	Mid	Deep	Bomb
2006	ATL	16	30	64	506	47%	16.9	0	2.2	78	-12.6%	65	0	65	6	15%	45%	13%	27%
2007	ATL	16	83	137	1202	61%	14.5	6	5.5	7	1.3%	45	149	29	167	34%	41%	16%	10%
2008	ATL	16	88	148	1382	59%	15.7	7	4.1	33	22.1%	6	399	3	361	27%	45%	17%	12%
2009	ATL		84	156	1183	54%	14.1	8			11.0%								

Perhaps the only useful thing Joe Horn did as a Falcon was instill the work ethic in White that he needed to take his game to the next level. As White recalled in an interview with Yahoo's Michael Silver, Horn said "… you can't just come to work every day — you've got to come to work and work every day." Since 2007, White's been among the best receivers in football. He was always fast, but the time spent honing his craft has resulted in dramatically increased route-running, opening up opportunities for big plays on the second level with double moves. Indeed, White's success rate of 47 percent on passes thrown 30 or more yards down the field was second in the league to Steve Smith (minimum: 10 attempts). The Falcons star wasn't part of the "Best Receiver In Football" discussion that raged during the playoffs, but only Larry Fitzgerald and Andre Johnson were superior in our advanced metrics a year ago. In the final year of his rookie deal, White's deserving of the huge contract he's about to receive.

Demetrius Williams

Height: 6-2 Weight: 191 College: Oregon   Draft: 2006/4 (111) Born: 28-Mar-1983 Age: 26 Risk: Red

Year	Team	G	Rec	Pass	Yds	C%	Yd/C	TD	YAC	Rk	DVOA	Rk	DYAR	Rk	YAR	Short	Mid	Deep	Bomb
2006	BAL	16	22	45	396	49%	18.0	2	5.6	--	1.7%	--	49	--	53	11%	54%	22%	14%
2007	BAL	9	20	47	290	43%	14.5	0	1.5	--	-28.9%	--	-63	--	-47	16%	45%	20%	18%
2008	BAL	7	13	23	180	57%	13.8	1	4.1	--	-14.5%	--	-3	--	1	27%	45%	14%	14%
2009	BAL		27	49	511	55%	18.9	2			-1.7%								

The Ravens ran the ball 592 times and threw 121 passes to Derrick Mason. That left only a handful of footballs to distribute to the rest of the receivers, and Williams was the least-used third wideout in the NFL. Williams was targeted just 23 times; by contrast, Cardinals fourth wideout Jerame Urban got 51 targets, and Marty Booker, the fourth receiver on a run-oriented Bears team, got 49 targets. Williams missed the second half of last season with a foot injury, and he wasn't at full speed by the draft, but Ozzie Newsome said he didn't select a receiver early in the draft because he thought Williams was a legitimate number three. Considering how infrequently the Ravens use their third wideout, Newsome might just have been applying common-sense economics.

Reggie Williams

Height: 6-3 Weight: 223 College: Washington   Draft: 2004/1 (9) Born: 17-May-1983 Age: 26 Risk: N/A

Year	Team	G	Rec	Pass	Yds	C%	Yd/C	TD	YAC	Rk	DVOA	Rk	DYAR	Rk	YAR	Short	Mid	Deep	Bomb
2006	JAC	16	52	91	616	57%	11.8	4	4.7	17	-13.7%	66	-7	66	13	47%	36%	11%	5%
2007	JAC	15	38	60	629	63%	16.6	10	5.8	4	25.7%	7	183	26	183	33%	37%	23%	7%
2008	JAC	16	37	63	364	60%	9.8	3	2.0	75	-4.8%	54	40	59	39	35%	40%	20%	5%

Another primary culprit in the Great Jacksonville Receiver Disaster of 2008, Williams compounded his own limbo by managing to get himself arrested for DWI and marijuana possession just two hours into the free agency period. That he shares so many professional debits with fellow Washington Huskies alum Jerramy Stevens should come as no surprise to those familiar with Rick Neuheisel's teams in the early part of this decade; Williams' extracurricular activities were well-known way back when. Once again, Jacksonville's front office went for athleticism over football sense.

Roy Williams

Height: 6-2 Weight: 212 College: Texas   Draft: 2004/1 (7) Born: 20-Dec-1981 Age: 27 Risk: Yellow

Year	Team	G	Rec	Pass	Yds	C%	Yd/C	TD	YAC	Rk	DVOA	Rk	DYAR	Rk	YAR	Short	Mid	Deep	Bomb
2006	DET	16	82	151	1310	54%	16.0	7	4.2	28	8.7%	27	250	10	251	16%	39%	30%	15%
2007	DET	12	64	105	838	61%	13.1	5	4.6	23	1.0%	47	114	43	111	28%	42%	18%	12%
2008	DET/DAL	15	36	82	430	44%	11.9	2	3.5	47	-17.0%	75	-29	73	-74	20%	49%	17%	13%
2009	DAL		67	118	982	57%	14.7	9			14.7%								

The move to acquire Williams in the middle of the season was impossibly ill-advised, both on and off the field. With Terrell Owens already signed to a new long-term deal and the combination of Patrick Crayton and Miles Austin playing well across the field, the team didn't need another wide receiver. Without any connection to the Cowboys' scheme, it would obviously take Williams several weeks to simply learn the complexities of Jason Garrett's playbook. Furthermore, Williams was an unrestricted free agent following the season who played his college ball at Texas and high school football for the school featured in *Friday Night Lights*. Do you think he might have considered the Cowboys as an option? The team gave up a first-round pick for what essentially amounted to ten games of an underprepared receiver.

While Williams is considered the successful one of the three consecutive Matt Millen first-round wide receivers, there's reason to believe he's not quite a stud receiver. His 2006 season sticks out like a sore stumb statistically: It's the only season in which he was able to play all 16 games, and it came in Mike Martz's pass-happy system. Jerry Jones is expecting more seasons like that 2006 campaign, but it may have been Williams' peak as opposed to a sign of things to come.

Troy Williamson

Height: 6-1   Weight: 203 College: South Carolina   Draft: 2005/1 (7)   Born: 30-Apr-1983 Age: 26 Risk: Red

Year	Team	G	Rec	Pass	Yds	C%	Yd/C	TD	YAC	Rk	DVOA	Rk	DYAR	Rk	YAR	Short	Mid	Deep	Bomb
2006	MIN	14	37	76	455	49%	12.3	0	4.9	14	-23.8%	80	-68	81	-75	29%	41%	9%	21%
2007	MIN	11	18	38	240	47%	13.3	1	2.8	--	-19.5%	--	-21	--	-25	22%	54%	3%	22%
2008	JAC	8	5	13	30	38%	6.0	1	0.8	--	-45.0%	--	-33	--	-37	23%	38%	0%	38%
2009	JAC		21	41	327	51%	15.6	2			-10.7%								

Yet another first-round receiver bust that played for the Jaguars in 2008, but at least Jacksonville didn't draft this one. Williamson, who came to Jacksonville from Minnesota, gained more notoriety last season for his desire to fight Brad Childress at the 50-yard line before the November 23 contest between the Jags and Vikings. Childress countered with the notion that he would weigh in at "190 pounds of twisted steel and rompin', stompin' dynamite," according to the *Florida Times-Union*.

GOING DEEP

Sam Aiken, NE: Sam Aiken is a special teams standout and the occasional fourth read for Tom Brady. The Patriots didn't need two of those guys, which is why Kelley Washington now plays for Baltimore. (2008 stats: 8-for-11, 101 yards, 7.0% DVOA, 18 DYAR.)

Jake Allen, GB: The Mississippi College grad was a D-III All-American in 2008, and made the Packers' practice squad as an unrestricted free agent, where he stayed for the entire season. His given name is Jjathus Illimski Allen; Illimski would be our name if we were a Russian MC, so we approve.

Danny Amendola, PHI: When we talk about players like Wes Welker being easy to find — even if they're not as good as Welker — Amendola's the guy that comes to mind. Amendola replaced Welker at Texas Tech and played just as well, if not better, than Welker did; although he weighs eight pounds less than Welker, has two inches on him, and is slightly faster. Just like his predecessor, Amendola has great instincts for finding holes in zones and makes his cuts at a high speed, which allows him to embarrass linebackers and safeties in coverage. Most importantly, he went undrafted, which is our point: Guys like this simply aren't difficult to find, especially with the proliferation of spread offenses in college, so there's no reason to pay Welker $5.5 million (as the Patriots will this year) when you can get Amendola, who's realistically 85 to 90 percent of the same player, for the league minimum. He was on the Cowboys' practice squad and signed with the Eagles in the offseason; they could use him as a slot receiver and third-down weapon.

Devin Aromashodu, CHI: Aromashodu has bounced around practice squads for three years, with only seven catches for the Colts in 2007 to his name. He's a deep threat, as evidenced by his 94-yard touchdown catch in the preseason a year ago, but has no ability over the middle.

Adrian Arrington, NO: Last year's seventh-round pick struggled with turf toe as a rookie and then hamstring issues during OTAs; he is quickly gaining a rep as injury-prone. If he can stay healthy, the Saints' fifth receiver job is waiting for him.

Dallas Baker, PIT: A seventh-rounder in 2008, Baker lost his spot on the active roster to Limas Sweed after suffering a shoulder injury in Week 5, and spent the rest of the year on the practice squad. He may never get the opportunity to add to his lone NFL catch, a six-yard grab against the Colts.

Gary Banks, SD: It's never a good sign when Googling your name brings up your college profile page before your professional profile page. He's 28 and only in his second season as a pro, so let's figure out why he's on the roster. Banks was a fifth-round pick of the Cubs in the 2000 MLB Draft and hit .224/.299/.274 in four seasons without getting past Low-A. That led him to Troy, where he played four seasons as a wide receiver and part-time quarterba … ah, there it is. He'll backup LaDainian Tomlinson in the Wildcat if he makes it onto the active roster — and if the Chargers run any Wildcat-style plays, which they didn't in 2008.

Ramses Barden, NYG: An absolutely gigantic wideout, the 6-foot-6 Barden is tied with Matt Jones and Clarence Moore as the tallest wide receivers in recent NFL history, but his body type is closer to that of the man he could replace, Plaxico Burress. The problem? While Burress was, for better or worse, a very good receiver who was extremely tall, Barden is a raw athlete with good hands who just happens to be tall. New York's third-round pick struggled to get separation against FCS (I-AA) cornerbacks while playing at Cal Poly, so NFL corners should be able to make their living in his back pocket. He's got a lot of work to do before he might ever turn into something; at the moment, he's essentially a target on fade patterns in the end zone.

Taye Biddle, NYG: The former Panthers wideout bounced around the Lions and Giants' practice squads, but he became well-known after being randomly shot in his hometown of Decatur, Alabama, in January, only two months after he replaced a wounded Plaxico Burress on the roster. Biddle is expected to make a full recovery, but he's not likely to make the Giants roster in 2009.

D.J. Boldin, DET: A late-bloomer of sorts, Boldin (younger brother of Anquan) only caught 26 passes for 361 yards in 2005 and 2007 and sat out 2006 because of academic reasons. Last year, he came on strong as a possession receiver extraordinaire with 81 receptions for Wake Forest, but for his career he only averaged 11.2 yards per catch. He went undrafted and signed with Detroit.

John Broussard, CHI: Another of the Bears' undersized deep threats, the former Jaguar will be competing with Devin Aromashodu for a roster spot.

Freddie Brown, CIN: No, Eagles fans, don't worry; he's not the result of a bizarre experiment attempting to mate Freddie Mitchell with Reggie Brown. He's a Utah product who will fight with Quan Cosby for the last spot on the Bengals' roster.

Michael Bumpus, SEA: Washington State's all-time leader in pass receptions and punt return yards, Bumpus went undrafted, but was signed by his home-state team when every other receiver they had turned to dust. (Heck, the moving fees were low.) He soon joined them on the injured list, and as of April, was sitting out of team drills with foot injuries. (2008 stats: 5-for-8, 48 yards, 1 TD, 4.1% DVOA, 12 DYAR.)

Demetrius Byrd, SD: Byrd makes it to the NFL after two years at JuCo powerhouse Pearl River and two more at LSU, where he showed off the ability to be a good downfield receiver. His timed speed is better than his game speed, but he's a lanky six-footer with good hands. San Diego grabbed him in the seventh round and he's a likely candidate for the practice squad.

Kelly Campbell, TB: The former Minnesota receiver led the CFL last year with 22.6 yards per catch for the Edmonton Eskimos; he'll try to get back into the NFL with the Bucs, who don't exactly have scintillating wide receiver depth.

Drew Carter, FA: Carter's medical record includes not one, not two, but four ACL tears. He blew out his left knee in the first game of his sophomore year at Ohio State. He blew out his right knee near the end of his senior year, then tore it up again when he tried to get back on the field for 2004 rookie minicamps. After three years of nagging ankle issues in Carolina, he signed with Oakland as a free agent and promptly blew out the left knee again during the preseason. Technically there shouldn't be any reason why the fourth ACL tear is harder to rehab than the first ACL tear was, but it's pretty clear by now that Carter's joints and ligaments are simply not as strong as those of the average professional football player. Unsigned as of June. (2007 stats: 38-for-75, 517 yards, 4 TD, -6.6% DVOA, 38 DYAR.)

Jason Carter, CAR: Despite hanging around the league for three years without catching a regular season pass, Carter has had a big influence. In two preseason games as a rookie for Minnesota in 2006, Carter put up 155 yards and two touchdowns catching passes from a rookie quarterback. Who was the rookie quarterback? Yup, Tarvaris Jackson. The Vikings are still chasing that August 2006 magic. Carter has more realistic goals in his sights: first, not missing this season with a knee injury like 2008, and second, winning the fifth receiver spot in Carolina.

Brian Clark, TB: The Bucs picked Sammie Stroughter in the seventh round, and hope he has a career anywhere in the neighborhood of another Oregon State wideout picked in the final round, T.J. Houshmandzadeh. Regardless, the pick probably means the end for Clark in Tampa, although he was born and raised in the city, and teams often give a call to local guys when injuries hit.

Quan Cosby, CIN: Undrafted and undersized (5-foot-9), this Texas product is more quick than he is fast, but he knows how to use his body to shield defenders and he's a polished route-runner. That polish is the only thing that gives him a shot at the NFL. Thanks to four years spent in the Los Angeles Angels organization, Cosby will be 27 before the end of his rookie year in the NFL, which means he is now as good as he's ever going to get.

Keary Colbert, DET: In March of 2008, the Broncos signed Colbert to a three-year contract with a $2.5 million signing bonus. Two games into the season, they gave up on him, trading him to the Seahawks for a fifth-round pick. Seven weeks later, Seattle gave up on him, releasing him outright. The Lions promptly signed him, because they are the Lions and that is what they do. Colbert played on three teams in 2008, and those three teams combined to lose 36 games, which sounds like some kind of record from Hell. If he shows up on your team this fall, we won't think less of you for crying. (2008 stats: 12-for-27, 116 yards, 1 TD, -25.2% DVOA, -26 DYAR.)

Terrance Copper, KC: Just a guy. Played five games for New Orleans in 2008, then two for Baltimore, only on special teams. Signed with Kansas City but unlikely to make the team.

Jarret Dillard, JAC: The prototypical big fish in a small pond, Jacksonville's fifth-round pick had an explosive four years at Rice, catching 292 passes in four seasons (257 in the last three years) at 14.2 yards a catch. Dillard saved his best games for the biggest opponents, catching nine passes for 158 yards against Texas and seven passes for 105 yards against Vanderbilt in 2008, six for 90 yards against Texas Tech in 2007, and seven for 102 yards against UCLA in 2006.

Julian Edelman, NE: Like Josh Cribbs, Edelman is a Kent State quarterback turned NFL all-purpose prospect. The Patriots took him in the seventh round of the draft, and the next guy to say the word "Wildcat" gets a knuckle sandwich.

Dominique Edison, TEN: NFL teams struggle with translating the performance of receivers in spread offenses into a proper analysis of their NFL viability. Edison will see that bet and raise you the issue of playing at a lower level (Stephen F. Austin). Combine all that with the Titans' struggles to scout wide receivers effectively, and what do you get? Hopes so low they're buried underground, that's what.

Robert Ferguson, FA: Ferguson couldn't beat out Sidney Rice or Bobby Wade for the possession receiver spot in Minnesota, so he spent the majority of his time on special teams before being cut in December. He didn't catch on anywhere, and at 29 and having wound up with no one, it might be time for him to start singing "I Guess We're Done." (2008 stats: 3-for-5, 25 yards, -23.1% DVOA, -4 DYAR.)

Yamon Figurs, BAL: Figurs now has two career receptions for 78 yards. The NFL yards per reception record is held by Warren Wells, a Raiders speed merchant from the late 1960s who averaged 23.1 yards per catch. The record holder changes depending on where you set the reception minimum, but unfortunately for Figurs, no one is advocating setting the minimum to two. Figurs fell off as a return man last year. If he loses the return jobs to rookie cornerback Ladarius Webb, he could also lose his roster spot.

Joel Filani, TB: In 2006, Filani's senior season at Texas Tech, he caught 91 passes for around 1,300 yards; Michael Crabtree caught 93 passes for 1,135 yards last year. Filani stands about six-foot-two, weighs 210 pounds, and runs a 4.55 in the 40. Crabtree stands just under six-foot-two, weighs 215 pounds, and may or may not run a 4.5 in the 40. Obviously, Crabtree is a much better receiver than Filani — for one thing, he (Crabtree) had almost 2,000 yards receiving in his junior year — but on paper, the difference isn't nearly as big as you might imagine.

Brooks Foster, STL: Foster has an intriguing blend of size and speed, but his production dropped every year that he played at North Carolina. The Rams desperately need someone to play the role of possession receiver, but Foster is a development project, not an immediate starter.

Eric Fowler, DET: Fowler was waived off the Lions' active roster so that they could sign Drew Henson. To his credit, this didn't make him quit the pro game in disgust. The former Grand Valley State star went back to the practice squad and spent the year there, and he'll try again in 2009.

Will Franklin, OAK: The Chiefs aren't exactly swimming in receiver depth, so it was a little curious when the new administration waived a fourth-round wideout with potential after only one season. Franklin made his way to Detroit on waivers, only to be released around the draft, after which he caught on with Oakland. Franklin runs a 4.37 40-yard dash, so he should only pique Al Davis' interest mildly. (2008 stats: 7-for-17, 83 yards, -53.1% DVOA, -50 DYAR.)

Brandon Gibson, PHI: Gibson is your standard-issue Eagles receiver: 6-foot-1, good hands, decent route runner, good after the catch, can contribute on special teams, you know the type. You've seen one reserve Eagles receiver, you've seen them all. With seemingly 18 wideouts in camp, Gibson will struggle to make the active roster unless Reggie Brown makes himself scarce.

Skyler Green, NO: Green is a former sprint champion who spent two years on the Bengals roster before getting a cup of coffee with the Saints. He looked good in limited action as a return man last year. If he sees time at wide receiver, it means that 10 better receivers somehow vanished, so you should contact the proper authorities and keep your doors and windows locked.

Derek Hagan, NYG: Despite having an opportunity to emerge as a starting wide receiver against limited competition, Hagan failed to make an impact and quickly fell out of favor with Tony Sparano, leading to his release in November. After auditioning for receiver-needy teams like the Vikings and Lions, Hagan caught on with the Giants in December, but did not suit up. He's a big target with some upside, but his inability to play special teams and general obstinance makes it unlikely the light bulb will suddenly flip on.

Marques Hagans, WAS: The one-time Virginia quarterback has plenty of athletic talent, but he's never been able to transition to NFL wide receiver. St. Louis gave up on him before last season, so Kansas City grabbed him for a few weeks and mostly used him as a quarterback for some Wildcat-like trick plays before releasing him. He hooked up with Washington, but we're not sure why. The Redskins already have a college quarterback-turned-NFL wideout to run their trick plays.

Roy Hall, IND: The Peyton Manning/Tom Moore Colts have never developed a late-round receiver as a reliable weapon. Hall is an intriguing talent, but the Colts did not show much faith by drafting a presumptive slot receiver in Austin Collie. Hall had knee surgery early last season that set him back and limited his opportunities.

Chris Hannon, DET: A year in the life of a borderline NFL player: After spending time with the Chiefs and the Panthers in 2007, Hannon ended up with the Seahawks in training camp. He failed to make the team and was signed by the 49ers, who played the Seahawks two weeks later and wanted to know their audibles and other trade secrets. Hannon spent most of the year on their practice squad. After three days on the active roster, he was claimed off waivers by the Dolphins, who were playing the 49ers that week and wanted the same sort of information. He was waived a couple weeks later and signed by the Lions, who had him as one of their game-day inactives for the season-ending loss to the Packers. He's still yet to as much as suit up for an NFL regular season game.

Marcus Henry, NYJ: Henry was only the third player in Jayhawks history to gain more than 1,000 receiving yards in a season, and he left Kansas as the all-time leader in receiving touchdowns with 10. He is a big receiver on a team starved for size, but he didn't show much quickness or ability as a rookie, and he's probably destined for the practice squad.

Glenn Holt, CIN: Holt had a decent 2007, but regressed in 2008. His primary impact in Cincy came on special teams, but in Minnesota, where there is less wideout competition, he may get some time as a slot guy. (2008 stats: 3-for-11, 26 yards, 1 YD, -42.5% DVOA, -28 DYAR.)

Sam Hurd, DAL: Hurd struggled with a high ankle sprain in the preseason, only for it to recur in the regular season and force him into surgery. He wouldn't have had an impact on the offense, anyway. He'll be on special teams and serve as the fourth wide receiver this year, but there are three wide receivers, two tight ends, and three running backs ahead of him for touches, so he won't even see the ball as much as your standard fourth wideout would.

Chad Jackson, DEN: Chad Jackson does not exactly remind Josh McDaniels of the good times. The worst draft pick of the Belichick/Pioli era got cut by New England after just two seasons. Picked up by Denver at midseason, he had one catch for 19 yards and a few kickoff returns. It's hard to imagine him making the team in 2009, much less making an impact.

Adam Jennings, DET: Jennings was in Atlanta, but lost his punt return job to Harry Douglas and was released shortly thereafter. Since he was a consistently below-average punt returner, he caught on with the Lions shortly thereafter.

Manuel Johnson, DAL: We know Johnson's tough, missing only one game last year at Oklahoma after suffering a grotesque dislocation of his elbow. He's not particularly fast, so he's not going to have much upside, but he could stick as a fifth receiver and special teams player after Dallas made him their 12th second-day pick in this year's draft (229th overall).

C.J. Jones, KC: You might figure that a 29-year-old wide receiver who's yet to play in an NFL game would try something different, but Jones made it to the Patriots' active roster last year, five years after he last did so, as a member of the Browns. Scott Pioli brought him along to Kansas City, which makes us wonder whether Jones has compromising pictures.

Jacoby Jones, HOU: The Texans decided that Jones was a return man. Once a player gets that label, it proves hard to shake. In three years, Jones will leave as a free agent looking for playing time as a receiver, only to find out that the Texans were right, and he was best suited to be a full-time return man. (2008 stats: 3-for-5, 81 yards, 54.9% DVOA, 27 DYAR.)

Mark Jones, TEN: With Ryne Robinson out for the season, Jones was a pleasant surprise on punt and kickoff returns for Carolina last season. Even though he is no home-run threat, Jones has bounced from the Giants to the Bucs to the Panthers by following his blocks and protecting the ball. Jones is yet to lose a fumble in more than 200 career returns. Nevertheless, expect the Titans to see a drop-off in average from 2008 returner Chris Carr, who departed for the Ravens in free agency.

Derek Kinder, CHI: Kinder looked to be a top prospect after a great junior year for Pittsburgh in 2006, but he tore his ACL in August of 2007, missed the season, and wasn't all the way back last season. Taken in the seventh round by the Bears, it wouldn't be a surprise to see Kinder stashed on IR for a season while he digests the playbook, allowing Chicago to examine him as a receiver and special teams demon in 2010.

Johnny Knox, CHI: The Abilene-Christian product made his name at the Combine with a 40-yard dash timed as fast as 4.29, moving him all the way up to a fifth-round grade. Knox is a capable kick returner, but with Danieal Manning being the best regular kick returner in the league a year ago, it's hard to see a way for Knox to make it onto the roster.

Quinten Lawrence, KC: In a September 2008 interview with nfldraftblitz.com, Lawrence said that his best-case scenario in the NFL was Steve Smith, but with a twist: "Minus the off-the-field activities that some of these guys get into. I like the way they play on the field, I can't judge them off the field but I like the way they play on field." Weeks later, he broke his ankle and missed the rest of the season. We assume Smith was not responsible. The Chiefs think they got a steal when they took Lawrence in the sixth round, and will use him as a punt returner before attempting to expand his role.

Brandon London, MIA: Claimed off the waiver wire in August, London caught the eye of head coach Tony Sparano. "Just from them watching me out there in practice and seeing my progression in those games definitely caught some people's attention," London told the *Palm Beach Post* in January. "They want me back. I can't wait to come back." London's got a good chance to usurp Ernest Wilford in training camp and make a place for himself. (2008 stats: 3-for-6, 30 yards, -22.6% DVOA, -5 DYAR.)

Glenn Martinez, HOU: Martinez is the kind of guy who would have led NFL Europe in receiving yards if it were still around. He was waived in November when the Broncos had to make room for whatever healthy running backs they could scrounge up. Perhaps Mike Shanahan said nice things about Martinez to his son, because Houston picked him up on a futures contract. (2007 stats: 14-for-24, 175 yards, -2.0% DVOA, 19 DYAR.)

Kenny McKinley, DEN: A fifth-round pick out of South Carolina, McKinley was a four-year starter who caught 207 passes at school. His problem is staying healthy; he struggled with a turf toe as a junior and had hamstring issues as a senior. He looks like a classic Florida-era Spurrier receiver, which, from what we remember, usually meant bust.

Billy McMullen, SEA: Like many receivers on Seattle's 2008 squad, McMullen was signed off the street as a free agent when somebody else got hurt, before eventually going on the injured list himself. Unlike most of these training camp bodies turned regular season starters, McMullen remains on the Seahawks' roster, and will be given a chance to make the team in 2009. He'll be a long shot; the former third-round draft choice already washed out with the Eagles, Vikings, and Redskins. (2008 stats: 7-for-18, 124 yards, 1 TD, -35.2% DVOA, -32 DYAR.)

Brandon Middleton, FA: We covered Middleton's incredible trip through the miasma of suck in the Lions chapter; it's an arguable point that Middleton might have been the worst player on the first 0-16 team in NFL history. Middleton was a free agent at press time. (2008: 1-for-3 for 23 yards, -22.4% DVOA, -2 DYAR; -10.1 points below average on 38 kickoff returns.)

Marko Mitchell, WAS: At 6-foot-4 Mitchell was devastating in Nevada's Pistol attack, but he isn't fast enough to separate from defenders and fails to use his size effectively. Maybe the Redskins figured one Malcolm Kelly wasn't enough.

Kenneth Moore, CAR: In the fifth round of the 2008 draft, Matt Millen thought, "Hey, you know what we need? Another wide receiver." Cut to six months later, the Panthers signed Moore when Ryne Robinson was put on IR for the year. Moore was on the Panthers radar as a North Carolina native and first-team ACC selection at Wake Forest. Despite not catching a regular season pass last year, Moore could contribute due to Carolina's dearth of talent at the position.

Sean Morey, ARI: It says "wide receiver" by his name, and he has caught 11 passes in the decade since the Patriots drafted him out of Brown, but Morey is a special teams gunner first, a kick returner second, a swell teammate third, and a receiver somewhere way down the line. He made the play of his life last October, blocking a punt in overtime that teammate Monty Beisel returned for a touchdown to beat Dallas. He made the Pro Bowl as the NFC's special teamer. He lost Super Bowl XLIII to the Steelers; he won Super Bowl XL with them. His wife played professional hockey in Canada. Between the two of them, it's safe to say the kids never, ever misbehave.

Louis Murphy, OAK: You'll never guess. Louis Murphy is fast! He ran a 4.32 40-yard dash at the Combine, and he's got good size at 6-foot-2, but he failed to record even 40 receptions in a season at Florida. As a prospect, he makes Darrius Heyward-Bey look really, really good.

Ben Obomanu, SEA: Obamanu set a wretched precedent before last season began. When he broke his collarbone in a preseason game against the Raiders, he became the first Seahawks receiver to suffer a season-ending injury, a group that would grow by the week. He'll compete with the likes of Courtney Taylor and Logan Payne for a spot on the Seahawks roster.

Jake O'Connell, KC: O'Connell wasn't considered a prospect of any note after catching 46 passes during his career at Miami of Ohio, but a 4.66 40-yard dash at his Pro Day made him the 237th pick in this year's draft. His chances of becoming Marques Colston are, oh, one-in-300 or so.

Kevin Ogletree, DAL: Ogletree is one of only two receivers in Virginia history with two 50-catch seasons (the other is Billy McMullen), but whoever told him to come out as a junior is an idiot; his route-running and blocking are so raw that he slid all the way out of the draft. Dallas picked him up as a free agent and he could make some noise by 2011 or so.

Kassim Osgood, SD: After holding out last offseason in an attempt to get recognition and an opportunity to play wide receiver, Osgood didn't have a single catch last year and was put on the trade market voluntarily by San Diego in the offseason. He's a special teams demon, but he'll be 30 when his contract expires after the season, and has 32 career catches. That doesn't yield starting wide receiver.

Samie Parker, OAK: Parker was signed by Denver on April 14, released by Denver on August 25, signed by Carolina on August 26, released by Carolina on August 30, signed by Seattle on September 10, and released by Seattle on September 13. Naturally, the Oakland Raiders signed him to a contract this summer.

Logan Payne, SEA: With an STR of 92, Payne was the strongest wide receiver in Madden 09. How the makers of the game were able to measure the blocking prowess of Payne, who has played all of two games in his NFL career, is a mystery, but maybe he'll be able to move inside if the team's tight ends fall like the wideouts did last season. Payne's one of those who fell by the wayside last year, his season ended by a torn MCL in Week 2, but he was reportedly 100 percent at an April minicamp.

Darius Reynaud, MIN: The former West Virginia receiver and return man made it off the Vikings practice squad in November, and contributed 0.33 points of value on eight kickoff returns. Percy Harvin may very well take his role as a return man, which would put Reynaud out of a job.

Brandon Rideau, CHI: Rideau led the Bears in the preseason with 127 yards receiving and three touchdowns, but it wasn't enough for him to make the active roster. He spent the year on the practice squad and will fight with the bevy of rookies the Bears brought in for a roster spot this year.

Courtney Roby, NO: Resigned by the Saints in March, Roby is an adequate return man and special teamer who hasn't caught a pass since 2006. His ability to cover kicks and punts gives him an edge in the fifth wideout battle.

Micah Rucker, NYG: The 6-foot-6, 221-pound Rucker is as raw as it gets; he spent time on the Steelers and Giants practice squad in 2008, and will be in camp with the Giants this year, competing with Ramses Barden for the roster spot that goes to the 6-foot-6 guy.

Lorne Sam, GB: The brother of Bills receiver P.K. Sam, Lorne Sam was a part-time quarterback in college who shockingly did not play as a Wildcat quarterback at any point last year. (The Packers are too busy using two fullbacks at a time to use two quarterbacks at a time.) Sam is extremely raw and will have to put significant work in on his route-running and blocking before he becomes an NFL receiver — same story as his brother, who never did.

Steve Sanders, DET: An undrafted free agent out of Bowling Green, Sanders served a lengthy suspension for doping after he was caught spiking Brandon's drink AND taking steroids for added speed, while rumors have circulated regarding his attendance at illicit poker games. Although he doesn't have very high prospects of an NFL career, Sanders' experience running the Peach Pit After Dark should open up a lucrative career for him as a nightclub proprietor.

Arman Shields, OAK: Arman Shields saw his draft stock drop when a torn ACL cost him all but one game of the 2007 season. The knee was healthy enough for the University of Richmond prospect to run the third-fastest 40 of any wide receiver at the 2008 combine (4.374 seconds), which of course intrigued the Raiders enough for Oakland to grab him in the fourth round. Then the knee went gimpy again; Shields could not get on the practice field consistently, spent all of 2008 on injured reserve, and was still having problems as of this year's minicamp. You know, if the Raiders keep signing all the fast receivers with constant knee issues, there won't be any left for the rest of the league.

Marcus Smith, BAL: The 2008 fourth-round pick spent a fair amount of the year on the active roster, but failed to catch a pass. Smith is a favorite of the coaching staff thanks to his work on special teams, and has a shot at winning the Ravens' third receiver spot.

Isaiah Stanback, DAL: Stanback missed most of the year with multiple shoulder injuries, catching only two passes for 24 yards. He hasn't made much progress in his first two years removed from Washington, but he's the ideal Wildcat quarterback and will likely take some snaps out of that formation (we're sorry, the *"Razorback"*) for Dallas in 2009.

Derek Stanley, STL: Stanley tore his ACL in a Week 15 loss to the Seattle Seahawks, thus proving that any wide receiver within 100 miles of the Seattle Seahawks was potentially subject to the voodoo hex placed on them last year. He was unable to participate in the Rams' April minicamps and may be the odd man out come roster cutdowns in August; if he makes the team, he'll mostly play special teams. (2008 stats: 6-for-12, 119 yards, 1 TD, -29.3% DVOA, -15 DYAR.)

Sammie Stroughter, TB: Stroughter had an up-and-down career at Oregon State, sandwiching two 70-catch, 1,000-plus-yard seasons (2006, 2008) between a harrowing 2007 that saw him fight through depression after losing three loved ones in the offseason, then suffer a lacerated kidney after just two games. Undersized but tough, Stroughter doesn't possess top-end speed but is extremely tough and runs good routes.

Brett Swain, GB: The poor man's Jordy Nelson, Swain is stuck on the practice squad of a team that has the real deal. He needs a change of scenery to have a chance at making an impact at this level.

Brandon Tate, NE: The NCAA's all-time leader in kick return yardage (six career return touchdowns), Tate could be a major big-play threat if he returns to 100 percent after tearing his ACL and MCL midway through 2008. He never put up large reception totals in North Carolina (46 catches in 23 career games), but he averaged 20.2 yards per reception. The Patriots drafted him in the third round with an eye on 2010, and he'll likely take an NFL redshirt year on IR.

Courtney Taylor, SEA: You know how our college football section lists the number of returning players for each team? With a whopping 10 games played, Taylor is the top returning wideout for Seattle this season. Only Bobby Engram (13) and Koren Robinson (12) played in more games, and they're both gone now. In those ten games, Taylor could only manage nine receptions. If he's still on the roster this fall, it means he's one of the few Seahawks receivers who can get around without the use of a cane. (2008 stats: 9-for-25, 98 yards, -46.7% DVOA, -67 DYAR.)

Travis Taylor, DET: Taylor's bounced around the practice squads of Carolina, Seattle, and now Detroit, who signed him in December. He has no qualities an NFL team would want on their active roster at this point. On the bright side, he wasn't tased last year.

Mike Thomas, JAC: As part of their move away from taking athletic projects at wide receiver, the Jags used a fourth-round pick on Thomas, a 5-foot-8 receiver out of Arizona who set the Pac-10 conference record with 259 receptions. His skill set is reminiscent of Jordy Nelson's, and although he lacks Nelson's size, Thomas could be a slot receiver and return man for Jacksonville relatively quickly.

James Thrash, FA: At 34, Thrash is more a special-teamer than anything else — his yards per game and yards per catch have decreased every year since 2004. He suffered with a bulging disc in his neck for most of the offseason, and the Redskins cut him in June when he failed his physical. (2008 stats: 9-for-22, 81 yards, 1 TD, -43.8% DVOA, -50 DYAR.)

Patrick Turner, MIA: Turner is big, tall, and runs good routes, but he's not particularly fast (career long reception at USC: 42 yards). He was a consistent target for John David Booty and Mark Sanchez from 2006 to 2008, and his skills complement Ted Ginn well if both players can reach their full potential.

David Tyree, NYG: The hero of Super Bowl XLII missed the entire season with a knee injury; his primary impact would have been on special teams, and the Giants didn't show any significant shift in their return performance without him on the roster. The addition of two wideouts in the draft numbers Tyree's days in New York; he always has the option of taking a job at Patriots Place, where Patriots fans could come and swat the ball out of the air before it gets to him for $15. Polaroid included.

Tiquan Underwood, JAC: Like Thomas, Underwood's a productive college receiver who the Jaguars hope will contribute on special teams and after the catch. He had a somewhat disappointing senior season, falling from 65 catches as a junior to 40 as a senior, with Kenny Britt siphoning away his targets.

Kelley Washington, BAL: The Patriots always valued Washington as a special teams maven, but he'll get a real shot with the Ravens' undermanned receiver corps. If he can score a few more touchdowns, we might see the Squirrel Dance again (let YouTube be your guide).

Jeff Webb, KC: At the start of the season, Webb had a shot to earn the starting job across from Dwayne Bowe. By the end of the season, he had only been active for five games. Nonetheless, the release of Will Franklin suggests Webb will stick around for another year as a depth receiver. (2008 stats: 5-for-13, 46 yards, -53.1% DVOA, -46 DYAR.)

Derrick Williams, DET: Williams was a prized recruit coming out of high school for Joe Paterno, but at Penn State, he didn't develop into a star wideout; instead, he became a max-effort, team leader type who contributed as an effective route runner and special teams stud. Essentially, he followed Peter Warrick's career path, just at a lower level. With Bryant Johnson arriving in Detroit over the offseason, Williams isn't likely to start across from Calvin Johnson, but he should make the team as a return man and third/fourth receiver.

Paul Williams, TEN: The Titans drafted Williams in the third round in 2007. Since then, he's been inactive for 27 of the team's 32 regular-season games and has just one career reception. With Kenny Britt and Nate Washington in the fold, Williams is about to lose his scholarship. "Once I heard we'd taken a receiver in the first round it was one of those things like, 'OK, it's time to work,'" Williams said in May. A little late for that, buddy.

Roydell Williams, WAS: Williams was a starter for the Tennessee Titans in 2007, catching 55 of 93 passes for 719 yards and four touchdowns (-1.1% DVOA, 85 DYAR). The Titans say that they cut Williams before the 2008 season because he wasn't playing at a high level. Williams said he was still dealing with a broken ankle suffered during the 2007 playoffs and should have gone on PUP. Either way, he missed the whole season but will try to make it back into the NFL with the Redskins.

Travis Wilson, DAL: The Browns' third-round pick in 2006, Wilson was cut in training camp and caught on with the Cowboys practice squad after Mike Jefferson violated the league's substance abuse policy. He appears to have peaked as a college junior, which wouldn't make him the only person in life to do so.

Wallace Wright, NYJ: Wright was a freshman walk-on at North Carolina who made his mark as a special teams star. He's taken the same approach in the pros, moving up from the practice squad to the active roster on the strength of his special teams play. Wright made 22 tackles last year, but didn't catch a single pass, and he's not likely to see the field as a receiver except in an emergency.

Dominique Zeigler, SF: A slot receiver who was called up from the practice squad last year, he is no relation to the Dominique Zeigler who played "le patron de la salle des jeux" in the French television series *Le Jardin Des Autres Roses*. (2008 stats: 5-for-8, 97 yards, 4.8% DVOA, 10 DYAR.)

Tight Ends

For an explanation of how to read the tight end statistics tables, see the Wide Receivers section.

Chris Baker
Height: 6-3   Weight: 258   College: Michigan State   Draft: 2002/3 (88)   Born: 18-Nov-1979   Age: 30   Risk: Green

Year	Team	G	Rec	Pass	Yds	C%	Yd/C	TD	YAC	Rk	DVOA	Rk	DYAR	Rk	YAR	Short	Mid	Deep	Bomb
2006	NYJ	16	31	45	300	67%	9.7	4	4.2	21	10.6%	9	53	12	47	53%	37%	9%	0%
2007	NYJ	15	41	61	409	67%	10.0	3	3.5	26	9.3%	15	70	16	62	51%	43%	7%	0%
2008	NYJ	11	21	30	194	70%	9.2	0	2.6	41	1.9%	22	18	26	17	39%	46%	14%	0%
2009	NE		26	42	272	62%	10.5	1			-2.0%								

Maybe the Border War isn't over just yet after all. Baker is a good receiver and a good blocker, but he's a little too short to be dominant in either area. He's a package guy who can provide some blocking either in-line or while lined up in the backfield in passing sets, and he can provide a short-area target when Randy Moss isn't open. Baker will split snaps with Alex Smith and Ben Watson, which means he'll put up very modest numbers.

Martellus Bennett
Height: 6-6   Weight: 259   College: Texas A&M   Draft: 2008/2 (61)   Born: 10-Mar-1987   Age: 22   Risk: Blue

Year	Team	G	Rec	Pass	Yds	C%	Yd/C	TD	YAC	Rk	DVOA	Rk	DYAR	Rk	YAR	Short	Mid	Deep	Bomb
2008	DAL	12	20	27	283	74%	14.2	4	6.1	5	58.8%	1	111	13	113	52%	22%	22%	4%
2009	DAL		18	28	223	64%	12.4	2			15.1%								

Bennett's great DVOA is a function of slipping open on plays where the defense simply ran out of guys to cover Cowboys, but hey, he still caught the ball. He even caught a touchdown pass from Brad Johnson in Johnson's most positive play of the entire season. While he was billed as a very good blocker and average receiver coming out of college, he was much better as a receiver than a blocker in 2008. If he can improve his route-running slightly and live up to his reputation as a blocker, he'll be as good as he says he is. His blog for the *Dallas Morning News* puts Chris Cooley's to shame.

Kevin Boss
Height: 6-7   Weight: 252   College: Western Oregon   Draft: 2007/5 (153)   Born: 11-Jan-1984   Age: 25   Risk: Yellow

Year	Team	G	Rec	Pass	Yds	C%	Yd/C	TD	YAC	Rk	DVOA	Rk	DYAR	Rk	YAR	Short	Mid	Deep	Bomb
2007	NYG	13	9	14	118	64%	13.1	2	3.7	--	44.5%	--	48	--	47	31%	46%	23%	0%
2008	NYG	12	33	55	384	60%	11.6	6	4.8	14	14.8%	15	84	16	68	45%	40%	15%	0%
2009	NYG		40	64	437	63%	10.9	4			9.0%								

The Bossman became the undisputed starter when Jeremy Shockey was dealt to New Orleans. He exceeded all expectations, even after a rocky start where he wasn't thrown the ball during the first two weeks of the season. He's most valuable on third down, where his 44.2% DVOA comes out of working with Steve Smith. The Giants love to cross the two and force linebackers to commit to one or the other, with Eli Manning exploiting the mismatch in man coverage and the holes in zone coverage. Boss also improved enough as a blocker that the Giants didn't miss Shockey whatsoever. He's an athletic, well-rounded tight end with ideal size that the Giants somehow picked up with the 153rd pick in the draft. If your child ever asks you where very good players come from, it's OK to just throw up your shoulders and shrug.

John Carlson   Height: 6-5   Weight: 251 College: Notre Dame   Draft: 2008/2 (38)   Born: 12-May-1984 Age: 25 Risk: Green

Year	Team	G	Rec	Pass	Yds	C%	Yd/C	TD	YAC	Rk	DVOA	Rk	DYAR	Rk	YAR	Short	Mid	Deep	Bomb
2008	SEA	15	55	80	627	69%	11.4	5	4.0	27	19.1%	10	143	8	147	32%	54%	14%	0%
2009	SEA		55	79	625	70%	11.4	3			17.8%								

Perhaps the sole bright spot of the 2008 Seahawks, Carlson became the first rookie tight end to lead his team in catches and receiving yards since Keith Jackson did it with the Eagles in 1988. Though that had as much to do with the havoc wreaked on the Seattle wide receiver depth chart as it did with Carlson's skill and ability, it was a very promising debut for the second-rounder. Carlson now finds himself playing for Jim Mora and Greg Knapp, whose top receiver in Atlanta was tight end Alge Crumpler, so he should have plenty of chances to repeat his success this season, although he will likely lose some red zone opportunities to T.J. Houshmandzadeh. Yes, KUBIAK really does project a virtually identical year.

Brent Celek   Height: 6-6   Weight: 260 College: Cincinnati   Draft: 2007/5 (162) Born: 25-Jan-1985 Age: 24 Risk: Green

Year	Team	G	Rec	Pass	Yds	C%	Yd/C	TD	YAC	Rk	DVOA	Rk	DYAR	Rk	YAR	Short	Mid	Deep	Bomb
2007	PHI	16	16	22	178	73%	11.1	1	4.5	--	23.5%	--	45	--	45	43%	43%	10%	5%
2008	PHI	16	27	38	318	71%	11.8	1	6.1	4	21.9%	8	77	17	68	53%	35%	12%	0%
2009	PHI		40	65	406	62%	10.1	3			1.4%								

Celek was 13th on last year's Top 25 Prospects list after a promising second half, and when L.J. Smith was too concussed to play against the Seahawks in Week 9, Celek filled in with a six-catch, 131-yard performance that should've netted him the starting job. Instead, Smith took his job back and Celek bided his time. Once the playoffs rolled around, though, Celek could not be contained any longer. He accrued 19 catches for 151 yards and three touchdowns during the Eagles' run, including a 10-catch performance against the Cardinals in the NFC Championship game. Celek will likely start this year, and he's the ideal West Coast Offense tight end: Quick enough to get off the line of scrimmage and into his routes, Celek is a reliable target with soft hands who can pick up first downs over the middle. He still needs to work on his blocking, but with the Eagles likely passing the ball even more thanks to Brian Westbrook's injury, Celek should be an effective player with some upside as a tight end in deep fantasy leagues.

Dallas Clark   Height: 6-3   Weight: 257 College: Iowa   Draft: 2003/1 (24)   Born: 12-Jun-1979 Age: 30 Risk: Green

Year	Team	G	Rec	Pass	Yds	C%	Yd/C	TD	YAC	Rk	DVOA	Rk	DYAR	Rk	YAR	Short	Mid	Deep	Bomb
2006	IND	12	30	57	367	53%	12.2	4	4.3	20	-4.8%	26	9	27	2	44%	31%	17%	8%
2007	IND	15	58	101	616	57%	10.6	11	3.7	24	1.8%	23	63	17	79	41%	38%	15%	5%
2008	IND	15	77	107	848	72%	11.0	6	4.7	16	18.4%	12	188	4	192	58%	25%	16%	1%
2009	IND		61	96	651	64%	10.7	5			14.3%								

Over the past two seasons, Clark has emerged as the Colts' second most-important skill position player behind Reggie Wayne. When Marvin Harrison missed much of the 2007 season, Clark basically became a wide receiver and was highly successful. Last year, he played much more tight end, where his versatility allowed the Colts' no-huddle to dominate. If teams play three linebackers, Clark splits out wide for mismatches. If they play five defensive backs, Clark shifts in for a power attack. Regression to the mean suggests he does not match last year's career high in receiving yards, but if neither Austin Collie nor Pierre Garcon wraps up the third receiver job, Clark could actually see his production go up.

Desmond Clark   Height: 6-3   Weight: 255 College: Wake Forest   Draft: 1999/6 (179) Born: 20-Apr-1977 Age: 32 Risk: Green

Year	Team	G	Rec	Pass	Yds	C%	Yd/C	TD	YAC	Rk	DVOA	Rk	DYAR	Rk	YAR	Short	Mid	Deep	Bomb
2006	CHI	16	45	80	626	56%	13.9	6	4.7	13	14.4%	7	117	5	135	37%	49%	10%	3%
2007	CHI	16	44	66	545	67%	12.4	4	5.3	10	16.3%	10	100	10	92	44%	40%	16%	0%
2008	CHI	16	41	73	367	56%	9.0	1	4.2	22	-28.7%	39	-109	43	-103	56%	35%	9%	0%
2009	CHI		29	48	285	60%	9.8	1			-13.7%								

Clark unsurprisingly gave way to Greg Olsen as the primary tight end in the passing game last year, but the Bears liked having him on the field enough to move to two-tight end sets on a regular basis; 35 percent of the Bears' offensive plays came out of sets involving two or more tight ends last year, up from just under 22 percent the year before. Having Clark at tight end also allows the team to split Olsen outside and still have an effective tight end on the interior. Clark's on the decline, but he remains an effective contributor in all facets of the game.

Chase Coffman

Height: 6-6   Weight: 245   College: Missouri   Draft: 2009/3 (98)   Born: 10-Nov-1986   Age: 23   Risk: Green

Year	Team	G	Rec	Pass	Yds	C%	Yd/C	TD	YAC	Rk	DVOA	Rk	DYAR	Rk	YAR	Short	Mid	Deep	Bomb
2009	CIN		21	28	162	74%	7.8	1			15.5%								

Coffman had amazing collegiate production at Missouri: 90 receptions in 2008, 247 in his career. The Tigers ran a spread offense, and Coffman caused a lot of mismatches by outrunning linebackers up the seam. He won't get open as easily in the NFL, but he's an intriguing size-speed-hands prospect for a Bengals team that needs possession weapons to replace T.J. Houshmandzadeh. Coffman broke a bone in his foot and missed most of OTAs. That will put him behind in his rookie development, but the Bengals will try to get him up to speed and on the field quickly.

Jared Cook

Height: 6-5   Weight: 242   College: South Carolina   Draft: 2009/3 (89)   Born: 7-Apr-1987   Age: 22   Risk: Green

Year	Team	G	Rec	Pass	Yds	C%	Yd/C	TD	YAC	Rk	DVOA	Rk	DYAR	Rk	YAR	Short	Mid	Deep	Bomb
2009	TEN		18	26	173	71%	9.4	1			-0.7%								

Cook ping-ponged between wide receiver and tight end at South Carolina; Steve Spurrier would put him at tight end, watch him miss a few blocks, throw his hands up, and split him wide. The shuffling continued at Titans camp, where the team worked him out with the wide receivers after drafting him as a tight end. Cook was the fastest tight end in the draft, or perhaps he was the biggest receiver … at any rate, he's a David Martin type with great measurables who doesn't like to block and doesn't read zones well enough to be a quality tight end. The Titans, who use lots of multi-tight end sets, will try to find some niche for him.

Chris Cooley

Height: 6-3   Weight: 265   College: Utah State   Draft: 2004/3 (81)   Born: 11-Jul-1982   Age: 27   Risk: Green

Year	Team	G	Rec	Pass	Yds	C%	Yd/C	TD	YAC	Rk	DVOA	Rk	DYAR	Rk	YAR	Short	Mid	Deep	Bomb
2006	WAS	16	57	95	734	57%	12.9	6	7.9	1	-2.6%	24	27	20	42	47%	33%	18%	3%
2007	WAS	16	66	110	786	60%	11.9	8	4.3	15	9.5%	14	121	7	114	40%	39%	17%	5%
2008	WAS	16	83	111	849	75%	10.2	1	5.7	8	7.6%	18	105	14	114	59%	30%	10%	1%
2009	WAS		85	120	781	71%	9.2	3			2.4%								

Two years ago, Jason Campbell could find nobody but Cooley in the end zone. Last year, Cooley caught one touchdown pass — from Antwaan Randle El on an option. According to the *Washington Post*, Cooley was double-teamed on nearly every play through the last 12 games of 2008. In those 12 games, he caught 66 passes for 670 yards. This tells us two things: First, Cooley is a very good player. Second, Washington's receiver corps might as well be re-named "Santana Moss and the Pips."

Brad Cottam

Height: 6-8   Weight: 270   College: Tennessee   Draft: 2008/3 (76)   Born: 28-Nov-1984   Age: 25   Risk: Green

Year	Team	G	Rec	Pass	Yds	C%	Yd/C	TD	YAC	Rk	DVOA	Rk	DYAR	Rk	YAR	Short	Mid	Deep	Bomb
2008	KC	4	7	11	63	64%	9.0	0	2.4	--	-10.2%	--	-2	--	2	40%	50%	10%	0%
2009	KC		36	57	386	63%	10.8	3			10.6%								

Scott Pioli will get the accolades when the Kansas City Chiefs are rebuilt, but Cottam is yet another example of how the previous administration set him up with a very smart draft in 2008. They knew Tony Gonzalez was itching to get out of town, but they also weren't planning on dealing him right away, so they could use a third-round pick to grab a raw tight end prospect who combined size, intelligence, and an excellent work ethic with very little collegiate experience. (Cottam missed his sophomore year after a car accident and lost most of his senior year to a dislocated wrist.) One year later, after apprenticing under Gonzalez, Cottam is ready to enter the starting lineup. Of course, it is hard to say how much actual playing time that means with Todd Haley running the show. Last year, Haley's Arizona offense had a tight end on the field only 58 percent of the time, while every other offense in the NFL used a tight end on at least 70 percent of plays. Cottam is a traditional tight end who blocks well and provides a big target to move the sticks on third down, not a receiver-first type.

Alge Crumpler
Height: 6-2   Weight: 262 College: North Carolina   Draft: 2000/2 (35)   Born: 23-Dec-1977   Age: 31   Risk: Blue

Year	Team	G	Rec	Pass	Yds	C%	Yd/C	TD	YAC	Rk	DVOA	Rk	DYAR	Rk	YAR	Short	Mid	Deep	Bomb
2006	ATL	16	56	103	780	51%	13.9	8	4.6	16	-2.4%	23	34	19	44	21%	55%	17%	7%
2007	ATL	14	42	70	444	60%	10.6	5	6.2	4	-0.4%	26	31	22	37	61%	31%	8%	0%
2008	TEN	16	24	41	257	59%	10.7	1	5.2	9	-8.6%	29	-3	29	-5	43%	38%	15%	5%
2009	*TEN*		*19*	*35*	*195*	*54%*	*10.3*	*1*			*-6.2%*								

The former Pro Bowler was supposed to take over from Bo Scaife as the primary tight end, but Crumpler's best days are clearly behind him, and he is basically a blocker at this point. His days as a viable fantasy tight end, much less an asset, are over.

Owen Daniels
Height: 6-3   Weight: 250 College: Wisconsin   Draft: 2006/4 (98)   Born: 9-Nov-1982   Age: 27   Risk: Green

Year	Team	G	Rec	Pass	Yds	C%	Yd/C	TD	YAC	Rk	DVOA	Rk	DYAR	Rk	YAR	Short	Mid	Deep	Bomb
2006	HOU	14	34	51	352	67%	10.4	5	5.2	8	15.1%	6	75	8	73	61%	27%	9%	2%
2007	HOU	16	63	94	768	67%	12.2	3	3.3	30	11.7%	13	121	8	118	33%	49%	17%	1%
2008	HOU	16	70	100	862	70%	12.3	2	5.8	7	19.3%	9	183	5	179	52%	42%	6%	0%
2009	*HOU*		*76*	*113*	*899*	*67%*	*11.8*	*3*			*14.4%*								

Arguably the most underrated tight end in football, Daniels consistently puts up good conventional numbers and very good advanced numbers. Daniels, like seemingly all Texans, failed to convert all his yardage into touchdowns. If the Texans offense is more consistent, Daniels could emerge as an elite fantasy tight end with six to eight touchdowns. Even if his fantasy value does not reach the upper echelon, he is now established as an upper echelon tight end in real football. A 1,000-yard, 8-touchdown season sometime in the next three years is possible. Daniels held out of OTAs looking for a new deal, but he should be in training camp.

Fred Davis
Height: 6-4   Weight: 248 College: USC   Draft: 2008/2 (48)   Born: 15-Jan-1986   Age: 23   Risk: Green

Year	Team	G	Rec	Pass	Yds	C%	Yd/C	TD	YAC	Rk	DVOA	Rk	DYAR	Rk	YAR	Short	Mid	Deep	Bomb
2008	WAS	4	3	10	27	30%	9.0	0	4.7	--	-53.2%	--	-31	--	-33	75%	0%	25%	0%
2009	*WAS*		*20*	*28*	*135*	*71%*	*6.8*	*1*			*-16.9%*								

It's too early to say that the Redskins whiffed an all three of their pass-catching draft picks in 2008, but Davis joined Malcolm Kelly and Devin Thomas as severe first-year disappointments. Coach Jim Zorn summed up Davis' rookie year with this *Washington Post* quote: "It makes no sense for me to put a guy out there who can run real fast, but not going in the right direction."

Vernon Davis

Height: 6-3   Weight: 253   College: Maryland   Draft: 2006/1 (6)   Born: 31-Jan-1984   Age: 25   Risk: Green

Year	Team	G	Rec	Pass	Yds	C%	Yd/C	TD	YAC	Rk	DVOA	Rk	DYAR	Rk	YAR	Short	Mid	Deep	Bomb
2006	SF	10	20	42	265	48%	13.3	3	7.5	2	-30.4%	42	-61	43	-47	47%	27%	20%	7%
2007	SF	14	52	85	509	61%	9.8	4	3.4	29	-8.9%	32	-9	32	6	45%	36%	13%	7%
2008	SF	13	31	49	358	63%	11.5	0	7.8	1	-24.6%	37	-54	37	-49	63%	7%	15%	15%
2009	SF		50	86	547	58%	10.9	4			-1.0%								

Another year, another offensive coordinator, another slew of promises to get Davis more involved in the offense. At this point, it's time to recognize Davis for what he is: an effective blocking tight end who is never going to develop into the downfield threat that 49ers' front office hoped for. And although that may not justify the sixth overall pick spent on him, the 49ers have plenty of young talent at wide receiver — but their offensive line remains highly suspect, so Davis's highest "use value" is at the line of scrimmage anyway.

Joel Dreessen

Height: 6-4   Weight: 260   College: Colorado State   Draft: 2005/6 (198)   Born: 26-Jul-1982   Age: 27   Risk: Green

Year	Team	G	Rec	Pass	Yds	C%	Yd/C	TD	YAC	Rk	DVOA	Rk	DYAR	Rk	YAR	Short	Mid	Deep	Bomb
2007	HOU	13	4	6	55	67%	13.8	2	2.0	--	69.0%	--	32	--	32	0%	83%	17%	0%
2008	HOU	14	11	17	77	65%	7.0	0	3.5	--	-35.0%	--	-31	--	-34	69%	23%	8%	0%
2009	HOU		16	26	132	62%	8.3	0			-22.7%								

Dreessen will battle rookies Anthony Hill and James Casey to be second-string behind Owen Daniels. Mark Bruener was the Titans' second tight end for years, and Hill best fits the Bruener mold as a blocking specialist. Dreesen is more useful as a receiver, but his role last season consisted of one five-yard reception per game, which Hill should be able to manage.

Greg Estandia

Height: 6-8   Weight: 255   College: UNLV   Draft: 2006/FA   Born: 18-Nov-1982   Age: 27   Risk: Green

Year	Team	G	Rec	Pass	Yds	C%	Yd/C	TD	YAC	Rk	DVOA	Rk	DYAR	Rk	YAR	Short	Mid	Deep	Bomb
2007	JAC	10	9	16	136	56%	15.1	0	4.1	--	15.6%	--	23	--	18	19%	44%	38%	0%
2008	JAC	8	10	15	113	67%	11.3	0	3.1	--	-5.3%	--	2	--	-3	29%	43%	14%	14%
2009	JAC		10	14	105	71%	10.5	3			13.7%								

A standout at UNLV, Estandia was an undrafted free agent who spent his rookie season on the practice squad. He's seen limited action in 2007 and 2008, with the top game being a four-catch special against the Packers last December. The Jags re-signed him as an exclusive-rights free agent, and he's got a chance for a few more reps in a changing tight end rotation.

Anthony Fasano

Height: 6-5   Weight: 255   College: Notre Dame   Draft: 2006/2 (53)   Born: 20-Apr-1984   Age: 25   Risk: Green

Year	Team	G	Rec	Pass	Yds	C%	Yd/C	TD	YAC	Rk	DVOA	Rk	DYAR	Rk	YAR	Short	Mid	Deep	Bomb
2006	DAL	16	14	24	126	58%	9.0	0	4.0	--	-23.7%	--	-25	--	-22	44%	44%	6%	6%
2007	DAL	16	14	21	143	67%	10.2	1	3.9	--	-2.3%	--	7	--	3	45%	45%	9%	0%
2008	MIA	13	34	53	454	64%	13.4	7	4.1	26	34.8%	4	156	6	164	28%	56%	16%	0%
2009	MIA		41	60	465	68%	11.3	2			12.9%								

Fasano followed Bill Parcells from Dallas and started his 2008 season with eight catches against the Jets and then a touchdown pass from Ronnie Brown in the Wildcat's debut against the Patriots in Week 3. The Dolphins see him just as more of a blocker, however, which makes him more of a standard tight end than a Gonzalez/Clark/Cooley-type threat.

Derek Fine

Height: 6-3   Weight: 245   College: Kansas   Draft: 2008/4 (132)   Born: 24-Aug-1983   Age: 26   Risk: Yellow

Year	Team	G	Rec	Pass	Yds	C%	Yd/C	TD	YAC	Rk	DVOA	Rk	DYAR	Rk	YAR	Short	Mid	Deep	Bomb
2008	BUF	5	10	12	94	83%	9.4	1	2.9	--	22.3%	--	25	--	28	45%	45%	9%	0%
2009	BUF		41	59	439	69%	10.7	1			1.8%								

Fine didn't see a lot of action in 2008, but he made the most of his opportunities, registering the second-best DVOA among tight ends with fewer than 50 passes. He is currently slated to be the starter, though he will likely split time with Derek Schouman and rookie Shawn Nelson.

Jermichael Finley

Height: 6-5   Weight: 243   College: Texas   Draft: 2008/3 (91)   Born: 26-Mar-1987   Age: 22   Risk: Green

Year	Team	G	Rec	Pass	Yds	C%	Yd/C	TD	YAC	Rk	DVOA	Rk	DYAR	Rk	YAR	Short	Mid	Deep	Bomb
2008	GB	14	6	12	74	50%	12.3	1	2.5	--	-21.8%	--	-13	--	-12	58%	17%	17%	8%
2009	GB		23	35	249	65%	10.9	1			11.6%								

Everyone agreed that Finley came out of school too early (he left Texas at 20 to support his two children), and as usual, everyone was right. While Finley is big and fast, he has neither the size nor the technique to block anyone he's going to go up against as a pro. As a result, the Packers' only real way of using him was to split him out wide and use him on fades and back-shoulder throws where he could use his frame to box out defenders; three of his six catches came with him split out. You know that top your girlfriend loves that she always complains doesn't go with anything? That's Jermichael Finley. He doesn't go with anything yet.

Bubba Franks

Height: 6-6   Weight: 263   College: Miami   Draft: 2000/1 (14)   Born: 6-Jan-1978   Age: 31   Risk: Blue

Year	Team	G	Rec	Pass	Yds	C%	Yd/C	TD	YAC	Rk	DVOA	Rk	DYAR	Rk	YAR	Short	Mid	Deep	Bomb
2006	GB	16	25	53	232	47%	9.3	0	4.6	15	-33.8%	43	-87	44	-98	57%	38%	2%	2%
2007	GB	8	18	32	132	56%	7.3	3	2.7	40	-18.3%	37	-24	37	-29	61%	25%	14%	0%
2008	NYJ	5	6	12	47	50%	7.8	0	4.2	--	-51.2%	--	-34	--	-33	55%	36%	9%	0%
2009	NYJ		10	19	116	53%	11.6	0			-16.7%								

Who would have guessed that Franks would outlast Brett Favre in New York? But the cupboard at tight end was perilously bare after releasing Chris Baker, so the Jets opted to re-up Franks for another season. Dustin Keller is going to suck up all the reception opportunities, so Franks is on board strictly to block.

Michael Gaines

Height: 6-2   Weight: 275   College: UCF   Draft: 2004/7 (232)   Born: 30-Mar-1980   Age: 29   Risk: Green

Year	Team	G	Rec	Pass	Yds	C%	Yd/C	TD	YAC	Rk	DVOA	Rk	DYAR	Rk	YAR	Short	Mid	Deep	Bomb
2006	CAR	16	15	28	146	57%	9.7	0	3.8	30	-13.2%	34	-11	34	-7	45%	45%	5%	5%
2007	BUF	15	25	35	215	71%	8.6	2	6.7	3	6.0%	18	32	21	33	74%	20%	6%	0%
2008	DET	16	23	36	260	64%	11.3	1	3.8	29	-16.1%	35	-21	34	-29	57%	31%	11%	0%
2009	CHI		15	23	159	65%	10.6	2			10.5%								

The Lions signed Gaines to a four-year, $10 million deal after the 2007 season because he was a decent blocker. Never mind that they already had Casey FitzSimmons. Gaines remained a nonentity in the passing game, was only an average blocker, and lost a fumble in opposition territory when the Lions were driving for the game-winning score against the Bears in Week 9. Gaines was released after the team drafted Brandon Pettigrew and signed with those same Bears, so maybe he knew what was coming.

Antonio Gates

Height: 6-4   Weight: 260 College: Kent State   Draft: 2003/FA   Born: 18-Jun-1980   Age: 29 Risk: Green

Year	Team	G	Rec	Pass	Yds	C%	Yd/C	TD	YAC	Rk	DVOA	Rk	DYAR	Rk	YAR	Short	Mid	Deep	Bomb
2006	SD	16	71	120	924	59%	13.0	9	4.1	24	10.0%	11	137	3	125	34%	42%	21%	2%
2007	SD	16	75	117	984	64%	13.1	9	3.5	27	30.1%	4	278	1	266	32%	39%	23%	6%
2008	SD	15	60	92	704	65%	11.7	8	3.7	31	15.6%	14	140	9	142	32%	50%	14%	4%
2009	SD		70	114	842	61%	12.0	9			21.3%								

An incomplete list of the injuries Gates went through last year: Toe, hip, ankle, foot. As you might suspect, this affected Gates' ability to create separation and use his best asset — his speed — to get open downfield. The result was a disappointing season for a player who otherwise has been markedly consistent as an NFL starter, but one that shouldn't stick as a new level of performance. One surprise: Gates is not as big a weapon in the red zone as you might think. Over the past three seasons, his red-zone DVOA has hovered between -10% and 15%.

John Gilmore

Height: 6-4   Weight: 260 College: Penn State   Draft: 2002/6 (196) Born: 21-Sep-1979   Age: 30 Risk: Green

Year	Team	G	Rec	Pass	Yds	C%	Yd/C	TD	YAC	Rk	DVOA	Rk	DYAR	Rk	YAR	Short	Mid	Deep	Bomb
2006	CHI	16	6	12	38	50%	6.3	2	3.7	--	-18.0%	--	-9	--	-10	78%	11%	11%	0%
2007	CHI	15	3	7	14	43%	4.7	0	3.0	--	-53.9%	--	-23	--	-22	60%	40%	0%	0%
2008	TB	11	15	21	147	71%	9.8	1	5.8	--	8.8%	--	23	--	22	75%	15%	10%	0%
2009	TB		10	18	97	56%	9.7	1			-24.3%								

Gilmore is primarily a blocker, but was effective when passes came his way. A high catch rate and solid DVOA suggest the Bucs can get some mismatches when they go to two-tight end sets and Winslow or Stevens draws attention.

Tony Gonzalez

Height: 6-4   Weight: 248 College: California   Draft: 1997/1 (13)   Born: 27-Feb-1976   Age: 33 Risk: Red

Year	Team	G	Rec	Pass	Yds	C%	Yd/C	TD	YAC	Rk	DVOA	Rk	DYAR	Rk	YAR	Short	Mid	Deep	Bomb
2006	KC	15	73	104	900	70%	12.3	5	3.7	32	28.7%	2	233	1	236	31%	52%	16%	0%
2007	KC	16	99	154	1172	64%	11.8	5	2.8	39	13.6%	12	201	3	208	32%	48%	18%	1%
2008	KC	16	96	155	1058	62%	11.0	10	2.6	40	16.4%	13	243	1	232	30%	57%	10%	3%
2009	ATL		83	121	924	69%	11.1	5			14.8%								

The astonishing Tony Gonzalez simply defies the effects of age. Last year he had 26 more receptions, 258 more yards, and four more touchdowns than any tight end had ever produced at age 32. He is the only tight end over the age of 30 to gain more than 1,000 receiving yards in a season, and he's now done it twice. There's no reason to expect the trade to Atlanta will hurt him, especially since it gives him a better quarterback. When his fantasy numbers take a hit, the culprit won't be age — it will be the Falcons' lower pass-to-run ratio and their preference to punch the ball in with Michael Turner at the goal line.

Daniel Graham

Height: 6-3   Weight: 257 College: Colorado   Draft: 2002/1 (21)   Born: 16-Nov-1978   Age: 31 Risk: Blue

Year	Team	G	Rec	Pass	Yds	C%	Yd/C	TD	YAC	Rk	DVOA	Rk	DYAR	Rk	YAR	Short	Mid	Deep	Bomb
2006	NE	12	21	34	235	62%	11.2	2	4.6	14	10.5%	10	42	14	49	53%	27%	20%	0%
2007	DEN	15	24	33	246	73%	10.3	2	4.3	18	15.9%	11	53	19	50	68%	19%	13%	0%
2008	DEN	14	32	50	389	64%	12.2	4	6.2	3	6.7%	19	48	20	60	48%	37%	11%	4%
2009	DEN		17	29	158	59%	9.3	1			-16.8%								

Graham is one of the league's better blocking tight ends, and while he's not considered a great receiver, he always manages to put up a positive DVOA. His basic receiving numbers went up last year, but Graham's game didn't really change. The Broncos threw him the ball more because they threw everyone the ball more; Denver's pass-run ratio went from 1.28 in 2007 to 1.63 in 2008. He had more yards after catch because the Broncos ran more tight end screens, and while Graham isn't a great route-runner, he's pretty agile when he gets the ball on a tight end screen. Luckily for him, it just so happens that Josh McDaniels likes to run tight end screens too.

Ben Hartsock   Height: 6-3   Weight: 264   College: Ohio State   Draft: 2004/3 (68)   Born: 5-Jul-1980   Age: 29   Risk: Yellow

Year	Team	G	Rec	Pass	Yds	C%	Yd/C	TD	YAC	Rk	DVOA	Rk	DYAR	Rk	YAR	Short	Mid	Deep	Bomb
2006	TEN	6	6	15	68	33%	11.3	0	6.3	--	-50.6%	--	-44	--	-44	36%	55%	9%	0%
2007	TEN	16	12	19	138	63%	11.5	0	5.9	--	-7.8%	--	-1	--	1	58%	37%	5%	0%
2008	ATL	6	3	6	26	50%	8.7	0	4.7	--	-38.6%	--	-12	--	-13	50%	50%	0%	0%
2009	ATL		11	18	102	61%	9.3	1			-7.3%								

Hartsock is a smart dude — he was All-Big Ten academically at Ohio State not once nor twice but thrice. Therefore, he is smart enough to know that with Tony Gonzalez in town, any pass that comes his way is either a fifth checkdown or has been deflected. He blocks well enough to stick around as the third tight end, assuming the Falcons keep three.

Todd Heap   Height: 6-5   Weight: 252   College: Arizona State   Draft: 2001/1 (31)   Born: 16-Mar-1980   Age: 29   Risk: Red

Year	Team	G	Rec	Pass	Yds	C%	Yd/C	TD	YAC	Rk	DVOA	Rk	DYAR	Rk	YAR	Short	Mid	Deep	Bomb
2006	BAL	16	73	116	765	63%	10.5	6	3.5	35	5.0%	16	92	6	91	45%	43%	10%	2%
2007	BAL	6	23	34	239	68%	10.4	1	2.9	38	3.2%	20	25	26	33	40%	43%	10%	7%
2008	BAL	14	35	64	403	55%	11.5	3	5.1	10	4.3%	20	49	19	36	38%	40%	15%	7%
2009	BAL		51	87	560	59%	11.0	3			0.2%								

Heap has lost a lot of athleticism to age and injuries. He can no longer turn and adjust quickly to throws away from his body, and he isn't much of a threat as a seam-splitter. He remains a viable third-down target (DVOA of 17.8% on 24 passes last year), but his primary asset is now his blocking. He did a fine job as a de facto right tackle on unbalanced line plays, which is no easy task; if L.J. Smith plays right tackle, the opposing left end will earn Defender of the Week honors.

Steve Heiden   Height: 6-5   Weight: 265   College: South Dakota State   Draft: 1999/3 (69)   Born: 21-Sep-1976   Age: 33   Risk: Green

Year	Team	G	Rec	Pass	Yds	C%	Yd/C	TD	YAC	Rk	DVOA	Rk	DYAR	Rk	YAR	Short	Mid	Deep	Bomb
2006	CLE	16	36	46	249	80%	6.9	2	4.4	18	0.7%	19	24	22	27	73%	19%	8%	0%
2007	CLE	16	12	21	104	57%	8.7	0	2.5	--	-33.0%	--	-33	--	-36	62%	29%	10%	0%
2008	CLE	9	23	42	249	55%	10.8	0	5.1	11	-11.6%	33	-12	32	-12	50%	40%	10%	0%
2009	CLE		25	40	258	63%	10.3	2			-8.3%								

When the Browns go through their regularly-scheduled painful paradigm shifts/regime changes/prostrate exams, Heiden hides in the bowels of the stadium with the equipment managers. When the fog of war clears, he introduces himself to the new coach as the Browns' second tight end, then sprints off to OTAs. Heiden was on the Butch Davis teams. He caught passes from Tim Couch and shared a lineup with William Green and Kevin Johnson. He survived the entire Kellen Winslow era. Now, he'll split time with Robert Royal in an offense that can be surprisingly tight end-friendly despite its spread tendencies. Heiden is a better blocker and more reliable receiver than Royal, so he should at least duplicate his 2008 numbers, and he'll probably be around in three years when the Browns fire Eric Mangini and hire Jim Harbaugh.

Dustin Keller   Height: 6-3   Weight: 242   College: Purdue   Draft: 2008/1 (30)   Born: 25-Sep-1984   Age: 25   Risk: Yellow

Year	Team	G	Rec	Pass	Yds	C%	Yd/C	TD	YAC	Rk	DVOA	Rk	DYAR	Rk	YAR	Short	Mid	Deep	Bomb
2008	NYJ	15	48	78	535	62%	11.1	3	3.5	33	2.2%	21	55	18	68	50%	31%	13%	6%
2009	NYJ		62	103	744	60%	12.0	3			9.0%								

The two consensus stars of the 2008 combine were Vernon Gholston and Dustin Keller; the Jets drafted both of them. Gholston was a disaster once he got on the field, but Keller proved to be the real deal, hauling in 48 catches and becoming Brett Favre's favorite target by the middle of the season. Keller is a tight end in the sense that Dallas Clark is — he's not going to block anyone, but he there to create mismatches in the passing game. There aren't many players on the Jets offense that scare defenses, but Keller does.

Reggie Kelly

Height: 6-4   Weight: 255   College: Mississippi State   Draft: 1999/2 (42)   Born: 22-Feb-1977   Age: 32   Risk: Blue

Year	Team	G	Rec	Pass	Yds	C%	Yd/C	TD	YAC	Rk	DVOA	Rk	DYAR	Rk	YAR	Short	Mid	Deep	Bomb
2006	CIN	16	21	33	254	64%	12.1	1	4.1	25	15.7%	5	51	13	42	52%	23%	26%	0%
2007	CIN	15	20	27	211	74%	10.6	0	2.5	42	9.0%	16	26	25	22	60%	16%	24%	0%
2008	CIN	13	31	42	207	74%	6.7	0	3.0	36	-28.2%	38	-55	38	-54	79%	13%	5%	3%
2009	CIN		10	18	78	56%	7.8	1			-28.6%								

Carson Palmer's best buddy maintains his roster spot by being a willing blocker and catching the few balls thrown his way. With Ben Utecht not helping the run game at all, Kelly will play, and his pal will ensure he catches enough passes to keep him around.

Jeff King

Height: 6-5   Weight: 253   College: Virginia Tech   Draft: 2006/5 (155)   Born: 19-Feb-1983   Age: 26   Risk: Green

Year	Team	G	Rec	Pass	Yds	C%	Yd/C	TD	YAC	Rk	DVOA	Rk	DYAR	Rk	YAR	Short	Mid	Deep	Bomb
2006	CAR	12	1	4	1	25%	1.0	1	0.0	--	-34.7%	--	-9	--	-10	67%	33%	0%	0%
2007	CAR	16	46	80	406	58%	8.8	2	3.0	37	-21.7%	39	-77	42	-76	55%	38%	5%	1%
2008	CAR	13	21	34	195	62%	9.3	1	3.8	28	-10.9%	31	-8	30	-12	60%	23%	17%	0%
2009	CAR		32	56	332	57%	10.4	2			-8.6%								

King's production as a receiver dropped off last year, thanks in part, to the emergence (tempered by the subsequent disappearance) of Dante Rosario. King is not a threat down the seam, but is a decent option on short routes. Where he really contributes is as a blocker in the run game. The Panthers signed him to a one-year deal in the offseason, likely hoping the combination of Rosario and second-year player Gary Barnidge can improve and eventually replace King.

Joe Klopfenstein

Height: 6-6   Weight: 245   College: Colorado   Draft: 2006/2 (46)   Born: 9-Nov-1983   Age: 26   Risk: Blue

Year	Team	G	Rec	Pass	Yds	C%	Yd/C	TD	YAC	Rk	DVOA	Rk	DYAR	Rk	YAR	Short	Mid	Deep	Bomb
2006	STL	16	20	34	226	62%	11.3	1	4.8	12	5.2%	15	27	21	27	48%	24%	28%	0%
2007	STL	16	2	3	37	67%	18.5	1	11.5	--	36.2%	--	9	--	11	67%	33%	0%	0%
2008	STL	9	11	19	123	58%	11.2	0	3.1	--	-41.0%	--	-41	--	-38	50%	33%	17%	0%
2009	STL		10	16	91	63%	9.1	1			-3.8%								

A season-ending injury to Randy McMichael forced Klopfenstein into the starting lineup in Week 5. Things did not go well, as "Klops" demonstrated limited pass-catching skills (despite tallying 468 yards receiving in his senior year at Colorado) and serious deficiencies as a blocker. In fact, Klopfenstein's -41 DYAR ranked him last in the league for tight ends catching fewer than 24 passes. As a result, the Rams signed former 49ers tight end Billy Bajema in the offseason, and Klopfenstein's roster spot is very much in doubt heading into the 2009 season.

Donald Lee

Height: 6-3   Weight: 255   College: Mississippi State   Draft: 2003/5 (156)   Born: 31-Aug-1980   Age: 29   Risk: Yellow

Year	Team	G	Rec	Pass	Yds	C%	Yd/C	TD	YAC	Rk	DVOA	Rk	DYAR	Rk	YAR	Short	Mid	Deep	Bomb
2006	GB	15	10	21	150	48%	15.0	0	8.0	--	-16.9%	--	-14	--	-12	29%	50%	21%	0%
2007	GB	15	48	63	575	76%	12.0	6	5.6	6	30.9%	3	167	5	168	54%	38%	5%	3%
2008	GB	16	39	50	303	78%	7.8	5	2.8	37	1.1%	23	27	24	31	65%	16%	16%	2%
2009	GB		38	71	381	54%	10.0	5			-2.3%								

Need a red zone target? Hit up Lee, who's been incredible close to the end zone. Last year, he caught eight of the nine passes thrown to him inside the 20, yielding five touchdowns and a DVOA of 64.6%. The year before,

Lee was 7-of-8 for four touchdowns, two first downs, and a 76.5% DVOA. Of course, flukes can happen in consecutive years, but maybe Lee really is just that good when he gets close to the goal line. With Greg Jennings, Donald Driver, Jordy Nelson, and even Jermichael Finley as viable options in the passing game so close to paydirt, Lee could be getting lost in the shuffle, but teams simply need to devote more resources to him or risk being burned for a third consecutive year.

Marcedes Lewis

Height: 6-6   Weight: 255 College: UCLA   Draft: 2006/1 (28)   Born: 19-May-1984 Age: 25 Risk: Yellow

Year	Team	G	Rec	Pass	Yds	C%	Yd/C	TD	YAC	Rk	DVOA	Rk	DYAR	Rk	YAR	Short	Mid	Deep	Bomb
2006	JAC	14	13	21	126	62%	9.7	1	4.4	--	6.9%	--	20	--	15	44%	39%	11%	6%
2007	JAC	16	37	57	391	65%	10.6	2	3.3	31	-0.3%	25	27	23	23	35%	44%	20%	0%
2008	JAC	15	41	71	489	58%	11.9	2	3.7	30	-1.8%	27	25	25	17	36%	44%	17%	3%
2009	JAC		46	69	531	67%	11.5	4			14.5%								

Few quarterbacks were plagued with more dropped passes than David Garrard, and Lewis' numbers were particularly horrible. His 10 drops (by far the worst for any tight end) on 71 targets explain a catch rate that nobody at his position should have. Lewis was one of four first-round busts David Garrard could throw to in 2008, and if he wants to transcend bust status, he'll have to embrace the concept of ball security. At least KUBIAK feels the love.

Brandon Manumaleuna

Height: 6-2   Weight: 288 College: Arizona   Draft: 2001/4 (129) Born: 4-Jan-1980   Age: 29 Risk: Green

Year	Team	G	Rec	Pass	Yds	C%	Yd/C	TD	YAC	Rk	DVOA	Rk	DYAR	Rk	YAR	Short	Mid	Deep	Bomb
2006	SD	16	14	17	91	82%	6.5	3	4.7	--	21.2%	--	30	--	27	88%	13%	0%	0%
2007	SD	16	10	15	86	67%	8.6	1	5.1	--	-7.9%	--	-1	--	0	83%	8%	8%	0%
2008	SD	11	15	19	127	79%	8.5	2	4.2	--	14.0%	--	27	--	26	58%	42%	0%	0%
2009	SD		15	20	146	75%	9.7	1			20.1%								

The Chargers' backup tight end beat out Scott Chandler for his job and had a positively Manumaleuna-esque season, finishing up with a touchdown in each of the final two games of the year. He remains a very good blocker with absolutely no upside; if Antonio Gates blows out his knee and misses the entire season, for example, it's not like Manumaleuna is going to suddenly get 70 catches and 1,000 yards. His catches are mostly of the "Oh, we forgot he was on the field" variety.

David Martin

Height: 6-4   Weight: 260 College: Tennessee   Draft: 2001/6 (198) Born: 13-Mar-1979 Age: 30 Risk: Green

Year	Team	G	Rec	Pass	Yds	C%	Yd/C	TD	YAC	Rk	DVOA	Rk	DYAR	Rk	YAR	Short	Mid	Deep	Bomb
2006	GB	11	21	36	198	58%	9.4	2	3.5	36	-1.9%	22	13	25	11	47%	28%	17%	8%
2007	MIA	15	34	50	303	68%	8.9	2	2.3	44	-8.7%	31	-5	31	-8	46%	46%	6%	2%
2008	MIA	15	31	45	450	69%	14.5	3	4.4	18	37.3%	3	131	10	131	34%	37%	22%	7%
2009	MIA		30	49	363	61%	12.1	2			7.4%								

Martin played the role of H-back and extra strongside blocker in the Wildcat, and he provided stability to an offense that experienced severe turnover in 2008. While he's had flashes of production, he had sports hernia surgery earlier this offseason, and reports indicate that the coaching staff isn't happy about his percentage of missed blocking assignments. That's a problem he's had since his days in Green Bay, and with Joey Haynos climbing up the depth chart, Martin might be the odd man out.

Randy McMichael

Height: 6-3   Weight: 250   College: Georgia   Draft: 2002/4 (114)   Born: 28-Jun-1979   Age: 30   Risk: Green

Year	Team	G	Rec	Pass	Yds	C%	Yd/C	TD	YAC	Rk	DVOA	Rk	DYAR	Rk	YAR	Short	Mid	Deep	Bomb
2006	MIA	16	62	96	640	66%	10.3	3	5.3	4	4.8%	18	70	9	62	55%	35%	8%	1%
2007	STL	16	39	67	429	58%	11.0	3	3.7	23	8.5%	17	70	15	63	55%	31%	13%	2%
2008	STL	4	11	21	139	52%	12.6	0	6.0	--	-2.2%	--	6	--	3	32%	42%	21%	5%
2009	STL		51	76	531	67%	10.4	5			12.8%								

The Rams were excited to reunite offensive coordinator Al Saunders with McMichael (who played under him in Miami) and finally get a tight end involved in the passing game. Unfortunately, McMichael suffered a broken tibia and torn ligament in his right leg in the Rams' 31-14 loss to Buffalo on September 28, and he was placed on IR for the rest of the season. He participated in April minicamps and should be ready to go when the season starts. He's also the only veteran pass catcher currently on the Rams roster, so he'll make a nice fantasy backup this year.

Billy Miller

Height: 6-3   Weight: 230   College: USC   Draft: 1999/7 (218)   Born: 24-Apr-1977   Age: 32   Risk: Green

Year	Team	G	Rec	Pass	Yds	C%	Yd/C	TD	YAC	Rk	DVOA	Rk	DYAR	Rk	YAR	Short	Mid	Deep	Bomb
2006	NO	10	14	22	129	55%	9.2	0	2.5	--	-30.5%	--	-33	--	-27	56%	31%	13%	0%
2007	NO	16	27	38	328	71%	12.1	2	7.0	2	21.6%	8	79	13	85	59%	24%	16%	0%
2008	NO	12	45	62	579	73%	12.9	1	4.2	24	28.8%	5	150	7	150	51%	27%	17%	5%
2009	NO		36	59	468	61%	13.0	1			18.6%								

Miller caught eight passes labeled as "deep middle" in the official play-by-play, the most of any tight end in the NFL. His numbers on these deep middle passes: 8-of-10, 200 yards. Jeremy Shockey was 3-of-4 on passes to the deep middle for 75 yards. Add them up, and the Saints threw to their tight ends in the deep middle more than any other team. That's not surprising in one sense: the Saints threw more of every type of pass than any other team. Still, it's odd for a team filled with offensive weapons to devote so much deep attention to a (then) 31-year-old who spent most of his career as a backup. Chalk it up to the scheme, to Miller's skills, and to Drew Brees, who only uncorked those deep passes when he knew his tight ends were open enough to catch them.

Heath Miller

Height: 6-5   Weight: 256   College: Virginia   Draft: 2005/1 (30)   Born: 22-Oct-1982   Age: 27   Risk: Green

Year	Team	G	Rec	Pass	Yds	C%	Yd/C	TD	YAC	Rk	DVOA	Rk	DYAR	Rk	YAR	Short	Mid	Deep	Bomb
2006	PIT	16	34	55	393	62%	11.6	5	5.3	5	4.9%	17	42	15	38	43%	39%	18%	0%
2007	PIT	16	47	61	566	77%	12.0	7	4.4	14	38.5%	1	193	4	201	40%	42%	18%	0%
2008	PIT	13	48	65	514	74%	10.7	3	4.8	13	22.1%	7	120	12	120	58%	33%	9%	0%
2009	PIT		42	71	459	59%	10.9	4			10.5%								

After catching 13 passes for 104 yards and six scores in the red zone in 2007, Miller caught just seven passes for 38 yards and three touchdowns a year ago. Once teams stopped fearing the Steelers running game in the red zone, they were able to pay more attention to Miller on play-action passes. Except for the touchdowns, Miller's 2008 numbers were a repeat of his 2007 production, and his role in the offense hasn't changed. Ironically, the presence of a real goal-line running back may make him more productive, not less.

Zach Miller

Height: 6-4   Weight: 256   College: Arizona State   Draft: 2007/2 (38)   Born: 12-Nov-1985   Age: 24   Risk: Green

Year	Team	G	Rec	Pass	Yds	C%	Yd/C	TD	YAC	Rk	DVOA	Rk	DYAR	Rk	YAR	Short	Mid	Deep	Bomb
2007	OAK	16	44	69	444	64%	10.1	3	3.3	32	-6.4%	30	4	30	13	44%	41%	13%	3%
2008	OAK	15	56	86	778	65%	13.9	1	4.3	21	9.2%	16	92	15	103	40%	35%	21%	4%
2009	OAK		55	100	704	55%	12.8	4			-6.6%								

His disappointing 2007 combine performance now a distant memory, Miller has taken advantage of Oakland's mess at wide receiver to establish himself as the Raiders' go-to guy — and he's a skilled blocker to boot. One thing Miller needs to improve is his ability to get open in the red zone; eight of his 11 targets in the red zone ended up incomplete, including two passes Miller dropped. The list of similar tight ends over their first two seasons features a lot of names to make Raiders fans excited, and one to scare them: Dan Ross (of the early-'80s Bengals), Ozzie Newsome, Owen Daniels, Rickey Dudley, Chris Cooley, Randy McMichael, and Tony Gonzalez.

Shawn Nelson   Height: 6-5   Weight: 245 College: Southern Miss   Draft: 2009/FA   Born: 5-Oct-1985   Age: 24 Risk: Green

Year	Team	G	Rec	Pass	Yds	C%	Yd/C	TD	YAC	Rk	DVOA	Rk	DYAR	Rk	YAR	Short	Mid	Deep	Bomb
2009	BUF		20	27	155	74%	7.8	1			3.6%								

The scouting report on Nelson is that he is fast, can separate and has the body control and soft hands to make catches in traffic. He's not a strong blocker, but that's not what the Bills drafted him to do. Nelson's job is to add some size and playmaking options in the red zone.

Greg Olsen   Height: 6-6   Weight: 254 College: Miami   Draft: 2007/1 (31)   Born: 11-Mar-1985   Age: 24 Risk: Green

Year	Team	G	Rec	Pass	Yds	C%	Yd/C	TD	YAC	Rk	DVOA	Rk	DYAR	Rk	YAR	Short	Mid	Deep	Bomb
2007	CHI	14	39	66	391	59%	10.0	2	3.8	22	-9.6%	33	-10	33	-18	48%	29%	22%	2%
2008	CHI	16	54	82	574	66%	10.6	5	4.6	17	0.0%	24	41	22	48	62%	24%	11%	4%
2009	CHI		61	95	738	64%	12.1	7			17.0%								

G-Reg became the Bears' most effective receiver in his sophomore campaign, showing off arguably the best hands of any tight end in the league on countless tough catches. He had only three drops on 82 attempts, the fifth-best percentage of any tight end (minimum: 75 targets). Because of his athleticism, the Bears lined him up in multiple locations, splitting him out with more frequency as the season went along and even spotting him time as the H-back. That DVOA isn't incredibly impressive, but a 31.6% DVOA on third down is a sign of how often he came through in tight situations. The weak points in Olsen's game come at the line of scrimmage; he's below average as a blocker, and struggles to beat press coverage. He'll get better at it, though, and with the arrival of Jay Cutler, should start a string of Pro Bowl selections this year.

Ben Patrick   Height: 6-3   Weight: 252 College: Delaware   Draft: 2007/7 (215) Born: 23-Aug-1984   Age: 25 Risk: Green

Year	Team	G	Rec	Pass	Yds	C%	Yd/C	TD	YAC	Rk	DVOA	Rk	DYAR	Rk	YAR	Short	Mid	Deep	Bomb
2007	ARI	8	7	12	73	58%	10.4	2	4.1	--	8.4%	--	15	--	21	60%	20%	20%	0%
2008	ARI	6	11	18	104	61%	9.5	0	4.1	--	-9.5%	--	-3	--	-2	54%	38%	8%	0%
2009	ARI		12	17	115	73%	9.6	1			0.8%								

Patrick's one-yard touchdown catch in the second quarter of the Super Bowl that pulled the Cardinals within a field goal of the Steelers will likely go down as his career highlight. A seventh-round pick out of Delaware two years ago, there's no guarantee he'll be on this or any other roster this season — especially since he pulled a four-game suspension for taking the ADD stimulant Adderall without league permission.

Justin Peelle   Height: 6-4   Weight: 255 College: Oregon   Draft: 2002/4 (103) Born: 15-Mar-1979   Age: 30 Risk: Green

Year	Team	G	Rec	Pass	Yds	C%	Yd/C	TD	YAC	Rk	DVOA	Rk	DYAR	Rk	YAR	Short	Mid	Deep	Bomb
2006	MIA	15	16	18	116	94%	7.3	1	3.9	--	13.7%	--	24	--	21	85%	15%	0%	0%
2007	MIA	16	29	47	228	62%	7.9	2	5.4	8	-19.4%	38	-39	39	-40	88%	12%	0%	0%
2008	ATL	16	15	23	159	65%	10.6	2	7.5	--	7.7%	--	25	--	26	71%	24%	5%	0%
2009	ATL		10	18	101	56%	10.1	1			-10.2%								

The steady blocking Peelle followed Cam Cameron from San Diego to Miami. When CamCam was fired after 2007, Peelle followed his offensive coordinator, Mike Mularkey, to the Falcons. Peelle rewarded his new sensai with a career in high yards per catch. Atlanta rewarded Peelle by acquiring Tony Gonzalez. Peelle should be the main blocking tight end — and his catch rate was much better than his main competition for the secondary role, Ben Hartsock.

Brandon Pettigrew
Height: 6-6   Weight: 280   College: Oklahoma State   Draft: 2009/1 (20)   Born: 23-Feb-1985   Age: 24   Risk: Red

Year	Team	G	Rec	Pass	Yds	C%	Yd/C	TD	YAC	Rk	DVOA	Rk	DYAR	Rk	YAR	Short	Mid	Deep	Bomb
2009	DET		45	69	463	65%	10.3	6			19.4%								

A throwback tight end, Pettigrew's an elite blocker who gives the Lions a sixth lineman on run plays, not to mention another blocker to keep Matthew Stafford from being slaughtered. He's capable of sealing a defensive end or a linebacker on the edge for tosses and sweeps, and he can cut back underneath on wham blocks to create holes at the point of attack on the interior. Pettigrew doesn't have great speed, so he's not the downfield threat on seam patterns that your dream tight end would be, but his soft hands and huge frame make him an ideal landing point on play-action. Think Daniel Graham, but three inches taller. That's a championship-caliber tight end.

Leonard Pope
Height: 6-8   Weight: 250   College: Georgia   Draft: 2006/3 (72)   Born: 9-Sep-1983   Age: 26   Risk: Green

Year	Team	G	Rec	Pass	Yds	C%	Yd/C	TD	YAC	Rk	DVOA	Rk	DYAR	Rk	YAR	Short	Mid	Deep	Bomb
2006	ARI	16	16	23	161	70%	10.1	0	4.0	--	-11.0%	--	-6	--	0	65%	35%	0%	0%
2007	ARI	13	23	34	238	68%	10.3	5	3.4	28	3.7%	19	26	24	27	50%	32%	9%	9%
2008	ARI	7	9	13	77	69%	8.6	0	1.8	--	-23.2%	--	-14	--	-11	50%	33%	8%	8%
2009	ARI		22	33	206	67%	9.4	4			6.0%								

Pope is probably the best tight end on the Arizona roster, which is not saying much. This is virtually a run-and-shoot team that only brings in tight ends for short-yardage and clock-killing plays. With the injury Stephen Spach suffered in the playoffs, Arizona is counting on Pope to get this part-time job done.

Richard Quinn
Height: 6-4   Weight: 264   College: North Carolina   Draft: 2009/2 (64)   Born: 6-Sep-1986   Age: 23   Risk: Blue

Year	Team	G	Rec	Pass	Yds	C%	Yd/C	TD	YAC	Rk	DVOA	Rk	DYAR	Rk	YAR	Short	Mid	Deep	Bomb
2009	DEN		22	35	210	62%	9.8	0			-17.3%								

Quinn told the *Colorado Springs Gazette* in May that he didn't expect to be drafted. "I thought maybe I'd be a free agent and be blessed to have the opportunity to come to a team and maybe try out," he said. Quinn only caught 12 passes in his entire college career, so his skepticism is understandable. Quinn's a heck of a blocker, as you might expect, and he showed in offseason workouts that he can catch pretty well. In case you missed the offseason, the Broncos are doing things in their own special way; they selected Quinn to play the Daniel Graham role as a blocking tight end, even though they already have the real deal. A designated blocker in the second round? The world is your oyster, Josh McDaniels.

Gijon Robinson
Height: 6-1   Weight: 255   College: Missouri Western   Draft: 2008/FA   Born: 12-Oct-1984   Age: 25   Risk: Yellow

Year	Team	G	Rec	Pass	Yds	C%	Yd/C	TD	YAC	Rk	DVOA	Rk	DYAR	Rk	YAR	Short	Mid	Deep	Bomb
2008	IND	9	19	24	166	79%	8.7	0	5.4	--	-4.2%	--	5	--	4	75%	25%	0%	0%
2009	IND		19	26	170	73%	8.9	2			17.4%								

Another example of the Colts making immediate use of undrafted free agents, Robinson leapfrogged Tom Santi and Jacob Tamme on the depth chart because he was the better blocker and Dallas Clark already manned the receiving tight end duties. Robinson still needs to improve his hands because Manning will throw to anyone who is open, but as the Colts look to revamp their rushing attack, Robinson should maintain his hold as the second starting tight end.

Dante Rosario

Height: 6-4   Weight: 250   College: Oregon   Draft: 2007/5 (155)   Born: 25-Oct-1984   Age: 25   Risk: Green

Year	Team	G	Rec	Pass	Yds	C%	Yd/C	TD	YAC	Rk	DVOA	Rk	DYAR	Rk	YAR	Short	Mid	Deep	Bomb
2007	CAR	16	6	7	108	86%	18.0	2	6.0	--	88.4%	--	54	--	54	29%	29%	43%	0%
2008	CAR	9	18	31	209	58%	11.6	1	3.3	35	-0.9%	26	13	27	21	27%	57%	13%	3%
2009	CAR		23	42	219	55%	9.5	1			-18.0%								

Fantasy football waiver wires blew up after Rosario's game-winning touchdown catch in Week 1 against the Chargers. Rosario was on so many "Hot Lists" in the first couple weeks of the season, you'd have thought he was Rosario Dawson. Unfortunately, he put up about the same numbers as Ms. Dawson the rest of the season. The fantasy red carpet had been rolled up and stowed away by Week 6. Rosario put up a grand total of three catches for 43 yards over the final 10 weeks of the season. If Rosario could be less of a blocking liability and learn the snap count (five false starts by Week 4), he would get more chances in the passing game too. Then we could stop calling him Ms. Dawson and everyone would be happy.

Robert Royal

Height: 6-4   Weight: 257   College: LSU   Draft: 2002/5 (160)   Born: 15-May-1979   Age: 30   Risk: Blue

Year	Team	G	Rec	Pass	Yds	C%	Yd/C	TD	YAC	Rk	DVOA	Rk	DYAR	Rk	YAR	Short	Mid	Deep	Bomb
2006	BUF	16	23	39	233	59%	10.1	3	4.5	17	0.7%	20	20	23	19	51%	31%	11%	6%
2007	BUF	16	25	38	248	66%	9.9	3	5.9	5	-14.7%	35	-19	36	-21	66%	23%	6%	6%
2008	BUF	13	33	57	351	58%	10.6	1	3.4	34	-30.3%	41	-85	42	-65	50%	33%	15%	2%
2009	CLE		15	26	167	58%	11.1	1			-15.2%								

Royal posted career highs in games started, receptions and yardage last year, and he was still the second-worst tight end in the league according to DVOA. Cleveland fans who were accustomed to watching Kellen Winslow do his thing should treat the news that Royal will be competing with Steve Heiden for the starting tight end job with a mixture of shock and disgust.

Bo Scaife

Height: 6-2   Weight: 249   College: Texas   Draft: 2005/6 (179)   Born: 6-Jan-1981   Age: 28   Risk: Green

Year	Team	G	Rec	Pass	Yds	C%	Yd/C	TD	YAC	Rk	DVOA	Rk	DYAR	Rk	YAR	Short	Mid	Deep	Bomb
2006	TEN	14	29	56	370	55%	12.8	2	5.0	10	-7.5%	30	-1	30	2	49%	31%	16%	4%
2007	TEN	16	46	78	421	59%	9.2	1	3.2	34	-24.4%	41	-88	43	-69	47%	35%	15%	3%
2008	TEN	12	58	84	561	69%	9.7	2	5.9	6	-0.3%	25	39	23	40	67%	24%	6%	3%
2009	TEN		45	75	503	60%	11.2	1			-1.7%								

Scaife was often viewed as Vince Young's personal receiver, since the two had played together at Texas, and Young relied heavily on him his first two seasons in Tennessee. Like the rest of the Tennessee offense, however, Scaife saw his performance improve with the switch from Young to Kerry Collins. In truth, his still-negative DVOA shows that the Titans continue to lean on him too heavily and are throwing too many short passes that provide little value. His lack of touchdowns show his inability to get separation in tight quarters, as he does better working into the flat or working down the field. The decision to franchise Scaife is probably wise, as he is still an asset, but it allows the Titans' to avoid making a long-term commitment to a good but not great tight end.

Tony Scheffler

Height: 6-6   Weight: 260   College: Western Michigan   Draft: 2006/2 (61)   Born: 15-Feb-1983   Age: 26   Risk: Green

Year	Team	G	Rec	Pass	Yds	C%	Yd/C	TD	YAC	Rk	DVOA	Rk	DYAR	Rk	YAR	Short	Mid	Deep	Bomb
2006	DEN	13	18	37	286	49%	15.9	4	3.9	28	7.5%	13	39	16	50	21%	45%	24%	9%
2007	DEN	16	49	65	549	75%	11.2	5	4.1	19	25.8%	5	147	6	145	45%	33%	15%	6%
2008	DEN	12	40	62	645	66%	16.1	3	5.0	12	22.2%	6	124	11	133	32%	30%	32%	7%
2009	DEN		47	72	582	65%	12.4	4			16.7%								

Like most one-hour television dramas, the Josh McDaniels/Jay Cutler soap opera in Denver had a smaller running subplot, "Tony Scheffler is unhappy." Various press rumors said Scheffler didn't like the Broncos trading his buddy Cutler, that he was unsure with his role in the McDaniels offense, and that the Broncos tried to deal him away on draft day. It's true that in the past, McDaniels has used his tight ends primarily as blockers — the Patriots last year used a tight end on 88 percent of plays (10th in the NFL) but threw only 65 passes to tight ends (27th). Then again, Scheffler is a better receiver than the tight ends on those Patriots teams. By minicamp, Scheffler was telling reporters that everything was fine, "water off a duck's back." That's how it normally works: While the main plot tends to have future consequences, like condemning the Broncos to a 4-12 season, the subplot gets wrapped up nicely by the 11 o'clock news (10 Central and Mountain).

Visanthe Shiancoe

Height: 6-4   Weight: 250   College: Morgan State   Draft: 2003/3 (91)   Born: 18-Jun-1980   Age: 29   Risk: Green

Year	Team	G	Rec	Pass	Yds	C%	Yd/C	TD	YAC	Rk	DVOA	Rk	DYAR	Rk	YAR	Short	Mid	Deep	Bomb
2006	NYG	16	12	14	81	85%	6.8	0	3.3	--	-12.5%	--	-4	--	-7	83%	17%	0%	0%
2007	MIN	16	27	43	323	63%	12.0	1	4.6	12	-5.8%	29	4	29	0	37%	39%	16%	8%
2008	MIN	16	42	59	596	71%	14.2	7	4.3	20	50.0%	2	220	2	215	26%	46%	25%	4%
2009	MIN		48	82	543	59%	11.3	3			5.2%								

Shiancoe became a headline name when he was shown naked on camera in a postgame segment. While one shudders at the thought of what might have happened had the player been Terrell Owens, Shiancoe took his national exposure in stride. "I didn't just get out of the pool," Shiancoe quipped. The incident obscured what was a breakout year for Shiancoe, who took advantage of Sidney Rice's injury and became a valued member of the offense as a possession receiver taking advantage of mismatches. Combined with his usual effective blocking, Shiancoe deserved to get the Pro Bowl nod ahead of Chris Cooley; we suppose the NFC gave Cooley the tie-breaker because he exposed himself first. Shiancoe reportedly got down to three percent body fat in the offseason; if he has a big year, KUBIAK will need to start busting out its calipers for 2010.

Jeremy Shockey

Height: 6-5   Weight: 253   College: Miami   Draft: 2002/1 (14)   Born: 18-Aug-1980   Age: 29   Risk: Green

Year	Team	G	Rec	Pass	Yds	C%	Yd/C	TD	YAC	Rk	DVOA	Rk	DYAR	Rk	YAR	Short	Mid	Deep	Bomb
2006	NYG	15	66	115	623	57%	9.4	7	2.9	39	-1.8%	21	39	17	54	36%	49%	14%	1%
2007	NYG	14	57	93	619	61%	10.9	3	4.1	20	2.9%	21	63	18	63	39%	40%	18%	2%
2008	NO	12	50	72	486	69%	9.7	0	4.2	23	-5.1%	28	11	28	14	50%	34%	16%	0%
2009	NO		40	66	460	65%	11.5	3			8.0%								

Shockey caught more passes than Billy Miller, but he gained fewer yards, and his stat profile now fits that of a second tight end or H-back. Second tight ends catch a large percentage of their passes on first down, when teams often line up in two-TE sets and it's safe and prudent for the quarterback to check down to pick up four quick yards. Half of Shockey's 72 passes were thrown to him on first down. Miller was more likely to be targeted on third down than Shockey (19 to 14 on fewer passes) and on deep passes (see Miller's comment). Shockey has lost much of his speed, so his blocking and ability to work short zones are now his greatest attributes. That could be a problem, because coaches want their blocking tight ends seen and not heard, and Shockey has a way of finding the center of attention.

Alex Smith

Height: 6-4   Weight: 258   College: Stanford   Draft: 2005/3 (71)   Born: 22-May-1982   Age: 27   Risk: Blue

Year	Team	G	Rec	Pass	Yds	C%	Yd/C	TD	YAC	Rk	DVOA	Rk	DYAR	Rk	YAR	Short	Mid	Deep	Bomb
2006	TB	14	35	53	250	66%	7.1	3	3.5	37	-23.3%	38	-55	40	-61	72%	15%	11%	2%
2007	TB	14	32	53	385	60%	12.0	3	4.3	17	1.8%	22	32	20	34	40%	33%	23%	5%
2008	TB	11	21	38	250	55%	11.9	3	6.2	2	8.7%	17	42	21	34	53%	31%	11%	6%
2009	NE		19	29	212	66%	11.2	1			1.9%								

Smith is a big deal in his native Bahamas, but his trade to New England caused a conundrum on the island nation. Apparently, Bahamanians generally prefer the geographically close Miami Dolphins. Now, one of their own is suiting up for the 'Phins' arch-rival. Oh, to be in Freeport for those two AFC East clashes! Smith was tough to tackle on third down, averaging 11.7 in YAC. Seems like a typical Pats pickup.

L.J. Smith Height: 6-3   Weight: 258 College: Rutgers   Draft: 2003/2 (61)   Born: 13-May-1980 Age: 29 Risk: Yellow

Year	Team	G	Rec	Pass	Yds	C%	Yd/C	TD	YAC	Rk	DVOA	Rk	DYAR	Rk	YAR	Short	Mid	Deep	Bomb
2006	PHI	16	50	80	611	63%	12.2	5	5.2	7	5.7%	14	64	10	71	51%	41%	5%	3%
2007	PHI	10	22	44	236	50%	10.7	1	3.2	35	-24.0%	40	-52	40	-53	34%	46%	15%	5%
2008	PHI	12	37	64	298	58%	8.1	3	4.8	15	-16.7%	36	-42	36	-46	61%	30%	9%	0%
2009	BAL		36	72	308	50%	8.6	1			-32.2%								

Smith became pejoratively known strictly as "Franchise Player" amongst FO authors and readers after the Eagles mysteriously gave him that tag in the 2008 offseason. Smith looks the part — he's got the size, has reasonable speed, and is capable of making the occasional very nice play — but he struggles to shrug off injuries and is just that half-step too slow to cradle a pass properly or effectively engage a blocker, leading to lots of plays where he almost succeeds, only to fail very obviously. He dropped six of the 64 passes thrown to him, simply too many for a receiver who doesn't get downfield. Our game charters' comments about him are full of quips like "I don't know who the pass was going to" and "Smith never looked back for the ball," indicating that he's running the wrong routes. He had the worst DVOA of any receiver in the Eagles' offense who was thrown more than three passes. The Eagles will be better off without him. Smith signed a one-year deal with Baltimore, where he'll split opportunities with Todd Heap.

Matt Spaeth Height: 6-7   Weight: 270 College: Minnesota   Draft: 2007/3 (77)   Born: 24-Nov-1983 Age: 26 Risk: Blue

Year	Team	G	Rec	Pass	Yds	C%	Yd/C	TD	YAC	Rk	DVOA	Rk	DYAR	Rk	YAR	Short	Mid	Deep	Bomb
2007	PIT	14	5	6	34	83%	6.8	3	2.8	--	70.0%	--	35	--	37	83%	17%	0%	0%
2008	PIT	9	17	26	136	65%	8.0	0	4.4	19	-15.1%	34	-13	33	-11	62%	38%	0%	0%
2009	PIT		13	24	96	54%	7.4	1			-31.6%								

Spaeth caught 12 passes for 108 yards in two games when Heath Miller was injured. He can be an adequate receiving option when called upon, and he could still fill a role as a "goal-line surprise" as he did in 2007. The most similar tight ends through two years: John (brother of Mike) Tice, Jim Kleinsasser, Justin Peelle, Michael Gaines, and Will Heller.

Jerramy Stevens Height: 6-7   Weight: 260 College: Washington   Draft: 2002/1 (28)   Born: 13-Nov-1979 Age: 30 Risk: Blue

Year	Team	G	Rec	Pass	Yds	C%	Yd/C	TD	YAC	Rk	DVOA	Rk	DYAR	Rk	YAR	Short	Mid	Deep	Bomb
2006	SEA	11	22	48	231	48%	10.5	4	1.7	44	-26.7%	41	-59	41	-51	28%	62%	7%	3%
2007	TB	15	18	21	189	86%	10.5	4	2.7	--	52.9%	--	87	--	87	60%	20%	15%	5%
2008	TB	11	36	59	397	61%	11.0	2	3.6	32	-9.7%	30	-10	31	-6	51%	28%	16%	5%
2009	TB		18	36	216	50%	12.0	1			-19.7%								

When your team brings in Kellen "F-in'" Soldier" Winslow to provide some character at your position, there is a problem. Stevens' production dropped precipitously after a monster 2007, and he won't be able to count on his football skills to paper over his sociopathy much longer. But he will probably spend another season in Tampa, much to the chagrin of the folks behind FireJerramyStevens.com.

Ben Utecht Height: 6-6   Weight: 249 College: Minnesota   Draft: 2004/FA   Born: 30-Jun-1981 Age: 28 Risk: Green

Year	Team	G	Rec	Pass	Yds	C%	Yd/C	TD	YAC	Rk	DVOA	Rk	DYAR	Rk	YAR	Short	Mid	Deep	Bomb
2006	IND	14	37	53	377	70%	10.2	0	4.9	11	12.0%	8	60	11	60	44%	48%	8%	0%
2007	IND	14	31	37	364	84%	11.7	1	5.3	9	32.9%	2	99	11	103	53%	39%	8%	0%
2008	CIN	8	16	28	123	57%	7.7	0	2.8	39	-41.0%	42	-62	39	-56	52%	28%	16%	4%
2009	CIN		22	36	196	61%	8.9	1			-5.3%								

Utecht has a reputation as a finesse player who doesn't like the physical elements of the game. That perception wasn't helped when his season came apart after a monster wallop to Utecht's heart (OK, chest) by Tennessee's David Thornton on the first play of the second game of the year. Sure, it was a foot problem that plagued Utecht for much of the year, but it was the blow to the thorax that screamed "metaphor!" Signed by Cincinnati in order to provide a much-needed receiving tight end, Peyton Manning's former toy grabbed only 16 passes, while missing seven games (counting the Titans tilt). Utecht, who once sang the national anthem before a game in Minnesota, released an album of Christian music during the offseason. That faith will be tested by draftee Chase Coffman.

Delanie Walker
Height: 6-2   Weight: 215   College: Central Missouri State   Draft: 2006/6 (175)   Born: 12-Aug-1984   Age: 25   Risk: Blue

Year	Team	G	Rec	Pass	Yds	C%	Yd/C	TD	YAC	Rk	DVOA	Rk	DYAR	Rk	YAR	Short	Mid	Deep	Bomb
2006	SF	7	2	4	30	50%	15.0	0	15.5	--	-7.7%	--	0	--	-3	50%	50%	0%	0%
2007	SF	16	21	42	174	50%	8.3	1	5.6	7	-39.4%	44	-90	44	-86	76%	12%	10%	2%
2008	SF	15	10	16	155	63%	15.5	1	10.8	--	-1.1%	--	7	--	15	38%	31%	25%	6%
2009	SF		15	26	153	58%	10.2	0			-1.6%								

Walker neither blocks nor catches particularly well, and is danger of losing his roster spot to rookie Bear Pascoe. On the other hand, Delanie Walker Red is a very drinkable whiskey.

Benjamin Watson
Height: 6-3   Weight: 253   College: Georgia   Draft: 2004/1 (32)   Born: 18-Dec-1980   Age: 28   Risk: Yellow

Year	Team	G	Rec	Pass	Yds	C%	Yd/C	TD	YAC	Rk	DVOA	Rk	DYAR	Rk	YAR	Short	Mid	Deep	Bomb
2006	NE	13	49	91	643	54%	13.1	3	4.1	23	-4.9%	27	14	24	0	38%	35%	16%	11%
2007	NE	12	36	49	389	73%	10.8	6	3.2	33	22.8%	7	103	9	101	54%	23%	23%	0%
2008	NE	10	22	47	209	47%	9.5	2	2.4	42	-29.4%	40	-73	41	-71	33%	45%	19%	2%
2009	NE		37	56	447	66%	12.1	4			14.1%								

Watson got a lot of reps in 2008, but mostly as a blocker. You usually think of tight ends as a good option on third down, but Watson had only two receptions there a year ago. The Patriots brought in Alex Smith and Chris Baker to challenge for production, and Watson will need more than a sub-zero DYAR and unspectacular Catch Rate to compete with the new guys. He's never quite produced like a first-round pick, and was probably a bit of an overdraft.

Kellen Winslow
Height: 6-4   Weight: 243   College: Miami   Draft: 2004/1 (6)   Born: 21-Jul-1983   Age: 26   Risk: Red

Year	Team	G	Rec	Pass	Yds	C%	Yd/C	TD	YAC	Rk	DVOA	Rk	DYAR	Rk	YAR	Short	Mid	Deep	Bomb
2006	CLE	16	89	120	875	76%	9.8	3	3.7	33	7.9%	12	118	4	111	48%	38%	10%	4%
2007	CLE	16	82	148	1106	55%	13.5	5	4.4	13	0.8%	24	78	14	85	29%	50%	19%	2%
2008	CLE	10	43	83	428	52%	10.0	3	2.8	38	-11.5%	32	-23	35	-31	34%	52%	14%	0%
2009	TB		69	114	858	61%	12.4	5			11.2%								

A high ankle sprain kept Winslow out of the final four games of last season, meaning that he missed most of the Ken Dorsey-Bruce Gradowski epoch. It was probably for the best: Winslow had just seven catches in three games before leaving the lineup. New Bucs offense coordinator Jeff Jagodzinski uses the tight end a lot in the passing game — Boston College tight end Ryan Purvis had 54 catches in 2007 — so Winslow will play a major role on his new team if he can stay healthy, infection-free, and non-controversial. The Bucs may well settle for two out of three.

Jason Witten
Height: 6-5   Weight: 257   College: Tennessee   Draft: 2003/3 (69)   Born: 6-May-1982   Age: 27   Risk: Yellow

Year	Team	G	Rec	Pass	Yds	C%	Yd/C	TD	YAC	Rk	DVOA	Rk	DYAR	Rk	YAR	Short	Mid	Deep	Bomb
2006	DAL	16	64	91	754	70%	11.8	1	3.9	29	20.6%	3	154	2	166	32%	49%	12%	6%
2007	DAL	16	96	141	1145	68%	11.9	7	3.9	21	21.3%	9	258	2	230	32%	53%	13%	2%
2008	DAL	16	81	120	952	68%	11.8	4	4.1	25	18.9%	11	203	3	194	41%	41%	15%	3%
2009	DAL		82	113	994	73%	12.1	5			22.2%								

No one ever minded when Mark Chmura was good friends with Brett Favre, but for some reason, Witten and Tony Romo being buddy-buddy ruins T.O.'s day. What probably upset Owens most is that he was being outplayed; Witten was the Cowboys' best receiver last year, and arguably their best offensive player altogether. He was Romo's go-to target on third down, with a DVOA of 38.4% (versus Owens' -6.3% DVOA with three more targets). His consistency since entering the league has been remarkable, never falling below 18th in DVOA and averaging between 11 and 12 yards per catch every year since his rookie campaign. He doesn't have that game-changing capability to really stand out as a potential Hall of Fame player, but he's already made five Pro Bowls and may very well have five more ahead of him.

GOING DEEP

Richard Angulo, JAC: Angulo's a blocking tight end and depth player whose size made him an attractive option in the season's last few games, as Jacksonville was just trying to make it through the season without any extra drama. (2008 stats: 8-for-11, 63 yards, -20.4% DVOA, -10 DYAR.)

Billy Bajema, STL: A pure blocking tight end and special teamer, Bajema's move from the 49ers to the Rams is proof that the teams in the NFC West are content to recycle marginal tight ends among themselves.

Gary Barnidge, CAR: Despite having a name worthy of a big ugly guard, Barnidge was more of a receiving than blocking tight end coming out of Louisville in 2008. After playing at around 230 pounds and running a 4.6 40 time at the combine, Barnidge spent last season bulking up (he's listed as 247 pounds on NFL.com now) and contributing on special teams. The fact that Jeff King was re-signed to only a one-year contract this offseason may bode well for Barnidge.

Anthony Becht, ARI: As of May, taking a page out of Denver's approach to running backs, the Cardinals were carrying six tight ends on their roster. The good news for Becht is that A) none of them are particularly good, and B) he's probably the best blocker among them. The bad news is that he's 31 and offers no help in the passing game, so if Stephen Spach recovers from the ACL injury he suffered in the playoffs, Becht may be looking for work in August. That's too bad, because the German version of the new Star Trek movie translates Bones at "Becht" and Spock as "Spach." It would be nice if they could stick together, ja? (2008 stats: 6-for-11, 39 yards, -48.7% DVOA, -31 DYAR.)

Travis Beckum, NYG: The Giants chose Beckum, a former walk-on defensive end at Wisconsin, with the 100th pick in the draft. Beckum has great hands and the versatility to play in the backfield, on the line, or even potentially split out. He suffered a series of injuries as a senior, culminating in a broken leg that wasn't healed by the time the Combine rolled around. Big Blue sees him as a player who can exploit linebackers in man coverage, but he'll need to get healthy before he can do anything like that. It wouldn't be a surprise to see the Giants stash him on the physically unable to perform list to start the season and even eventually move him to IR.

Dan Campbell, NO: The well-traveled Campbell pulled a hamstring in Week 1 and missed the rest of the season. We're afraid to ask how far he pulled it or where he pulled it to. He's moved back to New Orleans, where he and ex-Giants teammate Jeremy Shockey should be able to reunite their tag team, the Suicide Blondes.

Mark Campbell, FA: Random stat: Campbell was 7-of-8 for 90 yards and one touchdown on second downs. The Saints released Mark Campbell and signed Dan Campbell to be their third tight end in the offseason. The only plausible reason for such a switch is to confuse sportswriters or recycle the uniform. (2008 stats: 12-for-16, 121 yards, 2 TD, 25.1% DVOA, 41 DYAR.)

James Casey, HOU: Casey got a lot of hype before the draft as a 245-pounder who could do everything from play fullback in an I-Formation to flanker to quarterback in the Wildcat, but he ended up falling to the fifth round, where the

Texans snapped him up. At 24 and with three years as a White Sox pitcher behind him, the future's now for Casey, but he should be able to make the team as the third tight end.

Scott Chandler, FA: A 6-foot-7 specimen of an athlete, the Chargers' 2007 fourth-round pick was a project who San Diego hoped to turn into Antonio Gates lite. Instead, Chandler struggled with a toe injury and couldn't get on the field, leading to his release in April. He's a decent blocker with good hands, so Chandler should find a role somewhere else and could surprise.

Daniel Coats, CIN: Another contributor to Cincinnati's horrid rushing attack, Coats is a tight end hastily shifted to fullback when Jeremi Johnson's bloated frame proved too much for his knee to support. Coats was a pleasant surprise as an undrafted free agent in 2007, blocking well and being a solid special teamer, but he lacks the instincts and power to be an effective fullback. Plus, if his hands were as good as advertised, would he only catch two out of 10 passes? (19 yards, -70.3% DVOA, -48 DYAR.)

Tony Curtis, KC: Curtis lost his job as the Cowboys' second tight end once Martellus Bennett learned the playbook; he was a restricted free agent, but the Cowboys didn't even bother to tender him a contract, freeing him to sign with Kansas City. He'll compete with Sean Ryan to backup Brad Cottam. (2008 stats: 8-for-12, 37 yards, -59.8% DVOA, 40 DYAR.)

Kellen Davis, CHI: The Bears' fifth-round pick in 2008 played all 16 games on special teams without recording a catch. He's a good enough athlete to have seen some spot duty at Michigan State as a pass rusher; the Bears are hoping to mold him into a football player. They've got two more years.

Darnell Dinkins, NO: The best special teams performers have a certain statistical profile. First, they hang around for years, staying with teams for three or four seasons at a time, despite the fact that they are clearly second- or third-stringers. Second, they rack up five or six tackles per year; Dinkins has 31 in his seven-year career with the Ravens and Browns. Finally, the players who block for kickoff returns usually field a short kickoff or two per year; Dinkins has 15 returns for 160 yards. The Saints need all-purpose special teamers, so Dinkins probably has an edge over the dozen or so other third tight ends hanging around the Saints roster. (2008 stats: 5-for-11, 41 yards, 1 TD, -32.8% DVOA, -17 DYAR.)

Davon Drew, BAL: Drew was recruited as a quarterback by East Carolina; when he was moved to tight end at the end of the 2005 season, Drew refused the switch and left practice without permission, earning a two-day suspension. He eventually came around, bulked up to 254 pounds, and caught 43 balls for 695 yards and three touchdowns as a senior. Drew is not an in-line blocker, but he has good hands and enough speed to contribute in the passing game. He'll battle L.J. Smith for a role in the offense and should win one before the end of the season.

Jeff Dugan, MIN: Dugan is an H-Back who's had a total of 23 touches over the first five years of his career. There are inanimate objects with more fantasy value. Like, say, the pylon. Sure, it might always be out of bounds and can't break its own plane, but maybe you can convince someone in your league that it's due to score after being so consistently close to the goal line without getting in. If you tried to trade your friend Jeff Dugan, he'd assume that was the name of the guy at the draft he didn't know.

Casey FitzSimmons, DET: FitzSimmons is, by all accounts, a sweetheart of a guy who's stuck playing for an absolutely abysmal team. A blocking tight end/H-back, FitzSimmons not only made the NFL as an undrafted free agent from tiny Carroll College, but he got to play there after playing at such a small high school in Montana that the league played eight-a-side, with FizSimmons lining up at wide receiver, tight end, defensive end, and linebacker. You get the feeling the new coaching staff will take a liking to him. (2008 stats: 12-for-28, 85 yards, 1 TD, -44.1% DVOA, -70 DYAR.)

Dan Gronkowski, DET: The man chosen before Mr. Irrelevant, Gronkowski is Vernon Davis redux: He's ripped to shreds and is a solid blocker, but he struggles to turn his timed speed into game speed and is inconsistent. Gronkowski even replaced Davis at Maryland after the latter was drafted. The differences? Davis is better at getting off the line … and was selected 249 picks before Gronkowski.

Rodney Hannah, DAL: A former basketball player at Houston, Hannah's spent the last two years on the Cowboys practice squad. The departure of Tony Curtis frees up the third tight end spot for him, but as you might expect, he's raw enough to come with a USDA recommendation.

Joey Haynos, MIA: Haynos worked his way up from walk-on at Maryland to the Mackey Award Watch List in his senior season. Although he went undrafted in 2008, the Dolphins like his size and his potential — to whatever extent things progress contractually with Anthony Fasano and David Martin, you could see more of Haynos in the near future.

Will Heller, DET: Signed away from Seattle this offseason, Heller is less a tight end and more an undersized lineman who runs a lot of tackle-eligible plays. With the Lions taking Brandon Pettigrew 20th overall in the draft, Heller won't have to worry about reading coverages or running routes, and will be able to concentrate solely on putting defensive ends and linebackers on their backs. (2006-2008 stats: 21-for-37, 143 yards, 4 TD, -26.0% DVOA, -54 DYAR.)

Anthony Hill, HOU: As a block-first, -second, and -third tight end, the Texans drafted Hill with the intention that he'd be a direct replacement for Mark Bruener. As his skill set is the polar opposite of Owen Daniels', he'll beat out James Casey for the second tight end spot and see playing time in two-tight end sets, but he has no fantasy value.

Tory Humphrey, GB: Humphrey had seven starts from games where the Packers started out in a two-tight end set, but he was an inconsistent contributor in the passing game and isn't a good enough blocker to justify the roster spot. He wasn't tendered a contract by the Packers as an unrestricted free agent, but when no one bit on his bait, he went back to Green Bay on a one-year deal. (2008 stats: 11-for-16, 162 yards, 22.1% DVOA, 33 DYAR.)

Cornelius Ingram, PHI: Ingram was one of the most intriguing options in this year's draft. After playing several different positions at Florida and nearly quitting football altogether, Ingram settled in as a 245-pound junior tight end and showed off the ability to become a valuable receiver. He dipped his toes in the 2008 Draft, but changed his mind and returned to Florida for his senior year, only to tear his ACL in August and miss the entire season. Philly grabbed him with the hopes of using him in mismatches against linebackers when they go to four-wide sets. He's another candidate to be stashed on injured reserve for a season, a la Jeremy Bloom.

Darcy Johnson, NYG: With a work ethic forged from two decades of beating up punks who made fun of his first name, Johnson put on 15 pounds of muscle while playing one game over his first two NFL seasons. That gave him the strength he needed to become an effective blocker in two-tight end sets, and when teams forgot about him, he got open for a few passes. Any time half your receptions are touchdowns, you're doing something right. Johnson will split reps with Michael Matthews again this year. (2008 stats: 4-for-6, 46 yards, 2 TD, 48.9% DVOA, 28 DYAR.)

David Johnson, PIT: The 6-foot-2 Johnson prepared for the NFL by adding muscle as a senior year that put his weight in the 265-pound range, which makes him a misfit at tight end. He'll play fullback or H-Back at this level, and with the Steelers, that means he'll be competing with Sean McHugh for a roster spot. Maybe Pittsburgh will cut McHugh because his name sounds too much like Steely McBeam.

Jim Kleinsasser, MIN: Strictly a blocker at this point (17 catches over the past three seasons), the long-time Minnesota H-back signed a three-year, $9 million deal to stay with the team and clear out holes for Adrian Peterson. (2008 stats: 6-for-13, 92 yards, -2.0% DVOA, 4 DYAR.)

Nate Lawrie, FA: The Yale grad caught two passes from Harvard man Ryan Fitzpatrick in the season finale against KC, allowing the CBS Z team announcers relegated to the game to make condescending comments about how they were too smart to be playing football. They were the only passes Lawrie caught, and after five years and four catches, it's time to put that political science degree to use.

John Madsen, CLE: The Raiders signed Madsen as an undrafted free agent out of Utah and converted him from wide receiver to tight end. He was useful in 2006 and 2007, but barely played in 2008, and the Raiders cut him near the end of the season when they signed Ben Troupe. He signed in Cleveland, and there could be a place for him in the new Jets-influenced offense that will likely split tight ends out wide a good amount of the time. (Combined stats 2006-2008: 19-of-32, 248 yards, 2 TD, 0.9% DVOA, 19 DYAR.)

Michael Matthews, NYG: The 6-foot-4, 260-pound Matthews is strictly a blocking tight end who made the roster after Jeremy Shockey was dealt.

Sean McHugh, PIT: Two of McHugh's three receptions last year came when Heath Miller was hurt, making him the second tight end. He has limited value as an extra H-back or fullback; no one is going to give McHugh 17 touches, as the Lions did two years ago.

Zach Miller, JAC: The world really does not need two Zach Millers at tight end. This Miller is a 233-pound college quarterback the Jaguars are hoping to convert to receiver. You know, because everyone in Jacksonville just loved the Matt Jones era.

Garrett Mills, MIN: Some teams only carry two tight ends. Mills is Minnesota's fourth-string tight end. He had three catches for 49 yards against the Steelers in Week 1, making him a trendy waiver-wire pickup; he had two catches over the final 15 games, which is yet another reason why you shouldn't overreact when it comes to big performances in Week 1. Where's Frisman Jackson these days, anyway? (2008 stats: 5-for-11, 65 yards, -3.0% DVOA, 3 DYAR.)

Martrez Milner, NYJ: Milner was let go by the new Falcons front office in September, only a year after Bobby Petrino grabbed him out of Georgia in the fourth round. Milner caught on with the Giants and was on their practice squad the rest of the year, then got waived in May and picked up by the Jets. He's an athlete they hope to mold into a pass-catching tight end.

Cameron Morrah, SEA: This is harsh, but we're rooting against the Cal product just so we never have to hear Chris Berman yell "Cameron Sodom and Gomorrah" into a microphone on a cold, lonely Sunday night in November. He's a seventh-round pick who came out too early and is years away from making an impact.

Brandon Myers, OAK: An Iowa product, Myers should benefit from a weak depth chart behind Zach Miller (Raiders edition) and win a roster spot as the team's third tight end. A two-time All-Big Ten selection, Myers is an effective blocker with decent hands.

John Nalbone, MIA: Bill Parcells went to Monmouth three years ago and came away with Miles Austin; this year, he brought back Nalbone, who profiles as a tight end or H-back at this level. With excellent hands, he could carve out a role in the Miami offense as a safety valve with future upside as a starting tight end.

Buck Ortega, NO: A special teams gunner who caught one three-yard pass in three attempts last season, Ortega will probably lose his job to Darnell Dinkins.

John Owens, SEA: Detroit's third-string tight end signed with Seattle, where he'll move up to the second-string, but still remain a relatively anonymous blocker. (2008 stats: 8-for-12, 56 yards, 1 TD, -20.7% DVOA, -12 DYAR.)

Bear Pascoe, SF: The 49ers may have hit the sixth-round jackpot here. Much like the 49ers' overhyped starting tight end, Pascoe is a ferocious blocker, but unlike Davis, he also seems to be catching everything thrown to him in offseason minicamps. Plus, you have to love a guy who ropes cattle in his spare time and describes his playing style by saying, "I'm mean, yeah, but I'm playing nasty. I'm not playing dirty, I'm just playing nasty."

John Phillips, DAL: Heath Miller's replacement at Virginia lacks the athleticism to play a featured role, but as a max-effort blocker and gunner, he'll stick on the bottom of the Cowboys roster.

Jeb Putzier, DEN: Putzier returns to Denver, where his career started way back in 2002. His best years were in 2004 and 2005, when he ranked fifth and 10th among tight ends in DYAR. Those days are long gone, and it will be a struggle for Putzier to make the regular season roster.

Jason Rader, ATL: Rader only caught a single pass in 2008, and will be a victim of the numbers game in Atlanta — but he's 271 pounds, so teams needing a big blocker on the end of the line should give Rader a look.

Martin Rucker, CLE: Rucker started a game late in the season when both Kellen Winslow and Steve Heiden were hurt. Both of his receptions converted third downs. He was a productive receiver at Missouri and may get more opportunities this year if the Browns finally part ways with Steve Heiden. (2008 stats: 2-for-6, 17 yards, -29.7% DVOA, -9 DYAR.)

Sean Ryan, KC: Ryan bounced around the league last year, playing for Miami, New Orleans, and San Francisco, catching three of five passes for 15 yards (-12 DYAR, -43.2% DVOA). Kansas City signed him this offseason, but he doesn't really have a place in the Todd Haley offense outside of the goal-line package.

Tom Santi, IND: An offseason knee injury put Santi behind the curve in his rookie season. Midseason knee and shoulder injuries (and the Colts' need for a roster spot) led to a trip to injured reserve. Santi is a promising receiver, but he will need to be a more consistent blocker to play opposite Dallas Clark. (2008 stats: 10-for-13, 64 yards, 1 TD, -5.4% DVOA, 2 DYAR.)

Matt Schobel, PHI: Schobel's most prominent moment of the season was ignominious to say the least: It was he who missed the block on Alex Brown on fourth-and-goal from the Bears' 1-yard line in Week 4, costing Philly the game. He was phased out in favor of Brent Celek from there on out, and only had two receptions all season. At least he didn't get concussed again. Schobel will probably be back as the blocking tight end, which isn't a good thing.

Derek Schouman, BUF: Schouman made up one half of the Flying Dereks rotation, but at 6-foot-2 and 223 pounds, he's really more of an H-back than a traditional tight end. He'll be challenged for playing time by rookie Shawn Nelson, who is faster and more of a vertical threat. (2008 stats: 15-for-20, 153 yards, 1 TD, 0.6% DVOA, 11 DYAR.)

Stephen Spach, ARI: Spach signed with the Cardinals in October and soon became the team's top tight end, an indictment of incumbents Leonard Pope and Ben Patrick. His three receptions and 34 yards against Atlanta in the playoffs were both A) career single-game highs, and B) higher than his numbers for the entire regular season (two catches for 15 yards). Then against Carolina, he tore his ACL, MCL, and meniscus. He still hopes to be ready for the start of training camp, but we doubt he'll start, and if he does, he won't have any fantasy value.

Craig Stevens, TEN: Stevens is a blocking tight end in the perfect scheme for his talents: the Titans use lots of multi-TE sets and will give a glorified extra tackle 20 snaps per game, plus special teams. The team drafted Jared Cook, but Stevens is a real tight end, while Cook is a tall bodybuilder who was issued a two-digit uniform number beginning with an eight. Look for Stevens to find a role while Cook finds himself on the team's wide receiver treadmill.

Tony Stewart, OAK: Stewart is still a blocker first, a blocker second, and a receiver something like twenty-fifth, but he did get back on the stat sheet last year after going all of 2007 without a single pass thrown in his direction. (2008 stats: 11-for-15 for 81 yards, 1 DYAR, -6.1% DVOA.)

Quinn Sypniewski, BAL: Sypniewski suffered a freakishly-awful ACL injury in a 2008 minicamp. The description of the event uses words like "shredded ligament" and "shattered bone" in a way that makes you wince at the computer monitor. As of late May of this year, doctors were still performing meatball surgery to reattach various parts of the tight end's leg to each other. Sypniewski is doubtful for the start of camp, and his career may be over.

Jacob Tamme, IND: Tamme was an athletic fourth-round pick but lost a camp battle to Gijon Robinson, who is a better blocker. Tamme also fell behind Tom Santi on the depth chart, and his superior draft position means very little now that all three are in their second season.

David Thomas, NE: The Pats thought highly enough of Thomas to select him in the third round of the 2006 draft, but he's been a disappointment since he broke his foot in 2007. With Chris Baker and Alex Smith now on the roster, Thomas looks like the odd man out. (2008 stats: 9-of-17, 93 yards, -22.6% DVOA, -18 DYAR.)

Ben Troupe, FA: Cut by the Bucs after Jerramy Stevens got healthy, Troupe wound up in Oakland, where he injured his foot and didn't play a down. A second-round pick in 2004 by the Titans, Troupe has never lived up to that high draft status, and is strictly emergency fill-in material at this point.

Jerame Tuman, ARI: Honestly, can anyone in Phoenix learn how to spell "Jeremy?" The Cardinals cut Tuman after the season, and he has probably played his last game in the NFL after a ten-year career.

Daniel Wilcox, FA: Wilcox is now 32 and coming off a leg injury that ended his season in November. He had a fine little career as a second tight end for a team that loves its second tight end, but he has reached the end. (2008 stats: 5-for-7, 19 yards, 2 TD, 12.6% DVOA, 10 DYAR.)

Eddie Williams, WAS: A seventh-round pick out of Idaho, Williams tore his ACL at the end of the college season and is almost assuredly going to spend his rookie season on IR. He's expected to eventually replace Mike Sellers as the Redskins' H-back.

Kris Wilson, SD: The former Chiefs H-Back was cut by Philly in training camp and caught on as San Diego's third tight end, making it into three games. If Antonio Gates were to get hurt, Wilson might actually jump ahead of Brandon Manumaleuna on the depth chart because of his superior ability as a receiver, but that wouldn't mean he would be particularly good.

George Wrighster, NYG: At his "Catch This" blog (http://tightend.blogspot.com), you can read about Wrighster's exploits as one of Jacksonville's seemingly endless parade of tight ends, his release in early April, and his eventual signing with the Giants. It may not match Martellus Bennett's blog for sheer wackiness, but Wrighster does have some heartfelt thoughts about football, family and many other things. For the Giants, he'll back up Kevin Boss if he can stay healthy.

Todd Yoder, WAS: Yoder will have a job in Washington until Fred Davis gets the hang of the NFL — someone has to back up Chris Cooley, and right now, Yoder's the best bet. (2008 stats: 8-for-10, 50 yards, 1 TD, -5.9% DVOA, 1 DYAR.)

Kicker and Defense Projections

Listed below are the 2009 KUBIAK projections for kickers. Because of the inconsistency of field-goal percentage from year to year, kickers are projected almost entirely based on team forecasts, although a handful of individual factors do come into play:

• More experience leads to a slightly higher field-goal percentage in general, with the biggest jump between a kicker's rookie and sophomore seasons.

• Kickers with a better career field-goal percentage tend to get more attempts, although they are not necessarily more accurate.

• Field-goal percentage on kicks over 40 yards tends to regress to the mean.

Kickers are also listed with a Risk of Green, Yellow, or Red, as explained in the introduction to the section on quarterbacks. (There are Blue kickers in past seasons, but no kickers score as Blue for 2009.) Although there are a couple of camp battles for kicker positions, there is no significant difference between the projections for Steven Hauschka and Graham Gano in Baltimore, or those for Ryan Succop and Connor Barth in Kansas City.

2009 Kicker Projections

Kicker	Team	FG	Pct	XP	Pts	Risk	Kicker	Team	FG	Pct	XP	Pts	Risk
Stephen Gostkowski	NE	31-37	84%	49	141	Green	Jason Hanson	DET	27-32	84%	31	112	Green
Adam Vinatieri	IND	30-33	91%	48	138	Yellow	Kris Brown	HOU	26-31	84%	32	111	Yellow
Nate Kaeding	SD	25-29	86%	52	129	Yellow	Jason Elam	ATL	26-30	87%	33	110	Green
Olindo Mare	SEA	30-34	88%	37	127	Green	Lawrence Tynes	NYG	23-29	79%	40	108	Green
Robbie Gould	CHI	29-35	83%	41	127	Green	John Kasay	CAR	25-31	81%	34	108	Green
Phil Dawson	CLE	32-38	84%	28	126	Green	Steven Hauschka	BAL	27-36	75%	27	107	Red
Jeff Reed	PIT	26-30	87%	44	122	Green	Ryan Succop	KC	23-29	79%	37	105	Red
Josh Scobee	JAC	26-32	81%	43	121	Green	Nick Folk	DAL	21-29	72%	40	104	Green
Josh Brown	STL	28-34	82%	38	121	Green	Dan Carpenter	MIA	22-28	79%	35	102	Red
Garrett Hartley	NO	23-30	77%	48	118	Red	Jay Feely	NYJ	25-31	81%	27	102	Green
Ryan Longwell	MIN	25-29	86%	43	117	Yellow	Rian Lindell	BUF	24-28	86%	26	99	Green
David Akers	PHI	26-32	81%	38	117	Green	Neil Rackers	ARI	21-25	84%	33	97	Yellow
Mason Crosby	GB	26-32	81%	39	116	Red	Sebastian Janikowski	OAK	22-27	81%	30	97	Green
Rob Bironas	TEN	27-33	82%	36	116	Green	Matt Prater	DEN	22-27	81%	31	95	Yellow
Shayne Graham	CIN	28-36	78%	30	115	Green	Shaun Suisham	WAS	21-28	75%	28	91	Red
Joe Nedney	SF	26-29	90%	35	113	Green	Mike Nugent	TB	18-24	75%	27	81	Red

Listed below are the 2009 KUBIAK projections for fantasy team defense. The projection method is discussed in an essay in *Pro Football Prospectus 2006*, the key conclusions of which were:

• Schedule strength is very important for projecting fantasy defense.

• Categories used for scoring in fantasy defense have no consistency from year-to-year whatsoever, with the exception of sacks and interceptions.

Fumble recoveries and defensive touchdowns are forecast primarily based on the projected sacks and interceptions, rather than the team's totals in these categories from a year ago. This is why the 2009 projections will look very different from the fantasy defense values from the 2008 season. Safeties and shutouts are not common enough to have a significant effect on the projections, and team defense projections do not come with risk factors. Special teams touchdowns are not included. In addition to projection of separate categories, we also give an overall total based on our generic fantasy scoring formula: one point for a sack, two points for a fumble recovery or interception, and six points for a touchdown.

2009 Fantasy Team Defense Projections

Team	Fant Pts	Int	Sacks	Fum Rec	Def TD	Team	Fant Pts	Int	Sacks	Fum Rec	Def TD
CHI	135	24.0	42.0	11.7	3.7	MIA	93	10.2	40.6	7.5	2.8
SD	133	19.3	50.0	11.0	3.7	OAK	92	15.3	27.9	8.7	2.7
BAL	128	25.5	34.4	6.6	4.8	NYJ	89	13.9	31.3	7.9	2.4
MIN	116	19.2	33.5	12.7	3.1	ATL	88	13.4	28.6	9.1	2.4
NYG	115	17.0	42.0	10.9	2.8	NO	87	10.8	32.4	10.2	2.0
SEA	113	18.4	38.2	9.4	3.2	BUF	86	11.8	27.2	11.3	2.1
DAL	113	16.6	43.1	8.9	3.1	WAS	85	16.4	27.1	8.2	1.4
NE	111	18.1	39.6	9.2	2.7	HOU	84	12.8	28.5	6.5	2.9
CAR	107	17.1	36.4	10.3	2.7	GB	84	15.7	27.7	7.2	1.8
PHI	107	14.7	37.2	10.4	3.2	CIN	83	15.7	23.8	7.4	2.2
PIT	104	15.6	37.5	9.2	2.8	DET	83	13.7	25.3	8.6	2.1
STL	101	17.2	32.6	8.6	2.9	ARI	82	11.5	27.9	8.6	2.3
JAC	101	17.8	37.0	8.5	1.9	CLE	82	19.3	17.0	5.6	2.5
IND	100	14.0	34.8	10.5	2.6	SF	73	11.3	29.7	5.1	1.8
TEN	98	15.5	34.2	7.9	2.9	KC	72	15.0	16.9	6.6	1.9
TB	93	16.2	31.4	6.5	2.7	DEN	62	8.1	27.7	7.4	0.5

College Football Introduction and Statistical Toolbox

The fourth weekend of last September was a special one for college football fans. Jacquizz Rodgers of Oregon State juked through a USC defense overstocked with future NFL first-round draft picks en route to a 27-21 upset. Sam Bradford's Oklahoma Sooners lit up the top-ranked TCU defense for 35 points, twice as many as the Horned Frogs would surrender in any other game last season. Duke recorded its first conference victory in more than five years, a cathartic 31-3 spanking of Virginia. And following a stunning loss to Ole Miss, Florida's Tim Tebow shed tears at a podium in defeat, vowing to never allow the Gators to lose on his watch again — or something to that effect.

The Gators haven't lost since that heartbreaker against Mississippi, and they are poised to potentially run the table this fall. But the prophetic nature of Tebow's declaration isn't what made it memorable, and his fans didn't need him to demonstrate his passion for winning. It was the sincerity of the moment — not the athlete — that was remarkable. In college football, every game matters, and on that day, Tebow was just a quarterback testifying.

Of course, like everything else in college football, it's never that simple. In one sense, the fourth weekend in September is as important as the first weekend in December, and it matters as much to the Trojans as it does to the Blue Devils, Gators, and Sooners. But in other ways, the "every game matters" mantra can be awfully selective. The BCS system invites only two teams to its playoff bracket, and when everyone in consideration is flawed, the decision might come down to an opinion on which wins matter the most and which losses matter the least. And for non-BCS teams like Boise State and Utah, winning every game might never matter enough.

College football can be complicated, but it's also a lot of fun. At Football Outsiders, we're fans just like you. We tailgate on Saturday mornings every chance we get, and we marvel every weekend on campus or in our homes at the extraordinary spectacle of the college game. A gun-slinging team might complete an improbable sideline pass as time expires to alter the course of the national championship race. A service academy (or three) might win a game without completing a single pass. Every week, fans are motivated to storm the field, tee-pee the quad, and belt out the school alma mater in agony or ecstasy, and we're right there with them. Every game matters.

We actively celebrate the pageantry of college football and are inspired by its peculiarities. But as analysts, we also want to understand the game better than ever before. We want to know how it is that the No. 1 and No. 2 programs in college football lost to inferior opponents that weekend. Was Oregon State's success isolated to certain situational downs? Did its special teams unit outplay USC in terms of field position? How successful should Florida have expected to be on the critical fourth-and-short late in the game? Was the play of the Rebels defense on that day an outlier? Did the pace of either game have an impact, and if so, to what degree?

Two long-time polls — the Associated Press Poll and USA Today Coaches' Poll — have awarded national championships throughout college football history, so perhaps it is only fitting that we approach our stats analysis questions from two different perspectives. For the past six years, Brian Fremeau has been developing the Fremeau Efficiency Index (FEI) and its companion statistics based on drive-by-drive analysis. More recently, Bill Connelly's research has explored play-by-play data, developing new analysis of success rates and explosiveness to form the backbone of his S&P+ ratings.

The College Statistical Toolbox section that follows this introduction explains the methodology of FEI, S&P+, and other stats you'll encounter in the college chapters of this book. There are similarities to DVOA in both approaches, but college football presents a unique set of challenges different from the NFL. All football stats must be adjusted according to context, but how? Should Florida's performance be measured against that of an average SEC team or an average FBS team? If Texas and Idaho don't play one another and don't share any common opponents, how can their stats be effectively compared? We've only scratched the surface with FEI and S&P+, but we've learned a lot so far.

The book devotes a chapter to each of the six BCS conferences, with a seventh chapter covering the best of the non-BCS teams. The chapters provide a snapshot of each team's statistical profile in 2008 and projections for 2009, along with a summary of its keys to the upcoming season. Player and coaching personnel changes, offensive and defensive advantages and deficiencies, and schedule highlights and pitfalls are all discussed by our team of college football writers. The top NFL 2010 projected draft picks from each team

are included at the end of each team segment, with their most likely position in the draft (by round) listed in parentheses. Players with asterisks are juniors or redshirt sophomores who may or may not be available in the 2010 draft.

As we learned in 2008, settling arguments in college football is never cut and dry. From Big 12 conference tiebreakers and BCS title game uncertainties to go-for-it decisions and field position management, we're on it. We're pursuing the answers to college football's most important questions, and by taking two different statistical approaches, we think we'll better understand the terms of the debate. Hopefully, you will too. Enjoy the college football section of *Football Outsiders Almanac 2009*, and join us throughout the season at FootballOutsiders.com.

College Team Statistics Sample

No. 1 Florida Gators 11-1 (7-1)

2008: 13-1 (7-1)   **FEI:** No. 1   **S&P+:** No. 2   **F/+:** No. 1   **Program FEI:** No. 2   **Returning Starters:** OFF 7, DEF 11

2008 Offense		Rank	2008 Defense		Rank	2008 Field Position		Rank
Offensive FEI	0.816	1	Defensive FEI	-0.787	1	Field Position Advantage	0.558	2
Unadjusted Offense	0.615	9	Unadjusted Defense	-0.654	2	**2009 Projections**		**Rank**
Offensive S&P+	152.1	1	Defensive S&P+	135.1	4	FEI	0.340	1
Rushing S&P+	152.7	1	Rushing S&P+	124.0	15	Strength of Schedule	0.196	23
Passing S&P+	157.0	3	Passing S&P+	146.3	5	Offensive FEI	0.674	4
Standard Downs S&P+	156.8	1	Standard Downs S&P+	126.2	5	Defensive FEI	-0.868	1
Passing Downs S&P+	147.5	5	Passing Downs S&P+	122.3	19	**Mean Wins: 11.1 SEC: 7.3**		

COLLEGE STATISTICS TOOLBOX

Regular readers of FootballOutsiders.com may be familiar with the FEI and Varsity Numbers columns and their respective stats published throughout the year. Others may be learning about our advanced approach to college football stats analysis for the first time by reading this book. In either case, this College Statistics Toolbox section is highly recommended reading before getting into the conference chapters. The stats that form the building blocks for FEI and S&P+ have been updated, refined and in some cases renamed this offseason. Other stats are introduced for the first time in this volume.

One important note: 2008 records and 2009 projected records listed in each team capsule include results of games between FBS (formerly Division 1-A) and FCS (formerly Division 1-AA) teams. However, all of the statistics analysis for both FEI and S&P+ ignore data from these games.

Each team profile in the conference chapters begins

with a statistical snapshot (defending BCS champion Florida is presented here as a sample). Within each chapter, teams are organized by division (or conference in the final chapter) and Projected FEI rank. The projected overall and conference records — rounded from the team's projected Mean Wins — are listed alongside the team name in the header. The number of offensive and defensive starters returning in 2009 were collected from team and conference spring media guides. All other stats and rankings provided in the team snapshot are explained below.

FREMEAU EFFICIENCY INDEX

Fremeau Efficiency Index (FEI) analysis begins with drive data instead of play-by-play data, but FEI shares similar principles with DVOA. A team is rewarded for playing well against a strong opponent, win or lose, and is punished more severely for playing poorly against bad teams than it is rewarded for playing well against bad teams.

To calculate FEI, the nearly 20,000 possessions in every season of major college football are filtered to eliminate first-half clock-kills and end-of-game garbage drives and scores. A scoring rate analysis of the remaining possessions then determines the baseline possession efficiency expectations against which each team is measured. Game Efficiency is the composite possession-by-possession efficiency of a team over the course of a game, a measurement of the success of its offensive, defensive, and special teams units' essential goals: to maximize the team's own scoring opportunities and to minimize those of its opponent. Finally, each team's FEI rating synthesizes its season-long Game Efficiency data, adjusted for the strength of its opposition; special emphasis is placed on quality performance against good teams, win or lose.

OFFENSIVE AND DEFENSIVE FEI

Game Efficiency is a composite assessment of the possession-by-possession performance of a team over the course of a game. In order to isolate the relative performance of the offense and defense, more factors are evaluated.

First, we ran a regression on the national scoring rates of tens of thousands of college football drives according to starting field position. The result represents the value of field position in terms of points expected to be scored by an average offense against an average defense — 1.4 points per possession from its own 15-yard line, 2.3 points per possession from its own 40-yard line, and so on. These expected points are called Field Position Value (FPV).

Next, we ran a regression on the value of drive-ending field position according to national special teams scoring expectations. To determine the true national baseline for field-goal range, we took into account not only the 2200 field goals attempted annually, but also the 1400 punts kicked from opponent territory each year. In other words, if a team has an average field goal unit and a coach with an average penchant for risk-taking, the offensive value of reaching the opponent's 35-yard line is equal to the number of made field goals from that distance divided by the number of attempts plus the number of punts from that distance.

Touchdowns credit the offense with 6.96 points of drive-ending value, the value of a touchdown adjusted according to national point-after rates. Safeties have a drive-ending value of negative two points. All other offensive results are credited with a drive-ending value of zero.

Offensive efficiency is then calculated as the total drive-ending value earned by the offense divided by the sum of its offensive FPV over the course of the game. Defensive efficiency is calculated the same way using the opponent's offensive drive-ending value and FPV. Offensive and defensive efficiency are calibrated as a rating above or below zero — a good offense has a positive rating and a good defense has a negative one. These numbers are represented in the college chapters as Unadjusted Offense and Unadjusted Defense.

Offensive FEI and Defensive FEI are the opponent-adjusted values of offensive and defensive efficiency. As with FEI, the adjustments are weighted according to both the strength of the opponent and the relative significance of the result. Efficiency against a team's best competition is given more relevance weight in the formula.

FIELD POSITION ADVANTAGE (FPA)

FPA was developed in order to more accurately describe the management of field position over the course of a game. For each team, we calculate the sum of the FPV for each of its offensive series. Then, we add in a full touchdown value (6.96 points) for each non-offensive score earned by the team. (This accounts for the field position value of special teams and defensive returns reaching the end zone versus tripping up at the one-yard line.) Special teams turnovers and onside kicks surrendered have an FPV of zero. The sum of the FPV of every possession in the game for both teams represents the total field position at stake in the contest. FPA represents each given team's share of that total field position.

FPA is a description of which team controlled field position in the game and by how much. Two teams that face equal field position over the course of a game will each have an FPA of .500. Winning the field position battle is quite valuable. College football teams that play with an FPA over .500 win two-thirds of the time. Teams that play with an FPA over .600 win 90 percent of the time.

PROGRAM AND PROJECTED FEI

Relative to the pros, college football teams are more consistent in year-to-year performance. Breakout seasons and catastrophic collapses certainly occur, but generally speaking, teams can be expected to play within a reasonable range of their baseline program expectations. We introduced Program FEI last year in *Pro Football Prospectus 2008* as a way to represent those individual baseline expectations.

Program FEI is calculated from five years of possession efficiency data with a very similar formula as FEI. The only difference is that data from more recent performances is given more weight. The result not only represents the status of each team's program power, but provides an ideal rating on which to project future success. We adjust the Program FEI baseline with "transition factors" to produce our projections. The transition factors include returning offensive and defensive starters and, new this season, a small conference adjustment. The result, Projected FEI, is a more accurate predictor of next-year success than any other data we have tested (Table 1).

Table 1: Correlation of Stats, Year to Year+1

Statistic	Correlation
Conference Win Pct.	0.51
Win Pct.	0.59
Pythagorean Win Pct.	0.66
FEI	0.73
Program FEI (to FEI)	0.75
Projected FEI (to FEI)	0.78

STRENGTH OF SCHEDULE

Unlike other rating systems, our Strength of Schedule (SOS) calculation is not a simple average of the Projected FEI data of each team's opponents. Instead, it is calculated from a "privileged" perspective, representing the likelihood that an elite team (typical top-five team) would win every game on the given schedule. The distinction is valid. For any elite team, playing No. 1 Florida and No. 120 Idaho in a two-game stretch is certainly more difficult than playing No. 60 Northwestern and No. 61 Texas A&M. An average rating might judge these schedules to be equal.

The likelihood of an undefeated season is calculated as the product of Projected Win Expectations (PWE)

for each game on the schedule. PWEs are based on an assessment of five years of FEI data and the records of teams of varying strengths against one another. Roughly speaking, an elite team may have a 65 percent chance of defeating a team ranked No. 10, a 75 percent chance of defeating a team ranked No. 20, and a 90 percent chance of defeating a team ranked No. 40. Combined, the elite team has a 44 percent likelihood of defeating all three (0.65 x 0.75 x 0.90 = 0.439).

A lower SOS rating represents a lower likelihood of an elite team running the table — a stronger schedule. For our calculations of FBS versus FCS games, with all due apologies to Appalachian State, the likelihood of victory is considered to be 100 percent.

MEAN WINS

To project records for each team, we run an entirely new set of PWE numbers based on the likelihood of victory for the team itself in its individual games. These are combined to represent the average number of wins the team is expected to tally over the course of its scheduled games. Potential conference championship games and bowl games are not included.

The projected records listed next to each team name in the conference chapters are rounded from the mean wins data listed in the team capsule. Mean Wins are not intended to represent projected outcomes of specific matchups, rather they are our most accurate forecast for the team's season as a whole. The correlation of mean projected wins to actual wins is 0.69 for all games, 0.61 for conference games.

SUCCESS RATES

Our play-by-play analysis was introduced throughout the 2008 season in Bill Connelly's Varsity Numbers columns. More than 200,000 plays over two seasons in college football have been collected and evaluated to determine baselines for success for every situational down in a game. Similarly to DVOA, basic Success Rates are determined by national standards. The distinction for college football is in defining the standards of success. We use the following determination of a "successful" play:

- First down success = 50 percent of necessary yardage.
- Second down success = 70 percent of necessary

yardage.

• Third/Fourth down success = 100 percent of necessary yardage.

On a per-play basis, these form the standards of efficiency for every offense in college football. Defensive success rates are based on preventing the same standards of achievement.

EQUIVALENT POINTS AND POINTS PER PLAY

All yards are not created equal. A 10-yard gain from a team's own 15-yard line does not have the same value as a 10-yard gain that goes from the opponent's 10-yard line into the end zone. Based on expected scoring rates similar to FPV described above, we can calculate a point value for each play in a drive. Equivalent Points (EqPts) are calculated by subtracting the value of the resulting yard line from the initial yard line of a given play. This assigns credit to the yards that are most associated with scoring points, the end goal in any possession.

With EqPts, the game can be broken down and built back up again in a number of ways. With the addition of penalties, turnovers and special teams play, EqPts provides an accurate assessment of how a game was played on a play-by-play basis. We also use it to create a measure called Points Per Play (PPP), representative of a team's or an individual player's explosiveness.

S&P

Like OPS (on-base percentage plus slugging average) in baseball, we created a measure that combines consistency with power. S&P represents a combination of efficiency (Success Rates) and explosiveness (Points Per Play) to most accurately represent the effectiveness of a team or individual player.

A boom-or-bust running back may have a strong yards per carry average and PPP, but his low Success Rate will lower his S&P. A consistent running back that gains between four and six yards every play, on the other hand, will have a strong Success Rate but possibly low PPP. The best offenses in the country can maximize both efficiency and explosiveness on a down-by-down basis. Reciprocally, the best defenses can limit both.

S&P+

As with the FEI stats discussed above, context matters in college football. Adjustments are made to the S&P unadjusted data with a formula that takes into account a team's production, the quality of the opponent, and the quality of the opponent's opponent. To eliminate the noise of less-informative blowout stats, we filtered the play-by-play data to include only those that took place when the game was "close." This excludes plays where the score margin is larger than 24 points in the first quarter, 21 points in the second quarter, or 16 points in the second half.

The result is S&P+, representing a team's efficiency and explosiveness as compared to all other teams in college football. S&P+ values are calibrated around an average rating of 100. An above-average team, offensively or defensively, will have an S&P+ rating greater than 100. A below-average team will have an S&P+ rating lower than 100.

In the team capsules in each conference chapter, the S&P+ ratings are broken down further as follows:

• Rushing S&P+ includes only running plays, and unlike standard college statistics, does not include sacks.

• Passing S&P+ includes sacks and passing plays.

• Passing Downs S&P+ includes second-and-8 or more, third-and-5 or more, and fourth-and-5 or more. These divisions were determined based on raw S&P data showing a clear distinction in Success Rates as compared with Standard Downs.

• Standard Downs S&P+ includes all close-game plays not defined as Passing Downs.

F/+

The only other ranking provided in the team capsules represents a hybrid version of the FEI and S&P+ ratings for each team last season. Recognizing that there are clear distinctions in these two approaches, we'll be exploring the relationship of FEI and S&P+ this fall at FootballOutsiders.com. We do not have enough data to draw conclusions about the potential of F/+ as a predictive measure, but it may well represent the strength of our two-system approach.

Brian Fremeau and Bill Connelly

Atlantic Coast Conference

When the Atlantic Coast Conference joined the Big 12 and SEC as a 12-team mega-league in 2005, it was supposed to be Miami, Florida State and ten pelts for their respective walls. The Seminoles had won or shared 11 of the previous 13 ACC championships and the Hurricanes had dominated the old Big East for ten years. Either or both programs had won or contended for national championships on a yearly basis since the 1980s. Together, they would push each other to new heights and transform the premiere college basketball conference into a two-sport dynasty.

Or not. Combined, Miami and FSU have won only one conference title since 2005. Neither team has seriously factored into the national championship discussion since the expansion. If it were a case of other ACC teams taking over the national spotlight, it would be one thing. But the ACC is the only one of the six BCS conferences that hasn't sniffed a title game appearance since 2005. To many observers these days, it is a league populated by mediocre teams playing an uninspiring brand of football.

All but one team in the league finished within one game of .500 in conference play last season. The ACC sent a record 10 teams to bowl games, but only four were victorious. Its most prolific offense, Georgia Tech's, ranked only 50th nationally in yards per game. Add it all up and FEI rated the ACC as the most *underrated* conference in the nation in 2008. Huh?

The ratings were perplexing, but not totally inexplicable. Without much fanfare, the ACC won more games (17) against other BCS conferences (plus Notre Dame) than any other league in 2008 — the Big 12, SEC, and Big East defeated only 11 each. ACC teams played and beat more bowl teams in non-conference play than any other league, winning 18 of 32 games. None of those victories, however, came over teams rated in the Associated Press Top 10 at the time of the game or at season's end. Combine a lack of headline-grabbing non-conference victories with a lack of dominant play within the league and the disrespect in the polls is easy to understand.

There are several ways to view a league when its 11th-best team is nearly as strong on the field as its best — it's the most mediocre conference, the deepest and strongest, or somewhere in between. Get ready to rehash the arguments in 2009. We are projecting ten ACC teams to finish within a game of .500 in league play again. The national perception of the conference will hinge on games against Alabama (in Atlanta versus Virginia Tech on September 5), Oklahoma (at Miami on October 3), and Florida (hosting Florida State on November 28), but fans would be wise to pay attention to the rest of the games. The ACC's worst team, Duke, knocked off two bowl-bound teams in non-conference play in 2008.

COASTAL DIVISION

No. 4 Virginia Tech Hokies 10-2 (6-2)

2008: 10-4 (5-3) **FEI:** No. 9 **S&P+:** No. 41 **F/+:** No. 28 **Program FEI:** No. 7 **Returning Starters:** OFF 8, DEF 7

2008 Offense		Rank	2008 Defense		Rank	2008 Field Position		Rank
Offensive FEI	0.077	50	Defensive FEI	-0.394	17	Field Position Advantage	0.523	31
Unadjusted Offense	-0.253	90	Unadjusted Defense	-0.340	16	**2009 Projections**		**Rank**
Offensive S&P+	96.0	79	Defensive S&P+	116.4	22	FEI	0.226	4
Rushing S&P+	104.7	59	Rushing S&P+	125.3	13	Strength of Schedule	0.210	27
Passing S&P+	86.6	95	Passing S&P+	105.1	44	Offensive FEI	0.161	31
Standard Downs S&P+	93.0	89	Standard Downs S&P+	112.3	26	Defensive FEI	-0.427	13
Passing Downs S&P+	102.4	61	Passing Downs S&P+	110.3	39	**Mean Wins:** 9.7 **ACC:** 6.3		

Head coach Frank Beamer's 22nd season with the Hokies may have been his best to date. The third-longest tenured coach in college football squeezed an ACC championship and an Orange Bowl victory out of a team populated with underclass talent, particularly at the skill positions. Did we just say no teams have taken over the void left by Miami and Florida State? Virginia Tech joins only USC and Texas as teams that have registered at least 10 wins in each of the last five seasons. 2009 may be ripe for the plucking once again.

Everything will hinge on the health and development of junior quarterback Tyrod Taylor. He bounced in and out of the lineup last year while the offense sputtered. In the Orange Bowl victory over Big East champion Cincinnati, though, Taylor showed what his fleet feet are capable of, nimbly dancing past tacklers on a third-and-9 keeper for a 17-yard touchdown to set the tone early. His versatility in the backfield remind many in Blacksburg of Hokies legend Michael Vick, quarterback of the only Virginia Tech team to advance to the BCS national championship game. In order to repeat the feat ten years later, Taylor's decision-making will be just as critical as his improvisation skills. He threw seven interceptions and only two touchdown passes in 2008.

A big part of the offense's development should come from the surrounding cast. Tailback Darren Evans set an ACC record for most rushing yards (1,265) by a freshman in conference history last season. The top three Hokies receivers — Jarrett Boykin, Danny Coale, and Dyrell Roberts — were also freshmen in 2008. Adding in senior

tight end Greg Boone and three returning offensive linemen and the Hokies offense should finally be able to crack into another chapter in the playbook this year.

Expect the defense to dominate, as usual. Over the last five years, no team in college football has given up fewer yards per game than Virginia Tech. Seven starters return to a unit that ranked 17th nationally according to FEI. They were particularly dominant against the opponent's ground attack, ranking 13th in Rushing S&P+ last year, best in the conference. Keyed by returning defensive end Jason Worilds' 18.5 tackles for loss, Virginia Tech held opponents to fewer than 100 rushing yards on seven occasions in 2008.

As is the case with any contender, Virginia Tech will need to benefit from a few fortunate bounces to make another BCS-title run. In Blacksburg, those bounces are part of the game plan section entitled "Beamer Ball" — momentum swings and field position advantages created by ball-hawking defense and special teams. The Hokies' first opportunity to wreak havoc on a national stage in 2009 arrives September 5th against Alabama in the Georgia Dome.

Top 2010 NFL Prospects: DE Jason Worilds* (1-2), G Sergio Render (1-2), T Ed Wang (3-5), S Kam Chancellor (5-7).

No. 9 Georgia Tech Yellow Jackets 8-4 (5-3)

2008: 9-4 (5-3)	FEI: No. 17	S&P+: No. 49	F/+: No. 36	Program FEI: No. 17	Returning Starters: OFF 9, DEF 8		
2008 Offense		**Rank**	**2008 Defense**		**Rank**	**2008 Field Position**	**Rank**
Offensive FEI	0.333	16	Defensive FEI	-0.243	30	Field Position Advantage 0.503	53
Unadjusted Offense	-0.006	55	Unadjusted Defense	-0.152	39	**2009 Projections**	**Rank**
Offensive S&P+	109.8	40	Defensive S&P+	97.3	72	FEI 0.182	9
Rushing S&P+	117.9	24	Rushing S&P+	96.6	75	Strength of Schedule 0.133	11
Passing S&P+	95.8	75	Passing S&P+	98.1	66	Offensive FEI 0.409	11
Standard Downs S&P+	107.8	43	Standard Downs S&P+	95.4	76	Defensive FEI -0.251	31
Passing Downs S&P+	111.7	38	Passing Downs S&P+	99.2	67	**Mean Wins: 8.4 ACC: 5.3**	

When Paul Johnson took over the Yellow Jackets program, many wondered whether he would be able to successfully implement his triple-option offense with a major college program. At Navy, it had served as an equalizer when his undersized and under-recruited team took on the big boys. Could players with NFL aspirations be disciplined enough to buy in?

Thus far, the experiment appears to be working, and ahead of schedule. Georgia Tech enters 2009 as one of the favorites to contend for the ACC title. The league's best offense from last season returns nine starters, including junior quarterback Josh Nesbitt, sophomore

running back Roddy Jones, and junior running back Jonathan Dwyer, the ACC player of the year. The backfield exploded for more than 300 yards rushing in five games in 2008. The regular season concluded with back-to-back 40-point, 400-yard outbursts against Miami and Georgia, games in which the Yellow Jackets passed for only 65 total yards combined. One-time Georgia Tech coach John Heisman would have been proud.

The defensive line will feature several new faces in the fall, but the entire corps of starting linebackers and secondary all return. Things were hit or miss on the defensive side of the ball last year, but junior safety Morgan Burnett was a consistent force, leading the team in tackles (93) and interceptions (7). On the whole, the defense contributed 29 takeaways — a solid total upon which a ball-control offense should feast. The Yellow Jackets, however, coughed up 36 fumbles of their own, with 20 of them recovered by the opposing defense, second most in the country. If they can shore up this particular area in 2009, the schedule may be manageable enough for Johnson's team to pile up the Ramblin' Wreckage in its wake.

Top 2010 NFL Prospects: DE Derrick Morgan* (1-2), S Morgan Burnett* (1-2), RB Jonathan Dwyer* (3-5).

No. 18 Miami Hurricanes 7-5 (4-4)

2008: 7-6 (4-4)	FEI: No. 33	S&P+: No. 67	F/+: No. 54	Program FEI: No. 28		Returning Starters: OFF 8, DEF 8	
2008 Offense		**Rank**	**2008 Defense**		**Rank**	**2008 Field Position**	**Rank**
Offensive FEI	0.092	45	Defensive FEI	0.000	65	Field Position Advantage	0.503	52
Unadjusted Offense	-0.207	79	Unadjusted Defense	-0.012	63	**2009 Projections**	**Rank**
Offensive S&P+	101.5	58	Defensive S&P+	96.8	73	FEI	0.138	18
Rushing S&P+	104.6	60	Rushing S&P+	90.5	86	Strength of Schedule	0.122	10
Passing S&P+	98.9	66	Passing S&P+	102.8	54	Offensive FEI	0.179	27
Standard Downs S&P+	106.2	48	Standard Downs S&P+	102.1	55	Defensive FEI	-0.087	51
Passing Downs S&P+	92.8	85	Passing Downs S&P+	96.6	73	**Mean Wins: 7.3 ACC: 4.5**	

You are Randy Shannon, head coach of the Miami Hurricanes. In two seasons, you haven't exactly reversed the downward spiral of a once-frequent championship program and set it on a path to reclaim its past glory. There were certainly signs of life in 2008 — a victory over ACC champion Virginia Tech, a valiant battle against superior California in a bowl game. Still, you find yourself on the proverbial "hot seat," needing to prove that the reclamation project is well underway. With a ton of returning talent, you're feeling moderately confident, until you take a quick look at the opening schedule in 2009 — Florida State, Georgia Tech, Virginia Tech, Oklahoma. Awesome — four opponents among the FEI projected top 16.

It may be important to evaluate Shannon in 2009 on his ability to keep the team's chin up, at least for the first month. Miami could lose its first four games, then rip off eight straight, but it will require strong leadership both on the field and on the sidelines to make it happen. Sophomore quarterback Jacory Harris led two comeback victories last season, but may still be a year away from becoming a truly big-time playmaker. Sophomore receivers Aldarius Johnson, Thearon Collier and Travis Benjamin, plus junior running back Graig Cooper and senior Javarris James all showed flashes of potential as well. Benjamin led the conference in punt return yardage.

Like the offense, the defense returns eight starters, but they'll need to step up the production in key areas. According to S&P+, Miami ranked 11th in the ACC (86th nationally) defending the run last year, an area that is the strength of at least two of their opening gauntlet opponents. The Hurricanes defense was also particularly weak at collecting turnovers, intercepting a national-low four passes in 2008. They did, however, hold opponents to just a 51 percent completion rate, the second best rate nationally.

Top 2010 NFL Prospects: RB Javarris James (2-3), LB Darryl Sharpton (2-3), OT Jason Fox (3-4), LB Colin McCarthy (5-7)

No. 35 North Carolina Tar Heels 6-6 (3-5)

2008: 8-5 (4-4)	FEI: No. 6	S&P+: No. 46	F/+: No. 29	Program FEI: No. 47		Returning Starters: OFF 6, DEF 9	
2008 Offense		**Rank**	**2008 Defense**		**Rank**	**2008 Field Position**	**Rank**
Offensive FEI	0.209	31	Defensive FEI	-0.415	13	Field Position Advantage	0.553	4
Unadjusted Offense	-0.103	70	Unadjusted Defense	-0.287	21	**2009 Projections**	**Rank**
Offensive S&P+	109.3	42	Defensive S&P+	100.4	64	FEI	0.068	35
Rushing S&P+	103.0	62	Rushing S&P+	106.1	46	Strength of Schedule	0.167	17
Passing S&P+	116.2	23	Passing S&P+	95.2	77	Offensive FEI	-0.181	90
Standard Downs S&P+	108.4	39	Standard Downs S&P+	104.5	48	Defensive FEI	-0.214	34
Passing Downs S&P+	113.8	31	Passing Downs S&P+	91.3	84	**Mean Wins: 6.4 ACC: 3.2**	

UNC had a breakout year in 2008, winning eight games after six straight losing seasons against FBS competition. Four of their five losses came by a combined nine points. A big part of the turnaround was a boon in big plays. North Carolina tallied six non-offensive touchdowns and chipped in five blocked punts and kicks, helping the Heels rank fourth nationally in field position advantage.

Quarterback T.J. Yates returns to the starting role after an ankle injury sidelined him halfway through the season. Backup Cameron Sexton was effective in his absence, but not as versatile. The real identity crisis is at the wide receiver position. The top three pass catchers from 2008 — Hakeem Nicks, Brooks Foster, and Brandon Tate — are gone. Replacing Nicks' production — 68 receptions, 1,222 yards, 12 touchdowns —

will be an especially significant burden for head coach Butch Davis' new crop of heralded recruits.

The defense returns six of the starting front seven, led by ball-hawking/punt-blocking linebacker Bruce Carter. As good as they were turning in big plays, however, UNC finished last in the conference in 3rd-down defense. That stat is largely responsible for the discrepancy in the North Carolina FEI and S&P+ defensive ratings, and is part of the reason why a regression in performance may be in store for 2009. The Tar Heels also must face three of the ACC's top projected teams — Virginia Tech, Boston College and Georgia Tech — on the road.

Top 2010 NFL Prospects: DT Marvin Austin* (1-2), LB Wesley Flagg (5-7), DE E.J. Wilson (5-7).

No. 51 Virginia Cavaliers 5-7 (3-5)

2008: 5-7 (3-5) **FEI:** No. 43 **S&P+:** No. 60 **F/+:** No. 59 **Program FEI:** No. 40 **Returning Starters:** OFF 5, DEF 5

2008 Offense		Rank	2008 Defense		Rank	2008 Field Position		Rank
Offensive FEI	0.023	59	Defensive FEI	-0.085	51	Field Position Advantage	0.488	83
Unadjusted Offense	-0.285	97	Unadjusted Defense	-0.002	65	2009 Projections		Rank
Offensive S&P+	96.1	78	Defensive S&P+	104.0	53	FEI	0.041	51
Rushing S&P+	98.7	74	Rushing S&P+	102.7	57	Strength of Schedule	0.145	13
Passing S&P+	93.7	82	Passing S&P+	103.7	50	Offensive FEI	-0.048	69
Standard Downs S&P+	108.3	40	Standard Downs S&P+	106.8	43	Defensive FEI	-0.118	43
Passing Downs S&P+	88.2	100	Passing Downs S&P+	97.7	70	Mean Wins: 5.4 ACC: 2.8		

Four starters return to the offensive line, a unit that gave up a league-fewest 16 sacks a year ago. That solid experience will benefit either of three quarterbacks with varying levels of experience — dropback 2008 starter Mark Verica, pass/run threat and 2007 starter Jemeel Sewell, or run-first, 5-foot-9 converted cornerback Vic Hall, who took the reins against Virginia Tech in the finale last year. The problem is that, as well as the unit performed in quarterback protection, the offense was among the weakest in the ACC in actual production (74th rushing S&P+, 82nd passing S&P+, 115th nationally and last in the ACC in scoring offense). The leading rusher and five leading re-

ceivers from a year ago won't be around. Will young talent step up?

The defense is also thin on returning talent, with the exception of the secondary led by corners Chris Cook and Ras-I Dowling. The 2009 outlook might be more positive for Virginia if they are a little less cavalier with the football. In its seven losses last season, Virginia gave up the ball 22 times; they recorded only five turnovers in their four FBS victories.

Top 2010 NFL Prospects: OT Will Barker (3-4), DE Jeffrey Fitzgerald, RB Mikell Simpson (5-7).

No. 87 Duke Blue Devils 4-8 (1-7)

2008: 4-8 (1-7) **FEI:** No. 53 **S&P+:** No. 83 **F/+:** No. 69 **Program FEI:** No. 76 **Returning Starters:** OFF 5, DEF 5

2008 Offense		Rank	2008 Defense		Rank	2008 Field Position		Rank
Offensive FEI	-0.264	93	Defensive FEI	-0.193	36	Field Position Advantage	0.512	41
Unadjusted Offense	-0.487	116	Unadjusted Defense	-0.056	54	2009 Projections		Rank
Offensive S&P+	96.9	73	Defensive S&P+	93.8	80	FEI	-0.098	87
Rushing S&P+	85.8	103	Rushing S&P+	105.9	47	Strength of Schedule	0.222	33
Passing S&P+	105.1	48	Passing S&P+	80.6	111	Offensive FEI	-0.531	116
Standard Downs S&P+	94.3	84	Standard Downs S&P+	98.2	67	Defensive FEI	0.022	61
Passing Downs S&P+	95.4	75	Passing Downs S&P+	88.0	90	Mean Wins: 3.8 ACC: 1.0		

The Blue Devils have fewer wins versus FBS teams over the last six years (eight) than any other program in college football. The next closest BCS conference team, Baylor, has twice as many over the same span. So what's with the optimism in Durham? Duke did manage to record two wins over bowl teams in 2008 (Navy and Vanderbilt) and had three other single-score losses to bowl teams (Northwestern, Wake Forest and North Carolina). Head coach David Cutcliffe would like to be looking forward to building on that success in his second season this fall, but there will be much more rebuilding instead.

Duke returns fewer starters than any other ACC team in 2009, impacting both sides of the ball. In particular, departing linebacker Michael Tauiliili, the conference leader in tackles (140) a year ago, will be sorely missed. Critical to the team's success (and perhaps its psyche as it battles at the bottom of the standings yet again) will be senior quarterback Thaddeus Lewis, the most experienced member of the team (34 career starts).

Top 2010 NFL Prospects: DT Vince Oghobaase (2-3), LB Vincent Rey (3-4).

ATLANTIC DIVISION

No. 10 Clemson Tigers 9-3 (5-3)

| 2008: 7-6 (4-4) | FEI: No. 24 | S&P+: No. 30 | F/+: No. 25 | Program FEI: No. 14 | | Returning Starters: OFF 7, DEF 8 |

2008 Offense		Rank	2008 Defense		Rank	2008 Field Position		Rank
Offensive FEI	0.025	58	Defensive FEI	-0.529	6	Field Position Advantage	0.483	86
Unadjusted Offense	-0.274	95	Unadjusted Defense	-0.454	10	**2009 Projections**		Rank
Offensive S&P+	101.3	60	Defensive S&P+	117.8	17	FEI	0.178	10
Rushing S&P+	102.6	63	Rushing S&P+	120.0	22	Strength of Schedule	0.201	25
Passing S&P+	100.5	59	Passing S&P+	113.8	24	Offensive FEI	0.070	47
Standard Downs S&P+	102.2	58	Standard Downs S&P+	115.1	22	Defensive FEI	-0.643	2
Passing Downs S&P+	101.3	66	Passing Downs S&P+	113.4	36	**Mean Wins: 8.7 ACC: 5.2**		

Last season was awkward for Clemson fans. The Tigers began the year with national championship aspirations, but watched Alabama stomp its heart out on the opening weekend. The devastation lingered, Clemson sputtered to a 3-3 start, and longtime head coach/underachiever/scapegoat Tommy Bowden resigned midseason.

Enter Dabo Swinney with an interim title and a contagious energy. The team didn't exactly turn the tables — winning only four of its final seven games — but it certainly *felt* like progress. A whipping of archrival South Carolina in the regular season finale sealed up a permanent head coach title for Swinney; time will tell if he can produce the breakthrough season that eluded his predecessor.

Clemson will be breaking in a new starter at quarterback in either sophomore Willy Korn or redshirt freshman Kyle Parker. In either case, the surrounding cast is about as good as it gets for a first-time signal caller. The 2009 roster features returning starters across the entire offensive line, led by senior center Thomas Austin, a likely Outland Trophy candidate. A threat rushing, receiving, and returning kicks, senior tailback C.J. Spiller led the conference in all-purpose yardage last season and is eyeing the ACC career record this year.

Eight starters return to a defense that ranked 17th nationally in Close Game S&P+ in 2008, second only to Wake Forest in the conference. FEI rated the unit even higher nationally (No. 6), and with depth and experience back on the field, another outstanding season is projected for 2009. The Tigers gave up only six touchdowns on 76 opponent drives begun at or inside the opponent's own 30-yard line last season. With that kind of efficiency and a veteran offensive line creating field position advantages, Swinney may resurrect lofty expectations sooner rather than later.

Top 2010 NFL Prospects: RB C.J. Spiller (1-2), CB Crezdon Butler (3-5), C Thomas Austin (3-5), G Barry Humphries (5-7).

No. 14 Boston College Eagles 9-3 (5-3)

2008: 9-5 (5-3)　　**FEI:** No. 13　　**S&P+:** No. 35　　**F/+:** No. 27　　**Program FEI:** No. 11　　**Returning Starters:** OFF 7, DEF 7

2008 Offense		Rank	2008 Defense		Rank	2008 Field Position		Rank
Offensive FEI	0.108	43	Defensive FEI	-0.592	4	Field Position Advantage	0.478	91
Unadjusted Offense	-0.194	76	Unadjusted Defense	-0.552	5	2009 Projections		Rank
Offensive S&P+	105.2	47	Defensive S&P+	109.9	34	FEI	0.166	14
Rushing S&P+	110.5	42	Rushing S&P+	118.9	23	Strength of Schedule	0.192	20
Passing S&P+	99.6	62	Passing S&P+	102.2	57	Offensive FEI	0.076	44
Standard Downs S&P+	99.7	65	Standard Downs S&P+	106.6	45	Defensive FEI	-0.594	3
Passing Downs S&P+	103.5	57	Passing Downs S&P+	115.4	29	Mean Wins: 8.5　ACC: 5.1		

Over the past six years, Boston College has recorded more wins against FBS competition than all but nine other programs in the six major conferences. Don't believe it? Neither do the voters in the polls, who have ranked the Eagles in the preseason top 25 only once since 2003. This doesn't appear to be a team that has caught lightning in a bottle. BC has played in two different conferences, under two different coaches, and with four different starting quarterbacks over that stretch.

The common thread through it all has been longtime defensive coordinator and new Boston College head coach Frank Spaziani. The Eagles' Defensive FEI in 2008 ranked fourth nationally, and was remarkably stout at defending short fields. BC faced 27 opponent drives last season that started in Eagles territory, but only surrendered six touchdowns. To match that kind of performance in 2009, Boston College will need to replace three key contributors. Departing defensive tackles B.J. Raji and Ron Brace were both selected on the first day of the NFL draft this past spring. More stunning (and sobering) is the departure of ACC Defensive Player of the Year linebacker Mark Herzlich, who learned in late spring that he is battling a malig-

nant tumor in his left leg. His college playing career is over, but he's hoping chemo treatments won't prevent him from contributing to the team's weekly game planning and film study. Upperclassmen linebackers Alex Albright and Mike McLaughlin, safety Wes Davis, and cornerbacks DeLeon Gause and Roderick Rollins will be called upon to fill the void on the field.

Four starters return to the offensive line, which should help the development of young talent in the backfield. Running backs Montel Harris and Josh Haden shared most of the carries in 2008, both as freshmen, and combined for nearly 1,400 yards. The only quarterback with starting experience, Dominique Davis, transferred out of BC following an offseason academic suspension. Redshirt freshman Justin Tuggle and junior college transfer Codi Boek will compete for the role.

With several question marks, no one is picking BC to reach its third straight ACC title game. They've had a chip on their shoulder for most of their history, though, and they would probably want it no other way.

Top 2010 NFL Prospects: LB Alex Albright (5-7), C Matt Tennant (5-7).

No. 16 Florida State Seminoles 7-5 (5-3)

2008: 9-4 (5-3)　　**FEI:** No. 10　　**S&P+:** No. 37　　**F/+:** No. 23　　**Program FEI:** No. 15　　**Returning Starters:** OFF 8, DEF 5

2008 Offense		Rank	2008 Defense		Rank	2008 Field Position		Rank
Offensive FEI	0.322	17	Defensive FEI	-0.343	23	Field Position Advantage	0.507	46
Unadjusted Offense	0.002	53	Unadjusted Defense	-0.228	28	2009 Projections		Rank
Offensive S&P+	111.9	33	Defensive S&P+	103.1	55	FEI	0.148	16
Rushing S&P+	122.3	15	Rushing S&P+	100.6	64	Strength of Schedule	0.068	3
Passing S&P+	101.8	57	Passing S&P+	105.7	43	Offensive FEI	0.313	16
Standard Downs S&P+	111.3	31	Standard Downs S&P+	102.1	56	Defensive FEI	-0.179	36
Passing Downs S&P+	114.0	29	Passing Downs S&P+	109.7	42	Mean Wins: 7.1　ACC: 4.6		

The Seminoles engineered one of the biggest blowouts of last year's bowl season, a 42-13 thrashing of Wisconsin in the Champs Sports Bowl. That's the kind of performance that gets everyone associated with the program excited for the new year, but often also raises lofty and unrealistic ex-

pectations. Florida State might be better in 2009 and still be saddled by a frustrating record. They'll face 11 teams that played in bowl games last season.

The good news is that junior quarterback Christian Ponder returns along with the entire starting offensive line from 2008. Ponder was a solid performer a year ago, rushing for more than 400 yards and adding 2,000 through the air. FSU had the best offense in the conference according to S&P+ and ranked 15th nationally running the football. A slew of new athletes take over the skill positions, but the veteran core should be able to take a few steps forward.

The rest of the team has its work cut out for it. Second team All-American defensive end Everette Brown passed up his senior season for the pros. Safety (and Rhodes Scholar) Myron Rolle passed up a final year of eligibility to go pro (for now) in something other than sports. Only five starters return to a defense that led the nation last year in third-down efficiency. The biggest missing piece may,

in fact, be the leg of punter/placekicker Graham Gano. He was 5-of-7 on field goals kicked from distances of at least 49 yards last year. For FSU in 2009, those kicks will likely be punts or fourth-down conversion attempts.

In addition to facing the brutal schedule with green talent, head coach Bobby Bowden will be pestered all season long with questions regarding his plans for retirement. If the Seminoles stumble out of the gate, the calls for coach-in-waiting Jimbo Fisher to take over will be louder than the Tomahawk War Chant in Tallahassee.

Top 2010 NFL Prospects: CB Patrick Robinson (2-3), DT Budd Thacker (5-7), WR Preston Parker (5-7).

No. 26 Wake Forest Demon Deacons 7-5 (4-4)

| 2008: 8-5 (4-4) | FEI: No. 18 | S&P+: No. 39 | F/+: No. 31 | Program FEI: No. 23 | Returning Starters: OFF 9, DEF 4 |

2008 Offense		Rank	2008 Defense		Rank	2008 Field Position		Rank
Offensive FEI	-0.079	70	Defensive FEI	-0.528	7	Field Position Advantage	0.553	3
Unadjusted Offense	-0.305	100	Unadjusted Defense	-0.315	18	2009 Projections		Rank
Offensive S&P+	92.0	90	Defensive S&P+	120.9	12	FEI	0.096	26
Rushing S&P+	88.8	94	Rushing S&P+	122.2	17	Strength of Schedule	0.196	24
Passing S&P+	95.0	77	Passing S&P+	120.2	11	Offensive FEI	-0.064	72
Standard Downs S&P+	91.8	91	Standard Downs S&P+	116.5	18	Defensive FEI	-0.270	28
Passing Downs S&P+	95.1	76	Passing Downs S&P+	112.0	38	Mean Wins: 7.0 ACC: 3.8		

Senior quarterback Riley Skinner enters 2009 as the most accurate passer in ACC history. In a high-octane spread offense, his 67 percent completion rate might light up the scoreboard. Not many passes are thrown downfield at Wake, however — D.J. Boldin led the conference in pass receptions last year, but was outpaced in yards per reception by the leading pass catcher from every other team.

Boldin won't be back this year, but nearly every other member of the offense returns. The overall experience will be critical in improving upon a worst-in-the-ACC S&P+ rating from a year ago. The running game was particularly anemic last year — Wake Forest was held to fewer than 100 yards on seven occasions. Sophomore backs Brendan Pendergrass and junior Josh Ad-

ams will share the load again in 2009. The defense was a bright spot a year ago, but it will feature an almost entirely new set of faces this fall. Senior nose tackle Boo Robinson is the most experienced, but was only ranked sixth on the team in tackles last year.

One area to expect consistency is field position, an advantage created by head coach Jim Grobe's conservative decision-making and the team's terrific punt unit — Wake Forest opponents had only nine total punt return yards combined over all of last season. Doing the little things well may keep the Demon Deacons in games while their defense gains confidence.

Top 2010 NFL Prospects: CB Brandon Ghee (3-5), DT Boo Robinson (5-7).

No. 44 North Carolina State Wolfpack 6-6 (3-5)

2008: 6-7 (4-4)   **FEI:** No. 31   **S&P+:** No. 62   **F/+:** No. 47   **Program FEI:** No. 48   **Returning Starters:** OFF 7, DEF 7

2008 Offense		Rank	2008 Defense		Rank	2008 Field Position		Rank
Offensive FEI	0.253	23	Defensive FEI	-0.015	62	Field Position Advantage	0.502	57
Unadjusted Offense	-0.091	68	Unadjusted Defense	0.016	68	2009 Projections		Rank
Offensive S&P+	109.6	41	Defensive S&P+	90.2	91	FEI	0.055	44
Rushing S&P+	115.2	30	Rushing S&P+	89.5	89	Strength of Schedule	0.163	15
Passing S&P+	104.1	49	Passing S&P+	91.2	86	Offensive FEI	0.164	29
Standard Downs S&P+	102.3	56	Standard Downs S&P+	90.9	95	Defensive FEI	0.056	65
Passing Downs S&P+	124.0	22	Passing Downs S&P+	84.8	96	Mean Wins: 6.0 ACC: 3.1		

Very little went right for the Wolfpack over the first half of 2008. They lost six of their first seven games against FBS competition, three by blowout margins. The biggest culprit was the defense, rated ahead of only Miami according to FEI and last in the conference according to S&P+. NC State couldn't stop the run or pass throughout the stretch, surrendering more than 500 total yards to both Florida State and Boston College. They bounced back in November, winning four in a row to become bowl eligible. But two of those victories came against the worst offenses in the ACC (Wake Forest and Duke), and the Wolfpack were plus-nine in turnovers in the other two wins (against Miami and North Carolina).

One bright spot was the play of freshman quarterback Russell Wilson, who returns this fall along with six other offensive starters. Wilson was especially solid in limiting mistakes, throwing only one interception in 275 pass attempts. With two FCS teams on the schedule, another bowl-eligible season won't be a monumental task in 2009. But unless the offense and defense make significant strides, NC State is going to be staring up again at too many other ACC contenders.

Top 2010 NFL Prospects: DE Willie Young (5-7), DT Alan Michael Cash (5-7).

No. 54 Maryland Terrapins 5-7 (3-5)

2008: 8-5 (4-4)   **FEI:** No. 49   **S&P+:** No. 52   **F/+:** No. 44   **Program FEI:** No. 45   **Returning Starters:** OFF 6, DEF 4

2008 Offense		Rank	2008 Defense		Rank	2008 Field Position		Rank
Offensive FEI	0.048	53	Defensive FEI	-0.049	56	Field Position Advantage	0.498	62
Unadjusted Offense	-0.212	81	Unadjusted Defense	0.046	72	2009 Projections		Rank
Offensive S&P+	107.9	44	Defensive S&P+	97.4	71	FEI	0.024	54
Rushing S&P+	112.9	36	Rushing S&P+	105.2	49	Strength of Schedule	0.140	12
Passing S&P+	104.1	50	Passing S&P+	88.8	90	Offensive FEI	0.045	54
Standard Downs S&P+	115.0	22	Standard Downs S&P+	98.1	68	Defensive FEI	0.022	62
Passing Downs S&P+	89.9	93	Passing Downs S&P+	99.1	68	Mean Wins: 4.9 ACC: 2.7		

If the Terrapins didn't have the strangest season in college football last year, who did? A week after suffering a double-digit loss to Middle Tennessee (3-4 in the Sun Belt Conference), Maryland shocked California (6-3 in the Pac-10 Conference). A week after being obliterated by 31 points against Virginia (1-3 at the time of the game), the Terrapins laid a 26-point beat down on Wake Forest (4-1 at the time of the game). The only thing you could count on with Maryland in 2008 was its inconsistency.

Remarkably, junior quarterback Chris Turner has been at his best and most consistent in his career against ranked opponents (6-1 record, 9 TD, 2 INT). Maintaining that production will be challenging this season, however, as Maryland will replace three offensive line starters and speedy wide receiver Darrius Heyward-Bey. Worse, only four starters return to the defensive side of the ball. Sophomore punter Travis Baltz should be a bright spot. He led the ACC in punt distance last season, pinning opponents inside their own 20-yard line 24 times.

Top 2010 NFL Prospect: FB Cory Jackson (5-7).

Brian Fremeau

Big East

While conferences like the Big Ten and Pac-10 have fallen under one-party rule, the Big East has become a true democracy. A couple of years ago, it appeared that West Virginia and Louisville were ready to run away with the power, but things have balanced out quickly. The Moutaineers may be able to bounce back to dominance in 2009, but the conference could very well be up for grabs. Any of four to seven teams could challenge for supremacy, with last year's standings stirred up by the departure of so much talent from the 2008 season.

Gone are Pat White from West Virginia; Kenny Britt and Mike Teel from Rutgers; LeSean McCoy from Pittsburgh; Donald Brown and Darius Butler from Connecticut; and Cincinnati's Connor Barwin (and nine other defensive starters). While star power still remains with players such as Noel Devine, Mardy Gilyard, George Selvie, and Arthur Jones, the league is reshuffling itself a bit. There probably isn't a national title contender in the bunch, but that doesn't mean there won't be an exciting conference title race.

No. 12 West Virginia Mountaineers 10-2 (6-1)

2008: 9-4 (5-2) FEI: No. 21 S&P+: No. 75 F/+: No. 49 Program FEI: No. 9 Returning Starters: OFF 5, DEF 8

2008 Offense		Rank	2008 Defense		Rank	2008 Field Position		Rank
Offensive FEI	0.206	32	Defensive FEI	-0.277	28	Field Position Advantage	0.491	77
Unadjusted Offense	-0.061	62	Unadjusted Defense	-0.308	20	2009 Projections		Rank
Offensive S&P+	114.8	27	Defensive S&P+	79.7	113	FEI	0.172	12
Rushing S&P+	120.9	17	Rushing S&P+	78.7	111	Strength of Schedule	0.400	72
Passing S&P+	110.9	30	Passing S&P+	81.2	109	Offensive FEI	0.148	35
Standard Downs S&P+	109.7	34	Standard Downs S&P+	80.4	115	Defensive FEI	-0.425	15
Passing Downs S&P+	126.4	19	Passing Downs S&P+	77.1	111	Mean Wins: 9.6 Big East: 5.6		

The transition from Rich Rodriguez to Bill Stewart in 2008 was not a particularly smooth one for West Virginia. Stewart tried to implement more passing into the offensive attack, and while Pat White responded with decent numbers, what was supposed to be a team with dark horse national title capabilities ended up a bit of a disappointment. The Mountaineers scored just 17 combined points in early losses to East Carolina and Colorado before winning eight of ten to end the season, including a 31-30 win over North Carolina in the Meineke Car Care Bowl, possibly the most entertaining game of bowl season.

The good news for the Mountaineers is that they return more playmakers than anybody else in the conference. The bad news is that they are lacking in beef.

White's departure leaves 6-foot-4, 220-pound Jarrett Brown in charge of the WVU offense. In three years of substitute work behind White, Brown has put together decent numbers, completing 65 percent of his passes with five touchdowns to four interceptions. He has also proven to be a strong running threat, averaging 5.7 yards per carry and scoring seven touchdowns. He will have nice weapons around him, namely shifty, explosive running back Noel Devine and wide receivers Jock Sanders, Alric Arnett, Bradley Starks, and Wes Lyons. The bad news for Brown, however, is that he will be protected by the least experienced offensive line in the conference.

Eight starters return to a defense that fell a long way after ranking ninth in Defensive S&P+ in 2007. The numbers were not particularly kind to the Mountaineers in any category, but they are much more experienced in 2009, and the linebacker corps could be outstanding. J.T. Thomas returns, as does 2007 leader Reed Williams, who missed all but two games in 2008. Combined with a solid tackle in Scooter Berry, the Mountaineer front seven should improve. Cornerback Brandon Hogan leads the secondary.

All eyes will be on the offense in Morgantown. Stewart earned some naysayers in his first season by tinkering with an explosive offense, and he needs a young offensive line to create opportunities for WVU's playmakers.

Top 2010 NFL Prospects: RB Noel Devine* (2-3), QB Jarrett Brown (5-6), OT Selvish Capers (6-7).

No. 29 Rutgers Scarlet Knights 9-3 (4-3)

2008: 8-5 (5-2)	FEI: No. 22	S&P+: No. 29	F/+: No. 24	Program FEI: No. 32		Returning Starters: OFF 8, DEF 6	

2008 Offense		Rank	2008 Defense		Rank	2008 Field Position		Rank
Offensive FEI	0.250	25	Defensive FEI	-0.195	34	Field Position Advantage	0.507	45
Unadjusted Offense	0.203	30	Unadjusted Defense	-0.175	36	2009 Projections		Rank
Offensive S&P+	114.1	29	Defensive S&P+	105.1	48	FEI	0.087	29
Rushing S&P+	106.1	53	Rushing S&P+	118.3	25	Strength of Schedule	0.472	78
Passing S&P+	120.4	17	Passing S&P+	90.8	88	Offensive FEI	0.183	26
Standard Downs S&P+	117.9	15	Standard Downs S&P+	105.9	46	Defensive FEI	-0.025	57
Passing Downs S&P+	106.2	49	Passing Downs S&P+	106.1	50	Mean Wins: 8.8 Big East: 4.3		

In the decade between 1993 and 2002, Rutgers won 27 games. In the last four seasons, they have won 34, including a span of 14 wins in 16 games in 2006-07. But the 2008 season initially looked like a return to the impotent Scarlet Knights of yore, as Rutgers adjusted to life without running back Ray Rice. RU started 1-5, but riding the arm of Mike Teel, they won their last seven games, averaging 43 points per game over the last six and finishing 17th in Passing S&P+. As alcohol is to Homer Simpson, Teel was the cause of and solution to most of Rutgers's problems in 2008, but he is gone, as are receivers Kenny Britt, a first-round pick, and Tiquan Underwood.

Life after Teel and Britt will center around explosive receiver Tim Brown, an experienced offensive line (five returning starters, 83 career starts), and a combination of running backs, including Joe Martinek, Jourdan Brooks, and injury-prone Kordell Young. Dom Natale is the likely starter at quarterback, though highly-touted freshman Tom Savage will be given the chance to make noise in the fall. In all, the experienced offensive line will help Natale (or Savage) tremendously, but a lot will be expected of Brown to play at Britt's level to make the offense click.

The Scarlet Knight defense was decent against the run (25th) and atrocious against the pass (88th) in 2008. The line has to replace Pete Tverdov and Jamaal Westerman (23.5 tackles for a loss combined), but end George Johnson returns, as does star linebacker Ryan D'Imperio. They should provide stability up front, but the secondary remains shaky — particularly when opponents spread the field. Corner Devin McCourty and safety Joe Lefeged are solid, but they are the only proven commodities on the Scarlet Knight pass defense in 2009.

Top 2010 NFL Prospects: OT Anthony Davis (1-2), LB Ryan D'Imperio (5-7), DE George Johnson (6-7)

No. 30 Pittsburgh Panthers 8-4 (4-3)

2008: 9-4 (5-2)	FEI: No. 12	S&P+: No. 22	F/+: No. 17	Program FEI: No. 33		Returning Starters: OFF 7, DEF 7	

2008 Offense		Rank	2008 Defense		Rank	2008 Field Position		Rank
Offensive FEI	0.250	24	Defensive FEI	-0.312	26	Field Position Advantage	0.506	49
Unadjusted Offense	0.080	43	Unadjusted Defense	-0.180	34	2009 Projections		Rank
Offensive S&P+	110.3	38	Defensive S&P+	117.9	16	FEI	0.087	30
Rushing S&P+	122.0	16	Rushing S&P+	116.1	30	Strength of Schedule	0.360	60
Passing S&P+	100.4	60	Passing S&P+	118.2	12	Offensive FEI	0.063	49
Standard Downs S&P+	106.6	47	Standard Downs S&P+	110.1	29	Defensive FEI	-0.143	40
Passing Downs S&P+	112.6	33	Passing Downs S&P+	140.9	8	Mean Wins: 7.8 Big East: 4.3		

Beleaguered head coach Dave Wannstedt finally brought Pittsburgh back to respectability in 2008. Second-round NFL draft pick LeSean McCoy carried the Panthers on his back to a 9-4 record and Sun Bowl berth. Without McCoy and solid quarterback play, the Pitt offense could take a step backwards in 2009, but the defense could be dominant. The offense won't have to score too many points to give the Panthers a chance.

The Pittsburgh offense is littered with potential and inconsistency. Even with an extreme rushing threat in McCoy, Panther quarterbacks only managed nine touchdowns against ten interceptions and a 56 percent completion rate. Bill Stull returns as the starter, but he was pushed by Pat Bostick and Tino Sunseri in the spring. Whoever wins the battle will have a nice thunder-lightning receiving combination in tight end Nate Byham and receivers Oderick Turner and Jonathan Baldwin. Turner and Baldwin combined for just 39 catches in 2008, but averaged 18 yards per catch. Meanwhile, a relatively experienced line will be blocking for Stull and whoever wins the running back battle, potentially freshman Dion Lewis or sophomore Shariff Harris.

For the defense, the goal in 2008 was to leverage the offense into passing downs, then unleash the fury (ninth Passing Downs S&P+). Ends Greg Romeus and Jabaal Sheard combined for 13 sacks and 26 tackles for loss, and both return for 2009. So do cornerbacks Aaron Berry (all-conference) and Jovani Chappel and safety Dom DeCicco (a Pittsburgh name if ever one existed).

Top 2010 NFL Prospects: G/OT Joe Thomas (4-5), WR Oderick Turner (6-7), TE Nate Byham (6-7), CB Aaron Berry (6-7)

No. 47 South Florida Bulls 7-5 (4-3)

2008: 8-5 (2-5)   **FEI:** No. 29   **S&P+:** No. 23   **F/+:** No. 21   **Program FEI:** No. 35   **Returning Starters:** OFF 5, DEF 6

2008 Offense		Rank	2008 Defense		Rank	2008 Field Position		Rank
Offensive FEI	0.088	48	Defensive FEI	-0.157	39	Field Position Advantage	0.525	27
Unadjusted Offense	0.045	48	Unadjusted Defense	-0.196	31	**2009 Projections**		Rank
Offensive S&P+	117.4	21	Defensive S&P+	109.1	38	FEI	0.051	47
Rushing S&P+	113.3	34	Rushing S&P+	127.9	10	Strength of Schedule	0.315	53
Passing S&P+	120.8	16	Passing S&P+	93.7	78	Offensive FEI	-0.064	71
Standard Downs S&P+	108.7	37	Standard Downs S&P+	111.4	27	Defensive FEI	-0.108	46
Passing Downs S&P+	131.0	14	Passing Downs S&P+	109.7	43	**Mean Wins: 7.1 Big East: 3.6**		

For quite a few years in a row, South Florida seemed poised to make a move into the national scene. It almost happened in 2007, when the Bulls started 6-0 and advanced to No. 2 in the national polls before losing three in a row and falling to Oregon in the Sun Bowl. In 2008, although they salvaged another winning season with an undefeated non-conference slate, they fell to 2-5 in conference after three straight years at 4-3.

Coach Jim Leavitt's 13th season is a bit of a desperate time in St. Petersburg. South Florida has been to four straight bowl games, a fine accomplishment for such a young program (Leavitt is the only coach USF has ever had), but quarterback Matt Grothe and defensive end George Selvie, the two most notable USF players ever, are both seniors, and the clock is ticking before the Bulls have to do a little rebuilding.

Injuries and double-teams slowed Selvie down in 2008, but he remains the anchor of a defense that was great against the run (tenth in Rushing S&P+) and pretty bad against the pass (78th). New defensive coordinator Joe Tresey will attempt to piece together a better secondary, with safety Nate Allen an anchor. An improved pass rush would certainly help, and a healthy Selvie should assure that.

On offense, the feast or famine career of Grothe will come to an end in 2009. The gunslinger has thrown 42 interceptions in three seasons but still managed a respectable passer rating each year thanks to the big play. He has a big-play weapon in receiver Jessie Hester, Jr., but an inexperienced offensive line and the lack of a breakout running back could force him to improvise a bit too much.

Top 2010 NFL Prospects: DE George Selvie (1), S Nate Allen (2-3), QB Matt Grothe (6-7)

No. 49 Louisville Cardinals 7-5 (3-4)

2008: 5-7 (1-6)   **FEI:** No. 84   **S&P+:** No. 65   **F/+:** No. 74   **Program FEI:** No. 31   **Returning Starters:** OFF 5, DEF 4

2008 Offense		Rank	2008 Defense		Rank	2008 Field Position		Rank
Offensive FEI	-0.191	84	Defensive FEI	0.096	71	Field Position Advantage	0.474	96
Unadjusted Offense	-0.215	82	Unadjusted Defense	0.141	82	**2009 Projections**		Rank
Offensive S&P+	98.2	69	Defensive S&P+	100.8	63	FEI	0.043	49
Rushing S&P+	106.3	52	Rushing S&P+	107.8	42	Strength of Schedule	0.376	64
Passing S&P+	90.8	87	Passing S&P+	95.4	75	Offensive FEI	0.059	50
Standard Downs S&P+	102.5	55	Standard Downs S&P+	95.0	80	Defensive FEI	-0.154	39
Passing Downs S&P+	94.9	77	Passing Downs S&P+	91.2	85	**Mean Wins: 6.8 Big East: 3.5**		

From 2003-06, Louisville went 41-9, a ridiculously good mark for a team with no discernible football history. They appeared ready to break through. They were signing national-level recruits like Brian Brohm and Michael Bush, they were upgrading their facilities, and they were winning the 2007 Orange Bowl. And then Bobby Petrino left for (a few games with) the Atlanta Falcons. Steve Kragthorpe, who had been outstanding with Tulsa, took the job, and Louisville has quickly fallen off the national radar.

For an offense that had so recently featured one of the nation's best passing attacks, the Cardinals were shockingly mediocre in the passing game in 2008 (87th Passing S&P+) and not much better running (52nd). Victor Anderson is a potential star at running back, and Louisville certainly has good receiver prospects with Doug Beaumont, Josh Chichester, and Scott Long, who tore his ACL midway through 2008. Yet the Cardinals are inexperienced on the offensive line, and spring did

nothing to answer the question of who will replace Hunter Cantwell at quarterback.

Meanwhile, the defense has given up 30.6 points per game over the last two seasons. Athletes like linebacker Jon Dempsey and linebacker/safety Brandon Heath could become stars in 2009, but depth remains a lingering problem.

Thus far, Steve Kragthorpe's tenure as Louisville coach has been far from successful. In Kragthorpe's third season, Louisville will possess as much athleticism as anybody in the conference, but inexperience at quarterback and potential depth problems in the trenches could hold them back. If either Justin Burke or Adam Froman emerges as a strong quarterback and Scott Long gets back to 100 percent, Louisville could be solid. But that is anything but a given.

Top 2010 NFL Prospects: G Brian Roche (6-7), LB Jon Dempsey (6-7), WR Scott Long (6-7)

No. 55 Connecticut Huskies 6-6 (3-4)

2008: 8-5 (3-4)	FEI: No. 26		S&P+: No. 26	F/+: No. 26	Program FEI: No. 53		Returning Starters: OFF 7, DEF 7	
2008 Offense		**Rank**	**2008 Defense**		**Rank**	**2008 Field Position**		**Rank**
Offensive FEI	-0.035	67	*Defensive FEI*	-0.503	9	Field Position Advantage	0.481	89
Unadjusted Offense	-0.083	65	*Unadjusted Defense*	-0.423	11	**2009 Projections**		**Rank**
Offensive S&P+	101.8	57	Defensive S&P+	120.7	13	FEI	0.023	55
Rushing S&P+	119.5	19	Rushing S&P+	113.0	33	Strength of Schedule	0.340	57
Passing S&P+	81.9	103	Passing S&P+	128.3	8	Offensive FEI	-0.221	97
Standard Downs S&P+	105.6	51	Standard Downs S&P+	112.7	25	Defensive FEI	-0.334	22
Passing Downs S&P+	87.2	104	Passing Downs S&P+	146.0	3	**Mean Wins: 6.2 Big East: 3.1**		

Few teams in the country had as big a run-pass contrast as Connecticut did in 2008. They were 19th in Rushing S&P+ and 103rd in Passing S&P+. In this sense, the loss of quarterback Tyler Lorenzen might not spell doom for the Huskies, but do not underestimate the loss of first-round pick Donald Brown. Brown was both durable (28 carries a game) and explosive (5.7 yards per carry, 18 touchdowns), and he helped carry the Huskies to eight wins despite a passing attack that produced a 5-17 TD-INT ratio.

So if the Huskies lose their star runner and haven't done much to bolster their passing game, how are they going to score points? Hope lies in the youth of players like new starting quarterback Zach Frazer, sophomore back Jordan Todman and sophomore receiver Kashif Moore, and the experience of an offensive line, led by tackle Will Beatty, that returns more career starts (91) than any team in the conference. Whether UConn will be explosive remains

to be seen, but they should be able to play a decent ball control game.

Ball control is important because if the offense can avoid losing the game, the defense can win it. Sophomore tackles Kendall Reyes and Twyon Martin should team with senior end Lindsey Witten to form one of the best defensive lines in the conference. Cornerback Darius Butler departs, but Jasper Howard and Robert Vaughn return to a secondary that was eighth in Passing S&P+ last season. In between is Scott Lutrus, an underrated force at linebacker.

Despite the loss of some big-time talent in Brown, Butler, and others, the Huskies could be strong and surprising in 2009. However, they will have to find an explosive weapon on offense to challenge for the conference title.

Top 2010 NFL Prospects: S Robert Vaughn (5-7), OT Mike Hicks (6-7), RB Andre Dixon (6-7)

No. 63 Cincinnati Bearcats 6-6 (3-4)

2008: 11-3 (6-1)   **FEI:** No. 25   **S&P+:** No. 19   **F/+:** No. 19   **Program FEI:** No. 38   Returning Starters: OFF 8, DEF 1

2008 Offense		Rank	2008 Defense		Rank	2008 Field Position		Rank
Offensive FEI	-0.034	66	Defensive FEI	-0.307	27	Field Position Advantage	0.532	19
Unadjusted Offense	-0.131	72	Unadjusted Defense	-0.286	22	2009 Projections		Rank
Offensive S&P+	110.7	34	Defensive S&P+	120.7	14	FEI	-0.007	63
Rushing S&P+	105.1	57	Rushing S&P+	122.3	16	Strength of Schedule	0.403	73
Passing S&P+	112.9	26	Passing S&P+	117.9	14	Offensive FEI	-0.125	82
Standard Downs S&P+	106.1	49	Standard Downs S&P+	115.8	20	Defensive FEI	0.143	80
Passing Downs S&P+	112.0	37	Passing Downs S&P+	119.9	22	Mean Wins: 5.8 Big East: 2.6		

The Bearcats took major strides in 2008, winning 11 games and playing in their first ever Orange Bowl. They return a good quarterback, a couple of decent running backs, a great wide receiver, 64 career starts on the offensive line … and one defensive starter.

The Bearcats ranked 16th in rushing defense and 14th in passing defense, but were decimated by graduation. Coach Brian Kelly has brought in new defensive coordinator Bob Diaco and switched to a 3-4 scheme. When you have to start over on defense anyway, why not a scheme change? Safety Aaron Webster was solid in 2008 and now becomes the de facto defensive leader. Nose guard Derek Wolfe had a great spring and will be counted on to anchor the line.

The Bearcats will likely be involved in a few shootouts in 2009; while the defense will probably experience some growing pains, the offense could be the best in the Big East. Tony Pike (2,407 passing yards, 19 touchdowns, 11 interceptions) returns and will have the league's best receiving corps at his disposal. The main man is the explosive Mardy Gilyard (1,276 receiving yards, 11 touchdowns), a potential All-American. He is joined in the receiving corps by a potential weapon in sophomore D.J. Woods. In the backfield, last year's leading rushers Jacob Ramsey and John Goebel return; they will be pushed by sophomore Isaiah Pead, who had a nice spring. The offense is as deep as the defense is thin.

Needless to say, statistical projections don't smile on the loss of ten starters; Kelly will be challenged to repeat 2008's success.

Top 2010 NFL Prospects: WR Mardy Gilyard (2-3), QB Tony Pike (6-7), S Aaron Webster (6-7)

No. 93 Syracuse Orange 3-9 (1-6)

2008: 3-9 (1-6)   **FEI:** No. 87   **S&P+:** No. 87   **F/+:** No. 90   **Program FEI:** No. 91   Returning Starters: OFF 7, DEF 7

2008 Offense		Rank	2008 Defense		Rank	2008 Field Position		Rank
Offensive FEI	-0.193	85	Defensive FEI	0.176	80	Field Position Advantage	0.459	110
Unadjusted Offense	-0.362	104	Unadjusted Defense	0.300	100	2009 Projections		Rank
Offensive S&P+	96.2	77	Defensive S&P+	92.7	83	FEI	-0.111	93
Rushing S&P+	110.9	41	Rushing S&P+	91.7	84	Strength of Schedule	0.326	54
Passing S&P+	80.8	104	Passing S&P+	93.5	80	Offensive FEI	-0.219	96
Standard Downs S&P+	86.8	101	Standard Downs S&P+	93.9	86	Defensive FEI	0.184	81
Passing Downs S&P+	114.7	28	Passing Downs S&P+	86.4	93	Mean Wins: 3.0 Big East: 1.1		

How did such a proud program get here? From 1983 to 2001, Syracuse had one losing season. They have now suffered four in a row and haven't finished above an even .500 since 2001. In four seasons under Greg Robinson, the Orange won ten games. *Ten.*

Robinson is gone now, replaced by Syracuse alum Doug Marrone. He inherits a squad that was actually decent running the football in 2008, but couldn't pass, and despite the presence of an All-American talent in defensive tackle Arthur Jones, couldn't actually stop anybody. Syracuse could quickly field a competent offense with either Ryan Nassib, Cameron Dantley, or former Duke point guard Greg Paulus throwing to Mike Williams and Donte Davis, but the defense has a long way to go.

Top 2010 NFL Prospects: DT Arthur Jones (2-3), QB Greg Paulus (4-6), WR Mike Williams (5-7)*

Bill Connelly

Big Ten

Remember the good old days, when anybody could win the Big Ten? Northwestern did it in 1995, Purdue in 2000, Illinois in 2001 — heck, Wisconsin did it twice (1998-99)! Alas, those days are gone. We have entered a gilded age in the Big Ten, where the rich are rich, the poor are poor, and while there may be a lot of shuffling in the middle from year to year, everybody pretty much stays in their given class. In this example, Ohio State is both the Vanderbilts and the Carnegies, while Michigan, Penn State, and Iowa take turns being the Rockefellers. Meanwhile, everyone else at some point or another (even Indiana, however briefly) has jumped up and taken a tour of the middle class before falling on hard times. The latest example was Wisconsin, which threatened to break through to upper middle class for a while before forgetting how to play defense in 2008.

The real Gilded Age resulted in technological advances and the formation of unions for fairness. The Big Ten already has its own network and evenly shares revenue from it, and yet the inequality persists, so this analogy begins to fall apart. It must be just plain recruiting, coaching, and money.

Has this stratified society served the conference well? Not really. Not only has Ohio State made headlines for losing three consecutive BCS bowl games, including back-to-back BCS Championship Game losses, but the conference has only managed one winning record in the last six bowl seasons, going just 18-

Table 1: Big Ten Standings and Point Differential, 2002-2008

Team	W-L	PF	PA	Win%	Pt Dif
Ohio State	47-9	1607	794	.839	+813
Penn State	31-25	1435	1010	.554	+425
Iowa	36-20	1482	1081	.643	+401
Michigan	40-16	1568	1192	.714	+376
Wisconsin	32-24	1507	1326	.571	+181
Purdue	27-29	1415	1289	.482	+126
Michigan State	23-33	1560	1689	.411	-129
Minnesota	21-35	1466	1689	.375	-223
Northwestern	25-31	1262	1720	.446	-458
Illinois	15-41	1153	1705	.268	-552
Indiana	11-45	1085	2045	.196	-960

28 in that span. Are bowls the best indicator of conference strength? Of course not. But the marquee losses, the lack of national titles (the Big Ten has won fewer national titles in the last decade than LSU, USC, or Florida alone), and the lack of a consistent second power has hurt the perceptions of this historically powerful conference.

If teams are ever going to successfully shift the balance of power a few degrees away from Ohio State, now is the time. Every conference contender has defined liabilities, many in the area of skill positions, and though Ohio State is still the favorite, any of about ten teams (sorry, Indiana) could make a run to, or near, the top of the Big Ten standings in 2009.

No. 8 Ohio State Buckeyes 9-3 (6-2)

2008: 10-3 (7-1)		FEI: No. 14	S&P+: No. 8	F/+: No. 8	Program FEI: No. 4	Returning Starters: OFF 5, DEF 7	
2008 Offense		**Rank**	**2008 Defense**		**Rank**	**2008 Field Position**	**Rank**
Offensive FEI	0.213	30	Defensive FEI	-0.399	15	Field Position Advantage	0.550	6
Unadjusted Offense	0.019	51	Unadjusted Defense	-0.398	13	**2009 Projections**		**Rank**
Offensive S&P+	120.5	16	Defensive S&P+	132.3	6	FEI	0.195	8
Rushing S&P+	123.3	12	Rushing S&P+	114.4	32	Strength of Schedule	0.236	35
Passing S&P+	119.9	18	Passing S&P+	150.0	2	Offensive FEI	0.185	25
Standard Downs S&P+	112.0	29	Standard Downs S&P+	123.6	10	Defensive FEI	-0.526	7
Passing Downs S&P+	127.1	18	Passing Downs S&P+	144.8	5	Mean Wins: 9.5 Big Ten: 6.3		

Three consecutive BCS bowl losses and two underwhelming national title game appearances have taken

the shine off of what has been an absolutely outstanding tenure for Jim Tressel in Columbus. Yes, they have lost a series of games that would have earned them more respectability — Florida in 2006, LSU in 2007, USC and Texas in 2008 — but the last time the Buckeyes lost a game to a team that won fewer than nine games in a season was 2004 (with 34 straight wins since). While every other team in the country has suffered costly losses at the hands of mediocre teams, Ohio State has not. The Ohio State University has won 83 games in Tressel's eight years, and they will likely continue at that pace.

For the Buckeyes to continue their conference hot streak (29-3 over the last four seasons), quite a few unknowns need to become known in the first half of the season. Buckeye fans are excited about the potential "Boom and Zoom" combination of the physical Dan Herron and explosive Brandon Saine, but neither came close to the 5.8 yards per carry Beanie Wells averaged in 2008. Meanwhile, hopes are high that DeVier Posey is ready for a breakout season catching passes, but the sophomore is still more raw than polished. The offensive line, led by Michael Brewster and Michigan transfer (yes, you read that correctly) Justin Boren, should be solid.

Of course, nobody matters to the Buckeyes' success as much as the man at quarterback. Eased into the lineup during his freshman season, Terrelle Pryor showed glimpses of both athleticism and game management abilities. His 146.5 pass efficiency rating balanced nicely with his 631 rushing yards (4.5 per carry). In 2009, he will carry 100 percent of the load, and due to the host of unproven skill position players around him, he will be asked to do a lot.

On defense, star linebackers James Laurinaitis and Marcus Freeman are gone, as are cornerback Malcolm Jenkins and tackle Nader Abdallah. The last time Tressel had to replace this much star quality on defense was 2006, and the Buckeyes responded by allowing just 12.8 points per game. While their pass defense (second in S&P+) could suffer in 2009, their run defense (32nd) could improve with the emergence of ends Thaddeus Gibson and Cameron Hayward and tackle Doug Worthington.

Top 2010 NFL prospects: S Anderson Russell (3-4), C Jim Cordle (4-5), DE Doug Worthington (4-5), DE Lawrence Wilson (5-6).

No. 19 Penn State Nittany Lions 9-3 (5-3)

2008: 11-2 (7-1)	FEI: No. 5		S&P+: No. 6	F/+: No. 5		Program FEI: No. 10		Returning Starters: OFF 5, DEF 4	
2008 Offense		Rank	**2008 Defense**		Rank	**2008 Field Position**			Rank
Offensive FEI	0.671	5	Defensive FEI	-0.332	24	Field Position Advantage	0.549		9
Unadjusted Offense	0.550	11	Unadjusted Defense	-0.408	12	**2009 Projections**			Rank
Offensive S&P+	145.7	4	Defensive S&P+	120.5	15	FEI		0.136	19
Rushing S&P+	152.0	2	Rushing S&P+	130.3	8	Strength of Schedule		0.361	62
Passing S&P+	139.6	6	Passing S&P+	111.4	29	Offensive FEI		0.445	9
Standard Downs S&P+	131.5	5	Standard Downs S&P+	118.4	15	Defensive FEI		-0.106	48
Passing Downs S&P+	159.5	1	Passing Downs S&P+	131.7	12	Mean Wins: 9.1 Big Ten: 5.3			

After starting the decade with four losing seasons in five years, Joe Paterno has apparently found his second (fifth? sixth?) wind. Beginning in 2005, when recruiting began to pick up again, the Nittany Lions have won 40 games in four seasons and two conference titles (2005 and 2008). Paterno appears to still be going strong for now (he even spent part of his offseason yelling at the old fuddy-duddies in the conference about adding a 12th team and instituting a conference championship game), and Penn State remains built for the long haul.

Penn State enters 2009 with both savvy veterans and green newcomers. They are loaded at quarterback, running back, and linebacker, and quite inexperienced at receiver, offensive line, and de-

fensive back. However, the schedule is favorable, with eight home games and both Iowa and Ohio State visiting State College. Win out at home, and they will be directly in the hunt for another Big Ten crown despite inexperience.

Quarterback Daryll Clark (2,592 passing yards, 19 touchdowns, six interceptions) was outstanding in 2008. He returns to the Penn State backfield, as do rushers Evan Royster and Stephfon Green, who combined for 1,800 rushing yards last year. Unfortunately, a host of four-year contributors in the receiving corps are gone, particularly Deon Butler and Derrick Williams. Derek Moye and Graham Zug lead a sparkly new corps, and while they are talented, they are quite unproven.

Also unproven: a relatively inexperienced, reshuffled offensive line. Paterno teams are usually fine in the trenches, and this team may be no different, but their 39 returning career starts are the lowest in the Big Ten, and there will likely be some growing pains over the first half of the season.

Defensively, PSU is shaping up to potentially be as good as ever. The Nittany Lions are raw at defensive end, where Maurice Evans and Aaron Maybin are both gone, but they are strong at tackle and as stacked as ever at linebacker, where 2007 star Sean Lee returns from a knee injury to join Navorro Bowman and Josh Hull. The front seven is loaded.

The secondary, however, is a concern. It was the weaker link of last year's defense (29th in S&P+ against the pass, compared to eighth against the run), and all four starters needed replacing. Safety Drew Astorino looks like a keeper, but after that it gets iffy.

Top 2010 NFL prospects: LB Sean Lee (1-2), RB Evan Royster* (2-3), CB A.J. Wallace (5-6), QB Daryll Clark (6-7).

No. 20 Michigan Wolverines 8-4 (5-3)

2008: 3-9 (2-6)		FEI: No. 71	S&P+: No. 68	F/+: No. 68	Program FEI: No. 21		Returning Starters: OFF 10, DEF 5	
2008 Offense		**Rank**	**2008 Defense**		**Rank**	**2008 Field Position**		**Rank**
Offensive FEI	-0.153	80	Defensive FEI	-0.130	45	Field Position Advantage	0.474	95
Unadjusted Offense	-0.292	98	Unadjusted Defense	-0.142	44	**2009 Projections**		**Rank**
Offensive S&P+	89.2	95	Defensive S&P+	108.6	42	FEI	0.121	20
Rushing S&P+	98.9	72	Rushing S&P+	111.5	36	Strength of Schedule	0.282	48
Passing S&P+	77.5	112	Passing S&P+	104.3	45	Offensive FEI	0.302	18
Standard Downs S&P+	94.2	85	Standard Downs S&P+	117.6	17	Defensive FEI	-0.294	26
Passing Downs S&P+	80.5	110	Passing Downs S&P+	95.2	77	**Mean Wins: 8.3 Big Ten: 5.0**		

Rich Rodriguez inherited a difficult situation when he moved from Morgantown to Ann Arbor following the 2007 season. Not only was the remaining personnel from Lloyd Carr's Wolverines rather incompatible with the Rodriguez system, but there was almost no experience whatsoever on the offensive side of the ball. Consequently, Michigan struggled to move the ball in 2008, finishing 70th or worse in every major Football Outsiders offensive category; this includes a dismal 112th out of 120 FBS teams in passing S&P+. Michigan's 3-9 record in 2008 was their worst since 1962.

The good news is, Michigan will be more experienced in 2009. But are they experienced enough? Does the talent fit the system yet?

In 2008, Michigan's offense possibly suffered from the lack of a quarterback meant for Rodriguez's system. Pro-style Steven Threet did his best, but he was not the necessary running threat. Threet saw the writing on the wall and transferred. That left junior Nick Sheridan and heralded true freshman Tate Forcier, in for spring practice after graduating early from high school, to battle for the top position. Forcier showed great promise with both his arm and legs, but he still made rookie mistakes. Rodriguez will have a decision to make between the steady Sheridan and the explosive Forcier.

Whoever wins the job will hand the ball quite a bit to Brandon Minor, Vincent Smith, and a host of talented backs. The wide receiver position, however, remains a bit lackluster. Neither Martavious Odoms nor Greg Mathews proved to be explosive forces in the passing game.

While ten starters return on offense, only five return to a defensive unit that was solid though unspectacular. The Wolverine defense ranked 36th against the run and 45th against the pass in 2008; they struggled most by giving up big plays on passing downs. A more mature secondary led by safety Stevie Brown and cornerbacks Donovan Warren and Boubacar Cissoko could lead to fewer breakdowns, as could an improved pass rush if the Wolverines can find a complement to outstanding senior Brandon Graham (10 sacks in 2008). Linebacker Obi Ezeh is a tackling machine.

Michigan always recruits well, and teams have tended to take off offensively in Rodriguez's second year in a job (West Virginia as head coach, Clemson and Tulane as offensive coordinator). Things bode relatively well in Ann Arbor, but the Wolverines will likely only go as far as the quarterback position will take them.

Top 2010 NFL prospects: CB Donovan Warren* (1-2), LB Obi Ezeh* (1-2), DE Brandon Graham (2-3), WR Greg Matthews (4-5).

No. 22 Iowa Hawkeyes 8-4 (5-3)

2008: 9-4 (5-3)   FEI: No. 16   S&P+: No. 13   F/+: No. 10   Program FEI: No. 22   Returning Starters: OFF 6, DEF 8

2008 Offense		Rank	2008 Defense		Rank	2008 Field Position		Rank
Offensive FEI	0.134	39	Defensive FEI	-0.471	10	Field Position Advantage	0.535	17
Unadjusted Offense	0.053	47	Unadjusted Defense	-0.527	7	2009 Projections		Rank
Offensive S&P+	115.3	25	Defensive S&P+	122.2	11	FEI	0.116	22
Rushing S&P+	123.7	11	Rushing S&P+	140.5	4	Strength of Schedule	0.295	50
Passing S&P+	107.2	40	Passing S&P+	110.5	30	Offensive FEI	-0.028	65
Standard Downs S&P+	116.8	17	Standard Downs S&P+	113.5	24	Defensive FEI	-0.447	11
Passing Downs S&P+	110.4	41	Passing Downs S&P+	149.9	2	Mean Wins: 8.1 Big Ten: 4.7		

After 31 wins from 2002-04, Kirk Ferentz's Iowa Hawkeyes took a break from elite football, going just 19-18 from 2005-07. In 2008, however, Iowa snuck back onto the national scene when nobody was looking. They started slow, with three consecutive losses to Pittsburgh, Northwestern, and Michigan State, leaving them at 3-3 in early October. The mediocre record, combined with a series of off-field player problems, had Ferentz in a bit of hot water despite the fantastic turnaround he had engineered in the early part of the decade.

However, the Hawkeyes got mean again in the trenches, locked down opposing offenses, and found themselves a solid quarterback in Ricky Stanzi; they finished 2008 winning six of seven, including a win over Penn State that knocked the Nittany Lions from the ranks of the undefeated and a January 1 romp over South Carolina in the Outback Bowl. As an added bonus, they embarrassed Minnesota in the Gophers' final home game at the Metrodome, winning 55-0 and watching their visiting fans tear down the goalposts. They were 11th nationally in rushing offense and fourth in rushing defense, and Stanzi's new-found game-management ability led to a nine-win season.

Even without star running back Shonn Greene, now with the New York Jets, Iowa appears to be ready to look like Iowa again. That means a rugged, mean offensive line — and an experienced one at that — and a hard-hitting front seven with run-stuffing linebackers. Juniors Pat Angerer and A.J. Edds appear ready to be Iowa's newest great linebacker tandem; combined with potential stud ends Adrian Clayborn and Christian Ballard, Iowa should be as tough as ever up front.

As for the offensive line part of the equation, Iowa returns a Big Ten-best 98 career starts up front, led by bookend tackles Kyle Calloway and Bryan Bulaga. Stanzi and likely starting running back Jewel Hampton will likely feel quite well-protected by the hosses up front. Meanwhile, safety Tyler Sash leads an experienced secondary.

The main question mark for the Hawkeyes is lined up wide. Receiver Derrell Johnson-Koulianos fell out of favor with the coaching staff in the spring, opening the door for converted quarterback Marvin McNutt to lead the way in the receiving corps. There are few proven commodities outside of Johnson-Koulianos.

Top 2010 NFL prospects: C Rafael Eubanks (2-3), OT Bryan Bulaga* (2-3), OL Dan Doering (4-5).

No. 31 Michigan State Spartans 7-5 (4-4)

2008: 9-4 (6-2)   FEI: No. 44   S&P+: No. 31   F/+: No. 37   Program FEI: No. 39   Returning Starters: OFF 7, DEF 8

2008 Offense		Rank	2008 Defense		Rank	2008 Field Position		Rank
Offensive FEI	-0.016	63	Defensive FEI	-0.081	53	Field Position Advantage	0.535	16
Unadjusted Offense	-0.222	86	Unadjusted Defense	-0.098	49	2009 Projections		Rank
Offensive S&P+	102.5	55	Defensive S&P+	116.1	23	FEI	0.085	31
Rushing S&P+	102.6	64	Rushing S&P+	117.0	28	Strength of Schedule	0.332	56
Passing S&P+	106.8	41	Passing S&P+	114.8	20	Offensive FEI	0.016	57
Standard Downs S&P+	104.5	53	Standard Downs S&P+	115.2	21	Defensive FEI	-0.183	35
Passing Downs S&P+	96.0	73	Passing Downs S&P+	119.3	23	Mean Wins: 7.5 Big Ten: 4.4		

It is said that teams and coaches are remembered for what they do in November and later. No coach proved that more than former Michigan State head John L.

Smith. In four seasons in East Lansing, Smith's teams went 2-13 after Halloween. State had the reputation of a team that would inevitably collapse down the stretch, when games became twice as important.

In two seasons since replacing Smith, Mark Dantonio has begun to change that defeatist mindset. Granted, the Spartans have gone only 4-4 post-October, but even treading water has allowed them to reach heights not seen since Nick Saban was prowling the sideline in the 1990s, namely a January 1 bowl (they lost to Georgia in the 2009 Capital One Bowl).

In 2009, Michigan State returns eight starters from a defense that ranked in the S&P+ Top 30 in defending both the run and the pass last season. Linebackers Greg Jones and Eric Gordon were outstanding in 2008, combining for 212 tackles and 21.5 tackles for loss. They bring attitude to a defense that is pretty set everywhere but at the safety position.

The State offense, on the other hand, will undergo an identity change despite seven returning starters. Bigtime playmaking receivers Blair White (659 receiving yards, 15.3 yards per catch) and Mark Dell (679, 18.9) return, but a different quarterback will be throwing to them in the fall. Gone is Brian Hoyer; the battle to replace him has been a fierce one between sophomores Kirk Cousins and Keith Nichol.

The biggest change in State's identity, however, will come in the backfield, where Javon Ringer departs after toting the ball an insane 390 times in 2008. His explosiveness can be replaced, but his durability likely cannot.

Top 2010 NFL prospects: LB Greg Jones* (1-2), LB Eric Gordon* (3-5), C/G Joel Nitchman (6-7).

No. 33 Wisconsin Badgers 8-4 (4-4)

2008: 7-6 (3-5)	**FEI:** No. 57		**S&P+:** No. 64	**F/+:** No. 62		**Program FEI:** No. 25		**Returning Starters:** OFF 6, DEF 5	
2008 Offense		Rank	**2008 Defense**		Rank	**2008 Field Position**			Rank
Offensive FEI	-0.077	69	Defensive FEI	-0.194	35	Field Position Advantage	0.477		92
Unadjusted Offense	-0.090	67	Unadjusted Defense	-0.152	40	**2009 Projections**			Rank
Offensive S&P+	114.8	28	Defensive S&P+	84.2	107	FEI	0.079		33
Rushing S&P+	126.2	9	Rushing S&P+	84.6	101	Strength of Schedule	0.341		58
Passing S&P+	102.4	56	Passing S&P+	85.1	101	Offensive FEI	-0.293		106
Standard Downs S&P+	117.8	16	Standard Downs S&P+	85.5	108	Defensive FEI	-0.029		54
Passing Downs S&P+	110.2	42	Passing Downs S&P+	80.2	107	**Mean Wins:** 7.6 **Big Ten:** 4.2			

Long considered a stalwart defensive squad, Wisconsin went from giving up 12.1 points per game to 26.5 in just two seasons. The Badgers struggled at times on offense in 2008, but the defense let them down tremendously in a rather disappointing 7-6 season, giving up more than 24 points seven times.

Wisconsin was mediocre on both sides of the ball, struggling with consistency and the lack of playmakers. If things are to change in 2009, it will be because of a couple of new faces on defense and a couple of more mature athletes on offense. Defensively, the biggest impact could be made by newcomer J.J. Watt, a 6-foot-6, 285-pound sophomore transfer from Central Michigan. He and O'Brien Schofield could make for a disruptive force on the line. The secondary is a hodgepodge of experienced starters like Niles Brinkley and Jay Valai and new names like Devin Smith and Marcus Cromartie. The Badgers' most proven overall defensive player

is probably linebacker Jaevery McFadden.

On offense, a beefy, young offensive line (average weight: 314 pounds) will be blocking for a beefy, young running back named John Clay. As a freshman, Clay gained 884 yards (5.7 yards per carry) in backup work. He was listed at 247 pounds in the spring — keeping his weight in the 240- to 245-pound range could make him quite a force.

Meanwhile, inconsistent quarterback Dustin Sherer may have found a new, big-time target in the spring by the name of Nick Toon, son of former Badgers (and New York Jets) great Al Toon. He and David Gilreath (16.8 yards per catch in 2008) could make a nice 1-2 punch to go with a solid tight end in Garrett Graham. Toon and Clay are both sophomores, and they could lead Wisconsin to good things in the future.

Top 2010 NFL prospects: TE Garrett Graham (4-5), S Shane Carter (6-7), LB Jaevery McFadden (6-7).

No. 42 Minnesota Golden Gophers 7-5 (4-4)

2008: 7-6 (3-5)   FEI: No. 73   S&P+: No. 63   F/+: No. 66   Program FEI: No. 59   Returning Starters: OFF 10, DEF 8

2008 Offense		Rank	2008 Defense		Rank	2008 Field Position		Rank
Offensive FEI	-0.180	82	Defensive FEI	0.018	66	Field Position Advantage	0.512	42
Unadjusted Offense	-0.269	94	Unadjusted Defense	-0.042	56	2009 Projections		Rank
Offensive S&P+	103.0	54	Defensive S&P+	96.7	74	FEI	0.059	42
Rushing S&P+	97.5	77	Rushing S&P+	107.2	44	Strength of Schedule	0.265	43
Passing S&P+	108.4	37	Passing S&P+	87.7	95	Offensive FEI	0.088	42
Standard Downs S&P+	99.1	69	Standard Downs S&P+	98.1	69	Defensive FEI	-0.113	44
Passing Downs S&P+	113.1	32	Passing Downs S&P+	100.6	62	Mean Wins: 6.6 Big Ten: 3.8		

In Tim Brewster's first season after taking over for Glen Mason in 2007, the Golden Gophers were a terrible 1-11. They were bad on offense (57th in Close-Game S&P+) and atrocious on defense (114th). Twelve months later, they were playing in the Insight Bowl. A 7-1 start was followed by a five-game losing streak to end the season, but that 7-6 record was still a significant improvement.

Streakiness aside, Minnesota was distinctly average in 2008, on both offense and defense. Of course, average was a significant improvement from 2007, especially with so much youth on the field. The Gophers return quarterback Adam Weber (2,761 passing yards, 15 touchdowns, eight interceptions) and receiver Eric Decker (1,074 receiving yards), who it appears will be forgoing a professional baseball career for his senior season on the football field. Sophomore Troy Stoudermire is a potentially explosive threat at receiver as well. In all, ten starters return on offense, including an outstanding 96 career starts on the offensive line. A stronger rushing threat needs to emerge, but components are in place for significant offensive improvement.

Eight starters return on the defensive side of the ball. Minnesota was decent versus the run (44th Rushing S&P+), and the defensive line should be a threat with tackles Eric Small and Garrett Brown. The secondary, however, is a concern. UM was terrible against the pass (95th Passing S&P+) in 2008 despite the six combined interceptions from corners Traye Simmons and Marcus Shereis, and if the Gophers want to make another leap up the standings, they must allow fewer big plays.

Also worth noting: Brewster has made significant recruiting strides in the last two years, and that should start to pay off. Former blue-chip quarterback MarQueis Gray could make a difference sooner than later.

Top 2010 NFL prospects: WR Eric Decker (5-7), DT Garrett Brown (5-7), DT Eric Small (6-7).

No. 58 Purdue Boilermakers 5-7 (3-5)

2008: 4-8 (2-6)   FEI: No. 67   S&P+: No. 59   F/+: No. 63   Program FEI: No. 49   Returning Starters: OFF 4, DEF 7

2008 Offense		Rank	2008 Defense		Rank	2008 Field Position		Rank
Offensive FEI	-0.186	83	Defensive FEI	-0.183	37	Field Position Advantage	0.468	103
Unadjusted Offense	-0.223	87	Unadjusted Defense	-0.058	53	2009 Projections		Rank
Offensive S&P+	96.7	76	Defensive S&P+	104.3	51	FEI	0.009	58
Rushing S&P+	102.0	66	Rushing S&P+	100.9	62	Strength of Schedule	0.274	46
Passing S&P+	93.8	79	Passing S&P+	106.8	39	Offensive FEI	-0.229	100
Standard Downs S&P+	98.6	70	Standard Downs S&P+	103.3	52	Defensive FEI	-0.363	18
Passing Downs S&P+	111.6	39	Passing Downs S&P+	99.9	64	Mean Wins: 5.1 Big Ten: 3.2		

With the way his tenure ended, it is easy to forget just how successful Joe Tiller was at Purdue. He inherited a program that had not experienced a winning record in 12 seasons and immediately turned things around. The Boilermakers did not have a losing record until Tiller's ninth season and had only two during his 12 years in West Lafayette. Unfortunately, his worst team was probably his last. Tiller was known as an offensive innovator, bringing the spread offense to the Big Ten, but Purdue scored in single digits four times in a six-game span during conference play in 2008.

Danny Hope now takes over the reins; he was an offensive assistant for six years under Tiller. With a reasonably experienced offensive line and options at running back in Jaycen Taylor (who redshirted in

2008 following a torn ACL), Dan Dierking, and Ralph Bolden, they should get a good ground game going to take the pressure off of likely starting quarterback Joey Elliott.

The Boiler defense, an average unit in 2008, will feature a strong defensive line anchored by potential stars Ryan Kerrigan, a junior end, and Mike Neal, a senior tackle. Three members of a solid secondary return as well, though question marks exist at linebacker, where Anthony Heygood was their steadiest player but used up his eligibility.

Top 2010 NFL prospects: G Zach Reckman (5-7), DT Mike Neal (6-7), RB Jaycen Taylor (6-7).

No. 60 Northwestern Wildcats 6-6 (3-5)

2008: 9-4 (5-3)　　**FEI:** No. 51　　**S&P+:** No. 44　　**F/+:** No. 43　　**Program FEI:** No. 58　　**Returning Starters:** OFF 5, DEF 8

2008 Offense		Rank	2008 Defense		Rank	2008 Field Position		Rank
Offensive FEI	0.194	35	Defensive FEI	-0.082	52	Field Position Advantage	0.495	66
Unadjusted Offense	-0.060	61	Unadjusted Defense	-0.204	29	2009 Projections		Rank
Offensive S&P+	102.1	56	Defensive S&P+	108.4	43	FEI	0.001	60
Rushing S&P+	97.7	76	Rushing S&P+	109.1	40	Strength of Schedule	0.440	75
Passing S&P+	106.3	44	Passing S&P+	107.5	36	Offensive FEI	0.017	56
Standard Downs S&P+	102.2	57	Standard Downs S&P+	100.8	58	Defensive FEI	-0.111	45
Passing Downs S&P+	102.5	60	Passing Downs S&P+	120.4	21	Mean Wins: 6.5　Big Ten: 3.2		

In playing seven games decided by a possession or less, Northwestern came close to a wonderful season and close to a wholly mediocre one. They only beat Duke and Ohio by a combined 12 points and suffered a disappointing road loss at Indiana, but they also won at Iowa, Minnesota, and Michigan (all by a touchdown or less) and managed to go 9-4 despite only being ranked in the top 30 in one major statistical category (21st in Defensive Passing Downs S&P+). In the Alamo Bowl, Northwestern almost upset Missouri for its first bowl victory ever before falling in overtime. While the Wildcats were a competitive team in 2008, they played over their heads at times and should fall back to earth a bit in 2009.

Offensively, Northwestern is unknown at the skill positions — they have to replace a solid running back (Tyrell Sutton) and all three starting receivers, along with quarterback C.J. Bacher. However, new starting quarterback Mike Kafka looked good when Bacher was injured in 2008, and the Wildcats return a deep, experienced offensive line. On defense, the Wildcats look to improve with three potential stars in corner Sherrick McManis and safeties Brad Phillips and Brendan Smith. End Corey Wootton is a star on the defensive line if he returns healthy from a bowl-game injury. If the offense can produce, the defense could be good enough to win another batch of close games.

Top 2010 NFL prospects: DE Corey Wootton (2-4), CB Sherrick McManis (6-7), S Brad Phillips (6-7).

No. 76 Illinois Fighting Illini 4-8 (2-6)

2008: 5-7 (3-5)　　**FEI:** No. 56　　**S&P+:** No. 25　　**F/+:** No. 35　　**Program FEI:** No. 61　　**Returning Starters:** OFF 8, DEF 3

2008 Offense		Rank	2008 Defense		Rank	2008 Field Position		Rank
Offensive FEI	0.049	52	Defensive FEI	-0.142	41	Field Position Advantage	0.473	99
Unadjusted Offense	0.010	52	Unadjusted Defense	-0.038	58	2009 Projections		Rank
Offensive S&P+	112.8	31	Defensive S&P+	111.8	31	FEI	-0.046	76
Rushing S&P+	109.8	44	Rushing S&P+	110.8	39	Strength of Schedule	0.298	51
Passing S&P+	115.8	24	Passing S&P+	109.3	34	Offensive FEI	0.055	52
Standard Downs S&P+	116.2	18	Standard Downs S&P+	114.5	23	Defensive FEI	0.109	74
Passing Downs S&P+	120.7	24	Passing Downs S&P+	97.1	72	Mean Wins: 4.1　Big Ten: 2.1		

Illinois had the distinct honor of being the highest-ranked (via S&P+ and F/+) team with a losing record in 2008. They had a decent offense and defense but struggled mightily in special teams and significantly lost the field position (99th FPA) and turnover battles (89th in turnover margin). Such a strange team of extremes can expect to see more of the same in 2009. The Illini could be better offensively, worse defensively, and potentially no better at special teams.

First, the good news: Ron Zook continues to stockpile more weapons around quarterback Juice Williams, who is returning for his final go-round in orange and white. Williams is an adept runner (719 rushing yards) and at least a competent passer (3,173 passing yards, 22 touchdowns, 16 interceptions). His main target will once again be Arrelious Benn (1,055 receiving yards), but the hope is that Florida transfer Jarred Fayson will be healthy and ready to provide a serious threat opposite Benn. The running game is a question mark with sophomores Jason Ford and Mikel LeShoure.

Now, the bad news: A decent defense has to replace a lot of strong talent. Cornerback Vontae Davis was drafted in the first round by the Miami Dolphins, and leading tackler Brit Miller is gone, along with UI's top four sack leaders and eight total starters. Zook has stocked up on raw, athletic players over the last couple of seasons, but they need to start producing.

Top 2010 NFL prospects: WR Arrelious Benn* (1), QB Juice Williams (6-7), TE Michael Hoomanawanui (6-7).

No. 77 Indiana Hoosiers 4-8 (2-6)

2008: 3-9 (1-7) **FEI:** No. 108 **S&P+:** No. 71 **F/+:** No. 88 **Program FEI:** No. 84 **Returning Starters:** OFF 8, DEF 8

2008 Offense		Rank	2008 Defense		Rank	2008 Field Position		Rank
Offensive FEI	-0.147	79	Defensive FEI	0.331	97	Field Position Advantage	0.463	108
Unadjusted Offense	-0.230	88	Unadjusted Defense	0.385	107	2009 Projections		Rank
Offensive S&P+	100.9	61	Defensive S&P+	96.0	75	FEI	-0.061	77
Rushing S&P+	113.3	35	Rushing S&P+	96.8	74	Strength of Schedule	0.299	52
Passing S&P+	90.8	88	Passing S&P+	95.4	74	Offensive FEI	0.063	48
Standard Downs S&P+	94.5	83	Standard Downs S&P+	94.3	85	Defensive FEI	0.121	75
Passing Downs S&P+	96.0	74	Passing Downs S&P+	88.4	88	Mean Wins: 4.3 Big Ten: 1.8		

After an exciting 2007 season that saw Indiana go to its first bowl since 1993, Indiana fell off the proverbial cliff in 2008. Troubled quarterback Kellen Lewis couldn't keep from getting into trouble, and the Hoosiers plunged to 3-9, getting outscored 328-116 in conference play.

Indiana was pretty bad across the board in 2008, but its running game (35th S&P+) was decent. Unfortunately, that was due primarily to Marcus Thigpen, who is out of eligibility. Plus, Lewis, a running threat at quarterback, was dismissed from the team. The running game will likely suffer despite a pretty experienced offensive line, and the passing threat (88th S&P+) is shaky, although junior Ben Chappell will be throwing to a young receiving corps that has some potential.

On defense, the good news is that eight starters return. The bad news is that they were part of a pretty bad unit in 2008. Defensive end Greg Middleton, the one standout, is consistently double-teamed, a big reason why his sack total fell from 16 as a sophomore in 2007 to just four a year ago.

Top 2010 NFL prospects: DE Greg Middleton (1-3), S Austin Thomas (5-6), LB Will Patterson (5-7).

Bill Connelly

Big 12

One could tell as far back as 2006 that the Big 12 was going to have a great year in 2008. Colt McCoy was excelling as a redshirt freshman at Texas, and Josh Freeman was getting by as a true freshman at Kansas State. Chase Daniel (Missouri), Graham Harrell (Texas Tech), Stephen McGee (Texas A&M), and even Bobby Reid (Oklahoma State) were all good-looking sophomores piling up the experience. In a league already dominated by offense and quarterbacks, half the teams in the league would be starting a three-year starter in 2008 — and this doesn't even count future 2008 Heisman winner Sam Bradford, who was redshirting in 2006.

In all, the season lived up to expectations. Thanks to both experience and mostly easy non-conference schedules, the league produced four teams with at least ten wins and two more with nine. It also produced a fair share of controversy when Oklahoma, Texas, and Texas Tech all tied for the South title with a 7-1 record, having gone 1-1 versus each other and 6-0 versus everybody else in the conference. To break the tie, the Big 12 had to go to its fifth tie-breaker procedure ("The highest ranked team in the first Bowl Championship Series Poll following the completion of Big 12 regular season conference play shall be the representative") to choose Oklahoma for the Big 12 title game. Naturally, Texas fans screaming "45-35!!" were appalled by the process, but let's face it: If you have to get down to the fifth tie-breaker to determine a champion, the losing schools are inevitably going to feel pretty raw about it.

In 2009, the Big 12 returns plenty of familiar faces — Bradford and McCoy to name just two — but the balance of power in the rest of the conference may shift. Gone are Freeman, Daniel, Harrell, McGee, and Nebraska's Joe Ganz. (Reid was already gone a year ago, transferring to Texas Southern when he lost his job to Zac Robinson.) Gone are two-time Biletnikoff Award winner Michael Crabtree from Texas Tech, as well as Missouri All-Americans Jeremy Maclin and Chase Coffman. Gone is most of Oklahoma's offensive line, and all of Kansas's linebackers.

New faces — just as heavily recruited as the last batch of stars — abound in the Big 12, but the race for the conference title will still probably be decided by some names you recognize.

BIG 12 SOUTH

No. 3 Texas Longhorns 11-1 (7-1)

2008: 12-1 (7-1)   **FEI:** No. 4   **S&P+:** No. 5   **F/+:** No. 4   **Program FEI:** No. 3   **Returning Starters:** OFF 8, DEF 6

2008 Offense		Rank	2008 Defense		Rank	2008 Field Position		Rank
Offensive FEI	0.774	3	Defensive FEI	-0.616	3	Field Position Advantage	0.529	21
Unadjusted Offense	1.068	1	Unadjusted Defense	-0.247	27	**2009 Projections**		**Rank**
Offensive S&P+	124.6	10	Defensive S&P+	146.4	2	FEI	0.245	3
Rushing S&P+	115.4	29	Rushing S&P+	147.1	2	Strength of Schedule	0.349	59
Passing S&P+	133.3	9	Passing S&P+	148.9	3	Offensive FEI	0.774	1
Standard Downs S&P+	114.4	24	Standard Downs S&P+	130.6	3	Defensive FEI	-0.513	8
Passing Downs S&P+	152.8	2	Passing Downs S&P+	145.0	4	**Mean Wins: 10.6 Big 12: 6.8**		

There were 780 minutes of game time in Texas' 2008 season; oh, what a difference only 15 seconds can make. The final 15 seconds of the Texas-Texas Tech game — just 0.03 percent of the Longhorns' season — changed the 2008 fate of both Texas and Oklahoma. A dropped interception was followed by the national play of the year, Graham Harrell to Michael Crabtree for the touchdown with 0:01 left, and both the win and eventually a shot at the national title disappeared. Alas, 100 percent of the season needs to go your way sometimes, not just 99.97 percent.

The good news for Texas is, they return as much talent as anybody else in the country. Colt McCoy returns for his senior season, his favorite target Jordan Shipley was granted a sixth year of eligibility, his offensive line looks great, the defense returns playmakers like Sergio Kindle, and a secondary that was green in 2008, returns deep and intact.

Three main obstacles stand between Mack Brown's Longhorns and a spot in the national title game:

1) As yet, nobody has emerged as the No. 1 running back. Cody Johnson (short yardage specialist), Vondrell McGee (steady, consistent), and Fozzy Whitaker (shifty and explosive) all have particular strengths, but none have seized the job yet. The loss of Chris Ogbonnaya — a great receiving threat and, like McGee, a steady performer — might end up hurting Texas in close games.

2) Quan Cosby has departed from the receiving corps, and while his potential replacements — namely, Malcolm Williams, Brandon Collins, Dan Buckner, and James Kirkendoll — are all more explosive than Cosby, none have proven to be a consistent force yet. Ogbonnaya and Cosby were both great bailout options for McCoy when a play broke down.

3) In 2008, Texas' offense actually performed better on Passing Downs than Standard Downs. They were one of only two teams in the country able to claim that (the other: East Carolina), and it raises a concern that their disproportionate success on Passing Downs may not be duplicable from one season to another. (In fact, this is so rare that right now we don't have a big enough sample of teams in our college database to do a study on it.)

At this stage, however, these concerns are minor. The Longhorns are loaded with athletes at the skill positions, their offensive line returns more career starts (91) than anybody else in the country, their defense is deeper and more experienced than in recent years, and they have fewer question marks than anybody else in the conference. They are the favorites heading into the fall.

Top 2010 NFL Prospects: QB Colt McCoy (1), LB Sergio Kindle (1), OT Adam Ulatoski (1-2) DE Lamarr Houston (2-3).

No. 5 Oklahoma Sooners 10-2 (6-2)

2008: 12-2 (7-1)	FEI: No. 3	S&P+: No. 3	F/+: No. 3	Program FEI: No. 5	Returning Starters: OFF 5, DEF 9

2008 Offense		Rank	2008 Defense		Rank	2008 Field Position		Rank
Offensive FEI	0.786	2	Defensive FEI	-0.433	11	Field Position Advantage	0.532	18
Unadjusted Offense	0.894	3	Unadjusted Defense	-0.036	59	2009 Projections		Rank
Offensive S&P+	151.7	2	Defensive S&P+	129.2	7	FEI	0.219	5
Rushing S&P+	133.4	6	Rushing S&P+	129.8	9	Strength of Schedule	0.251	39
Passing S&P+	170.5	1	Passing S&P+	129.3	7	Offensive FEI	0.545	6
Standard Downs S&P+	128.6	6	Standard Downs S&P+	124.8	8	Defensive FEI	-0.450	10
Passing Downs S&P+	151.3	3	Passing Downs S&P+	139.6	9	Mean Wins: 9.9 Big 12: 6.5		

Oklahoma returns only 29 career starts on the offensive line in 2009 — second-worst in the conference — but if a new line gels around star tackle Trent Williams, the offense should click, and the Sooners could be as good as ever.

Heisman winner Sam Bradford surprised many by returning for his junior season to defend both the Heisman and Oklahoma's three straight South division titles. If Bradford is not running for his life behind a thin, patchwork offensive line, he will have plenty of weapons surrounding him. Backs DeMarco Murray and Chris Brown should both be healthy in the fall after rehabilitating from injuries most of the offseason; behind them are former high school stars Justin Johnson and Jermie Calhoun. The receiving corps is raw behind star tight end Jermaine Gresham and receiver Ryan Broyles, but

the Sooners are optimistic about injury-prone senior Adron Tennell, junior Brandon Caleb, and sophomore Jameel Owens. The offensive line is a large concern, but against most teams the Oklahoma offense should click along without missing much of a beat from 2008.

Oklahoma's defense was much-maligned through portions of 2008, but the criticism was overblown. After struggling briefly to compensate for an injury that sidelined linebacker Ryan Reynolds, the Sooners were almost as dominant as ever, finishing seventh in the Close-Game S&P+ rankings and allowing some of the lowest Success Rate+ figures across the board. Every key figure on this defense will be back in 2009.

Oklahoma should have one of the best defensive lines in the game behind star tackles Gerald McCoy and DeMarcus Granger and ends Auston English,

Jeremy Beal and Frank Alexander. Linebacker Travis Lewis was a revelation as a redshirt freshman, and Austin Box got valuable experience in Reynolds' absence. Reynolds also returns, but with the experience around him, not as much will be required of him. In the defensive backfield, the Sooners will miss departed safeties Nic Harris and Lendy Holmes, but the cornerback tandem of Dominique Franks and Brian Jackson should be rock solid.

In all, Oklahoma's national title hopes will come down to blocking and a random slip-up. If OU loses to Texas but goes 11-1, they will be in the national title hunt, as they were in 2008. But if another team gets to Bradford — and tricky road trips to Miami, Kansas, Nebraska and Texas Tech do loom — then the Sooners' 2009 goals will not include a national title.

Top 2010 NFL Prospects: QB Sam Bradford* (1), DT Gerald McCoy* (1), OT Trent Williams (1), TE Jermaine Gresham (1).

No. 24 Oklahoma State Cowboys 8-4 (5-3)

2008: 9-4 (5-3)	FEI: No. 36	S&P+: No. 14	F/+: No. 18	Program FEI: No. 41	Returning Starters: OFF 9, DEF 7

2008 Offense		Rank	2008 Defense		Rank	2008 Field Position		Rank
Offensive FEI	0.552	7	Defensive FEI	0.155	77	Field Position Advantage	0.526	26
Unadjusted Offense	0.672	7	Unadjusted Defense	0.296	98	2009 Projections		Rank
Offensive S&P+	123.5	13	Defensive S&P+	113.2	27	FEI	0.100	24
Rushing S&P+	123.2	13	Rushing S&P+	108.6	41	Strength of Schedule	0.185	19
Passing S&P+	129.4	11	Passing S&P+	115.8	17	Offensive FEI	0.634	5
Standard Downs S&P+	118.5	14	Standard Downs S&P+	104.2	49	Defensive FEI	0.194	83
Passing Downs S&P+	136.9	10	Passing Downs S&P+	117.7	27	Mean Wins: 7.6 Big 12: 4.7		

For a while last October, the Big 12 South was looking at not only a three-way race for the title, but a four-way race. Oklahoma State had followed up a surprising upset of Missouri in Columbia by coming within four points of Texas in Austin. Their QB-RB-WR combo of Zac Robinson, Kendall Hunter and Dez Bryant looked like OSU's best since Mike Gundy was handing to Thurman Thomas and throwing to Hart Lee Dykes. Meanwhile, defensive coordinator Tim Beckman was unloading a bag of tricks on opponents, confusing both Chase Daniel and Colt McCoy, and completely confounding Baylor's Robert Griffin.

Unfortunately, Beckman's bag of tricks fell empty, and the Cowboys finished the season by giving up 59 points to Texas Tech, 61 to Oklahoma, and 42 in a Holiday Bowl loss to Oregon. All three of these opponents had Top 10 offenses, but regardless, Oklahoma State finished the year losing three of four after an 8-1 start.

No disappointment, however, can quell runaway optimism in Stillwater for 2009. Robinson (3,000 yards passing, 500 rushing), Hunter (1,555 yards rushing, 17 total touchdowns), and Bryant (1,480 yards receiving, 21 total touchdowns) all return, and the OSU offensive line, led by potential 2010 Top 10 pick Russell Okung, is the second-most experienced in the conference behind Texas. The only offensive question mark comes at wide receiver, where the Cowboys are thin and inexperienced behind Bryant, and Brandon Pettigrew has departed for the NFL. Early indications say redshirt freshman Juston Blackmon could be a strong player, but clearly the answers here will not come until the fall.

The defense is highlighted by All-American candidate Andre Sexton and a strong, experienced linebacker corps. The secondary has been shaken up with the losses of cornerback Jacob Lacey and safety Ricky Price, but the biggest adjustment will come on the sidelines. Defensive Coordinator Beckman accepted the head coaching job at Toledo, and while replacement Bill Young has put together a strong resume at Kansas and Miami, it sometimes takes a defense a while to adapt to a new coordinator.

Oklahoma State has become this year's Texas Tech — the choice of many preseason prognosticators to have a breakthrough season. If the stars stay healthy and the defense adapts well to Young's defensive philosophy, they will have a chance. But a tough home schedule — Georgia, Missouri, Texas, and Texas Tech all visit Stillwater — and a Thanksgiving weekend trip to Norman await.

Top 2010 NFL Prospects: OT Russell Okung (1), WR Dez Bryant (2-3), CB Perrish Cox (5-7), S Andre Sexton (5-7).

No. 25 Texas Tech Red Raiders 8-4 (5-3)

2008: 11-2 (7-1)   FEI: No. 15   S&P+: No. 15   F/+: No. 16   Program FEI: No. 20   Returning Starters: OFF 4, DEF 7

2008 Offense		Rank	2008 Defense		Rank	2008 Field Position		Rank
Offensive FEI	0.716	4	Defensive FEI	-0.364	21	Field Position Advantage	0.494	69
Unadjusted Offense	1.026	2	Unadjusted Defense	0.103	78	2009 Projections		Rank
Offensive S&P+	128.0	7	Defensive S&P+	105.7	45	FEI	0.098	25
Rushing S&P+	138.9	4	Rushing S&P+	96.1	77	Strength of Schedule	0.261	41
Passing S&P+	121.7	15	Passing S&P+	114.4	21	Offensive FEI	0.470	7
Standard Downs S&P+	121.4	11	Standard Downs S&P+	98.7	63	Defensive FEI	-0.341	19
Passing Downs S&P+	143.5	7	Passing Downs S&P+	142.3	7	Mean Wins: 8.1 Big 12: 4.5		

If Oklahoma State is this year's Texas Tech, what does that leave for this year's Texas Tech? Before 2008, the Red Raiders under Mike Leach had been almost boringly consistent, winning between seven and nine games every year of the 2000s. Tech broke through with 11 wins and a South co-title in 2008, but they will likely take a step back into eight-win land in 2009 as they attempt to replace three-year starting quarterback Graham Harrell and two-time All-American receiver Michael Crabtree.

Harrell and Crabtree proved that if you put elite talent into Mike Leach's wide-open offense, the yards and wins will pile up in unprecedented fashion. But it is a given that Tech will move the ball at will against a majority of teams, no matter who is slinging the ball around. This year, those honors will likely go to senior Taylor Potts, long-time backup to Harrell.

Though Crabtree is gone, there is no shortage of decent options in the receiving corps — Detron Lewis (71 catches), Tramain Swindall (42), Edward Britton (30), and Lyle Leong (17) have all shown flashes of talent, and walk-on Alex Torres looked great in the spring. At running back — yes, Tech uses a running back sometimes — Baron Batch was outstanding in 2008 (742 rushing yards, 6.7 yards per carry). Even though the Red Raiders only use the run to keep teams off-balance, he is a tremendous weapon.

Harrell and Crabtree were great, but the other reason Tech was so successful in 2008 was that their defense, while not great, was not the liability it had been in years past with Leach. Their Close-Game S&P+ ranked only 45th in the country, but they were seventh on Passing Downs. Their offense would put the pressure on opponents to pile up points, and the defense would leverage desperate opponents into passing situations, then light them up. (For you NFL fans reading, consider the defensive philosophy of the Indianapolis Colts.)

The strength of Tech's defense was on the defensive line, where Brandon Williams and McKinner Dixon combined for 19 sacks and Colby Whitlock was one of the league's best tackles. Whitlock returns, as does improving tackle Richard Jones, but replacements need to be found at defensive end. Tech also needs a new anchor in the secondary with the departure of Darcel McBath and Daniel Charbonnet.

Top 2010 NFL Prospects: CB Jamar Wall (4-5), OT/G Brandon Carter (6-7), DE Rajon Henley (6-7).

No. 61 Texas A&M Aggies 5-7 (3-5)

2008: 4-8 (2-6)   FEI: No. 113   S&P+: No. 98   F/+: No. 101   Program FEI: No. 70   Returning Starters: OFF 9, DEF 7

2008 Offense		Rank	2008 Defense		Rank	2008 Field Position		Rank
Offensive FEI	0.033	56	Defensive FEI	0.567	116	Field Position Advantage	0.461	109
Unadjusted Offense	-0.021	57	Unadjusted Defense	0.584	114	2009 Projections		Rank
Offensive S&P+	93.6	85	Defensive S&P+	92.4	84	FEI	-0.004	61
Rushing S&P+	88.7	95	Rushing S&P+	88.2	93	Strength of Schedule	0.217	31
Passing S&P+	97.8	70	Passing S&P+	96.4	72	Offensive FEI	0.456	8
Standard Downs S&P+	94.0	87	Standard Downs S&P+	94.3	83	Defensive FEI	0.263	91
Passing Downs S&P+	117.1	26	Passing Downs S&P+	86.9	92	Mean Wins: 5.4 Big 12: 3.0		

Former Green Bay Packers coach Mike Sherman took over the Texas A&M head coaching job before the 2008 season, and to say the Aggies struggled would be an understatement. Never mind that they lost to Ar-kansas State in the season opener, and never mind that they gave up a combined 188 points to Oklahoma State, Kansas State, Texas Tech, and Iowa State in October.

No, the most jarring, telling loss of the season came

in a 41-21 shellacking at the hands of Baylor in mid-November. Baylor had more young talent and athleticism than the Aggies, and it sent warning signals of the road ahead.

If Texas A&M has any hope for a bounce-back season in 2009, it is because of the developing connection between junior quarterback Jerrod Johnson and sophomore receivers Ryan Tannehill and Jeff Fuller; that is, unless Tannehill overtakes Johnson for his starting job.

Meanwhile, both leadership and an influx of speed are needed on a defense that was almost equally iffy at defending the run (93rd in Rushing S&P+) and pass (72nd). Hope is high that linebacker Von Miller can provide both.

Top 2010 NFL Prospects: OT/G Michael Shumard (6-7), LB Anthony Lewis (6-7).

No. 73 Baylor Bears 4-8 (2-6)

2008: 4-8 (2-6)	FEI: No. 78	S&P+: No. 40	F/+: No. 57	Program FEI: No. 92	Returning Starters: OFF 9, DEF 9	

2008 Offense		Rank	2008 Defense		Rank	2008 Field Position		Rank
Offensive FEI	0.286	21	Defensive FEI	0.285	95	Field Position Advantage	0.491	76
Unadjusted Offense	0.350	18	Unadjusted Defense	0.409	108	2009 Projections		Rank
Offensive S&P+	110.4	37	Defensive S&P+	102.1	58	FEI	-0.040	73
Rushing S&P+	116.0	28	Rushing S&P+	100.4	65	Strength of Schedule	0.203	26
Passing S&P+	105.1	47	Passing S&P+	102.4	56	Offensive FEI	0.318	14
Standard Downs S&P+	102.1	59	Standard Downs S&P+	107.0	42	Defensive FEI	0.270	92
Passing Downs S&P+	109.2	44	Passing Downs S&P+	99.8	65	Mean Wins: 4.4 Big 12: 2.1		

Is this the year Baylor returns to the land of the living? Following a season that saw the Bears finish 4-8 while going 0-3 in games decided by a touchdown or less, with an offense that finished 37th in Close-Game S&P+ (28th rushing) and a young defense that was solid on Standard Downs (42th), there is hope.

More specifically, there is Robert Griffin III. A true freshman in 2008, Griffin — who bears a striking resemblance to SNL-era, "James Brown's Celebrity Hot Tub Party" Eddie Murphy — was eased into the lineup during nonconference play but still finished with 2,091 yards passing (15-3 TD-INT, 59.9% completion rate) and 843 yards rushing (13 TD). Barring a sophomore slump, Griffin seems a lock for a 2,000-1,000 season, but in BU's quest for their first bowl since 1994, coach Art Briles needs to find more complementary talent for Griffin. Nine offensive starters return, including intriguing junior running back Jay Finley (865 rushing yards,

5.8 yards per carry). Much hope resides in sophomore receiver Kendall Wright turning into a big-time threat.

An experienced defense (nine starters returning) hopes to build around the up-the-middle trifecta of All-Big 12 safety Jordan Lake, three-year starting linebacker Joe Pawelek, and defensive tackles Trey Bryant and Phil Taylor. Taylor, a Penn State transfer, is particularly intriguing after a dominating spring.

If there is a red flag for the Bears, it is that they benefitted tremendously from turnovers. Their +16 turnover margin was fourth-best in the country, and a margin that high is hard to duplicate from one year to another. Defenses will start to figure out Griffin's tendencies as well, meaning he will potentially throw more than just three interceptions in 2009.

Top 2010 NFL Prospects: LB Joe Pawelek (4-5), S Jordan Lake (4-5), TE Justin Akers (6-7).

BIG 12 NORTH

No. 38 Kansas Jayhawks 7-5 (4-4)

2008: 8-5 (4-4)   **FEI:** No. 61   **S&P+:** No. 20   **F/+:** No. 33   **Program FEI:** No. 46   Returning Starters: OFF 7, DEF 7

2008 Offense		Rank	2008 Defense		Rank	2008 Field Position		Rank
Offensive FEI	0.264	22	Defensive FEI	0.134	75	Field Position Advantage	0.493	71
Unadjusted Offense	0.318	22	Unadjusted Defense	0.119	80	**2009 Projections**		**Rank**
Offensive S&P+	118.1	19	Defensive S&P+	111.9	30	FEI	0.065	38
Rushing S&P+	118.8	21	Rushing S&P+	111.1	38	Strength of Schedule	0.246	38
Passing S&P+	115.2	25	Passing S&P+	113.3	27	Offensive FEI	0.395	12
Standard Downs S&P+	110.0	33	Standard Downs S&P+	107.2	41	Defensive FEI	-0.014	59
Passing Downs S&P+	128.0	16	Passing Downs S&P+	113.5	35	**Mean Wins: 7.2 Big 12: 4.1**		

The 2008 season saw Kansas take a step backwards after their dramatic 12-1 run in 2007. As the conference slate got much harder in 2008, wins were much more difficult to accumulate, and Kansas went 8-5 with a series of losses to highly-ranked teams.

The Jayhawks return more recognizable names in 2009 than any other North division team, which is why many are deeming them North favorites. Quarterback Todd Reesing returns for his senior season, and the skill position talent surrounding him is both plentiful and experienced. Senior Jake Sharp (1,143 rushing and receiving yards in 2008, 13 TDs) is the starter in the backfield. He is a productive but not especially flashy runner, with good receiving skills.

The receiving corps is a strength. Returning are junior Dezmon Briscoe (1,407 yards, 15 TDs) and senior Kerry Meier (1,045 yards, 8 TDs), potentially the most proven 1-2 punch in the Big 12. Reesing, Sharp, Briscoe, and Meier have two years of experience together, and when a play breaks down and Reesing has to improvise, good things often happen. This experienced connection explains how Kansas ranked higher in Passing Downs S&P+ (16th) than Standard Downs (33th).

If there is a concern on the offense, it is the glaring lack of experience on the offensive line. Returning players have just 26 career starts, the lowest figure in the Big 12. Reesing excels when running for his life, but that does not mean he needs to be doing it on every pass play. If Kansas doesn't win the North in 2009, it is likely because either the offensive line failed, or their schedule (South opponents: Oklahoma, Texas, Texas Tech) was too brutal.

On defense, KU benefitted from great experience in the linebacker corps in both 2007 and 2008, when the trio of James Holt, Joe Mortensen, and Mike Rivera played just about every snap — but they all depart for 2009. They return experience in the secondary — led by all-Big 12 safety Darrell Stuckey — and decent talent on the defensive line in the form of tackles Caleb Blakesley and Richard Johnson, but such a drop-off at linebacker means a likely overall dropoff, particularly against the run, where Kansas only ranked 38th to begin with in 2008.

Top 2010 NFL Prospects: S Darrell Stuckey (2-4), WR Dezmon Briscoe* (4-6), S Justin Thornton (6-7).

No. 40 Missouri Tigers 8-4 (5-3)

2008: 10-4 (5-3)   **FEI:** No. 28   **S&P+:** No. 10   **F/+:** No. 13   **Program FEI:** No. 30   Returning Starters: OFF 5, DEF 4

2008 Offense		Rank	2008 Defense		Rank	2008 Field Position		Rank
Offensive FEI	0.396	12	Defensive FEI	-0.037	59	Field Position Advantage	0.548	10
Unadjusted Offense	0.584	10	Unadjusted Defense	0.187	88	**2009 Projections**		**Rank**
Offensive S&P+	124.4	11	Defensive S&P+	116.7	20	FEI	0.063	40
Rushing S&P+	116.8	27	Rushing S&P+	124.5	14	Strength of Schedule	0.392	69
Passing S&P+	127.4	12	Passing S&P+	113.4	26	Offensive FEI	0.315	15
Standard Downs S&P+	123.8	8	Standard Downs S&P+	109.1	33	Defensive FEI	0.043	63
Passing Downs S&P+	124.1	21	Passing Downs S&P+	113.7	32	**Mean Wins: 8.0 Big 12: 4.6**		

An era is over in Columbia. Chase Daniel has handed the reins over after 30 wins in three seasons as Missouri starter. In his place: Blaine Gabbert. Gabbert, a high school All-American and understudy under

Chase Daniel in 2008, is everything Daniel wasn't: tall, highly-recruited, with a million-dollar arm. However, Daniel departs Missouri after making a very good case for having been Missouri's best quarterback ever. Expect growing pains from Gabbert in 2009, and the amount of growth could make the difference between five wins and ten.

Gabbert will have a talented cast of characters surrounding him despite the losses of All-Americans Jeremy Maclin and Chase Coffman. Derrick Washington was one of the best running backs in the Big 12 in 2008, while the offensive line is potentially the best in the Big 12 North. Question marks exist at wide receiver and tight end, where Maclin and Coffman were by far the top two targets. Receivers Jared Perry and Danario Alexander bring experience to the table, while youngsters Jerrell Jackson and Wes Kemp looked good in the spring. At tight end, tough Andrew Jones and sleek

Michael Egnew will try to give Gabbert as much of a Martin Rucker-Chase Coffman imitation as possible.

Defensively, the Tigers are an unknown. Gone are draftees Ziggy Hood, William Moore, and Stryker Sulak. Returning, however, are Sean Weatherspoon and quite a few strong athletes. However, experience is a concern, especially on the defensive line. Missouri's pass defense was not as bad as the total yardage figures suggest — when strength of opponent is taken into account, Missouri ended up with a respectable No. 26 ranking in Pass Defense S&P+, and while they could approximate that in 2009 with a more athletic secondary, the Run Defense S&P+ (14th) could suffer with the loss of Hood.

Top 2010 NFL Prospects: LB Sean Weatherspoon (1-2), WR Danario Alexander (5-7), OL Kurtis Gregory (5-7), DT Jaron Baston (5-7).

No. 62 Nebraska Cornhuskers 6-6 (3-5)

2008: 9-4 (5-3)	FEI: No. 59	S&P+: No. 21	F/+: No. 32	Program FEI: No. 57	Returning Starters: OFF 5, DEF 6	
2008 Offense		**Rank**	**2008 Defense**		**Rank**	**2008 Field Position**	**Rank**

2008 Offense		Rank	**2008 Defense**		Rank	**2008 Field Position**		Rank
Offensive FEI	0.291	20	*Defensive FEI*	0.121	73	Field Position Advantage	0.500	59
Unadjusted Offense	0.282	23	*Unadjusted Defense*	0.106	79	**2009 Projections**		**Rank**
Offensive S&P+	119.9	18	Defensive S&P+	108.8	41	FEI	-0.006	62
Rushing S&P+	107.0	50	Rushing S&P+	102.0	60	Strength of Schedule	0.266	44
Passing S&P+	131.3	10	Passing S&P+	112.2	28	Offensive FEI	0.225	23
Standard Downs S&P+	120.1	13	Standard Downs S&P+	103.9	51	Defensive FEI	0.084	69
Passing Downs S&P+	119.1	25	Passing Downs S&P+	114.0	31	**Mean Wins: 5.9 Big 12: 3.3**		

When Nebraska lost back-to-back games to Virginia Tech and Missouri (in dominant 52-17 fashion) in late September and early October, most wrote them off. It looked as if they were still a year away from returning to truly competitive form in the Big 12. However, after a competitive overtime loss at Texas Tech, the Huskers quietly got rolling. They would roll through the rest of the Big 12 North and finish the season winning six of their last seven games. Granted, the only decent teams they beat in that span were Kansas (33rd in F/+) at home and Clemson (25th) in the Gator Bowl, but they did show significant improvement.

The good news for the Huskers is that most of their defensive playmakers return for another season under defense-centric head coach Bo Pelini. Defensive tackle Ndamukong Suh is an All-American candidate and likely high draft pick in 2010. He joins solid ends Pierre Allen and Barry Turner to form what should be the best defensive line in the Big 12 North — they

should improve on their 60th-ranked run defense in 2009, but their improvement will be limited unless the linebacker corps improves. The secondary is unspectacular but very experienced.

The bad news for Nebraska's 2009 North title hopes is that while the defense could improve, the offense could regress. Quarterback Joe Ganz is gone after a solid 2008 season, as are multi-year starting back Marlon Lucky and receivers Todd Peterson and Nate Swift. In their place are sophomore signal-caller Zac Lee, a solid rushing tandem in Roy Helu, Jr., and Quentin Castille, and receivers Menelik Holt and Niles Paul. Like Missouri, they lose a lot of offensive playmakers, and while their replacements could be quite solid, other than Helu they are relatively unproven.

Top 2010 NFL Prospects: DT Ndamukong Suh (1), OL Jacob Hickman (5-7), LB Phillip Dillard (5-7).

No. 65 Kansas State Wildcats 6-6 (3-5)

2008: 5-7 (2-6)   FEI: No. 91   S&P+: No. 79   F/+: No. 89   Program FEI: No. 69   Returning Starters: OFF 7, DEF 8

2008 Offense		Rank	2008 Defense		Rank	2008 Field Position		Rank
Offensive FEI	-0.025	64	Defensive FEI	0.336	98	Field Position Advantage	0.510	43
Unadjusted Offense	0.330	21	Unadjusted Defense	0.463	110	**2009 Projections**		Rank
Offensive S&P+	98.0	70	Defensive S&P+	94.3	79	FEI	-0.015	65
Rushing S&P+	94.2	85	Rushing S&P+	90.1	88	Strength of Schedule	0.379	65
Passing S&P+	101.5	58	Passing S&P+	96.6	71	Offensive FEI	0.153	33
Standard Downs S&P+	96.6	78	Standard Downs S&P+	96.1	72	Defensive FEI	0.090	70
Passing Downs S&P+	87.3	102	Passing Downs S&P+	104.0	54	Mean Wins: 6.1 Big 12: 3.1		

It is a new day in Manhattan now that Ron Prince is gone after three iffy years in the Little Apple. Kansas State fans hope this new day looks a lot like days they have seen before. Bill Snyder returns for his second run as Wildcat coach. His first time around, he took one of the most moribund programs in the country — KSU had won nine games their previous seven seasons — and turned them into a Big 8/12 powerhouse.

Snyder's recruiting had tailed off the first time around, and KSU went just 9-13 his last two seasons. There is no questioning that the man can coach, and there is little question that a defense that ranked 79th in Close-Game S&P+ in 2008 will see at least moderate immediate improvement. But how much success Snyder will have this time around will depend on how much talent he can attract next door to resurgent Kansas and Missouri programs. The cupboard isn't as bare as it was the first time around, but it certainly isn't loaded. Look for quarterback Cameron Coffman to lead a nondescript offense while sophomore Alex Hrebec hopes to become the next great linebacker coached by Snyder.

Top 2010 NFL Prospects: S Courtney Herndon (6-7), WR Brandon Banks (6-7).

No. 68 Colorado Buffaloes 5-7 (3-5)

2008: 5-7 (2-6)   FEI: No. 88   S&P+: No. 82   F/+: No. 86   Program FEI: No. 64   Returning Starters: OFF 9, DEF 4

2008 Offense		Rank	2008 Defense		Rank	2008 Field Position		Rank
Offensive FEI	-0.273	94	Defensive FEI	-0.106	50	Field Position Advantage	0.492	73
Unadjusted Offense	-0.222	85	Unadjusted Defense	0.087	77	**2009 Projections**		Rank
Offensive S&P+	82.0	113	Defensive S&P+	110.0	33	FEI	-0.024	68
Rushing S&P+	85.9	101	Rushing S&P+	103.1	56	Strength of Schedule	0.274	47
Passing S&P+	78.9	108	Passing S&P+	115.3	18	Offensive FEI	0.024	55
Standard Downs S&P+	84.0	108	Standard Downs S&P+	108.6	36	Defensive FEI	-0.128	42
Passing Downs S&P+	79.9	111	Passing Downs S&P+	124.0	15	Mean Wins: 5.0 Big 12: 2.8		

The 2009 season will signal a turning point, one way or another, for the Colorado football program. In three seasons under Nick Nolte look-alike Dan Hawkins, the Buffaloes have gone just 13-24, and Hawkins is feeling some heat. In 2008, the Buffalos offense regressed significantly after making strides in 2007. They ranked 114th in Close-Game S&P+, equally bad in virtually every possible category — rushing (102nd), passing (111th), Standard Downs (110th), Passing Downs (114th), first quarter (98th), fourth quarter (89th), and everything in between.

Injuries played a key role in Colorado's extreme struggles — multiple injuries on the offensive line caused setbacks, plus young running backs Rodney Stewart and Darrell Scott were both hobbled and limited at times. A healthy Buff offense should see improvement, but how much can an offense improve in one offseason? In a league full of great offenses, Colorado has a ton of ground to make up to compete.

Hawkins' fate in Boulder will be determined primarily by two players: beleaguered quarterback (and coach's son) Cody Hawkins, and sophomore running back Darrell Scott, former blue-chipper. Hawkins looked steely and steady in 2007, defeating Oklahoma as a redshirt freshman, but he was average at best in 2008, showing iffy mobility and averaging just 5.9 yards per pass. Scott, on the other hand, has a world of potential if he can stay healthy, get some decent blocking, and continue learning the college game. He is the main reason many are once again naming Colorado as a Big 12 sleeper.

The offense needs to improve, but the defense faces its own problems. Their No. 18 pass defense could be solid with the return of three solid cornerbacks (led by Cha'pelle Brown), but the Buffs are starting over on the defensive line with the losses of George Hypolite and Maurice Lucas.

Top 2010 NFL Prospects: TE Riar Geer (6-7), FB Jake Behrens (6-7), LB Jeff Smart (6-7), CB Benjamin Burney (6-7).

No. 79 Iowa State Cyclones 5-7 (3-5)

2008: 2-10 (0-8)   **FEI:** No. 105   **S&P+:** No. 104   **F/+:** No. 107   **Program FEI:** No. 82   **Returning Starters:** OFF 9, DEF 6

2008 Offense		Rank	2008 Defense		Rank	2008 Field Position		Rank
Offensive FEI	-0.141	78	Defensive FEI	0.445	110	Field Position Advantage	0.490	79
Unadjusted Offense	-0.105	71	Unadjusted Defense	0.630	117	**2009 Projections**		**Rank**
Offensive S&P+	88.1	100	Defensive S&P+	89.6	93	FEI	-0.065	79
Rushing S&P+	88.4	96	Rushing S&P+	96.6	76	Strength of Schedule	0.504	82
Passing S&P+	87.5	93	Passing S&P+	81.8	108	Offensive FEI	0.131	37
Standard Downs S&P+	92.1	90	Standard Downs S&P+	91.0	94	Defensive FEI	0.345	98
Passing Downs S&P+	92.8	87	Passing Downs S&P+	82.3	102	**Mean Wins:** 5.0 **Big 12:** 2.5		

After Gene Chizik bolted for Auburn after just two years (and five wins) in Ames, Iowa State was left looking for their third head coach in four seasons. Enter Paul Rhoads, born and bred in Iowa, and a nine-year Division I defensive coordinator. Rhoads could very well be a good head coach — his background suggests he is more likely to consider ISU a destination job rather than a jumping-off point — but he is going to need to bring in a lot more talent than what the Cyclones currently have.

If ISU is to have any success in 2009, it will be on the arm of Austen Arnaud (2,792 yards passing, 15-10 TD-INT) and the legs of Alexander Robinson (703 rushing yards, 4.3 yards per carry). It will take the defensive-minded Rhoads a while to mold into shape a Cyclone defense that ranked 93rd in Close-Game S&P+ (108th versus the pass).

Top 2010 NFL Prospects: OL Reggie Stephens (5-7), P Mike Brandtner (6-7), DT Nate Frere (6-7), TE Derrick Catlett (6-7).

Bill Connelly

Pac-10

The 2001 Oregon Ducks went 11-1 and defeated Colorado in the Fiesta Bowl, finishing No. 2 in the AP and *USA Today* polls behind Miami. They sent a number of players to the NFL, most notably first-round quarterback Joey Harrington, but also Maurice Morris, Justin Peelle, and the best of the bunch, Igor Olshansky. Their most stellar achievement, however, can only be seen in hindsight: They were the last Pac-10 team to finish ahead of USC in the standings.

In the seven seasons that have followed, the Trojans have won four conference championships outright and tied for three others. They've gone 52-7 in conference games over that span. The next-best team over that time: Oregon, at 35-24.

Though USC has dominated its conference like no other school in recent history, it is far from the only strong team to be found in the Pac-10. Since 2002, Pac-10 teams have gone 177-96 against out-of-conference foes. Only two schools (Stanford and Washington) have posted losing records outside the conference; five have won at least two-thirds of their non-conference games.

That being said, we're projecting a down year for the conference — except for USC, of course, who should contend for a spot in the BCS Championship game. Other than a solid California team, we're not projecting any other Pac-10 schools to finish in the Top 25, with only one more (Oregon) in the Top 40. The Pac-10 may be too tough for its own good in 2009, as a bunch of good schools in the middle of the conference beat each other up and leave few survivors playing in bowl games.

No. 2 USC Trojans 10-2 (8-1)

2008: 12-1 (8-1)　　**FEI:** No. 2　　**S&P+:** No. 1　　**F/+:** No. 2　　**Program FEI:** No. 1　　**Returning Starters:** OFF 9, DEF 3

2008 Offense		Rank	2008 Defense		Rank	2008 Field Position		Rank
Offensive FEI	0.617	6	Defensive FEI	-0.647	2	Field Position Advantage	0.550	7
Unadjusted Offense	0.535	12	Unadjusted Defense	-0.662	1	**2009 Projections**		**Rank**
Offensive S&P+	146.3	3	Defensive S&P+	141.7	3	FEI	0.250	2
Rushing S&P+	132.5	7	Rushing S&P+	133.5	6	Strength of Schedule	0.257	40
Passing S&P+	161.3	2	Passing S&P+	147.9	4	Offensive FEI	0.716	2
Standard Downs S&P+	137.4	2	Standard Downs S&P+	137.5	2	Defensive FEI	-0.420	16
Passing Downs S&P+	151.1	4	Passing Downs S&P+	172.2	1	**Mean Wins:** 10.3　**Pac-10:** 7.9		

As dominant as USC has been against Pac-10 foes, it's done even better against other opponents, going 6-1 in BCS bowl games and 30-2 overall outside the Pac-10 since 2002. So why is it Florida and not USC that has won multiple BCS titles this decade? Because every year, the Trojans lose a game to an opponent that they should blow off the field. Last year, they were done in by Oregon State, which lost four games by a combined 69 points. In 2007, they fell to Stanford, a team that gave up nearly twice as many points as it scored on the season. The year before that, they dropped their Pac-10 finale to UCLA, which finished 5-4 in the conference. People in Los Angeles joke that they don't need the NFL because they have USC, but someone needs to tell the Trojans that the BCS doesn't let you lose a couple games and make up for it with a hot playoff run.

If the Trojans fall into a similar trap this season, it will likely be due to an inexperienced defense that returns only three starters: linemen Averell Spicer and Everson Griffen, and free safety Taylor Mays. Last year's Trojans defense was second in the nation in FEI, and sixth or better in S&P+ against both run and pass, and on Standard and Passing Downs. There's nowhere to go but down here.

On offense, things look much better. All five linemen from last year's robust rushing attack (seventh in Rushing S&P+) return, as do tailbacks Stafon Johnson, Joe McKnight, and C.J. Gable, who combined for 1,981 yards and 19 touchdowns on the ground in

2008. Leading wide receiver Damian Williams is also back, but he'll be catching balls from a new passer: sophomore Aaron Corp, who won the quarterback job in spring camp. He's got big shoes to fill; Mark Sanchez and company were second in the nation in Passing S&P+ last year.

When looking for big games on a schedule, you usually look for tough road trips like the Trojans will make to Ohio State, California, or Notre Dame. Given USC's penchant for falling to suspect teams, though, you may want to watch out for games at Arizona State or hosting Oregon State. And if they get through all those, you can look for them to make a final road trip to Pasadena and the BCS title game.

Top 2010 NFL prospects: S Taylor Mays (1), DE Everson Griffen* (2-3), TE Anthony McCoy (2-3), RB Joe McKnight* (2-3), OLB Michael Morgan* (2-3), C Kristofer O'Dowd* (2-3), OLB Malcolm Smith* (2-3), WR Damian Williams* (2-3), OT Charles Brown (3), RB Stafon Johnson (3-4), LB Luthur Brown (4-5).

No. 15 California Bears 9-3 (6-3)

2008: 9-4 (6-3)		FEI: No. 34	S&P+: No. 27	F/+: No. 30	Program FEI: No. 16		Returning Starters: OFF 7, DEF 8	
2008 Offense		**Rank**	**2008 Defense**		**Rank**	**2008 Field Position**		**Rank**
Offensive FEI	-0.029	65	Defensive FEI	-0.397	16	Field Position Advantage	0.525	28
Unadjusted Offense	-0.038	60	Unadjusted Defense	-0.457	9	**2009 Projections**		**Rank**
Offensive S&P+	104.5	50	Defensive S&P+	117.8	18	FEI	0.154	15
Rushing S&P+	112.7	38	Rushing S&P+	116.1	29	Strength of Schedule	0.293	49
Passing S&P+	99.5	64	Passing S&P+	118.2	13	Offensive FEI	0.059	51
Standard Downs S&P+	112.7	28	Standard Downs S&P+	118.7	14	Defensive FEI	-0.553	6
Passing Downs S&P+	106.4	48	Passing Downs S&P+	118.3	25	**Mean Wins: 9.0 Pac-10: 6.5**		

If any team can knock USC off the Pac-10 throne, it figures to be California, led by a defense that will keep the Trojans from running away with things. Eight starters return on a unit that was 16th in the nation in FEI. Like USC, the Bears are weakest at linebacker, losing three starters to graduation. Unlike USC, the Bears have experience everywhere else. All four starters in the secondary return, led by cornerback Syd'Quan Thompson. California is also strong along the line. If there aren't enough linebackers to be found, the team may switch back to a 4-3 look.

Coach Jeff Tedford did not name a starting quarterback after spring practice, but the favorite for the job is Kevin Riley, who split time with Nate Longshore last year. Leading wideout Nyan Boateng returns, but this figures to be a rushing team, with one of the best one-two tailback combos in the country. Top man Jahvid Best rushed for 1,580 yards last year on only 194 carries, a ridiculous 8.1-yard average. His backup, sophomore Shane Vereen, chipped in 715 yards, 5.0 per carry. Expect them to do most of their damage on the left side, where tackle Mike Tepper and guard Mark Boskovich add up to 623 pounds of returning starters. They figure to be weaker up the middle, with center Alex Mack drafted in the first round by Cleveland.

The fate of the Bears will likely be decided early in the year. Their conference opener comes September 26 at Oregon. They host USC the following week. If they can win those two contests, they'll have a clear path to the Pac-10 crown. Go 0-2 however, and their fate may be sealed. The non-conference schedule consists of Maryland, Minnesota, and Eastern Washington. Wins in those games won't help the Bears much, but losses could doom them come bowl season.

Top 2010 NFL prospects: RB Jahvid Best* (1-2), CB Syd'Quan Thompson (2-3), DE Tyson Alualu (5-7), OT Mike Tepper (6-7) .

No. 27 Oregon Ducks 7-5 (5-4)

| 2008: 10-3 (7-2) | FEI: No. 27 | S&P+: No. 11 | F/+: No. 14 | Program FEI: No. 18 | Returning Starters: OFF 5, DEF 5 |

2008 Offense		Rank	2008 Defense		Rank	2008 Field Position		Rank
Offensive FEI	0.335	15	Defensive FEI	-0.162	38	Field Position Advantage	0.517	36
Unadjusted Offense	0.345	19	Unadjusted Defense	-0.147	42	2009 Projections		Rank
Offensive S&P+	127.9	8	Defensive S&P+	112.5	29	FEI	0.095	27
Rushing S&P+	142.5	3	Rushing S&P+	121.1	21	Strength of Schedule	0.236	34
Passing S&P+	109.6	32	Passing S&P+	107.5	37	Offensive FEI	0.285	20
Standard Downs S&P+	131.9	4	Standard Downs S&P+	109.5	31	Defensive FEI	-0.164	37
Passing Downs S&P+	128.0	15	Passing Downs S&P+	118.3	24	Mean Wins: 7.1 Pac-10: 5.3		

It's one of the strangest coaching transitions you'll ever see, but it seems to be working. When Mike Bellotti, third in Pac-10 history with 72 conference wins, stepped into the athletic director's shoes at Oregon this offseason, offensive coordinator Chip Kelly was moved up to head coach. That's fairly standard operating procedure. What makes it unusual is that Bellotti has also retained himself as the school's quarterback coach. If the Ducks get off to a slow start, there are going to be calls for Bellotti to promote himself.

Most teams would suffer when losing a player like Jeremiah Johnson, and the 1,201 yards and 13 touchdowns he produced last season. Not Oregon, where LeGarrette Blount hopes to top his 1,002-yard, 17-touchdown junior season. Blount was the best running back in the country in terms of Points Per Play. He'll join quarterback Jeremiah Masoli, who was effective through the air (13 touchdowns, only five interceptions) and on the ground (718 yards, 10 scores) as a sophomore. They'll need younger players on offense to step up, however; the team lost two of its three leading receivers to graduation, while center Max Unger was drafted by Seattle in the second round. If Oregon is going to contend for the Pac-10 crown, they'll need to find balance on offense — in S&P+, they were third in the nation in rushing, but only 32nd in passing.

Even though rover Patrick Chung is now with the Patriots, the strength on defense is still the back seven, where four starters return. Expect an improvement in pass defense, which ranked 37th in S&P+ last year.

The good news for the Ducks is that they play their three toughest conference games — California, USC, and the Civil War against Oregon State — at home. Their non-conference slate includes a couple of top non-BCS teams — at Boise State, hosting Utah — so a good record there would pay off in January.

Top 2010 NFL prospects: RB LeGarrette Blount (2-3), CB Walter Thurmond (2-3), TE Ed Dickson (3-4), DE Will Tukuafu (4-6).

No. 41 UCLA Bruins 7-5 (5-4)

| 2008: 4-8 (3-6) | FEI: No. 90 | S&P+: No. 66 | F/+: No. 79 | Program FEI: No. 52 | Returning Starters: OFF 9, DEF 7 |

2008 Offense		Rank	2008 Defense		Rank	2008 Field Position		Rank
Offensive FEI	-0.423	110	Defensive FEI	-0.133	44	Field Position Advantage	0.451	111
Unadjusted Offense	-0.457	112	Unadjusted Defense	-0.150	41	2009 Projections		Rank
Offensive S&P+	89.1	96	Defensive S&P+	109.2	37	FEI	0.063	41
Rushing S&P+	82.1	109	Rushing S&P+	111.2	37	Strength of Schedule	0.238	36
Passing S&P+	93.7	80	Passing S&P+	106.5	40	Offensive FEI	-0.010	64
Standard Downs S&P+	89.5	99	Standard Downs S&P+	107.7	40	Defensive FEI	-0.427	14
Passing Downs S&P+	82.6	107	Passing Downs S&P+	129.3	14	Mean Wins: 6.6 Pac-10: 4.6		

How bleak are things for the Bruins on offense? They ranked 110th in Offensive FEI, 109th in Offensive Rushing S&P+. Even though there are a number of players on both sides of the ball with some starting experience, this team still has holes to fill. One of those starters is senior quarterback Kevin Craft, a last-second injury replacement who threw 21 interceptions with only 7 touchdowns. (Keep in mind, the passing game was the *strength* of this offense.) The other diehard: senior right guard Nick Ekbatani. On the flip side of the spectrum are the left tackle and tailback positions. Between those two spots, the Bruins list 10 players on the depth chart, with a combined total of one start. Top right tackle Nate Chandler, a sophomore, has two starts on his record — both at tight end.

Fortunately for UCLA, there are two sides to the line of scrimmage, and they have five returning defenders who started 12 games last season. The best of the bunch may be free safety Rahim Moore, who started a dozen games as a freshman. The Bruins excel when they can hold opponents to third-and-long, ranking 14th in S&P+ on Passing Downs.

Given the way Southern Cal has dominated the league, the best the Bruins can realistically hope for is to be the second-best team in California. With conference games against Stanford and California, plus a game with San Diego State in September, they'll have the chance to prove it — unless the Fresno State Bulldogs have anything to say about it. Other non-conference foes include Tennessee and Kansas State, two teams that figure to join UCLA on the bowl bubble.

Top 2010 NFL prospects: DT Brian Price* (1-2), LB Reggie Carter (3-4), CB Alterraun Verner (4), TE Ryan Moya (5).

No. 43 Arizona Wildcats 7-5 (5-4)

2008: 8-5 (5-4)	FEI: No. 40	S&P+: No. 28	F/+: No. 34	Program FEI: No. 43		Returning Starters: OFF 6, DEF 7	
2008 Offense		**Rank**	**2008 Defense**		**Rank**	**2008 Field Position**	**Rank**
Offensive FEI	0.244	27	Defensive FEI	-0.141	42	Field Position Advantage 0.523	32
Unadjusted Offense	0.378	16	Unadjusted Defense	-0.270	24	**2009 Projections**	**Rank**
Offensive S&P+	115.4	24	Defensive S&P+	105.0	49	FEI 0.057	43
Rushing S&P+	118.8	22	Rushing S&P+	94.5	80	Strength of Schedule 0.241	37
Passing S&P+	111.6	29	Passing S&P+	114.1	22	Offensive FEI 0.150	34
Standard Downs S&P+	115.6	20	Standard Downs S&P+	109.1	34	Defensive FEI -0.133	41
Passing Downs S&P+	107.0	47	Passing Downs S&P+	109.3	44	**Mean Wins: 6.6 Pac-10: 4.5**	

It's been a string of mediocre seasons for the Wildcats, who have gone 4-5, 5-4, and 5-4 in the Pac-10 over the last three years. Naturally, we're projecting another 5-4 finish in 2009.

Matt Scott takes over at quarterback from the departed Willie Tuitama, who threw for 9,216 yards and 67 touchdowns in his Arizona career. Other new starters include tackle Adam Grant and guard Vaughn Dotsy. Grant will be under the spotlight — he's taking the spot of Eben Britton, who was drafted in the second round by Jacksonville.

The experience on offense comes from the wide receivers. Although the team lost Mike Thomas (74 catches for 826 yards last year), Terrell Turner, Chris Gronkowski, and Delashaun Dean return to Arizona's spread offense. The trio notched 143 catches for 1,845 yards and 15 scores last season. Also returning is a pair of tailbacks: Nicholas Grigsby (1,153 yards, 13 touchdowns in 2008) and Keola Antolin (525 yards, 10 touchdowns).

Things are more stable on defense, where seven starters return, including all four linemen: ends Brooks Reed and Ricky Elmore, and tackles Donald Horton and Earl Mitchell. Arizona's biggest weakness last year was its run defense (80th in Rushing S&P+), so these four gentlemen must play better in 2009.

If the Wildcats are going to break into the Pac-10's upper crust, they're going to have to beat other on-the-bubble teams. That means important games will come at home against UCLA and Oregon, and on visits to Oregon State and Arizona State. Before conference play starts, Arizona hosts "games" against Central Michigan and Northern Arizona, then travels to Iowa City to take on the Hawkeyes.

Top 2010 NFL prospects: TE Rob Gronkowski* (2-3), C Colin Baxter* (3-4), CB Devin Ross (5-7), SS Cam Nelson (6-7), DT Earl Mitchell (6-7), WR Terrell Turner (6-7).

No. 45 Arizona State Sun Devils 7-5 (4-5)

2008: 5-7 (4-5)   FEI: No. 74   S&P+: No. 69   F/+: No. 70   Program FEI: No. 44   Returning Starters: OFF 7, DEF 6

2008 Offense		Rank	2008 Defense		Rank	2008 Field Position		Rank
Offensive FEI	-0.046	74	Defensive FEI	-0.123	46	Field Position Advantage	0.524	29
Unadjusted Offense	-0.253	89	Unadjusted Defense	-0.136	46	2009 Projections		Rank
Offensive S&P+	88.2	99	Defensive S&P+	109.0	40	FEI	0.054	45
Rushing S&P+	75.1	116	Rushing S&P+	127.5	11	Strength of Schedule	0.194	21
Passing S&P+	99.9	61	Passing S&P+	96.6	70	Offensive FEI	-0.038	68
Standard Downs S&P+	90.2	98	Standard Downs S&P+	119.8	12	Defensive FEI	-0.304	25
Passing Downs S&P+	88.7	99	Passing Downs S&P+	103.1	57	Mean Wins: 6.5 Pac-10: 4.5		

The Sun Devils have not had a winning conference record since 2004; a fifth non-winning year may mean the end of the road for coach Dennis Erickson. It would not be the first dead end Erickson has found in his career.

There will be plenty of new faces on an offense that lost its leading passer (Rudy Carpenter) and receiver (Michael Jones). Senior quarterback Danny Sullivan hasn't played much in his career, but his receivers — led by seniors Chris McGaha and Kyle Williams — have. There's also tailback Dimitri Nance, who led the team with a mere 410 rushing yards last season. The line also returns a pair of starters: tackle Shaun Lauvao and guard Jon Hargis.

The most stable position on defense is cornerback, where starters Omar Bolden and Terrell Carr are both back. Linebacker Travis Goethel is also returning, but he's moving inside after playing strongside linebacker in 2008. Speaking of position switches, Ryan McFoy is moving from weakside linebacker to strong safety. At just 209 pounds, that position should be a much better fit for him.

Don't expect a lot of long runs when the Sun Devils play. Their offense ranked last in the conference and 116th in the country (out of 120 teams) in Rushing S&P+, but their defense ranked 11th in the same statistic.

Cal comes trick-or-treating to Sun Devil Stadium on Halloween, with USC coming to town the following week. With the Pac-10 heavyweights playing in Tempe, there may be no unwinnable games on the Sun Devils' conference slate.

Top 2010 NFL prospects: LB Dexter Davis (2-3), WR Chris McGaha (2-3), CB Omar Bolden* (2-3), G Shawn Lauvao (6-7), WR Kyle Williams (6-7), LB Mike Nixon (6-7).

No. 50 Oregon State Beavers 7-5 (4-5)

2008: 9-4 (7-2)   FEI: No. 32   S&P+: No. 17   F/+: No. 20   Program FEI: No. 36   Returning Starters: OFF 6, DEF 3

2008 Offense		Rank	2008 Defense		Rank	2008 Field Position		Rank
Offensive FEI	0.198	34	Defensive FEI	-0.060	55	Field Position Advantage	0.540	14
Unadjusted Offense	-0.008	56	Unadjusted Defense	-0.078	51	2009 Projections		Rank
Offensive S&P+	115.1	26	Defensive S&P+	117.7	19	FEI	0.043	50
Rushing S&P+	112.4	40	Rushing S&P+	118.0	27	Strength of Schedule	0.273	45
Passing S&P+	117.6	21	Passing S&P+	116.5	16	Offensive FEI	0.157	32
Standard Downs S&P+	115.2	21	Standard Downs S&P+	124.2	9	Defensive FEI	0.101	73
Passing Downs S&P+	143.9	6	Passing Downs S&P+	106.4	49	Mean Wins: 6.7 Pac-10: 4.2		

Though there were concerns about the health of senior quarterback Lyle Moevao and the Rodgers brothers — junior wideout James and sophomore tailback Jacquizz — all three should be ready to get on the field in August. The trio had been banged up with various shoulder and collarbone injuries in spring. The younger Rodgers (a.k.a. "Pocket Herculizz") is the star of the show, setting a Pac-10 freshman record with 1,253 rushing yards and becoming the first frosh to be named Pac-10 Offensive Player of the year, despite missing the last 11 quarters of the season. He'll have a trio of returning linemen clearing running lanes for him.

On the other side of the ball, new faces will be everywhere. The most turnover is in the secondary, home of four new starters. In contrast, a pair of impact linebackers are returning: junior Keith Pankey on the weak side and senior Keaton Kristick in the middle. Although the Beavers' offense excelled on third downs last season (sixth in the nation S&P+ on

Passing Downs), the defense struggled (49th, compared to ninth on Standard Downs).With a pathetic non-conference schedule consisting of home games against Portland and Cincinnati sandwiched around a trip to UNLV, the Beavers seem destined to play in the postseason, where they'll go for their fourth bowl win in as many seasons. In conference, all their tough games — against USC, California, and Oregon — are on the road, but even if they lose all three, they'll gain valuable experience for 2010. Only five of this year's 22 starters will be seniors.

Top 2010 NFL prospects: DT Stephen Paea* (2-3), LB Keaton Kristick (7).

No. 59 Stanford Cardinal 5-7 (3-6)

2008: 5-7 (4-5)   **FEI:** No. 66   **S&P+:** No. 43   **F/+:** No. 51   **Program FEI:** No. 67   **Returning Starters:** OFF 8, DEF 8

2008 Offense		Rank	2008 Defense		Rank	2008 Field Position		Rank
Offensive FEI	0.144	37	Defensive FEI	0.132	74	Field Position Advantage	0.494	67
Unadjusted Offense	0.067	46	Unadjusted Defense	0.079	76	2009 Projections		Rank
Offensive S&P+	124.3	12	Defensive S&P+	86.6	103	FEI	0.008	59
Rushing S&P+	125.1	10	Rushing S&P+	89.0	91	Strength of Schedule	0.195	22
Passing S&P+	124.8	13	Passing S&P+	84.7	102	Offensive FEI	0.192	24
Standard Downs S&P+	123.7	9	Standard Downs S&P+	91.2	92	Defensive FEI	0.084	68
Passing Downs S&P+	135.1	13	Passing Downs S&P+	88.0	89	Mean Wins: 4.8 Pac-10: 3.5		

Senior quarterback Tavita Pritchard is listed among the team's returning starters, but he's not guaranteed to be under center when the Cardinal season opens at Washington State. Freshman Andrew Luck outplayed Pritchard in the spring game, going 18-for-25 for 352 yards. Even worse for Pritchard, the coaching staff made it clear that Luck was the "top draft pick" among the red and white rosters for that game, and Pritchard was the second choice. Whoever eventually wins the quarterback job, he'll have a pair of junior wideouts ready and waiting. Ryan Whalen and Doug Baldwin started as sophomores and both are back in 2009. Also returning is senior tailback Toby Gerhart; he ran for 1,136 yards and 15 touchdowns last season.

The offense is coach Jim Harbaugh's specialty, and under his watch the team has found the end zone far more often. They scored only 15 touchdowns in 2006. That number climbed to 27 in 2007, then 39 last year. They ranked 13th or better in Rushing and Passing S&P+, and on both Standard and Passing Downs.

On defense, however, they were 103rd overall, and no better than 89th in any of those categories. Most of the experience here is in the backfield, with senior cornerback Kris Evans, senior strong safety Bo McNally, and junior free safety Sean Wiser.

Will Stanford play in its first bowl game since 2001? Non-conference wins at Wake Forest and against Notre Dame and San Jose State would help. In conference, they'll probably need to win at least three games in October, when they play UCLA and Arizona State in Palo Alto, and travel to Oregon State and Arizona.

Top 2010 NFL prospects: RB Toby Gerhart (2-3), LB Clinton Snyder (3), TE Konrad Reuland* (3-4), OT Chris Marinelli (4-5), DT Ekom Udofia (4-5).

No. 69 Washington Huskies 4-8 (3-6)

2008: 0-12 (0-9)   **FEI:** No. 117   **S&P+:** No. 111   **F/+:** No. 116   **Program FEI:** No. 87   **Returning Starters:** OFF 8, DEF 10

2008 Offense		Rank	2008 Defense		Rank	2008 Field Position		Rank
Offensive FEI	-0.286	98	Defensive FEI	0.449	112	Field Position Advantage	0.438	114
Unadjusted Offense	-0.466	113	Unadjusted Defense	0.637	118	2009 Projections		Rank
Offensive S&P+	80.5	114	Defensive S&P+	88.6	99	FEI	-0.033	69
Rushing S&P+	88.2	97	Rushing S&P+	79.4	110	Strength of Schedule	0.150	14
Passing S&P+	73.5	116	Passing S&P+	95.5	73	Offensive FEI	0.101	41
Standard Downs S&P+	90.5	96	Standard Downs S&P+	90.7	97	Defensive FEI	-0.041	53
Passing Downs S&P+	89.5	96	Passing Downs S&P+	83.4	99	Mean Wins: 3.9 Pac-10: 2.7		

It is hard to believe this team was once considered a national powerhouse; they've finished last or second-to-last in the conference four years in a row. New coach Steve Sarkisian has been charged with bringing back former glory. He's probably learned by now that as USC's offensive coordinator, he had access to better talent and facilities.

Sarkisian's first task will be to develop the skills of junior Jake Locker, a ridiculously athletic quarterback (97 yards per game on the ground for his career) who has had little luck as a passer, with a completion rate below 50 percent. Locker should be the main ground threat again for the Huskies — the tailbacks have a combined total of 242 career rushing yards. Junior D'Andre Goodwin was the only reliable receiver for Washington last year, collecting more than one-third of their catches and yards. The numbers here reflect Locker's strengths and weaknesses — Washington ranked 97th in Rushing S&P+, 116th in Passing S&P+.

On defense, the good news is that a plethora of starters return. The bad news is, they're the same starters who finished 112th in Defensive FEI last season.

After a winless season, any chance for a victory seems like a big game. We're betting on September 12, when the Idaho Vandals come to Husky Stadium, as the day the Huskies win their first game since November 17, 2007.

Top 2010 NFL prospects: QB Jake Locker* (3-4), DE Daniel Te'o-Nesheim (4), LB E.J. Savannah (5-6), OT Ben Ossai (6).

No. 98 Washington State Cougars 2-10 (1-8)

2008: 2-11 (1-8)   **FEI:** No. 118   **S&P+:** No. 118   **F/+:** No. 119   **Program FEI:** No. 95   **Returning Starters:** OFF 8, DEF 5

2008 Offense		Rank	2008 Defense		Rank	2008 Field Position		Rank
Offensive FEI	-0.537	116	Defensive FEI	0.367	105	Field Position Advantage	0.420	118
Unadjusted Offense	-0.635	120	Unadjusted Defense	0.504	112	**2009 Projections**		**Rank**
Offensive S&P+	69.9	118	Defensive S&P+	84.5	105	FEI	-0.123	98
Rushing S&P+	77.9	113	Rushing S&P+	81.6	107	Strength of Schedule	0.214	29
Passing S&P+	62.8	117	Passing S&P+	87.5	96	Offensive FEI	-0.096	77
Standard Downs S&P+	81.2	115	Standard Downs S&P+	86.8	106	Defensive FEI	0.081	67
Passing Downs S&P+	58.8	118	Passing Downs S&P+	82.0	103	**Mean Wins: 2.3 Pac-10: 1.2**		

It's astounding how bad this team was in 2008. Between offense and defense, rushing and passing, Standard Downs and Passing Downs, we track eight different varieties of S&P+, and the Cougars were 103rd or worse in seven of them. The exception was Defensive Pass S&P+, where they ranked 96th.

Looking for signs of optimism here? You won't find them. The Cougars' offensive line was supposed to be a strength, with three starters returning. But then senior center Kenny Alfred, junior guard Brian Danaher, and junior tackle Micah Hannam all missed spring practice with injuries. The news is hardly any better on the other side of the ball. The healthy members of the front seven have a combined total of just 23 starts. They're led by the nine starts of weakside linebacker Louis Bland, a sophomore.

Still, one assistant coach was excited that at least you could hear pads popping in April, noting the prior spring practice had sounded like "a pillow fight."

The Cougars open with three straight home games against Stanford, Hawaii, and Southern Methodist. If they can't beat any of those teams, they may not win all year. They probably won't beat Notre Dame on Halloween afternoon in San Antonio, but at least they'll be on TV.

Top 2010 NFL prospect: WR Jeshua Anderson* (3-4), C Kenny Alfred (5-6).

Vince Verhei

Southeastern Conference

2008 was a tricky year for those who believe the SEC is the uberconference. Yes, there was another BCS title — the SEC's third in a row, courtesy of Florida. And Alabama leapt back into national prominence sooner than expected. But the traditional strength simply wasn't there. Defending champion LSU had quarterback issues. Georgia, the consensus preseason number one team, struggled with injuries and inconsistency and lost three games. Auburn and Tennessee cratered, and longtime coaches Tommy Tuberville and Philip Fulmer lost their jobs as a result.

2009 should restore some luster. FEI projects nine conference schools in the top 34, and a tenth, Ole Miss, has the potential first overall NFL draft pick in 2010. Florida is at the top, and with Tim Tebow and all 11 defensive starters returning to Gainesville, the Gators have an excellent chance to win another football-shaped crystal. Conference-wide, the defenses should be excellent, which would be a return to normalcy in Athens and Baton Rouge.

It is difficult to see any program challenging Florida, due to unsettled quarterback situations. Georgia, Alabama, and LSU will be breaking in new signal-callers. At Auburn, Tennessee, and Vanderbilt, the competition is wide-open. Beyond Tebow, only Jevan Snead at Ole Miss is a returning starter with credibility. Snead is a borderline All-American and makes the Mel Kiper types quiver in ecstasy. The rest of the conference is littered with untested players like Georgia's Joe Cox or Greg McElroy at Alabama, or proven mediocrities like Kodi Burns in Auburn or Tennessee's Jonathan Crompton. They make the alumni quiver — in fear.

As always, the league's coaches are fascinating. The three newbies are especially interesting. Lane Kiffin did a cannonball into the SEC pool upon arriving in Knoxville, talking smack and alleging his new rivals of recruiting improprieties. Kiffin has sucked up so much media oxygen that the Auburn fanbase's dissatisfaction with the hiring of Gene Chizik (record at Iowa State: 5-19) has been mostly buried. Ex-Florida offensive coordinator Dan Mullen, meanwhile, will try to breathe some spread-oriented life into the moribund attack at Mississippi State. If any can resuscitate their programs, they may command similar fealty and paydays to those of the league's emperors, Urban Meyer and Nick Saban.

SEC EAST

No. 1 Florida Gators 11-1 (7-1)

2008: 13-1 (7-1)   FEI: No. 1   S&P+: No. 2   F/+: No. 1   Program FEI: No. 2   Returning Starters: OFF 7, DEF 11

2008 Offense		Rank	2008 Defense		Rank	2008 Field Position		Rank
Offensive FEI	0.816	1	Defensive FEI	-0.787	1	Field Position Advantage	0.558	2
Unadjusted Offense	0.615	9	Unadjusted Defense	-0.654	2	2009 Projections		Rank
Offensive S&P+	152.1	1	Defensive S&P+	135.1	4	FEI	0.340	1
Rushing S&P+	152.7	1	Rushing S&P+	124.0	15	Strength of Schedule	0.196	23
Passing S&P+	157.0	3	Passing S&P+	146.3	5	Offensive FEI	0.674	4
Standard Downs S&P+	156.8	1	Standard Downs S&P+	126.2	5	Defensive FEI	-0.868	1
Passing Downs S&P+	147.5	5	Passing Downs S&P+	122.3	19	Mean Wins: 11.1 SEC: 7.3		

Well, let's see, there must be a few weaknesses here someplace … ah, yes, the ultra-explosive Percy Harvin has gone to the Minnesota Vikings. The Gators will have to break in a new kicker with Jonathan Phillips graduated, and tackle Phil Trautwein has traded in blue and orange for St. Louis blue and gold. So the Gators may have some challenges this season.

Actually, Florida has the highest Projected FEI ever recorded by the system (factoring in that five-year possession data isn't fully available prior to 2003). The margin between Florida and No. 2 USC is greater than the margin between the Trojans and No. 14 Boston College. This is what happens when all 11 defensive starters and reams of playmakers return to defend the national championship.

Of those coming back, first among equals is quarterback/fullback/messiah Tim Tebow. All Tebow has done through three seasons is win two national titles, the Heisman Trophy, and the undying worship of Gator fans and broadcasters everywhere. He even has a postgame tantrum memorialized in plaque form at the entrance to Florida Field.

It will be interesting to see if coach Urban Meyer changes the attack to showcase Tebow's passing this season, in an effort to convince NFL scouts of his viability as a pro quarterback. Tebow glanced briefly at the draft after 2008, but the lukewarm reception he received was enough to send him back to the warm bosom of campus life (he doubtless sees plenty of bosoms, though the devout Tebow prefers his hidden under several layers of sackcloth). While Meyer's prime purview is to win games, not ensure Sunday pay for his graduates, the coach is likely to do whatever he can for his best player.

Weaponry abounds in the backfield and on the flanks. Slot backs Jeff Demps, Brandon James, and Chris Rainey are all burners with a gear unmatchable by enemy defenders, and while traditional running back Emmanuel Moody didn't do much a year ago, he remains a power option when Tebow gets tired. Riley Cooper leads a steady group of receivers, and Aaron Hernandez is a Mackey Award possibility at tight end. Meyer's outstanding recruiting classes over the past couple of seasons has left the depth chart stacked with talents ready to show their wares. Look for sophomore Deonte Thompson and freshman Andre Dubose

to catch some balls and make some plays this season.

Offensive line — tackle specifically — is the only question mark on the team. The Pouncey twins, Mike and Maurkice, handle the guard spots, and Sam Robey, son of former NBA big man Rick Robey, was outstanding in the spring at center. Carl Johnson was expected to take over one tackle spot, but a February arrest for violating a restraining order clouds his future. Matt Patchan will flop from defensive tackle to the offensive side, and may earn a starting role. Meyer's chief function will be to shape the line and get the unit sharp on the intricacies of spread blocking. If he can't, there is hope for the rest of the SEC.

Regardless, it will be difficult to score on the Gators, who were 15th in Rushing S&P+ and 5th in Passing S&P+ in 2008. The defense that held the Globetrotter-like scoring machine of Oklahoma to 14 points in the BCS Championship game is back intact. The Gators surrendered just five touchdowns over the final eight games, and set a school record with 25 interceptions. Brandon Spikes is the cornerstone player at middle linebacker, a consensus first team All-American. Carlos Dunlap is the pass rush threat on the end. The deep secondary includes strong press corners Joe Haden and Janoris Jenkins. The talent and experience combine to form a unit that has an astounding projected FEI of -0.868, miles ahead of the second-best projected defense, Clemson, well back at -0.643.

Top 2010 NFL Prospects: QB (?) Tim Tebow (1-4), DE Carlos Dunlap* (1), LB Brandon Spikes (1), CB Joe Haden* (1), DE Jermaine Cunningham (2-3).

No. 6 Georgia Bulldogs 8-4 (5-3)

2008: 10-3 (6-2)	FEI: No. 23	S&P+: No. 12	F/+: No. 12	Program FEI: No. 6		Returning Starters: OFF 7, DEF 6	
2008 Offense		Rank	**2008 Defense**		Rank	**2008 Field Position**	Rank
Offensive FEI	0.516	8	Defensive FEI	-0.121	48	Field Position Advantage	0.489	81
Unadjusted Offense	0.217	28	Unadjusted Defense	-0.137	45	**2009 Projections**	Rank
Offensive S&P+	135.4	5	Defensive S&P+	102.5	57	FEI	0.211	6
Rushing S&P+	117.5	26	Rushing S&P+	97.7	70	Strength of Schedule	0.061	1
Passing S&P+	153.3	4	Passing S&P+	109.8	32	Offensive FEI	0.676	3
Standard Downs S&P+	136.5	3	Standard Downs S&P+	100.8	59	Defensive FEI	-0.247	33
Passing Downs S&P+	140.6	9	Passing Downs S&P+	92.4	83	**Mean Wins:** 8.4 **SEC:** 5.2	

2008 was a severe disappointment between the hedges, even though the Dawgs went 10-3 and won the Capital One Bowl. Crushing injuries, especially along the offensive and defensive lines, hampered a team that featured the sensational Knowshon Moreno running the ball plus the NFL's top overall draft pick, Matthew Stafford, at quarterback.

The 2009 team won't have the sizzle, but could be bet-

ter — or at least more consistent. Better tackling would be a start. The usually disciplined defense (59th in Defensive S&P+) fell off last year, allowing almost 25 points per game, and the projection sees more erosion. The talent is there to improve, however, especially tackle Geno Atkins and linebackers Rennie Curran and Akeem Dent. Atkins and Jeff Owens (back from knee surgery) form the best tackle combo in the league, and they will have to get to the quarterback. Georgia was tenth in the SEC in sacks last season, a ranking that seems certain to rise.

With the end of the Stafford Era, senior Joe Cox takes over. The situation is reminiscent of 2005, when D.J. Shockley stepped in for longtime starter David Greene and led the Dogs to an unexpected SEC title. Cox doesn't have an arm like Stafford or wheels like Shockley, but he is a veteran who has played well in limited opportunities. He'll surely be looking to A.J. Green, who was Randy Moss Lite during his freshman season, galloping downfield on long, thin legs to score eight touchdowns and approach 1,000 receiving yards. The rest of the offense is a

question mark. Caleb King (4.0 yards per carry as a freshman) and several others will rotate in order to approach Moreno's lost production. No back stood out in the spring. And the offensive line is made up of players who are either inexperienced, returning from injury, or both. If the unit finds some cohesion, 2009 could be as mellow as 2008 was a bummer. If not, the Dawgs could slip behind hated rival Georgia Tech as in-state bully.

Top 2010 NFL Prospects: S Reshad Jones* (1-2), LB Rennie Curran* (2-3), DT Geno Atkins (2-4), DT Kade Weston (6-7).

No. 23 Tennessee Volunteers 7-5 (4-4)

2008: 5-7 (3-5)	FEI: No. 58	S&P+: No. 32	F/+: No. 40	Program FEI: No. 24		Returning Starters: OFF 7, DEF 6	

2008 Offense		Rank	2008 Defense		Rank	2008 Field Position		Rank
Offensive FEI	-0.228	88	Defensive FEI	-0.377	19	Field Position Advantage	0.505	50
Unadjusted Offense	-0.386	105	Unadjusted Defense	-0.499	8	2009 Projections		Rank
Offensive S&P+	95.4	80	Defensive S&P+	122.8	10	FEI	0.113	23
Rushing S&P+	107.9	48	Rushing S&P+	146.0	3	Strength of Schedule	0.088	8
Passing S&P+	84.3	100	Passing S&P+	103.8	49	Offensive FEI	0.002	61
Standard Downs S&P+	102.8	54	Standard Downs S&P+	125.7	6	Defensive FEI	-0.572	4
Passing Downs S&P+	85.8	106	Passing Downs S&P+	118.1	26	Mean Wins: 7.1 SEC: 3.7		

It's hard to imagine Phil Fulmer ripping off his shirt to fire up a group of recruits. Or calling out Urban Meyer for supposed recruiting violations (Phil preferred to drop a dime on Alabama surreptitiously). That sort of fiery, lunatic energy is what Lane Kiffin has brought to Knoxville, and it has paid off in attention and new blood pumping through the program. Now it remains to be seen whether that translates to winning.

Despite the change at the top, the problem with the Vols remains the same as the past few seasons — quarterback play. Jonathan Crompton (889 passing yards, 51.5% completion rate, four touchdowns, five interceptions) looks to be the starter again by default, a thought that surely fills the Volunteer Navy with dread. Running back is a future, and perhaps immediate, strength, with freshmen Bryce Brown and David Oku committing to Tennessee from the Midwest (Kansas and Nebraska, respectively). They'll apprentice behind Montario Hardesty (271 yards, 3.6 per

carry) for the moment.

There will be a swarming defense in orange in 2009, potentially one of the best in the country (it was already pretty good in 2008 — tenth in Defensive S&P+, sixth on Standard Downs). Lane's old man Monte has abandoned the pro game to work with his son, and brings his years of experience to the Vols' sideline. He has plenty of talent to work with, including All-American defensive back Eric Berry, linebacker Rico McCoy, and ferocious defensive end Chris Walker. Walker has the potential to be a Dwight Freeney-like edge presence in Kiffin's Cover-2 system. Mammoth tackles aren't a necessity under Kiffin, but Montori Hughes evoked comparisons to space eaters like Albert Haynesworth during spring practice.

Top 2010 NFL Prospects: CB Eric Berry* (1), OLB Rico McCoy (2-4), DT Dan Williams (3-4), OLB Gerald Williams (4-5).

No. 28 Vanderbilt Commodores 7-5 (4-4)

2008: 7-6 (4-4)   **FEI:** No. 42   **S&P+:** No. 57   **F/+:** No. 56   **Program FEI:** No. 54   **Returning Starters:** OFF 9, DEF 9

2008 Offense		Rank	2008 Defense		Rank	2008 Field Position		Rank
Offensive FEI	-0.104	72	Defensive FEI	-0.319	25	Field Position Advantage	0.488	82
Unadjusted Offense	-0.392	106	Unadjusted Defense	-0.258	26	**2009 Projections**		**Rank**
Offensive S&P+	94.4	83	Defensive S&P+	106.6	44	FEI	0.090	28
Rushing S&P+	104.9	58	Rushing S&P+	98.6	67	Strength of Schedule	0.082	6
Passing S&P+	84.1	102	Passing S&P+	114.9	19	Offensive FEI	-0.037	67
Standard Downs S&P+	95.4	81	Standard Downs S&P+	104.5	47	Defensive FEI	-0.370	17
Passing Downs S&P+	87.7	101	Passing Downs S&P+	113.6	33	**Mean Wins:** 6.8 **SEC:** 3.7		

The Commodores had an amazing start to 2008, winning their first five games, including a national TV stunner of Auburn in front of a full-throated house at Dudley Field. Then the bottom fell out, as Vandy lost six of seven games before upsetting Boston College in the Music City Bowl. Nevertheless, by Vanderbilt standards, it was a breakthrough season for head coach Bobby Johnson.

But building on that success may prove tough in 2009. The team's best two players, quarterback Chris Nickson and cornerback D.J. Moore, are gone — Nickson to graduation, Moore to the NFL. Sophomore Larry Smith (167 yards, 55.9 percent completion rate in 34 pass attempts) took over for the injured Nickson and won the bowl game; he looks like the starter. Smith won an Alabama state title at powerful Prattville High, and has good speed, but his throwing ability is in question. Senior Mackenzi Adams could wrest away the position with a strong camp.

Wideout Terence Jeffers, a Connecticut transfer (582 receiving yards, 13.2 yards per catch, 5 touchdowns in 2007), is a playmaker on offense, something that is in short supply in Nashville. Most of the best athletes are on a defense that ranked 44th in Defensive S&P+ (19th in Passing S&P+), including Chris Marve, who had a dynamic freshman season at linebacker, and Myron Lewis, a rock-steady corner. Vandy could find depth to be a real issue again this season — it was a key factor in the team's swoon in 2008.

Top 2010 NFL Prospects: CB Myron Lewis (2-3), DE Broderick Stewart (2-3).

No. 34 South Carolina Gamecocks 6-6 (3-5)

2008: 7-6 (4-4)   **FEI:** No. 41   **S&P+:** No. 34   **F/+:** No. 38   **Program FEI:** No. 37   **Returning Starters:** OFF 5, DEF 6

2008 Offense		Rank	2008 Defense		Rank	2008 Field Position		Rank
Offensive FEI	-0.105	73	Defensive FEI	-0.391	18	Field Position Advantage	0.521	33
Unadjusted Offense	-0.359	103	Unadjusted Defense	-0.283	23	**2009 Projections**		**Rank**
Offensive S&P+	100.8	62	Defensive S&P+	115.1	24	FEI	0.069	34
Rushing S&P+	99.7	71	Rushing S&P+	112.9	34	Strength of Schedule	0.072	4
Passing S&P+	103.4	53	Passing S&P+	117.6	15	Offensive FEI	-0.156	83
Standard Downs S&P+	97.3	74	Standard Downs S&P+	110.7	28	Defensive FEI	-0.443	12
Passing Downs S&P+	113.9	30	Passing Downs S&P+	133.2	11	**Mean Wins:** 5.7 **SEC:** 3.0		

Steve Spurrier's arrival in Columbia four years ago was supposed to be a defining moment in Gamecocks history. Instead, not much has changed under the Ol' Ballcoach. South Carolina still gets beat on top in-state recruits by the likes of Georgia (see A.J. Green). The offense (62nd in Offensive S&P+, 72nd in PPP+, suggesting little explosive talent) still remains challenged, especially at quarterback, despite Spurrier's reputation as a guru. And The Other USC remains an SEC East also-ran.

Stephen Garcia's development at quarterback is crucial for the Cocks, or they might slip further in the conference pecking order. His last outing was an awful three-pick performance in the Outback Bowl. Garcia (832 passing yards, 53.3% completion rate, six touchdowns, eight interceptions) reportedly had a solid group of spring practices. But if he doesn't play well, or gets hurt, there is little behind him. Chris Smelley is gone, ruining things for those of us who enjoyed chalking up another futile South Carolina afternoon to "Smelley play." He didn't merely transfer, he dropped football entirely — Smelley is now catching for the Alabama baseball team.

The rest of the offense is inexperienced. New line coach Eric Woford was hired from Illinois to improve upon last year's shoddy play upfront. If that happens, the rest of the offense should follow suit, regardless of age.

The defense — stop me if you've heard this before — is way ahead of the offense. Eric Norwood is a pro-caliber linebacker who came back for his senior year. He keys a strong, fast unit (24th in Defensive S&P+, 18th in Defen-

sive PPP+) that will keep the Cocks in games while they cast about for some first downs.

Top 2010 NFL Prospects: DE/OLB Eric Norwood (1-2), DE Clifton Geathers* (2-3).

No. 64 Kentucky Wildcats 5-7 (2-6)

| 2008: 7-6 (2-6) | FEI: No. 68 | S&P+: No. 74 | F/+: No. 71 | Program FEI: No. 60 | Returning Starters: OFF 7, DEF 5 |

2008 Offense		Rank	2008 Defense		Rank	2008 Field Position		Rank
Offensive FEI	-0.262	91	Defensive FEI	-0.036	61	Field Position Advantage	0.549	8
Unadjusted Offense	-0.448	111	Unadjusted Defense	-0.155	38	2009 Projections		Rank
Offensive S&P+	92.5	87	Defensive S&P+	102.8	56	FEI	-0.013	64
Rushing S&P+	98.8	73	Rushing S&P+	105.8	48	Strength of Schedule	0.085	7
Passing S&P+	87.0	94	Passing S&P+	101.3	59	Offensive FEI	-0.186	91
Standard Downs S&P+	100.8	63	Standard Downs S&P+	109.3	32	Defensive FEI	-0.026	56
Passing Downs S&P+	80.7	109	Passing Downs S&P+	95.4	75	Mean Wins: 4.7 SEC: 1.8		

The 'Cats have the lowest projection in the conference in Defensive FEI, based on the graduation of several key starters. But there are some studs left, and reports out of spring practice indicate that Rich Brooks' defense may simply reload. Linebacker Micah Johnson (13.0 tackles for loss, 2.5 sacks) and corner Trevard Lindley (four interceptions, 11 passes broken up) are pro prospects the unit can build around.

Offensively, run-first quarterback Randall Cobb is now a full-time wideout. That leaves Mike Hartline

(1,666 passing yards, 55.3% completion rate, nine touchdowns, eight interceptions) as the man behind center. Hartline had a strong Liberty Bowl, leading Kentucky to an upset win over East Carolina. Hartline was up and down last year, but the junior will have every chance to lead the team back to a bowl game — or straight into the ground.

Top 2010 NFL Prospects: CB Trevard Lindlay (2), LB Micah Johnson (3-5), OLB Sam Maxwell (5-7).

SEC WEST

No. 7 Louisiana State Tigers 9-3 (5-3)

| 2008: 8-5 (3-5) | FEI: No. 35 | S&P+: No. 24 | F/+: No. 22 | Program FEI: No. 8 | Returning Starters: OFF 7, DEF 6 |

2008 Offense		Rank	2008 Defense		Rank	2008 Field Position		Rank
Offensive FEI	0.132	40	Defensive FEI	-0.121	49	Field Position Advantage	0.528	22
Unadjusted Offense	0.031	50	Unadjusted Defense	-0.176	35	2009 Projections		Rank
Offensive S&P+	116.4	23	Defensive S&P+	109.7	35	FEI	0.208	7
Rushing S&P+	122.9	14	Rushing S&P+	104.0	54	Strength of Schedule	0.089	9
Passing S&P+	111.9	28	Passing S&P+	113.9	23	Offensive FEI	0.380	13
Standard Downs S&P+	113.9	26	Standard Downs S&P+	109.7	30	Defensvie FEI	-0.335	20
Passing Downs S&P+	110.4	40	Passing Downs S&P+	122.5	18	Mean Wins: 9.0 SEC: 5.1		

The Chick-Fil-A (née Peach) Bowl last New Year's Eve was LSU in microcosm. Underdogs to Georgia Tech in Atlanta, the Tigers came out focused and intense, and destroyed the Jackets 38-3. Over the past few seasons, even during the championship run in 2007, the knock on the Bayou Bengals has been lackadaisical play. Coach Les Miles has brought oodles of talent to Baton Rouge, but can't seem to recruit consistency.

FEI likes LSU to win the stacked SEC West. Much of that projection leans on Jordan Jefferson (419 passing yards, 49.3% completion rate, four touchdowns, one interception in part-time work), the sophomore quarterback who played so brilliantly in the bowl game. One game does not a steady starter make, and the recruitment of super prospect Russell Shepard indicates the staff thinks an upgrade may be in the future. Jefferson is tall and strong, and the surprise return to school of wideout Brandon LaFell (63 receptions, 929 yards, eight touchdowns) will make the game easier for him. Even better for Jefferson's development will be turning and handing off 20 times a game to Charles Scott, who had 18 touchdowns a year ago. Offensive tackle Ciron Black thought about turning pro, but will be back for his senior season, which will help Scott immensely. Black has started the last 40 games for the Tigers, and is not only a great player but a tremendous leader.

Defensively, the front four that has been so spectacu-lar over the past few years is in rebuilding mode. The back seven will have to carry the unit. Harry Coleman (71 tackles, 7 passes broken up) moves from safety to linebacker, leaving Chad Jones and Ron Brooks, two versatile athletes, at safety. Cornerback Patrick Peterson is young, but is already turning heads with his next-level athleticism and cover skills.

Top 2010 NFL Prospects: WR Brandon LaFell (1), S Chad Jones (1), RB Charles Scott (1-2), OT Ciron Black (1-2), DE Rahim Alem (2-4).*

No. 11 Auburn Tigers 9-3 (5-3)

| 2008: 5-7 (2-6) | FEI: No. 54 | S&P+: No. 73 | F/+: No. 64 | Program FEI: No. 12 | Returning Starters: OFF 7, DEF 7 |

2008 Offense		Rank	2008 Defense		Rank	2008 Field Position		Rank
Offensive FEI	-0.295	100	Defensive FEI	-0.260	29	Field Position Advantage	0.528	24
Unadjusted Offense	-0.524	117	Unadjusted Defense	-0.265	25	2009 Projections		Rank
Offensive S&P+	85.4	108	Defensive S&P+	110.4	32	FEI	0.176	11
Rushing S&P+	87.1	99	Rushing S&P+	118.0	26	Strength of Schedule	0.164	16
Passing S&P+	85.2	98	Passing S&P+	103.4	53	Offensive FEI	-0.001	62
Standard Downs S&P+	84.0	107	Standard Downs S&P+	108.1	39	Defensive FEI	-0.572	5
Passing Downs S&P+	93.2	84	Passing Downs S&P+	113.5	34	Mean Wins: 8.7 SEC: 5.2		

Last season's flirtation with spread offense guru Tony Franklin blew up in Auburn's face. The team didn't fully commit, the players were slow to pick up the scheme, several coaches openly scorned Franklin's credentials and methods, Franklin was fired in midseason, and coach Tommy Tuberville lost his job at the end of the year. If Nick Saban himself had drawn up the plans for removing his in-state rivals from competition, he couldn't have done a better job than Auburn did to itself.

War Eagle Nation wasn't dancing on the Plains when Gene Chizik was hired as coach. Even Charles Barkley voiced his outrage at the hiring, and we all know how reticent he is about public controversies. Yes, Chizik has Auburn ties (he was defensive coordinator for the unbeaten 2004 season), but he was underwhelming as head man at Iowa State. On the other hand, he'll have far more talent to work with at Auburn, especially on defense, where he made his bones. The Tigers project to having the fifth best defense in the nation according to FEI.

On offense (109th Offensive S&P+), the Tigers will try to go the spread route once again, this time with former Tulsa assistant Gus Malzahn bringing his high-scoring wizardry to the rugged SEC West. His Golden Hurricane offense last year led FBS schools in yards per game and ranked ninth in offensive FEI. Auburn's quarterback situation, while not dreamy, at least cleared somewhat with the injury to Barrett Trotter. That leaves Kodi Burns (1,050 passing yards, 52.5 percent completion rate, two touchdowns, seven interceptions, 411 rushing yards), who played to less than full effect in 2008 and was awful in the spring game, to duel with Neil Caudle, who had a better spring. As usual, Auburn has a good stable of runners, but just how they will be used in Malzahn's spread remains to be seen.

Top 2010 NFL Prospects: DE Antonio Coleman (2-4), RB Ben Tate (4-6), OLB Troy Blackmon (5-6).

No. 13 Alabama Crimson Tide 9-3 (5-3)

2008: 12-2 (8-0)	FEI: No. 8	S&P+: No. 9	F/+: No. 7	Program FEI: No. 13		Returning Starters: OFF 5, DEF 9	
2008 Offense		**Rank**	**2008 Defense**		**Rank**	**2008 Field Position**	**Rank**
Offensive FEI	0.321	18	Defensive FEI	-0.425	12	Field Position Advantage	0.548	11
Unadjusted Offense	0.070	44	Unadjusted Defense	-0.547	6	**2009 Projections**	**Rank**
Offensive S&P+	126.6	9	Defensive S&P+	123.5	8	FEI	0.167	13
Rushing S&P+	136.0	5	Rushing S&P+	139.6	5	Strength of Schedule	0.183	18
Passing S&P+	117.0	22	Passing S&P+	113.6	25	Offensive FEI	0.109	40
Standard Downs S&P+	127.4	7	Standard Downs S&P+	126.8	4	Defensive FEI	-0.470	9
Passing Downs S&P+	116.4	27	Passing Downs S&P+	123.8	16	Mean Wins: 8.7 SEC: 5.4	

Coaches often talk about their second season with a program as being special. They are settled in, have systems and practice regimens fully installed, and the players have fully bought in to the program (the ones who haven't usually transfer). Nick Saban rode that second-year karma to an undefeated regular season and a restored pride in Alabama football, until losses in the SEC title game and the Sugar Bowl swept away some of the good tidings.

'Bama should be strong again, with a powerful defense ranked ninth in our projections. Nine starters return, including corner Javier Arenas, linebackers Cory Reamer and Rolando McClain, and tackle Terrence "Mount" Cody, a continent-sized landmass over center. Saban loves to win with defense and special teams, and should have no problem with a conservative style in 2009.

That's good, because scoring points won't be easy. It only felt as though John Parker Wilson was in Tuscaloosa for as long as Bear Bryant, but the three-year starter is finally gone. Greg McElroy is his replacement, though prize recruit Star Jackson will be asked to make plays in the running game while under center. The offensive line loses superstar tackle Andre Smith and center Antoine Caldwell, but is still big and talented. Receiver Julio Jones (58 receptions, 924 yards, 4 touchdowns) had an immediate impact as a freshman, and should only improve. Runners Mark Ingram (5.1 yards per carry) and Roy Upchurch (6.0) should find plenty of running room in the ground-based attack.

The Tide kick-started its 2008 campaign with a blowout of Clemson in the Georgia Dome. Atlanta will be running red again for this year's opener, as Alabama returns to face Virginia Tech in another early test of SEC-ACC power. If 'Bama can survive that one, the schedule is very user-friendly the rest of the way.

Top 2010 NFL Prospects: DT Terrence Cody (1), ILB Rolando McClain* (1), CB Javiar Arenas (1-2), G Mike Johnson (2-3), CB Kareem Jackson* (2-3).

No. 21 Arkansas Razorbacks 7-5 (4-4)

2008: 5-7 (2-6)	FEI: No. 81	S&P+: No. 38	F/+: No. 52	Program FEI: No. 42		Returning Starters: OFF 8, DEF 9	
2008 Offense		**Rank**	**2008 Defense**		**Rank**	**2008 Field Position**	**Rank**
Offensive FEI	0.103	44	Defensive FEI	0.053	67	Field Position Advantage	0.445	113
Unadjusted Offense	-0.069	63	Unadjusted Defense	0.180	87	**2009 Projections**	**Rank**
Offensive S&P+	110.7	35	Defensive S&P+	104.0	52	FEI	0.116	21
Rushing S&P+	115.0	31	Rushing S&P+	99.0	66	Strength of Schedule	0.074	5
Passing S&P+	107.9	39	Passing S&P+	109.3	35	Offensive FEI	0.420	10
Standard Downs S&P+	108.5	38	Standard Downs S&P+	102.3	54	Defensive FEI	-0.316	23
Passing Downs S&P+	112.5	34	Passing Downs S&P+	109.8	41	Mean Wins: 7.1 SEC: 3.5	

It beggars belief that the hiring of Bobby Petrino would be a stabilizing force for a team, but after the madness of the Houston Nutt years, things were contextually calm in Sooey Nation. Unfortunately, the Razorbacks weren't as good, either.

That could change rapidly, however. Arkansas is an intriguing squad with an explosive offense. Ryan Mallett (43.3 percent completion rate, seven touchdowns, five interceptions at Michigan in 2007) was a poor fit in Ann Arbor under Rich Rodriguez' spread scheme, but has looked sensational in practices with the Hogs. He has a surfeit of targets. Receivers Joe Adams, London Crawford, and Jarius Wright are speedy and break a lot of tackles. Tight end D.J. Williams (699 receiving yards) may be the best at his position in college football. He returns for his junior year as the returning team leader in receptions, yards, and touchdowns.

Petrino's passing attack should open space for the running game, as it did in Louisville. Michael Smith (1,072 rushing yards, 5.2 yards per carry, 32 receptions) isn't the talent Darren McFadden or Felix Jones was in college, but he proved more of a receiving threat than either. Smith suffered a bad hamstring injury at the end of the season, so the Hogs' strong depth behind him may come into play.

Unlike most SEC squads, the defense lags behind in Arkansas. The unit (52nd in Defensive S&P+, 66th in Rushing S&P+) was poor in 2008, giving up 139 points in a grim three-game stretch against Texas, Alabama, and Florida. Petrino needs to gin up the recruiting on the defensive end if the 'Backs are to rejoin the SEC West elite.

Top 2010 NFL Prospects: TE D.J. Williams* (1), CB Jerrell Norton (2-3).

No. 46 Ole Miss Rebels 6-6 (3-5)

2008: 9-4 (5-3)	FEI: No. 17		S&P+: No. 18	F/+: No. 11		Program FEI: No. 50		Returning Starters: OFF 6, DEF 8	
2008 Offense		**Rank**	**2008 Defense**		**Rank**	**2008 Field Position**			**Rank**
Offensive FEI	0.434	10	*Defensive FEI*	-0.505	8	Field Position Advantage	0.521		34
Unadjusted Offense	0.184	34	*Unadjusted Defense*	-0.357	15	**2009 Projections**			**Rank**
Offensive S&P+	122.8	14	Defensive S&P+	109.6	36	FEI	0.052		46
Rushing S&P+	108.9	45	Rushing S&P+	121.9	19	Strength of Schedule	0.210		28
Passing S&P+	140.6	5	Passing S&P+	102.8	55	Offensive FEI	0.045		53
Standard Downs S&P+	114.3	25	Standard Downs S&P+	116.1	19	Defensive FEI	-0.253		30
Passing Downs S&P+	141.9	8	Passing Downs S&P+	105.8	51	**Mean Wins: 6.4 SEC: 2.9**			

The FEI projections consider a ranking of program strength over a five-year span, not just a team's recent performance. That factor weighs down Ole Miss' ranking, even though they are a sexy preseason Top Ten choice, with some thinking they have a shot at the SEC West title. The numbers took a similar tough love stance with Illinois last season after a stunning turnaround in 2007. FEI correctly predicted the Illini would come nowhere near the Top 25.

The Rebels also return only 14 starters, and the ones that left were very high quality, including first-round draft picks Michael Oher and Peria Jerry. Losing your best offensive and defensive linemen is usually a good indicator that struggles are ahead, regardless of how the media fancies your chances.

The X factor is that Ole Miss has an All-American caliber quarterback in Jevan Snead. That tends to make up for a lot of weaknesses elsewhere. Snead entered Texas the same year Colt McCoy came to Austin. After a spirited battle, McCoy won the starting role, and Snead transferred to Oxford. He has the strongest arm in the conference, threw for 26 touchdowns last season, and outgunned Graham Harrell and the Texas Tech flyboys in the Cotton Bowl.

His receiving corps is senior-laden and top notch.

Dexter McCluster (655 rushing yards, 625 receiving yards) is a poor man's Percy Harvin, lining up all over and making explosive plays everywhere. Shay Hodge and tight end Gerald Harris are two other steady seniors. Brandon Bolden (542 rushing yards, 5.5 yards per carry) will likely start at running back, but there are plenty of others pushing him, including prep sensation Enrique Davis. Peria's brother John Jerry is the best returning lineman.

Defensively, however, Houston Nutt needs to find some guys to make plays. Greg Hardy is an excellent situational pass rusher — he had 8.5 sacks last year despite playing hurt most of the year. He single-handedly destroyed Florida's blocking in the Rebs' upset win at Gainesville. The rest of the defense is enigmatic, however.

Nutt himself may be the key figure. His teams tend to outperform low expectations, but then fail to break through to the next level. The Rebels are at the cusp of success, but a backwards step is more likely than a trip to Atlanta in December.

Top 2010 NFL Prospects: QB Jevan Snead* (1), DE Greg Hardy (1), WR Dexter McCluster (3-5), G John Jerry (4-6).

No. 78 Mississippi State Bulldogs 3-9 (1-7)

| 2008: 4-8 (2-6) | FEI: No. 89 | S&P+: No. 92 | F/+: No. 91 | Program FEI: No. 72 | Returning Starters: OFF 9, DEF 4 |

2008 Offense		Rank	2008 Defense		Rank	2008 Field Position		Rank
Offensive FEI	-0.343	106	Defensive FEI	-0.141	43	Field Position Advantage	0.447	112
Unadjusted Offense	-0.476	115	Unadjusted Defense	-0.099	48	2009 Projections		Rank
Offensive S&P+	88.0	101	Defensive S&P+	99.8	66	FEI	-0.063	78
Rushing S&P+	100.7	67	Rushing S&P+	104.5	51	Strength of Schedule	0.067	2
Passing S&P+	78.4	110	Passing S&P+	93.7	79	Offensive FEI	-0.117	80
Standard Downs S&P+	84.8	106	Standard Downs S&P+	96.0	73	Defensive FEI	-0.092	50
Passing Downs S&P+	94.2	81	Passing Downs S&P+	97.6	71	Mean Wins: 3.2 SEC: 1.2		

Dan Mullen replaces Sylvester Croom, a sentimental favorite who appeared to get the program going in 2007, when the Bulldogs made the Liberty Bowl. But last year's 4-8 record and a 45-0 humbling in the Egg Bowl against Ole Miss was too much for the cowbell ringers. Racial progress was sacrificed for pigskin progress.

Mullen will have his work cut out rebuilding the offense (102nd in Offensive S&P+, 114th in Passing S&P+), although steady running back Anthony Dixon (869 rushing yards, 4.4 yards per carry) has dropped weight and is poised to line up at various positions.

Mullen hopes prize recruit Tyler Russell becomes his Tim Tebow in the Starkville Spread. Russell will challenge senior Tyson Lee and sophomore Chris Reif for the starting gig. As with many of the Bulldogs' rivals, the defense (66th in Defensive S&P+) is stronger, and will be looked to carry the team while the offense comes together. JuCo transfer Pernell McPhee looks like an immovable force at tackle.

Top 2010 NFL Prospects: DT Pernell McPhee* (3-4), RB Anthony Dixon (4-5).

Robert Weintraub

Non-BCS Conferences, Independents

College football gets a bad rap among playoff enthusiasts, but there is one thing the current system affords that no other major sport can match — the opportunity for teams to go undefeated. The NBA, NHL and MLB play way too many games for the feat to be possible. The 2007 New England Patriots were the only NFL team in 35 years to win all of its regular season games, and they couldn't close the deal in the Super Bowl. But at the college level, an undefeated football season is a realistic goal for teams with national championship aspirations, year in and year out.

Or is it? In the last three seasons, four teams — Boise State (2006 and 2008), Hawaii (2007), and Utah (2008) — completed undefeated regular seasons and none were even considered for participation in the national championship game. Five of the six BCS title game participants in that span had at least one loss, and one — LSU in 2007 — had lost two regular season games.

The snubbing isn't about to change anytime soon for teams from non-BCS-qualifying conferences. Human polls are the most important factor in the BCS formula, and the general consensus is that undefeated teams from the Mountain West or WAC simply wouldn't be able to post similarly gaudy records if they were subjected to weekly BCS conference slugfests. That consensus is backed up by head-to-head records between the haves and have-nots (Table 1), though the imbalance is shrinking.

Table 1: Non-BCS Teams vs. BCS Teams*

Year	W	L	Win%
2005	13	96	11.9%
2006	23	114	16.8%
2007	25	117	17.6%
2008	27	96	22.0%

*including Notre Dame

Last year, Mountain West teams were 6-2 against Pac-10 teams, 2-0 against the SEC, and 1-0 against the Big Ten. Six of those victories came against teams with losing records, though, and those results were enough for FEI and other ranking systems to temper enthusiasm. Nevertheless, four non-BCS teams — Utah, Boise State, Brigham Young, and Texas Christian — rank among the top 40 in Program FEI, and each is on the rise. Such accolades for so-called inferior teams would have been unthinkable five years ago.

In the polls, only Notre Dame gets the benefit of the doubt outside of the major conferences, and mostly because of its prestige in the history books. The key to earning more respect for the rest is to maintain high-level performances over a number of years. That challenge is made all the more difficult by the fact that elite coaches at lesser conferences are poached each season for higher-paying gigs at BCS schools. For their part, the best of the non-BCS teams have created some stability lately at the head coaching position, and that has made all the difference.

No. 17 Notre Dame Fighting Irish 8-4 (-)

2008: 7-6 (-) **FEI:** No. 50 **S&P+:** No. 54 **F/+:** No. 58 **Program FEI:** No. 34 **Returning Starters:** OFF 10, DEF 7

2008 Offense		Rank	2008 Defense		Rank	2008 Field Position		Rank
Offensive FEI	-0.016	62	Defensive FEI	-0.212	32	Field Position Advantage	0.524	30
Unadjusted Offense	0.038	49	Unadjusted Defense	-0.198	30	2009 Projections		Rank
Offensive S&P+	100.3	63	Defensive S&P+	101.8	60	FEI	0.139	17
Rushing S&P+	86.7	100	Rushing S&P+	100.8	63	Strength of Schedule	0.219	32
Passing S&P+	108.8	35	Passing S&P+	103.9	48	Offensive FEI	0.270	21
Standard Downs S&P+	96.8	77	Standard Downs S&P+	102.5	53	Defensive FEI	-0.310	24
Passing Downs S&P+	105.3	52	Passing Downs S&P+	100.0	63	Mean Wins: 8.3		

Most of the college football world wonders why so much attention is paid to a team 15 years removed from serious national title contention. Brace yourselves. America's love-'em-or-hate-'em program is being hyped (again) for the latest chapter in an ongoing "return to glory" saga.

Head coach Charlie Weis earned a great deal of goodwill in ND circles along with back-to-back BCS bowl berths in 2005 and 2006. But a catastrophic 2007 and an underwhelming 2008 season — the Irish lost three games last year in which they held a double-digit second-half lead — have him teetering on the brink. He kept his job in large part because of his knack for delivering highly-recruited talent to South Bend. Now that the roster finally features depth and experience, the restless fan base demands performance.

Junior quarterback Jimmy Clausen will be central to Notre Dame's success in 2009. His near-perfect Hawaii Bowl (22-of-26 with four dropped passes, five touchdowns, 401 yards) offered a glimpse of his potential, though it came against a Warriors team ranked 94th nationally against the pass according to S&P+. Nevertheless, he'll likely run up gaudy statistics throughout the fall playing pitch-and-catch with playmaking receivers Michael Floyd and Golden Tate and tight end Kyle Rudolph. The offensive line is among the most experienced in the nation. A consistent rushing attack has eluded the Irish under Weis, but three returning backs — Armando Allen, James Aldridge, and Robert Hughes — are all capable of carrying the load.

The defense has question marks along the front line but boasts experience everywhere else. Expect defensive coordinator Jon Tenuta to ramp up a blitz-happy scheme featuring an experienced corps of linebackers and defensive backs. The Irish defense was at its best last year defending the pass according to S&P+, and the secondary returns starters at every position including a rising star, sophomore cornerback Robert Blanton.

Much will be made about Notre Dame's schedule in 2009, which may be its weakest in years. But our projections aren't particularly pessimistic about the fortunes of Michigan, Boston College, Pittsburgh, and Michigan State, not to mention perennial contender USC. A BCS bowl berth is plausible, but there are probably enough stumbling blocks to keep ND's win total in the single digits.

Top 2010 NFL Prospects: OT Sam Young (1-2), QB Jimmy Clausen* (2-3), G Eric Olsen (3-5), RB James Aldridge (6-7).

No. 56 Navy Midshipmen 8-5 (-)

2008: 8-5 (-)		FEI: No. 37	S&P+: No. 77	F/+: No. 61	Program FEI: No. 51		Returning Starters: OFF 4, DEF 7	
2008 Offense		**Rank**	**2008 Defense**		**Rank**	**2008 Field Position**		**Rank**
Offensive FEI	0.370	14	Defensive FEI	0.233	86	Field Position Advantage	0.501	58
Unadjusted Offense	0.196	32	Unadjusted Defense	0.043	71	**2009 Projections**		**Rank**
Offensive S&P+	112.1	32	Defensive S&P+	80.9	109	FEI	0.015	56
Rushing S&P+	117.7	25	Rushing S&P+	81.2	108	Strength of Schedule	0.392	68
Passing S&P+	112.0	27	Passing S&P+	78.2	115	Offensive FEI	0.121	39
Standard Downs S&P+	108.1	42	Standard Downs S&P+	89.3	101	Defensive FEI	0.259	90
Passing Downs S&P+	101.9	64	Passing Downs S&P+	67.9	119	**Mean Wins: 8.4**		

Head coach Ken Niumatalolo didn't need to rock the boat in his first season at the helm. Running the football out of a triple-option attack is pretty much the one thing Navy does really well, and 2008 marked the fourth straight season the Midshipmen led the nation in rushing yards per game. In a 34-7 victory over Southern Methodist, in fact, Navy didn't even attempt a pass.

More of the same should be in store for 2009, even with a number of new faces in the lineup. Junior quarterback Ricky Dobbs saw limited action a year ago, but made the most of his opportunities. Off the bench, he spearheaded the SMU blowout (42 carries, 224 yards) and led two late rallies against Temple and Notre Dame. There weren't many stars on the other side of the ball, but defensive end Jabaree Tuani had a breakout freshman season (42 tackles, nine tackles for a loss, three forced fumbles).

Navy was the second-least penalized team in college football last year and scored on its first possession in all but one game. Combined with the rushing attack, these stats form the blueprint for a ball control advantage that can disguise other deficiencies, like the inability to shut teams down defensively. Navy games featured only 22.5 possessions in 2008, fewest in the country and 3.4 below the national average. Patience and discipline probably won't be enough to win the opener at Ohio State, but it will be the key for a run at a seventh-straight winning season, seventh-straight bowl berth, and seventh-straight Commander-in-Chief trophy.

Top 2010 NFL Prospects: None.

MOUNTAIN WEST CONFERENCE

No. 32 Utah Utes 9-3 (6-2)

2008: 13-0 (8-0)   **FEI:** No. 11   **S&P+:** No. 16   **F/+:** No. 15   **Program FEI:** No. 19   **Returning Starters:** OFF 4, DEF 7

2008 Offense		Rank	2008 Defense		Rank	2008 Field Position		Rank
Offensive FEI	0.205	33	Defensive FEI	-0.372	20	Field Position Advantage	0.547	12
Unadjusted Offense	0.203	31	Unadjusted Defense	-0.375	14	2009 Projections		Rank
Offensive S&P+	116.6	22	Defensive S&P+	116.5	21	FEI	0.083	32
Rushing S&P+	109.9	43	Rushing S&P+	122.0	18	Strength of Schedule	0.599	94
Passing S&P+	119.7	20	Passing S&P+	110.1	31	Offensive FEI	-0.102	78
Standard Downs S&P+	121.1	12	Standard Downs S&P+	117.8	16	Defensive FEI	-0.288	27
Passing Downs S&P+	107.7	46	Passing Downs S&P+	108.2	46	**Mean Wins:** 9.4 **Mountain West:** 6.4		

There may not be any crystal footballs in the trophy case in Salt Lake City, but Utah fans can't ask much more of their program. Only six FBS teams have completed an undefeated season since 2004, and the Utes have accomplished the feat twice. Following a Sugar Bowl smackdown of Alabama, Utah collected some national respect and admiration instead of hardware. In order to keep the nation's longest winning streak (14 games) alive in 2009, they'll have to fill several holes.

Utah's top three receivers from last season graduated, but the bigger question mark is at quarterback. Last year's now-graduated starting quarterback, Brian Johnson, was the Mountain West Offensive Player of the Year, leading the team to the second-best offensive S&P+ rating in the conference. A three-way competition for the vacancy under center between Corbin Louks, Terrance Cain, and Jordan Wynn in the spring didn't settle matters. Senior left tackle Zane Beadles, a three-year starter, will make the transition for any of the three somewhat easier. Senior tailback Matt Asiata

(716 yards, 12 touchdowns) led the team in rushing, but may need to shoulder a greater burden this fall.

The defense anchored several victories in 2008, and the top four tacklers return. Linebacker Stevenson Sylvester was a menace against the Crimson Tide last January, recording three sacks and a fumble recovery. Defensive end Koa Misi forced a team-best three fumbles on the season and chipped in 8.5 tackles for loss. Field position doesn't show up on the defensive stat sheet, but senior kicker Ben Vroman ranked second in the nation in kickoff touchback percentage. If their opponents have to face 80-yard fields consistently, it will make life easier for the Utes.

Utah is projected to be better than all but one team on its schedule in 2009 (No. 27 Oregon). But in addition to a September 19 trip to Eugene, they'll have to be road warriors against Mountain West contenders BYU and TCU to make another run at the BCS.

Top 2010 NFL Prospects: LB Stevenson Sylvester (1-2), OT Zane Beadles (2-3), DE Koa Misi (6-7).

No. 36 BYU Cougars 9-3 (6-2)

2008: 10-3 (6-2)   **FEI:** No. 52   **S&P+:** No. 33   **F/+:** No. 39   **Program FEI:** No. 27   **Returning Starters:** OFF 4, DEF 8

2008 Offense		Rank	2008 Defense		Rank	2008 Field Position		Rank
Offensive FEI	0.293	19	Defensive FEI	0.190	83	Field Position Advantage	0.546	13
Unadjusted Offense	0.478	13	Unadjusted Defense	-0.017	61	2009 Projections		Rank
Offensive S&P+	130.3	6	Defensive S&P+	87.6	101	FEI	0.066	36
Rushing S&P+	118.6	23	Rushing S&P+	90.5	87	Strength of Schedule	0.381	66
Passing S&P+	136.2	8	Passing S&P+	86.8	98	Offensive FEI	0.230	22
Standard Downs S&P+	121.6	10	Standard Downs S&P+	97.8	70	Defensive FEI	-0.021	58
Passing Downs S&P+	135.7	11	Passing Downs S&P+	74.6	115	**Mean Wins:** 8.5 **Mountain West:** 6.2		

It isn't often that 10-win seasons disappoint a fan base, but 2008 was that kind of year for BYU. The Cougars were in the top 20 at the start of the year and ascended to eighth in the Associated Press poll in mid-October after winning their first six games by a cumulative score of 227-51. If

anyone was going to crash the BCS, this was the team.

Then the wheels came off the defense. The Cougars gave up 31 points or more in five of their last seven games, and simply couldn't stop either of the other Mountain West contenders, TCU and rival Utah. BYU was the league's worst defense on Passing Downs S&P+, in large part because they had new starters all over the field. This year, the experience will help turn those numbers around, starting with the pass rush led by senior defensive end Jan Jorgensen (five sacks, 11 quarterback hurries in 2008).

Offensively, BYU is loaded at the skill positions. Quarterback Max Hall ranked sixth in the nation last season in yards per game (304) and fifth in completion percentage (69.2). He'll be joined by both a 1,000-yard rusher (Harvey Unga) and a 1,000-yard receiver (Dennis Pitta). The offensive line will be entirely rebuilt, however, and the early departure of wide receiver Austin Collie is a blow. The Cougars had the second-best third-down conversion rate in the nation last year (55.7 percent), and Collie was a frequent target in those situations.

Utah and TCU each have personnel losses to contend with as well, and both will visit Provo this year. The nonconference schedule is a killer, featuring games against Oklahoma and Florida State.

Top 2010 NFL Prospects: TE Dennis Pitta (1-2), DE Jan Jorgensen (3-5), QB Max Hall (3-5).

No. 48 TCU Horned Frogs 9-3 (6-2)

2008: 11-2 (7-1)	FEI: No. 20		S&P+: No. 4	F/+: No. 6	Program FEI: No. 29		Returning Starters: OFF 6, DEF 4	
2008 Offense		**Rank**	**2008 Defense**		**Rank**	**2008 Field Position**		**Rank**
Offensive FEI	0.091	46	Defensive FEI	-0.570	5	Field Position Advantage	0.553	5
Unadjusted Offense	0.233	27	Unadjusted Defense	-0.620	3	**2009 Projections**		**Rank**
Offensive S&P+	103.5	52	Defensive S&P+	170.3	1	FEI	0.051	48
Rushing S&P+	112.5	39	Rushing S&P+	165.9	1	Strength of Schedule	0.500	81
Passing S&P+	94.8	78	Passing S&P+	176.4	1	Offensive FEI	-0.076	74
Standard Downs S&P+	108.2	41	Standard Downs S&P+	159.6	1	Defensive FEI	-0.335	21
Passing Downs S&P+	101.6	65	Passing Downs S&P+	144.7	6	**Mean Wins: 8.5 Mountain West: 5.9**		

The Horned Frogs' defense was virtually impenetrable last season, surrendering a touchdown or less on seven occasions. TCU gave up the fewest rushing yards and total yards in the NCAA and ranked fifth in defending third-down conversions (28.7 percent). According to S&P+, they were the best defense in college football by far.

The bad news is that only four of the top 12 tacklers from a year ago are back. Defensive end Jerry Hughes was a standout in 2008, leading the nation in sacks (15) and forced fumbles (6). With unproven talent across the rest of the line, though, he'll face more double teams this fall. Defensive backs Tejay Johnson, Rafael Priest and Nick Sanders will need to step up in order to reproduce the plus-13 turnover margin from a year ago.

Junior quarterback Andy Dalton is a two-year starter, and is joined by leading receiver Jimmy Young in the passing game. Running back Joseph Turner (577 yards, 11 touchdowns in 2008) helped TCU to the third-best rushing S&P+ in the conference. His production in 2009 will be critical for controlling the line of scrimmage and giving the young Horned Frogs defense more breathing room.

Top 2010 NFL Prospects: DE/LB Jerry Hughes (1-2), LB Daryl Washington (3-5), G Marshall Newhouse (6-7).

WESTERN ATHLETIC CONFERENCE

No. 39 Boise State Broncos 11-2 (7-1)

2008: 12-1 (8-0)	FEI: No. 19		S&P+: No. 7	F/+: No. 9	Program FEI: No. 26		Returning Starters: OFF 5, DEF 5	
2008 Offense		**Rank**	**2008 Defense**		**Rank**	**2008 Field Position**		**Rank**
Offensive FEI	0.126	42	Defensive FEI	-0.406	14	Field Position Advantage	0.539	15
Unadjusted Offense	0.398	15	Unadjusted Defense	-0.587	4	**2009 Projections**		**Rank**
Offensive S&P+	120.5	15	Defensive S&P+	133.0	5	FEI	0.065	39
Rushing S&P+	100.1	69	Rushing S&P+	132.1	7	Strength of Schedule	0.680	111
Passing S&P+	139.4	7	Passing S&P+	128.1	9	Offensive FEI	-0.075	73
Standard Downs S&P+	111.5	30	Standard Downs S&P+	125.1	7	Defensive FEI	-0.257	29
Passing Downs S&P+	126.2	20	Passing Downs S&P+	134.1	10	**Mean Wins: 10.7 WAC: 7.1**		

Over the last ten seasons, Boise State has the best overall, conference, and home field winning percentage in college football. The blue stadium turf may be partly responsible, on top of the relative weakness of most of their WAC brethren. The conference has a high-octane reputation, and the Broncos have led the way this decade, averaging more than 40 points per game since 2000. But recently, and especially in 2008, the secret to their success is actually on the other side of the ball.

Eleven Broncos opponents were held to fewer 20 points a year ago, with six held to a touchdown or less. The Broncos will have a tough time maintaining that stalwart defense in 2009, as they're replacing all but one of their front seven. Returning senior cornerback Kyle Wilson led the team in interceptions (five) and passes defended (15) and will anchor an experienced secondary. Wilson was also a force on special teams, leading the WAC in punt return yardage (third nationally) and chipping in three punt return touchdowns, most in the nation.

The offense must also fill holes, graduating both starting receivers and, more crucially, running back Ian Johnson. Johnson had been the face of the program for three years after his two-point conversion and marriage proposal capped the thrilling Fiesta Bowl shocker over Oklahoma. He had been the legs of the program as well, leading the team for three straight seasons in all-purpose yards. The new face of the program, quarterback Kellen Moore, was a standout freshman in 2008, setting a Boise State record in completion percentage (69.1 percent), racking up nearly 3500 yards through the air, and finishing first in the WAC and 12th nationally in passing efficiency (25 touchdowns, ten interceptions).

Boise State far outpaced the rest of the conference in nearly every S&P+ category a year ago. Unlike his predecessors, head coach Chris Petersen has shown no interest in leaping to bigger and better things. That stability above all else bodes well as Boise State reloads for a run at its seventh conference championship in the last eight years.

Top 2010 NFL Prospects: CB Kyle Wison (2-3), FB Richie Brockel (6-7).

No. 57 Fresno State Bulldogs 9-3 (6-2)

2008: 7-6 (4-4)	FEI: No. 82		S&P+: No. 61	F/+: No. 73		Program FEI: No. 63		Returning Starters: OFF 7, DEF 9	
2008 Offense		**Rank**	**2008 Defense**		**Rank**	**2008 Field Position**			**Rank**
Offensive FEI	0.040	55	*Defensive FEI*	0.346	100	Field Position Advantage		0.497	63
Unadjusted Offense	0.132	38	*Unadjusted Defense*	0.157	83	**2009 Projections**			**Rank**
Offensive S&P+	107.0	45	Defensive S&P+	92.9	81	FEI		0.012	57
Rushing S&P+	106.7	51	Rushing S&P+	87.4	96	Strength of Schedule		0.689	112
Passing S&P+	108.9	34	Passing S&P+	98.8	64	Offensive FEI		0.138	36
Standard Downs S&P+	108.9	35	Standard Downs S&P+	90.2	98	Defensive FEI		0.128	76
Passing Downs S&P+	105.2	53	Passing Downs S&P+	81.7	105	**Mean Wins: 9.0 WAC: 6.4**			

Head coach Pat Hill has an "anyone, anywhere" philosophy with regard to scheduling, and for the second straight season, Fresno State will play seven games on the road. Unlike last year, they'll be boarding those buses as an experienced pack of Bulldogs looking to take a bite out of conference behemoth Boise State.

Four running backs — Anthony Harding, Lonyae Miller, Ryan Matthews, and Jamaal Rashad — combined last season for almost 2,400 yards and 19 touchdowns on the ground, and all will be battling for carries again this fall. They may need to ramp up the production, in fact, to help a new starting quarterback get his bearings. Junior Ryan Coburn is the only one with game experience, but freshman Derek Carr (brother of David Carr) has the pedigree. Last year's defense didn't have much to celebrate, but this year there is more experience, starting with junior linebacker Ben Jacobs (113 tackles). There are two key areas of focus for improvement. Fresno State collected a league-worst 13 turnovers last year (second-worst in the country), and ranked second to last in the WAC in sacks (18).

Special teams are the X-factor for make-or-break seasons, and Fresno State may have the nation's best. A.J. Jefferson ranked fourth nationally in kick return average and leads all active college football players with three kickoff return touchdowns. Three other Bulldogs returned punts for touchdowns in 2008, and Fresno State led the nation in punt return average as a team.

Road trips to Wisconsin, Cincinnati, and Illinois are on the docket, but the conference schedule begins (and, for all intents and purposes, ends) September 18 when Boise State comes to town.

Top 2010 NFL Prospects: WR Seyi Ajirotutu (6-7), FB Anthony Harding (6-7).

CONFERENCE USA

No. 37 Southern Mississippi Golden Eagles 8-4 (6-2)

2008: 7-6 (4-4)   **FEI:** No. 45   **S&P+:** No. 50   **F/+:** No. 46   **Program FEI:** No. 55   **Returning Starters:** OFF 8, DEF 8

2008 Offense		Rank	2008 Defense		Rank	2008 Field Position		Rank
Offensive FEI	0.131	41	Defensive FEI	0.081	69	Field Position Advantage	0.513	39
Unadjusted Offense	0.262	25	Unadjusted Defense	-0.072	52	**2009 Projections**		**Rank**
Offensive S&P+	108.2	43	Defensive S&P+	98.3	69	FEI	0.065	37
Rushing S&P+	120.1	18	Rushing S&P+	97.9	69	Strength of Schedule	0.599	93
Passing S&P+	97.6	71	Passing S&P+	97.8	67	Offensive FEI	0.161	30
Standard Downs S&P+	107.6	46	Standard Downs S&P+	104.0	50	Defensive FEI	0.050	64
Passing Downs S&P+	108.3	45	Passing Downs S&P+	85.3	94	**Mean Wins:** 8.4 **Conference USA:** 5.8		

Heading into the month of November last season, Southern Miss was winless in league play and had a 2-6 overall record. Such is the nature of teams breaking in young talent. The Golden Eagles matured in a hurry, however, and won their last four regular season games by a cumulative score of 136-35, highlighted by a smackdown of eventual Conference USA champion East Carolina. A bowl victory over Sun Belt champion Troy sets the stage for a promising 2009.

Quarterback Austin Davis was a standout dual threat as a freshman, passing for 23 touchdowns and rushing for nine more. His number one target, wide receiver DeAndre Brown, led the nation's freshmen in yards (1,117) and touchdowns (12). His playing future looked bleak after he suffered a nasty leg fracture in the bowl game, but after a successful surgery and off-season rehab, the injury isn't expected to keep him off the field this fall. Veteran running back Damion Fletcher will be setting his sights on a fourth-straight

1,000-yard season. Southern Miss led the conference in rushing S&P+ a year ago.

The defense wasn't as impressive statistically, but most of that damage was done in the first half of the year. In conference play, Southern Miss ranked second in the league in scoring defense. Eight starters return this year, including all four in the secondary. Defensive backs Eddie Hicks and Justin Wilson picked off four passes apiece in 2008, helping the Golden Eagles to the second-best turnover margin in Conference USA.

There isn't a single team on the Southern Miss schedule projected ahead of the Golden Eagles. Still, in order to make some national noise, they'll need to catch breaks in several toss-up games — Virginia, Kansas, and Louisville out of conference, plus Tulsa and East Carolina to close out the season.

Top 2010 NFL Prospects: RB Damion Fletcher (4-6), OT Calvin Wilson (6-7).

No. 52 Tulsa Golden Hurricane 8-4 (6-2)

2008: 11-3 (7-1)   **FEI:** No. 39   **S&P+:** No. 48   **F/+:** No. 42   **Program FEI:** No. 56   **Returning Starters:** OFF 6, DEF 8

2008 Offense		Rank	2008 Defense		Rank	2008 Field Position		Rank
Offensive FEI	0.450	9	Defensive FEI	0.117	72	Field Position Advantage	0.490	78
Unadjusted Offense	0.833	4	Unadjusted Defense	-0.013	62	**2009 Projections**		**Rank**
Offensive S&P+	117.7	20	Defensive S&P+	91.4	86	FEI	0.038	52
Rushing S&P+	112.8	37	Rushing S&P+	101.2	61	Strength of Schedule	0.452	76
Passing S&P+	124.5	14	Passing S&P+	82.8	106	Offensive FEI	0.291	19
Standard Downs S&P+	116.0	19	Standard Downs S&P+	94.7	81	Defensive FEI	0.138	78
Passing Downs S&P+	135.6	12	Passing Downs S&P+	87.7	91	**Mean Wins:** 8.0 **Conference USA:** 5.6		

Tulsa likes to play fast. During their few national TV appearances last year, you had to feel a little bit bad for the TV crew, trying to speak intelligently about a replay while the Tulsa offense was halfway downfield on the next snap. The Golden Hurricane offense ran 1,097 plays last year — second nationally behind Oklahoma and 250 more than an

average team — and ranked first in yards per play.

That kind of pace requires hyper-precision from the offense, but 2009 won't provide head coach Todd Graham with the luxury of an experienced starter at quarterback. Then again, graduating senior David Johnson threw for more than 4,000 yards last season as a first-year starter, and three of the four leading receivers are back. Tulsa also lost 1,500-yard running back Tarrion Adams, but Jamad Williams was a solid backup and fullback Charles Clay is a dangerous second option rushing and receiving out of the backfield. The defense was hit-or-miss last season, perhaps in part because of the frenetic pace set by the offense. Consistency should be expected with eight returning starters. Linebackers Mike Bryant, Tanner Antle, and George Clinkscale combined for 235 tackles and 10.5

sacks in 2008. Tulsa finished second to last in the conference defending the pass, and the 2009 starting secondary combined for only one interception a year ago. The non-conference schedule is daunting, with games against Oklahoma and Boise State, but Tulsa plays in Conference USA's weaker West Division and should return to the conference title game.

Top 2010 NFL Prospects: FB Charles Clay* (2-3), C Jody Whaley (6-7).

No. 53 East Carolina Pirates 7-5 (5-3)

2008: 9-5 (6-2)   **FEI:** No. 38   **S&P+:** No. 56   **F/+:** No. 48   **Program FEI:** No. 62   **Returning Starters:** OFF 8, DEF 8

2008 Offense		Rank	2008 Defense		Rank	2008 Field Position		Rank
Offensive FEI	-0.106	74	Defensive FEI	-0.346	22	Field Position Advantage	0.482	87
Unadjusted Offense	-0.026	58	Unadjusted Defense	-0.327	17	2009 Projections		Rank
Offensive S&P+	92.6	86	Defensive S&P+	109.0	39	FEI	0.036	53
Rushing S&P+	88.9	93	Rushing S&P+	112.3	35	Strength of Schedule	0.330	55
Passing S&P+	97.5	72	Passing S&P+	105.9	41	Offensive FEI	-0.203	92
Standard Downs S&P+	86.5	103	Standard Downs S&P+	108.4	38	Defensive FEI	-0.249	32
Passing Downs S&P+	102.8	59	Passing Downs S&P+	114.9	30	Mean Wins: 7.0 Conference USA: 5.3		

The Pirates knocked off two top 15 teams — Virginia Tech and West Virginia — in back-to-back games to open their 2008 season. The victories set the stage for a Conference USA championship run fueled by opportunism. East Carolina picked off 22 passes and collected 11 fumble recoveries, the eighth-best total in takeaways nationally.

The offense capitalized on turnovers, but didn't do much else, ranking ninth in the conference according to S&P+. Like many young starters, quarterback Patrick Pinkney wasn't spectacular, but proved he could be effective by not forcing anything. The defense returns key starters throughout, particularly along the defensive line. Defensive end C.J. Wilson ranked second in

the conference in sacks (10.5) and tied for first in tackles for loss (18.5). Kicker Ben Hartman was called on often, leading the nation in field goal attempts (31) and ranking sixth in field goals made (24).

Head coach Skip Holtz likes challenges and thus far he has met them, improving the Pirates' win total every year since taking over in 2005. Continuing that trend will be a monumental feat this season, with a non-conference schedule that includes North Carolina plus both Virginia Tech and West Virginia seeking revenge.

Top 2010 NFL Prospects: DE C.J. Wilson (1-2), FS Van Eskridge (3-5), OG Doug Palmer (5-7), DT Jay Ross (5-7).

MID-AMERICAN CONFERENCE

No. 72 Central Michigan Chippewas 7-5 (5-3)

2008: 8-5 (6-2)   **FEI:** No. 63   **S&P+:** No. 80   **F/+:** No. 76   **Program FEI:** No. 77   **Returning Starters:** OFF 6, DEF 10

2008 Offense		Rank	2008 Defense		Rank	2008 Field Position		Rank
Offensive FEI	0.248	26	Defensive FEI	0.431	109	Field Position Advantage	0.496	65
Unadjusted Offense	0.343	20	Unadjusted Defense	0.352	104	2009 Projections		Rank
Offensive S&P+	100.1	65	Defensive S&P+	92.1	85	FEI	-0.038	72
Rushing S&P+	88.0	98	Rushing S&P+	86.0	99	Strength of Schedule	0.519	83
Passing S&P+	110.0	31	Passing S&P+	97.4	68	Offensive FEI	0.075	45
Standard Downs S&P+	97.8	72	Standard Downs S&P+	90.8	96	Defensive FEI	0.364	101
Passing Downs S&P+	102.9	58	Passing Downs S&P+	90.9	86	Mean Wins: 6.9 Mid-American: 5.3		

Yes, Mid-American Conference, Dan LeFevour still has one more year of eligibility. The quarterback enters the 2009 season ranked 14th in college football history in total offense (11,702 yards), an average of more than 300 yards per game passing and rushing over 39 career games. He'll blow past Byron Leftwich's career conference record in the category early this fall, but he'll need a freakishly productive season to threaten the NCAA record. Though injuries held back his production in 2008, he still led the team in both rushing and passing, and posted career bests in completion percentage (66.8) and touchdown-to-interception ratio (21-to-6). Bryan Anderson and Antonio Brown return as the top two receivers in CMU history. Brown was also a special teams star, leading the nation in punt return average (20.5 yards per return) and finishing third nationally in all-purpose yards.

All that firepower went to waste in key games down the stretch a year ago. The defense finished last in the conference in defensive FEI, giving up 87 points in their final two conference games after ripping off six

straight. The unit has an opportunity for redemption, though, returning ten starters to the lineup with a year of experience under their belts and a bitter taste in their mouths. They'll be led by linebacker Nick Bellore, who ranked third in the nation last year with 148 tackles.

To break out as Ball State did a year ago will be a daunting challenge for CMU, with road games at Michigan State, Arizona, and Boston College. CMU should be the class of the MAC, but the league is as competitive as it gets. The Chippewas are the only team in the last five years to make back-to-back trips to the conference championship game, doing so with LeFevour under center in 2006 and 2007. In 2009, we're projecting all 13 teams to finish within a game of .500 in conference play, with Toledo, Bowling Green, Northern Illinois, and Ball State all projected with FEI ranks between 80th and 85th.

Top 2010 NFL Prospects: QB Dan LeFevour (2-3), WR Bryan Anderson (3-5), DE Frank Zombo (6-7).

SUN BELT CONFERENCE

No. 81 Middle Tennessee Blue Raiders 7-5 (6-2)

| 2008: 5-7 (3-4) | FEI: No. 92 | S&P+: No. 105 | F/+: No. 104 | Program FEI: No. 98 | Returning Starters: OFF 10, DEF 7 |

2008 Offense		Rank	2008 Defense		Rank	2008 Field Position		Rank
Offensive FEI	-0.280	97	Defensive FEI	0.348	103	Field Position Advantage	0.504	51
Unadjusted Offense	-0.075	64	Unadjusted Defense	0.057	74	2009 Projections		Rank
Offensive S&P+	87.7	102	Defensive S&P+	89.5	94	FEI	-0.073	81
Rushing S&P+	77.1	114	Rushing S&P+	97.4	71	Strength of Schedule	0.603	95
Passing S&P+	96.7	74	Passing S&P+	81.0	110	Offensive FEI	-0.083	76
Standard Downs S&P+	87.8	100	Standard Downs S&P+	95.4	77	Defensive FEI	0.340	97
Passing Downs S&P+	92.8	86	Passing Downs S&P+	85.0	95	Mean Wins: 7.0 Sun Belt: 5.6		

Middle Tennessee's defeat of Maryland last year was the Sun Belt's only regular-season non-conference victory over a team with a winning record. In the worst conference in FBS, such accomplishments are worth celebrating. The team was last in the league rushing the ball in 2008 according to S&P+, but running back Philip Tanner romped for five scores against North Texas late in the year, and should be able to build on that momentum behind an experienced line. Defensively, three of the top four tacklers return, including linebacker Danny Campbell (89 tackles, 11.5 tackles

for loss). Additionally, all but one other team in the Sun Belt is projected to decline offensively according to FEI.

The Blue Raiders will make non-conference trips to Clemson and Maryland, but the Sun Belt will likely be decided on October 6, when Middle Tennessee visits defending conference champion Troy. With five of their final seven games at home, however, the Blue Raiders may be able to survive even if they trip up.

Top 2010 NFL Prospects: DE Jarrett Crittenton (6-7).*

No. 82 Troy Trojans 7-5 (6-2)

2008: 8-5 (6-1)   **FEI:** No. 65   **S&P+:** No. 42   **F/+:** No. 55   **Program FEI:** No. 78   **Returning Starters:** OFF 8, DEF 5

2008 Offense		Rank	2008 Defense		Rank	2008 Field Position		Rank
Offensive FEI	-0.128	76	Defensive FEI	0.141	76	Field Position Advantage	0.518	35
Unadjusted Offense	0.155	36	Unadjusted Defense	-0.155	37	**2009 Projections**		**Rank**
Offensive S&P+	96.9	72	Defensive S&P+	114.1	25	FEI	-0.077	82
Rushing S&P+	97.1	79	Rushing S&P+	118.7	24	Strength of Schedule	0.262	42
Passing S&P+	97.3	73	Passing S&P+	109.5	33	Offensive FEI	-0.170	86
Standard Downs S&P+	97.2	76	Standard Downs S&P+	108.6	37	Defensive FEI	0.338	96
Passing Downs S&P+	92.5	88	Passing Downs S&P+	116.9	28	Mean Wins: 6.5 Sun Belt: 5.5		

The Trojans of Troy University have won three consecutive conference championships, but 2008 might best be remembered for what they *almost* accomplished. On November 15th, Troy led defending national champion LSU by four touchdowns late in the third quarter. But instead of finishing off the most significant victory in the program's history, Troy gave up a 37-point rally, the biggest comeback in LSU's storied history.

It is a testament to head coach Larry Blakeney that Troy didn't wallow in defeat, but rather took out their frustration on the final two Sun Belt opponents of the year by a combined score of 83-12. Troy averaged more than 400 yards and 33 points offensively in quarterback Levi Brown's eight starts last season, and he'll be joined this fall by 1,000-yard running back DuJuan Harris and leading receiver Jerrel Jernigan. The Trojans' strength was their defense last year, but linebacker Boris Lee (112 tackles) and defensive end Brandon Lang (11.5 sacks) are among the few returning starters. Troy will visit this year's defending national champion Florida on September 12.

Top 2010 NFL Prospects: DE Brandon Lang (1-2), LB Boris Lee (5-7).

OTHER TOP 2010 NFL PROSPECTS

Division I-A (FBS): *Hawaii C John Estes (2), Buffalo WR Naaman Roosevelt (2-3), New Mexico C Erik Cook (3-4), Western Michigan QB Tim Hiller (3-5), Marshall TE Cody Slate (3-5), Nevada OT Alonzo Durham (4-5).*

Division I-AA (FCS): *Western Illinois CB Patrick Stoudamire (2-4), Elon WR Terrell Hudgins (4-5), Appalachian State WR Armanti Edwards (4-7).*

Brian Fremeau

For a table featuring the projections for all 120 FBS teams, visit http://www.footballoutsiders.com/stats/fei2009projections.

Recruiting and the Ruling Class

This spring, South Carolina defensive line coach Brad Lawing told South Carolina's *The State* that recruiting services and rankings are ridiculous, and that, among other things, he could make one call and change a recruit's ranking from two to three stars, or from three to four. It encapsulated the feeling a lot of people have toward football recruiting: It is overhyped and overblown, and its legitimacy is underwhelming.

Then why does following it continue to become more and more popular? Is it just a way to kill the empty space between early January and late August, or is there actually some substance here?

Here's an even better question: Are recruiting and recruiting rankings legit enough for Football Outsiders to analyze them?

Despite the sometimes legitimate complaints about the politics involved in the rankings, and the general queasiness associated with grown men following every move of a 17-year-old kid, recruiting reports and analysis are not going away. The business is only going to become bigger, the hat ceremonies* more grandiose, the all-star games more political. It continues to go down the road of basketball recruiting, where players start to get ranked in junior high ("He's 5-foot-11, 200 pounds, and 13 years old. He's going to be a monster!"), and participation in certain camps and/or all-star games enhances both a high schooler's face time and recruiting ranking.

In the 2009 NFL Draft, 14 schools produced at least five picks. Among them were traditional powers like USC (11 picks), Ohio State (7), Georgia (6), LSU (6), and Penn State (5). Also among them: Oregon State (7), Cincinnati (6), Missouri (6), and Rutgers (5). While USC and the other power programs consistently rack up highly-ranked recruiting classes, the average rank of Missouri's recruiting class by Rivals.

com over the past eight years has been 34.1. Oregon State (46.5), Rutgers (47.3) and Cincinnati (85.5, below that of Arkansas State, Middle Tennessee, and Troy), have brought in classes perceived to be even worse. And yet they all produced a large number of draft picks. Not only that, but Cincinnati went to the Orange Bowl in 2008, Oregon State has beaten USC in two of the last three years, and Missouri and Rutgers have averaged ten and nine wins, respectively, over the last three seasons.

These four programs are making noise despite the lack of big-time recruiting success, but in the grand scheme of things, they are only making so much noise. Of the four, only Missouri has finished a season (2007) in the Top 5 since 2000. It has been since at least 2001 (Nebraska), and potentially 1999 (Virginia Tech), that a team without top recruiting classes has played for the national championship. And in both 1999 and 2001, those teams lost to recruiting powerhouses (Miami, Florida State). As it turns out, when you are talking about college football's ruling class, recruiting does matter.

Big-time recruiting didn't start with the creation of Rivals.com. It has been around since the beginning of college football itself. For decades, coaches (and boosters) have been trying to figure out the fine art of legally (or otherwise) wooing top-flight talent to their school. But as it pertains to Football Outsiders, the question here is, how much can the recruiting services tell us about how good a player, or a team, is going to be?

Let's compare recruiting success to in-game success at a macro level, using annual Rivals class rankings from 2002-08 and final AP poll rankings from that span. (Table 1) As one would expect, most of the names atop the recruiting rankings have also had ma-

---

* For Football Outsiders readers familiar only with the NFL and not the college ranks, A) thanks for reading the college section of the book, and B) a "hat ceremony" in this instance is not an ancient Asian custom, but the new ceremony among top recruits, in which they sit at a table with a series of hats representing the schools from which they are choosing. Sometimes, it is as simple as the recruit grabbing a hat, putting it on, and announcing they are choosing that given school. Sometimes, it borders on ridiculous. The most familiar example was that of Maryland high schooler Antonio Logan-El, a four-star recruit, whose announcement was televised from the Baltimore ESPN Zone. He wore a red tie, reportedly invited Maryland coach Ralph Friedgen's wife to the ceremony, pulled out a red Maryland hat …and then put it down in favor of a Penn State hat. (Within two years, he had first transferred from Penn State to Towson, then quit football altogether.)

jor on-field success. In fact, **the top 14 teams according to cumulative Rivals rankings over that span have also finished in the top 25 according to cumulative AP rankings.**

Sure, some have not fared as well on the field — South Carolina is 15th in recruiting and 75th in performance, while North Carolina is 29th in recruiting and has not finished a season with a single AP vote. Meanwhile, some have seen the opposite effect — teams like Boise State (11th in performance, 78th in recruiting) and Utah (17th, 65th) continue to garner national respect without landing blue-chippers by the handful.

It is certainly important to take the outliers into consideration and acknowledge the impact big-name schools indirectly play in recruiting rankings. For instance, if Florida or USC offers a player, chances are recruiting services are going to assume they're pretty good and raise their ranking. An offer from Boise State does not have the same effect.

Acknowledging this, however, does not change the fact that the top teams draw the top talent, and on average they win the most games. The 14 teams that have finished in the top 25 of both Rivals and AP rankings over the last eight years each gathered between 1.85 percent and 2.85 percent of all Rivals recruiting points over that eight-year span. Combined, they make up 11 percent of all teams in the Bowl Subdivision of Division I, and yet they have pulled in 31 percent of all recruiting points doled out by Rivals.

After that, however, the water gets a bit muddy.

The next 14 teams in terms of cumulative Rivals rankings only gathered between 1.31 percent and 1.69 percent, a gap of 0.38 percent. The next 14: between 1.07 percent and 1.28 percent (gap: 0.21 percent). After the top teams, the difference between each recruiting class is progressively smaller. There is simply not much difference between the recruiting classes ranked 20th and 40th. And when you take into account coaching, momentum, relative experience, and other factors, it is not much of a surprise to see a team like West Virginia or Missouri — who have finished with recruiting classes mostly in the 30s — finishing in the Top 25, or, on the flipside, teams like Clemson or Nebraska finishing *outside* the Top 25 with recruiting classes in the lower teens and high 20s.

However, it *should* be a surprise to see teams like the Mountaineers or Tigers making their way into the Top 10 or even the Top 5. Both were one game away from the BCS Championship Game in 2007. But even

in 2007, one of the craziest years on record (a Top 5 team lost to an unranked opponent 13 times, five more times than in any other season) it was LSU (average recruiting ranking in the last eight years: third) versus

Table 1: Recruiting Rankings versus Final AP finishes

Team	Cumulative Rivals Rank*	% of all Rivals Pts	Cumulative AP Rank	% of all Final AP votes
USC	1	2.85%	1	7.18%
Florida	2	2.55%	7	3.41%
LSU	3	2.45%	6	4.54%
Florida State	4	2.44%	22	1.62%
Oklahoma	5	2.41%	4	5.47%
Georgia	6	2.37%	5	5.12%
Texas	7	2.31%	3	5.66%
Miami	8	2.27%	12	3.02%
Michigan	9	2.15%	8	3.33%
Tennessee	10	2.12%	21	1.77%
Ohio State	11	2.10%	2	5.93%
Auburn	12	1.92%	10	3.30%
Alabama	13	1.91%	16	2.22%
Notre Dame	14	1.85%	24	1.49%
S. Carolina	15	1.69%	75	0.00%
Texas A&M	16	1.62%	66	0.03%
Nebraska	17	1.56%	43	0.51%
Clemson	18	1.55%	39	0.62%
UCLA	19	1.55%	42	0.52%
California	20	1.48%	29	1.29%
Penn State	21	1.47%	15	2.37%
Oregon	22	1.41%	28	1.38%
Maryland	23	1.35%	33	0.96%
Virginia Tech	24	1.35%	9	3.31%
Ole Miss	25	1.34%	31	1.14%
Arkansas	26	1.34%	44	0.51%
Arizona State	27	1.31%	36	0.70%
Oklahoma St.	28	1.31%	46	0.48%
N. Carolina	29	1.28%	N/A**	0.00%
Arizona	30	1.28%	73	0.00%
Virginia	31	1.27%	50	0.34%
Colorado	32	1.25%	53	0.21%
Washington	33	1.21%	80	0.00%
Kansas State	34	1.20%	25	1.46%
Pittsburgh	35	1.20%	45	0.49%
Illinois	36	1.16%	51	0.30%
N.C. State	37	1.16%	37	0.64%
Missouri	38	1.13%	30	1.19%
Iowa	39	1.12%	14	2.60%
Michigan State	40	1.10%	59	0.09%

This is a combined ranking of all recruiting classes from 2002 to 2008.

** *North Carolina has not finished a season between 2002 and 2008 with any AP votes.*

Ohio State (11th) for the crystal football.

When it comes down to it, college football is basically one giant oligarchy. If recruiting rankings actually mean something — and it appears that at least the top ones do — and if the same schools always land the top recruits, how does a team from the outside that top-tier ever break through to the big time? Well, the short answer is, they don't, at least not for very long. In the last decade, the only major conference teams who have found steady success without top-ranked recruiting classes at a high level are Virginia Tech, West Virginia, and Iowa, and even their forays into the final Top 5 have been limited (VT did it in 1999, WVU in 2005). Plus, with less margin for error, it only takes a small bout of iffy recruiting or player development to fall. Virginia Tech has managed to consistently win, but Iowa went just 19-18 between 2005 and 2007 before bouncing back with nine wins in 2008, and West Virginia might fall after losing Pat White last year and Noel Devine soon.

It is not at all uncommon to see schools experience a one- or two-year "nouveau riche" breakthrough and then plummet back to earth. There are a number of reasons this could happen — maybe an up-and-coming coach succeeds before leaving for a more big-time job; or there is a perfect confluence of experience and unique talent, never to be duplicated.

Oregon State exploded for double-digit wins and a Fiesta Bowl berth early in this decade, then their coach (globetrotter Dennis Erickson) left for a better job. Kansas did the same in the mid-'90s, and their coach (Glen Mason) left for a marginally better job at Minnesota. Arizona State went to the 1997 Rose Bowl and was one Daryl Boston touchdown away from a possible national title, but they fell to 9-3 the next year, and then three seasons near .500 got coach Bruce Snyder canned. Arizona came out of nowhere to go 12-1 in 1998, then caved under high expectations in 1999 and didn't see another bowl game until last season's Las Vegas Bowl.

And finally, after 30 wins in three years, Missouri now has to attempt to reload without a trifecta of big-time offensive players from the past few seasons — quarterback Chase Daniel, two-time All-American receiver Jeremy Maclin, and Mackey Award-winning tight end Chase Coffman.

When a breakthrough coach or player(s) leaves, you roll the dice again, and you likely land back in the middle when all is said and done. And the blue-chippers still end up going to the same schools as before.

How hard is it to break into college football's ruling class? Most of the teams in this class — USC, Oklahoma, Georgia, Texas, Michigan, Tennessee, Ohio State, Alabama, Notre Dame — have been national powers for decades. The most recent additions to the club, really, are Florida and LSU, and they have been established for quite a while now.

The same thing basically happens with the rankings of individual players. Skeptics can point out that Baylor's Jason Smith, the second pick in the 2009 draft, was just a two-star recruit, as were fellow first-rounders Aaron Curry, B.J. Raji, and Brandon Pettigrew. Meanwhile, USC's Clay Matthews was a mere walk-on. But these players are exceptions; while there are certainly outliers every year, but the percentages tell the story.

Depending on how you want to calculate odds, the facts are this:

• For a Rivals five-star recruit — of which there are roughly 25 to 30 each year — the odds of being a first-round pick are between about 10 and 15 percent.

• For a four-star recruit, the odds are about 3 to 8 percent.

• For a three-star recruit, the odds are about 0 to 2 percent.

• For a recruit with two stars or fewer, the odds are less than 0.5 percent.

About one in every four five-star recruits ends up drafted in the first three rounds. Sure, that leaves three of four who *aren't* top draft picks, but the odds are almost exponentially better for the top recruits.

As shown in Table 2, only a small handful of schools sign most of these five-star recruits.. In the last four recruiting classes (2006-09), four schools (USC, Florida, LSU, Alabama) have landed 35 percent of them. Meanwhile, 12 (those four, plus Tennessee, Ohio State, Texas, Notre Dame, Florida State, Oklahoma, Michigan, and Georgia) have landed 70 percent of them. **Think about this for a second: There are 120 FBS schools. Twelve of them land 70 percent of the bluest of blue-chippers, leaving the other 108 to fight over the remaining 30 percent.** Scholarship limits have helped even the overall college football playing field a smidge, but college football truly is the most dynastic of all major sports.

All the predictable disclaimers apply here. 1) Racking up five-star recruits doesn't guarantee success. Just ask Notre Dame. 2) A five-star recruit is not guaranteed to be successful. Just ask Mike D'Andrea or Chris Patterson. (Who? Exactly.) 3) There are only 25

Table 2: Rivals Five-Star Signees (2006-09)

Team	5-star signees	% of all 5-star recruits	Cumulative Pct.	% of all Final AP votes
USC	17	11.7%	11.7%	7.18%
Florida	15	10.3%	22.1%	3.41%
LSU	10	6.9%	29.0%	4.54%
Alabama	9	6.2%	35.2%	1.62%
Ohio State	8	5.5%	40.7%	5.47%
Tennessee	8	5.5%	46.2%	5.12%
Notre Dame	7	4.8%	51.0%	5.66%
Texas	7	4.8%	55.9%	3.02%
Florida State	6	4.1%	60.0%	3.33%
Georgia	5	3.4%	63.4%	1.77%
Michigan	5	3.4%	66.9%	5.93%
Oklahoma	5	3.4%	70.3%	3.30%
Miami	4	2.8%	73.1%	2.22%
Ole Miss	4	2.8%	75.9%	1.49%
Auburn	3	2.1%	77.9%	0.00%
Clemson	3	2.1%	80.0%	0.03%
North Carolina	3	2.1%	82.1%	0.51%

to 40 five-star recruits each year, so even the biggest programs have to fill out their classes with three- and four-star guys, and if none of the three- and four-star guys work out, the team will fail.

Nevertheless, recruiting rankings are all about margin for error. The more stars a recruit has, the more likely it is that he will be successful. The more big-time recruits you get, the more margin for error you have. A program can succeed with two- and three-star recruits — aforementioned teams like Missouri and West Virginia have made a recent living off of the diamonds in the rough, and they will continue to try to do just that — but as a whole, teams are a lot more likely to succeed at the highest level with four- and five-star athletes. And all it takes is one batch of rough products that *don't* turn into diamonds, and you will fall back to the pack quickly and violently.

Teams that are trying to find diamonds in the rough are essentially trying to exploit "inefficiencies in the market," so to speak, like Billy Beane in *Moneyball* and other small-market baseball general managers. If one team finds a method that works, others will emulate it. If one team finds a hidden source of talent, others will try to tap it. Both finding and landing those diamonds in the rough will get harder, and it will be imperative to have a nice bank of talent to fall back on when those methods begin to fail.

While it is almost impossible to break into football's

ruling class, on the flipside, all it takes is a couple of bad hires, or maybe just one egregiously bad hire, and a team can fall out of the ruling class quite easily. All of today's top teams are at the top because they made a great hire following a bad one. Oklahoma is great because John Blake made way for Bob Stoops. USC thrived under Pete Carroll after going 19-18 in three seasons under Paul Hackett. Urban Meyer is at Florida because Ron Zook only lasted three seasons. John Mackovic went 12-12 in his final two seasons at Texas, paving the way for Mack Brown. Les Miles followed Nick Saban at LSU, and while Saban was clearly a great coach, he was only there because Gerry DiNardo got dumped.

When Mack Brown retires, or Bob Stoops moves on to the NFL (not that that will happen), or Urban Meyer leaves for Notre Dame (ditto), or Pete Carroll leaves for another shot at the NFL, their respective programs will only continue to succeed if they hire quality successors. One bad hire, and you could fall out of the ruling class. Just ask Nebraska, or Notre Dame.

Right now, Michigan fans are anxiously waiting to see if Rich Rodriguez just needed to get more of his own style of recruits to succeed, or if he is their ticket out of the ruling class.

But back to the matter at hand: recruiting and Football Outsiders. If there is a purpose and benefit to recruiting rankings, then FO should be exploring it for predictive, and possibly evaluative, purposes.

Our college football play-by-play database will never match our NFL database (which currently goes back to 1994), but by the end of this year we'll have four seasons of college data. The performance of every player can eventually be tied to his recruiting ranking, be it Rivals, or Scout, or ESPN, or Phil Steele's compilation. Comparisons can be made of the accuracy of one recruiting service over another, and even more interesting than that, projections for a given player and his chosen team can be made based on his recruiting ranking. How does the average five-star running back recruit perform his freshman year? What about a four-star wide receiver? Or a five-star quarterback thrown into the fire his first month or two on campus? As the sample sizes get bigger, a much more quantifiable approach can be taken to the blitz of hype and hat ceremonies.

Plus, recruiting services are still tinkering with their methods, looking for better, more elaborate methods of evaluating prospects. Rivals.com has gone to some lengths to improve the informative nature of their recruiting rankings — instead of just a star rating of 1 to 5, a high school recruit also receives a "Rivals Rating," which breaks out each star rating further. A three- or four-star recruit is divvied into one of three tiers. What this means is, with more outcomes data in the future, FO can begin to explore potentially more intricate college player projections from one year to another.

Every year, it seems that everything about recruiting gets bigger, louder, and more televised. The reason is simple: There's an audience. The NFL has turned itself into a year-round sport; why not the NCAA? Signing Day comes, and everybody is excited or enraged by their team's class, and then the next year's coverage kicks up immediately, the all-star game rosters start filling out, and the entire process begins again.

Whether you like it or not, the glitz and superficial glamour of football recruiting are part of the fabric of college football, and it is not going to change. We might as well figure out ways to analyze it accurately. And enjoy the unintentional comedy of the hat ceremonies.

Bill Connelly

Enter the Wildcat

In 2008, Pat White would not have been a hot draft commodity. As a short quarterback who was better known for his running than his passing at West Virginia, White would have gone in the later rounds after trying to prove to teams that he could change positions to wide receiver. But that was before the Wildcat became the NFL's hottest trend.

Miami's variation on the classic single-wing offense worked so well that similar direct-snap plays were spreading around the league within weeks. Over half the NFL's teams ran at least one play last year featuring a direct snap to a non-quarterback, or two quarterbacks on the field at once. Teams like Dallas, Philadelphia, and New England displayed an interest in White's specific skills as they related to the formation set. As a result, White wasn't just another spread-option quarterback designated for the NFL scrap heap — he was the talk of the 2009 Scouting Combine.

Atlanta Falcons GM Thomas Dimitroff, fresh from his own Miami-style one-season miracle turnaround, had his eye on White's abilities from the start. "Obviously, Pat White is an incredible athlete," Dimitroff said at the Combine. "I think the Wildcat situation is something that a lot of us are trying to figure out what's the best way to defend it and use it. I think (offensive coordinator) Mike Mularkey has a very good understanding of that as well. I think it will continue to bring players to the forefront that are a little bit of that 'Slash' ability (referring for former Steelers quarterback Kordell 'Slash' Stewart, known for his versatility), where they can also toss the ball. If you can get that runner who can run as well as be a receiver, versatility in this league is huge at any position. But when you get a receiver-slash-skill position, a guy who has the versatility to run it out of the backfield, to me, that adds a whole different dimension."

But did the Wildcat actually work for other teams? The answer is yes, but not always as well as you might expect — and part of the reason why the Wildcat works explains why teams are interested in White and players like him.

Miami's Wildcat is a very specific formation design. The left tackle (Jake Long, for the Dolphins) moves over to the right side. The left guard (Justin Smiley) frequently pulls right. One running back is behind the center, while another is on the wing, sweeping across before the snap. You can't just direct-snap the ball to your running back and call it "Wildcat," although apparently nobody told the television play-by-play guys. To most of them, any odd formation was automatically designated as such.

When they ran it against the Patriots in Week 3, the Dolphins used three formations — described as "Steeler," "Power," and "Counter" by quarterbacks coach David Lee, who ran the very same plays at Arkansas with Darren McFadden and Felix Jones in 2007.

"Steeler," in which the halfback (Ricky Williams) moves from left to right after the snap and takes the ball from the quarterback (Ronnie Brown). (Figure 1) The running back then blasts off to the right behind a pulling left guard, an unbalanced right offensive line, and an H-back either between and behind the two right tackles or just outside the right tackle to block.

Figure 1: Wildcat "Steeler"

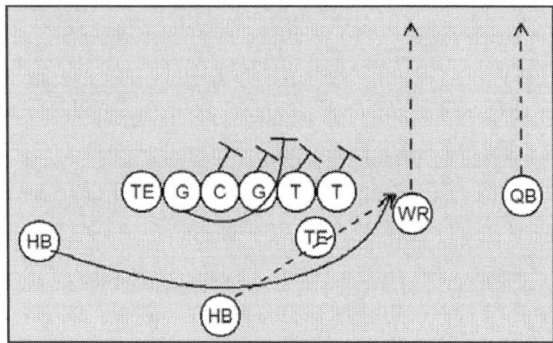

"Power," in which the fake to the running back in the "Steeler" formation leaves the quarterback to (hopefully) blow through any one of four different holes to the right. (Figure 2) The H-back will stay in to block, and the pulling guard is the key. Left guard Justin Smiley was money for the Dolphins on this play until a leg injury ended his season early (dashed arrows indicate Brown's secondary running options

Figure 2: Wildcat "Power"

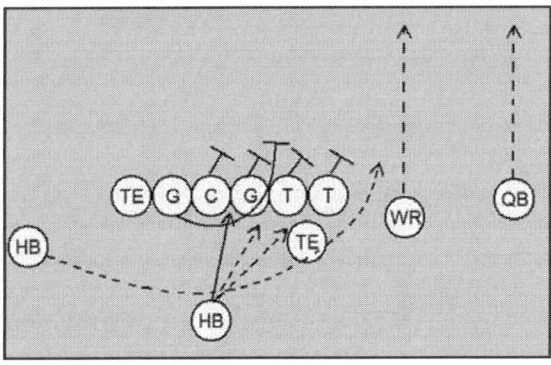

or, for other players, dummy routes.).

"Counter", in which the running back fake leaves the defense biting on "Power," only to watch helplessly as the back runs left through a huge open cutback lane. (Figure 3) The line can go with slide protection at times instead of a pulling guard. There's a passing option out of the Counter, as Miami running back Ronnie Brown showed against the Pats in Week 3 when he hit tight end Anthony Fasano for a 19-yard touchdown.

Figure 3: Wildcat "Counter"

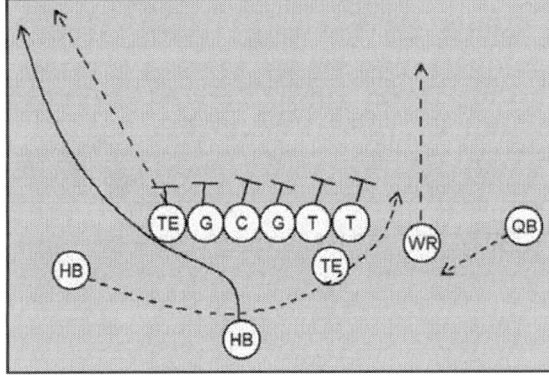

The effectiveness of the specific formation design begins with pre-snap sameness — Wildcat plays look similar at the start, though they might end up with a sweep, a plunge up the middle, or even a pass. Brown's touchdown pass to Fasano out of the Counter was enough to set up the possibility of the pass for the rest of the season.

One Steeler option was a handoff to the quarterback (Chad Pennington) from wide right, from which Pennington would throw downfield. The Dolphins started playing against defenses that were cheating up to nine in the box, and this really came to life against the Tex-

ans in Week 6. On Miami's second drive, Houston crashed through and killed the game's first Wildcat play, a Williams Steeler/Power read option that went nowhere. On the next play, Miami lined up the same way and started the Steeler sweep, only to add the extra wrinkle of the Williams handoff to Pennington. The Texans were practically bringing players from the sideline to overload the left side. As a result, Pennington had a wide-open man, and tossed a lob to running back Patrick Cobbs, who sauntered into the end zone for a 58-yard touchdown. (Figure 4) Pennington confirmed after the game that the Dolphins were reading Houston with the first play to see how much they'd bite on the inside run.

Figure 4: Wildcat Pass to Cobbs

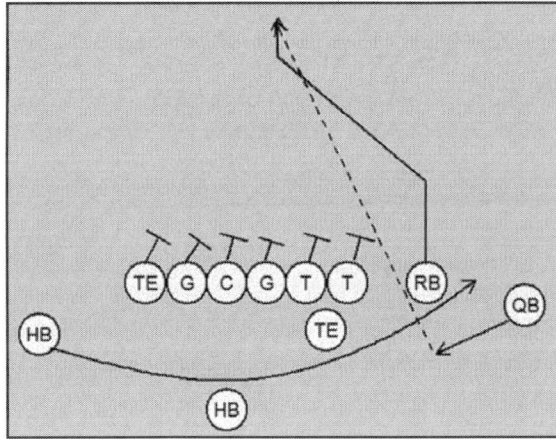

While the Dolphins were fooling the Texans, other teams were trying different formations on that same Sunday. The 49ers gave it a shot against the Eagles, but messed up the timing of the sweep as center Eric Heitmann was called for a false start. The Falcons tried a few bursts into the line with Matt Ryan and Jerious Norwood in the backfield. Atlanta had a potentially lethal combination with Norwood's cutback speed and the option misdirection, and the Falcons might be the team to watch when it comes to odd formations in 2009.

The Cleveland Browns had some interesting angles in what they call their "Flash" package. Receiver Josh Cribbs, who was a quarterback at Kent State and is now the best return man in football, took a handoff in that same Week 6 from quarterback Derek Anderson. Cribbs, sweeping right, then pitched the ball to running back Jerome Harrison going the other way. You could see about nine Giants defenders trying to put on the brakes to no avail, as Harrison gained 33 yards down the left side. The successful play had the snap going to Anderson, but the Browns had run read-options with direct snaps to Cribbs earlier in the game — one where Cribbs darted upfield for 12 yards, and a two-yard handoff to Jamal Lewis.

The more the direct snap presents the threat of a pass, the more likely it is to gain serious yardage. Kansas City's numbers looked good primarily because one of its nine direct-snap plays was a pass, in Week 9 against Tampa Bay. Running back Jamaal Charles took the snap and handed off to wide receiver Mark Bradley, who threw downfield to quarterback Tyler Thigpen (who had lined up as a receiver) for a 37-yard touchdown. That's the kind of trick play where confusion pays off, leaving a man wide open for six.

The Rams also had success by mixing passes into their version of the Wildcat. In Weeks 15 and 16, wide receiver Dane Looker took the ball from Steven Jackson on an end-around and completed passes to quarterback Marc Bulger (who had lined up at receiver) for 11 yards on first-and-15 and six yards on first-and-10. Thanks to those passes, defenses couldn't just load up the middle when Jackson took a direct snap.

Contrast that to the lack of creativity shown by the Cincinnati Bengals in their two "Wildcat" plays last year. On one, wide receiver Andre Caldwell lined up under center on third-and-2, took the snap, and ran a simple sweep to the left for just one yard. On the other, Cedric Benson took a direct snap on second-and-10 and went straight up into the line for four yards, setting up… third-and-long. Not a play teeming with excitement or productivity.

Other than Kansas City and Miami, the teams that had the most success with "Wildcat" style plays were Baltimore and the New York Jets (Table 1), and they show why a team that wants to run similar unconventional plays might want the extra passing option. Neither team's "Wildcat" was really the Wildcat at all, because neither team snapped the ball to a running back. The Ravens ran a series of plays with two quarterbacks on the field at once, lining up either Joe Flacco or Troy Smith under center with the other lined up as a wide receiver. The Jets snapped to former Missouri option quarterback-turned-NFL wideout Brad Smith.

Trick plays work because the defense doesn't know what's coming. Whether you are talking about the true Miami "Wildcat" or Baltimore's two-quarterback package, the threat of the pass plays an important role.

On the other hand, when the offense just direct-snaps to the running back and runs him up into the middle of the offensive line, you end up with a "Wildcat" that isn't really that wild — or useful. Baltimore's Smith had his big option play when he threw a 43-yard pass to quarterback Joe Flacco in the third quarter of a 29-10 Week 8 win over the Raiders. Successful option plays like these bring new chances for dual-threat quarterbacks like Smith and White, whose predecessors generally washed out in the NFL.

Baltimore's defense was the Wildcat's Kryptonite, proving the need for more diversity. The Dolphins played the Ravens twice last season, lost both games, and gained a grand total of six yards out of the formation on seven running plays and one false start penalty. Baltimore's lethal combination of team speed and gap control proved too much for the simple plays. The Dolphins gained 580 yards on their 90 Wildcat plays, a 6.4 yard-per-play average. Take out the Baltimore games, and that average jumps up to 7.0. Enter Pat White, and the specter of the aerial Wildcat.

Even before the Dolphins drafted White in the second round, head coach Tony Sparano was aware of what players like White could do for his offense — and the offenses of others. As he said at the Combine, the Dolphins were going to scout with the Wildcat in

Table 1: Wildcat and other Direct Snaps to non-QBs in 2008

Team	Plays	Yd/Play	Suc Rate*
MIA	90	6.4	47%
CLE	21	4.8	43%
BAL	18	6.3	50%
SF	12	4.6	42%
CAR	11	4.5	36%
ATL	11	5.5	36%
BUF	10	4.0	60%
KC	9	8.1	56%
OAK	8	5.6	63%
STL	8	6.0	63%
PHI	5	4.8	60%
NYJ	4	6.8	75%
CHI	3	5.3	33%
ARI	3	6.3	33%
NE	2	1.5	50%
CIN	2	2.5	0%
TB	2	2.5	0%
HOU	1	-5.0	0%

*Percent of successful plays: 45% of needed yards on first down, 60% on second down, or 100% on third/fourth down.

mind. "I'm sure of that. I'm sure that there are some people that are looking at those pieces right now," he said. " I don't know how committed other teams are to it, but there are a lot of those kinds of players out there, the potential Wildcat guys, whether they're different positional players that have the skill to run the football, or maybe have thrown the football."

White, who spent his time between the Combine and the draft trying to dissuade people of the notion that he could only make the NFL as a receiver, seems excited about his options in Miami. "I fit fairly well in the Wildcat, so I hope that is my quickest way onto the field. ... I am excited to see how they can utilize my talent," he said shortly after he was selected. In mini-camps, White has both taken shotgun snaps and lined up wide as a receiver. And you can bet that the rest of the NFL is watching.

The Cowboys want to run what they call the "Razorback" with Felix Jones, who ran the original Wildcat with David Lee in Arkansas. Vikings head coach Brad Childress has used Florida receiver Percy Harvin, Minnesota's first-round pick, in different option sets with quarterback Tarvaris Jackson split wide. That Childress, the former bastion of playbook conservatism, has embraced the concept to that degree tells you all you need to know about its popularity. Other teams, like the Jaguars and Chargers, are running Wildcat looks in practice simply to learn how to defend it — or, at least that's what they're telling the media.

Announcers may struggle to understand it, and many talking heads dismiss it as a gimmick, but the NFL is trying to come to terms with this latest trend. If the Dolphins are able to lead the way to a new level where the Wildcat becomes a major part of an offense, you'll see CopyCats of every stripe — and as it is with the recent predominance of the shotgun or the 3-4 defense, personnel and proper coaching will decide how successful each team is with the new wrinkles. Just as surely, some teams will be better off sticking with the basics.

Aaron Schatz and Doug Farrar

The Red Menace

The red zone: It's the most valuable expanse of real estate in the game, the place where bending defenses don't break and great offenses put the ball in the end zone. A team's red zone efficiency holds almost mythical status; even famously anti-statistics defensive coordinator Greg Blache looks at red zone performance as a sign of how well his Redskins defense is playing, while Bill Belichick may have put it best in a 2004 *USA Today* piece: "There is no way to overstate the importance of the red zone…It's impossible."

Far be it from us to disagree with Belichick with regards to that point; offensive red zone DVOA bears a .52 correlation with wins, while defensive red zone DVOA is at -.39.

The implication made in most commentaries on red zone performance, though, is that great teams *rise to the occasion* inside the red zone, that they improve on their normal level of performance in this clutch situation and do so on a regular basis.

If we look at 2008, the teams that overachieved defensively in the red zone are Baltimore, Pittsburgh, San Diego, Minnesota, and Miami, none of whom are slouches on the defensive side of the ball. The New England Patriots, ironically, had the worst red zone defense in the league, and were the biggest underachievers inside their own 20.

It's on the offensive side where the validity of Belichick's statement really comes to light, though. A struggling offense that ranked 30th in the league with an overall DVOA of -20.6% came to life near the opposition end zone, putting up a 14.0% DVOA that was ninth in the NFL. That team that rode their red zone efficiency to a perfect season was … the Detroit Lions.

You might be able to figure out where we're going with this.

On a year-to-year basis, there's essentially no relationship with regards to the difference between a team's red zone DVOA and their overall DVOA, on either side of the ball (Table 1). That means that a team which grossly outplays its red zone DVOA in a given season, while likely deriving significant success from doing so, is no more likely to do so in the subsequent campaign than a team which dramatically underperformed their standard performance inside the red zone.

If a team really retained the ability to be effective in the red zone over a multi-year period, we'd see a specific organization or perhaps a particular scheme appearing repeatedly amongst those teams with the biggest gaps between red zone performance and overall performance; at the very least, the teams that had the biggest gaps between the two would remain above-average in the red zone in the subsequent campaign.

That's not the case. Of the 20 offenses that overachieved the most in the red zone, 13 actually underachieved in the subsequent season. Eight of the 20 most overachieving defenses had a higher DVOA inside the red zone than they did outside a year later.

Even more damning is a comparison of the red zone overachievers on defense to the 20 teams who *under*achieved their regular performance the most inside their own 20. In the subsequent season, those red zone underachievers were nearly 11 percentage points of DVOA better in the red zone than they were over the rest of the field; meanwhile, the 20 DVOA overachievers were only two percentage points of DVOA better in the red zone than over the rest of the field. In other words, if you were trying to pick the defenses that would raise their game the most inside the red zone in 2009, you would be better off looking at last year's worst teams in the red zone than you would be looking at the teams that were at their best in the red zone.

Just looking at 2007 and 2008, the dramatic variance on a year-to-year basis is obvious. In 2007, the Patriots were the best offense in the league *and* were the biggest overachievers in the red zone; in 2008, after

Table 1: The Difference Is...

Year-To-Year Correlation	Offense	Defense
Overall DVOA	0.47	0.39
Red Zone DVOA	0.32	0.21
Difference Between Two	0.09	0.01

losing Tom Brady, they were -2.9% worse in the red zone than they were overall. The Colts were second and effective both years, but the Jaguars went from third in 2007 (with a quarterback who knew how to manage the game and avoid turnovers in David Garrard) to 24th a year ago (with a quarterback who knew how to manage the game but didn't avoid quite as many turnovers, still named David Garrard).

Defensively, the two teams with the worst red zone performance in 2007 (in relation to their overall defense) were the Dolphins and the Giants. So much for the idea about red zone defense being the reliable mark of a champion. The Giants were about the same in the red zone as they were elsewhere in 2008, but only the Chargers, Vikings, and Ravens overachieved more in the red zone than the Dolphins did a year ago.

You'll note that those teams also saw improvement in the win column a year ago, and that's not surpris-

ing; the 20 worst defensive underachievers increased their win totals by an average of 1.5 games in the subsequent season, nearly mirroring a two-win drop by the top 20 defensive overachievers. The effects on offense aren't as severe, but still represent some regression to the mean (and are discussed further in the St. Louis chapter).

Is red zone performance important? Absolutely. Are there teams who have the red zone figured out and successfully employ offensive schemes and defensive schemes that consistently rank them above the league average? Not whatsoever. The last offense to outplay their standard scheme in the red zone in each year of a five-year stretch was the 2001-2005 49ers; no one's breaking those teams' doors down with Hall of Fame nominations. A team almost always needs to be good in the red zone to succeed, but the best way to ensure success in the red zone is to have a good team.

Bill Barnwell

Table 2: Offensive DVOA Overachievers in Red Zone, 1995-2007

Year	Team	Red	Total	Diff	Next Yr Red	Next Yr DVOA	Next Yr Diff	Wins	Wins+1	Diff
1997	CIN	55.5%	15.4%	40.1%	-17.6%	-8.4%	-9.2%	7	3	-4
2006	SD	63.0%	23.3%	39.7%	31.3%	4.8%	26.5%	14	11	-3
1997	NO	-9.5%	-47.6%	38.1%	-27.4%	-20.4%	-7.0%	6	6	0
2003	KC	62.5%	24.4%	38.1%	12.1%	28.6%	-16.5%	13	7	-6
2005	SEA	60.1%	23.3%	36.8%	3.0%	-11.1%	14.1%	13	9	-4
2003	GB	45.4%	8.8%	36.6%	20.3%	17.5%	2.8%	10	10	0
2004	BAL	30.1%	-5.7%	35.9%	-39.9%	-15.7%	-24.3%	9	6	-3
2002	NE	42.8%	7.0%	35.8%	3.3%	-0.9%	4.2%	9	14	5
1999	KC	41.1%	5.5%	35.6%	1.2%	10.1%	-9.0%	9	7	-2
2000	SEA	27.2%	-7.7%	34.9%	0.7%	-5.0%	5.7%	6	9	3
Average		41.8%	4.7%	37.2%	-1.3%	0.0%	-1.3%	9.6	8.2	-1.4

Table 3: Offensive DVOA Underachievers in Red Zone, 1995-2007

Year	Team	Red	Total	Diff	Next Yr Red	Next Yr DVOA	Next Yr Diff	Wins	Wins+1	Diff
1996	SEA	-41.3%	-7.3%	-34.0%	-6.3%	5.9%	-12.1%	7	8	1
2000	BAL	-42.9%	-7.0%	-35.9%	-35.8%	-12.9%	-22.9%	12	10	-2
2001	ATL	-47.0%	-9.6%	-37.4%	4.5%	8.2%	-3.6%	7	9.5	2.5
1999	DEN	-43.3%	-5.3%	-38.0%	7.8%	19.1%	-11.4%	6	11	5
2006	GB	-47.4%	-5.4%	-42.0%	18.6%	17.3%	1.4%	8	13	5
2005	ARI	-53.2%	-10.0%	-43.2%	-12.6%	-6.6%	-6.0%	5	5	0
1999	MIN	-31.9%	13.4%	-45.2%	34.4%	22.2%	12.3%	10	11	1
2000	ATL	-71.6%	-25.4%	-46.2%	-47.0%	-9.6%	-37.4%	4	7	3
1997	SD	-82.1%	-28.4%	-53.7%	-31.0%	-36.0%	5.0%	4	5	1
2000	ARI	-83.4%	-21.6%	-61.8%	-11.8%	-0.2%	-11.6%	3	7	4
Average		-54.4%	-10.6%	-43.8%	-7.9%	0.7%	-8.6%	6.6	8.7	2.1

Table 4: Defensive DVOA Overachievers in Red Zone, 1995-2007

Year	Team	Red	Total	Diff	Next Yr Red	Next Yr DVOA	Next Yr Diff	Wins	Wins+1	Diff
1997	KC	-54.8%	-24.6%	-30.2%	6.0%	-3.3%	9.3%	13	7	-6
2001	NYJ	-40.4%	-10.0%	-30.4%	18.0%	11.0%	7.0%	10	9	-1
1996	CIN	-40.1%	-8.4%	-31.7%	18.8%	13.1%	5.6%	8	7	-1
2004	BAL	-50.4%	-18.2%	-32.2%	-18.4%	-10.3%	-8.1%	9	6	-3
1997	TB	-34.0%	-1.4%	-32.7%	-21.6%	-13.0%	-8.6%	10	8	-2
2000	PHI	-45.2%	-12.0%	-33.2%	-59.1%	-21.5%	-37.6%	11	11	0
2001	CHI	-49.2%	-14.8%	-34.4%	-8.6%	4.5%	-13.2%	13	4	-9
1999	TEN	-39.7%	-4.6%	-35.1%	-21.9%	-28.4%	6.6%	13	13	0
2001	NYG	-37.9%	-2.4%	-35.5%	23.1%	0.3%	22.8%	7	10	3
2001	PHI	-59.1%	-21.5%	-37.6%	-16.8%	-13.8%	-3.0%	11	12	1
Average		-45.1%	-11.8%	-33.3%	-8.1%	-6.1%	-1.9%	10.5	8.7	-1.8

Table 5: Defensive DVOA Underachievers in Red Zone, 1995-2007

Year	Team	Red	Total	Diff	Next Yr Red	Next Yr DVOA	Next Yr Diff	Wins	Wins+1	Diff
1999	OAK	18.1%	-9.6%	27.7%	-2.1%	-6.7%	4.5%	8	12	4
2003	BAL	-2.4%	-29.9%	27.5%	-50.4%	-18.2%	-32.2%	10	9	-1
2002	CAR	13.3%	-13.9%	27.2%	-1.7%	-9.4%	7.8%	7	11	4
2007	MIA	43.7%	16.7%	27.0%	-21.9%	-1.4%	-23.5%	1	11	10
2000	CHI	30.4%	4.7%	25.7%	-49.2%	-14.8%	-34.4%	5	13	8
1997	IND	37.4%	11.7%	25.7%	7.7%	18.0%	-10.3%	3	3	0
2007	NYG	22.3%	-2.9%	25.2%	-0.7%	-6.9%	-26.0%	10	12	2
1999	BAL	3.4%	-21.5%	24.9%	-83.1%	-30.0%	-53.1%	8	12	4
2005	TEN	38.5%	14.5%	24.0%	7.1%	6.1%	1.0%	4	8	4
2004	CLE	32.1%	8.3%	23.8%	0.8%	6.5%	-5.7%	4	6	2
Average		23.7%	-2.2%	25.9%	-19.3%	-5.7%	-17.2%	6.0	9.7	3.7

Introducing Playmaker Score

Baseball analysts have it easy. At its heart, baseball is a series of one-on-one matchups between batters and pitchers. If you know how a batter performed in the minor leagues, you can just tweak his numbers to adjust for the pitchers he faced and the parks he played in, and you'll get a reasonable estimate of how he'll do as a major leaguer.

Not so in football, and especially not with wide receivers. Beyond the location and opposition, a player's numbers are affected by the quality of his teammates and coaches, the offensive system, whether the player's team was usually ahead or behind, and more.

Still, some trends do carry over from the college game to the pros. If you can't get open downfield or find the end zone in the ACC or the SEC, you're not likely to have much luck in the NFL.

From 2001 to 2006, 53 wide receivers were drafted in the first or second round. Two of those — Matt Jones and Antwaan Randle El — primarily played quarterback in college; we're ignoring them here. We took the remaining 51 receivers and looked at college stats to find the strongest indicator of NFL success (as measured by receiving yards in a player's first three years). The highest correlation belonged to average gain per catch, followed by touchdowns scored, total yards, and receptions.

Not surprisingly, the numbers get more accurate if we use per-game figures instead of career totals. This boosts underclassmen who leave early for the NFL ahead of lesser four-year players who hang around racking up higher totals. In fact, touchdowns per game is an even stronger indicator than average yards gained per catch.

Why would those two statistics be more indicative than either total yards or receptions? Total stats likely say more about where a receiver played than how he played; the top receiver at Texas Tech is going to catch more passes than the top receiver at Navy. Judging a receiver on a per-catch basis, however, shows when a player can dominate the lower levels with speed, leaping ability, or the skill to make tacklers miss. If your only strength is to find the holes in college zones and catch six-yard curls, your pro future is likely bleak. As for touchdowns, consider that successful NFL receivers are likely to have been the best players on their teams in college, and would probably be the top targets on the most important area of the field.

For an even stronger indicator, we can multiply touchdowns per game by average gain. The resulting product is more accurate than either statistic by itself. For example, multiplying Michael Crabtree's 1.6 touchdowns per game at Texas Tech by his 13.5 yards per catch gives us a product of 21.3, the best among this year's first-day receivers. That score — we'll call it the Playmaker Score — matches Crabtree's elite reputation; among first-day draft picks, only Larry Fitzgerald (22.6), Ashley Lelie (22.3), and Charles Rogers (22.2) produced higher numbers.

The presence of Charles Rogers and Ashley Lelie at the top of the rankings is a good hint that when it comes to picking out superstars, Playmaker Score is less accurate than either the Lewin Career Forecast for quarterbacks or Speed Scores for running backs. Playmaker Score predicted big things for Fitzgerald, Reggie Wayne (Playmaker Score of 16.0), and Andre Johnson (16.5), but it also saw bright futures for Rogers, Mike Williams (16.9), and David Terrell (18.6).

No, the real value of Playmaker Score is not its ability to tell us which wide receivers are likely to be productive. It's real value comes in its ability to tell us which wide receivers are likely to be *un*productive.

We sorted the 51 receivers in this study into four relatively even groups, sorted by Playmaker Score. There's confusion on top of the pile, but clarity on the bottom (Table 1).

As noted earlier, the top two groups are a pretty even mix of stars, good players, and busts. The third group

Table 1: Playmaker Profile

Playmaker Score	Number	Receptions	Yards
Over 15	13	117	1649
11-15	15	142	2103
8-11	11	84	1170
Below 8	13	77	1029

*Average stats per receiver over first three seasons.

Table 2: Crabtree and the Seven Dwarves

Name	College	Round	Overall	Team	G	Rec	Yds	TD	Yd/Rec	TD/G	Playmaker
Michael Crabtree	Texas Tech	1	10	SF	26	231	3127	41	13.5	1.58	21.3
Jeremy Maclin	Missouri	1	19	PHI	28	182	2315	22	12.7	0.79	10.0
Hakeem Nicks	North Carolina	1	29	NYG	36	181	2840	21	15.7	0.58	9.2
Kenny Britt	Rutgers	1	30	TEN	32	178	3043	17	17.1	0.53	9.1
Brian Robiskie	Ohio State	2	36	CLE	40	127	1866	24	14.7	0.60	8.8
Percy Harvin	Florida	1	22	MIN	36	133	1929	13	14.5	0.36	5.2
Darrius Heyward-Bey	Maryland	1	7	OAK	39	138	2089	13	15.1	0.33	5.0
Mohamed Massaquoi	Georgia	2	50	CLE	51	158	2282	16	14.4	0.31	4.5

(Playmaker Score 8-11) is boosted by Chris Chambers and Rod Gardner, but the rest of the group consists of first-round disappointments or complete wipeouts like Rashaun Woods, Taylor Jacobs, and Chad Jackson.

The final group, the players with Playmaker Score below eight, is a complete disaster. Only two receivers in this group had more than 125 receptions in their first three seasons: Reggie Brown, who is in the process of losing his job in Philadelphia, and one-year wonder Michael Clayton. The rest of the group reads like a murderer's row of failed receivers. Keary Colbert! Bethel Johnson! Tyrone Calico! Terrence Murphy! Sinorice *and* Santana Moss! (OK, Santana turned out to be a decent player, but he got off to a very slow start.)

It's important to remember that this formula, like the Lewin Career Forecast, is intended to forecast the futures of first- and second-round draft picks only. Ramses Barden put up sick numbers in college — 20.4 yards per catch, 1.14 touchdowns per game, Playmaker score of 23.2 — but there is a reason he was available when the Giants took him in the third round with the 85th overall pick. Most likely, it's because Barden put that resume together while playing for the Cal Poly Mustangs, whose 2008 schedule included wins over South Dakota, South Dakota State, and North Carolina Central.

When you look at this year's first- and second-round receivers, however, keep our four Playmaker Score groups in mind. While Michael Crabtree is light years ahead of the rest of his class, players like Jeremy Maclin, Hakeem Nicks, and Kenny Britt are perilously close to the minimum threshold of productive receivers. The list of first-round receivers with a Playmaker under 10.0 isn't pretty: Troy Williamson, Reggie Williams, Mark Clayton, Michael Clayton, Santana Moss, Michael Jenkins, and Bryant Johnson. Percy Harvin and Mohamed Massaquoi seem like longshots, although Harvin comes with an asterisk since he spent so much time in the backfield.

And then there's Darrius Heyward-Bey, whom Oakland selected with Crabtree still on the board. Only seven receivers posted a lower Playmaker Score than Heyward-Bey's 5.0: Bethel Johnson, Sinorice Moss, Bryant Johnson, Terrence Murphy, Andre Davis, Reggie Brown, and Tim Carter. Those seven players averaged less than a thousand yards in their first three seasons combined. The Raiders may have passed on the next Andre Johnson to select the next Andre Davis.

Vince Verhei

They Try To Make Me Go To Rehab:
The Hidden Process of Getting a Player Back

There's an information gap in injury analysis. If we look at the stories, things go from point A to point B, from injury to return, but the intervening weeks and months are lost. At best, there will be a passing reference to rehab, a note in a beat writer's column that the player is back at the practice facility, happy to see his teammates, and looking good. The coach and player will say all the right things, while the doctors and Trainers will give vague timelines. There's a reason why writers skip this stuff. It's long, tedious, repetitive, and painful. I can only hope this article isn't the same.

Most of what you'll hear about rehab — if it's anything at all — won't have any value to anyone but the player himself. It's the jargon of the trade that nobody explains, like "Tom Brady is doing lateral plyometrics, spending time on a wobble board, and contrast soaks." To most football fans, that means next to nothing. They're just concerned with overall process and the timeline, and this is one place where the fans and the head coaches aren't too different. A head coach doesn't want specifics; he just wants to know if the player is able to play or not able to play. He'll have a board on their office wall, charts and spreadsheets from the medical staff, and other techniques for managing their roster, but most couldn't tell a Swiss ball from a Swedish meatball.

It should be that way for fans and fantasy players as well, but they seem to be a twitchy, paranoid sort. This piece will give me something to point to and to show you just how much goes into the process that is essentially invisible, not just to the outside world, but even inside the game. For those not in Training Rooms, they just don't know. For those players that have been through the process, they give that knowing nod. Last season I crossed paths with Andre Johnson. I was on the Lucas Oil Stadium field for the first time, before a Colts-Texans game and was testing out the turf. I squished it a bit and tried to start running a few steps, but as I did, my knee reminded me how old I was and I hobbled a couple steps. Johnson nodded and said "Yeah, I know what that feels like."

In order to take you through this process, I talked with the professionals who do this day in, day out. The rehab process may be ignored, but all of it — from the best known players and most gruesome injuries down to the tedium of practice squad players getting preventative care in the training room — is an important factor in determining the W's and L's each Sunday. Getting a player back a week early or having him at 90 percent instead of 80 percent can be the difference between a trip to the Super Bowl and another long wait for minicamp. Throughout this article, I'll be referring to ACL reconstruction, one of the most common injuries in the NFL, but the process is much the same for any major surgery.

Athletes in any sport have a low "action tolerance." An NFL strength and conditioning coach (who remains anonymous due to league rules) told me that the biggest worry for any rehabbing athlete is the loss of structure and action. "Getting them to show up isn't an issue, since they're getting paid. The difference is often how much and how they work. I don't pay a lot of attention to the draft, but I've gone back and taken a look at some of the comments on our injured guys and there's some predictive stuff in there. I know you guys wave off 'heart' and 'guts' but that's the kind of guys that succeed in rehab. I want the self-motivated gym rat. I want the guy who was already spending extra time in the weight room."

The rehab starts before the injury has even occurred. "Prehab" is a word that's somewhat hashed together, but it's an important component of every single team's strength and conditioning programs. "We know what the injuries are likely to be," said the strength and conditioning coach, "and for each position, we'll not only do what makes them functional, but will support them in both preventing and rehabbing an injury." Strong quad muscles are key in supporting the knee and allowing for "deeper" cuts. Deeper? Think squats. "Maurice Jones-Drew and Barry Sanders are two guys I think of when I'm talking about deep cuts," Edgerrin James told me during his rehab from an ACL tear. "They're down low, letting the big muscles work." James may not be a biomechanist, but his adjustment is correct. By dipping down lower, a back reduces the risk of an ACL tear if hit from any side. Try it yourself.

When the injury does occur, the medical staff is quickly out there. "I can usually tell what's happened before I get to the athlete," said an NFL team physician. Just watching the game can often tell us what the injury is (though we can be wrong, as I was due to camera angle after the Tom Brady injury last season.) The trainers and doctors have experience and training, in addition to a better seat. "The guy gets hit, he's grabbing at his knee; I don't need an MRI to know when a guy's blown it out and we can begin the prep right there." For clear surgical cases, teams will focus on reduction of pain and swelling in the short term as well as supporting the structures that could be endangered by the failure of one system. "While we don't repair MCL's much," the doctor explained, "we still want to minimize the collateral damage (no pun intended). That can be as simple as getting him properly immobilized and breaking the pain cycle, but at times we also have to get range of motion issues from getting in there."

Of course, athletes get the very best of care. They don't wait in lines or have much of a problem getting scheduled quickly. Top surgeons like Dr. James Andrews keep some time available early in the week to make sure that they can fit in players who were injured on Sunday afternoon. The surgeries are relatively the same, which isn't to say surgery is an assembly line. It's just all too routine. While what happens on the table is the same as it was a few years ago (aside from often being observed by team trainers or other personnel), what happens just afterwards is now different. The state of the art currently calls for using transplanted tendons, usually Achilles tendons. While the use of these harvested parts is easier on the body than harvesting part of the patient's own body, there can be some psychological effects. Most famously, Carson Palmer was thrown off a bit when it was discovered that his new ACL had been the Achilles of a 24-year-old woman killed by a drunk driver.

The incision is barely closed when the work begins again. "Weight bearing is the new hotness," said one sports orthopaedist who has worked on several NFL and MLB players. "When Alex Rodriguez had his hip done, [Dr. Marc] Phillipon had him on a stationary bike before he'd fully woken up. I've heard he was puking while he was pedaling." That may sound a bit harsh and certainly isn't something most surgeons would be doing when Grandma gets her hip replaced, but these are well-tuned athletes. One of the hardest things about assessing an injury or rehab is that we think about this players as people. It's easier to think of them as a different species with many of the same parts, *homo footballus* or something.

The first three weeks of rehabilitation focus on inflammation control and range of motion. While a physical therapist is spending a couple hours a day following charts and protocols to free up the knee's full range of motion, the athlete is usually working on upper body strength, cardiovascular conditioning, and maintaining the opposite leg. It's that last part that can often be a problem. "They're on crutches and well below their normal activity level," said the strength and conditioning coach, who monitors all rehabs throughout the process. "We have to adjust things they don't even think about in order to keep atrophy from setting in." This doesn't just involve making sure that the athlete doesn't get lazy; it also diet adjustments that compensate for lower caloric demands while making sure there is enough protein to support healing.

Athletes then move to the "strength phase," which takes another three weeks. For weeks four through six, the athlete is focused on strengthening the secondary stabilizers and making sure that any atrophy of other muscles is handled quickly. For an ACL repair, the focus stays on the hamstring, quadriceps, and calf bilaterally, but there's also some additional focus put on the hips and back. "You call them cascade injuries, right?" said an NFL Certified Athletic Trainer (ATC)*, laughing a bit. "We call them preventable and predictable, and it's a big, big part of the process." At this point, the knee hasn't healed. The scar is pink and raw, a symbol of the process. In many cases, the season is still going on and a player has to watch his replacement, wondering if he'll ever play again. This is the time when the rehab team often feels like a troupe of amateur psychologists. "We get the coaches involved here," said one rehab coordinator. "They'll see improvements and usually haven't had a lot of involvement with the player, so it's a double reinforcement for the player." This part is usually harder for the fringe player, but not always. "Some of the [backups] have a resignation to it and realize the dream is done," the coordinator told me, "but others, especially the ones

---

* No, don't ask us why Certified Athletic Trainer is not abbreviated CAT.

that weren't physically gifted to begin with, can use it as a springboard. Some of the players that weren't gym rats before become that in rehab."

Once strength around the injury is up, the rehab moves to a phase focused on proprioception. Proprioception is defined as the ability to sense the position of the body in space. (A simple example: Close your eyes and you still know where your hands are, even if they're moving.) This is perhaps the most difficult phase as the body begins to sense itsnewly repaired part, but while that replacement part has been integrated, the worry is still there. "I didn't want to cut," Deuce McAllister said a year after his second knee reconstruction, speaking of his reluctance to test the repaired knee. The problem often is solved by some random event. In McAllister's case, he had a linebacker heading at him in Week 6 of the season, cut out of instinct, and while rushing for the touchdown, realized that his knee was just fine. While a greater focus on proprioception in early rehab appears to be helping, this is still the most unpredictable part of rehabilitation.

The rehab moves out of the Training Room and/or clinic somewhere in the four- to five-month range, depending on how severe the injury was and how the rehab has progressed to this point. "It's important to remember that rehab is like fingerprints or snowflakes," said an NFL ATC. "It's never the same because the person isn't the same. The injury didn't happen the same way. I don't know, the barometric pressure is different. There's always something that changes and we have to be conscious of that, adjusting from week to week and moment to moment to make sure that the guy is getting back not getting set back." At this stage, functional work comes in and rehabilitation begins to look more like football and less like therapy. While some of the strength and agility work is the same, there are going to be variations based on position and body type. "Tom Brady doesn't have the same physical demands on his body as some defensive back or lineman. For a QB, you're looking at stability first and the ability to get through all his footwork. Defensive backs are the toughest for me," said the NFL rehab coordinator, "because they're Ginger [Rogers] and everyone else is Fred [Astaire]. They have to backpedal and swivel rather than just run, but they do have to run too."

That specificity is actually new. While some would say that it's common sense that specific activities would help a rehab process, it was only about 20 years ago that rehabilitation became sport-specific. The shift to position specificity has come in over the last dozen years, and the trend is accelerating. One NFL ATC told me that his staff actually preps for the possibility of rehab by testing all of their players for rehab style activities in order to establish a baseline. "It sounds like the Combine," he told me at the Combine. "All it is really is making sure we have some measureables to work with. I want to know the goal and what to actually get that guy back to 40 times, how they work through some of their drills, so forth. We just tested a bunch of linemen — both sides — with a machine that tells us how hard they pop someone with their hands. I wanted to try a full-on hit with the shoulder, but the guy with the machine said we'd break it!"

At some point, the athlete has progressed enough that the ATC, the rehab coordinator, and the allied professionals on the medical team feel comfortable handing him back to the team. "That's always the goal," said an NFL ATC, "but we spend so much time and effort on these guys through the process that we joke about it. I told one guy that I was sorry, but that we had to break up because his [leg] was better." One estimate by a group of NFL medical staffers that I spoke with in February was that an ACL rehab costs somewhere in the vicinity of 1,200 man-hours for the medical staff. Add that to their already overtaxed schedules and it's a wonder that anyone comes back at all.

Even as the athlete leaves the rehab process and returns to activity, he's not done with the medical staff. He'll be in daily for treatment before and after activity. He'll possibly need fitted for a brace or need extra protective taping prior to activity. He'll need constant monitoring to make sure that the rehabbed part is functioning normally and that there's no compensation taking place that will put another body part at risk, ruining all that time and work with another injury. Rehabilitation is never really over.

In the end, the best reward for the medical staff is seeing their player out on the field. The Pittsburgh medical staff felt every step that Hines Ward took in the Super Bowl was partly theirs; that's what motivates the trainers that give a large portion of their lives to the game. They look out on the field and where most see a player, they see a rebuilt knee that's going to lead to a renewed career. They turn hours of work into wins. Seeing how the sausage is made isn't glamorous, but rehab is one area of sports where there's a clear difference from team to team, doctor to doctor, and player to player. There's no area more ignored by fans, and perhaps no area more important.

Will Carroll

Rating the 32 Medical Staffs

The rules of the NFL make Athletic Trainers defenseless. When Jerry Jones told the press he was shocked that Marion Barber was unavailable a week after dislocating his toe, it may have made Jim Maurer's fantastic staff in Dallas look bad — but since Maurer's not allowed to talk to the media (and Jones is his boss), there was no defense.

While every staff in the league spends hours at work keeping players on the field through the assorted injuries that make up an NFL season, there was some miraculous work done last year to keep teams at the top of the standings. In Baltimore, Bill Tessendorf's crew may have saved the Ravens' season by ensuring the availability of players like Derrick Mason (separated shoulder) and Ed Reed (assorted injuries). Philly eked their way into the playoffs on the final day of the season, but it never would have happened without the work of Rick Burkholder to keep Brian Westbrook's knees and ankles functional.

At Football Outsiders, we're aware of just how huge a part injury — or the absence of injury — plays in a team's success, so it only makes sense for us to acknowledge the efforts of the better training staffs around the league by ranking their ability to keep players on the field over the last three seasons. Using the injury report, historical rates of player participation at each injury status, and our research into a player's role on the team, we summate our findings into a metric known as Adjusted Games Lost (AGL). For the purposes of these rankings, we measure AGL over a three-year period.

The team that rose to the top of the health standings has had a dramatic back-and-forth shift in their player availability over the past several years, one that correlates perfectly with their performance on the field. They were able to ride their health into the postseason in 2006, but came up one game short in 2008.

New York Jets

Head ATC: John Mellody
Adjusted Games Lost, 2008: 17.9 (1)
Three-Year Rank: 1

Trend: Unsustainably positive. Eric Mangini's famed for his manipulation of injury information — Alan Schwarz wrote a piece about it for the *New York Times* in December — but even considering the absence of Brett Favre on the injury report, what Mellody and his team did in 2008 was incredible. The Jets' 11 offensive starters made it through all 16 games, while the defensive starters missed a combined 11 games. Their work managing issues like Laveranues Coles' hamstring and Kris Jenkins' back was masterful and deserving of such a top spot. The odds of this team staying this healthy for back-to-back years — especially while learning a new defensive scheme from a head coach who likes a little reckless abandon — are extremely low, which is why we're saying it's unsustainably good work.

Tennessee Titans

Head ATC: Brad Brown
Adjusted Games Lost, 2008: 23.4 (3)
Three-Year Rank: 2

Trend: Plateau. Last year's healthiest group of starters made it through an extremely healthy first half (and went 8-0) before things began to break down in the second half. Injuries rise for all teams as the season goes along, but Tennessee suffered more than twice as many injuries in the second half as they did in the first. It started with Nick Harper's aggravation of a sprained ankle, but as the season went along, more players started to go down, culminating with the injuries to Albert Haynesworth and Kyle Vanden Bosch, as well as the unknown ailment that knocked Chris Johnson out of the team's season-ending playoff loss to Baltimore. That suggests fatigue as the main culprit, in case those asking for an 18-game schedule are reading. Similar issues are more likely to crop up in 2009 as the roles of players like Johnson and Jason Jones expand, while aging veterans like Harper and Kerry Collins remain in key roles.

Minnesota Vikings

Head ATC: Eric Sugarman
Adjusted Games Lost, 2008: 34.0 (8)
Three-Year Rank: 3

Trend: Rising. Masterful work on the separated shoulder of Jared Allen and hamstring of Adrian Peterson kept the team's top players on the field for 16 and 15 games, respectively. Furthermore, the most prominent injury affecting the team was E.J. Henderson's dislocated toes (yes, plural), which was a freak injury and out of the staff's control. The team actually shouldn't see as many traumatic events in 2009, which makes Minnesota the early favorite to be the healthiest team in the league.

Carolina Panthers

Head ATC: Ryan Vermillion
Adjusted Games Lost, 2008: 19.9 (2)
Three-Year Rank: 4

Trend: Strange. 14 of the 16 games missed by Carolina starters came on the offensive line, an odd figure. Those injuries ranged from an irregular heartbeat to a severe concussion, the latter of which was suffered by star left tackle Jordan Gross. Gross only missed a single game despite suffering a Grade-3 concussion, the same level as the one that nearly ended Trent Green's career during the opening game of the 2006 season. That Gross only missed a single week was shocking, for better or worse.

Kansas City Chiefs

Head ATC: David Price
Adjusted Games Lost, 2008: 47.3 (15)
Three-Year Rank: 5

Trend: Negative. Kansas City was one of the healthiest teams in the league in 2006 and 2007, but began to see veterans like Damon Huard, Donnie Edwards, and Patrick Surtain go down last year as they were extended beyond the limits of what their bodies can handle at their respective ages. Of course, it's hard to spot a quarterback's playing time, but without the depth around them to properly let them get off the field for a few downs each game, it's more likely for guys like Edwards or Surtain to get hurt. While Scott Pioli will further a youth movement here, the implementation of two new schemes and the arrival of a bunch of new players with imperfect technique should result in a steady stream of injuries. The injury report in Kansas City is going to be an interesting story this year.

Houston Texans

Head ATC: Geoff Kaplan
Adjusted Games Lost, 2008: 43.1 (14)
Three-Year Rank: 6

Trend: Neutral. The organization did a remarkable job of keeping their players healthy once the season began. Most of their AGL came on season-ending injuries to Fred Weary (preseason) and C.C. Brown (Week 4), the latter of which may have been addition by subtraction. The team deserves credit for keeping an undersized offensive line healthy (besides Weary). One concern is Matt Schaub; he's missed five games in each of his two seasons as the Houston starting quarterback with assorted maladies, including a separated shoulder and a torn ACL.

San Francisco 49ers

Head ATC: Jeff Ferguson
Adjusted Games Lost, 2008: 30.3 (6)
Three-Year Rank: 7

Trend: Slightly positive. Their biggest issue was with Jonas Jennings, who reportedly sprained his shoulder in Week 3, spent six weeks inactive, and then had season-ending surgery when it was clear he wasn't going to be able to come back. Jennings' release in the offseason is a positive move, as the troubled tackle made it to more than five games only once over his four years by the Bay. The defense only missed a total of four starts, which isn't likely to happen again.

San Diego Chargers

Head ATC: James Collins
Adjusted Games Lost, 2008: 34.7 (9)
Three-Year Rank: 8

Trend: Positive. The very public deliberations regarding Shawne Merriman's injury wasn't the medical staff's fault; Merriman was simply not listening to them. The staff might have identified Merriman's torn LCL and PCL earlier in his rehab from offseason cartilage surgery, but once it was found, both they and the four doctors Merriman went to in order to try and find an option that didn't involve season-ending surgery agreed that it was necessary to keep him off the field. Their biggest task this year will be monitoring Merriman's knee and protecting it from its owner, especially considering that "Lights Out" is in a contract year.

Green Bay Packers

Head ATC: T. Pepper Burruss
Adjusted Games Lost, 2008: 49.6 (17)
Three-Year Rank: 9

Trend: Negative. Green Bay's defense fell apart in 2008, particularly in the secondary, where the team spent a fair amount of the season without half its starters. We'd normally expect them to be healthier, but the move to a 3-4 puts them all in new situations with different responsibilities.

Dallas Cowboys

Head ATC: Jim Maurer
Adjusted Games Lost, 2008: 53.3 (18)
Three-Year Rank: 10

Trend: Negative. The other shoe had to fall eventually, and that was 2008; the staff still did remarkable work keeping players like Jason Witten (separated shoulder, fractured rib, and sprained ankle) on the field while getting Tony Romo back under center as quickly as possible in an attempt to save Dallas' season. Nonetheless, a misdiagnosis of Terence Newman's sports hernia in the preseason cost him a large part of the year, and a cascade injury suffered by Felix Jones during his rehab from a partially torn hamstring cost them their most dynamic offensive weapon and return man over the final few games of the season.

Pittsburgh Steelers

Head ATC: John Norwig
Adjusted Games Lost, 2008: 54.2 (19)
Three-Year Rank: 11

Trend: Negative. Their injury rate nearly doubled relative to 2006 and 2007, with manageable issues like Brett Keisel's calf strain and Marvel Smith's back spasms growing into significant problems. All three of their starters up front missed time for the first time since 1999.

Atlanta Falcons

Head ATC: Ron Medlin
Adjusted Games Lost, 2008: 28.7 (5)
Three-Year Rank: 12

Trend: Positive. Outside of a couple players rested in Week 17, the only starters to miss time were Sam Baker and Ben Hartsock. That's remarkable, and the work done in keeping elder statesmen like Grady Jackson and Todd Weiner (Baker's replacement) healthy through knee issues is what will stick, even if the flukishly-low injury rate won't.

New York Giants

Head ATC: Ronnie Barnes
Adjusted Games Lost, 2008: 35.9 (10)
Three-Year Rank: 13

Trend: Positive. Their work would look even better had the team not placed Osi Umenyiora on injured reserve prematurely; Umenyiora's rehab from a torn meniscus went so well that he could've made it back into the rotation at defensive end by the playoffs. Now that Brandon Jacobs is locked up with a long-term deal, carefully monitoring and maintaining his knee is doubly important.

Philadelphia Eagles

Head ATC: Rick Burkholder
Adjusted Games Lost, 2008: 39.0 (12)
Three-Year Rank: 14

Trend: Slightly negative. Obviously, Westbrook's sprained ankle (suffered under somewhat murky circumstances) puts them behind the eight-ball to start the season, and they'll be working with an injury-prone quarterback and offensive line to go with a defense that was extraordinarily healthy last year. A huge part of our projected decline in their performance is an expected increase in injury — it will be on Burkholder and his team to minimize many potential flashpoints for another year.

Arizona Cardinals

Head ATC: Tom Reed
Adjusted Games Lost, 2008: 37.8 (11)
Three-Year Rank: 15
Trend: Positive. The Arizona medical staff was most prominently discussed in relation to Anquan Boldin and his recovery from the fractured sinuses he suffered against the Jets, but their work on Boldin's shoulder later in the season was just as notable, since it allowed him to appear in three of the Cardinals' four playoff games. They also did better work than that AGL number indicates, since the Cardinals gave more than one player an extra week off during their coast into the playoffs over the last few weeks of the season.

Oakland Raiders

Head ATC: Rod Martin
Adjusted Games Lost, 2008: 54.3 (20)
Three-Year Rank: 16

Trend: Negative. Their AGL has risen from 29.8 in 2006 to 43.4 in 2007 and then 54.3 last year, although they should be commended for doing good preventative work on the turf toe of Darren McFadden. To an extent, the medical staff was limited by the players who were brought in — there's not much any staff could do to keep Javon Walker healthy. We feel for them, but the numbers are overwhelmingly negative.

Washington Redskins

Head ATC: John Burrell
Adjusted Games Lost, 2008: 55.0 (21)
Three-Year Rank: 17

Trend: Neutral. They've ranked between 21st and 23rd each of the last three seasons, so they're absolutely stagnant in slightly below-average performance. They had to deal with a rarely-seen issue in Jason Taylor's compartmental syndrome, potentially saving Taylor's life by identifying the problem and insisting on immediate surgery. (This rare condition is a reaction to trauma, where the body traps fluid underneath the fascia. Swelling can lead to pain, tissue and nerve damage, and even necrosis, although it is easily corrected by releasing the pressure with small incisions.) Washington will miss Director of Sports Medicine Bubba Tyer, a 37-year veteran of the Redskins organization who came out of retirement with Joe Gibbs in 2004, but decided to call it quits for a second time in January.

Buffalo Bills

Head ATC: Bud Carpenter
Adjusted Games Lost, 2008: 48.2 (16)
Three-Year Rank: 18

Trend: Neutral. Angelo Crowell was placed on IR after a preseason knee scope, but it wasn't for purely medical reasons. With the Bills strapped for cash, it would be no surprise if they put Crowell on IR to get an insurance payout to make up the $1.725 million in salary they owed him. They cut Troy Vincent in a similarly dubious fashion in 2006. While the decision to place Crowell on IR was almost assuredly not the decision of the Bills' medical staff, the injury is added to their totals anyway. Take that figure away and the Bills are at an above-average total of 32.2, although the players who got hurt (Aaron Schobel, Donte Whitmer, Marshawn Lynch, Jason Peters) were arguably also the team's best players.

Miami Dolphins

Head ATC: Kevin O'Neill
Adjusted Games Lost, 2008: 25.7 (4)
Three-Year Rank: 19

Trend: Extremely positive. Tony Sparano willfully ignored the injury report last year, listing only seven players as Probable all season. AGL looks primarily at players missing games, though, and the Dolphins didn't have many of them, a Bill Parcells trademark; his teams almost always rank amongst league's best with regards to health. Miami only had four starters miss time last year, and they were almost exclusively from traumatic incidents (Greg Camarillo's torn ACL, Justin Smiley's broken ankle and fibula); they'll have more players miss time due to wear-and-tear in 2009, regardless of whether Sparano lists them on the injury report or not.

New Orleans Saints

Head ATC: Scottie Patton
Adjusted Games Lost, 2008: 57.4 (22)
Three-Year Rank: 20

Trend: Slightly negative. They had some trouble with the knee injuries of Reggie Bush and Marques Colston, with the latter quietly undergoing microfracture surgery this offseason. They were also unable to get Deuce McAllister back to his previous level of performance, although that has something to do with McAllister being 30. The secondary will be healthier; it's hard to imagine that they'll have seven different players miss time again.

New England Patriots

Head ATC: Jim Whalen
Adjusted Games Lost, 2008: 78.5 (28)
Three-Year Rank: 21

Trend: Negative. As you might suspect, you need to be pretty healthy to go 16-0, and while we expected them to suffer more injuries in 2008, no one could've expected Tom Brady to go down before halftime of Week 1. Beyond that, it was roughly your standard-issue Belichick-era Patriots season of injuries; Laurence Maroney went down, the secondary was injury-riddled, and the aging linebackers couldn't make it through a full season without a couple of breakdowns.

Tampa Bay Buccaneers

Head ATC: Todd Toriscelli
Adjusted Games Lost, 2008: 42.8 (13)
Three-Year Rank: 22

Trend: Positive. That figure's an improvement from their mid-twenties ranks from 2006 and 2007; they've also gotten rid of most of their veterans, including injury-prone players like Jeff Garcia and Joey Galloway. Expecting little out of Cadillac Williams when it comes to health is an added bonus.

Seattle Seahawks

Head ATC: Sam Ramsden
Adjusted Games Lost, 2008: 78.9 (29)
Three-Year Rank: 23

Trend: Negative. What are the odds that a team's top five options at wide receiver would go down with injuries at once? It's hard to say, but the odds of a starting receiver being unavailable for a game are about 11.7 percent. The odds of that happening to five receivers at once are in the range of 0.0023 percent, or one in 43,478.

Chicago Bears

Head ATC: Tim Bream
Adjusted Games Lost, 2008: 33.8 (7)
Three-Year Rank: 24

Trend: Positive. Obviously, the big concern is keeping Tommie Harris healthy on the interior; although he's arguably the team's best pass rusher (and creates the pass rush by occupying two men), the medical staff could get help from Lovie Smith and company by giving Harris some snaps off on obvious passing downs. You have to wonder what the communication is like within the organization after Jerry Angelo selected Chris Williams in the first round of the 2008 draft despite the presence of an existing back injury.

Detroit Lions

Head ATC: Al Bellamy
Adjusted Games Lost, 2008: 104.9 (31)
Three-Year Rank: 25

Trend: Negative. Much like a lot had to go right to allow the Patriots to go 16-0, a lot had to go wrong on the injury front for the Lions to go 0-16. No team had more injuries on the defensive side of the ball than Detroit did a year ago; they had all four of their starting defensive linemen and four of their top six defensive backs miss time with injuries. They also won't go down to their fourth-string quarterback in 2009.

Jacksonville Jaguars

Head ATC: Michael Ryan
Adjusted Games Lost, 2008: 64.2 (23)
Three-Year Rank: 26

Trend: Neutral. Jacksonville's been around this range each of the last three years, but the makeup was different in 2008; they had more injuries on the offensive line than any team in football, with starters Maurice Williams and Vince Manuwai each missing the final 15 games of the season. The rest of the team was relatively healthy, so while the offensive line might be healthier, there's reason to think the rest of the team will miss more time than they did a year ago.

St. Louis Rams

Head ATC: Jim Anderson
Adjusted Games Lost, 2008: 80.3 (30)
Three-Year Rank: 27

Trend: Negative with extreme prejudice. The days when the Rams were among the healthiest teams in football — 2006 — seem so long ago. Of particular concern is the health of Steven Jackson — the team's star back has missed four games in consecutive seasons. The team had five different starters suffer season-ending injuries in the first six weeks of the season; that's unlucky, and it's hard to envision it happening again. If any team's likely to see the sort of drastic reversal of injury fortune that the Falcons and Dolphins enjoyed last year, it's the Rams.

Denver Broncos

Head ATC: Steve Antonopulus
Adjusted Games Lost, 2008: 75.4 (26)
Three-Year Rank: 28

Trend: Negative. Denver's been on a steady decline the last three seasons; their issues in 2008 were driven by running back, where they had the most injuries at the position of any team in our database. Obviously, no team has that sort of injury redundancy, and that sort of absurd injury stack doesn't happen consistently. This would normally point to an improvement in the Broncos' AGL, but with a scheme change up front, who knows? Their rushing DVOA already can't go much higher; it was number one last year despite all the running back injuries because the offensive line stayed completely healthy.

Baltimore Ravens

Head ATC: Bill Tessendorf
Adjusted Games Lost, 2008: 77.3 (27)
Three-Year Rank: 29

Trend: Negative. The most remarkable part about the Ravens' playoff run was that it came with such injury issues; at one point, the team was down two starting defensive linemen and three of their four starters in the secondary, but the play of studs like Ed Reed and Haloti Ngata allowed Baltimore to maintain their elite level of defense. This number would be even higher if we considered Kyle Boller, who missed the whole season, the "starter" at quarterback.

Indianapolis Colts

Head ATC: Hunter Smith
Adjusted Games Lost, 2008: 71.4 (24)
Three-Year Rank: 30

Trend: Neutral. No, he isn't leaving for Washington with the punter Hunter Smith, but the Colts' Head ATC has had to put up with a consistently high level of injuries during the Bill Polian era. It's the accepted downside to a draft philosophy which doesn't shy away from taking smaller players. Expect that to continue for a year or two more, as the team slowly starts shifting away from the Cover-2. Smith left the team after a long stay, one of two ATC changes made in the NFL; he'll be replaced by Dave Hammer.

Cleveland Browns

Head ATC: Marty Lauzon
Adjusted Games Lost, 2008: 74.5 (25)
Three-Year Rank: 31

Trend: Negative. The 2004 and 2006 Browns were the most-injured teams in football, so only finishing 25th out of 32 is getting off relatively easy. Their only above-average year of health was 2007 — it's no coincidence that it was their only year of success as a team. Mangini will artificially drop their AGL some with injury report shenanigans, but as anyone who has monitored the continuing health issues related to this organization knows, something is broken here and has been for a long time. Lauzon was replaced by Joe Sheehan, who comes to the Browns from the University of Arkansas. It's an odd path to the top medical job and one that bears watching.

Cincinnati Bengals

Head ATC: Paul Sparling
Adjusted Games Lost, 2009: 108.1 (32)
Three-Year Rank: 32

Trend: Negative. The Bengals were two offensive linemen, one defensive lineman, and one linebacker short of having a full team of starters that missed time in 2008. That's astounding. Losing Carson Palmer hurt, obviously, but it's hard to imagine him making the difference given the accumulation of injuries this team suffered. The good news? The last team to suffer anywhere near this many injuries was the 1998 Redskins (91.3 AGL); they went 6-10 in 1998, but improved to 13-3 in 1999.

Bill Barnwell and Will Carroll

Top 25 Prospects

efining a "prospect" in football terms is very different from prospects in baseball, where cottage industries and careers are seemingly staked on the compilation of top prospect lists. While college baseball players spend their days in relative obscurity, college football is one of the most popular spectator sports on the planet. We don't need to tell you about Matthew Stafford or Michael Crabtree; they're already prominent names, and paid as such.

Instead, our Top 25 Prospects list looks to highlight the players you haven't heard of yet. It's a mix of backups who have shown flashes of brilliance in situational play and young players who are an injury or an opportunity away from potentially busting out on the league. As with baseball prospect lists, there's a fair amount of projection that comes into play, and we consider statistics as well as measurables.

Our first two prospect lists yielded a mix of hits and misses. In the past, we've highlighted players like Cortland Finnegan, Marion Barber, Brandon Marshall, and Stacy Andrews as players with serious potential. On the other hand, we've called attention to guys like Junior Glymph, Marques Hagans, and James Marten. Hey, no one's perfect.

To be considered for our top prospects list, players have to meet the following criteria:
- Drafted or signed between 2006 and 2008.
- Drafted in rounds three through seven, or undrafted.
- Fewer than five career games started.
- Still on either a free agent contract or their original contract.

Our number one prospect this year managed to make it through the entire 2006 draft without being selected, and only has 18 career catches. Of course, it's what he's done with those 18 catches — and what he could do on the next 100 — that make him our top prospect.

1. Miles Austin, WR, Cowboys
Austin got our attention with a 33.8% DVOA in 2007 and 48.7% DVOA in 2008; apparently, it also got the Cowboys' attention, since they released Terrell Owens and didn't bring in any veterans at wideout, opening up a starting spot for Austin across from Roy Williams. An undrafted free agent in 2006 out of Monmouth, the 6-foot-3 Austin was a clump of clay that the Dallas coaching staff molded. They have applied enough technique to allow Austin to take advantage of his prototypical size and speed. The only thing holding Austin back from emerging on the league as a receiver with Pro Bowl potential is a hamstring issue; he'll need to heal up before training camp to keep Patrick Crayton in the slot. There's some boom-or-bust here, but there are few players on this list who could potentially become one of the best players in football at their position. Austin's not there yet, but he has that sort of ability.

2. Jacob Ford, DE, Titans
Ford spent his rookie year with the Titans on IR after tearing his Achilles in training camp; in his "second year," though, Ford had a huge impact as a pass rusher. Ford picked up seven sacks over the final eight games of the year, despite starting only three times. He was also stout against the run, putting up the best Stop Rate of any Titans end. He should be able to beat out Jevon Kearse and Dave Ball across from Kyle Vanden Bosch, and with attention focused on KVB, Ford has double-digit sack potential.

3. Jerious Norwood, RB, Falcons
Norwood was our number one prospect in both 2007 and 2008, but he falls off the top of this list in his final year of eligibility because of a 2008 that didn't meet the standards of his first two seasons. Last year, Norwood was merely a very good change-of-pace back as opposed to an elite one. It's not a sign that he was overhyped; the variance between his 2007 and 2008 is wholly reasonable for a player of his talent. If Michael Turner succumbs to the Curse of 370, Norwood's role should expand. That comes just in time for him to become a free agent (assuming the CBA is renewed), creating an

opportunity for him to carve out a bigger chunk of the carries — and the salary cap — elsewhere.

4. Cliff Avril, DE, Lions

Much like Ford, Avril was a dynamic pass rusher at the end of the season; unlike Ford, though, Avril did so on a terrible team, which meant fewer pass attempts for him to even get a chance to sack the quarterback on. The Lions will be better this year, and Avril will most likely be a starter from Day One. The increase in opposition pass attempts and the arrival of Jim Schwartz gives us high hopes for Avril next year — he could really be something special.

5. William Gay, CB, Steelers

The Steelers' dime back was pushed into service by injuries to Bryant McFadden and DeShea Townsend, but he didn't look like a fill-in; he led the league in Adjusted Yards per Pass and had the fourth-best Success Rate amongst corners that were targeted more than 40 times. That was promising enough for Pittsburgh to let McFadden head to Arizona in free agency; Gay's expected to start across from Ike Taylor, ensuring his departure from this list next year.

6. Jerome Harrison, RB, Browns

Truthfully, it's ridiculous that Harrison's a "prospect" and not the Browns' starting running back. While Jamal Lewis has plodded his way to 4.0 yards per carry over the past two years, Harrison's averaged an eye-popping 6.8 yards each time he's been handed the ball. He's also a superior receiver out of the backfield. Harrison is slightly undersized at 5-foot-9 and 195 pounds, but his Speed Score is 100.7, indicating that he has the athletic ability to play at this level. Even if he doesn't become the starter this year, he could play the same role for Eric Mangini's Browns that Leon Washington played for Mangini's Jets teams — and if our KUBIAK projection system is correct about a Lewis breakdown, Harrison is one of the top fantasy sleepers out there.

7. Orlando Scandrick, CB, Cowboys

Scandrick often looked like the best corner the Cowboys had last year, which was impressive when you consider that he was playing behind three first-round picks and Anthony Henry, who's been a starting corner in the league since 2002. Even fifth on the depth chart, Scandrick was on the field enough to get ranked in our game charting stats, and he finished in the top 20 for both Success Rate and Adjusted Yards per Pass. Scandrick is undersized, but he's smooth in and out of cuts and has a nice habit of getting his fingers on the ball at the last possible second to knock it away. If he's this good again next year, it won't matter what round he was drafted in.

8. Josh Sitton, G, Packers

Sitton actually won a starting job in training camp last year, but sprained his knee and was never 100 percent the rest of the way. He's fully healed now, and with the Packers moving to a man blocking scheme, they'll require more heft up front; Sitton's 320-pound frame makes him the favorite to win the job at right guard.

9. Tashard Choice, RB, Cowboys

No, it's not just hype; the Cowboys really do have three candidates worthy enough to appear in our top ten. Choice only got his opportunity after Marion Barber and Felix Jones both went down with injuries, but he showed off a skill set similar to Barber's with, arguably, superior receiving skills out of the backfield. He doesn't "run nasty" like Barber does, nor does he have the blazing speed and acceleration of Jones, but he's simply an above-average running back who will allow the Cowboys to keep Barber fresh.

10. Charles Johnson, DE, Panthers

Johnson is another one of those players who was an absolute monster in limited time, accruing six sacks and a 90 percent Stop Rate subbing in for Tyler Brayton. He'll suffer some if Julius Peppers doesn't return, but the possibility also exists for Johnson to emerge as a star by nabbing some of Peppers' playing time.

11. Harry Douglas, WR, Falcons

The brash Louisville product backed up his words as a rookie, scoring touchdowns as a rusher, receiver, and punt returner. He showed enough promise in that versatility to get him onto this list, but we could have said the same thing about Brad Smith two years ago, and he never improved. That's not to say that the same thing will happen to Douglas; it's just a reminder that we'll know a lot more about his potential a year from now.

12. Stephen Nicholas, LB, Falcons

Continuing the Falcons theme, Nicholas is a fantastic athlete and one of the few holdovers from the old regime that Mike Smith and Thomas Dimitroff actually like. Nicholas won't pick up huge statistics as the Falcons' strongside linebacker, but he's stout against the run and will likely be a starting two-down linebacker from Week 1 on.

13. Jamaal Charles, RB, Chiefs

We were sanguine on Charles' chances of succeeding in the NFL thanks to his 108.7 Speed Score coming out of Texas, but concerned about his chances behind a rebuilding Kansas City offensive line and with Larry Johnson in front of him. Instead, Charles put up a 12.5% rushing DVOA for a team that didn't have another back put up anything better than a -12.7% rushing DVOA. He's also an effective receiver out of the backfield, which makes him a better fit for Todd Haley's spread shotgun offense. His role in 2009 starts as third-down back and, depending on Larry Johnson's mood, could end as unquestioned starter.

14. Josh Morgan, WR, 49ers

Morgan had a whirlwind season, starting with a staph infection that cost him 15 pounds. His role in the offense expanded as the season went along, and after accruing 86 yards and a touchdown in Week 7 against the Giants, he got his first start against the Seahawks a week later, but was pulled from the game by debuting head coach Mike Singletary after dropping the first slant thrown to him. (Way to build up a guy's confidence.) He came back against the Cardinals following the team's bye and scored another touchdown, but went down with a groin injury and missed the better part of five games before contributing in the 49ers' final two games of the year. If he can stay healthy and on Singletary's good side, he's a great athlete who has serious upside as the flanker across from Michael Crabtree in 2009.

15/16. Chansi Stuckey/David Clowney, WR, Jets

We tried mashing their names up, but it doesn't work. Chansid Clowey? Davisi Stuney? Stuckey and Clowney should never become a celebrity couple, but they're joined on this list because only one will have the opportunity to break out next year as the starter across from Jerricho Cotchery. Clowney's a speed demon, but he drops too many passes; Stuckey is more of the sure-and-steady type. We could see Stuckey starting as the split end and Clowney working out of the slot, roles that would fit each player well.

17. Pierre Woods, LB, Patriots

Plenty of young linebackers have come and gone through New England under Bill Belichick, but very few have stuck around on the fringes of the roster for several seasons with the hopes that they'd eventually turn into a starter. Woods is one, and it appears that he'll have the opportunity to do just that in 2009. After the Patriots chose to pass on Jason Taylor and Greg Ellis in free agency, Woods (undrafted out of Michigan in 2006) will need to beat out only 2008 third-round pick Shawn Crable for a starting gig as right outside linebacker.

18. Pierre Garcon, WR, Colts

The back-to-back Pierres on this list are a coincidence, we swear. We were high on Garcon coming out of Division III Mount Union as a great blocker with NFL-caliber hands, and the Colts share our enthusiasm; the organization absolutely loves him, making him the favorite for the team's third receiver job. He even looked good in Week 17 against the Titans. From D-III to an injury away from starting in one of the league's best offenses in two years? Not bad.

19. Martin Rucker, TE, Browns

Rucker was buried behind Kellen Winslow as a fourth-round rookie, but was an effective receiver at Missouri. He'll have to compete with Steve Heiden and Robert Royal for time, but Heiden's coming off of knee surgery and is likely to see the PUP list, while Robert Royal is Robert Royal. Rucker has the hands to have an impact in the passing game, making him a sleeper in deep fantasy leagues — particularly dynasty leagues.

20. Michael Bush, RB, Raiders

After missing the better part of two years with a broken leg, Bush had the best year of the Raiders' three-headed hydra at halfback, culminating in the 177-yard, two-touchdown upset of the Buccaneers in Week 17 that pushed Philly into the playoffs. For a 243-pound back, he showed surprising acceleration and big-play ability; he should see a relatively similar workload in 2009, losing some carries to Darren McFadden, but making up for it by taking some from Justin Fargas. He should, at the very least, be a good goal-line back.

21. Chauncey Washington, RB, Jaguars

If you're worried about Maurice Jones-Drew's viability as the primary back, you're probably interested in Washington, who profiles as MJD's backup and change of pace. At 224 pounds, he has the muscle to be an effective North-South runner; we say muscle and not bulk because of the 25 pounds of fat Washington dropped before his senior year at USC in 2007. He has serious potential as a touchdown vulture.

22. Quintin Demps, S, Eagles

Admittedly, our last memories of Demps are of his ridiculous late hit on Kurt Warner during the NFC Championship Game, but he showed enough promise to usurp Sean Considine's playing time as the season went along. He'll need to beat out Sean Jones for a starting job, but even if he loses the race, Jones' propensity for injury makes Demps the favorite to be the starter by the end of 2009.

23. Tavares Gooden, LB, Ravens

A member of Miami's seminal hip-hop heroes Seventh Floor Crew (T-Good, natch), Gooden showed flashes of brilliance in the four games he played as a rookie. The Ravens think enough of his athleticism to stick him inside and put him next to Ray Lewis as Bart Scott's replacement. It's a move that fits Gooden's strengths; he's not great at attacking the line of scrimmage, but he's an effective sideline-to-sideline linebacker. Gooden is a big-time sleeper if you play in an IDP fantasy league.

24. Dan Federkeil, G, Colts

The Colts' line went through many a backup lineman last year, but by the end of the year, it was Federkeil who was replacing an injured Mike Pollak at right guard. At 290 pounds, the Canadian national (undrafted out of the University of Calgary in 2006) wouldn't fit on a power-blocking line, but the Colts' scheme fits him perfectly. He'll have to hope for an injury again this year to get playing time (and avoid his concussion issues in the process), but with the Colts, injury is to be expected.

25. Colt Brennan, QB, Redskins

Brennan was a bit of a punchline after his awful Sugar Bowl against Georgia, but the sixth-round pick looked fantastic in the preseason; he led all rookies in completion percentage, quarterback rating and passing yards, and threw three touchdowns without an interception. He's expected to pass Todd Collins and move into the Redskins' backup job during training camp, and if Jason Campbell gets benched or injured, Brennan could have a job open up for him in a West Coast offense that fits his skill set.

Honorable Mention

Zackary Bowman, CB/S, Bears
Ahmad Bradshaw, RB, Giants
Shawn Crable, LB, Patriots
Mike Devito, DE/DT, Jets
Early Doucet, WR, Cardinals
Justin Forsett, RB, Seahawks
Jason Shirley, DT, Bengals
Jonathan Wilhite, CB, Patriots

Bill Barnwell

Statistical Appendix A: Fantasy Projections

Here are the top 240 players according to the KUBIAK projection system, ranked by projected fantasy value (**FANT**) in 2009. We've used the following generic scoring system:

• 1 point for each 10 yards rushing, 10 yards receiving, or 20 yards passing

• 6 points for each rushing or receiving TD, 4 points for each passing TD

• -2 points for each interception or fumble lost

• 1 point for each extra point, 3 points for each field goal

• Team defense: 2 points for a fumble recovery, interception, or safety, 1 point for a sack, and 6 points for a touchdown.

These totals are then adjusted based on each player's listed **Risk** for 2009:

• Green: Standard risk, no change

• Yellow: Higher than normal risk, value dropped by 5 percent

• Red: Highest risk, value dropped by 10 percent

• Blue: Significantly lower than normal risk, value increased by 5 percent

Note that fantasy totals may not exactly equal these calculations, because each touchdown projection is not necessarily a round number. (For example, a quarterback listed with 2 rushing touchdowns may actually be projected with 2.4 rushing touchdowns, which will add 14 fantasy points to the player's total rather than 12.) Fantasy value does not include adjustments for week-to-week consistency.

Players are ranked in order based on marginal value of each player, the idea that you draft based on how many more points a player will score compared to the worst starting player at that position, not how many points a player scores overall. The ranks in this table are based on a 12-team league that starts 1 QB, 2 RB, 2 WR, 1 FLEX (RB/WR), 1 TE, 1 K, and 1 DEF. The rankings also include half value for the first running back on the bench, and reduce the value of kickers and defenses to reflect the general drafting habits of fantasy football players. We urge you to draft using common sense, not a strict reading of these rankings.

A customizable spreadsheet featuring these projections is also available at FootballOutsiders.com for a $20 fee. This spreadsheet is updated based on injuries and changing forecasts of playing time during the preseason, and also has a version which includes individual defensive players.

Rk	Player	Team	Bye	Pos	PaYd	PaTD	INT	Ru	RuYd	RuTD	Rec	RcYd	RcTD	Fum	XP	FG	Fant	Risk
1	Maurice Jones-Drew	JAC	7	RB	0	0	0	303	1421	14	55	457	3	1	0	0	258	Red
2	Adrian Peterson	MIN	9	RB	0	0	0	373	1837	12	23	189	1	3	0	0	242	Red
3	Matt Forte	CHI	5	RB	0	0	0	322	1272	14	68	417	2	2	0	0	236	Red
4	Steven Jackson	STL	9	RB	0	0	0	265	1298	11	48	389	2	1	0	0	231	Yellow
5	LaDainian Tomlinson	SD	5	RB	20	1	0	233	893	13	59	513	1	1	0	0	227	Green
6	Randy Moss	NE	8	WR	0	0	0	7	33	0	95	1391	13	1	0	0	211	Yellow
7	Steve Slaton	HOU	10	RB	0	0	0	285	1214	8	55	405	3	2	0	0	210	Yellow
8	Drew Brees	NO	5	QB	4248	33	11	24	51	0	0	0	0	4	0	0	323	Green
9	Tom Brady	NE	8	QB	4040	34	9	33	68	1	0	0	0	4	0	0	323	Green
10	Brandon Jacobs	NYG	10	RB	0	0	0	292	1417	10	10	48	0	2	0	0	201	Green
11	Andre Johnson	HOU	10	WR	0	0	0	2	14	0	93	1336	11	1	0	0	201	Green
12	Peyton Manning	IND	6	QB	4045	31	10	21	37	1	0	0	0	2	0	0	314	Green
13	Frank Gore	SF	6	RB	0	0	0	246	1129	7	45	356	2	2	0	0	200	Green
14	Larry Fitzgerald	ARI	4	WR	0	0	0	0	0	0	100	1285	11	1	0	0	191	Green
15	Julius Jones	SEA	7	RB	0	0	0	232	1023	11	31	219	3	1	0	0	192	Yellow
16	Chris Johnson	TEN	7	RB	0	0	0	268	1225	8	37	304	1	2	0	0	191	Yellow

Rk	Player	Team	Bye	Pos	PaYd	PaTD	INT	Ru	RuYd	RuTD	Rec	RcYd	RcTD	Fum	XP	FG	Fant	Risk
17	Marion Barber	DAL	6	RB	0	0	0	217	883	8	52	468	2	1	0	0	190	Green
18	DeAngelo Williams	CAR	4	RB	0	0	0	225	1121	11	19	114	0	2	0	0	187	Green
19	Ronnie Brown	MIA	6	RB	21	0	0	238	1131	7	38	260	1	2	0	0	187	Green
20	Brian Westbrook	PHI	4	RB	0	0	0	205	904	6	66	562	4	1	0	0	185	Red
21	Philip Rivers	SD	5	QB	3724	31	10	25	48	1	0	0	0	2	0	0	297	Green
22	Clinton Portis	WAS	8	RB	10	0	0	282	1218	7	21	144	0	1	0	0	179	Green
23	Reggie Wayne	IND	6	WR	0	0	0	0	0	0	92	1153	10	1	0	0	175	Green
24	Marques Colston	NO	5	WR	0	0	0	2	11	0	85	1261	11	1	0	0	174	Red
25	Greg Jennings	GB	5	WR	0	0	0	2	13	0	81	1245	10	0	0	0	174	Yellow
26	Calvin Johnson	DET	7	WR	0	0	0	3	18	0	69	1092	12	0	0	0	173	Yellow
27	Dwayne Bowe	KC	8	WR	0	0	0	0	0	0	84	1194	10	1	0	0	172	Yellow
28	Knowshon Moreno	DEN	7	RB	0	0	0	225	1025	10	39	303	0	1	0	0	172	Red
29	Vincent Jackson	SD	5	WR	0	0	0	2	14	0	68	1040	10	0	0	0	165	Green
30	Steve Smith	CAR	4	WR	0	0	0	9	39	0	74	1057	9	0	0	0	166	Green
31	Roddy White	ATL	4	WR	0	0	0	0	0	0	84	1183	8	1	0	0	163	Green
32	Pierre Thomas	NO	5	RB	0	0	0	196	882	8	63	428	2	3	0	0	164	Red
33	Michael Turner	ATL	4	RB	0	0	0	291	1183	10	10	82	0	2	0	0	163	Red
34	Anthony Gonzalez	IND	6	WR	0	0	0	0	0	0	74	1183	9	0	0	0	161	Yellow
35	Aaron Rodgers	GB	5	QB	3696	24	13	48	173	3	0	0	0	6	0	0	275	Green
36	Kevin Smith	DET	7	RB	0	0	0	254	1064	9	30	200	0	1	0	0	161	Red
37	Donovan McNabb	PHI	4	QB	3761	21	8	50	174	2	0	0	0	6	0	0	273	Green
38	LenDale White	TEN	7	RB	0	0	0	201	875	13	6	36	1	2	0	0	160	Yellow
39	Thomas Jones	NYJ	9	RB	0	0	0	219	904	8	25	157	1	1	0	0	159	Green
40	Chad Johnson	CIN	8	WR	0	0	0	2	12	0	75	1046	10	0	0	0	157	Yellow
41	T.J. Houshmandzadeh	SEA	7	WR	0	0	0	3	22	0	87	1004	9	1	0	0	156	Green
42	Felix Jones	DAL	6	RB	0	0	0	151	732	5	52	556	1	2	0	0	157	Yellow
43	Brandon Marshall	DEN	7	WR	0	0	0	3	48	0	86	1024	10	1	0	0	157	Yellow
44	Antonio Gates	SD	5	TE	0	0	0	0	0	0	70	842	9	0	0	0	137	Green
45	Wes Welker	NE	8	WR	0	0	0	5	38	0	107	1113	8	1	0	0	155	Yellow
46	Hines Ward	PIT	8	WR	0	0	0	2	12	0	91	1127	8	1	0	0	152	Yellow
47	Ben Roethlisberger	PIT	8	QB	3639	25	12	29	87	1	0	0	0	4	0	0	265	Green
48	Anquan Boldin	ARI	4	WR	10	0	0	8	61	0	90	1112	7	1	0	0	152	Yellow
49	Donnie Avery	STL	9	WR	0	0	0	6	28	0	79	1081	10	1	0	0	151	Red
50	Derrick Mason	BAL	7	WR	0	0	0	0	0	0	85	1022	8	1	0	0	149	Green
51	Torry Holt	JAC	7	WR	0	0	0	3	22	0	81	1119	7	1	0	0	149	Yellow
52	Ryan Grant	GB	5	RB	0	0	0	270	1014	9	18	139	0	2	0	0	149	Red
53	Roy Williams	DAL	6	WR	0	0	0	2	12	0	67	982	9	0	0	0	146	Yellow
54	Jason Witten	DAL	6	TE	0	0	0	0	0	0	82	994	5	0	0	0	128	Green
55	Matt Hasselbeck	SEA	7	QB	3857	20	9	36	91	0	0	0	0	3	0	0	259	Green
56	Cedric Benson	CIN	8	RB	0	0	0	227	839	3	41	318	2	1	0	0	146	Green
57	Jonathan Stewart	CAR	4	RB	0	0	0	186	975	10	12	59	0	1	0	0	145	Red
58	Larry Johnson	KC	8	RB	0	0	0	214	946	10	19	83	0	2	0	0	144	Red
59	Domenik Hixon	NYG	10	WR	0	0	0	2	14	0	81	1051	9	1	0	0	143	Red
60	Derrick Ward	TB	8	RB	0	0	0	197	815	7	31	204	0	1	0	0	141	Green
61	Santonio Holmes	PIT	8	WR	0	0	0	4	42	0	71	1104	7	0	0	0	141	Red
62	Jay Cutler	CHI	5	QB	3409	20	12	63	190	3	0	0	0	5	0	0	254	Green
63	Jerome Harrison	CLE	9	RB	0	0	0	162	793	6	44	397	1	2	0	0	140	Red
64	Tony Romo	DAL	6	QB	3666	25	12	38	96	1	0	0	0	5	0	0	253	Yellow
65	Donald Driver	GB	5	WR	0	0	0	0	0	0	72	1018	8	0	0	0	139	Yellow
66	Reggie Bush	NO	5	RB	0	0	0	113	493	3	82	714	3	3	0	0	140	Yellow
67	Rashard Mendenhall	PIT	8	RB	0	0	0	157	716	5	49	382	2	1	0	0	139	Red
68	Darren Sproles	SD	5	RB	0	0	0	158	690	4	38	397	2	1	0	0	136	Yellow
69	Tarvaris Jackson	MIN	9	QB	3128	21	13	70	292	4	0	0	0	3	0	0	248	Yellow

Rk	Player	Team	Bye	Pos	PaYd	PaTD	INT	Ru	RuYd	RuTD	Rec	RcYd	RcTD	Fum	XP	FG	Fant	Risk
70	David Garrard	JAC	7	QB	3290	19	11	77	305	3	0	0	0	4	0	0	248	Yellow
71	Ted Ginn	MIA	6	WR	0	0	0	6	29	0	66	930	8	0	0	0	136	Yellow
72	Braylon Edwards	CLE	9	WR	0	0	0	0	0	0	59	948	8	0	0	0	135	Yellow
73	Lee Evans	BUF	9	WR	0	0	0	0	0	0	66	1006	7	0	0	0	134	Yellow
74	Darren McFadden	OAK	9	RB	0	0	0	171	813	3	47	395	1	2	0	0	134	Yellow
75	Bears D	CHI	5	D	0	0	0	0	0	0	0	0	0	0	0	0	140	N/A
76	Terrell Owens	BUF	9	WR	0	0	0	3	18	0	66	935	7	0	0	0	132	Yellow
77	Antonio Bryant	TB	8	WR	0	0	0	0	0	0	75	974	7	0	0	0	130	Yellow
78	Matt Ryan	ATL	4	QB	3184	21	11	47	247	2	0	0	0	6	0	0	244	Green
79	Greg Olsen	CHI	5	TE	0	0	0	0	0	0	61	738	7	0	0	0	112	Green
80	DeSean Jackson	PHI	4	WR	0	0	0	3	21	0	63	1006	7	0	0	0	129	Red
81	Tony Gonzalez	ATL	4	TE	0	0	0	0	0	0	83	924	5	0	0	0	112	Red
82	Ray Rice	BAL	7	RB	0	0	0	171	715	6	33	253	2	2	0	0	129	Red
83	Stephen Gostkowski	NE	8	K	0	0	0	0	0	0	0	0	0	0	49	31	141	Green
84	Chargers D	SD	5	D	0	0	0	0	0	0	0	0	0	0	0	0	134	N/A
85	Eli Manning	NYG	10	QB	3356	21	13	21	37	1	0	0	0	3	0	0	241	Blue
86	Jerricho Cotchery	NYJ	9	WR	0	0	0	0	0	0	68	930	7	0	0	0	126	Yellow
87	Bernard Berrian	MIN	9	WR	0	0	0	2	10	0	46	762	9	0	0	0	125	Yellow
88	Nate Burleson	SEA	7	WR	0	0	0	2	11	0	63	896	6	0	0	0	125	Green
89	Joseph Addai	IND	6	RB	0	0	0	175	687	4	37	276	1	1	0	0	125	Green
90	Ravens D	BAL	7	D	0	0	0	0	0	0	0	0	0	0	0	0	132	N/A
91	Willie Parker	PIT	8	RB	0	0	0	211	704	9	14	88	1	1	0	0	125	Red
92	Owen Daniels	HOU	10	TE	0	0	0	0	0	0	76	899	3	0	0	0	105	Green
93	Michael Crabtree	SF	6	WR	0	0	0	6	35	0	70	928	7	0	0	0	122	Red
94	Santana Moss	WAS	8	WR	0	0	0	3	17	0	74	873	6	0	0	0	121	Green
95	Chris Wells	ARI	4	RB	0	0	0	187	627	7	17	149	2	1	0	0	124	Yellow
96	Kellen Winslow	TB	8	TE	0	0	0	0	0	0	69	858	5	0	0	0	103	Red
97	Matt Schaub	HOU	10	QB	3633	19	11	45	147	1	0	0	0	5	0	0	234	Yellow
98	Donald Brown	IND	6	RB	0	0	0	147	623	5	42	349	0	1	0	0	120	Yellow
99	Matt Cassel	KC	8	QB	3277	20	14	40	132	3	0	0	0	7	0	0	230	Green
100	Adam Vinatieri	IND	6	K	0	0	0	0	0	0	0	0	0	0	48	30	131	Yellow
101	Kurt Warner	ARI	4	QB	4036	25	14	12	15	0	0	0	0	10	0	0	230	Red
102	Olindo Mare	SEA	7	K	0	0	0	0	0	0	0	0	0	0	37	30	127	Green
103	Devin Hester	CHI	5	WR	0	0	0	6	42	0	62	858	5	0	0	0	116	Yellow
104	Phil Dawson	CLE	9	K	0	0	0	0	0	0	0	0	0	0	28	32	126	Green
105	Vikings D	MIN	9	D	0	0	0	0	0	0	0	0	0	0	0	0	119	N/A
106	Robbie Gould	CHI	5	K	0	0	0	0	0	0	0	0	0	0	41	29	127	Green
107	Chris Cooley	WAS	8	TE	0	0	0	0	0	0	85	781	3	1	0	0	95	Green
108	Giants D	NYG	10	D	0	0	0	0	0	0	0	0	0	0	0	0	117	N/A
109	Marshawn Lynch	BUF	9	RB	0	0	0	167	655	3	32	224	1	1	0	0	110	Green
110	Zach Miller	OAK	9	TE	0	0	0	0	0	0	55	704	4	0	0	0	94	Green
111	Dallas Clark	IND	6	TE	0	0	0	0	0	0	61	651	5	0	0	0	93	Green
112	Jeff Reed	PIT	8	K	0	0	0	0	0	0	0	0	0	0	44	26	122	Green
113	Seahawks D	SEA	7	D	0	0	0	0	0	0	0	0	0	0	0	0	115	N/A
114	Nate Kaeding	SD	5	K	0	0	0	0	0	0	0	0	0	0	52	25	122	Yellow
115	Ladell Betts	WAS	8	RB	0	0	0	139	649	6	19	184	1	1	0	0	110	Red
116	Cowboys D	DAL	6	D	0	0	0	0	0	0	0	0	0	0	0	0	114	N/A
117	Josh Scobee	JAC	7	K	0	0	0	0	0	0	0	0	0	0	43	26	121	Green
118	Patriots D	NE	8	D	0	0	0	0	0	0	0	0	0	0	0	0	112	N/A
119	Chad Pennington	MIA	6	QB	3576	22	14	29	105	1	0	0	0	4	0	0	221	Red
120	Josh Brown	STL	9	K	0	0	0	0	0	0	0	0	0	0	38	28	121	Green
121	Eddie Royal	DEN	7	WR	0	0	0	8	85	0	65	745	4	0	0	0	106	Green
122	Panthers D	CAR	4	D	0	0	0	0	0	0	0	0	0	0	0	0	110	N/A

Rk	Player	Team	Bye	Pos	PaYd	PaTD	INT	Ru	RuYd	RuTD	Rec	RcYd	RcTD	Fum	XP	FG	Fant	Risk
123	Justin Gage	TEN	7	WR	0	0	0	4	29	0	56	756	7	0	0	0	106	Red
124	Kevin Walter	HOU	10	WR	0	0	0	2	10	0	65	819	5	0	0	0	105	Yellow
125	Fred Jackson	BUF	9	RB	0	0	0	141	622	3	53	330	1	1	0	0	105	Red
126	Jerious Norwood	ATL	4	RB	0	0	0	117	547	1	41	385	1	1	0	0	105	Green
127	Eagles D	PHI	4	D	0	0	0	0	0	0	0	0	0	0	0	0	109	N/A
128	LeSean McCoy	PHI	4	RB	0	0	0	122	594	5	27	213	0	2	0	0	105	Yellow
129	Dustin Keller	NYJ	9	TE	0	0	0	0	0	0	62	744	3	0	0	0	87	Yellow
130	Joe Nedney	SF	6	K	0	0	0	0	0	0	0	0	0	0	33	28	117	Green
131	Laveranues Coles	CIN	8	WR	0	0	0	2	16	0	59	753	4	0	0	0	102	Green
132	David Akers	PHI	4	K	0	0	0	0	0	0	0	0	0	0	38	26	117	Green
133	Steelers D	PIT	8	D	0	0	0	0	0	0	0	0	0	0	0	0	106	N/A
134	Tony Scheffler	DEN	7	TE	0	0	0	0	0	0	47	582	4	0	0	0	84	Green
135	Rob Bironas	TEN	7	K	0	0	0	0	0	0	0	0	0	0	36	27	116	Green
136	Justin Fargas	OAK	9	RB	0	0	0	150	693	5	10	84	1	1	0	0	99	Red
137	Jaguars D	JAC	7	D	0	0	0	0	0	0	0	0	0	0	0	0	104	N/A
138	Rams D	STL	9	D	0	0	0	0	0	0	0	0	0	0	0	0	104	N/A
139	John Carlson	SEA	7	TE	0	0	0	0	0	0	55	625	3	0	0	0	82	Green
140	Carson Palmer	CIN	8	QB	3554	22	12	14	45	0	0	0	0	4	0	0	214	Red
141	Kevin Faulk	NE	8	RB	0	0	0	61	288	2	44	464	2	1	0	0	99	Green
142	Randy McMichael	STL	9	TE	0	0	0	0	0	0	51	531	5	0	0	0	80	Green
143	Lance Moore	NO	5	WR	0	0	0	0	0	0	54	715	4	0	0	0	97	Green
144	Vernon Davis	SF	6	TE	0	0	0	0	0	0	50	547	4	0	0	0	80	Green
145	Steven Smith	NYG	10	WR	0	0	0	0	0	0	74	800	4	0	0	0	96	Yellow
146	Jamaal Charles	KC	8	RB	0	0	0	144	605	3	31	214	0	1	0	0	96	Green
147	Steve Breaston	ARI	4	WR	0	0	0	4	19	0	57	781	4	0	0	0	96	Yellow
148	T.J. Duckett	SEA	7	RB	0	0	0	151	727	4	5	45	0	2	0	0	97	Green
149	Jamal Lewis	CLE	9	RB	0	0	0	150	488	5	22	180	1	1	0	0	97	Green
150	Byron Leftwich	TB	8	QB	3499	12	15	45	205	3	0	0	0	4	0	0	209	Yellow
151	Marc Bulger	STL	9	QB	3211	16	13	22	56	1	0	0	0	2	0	0	208	Green
152	Trent Edwards	BUF	9	QB	3221	16	16	62	253	2	0	0	0	7	0	0	208	Yellow
153	Chris Chambers	SD	5	WR	0	0	0	4	45	0	44	606	5	0	0	0	94	Green
154	Earl Bennett	CHI	5	WR	0	0	0	4	22	0	49	663	6	0	0	0	94	Red
155	Mark Bradley	KC	8	WR	0	0	0	9	39	0	52	705	5	0	0	0	94	Red
156	Joey Galloway	NE	8	WR	0	0	0	2	10	0	44	720	3	0	0	0	93	Green
157	Kevin Curtis	PHI	4	WR	0	0	0	2	14	0	49	710	4	0	0	0	90	Yellow
158	Kenneth Darby	STL	9	RB	0	0	0	101	459	4	29	274	1	2	0	0	91	Red
159	Fred Taylor	NE	8	RB	0	0	0	160	679	3	7	58	0	1	0	0	91	Green
160	Marcedes Lewis	JAC	7	TE	0	0	0	0	0	0	46	531	4	0	0	0	72	Yellow
161	Brandon Pettigrew	DET	7	TE	0	0	0	0	0	0	45	463	6	0	0	0	72	Red
162	Visanthe Shiancoe	MIN	9	TE	0	0	0	0	0	0	48	543	3	0	0	0	72	Green
163	Heath Miller	PIT	8	TE	0	0	0	0	0	0	42	459	4	0	0	0	71	Green
164	Kyle Orton	DEN	7	QB	3473	17	15	16	38	0	0	0	0	7	0	0	201	Green
165	Devery Henderson	NO	5	WR	0	0	0	2	23	0	35	706	4	0	0	0	87	Red
166	Joe Flacco	BAL	7	QB	3026	15	10	37	167	1	1	15	0	7	0	0	200	Green
167	Todd Heap	BAL	7	TE	0	0	0	0	0	0	51	560	3	0	0	0	67	Red
168	Miles Austin	DAL	6	WR	0	0	0	0	0	0	41	687	4	0	0	0	83	Red
169	Jeremy Shockey	NO	5	TE	0	0	0	0	0	0	40	460	3	0	0	0	66	Green
170	Brian Robiskie	CLE	9	WR	0	0	0	5	32	0	63	657	4	0	0	0	82	Red
171	Michael Jenkins	ATL	4	WR	0	0	0	0	0	0	48	684	3	0	0	0	81	Yellow
172	Greg Camarillo	MIA	6	WR	0	0	0	0	0	0	53	695	3	0	0	0	82	Yellow
173	JaMarcus Russell	OAK	9	QB	3235	14	9	38	139	2	0	0	0	5	0	0	195	Red
174	Michael Clayton	TB	8	WR	0	0	0	2	12	0	48	655	3	0	0	0	81	Yellow
175	Pierre Garcon	IND	6	WR	0	0	0	3	13	0	37	553	6	0	0	0	80	Red

Rk	Player	Team	Bye	Pos	PaYd	PaTD	INT	Ru	RuYd	RuTD	Rec	RcYd	RcTD	Fum	XP	FG	Fant	Risk
176	Willis McGahee	BAL	7	RB	0	0	0	131	504	4	20	160	0	2	0	0	82	Yellow
177	Benjamin Watson	NE	8	TE	0	0	0	0	0	0	37	447	4	0	0	0	65	Yellow
178	Earnest Graham	TB	8	RB	0	0	0	81	401	5	18	165	0	1	0	0	80	Red
179	Kevin Boss	NYG	10	TE	0	0	0	0	0	0	40	437	4	0	0	0	64	Yellow
180	Davone Bess	MIA	6	WR	0	0	0	2	12	0	50	601	4	0	0	0	79	Yellow
181	Donald Lee	GB	5	TE	0	0	0	0	0	0	38	381	5	0	0	0	61	Yellow
182	Mike Walker	JAC	7	WR	0	0	0	2	11	0	53	679	3	0	0	0	78	Red
183	Ricky Williams	MIA	6	RB	0	0	0	125	524	2	15	151	0	2	0	0	80	Blue
184	Laurence Maroney	NE	8	RB	0	0	0	134	539	4	8	75	0	2	0	0	79	Yellow
185	Antwaan Randle El	WAS	8	WR	0	0	0	2	12	0	50	638	2	0	0	0	76	Green
186	Kenny Britt	TEN	7	WR	0	0	0	4	23	0	49	560	4	0	0	0	77	Yellow
187	Matthew Stafford	DET	7	QB	2882	16	18	42	244	2	0	0	0	4	0	0	191	Yellow
188	Brady Quinn	CLE	9	QB	3411	15	16	30	135	0	0	0	0	7	0	0	191	Yellow
189	Hakeem Nicks	NYG	10	WR	0	0	0	4	19	0	47	664	3	0	0	0	77	Red
190	Harry Douglas	ATL	4	WR	0	0	0	6	30	0	32	437	6	0	0	0	76	Yellow
191	Percy Harvin	MIN	9	WR	0	0	0	37	181	1	44	457	2	0	0	0	76	Yellow
192	Anthony Fasano	MIA	6	TE	0	0	0	0	0	0	41	465	2	0	0	0	58	Green
193	Jason Campbell	WAS	8	QB	3182	12	12	63	246	2	0	0	0	5	0	0	189	Red
194	Brad Cottam	KC	8	TE	0	0	0	0	0	0	36	386	3	0	0	0	57	Green
195	Laurent Robinson	STL	9	WR	0	0	0	2	20	0	47	593	3	0	0	0	74	Yellow
196	Johnnie Lee Higgins	OAK	9	WR	0	0	0	3	14	0	43	633	2	0	0	0	74	Yellow
197	Bo Scaife	TEN	7	TE	0	0	0	0	0	0	45	503	1	0	0	0	56	Green
198	Shaun Hill	SF	6	QB	3032	19	18	39	167	0	0	0	0	7	0	0	187	Yellow
199	Bryant Johnson	DET	7	WR	0	0	0	2	11	0	45	595	4	0	0	0	73	Red
200	Brent Celek	PHI	4	TE	0	0	0	0	0	0	40	406	3	0	0	0	56	Green
201	Malcom Floyd	SD	5	WR	0	0	0	2	19	0	38	504	4	0	0	0	72	Yellow
202	Chaz Schilens	OAK	9	WR	0	0	0	0	0	0	56	538	4	0	0	0	72	Red
203	Muhsin Muhammad	CAR	4	WR	0	0	0	0	0	0	45	572	2	0	0	0	71	Green
204	Patrick Crayton	DAL	6	WR	0	0	0	2	15	0	36	584	2	0	0	0	71	Green
205	Billy Miller	NO	5	TE	0	0	0	0	0	0	36	468	1	0	0	0	55	Green
206	Deion Branch	SEA	7	WR	0	0	0	2	11	0	43	571	2	0	0	0	70	Green
207	Tim Hightower	ARI	4	RB	0	0	0	105	291	1	42	370	1	2	0	0	72	Yellow
208	Brandon Jackson	GB	5	RB	0	0	0	108	461	1	18	180	0	1	0	0	70	Green
209	Chester Taylor	MIN	9	RB	0	0	0	54	266	1	32	315	1	1	0	0	71	Blue
210	Ronald Curry	DET	7	WR	0	0	0	0	0	0	53	639	2	0	0	0	69	Red
211	Chris Henry	CIN	8	WR	0	0	0	0	0	0	37	511	4	0	0	0	69	Yellow
212	Nate Washington	TEN	7	WR	0	0	0	3	27	0	38	588	2	0	0	0	70	Yellow
213	Tashard Choice	DAL	6	RB	0	0	0	71	331	2	25	225	1	2	0	0	70	Green
214	Leon Washington	NYJ	9	RB	0	0	0	60	288	1	44	325	1	1	0	0	69	Yellow
215	Mark Clayton	BAL	7	WR	0	0	0	7	34	0	43	493	2	0	0	0	67	Green
216	Antonio Pittman	STL	9	RB	0	0	0	73	355	4	8	71	0	1	0	0	68	Green
217	Mewelde Moore	PIT	8	RB	0	0	0	76	307	2	28	254	1	1	0	0	68	Yellow
218	David Martin	MIA	6	TE	0	0	0	0	0	0	30	363	2	0	0	0	50	Green
219	Limas Sweed	PIT	8	WR	0	0	0	0	0	0	29	470	4	0	0	0	66	Red
220	Bobby Engram	KC	8	WR	0	0	0	4	19	0	44	600	2	0	0	0	66	Red
221	Derek Fine	BUF	9	TE	0	0	0	0	0	0	41	439	1	0	0	0	49	Yellow
222	Jeremy Maclin	PHI	4	WR	0	0	0	0	0	0	42	546	3	0	0	0	66	Red
223	Kerry Collins	TEN	7	QB	2986	13	11	25	49	0	0	0	0	3	0	0	178	Green
224	Shayne Graham	CIN	8	K	0	0	0	0	0	0	0	0	0	0	30	28	115	Green
225	Sidney Rice	MIN	9	WR	0	0	0	2	29	0	43	481	3	0	0	0	64	Red
226	Leonard Weaver	PHI	4	RB	0	0	0	36	154	2	40	359	1	1	0	0	65	Red
227	Mark Sanchez	NYJ	9	QB	2981	13	16	23	83	1	0	0	0	3	0	0	176	Green
228	Jason Hanson	DET	7	K	0	0	0	0	0	0	0	0	0	0	31	27	112	Green

Statistical Appendix B

This section contains a number of lists based on stats from either game charting or play-by-play analysis. Many of these statistcs are defined in the "Statistical Toolbox" near the front of the book. All stats are for 2008 only except where noted.

Top 20 Players in Offensive Penalties

Rk	Player	Team	Penalties
1	K.Harris	OAK	17
2	F.Adams	DAL	14
3	J.Gaither	BAL	13
3	W.Colon	PIT	13
3	D.Lutui	ARI	13
6	R.Incognito	STL	12
7	K.Warner	ARI	11
7	K.Barnes	JAC	11
7	J.Backus	DET	11
7	A.Barron	STL	11
7	T.Pashos	JAC	11
12	G.Cherilus	DET	10
12	J.Trueblood	TB	10
12	V.Davis	SF	10
12	J.Brown	NO	10
16	C.Green	OAK	9
16	C.Clifton	GB	9
16	R.Cook	MIN	9
16	P.Rivers	SD	9
16	B.Edwards	CLE	9
16	J.Gross	CAR	9
16	J.Peters	BUF	9

Includes declined and offsetting, but not special teams.

Top 20 Players in Defensive Penalties

Rk	Player	Team	Penalties
1	T.Brown	TEN	14
2	A.Cromartie	SD	11
3	S.Rogers	CLE	9
3	R.Barber	TB	9
3	T.Cole	PHI	9
6	N.Asomugha	OAK	8
6	D.Dockett	ARI	8
6	C.Johnson	CAR	8
6	G.Adams	TB	8
6	R.McDonald	SF	8
6	K.Edwards	OAK	8
12	T.Williams	GB	7
12	A.Harris	GB	7
12	D.Ware	DAL	7
12	R.Harper	NO	7
12	C.Finnegan	TEN	7
12	F.Robbins	NYG	7
12	K.Williams	MIN	7
12	T.Suggs	BAL	7
20	10 tied with		6

Includes declined and offsetting, but not special teams.

Top 20 Players in Passes Defensed

Rk	Player	Team	Defensed
1	C.Webster	NYG	25
2	C.Rogers	WAS	24
2	A.Samuel	PHI	24
4	C.Houston	ATL	22
5	A.Goodman	MIA	21
6	Q.Jammer	SD	19
6	R.Bartell	STL	19
8	W.Allen	MIA	18
8	C.Gamble	CAR	18
8	L.Hall	CIN	18
8	J.Reeves	HOU	18
8	D.Rodgers-Cromartie	ARI	18
8	C.Finnegan	TEN	18
14	T.McGee	BUF	17
14	D.Hall	OAK/WAS	17
16	R.Gay	NO	16
16	D.Lowery	NYJ	16
16	C.Tillman	CHI	16
16	B.McDonald	CLE	16
16	C.Woodson	GB	16

Based on the definition given in the Statistical Toolbox, not NFL totals.

Top 20 Defenders in Defeats

Rk	Player	Team	Dfts
1	T.Suggs	BAL	36
2	D.Ware	DAL	35
3	L.Briggs	CHI	34
4	T.Davis	CAR	30
5	J.Harrison	PIT	29
5	T.Cole	PHI	29
7	J.Tuck	NYG	28
8	J.Farrior	PIT	27
8	R.Lewis	BAL	27
8	A.Winfield	MIN	27
11	D.Jackson	CLE	26
11	K.Dansby	ARI	26
11	S.Bradley	PHI	26
11	B.Urlacher	CHI	26
11	A.Ogunleye	CHI	26
11	L.Woodley	PIT	26
17	T.Polamalu	PIT	25
17	J.Peppers	CAR	25
17	J.Allen	MIN	25
20	Six tied with		24

Top 20 Defenders in Quarterback Hits

Rk	Player	Team	Hits
1	A.Kampman	GB	20
2	J.Allen	MIN	18
2	S.Rogers	CLE	18
4	J.Abraham	ATL	16
5	M.Williams	HOU	15
6	D.Dockett	ARI	14
6	R.Edwards	MIN	14
6	K.Vanden Bosch	TEN	14
6	A.Haynesworth	TEN	14
10	B.Mebane	SEA	13
10	D.Ware	DAL	13
10	A.Carter	WAS	13
10	D.Freeney	IND	13
14	T.Pryce	BAL	12
14	G.Adams	TB	12
14	T.Cole	PHI	12
17	T.Brown	TEN	11
17	J.Smith	SF	11
17	A.Brown	CHI	11
17	T.Suggs	BAL	11

Adjusted based on official scorer tendencies

Top 20 Defenders in QB Knockdowns (Sacks+Hits)

Rk	Defender	Team	Adj KD
1	J.Abraham	ATL	33
2	D.Ware	DAL	32
3	A.Kampman	GB	31
4	J.Allen	MIN	30
5	J.Porter	MIA	25
6	J.Peppers	CAR	24
7	M.Williams	HOU	23
7	S.Rogers	CLE	23
7	A.Haynesworth	TEN	23
10	D.Freeney	IND	22
11	J.Tuck	NYG	21
12	R.Edwards	MIN	20
12	G.Adams	TB	20
12	T.Suggs	BAL	20
12	T.Cole	PHI	20
16	M.Kiwanuka	NYG	19
16	D.Dockett	ARI	19
16	K.Williams	MIN	19
16	J.Harrison	PIT	19
20	B.Mebane	SEA	18

Adjusted based on official scorer tendencies

Top 20 Defenders in Hurries

Rk	Defender	Team	Hur
1	D.Freeney	IND	28
2	J.Allen	MIN	27
3	J.Peppers	CAR	24
4	T.Cole	PHI	23
5	M.Williams	HOU	22
6	T.Suggs	BAL	20
6	J.Abraham	ATL	20
6	K.Williams	MIN	20
9	J.Tuck	NYG	19
10	D.Burgess	OAK	18
10	C.Pace	NYJ	18
12	E.Dumervil	DEN	17
12	J.Harrison	PIT	17
14	S.Phillips	SD	16
14	T.Pryce	BAL	16
14	A.Ogunleye	CHI	16
14	D.Ware	DAL	16
18	T.Hali	KC	15
18	B.Scott	BAL	15
18	J.Smith	SF	15
18	C.Grant	NO	15

Adjusted based on game charter tendencies

Top 20 Players in Blown Blocks

Rk	Defender	Team	Hur
1	D.Brown	HOU	10
2	L.Brown	ARI	8
2	K.Harris	OAK	8
2	J.Clary	SD	8
5	J.Peters	BUF	7.5
5	L.Jones	CIN	7.5
7	E.Winston	HOU	7
7	M.Light	NE	7
9	J.Staley	SF	6.5
10	J.St.Clair	CHI	6
10	F.Adams	DAL	6
10	J.Backus	DET	6
10	K.Barnes	JAC	6
10	D.McIntosh	KC	6
10	A.Snyder	SF	6
16	M.Gandy	ARI	5.5
16	C.Clifton	GB	5.5
16	A.Barron	STL	5.5
19	Eight tied with		5

Top 20 Quarterbacks in QB Hits

Rk	Player	Team	Adj Hits
1	K.Warner	ARI	76
2	D.Garrard	JAC	73
3	T.Romo	DAL	49
4	J.Garcia	TB	48
5	J.Campbell	WAS	47
6	D.Brees	NO	44
7	M.Cassel	NE	43
7	M.Schaub	HOU	43
9	P.Manning	IND	41
10	A.Rodgers	GB	40
10	E.Manning	NYG	40
12	B.Roethlisberger	PIT	38
13	D.McNabb	PHI	35
13	J.Flacco	BAL	35
13	M.Ryan	ATL	35
16	B.Favre	NYJ	32
17	D.Anderson	CLE	31
18	C.Pennington	MIA	29
19	J.Russell	OAK	28
19	J.Delhomme	CAR	28

Adjusted based on official scorer tendencies

Top 20 QBs in QB Knockdowns (Sacks + Hits)

Rk	Player	Team	Adj KD
1	D.Garrard	JAC	110
2	K.Warner	ARI	101
3	M.Cassel	NE	88
3	J.Campbell	WAS	88
5	B.Roethlisberger	PIT	81
6	A.Rodgers	GB	72
7	T.Romo	DAL	70
7	J.Garcia	TB	70
9	E.Manning	NYG	69
10	M.Schaub	HOU	64
11	J.Flacco	BAL	62
12	B.Favre	NYJ	60
13	J.Russell	OAK	57
13	D.Brees	NO	57
13	M.Bulger	STL	57
16	D.McNabb	PHI	56
16	R.Fitzpatrick	CIN	56
18	P.Manning	IND	55
19	K.Orton	CHI	54
20	C.Pennington	MIA	52

Adjusted based on official scorer tendencies

Top 10 Quarterbacks in Knockdowns per Pass

Rk	Player	Team	KD	Pct
1	T.Jackson	MIN	39	23.9%
2	J.P.Losman	BUF	24	20.6%
3	D.Culpepper	DET	25	19.3%
4	D.Garrard	JAC	110	19.0%
5	J.Garcia	TB	70	17.7%
6	B.Griese	TB	33	17.3%
7	M.Hasselbeck	SEA	39	16.7%
8	J.Campbell	WAS	88	16.2%
9	K.Warner	ARI	101	16.1%
10	B.Roethlisberger	PIT	81	15.7%
10	M.Schaub	HOU	64	15.7%

Min. 100 passes; adjusted based on official scorer tendencies

Bottom 10 Quarterbacks in Knockdowns per Pass

Rk	Player	Team	KD	Pct
32	B.Favre	NYJ	60	10.7%
33	C.Pennington	MIA	52	10.4%
34	P.Manning	IND	55	9.6%
35	D.McNabb	PHI	56	9.5%
36	D.Brees	NO	57	8.8%
37	S.Rosenfels	HOU	16	8.5%
38	T.Thigpen	KC	36	8.0%
39	P.Rivers	SD	40	7.9%
40	K.Collins	TEN	30	7.0%
41	J.Cutler	DEN	25	4.0%

Min. 100 passes; adjusted based on official scorer tendencies

Top 10 Quarterbacks, DVOA When Hurried

Rk	Player	Team	Plays	Yds	DVOA
1	J.Garcia	TB	58	7.8	70.7%
2	J.Campbell	WAS	78	6.3	39.6%
3	K.Warner	ARI	91	5.4	26.1%
4	C.Pennington	MIA	66	6.2	25.4%
5	D.Culpepper	DET	27	5.7	21.1%
6	T.Edwards	BUF	65	5.0	19.7%
7	T.Jackson	MIN	26	5.2	11.7%
8	P.Rivers	SD	70	5.1	1.2%
9	J.Cutler	DEN	61	6.5	0.8%
10	T.Romo	DAL	100	5.4	-0.9%

Min. 20 hurries

Bottom 10 Quarterbacks, DVOA When Hurried

Rk	Player	Team	Plays	Yds	DVOA
31	M.Schaub	HOU	50	2.5	-65.2%
32	G.Frerotte	MIN	28	6.0	-66.7%
33	B.Favre	NYJ	47	2.9	-72.4%
34	K.Orton	CHI	54	2.1	-77.3%
35	M.Bulger	STL	39	1.6	-78.5%
36	J.Delhomme	CAR	34	3.3	-88.9%
37	J.P.Losman	BUF	21	2.1	-107.9%
38	D.Orlovsky	DET	32	1.0	-117.5%
39	M.Hasselbeck	SEA	31	1.7	-145.7%
40	S.Rosenfels	HOU	23	3.5	-153.8%

Min. 20 hurries

Quarterback Accuracy

Rk	Player	Team	Accuracy	Rk	Player	Team	Accuracy
1	D.Brees	NO	90.2%	18	A.Rodgers	GB	82.4%
2	P.Manning	IND	87.0%	19	T.Romo	DAL	81.9%
3	B.Favre	NYJ	86.7%	20	K.Orton	CHI	81.6%
4	K.Warner	ARI	86.5%	21	J.Flacco	BAL	81.5%
5	J.Garcia	TB	86.0%	22	P.Rivers	SD	81.5%
6	J.Cutler	DEN	85.8%	23	D.McNabb	PHI	81.2%
7	J.Campbell	WAS	85.7%	24	S.Hill	SF	81.1%
8	J.Delhomme	CAR	84.7%	25	K.Collins	TEN	80.9%
9	M.Cassel	NE	84.6%	26	E.Manning	NYG	80.8%
10	C.Pennington	MIA	84.5%	27	S.Wallace	SEA	80.3%
11	M.Bulger	STL	84.4%	28	T.Thigpen	KC	79.3%
12	D.Garrard	JAC	84.4%	29	M.Ryan	ATL	79.0%
13	M.Schaub	HOU	84.1%	30	J.T.O'Sullivan	SF	78.6%
14	T.Edwards	BUF	83.9%	31	D.Anderson	CLE	77.9%
15	B.Roethlisberger	PIT	83.5%	32	D.Orlovsky	DET	77.8%
16	R.Fitzpatrick	CIN	83.3%	33	M.Hasselbeck	SEA	77.0%
17	G.Frerotte	MIN	82.8%	34	J.Russell	OAK	73.5%

Definition: Percentage of Passes which are not marked as Thrown Ahead, Thrown Behind, Overthrown, Underthrown, or Out of Bounds. Does not include passes marked Thrown Away, Tipped at Line, or Hit in Motion. NFL average is 82.6%. Min. 200 passes.

Top 10 QBs in Rate of Passes Overthrown

Rk	Player	Team	Total	Pct
1	D.Anderson	CLE	25	9.0%
2	G.Frerotte	MIN	24	8.1%
3	B.Roethlisberger	PIT	36	7.8%
4	M.Hasselbeck	SEA	16	7.8%
5	S.Hill	SF	21	7.5%
6	D.McNabb	PHI	39	7.0%
7	J.T.O'Sullivan	SF	15	6.9%
8	J.Russell	OAK	24	6.6%
9	M.Schaub	HOU	22	6.0%
10	D.Orlovsky	DET	14	5.6%

Min. 200 passes. Includes plays marked "Overthrown" or "Thrown Ahead."

Bottom 10 QBs in Rate of Passes Overthrown

Rk	Player	Team	Total	Pct
25	M.Ryan	ATL	18	4.2%
26	S.Wallace	SEA	10	4.2%
27	K.Collins	TEN	17	4.1%
28	A.Rodgers	GB	20	3.8%
29	J.Campbell	WAS	18	3.6%
30	J.Cutler	DEN	20	3.3%
31	C.Pennington	MIA	15	3.2%
32	J.Delhomme	CAR	13	3.2%
33	P.Rivers	SD	14	3.0%
34	D.Brees	NO	16	2.6%

Min. 200 passes. Includes plays marked "Overthrown" or "Thrown Ahead."

Top 10 QBs in Rate of Passes Underthrown

Rk	Player	Team	Total	Pct
1	J.Russell	OAK	60	16.5%
2	E.Manning	NYG	62	13.1%
3	T.Thigpen	KC	54	13.1%
4	D.Anderson	CLE	36	12.9%
5	M.Hasselbeck	SEA	25	12.1%
6	S.Wallace	SEA	29	12.1%
7	K.Collins	TEN	50	12.1%
8	J.Delhomme	CAR	48	11.7%
9	M.Ryan	ATL	50	11.6%
10	D.Orlovsky	DET	28	11.2%

Min. 200 passes. Includes plays marked "Underthrown" or "Thrown Behind."

Bottom 10 QBs in Rate of Passes Underthrown

Rk	Player	Team	Total	Pct
25	A.Rodgers	GB	44	8.3%
26	J.Cutler	DEN	50	8.2%
27	D.Garrard	JAC	41	7.8%
28	B.Roethlisberger	PIT	35	7.6%
29	P.Manning	IND	41	7.5%
30	D.Brees	NO	45	7.3%
31	K.Warner	ARI	40	6.9%
32	J.Garcia	TB	25	6.8%
33	J.Campbell	WAS	32	6.4%
34	M.Schaub	HOU	18	4.9%

Min. 200 passes. Includes plays marked "Underthrown" or "Thrown Behind."

Top 20 Quarterbacks, Passes Dropped

Rk	Player	Team	Dropped
1	J.Campbell	WAS	39
2	A.Rodgers	GB	38
3	D.Brees	NO	36
3	P.Manning	IND	36
5	B.Roethlisberger	PIT	35
5	D.McNabb	PHI	35
7	D.Garrard	JAC	34
7	K.Orton	CHI	34
9	J.Cutler	DEN	33
10	M.Bulger	STL	32
11	M.Ryan	ATL	31
12	E.Manning	NYG	30
12	M.Cassel	NE	30
14	K.Warner	ARI	29
15	K.Collins	TEN	28
16	D.Anderson	CLE	27
16	T.Romo	DAL	27
18	J.Delhomme	CAR	24
19	J.Russell	OAK	23
19	G.Frerotte	MIN	23

Top 20 Quarterbacks, Passes Defensed

Rk	Player	Team	Defensed
1	J.Cutler	DEN	83
2	D.Brees	NO	72
3	T.Thigpen	KC	64
4	D.Garrard	JAC	57
5	M.Bulger	STL	55
6	D.McNabb	PHI	53
6	B.Favre	NYJ	53
8	J.Flacco	BAL	51
8	J.Delhomme	CAR	51
10	J.Campbell	WAS	50
11	B.Roethlisberger	PIT	45
12	M.Cassel	NE	44
13	P.Manning	IND	42
13	K.Warner	ARI	42
15	E.Manning	NYG	40
16	A.Rodgers	GB	39
17	C.Pennington	MIA	37
18	K.Collins	TEN	36
19	T.Romo	DAL	35
19	K.Orton	CHI	35

Top 10 QBs, Yards from Pass Interference

Rk	Player	Team	Plays	Yards
1	P.Rivers	SD	7	143
1	G.Frerotte	MIN	6	143
3	E.Manning	NYG	10	134
4	D.Garrard	JAC	6	122
5	B.Favre	NYJ	10	107
6	J.T.O'Sullivan	SF	5	101
7	K.Collins	TEN	4	100
8	K.Warner	ARI	7	98
8	J.Russell	OAK	4	98
10	B.Roethlisberger	PIT	3	93

Top 20 Players, Passes Dropped

Rk	Player	Team	Total
1	B.Edwards	CLE	15
2	M.Lynch	BUF	12
2	S.Moss	WAS	12
2	R.White	ATL	12
5	D.Bowe	KC	10
5	C.Johnson	CIN	10
5	M.Lewis	JAC	10
5	D.Driver	GB	10
9	B.Marshall	DEN	9
9	T.Owens	DAL	9
9	A.Randle El	WAS	9
9	R.Wayne	IND	9
9	M.Colston	NO	9
14	D.Jackson	DEN	8
14	S.Holmes	PIT	8
14	Ro.Williams	DET/DAL	8
14	B.Wade	MIN	8
14	H.Ward	PIT	8
14	D.Hester	CHI	8
14	G.Jennings	GB	8

Top 20 Players, Pct. Passes Dropped

Rk	Player	Team	Drops	Pct
1	A.Pittman	STL	7	27%
2	M.Lynch	BUF	12	19%
3	C.Portis	WAS	6	17%
4	J.Lewis	CLE	5	16%
5	A.Peterson	MIN	5	15%
6	M.Lewis	JAC	10	15%
7	B.Celek	PHI	5	15%
8	B.Watson	NE	6	14%
9	J.Addai	IND	5	14%
10	J.Charles	KC	5	13%
11	H.Douglas	ATL	5	13%
12	J.Morgan	SF	5	13%
13	B.Edwards	CLE	15	11%
14	T.Hightower	ARI	5	11%
15	R.Davis	CHI	7	11%
16	A.Randle El	WAS	9	11%
17	S.Jackson	STL	6	11%
18	M.Clayton	TB	6	11%
19	C.Johnson	CIN	6	11%
20	J.Gaffney	NE	6	10%

Min. five drops

Top 10 Intended Receivers on Interceptions

Rk	Player	Team	Total
1	A.Johnson	HOU	10
2	B.Edwards	CLE	9
2	T.Owens	DAL	9
2	J.Cotchery	NYJ	9
5	C.Johnson	CIN	8
5	D.Avery	STL	8
7	R.White	ATL	7
7	B.Marshall	DEN	7
7	J.Witten	DAL	7
7	L.Evans	BUF	7

Top 20 First Downs/Touchdowns Allowed in Coverage

Rk	Player	Team	Total	Rk	Player	Team	Total
1	C.Tillman	CHI	44	10	B.Carr	KC	36
2	L.Hall	CIN	41	14	M.Trufant	SEA	35
2	D.Bly	DEN	41	14	L.Bodden	CLE	35
2	J.Reeves	HOU	41	16	B.Williams	JAC	34
5	B.McDonald	CLE	39	17	R.Barber	TB	33
6	T.McGee	BUF	38	17	K.Lucas	CAR	33
7	C.Griffin	MIN	37	19	C.Gamble	CAR	32
7	A.Cromartie	SD	37	20	K.Jennings	SEA	31
7	D.Lowery	NYJ	37	20	I.Taylor	PIT	31
10	Q.Jammer	SD	36	20	F.Smoot	WAS	31
10	E.Wright	CLE	36	20	P.Buchanon	TB	31
10	J.Wilson	SEA	36				

Top 20 Passing Yards Allowed in Coverage

Rk	Player	Team	Yards
1	J.Reeves	HOU	1532
2	T.McGee	BUF	1341
3	L.Hall	CIN	1287
4	A.Goodman	MIA	1262
5	C.Gamble	CAR	1245
6	C.Tillman	CHI	1240
7	R.Bartell	STL	1223
8	B.McDonald	CLE	1219
9	C.Rogers	WAS	1194
10	M.Trufant	SEA	1178
11	D.Hall	OAK/WAS	1137
12	I.Taylor	PIT	1120
13	N.Harper	TEN	1115
14	R.Hood	ARI	1107
15	C.Griffin	MIN	1099
16	L.Bodden	CLE	1098
17	T.Williams	GB	1083
18	C.Houston	ATL	1056
19	W.Harris	SF	1045
20	K.Lucas	CAR	1022

Top 20 Yards After Catch Allowed in Coverage

Rk	Player	Team	YAC
1	C.Griffin	MIN	332
2	B.Williams	JAC	321
3	R.Barber	TB	293
4	W.Allen	MIA	288
5	C.Greenway	MIN	285
6	A.Cromartie	SD	267
7	D.Bly	DEN	254
8	A.Ross	NYG	251
9	N.Clements	SF	226
10	L.Bodden	CLE	225
11	B.Carr	KC	212
12	K.Jennings	SEA	207
12	L.Hall	CIN	207
14	R.Hood	ARI	206
14	J.Reeves	HOU	206
16	C.Tillman	CHI	203
17	D.Rogers-Cromartie	ARI	200
18	T.Williams	GB	197
19	D.Lowery	NYJ	193
19	J.Farrior	PIT	193

Most Dropped Interceptions, 2007-2008

Rk	Player	Team	Drops
1	I.Taylor	PIT	7
1	N.Collins	GB	7
3	T.McGee	BUF	6
3	A.Samuel	NE/PHI	6
5	C.Gamble	CAR	5
5	C.Rogers	WAS	5
5	D.Grant	SEA	5
8	R.Barber	TB	4
8	E.Hobbs	NE	4
8	L.Landry	BAL	4
8	A.Bethea	IND	4
8	C.Griffin	MIN	4
8	B.Williams	JAC	4

Fewest Avg Yards on Run Tackle, DL

Rk	Player	Team	Tkl	Avg
1	F.Robbins	NYG	27	0.3
2	A.Brown	CHI	37	0.7
3	B.Mebane	SEA	30	1.1
4	R.Meier	JAC	27	1.1
5	G.Jackson	ATL	26	1.2
6	M.Douglas	BAL	33	1.2
7	T.Brown	TEN	37	1.3
8	K.Jenkins	NYJ	44	1.4
9	J.Babineaux	ATL	30	1.4
10	J.Engelberger	DEN	27	1.4
11	B.Keisel	PIT	34	1.5
12	A.Haynesworth	TEN	38	1.5
13	R.Edwards	MIN	40	1.5
13	G.Dorsey	KC	40	1.5
15	J.Williams	SD	49	1.5
16	H.Ngata	BAL	47	1.5
17	C.Kelsay	BUF	37	1.5
18	K.Williams	MIN	44	1.6
19	J.Tuck	NYG	47	1.6
20	A.Ogunleye	CHI	48	1.6
20	K.Williams	BUF	48	1.6

Min. 25 run tackles

Fewest Avg Yards on Run Tackle, LB

Rk	Player	Team	Tkl	Avg
1	D.Brooks	TB	49	1.0
2	Dh.Jones	CIN	27	1.8
3	G.Brackett	IND	49	1.9
4	A.Ayodele	MIA	44	2.1
5	S.Tulloch	TEN	52	2.3
6	K.Bulluck	TEN	35	2.3
7	C.June	TB	53	2.3
8	G.Hayes	ARI	26	2.3
9	K.Morrison	OAK	39	2.3
10	K.Rivers	CIN	39	2.4
11	C.Pace	NYJ	43	2.4
12	S.Cooper	SD	29	2.5
13	B.Poppinga	GB	57	2.6
14	R.Jeanty	CIN	52	2.6
15	P.Thomas	KC	85	2.6
16	J.Durant	JAC	53	2.7
17	E.Barton	NYJ	66	2.7
18	R.Lewis	BAL	56	2.7
18	D.Smith	JAC	42	2.7
20	S.Fujita	NO	31	2.8

Min. 25 run tackles

Fewest Avg Yards on Run Tackle, DB

Rk	Player	Team	Tkl	Avg
1	B.Scott	BUF	39	2.5
2	A.Winfield	MIN	31	2.7
3	M.Johnson	NYG	31	3.0
4	R.Barber	TB	24	3.5
5	C.Horton	WAS	41	3.8
6	J.Phillips	TB	37	4.0
7	A.Wilson	ARI	42	4.2
8	M.Bullitt	IND	27	4.2
9	Q.Mikell	PHI	50	4.2
10	N.Asomugha	OAK	25	4.5
11	T.Polamalu	PIT	43	4.5
12	C.Graham	CHI	29	4.5
13	B.Williams	JAC	30	4.5
14	G.Wilson	OAK	86	4.6
15	C.Ndukwe	CIN	32	4.6
16	C.Gamble	CAR	26	4.7
16	C.Griffin	MIN	26	4.7
18	M.Brown	CHI	34	4.9
19	A.Rouse	GB	35	5.0
20	C.Crocker	MIA/CIN	23	5.0

Min. 20 run tackles

Top 10 Kickers, Gross Kickoff Value over Average

Rk	Player	Team	Kick Pts+	Net Pts+	Kicks
1	O.Mare	SEA	8.69	5.84	67
2	R.Lloyd	CAR	7.68	17.31	86
3	R.Bironas	TEN	5.72	1.42	82
4	S.Janikowski	OAK	5.26	-1.37	64
5	J.Brown	STL	3.84	2.33	64
6	D.Akers	PHI	3.68	2.53	87
7	A.Vinatieri	IND	3.59	2.29	72
8	S.Gostkowski	NE	3.30	-0.22	89
9	S.Hauschka	BAL	2.17	-0.03	42
10	M.Koenen	ATL	1.71	9.18	85

Min. 20 kickoffs; squibs and onside not included

Bottom 10 Kickers, Gross Kickoff Value over Average

Rk	Player	Team	Kick Pts+	Net Pts+	Kicks
24	S.Suisham	WAS	-2.70	5.69	64
25	C.Barth	KC	-2.72	-13.37	44
26	M.Stover	BAL	-2.76	-6.82	41
27	R.Lindell	BUF	-2.99	6.42	71
28	R.Longwell	MIN	-3.35	-5.52	79
29	D.Carpenter	MIA	-3.94	-9.39	71
30	N.Kaeding	SD	-4.76	-5.86	88
31	M.Bryant	TB	-6.61	4.49	78
32	N.Folk	DAL	-6.79	-7.46	67
33	J.Carney	NYG	-8.76	-11.29	75

Min. 20 kickoffs; squibs and onside not included

Top 10 Punters, Gross Punt Value over Average

Rk	Player	Team	Punt Pts+	Net Pts+	Punts
1	S.Lechler	OAK	16.61	13.94	90
2	S.Koch	BAL	14.09	20.86	84
3	D.Jones	STL	11.85	3.95	82
4	B.Moorman	BUF	10.98	7.31	58
5	H.Smith	IND	7.75	8.98	53
6	D.Zastudil	CLE	7.36	16.92	75
7	A.Lee	SF	6.48	5.57	67
8	J.Ryan	SEA	5.59	8.60	78
9	J.Feagles	NYG	5.14	11.70	64
10	M.Scifres	SD	4.77	10.07	51

Min. 20 punts

Bottom 10 Punters, Gross Punt Value over Average

Rk	Player	Team	Punt Pts+	Net Pts+	Punts
29	M.McBriar	DAL	-3.79	-6.16	25
30	M.Berger	PIT	-4.83	8.76	66
31	R.Plackemeier	SEA/WAS	-5.08	-9.93	67
32	A.Podlesh	JAC	-5.16	-3.19	46
33	M.Koenen	ATL	-5.51	4.82	65
34	D.Frost	GB	-6.05	0.54	49
35	C.Hentrich	TEN	-7.89	-2.38	88
36	S.Weatherford	NO/JAC/KC	-8.06	-6.22	59
37	J.Baker	CAR	-10.36	-10.54	76
38	K.Larson	CIN	-12.17	-8.78	101

Min. 20 punts

Top 10 Kick Returners, Value over Average

Rk	Player	Team	Pts+	Returns
1	D.Manning	CHI	16.59	36
2	L.McKelvin	BUF	13.91	52
3	E.Hobbs	NE	12.00	45
4	L.Washington	NYJ	9.83	47
5	J.Miller	NYJ/OAK	8.38	32
6	D.Sproles	SD	7.97	53
7	A.Rossum	SF	7.79	48
8	J.Cribbs	CLE	7.35	42
9	C.Smith	TB	7.02	36
10	R.Cartwright	WAS	6.79	50

Min. eight returns

Bottom 10 Kick Returners, Value over Average

Rk	Player	Team	Pts+	Returns
55	D.Bess	MIA	-3.69	14
56	D.Walker	SF	-3.90	13
57	D.Hester	CHI	-3.97	31
58	M.Austin	DAL	-4.15	29
59	B.Witherspoon	JAC	-5.03	52
60	Y.Figurs	BAL	-5.43	28
61	W.Blackmon	GB	-6.03	53
62	S.Breaston	ARI	-6.18	33
63	D.Hall	STL	-7.37	36
64	B.Middleton	DET	-10.14	38

Min. eight returns

Top 10 Punt Returners, Value over Average

Rk	Player	Team	Pts+	Returns
1	J.Higgins	OAK	15.19	44
2	R.Bush	NO	13.35	20
3	C.Smith	TB	8.26	23
4	R.Parrish	BUF	6.91	21
5	D.Hixon	NYG	6.39	24
6	J.Jones	HOU	6.25	32
7	A.Rossum	SF	5.22	14
8	M.Jones	CAR	4.73	39
9	W.Blackmon	GB	4.01	36
10	H.Douglas	ATL	3.73	19

Min. eight returns

Bottom 10 Punt Returners, Value over Average

Rk	Player	Team	Pts+	Returns
34	A.Jennings	ATL	-4.87	23
35	Y.Figurs	BAL	-5.00	23
36	Dex.Jackson	TB	-5.24	20
37	S.Holmes	PIT	-6.32	34
38	S.Breaston	ARI	-6.52	33
39	C.Gordon	MIN	-6.58	15
40	A.Randle El	WAS	-7.47	39
41	A.Jones	DAL	-7.55	21
42	D.Hester	CHI	-7.94	32
43	K.Ratliff	IND	-8.74	16

Min. eight returns

Top 10 Offenses, 3-and-out per drive

Rk	Team	Pct
1	IND	13.2%
2	HOU	15.2%
3	DEN	15.2%
4	NO	16.0%
5	BUF	16.4%
6	NE	16.9%
7	SD	17.8%
8	ARI	19.0%
9	MIN	19.5%
10	NYG	19.6%

Bottom 10 Offenses, 3-and-out per drive

Rk	Team	Pct
23	STL	26.6%
24	CLE	27.2%
25	SEA	28.0%
26	KC	28.7%
27	DAL	28.8%
28	TEN	29.0%
29	OAK	29.4%
30	DET	29.6%
31	CHI	29.8%
32	CIN	34.6%

Top 10 Offenses, avg LOS to start drive

Rk	Team	LOS
1	CHI	33.5
2	NE	33.1
3	BUF	32.4
4	TEN	32.2
5	TB	32.1
6	NYG	32.0
7	BAL	31.8
8	NYJ	31.7
9	WAS	31.3
10	CAR	31.3

Bottom 10 Offenses, avg LOS to start drive

Rk	Team	LOS
23	MIN	29.1
24	SF	28.5
25	MIA	28.2
26	IND	28.1
27	GB	28.0
28	DET	27.9
29	KC	27.8
30	JAC	27.5
31	STL	27.3
32	DEN	25.8

Top 10 Defenses, 3-and-out per drive

Rk	Team	Pct
1	WAS	32.7%
2	BAL	31.7%
3	NE	31.1%
4	PIT	30.1%
5	PHI	29.7%
6	TB	27.5%
7	NYG	26.0%
8	JAC	25.5%
9	GB	24.5%
10	DAL	24.2%

Bottom 10 Defenses, 3-and-out per drive

Rk	Team	Pct
23	STL	19.7%
24	MIA	19.5%
25	IND	19.2%
26	DET	19.2%
27	SD	19.2%
28	DEN	18.5%
29	ARI	18.4%
30	NYJ	18.4%
31	KC	16.0%
32	CLE	14.6%

Top 10 Defenses, avg LOS to start drive

Rk	Team	LOS
1	ATL	27.2
2	IND	27.3
3	CAR	27.7
4	MIA	27.8
5	WAS	27.8
6	NE	27.9
7	BAL	28.3
8	SEA	28.8
9	NYG	29.0
10	HOU	29.0

Bottom 10 Defenses, avg LOS to start drive

Rk	Team	LOS
23	BUF	31.1
24	JAC	31.1
25	CHI	31.2
26	MIN	31.5
27	STL	31.9
28	GB	32.1
29	DAL	32.5
30	ARI	32.8
31	KC	33.3
32	SF	33.8

Top 10 Offenses, Yards per drive

Rk	Team	Yds/Dr
1	DEN	38.38
2	IND	37.40
3	NO	36.55
4	NE	35.67
5	HOU	35.67
6	ATL	34.83
7	SD	34.20
8	NYG	34.10
9	MIA	33.05
10	ARI	32.99

Bottom 10 Offenses, Yards per drive

Rk	Team	Yds/Dr
23	PIT	27.53
24	BAL	27.35
25	TEN	26.62
26	SEA	24.90
27	CHI	23.90
28	STL	23.51
29	CLE	23.14
30	DET	22.52
31	OAK	22.47
32	CIN	21.74

Top 10 Offenses, Points per drive

Rk	Team	Pts/Dr
1	NO	2.54
2	SD	2.52
3	NE	2.42
4	IND	2.41
5	NYG	2.39
6	ARI	2.24
7	ATL	2.20
8	CAR	2.17
9	DEN	2.16
10	NYJ	2.13

Bottom 10 Offenses, Points per drive

Rk	Team	Pts/Dr
23	JAC	1.67
24	CHI	1.67
25	KC	1.56
26	SEA	1.53
27	WAS	1.49
28	DET	1.39
29	CLE	1.24
30	OAK	1.21
31	STL	1.20
32	CIN	1.02

Top 10 Defenses, Yards per drive

Rk	Team	Yds/Dr
1	PIT	20.60
2	BAL	21.68
3	PHI	22.77
4	MIN	24.34
5	TEN	24.87
6	CHI	25.75
7	DAL	25.88
8	TB	26.11
9	WAS	26.53
10	NYG	27.46

Bottom 10 Defenses, Yards per drive

Rk	Team	Yds/Dr
23	HOU	32.07
24	MIA	32.22
25	STL	32.50
26	SEA	32.91
27	IND	33.29
28	CLE	33.31
29	SD	33.75
30	KC	35.82
31	DEN	36.86
32	DET	37.20

Top 10 Defenses, Points per drive

Rk	Team	Pts/Dr
1	BAL	1.11
2	PIT	1.12
3	TEN	1.22
4	PHI	1.30
5	MIN	1.44
6	WAS	1.57
7	NYG	1.62
8	TB	1.65
9	CHI	1.68
10	CAR	1.69

Bottom 10 Defenses, Points per drive

Rk	Team	Pts/Dr
23	GB	2.01
24	NO	2.03
25	SEA	2.09
26	JAC	2.15
27	HOU	2.20
28	ARI	2.27
29	STL	2.33
30	KC	2.41
31	DEN	2.58
32	DET	2.72

Top 10 Offenses, Better DVOA with Shotgun

Rk	Team	% Plays Shotgun	DVOA Shot	DVOA Not	Yd/Play Shot	Yd/Play Not	DVOA Dif
1	NO	31%	51.9%	9.8%	7.9	5.7	42.2%
2	SF	15%	20.3%	-15.8%	7.7	4.9	36.1%
3	NYG	39%	45.8%	12.6%	6.5	5.3	33.2%
4	TB	37%	26.5%	-6.6%	6.3	4.7	33.1%
5	IND	47%	36.2%	3.5%	6.6	4.8	32.8%
6	JAC	34%	34.8%	4.0%	5.7	5.0	30.8%
7	CAR	12%	43.7%	15.3%	6.3	6.0	28.4%
8	PHI	41%	29.5%	1.5%	6.3	4.9	28.0%
9	WAS	19%	35.6%	9.1%	6.1	4.9	26.5%
10	DAL	44%	22.5%	-3.5%	6.2	5.2	25.9%

Bottom 10 Offenses, Better DVOA with Shotgun

Rk	Team	% Plays Shotgun	DVOA Shot	DVOA Not	Yd/Play Shot	Yd/Play Not	DVOA Dif
23	PIT	31%	4.4%	3.5%	5.7	4.8	0.9%
24	TEN	21%	4.4%	10.0%	6.0	5.2	-5.6%
25	DET	35%	-28.4%	-17.2%	4.7	4.8	-11.2%
26	MIA	28%	6.8%	20.1%	5.8	5.9	-13.2%
27	CLE	29%	-34.5%	-10.5%	3.9	4.6	-24.0%
28	CHI	24%	-26.1%	0.6%	5.0	4.8	-26.7%
29	NYJ	38%	-14.9%	15.4%	5.2	5.7	-30.3%
30	HOU	11%	-24.4%	14.4%	4.8	6.3	-38.9%
31	OAK	22%	-62.6%	-12.7%	4.1	5.1	-49.9%
32	SEA	6%	-64.5%	-6.9%	4.6	4.8	-57.6%

Top 10 Defenses, Better DVOA vs. Shotgun

Rk	Team	% Plays Shotgun	DVOA Shot	DVOA Not	Yd/Play Shot	Yd/Play Not	DVOA Dif
1	TB	27%	-34.7%	1.2%	4.7	5.5	-35.9%
2	MIN	37%	-32.6%	-10.2%	4.9	5.1	-22.4%
3	IND	30%	-14.0%	5.1%	5.2	5.1	-19.0%
4	STL	30%	9.7%	28.2%	6.2	6.4	-18.6%
5	PIT	35%	-35.2%	-23.2%	4.6	3.8	-12.0%
6	CHI	31%	-14.8%	-3.9%	5.1	5.0	-10.9%
7	CIN	30%	-2.0%	5.9%	5.4	5.2	-8.0%
8	NE	31%	4.1%	10.1%	5.6	5.4	-6.0%
9	PHI	34%	-24.4%	-18.4%	5.0	4.3	-6.0%
10	BAL	37%	-27.0%	-23.2%	4.4	4.7	-3.8%

Bottom 10 Defenses, Better DVOA vs. Shotgun

Rk	Team	% Plays Shotgun	DVOA Shot	DVOA Not	Yd/Play Shot	Yd/Play Not	DVOA Dif
23	ATL	33%	25.8%	4.4%	6.4	5.3	21.4%
24	SEA	33%	30.9%	7.8%	6.8	5.4	23.1%
25	DAL	30%	17.5%	-6.7%	5.8	4.7	24.2%
26	OAK	34%	27.9%	-0.9%	6.6	5.2	28.8%
27	SF	35%	27.7%	-1.9%	6.4	4.5	29.6%
28	JAC	29%	32.4%	2.5%	7.3	5.3	29.9%
29	CLE	27%	31.5%	-0.4%	7.3	5.3	32.0%
30	DET	19%	58.9%	23.3%	9.0	6.2	35.7%
31	NYJ	39%	28.1%	-11.4%	6.6	4.4	39.5%
32	ARI	28%	51.1%	-3.8%	6.6	4.9	54.9%

Top 10 Offenses, Better DVOA with Play-Action

Rk	Team	% PA	DVOA PA	DVOA No PA	Yd/Play PA	Yd/Play No PA	DVOA Dif
1	OAK	25%	37.9%	-39.3%	8.2	4.5	77.2%
2	HOU	22%	77.3%	10.1%	11.0	6.2	67.1%
3	GB	17%	84.2%	17.1%	10.0	5.9	67.1%
4	SEA	23%	35.2%	-11.1%	6.3	5.0	46.3%
5	DET	12%	22.9%	-22.3%	6.9	5.1	45.2%
6	SD	20%	85.1%	45.5%	10.7	7.0	39.5%
7	TB	13%	47.9%	14.6%	7.7	5.9	33.2%
8	TEN	18%	43.5%	11.2%	7.5	5.9	32.3%
9	NYJ	14%	30.5%	1.1%	7.9	5.6	29.4%
10	CAR	23%	52.0%	23.7%	10.9	6.2	28.4%

Bottom 10 Offenses, Better DVOA with Play-Action

Rk	Team	% PA	DVOA PA	DVOA No PA	Yd/Play PA	Yd/Play No PA	DVOA Dif
23	MIN	18%	-0.5%	2.4%	7.7	6.1	-3.0%
24	NO	22%	35.2%	39.1%	8.9	7.2	-3.9%
25	DEN	19%	26.4%	33.6%	8.2	7.0	-7.1%
26	BAL	26%	7.8%	16.7%	5.9	6.4	-8.9%
27	KC	11%	-2.8%	7.4%	5.0	5.8	-10.2%
28	IND	18%	23.9%	46.2%	7.7	6.7	-22.3%
29	JAC	15%	0.1%	32.7%	6.7	5.9	-32.6%
30	CIN	9%	-38.5%	1.1%	3.3	4.7	-39.5%
31	DAL	12%	-20.8%	22.8%	6.5	6.4	-43.6%
32	SF	11%	-49.1%	3.2%	6.9	6.1	-52.3%

Top 10 Defenses, Better DVOA vs. Play-Action

Rk	Team	% PA	DVOA PA	DVOA No PA	Yd/Play PA	Yd/Play No PA	DVOA Dif
1	GB	17%	-33.1%	2.3%	5.6	6.2	-35.3%
2	SD	14%	-9.9%	21.5%	6.0	6.5	-31.4%
3	CLE	20%	-7.3%	20.5%	8.1	6.8	-27.8%
4	BAL	13%	-34.0%	-16.7%	8.4	4.8	-17.4%
5	MIA	13%	-4.7%	8.7%	6.0	6.4	-13.4%
6	KC	23%	19.0%	29.4%	8.1	6.8	-10.4%
7	PHI	16%	-27.7%	-17.5%	4.8	5.2	-10.2%
8	NYG	14%	-3.0%	6.4%	6.9	5.8	-9.4%
9	JAC	18%	19.8%	26.7%	6.9	7.4	-6.9%
10	ARI	18%	19.0%	25.0%	7.6	6.2	-6.1%

Bottom 10 Defenses, Better DVOA vs. Play-Action

Rk	Team	% PA	DVOA PA	DVOA No PA	Yd/Play PA	Yd/Play No PA	DVOA Dif
23	DAL	14%	28.1%	-2.1%	6.6	5.2	30.2%
24	TEN	16%	9.1%	-23.4%	6.9	4.9	32.6%
25	NYJ	11%	44.5%	11.1%	7.8	6.1	33.4%
26	TB	17%	18.6%	-17.8%	8.1	5.4	36.4%
27	NE	16%	54.5%	18.0%	9.1	6.0	36.5%
28	ATL	18%	47.7%	7.2%	8.6	5.8	40.5%
29	NO	18%	59.2%	12.0%	9.9	6.0	47.2%
30	HOU	18%	67.3%	11.8%	9.3	6.6	55.5%
31	STL	19%	73.1%	15.3%	11.1	6.5	57.8%
32	BUF	19%	70.2%	7.9%	10.2	5.7	62.3%

Author Biographies

Editor-in-Chief and Statistician

Aaron Schatz is the creator of FootballOutsiders.com and the proprietary NFL statistics within *Football Outsiders Almanac*. He writes regularly for ESPN.com and *ESPN the Magazine*. During the 2007 season, he also wrote simultaneously for FOXSports.com and AOL Sports, thus establishing himself as the greatest crossover artist since Ray Charles topped the *Billboard* Country and Western charts. His work has also appeared in *The New York Times*, *The Boston Globe*, *The New York Sun*, The New Republic Online, and Slate.com, and has done custom research for a number of NFL teams. Before creating Football Outsiders, he was a radio disc jockey and spent three years tracking search trends online as the writer and producer of the Internet column "The Lycos 50." He has a BA in Economics from Brown University and lives in Framingham, Massachusetts, with his wife Kathryn and daughter Mirinae.

Managing Editor

Bill Barnwell serves as the Managing Editor of FootballOutsiders.com, and writes regularly for ESPN.com and *ESPN The Magazine*. When not managing the FO forums and writing about football, he can be found trying too hard at trivia nights and micro stakes poker games around Boston. Like most people born during the Reagan administration, Bill is only capable of forming meaning through intertextuality, so he'd like to thank *The Nightman*, Pavement's *Watery, Domestic* EP, Pepsi One, and the VLOOKUP function in Excel for helping him complete his work on this year's book.

Layout and Design

Vince Verhei is a jack of all trades for Football Outsiders. He did the majority of layout for *Football Outsiders Almanac 2009*, along with writing a number of chapters. As copy editor for FootballOutsiders.com, he reads, proofs and lays out nearly every story that appears on the Web site. As a writer, he co-wrote Scramble for the Ball this past season and has written numerous other columns for FO. As an avid game watcher, he has been involved with the game charting project since 2005. A graduate of Western Washington University, a school that canceled its football program last year, Verhei worked on the editorial staff of an outdoors magazine in the Seattle area for more than eight years despite the fact that his last fishing trip came in elementary school. His other night job is as a writer and podcast host for pro wrestling/MMA website Figurefouronline.com.

Further layout and cover design were contributed by **Jason Beattie**, who has also been providing his unique perspective on the NFL in weekly cartoons on FootballOutsiders.com since 2003. He lives in Denver and really hopes our numbers are wrong about the 2009 Broncos.

Contributors

Dr. Benjamin Alamar is the founding editor of the *Journal of Quantitative Analysis in Sports* and has consulted for various NFL and NBA franchises. He holds a doctorate in Economics from the University of California at Santa Barbara.

Will Carroll is a fantasy owner's best friend and a thorn in the side of the NFL's control over injury information. A three-time Fantasy Sports Writers Association award winner, Will came over to Football Outsiders and brought the same edge to the funny-shaped pigskin ball that he did to the spherical horsehide one. He lives in Indianapolis, where he also writes the Baseball Prospectus column "Under the Knife" and manages their new hockey Web site, Puck Prospectus.

Bill Connelly analyzes the ins and outs of college football play-by-play data in the weekly Football Outsiders column, Varsity Numbers. He grew up a numbers and sports nerd in western Oklahoma. His favorite teams growing up were, in no particular order, the Missouri Tigers, Miami Dolphins, Pittsburgh Pirates, and Portland Trailblazers. Perhaps he should have taken the hint and given up on sports a decade ago. Instead, he spends his time creating Excel files full of play-by-plays and attempting to create the perfect, most all-encompassing football statistic ever. The S&P+ is as close as he's come so far. He lives in Missouri with his wife and pets, working for his alma mater, and writing for the Missouri blog, Rock M Nation.

Born in Milan, Italy, and reared in Denver, **Doug Farrar** fell in love with pro football as a wee lad, when Broncomania filled the mile-high air, Lyle Alzado was more than a cautionary tale, and Woody Paige wrote books. Though he once dreamed of returning punts like Rick Upchurch, it was the allure of the guitar and pen that took Doug through his adolescent years. A Seattleite since 1985, Doug now holds true allegiance to the Emerald City and all she possesses. He was Football Outsiders' first West Coast draft pick in 2006, and his responsibilities include the weekly column Cover-3 and compiling Audibles at the Line each Monday morning. He also writes online for ESPN.com and the Web sites of the *Washington Post* and *Seattle Times*. In his non-existent free time, Doug runs the Atlanta Falcons and Seattle Seahawks Web sites for Scout.com.

Brian Fremeau contributes the Fremeau Efficiency Index (FEI) and other college football stats and analysis to FootballOutsiders.com. His work has also recently appeared on ESPN.com and in several Maple Street Press college football publications, including *Here Come the Irish 2009*, *Buckeye Battle Cry 2009*, and *Yea Alabama 2009*. He lives in South Bend, Indiana, with his wife and daughter and spends every home Saturday cheering his beloved alma mater, Notre Dame, from the South end zone, Touchdown Jesus' outstretched arms signaling into the blue, gray sky.

Ned Macey is a recent University of Michigan law school graduate who hopes to delay inevitably earning the actual title of lawyer in a desperate attempt to stay young. He writes the weekly column "Any Given Sunday," analyzing the week's biggest upset Football Outsiders' style. His work has appeared in various places connected to Football Outsiders, including ESPN.com over this past year. He lives with his wife Melanie and daughter Katie in Indianapolis.

Sean McCormick is a graduate of the University of Pennsylvania and holds an MFA in Creative Writing from Arizona State University. In addition to being a regular contributor at FootballOutsiders.com, his draft coverage has appeared at FOXSports.com. He also indulges his inner masochist as a contributing writer for TheJetsBlog.com and is the proud owner of the lone Richard Todd jersey still in existence. He lives in Brooklyn, New York.

Boston-native **Bill Moore** currently commutes between New York and Minneapolis, where his office overlooks the Metrodome. He graduated from Babson College and is employed in finance when he is not coordinating the activities of more than two dozen volunteers each week for the Football Outsiders Game Charting Project. Although his probation period expired long ago, his wife has still not completely forgiven him for kicking a hole in their couch during Super Bowl XXXI.

Mike Tanier has been part of the Football Outsiders team since 2005. He writes the weekly Rundown column for FOXSports.com and has also written for *ESPN the Magazine*, *Maxim*, Rotoworld, Deadspin, and other outlets. He lives in South Jersey with his wife Karen, sons C.J. and Michael, and dog Rosie. He teaches at Audubon High School, and is proud to have known Joe Flacco when he was only 6-foot-3.

Robert Weintraub bleeds orange, both because of his inexplicable passion for the Cincinnati Bengals (he grew up in suburban New York, not Ohio) and because of his alma mater, Syracuse University. He now lives in Atlanta, the epicenter of college football hyper-allegiance, so that Syracuse degree comes in handy (maintaining plausible deniability when writing about Georgia and Florida and Alabama is crucial). When not watching games in his ancient Boomer Esiason jersey, Robert contributes regularly to Slate, ESPN.com, and *The Guardian*, and works as a freelance television producer.

Mark Zajack confesses that despite growing up in New York State he didn't see his beloved G-men play in person until his first job took him to Oakland in September 1998. After a close encounter with the Black Hole and a Giants loss he learned two things: 1) the heartbreak of losing is multiplied by the number of carousing costumed humanoids heckling you; 2) getting shanked hurts. He currently resides in Clemson, South Carolina, where he is pursuing a Ph.D. in Industrial-Organizational Psychology, an excuse to study a statistical approach to predicting performance. He spent much of the past year traveling the "series of tubes" and compiling material for "This Week in Quotes."

Acknowledgements

We want to thank all the Football Outsiders readers, all the people in the media who have helped to spread the word about our Web site and books, and all the people in the NFL who have shown interest in our work. This year, instead of the never-ending long list naming everyone who's ever acknowledged our existence, we wanted to give a few specific acknowledgements:

• FO techmaster Elias Holman, who masterminded last year's redesign and this summer's premium expansion, and Benjy Rose, the original designer of FootballOutsiders.com.

• The FO folks whose work is not in the book: salary cap expert J.I. Halsell, programmers Pat Laverty and Sean McCall, Excel stat report guru John Argentiero, and drive stats guru Jim Armstrong.

• David Lewin, creator of the Lewin Career Forecast, and Jason McKinley, creator of O-Line Continuity Score.

• Al Bogdan, Russell Levine, Michael David Smith, and Ryan Wilson, for all they did for FO in our first few years. We miss you guys.

• Chris Povirk, the greatest Internet data-scraper in the history of Internet data-scraping.

• Roland Beech of TwoMinuteWarning.com and 82games.com, who came up with the original ideas behind our individual defensive stats.

• The people at Prospectus Entertainment Ventures, still our buddies even if we changed the name of the book. Thanks for all your support over the past few years.

• Our editors at ESPN.com and *ESPN the Magazine*, particularly Scott Burton, Jon Scher, Daniel Kaufman, and Jamar Hudson.

• Bill Simmons, for constantly promoting us on his podcast, and Peter King, for lots of promotion in his SI.com column.

• Ron Jaworski, Greg Cosell, and the entire *NFL Matchup* production team, for the annual film-study lessons.

• Chris Hoeltge at the NFL, for responding to our endless questions about specific items in the official play-by-play, and for collecting old gamebooks and making them available to us.

• All the media relations people at various NFL teams who have helped with our search for old play-by-play, plus Jon Kendle at the Hall of Fame for filling in the gaps and Corey Rubin for going to Canton to get those gamebooks.

• Russ Lande, whose draft guide was extremely helpful in researching this year's rookies.

• Our comrades in the revolution: Doug Drinen (creator of the indispensible pro-football-reference.com), Jason Lisk, Chase Stuart, and K.C. Joyner.

• Interns who helped prepare data over the past year or for this book specifically: Beth Dewey, James Doyle, Dan Haverkamp, Rory Hickey, Stephen Lauer, Andy Lithio, Chris McCown, Marcus Mueller, Jim O'Hearn, Kyle Prince, Megan Rudebeck, Jesse Schupack, Joe Skolnik, Devon Teeple, Dan Waechter, Gavin Weiss, Parker Woodard.

• All those who have volunteered their time and effort for the Football Outsiders game charting project, particularly those people who have been consistently charting for multiple seasons: Sergio Becerril Lopez, Dave DuPlantis, Tom Gower, Peter Koski, Shawn Krest, Dave Nicoloro, Matt Raymond, Nate Richards, Michael Rutter, and Nevin Sharma.

• Everyone who has participated in the old play-by-play transcription project, particularly the absurdly prolific Jeremy Snyder.

Infinite gratitude goes to our wives and children, for putting up with this silliness.

Football Outsiders Almanac 2009 is dedicated to the memory of John L. Tanier, Jr. (1937-2009).

2926746